The Shipmaster's BUSINESS COMPANION

Malcolm Maclachlan
MICS, FNI, Master Mariner
Lecturer in Business and Law, Glasgow College of Nautical Studies

The Nautical Institute

THE SHIPMASTER'S
BUSINESS COMPANION

Published by The Nautical Institute
202 Lambeth Road, London SE1 7LQ, England
TEL: +44 (0)20 7928 1351
FAX: +44 (0)20 7401 2817
Web: www.nautinst.org

First edition published 1996
Second edition 1997
Third edition 1998
Fourth edition 2004
Reprinted 2005

The author and publisher have used their best efforts in collecting and preparing material for inclusion in The Shipmaster's Business Companion. They do not assume, and hereby disclaim, any liability to any party for any loss or damage caused by errors or omissions in The Shipmaster's Business Companion, whether such errors or omissions result from negligence, accident or any other cause.

Readers of The Shipmaster's Business Companion are advised to make themselves aware of any applicable local, national or international legislation or administrative requirements or advice which may affect decisions taken by them in their professional capacities.

A CD is provided with this book which is designed to run on PC and Apple Mac based systems.
The data is filed in portable digital format (pdf) and the searching is carried out through Adobe software.

This disc is designed to run on computers with the following specification:
PC: Windows 98, NT, 2000, XP, Pentium 300 MHz, 120 MB Ram 1024 x 786 colour display. 4 x CDRom drive. Installation of Adobe Reader may be required.
MAC: OS 8.6 or OS 9 G3 300 MHz, 128 MB Ram, 1024 x 767 colour display, 4 x CDRom drive. Installation of Adobe Reader may be required. To be reviewed with future updates.

Printed in England
by O'Sullivan Printing Corporation, Southall, Middlesex U.K.

ISBN 1 870077 45 8

Contents

The Author

Malcolm Maclachlan was born in Dover in 1947 and first worked at sea - illegally - as a 14-year old pantry boy in the Townsend car ferry *Halladale*. In the early 1960s he trained as a cadet on the training ship HMS *Worcester* before serving a deck apprenticeship with Alfred Holt & Company, sailing as midshipman in general cargo liners of the Blue Funnel Line and Glen Line.

Deep sea and coastal service as a deck officer with several British and Danish liner, reefer, tramp and tanker companies, and a spell in Scottish fishery protection vessels, culminated in 1980 in an appointment as master in Bell Lines' fleet of short-sea containerships.

Redundancy in 1982 led to a year of lecturing at the ill-fated Leith Nautical College, followed by four years as control room operator on North Sea drilling rigs. The 1986 oil slump and a second redundancy prompted the author to become a freelance marine journalist, writing and cartooning for *Fairplay*, *Seascape* and *The Sea*. During this period he wrote *An Introduction to Marine Drilling*, compiled *The North Sea Field Development Guide* (both published by OPL) and drew monthly cartoons for the NUMAST *Telegraph*, a collection of which NUMAST published as *A Laugh on the Ocean Wave*.

In 1989 the author returned to teaching, this time at Glasgow College of Nautical Studies, where he teaches Shipmaster's Business and related subjects. Shipbroking studies and growing pressure of college work forced him to stop cartooning, but in compensation he won the 1995 *Fairplay Prize* for his Ship Management paper in the annual Institute of Chartered Shipbrokers examinations. He became an MICS in that year.

The author self-publishes - under his own North Sea Books houseflag - *The Shipmaster's Business Self-Examiner*, a question-and-answer "orals" primer used by many "orals" candidates as well as seagoing officers, and is compiling a *Dictionary of Merchant Shipping Terminology*.

Malcolm Maclachlan is married and has a son - an engineer officer with Teekay Shipping (Canada) - and two daughters, one of whom sailed as a deck officer with BP Shipping and is now a bunker broker. He and his wife live in a small town in the Southern Uplands of Scotland. In his spare time he runs on the Scottish hills and plays blues harmonica.

Preface to the 1998 edition

In an increasingly litigious world where environmental concerns often place ships and their masters under official and public scrutiny, every serving and aspiring shipmaster needs to be fully aware of his obligations to his owners, managers, charterers, shippers, flag state, port state, coastal states, and crew. He can only know what his numerous obligations are, however, if he is armed with a sound knowledge of current 'Shipmaster's Business and Law'.

Most masters find it difficult, if not impossible, to keep abreast of current Business and Law while at sea. Few ships carry a good reference library, and even when they do, today's maritime law and commercial practice is embodied in so many texts published by different organisations that a master may well be at a loss to know even what the relevant document is, far less what it states. Moreover, shipping legislation changes frequently and sometimes radically. The *Merchant Shipping Act 1995* consolidated much of the primary British shipping legislation of the previous 101 years, while *STCW 95* has brought radically new requirements for training, certification and safe manning, sweeping away old provisions with which masters were reasonably familiar, such as the deck and engineer officer manning scales, the European trading areas, and the 'short-handed' manning provisions. (Readers will find notes on the new *STCW 95*-based regulations in Section E along with notes on the 'old' provisions for comparison, where relevant.)

Shipmasters with enough on their plates do not usually welcome totally new legislation, but the *Master's Discretion Regulations 1997* (described in Section H) should be greeted warmly by all in command. No more need a safety-conscious master feel uneasy about resisting 'commercial' pressure to sail, or to increase speed in fog, or to take any suggested course of action of which he disapproves on grounds of navigational safety. This SI is long overdue.

Merchant Shipping Notices have now passed MSN1700, Marine Guidance Notes have reached their half-century and Marine Information Notes are at MIN17. It is clear that officers can no longer be expected to have even a working knowledge (as they once could) of M Notices in force, and references are therefore included in the text to any relevant MSN, MGN or MIN.

This book makes no pretence to be a definitive work on any particular aspect of maritime law or shipping business practice, and readers will not find tables of leading cases, annotations, footnotes or references. It is simply a compendium of Business and Law notes that may prove of some value to professional mariners in their day-to-day work. If it contributes anything to the commercial success of a voyage, or is useful to officers in their studies for higher certificates, or to shore-based shipping practitioners in some way, it will have exceeded my hopes and expectations.

A reference book for maritime professionals clearly needs to be up to date, and to this end the Nautical Institute intends to publish an annual supplement in its journal *Seaways*, and a fully revised edition in about three years' time.

Malcolm Maclachlan
Biggar, Scotland
December 1997

Preface to the 2003 edition

This new edition is corrected to the end of June 2003. It incorporates the amendments contained in the two supplements to the 1998 edition, published by the Nautical Institute in 1999 and 2000, and includes much new information, as evidenced by the considerable increase in size.

Topics introduced include the revised SOLAS chapter V and the UK's Merchant Shipping (Safety of Navigation) Regulations 2002, the International Ship and Port Facility Security (ISPS) Code (due to enter into force in July 2004), the revised ISM Code, the UK's Domestic Safety Management (DSM) Code, EU passenger ship classes, operational requirements applicable to the principal vessel types, MCA codes of practice for small vessels, Shipboard Marine Pollution Emergency Plans (SMPEPs), the European Working Time Directive and the Merchant Shipping (Hours of Work) Regulations 2002, LOF 2002, the revised Scopic Clause and the International Hull Clauses (01/11/02). An extensive UK ship documentation index and a detailed table of mandatory Official Log Book entries are added to Section D, while the key points of the MCA's Training and Certification Guidance are added to Section E. Numerous cross-references have been added throughout the text, and there are more references to relevant M Notices. The index – so important in a book of this size and scope - has been greatly expanded.

Users of the 1998 edition will find that much of the text has been rearranged and - hopefully - improved. Key words are highlighted in bold type, and footnotes have been added where relevant. Hyperlinks, originally added for the author's own convenience whilst editing disc files, are left in the hard copy text as a guide to section contents. The value obtained from using hyperlinks whilst editing this edition led to the idea of a searchable CD-ROM edition, and I would like to record my thanks to Julian Parker, retiring Secretary of the Nautical Institute, for so enthusiastically embracing and pursuing this idea.

In the five years since publication of the last edition there has been a slight reduction in the annual output of new UK merchant shipping legislation, but the MCA has in that period published no less than 63 Merchant Shipping Notices, 110 Marine Information Notes and 151 Marine Guidance Notes. Meanwhile, external and "company" ISM audits have become part of routine shipboard operations and seafarers have had to adapt to the STCW 95 regime, including its on-board training requirements. With the ISPS Code now about to add in no small measure to the proliferation of paperwork and disruption of life on board, shipmasters and officers clearly need up-to-date guidance as to their numerous statutory and commercial obligations. In this respect, I sincerely hope that this new edition will be found of some help on board, and in the owners' or managers' office.

Malcolm Maclachlan
Biggar, Scotland
June 2003

Foreword

International shipping is a highly competitive industry that provides an essential service for Society through the economic transportation of goods, commodities and passengers. Because there are so many stakeholders, it is essential to have agreed and shared rules. For example - Shipping is a capital-intensive industry and companies need to finance their operations. This finance largely comes from banks that derive their own finance from loans and the investments of their shareholders. Banks and their shareholders, who might even guard our own pension funds, need a rule-based system to protect their risks. Similarly the carriage of cargo depends upon well-tested contracts and expertise, which in turn are used to determine the outcome of an insurance claim in the event of loss or damage.

Seafarers are also bound by contracts of employment and owners have obligations to provide seaworthy ships. Not only does this cover the physical condition of the vessels but the human element, the manning and qualifications of the crew, navigational outfit, fire protection, life saving capability and watertight integrity. It must not be forgotten that ships have to enter and work in ports. They require pilots, interact with stevedores and share facilities; they need services; stores; bunkers and water. The seafarers themselves become visitors with immigration and health controls, which are quite widely different in the various countries they visit. Customs too have a direct interest in ships, their cargo, crew and passengers for duties, contraband and drugs.

There is an understanding that the seas are used for many purposes, which include exploration, fishing, fish farming and leisure activities. The littoral is used for economic activities such as tourism and can also contain sensitive ecological habitats. How then is it possible to satisfy the needs of society for cheap efficient transport with the demands for safety and environmental protection.

The answer of course lies in the complex regulatory mechanisms, which have evolved over centuries. If laws stayed the same it would be possible to provide training in their use, but the situation is much more dynamic with new developments taking place at an increasing pace. New regulation, like the ISM Code do not yet have a body law tested in court concerning the commercial consequences of mismanagement and governments have not yet invoked their statutory powers: so the interpretation of specific clauses may lack precise definition. Operators, however, have to manage and run their ships and shipmasters in particular have to be aware of their legal obligations. The task is formidable.

When the first edition of the Shipmasters Business Companion was published in 1996 it contained 470 pages. In 2004 just 7 years later the current volume is expanded to some 900 pages. It is not until the full range of maritime legislation from portage bills to port state control, is put "on the table" that we can appreciate just how prescribed our industry has become.

The oil industry recognised some time ago that rule based behaviour had limitations and that sector of maritime activity undertook a complete revision of its operating practices following the Piper Alpha platform accident in 1988. This change was based mainly on self regulated Operational Industry Guidelines. They were to become guidelines, however, that could only be ignored at the operator's peril.

The time has surely come in shipping when the burden of regulations should be lifted and turned into a similar culture with accepted industry codes of practice that will offer real support. If industry guidelines are ignored this would lead bad owners and operators into courts of law through failing to operate within an accepted "Duty of Care". The bad owner or manager would then land up where they belong, brought to the courts by charterer, cargo owner, flag state, underwriter or even by their own staff.

This book tells us much about the way all aspects of shipping have become codified and the enormous burden placed upon those in responsible positions to know, understand and implement correct practices.

Malcolm Maclachlan has undertaken the Herculean task of compiling international, commercial and national legislation into one great volume with a style and precision which will be readily appreciated by all who need to know the current regulations covering maritime operations. His outstanding work has been recognised by the UK Government's Maritime and Coastguard Agency who have made this book essential reading for certificates of competency.

The new package with the Compact Disc will enable supplements to be produced more economically in future: so enhancing this authoritative and practical reference work.

Nobody can keep the whole spectrum of maritime law in their heads any more. Surveyors, owners, managers, sea staff educationalists, lawyers and those concerned with maritime operations will find this book with its comprehensive index the perfect reference.

Captain R. B. Middleton FNI,
President, The Nautical Institute

Section A

MARITIME TREATIES

A01 International maritime law

A01a SOURCES OF INTERNATIONAL MARITIME LAW

* Sources of international law include **international law**, **customary law** and **treaties**.

A01a.1 International law

- is the system of law regulating the relations between sovereign States and their rights and duties with respect to each other. It derives mainly from **customary law** and **treaties**.

A01a.2 Customary law

- derives from **practice followed continuously in a particular location**, or by **particular States**, such that the practice becomes accepted as part of the law in that location or of those States.
- is ascertained from the **customary practice of States** together with evidence that States regard these practices as a legal obligation.
- is sometimes regarded as the **foundation stone of international law**.

A01a.3 Treaties

* A **treaty** is a written international agreement between two States (a bilateral treaty) or between a number of States (a multilateral treaty), which is binding in international law.
* Treaties are usually made under the auspices of an internationally accepted organisation such as the United Nations or one of its agencies, such as IMO or ILO.
* Treaties are **binding** only on those States which are parties to the treaty (sometimes called "convention countries"), but they may be binding even on non-party States if their provisions are also a part of customary law.
* Treaties are generally first **drafted** (often by a specialist committee), then **considered for adoption** by a formally convened conference attended by representatives of States which are members of the sponsoring organisation. Drafting and adoption may take several years, although where quick responses are required in urgent cases, governments may be willing to accelerate this process.
* Once the conference has formally **adopted** a treaty it will be **opened for signature** by States, often for 12 months, after which it will remain **open for accession**.
* A treaty will often contain provisions wherein a State may become a party by either:
  * **signature alone** (without reservation as to ratification, acceptance or approval); or
  * **signature subject to ratification, acceptance or approval**, followed by ratification, acceptance or approval; or
  * **accession**.
* Where a State chooses the "signature subject to ratification" option the signature must be followed by **deposit of an instrument of ratification** with the host organisation (called the "depositary"). The words "acceptance" and "approval" basically mean the same as ratification, but pose fewer legal or constitutional problems. Many States choose the "subject to ratification" option since it gives them the chance to enact national legislation to give legal effect to the treaty's provisions before entering into treaty commitments.
* **Accession** is the method used by a State to become a party to a treaty which it did not sign while it was open for signature. Technically, the State must deposit an **instrument of accession** with the depositary before the treaty becomes binding on the State.
* It may take several years before an adopted treaty **enters into force** (i.e. becomes binding on those governments which have formally accepted it by one of the above methods). A treaty normally enters into force in accordance with criteria incorporated into the treaty itself, e.g. 12 months after a stipulated number of States have become parties to it.
* A treaty usually has no legal effect in an accepting State until it has been incorporated by statute into the **national law** of the State (although some States give direct effect to treaties without national legislation). The duties of salvors in the UK would not be legally affected by the International Convention on Salvage 1989, for example, had the terms of the Convention not been embodied in the Merchant Shipping Act 1995 (see H05c).
* The more States that become parties to a treaty, the greater the influence that treaty will have on the development of **customary law**.

* The **law of the sea** has been made at various UN Conferences on the Law of the Sea (**UNCLOS**) (see A02a).
* The **chief international treaty-making bodies** making provisions which regulate merchant shipping are:
  * the International Maritime Organization (**IMO**) (see A03);
  * the International Labour Organization (**ILO**) (see A04);
  * the World Health Organization (**WHO**) (see A06a); and
  * the International Telecommunications Union (**ITU**) (see A06b).

A02 UN Conferences on the Law of the Sea

A02a UNCLOS

A02a.1 UNCLOS conferences and Convention

* Three **"UNCLOS" conferences** have been convened: UNCLOS I, at Geneva in 1958; UNCLOS II, at Geneva in 1960; and UNCLOS III, at Geneva in 1974.
* The outcome of UNCLOS III was the **United Nations Convention on the Law of the Sea** (catalogued by HMSO as Cmnd. 8941), commonly known as "**UNCLOS**".
* **UNCLOS** -
  - attempts to codify the international law of the sea.
  - is a treaty document of **320 articles** and **9 annexes**, governing all aspects of ocean space, such as delimitation, environmental control, marine scientific research, economic and commercial activities, transfer of technology and the settlement of disputes relating to ocean matters.
  - came into force internationally on 16 November 1994.

A02a.2 UNCLOS provisions relating to zones of coastal State jurisdiction and the High Seas

* UNCLOS sets the width of the **territorial sea** at 12 nautical miles, with a **contiguous zone** at 24 nautical miles from the baseline. It defines **innocent passage** through the territorial sea and defines **transit passage** through international straits. It defines **archipelagic States** and allows for passage through **archipelagic waters**.
* UNCLOS establishes **exclusive economic zones** (EEZs) extending to 200 nautical miles from baselines. It defines the **continental shelf** and extends jurisdiction over the resources of the shelf beyond 200 miles where appropriate.
* UNCLOS defines the legal status of the **high seas** and establishes regulations for the control of marine pollution.
* States in dispute about their interpretation of UNCLOS may submit their disagreements to competent courts such as the **International Court of Justice** (in The Hague), or the **Law of the Sea Tribunal** (in Hamburg).
* For notes on the different **zones of coastal State jurisdiction**, and on the **high seas** see H01e.

A02a.3 UNCLOS provisions relating to port State, coastal State and flag State control of shipping

* Responsibility for **enforcement of regulations** rests mainly with flag States, but as vessels enter zones closer to the coast the influence of **coastal State jurisdiction** and, ultimately, **port State jurisdiction**, gradually increases.
* **Article 94** deals with **duties of the flag State**, while **Article 217** deals with **enforcement by flag States** (see Section B: The Flag State).
* **Article 218** deals with **port State jurisdiction**. When a vessel is voluntarily within a port or at an offshore terminal, the port State may, where the evidence warrants, begin proceedings in respect of discharges in violation of international rules (i.e. regulations in MARPOL 73/78). Another State in which a discharge violation has occurred, or the flag State, may request the port State to investigate the violation.
* **Article 200** deals with **coastal State jurisdiction** as applied in relation to pollution provisions. Where there are clear grounds for believing that a vessel navigating in the territorial sea of a State has violated laws and regulations of the coastal State adopted in accordance with UNCLOS or applicable international pollution regulations, the **coastal State may inspect the vessel** and, where evidence warrants, **institute proceedings including detention** of the vessel. Vessels believed to have violated pollution laws in an EEZ may be required to give identification and voyage information to the coastal State.

A02a.4 UNCLOS provisions relating to pollution prevention

* States must agree international rules and standards to **prevent pollution from vessels** (Article 211). (This obligation is currently met by **MARPOL 73/78**.)
* Coastal States may also promulgate and enforce **pollution regulations in their own EEZs** which may, in some circumstances, include imposition of routeing restrictions.
* **In the territorial sea** additional navigational restraints (e.g. traffic separation schemes and sea lanes) may be imposed on vessels with dangerous and hazardous cargoes.
    * Coastal States and ports may make **entry to internal waters and harbours** conditional on meeting additional pollution regulations.

A02b IMPLEMENTATION OF UNCLOS PROVISIONS BY UK

* The MS (Prevention of Pollution) (Law of the Sea Convention) Order 1996 (SI 1996/282) enables UK regulations to be made -
    - implementing provisions in UNCLOS 1982 (Cmnd. 8941) relating to pollution of the sea by ships; and
    - relating to the protection and preservation of the marine environment from pollution from ships caused beyond the UK's territorial sea.
* The **MS (Prevention of Pollution) (Limits) Regulations 1996** (SI 1996/2128) and the **MS (Prevention of Pollution) (Limits) Regulations 1997** (SI 1997/506), which were made under powers conferred by the above Order, specify sea areas, called "**controlled waters**", within which the **jurisdiction and rights of the UK are exercisable in accordance with part XII of UNCLOS** for the protection and preservation of the marine environment, i.e. in order to prevent pollution by discharges from ships. For a notes on **controlled waters** see I01a.1b.

A03 International Maritime Organization (IMO)

A03a NATURE AND PURPOSES OF IMO

* IMO is a specialised **agency of the United Nations** dealing with maritime affairs. Its **membership** consists of 162 signatory States that include the UK and every other major maritime country, and three Associate Members[1]. Together, IMO Member States control more than 96% of world merchant tonnage.
* **IMO's purposes** are stated in Article 1 of the Convention on the International Maritime Organization. The chief purposes can be summarised as:
    * to facilitate inter-governmental co-operation on State regulation and practices relating to maritime technical matters; and
    * to encourage and facilitate the adoption of the highest practicable standards of maritime safety, efficiency of navigation and prevention and control of marine pollution from ships.
* **Address**: 4 Albert Embankment, London SE1 7SR, England.
* **Website**: www.imo.org

A03b IMO PROCEDURES

A03b.1 IMO organs

* IMO's main organs are its **Assembly, Council, Maritime Safety Committee** (MSC), **Marine Environment Protection Committee** (MEPC), **Legal Committee**, and **Technical Co-operation Committee**. There is also a **Facilitation Committee** and a number of **sub-committees** of the main technical committees.
* IMO's work is mostly technical, and is carried out by the committees and sub-committees on which sit representatives of the governments of Member States. (For a note on the UK's **IMO Liaison Team** and **Permanent Representative to IMO** see B05b.2a).

---

[1] At 24 April 2003.

A03b.1a Assembly

- is the **highest governing body of IMO**. It consists of all Member States and meets once **every 2 years** in regular sessions, and in extraordinary sessions if necessary. The Assembly is responsible for approving IMO's work programme, for voting IMO's budget and for determining IMO's financial arrangements. It elects IMO's Council. Plenary sessions of the Assembly are open to the press and public, but the majority of its work is done in Committee.

A03b.1b Council

- is composed of 40 Member States elected by the Assembly for 2-year terms beginning after each regular session. 10 Council members are Member States with the largest interest in providing international shipping services, e.g. Greece and Norway. 10 are other States with the largest interest in international seaborne trade. 20 are other States with special interests in maritime transport or navigation and whose election to the Council will ensure the representation of all major geographic areas of the world[2].
* Council is the **executive organ of IMO**, responsible under the Assembly for supervising IMO's work. It performs the functions of Assembly between sessions, except for making recommendations to governments on maritime safety and pollution.

A03b.1c Main committees

- include the **Maritime Safety Committee** (MSC), the **Marine Environment Protection Committee** (MEPC) and the Legal Committee.
- each have **sub-committees** which deal with detailed technical matters.
- may produce **resolutions** (see A03b.2d).

A03b.1d Secretariat

- consists of the **Secretary-General** and nearly 300 personnel, based at IMO's London headquarters (for address see A03a).

A03b.2 IMO instruments

- include:
  • **Conventions**;
  • **Protocols**;
  • **Amendments**;
  • **Recommendations**, **Codes** and **Guidelines**; and
  • **Resolutions**.
* Amendments, guidelines and other measures are promulgated by the **main committees** (including the MSC and MEPC) by means of **circulars**, e.g. MSC/Circ. 666: Loading and unloading of bulk cargoes.

A03b.2a Conventions

- are **multilateral treaty documents**. (For notes on treaties see A01a.3.)
- are the **chief instruments** of IMO, being **binding legal instruments** regulating some aspect of maritime affairs of major concern to IMO, e.g. safety of life at sea or marine pollution.
- are identified by a **name** and the **year of adoption by the Assembly**, e.g. the "International Convention on the Safety of Life at Sea, 1974".
- may have **detailed technical provisions** attached in **annexes**, e.g. the six annexes to the MARPOL Convention, each dealing with a different aspect of marine pollution.
- may also have detailed technical provisions in an associated **code**, e.g. the LSA Code, which contains technical provisions of equipment required under the provisions of SOLAS.
- are commonly referred to by a single-word **code-name**, e.g. "COLREG", more correctly called "COLREG 1972" to indicate the year of adoption.

---

[2] The composition of the Council was changed by the 1993 amendments to the IMO Convention which came into effect on 7 November 2002.

* A Member State which ratifies or accedes to an IMO convention is obliged to **give effect to it** by making its requirements part of its **national law**. Ratification involves a dual obligation for a Member State; it is both a formal commitment to apply the provisions of the convention, and an indication of willingness to accept a measure of international supervision.

A03b.2b Protocols

- are important treaty instruments made when **major amendments** are required to be made to a convention which, although already adopted, has not yet entered into force.
* The SOLAS Convention, 1974 has been amended twice by means of protocols: by the **1978 SOLAS Protocol** (which entered into force on 1 May 1981) and by the **1988 SOLAS Protocol** (which entered into force on 3 February 2000 and replaced and abrogated the 1978 Protocol as between Parties to the 1988 Protocol). The combined instruments, formerly known as **SOLAS 74/78**, are now collectively called **SOLAS 74/88**.
* The MARPOL Convention, 1973 has also been amended by means of protocols. The **1978 MARPOL Protocol** made major changes to MARPOL in the wake of several large-scale pollution incidents in the 1970s, even though the 1973 Convention had not yet come into force; it also absorbed the parent Convention and ensured that the combined Convention/Protocol instrument (called **MARPOL 73/78**) would enter into force at an earlier date than the parent Convention would have done alone. (MARPOL 73/78 came into force on 2 October 1983.) The **1997 MARPOL Protocol** (containing Annex VI – Regulations for the Prevention of Air Pollution from Ships) was adopted on 26 September 1997 and will enter into force 12 months after being accepted by at least 15 States with not less than 50% of world merchant shipping tonnage. (After that date MARPOL 73/78 may be referred to as MARPOL 73/78/97.)
* The International Convention on Load Lines, 1966 (LL 66) has been amended by a 1988 Protocol (which entered into force on 3 February 2000) and may now be referred to as **LL 66/88**.

A03b.2c Recommendations, Codes and Guidelines

* In addition to Conventions and other formal treaty instruments, IMO has adopted several hundred **Recommendations** and a number of **Codes** and **Guidelines** dealing with a wide range of subjects, most of them technical in nature. Each of these instruments is agreed by adoption of a Resolution, either of the Assembly or a main committee.
* **Recommendations** are not formal treaty documents like Conventions and Protocols and are not subject to ratification. They provide more specific guidelines than treaty documents. Although Recommendations are not legally binding on governments, they provide guidance in framing national regulations and requirements. Many governments do in fact apply the provisions of recommendations by incorporating them, in whole or in part, national legislation or regulations. Recommendations are generally intended to supplement or assist the implementation of the relevant provisions of conventions and, in some cases, the principal codes, guidelines, etc.
* Many Recommendations are closely linked to Conventions and are designed to assist in their implementation. For example, Resolution A.526(13) which was adopted in at the 13th Session of the Assembly in 1983 and lays down minimum performance standards for rate-of-turn indicators. (Where required to be fitted under SOLAS Regulation V/12, rate-of-turn indicators must meet or exceed the performance standards established by Resolution A.526(13).)
* Some Recommendations constitute Codes, Guidelines or Recommended Practices on important matters not considered suitable for regulation by formal treaty instruments such as Conventions or Protocols.
* **Codes** are named, e.g. the International Code of Signals (1969) and the ISM Code. Many Codes, such as the Timber Deck Cargoes Code, are non-mandatory but may be used by Governments as the basis for national regulations. Other codes, such as the ISM Code, the IBC Code and the IGC Code, are mandatory under a regulation of a "parent" Convention. For a list of the **chief codes** see A03c.5.

A03b.2d Resolutions

- are the final documents resulting from the agreement by the IMO **Assembly** or a **main committee** (e.g. MSC or MEPC) of some matter such as an Amendment or Recommendation.
- may be:
  • Resolutions of the Assembly, e.g. Resolution A.586(XIV), where "A" refers to the Assembly, "586" is the serial number of the resolution, and "XIV" indicates that it was made by the 14th Session of the Assembly; or
  • Resolutions of a main IMO committee, e.g. MEPC.54(32), where "MEPC" stands for "Marine Environment Protection Committee", "54" is the serial number of the resolution, and "32" indicates that it was made by the 32nd session of the Committee.

* Where a Resolution is made by one of IMO's main committees to take account of amendments to the provisions of a convention, a member State which has ratified the convention **may enforce** the Resolution through domestic legislation. For example, the UK Government made the (now revoked) MS (Pilot Ladders and Hoists) (Amendment) Regulations 1993 to take account of amendments made to regulation 17 of chapter V of SOLAS 74 by Resolution MSC.22(59) of the Maritime Safety Committee of IMO.

A03b.3 Development of IMO Conventions

* Developments in shipping and related industries are **discussed** by Member States in main IMO organs (Assembly, Council and 4 main committees). The need for a new convention or amendments to an existing convention can be raised in any of these, but is usually raised in one of the committees. The **proposal** goes to Council and, as necessary, to Assembly.
* With authorisation of Council or Assembly, the committee concerned **considers** the matter in greater detail and draws up a **draft Convention**. Detailed consideration may be given in a **sub-committee**. **Inter-governmental and non-governmental organisations** with a working relationship with IMO assist committees and sub-committees with views and advice.
* The draft Convention is **reported to Council and Assembly** with a recommendation that a conference be convened to consider draft for formal adoption.
* Invitations to attend a conference are sent to all Member States, all member States of the UN, and specialised agencies of the UN. The draft Convention is circulated for comment by governments and organisations.
* Conference examines the draft Convention and comments. Necessary changes are made before producing a draft acceptable to the majority of governments present. The Convention thus agreed on is adopted by the conference and deposited with the Secretary-General, who sends copies to all governments of Member States.
* The Convention is **opened for signature** by States, usually for 12 months. Signatories may **ratify or accept** the Convention. Non-signatories may **accede** to the Convention. (For notes on **ratification and acceptance** see A01a.3.)
* The Convention is not binding on any ratifying State until **formally accepted** by that State.

A03b.4 Entry into force of IMO Conventions

* Each Convention includes provisions stipulating **conditions to be met before it enters into force**. The more important and complex the document, the more stringent the conditions for entry into force. E.g. TONNAGE 1969 required acceptance by 25 States with combined merchant tonnage totalling at least 65 per cent of world gross tonnage, whereas the International Convention for Safe Containers (CSC) only required acceptance by 10 States.
* Governments take measures to comply with Convention's requirements. In many cases this means **enacting or changing national legislation** to enforce Convention provisions. (E.g. the UK made the Merchant Shipping (Safety of Navigation) Regulations 2002 to give effect to the revised Chapter V of SOLAS.)
* Governments deposit a **formal instrument of acceptance** and become **Contracting States**.
* When stipulated entry conditions have been met, the Convention **enters into force** for all States which have accepted it, generally after a period of grace to enable States to take measures for implementation.

A03b.5 Amendment of IMO Conventions and other instruments

* Amendments may be made to conventions, protocols or their annexes after discussion, agreement and adoption by the IMO Assembly.
* Amendments are made by adoption of a **Resolution**, such as MEPC.51(32) - Amendments to the Annex of the Protocol of 1978 relating to the International Convention for the Prevention of Pollution by Ships, 1973 (Discharge criteria of Annex I of MARPOL 73/78).
* Amendments are suggested, discussed, agreed as with Conventions, described in A03b.3.
* The major IMO conventions such as SOLAS and MARPOL have been amended on numerous occasions.
* In early Conventions, amendments came into force only after a percentage of Contracting States, usually two thirds, had accepted them. This took several, and sometimes many, years. Newer Conventions incorporate procedure for **tacit acceptance** of amendments by States, which speeds up the amendment process. Under the tacit acceptance procedure, an amendment enters into force at a particular time unless, before that date, objections to the amendment are received from a specified number of Parties.

A03b.6 Enforcement of IMO conventions

* See A05.

A03c IMO INSTRUMENTS

* The "parent" instrument of IMO is the **IMO Convention**, which entered into force on 17 March 1958 and has (at 31 April 2003) 162 contracting States with 98.52% of world tonnage.
* The majority of other conventions and other instruments adopted under the auspices of IMO fall into three main categories:
   • **maritime safety instruments** (see A03c.1);
   • **marine pollution instruments** (see A03c.2); and
   • **liability and compensation instruments**, especially in relation to damage caused by pollution (see A03c.3).
* In addition there are several instruments concerning **other subjects** (see A03c.4) and many IMO **Codes** (see A03c.5).

A03c.1 IMO maritime safety instruments

Instrument name *Abbreviated name*	Notes *Entry into force date. Number of Contracting Parties with percentage of world gross tonnage at 31 May 2003.*	SBC ref.
International Convention for the Safety of Life at Sea, 1974 *SOLAS 1974*	Chief maritime safety convention. Replaced SOLAS 1960 and introduced "tacit acceptance" amendment procedure to speed up introduction of amendments. Technical provisions in 12 chapters (see A03c.1a). Amended numerous times. Given effect in UK by several SIs (see A03c.1a). *In force 25 May 1980. 146 Contracting States (98.49% world tonnage).* *1978 Protocol in force 1 May 1981. 100 Contracting States (94.64% world tonnage).* *1988 Protocol in force 3 Feb 2000. 62 Contracting States (63.27% world tonnage).*	A03c.1a
International Convention on Load Lines, 1966 *LL 1966*	Limits, by means of minimum freeboards, draughts to which ships may be loaded, taking into account hazards in different zones and seasons. Prescribes minimum standards for external weathertight and watertight integrity. Currently under revision. Given effect in UK by MS (Load Line) Regulations 1998 (SI 1998/2241), as amended. *In force 21 Jul 1968. 151 Contracting States (98.46% world tonnage).* *1988 Protocol in force 3 Feb 2000. 64 Contracting States (63.26% world tonnage).*	D04i I07b.1
Special Trade Passenger Ships Agreement, 1971 *STP 1971*	Regulates carriage of large numbers of unberthed passengers in special trades such as the pilgrim trade. Annexed Special Trade Passenger Ships Rules, 1971 modify regulations of Chapters II and III of SOLAS 1960 Convention. Complemented by Protocol on Space Requirements for Special Trade Passenger Ships, 1973. *In force 2 Jan 1974. 17 Contracting States (22.30% world tonnage).*	-
Convention on the International Regulations for Preventing Collisions at Sea, 1972 *COLREG 1972*	Replaced 1960 Convention and Rules. Technical provisions in 38 Rules and 4 Annexes ("Colregs") which apply to all ships on the high seas, etc. Amended 1981, 1987, 1989, 1993. Gives recognition to traffic separation schemes. Given effect in UK by MS (Safety of Navigation) Regulations 2002 (SI 2002/1473). *In force 15 Jul 1977. 142 Contracting States (97.30% world tonnage).*	H02a
International Convention for Safe Containers, 1972 *CSC 1972*	Aims to ensure safety in transport and handling of containers through acceptable test procedures and strength requirements. Also aims to facilitate international transport of containers by providing uniform international safety regulations, equally applicable to all modes of surface transport, so as to avoid proliferation of divergent national safety regulations. *In force 6 Sep 1977. 72 Contracting States (59.75% world tonnage).*	-
Convention on the International Maritime Satellite Organization, 1976 *INMARSAT C 1976*	Parent of INMARSAT organisation. Defines purposes of INMARSAT as being to improve maritime communications, thereby assisting in improving distress and safety of life at sea communications, the efficiency and management of ships, maritime public correspondence services, and radio-determination capabilities. INMARSAT'S obligation to provide maritime distress and safety services via satellite were enshrined within 1988 (GMDSS) amendments to SOLAS. *In force 16 Jul 1979. 88 Contracting States (92.30% world tonnage).*	-
Torremolinos Protocol of 1993 relating to the Torremolinos International Convention for the Safety of Fishing Vessels, 1993 *SFV Protocol 1993*	Updates, amends and absorbs parent SFV Convention 1977. Applies to fishing vessels of 24 metres in length and over including those vessels also processing their catch. Safety provisions in 10-chapter Annex. *Not yet in force. 9 Contracting States with 9.03% of world tonnage.*	-

International Convention on Standards of Training, Certification and Watchkeeping for Seafarers, 1978 *STCW 1978*	Provides minimum international requirements for training, certification and watchkeeping, replacing nationally-set standards. Applies to ships of non-party States when visiting ports of Party States. Given effect in UK by MS (Training and Certification) Regulations 1997 (SI 1997/348) and MS (Safe Manning, Hours of Work and Watchkeeping) Regulations 1997 (SI 1997/1320). *In force 28 Apr 1984. 144 Contracting States (98.47% world tonnage).* *1995 amendments (STCW 95, including STCW Code) in force 1 Feb 2002.*	E01a
International Convention on Maritime Search and Rescue, 1979 *SAR 1979*	Aims at developing an international SAR plan, so that no matter where an accident occurs, rescue of persons in distress at sea will be co-ordinated by a SAR organisation and, when necessary, by co-operation between neighbouring SAR organisations. Parties must ensure arrangements are made for provision of adequate SAR services in their coastal waters and are encouraged to enter into SAR agreements with neighbouring States. *In force 22 Jun 1985. 75 Contracting States (51.83% world tonnage).*	H04b.12
International Convention on Standards of Training, Certification and Watchkeeping for Fishing Vessel Personnel, 1995 *STCW-F 1995*	Aims to make standards of safety for crews of fishing vessels mandatory. Will apply to crews of seagoing fishing vessels of 24 metres in length and above. Short convention has an annex containing technical regulations. *Will enter into force 12 months after being accepted by 15 States. 4 Contracting States (3.30% world tonnage).*	-

*STCW 1978 was revised at a conference in London in July 1995; the revised convention is generally known as **STCW 95** (see E01a).

A03c.1a SOLAS chapters

*   SOLAS 1974, as amended, comprises **chapters** as shown in the following table.

Ch.	Title	Related IMO Code(s)	Notes	Principal regulations giving effect in UK	SBC ref.
I	General provisions	-		MS (Survey and Certification) Regulations 1995	D04f
II-1	Construction – Structure, subdivision and stability, machinery and electrical installations	-		MS (Passenger Ship Construction: Ships of Classes I, II and II(A)) Regulations 1998 MS (Cargo Ship Construction) Regulations 1997	D02a.1 D02a.1
II-2	Construction – Fire protection, fire detection and fire extinction	FSS Code FTP Code	Revised chapter in force from 1 July 2002. Technical requirements contained in associated codes	MS (Fire Protection: Large Ships) Regulations 1998	D04l
III	Life-saving appliances and arrangements	LSA Code		MS (Life-Saving Appliances for Ships Other Than Ships of Classes III to VI(A)) Regulations 1999	D04k
IV	Radiocommunications	-		MS (Radio Installations) Regulations 1998	D04m
V	Safety of navigation	International Code of Signals	Revised chapter in force from 1 July 2002.	MS (Safety of Navigation) Regulations 2002	H01f
VI	Carriage of cargoes	BC Code; CSS Code; International Grain Code; Timber Deck Cargoes Code		MS (Carriage of Cargoes) Regulations 1999	F07g
VII	Carriage of dangerous goods	IMDG Code; IBC Code; IGC Code; INF Code		MS (Dangerous Goods and Marine Pollutants) Regulations 1997 MS (Gas Carriers) Regulations 1994 MS (Carriage of Packaged Irradiated Nuclear Fuel etc.) (INF Code) Regulations 2000	F07f.2 D03d.2a F07h
VIII	Nuclear ships	Code of Safety for Nuclear Ships	Applies to all nuclear ships except warships	-	-
IX	Management for the safe operation of ships	ISM Code		MS (International Safety Management (ISM) Code) Regulations 1998	C04b D03a.1
X	Safety measures for high-speed craft	HSC Code	Applies to high-speed craft built on/after 1 Jan 1996	MS (High Speed Craft) Regulations 1996	D03i.1 D04f.3b D04v.2a
XI-1	Special measures to enhance maritime safety	-	Contains regulations on (1) Authorisation of recognised organisations; (2) Enhanced surveys; (3) Ship identification number; (4) Port State control on operational requirements.	MS (Port State Control) Regulations 1995	D01h D04f.1a I02c.3

| XI-2 | Special measures to enhance maritime security | ISPS Code | Regulation 2/3 enshrines new ISPS Code. Regulation 2/5 requires all ships to be provided with a ship security alert system. | Regulations to be announced before July 2004 | A03c.5
C03c.8
D03a.6
H04e.2
I01k |
| XII | Additional safety measures for bulk carriers | BLU Code | Applies to bulk carriers as defined in regulation IX/1.6 | MS (Additional Safety Measures for Bulk Carriers) Regulations 1999 | D03f.2
D03f.3a
F07g.1g
F07i1
I05d.4 |

A03c.2 IMO marine pollution instruments

Instrument name *Abbreviated name*	Notes *Entry into force date. Number of Contracting Parties with percentage of world gross tonnage at 31 May 2003.*	SBC ref.
International Convention Relating to Intervention on the High Seas in Cases of Oil Pollution Casualties, 1969 *INTERVENTION 1969* *INTERVENTION Protocol 1973*	Affirms the right of a coastal State to take such measures on the high seas as may be necessary to prevent, mitigate or eliminate danger to its coastline or related interests from pollution by oil or the threat thereof, following a maritime casualty. 1973 Protocol extends Convention to cover substances other than oil. *In force 6 May 1975. 78 Contracting States (71.10% world tonnage).* *1973 Protocol in force 30 Mar 1983. 44 Contracting States (44.51% world tonnage).*	H03i H05c.2
Convention on the Prevention of Marine Pollution by Dumping of Wastes and Other Matter, 1972 *LC 1972* *LC Protocol 1996*	Known as "London Convention". Prohibits dumping of certain hazardous materials. Requires a prior special permit for dumping of a number of other identified materials and a prior general permit for other wastes or matter. Defines "dumping" as deliberate disposal at sea of wastes or other matter from vessels, aircraft, platforms or other man-made structures, as well as the deliberate disposal of these vessels or platforms themselves. (Definition excludes wastes derived from exploration and exploitation of sea-bed mineral resources.) Contracting Parties undertake to designate an authority to deal with permits, keep records, and monitor the condition of sea. *In force 30 Aug 1975. 80 Contracting States (70.44% world tonnage).* *1996 Protocol not yet in force. 17 Contracting States (10.67% world tonnage).*	-
International Convention for the Prevention of Pollution from Ships, 1973, as modified by the Protocol of 1978 relating thereto *MARPOL 73/78* *Annexes I/II*	Chief convention aimed at prevention of pollution of marine environment by ships from operational or accidental causes. Combination of two treaties, adopted 1973 and 1978. Annexes I and II are mandatory. Amended many times. Annex I given effect in UK by MS (Prevention of Oil Pollution) Regulations 1996 (SI 1996/2154); Annex II given effect in UK by MS (Dangerous or Noxious Liquid Substances in Bulk) Regulations 1996 (SI 1996/3010). *In force 2 Oct 1983. 125 Contracting States (97.00% world tonnage).*	D04g.1 D04g.2 D04g.3 H03a.1 H03b.1
International Convention for the Prevention of Pollution from Ships, 1973, as modified by the Protocol of 1978 relating thereto *MARPOL 73/78* *Annex III*	Provides controls for prevention of pollution by packaged harmful substances, i.e. dangerous goods and marine pollutants. Optional annex. Given effect in UK by MS (Dangerous Goods & Marine Pollutants) Regulations 1997 (SI 1997/2367). *In force 1 Jul 1992. 107 Contracting States (83.03% world tonnage).*	F07f.1 H03c.1
International Convention for the Prevention of Pollution from Ships, 1973, as modified by the Protocol of 1978 relating thereto *MARPOL 73/78* *Annex IV*	Provides controls for prevention of pollution from ships' sewage. Optional annex. Will be given effect in UK by new MS (Prevention of Pollution by Sewage) Regulations. *In force 27 Sep 2003. 91 Contracting States (51.22% world tonnage).*	D04g.8 H03d.1
International Convention for the Prevention of Pollution from Ships, 1973, as modified by the Protocol of 1978 relating thereto *MARPOL 73/78* *Annex V*	Provides controls for prevention of pollution from ships' garbage. Optional annex. Given effect in UK by MS (Prevention of Pollution by Garbage) Regulations 1998 (SI 1998/1377). *In force 31 Dec 1988. 112 Contracting States (89.34% world tonnage).*	D04g.9 H03e.1
International Convention for the Prevention of Pollution from Ships, 1973, as modified by the Protocol of 1978 relating thereto *MARPOL Protocol 1997* *(Annex VI)*	Provides controls for prevention of air pollution from ships. *Will enter into force 12 months after ratification by 15 States with at least 50% world tonnage. 10 Contracting States (52.56% world tonnage).*	D04g.10 H03f.1

International Convention on Oil Pollution Preparedness, Response and Co-operation, 1990 *OPRC 1990*	Parties must establish measures for dealing with pollution incidents, either nationally or in co-operation with other countries. Ships must carry a shipboard oil pollution emergency plan (SOPEP). Ships must report incidents of pollution to coastal authorities. Provides for establishment of stockpiles of oil spill combating equipment, holding of oil spill combating exercises and the development of detailed plans for dealing with pollution incidents. Parties must provide assistance to others in the event of a pollution emergency and provision is made for the reimbursement of any assistance provided. Given effect in UK by MS (Oil Pollution Preparedness, Response and Co-operation Convention) Regulations 1998 (SI 1998/1056), as amended. *In force 13 May 1995. 71 Contracting States (58.61% world tonnage).*	H06e.2
Protocol on Preparedness, Response and Co-operation to Pollution Incidents by Hazardous and Noxious Substances, 2000 *OPRC/HNS 2000*	Aims to provide a global framework for international co-operation in combating major incidents or threats of marine pollution. Parties must establish measures for dealing with pollution incidents, either nationally or in co-operation with other countries. Ships must carry a shipboard pollution emergency plan to deal specifically with incidents involving HNS. *Will enter into force 12 months after ratification by 15 States party to OPRC Convention. 5 Contracting States (11.46% world tonnage).*	-
International Convention on the Control of Harmful Anti-fouling Systems on Ships, 2001 *AFS 2001*	Prohibits use of harmful organotins in anti-fouling paints used on ships and establishes a mechanism to prevent potential future use of other harmful substances in anti-fouling systems. *Will enter into force 12 months after ratification by 25 States with 25% of world tonnage. 3 contracting States (2.12% world tonnage).*	-

A03c.3 IMO liability and compensation instruments

Instrument name *Abbreviated name*	Notes *Entry into force date. Number of Contracting Parties with percentage of world gross tonnage at 31 May 2003.*	SBC ref.
International Convention on Civil Liability for Oil Pollution Damage, 1969 *CLC 1969* *CLC Protocol 1976* *CLC Protocol 1992 (often called CLC Convention 1992)*	Aims at ensuring that adequate compensation is available to persons suffering oil pollution damage from maritime casualties involving oil-carrying ships. Applied to seagoing vessels carrying bulk oil cargoes. Ships carrying more than 2,000 tons of oil as cargo must maintain oil pollution insurance. Spills from tankers in ballast or bunker spills from ships other than other than tankers were not covered. 1969 convention replaced by 1992 Protocol, which extended cover to both loaded and unladen tankers, including bunker oil spills. CLC 1992 intended to eventually replace the CLC 1969. Some States Party to 1969 CLC have not yet ratified the 1992 Protocol; for the time being, therefore, both regimes are co-existing. Given effect in UK by Chapter III of the Merchant Shipping Act 1995. *In force 19 Jun 1975. 43 Contracting States (4.83% world tonnage).* *1976 Protocol in force 8 Apr 1981. (55 Contracting States (57.53% world tonnage).* *1992 Protocol in force 30 May 1996. 91 Contracting States (91.29% world tonnage).*	G04d.1 G04d.2
International Convention on the Establishment of an International Fund for Compensation for Oil Pollution Damage, 1971 *FUND 1971* *FUND Protocol 1976* *FUND Protocol 1992(often called Fund Convention 1992)* *FUND Protocol 2003*	Aims mainly at providing compensation for pollution damage to the extent that the protection afforded by 1969 Civil Liability Convention (CLC) is inadequate, and to give relief to shipowners in respect of additional financial burden imposed on them by the 1969 CLC. 1971 Convention ceased to be in force, following denunciations, on 24 May 2002; superseded by FUND Protocol 2000. Given effect in UK by Chapter IV of the Merchant Shipping Act 1995. *1976 Protocol in force 22 Nov 1994. 33 Contracting States (46.85% world tonnage).* *1992 Protocol in force 30 May 1996. 85 Contracting States (87.18% world tonnage).* *2000 Amendments in force 1 Nov 2003.* *2003 Protocol not in force. No Contracting States.*	G04d.2
Convention relating to Civil Liability in the Field of Maritime Carriage of Nuclear Materials, 1971 *NUCLEAR 1971*	Aims to resolve difficulties and conflicts arising from simultaneous application to nuclear damage of certain conventions dealing with shipowners' liability, as well as other conventions which placed liability arising from nuclear incidents on the operators of the nuclear installations from which or to which the material in question was being transported. Provides that a person otherwise liable for damage caused in a nuclear incident will be exonerated for liability if the operator of the nuclear installation is also liable for such damage under the Paris Convention, 1960 or the Vienna Convention, 1963, or national law similar in the scope of protection given to the persons suffering damage. *In force 15 Jul 1975. 16 Contracting States (20.26% world tonnage).*	-
Convention relating to the Carriage of Passengers and their Luggage by Sea, 1974 *PAL 1974* *PAL Protocol 1976* *PAL Protocol 1990* *PAL Protocol 2002*	Usually called the Athens Convention. Establishes liability regime for damage suffered by passengers carried on a seagoing vessel. Makes carrier liable for damage or loss suffered by a passenger if the incident causing the damage occurred in the course of the carriage and was due to the fault or neglect of the carrier. Unless carrier acted with intent to cause such damage, or recklessly and with knowledge that such damage would probably result, he can limit his liability. Sets limits of carrier's liability. Given effect in UK by section 183 and Schedule 6 of Merchant Shipping Act 1995. *In force 28 Apr 1987. 29 Contracting States (34.64% world tonnage).* *1976 Protocol in force 30 Apr 1989. 23 Contracting States (34.33% world tonnage).* *1990 Protocol not yet in force. 3 Contracting States (0.74% world tonnage).* *2002 Protocol not yet in force. No contracting States.*	F08a.2

Convention on Limitation of Liability for Maritime Claims, 1976 *LLMC 1976* *LLMC Protocol 1996*	Specifies limits of liability for claims for loss of life or personal injury, and property claims (such as damage to other ships, property or harbour works). Limitation amounts are expressed in terms of "units of account", each unit being equivalent in value to the Special Drawing Right (SDR) as defined by the International Monetary Fund (IMF). For personal claims, liability for ships not exceeding 500 tons is limited to 330,000 SDR (equivalent to around US$422,000). For larger ships, additional amounts are based on a tonnage scale. Provides for a virtually unbreakable system of limiting liability. Declares that a person will not be able to limit liability only if "it is proved that the loss resulted from his personal act or omission, committed with the intent to cause such a loss, or recklessly and with knowledge that such loss would probably result". Given effect in UK by section 185 and Schedule 7 of Merchant Shipping Act 1995. *In force 1 Dec1986. 40 Contracting States (43.78% world tonnage).* *1996 Protocol not yet in force. 8 Contracting States (9.71% world tonnage).*	-
International Convention on Liability and Compensation for Damage in Connection with the Carriage of Hazardous and Noxious Substances, 1996 *HNS 1996*	Aims at ensuring that compensation is available to victims of accidents involving HNS, which include oils; other liquid substances defined as noxious or dangerous; liquefied gases; liquid substances with a flashpoint not exceeding 60°C; dangerous, hazardous and harmful materials and substances carried in packaged form; and solid bulk materials defined as possessing chemical hazards. Also covers residues left by the previous carriage of HNS, other than those carried in packaged form. Based on 2-tier system established under CLC and Fund Conventions but covers not only pollution damage but also risks of fire and explosion, including loss of life or personal injury and loss of or damage to property. *Will enter into force 18 months after 12 States have accepted the Convention, 4 of which have not less than 2 million gross tonnage, provided that persons in these States who would be responsible to pay contributions to the general account have received a total quantity of at least 40 million tonnes of contributing cargo in the preceding calendar year. 3 Contracting States (1.87% world tonnage).*	-
International Convention on Civil Liability for Bunker Oil Pollution Damage, 2001 *BUNKERS 2001*	Aims at ensuring that compensation is available to persons who suffer damage caused by bunker oil spills. Applies to damage caused on the territory, including the territorial sea, and in exclusive economic zones of Party States. *Will enter into force 12 months after signature by 18 States, including 5 States each with ships whose combined gross tonnage is not less than 1 million gt. 2 contracting States (0.38% world tonnage).*	-

A03c.4 IMO instruments concerning other subjects

Instrument name *Abbreviated name*	Notes *Entry into force date. Number of Contracting Parties with percentage of world gross tonnage at 31 May 2003.*	SBC ref.
Convention on Facilitation on International Maritime Traffic, 1965 *FAL 1965*	Aims to facilitate maritime transport by simplifying and minimising the formalities, documentary requirements and procedures associated with the arrival, stay and departure of ships engaged on international voyages, including all documents required by customs, immigration, health and other public authorities pertaining to the ship, its crew and passengers, baggage, cargo and mail. *In force 5 Mar 1967. 94 Contracting States (60.53% world tonnage).*	
International Convention on Tonnage Measurement of Ships, 1969 *TONNAGE 1969*	Introduced a universal tonnage measurement system. Provides for gross and net tonnages, both of which are calculated independently. Given effect in UK by MS (Tonnage) Regulations 1997 (SI 1997/1510). *In force 18 Jul 1982. 136 Contracting States (98.20% world tonnage).*	D04h.1
Convention for the Suppression of Unlawful Acts Against the Safety of Maritime Navigation, 1988 *SUA 1988*	Aims at ensuring that appropriate judicial action is taken against persons committing acts against ships, which include the seizure of ships by force, acts of violence against persons on board ships, and the placing of devices on board a ship which are likely to destroy or damage it. Obliges Contracting Governments either to extradite or prosecute alleged offenders. The Protocol for the Suppression of Unlawful Acts against the Safety of Fixed Platforms Located on the Continental Shelf, 1988 provides similar regulations relating to fixed platforms located on the Continental Shelf. Both instruments under review (at time of writing) following terrorist attacks in USA on 11 September 2001. *In force 1 Mar 1992. 89 Contracting States (76.85% world tonnage).* *SUA Protocol 1988 in force 1 Mar 1992. 80 Contracting States (75.41% world tonnage).*	H04e.2
International Convention on Salvage, 1989 *SALVAGE 1989*	Replaced 1910 convention on salvage law which incorporated "no cure, no pay" principle but gave no incentive for salvors to attempt to preserve the environment where the prospect of saving property was small. Provides for an enhanced salvage award, taking into account skill and efforts of salvors in preventing or minimising damage to environment. Given effect in UK by section 224(1)(2) and Schedule 11 of Merchant Shipping Act 1995. *In force 14 Jul 1996. 43 Contracting States (33.44% world tonnage).*	H05c.1

A03c.5 Chief IMO Codes

Code name *Abbreviated name*	Notes	SBC ref.
Code for Existing Ships Carrying Liquefied Gases in Bulk *GC Code for Existing Ships*	Provides international standard for safe carriage of liquefied gases in bulk by gas carriers already in service at 31 December 1976 or which otherwise fall outside the scope of the more extensive standards in resolution A.328(IX) and the IGC Code.	D03d.1a
Code for the Construction and Equipment of Mobile Offshore Drilling Units *MODU Code*	Adopted by resolution A.649(16) to supersede 1979 MODU Code, which was adopted by resolution A.414(XI). Applies to MODUs built since 1 May 1991.	D03h.5
Code for the Construction and Equipment of Ships Carrying Dangerous Chemicals in Bulk *BCH Code*	Provides international standard for safe carriage by sea of dangerous and noxious liquid chemicals in bulk in chemical tankers built after 1 July 1986. Prescribes design and construction standards of chemical tankers and equipment they should carry.	D03e.1a
Code for the Construction and Equipment of Ships Carrying Liquefied Gases in Bulk *GC Code*	Provides international standard for safe carriage by sea in bulk of liquefied gases and certain other substances in gas carriers built on or after 31 December 1976 but prior to 1 July 1986. Prescribes design and constructional features of gas carriers and equipment they should carry.	D03d.1b
Code of Practice for the Safe Loading and Unloading of Bulk Carriers *BLU Code*	Adopted by resolution A.862(20). Provides guidance to bulk carrier masters, terminal operators and other parties concerned with dry bulk cargo operations on the suitability of ships and terminals, procedures for the safe loading and unloading of solid bulk cargoes and model forms for loading and unloading plans and a ship/shore safety checklist. Linked to SOLAS regulation VI/7, as amended by resolution MSC.47(66). Non-mandatory.	F07g.3
Code of Safe Practice for Cargo Stowage and Securing *CSS Code*	Adopted by resolution A.714(17). Provides general principles to be followed by shipowners and operators to minimise risks to ships and personnel. Offers advice on equipment and techniques, details cargoes known to create hazards and difficulties, and advises on actions to be taken in heavy seas and to remedy effects of cargo shifting.	F0g.1b
Code of Safe Practice for Ships Carrying Timber Deck Cargoes *TDC Code*	Applies to ships carrying timber deck cargoes. Aimed at preventing casualties involving shifting and loss of timber cargoes. Adopted by resolution A.715(17). Contains chapters as follows: 1. General; 2. Stability; 3. Stowage; 4. Securing; 5. Personnel protection and safety devices; 6. Action to be taken during the voyage; Appendix A. Advice on stowage practices; Appendix B. General guidelines for the underdeck stowage of logs. Non-mandatory.	F0g.1b
Code of Safe Practice for Solid Bulk Cargoes *BC Code*	Provides guidance on standards for safe stowage and shipment of solid bulk cargoes (excluding grain). Aims to highlight dangers associated with shipment of certain types of bulk cargoes, listing cargoes which may liquefy and those which possess chemical hazards, and providing advice on their properties and handling. Includes revised test procedures for determining various characteristics of bulk cargo materials, emergency schedules, and safety precautions for entering enclosed spaces. Related to SOLAS chapter VI.	F07i.2 F07g.1b
Code of Safe Practice for the Carriage of Cargoes and Persons by Offshore Supply Vessels *OSV Code*	Adopted by resolution A.863(20). Aims to provide, for both operator and contractor, an international standard to avoid or reduce to a minimum the hazards which affect OSVs in their daily operation of carrying cargoes and persons from and between offshore installations. This standard should be considered when implementing a safety management system within the meaning of paragraph 1.4 of the International Safety Management (ISM) Code. Non-mandatory.	D03h.1
Code of Safety for Diving Systems -	Aims to minimise risks to ships and floating structures equipped with diving systems and their divers and personnel, and to facilitate international movement of these ships and floating structures in the context of diving operations. Recommends design criteria and construction, equipment and survey standards for diving systems. Adopted by resolution A.536(13). Amended by resolution A.831(19)). Non-mandatory.	D03h.6
Code of Safety for Dynamically Supported Craft *DSC Code*	Adopted by resolution A.373(X)). Concerns dynamically supported craft primarily engaged in high-speed, high-passenger-density operations. Provides minimum safety requirements for craft carrying up to 450 passengers and operating within 100 nautical miles from a place of refuge.	D03i.4 D04f.3b
Code of Safety for Special Purpose Ships *SPS Code*	Recommends design criteria, construction standards and other safety measures for special purpose ships (such as research ships and polar supply ships which carry "special personnel"). Adopted by resolution A.534(13)). Non-mandatory.	D03j.1
International Code for Application of Fire Test Procedures *FTP Code*	Contains technical requirements of revised SOLAS chapter II-2 for fire test procedures. Intended to be used by Administrations and competent authorities of flag States when approving products for installation in ships in accordance with requirements of SOLAS and by testing laboratories when testing and evaluating products under the Code. Mandatory from 1 July 2002 under revised SOLAS chapter II-2.	A03c.1a
International Code for Fire Safety Systems *FSS Code*	Contains detailed technical requirements of revised SOLAS chapter II-2. Mandatory from 1 July 2002.	A03c.1a
International Code for the Construction and Equipment of Ships Carrying Dangerous Chemicals in Bulk *IBC Code*	Adopted by resolution MSC.4(48). Provides an international standard for the safe carriage by sea of dangerous and noxious liquid chemicals in bulk in chemical tankers built after 1 July 1986. Prescribes design and construction standards of chemical tankers and the equipment they should carry, with due regard to the nature of the products involved. Mandatory under SOLAS chapter VII.	D03e.1b

International Code for the Construction and Equipment of Ships Carrying Liquefied Gases in Bulk *IGC Code*	Adopted by resolution MSC.5(48). Applies to ships built after 1 July 1986. Provides an international standard for safe carriage by sea of liquefied gases (and other substances listed in the Code) in bulk. Prescribes design and constructional standards of gas carriers and equipment they should carry. 1993 edition incorporates amendments adopted by resolution MSC.30(61). Mandatory under SOLAS chapter VII.	D03d.1c
International Code for the Safe Carriage of Grain in Bulk *International Grain Code*	Adopted by resolution MSC.23(59). Contains detailed regulations on carriage of grain in bulk, leaving more general requirements in SOLAS chapter VI. Mandatory under SOLAS chapter VI.	F07g.1b F07g.2
International Code for the Safe Carriage of Packaged Irradiated Nuclear Fuel, Plutonium and High-Level Radioactive Wastes in Flasks on board Ships *INF Code*	Applies to ships carrying packaged irradiated nuclear fuel, plutonium and high-level radioactive wastes in flasks, e.g. for reprocessing. Adopted May 1999 by resolution MSC.88(71). Mandatory from 1 January 2001 under SOLAS regulation VII/13.	F07h
International Code of Safety for High-Speed Craft, 1994 and 2000 *HSC Codes*	1994 HSC Code developed following a revision of the Code of Safety for Dynamically Supported Craft (DSC Code) and in recognition of growth in size and types of high-speed craft. Adopted May 1994 by resolution MSC.36(63); mandatory under SOLAS chapter X. 2000 HSC Code adopted by resolution MSC.97(73) and in force 1 July 2002 for new craft.	D03i.1
International Code of Signals -	Intended for communications between ships, aircraft and authorities ashore during situations related essentially to the safety of navigation and persons; especially useful when language difficulties arise. Suitable for transmission by all means of communication. Mandatory under SOLAS chapter V.	D04o
International Life-Saving Appliance Code *LSA Code*	Provides international standards for personal life-saving appliances, visual signals, survival craft, rescue boats, launching and embarkation appliances, line-throwing appliances and general alarms and public address systems. Adopted June 1996. Mandatory under amendments to SOLAS chapter III.	D04k.4
International Maritime Dangerous Goods Code *IMDG Code*	Amplifies requirements of part A of chapter VII of SOLAS 74 relating to dangerous goods, and of Annex III of MARPOL 73/78 relating to marine pollutants. Standard guide to all aspects of handling dangerous goods and marine pollutants in sea transport. Lays down basic principles; detailed recommendations for individual substances, materials and articles; and a number of recommendations for good operational practice including advice on terminology, packing, labelling, stowage, segregation and handling, and emergency response action. 2000 edition, incorporating Amendment 30-00, is in two A4 paperback volumes. Supplement contains several related texts including a revised Medical First Aid Guide and mandatory INF Code. Originally recommended to Governments for adoption or for use as basis for national regulations to give effect to SOLAS 1974 and MARPOL 73/78. Becoming mostly mandatory under SOLAS amendments with effect from 1 January 2004.	F07f.3
International Safety Management Code *ISM Code*	Introduced under new SOLAS chapter IX in 1994 SOLAS amendments, effective 1 July 1998, to address poor management standards in shipping. Current form, adopted in 1993 as resolution A.741(18), evolved through development of Guidelines on management for the safe operation of ships and for pollution prevention, adopted 1989 as resolution A.647(16), and revised Guidelines, adopted as resolution A.680(17). Mandatory under SOLAS chapter IX. 2002 edition in force 1 July 2002.	C04b D03a.1
International Ship and Port Facility Security Code *ISPS Code*	Contains detailed security-related requirements for governments, port authorities and shipping companies in a mandatory section (Part A), together with guidelines on how to meet these requirements in a non-mandatory section (Part B). Essentially requires security to be treated as a risk management problem. Requirements for ships include Ship Security Plans, Ship Security Officers, Company Security Officers, and certain on-board equipment. Applies to all passenger ships and cargo ships of 500gt or over, including high-speed craft, MODUs and port facilities serving such ships engaged on international voyages. Adopted December 2002 under new SOLAS chapter XI-2 (Special measures to enhance maritime security). In force 1 July 2004.	C03c.8 D03a.6 D04t.10 D05b.9 E02d.9 E03d.10 E04h.7 H04e.2 I01k

A03d IMO ACTION DATES

* The following list outlines the chief amendments to IMO instruments coming into effect during the next 4 years.

Date	Action
27 Sep 2003	Entry into force of **MARPOL Annex IV**, dealing with ship sewage (see D04g.8).
1 Nov 2003	Entry into force of October 2000 amendments to **CLC and Fund Conventions** (see G04d.2), raising by 50% the limits of compensation payable to victims of pollution by oil from oil tankers.
29 Nov 2003	Entry into force of **November 2001 amendments to Colregs**, including: new rules relating to wing-in-ground (WIG) craft; amendments to rules relating to positioning and technical details of lights and shapes (Annex I): vertical separation of high-speed craft masthead lights; technical details of sound signal appliances (Annex III); and whistles and bell or gong for small vessels.
1 Jan 2004	Entry into force of **May 2002 Amendments to SOLAS chapter VII** (Carriage of Dangerous Goods) make the **IMDG Code** mandatory, but the provisions of certain parts of the Code remain recommendatory (see F07f.3).
1 Jul 2004	Entry into force of **SOLAS chapter XI-2** and **International Ship and Port Facility Security Code** (ISPS Code) (see D03a.6).

| 1 Jul 2004 | Entry into force of **December 2002 Amendments to SOLAS**, including amendments to Chapter XII (Additional Safety Measures for Bulk Carriers), chapter II-1 (Construction - structure, subdivision and stability, machinery and electrical installations), chapter II-2 (Fire protection, fire detection and fire extinction), chapter III (Life-saving appliances and arrangements). INF Code also amended to reflect SOLAS Amendments. |
| Date unknown | **MARPOL Annex VI**, dealing with air pollution from ships, was adopted in a Protocol in September 1997 and will enter into force 12 months after the date on which not less than 15 States with combined merchant tonnage totalling 50% of world gross tonnage, have become parties to the 1997 Protocol. For an outline of technical details of Annex VI, see H03f.1. |

A03e IMO PUBLICATIONS

* Much useful IMO literature can viewed online at www.imo.org/index.htm including:
  * a magazine, **IMO News**, which contains a great deal of information on the development and amendment of IMO instruments, and is published three or four times a year online (as well as on paper);
  * a complete **Index of Resolutions**;
  * **IMO Circulars**;
  * IMO Press **Briefings**;
  * IMO **Current Awareness Bulletin**;
  * **papers and articles** by IMO staff;
  * Answers to **Frequently Asked Questions**; and
  * **Focus on IMO**.
* **Focus on IMO** is a series of background papers, each covering covering an individual aspect of IMO's work. New papers are added from time to time and each paper is revised periodically to keep up to date with developments. All papers are available in English and the majority have been translated into French and Spanish. The series currently consists of the following titles:

Title	Latest edition
Alien invaders – putting a stop to the ballast water hitch-hikers	Oct 98
Anti-fouling systems	Apr 99
A summary of IMO Conventions	Apr 2001
Basic facts about IMO	Mar 2000
Cutting red tape: IMO and the facilitation of maritime travel and transport	Dec 96
Dumping at sea	Jul 97
IMO 1948-1998: a process of change	Sep 98
IMO and dangerous goods at sea	May 96
IMO and ro-ro safety	Jan 97
IMO and the safety of bulk carriers	Sep 99
IMO and the safety of navigation	Jan 98
Liability and compensation	Jun 98
MARPOL 73/78	Oct 97
MARPOL – 25 years	Oct 98
Piracy and armed robbery at sea	Jan 2000
Preventing marine pollution - the environmental threat	Mar 98
Shipping Emergencies – Search and Rescue and the GMDSS	Mar 99
SOLAS: the International Convention for the Safety of Life at Sea, 1974	Oct 98
Surviving disaster – life saving at sea	Jan 2000
Tanker safety: the work of the International Maritime Organization	Mar 96
The new STCW Convention	Apr 97

* IMO publishes (for sale) numerous texts of conventions, codes, regulations, recommendations, guidelines, etc., each translated from the original English version into French and Spanish, and an increasing number also into Arabic, Chinese and Russian. Some publications are available on CD-ROM. About 250 titles are available in English, all listed in the IMO Publications catalogue, available at the address below. The **catalogue** is available online at www.imo.org/index.htm
* IMO maintains a large library of maritime **Internet links** at www.imo.org/index.htm
* **Address**: International Maritime Organization, 4 Albert Embankment, London SE1 7SR, England. Tel: 0171 735 7611. Telex: 23588 IMOLDN G Fax (general enquiries): 0171 587 3210. Fax (publications sales): 0171 587 3241. E-mail: publications.sales@imo.org
* **Website**: www.imo.org

A04 International Labour Organization (ILO)

A04a NATURE AND PURPOSES OF ILO

* Like IMO, ILO is a specialised **agency of the United Nations**. Its membership consists of signatory States, of which there are **175.**
* ILO's main purpose is to **raise world labour standards** by building up a **code of international law and practice**. It forms policies and programmes to help **improve working and living conditions**, **enhance employment opportunities** and **promote basic human rights**.
* ILO's labour standards, when adopted, serve as **guidelines** for individual countries to put these policies into action.
* **Website**: www.ilo.org
* **ILO London Office**: www.ilo.org/public/english/region/eurpro/london

A04b ILO PROCEDURES

* The **ILO Conference** convenes **annually**. Each Member State is represented by **two government delegates** plus an **employer delegate** and a **worker delegate**.
* Conference's main job is to examine social problems and adopt **international labour standards** in the form of ILO **conventions** and **recommendations**.

A04c ILO MARITIME CONVENTIONS

* Of over 160 adopted ILO conventions, more than 30 have been maritime conventions, the most important being the **Merchant Shipping (Minimum Standards) Convention, 1976** (No. 147), known as **ILO 147**.
* ILO maritime conventions usually require ratification measured by a certain percentage of world tonnage.
* As with IMO conventions, a great deal of merchant shipping legislation has been enacted by member nations specifically to give effect to ILO Conventions.
* ILO Conventions adopted are binding on every member State which ratifies them.
* ILO has **no enforcement powers** of its own, but provisions are contained in ILO 147 to allow for **port State control** measures (see A05).
* Texts of ILO Conventions and Recommendations, and comments of the Supervisory Bodies ("ILOLEX") can be accessed at the ILO website (www.ilo.org) by clicking on "International Labour Standards".

A04c.1 ILO Convention No. 147

- is commonly known as the **Minimum Standards Convention**.
- is one of a number of important conventions (the others being IMO Conventions) compliance with which is checked in Port State Control inspections of ships under existing MOUs (see A05 and I02c).
- aims at ensuring observance of a wide range of standards including those laid down in many other Conventions. E.g., the UK's Merchant Shipping (Means of Access) Regulations, Merchant Shipping (Safe Movement On Board Ship) Regulations, and various other "health and safety" regulations were introduced to give effect to parts of Convention 147, since this requires provisions to be made more or less equivalent to those in the Prevention of Accidents (Seafarers) Convention 1970 (Convention No. 134) and several other ILO Conventions. Entry into force of the UK safety regulations meant that Convention No. 134 could then be ratified by the UK Parliament.
- applies to every sea-going merchant ship, whether publicly or privately owned, engaged in the transport of cargo or passengers for trade or for any other commercial purpose (Article 1).
- does not apply to sailing or auxiliary sailing vessels, fishing vessels, or to small vessels and vessels such as oil rigs and drilling platforms when not engaged in navigation.
- requires ratifying States to have regulations laying down for ships registered in their territory:
  * safety standards, including standards of competency, hours of work and manning;
  * appropriate social security measures;
  * shipboard conditions of employment and living arrangements where these are not already provided for by collective agreements or courts;

- requires ratifying States to agree:
    - to exercise effective control over its ships in respect of the above matters;
    - to ensure that measures for the effective control of other shipboard conditions of employment and living arrangements, where the State has no effective jurisdiction, are agreed;
    - to ensure that adequate procedures exist for the engagement of seafarers on its ships and for investigation of
    - complaints in this connection and that adequate procedures exist for the investigation of complaints about engagement of its own seafarers on foreign ships, or foreign seafarers on foreign ships in its territory;
    - to ensure that seafarers employed on its own flag ships are properly qualified or trained;
    - to verify by inspection, etc. that its flag ships comply with applicable international labour Conventions which it has ratified;
    - to hold an official inquiry into any serious marine casualty involving its flag ships, particularly those involving injury and/or loss of life, the final report of the inquiry normally to be made public (Article 2).
- requires ratifying States to advise their nationals of the possible problems of signing on a ship of a non-ratifying State, if non-equivalent standards apply on it (Article 3).
- allows ratifying States to report complaints or evidence received that ships calling in its ports do not conform to Convention standards, the report to go to the ship's flag Administration with a copy to the ILO, and may take steps to rectify any conditions onboard which are hazardous to health or safety (Article 4). (In taking these measures, the port State must notify the flag State, and must not unreasonably detain or delay the ship.) ("Complaint", in this connection, means information from a crew member, a professional body, a trade union or any person with an interest in the safety of the ship, including the health and safety of the crew.)
- is open to ratification by ILO Members which are parties to SOLAS, the Load Line Convention 1966 and Colreg 1972 (Article 5).
- has as an Annex Convention No. 180 (see A04c.2).

A04c.2 Other ILO maritime conventions

* **No 7 - the 1920 Minimum Age (Sea) Convention** provides that children under the age of 14 shall not be employed on vessels (except where members of the same family are employed and except on approved schoolships or training ships, and that every shipmaster shall keep a register of all persons under the age of 16 employed on his vessel.

* **No 9 - the 1920 Placing of Seamen Convention** provides for the abolition of systems of finding employment for seamen as a commercial enterprise conducted for pecuniary gain and for their replacement by public employment offices finding employment for seamen free of charge, and also for freedom of choice of ship to be assured to seamen and freedom of choice of crew to shipowners.

* **No 22 - the 1926 Seamen's Articles of Agreement Convention** lays down exact procedures for drawing up articles of agreement between shipowners and seamen, as well as their scope, in terms of the applicable national laws.

* **No 23 - the 1926 Repatriation of Seamen Convention** defines a seaman's right to repatriation after being landed during the period of his engagement or after its expiry.

* **No 53 - the 1936 Certificates of Competency Convention** lays down the minimum conditions for the granting of certificates of competency to masters and officers on board merchant ships.

* **No 55 - the 1936 Shipowners' Liability (Sick and Injured Seamen) Convention** defines shipowners' liability in the event of injury, sickness and resultant death of persons employed on board a vessel (within the scope of national laws and regulations).

* **No. 56 - the 1936 Sickness Insurance (Sea) Convention** provides compulsory sickness insurance for all persons employed in the service of the ship and lays down the details and scope of such insurance.

* **No. 58 - the Minimum Age (Sea) Convention** revises Convention No. 7 of 1920 by fixing the minimum age of children for employment on vessels at 15 years (instead of 14), except when only members of the same family are employed or where children work on approved school- or training ships. However, children of not less than 14 years of age may be employed if it is officially certified that such employment will benefit them.

* **No. 68 - the 1946 Food and Catering (Ships' Crews) Convention** provides that States party to the Convention are obliged to promote a proper standard of food supply and services for crews on sea-going vessels under the supervision of a competent authority whose inspectors have wide-ranging powers and which has to submit an annual report to the ILO.

* **No. 69 - the 1946 Certification of Ships' Cooks Convention** provides that a certificate of qualification must be held by any person engaged as a ship's cook.

* **No. 71 - the 1946 Seafarers' Pensions Convention** provides for the establishment of a pensions scheme for retiring seafarers.

* **No. 73 - the 1946 Medical Examination (Seafarers) Convention** requires each would-be crew member to produce a medical certificate affirming his fitness for the work for which he wishes to be engaged, such certificates normally remaining in force for two years.

* **No. 74 - the 1946 Certification of Able Seamen Convention** provides that no person shall be employed as an able seaman unless deemed competent under national law and regulations and in possession of a certificate of qualification as an able seaman attesting to his previous period of service (normally of 3 years) and the passing of an examination.
* **No. 91 - the 1949 Paid Vacations (Seafarers) Convention** lays down periods of paid vacations for each year of service (18 days for masters, officers and radio operators and 12 days for other crew members) subject to specified conditions and laws, regulations and/or collective agreements.
* **No. 92 - the 1949 Accommodation of Crews Convention (Revised)** lays down detailed accommodation requirements with regard to the safety of the crew.
* **No. 108 - the 1958 Seafarers' Identity Documents Convention** requires convention States to issue an identity document to each seafarer, but when such a document is issued to a foreigner it shall not constitute proof of his nationality.
* **No. 133 - the 1970 Accommodation of Crews (Supplementary Provisions) Convention** expands the provisions of Convention No 92.
* **No. 134 - the 1970 Prevention of Accidents (Seafarers) Convention** requires all occupational accidents to be adequately reported and investigated, with statistics of such accidents to be kept, and provisions to be made for the prevention of accidents.
* **No. 146 - the 1976 Seafarers' Annual Leave with Pay Convention** provides that seafarers shall be entitled to annual leave with pay of specific minimum length (of not less than 30 calendar days for one year's service). It revises Convention No. 91).
* **No. 163 - the 1987 Seafarers' Welfare at Sea and in Port Convention** lays down provisions for welfare facilities and services for seafarers both at sea and in port.
* **No. 164 - the 1987 Health Protection and Medical Care (Seafarers) Convention** provides for standards on board ship for the protection of the health of seafarers.
* **No. 165 - the 1987 Social Security for Seafarers (Revised) Convention** revises the 1946 Convention by providing that seafarers should have social security protection not less favourable than that enjoyed by shore workers in respect of each of the branches of social security.
* **No. 166 - the 1987 Repatriation of Seafarers (Revised) Convention** revises the 1926 Convention and brings up to date the seafarer's entitlement to repatriation.
* **No. 178 – the Labour Inspection (Seafarers) Convention, 1996.**
* No. 179 – the Recruitment and Placement of Seafarers Convention, 1996.
* **No. 180 – Seafarers' Hours of Work and Manning of Ships Convention, 1996** lays down maximum hours of work and minimum hours of rest, and requires sufficient and efficient manning of vessels. Requirements of the convention may be checked for compliance during Port State Control inspections. Working time is restricted to a maximum of 14 hours in any 24-hour period, and to 72 hours in any 7-day period. There must be a minimum of 10 hours of rest in any 24-hour period, or 77 hours in any 7-day period. Records must be kept of hours worked. This accords with the European Agreement on the Organisation of Working Time of Seafarers (see E03c.2).

A04c.3 Non-maritime ILO conventions affecting seafarers

* Seafarers are also covered by non-maritime general ILO conventions. The two most important - which are also the most commonly violated - cover general collective and trade union rights.
* **No. 87 - the 1948 Freedom of Association and Protection of the Right to Organise Convention** concerns the rights of workers to form and join their own organisations free from administrative or outside control. Governments which refuse to allow their citizens to join the unions of their choice violate this Convention. It is also illegal to prevent unions from affiliating to international federations (such as the ITF). It is a breach of this Convention, for example, for seafarers to be prohibited from contacting the ITF or ITF unions.
* **No. 98 - the 1949 Right to Organise and Collective Bargaining Convention** guarantees freedom for workers from anti-union discrimination, such as being sacked or blacklisted for union membership. It prohibits employers from making non-union membership a condition of employment. It requires national Administrations to protect the "right to organise" in national law and specifically opposes State interference in union organisation.
* **No. 111 - the 1958 Discrimination (Employment and Occupation) Convention** commits governments to ensuring "equality of opportunity and treatment in respect of employment...with a view to eliminating any discrimination". Discrimination includes any "distinction, exclusion or preference made on the basis of sex, religion, political opinion, national extraction or social origin". Paying different rates of pay to different people who do the same job because of their race or sex is a violation of this Convention.
* **No. 138 – the Minimum Age Convention, 1973.**

A05 Enforcement of IMO and ILO conventions

A05a CONVENTION PROVISIONS CONCERNING ENFORCEMENT

* Neither IMO nor ILO have enforcement powers of their own, other than limited powers under the revised STCW Convention (STCW 95). Contracting Governments enforce the provisions of IMO and ILO conventions in respect of their own ships and set penalties for offences. They may have limited powers of **port State control** in respect of ships flying the flags of other States when these ships are in ports and waters under their jurisdiction (see I02c). Enforcement thus depends on Governments of Member States, i.e. **flag States** and **port States**.
* **Port State control** provisions are contained in several of the main conventions. For example, **SOLAS regulation I/19** provides that:
    * every ship in a port of another SOLAS country is subject to control by authorised officers of the port State for the purpose of verifying that SOLAS certificates carried are valid (regulation 19(a));
    * certificates, if valid, will be accepted unless there are clear grounds for believing that the condition of the ship or its equipment does not correspond substantially with the particulars on any of the certificates or that the ship and its equipment do not comply with SOLAS (regulation 19(b));
    * where a certificate has expired or ceased to be valid, the port State control officer will detain the ship until it can proceed to sea or to a repair port without danger to the persons on board (regulation 19(c));
    * in event of detention, the flag State's consul, IMO, and surveyors of the organisations issuing the certificates will be informed (regulation 19(d));
    * where the port State is unable to take action, or where it allows a ship to proceed despite defects or deficiencies, it will notify the authorities at the next port of call (regulation 19(e));
    * when exercising control, all possible efforts will be made to avoid a ship being unduly detained or delayed (regulation 19(f)).
* **MARPOL 73/78, ILO 147 and several other conventions** contain similar port State control provisions to those in SOLAS chapter I.
* **Offences** discovered during port State control inspections may result in **detention** by the port State, if it is a Contracting Party to the convention being breached.
* When an **offence occurs within the jurisdiction of another State**, that State can either instigate proceedings in accordance with its own laws or give details of the offence to the flag State so that it can take action.
* **Offences committed in international waters** may be reported to the flag State.
* Under the terms of the **Intervention Convention 1969**, Contracting States are empowered to act against **ships of other countries** which have been involved in an **accident or have been damaged on the high seas** if there is a **grave risk of oil pollution** occurring. These powers are exercised in the UK under section 137 of Merchant Shipping Act 1995 (see H03i).

A05b REGIONAL PORT STATE CONTROL AGREEMENTS

* For notes on the various **regional port State control agreements** in force or under development see I02c.2.

A06 Other treaty provisions affecting shipping

A06a INTERNATIONAL HEALTH REGULATIONS

* The **World Health Organization (WHO)** is a specialised agency of the United Nations, based in Geneva, Switzerland. It collaborates with Member Governments, UN agencies and other bodies to develop health standards, control communicable diseases and promote all aspects of family and environmental health.
* The member States of WHO made and adopted the **International Health Regulations (1969)**, which are a revised and consolidated version of the old International Sanitary Regulations. The Regulations have been amended at various subsequent World Health Assemblies.
* The current **International Health Regulations (IHRs)** have been in force since 1971, replacing the International Sanitary Regulations, which were adopted by the World Health Assembly in 1951. They were first introduced to

help monitor and control four serious diseases that had significant potential to spread between countries. The goals of the IHRs are to:

- detect, reduce or eliminate sources from which infection spreads;
- improve sanitation in and around ports and airports; and
- prevent dissemination of vectors.

* The IHRs require mandatory declaration of **cholera**, **plague** and **yellow fever**. (**Smallpox** was removed in 1981.) They do not cover several diseases of international importance including ebola and other haemorrhagic fevers. The IHRs are therefore currently (as at November 2001) being revised to make them more appropriate to control infectious diseases of international importance at the start of the 21st century.

* **Article 81 of the IHRs** provides that "no health document, other than those provided for in these Regulations, shall be required in international traffic".

* Separate **vaccination certificates** were once required for smallpox, cholera and yellow fever. WHO's publication *International Travel and Health*, published in 1995, states that the eradication of smallpox was confirmed by WHO "more than 10 years ago" and that smallpox vaccination is no longer indicated, and may be dangerous to those who are vaccinated and those in close contact with them. It also states that vaccination against cholera cannot prevent the introduction of the infection into a country and the WHO therefore amended the International Health Regulations in 1973 so that cholera vaccination should no longer be required of any traveller.

* A **certificate of vaccination against yellow fever** is the only certificate that should now be required, if any, for international travel. Most European countries have **no vaccination requirements** for international travellers, while most Asian and African countries require a **yellow fever vaccination**.

* Provisions of the IHRs also cover **seafarers' vaccinations**. (See E04b for notes on seafarers' health and medical documents.)

* **Article 54 of the IHRs** requires every ship to be either -
- **permanently kept** in such a condition that it is **free of rodents and the plague vector**; or
- **periodically deratted**.

* For notes on **Deratting and Deratting Exemption Certificates** see D04q and I01e.1g. For notes on **deratting**, see I01e.1i.

* **WHO website**: www.who.int/home-page

* **IHRs website**: http://policy.who.int/cgi-bin/om_isapi.dll?infobase=Ihreg&softpage=Browse_Frame_Pg42

A06b INTERNATIONAL TELECOMMUNICATION REGULATIONS

* The **International Telecommunications Union (ITU)** is a specialised agency of the UN, based in Geneva, Switzerland. It promotes international co-operation and sets **standards and regulations** for telecommunications operations of all kinds. It allocates the radio frequency spectrum, registers radio frequency assignments so as to avoid harmful interference between radio stations in different countries, makes international agreements on radiocommunication matters (including marine radiocommunications) and publishes **books and documents used by ships' radio operators** (see D04m.3), including:
- ITU Manual for use by the Maritime Mobile and Maritime Mobile-Satellite Services 1992;
- ITU List of Coast Stations;
- ITU List of Ship Stations;
- ITU List of Radiodetermination and Special Services; and
- ITU List of Callsigns and Numerical Table of Identities of Stations used by the Maritime Mobile and Maritime Mobile-Satellite Services.

* **ITU website**: www.itu.int/home/index.html

* The part of the ITU website of most professional interest to mariners is the Maritime mobile Access & Retrieval System (MARS) section at www.itu.int/cgi-bin/htsh/mars/mars_index.sh,

* The **Maritime mobile Access & Retrieval System** (MARS) is a database retrieval system, developed by the ITU, which allows the maritime community to consult the current contents of the master **ITU Ship station database**. This contains **ship station particulars** as specified by the Radio Regulations and provided in Part III of the List of ship stations, as well as the following:
- **Particulars of Administrations and Geographical Areas** that have data in the ITU Ship Station database, including addresses, call sign series, maritime identification digits (MIDs), the telegraph transmission code allocated to the Administration and the accounting authorities, by AAICs code.
- **Accounting Authorities particulars** including the complete available address of the Accounting Authority.

* In addition the site contains the following allocation tables in accordance with the Radio Regulations:
- Table of International Call Sign Series (Appendix S42 to the Radio Regulations);

- Table of Maritime Identification Digits (MIDs);
- Table of coast station identification numbers;
- Table of ship station selective call numbers;
- Table of selective call numbers for predetermined groups of ship stations; and
- Summary of allocations.

Section B

THE FLAG STATE

B01 Ship's flag
B01a UNCLOS provisions relating to ship's flag and nationality
B01b Types of ship register

B02 Flag States
B02a UNCLOS provisions relating to duties of flag States
B02b UNCLOS provisions relating to enforcement by flag States
B02c Flag State Administrations
B02d Overseas representation of flag State Administrations

B03 English law
B03a Classes of law concerning shipmasters
B03b UK courts, legal proceedings and penalties
B03c Law of contract
B03d Agency
B03e Law of torts
B03f Law of carriage by sea
B03g Liens
B03h Arrest of ships
B03i Arbitration and mediation

B04 Merchant shipping legislation
B04a Types of UK legislation
B04b Legislation in force
B04c Chief shipping-related Acts of Parliament of concern to shipmasters
B04d EC Directives

B05 Department for Transport (DfT) and its agencies
B05a Department for Transport (DfT)
B05b Maritime and Coastguard Agency (MCA)
B05c Registry of Shipping and Seamen (RSS)
B05d Marine Accident Investigation Branch (MAIB)
B05e Health and Safety Commission (HSC) and Health and Safety Executive (HSE)
B05f Sharing of responsibilities between HSE, MCA and MAIB

B06 Radiocommunications Agency and associated organisations
B06a Functions of Radiocommunications Agency
B06b Organisations associated with Radiocommunications Agency

B01 Ship's flag

B01a UNCLOS PROVISIONS RELATING TO SHIPS' FLAG AND NATIONALITY

* Every State, whether coastal or land-locked, has the **right** to have **ships flying its flag on the high seas** (Article 90).
* Every State must fix the conditions for the **grant of its nationality** to ships, for the **registration of ships** in its territory, and for the **right to fly its flag** (Article 91).
* Ships have the **nationality** of the State whose flag they are entitled to fly (Article 91).
* There must be a **genuine link** between the State and the ship (Article 91).
* Every State must issue to ships to which it has granted the right to fly its flag **documents** to that effect (Article 91).
* Ships must sail under the flag of **one State** only and, save in exceptional cases expressly provided for in international treaties and UNCLOS, must be subject to its **exclusive jurisdiction** on the high seas (Article 92).
* A ship may **not change its flag** during a voyage or while in a port of call, save in the case of a **real transfer of ownership** or **change of registry** (Article 92).
* A ship which sails under the flags of two or more States, using them according to convenience, **may not claim any of the nationalities** in question with respect to any other State, and may be regarded as similar to a **ship without nationality** (Article 92).

B01b TYPES OF SHIP REGISTER

B01b.1 National registers

- are registers where there is a **genuine link** between the vessel's flag State and the owner or operator (as required by UNCLOS).
- are known also as "**closed registers**" and "**first registers**".
- include the first registers of most of the "traditional" shipowning nations including the UK, Norway, France, Denmark, Germany and many others.

B01b.2 Flags of convenience (FOCs)

- are also known (by shipowners) as "flags of necessity", "open registers" and "free flags".
- are deemed by the International Transport Workers' Federation (ITF) (see C05) to exist where **beneficial ownership and control** of the vessel is found to lie elsewhere than in the country of the flag the vessel is flying[1].
- are designated by the **ITF Fair Practices Committee**, which decides which flags are FOCs and which are not. This committee maintains a list of countries offering FOC facilities and from time to time adds countries to or deletes them from the list. The criteria for entry in the list are the "Rochdale Criteria", which were laid down by a British Committee of Inquiry into Shipping in 1970. The criteria include:
  * whether the country allows non-citizens to own and control vessels;
  * whether access to and transfer from the registry is easy;
  * whether taxes on shipping income are low or non-existent;
  * whether the country of registration does not need the shipping tonnage for its own purposes but is keen to earn the tonnage fees;
  * whether manning by non-nationals is freely permitted;
  * whether the country lacks the power (or the willingness) to impose national or international regulations on the shipowners using its flag.
* In defining an FOC register, the ITF takes as the most important factor whether the nationality of the shipowner is the same as the nationality of the flag.
* FOC ships are **beneficially owned** mainly in the USA, Greece, Hong Kong, and Western European States.
* The list of **ITF-designated FOCs** can be viewed at www.itf.org.uk/seafarers/foc/foc.htm In April 2002 it included the following 30 flags: **Antigua and Barbuda**, **Aruba** (Netherlands), **Bahamas**, **Barbados**, **Belize**, **Bermuda**

---

[1] UNCLOS Article 91 provides that there must be a **genuine link** between the ship and the State whose flag the ship is entitled to fly, but fails to say what this means in practice.

(UK), **Bolivia, Burma/Myanmar, Cambodia, Canary Islands** (Spain), **Cayman Islands** (UK), **Cook Islands** (New Zealand), **Cyprus, Equatorial Guinea, German International Ship Register** (GIS), **Gibraltar** (UK), **Honduras, Lebanon, Liberia, Luxembourg, Malta, Marshall Islands** (USA), **Mauritius, Netherlands Antilles, Panama, São Tomé and Príncipe, Sri Lanka, St Vincent, Tuvalu and Vanuatu.**

* Ships registered in the above countries which can demonstrate that they are **genuinely owned** in that country are not treated as FOCs. Equally, ships from countries not on the list will be treated as FOCs if the ITF receives information that they are beneficially owned in another country.
* In deciding whether a particular ship is operating under a FOC, the ITF will **additionally consider on an individual basis** ships flying the flags of Hong Kong, Philippines (foreign-owned ships bareboat-chartered to the Philippines), and Singapore (foreign-owned ships without approved crew agreements). 18 ships flying the Kerguelen flag were declared in 2001 to be flying a flag of convenience.

B01b.3 Second registers

- are also known as **offshore registers** and **international ship registers**.
- are in some cases established under **separate legislation** as a second register in the "parent" State, e.g. the Norwegian International Shipregister (NIS), which is established in Norway to run alongside the Norwegian "first" register.
- are in other cases established in an **offshore territory** with legal links to the "parent" State, e.g. Kerguelen (linked to France), Isle of Man (linked to the UK); these registers may be termed **offshore registers**.
- first appeared in June 1987 with the establishment of NIS, immediate success of which prompted other countries to follow its example.
- are different from FOCs in that, while manning, taxation and other laws may be relaxed under the second register, shipowners must still have a **genuine link** with the flag State.
- have their **status** determined by the ITF (see C05), which considers whether ownership is genuinely from the flag "parent" State and whether there are agreements acceptable to that country's trades unions.
- include the following **registers**: **Danish International Ship Register** (DIS) (Denmark), **Isle of Man** (UK), **Kerguelen** (France), **Madeira** (Portugal) and **Norwegian International Ship Register** (NIS) (Norway).

B01b.4 Bareboat charter registers

* Several States, including the UK, have relaxed their ship registration legislation to allow for the bareboat chartering of ships into or out of the national flag. For the duration of the bareboat charter, but usually subject to a specified maximum term, the vessel is entered on the register of the bareboat charterer's State (the "**bareboat charter registry**") and flies that State's flag, whilst **retaining her primary registration**. On the termination of the bareboat charter, the bareboat charter registry is cancelled and the vessel **reverts to her primary registry**[2].
* BIMCO has warned owners[3] that **serious consequences** may be faced by vessels sailing under more than one registry. Both international treaties (e.g. UNCLOS) and customary international law require that ships sail under the flag of **only one State**. (For UNCLOS Article 92 provisions see B01a.) A ship which sails under the flags of two or more States may not claim any of the nationalities in question with respect to any other State and may be treated as **a ship without nationality**. Consequently, in the course of enforcement of UN sanctions by multi-national naval fleets, any merchant ship which misrepresents its flag or registry to the Maritime Interception Forces will be treated as a **stateless vessel** and will be subject to the jurisdiction of the Maritime Interception Operation vessel's flag State.
* Ships on bareboat charter registers are sometimes known as "**dual register ships**".

B02 Flag States

B02a DUTIES OF FLAG STATES

* **UNCLOS Article 94** requires the flag State to effectively exercise its jurisdiction and control in administrative, technical and social matters over ships flying its flag (i.e. to exercise "**flag State control**" over its ships), and to:
  - maintain a register of ships;

---

[2] For notes on bareboat charter registry under UK law, see D01f.
[3] BIMCO Bulletin, February 1995.

- assume jurisdiction under its internal law over each ship flying its flag and its master, officers and crew in respect of administrative, technical and social matters concerning the ship; and
- take such measures for ships flying its flag as are necessary to ensure safety at sea with regard, *inter alia*, to:
  * the construction, equipment and seaworthiness of ships;
  * the manning of ships, labour conditions and the training of crews, taking into account the applicable international agreements (e.g. STCW and ILO conventions);
  * the use of signals, the maintenance of communications and the prevention of collisions.

* The above measures must include those necessary to ensure the following:
  * that the ship is surveyed by a qualified surveyor of ships and has on board such charts, nautical publications and navigational equipment and instruments as are appropriate for the navigation of the ship;
  * that the ship is in the charge of a master and officers who possess appropriate qualifications, in particular in seamanship, navigation, communications and marine engineering, and that the crew is appropriate in qualifications and numbers for the type, size, machinery and equipment of the ship;
  * that the master, officers and, to the extent appropriate, the crew are fully conversant with and required to observe the applicable international regulations concerning the safety of life at sea, the prevention of collisions, the prevention, reduction and control of marine pollution, and the maintenance of communications by radio.

* In taking the above measures, the State is required to conform to generally accepted international regulations, procedures and practices and to take any steps which may be necessary to secure their observance.

* A State which has clear grounds to believe that proper jurisdiction and control with respect to a ship have not been exercised may report the facts to the flag State. Upon receiving such a report, the flag State must investigate the matter and, if appropriate, take any action necessary to remedy the situation.

* Each State must cause an inquiry to be held by or before a suitably qualified person or persons into every marine casualty or incident of navigation on the high seas involving a ship flying its flag and causing loss of life or serious injury to nationals of another State or serious damage to ships or installations of another State or to the marine environment. The flag State and the other State must co-operate in the conduct of the inquiry.

* **IMO resolution A.912(22)** on Self-Assessment of Flag State performance provides (in Annex 1 paragraph 4) that a **flag State should**:
  * take measures to ensure safety at sea and pollution prevention for ships entitled to fly its flag with regard to:
    ▪ the construction, equipment and management of ships;
    ▪ the principles and rules with respect to the limits to which ships may be loaded;
    ▪ the prevention, reduction and control of pollution of the marine environment and the minimisation of the impact of accidental discharges of pollutants;
    ▪ the manning of ships and the training of crews; and
    ▪ the safety of navigation (including taking part in mandatory reporting and routeing systems), maintenance of communications and prevention of collisions;
  * promulgate laws which permit effective jurisdiction and control in administrative, technical and social matters over ships flying its flag and, in particular, relating to the inspection of ships, safety and pollution-prevention laws applying to such ships and the making of associated regulations; and
  * promulgate laws providing the legal basis for the establishment of a registry and maintain a register of ships flying its flag.

B02b ENFORCEMENT BY FLAG STATES

* **UNCLOS Article 217** makes the following provisions.
  1. States must ensure compliance by vessels flying their flag or of their registry with applicable international rules and standards, established through the competent international organisation or general diplomatic conference, and with their laws and regulations adopted in accordance with UNCLOS for the prevention, reduction and control of pollution of the marine environment from vessels and must accordingly adopt laws and regulations and take other measures necessary for their implementation. Flag States must provide for the effective enforcement of such rules, standards, laws and regulations, irrespective of where a violation occurs.
  2. States must, in particular, take appropriate measures in order to ensure that vessels flying their flag or of their registry are prohibited from sailing, until they can proceed to sea in compliance with the requirements of the international rules and standards referred to above, including requirements in respect of design, construction, equipment and manning of vessels.
  3. States must ensure that vessels flying their flag or of their registry carry on board certificates required by and issued pursuant to international rules and standards referred to above. States must ensure that vessels flying their flag are periodically inspected in order to verify that such certificates are in conformity with the actual condition of the vessels. These certificates must be accepted by other States as evidence of the condition of the

vessels and must be regarded as having the same force as certificates issued by them, unless there are clear grounds for believing that the condition of the vessel does not correspond substantially with the particulars of the certificates.

4. If a vessel commits a violation of rules and standards established through the competent international organisation or general diplomatic conference, the flag State, without prejudice to Articles 218, 220 and 228, must provide for immediate investigation and where appropriate institute proceedings in respect of the alleged violation irrespective of where the violation occurred or where the pollution caused by such violation has occurred or has been spotted.

5. Flag States conducting an investigation of the violation may request the assistance of any other State whose co-operation could be useful in clarifying the circumstances of the case. States must endeavour to meet appropriate requests of other States.

6. States must, at the written request of any State, investigate any violation alleged to have been committed by vessels flying their flag. If satisfied that sufficient evidence is available to enable proceedings to be brought in respect of the alleged violation, flag States must without delay institute such proceedings in accordance with their laws.

7. Flag States must promptly inform the requesting State and the competent international organisation of the action taken and its outcome. Such information must be available to all States.

8. Penalties provided for by the laws and regulations for States for vessels flying their flag must be adequate in severity to discourage violations wherever they occur.

* **IMO resolution A.912(22)** on Self-Assessment of Flag State performance provides (in Annex 1 paragraph 5) that a **flag State should**:
  * provide for the enforcement of its national laws, including the associated investigative and penalty processes;
  * take appropriate action against ships flying its flag that fail to comply with applicable requirements;
  * ensure the availability of sufficient personnel with maritime and technical expertise to carry out its flag State responsibilities, including:
    * the development and enforcement of necessary national laws;
    * the establishment and maintenance of minimum safe manning levels on board ships flying its flag and the provision of effective certification of seafarers;
    * the inspection of ships flying its flag to ensure compliance with the requirements of international instruments to which the flag State is a Party;
    * the reporting of casualties and incidents as required by the respective instruments; and
    * the investigation of circumstances following any detention of ships flying its flag.

B02c FLAG STATE ADMINISTRATIONS

* Most flag States regulate their merchant shipping and enforce international maritime treaty obligations and national laws through the agency of a **marine Administration**. This is usually a national governmental organisation, e.g. US Coast Guard (USCG) in the case of the USA, Department for Transport (DfT) (UK), Australian Maritime Safety Authority (AMSA) (Australia), Norwegian Maritime Directorate (NMD) (Norway).

* Flag of convenience countries sometimes **delegate** their marine administrative duties to a **commercial organisation**, e.g:
  * Liberian International Ship & Corporate Registry (LISCR) operating the **Liberian register** from Viginia, USA;
  * International Registries, Inc. (IRI), operating the **Marshall Islands register** from Renton, Washington DC, USA; and
  * Vanuatu Maritime Services Ltd (VMSL), operating the **Vanuatu register** from New York, USA.

* The **functions of a flag State Administration** are chiefly:
  * to set, monitor and enforce standards of safety and pollution prevention on vessels flying the State's flag;
  * to enforce international standards of safety and pollution prevention on foreign ships visiting the State's ports;
  * to draw up, set and enforce statutory merchant shipping regulations for the flag State;
  * to survey and inspect vessels in accordance with domestic and international regulations;
  * to set and enforce standards of competency amongst seafarers;
  * to investigate accidents involving ships flying the State's flag and ships of other flags when in the State's waters;
  * to approve equipment types for vessels under international regulations;
  * to advise on matters such as the loading of hazardous cargoes and many other safety matters;
  * to maintain a register of ships flying the State's flag.

* Many flag State Administrations will, in addition, take on a responsibility to work for the **raising of standards** internationally and will lead the national delegation at international committees on which the flag State is

represented, e.g. IMO's Maritime Safety Committee (MSC) and Marine Environment Protection Committee (MEPC).

B02c.1 Flag State obligations relating to ship security

* SOLAS regulation XI-2/3.1 provides that flag State Administrations must **set security levels** and ensure the **provision of security level information** to ships entitled to fly their flag. When changes in security level occur, security level information must be **updated** as the circumstance dictates.
* Flag State Administrations have a number of **security-related responsibilities** for ships registered under their flags. These include:
    * **setting security levels** for ships entitled to fly their flag and **notifying** ships of the current security level;
    * providing **guidance** on the development of **Ship Security Plans**;
    * providing **guidance** on **security measures** for ships to implement at each security level;
    * providing **guidance** on the **reporting of attacks** on ships;
    * **approval of Ship Security Plans**;
    * **issuing International Ship Security Certificates** (ISSCs) to ships;
    * **notifying** other governments of **ship security alerts** from ships within their jurisdiction;
    * **specifying** requirements for **Declarations of Security**;
    * agreeing to **temporary measures** to be implemented if **security equipment fails**;
    * deciding whether or not to **delegate approval** of Ship Security Plans, verification of ship security systems, and issue of International Ship Security Certificates to Recognised Security Organisations (RSOs), and overseeing such delegations.
* Flag State Administrations are permitted to delegate some of their responsibilities to **Recognised Security Organisations** (RSOs). A **Recognised Security Organisation** means an organisation with appropriate expertise in security matters and with appropriate knowledge of ship and port operations authorised to carry out an assessment, or a verification, or an approval or a certification activity, required by SOLAS chapter XI-2 or by part A of the ISPS Code (SOLAS regulation XI-2/1.1). In practice, RSOs will normally include those **classification societies** authorised by the flag State Administration to carry out certain surveys and issue ship certificates on its behalf.

B02d OVERSEAS REPRESENTATION OF FLAG STATE ADMINISTRATIONS

B02d.1 Diplomatic missions and officials

* A **diplomatic mission** is the office of a country's diplomatic representatives in another country. Major States generally maintain a diplomatic mission in each foreign State capital with which they have full diplomatic relations. The diplomatic mission of one Commonwealth member country, such as the UK, in another Commonwealth member country is a **High Commission**. In non-Commonwealth countries the diplomatic mission is generally an **Embassy**. High Commissions and Embassies perform the same functions and have the same status.
* The **head of mission** in Commonwealth countries is a **High Commissioner** and in non-Commonwealth member countries is normally an **Ambassador**.
* A **consular mission** is the office of a country's consular representative in another country, either in the capital city or is some other significant place. **Consulates** will generally be maintained by the more prosperous countries in each foreign capital where it is represented and in the more important cities and towns with which the country maintains trade links. Many consulates are therefore located in major ports, while the nearest consulate to a minor port may be in a distant inland town.
* Consular missions are established in accordance with the provisions of the Vienna Convention on Consular Relations, 1963 which provides four different grades of consular representatives (in descending order of importance): **Consul-General**; **Consul**; **Vice-Consul**; and **Consular Agent**. Their offices are called Consulate-General, Consulate, Vice-Consulate and Consular Agency, respectively.[4] In many ports the consulate of a foreign country is a commercial enterprise such as a shipping agency, and may have the status of **Honorary Consulate**.
* **Consular representatives** undertake a more restricted range of duties than diplomatic representatives, their prime duty being to protect the interests of the nationals of their country in the host country. A **consul** is defined in The

---

[4] In some Commonwealth countries, the senior consular missions of other Commonwealth countries are called Deputy High Commissions and the heads of these offices are called Deputy High Commissioners. However, the trend is for such offices to be called Consulate-General, etc.

Shorter Oxford English dictionary as "an agent, commissioned by a sovereign State to reside in a foreign town or port, to protect the interests of its subjects there, and to watch over its commercial rights and privileges".

* Consular representatives may be career officers (i.e. full-time employees of their government) or honorary officers (i.e. officers paid only an honorarium by the country they represent). Career officers are normally nationals of the country they represent and members of that country's diplomatic or consular service. Honorary officers are usually permanent residents of the country in which they work and may be nationals of the country in which they live or of the country that they represent.
* It is important for the master of a ship of any flag when at a foreign port to be able to be able to identify and locate the **nearest consular mission of the flag State**, since he may require consular assistance in a variety of circumstances (see B02d.2 and I01j.1). Port agents maintain lists of local consular missions.
* In some situations (e.g. loss of personal national identity documents, or personal arrest), where the master is not of the same nationality as the ship's flag, the appropriate diplomatic mission to contact will be that of his **own country**.
* A full list of **British Diplomatic Missions** can be viewed at: www.fco.gov.uk/directory/posts.asp

B02d.2 British Consuls

* A **British Consul** is an official appointed by the Foreign and Commonwealth Office of Her Majesty's Government to reside in a foreign port or place in order to protect the commercial interests of British subjects locally. The British Consul in a particular place should not be confused with the **British Council**[5].
* A British Consul also has a **duty to protect the interests of a British ship**, regardless of the nationality of its master or crew.
* As "**proper officers**" under Merchant Shipping Acts and regulations (see B05b.3d), British Consuls have a wide range of **statutory duties in connection with merchant shipping**, including duties concerning:
  * engagement and discharge of crew, crew agreements, list of crew, and exemption provisions;
  * seamen's wages and wages disputes;
  * relief and repatriation of seamen left behind;
  * returns and reports of births and deaths at sea;
  * inquiries into deaths;
  * Official Log Books;
  * manning of ships;
  * health, provisions and water;
  * seamen's documents;
  * depositions (protests) and certified log extracts; and
  * many other matters.
* British Consuls are **the representatives of British law** at their ports. They are also often in a position to render to British shipping interests valuable services which lie outside the administration of the law.
* British Consuls have a duty to **report to the Department for Transport** (DfT) matters of **general commercial interest** to the UK Government such as changes in port regulations, port charges or general dues on shipping, strikes affecting shipping, new trading facilities, impending developments in commerce of any kind, epidemic diseases or conditions making it unsafe for British ships to enter or stay at the port. They also have a duty to **report to the Foreign and Commonwealth Office** when a British ship is **detained** or **arrested** by any foreign authority, and to adopt all suitable means for obtaining its release and indemnity.
* British Consuls have a duty to **warn British shipmasters** of dangers in their ports, and to help masters by advising them of all **regulations in force** at their ports.
* Whenever the master of a British ship attends the British Consulate at a large port to transact business, it is appropriate for the **Consul himself**, or the **Vice-Consul**, to deal with him.
* In business transactions the consul has the powers of a **notary public** and of a **commissioner for oaths**. He is thus empowered to register **protests** by masters.
* Consuls and Vice-Consuls are referred to as **proper officers** throughout British merchant shipping legislation. Broadly, a proper officer is any official performing the duties of a DfT Marine Office superintendent.
* The equivalent official to a Consul at a port in a **British Overseas Territory**, such as Gibraltar, Port Stanley (Falkland Islands), etc., is a **Shipping Master**. Shipping Masters are also **proper officers** and carry out the same functions as Consuls under the Merchant Shipping Acts.

---

[5] The **British Council** is the UK's international organisation for educational and cultural relations, operating from 227 towns and cities in 109 countries worldwide. It connects people in those countries with learning opportunities and creative ideas from the UK, thus helping to build lasting relationships between the UK and other countries. It is a national, non-departmental public body, sponsored by the Foreign and Commonwealth Office and registered as a charity in the UK. Foreign seafarers may sit certain UK-administered examinations, including Certificate of Equivalent Competency examinations (see E02c.19), at their local British Council office.

* A **Consular Fees Order** prescribes the current level of **fees** to be levied by consular officers in the exercise of their duties. The Order currently in force is **The Consular Fees Order 1999** (SI 1999/655), as amended by The Consular Fees (Amendment) Order 1999 (SI 1999/3132). In connection with **ships and shipping**, fees were levied at the time of writing as follows:

- Granting or considering whether to grant a **provisional certificate of registry**, whether the owner is a private individual or body corporate: £210.00.
- Receiving a **return of the birth or death** of any person on board a ship and endorsing the agreement with the crew accordingly: £30.00.
- Examining or arranging for the **examination of provisions or water**, payable by the party who proves to be in default in addition to the cost, if any, of survey: £30.00.
- **Noting a marine protest** and furnishing one certified copy if required: £25.00; and for every further copy: £25.00.
- **Extending a marine protest**, filing the original and furnishing one certified copy if required -
  (a) for any number of words up to 200, excluding the declaratory clause: £60.00
  (b) for every subsequent 100 words or less, in addition to the foregoing fees where applicable: £25.00
- Making a **request**, or issuing or arranging for the **issue of a document**, in connection with a **survey of a ship** -
  (a) for the purposes of SOLAS 74 or of MARPOL 73/78: £40.00.
  (b) for any other purpose in addition to fee where applicable: £72.00.
- Issuing a **bill of health**: £25.00.
- **Preparing or signing, or both, any document**, whether required by the Merchant Shipping Acts or by the local authorities, **relating to the master or the members of the crew** of a ship, to their numbers, names or other details, or to their engagement, discharge, desertion or death except where -
  (a) fee 43 is taken in addition to fee 35, or
  (b) a death inquiry is held under section 271 of the Merchant Shipping Act 1995: £40.00.
- **Signing and, if required, sealing any documents** at the request of the master of the ship except where-
  (a) this is required under the Merchant Shipping Acts, or
  (b) fee 49 is taken: £40.00.
- **Inspecting** -
  (a) a **ship's papers** when required to enable a consular officer to do any matter or thing in respect of a ship except where fee 49 is taken in addition to fee 35: £30.00;
  (b) the **marking of a ship**, irrespective of the number of visits, in addition to fee 35: £30.00.

B03 English law

English law has formed the model for the law of many flag States, especially Commonwealth countries. It is the preferred jurisdiction of many foreign parties to maritime contracts who wish to resolve their disputes. Aspects of English law that are relevant to shipmasters are outlined in this section. Since offences under UK merchant shipping legislation may in certain circumstances be tried in Scottish courts, the structure and procedures of Scottish courts are also outlined in this section.

B03a CLASSES OF LAW CONCERNING SHIPMASTERS

- include **common law**, **equity**, **statute law**, **case law**, **civil law**, **criminal law**, **European Community law**, and **Admiralty law**.

B03a.1 Common law

- is defined in The Shorter Oxford English Dictionary as "the unwritten law of England, administered by the King's courts, based on ancient and universal usage, and embodied in commentaries and reported cases. (Opp. to *statute law*)".
- comprises **ancient customs**, **judicial decisions** (or **precedents**) and **enacted laws**.
- is recorded in **law reports** and **legal textbooks**, but not in statutes.
- * A **judicial precedent** is a decision of a court (i.e. a judgement), normally recorded in a **law report**, and often in legal textbooks, and used as an authority in reaching a similar decision in a subsequent case. A decision of the House of Lords is binding on the Court of Appeal and all lower courts and a decision of the Court of Appeal is

binding on all lower courts. A decision of the High Court is binding on all lower courts, but a decision of any lower court does not create a binding precedent. By the **doctrine of precedent**, where a lower court is bound by a previous decision of a higher court, it is only bound by those parts of the judgement forming the **principle** of the decision (called by lawyers the *ratio decidendi*), and is not bound by additional comments of the judge.

* The body of law as set out in **judicial decisions** is sometimes referred to as **case law**. A case, the decision in which establishes an important principle of the law, becomes known as a **leading case** and will usually be quoted in legal textbooks. For example, a leading case concerning the definition of an "arrived ship" was *Oldendorff (E.L.) and Co. v. Trader Export SA (1973)*, in which was established the test: "Had the ship reached a position within the port where she was at the immediate and effective disposition of the charterers?"

B03a.2 Equity

- is **law based on principles** formulated by early Chancellors **for correcting injustices** arising where the common law was strictly adhered to.
- supplements the common law.
- is applied in all civil courts where it takes precedence in the event of a conflict with common law.

B03a.3 Statute law

- is the body of UK **law contained in statutes**, i.e. Acts of Parliament and orders, rules and regulations made under statutes. (These are printed and published by the government's stationery office, HMSO[6] and sold at Stationery Office bookshops.)
  - is now the chief source of English law.

B03a.4 Civil law

- is law primarily concerned with the **rights and duties of individuals and companies** towards each other. It is made by judges in the civil courts and includes the **law of contract**, the **law of tort**, the **law of property**, the **law of succession**, **family law**, and **admiralty law**.
- is dealt with mostly by the **civil courts** which have a separate system and procedure from the criminal court system and procedure. Its object is not the punishment of the wrongdoer but to give a remedy to the persons wronged. There are no penalties in civil law, but the "losing" party could be ordered to pay damages, or perform a contract, or not do something that he would otherwise do, etc.

B03a.5 Criminal law

- is that part of the law which characterises certain kinds of wrongdoings as **offences against the State** which are punishable by the State. These offences do not necessarily violate the rights of any individual.
- is mostly **laid down in parliamentary statutes** (i.e. primary legislation) such as the Merchant Shipping Acts, and **secondary legislation** such as Merchant Shipping Regulations.
- is recorded for the reference of lawyers, judges and academics in textbooks such as *Archbold*.
- is mostly enforced in the UK by the police and is dealt with by the **criminal courts**.

---

[6] **HMSO** should not be confused with **The Stationery Office** Limited (tSO) the private sector company which acquired the trading functions of HMSO following privatisation in 1996. HMSO oversees the printing and publication of all UK legislation and related official materials in traditional print formats and via the internet. It also regulates the use, licensing of re-use of all information produced by government which is protected by Crown copyright.

B03a.6 European Community legislation

- **applies in the UK** as a consequence of the UK's membership (since 1 January 1973) of the European Union[7] (EU).
- is applied in all EU member States by the **European Court of Justice** (ECJ) in accordance with the provisions of various treaties, e.g. the Treaty of Rome, which are binding on member States. The ECJ plays an important part in the UK's judicial system, most notably in the field of employment law. Under Article 234 of the Treaty of Rome, any UK court may refer questions on points of EU law to the ECJ, and the decision of the ECJ will be binding on the national court and in other, future cases. A decision of the ECJ relating to a case in one EU member States will be binding in all other member States. The ECJ is not bound by its own previous decisions, however.
- stands alongside UK statute law, common law and equity in the UK, but **takes precedence** over them where there is any conflict.
- can be viewed on the **Eur-Lex website** at http://europa.eu.int/eur-lex/index.html
* Chief instruments of EC law include **Regulations**, **Directives** and **Decisions**.
* **EC Regulations** are binding in all EU member States without requiring any implementation or adoption by national parliaments. They apply directly and take precedence over national law. They may create rights which are enforceable by individuals in their national courts. An example is Council Regulation (EC) No 3051/95 of 8 December 1995 on the safety management of roll-on/roll-off passenger ferries (ro-ro ferries).
* **EC Directives** are instructions to EU member States to adapt their national law to conform with EC requirements. EC Directives (and their forerunners, EEC Directives) are binding, but leave EU member States a choice as to the method by which the requirements of the Directive are met. In the UK this may be through an Act of Parliament or through delegated legislation, such as a Statutory Instrument. Several **EC Directives concerning merchant shipping** have been implemented in the UK by Merchant Shipping regulations, e.g. EC Directive 95/21/EC concerning the port State control of shipping in EC ports, implemented by the MS (Port State Control) Regulations 1995 and Council Directive 98/18/EC on Safety Rules and Standards for Passenger Ships, implemented by the MS (Passenger Ships on Domestic Voyages) Regulations 2000 (SI 2000/2687). For an **index of Directives** referred to in the text of this book, see B04d.
* **EC Decisions** are binding in their entirety on those to whom they are addressed, whether they be EU member States, companies or individuals. Decisions of the European Court of Justice are binding on the highest courts of EU member States; thus the UK House of Lords must accept a European Court Decision as binding. An example is Commission Decision of 30 September 1996 on the publication of the list of recognised organisations which have been notified by member States in accordance with Council Directive 94/57/EC.

B03a.7 Admiralty law

- is the distinct body of civil law (both substantively and procedurally) that deals mainly with **navigation and shipping** matters including **collisions**, **salvage**, **damage to cargo**, **maritime liens** and **arrest** of ships. **Piracy** is also a matter of admiralty law.
- is dealt with in the UK by the **Admiralty Court** (see B03b.7). The word "admiralty" in this context has nothing to do with the Ministry of Defence.
* The law of many maritime nations includes a body of admiralty law, and in some countries, e.g. South Africa and Canada, it is very similar to English admiralty law. In the admiralty law of certain other countries, e.g. China, there are marked differences from what is considered the international norm. P&I club bulletins occasionally draw the attention of club members to these differences, where relevant to members' operations.

---

[7] **EU member States** are currently Austria, Belgium, Denmark, Finland, France, Germany, Greece, Ireland, Italy, Luxembourg, Netherlands, Portugal, Spain, Sweden, United Kingdom (15). Cyprus, the Czech Republic, Estonia, Hungary, Latvia, Lithuania, Malta, Poland, the Slovak Republic and Slovenia (10) are scheduled to join the EU in June 2004. The EU is the result of a process of co-operation and integration, which began in 1951 between 6 countries. After four waves of accessions there are now 15 Member States in the EU and it is preparing for its fifth enlargement. The name "EU" came into use on 1 November 1993 when the Maastricht Treaty entered into force. The EU unites under one "roof" the three "pillars" of European co-operation: the European Community (EC) (including the single market and single currency), the Common Foreign and Security Policy, and the area of Justice and Home Affairs (JHA) co-operation. **European Community (EC) law** is applicable in all EU Member States.

B03b UK COURTS, LEGAL PROCEEDINGS AND PENALTIES

B03b.1 Criminal courts and procedures

- administer and apply the existing **criminal law** but **cannot make new criminal law**, since it can only be made by Parliament.
- use two **procedures** for dealing with criminal cases: **summary procedure** and **solemn procedure**.
* The legislation creating a particular offence will also determine how that offence may be tried. Certain offences are triable only by lower courts, using summary procedure while other offences are triable by either higher or lower courts (these offences being known as "**either way offences**"). Many breaches of UK merchant shipping legislation are "either way offences".

B03b.1a Summary procedure and summary conviction

* **Summary procedure** is used for trying cases involving relatively minor offences, such as minor breaches of road traffic regulations or merchant shipping regulations. A criminal prosecution is normally begun in the name of the **Crown** (i.e. the State) through the **police** and the **Crown Prosecution Service** (CPS) or, in Scotland, the **Procurator-Fiscal**. The decision whether or not to press the prosecution is not the concern of the victim. For an offence to be summarily triable, the legislation creating the offence must provide for a penalty on **summary conviction**; most merchant shipping offences are summarily triable.
* If it is decided by the CPS or Procurator-Fiscal that there is sufficient evidence to take the case to court, the case might cited as: *R. v. Munro.* ("R" stands for Regina, i.e. the Queen.) The Crown, signified by Regina, **prosecutes** Munro (the defendant, or, in Scotland, defender). The defendant, if not already in custody, is **summonsed** to appear before the court, which consists of magistrates (or in Scotland, usually a sheriff but in some cases magistrates) sitting without a jury. The **magistrates or sheriff decide questions of both fact and law**. Magistrates (who are Justices of the Peace or JPs) are not usually qualified in law and are mostly lay persons who may hear only minor cases and may impose lesser sentences than may judges or sheriffs. Magistrates and sheriffs may **commit** an accused for **trial at a higher court** (e.g. the Crown Court in England or Wales, or the High Court in Scotland).
* If the defendant is found guilty of the offence there is a **summary conviction**. The defendant may then be punished by one of a range of sentences that the court is allowed by statute to impose. For most criminal offences a magistrate or sheriff may impose a maximum fine of £5,000 (the "**statutory maximum**" for many merchant shipping offences) or a maximum prison sentence of 3 months (but in some circumstances, 6 months).
* Numerous provisions of merchant shipping legislation provide for a **fine on summary conviction**. This may be stated as a particular sum (e.g. "£1000"), or as "**fine of the statutory maximum**" (meaning the maximum allowed to be imposed for the particular offence being tried), or as a certain "**level on the standard scale**" (see B03b.3c).
* For **two offences** a shipmaster may be fined up to **£250,000** on summary conviction (see B03b.3d).
* For **eleven offences** a shipmaster may be fined up to **£50,000** on summary conviction (see B03b.3e).
* For **two offences** a shipmaster may be fined up to **£25,000** on summary conviction (see B03b.3f).

B03b.1b Solemn procedure and conviction on indictment

* **Solemn procedure** is used for trying cases involving the more serious offences. Breaches of some pieces of legislation does not carry a sentence on **conviction on indictment**, and can therefore only be dealt with by summary procedure.
* The defendant is **indicted** to appear before the court, which consists of a **judge** sitting with a **jury** of 12 members of the public (or 15 in Scotland). The judge decides questions of law and directs the jury accordingly. The jury decides questions of fact (i.e. whether the defender is telling the truth) and whether he is guilty of the charge, or not.
* If the jury find the defendant guilty, a **conviction on indictment** results and the judge passes a sentence. Acts of Parliament and statutory instruments (SIs) lay down the maximum sentence for most criminal offences. For breaches of merchant shipping legislation a judge may normally impose an **unlimited fine** and/or a maximum sentence of **2 years' imprisonment** on summary conviction.
* **Penalties** for breaches of particular regulations are prescribed in the SI, e.g. regulation 15(1) of the MS (Musters, Training and Decision Support Systems) Regulations 1999 (SI 1999/2722), which provides that "if, in respect of a ship, there is a breach of any of the requirements of these Regulations the master and the owner shall each be guilty of an offence punishable on summary conviction by a fine not exceeding the statutory maximum or, on conviction on indictment, by imprisonment for a term not exceeding two years, or an unlimited fine, or both".
* If the case merits a more severe penalty than the judge can impose, he can send the case to a **higher court**.

* **Appeals** against sentence are heard in a higher court than that passing the sentence. The **appeal judges** can lower or raise the sentence, or quash it.
* Information on the work of certain courts in England and Wales, including the High Court and Crown Courts, is provided on the **Court Service website** at www.courtservice.gov.uk
* Information on **Scottish courts** can be viewed at www.scotcourts.gov.uk and www.district-courts.org.uk

B03b.1c Ranking of criminal courts in England and Wales

* In ascending order of authority the ranking of criminal courts in England and Wales is:
  1. Magistrates' Court;
  2. Crown Court;
  3. Court of Appeal (court of appeal only);
  4. House of Lords (court of appeal only).

B03b.1d Ranking of criminal courts in Scotland

* In ascending order of authority the ranking of criminal courts in Scotland is:
  1. District Court[8];
  2. Sheriff Court;
  3. High Court of Justice;
  4. High Court of Justiciary in Edinburgh.

B03b.2 Legal proceedings in criminal cases under Merchant Shipping Act 1995

* **Primary legislation relating to legal proceedings** against persons committing offences on or in connection with UK ships is contained in Part XII of the Merchant Shipping Act 1995, sections 274 to 291, as shown in the following table.

Section	Section title	SBC reference
274	Time limit for summary offences	B03b.2a
275	Time limit for summary orders	-
276	Summary offences: Scotland	B03b.2b
277	Offences by officers of bodies corporate	B03b.2c
278	Offences by partners, etc. in Scotland	B03b.2c
279	Jurisdiction in relation to offences	B03b.2e
280	Jurisdiction over ships lying off coasts	B03b.2f
281	Jurisdiction in case of offences on board ship	B03b.2g
282	Offences committed by British seamen	B03b.2h
283	Return of offenders	B03b.2i
284	Enforcing detention of ship	B05d.4d
285	Sums ordered to be paid leviable by distress on the ship	I02f
286	Depositions of persons abroad admissible	B05f.2
287	Admissibility in evidence and inspection of certain documents	D05d.1
288	Admissibility of documents in evidence	D05d.1
289	Inspection and admissibility in evidence of copies of certain documents	D05d.1
290	Proof, etc of exemptions	-
291	Service of documents	I02e

B03b.2a Time limit for summary offences

* **Section 274(1) of Merchant Shipping Act 1995** provides that, subject to sections 274(2) and 274(3) no person may be convicted of an offence under the Act in **summary proceedings** unless the proceedings were commenced within **six months** beginning with the date on which the offence was committed, or in a case where the accused was out of the UK during that period, the proceedings were commenced within **two months of his first arrival in the UK** and within **three years** from the date on which the offence was committed. Section 274(2) provides that section 274(1) does not apply in relation to any **indictable offence**.
* Under section 274(3), the time limits in section 274(1) will not prevent a conviction for an offence in summary proceedings begun within **three years** from the date on which the offence was committed and within -
  * **six months** from the day when evidence which the MCA considers is sufficient to justify a prosecution for the offence came to their knowledge; or

---

[8] For a note on section 276, Merchant Shipping Act 1995 relating to the district court, see B03b.2b.

- **two months** from the day when the accused was first present in the UK after the end of the six-month period mentioned in the last sub-paragraph if throughout that period the accused was absent from the UK.

B03b.2b Summary offences in Scotland

* **Section 276 of the Merchant Shipping Act 1995** provides that, in Scotland, all prosecutions in respect of offences under the Act in respect of which the maximum penalty which may be imposed does not exceed imprisonment for a period of three months or a fine of level 4 on the standard scale, or both, may be tried in "a summary manner" (i.e. summary proceedings) before the district court.

B03b.2c Offences by officers of bodies corporate and Scottish partners

* **Section 277(1) of the Merchant Shipping Act 1995** provides that where a body corporate is guilty of an offence under the Act or any instrument made under it, and the offence is proved to have been committed with the consent or connivance of, or to be attributable to any neglect on the part of, a director, manager, secretary or other similar officer of the body corporate, he as well as the body corporate will be guilty of that offence and will be liable to be proceeded against and punished accordingly. Section 277(2) provides that where the affairs of a body corporate are managed by its members, section 277(1) will apply in relation to the acts and defaults of a member in connection with his functions of management as if he were a director of the body corporate. These provisions are found (usually immediately after the main "Offences and Penalties" regulation) in a few modern SIs, notably Regulations giving effect to EC Directives on health and safety matters applying to ships operating in the EU[9].
* **Section 278** makes a similar extension of criminal liability where a partnership or unincorporated association in Scotland is guilty of an offence under the Act.

B03b.2d Offences committed due to the act or default of another person

- Some SIs[10] contain a regulation (usually found immediately after the main Offences and Penalties regulation) providing that where the commission by any person of an offence is due to the act or default of **some other person**, that other person will be guilty of the offence and may be charged with and convicted of the offence whether or not proceedings are taken against the first-mentioned person.

B03b.2e Jurisdiction in relation to offences

* **Section 279(1) of the Merchant Shipping Act 1995** provides that, for the purpose of conferring jurisdiction, any offence under the Act (e.g. an offence committed on a ship outside the UK, perhaps in waters under the jurisdiction of another State) will be deemed to have been committed in any place in the UK where the offender may be for the time being, and any matter of complaint will be deemed to have arisen where the person complained against may be for the time being.

B03b.2f Jurisdiction over ships lying off coasts

* **Section 280(1) of the Merchant Shipping Act 1995** provides that where the area within which a court in any part of the UK has jurisdiction is situated on the coast of any sea or abuts on or projects into any bay, channel, lake, river or other navigable water the court will have jurisdiction as respects offences under the Act over any vessel being on, or lying or passing off, that coast or being in or near that bay, channel, lake, river or navigable water and over all persons on board that vessel or for the time being belonging to it.

B03b.2g Jurisdiction in case of offences on board ship

* **Section 281 of the Merchant Shipping Act 1995** provides that where any person is charged with having committed any offence under the Act, then -
    - if he is a **British citizen** and is charged with having committed the offence **on any UK ship on the high seas, in any foreign port or harbour, or on any foreign ship to which he does not belong**; or

---

[9] Examples of such SIs are the MS & FV (Manual Handling Operations) Regulations 1998 (SI 1998/2857), the MS & FV (Personal Protective Equipment) Regulations 1999 (SI 1999/2205) and the MS & FV (Safety Signs and Signals) Regulations 2001 (SI 2001/3444).
[10] Examples are the MS (Prevention of Oil Pollution) Regulations 1996 (SI 1996/2154), the MS (Dangerous Goods and Marine Pollutants) Regulations 1997 (SI 1997/2367) and the MS (Carriage of Cargoes) Regulations 1999 (SI 1999/336).

- if he is **not a British citizen** and is charged with having committed the **offence on any UK ship on the high seas**,

- and he is found within the jurisdiction of any court in the UK which would have had jurisdiction if the offence had been committed on a UK ship (within the limits of its ordinary jurisdiction to try the offence), that court will have jurisdiction to try the offence.

B03b.2h Offences committed by British masters and seamen

* Under **Section 282(1) of the Merchant Shipping Act 1995**, any act in relation to property or person done in or at any place (ashore or afloat) **outside the UK** by any master or seaman employed in a UK ship, which, if it had been done in any part of the UK, would be an offence under the law of any part of the UK, will -
- be an offence under that law; and
- will be treated for the purposes of jurisdiction and trial, as if it had been done within the jurisdiction of the Admiralty of England.

* This provision also applies in relation to a person who **had been employed** as a master or seaman in a UK ship within the period of **three months** expiring with the time when the act was done. It also applies to **omissions** (e.g. omissions to perform specified duties under regulations) as they apply to acts.

B03b.2i Return of offenders

* **Section 283 of the Merchant Shipping Act 1995** gives powers to proper officers to return to the UK masters and seamen who are alleged to have committed offences outside the UK.

* **Section 283(1)** provides that the powers conferred on a British consular officer by subsection 282(2) are exercisable in the event of any complaint being made to him -
- that any offence against property or persons has been committed at any place (ashore or afloat) outside the UK by any master or seaman who at the time when the offence was committed, or within three months before that time, was employed in a UK ship; or
- that any offence on the high seas has been committed by any master or seaman belonging to any UK ship.

* Section 283(2) gives the proper officer power to **inquire** into the case upon oath, and if the case requires it, to take **any steps in his power** for the purpose of placing the offender under the necessary **restraint** and **sending him by UK ship** as soon as practicable in safe custody **to the UK** for proceedings to be taken against him.

* Under section 283(3) the consular officer may, subject to subsections 283(4) and (5), **order the master of any UK ship which is bound for the UK** to receive and carry **the offender and witnesses to the UK**. The proper officer must endorse any relevant particulars on the ship's **Crew Agreement** as required by the MCA.

* Under section 283(4) a consular officer may not exercise the power conferred by subsection 283(3) unless **no more convenient means of transport** is available or it is available only at **disproportionate expense**.

* Under section 283(5) no master of a ship may be required under subsection 283(3) to receive more than **one offender for every 100 tons of his ship's registered tonnage** (i.e. net tonnage) or **more than one witness for every 50 tons** of his ship's registered tonnage.

* Section 283(6) provides that the master of any ship to whose charge an offender has been committed under subsection 283(3) must, on his ship's arrival in the UK, give the offender into the custody of some **police officer or constable**.

* Section 283(8) provides that the **expense** of imprisoning an offender and of **carrying him and witnesses** to the UK otherwise than in the ship to which they respectively belong must be paid out of **money provided by Parliament**.

* Under section 283(9) references in section 283 to carrying a person in a ship include affording him **subsistence** during the voyage.

B03b.2j Restriction on UK jurisdiction over oil pollution offences outside UK limits

* **Regulation 38(1) of the MS (Prevention of Oil Pollution) Regulations 1996** (SI 1996/2154) provides that no proceedings for breaches of the "discharge regulations" (regulations 12, 13 or 16) by a non-UK ship, where the discharge was in the internal waters, territorial waters or EEZ of another State will be instituted (in the UK) unless:
- that State, the flag State or a State damaged or threatened by the discharge requests proceedings to be taken; or
- the discharge has caused or is likely to cause pollution in the internal waters, territorial sea or controlled waters of the UK.

* Where proceedings as above in respect of an offence by a non-UK ship have been commenced but not concluded, and the State concerned requests their suspension, then the proceedings will be suspended and the DfT will send all the case documents, etc. to the other State (regulation 38(2)).

* It will be a **defence** under regulation 38(3) for a person charged with an offence as above to show:

- that the ship is not a UK ship; and
- the discharge took place outside the UK, its territorial waters and the controlled waters of the UK; and
- the ship was in a port in the UK at the time of institution of proceedings due to stress of weather or other reason beyond the control of the master, owner or charterer.

B03b.2k Admissibility of depositions of persons abroad

* **Section 286** provides that if the **evidence** of any person is required in the course of legal proceedings but that person cannot be found in the UK, any **deposition** that he may previously have made outside the UK in relation to the same matter will, subject to certain conditions, be admissible in evidence. For a deposition to be admissible in evidence it must have been taken on oath before a justice or magistrate in any colony or a British consular officer in any other place, must be authenticated by the signature of the justice, magistrate or consular officer, and must, in the case of criminal proceedings, have been taken in the presence of the accused.
* For notes on the **use of documents in legal proceedings**, see D05d.

B03b.3 Penalties

B03b.3a Penalties provisions in Merchant Shipping legislation

* A vast number of provisions of Merchant Shipping legislation, whether sections of Acts or regulations in statutory instruments, create offences that carry a **criminal penalty**. Where several duties are laid down in the legislation there may be different penalties for breach of different duties. Any penalty must be clearly stated before it can be enforced by the courts.
* Any section of an Act containing duties will probably carry a penalty for breach of those duties, but the penalty will not usually be in a clearly-headed and separate section of the Act; the relevant section must therefore be carefully read to ascertain the penalty, if any.
* In Merchant Shipping and other statutory instruments the regulation containing the penalty or penalties is usually clearly headed "**Offences and Penalties**" or in some cases "**Penalties**", and is most often found at the end of the regulations, often preceding a further regulation allowing one or more **defences**.
  - Every offence must be **triable** in some form of court proceedings, i.e. either summary procedure (see B03b.1a) or solemn procedure (see B03b.1b). Some offences are triable only in summary proceedings in which case the penalty will refer to "**summary conviction**". Many offences are indictable and are therefore triable "either way", i.e. either in summary procedure or solemn procedure, and in this case the penalty provision will also lay down a penalty "**on conviction on indictment**".

B03b.3b Fines not exceeding the statutory maximum

  - The penalty on summary conviction for breach of a statutory provision may be specified in the relevant piece of legislation as "**a fine not exceeding the statutory maximum**". The **statutory maximum** is currently **£5000**.

B03b.3c Standard scale of fines

* For breaches of most pre-1982 UK legislation a **fixed sum penalty** on summary conviction, e.g. a maximum fine of £50, was prescribed. Whenever amendment became necessary in order to raise the specified fines to realistic sums reflecting current levels of wealth, numerous pieces of legislation required individual amendment, which was difficult, slow and costly.
* **Section 37 of the Criminal Justice Act 1982** (CJA 1982) introduced a **standard scale of fines** consisting of **five levels**, each equating to a monetary sum which could be amended periodically to reflect changes in national income levels. Every piece of legislation providing for a fine of a specified level on the standard scale can be amended by means of one piece of legislation which amends the CJA 1982. In post-1982 legislation, fines specified as penalties on summary conviction are either a fine of the **statutory maximum** (see B03b.3b) or a fine of a specified level on the standard scale.
* The current levels of the standard scale came into effect on 1 October 1992 and are as follows:
    Level 1: £200;
    Level 2: £500;
    Level 3: £1000;
    Level 4: £2500;
    Level 5: £5000.

* The courts are required by law to have regard to the **means of the accused** when determining the level of the fine to be imposed in any particular case.

B03b.3d £250,000 offences by masters

* Masters breaching UK merchant shipping legislation are liable to a maximum fine on summary conviction of **£250,000** for **two offences** which are both related to oil pollution, as shown in the following table.

Offence (with offender shown in bold)	Legislation contravened	Penalties provision and penalties on summary conviction (SC) & conviction on indictment (COI)
Failure by ship to comply with any requirement of regulation 12, 13 or 16 (the "discharge regulations"). (**Owner and master**)	Regulations 12, 13 or 16, MS (Prevention of Oil Pollution) Regulations 1996	Reg. 36(2), as amended by reg. 8, MS (Prevention of Oil Pollution) (Amendment) Regulations 1997. SC: A fine not exceeding £250,000. COI: A fine.
Oil or mixture containing oil is discharged into UK national waters which are navigable by sea-going ships. ((a) **Owner or master**, unless he proves that the discharge took place and was caused as in (b). (b) If the discharge is from a ship but takes place in the course of a transfer of oil to or from another ship or a place on land and is caused by the act or omission of any person in charge of any apparatus in that other ship or that place, the **owner or master of that other ship** or, as the case may be, the **occupier of that place**.)	Section 131(1), Merchant Shipping Act 1995	S.131(3), Merchant Shipping Act 1995 as amended by s.7(1), Merchant Shipping and Maritime Security Act 1997. SC: A fine not exceeding £250,000. COI: A fine.

B03b.3e £50,000 offences by masters

* Masters breaching UK merchant shipping legislation are liable to a maximum fine on summary conviction of **£50,000** for **eleven offences**, as shown in the following table. Five of these are listed in **M.1255** as being offences under Merchant Shipping Act 1979; these have been transferred to, and added to by, the Merchant Shipping Act 1995 and the Merchant Shipping and Maritime Security Act 1997.

Offence (with offender shown in bold)	Legislation contravened	Penalties provision and penalties on summary conviction (SC) & conviction on indictment (COI)
Master or owner of a ship which is not a British ship does anything, or permits anything to be done, for the purpose of causing the ship to appear to be a British ship.	Section 3(1), Merchant Shipping Act 1995	Section 3(6). SC: A fine not exceeding £50,000. COI: Max. 2 years imprisonment or a fine or both. Ship liable to forfeiture under section 3(1).
Master or owner of a British ship does anything, or permits anything to be done, for the purpose of concealing the nationality of the ship. (**Master, owner and any charterer**)	Section 3(1), Merchant Shipping Act 1995	Section 3(6). SC: A fine not exceeding £50,000. COI: Max. 2 years imprisonment or a fine or both. Ship liable to forfeiture under section 3(4).
Master fails to render assistance to and stay by the other ship following a collision.	Section 92(1)(a), Merchant Shipping Act 1995	Section 92(4)(a). SC: A fine not exceeding £50,000 or max. 6 months imprisonment or both. COI: Max. 2 years imprisonment or a fine or both.
Ship in a UK port, or a UK ship in any other port, is dangerously unsafe. (**Master and owner/charterer/manager**)	Section 98(1), Merchant Shipping Act 1995	Section 98(3). SC: A fine not exceeding £50,000. COI: Max. 2 years imprisonment or a fine or both.
Ship enters or remains in a temporary exclusion zone or a part of such a zone in contravention of Section 100B(1) or (3). (**Owner and master**)	Section 100B(1) or (3), Merchant Shipping Act 1995.	Section 100B(6)[11]. SC: A fine not exceeding £50,000. COI: Max. 2 years imprisonment or a fine or both.
Contravention of, or failure to comply with, a section 137 direction[12] as respects ship or cargo given following a shipping casualty. (**Person** to whom direction was given)	Section 139(1), Merchant Shipping Act 1995	Section 139(4). SC: A fine not exceeding £50,000. COI: A fine.
Intentionally obstructing any person (a) acting on behalf of the Secretary of State in connection with the giving or service of a section 137 direction or (b) acting in compliance with the direction or (c) acting under section 137(4) or (5). (**Any person so obstructing**)	Section 139(2), Merchant Shipping Act 1995	Section 139(4). SC: A fine not exceeding £50,000. COI: A fine.

---

[11] Section 100B was added to MS Act 1995 by virtue of Section 1 of the Merchant Shipping and Maritime Security Act 1997 (c.28).
[12] This means directions given by the Secretary of State's Representative (SOSREP) in a salvage/pollution incident affecting in UK waters.

Ship enters or leaves, or attempts to enter or leave, a port or arrives at or leaves, or attempts to arrive at or leave, a terminal in the UK (or, if the ship is a UK ship, in any other country), without having a valid OPIC certificate in force. (**Master or owner**)	Section 163(5), Merchant Shipping Act 1995	Section 163(5). SC: A fine not exceeding £50,000. COI: A fine. Ship attempting to leave a port in the UK in contravention of section 163 may be detained.
Ship which has been detained, or as respects which notice of detention or an order for detention has been served on the master, proceeds to sea before it is released by a competent authority. (**Master**)	Section 284(2), Merchant Shipping Act 1995	Section 284(2). SC: A fine not exceeding £50,000. COI: A fine.
Failure to ensure that there is not on board a greater number of passengers than that stated on the ship's Passenger Ship Safety Certificate or Passenger Certificate. (**Owner and master**)	Regulation 23, MS (Survey and Certification) Regulations 1995	Reg. 24(5). SC: A fine not exceeding £50,000. COI: Max. 2 years imprisonment or a fine or both.
Infringement of Rule 10(b)(i) (duty to proceed with traffic flow in lanes of separation schemes). (**Owner, master and any person for the time being responsible for the conduct of the vessel**)	Regulation 4(1), MS (Distress Signals and Prevention of Collision Regulations 1996.	Regulation 6(1). SC: A fine not exceeding £50,000. COI: Max. 2 years imprisonment or a fine or both.

B03b.3f £25,000 offences by masters

* Masters breaching UK Merchant Shipping legislation[13] are liable to a maximum fine on summary conviction of **£25,000** for **three offences** which are all related to pollution, as shown in the following table.

Offence (with offenders shown in bold)	Legislation contravened	Penalties provision and penalties on summary conviction (SC) & conviction on indictment (COI)
Breach of the requirements of regulations 4, 5. 6 or 7 (i.e. prohibited disposal of garbage outside Special Areas, prohibited disposal of garbage within Special Areas, prohibited disposal of garbage within 500 metres of fixed or floating installations, and breach of restriction on UK ships entering the Antarctic area). (**Owner, manager, demise charterer and master**)	Regulation 4, 5, 6 or 7, MS (Prevention of Pollution by Garbage) Regulations 1998	Reg. 14(2). SC: A fine not exceeding £25,000. COI: A fine.
Prohibited discharge of any noxious liquid substance, except where permitted by Schedule 2 of M.1703/NLS1. (**Owner and master**)	Regulation 5(a), MS (Dangerous or Noxious Liquid Substances in Bulk) Regulations 1996	Reg. 14(1), MS (Dangerous or Noxious Liquid Substances in Bulk) Regulations 1996 as amended by reg. 2, MS (Dangerous or Noxious Liquid Substances in Bulk) (Amendment) Regulations 1998. SC: A fine not exceeding £25,000. COI: A fine.
Contravention of requirement that tanks shall be washed, or prewashed, and the tank washings shall be dealt with, as prescribed in Schedule 2 of M.1703/NLS1. (**Owner and master**)	Regulation 5(b), MS (Dangerous or Noxious Liquid Substances in Bulk) Regulations 1996	Reg. 14(1), MS (Dangerous or Noxious Liquid Substances in Bulk) Regulations 1996 as amended by reg. 2, MS (Dangerous or Noxious Liquid Substances in Bulk) (Amendment) Regulations 1998. SC: A fine not exceeding £25,000. COI: A fine.

B03b.4 Civil courts

- deal with disputes involving **civil law**, e.g. concerning marriages, child custody, contractual breaches, copyright infringements, etc., i.e. non-criminal cases. The vast majority of cases heard are, in fact, divorce cases.
- **apply existing civil law** and, in some cases, **make new civil law**.

B03b.4a Civil court procedure

* A **civil action** is started by a private individual or firm. They have the right to determine how far the action should continue.
* A civil action might be cited as: *Jones v. Smith*. Jones (the plaintiff) sues Smith (defendant) for breach of contract, for example.
* In England and Wales, civil cases are heard by circuit judges in the **county courts**. In Scotland, sheriffs and judges of the **Outer House of the Court of Session** usually sit alone, but may very occasionally sit with a jury of 12. The **plaintiff** (or pursuer in Scotland) brings an action against (i.e. sues) the **defendant** (defender in Scotland). In most cases, the remedy sued for is monetary damages.

---

[13] A £25,000 fine on summary conviction is also provided for by section 5(1) of the Dangerous Vessels Act 1985 (see B04c.8) where a person (e.g. a master) contravenes or fails to comply with any directions given by a harbour master under section 1 (e.g. prohibiting entry or requiring removal of a ship).

* A civil court cannot impose a fine or custodial sentence. If the action is successful, the result is a **judgement for the plaintiff** which may order the defendant to:
  * pay the plaintiff monetary **damages**;
  * **transfer property** to him;
  * refrain from doing something (**injunction** or, in Scotland, **interdict**); or
  * enforce the performance of a contract (**specific performance**).
* An **appeal** against a judgement of a lower court may generally be heard by the next higher court.

B03b.4b Ranking of civil courts in England and Wales

* In ascending order of authority the ranking is:
  * County Court;
  * High Court (of which the Admiralty Court is part);
  * Court of Appeal;
  * House of Lords.

B03b.4c Ranking of civil courts in Scotland

* In ascending order of authority the ranking is:
  * Sheriff Court;
  * Outer House of the Court of Session;
  * Inner House of the Court of Session.

B03b.5 Differences in rules of evidence, etc. between criminal and civil systems

* There are differences in the rules of evidence and procedure in the two systems. A criminal prosecution is more damaging to a person's character than failure in a civil action. Rules of evidence are therefor more strict in criminal cases, e.g. a confession is more carefully examined. In civil cases, by contrast, an admission is freely accepted.
* The **standard of proof** is greater in criminal cases, but the accused must be proved **guilty beyond all reasonable doubt**. The plaintiff in a civil action will succeed **on the balance of probabilities**, i.e. if he can convince the court that he has only a marginally stronger case than that of the defendant.

B03b.6 Civil and criminal consequences of a wrong

* The same series of events may give rise to both types of case. For example, a shipowner, as an employer, may be alleged to have left dangerous engine room machinery unguarded, causing injury to a seaman. Two types of issue arise. On one hand, failure to guard machinery, as a breach of a statutory requirement (see E08e.1), is a **criminal offence**: the employer may be prosecuted in a criminal court and if found guilty, may be punished. On the other hand, whether the employer caused loss to the injured seaman through negligence or failure to comply with his statutory duty may be determined in a separate **civil action** brought by the seaman in a civil court, where the seaman may claim damages from his employer.

B03b.7 The Admiralty Court

* The **Admiralty Court of the Queen's Bench Division of the High Court of Justice** -
  - is a court in London with jurisdiction embracing **civil shipping matters**.
  - deals with cases concerning **collisions, salvage, navigation, loss of life or injury caused by ships, cargo loss, damage or delay, claims *in rem*, marine insurance, piracy**, etc.
* The jurisdiction of the Admiralty Court does not extend to non-maritime matters.
* A distinctive feature of the Admiralty Court's procedure is **action *in rem***, i.e. against the thing, rather than action *in personam*, i.e. against a person or group of persons. For notes on **maritime liens**, see B03g.3.

B03c LAW OF CONTRACT

B03c.1 Nature of contracts

* A **contract** is a legally binding agreement, i.e. one that will be enforced by the courts.
* Everyday **domestic agreements** are not usually intended to be legally binding, and are therefore not contracts.
* In a contract there must be *consensus ad idem* ("agreement on the same thing"), i.e. the contracting parties must agree to identical terms.
* Agreement arises from **offer and acceptance**, but to be enforceable at law a number of **other elements** must be present (see B03c.3).

B03c.2 Categories of contract

* A **voidable** contract is one that, because of misrepresentation, mistake, non-disclosure or undue influence, may be set aside by one of the parties, subject to certain restrictions (e.g. that both parties can be restored to their original positions and that the rights of a third party will not be upset if the contract is ended). A buyer of goods cannot, therefore, rescind the sale contract unless he can return the goods, and the seller cannot rescind if he has already sold the goods to a third party.
* A **void** contract is one that has no legal force from the moment of its making, e.g. because of lack of capacity of the parties, or mistake.
* An **illegal** contract is one that is prohibited by statute or is illegal at common law on the grounds of public policy and is automatically void since it is impossible to perform within the law.
* An **unenforceable** contract, although valid, cannot be enforced because it is neither evidenced in writing not supported by a sufficient act of part performance. The contract might be not capable of proof, or not stamped (where stamping is required), or legal remedy may be barred by lapse of time.
* A **valid** contract is one that does not fall into one of the above categories.

B03c.3 Elements of a contract

* Every contract must be **entered into voluntarily** by **two or more parties** having legal **capacity** to contract and **intending** thereby to create a **legally binding relationship** between them.
* Of the several **essential elements** in any contract, the most vital are:
  * **offer**;
  * **acceptance**; and
  * **consideration** (unless the contract is by deed).
* The contract is concluded when one party makes an offer that is unconditionally accepted by the other party. The offer and acceptance may be made through the agency of one or more **brokers**.
* If one party fails to keep its promise, the other is entitled to legal **remedy**.
* Other **necessary elements** include
  * intention to create legal relations;
  * legal capacity;
  * legality;
  * possibility of performance;
  * sufficient certainty of terms; and
  * prescribed form.
* **Intention to create legal relations**, i.e. to enter into a legally enforceable agreement, is necessary in a formal contract . (A purely social or domestic arrangement or agreement does not constitute a contract.)
* **Legal capacity** is the legal right to enter into contracts. Under English common law some parties, including enemy aliens, convicts, infants and minors, lunatics and drunks, may not have the full legal capacity to contract, and a contract agreed by them may be unenforceable.
* **Legality** of the contract is an important requirement. A contract that is prohibited by statute (e.g. a contract for the sale of prohibited goods, or a contract for the sale of goods to a country that is subject to an embargo) is an illegal contract. A contract that is illegal at common law on the grounds of public policy (e.g. a contract to commit a crime or a tort or to defraud the Inland Revenue, or a contract that prejudices national safety or the administration of justice) is an illegal contract. Illegal contracts are totally void, but neither party can recover any money paid or property transferred under it.

* **Possibility of performance** If the performance of a contract is impossible when it was entered into, the whole contract becomes void.
* **Sufficient certainty of terms** means that details of the contract must be stated (i.e. expressed) or ascertainable. There must be a precise meaning to the words, with no ambiguous clauses.
* **Prescribed form** is necessary to make some contracts valid. In general no particular formality is required for the creation of a valid contract, and it may be oral, written, part-oral, part-written, or even implied from conduct. Some transactions are valid only if effected by deed (e.g. a transfer of shares in a British ship) or in writing (e.g. marine insurance contracts and promissory notes). Certain other contracts, although valid, can only be enforced at law if evidenced in writing.
* The agreement must not be rendered void either by some inherent defect, such as **operative mistake**. Certain contracts, though valid, may be liable to be set aside by one of the parties on grounds such as **misrepresentation** or the exercise of **undue influence**.
* A **misrepresentation** is an untrue statement of fact made by one party to the other in the course of negotiating a contract, that induces the other party to enter into the contract.
* **Mistake** is a misunderstanding or erroneous belief about a matter of fact (mistake of fact) or a matter of law (mistake of law). A **mistake of law** has no effect on the validity of a contract, but a **mistake of fact** may make the contract voidable, i.e. liable to be set aside by one of the parties, subject to certain conditions.
* **Duress** is pressure put on a person to act in a particular way, e.g. where a seafarer is ordered by the master of a ship changing articles during a voyage to sign a new crew agreement (i.e. a running agreement) before being discharged from the old one. Acts carried out under duress usually have no legal effect. A contract obtained by duress is voidable at law.
* **Undue influence** is influence that prevents someone from exercising an independent judgement with respect to any transaction.

B03c.4 Contract terms

* A written contract will usually set out the **rights, duties and obligations** of both parties in a set of terms dealing with matters of essential interest to the parties.
* In carriage of goods contracts terms mainly cover the transport of the goods from one place to another and the keeping of the goods safe and undamaged during transport. For notes on **matters required to be covered by contractual provisions in crew agreements**, see E07c.1b.
* Contract terms may usually be categorised as **conditions** (see B03c.4a) and **warranties** (see B03c.4b). A third, less important, categorisation is **innominate term** (see B03c.4c).

B03c.4a Conditions

* A **condition** is an essential contractual term going right to the root of the contract. If a condition is breached by one party, the contract becomes void and need not be fulfilled by the other party. In principle, if a condition is breached, the contract may be revoked by the injured party and he need not complete it.
* **Examples** of conditions are:
  * the (express) condition in a voyage charter that the vessel will be presented to the charterer at the agreed loading port during the agreed laydays; and
  * the (implied) condition in a marine insurance policy that the voyage will commence within a reasonable time of acceptance of the insurance and will be prosecuted with reasonable despatch throughout.

B03c.4b Warranties

* Except in insurance law, where it has a different meaning, a **warranty** is a contractual term less essential than a condition, such that its breach would not have the effect of frustrating the contract and cause the whole contract to be revoked.
* **Examples** of warranties are:
  * a charterer's warranty (to the shipowner) that the cargo loaded will not be dangerous to the ship; and
  * a shipowner's warranty (to his insurer) that the ship will be classed with a particular classification society and that class will be maintained.
* A **breach of warranty** will, however, entitle the injured party to claim **damages** from the party breaching the warranty. If a warranty is breached, the contract remains in force but the injured party is entitled to claim damages from the party breaching the warranty. In practice, the distinction between conditions and warranties is often unclear and depends to a large extent on the contract's wording.

B03c.4c Innominate terms

* An **innominate term** is a contractual term the identity of which as a condition or a warranty cannot be determined at the time the contract is made. Where an obligation in a contract is breached, the seriousness of that breach will determine the rights of the injured party, and only after that can it be determined whether the term was a condition or a warranty.

B03c.4d Implied terms

* An **implied term** is a contractual term considered so obvious that it is unnecessary to express it in the contract. E.g. in (English) common law, in every contract of carriage of goods by sea there is an implied term that the carrier will provide a seaworthy ship.

B03c.4e Express terms

* An **express term** is a contractual term which the parties consider materially affect their agreement, and is therefore expressed in the contract either **orally or in writing** (but most usually in writing). All the printed terms and conditions on a charter party form, in an employment contract document, etc. are thus express terms.

B03c.4f Standard terms and rider clauses

* **Standard terms** of a contract are usually those of the offeror (e.g. an oil company as charterer) and are printed on a form of his choice (e.g. SHELLVOY 3). They may be amended by deletion or the addition of side clauses and rider clauses.
* **Rider clauses** are typed clauses containing additional terms agreed by the parties. Charter parties commonly contain rider clauses covering matters not dealt with by the printed standard clauses. Where there is a conflict of terms, rider clauses supersede standard terms.

B03c.4g Side clauses, addenda and side letters

* **Side clauses** are additional clauses or words containing amendments to clauses that are typed in the margins of the printed text of a standard contract, each having a line running to the precise point of insertion in the main text. They can radically alter the meaning of a printed clause and therefore require close scrutiny when reading any contract containing them. Charter parties commonly contain side clauses amending the printed words (see F04c.1).
* **Addenda** to a contract, e.g. provisions of a charter party concerning the payment of freight or hire, may contain sensitive clauses that the parties do not, for reasons of security, want to be in the main charter party document.
* A **side letter** may concern matters relating to the contract, such as a charterer's instructions to the master relating to the charter.

B03c.5 Discharge of contracts

* "**Discharge**", with reference to contracts (including crew agreements) means release from a legal obligation.[14]
* A contract may be discharged by **performance**, **agreement**, **frustration** or **breach**.

B03c.5a Discharge by performance

- is the **carrying out** of the contractual obligations by both parties.

B03c.5b Discharge by agreement

- is where each party agrees that their obligations will be **waived**, e.g. where each party mutually agrees to cancel a future charter because of the non-availability of a ship or cargo.

---

[14] When a seaman is discharged from a ship he is, in fact, being discharged from the contractual obligations of the crew agreement.

B03c.5c Discharge by frustration

- is where something occurs which is **not the fault of either party**, and was **not contemplated** by either of them, and **prevents the contract from being performed** as intended. It makes the contract void, since it is **impossible to perform** and therefore lacks an essential element for validity.

B03c.5d Discharge by breach

- occurs when **one party repudiates his obligation**, or disables himself from performing his part of the contract, or **fails to perform** his part of the contract on or by the agreed date.
* A breach may be an **anticipatory breach**, i.e., occurring before the date for performance specified in the contract, or an **actual breach**.
* An **actual breach** may occur in three ways:
  • by **non-performance**, e.g. where a ship is not at the agreed place on the agreed date to start a charter;
  • by **defective performance**, e.g. where a ship arrives late when time is important; or
  • through **untruth** as regards a term of the contract, e.g. where the true condition of a ship is concealed from a charterer.

B03c.6 Privity and assignment of contracts

B03c.6a Doctrine of privity

* A contract is a private relationship between the parties to it, and no other party can acquire rights or incur liabilities under it. No party can acquire rights under a contract to which he is not a party, and no party can incur liabilities under a contract to which he is not a party. In other words, only the parties to a contract can sue and be sued on it. This is the common law **doctrine of privity**.

B03c.6b Transfer and assignment of contracts

* In some cases, **rights and liabilities under a contract** may be **assigned**, i.e. transferred to a third party. Where a contract is originally between parties A and B, B may transfer the contract to party C and drop out of the contract so that it will then be between A and C. Party B will generally have no further rights or liabilities under the contract. This happens, for example, where goods are sold by an original consignee to a third party to whom the bill of lading is transferred (see F07b.7). The new consignee, as holder of an original bill of lading, has the right to claim delivery of the goods from the carrier, but may also be liable for unpaid freight, demurrage, etc.

B03c.7 Law and jurisdiction governing a contract

* Every contract must be governed by the **law of some nation** or some set of **rules**. The governing law may be the law of the nation in which the contract was made or a nation mutually agreed by the parties to the contract. The nation or place in which disputes between the parties may be resolved is called the "**jurisdiction**", and should also be clearly specified in the contract terms. The choice of law and jurisdiction should be clearly stated in the contract terms in a **Law and Jurisdiction Clause**. A typical Law and Jurisdiction Clause might read "*This contract shall be governed by English law and any disputes shall be determined in the United Kingdom*".
* The **preferred law** of parties to contracts of international carriage by sea is in many cases **English law**, and the preferred jurisdiction is often England or the UK[15].
* Contracts for the supply of goods or services in a foreign port will probably be governed by the law of the port State, and disputes may have to be referred to a local court[16].
* An agreement is often made to resolve disputes by **arbitration** in, for example, London or New York, rather than litigation in the courts; in this case an **Arbitration Clause** will be inserted in the contract and this should indicate the agreed **place** for the arbitration (see B03i.1). Some charter parties offer a choice of clauses providing, on the one

---

[15] A Scottish ferry company's passenger ticket may provide that litigation arising out of the contract between a passenger and the company will be governed by Scottish law if the passenger brings the litigation in Scotland.
[16] For example, the Law and Arbitration Clause in a contract for the sale of marine fuels at an Estonian port provides that any dispute must be submitted for resolution by the Court of Tallinn and that the laws of Estonia will govern the contract.

hand, for dispute resolution under **English law and arbitration in London** or, on the other, under **US law and arbitration in New York**.
* Contracts of carriage evidenced by **bills of lading** usually contain a Paramount Clause (or "Clause Paramount") providing that the contract will be governed by either the **Hague Rules** or **Hague-Visby Rules**, depending on which rules are compulsorily applicable under national law. Where national law applies neither of these rules the carrier usually inserts a clause making the Hague-Visby Rules applicable to the bill of lading contract (see F07c.2).

B03d AGENCY

B03d.1 Nature of agency

* Any legal person (whether an individual, a firm, company, etc.) may appoint another legal person to **act on his behalf** in a particular matter, or in all his matters. The person thus appointed is an **agent**. The person on whose behalf the agent acts is his **principal**. The relationship between an agent and his principal is one of **agency**. The agency is created in most cases by **consent**, where the agent is given prior instructions to carry out a specific task or act in a certain capacity, but in some cases by later **ratification** of an act already performed (see B03d.3a).
* An agent only needs to state that he is acting for a principal, and does not have to name the principal. An unnamed principal is called an **undisclosed principal**.

B03d.2 Agent's authority

* The creation of an agency involves the giving of **authority** to the agent. The authority may be **actual authority** or **apparent authority** (also called **ostensible authority**).
* **Actual authority** may be **express** or **implied**. **Express authority** is given by words (spoken or written), such as when an officer is appointed by letter to command of a ship. Authority is **implied** when it is inferred by the conduct of the parties and the circumstances of the case, such as when a shipmaster is appointed to command by a shipowner, who thereby impliedly authorises him to carry out, on the owner's behalf, all the usual things that fall within the scope of a master's position, e.g. engagement and discharge of crew, signing of bills of lading, and purchasing of provisions. An exception to this would be where the principal has expressly placed a restriction on the implied authority of the agent, e.g. where the master is expressly prohibited from signing bills of lading.
* Where an agent's usual full authority is expressly restricted by his principal, but a third party, unaware of this restriction, is nevertheless brought by the agent into a contract with the principal, the agent has **apparent authority** (or **ostensible authority**) and the contract will (subject to the following conditions) be binding on the parties. There must be one or more representations (i.e. statements) by the principal or by the agent acting on his behalf. The representations must be of fact. They must be made to a third party, and the third party must rely on them.
* Most agencies are created by the principal giving his agent **express instructions**, e.g. where a port agent is appointed by a shipowner to act during the forthcoming visit of a vessel, and is given certain instructions.

B03d.2a Breach of warranty of authority

* An agent purporting to act on behalf of another party **impliedly warrants** that he has the authority to make contracts on behalf of his principal, i.e. he gives a **warranty of authority**.
* Where an agent brings a third party into a contractual relationship with his principal, the third party is entitled to rely on the agent's apparent authority. If the agent has **acted outside his authority**, the third party, although unable to enforce the contract with the principal, can sue the agent for **breach of warranty of authority**. (The agent will have no liability to his principal, since a principal cannot be bound by an act which he has not authorised.)

B03d.3 Types of agent and agency

* Agents are normally either **general agents** or **special agents**.
* A **general agent** is an agent who has authority to act for his principal in **all matters** concerning a particular trade or business, or of a particular nature. Many **liner agents**, for example, act as general agent in a particular city or country for one or more carriers.

* A **special agent** is an agent appointed for the carrying out of **particular duties** which are not part of his normal business activities. A special agent's authority is therefore limited by his actual instructions. Most **port agents** are special agents since their authority does not extend beyond their actual instructions. **Shipmasters** are similarly special agents for purposes of engaging and discharging crew, purchasing ships' stores and bunkers, and making salvage agreements in certain cases. If a special agent **acts outside his actual instructions** in some respect, his actions will not be binding on his principal.

* Other types of agent include **brokers, auctioneers, factors, mercantile agents**, and **del credere agents**. A **broker**, such as a shipbroker or stockbroker, is an intermediary employed by a principal to arrange a contract with a third party in return for a commission or brokerage. He does not take possession of goods and does not deal in his own name. An **auctioneer** is the agent of the seller, with authority to sell to the highest bidder. A **factor** is an agent entrusted with a principal's goods (or documents of title representing goods) for the purpose of sale. A **mercantile agent** is similar to a factor but may also have authority to buy goods, or to raise money for his principal on the security of goods. A **del credere** agent is an agent for the sale of goods who agrees to protect his principal against the risk of the buyer's insolvency by undertaking liability for the failure of the buyer to pay the price.

B03d.3a Agency by ratification

* A principal normally gives his agent the authority needed to act for him, and the authority thus comes before the act. Where an agent acts before obtaining the principal's authority, but the principal, on learning of the act, sanctions it, he thereby **ratifies** it and creates an **agency by ratification**. Certain conditions (which are not likely to be relevant to shipmasters) must be met for the ratification to be effective.

B03d.3b Agency of necessity

* In certain **emergency circumstances** an agent may **act beyond his authority** without liability for actions he takes on behalf of the principal. This form of agency is called "**agency of necessity**".
* Agency of necessity arises out of **exceptional circumstances**, e.g. fires, floods, war, imminent loss of a ship and/or cargo, etc. and **can only arise** when the following conditions are satisfied:
    1. there must be an **actual commercial necessity** for the agency (i.e. the **principal's property may be lost** if action on his behalf is not taken);
    2. there is **impossibility of communication** between agent and principal for the obtaining of instructions (e.g. cargo owners and owners of cargo containers cannot be contacted in the time available to the master of a disabled containership that is drifting towards a lee shore);
    3. the **agent acts** *bona fide* (i.e. in good faith) **in the best interests of the principal** (or **principals** where there is more than one, as in the case of many cargo-carrying ships).
* Agency of necessity will only be implied in favour of a person who is **already a duly appointed agent** for a principal (as is the case with a shipmaster), but who **must exceed his authority** in an emergency situation.
* It is for the **courts** to determine whether there was agency of necessity or not.
* For notes on the **master as an agent of necessity**, see E04f.2 and H04a.

B03d.4 Duties of an agent to his principal

* An **agent's duties** to his principal are:
    * to perform his duties **in person**[17], using **ordinary skill** and **diligence**, and if he purports to have special skills, to use his **special skills** also;
    * to **obey lawful instructions** of his principal, and when he is not instructed on a particular matter, to act in his principal's **best interests**;
    * to **disclose all information** relevant to the agency to the principal, avoiding any conflict of interest;
    * to **maintain confidentiality** about matters communicated to him as agent, and not to disclose them to prospective third parties;
    * to keep **proper accounts** of all transactions and render them to his principal on request;
    * not to make **extra profits** from the agency without disclosing them to his principal.

---

[17] It has been held that a person appointed as a sole agent has no authority to appoint a sub-agent. However, for normal business purposes an agent can delegate his duties to his own staff.

B03d.5 Duties of a principal to his agent

* A **principal's duties** to his agent are:
    * to **pay the agent's commission** or remuneration in accordance with the terms of the contract.
    * to **indemnify or reimburse the agent** for any expenses, losses or liabilities properly incurred in the course of the agency.

B03d.6 Liabilities of principal and agent

* A **principal** is generally liable for contracts arranged by his agent if within the agent's actual or apparent authority.
* Where the agent had authority, the principal will always bound by the agent's acts; this even includes acts involving **fraud** carried out by the agent within his actual authority. The principal will also be liable for **torts** such as misrepresentations, deceit, negligence, etc., committed by the agent within his apparent authority. In these cases, where the principal has had to compensate a third party he can claim an **indemnity** from the agent.

B03d.7 Termination of agency

* An agency may be **terminated** -
    - when the transaction for which the agent was hired is completed or the period for which the agent was hired is ended.
    - where either party gives notice that they are terminating the agency or where they both agree to end the agency. Certain types of agency cannot be revoked, however, e.g. where the agent has begun to perform his duty and has incurred a liability, or where a statute provides that the agency is not revocable.
    - by operation of law, such as on the death or the insanity of the principal or the agent, or on the bankruptcy of the principal or of the agent if it renders him incapable of performing his duties.

B03e LAW OF TORTS

B03e.1 Torts

* A "**tort**" is a wrongful act or omission by a person (other than a wrong that is purely a breach of contract), for which damages may be sued for in a civil court by the person wronged.
* **Torts recognised by law** include negligence, liability of occupiers of premises, strict liability, trespass to property, false imprisonment, nuisance, defamation, and miscellaneous torts of conspiracy, deceit and injurious falsehood.
* **Tortious liability** is quite separate from any liability under contract and generally arises from the breach of a duty under law (either common law or statute law). Where, for example, a ship causes damage to another person's property (e.g. collision damage[18] or pollution damage), the liability is tortious and the owner of the property suffering the damage may commence an **action in tort** to recover **damages** (i.e. he may **sue in tort**).
* **To succeed in an action for tort** it must usually be shown that the wrong was done intentionally or negligently, but there are some torts of **strict liability**.
* **The person chiefly liable** is the one who committed the tort, but under the **doctrine of vicarious liability** (see B03e.5) a person may be liable for a tort committed by another person.
* **The usual remedy** for a tort is an **action for damages**, but an **injunction** (or in Scotland, an **interdict**) can be obtained to prevent repetition of the injury, e.g. a libel by a newspaper.
* Some torts are also **breaches of contract**. Negligent navigation causing injury to a passenger, for example, is both the tort of negligence and breach of the contract to carry the passenger safely to the port of disembarkation. The passenger may sue the carrier either **in tort**, or **in contract**, or **both**.
* **Negligence** (see B03e.2) and **strict liability** (see B03e.6) are probably the torts of most concern to shipmasters. Collisions and damage to quays, etc. are torts. The negligent positioning of the gangway by the bosun of the *Himalaya* (for which the master was ultimately responsible) in Adler v. Dixon (1954) (The Himalaya) (see F07b.9a) was a tort. A master who wrongly uses his power of restraint may be liable in tort for **false imprisonment** (see E04h.4). Damage to cargo carried on board would not be a tort, but a pure breach of contract.
* **Many acts are crimes as well as torts**, assault being an obvious example. Reckless navigation is a crime but may also give rise to an action in tort if it causes injury to another person. The crime would be prosecuted like any other

---

[18] Several torts might apply to a collision between ships, the tort of negligence being by far the most important.

but it would be up to the injured person to seek compensation from the wrongdoer (i.e. the shipowner) by means of an action in tort.

* The following table compares procedures in cases dealing with contract, tort and crime.

Contract	Tort	Crime
Rights and duties arise under the terms of a contract.	Rights and duties arise under the civil law (i.e. statute law and common law).	Rights and duties arise under the criminal law.
A duty is owed to the other party (or parties) to the contract.	A duty is owed towards persons generally.	Criminal conduct is prescribed by the criminal law. A duty is owed to the general public.
A civil action is brought by the party alleging breach of contract against the other party to the contract.	A civil action is brought by the person wronged against the alleged wrong-doer.	A prosecution is brought by the Crown Prosecution Service or Procurator-Fiscal against the alleged offender.
The case is cited as *Smith v. Jones* (1996).	The case is cited as *Smith v. Jones* (1996).	The case is cited as *R. v. Jones* (1996).
The successful party is awarded damages or other remedy sought, e.g. injunction or specific performance.	The successful party is awarded damages or other remedy sought, e.g. an injunction.	The guilty party is punished by imprisonment, fine or non-custodial sentence, e.g. community service.

B03e.2 Negligence

* "**Negligence**" has been defined as "the omission to do something which a reasonable man....would do, or doing something which a prudent and reasonable man would not do". It is committed whenever a person owing a legal duty of care to another person breaches his duty with the result that damage of some kind (e.g. physical or financial harm) is caused to the other person.

* **Negligence** may also be described as "a failure to take reasonable care to avoid reasonably foreseeable risks of injury or damage to persons or property". Liability does not, therefore, arise simply from the causation of damage, but is based on unreasonable behaviour. (Damage may be caused without liability in negligence or, indeed, without any legal liability to compensate at all.)

* **To establish a claim for negligence** there must be:
  - a **plaintiff** who is entitled to claim;
  - a **defendant** who is responsible;
  - a **failure constituting negligence**; and
  - a **claimable damage** caused by that failure.

* **To succeed in an action for negligence**, the plaintiff has to prove:
  - a legal **duty of care**;
  - a **breach** of this duty; and
  - the **damage suffered** in consequence of the breach.

* In collision cases, **breach of the Collision Regulations** is likely to constitute good evidence of negligence.

B03e.3 Duty of care

* There is no standard legal definition of a "**duty of care**", and it has been held that "we may all be as careless (or negligent) as we wish, providing our carelessness does not cause harm, loss, injury or damage to another". Whether a party in a particular case had a duty of care or not is a question of law that may have to be decided by a judge in a court action.

* There are many situations where one person or party owes a duty of care to another, the most common arising on the **highways**. (All persons, whether drivers, riders or pedestrians, owe a duty of care to all other road users.) **Carriers** owe a duty of care to passengers and goods, **doctors** to their patients, **employers** to their employees, **teachers** to their students, etc. There are numerous situations where a duty of care arises, and thus **many forms of negligence**.

* **A shipmaster owes a duty of care** -
  - to the **shipowner**, for the care of his ship;
  - to every **owner** of goods carried by the ship;
  - to the **crew members** and supernumeraries (for their health, safety and well-being);
  - to the **passengers**, for their safety;
  - to other **persons who have business on board** the ship, such as stevedores, surveyors, pilots, agents and suppliers; and
  - to the **environment** (for its protection from pollution).

B03e.4 Employers' liability

* **A UK employer owes a duty of care to his employees** in that he must provide -
  * a reasonably **safe place of work**;
  * a reasonably **safe system of work**;
  * reasonably **safe machinery**; and
  * **competent fellow employees**.
* Liability can be in **tort** for negligence, and for **breach of statutory duty** under various statutes providing for health and safety at work, e.g. the MS (Health and Safety at Work) Regulations 1997.
* Under the **Employers' Liability (Compulsory Insurance) Act, 1969**, an employer (including a shipowner or manager) must obtain cover against liability for **bodily injury** or **disease** sustained by his employees in the course of, or arising from, their employment; this applies even where the injury is caused by defective equipment supplied by a third party[19]. A copy of the **insurance certificate** must be displayed at all premises where workers are employed. The employer is liable for **defective equipment** with which an employee is compelled to work in the course of his employment. Consequently a shipowner will be automatically liable to a crew member if he is injured by a defect in the ship, whether or not the shipowner has himself been negligent. For notes on the **Employers' Liability (Compulsory Insurance) Act, 1969** see C03c.4.
* In most countries a shipowner is only liable for injuries to a **stevedore** if the shipowner or his employees have been negligent.

B03e.5 Vicarious liability

* **"Vicarious liability"** is legal liability imposed on one person for torts or crimes committed by another, the aim of the doctrine being to ensure that employers pay the costs of damage caused by their business operations.
* Vicarious liability is dealt with under two headings:
  * the **liability of a master for the torts of his servant** ("master" in this sense meaning "employer"; and
  * the **liability of a principal for the torts of an independent contractor**.
* A **master-and-servant relationship** exists when one person employs another to do work for him on the basis that the servant is under the control of his employer as to the manner in which the work is to be done. Anyone employed under a "contract of service" (such as shipmasters and seamen) is a "servant", while their employers are "masters".
* **The general rule for masters and servants** is that a master is vicariously liable for the torts of his servants committed during the course of their employment, whether the master authorised them or not. The liability applies in respect of:
  * a wrongful act or omission expressly or impliedly authorised by the master;
  * a wrongful act or omission which is an unauthorised manner of doing something authorised by the master;
  * a wrongful and unauthorised act or omission which is ratified by the master.
* An **independent contractor** is under the control of his employer **as to what he must do**, but the employer cannot control the contractor's **method of work**. Independent contractors, e.g. stevedores, pilots, tug-owners, etc. work under a "contract for services", the principal in these examples usually being the shipowner or a charterer. The general rule here is that the principal is not liable for the torts of an independent contractor or of a servant employed by an independent contractor. (There are, however, some exceptions to this rule.)

B03e.6 Strict liability

* **"Strict liability"** is, in criminal law, liability for a crime which is imposed **whether the defendant was at fault or not**, i.e. without the need to prove *mens rea*, or "guilty mind". ("*Mens rea*" is the state of mind which, to secure a conviction, the prosecution in a criminal case must usually prove the defendant to have had when committing the crime. *Mens rea* varies from crime to crime, and is either established by precedent or defined in the statute creating the crime.)
* **An example of a crime of strict liability** is a breach of section 139 of the Merchant Shipping Act 1995, which provides that if a person given a Government direction under section 137 (following a shipping casualty threatening to cause harm to the environment, etc.) contravenes, or fails to comply with the direction, he shall be guilty of an offence. There are **no exceptions**, i.e. there is strict liability. Merchant shipping legislation creates numerous other offences of strict liability (sometimes called absolute liability) for such breaches of statutory duty.

---

[19] Most UK shipowners obtain cover against their liability for **crew claims** from their **P&I club** (see G02a.3).

* The rule of strict liability applies in certain civil cases also, where the defendant is liable for a tort or wrong regardless of whether there was any wrongful intent or negligence.
* **An example of a tort of strict liability** is oil pollution damage caused by a ship. **M.1577** explains that the victims of oil pollution damage do not have to prove fault on the part of the shipowner to obtain compensation; the **shipowner will be strictly liable** for any damage caused by oil pollution.

B03e.7 Breach of statutory duty

* An injured party may sue in tort for a breach of a duty imposed by legislation, i.e. a **statutory duty**. Most claims in this area concern industrial injuries arising under health and safety legislation. The employer may therefore be fined or imprisoned, as well as liable for damages.
* Whether the injured party will succeed in his action or not may depend whether the governing legislation imposed any **strict liability**; if so, **no proof of negligence or wrongful intent** will be required.
* Where a statute does not impose a strict liability, **negligence** will usually have to be proved by the plaintiff. He will have to prove:
  * that a statute was broken and the breach was a direct cause of the injury or damage;
  * that the plaintiff was a person from a class that the statute is intended to protect; and
  * that the injury complained of is one that the statute is intended to prevent.

B03f LAW OF CARRIAGE BY SEA

Certain aspects of general English law that are components of the law of carriage by sea (such as the laws of contract, agency, torts and liens), are covered elsewhere in Section B. Notes on aspects of English law that are particular to carriage of goods by sea, such as charter parties and bills of lading, can be found in Section F: The Ship's Employment.

B03g LIENS

B03g.1 Nature of and types of lien

* A "**lien**" is the right to retain possession of property, either as security for the performance of an obligation or to secure satisfaction of a claim.
* The lien may be **general**, when the property is held as security against all outstanding debts of the owner, or **particular**, when only the claims of the possessor in respect of the property held must be satisfied. Thus an unpaid seller may, in some contracts, be entitled to retain the goods until he receives the price, while a carrier may have a lien over goods he is transporting, and a repairer over goods he is repairing.
* **Whether a lien arises or not** depends on the **contract** and the usual practice of the trade.
* **A lien may be waived** by the holder.
* **A lien can be lost**, e.g. when goods on which a carrier has a possessory lien are delivered to another party through a mistake of a shore terminal in whose custody the goods have been left after the ship sails.
* If a purchaser of property is given notice of a lien, it binds him; otherwise he is not bound.
* **Two classes of lien concern shipmasters**:
  * **possessory liens** (see B03g.2) and
  * **maritime liens** (see B03g.3).

B03g.2 Possessory lien

* In common law **a carrier by sea has a possessory lien on goods in his possession** in three cases:
  * to recover **unpaid freight** (but not deadfreight, demurrage or damages for detention, for which a lien for recover must be specifically contracted for);
  * to recover **expenses incurred in protecting cargo** (since the master may have acted as an agent of necessity for the benefit of the cargo owner); and

- to recover **a General Average contribution due from cargo** (although in practice cargo is normally released once a General Average bond or guarantee has been signed, or security has been provided).

* Possession of the goods may be **actual** (i.e. where the goods are on board the carrier's vessel) or **constructive** (i.e. where they are not on his ship but still under his control, e.g. in a warehouse, tank, container compound etc. awaiting delivery).

* The common law right to exercise a possessory lien (i.e. a "**common law lien**") exists independently of contract. It is an **implied lien** and does not need to be expressly stated in the contract terms.

* A **contractual lien** is one incorporated by a term into a contract. By means of a contractual lien a carrier by sea may and often does - extend his common law lien for freight to include unpaid **deadfreight**, **demurrage** and (sometimes) **damages for detention**.

* A **Lien Clause**[20] is usually included in the terms of a **bill of lading** and a **charter party** (see F05e.2).

B03g.3 Maritime lien

- is a **claim against a ship**, her **cargo**, or **both**, as well as against the **freight** she will earn, in respect of **a service done to or injury caused by** any of them.
- is enforceable in the Admiralty Court (see B03b.7) by **proceedings *in rem*,** i.e. against the **property** involved (which is termed the *res*), and not against any person or persons who might own or manage or have possession of the property.
- can be enforced by **arrest** and **judicial sale**[21] of the property (unless security is given).
- **travels with the ship or cargo** whenever possession of it changes, and is good against a bona fide purchaser without notice.
- is **not dependent on possession**.

* **Examples** of maritime liens are:
  - the lien on a ship at fault in a **collision** in which property has been damaged;
  - the lien of a **salvor** on a ship and/or her cargo;
  - the lien of **seamen** on a ship for their wages;
  - the lien of a **master** on a ship for his wages and disbursements (i.e. his outgoings on behalf of the owners);
  - the lien of a **ship repairer** in respect of work done on a ship.

B03g.4 Seamen's lien for wages, etc.

* Section 39(1) of the Merchant Shipping Act 1995 provides that a seaman's lien, his remedies for the recovery of his wages, his right to wages in case of the wreck or loss of his ship, and any right he may have or obtain in the nature of salvage will not be capable of being renounced by any agreement. This does not affect such of the terms of any agreement made with the seamen of a ship which is to be employed on salvage service as provide for remuneration to be paid to them for salvage services rendered by the ship (section 39(2)).

B03g.5 Master's lien for remuneration, disbursements and liabilities

* The **master** of a ship will have the same lien for his **remuneration**, and all **disbursements** or **liabilities** properly made or incurred by him on account of the ship, as a seaman has for his wages (section 41, Merchant Shipping Act 1995).

B03g.6 Ranking of liens

* There may be several claims against a ship, each giving rise to a maritime lien or possessory lien. E.g., a ship may have been in **collision** with a second vessel, and **salvage services** may have been rendered by a third vessel. The owners of the salvaged vessel may become insolvent while the vessel is at a **repair yard** in the port of refuge and may fail to pay the **master's wages and disbursements**, the **crew's wages**, the **ship repairer's bill** and **other bills** incurred from **suppliers**, **port authority**, **agent**, etc. Meanwhile, there may be undischarged **mortgages** on the ship.

---

[20] **Lien clauses** can also be found in the standard terms of car hire agreements, road carriers' delivery notes, etc.

[21] Notices relating to "**judicial sales**" of ships, as a result of claimants exercising their liens, are sometimes carried in the back pages of *Lloyd's List*. Forthcoming sales are advertised, while some notices advertise for claimants to come forward in order to establish the priority of claims.

All these claimants may exercise **individual liens**, as outlined above, but the total of their claims may well exceed the value of the ship. In these circumstances, the vessel would probably be **arrested and sold** by order of the court.

* Obviously there will have to be some **priority** set for the discharging of the various liens when the sale proceeds are distributed to the claimants. There is **no statutory ranking** for maritime claims, and the priority is mainly at the discretion of the court.
* Normally, in the UK, the expenses of the **Admiralty Marshal** are paid first. **Maritime liens** will come next, before **mortgages** and **any statutory rights *in rem*** (i.e. against the ship or cargo, etc.) and **common law possessory liens**.
* A **salvage claim** will normally rank higher than other maritime liens, since the salvor has preserved the property and thereby the **fund** from which other claimants are claiming.
* **Wages liens** normally follow the salvor's lien, followed by **master's disbursements**.
* Among **several contractual liens**, and especially where there are several contractual liens for salvage services, the **later lien ranks first**, since it is the later act that has preserved the property for earlier claimants.
* Maritime liens arising for **damage arising from tort**, e.g. negligent navigation, normally rank equal to each other unless it can be proved that they arose at different times (e.g. where a ship has had a succession of collisions).
* Maritime liens arising from **tort** (e.g. negligent navigation) normally have priority over liens arising from **contracts agreed before the tort**, since contracts are entered into voluntarily. However, a **salvor's lien** attaching to a ship after a collision normally ranks higher than any damage liens resulting from the collision, for reasons explained above.
* The **ship repairer's lien**, which is a **common law possessory lien** and not a maritime lien, ranks lower than maritime liens attaching before the ship arrived at the repair yard. The repairer's lien will, however, rank before any later maritime liens arising while the ship is in his yard. His **lien will be lost** if the ship is allowed to leave the yard, but he will continue to have his statutory right *in rem*.

B03h ARREST OF SHIPS

B03h.1 Nature of arrest

* "**Arrest**", in relation to a ship, means "the detention of a ship by judicial process to secure a maritime claim, but does not include the seizure of a ship in execution or satisfaction of a judgment" (Article 1(2), Arrest Convention 1952).
  * The main **reason** for arresting a ship (or any other maritime property, such as cargo) is to obtain satisfaction of the judgement in an admiralty action *in rem*, i.e. against the property (see B03g.3).

B03h.2 Arrest Convention

* **The International Convention for the Unification of Certain Rules Relating to the Arrest of Seagoing Ships 1952** (the "**1952 Arrest Convention**") was intended to smooth out the differences between the approaches to ship arrest in countries which have common law legal systems (such as the UK) and countries which have civil law legal systems (such as France)[22]. The Convention contains Articles (amongst others) dealing with definitions, powers of arrest, exercise of right of arrest, release from arrest, right of re-arrest and multiple arrest and protection of owners and demise charterers of arrested ships.
* Article 2 of the 1952 Convention provides that a ship flying the flag of one of the contracting States to the Convention may be arrested in the jurisdiction of any of the contracting States in respect of any "maritime claim", but in respect of no other claim. "Maritime claim" is defined in Article 1 as a claim arising out of one or more of the following: damage caused by any ship either in collision or otherwise; loss of life or personal injury caused by any ship or occurring in connection with the operation of any ship; salvage; agreement relating to the use or hire of any ship whether by charterparty or otherwise; agreement relating to the carriage of goods in any ship whether by charterparty or otherwise; loss of or damage to goods including baggage carried in any ship; general average; bottomry; towage; pilotage; goods or materials wherever supplied to a ship for her operation or maintenance; construction, repair or equipment of any ship or dock charges and dues; wages of masters, officers or crew; master's disbursements, including disbursements made by shippers, charterers or agents on behalf of a ship or her owner; disputes as to the title to or ownership of any ship; disputes between co-owners of any ship as to the ownership, possession, employment or earnings of that ship; the mortgage or hypothecation of that any ship.

---

[22] While English admiralty law, for example, permits the arrest of a vessel only for a limited number of maritime claims, in civil law countries there is a *saisie conservatoire*, a discretionary right to detain all kinds of asset of the defendant until the final judgement is passed by the court.

* Article 3 permits "sister ship arrest" except where the dispute concerns ownership, possession, employment, earnings or mortgaging of a ship.
* Article 4 provides that a ship may only be arrested under the authority of a court or of the appropriate judicial authority of the Contracting State in which the arrest is made.
* A new, improved, **1999 Arrest Convention** has not yet entered into force. It permits several new maritime claims including claims for:
  * special compensation under Article 14 of the 1989 Salvage Convention;
  * environmental and similar claims;
  * wreck removal;
  * insurance premiums and P&I club calls;
  * commissions and brokerage, including agency fees;
  * sale contract disputes.

B03h.3 Ship arrest procedure in the UK

* **Arrest procedure** varies from nation to nation[23], but in many States, particularly those in which the law is based on English law, it is fairly similar to English procedure.
* The **injured party** (the **plaintiff**, e.g. the owner of a vessel collided with), if his claim is not satisfied, may issue against the ship a **writ of summons** in the Admiralty Court in London (see B03b.7) or, for relatively modest claims, in a county court.
* If the **defendant shipowner** fails to either satisfy the claim or to lodge an Acknowledgment of Service with the Court, the plaintiff can proceed with his court action to apply for a **warrant of arrest**. He must file an **affidavit** containing his grounds for arrest.
* Judgement may be given without further notice to the defendant shipowner and the court may issue the **warrant for arrest**.
* In actions for wages or possession of the ship where the ship is foreign, the **consul** representing the flag State is informed.
* The **Admiralty Marshal** instructs a Customs officer to **arrest the ship**. (In London the arrest is made by the Marshal's Officer in person.)
* The mere threat of arrest will often be sufficient to prompt owners into volunteering security to satisfy a claim. This will usually be a bank or insurance company **guarantee**, or a P&I club **letter of undertaking**, paid directly to the claimant, not to the court. In the absence of a guarantee or undertaking, the claimant can request a **bail bond** to be made, which would empower the court to "call it in". The amount of security must be reasonable.
* Unless security is provided and service of the writ accepted by the defendant's solicitors, so that the ship is released before receipt of the documents by Customs, the **Customs officer arrests the ship** by attaching a **Note of Action** to it, and carries out the Admiralty Marshal's instructions for keeping the ship safely under arrest. The **Writ**, along with a **warning notice** to potential removers of the property, is not "nailed to the mast" today but is generally posted on some conspicuous part of the ship such as the wheelhouse windows. The **Warrant** from the Court simultaneously prevents the vessel from sailing or being interfered with without written notice from the Admiralty Marshal on pain of proceedings for contempt of court.
* If the ship has not arrived, Customs will be instructed to arrest on arrival.
* Once the ship is under arrest she is in the **custody or possession of the Admiralty Marshal** on behalf of the court. The warrant of arrest on the ship covers everything belonging to it as part of its equipment, but excluding items which do not belong to the defendant shipowner such as the crew's property or passengers' luggage. Any **cargo** on board will not be under arrest, and arrangements can usually be made with the Admiralty Marshal to continue any discharge operations (unless the claim was for salvage and the cargo is also to be arrested). If the ship was loading, the Marshal will probably warn the agent not to continue loading if the writ has been issued by mortgagees, in view of the likelihood of the ship being sold on order of the court.

B03h.4 Release from arrest

* A ship under arrest can not be released unless the **plaintiff** agrees (which will normally be on the provision of adequate **security** for his claim) or the court orders the release. Release is normally granted on provision of a bank or insurance company **guarantee** or a P&I club's **letter of undertaking**. The plaintiff may, however, insist on bail or payment into the court. A guarantee will prevent re-arrest in respect of the same claim.

---

[23] P&I club bulletins occasionally carry articles on arrest procedure in a particular country.

B03i ARBITRATION AND MEDIATION

B03i.1 Arbitration

- may be defined as the **resolution of a dispute between contracting parties by one or more arbitrators appointed by the parties**.
- is often resorted to by contracting parties in shipping matters (e.g. a shipowner and charterer, a shipper and carrier, or a salvor and owner of salved property) **in preference to litigating** in the courts.
- usually has the following **benefits over litigation**:
  - parties' choice of arbitrator(s);
  - arbitrators are usually experts in the field, e.g. where a professional shipbroker arbitrates a charter party dispute, or a professional marine engineer arbitrates a fuel quality dispute;
  - confidentiality of hearing - only the parties, their witnesses and legal advisers are entitled to be present;
  - faster settlement;
  - lower costs;
  - less formality;
  - anonymity of parties and arbitrators (in a London arbitration);
  - enforceability of arbitrators' decisions abroad (whereas court judgements are not likely to be enforceable in foreign courts).
- has the following **disadvantages** in relation to litigation:
  - difficult points of law may need to be referred to a court;
  - right of appeal may be restricted (depending on wording of the Arbitration Clause in the contract between the disputing parties).
* The leading maritime arbitration centres are **London** and **New York**.
* New York arbitrations are generally **published**, while it is up to the parties in London arbitrations to decide whether the arbitration decision should be published.[24]
* London maritime arbitrations are usually conducted by members of the London Maritime Arbitrators Association (LMAA) and are on the LMAA Terms. They are subject to the provisions of the **Arbitration Act 1996**.
* **Appeals** from London arbitrations may usually made to a court (in most cases the Commercial Court).
* **LMAA website**: www.lmaa.org.uk

B03i.1a Arbitration clauses in shipping contracts

* An **Arbitration Clause** is included in most standard charter party forms and usually provides that the parties agree, in the event of a dispute under the contract, to refer the matter to arbitration at a named place, and that a specified number of arbitrators will be appointed. The clause may provide that the arbitration shall be conducted in accordance with the terms of a recognised dispute resolution service, such as the terms of the London Maritime Arbitrators Association (LMAA).
* BIMCO publishes a widely-used **Standard Law and Arbitration Clause**.

B03i.2 Mediation

* **Mediation** is a voluntary, confidential, "without prejudice" process that uses a neutral third party to help the parties in dispute come to a mutually agreed solution without having to go to court. It differs from arbitration and the courts in that a binding decision is not imposed on the parties by an arbitrator or judge. The process allows disputing parties to work out their solution assisted by the mediator.
* Mediation is, to the shipping industry, a relatively new "alternative dispute resolution" ("ADR") technique, but has gained widespread approval in other business sectors. To increase the shipping industry's awareness and use of mediation techniques in resolving disputes, BIMCO has developed a **Standard Dispute Resolution Clause** by incorporating a **Mediation Clause** into its widely used Standard Law and Arbitration Clause. Under the Mediation Clause either party may at any time, and from time to time, elect to refer the whole dispute or part of the dispute to mediation by serving on the other party a written notice calling on the other party to agree to mediation. If the other

---

[24] Summaries of London awards are published in Lloyd's Maritime Law Newsletter. Shipping journals such as *Fairplay International Shipping Weekly* and BIMCO Bulletin often feature reports of New York arbitrations, and occasionally of London arbitrations.

party does not agree to mediate, that fact may be brought to the attention of the arbitration tribunal and may be taken into account when the costs of the arbitration are allocated between the parties.

* **Clause 53 of the International Hull Clauses** (01/11/02) (Dispute resolution) provides that if disputes between the Assured and the Underwriters are not settled amicably by negotiation, they may be referred to **mediation** or some other form of alternative dispute resolution.

B04 Merchant shipping legislation

B04a TYPES OF UK LEGISLATION

B04a.1 Components of UK legislation

* **UK legislation** consists of laws made by, or under the authority of, Parliament, and comprises:
   • **statutes** or **primary legislation** (see B04a.2); and
   • **secondary legislation** (also called delegated or subordinate legislation) (see B04a.3).

B04a.2 Primary legislation

- **consists of statutes** known as **Acts**.
- **includes**:
  • **Acts of the UK Parliament**;
  • **Acts of the Scottish Parliament**; and
  • **Acts of the Northern Ireland Assembly**.
- **includes**:
  • **public acts**, such as the Merchant Shipping Act 1995 (c. 21);
  • **local acts**, such as the Mersey Docks and Harbour Act 1992 (c. x);
- may be **brought into force** either:
  • on such day as the relevant Secretary of State may appoint by order made by statutory instrument (i.e. called a **Commencement Order**). Different days may be appointed for different provisions or for different purposes. This was the procedure used for bringing Merchant Shipping Acts 1970 and 1988 into force; or
  • on the same day for all the sections of the act. (This was the procedure used for bringing the Merchant Shipping Act 1995 into force.)
* The **full title** of each Act of Parliament includes the **chapter number** occupied by the Act in the **statute book** for that year. The Merchant Shipping Act 1995 (c.21), for example, occupies the twenty-first chapter in the statute book for 1995.
* Since Acts do not always provide for the regulation of every detail of the subject dealt with, (especially where the subject is highly technical, such as shipping) the Act will often confer **powers** for the making of more detailed regulations, rules or orders by means of **statutory instrument** (see B04a.3a). Merchant Shipping Acts give the Secretary of State for Transport powers to make merchant shipping regulations concerning numerous matters in this way. Acts often specify details that need updating (fees, time limits, etc.) which is more easily done by statutory instrument.
* An Act may contain provisions giving effect in the UK to one or more **international treaties** to which the UK is a contracting State. Section 224 of the Merchant Shipping Act 1995, for example, gives effect to the International Salvage Convention 1989, as set out in Part I of Schedule 11 to the Act. Section 183 similarly gives effect to the Convention Relating to the Carriage of Passengers and Their Luggage by Sea (the Athens Convention), which is set out in Part I of Schedule 6, while section 185 gives effect to the Convention on Limitation of Liability for Maritime Claims 1976, as set out in Part I of Schedule 7.
* **Local acts** make statutory provisions that are applicable only within a particular locality in the UK. E.g. the Mersey Docks and Harbour Act 1992 is an Act to confer additional powers upon The Mersey Docks and Harbour Company; to amend the Mersey Docks and Harbour Act 1971 and the Mersey Docks and Harbour Act 1986; and for connected or other purposes.

* **Acts of the UK Parliament**[25] can be viewed on the **HMSO website** at www.legislation.hmso.gov.uk/acts.htm
* **Acts of the Scottish Parliament** (from 1999) can be viewed at www.scotland-legislation.hmso.gov.uk/legislation/scotland/s-acts.htm
* **Acts of the Northern Ireland Assembly** (from 2000) are at www.northernireland-legislation.hmso.gov.uk/legislation/northernireland/ni-acts.htm
* Courts cannot overturn the **validity** of an Act of Parliament, although judges may interpret the meaning of a provision of an Act.

B04a.3 Secondary, delegated or subordinate legislation

- is used to **supplement Acts** by prescribing the **detailed technical rules** required for the their operation.
- is mostly **governmental**, but also includes legislation made by a variety of **non-governmental bodies** who have been given certain powers by Parliament, e.g. **by-laws** made by local authorities, etc., **Rules of the Supreme Court**, and **codes of conduct** of certain professional bodies.
- can be made (and amended where necessary) without taking up parliamentary time, and is thus **more flexible** than Acts.
- **includes**:
  * **Orders in Council** (e.g. The General Medical Council (Interim Orders Committee) (Procedure) Rules Order of Council 2000 (SI 2000/2053);
  * **orders** (e.g. The Control of Pollution (SOLAS) Order 1998);
  * **regulations** (e.g. The Merchant Shipping (Carriage of Cargoes) Regulations 1999);
  * **rules** (e.g. The Merchant Shipping (Formal Investigations) Rules 1985);
  * **schemes** (e.g. The Merchant Shipping (Compensation to Seamen - War Damage to Effects) (Revocation) Scheme 1997); and
  * **byelaws** (e.g. Harwich Harbour Byelaws 1994).
* **Orders in Council** are **government orders of a legislative nature** made by the Crown and members of the Privy Council[26] and relate mainly to the regulation of certain professions and professional bodies (such as the General Medical Council). They include Orders amending the charters of various professional bodies, Orders approving Acts of British Overseas Territories, and Orders approving schemes of the Church Commissioners. Some Orders in Council are statutory instruments. Much Northern Ireland legislation is in the form of Orders in Council.
* **Orders, regulations and schemes** -
  - comprise the vast bulk of secondary legislation, with **regulations** being the most common form.
  - are published by HMSO as **statutory instruments**[27].
  - are **made under powers** conferred by an enabling Act. The Merchant Shipping (Section 63 Inquiries) Regulations 1997, for example, were made under the powers conferred by section 65(1) of the Merchant Shipping Act 1995.

B04a.3a UK statutory instruments

* **UK statutory instruments**, commonly referred to as "**SIs**" -
  - **consist** mostly of **Regulations** and **Orders**, a relatively small number being **Rules** or **Schemes** (see B04a.3a).
  - are **identified** by their **title** (e.g. The Merchant Shipping (Prevention of Oil Pollution) Regulations 1996), and the **year and number** of publication, e.g. 1996 No. 2154 (in the case of the Regulations referred to). SIs also have an ISBN number.
  - are **printed, published and sold** by **The Stationery Office** (TSO) under the authority and superintendence of the Controller of Her Majesty's Stationery Office, who is also the Queen's Printer of Acts of Parliament[28]. **TSO website**: www.tso.co.uk
  - are also published in **downloadable** form on the HMSO website (see below). At present only SIs published since 1 January 1987 are on the website.

---

[25] Full texts of all new Public General Acts from 1988 onwards, and all new Local Acts from 1991 onwards, are available on the HMSO website, as originally passed by the UK Parliament. New Acts are usually published on the website simultaneously with or, at least within 24 hours of their publication in printed form. Documents that are especially complex in terms of size or typography may take longer to prepare.

[26] The **Privy Council** is an ancient British body with limited statutory powers of legislation. It advises the Sovereign on certain judicial and other non-political matters, e.g. the grant of Royal Charters. At the meetings of the Privy Council, government ministers who are Privy Councillors obtain the Queen's formal approval to a number of Orders which have already been discussed and approved by them. Privy Council website: www.privy-council.org.uk

[27] Before 1948, instruments were known as Statutory Rules and Orders, abbreviated to SR & O.

[28] In 1987, 2279 United Kingdom SIs were published by HMSO. By 1997 the number had grown to 3114. In 2001, 4150 UK SIs were published. In 2002, just over 3047 were published up to 17 December.

* **Merchant shipping SIs** are usually drafted by DfT lawyers in consultation with MCA staff and are normally signed on behalf of the Secretary of State for Transport by the Parliamentary Under-Secretary of State for the DfT.
* Some SIs, such as Commencement Orders, are not subject to any Parliamentary procedure, and simply come into force on the date stated in them. However, most SIs are brought into effect only after they have been **laid before Parliament** in one of two procedures, i.e. negative or affirmative procedure. Under **negative procedure** the SI will become law on the date stated on it, but will be nullified if either House of Parliament passes a Motion calling for it annulment within a certain time (usually 40 days) from the date on which it was laid. This is the most common procedure. **Affirmative procedure** gives more stringent Parliamentary control, since the SI must receive the affirmative approval of both Houses before it can come into force. The applicable procedure for any SI is stated in its parent Act; e.g. section 306 of the Merchant Shipping Act 1995 provides that any SI containing regulations, orders or rules under the Act will be subject to annulment in pursuance of a resolution of either House of Parliament.
* **SIs are printed** by the Queen's Printer and are numbered consecutively for each calendar year in which he or she receives them; e.g. the first SI to be received in 2002 would be SI 2002 No. 1, regardless of its subject.
* There is **no statutory requirement** for any Act or SI to be carried on board any UK ship. The technical requirements of many modern Merchant Shipping SIs are contained in a **related Merchant Shipping Notice**; compliance with the MSN is made a statutory requirement by the SI.
* **HMSO website**: www.legislation.hmso.gov.uk/stat.htm

B04a.3b Byelaws

- are **local laws** which are made by a statutory public body such as a local authority or harbour authority, under an enabling power established by an Act of Parliament, for the good administration of their local area or undertaking. If there is general legislation (e.g. an Act or SI) to cover a subject, byelaws are not generally considered suitable.
- are a form of **delegated legislation**. They are not subject to the control of Parliament, but are made under powers conferred by an Act of Parliament or SI and take effect only after confirmation by a Government minister.
- are subject to **judicial control** (i.e. a court may order a change in or repeal of a byelaw).
- **create criminal offences** and may set **penalties** in the same way as any other legislation.
* **Byelaws concerning shipmasters** are mainly those made by **harbour authorities**. For notes **harbour byelaws**, see I02g.2.

B04a.3c Approved codes of practice

- are codes of practice **approved by relevant official bodies** such as the Health and Safety Commission (HSC) and the Maritime and Coastguard Agency (MCA).
- are bodies of **rules for practical guidance** only and **do not have the force of law** in themselves.
- provide **guidance** to employers, employees and their representatives **on the fulfilment of their statutory obligations** in relevant fields, such as health and safety, handling of certain types of cargo and operation of certain types of ship.
- **do not include IMO codes** such as the IMDG Code and STCW Code.
* Although **failure to observe any provision** of an approved code of practice is **not in itself an offence**, that failure may be taken by a court in criminal proceedings as proof that a person or company has contravened a regulation or section of an Act to which the provision relates, i.e. it may be **evidence** that the person or company has not fulfilled some statutory requirement. Non-compliance with the provisions in the Code of Safe Working Practices for Merchant Seamen on the rigging of accommodation ladders, for example, may be relied on by a court as evidence showing a breach of the MS (Means of Access) Regulations 1988. In such a case, however, it would be open to the person charged to satisfy the court that he has complied with the relevant regulation in some other way.
* **Statutory codes of practice** applying to UK vessels are shown in the following table. For detailed notes on each code see D03l.

Code title	Popular name	Related SI	Related M Notice	SBC ref.
The Safety of Small Commercial Motor Vessels – A Code of Practice	Yellow Code	1998/2771	-	D03l.2
The Safety of Small Commercial Sailing Vessels – A Code of Practice	Blue Code	1998/2771	-	D03l.3
The Safety of Small Workboats and Pilot Boats – A Code of Practice	Brown Code	1998/1609	MGN 50	D03l.4
The Code of Practice for the Safety of Small Vessels in Commercial Use for Sport or Pleasure operating from a Nominated Departure Point (NDP)	Red Code		MIN 77	D03l.6
The Code of Practice for Safety of Large Commercial Sailing and Motor Vessels	Megayacht Code or White Code	1998/2771	-	D03l.7
Code of Practice for Vessels Engaged in Oil Recovery Operations	Black Code	-	M.1663	D04g.11

B04a.4 M Notices

- disseminate safety, pollution prevention and other information of relevance to the shipping and fishing industries.
- are mostly issued by the MCA, although the MAIB may issue (and has issued) M Notices.
- have **no force of law** in themselves. An SI may, however, contain provisions requiring compliance with the provisions of a specified Merchant Shipping Notice; for example, the MS (Load Line) Regulations 1998 require compliance with the provisions in MSN 1752. Non-compliance with the provisions of the MSN would therefore constitute a breach of the SI's provisions, for which there is a criminal penalty.
- may contain directions that may in certain circumstances supersede directions in an SI. For example, the directions in M.1101 supersede the directions in SI 1960/1477 relating to passenger returns.
- since 11 March 1997 have been issued in three complementary series, as described below.
* **Merchant Shipping Notices** (MSNs) -
    - are used only to convey **mandatory information** that must be complied with under UK legislation.
    - **relate to SIs** and contain the **technical detail of regulations**.
    - are numbered in sequence, continuing the sequence in use prior to 11 March 1997, but with the prefix "MSN".
    - are printed on **white** paper.
    - can be viewed on the MCA website at www.mcga.gov.uk/publications/msn/default.htm
* **Marine Guidance Notes** (MGNs) -
    - provide **advice and guidance** to relevant parties in order to improve the safety of shipping and of life at sea, and to prevent or minimise pollution from shipping (in the manner of former "M" Notices).
    - are numbered in sequence from MGN 1.
    - are printed on **blue** paper.
    - can be viewed on the MCA website at www.mcga.gov.uk/publications/mgn/default.htm
* **Marine Information Notes** (MINs) -
    - provide **information for a more limited readership**, such as training establishments or equipment manufacturers, or which will only be of use for a **short period of time**, e.g. timetables for MCA examinations.
    - are numbered in sequence from MIN 1.
    - mostly have a fixed **cancellation date** which will typically be 12 months after publication.
    - are printed on **green** paper.
    - can be viewed on the **MCA website** at www.mcga.gov.uk/publications/min/default.htm
* A **suffix (M), (F), or (M+F)** is used to indicate whether a MSN, MGN or MIN is intended for merchant ships (M), or fishing vessels (F), or both (M+F).
* **SOLAS regulation V/19.2.1.4** provides that all ships, irrespective of size, must have **nautical charts and nautical publications** to plan and display the ship's route for the intended voyage and to plot and monitor positions throughout the voyage. This regulation is given effect in the UK by **regulation 5 of the MS (Safety of Navigation) Regulations 2002** (SI 2002/1473) (see H01f.2) and the MCA's **2002 SOLAS V publication** (see H01f.2a). **Guidance note 5 in Annex 3 to the 2002 SOLAS V publication** lists publications considered by the MCA to satisfy the requirements of SOLAS regulation V/19.2.1.4, and includes **Merchant Shipping Notices, Marine Guidance Notes and Marine Information Notes** published by the MCA. The Guidance Notes state that **only those parts** of the publication which are **relevant to the ship's voyage and operation** need be carried.
* As promulgated in **MIN 129**, copies of **individual MSNs, MGNs and MINs** and an **annual list** may be obtained from MCA Marine Offices or from the MCA's distribution agent: Mail Marketing (Scotland), Bloomsgrove Industrial Estate, Norton Street, Nottingham, NG7 3JG, England. Tel: 0115 901 3336. Fax: 0115 901 3334. E-mail: mca@promo-solution.com
* **Bound volumes** of M Notices can be bought at Stationery Office Bookshops (formerly known as Government Bookshops), addresses of which can be found at www.the-stationery-office.co.uk or in Yellow Pages.
* **Multiple copies** of MSNs, MGNs and MINs are available in a joint annual subscription. For details see **MIN 122**.
* A Marine Information Note is published annually by the MCA listing current MSNs, MGNs and MINs.

B04b LEGISLATION IN FORCE

* The following tables include all known Merchant Shipping legislation affecting shipmasters in force at the time of writing. In the titles, "MS" means "Merchant Shipping" and "FV" means "Fishing Vessels".
* Readers using the annually-issued Marine Information Note (MIN) entitled "Principal Acts and Regulations on Merchant Shipping" should note that the section headings of the MIN differ from those used below.

B04b.1 Acts of Parliament

Year	Chapter	Title	SBC references
1971	c.19	Carriage of Goods by Sea Act 1971	B04c.2, F07c.3
1971	c.60	Prevention of Oil Pollution Act 1971	B04c.9
1985	c.22	Dangerous Vessels Act 1985	B04c.8, I02g.3
1987	c.21	Pilotage Act 1987	B04c.4, I01b
1990	c.31	Aviation and Maritime Security Act 1990	B04c.6
1992	c.50	Carriage of Goods by Sea Act 1992	B04c.3, F07d
1995	c.21	Merchant Shipping Act 1995	B04c.1
1995	c.22	Shipping and Trading Interests (Protection) Act 1995	B04c.7
1997	c.28	Merchant Shipping and Maritime Security Act 1997	B04c.5, H04b.9

B04b.1a Commencement Orders

Year	SI No.	Title	SBC references
1996	1210 (C.20)	Merchant Shipping Act 1995 (Appointed Day No. 1) Order 1996	B04c.1
1997	1082 (C.39)	Merchant Shipping and Maritime Security Act 1997 (Commencement No.1) Order 1997	B04c.2
1997	1539 (C.62)	Merchant Shipping and Maritime Security Act 1997 (Commencement No.2) Order 1997	B04c.2
1997	3107 (C.114)	Merchant Shipping Act 1995 (Appointed Day No. 2) Order 1997	B04c.1

B04b.2 Statutory Instruments - General

Year	SI No.	Title	SBC references
1979	1519	MS (Increased Penalties) Regulations 1979	
1980	531	MS (Safety Convention) (Transitional Provisions) Regulations 1980	
1981	237	MS (Safety Convention 1974) (Countries) Order 1981	
1981	568	MS (Modification of Enactments) Regulations 1981	
1981	584	MS (Safety Convention) (Transitional Provisions) Regulations 1981	
1985	212	MS (Modification of Enactments) Regulations 1985	
1985	405	MS (Liner Conferences) (Conditions for Recognition) Regulations 1985	
1985	406	MS (Liner Conferences) (Mandatory Provisions) Regulations 1985	
1986	2285	General Lighthouse Authorities (Beacons: Hyperbolic Systems) Order 1986	
1987	37	Dangerous Substances in Harbour Areas Regulations 1987	I02g.4
1989	662	MS (Merchant Navy Reserve) Regulations 1989	
1989	1991	MS (Ministry of Defence Ships) Order 1989	D01c.5
1991	347	MS The General Lighthouse Authority (Beacons: Hyperbolic Systems) Order 1991	
1992	1293	MS (Ministry of Defence Commercially Managed Ships) Order 1992	D01c.5
1992	1294	MS (Ministry of Defence Yachts) Order 1992	D01c.5
1994	2788	MS (Sterling Equivalents) (Revocation) Order 1994	
1997	3016	The General Lighthouse Authorities (Beacons: Maritime Differential Correction Systems) Order 1997	
1998	209	MS (Compulsory Insurance: Ships Receiving Trans-shipped Fish) Regulations 1998	
1998	2771	MS (Vessels in Commercial Use for Sport or Pleasure) Regulations 1998	D03l.8
2000	482	MS (Vessels in Commercial Use for Sport or Pleasure) (Amendment) Regulations 2000	D03l.8
2001	1638	MS (Miscellaneous Amendments) Regulations 2001	
2002	1650	MS (Miscellaneous Amendments) Regulations 2002	

B04b.3 Cargo (including packaged dangerous goods and marine pollutants)

Year	SI No.	Title	SBC references
1997	2367	MS (Dangerous Goods and Marine Pollutants) Regulations 1997	A03c.1a, F07f.2
1999	336	MS (Carriage of Cargoes) Regulations 1999	A03c.1a, F07g
2000	3216	MS (Carriage of Packaged Irradiated Nuclear Fuel etc.) (INF Code) Regulations 2000	F07h

B04b.4 Construction, equipment and operation - cargo ships

Year	SI No.	Title	SBC references
1997	1509	MS (Cargo Ship Construction) Regulations 1997	A03c.1a, D02a.1, D04d.1
1999	643	MS (Cargo Ship Construction) (Amendment) Regulations 1999	D02a.1
1999	1644	MS (Additional Safety Measures for Bulk Carriers) Regulations 1999	A03c.1a, D03f.3a, F07g.1g, I05d.4

B04b.5 Construction, equipment and operation – passenger ships and ro-ro ships

Year	SI No.	Title	SBC references
1988	1275	MS (Weighing of Goods Vehicles and Other Cargo) Regulations 1988	D03b.2
1988	2272	MS (Emergency Equipment Lockers for Ro/Ro Passenger Ships) Regulations 1988	
1989	270	MS (Weighing of Goods Vehicles and Other Cargo) Regulations 1989	D03b.2
1989	568	MS (Weighing of Goods Vehicles and Other Cargo) (Application to Non-UK Ships) Regulations 1989	
1992	2356	MS (Categorisation of Waters) Regulations 1992	D04c.2a
1997	647	MS (Ro-Ro Passenger Ship Survivability) Regulations 1997	D03b.5c
1998	3022	MS (ISM Code - Ro-Ro Passenger Ferries) Regulations 1998	C04a, D03b.1a
1998	2514	MS (Passenger Ship Construction: Ships of Classes I, II and II(A)) Regulations 1998	A03c.1a, D02a.1
1998	2515	MS (Passenger Ship Construction: Ships of Classes III to VI(A)) Regulations 1998	D04d.1
2000	2687	MS (Passenger Ships on Domestic Voyages) Regulations 2000	D03b.6b
2001	152	MS (Mandatory Surveys for Ro-Ro Ferry and High Speed Passenger Craft) Regulations 2001	D04f.4
2001	3209	MS (Domestic Passenger Ships) (Safety Management Code) Regulations 2001	C04a, C04c, D03b.1b, D04c.2
2003	771	MS (Passenger Ships on Domestic Voyages) (Amendment) Regulations 2003	D03b.6b

B04b.6 Construction, equipment and operation - gas carriers and chemical tankers

Year	SI No.	Title	SBC references
1994	2464	MS (Gas Carriers) Regulations 1994	D03d.2a
1996	3010	MS (Dangerous or Noxious Liquid Substances in Bulk) Regulations 1996	B03b.3f, D03e.2a, D04g.3, D05b.3, H03b.2
1998	1153	MS (Dangerous or Noxious Liquid Substances in Bulk) (Amendment) Regulations 1998	D03e.2a, D04g.3, H03b.2

B04b.7 Construction, equipment and operation - high speed craft

Year	SI No.	Title	SBC references
1996	3188	MS (High Speed Craft) Regulations 1996	A03c.1a, D02a.1, D03i.2, D04v
2001	152	MS (Mandatory Surveys for Ro-Ro Ferry and High Speed Passenger Craft) Regulations 2001	D03i.3, D04f.4

B04b.8 Construction, equipment and operation – miscellaneous

Year	SI No.	Title	SBC references
1985	661	MS (Application of Construction and Survey Regulations to Other Ships) Regulations 1985	
1995	1210	MS (Survey and Certification) Regulations 1995	A03c.1a, B03b.3e, D04f.2
1995	1802	MS and FV (Medical Stores) Regulations 1995	D04p
1996	147	MS (Delegation of Type Approval) Regulations 1996	D04b.2
1996	2418	MS (Survey and Certification) (Amendment) Regulations 1996	D04f.2
1996	2821	MS and FV (Medical Stores) (Amendment) Regulations 1996	D04p
1996	2908	MS (Ship Inspection and Survey Organisations) Regulations 1996	D04d.2
1997	529	MS (Minimum Standards of Communications) Regulations 1997	D03a.4
1998	1561	MS (International Safety Management (ISM) Code) Regulations 1998	C04a, D03a.1
1999	1704	MS (Minimum Standards of Safety Communications) (Amendment) Regulations 1999	D03a.4
1999	1957	MS (Marine Equipment) Regulations 1999	D04b.1
2000	1334	MS (Survey and Certification) (Amendment) Regulations 2000	D04f.2
2002	1473	MS (Safety of Navigation) Regulations	D03a.5, D03l.8, D04n.1, D04n.2, D04o, D04t.7, D04w, H01a.6, H01a.11, H01f.2, H01f.3, H01f.4, H01f.5, H04b.1, H06d.2, I01b.9, I07i.2, I07i.4, I07i.7

B04b.9 Crew accommodation

Year	SI No.	Title	SBC references
1997	1508	MS (Crew Accommodation) Regulations 1997	E08g.1, E08h.3

B04b.10 Crew agreements

Year	SI No.	Title	SBC references
1977	45	MS (Crew Agreements, Lists of Crew and Discharge of Seamen) (Merchant Ships and Other Vessels) Regulations 1977	
1991	2144	MS (Crew Agreements, Lists of Crew and Discharge of Seamen) Regulations 1991	E07b

B04b.11 Crew - training, certification, manning, hours of work and watchkeeping

Year	SI No.	Title	SBC references
1970	294	MS (Certificate of Competency as AB) Regulations 1970	E02d.2
1981	1076	MS (Certification of Ships' Cooks) Regulations 1970	E02d.3
1987	408	MS (Seamen's Documents) Regulations 1987	E06a.2
1993	1213	MS (Local Passenger Vessels) (Masters' Licences and Hours, Manning and Training) Regulations 1993	E02d.1, E03c.5
1995	1427	MS (Officer Nationality) Regulations 1995	E03d.1a
1995	1803	MS (Ships' Doctors) Regulations 1995	E03d.4
1995	1900	MS (Seamen's Documents) (Amendment) Regulations 1995	E06a.2
1997	346	MS (Disqualification of Holder of Seaman's Certificates) Regulations 1997	E02d.8
1997	348	MS (Training and Certification) Regulations 1997	E02b
1997	1320	MS (Safe Manning, Hours of Work and Watchkeeping) Regulations 1997	E03b.1
1997	1911	MS (Training, Certification and Safe Manning) (Amendment) Regulations 1997	E02b.2
1998	2411	MS and FV (Health and Safety at Work) (Employment of Young Persons) Regulations 1995	E03c.4, E05c.1
1999	3281	MS (Seamen's Documents) (Amendment) Regulations 1999	E06a.2
2000	484	MS (Safe Manning, Hours of Work and Watchkeeping) (Amendment) Regulations 2000	E03b.1
2000	836	MS (Training and Certification) (Amendment) Regulations 2000	E02b.2
2002	2125	MS (Hours of Work) Regulations 2002	E03c.1

B04b.12 Crew - financial matters

Year	SI No.	Title	SBC references
1972	1304	Seamen's Savings Bank Regulations 1972	
1972	1635	MS (Maintenance of Seamen's Dependants) Regulations 1972	
1972	1698	MS (Seamen's Allotments) Regulations 1972	E09c.2
1972	1699	MS (Seamen's Wages) (Contributions) Regulations 1972	E09b.2c
1972	1700	MS (Seamen's Wages and Accounts) Regulations 1972	E09b.2
1972	1875	MS (Maintenance of Seamen's Dependants) (No. 2) Regulations 1972	
1978	1757	MS (Seamen's Wages and Accounts) (Amendment) Regulations 1978	E09b.2
1985	340	MS (Seamen's Wages and Accounts) (Amendment) Regulations 1985	E09b.2
1988	479	MS (Maintenance of Seamen's Dependants) (Amendment) Regulations 1988	
1994	791	MS (Seamen's Wages and Accounts) (Amendment) Regulations 1994	E09b.2
1997	1674	MS (Compensation to Seamen - War Damage to Effects) (Revocation) Scheme 1997	
1999	3360	MS (Seamen's Wages and Accounts) (Amendment) Regulations 1999	E09b.2

B04b.13 Crew – miscellaneous

Year	SI No.	Title	SBC references
1979	97	MS (Repatriation) Regulations 1979	E13c.1
1979	1577	MS (Returns of Births and Deaths) Regulations 1979	E14b
1982	1525	MS (Foreign Deserters) (Disapplication) Order 1982	
1983	1801	MS (Property of Deceased Seamen and Official Log Books) (Amendment) Regulations 1983	E14c
1985	174	MS (Foreign Deserters) (Disapplication) Order 1985	

B04b.14 Distress signals and prevention of collisions

Year	SI No.	Title	SBC references
1996	75	MS (Distress Signals and Prevention of Collisions) Regulations 1996	B03b.3e, H02a.2, H06b.1
2002	1473	MS (Safety of Navigation) Regulations 2002	H04b.1

B04b.15 Diving safety

Year	SI No.	Title	SBC references
2002	1587	MS (Diving Safety) Regulations 2002	D03h.7

B04b.16 Fees

Year	SI No.	Title	SBC references
1996	3243	MS (Fees) Regulations 1996	B05b.1
1998	531	MS (Fees) (Amendment) Regulations 1998	
1999	1063	MS (Fees) (Amendment) Regulations 1999	
1999	1923	MS (Fees) (Amendment No. 2) Regulations 1999	
2000	1683	MS (Fees) (Amendment) Regulations 2000	
2001	3340	MS (Fees) (Amendment) Regulations 2001	
2001	3628	MS (Fees) (Amendment No. 2) Regulations 2001	
2003	788	MS (Fees) (Amendment) Regulations 2003	

B04b.17 Fire

Year	SI No.	Title	SBC references
1998	1011	MS (Fire Protection: Small Ships) Regulations 1998	D04l.2
1998	1012	MS (Fire Protection: Large Ships) Regulations 1998	A03c.1a, D04l.1
1999	992	MS (Fire Protection) (Amendment) Regulations 1999	D04l.1

B04b.18 Inquiries and investigations

Year	SI No.	Title	SBC references
1982	1752	MS (Section 52 Inquiries) Rules 1982	B07c
1985	1001	MS (Formal Investigations) Rules 1985	B07b
1989	84	MS (Section 52 Inquiries) Rules (Amendment) Rules 1989	B07c
1990	123	MS (Formal Investigations) (Amendment) Rules 1990	B07b
1997	347	MS (Section 63 Inquiries) Rules 1997	B07d
2000	1623	MS (Formal Investigations) (Amendment) Rules 2000	B07b

B04b.19 Liability and indemnification of shipowners

Year	SI No.	Title	SBC references
1986	1040	MS (Liability of Shipowners and Others) (Calculation of Tonnage) Order 1986	C03d
1986	2224	MS (Limitations of Liability for Maritime Claims) (Parties to Convention) Regulations 1986	
1987	220	MS (Indemnification of Shipowners) Order 1987	
1994	3049	MS (Liability of Shipowners and Others) (Rate of Interest) Order 1994	
1998	1258	Convention on Limitation of Liability for Maritime Claims (Amendment) Order 1998	
1999	1922	MS (Liability of Shipowners and Others) (Rate of Interest) Regulations 1999	

B04b.20 Life-saving appliances

Year	SI No.	Title	SBC references
1999	2721	MS (Life-Saving Appliances for Ships Other Than Ships of Classes III to VI(A)) Regulations 1999	A03c.1a, D04k.1a
1999	2723	MS (Life-Saving Appliances for Passenger Ships of Classes III to VI(A)) Regulations 1999	D04k.1b
2000	2558	MS (Life-Saving Appliances for Passenger Ships of Classes III to VI(A)) (Amendment) Regulations 2000	D04k.1b
2001	2642	MS (Life-Saving Appliances) (Amendment) Regulations 2001	D04k.1a

B04b.21 Light dues

Year	SI No.	Title	SBC references
1997	562	MS (Light Dues) Regulations 1997	I07g.2
1998	495	MS (Light Dues) (Amendment) Regulations 1998	I07g.2
2002	504	MS (Light Dues) (Amendment) Regulations 2002	I07g.2

B04b.22 Load lines

Year	SI No.	Title	SBC references
1973	1979	MS (Metrication) Regulations 1973	
1998	2241	MS (Load Line) Regulations 1998	D04i.1, I07b.1
2000	1335	MS (Load Line) (Amendment) Regulations 2000	D04i.1

B04b.23 Musters and safety training

Year	SI No.	Title	SBC references
1999	2722	MS (Musters, Training and Decision Support Systems) Regulations 1999	E08l.1, I07f.2

B04b.24 Navigational safety

Year	SI No.	Title	SBC references
2002	1473	MS (Safety of Navigation) Regulations	A03c.1a, H01f.2, H06d.2

B04b.25 Occupational health and safety

Year	SI No.	Title	SBC references
1960	1932	The Shipbuilding and Ship-repairing Regulations 1960	I06e
1979	1435	Public Health (Ships) Regulations 1979	D04q.2, E06c.1, I01e.1
1988	1636	MS (Guarding of Machinery and Safety of Electrical Equipment) Regulations 1988	E08e.1
1988	1637	MS (Means of Access) Regulations 1988	E08e.2
1988	1638	MS (Entry into Dangerous Spaces) Regulations 1988	E08e.3
1988	1639	MS (Hatches and Lifting Plant) Regulations 1988	D04r.1, E08e.4
1988	1641	MS (Safe Movement on Board Ship) Regulations 1988	E08e.5
1988	2274	MS (Safety at Work Regulations) (Non-UK Ships) Regulations 1988	
1993	1213	MS (Local Passenger Vessels) (Masters' Licences and Hours, Manning and Training) Regulations 1993	E02d.1
1997	2962	MS and FV (Health and Safety at Work) Regulations 1997	E08b.2
1998	587	Suspension from Work on Maternity Grounds (Merchant Ships and Fishing Vessels) Order 1998	E08b.2h
1998	1838	MS (Code of Safe Working Practices for Merchant Seamen) Regulations 1998	E08c.3
1998	2411	MS (Health and Safety at Work) (Employment of Young Persons) Regulations 1998	E03c.4, E05c.1
1998	2857	MS and FV (Manual Handling Operations) Regulations 1998	E08e.8
1999	2205	MS and FV (Personal Protective Equipment) Regulations 1999	E08e.6
2000	2567	MS (Accident Reporting and Investigation) Regulations 1999	E08k.1
2001	54	MS and FV (Health and Safety at Work) (Amendment) Regulations 2001	E08b.2
2001	3444	MS and FV (Safety Signs and Signals) Regulations 2001	E08e.7
2002	2055	MS (Medical Examination) Regulations 2002	E06c.2

B04b.26 Official log books

Year	SI No.	Title	SBC references
1981	569	MS (Official Log Books) Regulations 1981	D05a.2, D05b.1, D05b.5, E08k.2, E14a.2, E14c, E14d, H04b.3, H04b.4, H04b.7, H04b.8, H04b.9, H04b.13, H04c.6, H04d
1985	1828	MS (Official Log Books) (Amendment) Regulations 1985	D05a.2
1991	2145	MS (Official Log Books) (Amendment) Regulations 1991	D05a.2
1997	1511	MS (Official Log Books for Merchant Ships and Fishing Vessels) (Amendment) Regulations 1997	D05a.2

B04b.27 Passengers

Year	SI No.	Title	SBC references
1960	1477	MS (Passenger Returns) Regulations 1960	I01i
1987	670	MS Carriage of Passengers and Their Luggage by Sea (Domestic Carriage) Order 1987	
1987	703	MS Carriage of Passengers and Their Luggage by Sea (Notice) Order 1987	
1987	855	MS Carriage of Passengers and Their Luggage by Sea (United Kingdom Carriers) Order 1987	
1989	1880	MS The Carriage of Passengers and Their Luggage by Sea (UK Carriers) (Amendment) Order 1989	
1990	660	MS (Emergency Information for Passengers) Regulations 1990	I07f.3
1999	1869	MS (Counting and Registration of Persons on Board Passenger Ships) Regulations 1999	I07f.1

B04b.28 Pilotage

Year	SI No.	Title	SBC references
1998	1609	MS (Small Workboats and Pilot Boats) Regulations 1998	D03l.5a
2002	1473	MS (Safety of Navigation) Regulations	H01f.2, I01b.9
2003	1230	The Pilotage (Recognition of Qualifications and Experience) Regulations 2003	

B04b.29 Pollution – garbage

Year	SI No.	Title	SBC references
1988	2252	MS (Prevention of Pollution by Garbage) Order 1988	
1993	1581	MS (Prevention of Pollution by Garbage) (Amendment) Order 1993	
1998	1377	MS (Prevention of Pollution by Garbage) Regulations 1998	B03b.3f, H03e.2

B04b.30 Pollution - dangerous and noxious liquid substances in bulk

Year	SI No.	Title	SBC references
1996	3010	MS (Dangerous or Noxious Liquid Substances in Bulk) Regulations 1996	B03b.3f, D03e.2a, D04g.3, D05b.3, H03b.1, H03b.2
1998	1153	MS (Dangerous or Noxious Liquid Substances in Bulk) (Amendment) Regulations 1998	D03e.2a, D04g.3, H03b.2

B04b.31 Pollution – oil

Year	SI No.	Title	SBC references
1957	358	Oil in Navigable Waters (Transfer Records) Regulations 1957	I06a.8
1967	710	Oil in Navigable Waters (Heavy Diesel Oil) Regulations 1967	
1981	612	Prevention of Oil Pollution (Convention Countries) Order 1981	
1983	1106	MS (Prevention of Oil Pollution) Order 1983	
1985	2002	MS (Prevention of Oil Pollution) (Amendment) Order 1985	
1986	2223	MS International Oil Pollution Compensation Fund (Parties to Convention) Order 1986	
1986	2225	MS (Oil Pollution) (Parties to Convention) Order 1986	
1990	2595	MP The Merchant Shipping (Prevention and Control of Pollution) Order 1990	
1991	2885	MS (Prevention of Oil Pollution) (Amendment) Order 1991	
1993	1580	MS (Prevention of Oil Pollution) (Amendment) Order 1993	
1996	282	MS (Prevention of Pollution) (Law of the Sea Convention) Order 1996	
1996	2154	MS (Prevention of Oil Pollution) Regulations 1996	B03b.2j, B03b.3d, B05b.4e, D03a.2, D04g.1, H03a.2, H03a.3, H03a.4, H03a.5, H03a.6, H03a.7, H03a.8, H03a.9
1997	1820	Oil Pollution (Compulsory Insurance) Regulations 1997	G04d.1b
1997	1910	MS (Prevention of Oil Pollution) (Amendment) Regulations 1997	D03a.2, H03a.2
1997	2566	MS (Liability and Compensation for Oil Pollution Damage) (Transitional Provisions) (Revocation) Order 1997	
1997	2567	MS (Oil Pollution Preparedness, Response and Cooperation Convention) Order 1997	
1998	1056	MS (Oil Pollution Preparedness, Response and Co-operation Convention) Regulations 1998	H06e.2
2000	483	MS (Prevention of Oil Pollution) (Amendment) Regulations 2000	D03a.2, H03a.2
2001	1639	MS (Oil Pollution Preparedness, Response and Co-operation Convention) (Amendment) Regulations 2001	

B04b.32 Pollution - jurisdiction and miscellaneous

Year	SI No.	Title	SBC references
1980	1093	MS (Prevention of Pollution) (Intervention) Order 1980	
1996	282	MS (Prevention of Pollution) (Law of the Sea Convention) Order 1996	A02b
1996	972	The Special Waste Regulations 1996	I06c.6
1996	2128	MS (Prevention of Pollution) (Limits) Regulations 1996	A02b, I01a.1b
1997	506	MS (Prevention of Pollution) (Limits) Regulations 1997	A02b, I01a.1b
1997	1869	MS (Prevention of Pollution) (Substances Other Than Oil) (Intervention) Order 1997	
1997	2568	MS (Prevention of Pollution) (Intervention) (Foreign Ships) Order 1997	
1997	2569	MS (Prevention of Pollution) (Amendment) Order 1997	
1998	254	Prevention of Pollution (Amendment) Order 1998	
1998	1500	MS (Control of Pollution) (SOLAS) Order 1998	
1998	3018	MS (Port Waste Reception Facilities) Regulations 1998	I06c.1

B04b.33 Port State control

Year	SI No.	Title	SBC references
1995	3128	MS (Port State Control) Regulations 1995	I01a.1c, I02c.3
1998	1433	MS (Port State Control) (Amendment) Regulations 1998	I02c.3
1998	2198	MS (Port State Control) (Amendment No. 2) Regulations 1998	I02c.3
2001	2349	MS (Port State Control) (Amendment) Regulations 2001	I02c.3

B04b.34 Provisions and water

Year	SI No.	Title	SBC references
1989	102	MS (Provisions and Water) Regulations 1989	E08h.1

B04b.35 Radio and navigational equipment

Year	SI No.	Title	SBC references
1998	2070	MS (Radio Installations) Regulations 1998	A03c.1a, D04m.1
2000	1850	MS (EPIRB Registration) Regulations 2000	D04b.5
2002	1473	MS (Safety of Navigation) Regulations	D04n.1, H01f.2

B04b.36 Registration of ships

Year	SI No.	Title	SBC references
1983	1470	MS (Small Ships Register) Regulations 1983	D01c.2
1993	3138	MS (Registration of Ships) Regulations 1993	D01c.1
1994	541	MS (Registration of Ships) (Amendment) Regulations 1994	D01c.1
1994	774	MS (Modification of Enactments) (Bareboat Charter Ships) Order 1994	D01f
1998	2976	MS (Registration of Ships) (Amendment) Regulations 1998	D01c.1
1999	3206	MS (Registration of Ships, and Tonnage) (Amendment) Regulations 1999	D01c.1
2003	1248	MS (Categorisation of Registries of Relevant British Possessions) Order 2003	D01c.2

B04b.37 Reporting and routeing

Year	SI No.	Title	SBC references
1995	2498	MS (Reporting Requirements for Ships Carrying Dangerous or Polluting Goods) Regulations 1995	F07f.5, H04b.4, H04d, H06e.1, I01a.7, I01b.7, I01b.10, I02g.4, I07d, I07d.1, I07d.2, I07d.3
1999	2121	MS (Reporting Requirements for Ships carrying Dangerous or Polluting Goods) (Amendment) Regulations 1999	H06f.1
2002	1473	MS (Safety of Navigation) Regulations	H01a.6, H06c.2

B04b.38 Statistical returns

Year	SI No.	Title	SBC references
1997	2330	Statistical Returns (Carriage of Goods and Passengers by Sea) Regulations 1997	

B04b.39 Tonnage

Year	SI No.	Title	SBC references
1982	1085	Tonnage (Various Countries) Order 1982	
1983	439	MS (Deck Cargo Tonnage) Regulations 1983	
1997	1510	MS (Tonnage) Regulations 1997	D04h.2
1999	3206	MS (Registration of Ships, and Tonnage) (Amendment) Regulations 1999	

B04c CHIEF SHIPPING-RELATED ACTS OF PARLIAMENT OF CONCERN TO SHIPMASTERS

B04c.1 Merchant Shipping Act 1995 (c.21)

- **consolidates** all Merchant Shipping Acts from 1894 to 1994 and various other enactments relating to merchant shipping.
- **replaced Merchant Shipping Act 1894** as the "**Principal Act**" in relation to UK merchant shipping legislation.
- **entered into force** in accordance with section 316(2) on 1 January 1996, with the exception of a small number of sections. Certain sections were brought into force by the Merchant Shipping Act 1995 (Appointed Day No. 1) Order 1996 (SI 1996/1210) and others by the Merchant Shipping Act 1995 (Appointed Day No. 2) Order 1997 (SI 1997/3107).
- **contains 316 sections** arranged in **13 parts**, and **14 schedules**. **Parts** are as follows: Part **I**. British ships; **II**. Registration; **III**. Masters and seamen; **IV**. Safety; **V**. Fishing vessels; **VI**. Prevention of pollution; **VII**. Liability of shipowners and others; **VIII**. Lighthouses; **IX**. Salvage and wreck; **X**. Enforcement officers and powers; **XI**. Accident investigations and inquiries; **XII**. Legal proceedings; **XIII**. Supplemental.
- **contains** numerous provisions which are referred to throughout the text of this book, and numerous powers to make regulations on matters covered by this book[29].
- * **Schedule 12** lists **repeals**, or partial repeals, of numerous sections and some schedules of Merchant Shipping Act 1894.
- * **Schedule 13** lists **consequential amendments** of other pieces of legislation.
- * **Acts totally repealed by the Merchant Shipping Act 1995** include the Merchant Shipping Act 1897, Merchant Shipping Act 1965, MS (Oil Pollution) Act 1971, Merchant Shipping Act 1981, Prevention of Oil Pollution Act 1986, MS (Registration etc) Act 1993, and Salvage and Pollution Act 1994. Some other acts are **partially repealed**.

B04c.2 Carriage of Goods by Sea Act 1971 (c.19)

- **is an act to amend the law** with respect to the carriage of goods by sea, principally by making the **Hague-Visby Rules** apply to the carriage of goods in certain circumstances. The Rules form the Schedule to the Act and by virtue of section 1(2) have the force of law in the UK.
- * For more detailed notes on the Act, see F07c.3.

B04c.3 Carriage of Goods by Sea Act 1992 (c.50)

- **is described** in its introduction as "an Act to replace the Bills of Lading Act 1855 with new provision with respect to bills of lading and certain other shipping documents".
- * For more detailed notes on the Act, see F07d.

---

[29] While many existing Merchant Shipping regulations were made under powers conferred by older acts, such as Merchant Shipping Act 1970, any replacing legislation will be made under powers conferred by the Merchant Shipping Act 1995.

B04c.4 Pilotage Act 1987 (c.21)

- **repealed the Pilotage Act 1983**, resulting a large-scale **reorganisation of pilotage service provision** in the UK.
- **provides** for certain masters and mates of ships using UK ports to obtain **Pilotage Exemption Certificates** (section 8).
- **contains** four parts (as detailed below) and three schedules. Parts I and II are of most concern to shipmasters.
- * **Part I** concerns Pilotage functions of competent harbour authorities, including Preliminary (section 1), Provision of pilotage services (sections 2 to 6), Compulsory pilotage (sections 7 to 9), Charging by authorities (section 10), Agents and joint arrangements (sections 11 to 13) and Accounts (section 14). **Part II** contains General Provisions Concerning Pilotage, including Compulsory pilotage (sections 15 and 16), Rights of pilots (sections 17 to 20), Misconduct by pilots (section 21), Limitation of liability (section 22) and Deep sea pilotage (section 23). **Part III** concerns the winding-up of the existing pilotage organisation. **Part IV** concerns Supplementary matters.
- * For notes on **port and canal pilotage**, see I01b.

B04c.5 Merchant Shipping and Maritime Security Act 1997 (c.28)

- **is described** in its introduction as "an Act to amend the Merchant Shipping Act 1995; to extend the powers of fire authorities to use fire brigades and equipment at sea; to make further provision about the protection of wrecks; to amend Part III of the Aviation and Maritime Security Act 1990; to make provision about piracy; to provide for the continuing application to the International Oil Pollution Compensation Fund of section 1 of the International Organisations Act 1968; to make provision about the International Tribunal for the Law of the Sea; and for connected purposes".
- **was brought into force** by the Merchant Shipping and Maritime Security Act 1997 (Commencement No.1) Order 1997 (SI 1997/1082 (C.39) and The Merchant Shipping and Maritime Security Act 1997 (Commencement No.2) Order 1997 (SI 1997/1539 (C.62).
- **amends** several sections and schedules of the Merchant Shipping Act 1995.
- **brings several sections of the Merchant Shipping Act 1995 into force** through the Merchant Shipping and Maritime Security Act 1997 (Commencement No.1) Order 1997 and the Merchant Shipping and Maritime Security Act 1997 (Commencement No.2) Order 1997.
- **contains** four parts, as follows: Part **I**. Aviation security; Part **II**. Offences against the safety of ships and fixed platforms. Part **III**. Protection of ships and harbour areas against acts of violence; Part **IV**. Miscellaneous and general.
- **contains** the following sections in Part II: **9**. Hijacking of ships; **10**. Seizing or exercising control of fixed platforms; **11**. Destroying ships or fixed platforms or endangering their safety; **12**. Other acts endangering or likely to endanger safe navigation; **13**. Offences involving threats; **14**. Ancillary offences; **15**. Master's power of delivery; **16**. Prosecution of offences and proceedings. **17**. Interpretation of Part II.
- **contains** the following sections in **Part III** of interest to shipmasters: **20**. Designation of restricted zones of harbour areas; **21**. Power to impose restrictions in relation to ships; **22**. Power to require harbour authorities to promote searches in harbour areas; **23**. Power to require other persons to promote searches; **24**. General power to direct measures to be taken for purposes to which Part III applies; **25**. Matters which may be included in directions under sections 21 to 24; **26**. Limitations on scope of directions under sections 21 to 24; **27**. General or urgent directions under sections 21 to 24; **28**. Objections to certain directions under section 24; **29**. Enforcement notices; **30**. Contents of enforcement notice; **31**. Offences relating to enforcement notices; **32**. Objections to enforcement notices; **33**. Enforcement notices: supplementary; **34**. Operation of directions under Part III in relation to rights and duties under other laws; **35**. Detention of ships; **36**. Inspection of ships and harbour areas; **37**. False statements relating to baggage, cargo etc.; **38**. False statements in connection with identity documents; **39**. Unauthorised presence in restricted zone; **40**. Offences relating to authorised persons; **41**. Sea cargo agents; **42**. Duty to report certain occurrences; **43**. Compensation in respect of certain measures taken under Part III; **45**. Service of documents.
- **contains** the following sections in **Part IV** of interest to shipmasters: **49**. Extradition by virtue of Orders in Council under section 2 of Extradition Act 1870; **50**. Offences by bodies corporate; **51**. Extension of Act outside the United Kingdom.

B04c.6 Aviation and Maritime Security Act 1990 (c.31)

- **is described** in its introduction as "an Act to give effect to the Protocol for the Suppression of Unlawful Acts of Violence at Airports Serving International Civil Aviation which supplements the Convention for the Suppression of Acts against the Safety of Civil Aviation; to make further provision with respect to aviation security and civil aviation; to give effect to the Convention for the Suppression of Unlawful Acts against the Safety of Maritime Navigation and to the Protocol for the Suppression of Unlawful Acts against the Safety of Fixed Platforms Located on the Continental Shelf which supplements that Convention; to make other provision for the protection of ships and harbour areas against acts of violence; and for connected purposes".

- **contains** four parts, as follows: Part **I**. Aviation Security; Part **II**. Offences against the security of ships and fixed platforms; Part **III**. Protection of ships and harbour areas against acts of violence; Part **IV**. Miscellaneous and general.
- **contains** the following sections in **Part II** of interest to shipmasters: **9**. Hijacking of ships; **10**. Seizing or exercising control of fixed platforms; **11**. Destroying ships or fixed platforms or endangering their safety; **12**. Other acts endangering or likely to endanger safe navigation; **13**. Offences involving threats; **14**. Ancillary offences; **15**. Master's power of delivery; **16**. Prosecution of offences and proceedings; **17**. Interpretation of Part II.

B04c.7 Shipping and Trading Interests (Protection) Act 1995 (c.22)

- **is described** in its introduction as "an Act to consolidate certain enactments for the protection of shipping and trading interests".
- * **Section 1** gives the UK Government powers to **regulate shipping services** in the event of "foreign action", i.e. where a foreign government or authority, or agency of either, is doing anything which damages or threatens to damage, the shipping or trading interests of the UK or a State to which the UK has some relevant obligations. A **protective order** may be issued to regulate matters such as the provision of shipping services, the type of shipping services provided, the admission to and departure from UK ports by ships and the making of charter-parties.
- * **Section 5** allows the UK Government to **prohibit by order certain shipping services**, including the carriage of goods or passengers between UK ports or between the UK and an offshore installation on the UK Continental Shelf, or between such installations, except where the services are provided from one or more permanent places of business maintained in the British Islands. The owner and **master** of a ship which breaches such an order is liable under section 6 to a fine on summary conviction not exceeding **£50,000**.

B04c.8 Dangerous Vessels Act 1985 (c.22)

- **is described** in its introduction as "an Act to empower harbour masters to give directions to prohibit vessels from entering the areas of jurisdiction of their respective harbour authorities or to require the removal of vessels from those areas where those vessels present a grave and imminent danger to the safety of any person or property, or risk of obstruction to navigation; to enable the Secretary of State to give further directions countermanding those first-mentioned directions; and for connected purposes".
- **contains** eight sections, of which sections 1 and 3 are of chief concern to shipmasters.
- * For notes on **sections 1 and 3** of the Act, see I02g.3.

B04d EC DIRECTIVES

- * For notes on **European Community legislation**, see B03a.6.
- * The EC Directives listed in the following table are referred to in the specified sections of this book.

Directive No./Name	Subject of Directive	SBC references
91/689/EEC "Hazardous Waste Directive"	Hazardous waste	I07c.6
1999/35/EC	System of mandatory surveys for the safe operation of regular ro-ro ferry and high-speed passenger craft services	D04f.4, I02c.3b
1999/63/EC	Concerning the Agreement on the organisation of working time of seafarers	E03b.4a, E03b.4d
1999/95/EC	Enforcement of working time restrictions on ships	E03b.4d
1999/32/EC	Sulphur content of certain liquid fuels	I06d.3
2000/34/EC	Amends Directive 93/104/EC	E03b.4d
79/115/EEC	Deep-sea pilotage in the North Sea and English Channel	H01a.8
89/391/EC	Introduction of measures to encourage improvements in the safety and health of workers at work	E08b.2
90/269/EEC	Minimum health and safety requirements for manual handling	E08e.8
91/383/EEC	Supplementing measures to encourage improvements in the safety and health of workers at work with a fixed-term or temporary employment relationship	E08b.2
92/29/EC	Minimum safety and health requirements for improved medical treatment on board vessels	D04p, E03c.4, H04c.3

92/58/EEC	Minimum requirements for the improvement of safety and/or health signs at work	E08e.7
92/85/EEC	Implementation of measures to encourage improvements in the safety and health at work of pregnant workers and workers who have recently given birth or are breastfeeding	E08b.2, E08b.2h
93/104/EC "Working Time Directive"	Certain aspects of the organisation of working time	E03b.4d
93/75/EEC "Hazmat Directive"	Minimum requirements for vessels bound for or leaving Community ports and carrying dangerous or polluting goods	B05b.2d, F07f.2, H06e.1, I01a.7, I02c.3d
94/33/EC	Protection of young people at work	E05c.1
94/57/EC	Common rules and standards of ship inspection and survey organisations and for the relevant activities of maritime Administrations	B03a.6 , D03i.2, D04d.1, D04d.2, I02c.3d
94/58/EC	Minimum level of training for seafarers (amended and repealed by Directive 2001/25/EC of the same name)	D03a.4
95/21/EC	Enforcement, in respect of shipping using Community ports and sailing in the waters under the jurisdiction of the Member States, of international standards for ship safety, pollution prevention and shipboard living and working conditions (port State control),	B03a.6, D04f.4, I02c.3
95/64/EC	Statistical returns in respect of carriage of goods and passengers by sea	C04c.5
96/98/EC "the MED"	Marine equipment	D04b.1
98/18/EC	Safety rules and standards for passenger ships	B03a.6, D03b.6a, D03b.6b, D04c.2a, D04f.2, D04f.2w, D04f.3, D04f.3a, D04f.3b, D04f.4
98/35/EC	Amendment of Directive 94/58/EC	D03a.4
98/41/EC	Registration of persons sailing on board passenger ships operating to or from ports of the Member States of the Community	I08f.1
98/55/EC	Amendment of Directive 93/75/EEC	H06e.1, I01a.7
98/85/EC	Amendment of Directive 96/98/EC	D04b.1

B05 Department for Transport (DfT) and its agencies

B05a DEPARTMENT FOR TRANSPORT (DfT)

- was **created** in May 2002 by the Labour Government of the UK, following a Cabinet reshuffle[30].
- is the UK government department **responsible for**:
  - road transport;
  - rail transport;
  - civil aviation;
  - merchant shipping;
  - health and safety.
- is **headed** by the **Secretary of State for Transport**, to whom the **Minister for Transport** has overall responsibility for Transport matters. An **Under-Secretary of State for Transport** is responsible for (*inter alia*) **shipping and ports** and the **Maritime and Coastguard Agency**, and is sometimes referred to as "the **Shipping Minister**".
- **is responsible**, in relation to merchant shipping, for:
  - Government policy towards the UK merchant fleet;
  - marine safety in general;
  - seaworthiness of ships;
  - safe construction and stability of ships;
  - safety and pollution aspects of ships' equipment;
  - safety of carriage of dangerous goods;
  - navigational safety;
  - safe manning;
  - certification of seafarers;
  - health, safety and welfare of seafarers;
  - civil marine search and rescue;

---

[30] In the year prior to the creation of the DfT, shipping was a responsibility of the Department for Transport, Local Government and the Regions (DTLR), which was created in June, 2001. The DTLR's predecessor was the Department for Environment, Transport and the Regions (DETR).

- prevention and combating of marine pollution;
- investigation of marine accidents; and
- representing the UK at international maritime conferences (e.g. IMO and ILO).
* **Website**: www.dft.gov.uk

B05b MARITIME AND COASTGUARD AGENCY (MCA)

B05b.1 The Maritime and Coastguard Agency

- is an **executive agency of the Department for Transport** (DfT).
- was created on 1 April 1998 by the merger of the **Marine Safety Agency** (**MSA**) with the **Coastguard Agency** (**CGA**), and carries out the functions of both former organisations.
- **is responsible** for:
  - developing, promoting and enforcing high standards of marine safety;
  - minimising loss of life amongst seafarers and coastal users;
  - responding to maritime emergencies 24 hours a day; and
  - minimising the risk of pollution of the marine environment from ships and where pollution occurs, minimising the impact on UK interests.
- **sets, monitors and enforces standards of safety and pollution prevention** on all UK merchant vessels and **enforces international standards** on foreign ships visiting UK ports.
- implements the **National Contingency Plan for Marine Pollution from Shipping and Offshore Installations**.
- has a wide range of **other duties** with a direct and indirect bearing on safety of life at sea and the prevention of pollution from ships.
- has various functions in connection with **crew matters** and documentation, death inquiries, etc.
- issues **directives and advice** on safety and other matters to masters and crews of ships, shipowners, fishermen and shipbuilders by means of **M Notices** (including Merchant Shipping Notices, Marine Guidance Notes and Marine Information Notes).
- has central **headquarters** at Southampton, England (see address below).
- maintains **Marine Offices** (MOs) in four administrative **regions** as follows:
  - Scotland and Northern Ireland Region: Aberdeen, Belfast, Glasgow, Leith, Shetland (Lerwick);
  - East of England Region: Beverley, Tyne (South Shields), Stockton, Thames (Walton-on-Naze), Yarmouth;
  - South of England Region: Southampton, Dover, Falmouth, Orpington, Plymouth;
  - Wales and West of England Region: Swansea, Cardiff, Liverpool, Milford Haven.
- employs **nautical, ship and engineer surveyors** who mainly work from Marine Offices and deal with:
  - statutory surveys for the issue and maintenance of validity of ship and fishing vessel certificates;
  - other surveys and inspections of UK and non-UK ships, e.g. of bulk cargoes, stowage of dangerous goods, etc.
  - Port State Control inspections of non-UK ships; and
  - sight tests and oral examinations of candidates for Certificates of Competency.
- charges **fees** for its services in accordance with the **MS (Fees) Regulations 1996** (SI 1996/3243), as amended (see B04b.16).
- operates the **Registry and Shipping and Seamen** (**RSS**) (see B05c).
- time-charters vessels for service as **Emergency Towing Vessels** (ETVs) around the UK coast (see B05b.2e).
- is a party, with the HSE and MAIB, to a **Memorandum of Understanding for health and safety enforcement activities** etc. at the water margin and offshore (see B05f).
* **MCA headquarters address**: Maritime and Coastguard Agency, Spring Place, 105 Commercial Road, Southampton SO15 1EG. Tel. 01703 329100. Fax 01703 329404.
* For notes on the **MCA website**, see B05b.6.

B05b.2 MCA structure and organisation

* The MCA's main component bodies of interest to seafarers are the **Directorate of Operations** (see B05b.2a) and the **Directorate of Quality and Standards** (see B05b.2d).

B05b.2a Directorate of Operations

* **The Directorate of Operations** consists of six separate parts:
  * Inspection Branch (including Port State Control);
  * Survey Branch;
  * Enforcement Unit;
  * SAR Prevention and Response (formerly Search and Rescue);
  * Counter Pollution and Response; and
  * Public Relations.
* The **Inspection Branch** supports Marine Offices in inspection of UK and foreign ships (ports State control). It is the contact point for procedures and case guidance, collates information on inspection activity, follows up ship detention with interested parties, manages the Survey and Inspection system (SIAS) and input to the Paris MOU system (SIRENAC), develops policy and represents the UK at national and international fora.
* The **Survey Branch** develops, promotes and monitors a consistent policy for survey operations; act as a focal point for Marine Office surveyors, Marine Accident Investigation Branch and classification societies when dealing with surveys overseas on behalf of the UK.
* The **Enforcement Unit** consists of a small team of **Enforcement Officers** who investigate breaches of Merchant Shipping legislation and prosecute offenders where appropriate. Offences investigates are mostly related to pollution, safety and manning, breaches of the Collision Regulations and forged certificates. **Prosecutions** (successful or otherwise) are publicised in the "Prosecutions" section of the **MCA website**.

B05b.2b HM Coastguard

- operates within the **Search and Rescue Branch** of the Directorate of Operations.
- maintains a **continuous distress watch** on international distress frequencies, digital selective calling (DSC) and satcoms.
- collates and broadcasts Maritime Safety Information on VHF and MF radio and NAVTEX.
- provides a **radio medical advice and assistance service** through six Maritime Rescue Co-ordination Centres (**MRCCs**) and fifteen Maritime Rescue Sub-Centres (**MRSCs**). Each Centre is continuously manned and is fitted with a comprehensive range and network of radio and telecommunications, satcoms, fax and telex together with emergency planning facilities, and is responsible for a District with a network of Auxiliary Coastguard Response Teams who are responsible for cliff rescues, mud rescues, coastal searches and patrol work.
- **initiates and co-ordinates all civil maritime search and rescue (SAR) operations** for vessels or persons requiring assistance in the **UK Search and Rescue Region**, i.e. around the 2,500 mile coastline of the UK and for 1,000 miles into the North Atlantic to 30°W.
- is responsible for **requesting the assistance** in distress situations of other appropriate **authorities and resources** including Coastguard helicopters, RNLI lifeboats, RN and RAF fixed wing aircraft, helicopters and ships, as well as merchant shipping, commercial aircraft and fishing vessels.
- **liaises** closely with adjacent foreign SAR organisations.
- maintains its own **coastal rescue teams**, **vehicles** and **boats**.
- operates three civil **helicopters** with full night- and all-weather rescue capability contracted to provide a SAR facility at Sumburgh Airport (Shetland), Stornoway (Isle of Lewis) and Lee-on-Solent for civil aviation and maritime rescue or medical evacuation from ships or offshore installations. Current aircraft are Sikorsky S61Ns with a typical endurance of 4 hours at 110 knots. 10 persons can be lifted by winch at about 150 miles radius or 20 persons at 80 miles radius depending on weather conditions.
* In particular, **HM Coastguard is responsible for**:
  * obtaining and evaluating all relevant information regarding an incident from appropriate sources;
  * initiating distress and urgency broadcasts as necessary;
  * alerting and tasking of appropriate resources to SAR incidents;
  * determining search areas, formulating search plans and tasking resources effectively;
  * where appropriate appointing an On-Scene Commander (OSC) or Aircraft Co-ordinator (ACO) to exercise local co-ordination at the scene of SAR operations;
  * co-ordinating the actions of all involved units;
  * deciding, after consideration of all the available information, that there is no longer any probability of survival of any missing persons, and that SAR action can be terminated.
* **HM Coastguard** is organised into six **Coastguard Search and Rescue Regions** (which are subdivisions of the UK Search and Rescue Region, or SRR). For SAR purposes, these Regions are each under the authority of Regional Inspectors, each based at a **Maritime Rescue Co-ordination Centre (MRCC)**. The six MRCCs are at Aberdeen, Yarmouth, Dover, Falmouth, Swansea and Clyde. Each Region is further subdivided into **Coastguard Districts**,

each under the authority of a District Controller. Each District is centred on either an MRCC or **Maritime Rescue Sub-Centre (MRSC)**.

* All **MRCCs and MRSCs** maintain a 24-hour communications watch system which together give coverage of the UK SRR. Within each District there are a number of Auxiliary Coastguard Rescue Teams grouped within Sectors under the management of regular Coastguard Officers.

* **MRCC Dover** is also the headquarters of the **Channel Navigation Information Service (CNIS)**, and operates a radar surveillance system in conjunction with its French counterpart at Cap Gris Nez to monitor the traffic flow through the Dover Strait. CNIS operates an aircraft to identify vessels which appear to be contravening the International Regulations for Preventing Collisions at Sea, 1972.

* **MRCC Dover and MRSC Portland** are also "reporting-in" stations for ships operating **the Ship Movement Reporting System (MAREP)**, and MRCC Dover is the collating station for information received as a result of the "Hazmat Directive" (see B04d). Vessels may also make voluntary Position and Intended Movement reports to MRCC Falmouth and MRSCs Shetland, Pentland and Stornoway when on passage through their areas of responsibility.

* In addition to regional responsibilities, **MRCC Falmouth** plays an important role in the GMDSS as the **UK SAR Point of Contact** for the International SAR Satellite System (SARSAT) and maintains links with foreign MRCCs to resolve incidents occurring worldwide. Liaison with countries nor covered by formal SAR liaison arrangements is also conducted through MRCC Falmouth.

B05b.2c Counter Pollution and Response Branch

- is a branch of the Directorate of Operations.
- fulfils the Government's commitment under international agreements to provide a **marine pollution response capability** by the maintenance of a **National Contingency Plan for Marine Pollution from Shipping and Offshore Installations** (which is on the MCA website).
- has the objective of **protecting the marine environment and minimising damage to UK interests from pollution** by maintaining an effective and efficient **response organisation** for the clean-up of oil and chemical spills from shipping casualties and offshore installations, using both **directly-owned and contracted resources** which include emergency cargo transfer equipment, dispersant-spraying and remote-sensing aircraft[31], dispersant-spraying tugs and some mechanical oil-recovery equipment. For onshore operations it holds stockpiles of specialised beach-cleaning equipment.
- **assesses reports of marine pollution** and potential pollution from oil and other hazardous substances (e.g. from vessels in difficulties) and takes **appropriate action**.
- provides **scientific and technical advice** on shoreline clean-up, and training for local authority oil pollution officers.
- manages the **Emergency Towing Vessel (ETV)** contract[32].
- seeks to detect **illegal discharges and offenders** through aerial surveillance.
- seeks to encourage **reporting of pollution** at sea.

* The Counter Pollution team based in MCA headquarters at Southampton manages the MCA stockpiles of **counter pollution equipment** and provides central and scientific support and back-up to the **Principal Counter Pollution and Salvage Officers (PCPSOs)** placed in each of the four MCA Regions. PCPSOs take responsibility for monitoring and dealing with pollution incidents in their regions, with support from Southampton HQ as needed.

* The Counter Pollution response was changed in March 1999 from a totally centralised organisation (which was known as the **Marine Pollution Control Unit**) to a **regional counter pollution organisation** supported by a central core of counter pollution officers, scientists and administrators. This was intended to improve the speed and performance of counter-pollution response in the Regions and to improve liaison with ports and harbours, harbourmasters and the oil industry located within the Regions.

---

[31] Aerial surveillance and dispersant spraying work is contracted out by the MCA to a commercial operator. Surveillance aircraft provided include a Cessna 406 and a Cessna 404, based at Coventry and Inverness. A Cessna 406, based at Inverness, is equipped for spraying 1.3 tonnes of dispersant. Two Lockheed Electras, each able to carry 13 tonnes of dispersant, are normally based at Coventry. Under a separate contract an Islander is based at Lydd (Kent) for Channel Navigation Information Service patrols operated by Dover MRCC; this aircraft, which has no pollution detection equipment, may also be tasked for counter-pollution visual observation and evidence recording in the Dover Strait.

[32] The MCA time-charters four ETVs to provide emergency towing cover in winter months in the four areas deemed to pose the highest risk of a marine accident, i.e. the Dover Strait, the Minches, the Western Approaches and the Fair Isle Channel. MCA delegates operational tasking of ETVs to local HMCG District Controllers. As part of the charter agreement, and at the discretion of MCA, any ETV may undertake such commercial towage as a shipowner and the ETV operator may agree. Any such "hire" agreement benefits both the ETV operator and MCA.

B05b.2d Directorate of Quality and Standards

- is responsible for: reviewing and developing standards for seafarers, ships and the environment; growing the business, including flagging-in work and the use of training skills within the MCA; internal and external quality assurance; developing the availability and the use of corporate information to support the operation of the MCA and its customers.
* Within the Directorate are branches responsible for: Fishing Vessel Safety; Code Vessel Safety; Shipping Safety; Environmental Quality; Communication and Innovation; Standards Setting; Seafarer Training and Certification; Formal Safety Assessment; International Standards; Seafarer Health and Safety; and the Registry of Shipping and Seamen (see B05c).

B05b.3 MCA personnel

* Duties and powers of the various **MCA personnel** with whom a shipmaster might have contact are outlined below.

B05b.3a Secretary of State's Representative (SOSREP)

- has the full title of **Secretary of State's Representative for Maritime Salvage and Intervention**.
- is a post created as part of the UK Government's response to *Command and Control: Report of Lord Donaldson's Review of Salvage and Intervention and their Command and Control*[33], commissioned in the wake of the *Sea Empress* grounding and published in March 1999. SOSREP commenced work at the MCA in October 1999 and is based at the MCA's Southampton headquarters.
- acts during a salvage operation on behalf of the Secretary of State for Transport, and in the public interest.
- has statutory powers to oversee, control and, if necessary, **intervene in salvage operations** within UK waters involving vessels or fixed platforms where there is a **significant risk of pollution**.
* During periods of emergency activity SOSREP will be based at an HM Coastguard MRCC or MRSC. At other times SOSREP is based at the MCA's HQ in Southampton, and is responsible to the MCA Chief Executive.
* The Government's **intervention powers** in shipping casualties are contained in section 137 of the Merchant Shipping Act 1995 (see H03i and H05c.2).

B05b.3b Receiver of Wreck

* The **Department for Transport** (DfT) has general superintendence of all matters relating to **wreck** found in the UK and in UK waters.
* **Wreck** is the subject of Part IX, Chapter II of the Merchant Shipping Act 1995. Under section 231 of the Act, sections 232, 233, 234 and 235 apply in circumstances where a UK or foreign vessel is wrecked, stranded, or in distress at any place on or near the coasts of the UK or any tidal water within UK waters.[34]
* **The official in charge of wreck** in the UK is the **Receiver of Wreck**, an MCA official appointed under section 248 of the Merchant Shipping Act 1995 and based at MCA's Southampton HQ.
* **The Receiver's main task** is to **process incoming reports of wreck** in the interest of both the salvor and owner. This involves researching ownership, liaising with the finder and owner, and liaising with other interested parties such as archaeologists and museums. Certain functions of the Receiver, e.g. taking charge at wreck scenes, are delegated to HM Customs and HM Coastguard officers around the UK coast.
* Under **section 231** of the Merchant Shipping Act 1995, **where a UK or foreign vessel is wrecked, stranded, or in distress** at any place on or near the coasts of the UK or in any tidal water within UK waters, the Receiver (or delegated official) must go to the scene, take command of all persons present and assign such duties and give such directions as he/she thinks are needed for the preservation of the vessel and the lives of the shipwrecked persons.
* Under **section 232(3)** the Receiver may not interfere between the master and crew of a vessel in reference to the management of the vessel unless he/she is requested to do so by the master.
* Under **section 233** the Receiver may, for the purpose of the preservation of shipwrecked persons or of the vessel, cargo and equipment:
  • require such persons as he/she thinks necessary to assist him/her;

---

[33] Available at the **DfT Shipping website**: www.shipping.dft.gov.uk/index.htm
[34] Sections 232, 233, 234 and 235 deal with: duty of the receiver where a vessel is in distress; powers of the receiver in case of a vessel in distress; power to pass over adjoining land; and liability for damage in case of plundered vessel, respectively.

- require the master, or any other person having the charge, of any vessel near at hand to give such assistance with his men, or vessel, as may be in his power;
- require the use of any vehicle that may be near at hand.
* **Section 234** confers on the Receiver considerable **powers to pass over land** adjoining a wreck scene. A land owner or occupier who hinders the Receiver will be liable to a level 3 fine on summary conviction.
* **Section 247** confers on the Receiver powers of entry, search and seizure (subject to a search warrant being granted) where he/she has reason to believe that wreck is being concealed or is in the possession of a non-owner, or is being improperly dealt with.
* **Section 226** requires the Receiver to detain wreck where salvage is due any person under Part IX, Chapter I of the Merchant Shipping Act 1995 and the wreck is not sold as unclaimed. The Receiver must detain the vessel and the cargo and equipment, or the wreck, until payment is made for salvage, or process is issued for the arrest or detention of the property by the court. The Receiver may release any property when satisfactory security is given.
* For notes on the **duties of a finder of wreck** and a definition of "**wreck**", see I02h.
* **Receiver of Wreck postal address**: Receiver of Wreck, Bay 1/05, Spring Place, 105 Commercial Road, Southampton SO15 1EG, England.
* **Receiver of Wreck web address**: www.mcga.gov.uk/row

B05b.3c Superintendents

- are properly called "**mercantile marine superintendents**".
- are **MCA officials**, based at **Marine Offices** in the UK.
- are **empowered** by section 296 of the Merchant Shipping Act 1995 to exercise the numerous functions conferred on superintendents by the Act, which include (but are not limited to) dealing with:
  * issue, endorsement and withdrawal, etc. of seamen's documents;
  * engagement of seamen and exemption provisions;
  * discharge of seamen;
  * seamen's wages and allotments;
  * resolution of wages disputes;
  * relief and repatriation of seamen left behind;
  * returns and reports of births and deaths at sea;
  * inquiries into deaths on board ships, etc.;
  * property of deceased seamen;
  * official log books;
  * manning of merchant ships;
  * seamen's health and safety;
  * receipt and onward delivery of ships' documents;
  * complaints by seamen about provisions or water;
  * complaints about seaworthiness of ships; and
  * inquiries into misconduct of seamen.

B05b.3d Proper officers

- are **defined** in section 313(1) of the Merchant Shipping Act 1995 as **consular officers** appointed by Her Majesty's Government in the UK and, in relation to a port in a country outside the UK which is not a foreign country, also any officer exercising in that port functions similar to those of a superintendent.
- have **powers in relation to merchant ships, masters and seamen** conferred by many provisions of Merchant Shipping legislation, many of which are referred to throughout this book, for example in connection with Official Log Books, returns of births and deaths, and repatriation of seamen.
* **In a foreign port**, the proper officer is a **consular officer** (i.e. the British consul or vice-consul). Consuls and vice-consuls are officials of the Foreign and Commonwealth Office (FCO) , and not the DfT, but carry out various official functions on behalf of the DfT.
* "Countries outside the UK which are not foreign countries" include Crown Dependencies and British Overseas Territories (see D01c.2).
* **In a port outside the UK which is not a foreign country** (e.g. in a Crown Dependency port such as Douglas, Isle of Man, or in a British Overseas Territory port such as Gibraltar), the proper officer is the port State government official who exercises similar functions to those of a mercantile marine superintendent in the UK. (These officials may be known locally as **Shipping Masters**.)
* For notes on **British consuls**, see B02d.2. For notes on **reasons for contacting a consul**, see I01j.i.

B05b.3e Inspectors

- are Department for Transport (DfT) **enforcement officers** appointed by the Secretary of State for Transport under **section 256(6)** of the Merchant Shipping Act 1995 to report to him –
  - upon the nature and causes of any accident or damage which any ship has or is alleged to have sustained or caused; whether any requirements, restrictions or prohibitions imposed by or under the Act have been complied with or contravened, as the case may be;
  - whether the hull and machinery of a ship are sufficient and in good condition; and
  - what measures have been taken to prevent the escape of oil or mixtures containing oil.
- have wide powers under several sections of the Merchant Shipping Act 1995, including the powers-
  - to require production of ships' documents (section 257);
  - to inspect ships and their equipment, etc. (section 258);
  - to enter premises and board ships, and make examinations, investigations, etc. (section 259);
  - to serve Improvement Notices (section 261);
  - to serve Prohibition Notices (section 262).
* **MAIB inspectors of marine accidents** are appointed separately under **section 267** of the Merchant Shipping Act 1995.
  - **HSE inspectors** are appointed separately under **section 267** of the Merchant Shipping Act 1995.

B05b.3f Surveyors of ships

- are **MCA** officials.
- include **nautical surveyors** (who are qualified as deck officers), **ship surveyors** (who are qualified as naval architects) and **engineer surveyors** (who are qualified as marine engineers).
- are **enforcement officers** appointed under section 256 of the Merchant Shipping Act 1995 for the purposes of the Act.
- have certain **powers as inspectors** (see B05b.3e).
- **enforce merchant shipping legislation** and **administer international maritime safety conventions** and related Codes of Practice.
- are **responsible for**:
  - the survey and certification of safety equipment on ships;
  - in some cases, the survey of ships' structures;
  - investigating shipping casualties and accidents to crew;
  - inspecting crew accommodation and related matters;
  - inspecting arrangements on ships for dealing with the prevention of marine pollution;
  - random general safety inspections of ships, both UK and foreign;
  - random inspections of the condition, loading and storage on ships of packaged dangerous goods, including tank containers and motor tank vehicles;
  - inspecting shipboard operational arrangements for the loading and unloading of oil, chemical and gas tankers and offshore support vessels;
  - inspecting arrangements relating to the occupational health and safety of seafarers;
  - safe manning and the certification of crews;
  - diving operation activities from UK flag vessels outside the jurisdiction of the Health and Safety Executive;
  - eyesight testing of deck officer candidates; and
  - oral examination of candidates for certificates of competency.
* For notes on functions of marine Administration surveyors generally, see I03b.3.

B05b.3g Customer Service Managers

* When a ship is to be "flagged in" to the UK Register, once the owner/manager decides to proceed with UK registration, a **Customer Service Manager** (CSM) will be appointed by RSS. The CSM is a fully qualified MCA surveyor who will be the owner's or manager's single point of contact with the RSS and will oversee the smooth transfer to the UK Register. For notes on **registration procedure in the UK**, see D01d.

B05b.3h MARPOL surveyors

- are surveyors appointed or authorised, and paid fees, by the MCA for the purposes of **exercising control procedures under MARPOL Annex II** (which covers noxious liquid substances carried in bulk).
- are mostly surveyors employed by marine survey firms, but also include individual marine consultants.
- do not have the same range of powers as MCA surveyors.
- are listed in **MIN 116**.
- will only attend of required by a shipowner or his agent.
- have duties which can be summarised as follows:
  - to attend the **completion of the unloading of all Category A substances** and verify that the pre-wash has been conducted;
  - to attend where the **unloading of Category B and C substances** cannot be carried out in accordance with the ship's Procedures and Arrangements Manual;
  - to attend vessels, such as **offshore supply vessels**, to verify that cargo tanks that have contained NLSs of Categories A, B or C have been **cleaned** and that the residues and washings have been **discharged** to port reception facilities in accordance with the ship's Procedures and Arrangements Manual;
  - to **exempt ships** from the requirements of paragraphs 1 to 10 of Schedule 2 of M.1703/NLS1 in accordance with paragraph 16 of Schedule 2;
  - to **endorse the ship's Cargo Record Book**;
  - to provide six-monthly **returns** (including nil returns) to the MCA.

B05b.4 Powers of MCA personnel

* **Various sections of the Merchant Shipping Act 1995** confer powers on MCA personnel and on proper officers, as outlined below.

B05b.4a Powers to require production of ships' documents

* **Section 257 of the Merchant Shipping Act 1995** confers certain powers on:
  - any Departmental officer (i.e. any Department for Transport (DfT) officer discharging functions under the Merchant Shipping Act 1995);
  - any commissioned naval officer;
  - any British consular officer;
  - the Registrar General of Shipping and Seamen or any person discharging his functions;
  - any chief officer of customs and excise; and
  - any superintendent -
    whenever the officer has reason to suspect that the Merchant Shipping Act 1995 or any law for the time being in force relating to merchant seamen or navigation is not complied with.
* The **powers** conferred are:
  - to require the owner, master, or any of the crew to produce any official log book or other documents relating to the crew or any member of the crew on their possession or control;
  - to require the master to produce a list of all persons on board his ship, and take copies or extracts from the official log books or other such documents;
  - to muster the crew; and
  - to require the master to appear and give any explanation concerning the ship or her crew or the official log books or documents produced or required to be produced.

B05b.4b Powers to inspect ships and their equipment, etc.

* **Section 258(1) of the Merchant Shipping Act 1995** allows, for the purposes of seeing that the Act and regulations are complied with, etc., a **surveyor of ships**, a **superintendent** or **any person appointed by the Secretary of State**, at all reasonable times go on board a ship and **inspect the ship and its equipment or any part thereof, any articles on board and any document carried in the ship** under the Act or any regulations or rules under it.
* These powers are also exercisable on a UK ship outside the UK by the above officers or by a **proper officer** (section 258(2)).

* A person exercising these powers shall not unnecessarily detain or delay a ship but may, if he considers it necessary following an accident or for any other reason, require a ship to be **taken into dock for a survey** of its hull or machinery (section 258(3)).
* Powers are also given under section 258 to **enter premises ashore** where there are reasonable grounds for believing that there are, on the premises, **provisions or water intended for supply to a UK ship** which, if provided on the ship would not be in accordance with relevant safety regulations.

B05b.4c Powers of inspectors in relation to premises and ships

* **Under section 259 of the Merchant Shipping Act 1995**, an inspector -
    - may at any reasonable time (or, in a situation which in his opinion is or may be dangerous, at any time) -
        * enter any premises in the UK; or
        * board any UK ship wherever it may be and any other ship which is in the UK or UK waters,
      if he has reason to believe that it is necessary for him to do so;
    - may, on entering the premises or boarding the ship, make such examination and investigation as he considers necessary;
    - may give a direction that the premises, ship, or anything in same shall be left undisturbed for as long as reasonably necessary during the examination or investigation;
    - may take measurements, photographs, recordings and samples as necessary;
    - may, in the interests of health or safety, have articles dismantled and tested;
    - may take temporary possession of articles or substances for certain purposes;
    - may require the giving of relevant information;
    - may require the production of, and inspect and take copies of books and documents which are required by the Act to be kept (including requiring a master to certify a copy of an oil record book as a true copy);
    - may require facilities and assistance.
* The powers to enter property and board ships, make examinations and investigations and require the production of and inspection and copying of books or documents are also exercisable in the UK under section 259 by **harbour masters**, for the purpose of ascertaining the circumstances relating to an **alleged discharge of oil or a mixture containing oil** from the ship into the harbour.
* Nothing in section 259 will be taken to compel the production by any person of a **document** of which he would on grounds of **legal professional privilege** be entitled to withhold production on an order for discovery in a High Court action or a Court of Session action, as the case may be. (Note: Masters should take advice from their company officials, P&I club or legal representatives before handing over such documents.) See also D06d.2 for notes on **legal professional privilege**.

B05b.4d Powers to detain ships

* **Section 284 of the Merchant Shipping Act 1995** gives powers of detention to:
    * any commissioned **naval or military officer**;
    * any **Departmental (i.e. Department for Transport (DfT)) officer**;
    * any **officer of Customs and Excise**; and
    * any **British consular officer**.
* Where a ship **breaches a detention order**, the master will be liable, on summary conviction, to a maximum fine of £50,000, or on conviction on indictment, an unlimited fine.
* For notes on **detention**, see I02e.

B05b.4e Power to deny entry to ports or offshore terminals

* **Regulation 35(1) of the MS (Prevention of Oil Pollution) Regulations 1996** (SI 1996/2154) gives the MCA the power to deny the entry to UK ports or offshore terminals of a ship which a harbour master has reason to believe proposes to enter the harbour but does not comply with the requirements of the Regulations, if the MCA is satisfied that the ship presents an unreasonable threat of harm to the marine environment.

B05b.4f Power to serve Improvement Notices

* **Section 261(1) of the Merchant Shipping Act 1995** provides that if an inspector appointed under section 256(6) is of the opinion that a person is **contravening one or more of the relevant statutory provisions**, or has contravened one or more of those provisions in circumstances that make it likely that the contravention will continue to be repeated, he may serve on that person an **Improvement Notice**.

* Holders of the above power include **MCA surveyors** and **HSE inspectors**.
* For notes on the **form and use of Improvement Notices**, see E08b.4.

B05b.4g Power to serve Prohibition Notices

* **Section 262(1)** of the Merchant Shipping Act 1995 provides that if, as regards any **relevant activities** which are being or are likely to be carried on **on board any ship** by or under the control of any person, an inspector appointed under section 256(6) is of the opinion that, as so carried on or as likely to be so carried on, the **activities involve** or (as the case may be) will involve the **risk of serious personal injury** to any person (whether on board the ship or not), or of **serious pollution of any navigable waters**, the inspector may serve on the first-mentioned person a **Prohibition Notice**.
* Section 262(2) provides that in section 262(1), "**relevant activities**" means activities to or in relation to which any of the relevant statutory provisions apply or will, if the activities are carried on as mentioned that sub-section, apply.
* Holders of the above power include **MCA surveyors** and **HSE inspectors**.
* **Section 263** of the Merchant Shipping Act 1995 provides that an Improvement Notice or a Prohibition Notice may (but need not) include **directions** as to the measures to be taken to remedy any contravention or matter to which the notice relates, and may give a choice between different ways of remedying the contravention or matter.
* **Section 264** of the Merchant Shipping Act 1995 provides for questions relating to notices served as above to be referred to **arbitration**.
* For notes on the **form and use of Prohibition Notices**, see E08b.4.

B05b.5 MCA publications

* The MCA publishes the publications listed in the following table (some of which were first published by a predecessor of the MCA).

Title	Publisher	Printed	ISBN
Carriage of Cargoes, Volume 2 - Solid Bulk Cargoes - Instructions for the Guidance of Surveyors	Maritime and Coastguard Agency	Stationery Office,	0 11 552127 5
Carriage of packaged dangerous goods by sea: Instructions for the Guidance of Surveyors	Department of Transport	HMSO, 1993	0 11 551167 9

Title	Publisher	Printed	ISBN
Code of practice for safety of large commercial sailing and motor vessels (the "Megayacht Code")	Marine Safety Agency	HMSO, 1997	0 11 551911 4
Code of practice for the construction, machinery, equipment, stability, operation and examination of sailing vessels, of up to 24 metres load line length, in commercial use and which do not carry cargo or more than 12 passengers (the "Blue Code")	Surveyor General's Organisation	HMSO, 1993	0 11 551184 9
Code of practice for the construction, machinery, equipment, stability, operation and examination of motor vessels, of up to 24 metres load line length, in commercial use and which do not carry cargo or more than 12 passengers (the "Yellow Code")	Surveyor General's Organisation	HMSO, 1993	0 11 551185 7
Code of practice for the safety of small workboats & pilot boats (the "Brown Code")	Maritime and Coastguard Agency	Stationery Office, 1998	0 11 552006 6
Code of practice for vessel engaged in oil recovery operations	Marine Safety Agency	HMSO, 1996	0 11 551811 8
Code of safe working practices for Merchant Seamen	Maritime and Coastguard Agency	Stationery Office, 1998	0 11 551836 3
Fire Protection Arrangements - Instructions for the Guidance of Surveyors	Maritime and Coastguard Agency	Stationery Office, 1999	0 11 552000 7
International Code of Safety for High Speed Craft (HSC Code) - Instructions for the Guidance of Surveyors	Maritime and Coastguard Agency	Stationery Office, 1999	0 11 552084 8
International Management Code for the Safe Operation of Ships and for Pollution Prevention, The ISM Code - Instructions for the Guidance of Surveyors	Maritime and Coastguard Agency	Stationery Office, 1999	0 11 551810 X
Load Line - Instructions for the Guidance of Surveyors	Maritime and Coastguard Agency	Stationery Office, 1999	0 11 551999 8
Merchant Shipping Navigational Equipment - Instructions for the Guidance of Surveyors	Maritime and Coastguard Agency	Stationery Office, 1999	0 11 552198 4
Passenger Ship Construction, Classes I, II & II(A): Instructions for the Guidance of Surveyors	Maritime and Coastguard Agency	Stationery Office, 1999	0 11 551998 X
Passenger Ship Construction, Classes III to VI(A): Instructions for the Guidance of Surveyors	Maritime and Coastguard Agency	Stationery Office, 1999	0 11 552114 3
Radio Installations on Fishing Vessels - Instructions for the Guidance of Surveyors	Maritime and Coastguard Agency		0 11 552199 2
Radio Installations on GMDSS Ships - Instructions to surveyors	Maritime and Coastguard Agency	Stationery Office, 1998	0 11 552010 4

Roll-on/roll-off ships - stowage and securing of vehicles - code of practice	Department of Transport	HMSO, 1991	0 11 550995 X
Survey of Chemical Tankers: Instructions for the Guidance of Surveyors	Maritime and Coastguard Agency	Stationery Office, 1999	0 11 552110 0
Survey of Crew Accommodation in Merchant Ships - Instructions for the Guidance of Surveyors	Maritime and Coastguard Agency	Stationery Office, 1998	0 11 552116 X
Survey of gas carriers: Instructions for the Guidance of Surveyors	Marine Safety Agency	HMSO, 1996	0 11 551696 4
Survey of Gas Carriers: Instructions for the Guidance of Surveyors	Maritime and Coastguard Agency	Stationery Office, 1999	0 11 552112 7
Survey of life-saving appliances Volume 1: Instructions for the Guidance of Surveyors	Maritime and Coastguard Agency	Stationery Office, 1999	0 11 552001 5
Survey of life-saving appliances Volume 2: Instructions of the Guidance of Surveyors - testing of life-saving appliances	Maritime and Coastguard Agency	Stationery Office, 1999	0 11 552002 3
Survey of Lights and Signalling Equipment - Instructions for the Guidance of Surveyors	Maritime and Coastguard Agency	Stationery Office, 1999	0 11 552173 9
The Carriage of Cargoes, Volume 1 - The carriage of packaged cargoes and cargo units (including containers and vehicles), Instructions for the Guidance of Surveyors	Maritime and Coastguard Agency	Stationery Office, 1998	0 11 552113 5
The Code of Practice for the Safety of Small Vessels in Commercial Use for Sport or Pleasure Operating from a Nominated Departure point (NDP) (the "Red Code")	Maritime and Coastguard Agency	Stationery Office, 1999	0 11 551812 6
The Prevention of Oil Pollution from Ships: Instructions for the Guidance of Surveyors	Maritime and Coastguard Agency	Stationery Office, 1999	0 11 552111 9
The Prevention of Pollution by Garbage from Ships and the provision and use of Port Waste Reception facilities: Instructions for the Guidance of Surveyors	Maritime and Coastguard Agency	HMSO, 1999	0 11 552107 0
The safety of sail training ships - stability information booklet	Department of Transport	HMSO, 1990	0 11 550956 9

B05b.6 MCA website

* The **MCA website** is at: www.mcga.gov.uk and contains[35] the following sections:
    * **homepage** – including "Solway" Safety Scheme; MCA training and advisory services; "Ensign" Large Yacht Safety; UK Flag & Registration; "CG66" ID Safety Scheme; Seafarer training and certification; MCA Business Plan; Consultations; "Sea Smart" Safety Scheme; History of HM Coastguard; Fishing vessel incidents; Code vessel safety; and "Coastwalk".
    * **About us** – including MCA Contacts; Receiver of Wreck; MCA business directory; IMO Committees; "How to find us"; Recruitment; and Dangerous goods;
    * **News** – including Press releases; Prosecutions; Detentions; and New statutory powers;
    * **Survey and Inspection** – including Seafarer Standards; Certification requirements for UK ships; Application for Survey and Inspection of Ships and Fishing Vessels; Code Vessel safety; Authorisation for issue of statutory certificates; Byelaws; Alternative Compliance Scheme; Standards setting; UK ship classification and EC equivalents; and Authorisation for Approval of Stability.
    * **Search and Rescue** – including Co-ordination; COMSAR Correspondence Group on Large Passenger Ship Safety; International SAR Co-operation Plans Index; Maritime Safety Information; UK Search and Rescue Framework; UK 406 MHz EPIRB registration form; and Firefighting at Sea Project.
    * **Counter Pollution and Response** – including Prevention; Information on Local Authority training course run by the MCA; Advisory Committee on Protection of the Sea (ACOPS) Annual Report; a Review of Emergency Towing Vessel (ETV) Provision Around the Coast of the UK; National Contingency Plan for Marine Pollution from Shipping and Offshore Installations; The Secretary of State's Representative (SOSREP); Oil Spill Contingency Guidelines; and STOp and INF Notices.
    * **Campaigns and Publications** – including: Regulations; Fishing Vessel Safety Survey; Fishing Vessel Engine Types Index; Corporate Information; Statutory Information; and Promotional Information.
    * a **Search** facility.
* The MCA's 2002 SOLAS V publication (see H01f.2a) is under the heading "Regulations" in the Campaigns and Publications pages.
* The complete text of the **Ship Captain's Medical Guide** can be downloaded from: www.mcga.gov.uk/publications/medical/index.htm
* A 24-hour **MCA Infoline** is maintained on telephone number 0870 6006505 or e-mail: infoline@mcga.gov.uk or by post to MCA Infoline, Tutt Head, Mumbles, Swansea SA3 4HW, Wales.

---

[35] In June 2003.

B05c REGISTRY OF SHIPPING AND SEAMEN (RSS)

- is a **branch of the MCA** co-located (as notified in **MIN 137**) with Cardiff Marine Office (see address below).
- **registers**, and maintains the **central register** of, UK merchant ships, pleasure vessels, fishing vessels and ships which are bareboat chartered ("bareboat charter ships") (see D01c.2).
- allocates **official numbers** and **approves names** of ships. (Radio call signs are allocated by the Radiocommunications Agency – see B06.)
- issues and revalidates **seafarers' certificates**.
- issues other **seamen's documents** such as discharge books and seamen's cards.
- issues **medals** to seamen and has custody of **records of medals and awards** to seamen.
- **registers all births and deaths** at sea.
- administers, on behalf of the Department for Transport, the **Crew Relief Scheme** (a scheme to assist shipowners with costs of flying UK seafarers to and from ships joined or left abroad).
- has **custody of Crew Agreements and Lists of Crew**, **Official Log Books**, and (for one year only) **Radio Logs** (although historic records are now kept in Newfoundland, Canada).
- has **custody of seamen's records** for verification of sea service.
- maintains the **central record of British Seamen's Cards and Discharge Books**.
- maintains **the Register of Certificates of Competency and Service** and issues copy certificates.
* **Address**: Registry of Shipping and Seamen, MCA Cardiff, Ground Floor, Anchor Court, Keen Road, Cardiff CF24 5JW, Wales; Tel 029 20448800; Fax: 029 20448820; E-mail rss@mcga.gov.uk

B05d MARINE ACCIDENT INVESTIGATION BRANCH (MAIB)

- is an **expert unit** within the **Department for Transport (DfT)**, based in Southampton, England.
- is responsible for **investigating marine accidents** for the UK government, **producing reports and recommendations** based on its findings, and **providing professional advice at public inquiries**.
- **investigates** accidents at sea and on board ships with the aim of determining what caused an accident in order to prevent it from happening again[36].
- **operates** under the requirements and powers of Part XI of the Merchant Shipping Act 1995 (Accident investigations and inquiries), which contains sections as follows: **267**. Investigation of marine accidents; **268**. Formal investigation into marine accidents; **269**. Re-hearing and appeal from investigation; **270**. Rules as to investigations and appeals; **271**. Inquiries into deaths of crew members and others; **272**. Reports of and inquiries into injuries; **273**. Transmissions of particulars of certain deaths on ships.
- **has duties** defined in the **MS (Accident Reporting and Investigation) Regulations 1999** (SI 1999/2567) (see E08k).
- operates **independently of the MCA**, and does not enforce Merchant Shipping legislation.
- **was established** in July 1989 (following the *Herald of Free Enterprise* disaster of 1987) under section 33 of the Merchant Shipping Act 1988.
- **is headed** by the **Chief Inspector of Marine Accidents**, who is appointed under section 267(1) of the Merchant Shipping Act 1995 and reports directly (and only) to the Secretary of State for Transport.
- **is staffed** by MAIB inspectors[37] whose powers and working framework are set out in Part XI of the Merchant Shipping Act 1995. (The MS (Accident Reporting and Investigation) Regulations 1999 put the framework into effect.)
- maintains a **computerised database** of marine accidents from 1991, which can be used to determine trends.
- is a party, with the MCA and HSE, to a **Memorandum of Understanding for health and safety enforcement activities** etc. at the water margin and offshore (see B05f).
* **MAIB inspectors** are appointed under and have powers conferred by section 267(1) of the Merchant Shipping Act 1995. Section 267(8) provides that for the purpose of discharging their investigative functions they have the powers of an **inspector** conferred by section 259.
* For notes on the **MS (Accident Reporting and Investigation) Regulations 1999** and procedures for reporting accidents, see E08k.

---

[36] MAIB received 1,453 accident and incident reports in 2000. Accidents to ships accounted for 621, with a further 631 involving accidents to people. 201 hazardous incidents (near-misses) were reported, a 25% increase on 1999.

[37] MAIB inspectors come from the three marine disciplines: nautical, engineering and naval architecture. Some are experienced former MCA surveyors; others have been recruited because of their recent seagoing or specialist knowledge. Inspectors are available to travel at short notice to wherever a ship has been involved in an accident. In the course of a year MAIB inspectors will provide assistance to various coroners, procurators fiscal, and the police in connection with marine accidents. Inspectors attended coroner's inquests in England, Wales and Northern Ireland, and fatal accident inquiries in Scotland, to give evidence.

* **MAIB address**: Marine Accident Investigation Branch, First Floor, Carlton House, Carlton Place, Southampton, Hampshire SO15 2DZ, UK. Tel (office hours): 023 8039 5500. Tel (24 hours): 023 8023 2527. Fax: 023 8023 2459. E-mail: maib@dft.gsi.gov.uk
* **Accident reporting line**: 023 8023 2527 (from outside UK: +44 23 8023 2527).
* **Website**: www.maib.dft.gov.uk

B05e HEALTH AND SAFETY COMMISSION (HSC) AND HEALTH AND SAFETY EXECUTIVE (HSE)

B05e.1 Functions, powers and jurisdiction of HSC and HSE

* The **Health and Safety Commission (HSC)** -
  - is responsible to the Secretary of State for Transport and to other Secretaries of State for the administration of the HSW Act throughout Great Britain and on installations on the UK Continental Shelf.
  - has the following **functions**:
    * to secure the health, safety and welfare of persons at work;
    * to protect the public generally against risks to health or safety arising out of work activities and to control the keeping and use of explosives, highly flammable and other dangerous substances;
    * to conduct and sponsor research; promote training and provide an information and advisory service;
    * to review the adequacy of health and safety legislation and submits to Government proposals for new or revised regulations and approved codes of practice.
  - has general oversight of the work of the Health and Safety Executive (HSE) and has power to delegate to the HSE any of its functions.
* The **Health and Safety Executive (HSE)** -
  - is the operating arm of the **Health and Safety Commission** (HSC).
  - is a **statutory body**, set up in 1975 with the main function of making arrangements to secure the health, safety and welfare of people at work and to protect the public from dangers arising from work activities.
  - **enforces**, in all premises in **Great Britain** and on **installations on the UK Continental Shelf**:
    * the Health and Safety at Work, etc. Act 1974 (HSWA), as amended (see E08b.1);
    * regulations made under HSWA;
    * other laws covering particular hazards, e.g. parts of the Food and Environment Protection Act, the COSHH Regulations and the Control of Pesticides Regulations; and
    * laws that cover a particular industry, such as the **ports** industry and the **offshore oil and gas industry**.
* **HSE inspectors** -
  - have **powers** derived principally from sections 20-23 of HSWA and associated legislation, including the **power of entry to all work places**, including docks and offshore installations, to **inspect health and safety conditions** and to **investigate accidents** to dock workers, etc. **working in a port** or while (on board) **loading or unloading a ship** in Great Britain.
  - have powers to **investigate accidents to a ship's crew** (see B05f).
  - have powers to **require transport** to, and **accommodation** on, **offshore installations**.
  - have powers to issue **Improvement Notices and Prohibition Notices** in any workplaces under their jurisdiction (including ships) (see E08b.4).
  - have the same powers to **inspect premises, ships and offshore installations** as Department for Transport (DfT) inspectors (see B05b.3e).
  - may bring **prosecutions** for breaches of relevant legislation.
* **HSE website**: www.hse.gov.uk
* **In Northern Ireland**, the Health and Safety Executive for Northern Ireland (**HSENI**) exercise similar powers to those of HSE. Website:

B05e.2 Legislation enforced by HSE applying to ships and offshore installations

* The following tables list the **chief health and safety legislation** applicable to ships in situations in which the HSE is the enforcing body.

Acts of Parliament

Year	Chapter	Title	SBC ref.
1974	c.37	Health and Safety at Work etc. Act 1974	E08b.1
1992	c.15	Offshore Safety Act 1992	
1992	c.24	Offshore Safety (Protection Against Victimisation) Act 1992	

Statutory Instruments

Year	SI No.	Title	SBC ref.
1987	37	The Dangerous Substances in Harbour Areas Regulations 1987	I02g.4
1987	1331	The Offshore Installations (Safety Zones) Regulations 1987	H01a.5
1988	1655	The Docks Regulations 1988	E08f
1989	971	The Offshore Installations (Safety Representatives and Safety Committees) Regulations 1989	
1992	2051	The Management of Health and Safety at Work Regulations 1992	
1992	2966	The Personal Protective Equipment at Work Regulations 1992	
1992	2932	The Provision and Use of Work Equipment Regulations 1992	
1992	2793	The Manual Handling Operations Regulations 1992	
1992	2885	The Offshore Installations (Safety Case) Regulations 1992	
1995	743	Offshore Installations (Prevention of Fire and Explosion, and Emergency Response) Regulations 1995	D03h.3
1997	2776	Diving at Work Regulations 1997	
2001	2127	The Health and Safety and Work etc. Act 1974 (Application Outside Great Britain Order) 2001	E08b.1a
2002	1355	The Offshore Chemicals Regulations 2002	
2002	1861	The Offshore Installations (Emergency Pollution Control) Regulations 2002	H03i

B05f SHARING OF RESPONSIBILITIES BETWEEN HSE, MCA AND MAIB

* **Areas of mutual interest** between HSE, MCA and MAIB include docks and harbours (including dry docks), coastal and inland waters, shipbuilding and ship repair, offshore, construction work, chain ferries, diving and hovercraft. In areas where there is an **overlap of responsibilities** between these bodies, e.g. at the water margin, in canals and offshore, effective co-ordination between the three organisations is ensured through a **Memorandum of Understanding for Health and Safety Enforcement Activities etc. at the Water Margin and Offshore**. ("the MOU"). The MOU identifies the organisation that will be the **lead authority** for inspection of vessels, investigation of accidents, etc. in different circumstances. The lead authority co-ordinates any joint inspection activities, accident investigation, etc. and notifies the other bodies if appropriate.
* The following notes outline some of the arrangements set out in the MOU. The full text of the **MOU** can be seen on the **MCA website** in the "Statutory information" section of the "Campaigns and publications" pages.

B05f.1 Enforcement

* **MCA** is responsible for enforcing all merchant shipping legislation in respect of occupational health and safety, the safety of vessels, safe navigation and operation (including manning levels and crew competency). Merchant shipping health and safety regulations extend to all those working on the ship at sea, and all shipboard activities carried out by the crew under the control of the ship's master (but not to shipboard activities in port, etc. carried out under the control of a land-based employer, such as stevedoring operations).
* For health and safety enforcement, MCA has powers over **non-UK vessels** only while they are moored, and not over such vessels exercising their right of transit through UK waters, which may include maintaining position by DP. (Vessels being moved using anchor winches are considered to be moored.)
* A **stacked offshore installation** is regarded in merchant shipping law as a ship. Under the MS (Port State Control) Regulations 1995, MCA's powers of inspection and detention extend to any non-UK stacked installation anchored off a port, but not if the installation is anchored off the coast unless the anchorage is a recognised port anchorage.
* **HSE** is responsible for enforcing the **Health and Safety at Work etc. Act 1974** (HSWA), and regulations made under it, in respect of **land-based and offshore work activities**, including loading and unloading of a ship, and for all work activities carried out in a **dry dock**.
* **MAIB** has no enforcement responsibilities or powers. MAIB inspectors observing serious contraventions of legislative requirements on vessels would, in practice, report them to MCA for possible prosecution.

* **HSE** is responsible for enforcement of HSWA in respect of **diving operations**, including certification of divers, equipment safety, etc. **MCA** is responsible for enforcement of relevant safety legislation applicable to diving support vessels.
* **MCA** is responsible for enforcement of legislation applicable to **hovercraft**, even when the craft has left the water. **HSE** is responsible for enforcement of HSWA in respect of the loading or unloading of passengers, vehicles and the handling of cargo.
* **HSE** has responsibility in respect of **standby vessels** only for enforcing the requirement on installation operators and owners for ensuring adequate provision of standby vessels where appropriate. **MCA** is responsible for enforcement of legislation concerning the safety of standby vessels and their crews.
* **HSE** has no responsibility in respect of survey vessels (except for diving operations), towing vessels, anchor handling vessels, dredging vessels or cable-laying vessels (unless cable-laying between installations).
* **In docks and harbours**, HSE is primarily responsible for enforcing legislation covering the safety of shore-based personnel and work equipment supplied by the shore, even when employed on a ship. **HSE** is also responsible for enforcing legislation covering the safety of passengers when on shore. (The dividing line between MCA and HSE responsibilities for passengers is at the gangway.) **MCA** is responsible for occupational health and safety of crews of ships in docks and harbours, for work equipment supplied by the ship, and for the safety of passengers on board ships in port.
* Merchant shipping legislation, enforced by **MCA**, applies to launches used for servicing lights and lightships in docks and harbours., including loading and unloading stores etc. at the light. HSWA, enforced by **HSE**, applies to maintenance work carried out on lights and lightships in docks and harbours.
* On **ships which are permanently moored** and have no master or crew, e.g. restaurant ships and museum ships, **HSE** has primary responsibility for enforcement in relation to shore-based workers and members of the public visiting the ship.
* For vessels on **inland waterways**, enforcement could be either under HSWA (by **HSE**) or merchant shipping legislation (by **MCA**). (The HSWA applies where there is no industry-specific legislation.)
* On **workboats** attending construction work such as bridge repairs, the **MCA** enforces the applicable statutory code regulating the boat's safety, while **HSE** enforces occupational health and safety legislation, since the work activity in land-based.
* Since the Merchant Shipping Act 1995 does not apply to **Crown-owned vessels** such as MOD vessels, Customs cutters and Coastguard craft, **HSE** is responsible for inspections and accident investigation, although they will seek assistance as required from MCA and MAIB.

B05f.2 Accident investigation

* **MAIB** investigates accidents relating to ships and their crews. **MAIB** may investigate any accident on any UK vessel anywhere, and on any vessel in UK territorial waters. For notes on the **MS (Accident Reporting and Investigation) Regulations**, within which the MAIB operates, see E08k.1.
* **HSE** investigates land-based and offshore accidents. Accidents must be reported under the **Reporting of Injuries, Diseases and Dangerous Occurrences Regulations 1995** ("RIDDOR") (SI 1995/3163), which came into force on 1 April 1996.
* In situations where an employer or a shipmaster has a **duty to report the same accident to both HSE** (under RIDDOR) **and MAIB** (under the ARI Regulations), the person filing the report with one organisation will be advised and the report passed on to the other.
* **HSE** would investigate **accidents involving shore-based workers**, such as linesmen falling from a quay during a mooring operation, in co-operation with **MAIB**.
* Where **access is provided by the ship**, MAIB leads in investigation of any accident involving access; where access is provided by the shore, HSE leads, and consults MCA if ship's personnel or passengers are involved.
* **MAIB** is responsible for investigating any accidents to or on diving support vessels. **MAIB** is also responsible for investigating accidents to or on hovercraft.

B06 Radiocommunications Agency and associated organisations

B06a RADIOCOMMUNICATIONS AGENCY

* The **Radiocommunications Agency (RA)** -
  - was established in London in 1990 as an executive agency of the Department of Trade and Industry (DTI).
  - **is responsible** for the issue (under the provisions of the **Wireless Telegraphy Act 1949**) of **Ship Radio Licences** of various categories (although this is contracted out to Wray Castle – see B06b.2);
  - **allocates radio call signs** to UK ships as part of the licensing function. The call sign is a unique identification for the vessel (unlike its name) and is registered by the RA with the ITU along with details given by the license applicant about the vessel.
  - **monitors** (from a station at Baldock, Hertfordshire) the **radio frequency spectrum** as an aid to management, enforcement and freedom from harmful interference.
  - **was formerly responsible** to the Secretary of State for Trade for the **certification of radio operators** and for the issue of Certificates of Competence and Authorities to Operate (ATO) in conformity with the Wireless Telegraphy Act 1949. (Since 1 April 1997 this function has been the responsibility of the MCA.)
  - is responsible for most **civil radio matters** in the UK other than those of telecommunications policy, broadcasting policy and the radio equipment market.
  - **allocates and assigns frequencies** to meet the needs of current and future users, service providers and manufacturers.
  - pursues a policy of **deregulation** where possible and appropriate.
  - **represents UK interests** in international negotiations on radio matters.
  - seeks to ensure that all UK users of radio equipment (as well as manufacturers and installers) comply with relevant **EC regulations and international agreements** to which the UK is a party.
* **Website**: www.radio.gov.uk
* Application forms and guidance notes for Ship Fixed Radio Licences and EPIRB registration are published on the RA website.

B06b ORGANISATIONS ASSOCIATED WITH THE RADIOCOMMUNICATIONS AGENCY

B06b.1 AMERC

* The **Association of Marine Electronics and Radio Colleges (AMERC)** -
  - **acts** as the **examining body** for a range of operator and maintenance certificates on behalf of the Radiocommunications Agency and MCA.
  - **provides**, as part of this examining agency status, a national network of **regional examination centres** for UK radio operator qualifications, with qualified examiners.
  - **sets examinations** and **maintains standards** for certificated personnel, as part of the above function.
  - **provides examination services to the MCA** for marine radio, radar and electronic navigation equipment maintenance certificates.
  - **operates**, in co-operation with the British Council, a limited number of **overseas examination centres**.
* **Website**: www.amerc.ac.uk

B06b.2 Wray Castle

- is an international **provider of telecoms training**, specialising in the design, development and delivery of high level technical training for RF, network and software engineers.
- **maintains databases** of ships' callsigns, Selcall numbers and Maritime Mobile Service Identities (MMSI).
- **issues radio operator certificates** (other than VHF-only certificates) on behalf of the Radiocommunications Agency.

- formerly distributed Ship Radio Licences on behalf of the Radiocommunications Agency; this is now done by Subscriptions Services Ltd.
* **Address**: Wray Castle Limited, Ambleside, Cumbria LA22 0JB, England. Tel: 015394 40200. Fax: 015394 40201.
* **Website**: www.wraycastle.com

B07 Statutory investigations and inquiries

B07a INSPECTOR'S INVESTIGATIONS

* **Under section 267(1) of the Merchant Shipping Act 1995** the Secretary of State must, for the purpose of the investigation of marine accidents, appoint inspectors of marine accidents, one of whom will be appointed as Chief Inspector of Marine Accidents.
* Section 267(2) identifies the "**accidents**" in subsection (1) as:
    * **any accident involving a ship or ship's boat**[38] where, at the time of the accident, the ship is a **UK ship**, or the ship or boat is **in UK waters**; and
    * such **other accidents** involving ships or ships' boats as the Secretary of State may determine.
* Under **regulation 6(1) of the MS (Accident Reporting and Investigation) Regulations 1999** (SI 1999/2567) **any accident** (as defined in regulation 2(1) may be investigated and the Chief Inspector of Marine Accidents must decide whether or not an investigation (known as an "Inspector's Investigation") should be carried out. Where a report of an accident or serious injury has been received under regulation 5, the MAIB must, within 28 days of receipt of the report or information, notify the master of any decision to have an Inspector's Investigation.
* Before making the decision whether or not to investigate an accident, the MAIB may, under regulation 6(2), require further information to be obtained, and the master or owner and any other relevant person or corporate body must provide this information to the best of their ability and knowledge.
* Under regulation 6(7) any initial decision not to investigate may later be reversed by the MAIB.
* Regulation 4 explains that the **fundamental purpose of investigating an accident** is to determine its circumstances and causes with the aim of improving the safety of life at sea and the avoidance of future accidents. It is not the purpose to apportion **liability** or, except so far as is necessary to achieve its fundamental purpose, to apportion **blame** (which are matters for the MCA and the courts).
* Regulation 8 makes the rules for the **conduct of Inspectors' Investigations**.
* Regulation 10 requires the Chief Inspector to produce **reports** of certain **Inspectors' Investigations** carried out under regulation 6(1).
* An investigation may be **reopened** under regulation 12.

B07b FORMAL INVESTIGATIONS

* **Under section 268 of the Merchant Shipping Act 1995** where any "**accident**" has occurred (as defined in the MS (Accident Reporting and Investigation) Regulations 1999), the Secretary of State for Transport may (whether or not an Inspector's Investigation into the accident has been carried out under section 267) cause a **Formal Investigation** to be held. In England, Wales or Northern Ireland a Formal Investigation will be held by a **wreck commissioner**, while in Scotland it will be held by a **sheriff**.
* Under section 268(3) the **Magistrates' Courts Act 1980** (which compels the attendance of witnesses and production of evidence) applies to a Formal Investigation held by a wreck commissioner **as if it were a magistrate's court** and the Formal Investigation was a "complaint". The wreck commissioner has the power to administer oaths for the Formal Investigation. In Scotland, a sheriff will dispose of a Formal Investigation as a "summary application", and his decision will be final (section 268(4)).
* Assistance will be given in the Formal Investigation by one or more suitably experienced and qualified **assessors** (usually mariners); if cancellation or suspension of an officer's certificate is likely to arise, not less than two assessors must be appointed.
* Under section 268(5) a wreck commissioner or sheriff may, if satisfied that an officer caused or contributed to an accident, **cancel or suspend any certificate** held by the officer, or censure him. On cancellation or suspension, the officer must deliver his certificate to the Department for Transport (DfT). Legal costs may also be awarded against an officer.

---

[38] References to an accident involving a ship or ship's boat include references to an accident occurring on board a ship or ship's boat. "Ship's boat" includes a life-raft.

* Section 269 provides for the **re-hearing** of all or part of a case where a formal investigation was held under section 268 and new and important evidence has been discovered or there appear to the Secretary of State to be other grounds for suspecting that a miscarriage of justice may have occurred. A re-hearing may be by a wreck commissioner or the High Court in England or Wales, or by a sheriff or the Court of Session in Scotland.
* The **rules for the conduct of Formal Investigations** are contained in the **MS (Formal Investigations) Rules 1985** (SI 1985/1001), as amended by SI 1990/123 and SI 2000/1623.

B07c INQUIRIES INTO THE FITNESS OR CONDUCT OF OFFICERS ("SECTION 61 INQUIRIES")

- may be held under powers given by **section 61 of the Merchant Shipping Act 1995**.
- were formerly known as "**section 52 Inquiries**", since they were formerly provided for under section 52 of the Merchant Shipping Act 1970.
* If it appears to the Department for Transport (DfT) that an officer -
  * is unfit to discharge duties, by reason of incompetence, misconduct or any other reason; or
  * has been seriously negligent in the discharge of his duties; or
  * has failed to render assistance and exchange information after a collision -
  then the DfT may hold an **inquiry** by one or more persons appointed by them and may, if they think fit, **suspend**, pending the outcome, **his certificate**.
* Where a certificate has been suspended the suspension may, on application of the officer, be terminated by the High Court, or if the inquiry is held in Scotland, by the Court of Session; the decision of the court will be final.
* The **Rules of the Inquiry** are laid down in the **MS (Section 52 Inquiries) Rules** (SI 1982/1752), as amended by SI 1989/84.

B07d INQUIRIES INTO THE FITNESS OR CONDUCT OF SEAMEN OTHER THAN OFFICERS ("SECTION 63 INQUIRIES")

- may be held under powers given by **section 63 of the Merchant Shipping Act 1995**.
* The Department for Transport (DfT) may, where it appears that a person who is the holder of a certificate other than an officer's, whether by reason of incompetence or misconduct or for any other reason, give him notice in writing that it is considering the suspension or cancellation of the certificate.
* The seaman may make written representations or claim to make oral representations to the DfT, and the DfT must decide whether to cancel the certificate.
* The holder of the certificate may, under section 63, require the case to be dealt with by an inquiry to be held by one or more persons appointed by the Secretary of State. They -
  * may confirm the DfT's decision and cancel or suspend the certificate;
  * where the decision was to cancel the certificate, may suspend it instead;
  * may, where the decision was to suspend the certificate, suspend it for a different period;
  * may, instead of confirming the decision of the Secretary of State, censure the seaman or take no further action;
  * may make an order with regard to the cost of the inquiry.
* The procedure to be followed at a Section 63 inquiry is prescribed by the **MS (Section 63 Inquiries) Rules 1997** (SI 1997/347).
* **Section 62** allows for the disqualification of the holder of a certificate other than an officer's (see E02d.8).

B07e POWER TO SUMMON WITNESSES

* **Section 68 of the Merchant Shipping Act 1995** gives the persons holding an inquiry under section 61 or section 62[39] powers to -
  * summon any person to attend to give evidence or to produce any documents in his custody or under his control which relate to the matter in question; and
  * take evidence on oath (and for that purpose administer oaths), or, instead of administering an oath, require the person examined to make a solemn affirmation.

---

[39] Section 62 actually deals with "Disqualification of holder of certificate other than officer's", whereas it is section 63 that provides for an "Inquiry into fitness or conduct of seaman other than an officer". Section 62(4) refers to "an inquiry under section 63".

* The persons holding an inquiry have powers to issue a warrant for the arrest of a person summoned but failing to attend, and to bring him before the inquiry, if it appears to them that there is no just excuse for the failure or if they are satisfied by evidence on oath that the absent person is likely to be able to give material evidence or produce a relevant document.

  • A person attending an inquiry but refusing to be sworn or to give evidence may be jailed for up to one month or fined up to £1000 by the persons holding the inquiry.

B07f DEATH INQUIRIES

* **Section 271 of the Merchant Shipping Act 1995** provides that, except where a coroner's inquest[40] is to be held, or, in Scotland, where a fatal accident inquiry is to be held, an **inquiry** into the cause of death shall be held by a superintendent or proper officer where -
  • any person dies in a UK ship or in a boat or liferaft from such a ship; or
  • the master of or a seaman employed in such a ship dies in a country outside the UK.
* The inquiry must be held **at the next port** where the ship calls after the death and where there is a superintendent or proper officer, or at such other place as the Secretary of State for Transport may direct.
* For the purposes of the inquiry the superintendent or proper officer will have the **powers of an inspector** under section 259 (see B05b.3e).
* For notes on **deaths of seafarers and other persons on board ships**, see E14.

---

[40] In England or Wales a **coroner's inquest** must be held if a death was violent or unnatural, was caused by an industrial disease, occurred in prison, or if the cause of death remains uncertain after post-mortem examination. Coroners hold inquests in these circumstances even if the death occurred abroad (and the body is returned to Britain). If a body has been destroyed or is unrecoverable, a coroner can hold an inquest by order of the Secretary of State provided the death is likely to have occurred in or near the coroner's jurisdiction. The inquest is an inquiry into the medical cause and circumstances of a death. It is held in public, sometimes with a jury. In Scotland, a **fatal accident inquiry** is held in similar circumstances.

Section C

THE SHIPOWNER, MANAGER AND OPERATOR

Section C Contents

C01 Ship ownership, management and operation

Many shipmasters rarely, and in some cases never, visit the owner's/manager's office. However tenuous their physical link with the shore office, however, the law views the shipmaster as the company's agent and representative. It may therefore benefit masters and other officers to know a little about the contractual relationships and legal obligations of their employers. A few relevant aspects of shipowning, managing and operation are described in this section.

C01a CONTRACTUAL RELATIONSHIPS IN SHIPPING

* **Separate contracts** exist between the **shipowner** and:
    * the **ship manager** (see C01c);
    * the **master** (see E04b);
    * the **crew** (see E05b);
    * the **classification society** (see D02c);
    * port **agents** (see I01h);
    * **suppliers, repairers, etc.** (see I03c);
    * **insurers**, including:
        * hull and machinery underwriters (see G04a);
        * his P&I club (see G04b);
        * insurers of risks not covered elsewhere (e.g. war and strikes risks) (see G01a).
* For notes on **contractual relationships related to the ship's employment**, see F02.

C01b SHIPPING COMPANY FUNCTIONS

C01b.1 Basic shipowning company functions

- include:
    * ship management or "husbandry" functions (see C01b.2);
    * ship operating functions (see C01b.3); and
    * various other functions (see C01b.4).

C01b.2 Ship management or "husbandry" functions

- include:
    * manning, including recruitment, training, travel and welfare;
    * fleet maintenance and repair, including routine drydocking and surveys;
    * documenting and implementing the Company's Safety Management System in conformity with ISM Code or, if applicable, DSM Code, including provision of Designated Person (DP or DPA);
    * ship supplies (sometimes called "purchasing");
    * ship insurance, including Hull & Machinery insurance and P&I cover.
* These functions comprise the major cost element in the formula PROFIT = REVENUE - COSTS.

C01b.3 Ship operating functions

- include:
    * obtaining employment for the company's ships (i.e. fixing vessels on charters);
    * scheduling the fleet;
    * ordering ("stemming") bunker fuel; and
    * arranging loading and discharge of cargoes and associated port activities.
- are concerned chiefly with maximising revenue.
- are designed to maximise the economic employment of the ship.

C01b.4 Other shipping company functions

- usually include:
  - finance, including budgeting, arranging loans and mortgages, sale and purchase of new vessels;
  - accounting, including producing financial figures for tax purposes, improving efficiency for clients;
  - administration, i.e. running company internal affairs, maintaining its buildings and equipment, security, etc.;
  - marketing/sales, including obtaining more business, advertising, etc.;
  - (sometimes) legal affairs;
  - (sometimes) research and development (R&D); and
  - (sometimes) quality assurance, including QA certification for ISO 9002, ISM Code certification, etc.

C01b.5 Operations Department functions

* The **Operations Department** -
  - should act as a **link** between:
    - the ship and its owner;
    - the owner and any charterer;
    - the owner and other cargo interests.
  - should ensure that the master knows and understands his **voyage instructions**.
  - should **monitor each voyage** with the aim of minimising expense and maximising profit.
  - should watch for and pre-empt **potential problems**.
  - should act as a **clearing house for information** sent to and from the ship.
  - will need to know, after the ship has been fixed on charter, the following **information**:
    - cargo type and quantity;
    - load and discharge ports and restrictions thereat;
    - notices of readiness required to be given by the master to charterers, shippers, agents or consignees;
    - any special instructions or advice in connection with the cargo.
  - should obtain a copy of the **charter party** from the broker and **discuss this** with the master. If the ship is time chartered, the master will need **information regarding delivery and redelivery** of the ship, etc.
  - should **contact agents** at the loading port(s). Agents should give the operations department:
    - a detailed pro-forma disbursements account;
    - confirmation of any restrictions at the port;
    - advice as to berthing and loading prospects;
    - any other relevant information.
  - should ensure that the following are **arranged** for the ship's voyage:
    - crew changes;
    - crew mailing arrangements;
    - engine and deck spares;
    - stores, lubricants, bunkers and water;
    - master's cash or other special requirements;
    - any surveys required.
  - should maintain close **contact with port agents** once the ship has arrived at the load port, to ensure:
    - that notice of readiness is tendered and accepted without problem;
    - that loading or discharge operations are progressing satisfactorily;
    - that agents are complying with instructions concerning bills of lading, freight collection, etc;
    - that the master's requirements are being met; and
    - that sufficient funds are sent to the agent for disbursements and master's cash requirements.

C01c TOTAL SHIP MANAGEMENT AND ITS FUNCTIONS

* Many shipowners entrust all or part of the management of their vessels to one or more ship managers.
* The **management agreement** (e.g. BIMCO's "SHIPMAN") may provide that the ship manager will be responsible for all or part of the management of the entire fleet, or part of the fleet, or a particular vessel.
* **Total ship management** includes the **functions** and **duties** shown in the following table. Different functions may be entrusted under separate contracts to different ship management companies. Technical management may, for

example, be provided by ship management company "A", crew management by ship manager "B", and commercial management (embracing chartering, operations and other functions) by ship manager "C".

Functions	Ship manager's duty
Technical management	1. Provision of competent personnel to supervise the maintenance and general efficiency of the vessel. 2. Arrangement and supervision of drydockings, repairs, alterations and the upkeep of the vessel to the standards required by the owner. 3. Arrangement of the supply of necessary stores, spares and lubricating oil. 4. Appointment of surveyors and technical consultants when considered necessary.
Crew management	1. Employment of master, officers and crew. 2. Arrangement of transportation of the crew, including repatriation. 3. Training of the crew. 4. Supervision of the efficiency of the crew and administration of all other crew matters such as planning for the manning of the vessel. 5. Payroll arrangement. 6. Arrangement and administration of pensions and crew insurance. 7. Discipline and union negotiations. 8. Enforcement of appropriate standing orders.
Insurance	Arranging such insurances as the owner has instructed or agreed, e.g. Hull & Machinery, P&I, war risks, etc.
Freight management	1. Provision of voyage estimates and accounts and calculation of hire and freights and/or demurrage and despatch moneys due from or due to the charterer, if any. 2. Arrangement of the proper payment to the owner of all hire and/or freight revenues or other moneys of any kind to which the owner may be entitled arising out of the employment of the vessel or otherwise in connection with the vessel.
Accounting	1. Establishing an accounting system meeting the requirements of the owner and providing regular accounting services, supplying regular reports and records in accordance therewith. 2. Maintaining the records of all costs and expenditures incurred under the management agreement as well as data necessary for the settlement of accounts between the owner and managers.
Chartering	Seeking and negotiating employment for the vessel and the conclusion (including the execution thereof) of charter parties or other contracts relating to the employment of the vessel.
Sale or purchase of vessel	Supervising the sale or purchase of vessels, including the performance of any sale or purchase agreement (but not the negotiation of same, which is usually left to a specialist S&P broker).
Provisions	Arranging for the supply of ships' provisions.
Bunkering	Arranging for the provision of bunker fuel of the quality specified by the owner as required for the vessel's trade.
Ship operation	1. Provision of voyage estimates and accounts. 2. Calculation of hire, freights, demurrage and/or despatch moneys due from or due to charterers. 3. Issue of voyage instructions. 4. Appointment of agents. 5. Appointment of stevedores. 6. Arranging for the surveying of cargoes.

C02 Ships' costs and budgets

C02a SHIPS' COST CLASSIFICATION

* The three **basic ship cost categories** are:
  * **capital costs**;
  * **voyage costs**;
  * **operating** or **running costs**.
* **Capital costs** -
  - are **fixed costs** associated with the ship's purchase.
  - include **pre-delivery costs**, **loan repayments**, **interest**, **leasing charges**, **initial registration fees**, **taxes** (sometimes), and any **bareboat charterhire** payable.
  - are the **owner's responsibility**.
* **Voyage costs** -
  - are **variable costs** associated with the commercial employment of the ship.
  - include costs of **bunkers**, **port** and **canal dues**, **pilotage**, **tug hire**, **agency fees** and **loading/discharge costs**.
  - are the responsibility of the ship's commercial operator. If the ship is let on a time charter, the charterer is liable for the voyage costs.
* **Operating** or **running costs** -
  - are **semi-variable costs** which fall between capital and voyage costs.
  - include costs of **crewing**, **storing**, **ship maintenance**, **insurance** and **administration**.
  - are the responsibility of the **ship owner or manager**.

C02b SHIPS' BUDGETS

The following notes may be useful to officers handling their ships' budgets.

* A ship manager is usually required under the management contract to present to the owner an annual 12-month budget. If the budget is agreed to, the managers will also produce a monthly comparison between the ship's budgeted and actual income and expenditure.
* The cost categories most likely to be used in pro-forma budget estimates and monthly reports are the **operating costs**, i.e. **crewing**, **storing**, **maintenance**, **insurance** and **administration**, as shown in the following table.

Operating cost	Items included in cost
Crewing	Officers' earnings and leave pay; ratings' earnings and leave pay; ratings' overtime; pension and insurance contributions; crew establishment costs (recruitment, training, cadets, etc.); crew travel expenses; and sundry/unrecoverable medical costs
Storing	Provisions; deck stores - general; engine stores - general; paint; cordage; lubricants; cabin stores/laundry; and fresh water.
Maintenance	Deck repairs and spares; engine repairs and spares; electronics and navaids; and surveys.
Insurance	Hull and machinery insurance; P&I calls; war risks insurance; loss of earnings insurance; and deductible allowance.
Administration	Communication expenses; owner's port costs; sundries; and management fee.

* The total of the above costs, added to the annual **drydocking allowance**, will give the grand total. (Some owners prefer to account for the drydocking allowance monthly.) The grand total divided by 365 gives the **vessel's daily rate**.
* A **Budget Analysis Statement**, which is generally prepared monthly or quarterly, will give the variance of "**Budget**" against "**Actual**" figures, with percentage variances.

C03 Shipowner's obligations and liabilities

C03a STATUTORY OBLIGATION OF OWNER AS TO SEAWORTHINESS IN CREW CONTRACTS

* **Section 42(1) of MSA 1995** provides that **in every contract of employment** between the owner of a UK ship and its **master** or **any seaman** employed in it, there will be implied an **obligation on the owner** -
  * that the owner, the master and every agent charged with loading the ship, preparing the ship for sea or sending the ship to sea **must use all reasonable means to ensure the seaworthiness of the ship** for the voyage at the time when the voyage commences; and
  * that **the ship will be kept in a seaworthy condition** for the voyage during the voyage.
* The obligation under section 42 applies notwithstanding any agreement to the contrary (i.e. it cannot be contracted out of) (section 42(2)).
* No liability on the owner arises under this obligation in respect of the ship being sent to sea in an unseaworthy state where, owing to **special circumstances**, the sending of the ship to sea in such a state was **reasonable and justifiable** (section 42(3)).

C03b OWNER'S LIABILITY FOR UNSAFE OPERATION OF SHIP

* **Section 100(1) of MSA 1995** provides that it will be the duty of the owner of a UK ship, and the owner of any other ship within UK waters while proceeding to or from a port in the UK, to take all reasonable steps to secure that the ship is operated in a safe manner, unless the ship would not proceeding to or from the port but for weather conditions or any other unavoidable circumstances.
* Where the ship is chartered by demise (i.e. bareboat chartered), or is managed (either wholly or in part) by a person other than the owner under the terms of a management agreement, reference to the owner should be construed as including a reference to the charterer or manager, or both, as the case may be (section 100(4)).

C03c OTHER LEGAL OBLIGATIONS AND LIABILITIES OF SHIPOWNERS

C03c.1 Owner's duty of care

* Shipowners have a **legal duty of care** -
  * to their **employees**;
  * to **shippers** and **owners of cargo**;
  * to **passengers**; and
  * to **other "neighbours"**, e.g. the owners of harbour property and other vessels (see B03e).
* Breach of this duty may result in either **criminal liability**, **civil liability**, or **both** (see B03b.6).

C03c.2 Criminal liabilities of owners

* Since most pieces of UK merchant shipping legislation that specify offences make the owner liable in addition to the master, the remarks in E04i.1 on the criminal liabilities of shipmasters apply equally to shipowners, and there can be few, if any, UK businesses more heavily burdened with potential criminal liabilities than shipowners.
* Numerous pieces of UK Merchant Shipping legislation apply to non-UK vessels while they are in UK ports and waters. In a similar way, a UK vessel will be subject to various pieces of foreign legislation when in the waters of any foreign State, especially those States with well-developed merchant shipping legislation. As with UK Merchant Shipping legislation, breaches of the foreign legislation will in most cases make the owner and/or the master liable. The USA's Oil Pollution Act 1990 is perhaps the most prominent example of a piece of foreign legislation affecting owners, but should not be thought of as the only US legislation the owner has to comply with. P&I Clubs, their correspondents and their club bulletins are probably the best source of information on foreign legislation.
* For notes on **offences by and criminal liability of a body corporate or Scottish partnership** see B03b.1e.
* For notes on the **criminal liabilities of shipmasters**, see E04i.1. Where a shipmaster is liable to a criminal penalty, the shipowner is, in most cases, also usually liable. Many Merchant Shipping regulations and much other legislation contains obligations a breach of which attracts a penalty on the **owner**.

C03c.3 Civil liabilities of owners

* Shipowners and operators may have **civil liabilities** to many parties including:
  * **shippers** (for breach of the contract of carriage);
  * **passengers** (for breach of the contract of passage);
  * **crew members** (for personal injuries, breaches of the crew agreement, etc.);
  * **relatives of crew members** killed during their employment and of persons killed by the owner's vessel;
  * **persons** (e.g. port authorities and other shipowners) **who suffer loss or damage to property** as a result of collision, etc.;
  * **customs and immigration authorities** (for fines on the vessel);
  * **harbour and coastal authorities** (for pollution);
  * **salvors** (for salvage rewards);
  * **co-adventurers** in the "common maritime adventure" (for general average contributions).

C03c.4 Employers' Liability (Compulsory Insurance) Act 1969

- requires every employer, unless exempt, to **insure against liability for bodily injury or disease sustained by his employees** in the course of their employment, and to maintain this insurance, and display a **Certificate of Insurance** at each place of business (e.g. on board a ship).
- applies to **owners of vessels in Great Britain** and in the areas within the baselines from which territorial waters are measured, i.e. inside all harbours and bays (up to a line not exceeding 24 miles long drawn across the bay), subject to certain exceptions.
- also applies to **employers of persons working on offshore installations** on the UK Continental Shelf and on vessels attendant on the installations, or any floating structure used in connection with it (e.g. a "floatel").
- does not apply to Northern Ireland, the Isle of Man or the Channel Islands, or outside Great Britain, except to employment on offshore installations and related structures.

* **Regulation 9 of The Employer's Liability (Compulsory Insurance) Regulations 1998** (SI 1998/2573) exempts any employer who is a member of a mutual insurance association of shipowners or of shipowners and others (e.g. a P&I club), in respect of any liability to an employee of the kind mentioned in section 1(1) of the Employers' Liability (Compulsory Insurance) Act 1969 against which the employer is insured for the time being with that association for an amount not less than that required by the 1969 Act and regulations under it, being an employer who holds a certificate issued by that association to the effect that he is so insured in relation to that employee.
* **M.757** explains that an exception to the general requirement of the Act that applies specifically to seafarers, concerns employers who are insured with a P&I club. This is an alternative to insurance under the Act. An employer must have one kind of insurance or the other, or he would be in breach of the Act.
* **Where the employer has insurance with a P&I club** there is no requirement to display a Certificate.

C03c.5 Statistical Returns (Carriage of Goods and Passengers by Sea) Regulations 1997

- implement EC Council Directive 95/64/EC.
- provide that the DfT may require any person carrying on business or trade in the maritime transport sector (i.e. shipping companies or their agents) or any harbour authority to **furnish data** including:
    * cargo, passenger and vessel movement information;
    * information about container and ro-ro unit numbers transported;
    * particulars of vessels and their operator and/or agent.

C03c.6 Oil pollution liability

* For notes on **compulsory oil pollution insurance requirements** in the UK, see G04d.1.
* For notes on the **Oil Pollution (Compulsory Insurance) Regulations**, see G04d.1b.
* For notes on **oil pollution liability schemes**, see G04d.2.
* For notes on **P&I pollution cover**, see G04d.3.

C03c.7 Carrier's liability for illegal immigration

* The **Immigration and Asylum Act 1999** contains a provision to extend the power to require information from carriers about their passengers and a new power to require advance notification by carriers of the arrival of passengers who are not nationals of the European Economic Area[1].
* The Act also strengthens previous **carriers' liability legislation** to facilitate the collection of any charges incurred by carriers by bringing inadequately documented passengers to the United Kingdom.
* The Act contains provisions for a new power to impose a **civil penalty** on persons responsible for the **transport of clandestine entrants to the UK**. The new civil penalty is additional to and separate from carriers' liability legislation, which the Act strengthens and replaces. The civil penalty applies to all vehicles, **ships**, or aircraft bringing clandestine entrants to the UK. The Act provides the power to detain vehicles, ships or aircraft as security until all charges for the carriage of illegal entrants have been paid.
* Information about **carrier's liability** can be found on the Immigration and Nationality Directorate **website** at: www.ind.homeoffice.gov.uk/default.asp?PageId=1275
* **Other States** may have similar, and perhaps more stringent, regulations. For a note on **carrier's liability in the USA** (affecting the master) see I01g.5.

C03c.8 Company obligations relating to ship security

* SOLAS chapter XI-2 relates to **Special Measures to Enhance Maritime Security**. In that chapter, **regulations 4 and 5** make requirements applicable to the **Company**. ("Company" means the owner, organization or person who is responsible for the operation of the ship.)

---

[1] The EEA is a free-trade area encompassing the member States of the European Union and the member States (excluding Switzerland) of the European Free Trade Association (EFTA), i.e. Norway, Iceland, and (from 1 May 1995) Liechtenstein.

* SOLAS regulation XI-2/4 (Requirements for Companies and ships) provides that **Companies** must comply with the relevant requirements of **SOLAS chapter XI-2** and of **part A of the ISPS Code**, taking into account the guidance in part B of the ISPS Code (regulation XI-2/4.1).
* SOLAS regulation XI-2/5 (Specific Responsibility of Companies) provides that the **Company** must ensure that the master has available on board, at all times, **information** through which officers duly authorized by a Contracting Government can establish:
1. Who is responsible for appointing the members of the crew or other persons currently employed or engaged on board the ship in any capacity on the business of that ship;
2. Who is responsible for deciding the employment of the ship; and
3. In cases where the ship is employed under the terms of charter, who are the parties to the charter.
* ISPS Code, part A, section 6 provides that -
   * the Ship Security Plan must contain a **clear statement emphasizing the master's authority**. The **Company** must establish in the Ship Security Plan that the master has the overriding authority and responsibility to make decisions with respect to the security of the ship and to request the **assistance of the Company** or of any SOLAS Contracting Government as may be necessary (section 6.1); and
   * the **Company** must ensure that the **company security officer** (CSO), the **master** and the **ship security officer** (SSO) are given the **necessary support to fulfil their duties and responsibilities** in accordance with SOLAS chapter XI-2 and part A of the ISPS Code (section 6.2).
* ISPS Code, part A, section 13 provides that the **company security officer and appropriate shore-based personnel** must have **knowledge** and have received **training**, taking into account the guidance given in part B of the ISPS Code (section 13.1). For other notes on **training requirements**, see E02d.9.
* Under SOLAS regulation XI-2/9.2.1, for the purpose of chapter XI-2, a SOLAS Contracting Government may require that **ships intending to enter its ports provide specified security-related information** (listed in D05b.9) to officers duly authorized by that Government to ensure compliance with chapter XI-2 **prior to entry into port** with the aim of avoiding the need to impose control measures or steps. If requested by the SOLAS Contracting Government, the ship or the **Company must provide confirmation**, acceptable to that Government, of the information.
* For notes on other **ship security requirements of SOLAS and the ISPS Code**, see D03a.6.

C03c.8a Company security officer

* ISPS Code, part A, section 11 provides that the Company must designate a **company security officer** (CSO). A person designated as the company security officer may act as the company security officer **for one or more ships**, depending on the number or types of ships the Company operates provided it is clearly identified for which ships this person is responsible. A Company may, depending on the number or types of ships they operate designate **several persons** as company security officers provided it is clearly identified for which ships each person is responsible (section 11.1).
* In addition to those specified elsewhere in part A of the ISPS Code, the duties and responsibilities of the company security officer include, but are not limited to:
   * **advising the level of threats** likely to be encountered by the ship, using appropriate security assessments and other relevant information;
   * ensuring that **ship security assessments** are carried out;
   * ensuring the development, the submission for approval, and thereafter the implementation and maintenance of the **ship security plan**;
   * ensuring that the **ship security plan** is modified, as appropriate, to correct deficiencies and satisfy the security requirements of the individual ship;
   * arranging for **internal audits and reviews** of security activities;
   * arranging for the **initial and subsequent verifications of the ship** by the flag State Administration or the Recognized Security Organisation (RSO);
   * ensuring that **deficiencies and non-conformities** identified during internal audits, periodic reviews, security inspections and verifications of compliance are promptly addressed and dealt with;
   * enhancing **security awareness and vigilance**;
   * ensuring adequate **training** for personnel responsible for the security of the ship;
   * ensuring **effective communication and co-operation** between the ship security officer and the relevant port facility security officers;
   * ensuring **consistency** between **security** requirements and **safety** requirements;
   * ensuring that, if **sister-ship or Fleet Security Plans** are used, the plan for each ship reflects the ship-specific information accurately; and

* ensuring that any **alternative or equivalent arrangements** approved for a particular ship or group of ships are implemented and maintained.
* ISPS Code, part B, section 4 provides that the **company security officer** or the ship security officer should **liaise** at the earliest opportunity with the **port facility security officer** (PFSO) of the port facility the ship is intended to visit **to establish the security level** applying for that ship at the port facility (section 4.11). For notes on the PFSO, see I01k.1.

C03c.8b Ship security assessments

* **ISPS Code, part A, section 8** contains requirements for **ship security assessments**.
* The ship security assessment is an essential and integral part of the process of developing and updating the Ship Security Plan (section 8.1).
* The **company security officer** must ensure that the ship security assessment is carried out by persons with appropriate skills to evaluate the security of a ship, in accordance with section 8, taking into account the guidance given in part B of the ISPS Code (section 8.2).
* Subject to the provisions of section 9.2.1, a Recognized Security Organisation (RSO) may carry out the ship security assessment of a specific ship (section 8.3).
* The ship security assessment must include an **on-scene security survey** and, at least, the following elements:
  * identification of existing security measures, procedures and operations;
  * identification and evaluation of key ship board operations that it is important to protect;
  * identification of possible threats to the key ship board operations and the likelihood of their occurrence, in order to establish and prioritise security measures; and
  * identification of weaknesses, including human factors in the infrastructure, policies and procedures (section 8.4).
* The ship security assessment must be **documented, reviewed, accepted and retained** by the Company (section 8.5).

C03d LIMITATION OF LIABILITY FOR MARITIME CLAIMS

* A shipowner who has unlimited liability might be faced with a claim of such magnitude (e.g. in cases involving great loss of life and/or property) that it would bankrupt him and discourage him (and other owners) from further participation in international trade. In respect of various types of maritime claim brought against shipowners, therefore, the shipowner, if found liable, is entitled in many countries to **limit his liability** to the claimant. This right has been enshrined in **international conventions**.
* The **Convention on the Limitation of Liability of Owners of Sea-going Ships 1957** was based on earlier conventions and was given effect in the UK and several other countries, some of which still give force to it.
* The **Convention on Limitation of Liability for Maritime Claims 1976** (sometimes called the "**London Convention**") made some radical changes from the 1957 convention. It was given effect in the UK by section 17 of the Merchant Shipping Act 1979, which was repealed and replaced by section 185 of the Merchant Shipping Act 1995. The text of most (but not all) of the 1976 Convention forms Part I of Schedule 7 to the Act, while Part II contains "Provisions having effect in connection with the Convention".
* Persons entitled to limit their liability under the 1976 Convention include shipowners and salvors, "shipowner" meaning the owner, charterer, manager or operator of a seagoing ship (Article 1).
* **Claims subject to limitation** are set out in Article 2 of the 1976 Convention and include:
  * claims in respect of loss of life or personal injury or loss of or damage to property (including damage to harbour works, basins and waterways and aids to navigation), occurring on board or in direct connection with the operation of the ship or with salvage operations, and consequential loss resulting therefrom;
  * claims in respect of loss resulting from delay in the carriage by sea of cargo, passengers or their luggage;
  * claims in respect of other loss resulting from infringement of rights other than contractual rights, occurring in direct connection with the operation of the ship or salvage operations;
  * claims in respect of the raising, removal, destruction or the rendering harmless of a ship which is sunk, wrecked, stranded or abandoned, including anything that is or has been on board such ship;
  * claims in respect of the removal, destruction or the rendering harmless of the cargo of the ship;
  * claims of a person other than the person liable in respect of measures taken in order to avert or minimise loss for which the person liable may limit his liability in accordance with the Convention, and further loss caused by such measures.
* **Claims not subject to limitation** are set out in Article 3 and include:
  * claims for salvage or for contribution in general average;

- claims for oil pollution damage within the meaning of the International Convention on Civil Liability for Oil Pollution Damage 1969 or of any amendment or Protocol thereto which is in force;
- claims subject to any international convention or national legislation governing or prohibiting limitation of liability for nuclear damage;
- claims against the shipowner of a nuclear ship for nuclear damage;
- claims by servants of the shipowner or salvor whose duties are connected with the ship or the salvage operations, including claims of their heirs, dependants or other persons entitled to make such claims, if under the law governing the contract of service between the shipowner or salvor and such servants the shipowner or salvor is not entitled to limit his liability in respect of such claims, or if he is by such law only permitted to limit his liability to an amount greater than that provided for in Article 6.

* Article 4 provides that **a person will not be entitled to limit his liability** if it is proved that the loss resulted from his personal act or omission, committed with the intent to cause such loss, or recklessly and with knowledge that such loss would probably result.

* Article 6 sets out the **limits of liability** for claims other than those mentioned in Article 7 (passenger claims). The amounts are specified in "Units of Account" for ships in various tonnage bands, "tonnage" meaning gross tonnage in accordance with the International Tonnage Convention 1969 and, in the UK, the MS (Liability of Shipowners and Others) (Calculation of Tonnage) Order 1986 (SI 1986/1040). The "Unit of Account" is defined in Article 8 as meaning the Special Drawing Right (SDR) as defined by the International Monetary Fund. (The current value of one SDR is given on the front page of Lloyd's List.)

* Article 7 provides that, in respect of claims arising on any distinct occasion for loss of life or personal injury to **passengers** of a ship, the limit of the shipowner's liability will be 46,666 Units of Account multiplied by the number of passengers which the ship is authorised to carry according to the "ship's certificate", but not exceeding 25 million Units of Account. The "ship's certificate" means the Passenger Ship Safety Certificate or Passenger Certificate, depending on which is in force. "Passengers" include those under a contract of passenger carriage as well as persons accompanying a vehicle or live animals which are covered by a contract of carriage of goods. The Convention relating to the Carriage of Passengers and their Luggage by Sea 1976 (the Athens Convention) (see F08a.2) sets limits of liability for claims made by passengers in respect of death, personal injury or loss of or damage to luggage. Where both the 1976 London Convention and the Athens Convention apply, the shipowner may limit his liability to the London Convention figure if lower.

* Article VIII of the Hague Rules (see F07c.4), Article VIII of the Hague-Visby Rules (see F07c.2), and Article 25(1) of the Hamburg Rules (see F07c.5) all contain provisions relating to **limitation of liability for cargo claims**. A UK shipowner may be able to further limit his liability for such claims where the limit under the 1976 Convention is lower than that set by the relevant rules.

* In claims where a UK shipowner has **liability for damage caused by oil pollution** under the Civil Liability Convention 1969 or the 1992 Liability Convention, the shipowner's right to limit his liability is governed by the relevant convention.

* **Section 186 of the Merchant Shipping Act 1995** excludes the owner of a UK ship from **liability for loss or damage by fire** of property on board, and from liability for loss of or damage to any gold, silver, watches, jewels or precious stones on board the ship by theft, robbery or other dishonest conduct if their nature and value were not at the time of shipment declared by their owner or shipper to the owner or master in the bill of lading or otherwise in writing.

C04 Safety management codes applicable to UK shipowners, operators and managers

C04a SAFETY MANAGEMENT CODES IN FORCE IN THE UK

* Two **safety management codes**, applicable to owners, operators and managers of UK ships and other ships operating to and from UK ports, are in force in the UK. The codes are:
  - the **International Management Code for the Safe Operation of Ships and for Pollution Prevention** (the **ISM Code**), which is mandatory under SOLAS chapter IX (see C04b.1) for certain ships on international voyages; and
  - the **Safety Management Code for Domestic Passenger Ships** (the **DSM Code**), which is not mandatory under any international instrument but is required to be complied with under UK national regulations on certain ships on domestic voyages.

- Regulations enforcing these codes in the UK, ship types to which the regulations apply, and relevant M Notices, are shown in the following table.

Code	UK regulations applying the Code	Ship types to which the Regulations apply	Relevant M Notice	SBC ref.
International Safety Management Code (ISM Code)	MS (International Safety Management (ISM) Code) Regulations 1998 (SI 1998/1561)	(1) Passenger ships of Classes I, II and II(A) (of any tonnage) (other than ro-ro passenger ferries on regular services to or from or within the UK); (2) oil tankers, chemical tankers, gas carriers, bulk carriers and cargo high-speed craft, of 500gt or more and which engage in international voyages; (3) other cargo ships and mobile offshore drilling units (MODUs) of 500gt or more which engage in international voyages.	MGN 40	C04b D03a.1
	MS (ISM Code) (Ro-Ro Passenger Ferries) Regulations 1997 (SI 1997/3022)	Ro-ro passenger ferries on regular services to or from or within the UK (i.e. ships to which Council Regulation (EC) No. 3051/95 on the safety management of roll-on/roll-off passenger ferries (ro-ro ferries) applies).	MGN 40	D03b.1a
Safety Management Code for Domestic Passenger Ships (DSM Code)	MS (Domestic Passenger Ships) (Safety Management Code) Regulations 2001 (SI 2001/3209)	Passenger ships of Classes III to VI(A) - other than ships to which Council Regulation (EC) No. 3051/95 on the safety management of roll-on/roll-off passenger ferries (ro-ro ferries) applies, i.e. ro-ro passenger ferries on regular services to or from or within the UK.	MSN 1754 MGN 158	C04c D03b.1b

C04b SOLAS CHAPTER IX AND THE ISM CODE

C04b.1 SOLAS Chapter IX

* SOLAS Chapter IX (Management for the safe operation of ships) -
  - **was adopted** by the 1994 SOLAS Conference and entered into force on 1 July 1998. The text was amended by resolution MSC.99(73), and the amended text entered into force on 1 July 2002.
  - **applies** to all ships, regardless of the date of construction (regulation 2.1).
  - **requires the company and the ship** to comply with the requirements of the ISM Code, which is mandatory (regulation 3.1).
  - **requires the ship** to be operated by a company holding a Document of Compliance (regulation 3.2).
  - **provides for the issue of a Document of Compliance** (DOC) to every company complying with the requirements of the ISM Code (regulation 4.1). The DOC may be issued by the flag State Administration, an organisation recognised by the Administration, or another SOLAS Contracting Government (regulation 4.1).
  - **provides that a copy of the DOC** must be kept on board so that the master can produce it for verification (regulation 4.2).
  - **provides for the issue of a Safety Management Certificate** (SMC) to every ship by the flag State Administration or an organisation recognised by the Administration following verification that the company and its shipboard management operate in accordance with the approved safety management system (regulation 4.3).
  - **requires the safety management system** to be maintained in accordance with the provisions of the ISM Code (regulation 5).
  - **requires the flag State Administration**, or another SOLAS Contracting Government at its request, or an organisation recognised by the flag State Administration, to **periodically verify the proper functioning of the ship's safety management system** (regulation 6.1).
  - requires a ship required to hold a Safety Management Certificate to be subject to **control in accordance with the provisions of SOLAS regulation XI/4**, and provides that for this purpose the SMC will be treated as a certificate issued under SOLAS regulation I/12 or I/13 (i.e. as a SOLAS passenger ship or cargo ship "safety certificate") (regulation 6.2). (SOLAS regulation XI/4 provides that a ship in a port of another SOLAS Contracting Government will be subject to port State control measures when there are clear grounds for believing that the master or crew are not familiar with essential shipboard safety procedures.)

C04b.2 Status of ISM Code

* The **International Management Code for the Safe Operation of Ships and for Pollution Prevention** (the **ISM Code**) -
  - **was adopted** by IMO Assembly Resolution A.741(18) in November 1993.
  - is **mandatory** under SOLAS regulation IX/3.1.
  - came into force on **1 July 1998** for:
    * **passenger ships** of any tonnage, including high-speed passenger ships, on international voyages;
    * **gas carriers** of 500gt or over on international voyages;
    * **oil tankers** of 500gt or over on international voyages;
    * **chemical tankers** of 500gt or over on international voyages;
    * **bulk carriers** of 500gt or over on international voyages; and
    * **high-speed cargo ships** of 500gt or over on international voyages.
  - came into force on **1 July 2002** for:
    * **other cargo ships** of 500gt or over on international voyages; and
    * **mobile offshore drilling units** (MODUs) of 500gt or over on international voyages.
  - **was amended** in December 2000 by resolution MSC.104(73) and **came into force in its revised form** on 1 July 2002.
* National regulations gave **earlier effect** in some countries to the ISM Code's requirements[2].
  * **Hull and machinery insurances** to which the International Hull Clauses (01/11/02) apply are conditional on a valid ISM **Document of Compliance** and **Safety Management Certificate** being held by the Owners or party assuming responsibility for operation of the vessel (see G04a.2i).

C04b.3 Contents of revised ISM Code

* **The revised ISM Code** (effective from 1 July 2002) contains a Preamble followed by 16 paragraphs arranged in two parts, A and B. The following table abbreviates the contents of each paragraph.
* In the table, **Co** = "the Company"; **IMO** = "the Organization"; **FSA** ("flag State Administration") = "the Administration"; **RO** ("recognised organisation") = "an organization recognized by the Administration"; **CG** = "Contracting Government"; **SMS** = Safety Management System; **DPA** = "designated person or persons ashore"; **DOC** = Document of Compliance; **IDOC** = Interim Document of Compliance; **SMC** = Safety Management Certificate; **ISMC** = Interim Safety Management Certificate.

Part or para.	Heading	Notes
-	**Preamble**	Sets out **ethos of Code**. Declares **purpose of Code** as being to provide an international standard for the safe management and operation of ships and for pollution prevention. Because no two shipping companies or owners are the same, and because ships operate under a wide range of different conditions, **Code is based on general principles and objectives**. **Code is expressed in broad terms** so it can have a widespread application. **Cornerstone of good safety management** declared to be **commitment from the top**. In matters of safety and pollution prevention it is **commitment, competence, attitudes and motivation of individuals** at all levels that determines the end result.
PART A	**IMPLEMENTATION**	
1	**General**	
1.1	**Definitions** (applicable to Parts A and B)	**International Safety Management (ISM) Code**: International Management Code for the Safe Operation of Ships and for Pollution Prevention, as adopted by IMO Assembly, as may be amended. **Company**: The owner of the ship or any other organisation or person such as a manager or bareboat charterer, who has assumed responsibility for operation of ship from the owner and who, on assuming that responsibility, has agreed to take over all duties and responsibility imposed by the Code. **Administration**: Government of the State whose flag the ship is entitled to fly. **Safety Management System**: a structured and documented system enabling Co personnel to implement effectively the Co safety and environmental protection policy. **Document of Compliance**: Document issued to a Company complying with Code's requirements. **Safety Management Certificate**: Document issued to a ship signifying that Co and its shipboard management operate in accordance with the approved SMS. **Objective evidence**: quantitative or qualitative information, records or statements of fact pertaining to safety or to the existence and implementation of a safety management system element, which is based on observation, measurement or test and which can be verified. **Observation**: A statement of fact made during a safety management audit and substantiated by objective evidence.

---

[2] The provisions of the ISM Code were given early effect in the UK (on 20 January 1998) in relation to ro-ro passenger ferries by the MS (ISM Code) (Ro-Ro Passenger Ferries) Regulations 1997 (SI 1997/3022) (see D03b.1a).

		Non-conformity: An observed situation where objective evidence indicates the non-fulfilment of a specified requirement. **Major non-conformity**: An identifiable deviation that poses a serious threat to the safety of personnel or the ship or a serious risk to the environment that requires immediate corrective action and includes the lack of effective and systematic implementation of a requirement of this Code. **Anniversary date**: The day and month of each year corresponding to expiry date of relevant document or certificate. **Convention**: SOLAS 74, as amended.
1.2	Objectives	Declares **objectives of Code** as being to ensure safety at sea, prevention of human injury or loss of life, and avoidance of damage to the environment, in particular, to the marine environment, and to property (1.2.1). **Safety management objectives of Co** should, *inter alia*: 1. provide for safe practices in ship operation and a safe working environment; 2. establish safeguards against all identified risks; and 3. continuously improve safety management skills of personnel ashore and aboard ships, including preparing for emergencies related both to safety and environmental protection (1.2.2). **SMS** should ensure: • compliance with mandatory rules and regulations; and • that applicable codes, guidelines and standards recommended by IMO, Administrations, classification societies and maritime industry organisations are taken into account (1.2.3).
1.3	Application	Requirements of ISM Code *may be applied to all ships*.
1.4	Functional requirements for a safety management system	Every **Co** should **develop, implement and maintain an SMS** which includes following **functional requirements**: 1. a safety and environmental protection policy; 2. instructions and procedures to ensure safe operation of ships and protection of the environment in compliance with relevant international and flag State legislation; 3. defined levels of authority and lines of communication between, and amongst, shore and shipboard personnel; 4. procedures for reporting accidents and non-conformities with the provisions of this Code; 5. procedures to prepare for and respond to emergency situations; and 6. procedures for internal audits and management reviews.
2	Safety and environmental-protection policy	**Co** should **establish a safety and environmental protection policy** which describes how the objectives, given in paragraph 1.2, will be achieved (2.1). **Co** should ensure that the **policy is implemented and maintained at all levels** of the organisation, both ship-based and shore-based (2.2).
3	Company responsibilities and authority	If entity responsible for operation of the ship is not the owner, **owner** must report full name and details of such entity to FSA (3.1). **Co** should define and document responsibility, authority and interrelation of all personnel who manage, perform and verify work relating to and affecting safety and pollution prevention (3.2). **Co** is responsible for ensuring adequate resources and shore based support are provided to enable DPA to carry out their functions (3.3).
4	Designated person(s)	To ensure safe operation of each ship and provide a link between Co and crew, every Co, as appropriate, should designate a person or persons ashore (**DPA**) with direct access to highest level of management. **Responsibility and authority of DPA** should include monitoring safety and pollution prevention aspects of operation of each ship and ensuring adequate resources and shore based support are applied, as required.
5	Master's responsibility and authority	**Co** should clearly define and document the master's responsibility with regard to: 1. implementing the safety and environmental protection policy of the Co; 2. motivating the crew in the observation of that policy; 3. issuing appropriate orders and instructions in a clear and simple manner; 4. verifying that specified requirements are observed; and 5. reviewing the SMS and reporting its deficiencies to shore based management (5.1). **Co** should ensure that SMS operating on ship contains a clear statement emphasising the master's authority. **Co** should establish in SMS that the master has overriding authority and responsibility to make decisions with respect to safety and pollution prevention and to request Co's assistance as may be necessary (5.2).
6	Resources and personnel	**Co** should ensure master is: 1. properly qualified for command; 2. fully conversant with Co's SMS; and 3. given the necessary support for safe performance of master's duties (6.1). **Co** should: 1. ensure each ship is manned with qualified, certificated and medically fit seafarers in accordance with national and international requirements (6.2). 2. establish procedures to ensure new personnel and personnel transferred to new assignments related to safety and environmental protection are given proper familiarisation with their duties. Essential pre-sailing instructions should be identified, documented and given (6.3). 3. ensure all personnel involved in the Co's SMS have adequate understanding of relevant rules, regulations, codes and guidelines (6.4). 4. establish and maintain procedures for identifying any training required in support of SMS and ensure such training is provided for personnel concerned (6.5). 5. establish procedures by which the ship's personnel receive relevant information on the SMS in a working language or languages understood by them (6.6). 6. ensure that the ship's personnel are able to communicate effectively in the execution of their duties related to the SMS (6.7).

7	Development of plans for shipboard operations	**Co** should establish procedures for preparation of plans and instructions, including checklists as appropriate, for key shipboard operations concerning the safety of the ship and pollution prevention. Tasks involved should be defined and assigned to qualified personnel.
8	Emergency preparedness	**Co** should establish procedures to identify, describe and respond to potential emergency shipboard situations (8.1). **Co** should establish programmes for drills and exercises to prepare for emergency actions (8.2). **SMS** should provide for measures ensuring that the Company's organisation can respond at any time to hazards, accidents and emergency situations involving its ships (8.3).
9	Reports and analysis of non-conformities, accidents and hazardous occurrences	**SMS** should include procedures ensuring that non-conformities, accidents and hazardous situations are reported to Co, investigated and analysed with objective of improving safety and pollution prevention (9.1). **Co** should establish procedures for implementation of corrective action (9.2).
10	Maintenance of the ship and equipment	**Co** should establish procedures to ensure ship is maintained in conformity with provisions of relevant rules and regulations and any additional requirements established by Co (10.1). In meeting these requirements **Co** should ensure that: 1. inspections are held at appropriate intervals; 2. any non-conformity is reported with its possible cause, if known; 3. appropriate corrective action is taken; and 4. records of these activities are maintained (10.2). **Co** should establish procedures in SMS to identify equipment and technical systems sudden operational failure of which may result in hazardous situations. SMS should provide for specific measures aimed at promoting reliability of such equipment or systems. These measures should include regular testing of stand-by arrangements and equipment or technical systems not in continuous use (10.3). **Inspections and measures** in 10.2 and 10.3 should be integrated into ship's operational maintenance routine (10.4).
11	Documentation	**Co** should establish and maintain procedures to control all documents and data relevant to SMS (11.1). **Co** should ensure that: 1. valid documents are available at all relevant locations; 2. changes to documents are reviewed and approved by authorised personnel; and 3. obsolete documents are promptly removed (11.2). Documents used to describe and implement SMS may be referred to as the "Safety Management Manual". Documentation should be kept in a form that Co considers most effective. Each ship should carry on board all documentation relevant to that ship (11.3).
12	Company verification, review and evaluation	**Co** should carry out internal safety audits to verify whether safety and pollution prevention activities comply with SMS (12.1). **Co** should periodically evaluate the efficiency of SMS and, when needed, review SMS in accordance with Co's established procedures (12.2). **Audits and any corrective actions** should be carried out in accordance with documented procedures (12.3). **Personnel carrying out audits** should be independent of the areas being audited unless this is impracticable due to the size and the nature of the Company (12.4). Results of audits and reviews should be brought to attention of all personnel with responsibility in areas involved (12.5). Management personnel responsible for area involved should take timely corrective action on deficiencies found (12.6).
PART B	**CERTIFICATION AND VERIFICATION**	
13	Certification and periodical verification	**Ship** should be operated by a Co issued with a DOC or IDOC in accordance with 14.1 (13.1). **DOC** should be issued by FSA, an RO or, at the request of FSA, by another CG, to any Co complying with Code's requirements for a period specified by FSA but note exceeding 5 years. **DOC or IDOC** should be accepted as evidence that Co is capable of complying with the requirements of Code (13.2). **DOC** is valid only for ship types it lists. List should be based on ship types on which initial verification was based. Other ship types should only be added after verification of Co's capability to comply with requirements applicable to them. In this context, ship types are those referred to in SOLAS regulation IX/1 (13.3). **DOC's validity** should be subject to annual verification by FSA, an RO or, at the request of FSA, by another CG within 3 months before or after anniversary date (13.4). **DOC** should be withdrawn by FSA or, at its request, by CG which issued it, when annual verification required in 13.4 is not requested, or on evidence of major non-conformities (13.5). **If DOC is withdrawn**, all associated SMCs and/or ISMCs should also be withdrawn (13.5.1). **Copy DOC** should be placed on board so that master, if requested, can produce it for verification by the FSA or organisation recognised by FSA, or for purposes of port State control on operational procedures. Copy DOC is not required to be authenticated or certified (13.6). **SMC** should be issued to ship for not more than 5 years by FSA, an RO or, at the request of FSA, by another CG. **SMC** should be issued after verifying that Co and its shipboard management operate in accordance with the approved SMS. **SMC** should be accepted as evidence that ship is complying with the requirements of Code (13.7). **Validity of SMC** should be subject to at least one intermediate verification by FSA, an RO or, at the request of FSA, by another CG. If only one intermediate verification is to be carried out and the SMC's period of validity is 5 years, it should take place between second and third anniversary date (13.8). In addition to requirements of 13.5.1, **SMC should be withdrawn** by FSA or, at the request of FSA, by the CG that issued it, when intermediate verification required in 13.8 is not requested or on

		evidence of major non-conformity (13.9). Notwithstanding requirements of 13.2 and 13.7, **when renewal verification is completed within 3 months before expiry date** of existing DOC or SMC, new DOC or SMC should be valid from date of completion of renewal verification for not more than 5 years from date of expiry of existing DOC or SMC (13.10). **When renewal verification is completed more than 3 months** before expiry date of existing DOC or SMC, new DOC or SMC should be valid from date of completion of renewal verification for not more than 5 years from date of completion of renewal verification (13.11).
14	Interim certification	**IDOC** may be issued to facilitate initial implementation of Code when: 1. a Co is newly established; or 2. new ship types will be added to an existing DOC, - following verification that Co has an SMS meeting Code's objectives, **provided** Co demonstrates plans to implement a SMS meeting full requirements of Code within IDOC's period of validity. **IDOC** should be issued for not more than 12 months by FSA, an RO or, at the request of FSA, by another CG. **Copy IDOC** should be placed on board so that master, if requested, can produce it for verification by the FSA or organisation recognised by FSA, or for purposes of port State control on operational procedures. Copy DOC is not required to be authenticated or certified (14.1). **ISMC** may be issued: 1. to new ships on delivery; 2. when a Company takes on responsibility for the operation of a ship which is new to the Company; or 3. when a ship changes flag . **ISMC** should be issued for not more than 6 months by FSA, an RO or, at the request of FSA, by another CG (14.2). **ISMC's validity may be extended** in special cases for not more than 6 months from expiry date by FSA or, at request of FSA, another CG (14.3). **ISMC** may be issued after verification that: 1. DOC or IDOC is relevant to the ship; 2. SMS provided by Co for the ship includes key elements of ISM Code and has been assessed during the audit for issuance of DOC or demonstrated for issuance of IDOC; 3. Co has planned a ship audit within 3 months; 4. master and officers are familiar with SMS and planned arrangements for its implementation; 5. essential pre-sailing instructions are provided; and 6. relevant information on SMS has been given in working language(s) understood by ship's personnel (14.4).
15	Verification	**All verifications** should be carried out in accordance with procedures acceptable to FSA, taking into account the IMO Guidelines adopted by resolution A.788(19).
16	Forms of certificates	**DOC, SMC, IDOC and ISMC** should be drawn up in a form corresponding to models in Code's appendix. If language used neither English nor French, text should include translation one or other (16.1). In addition to requirements of 13.3, ship types listed on DOC and IDOC may be endorsed to reflect any limitations in operations of ships described in the SMS (16.2).

C04c SAFETY MANAGEMENT CODE FOR DOMESTIC PASSENGER SHIPS (DSM CODE)

* The **Safety Management Code for Domestic Passenger Ships (DSM Code)**-
  - **must be complied with**, under regulation 5 of the MS (Domestic Passenger Ships) (Safety Management Code) Regulations 2001 (SI 2001/3209), by any company operating a passenger ship of **Classes III to VI(A)**, as defined in D04c.2, and to any ship of those classes **owned** by it or for which it has **operational responsibility**.
  - **is mandatory** for the above vessels under regulation 3(1) of the above Regulations.
  - **does not apply** (under regulation 3(2)) to ships to which Council Regulation (EC) No. 3051/95 on the safety management of roll-on/roll-off passenger ferries (ro-ro ferries) applies, i.e. ships subject to the MS (ISM Code) (Ro-Ro Passenger Ferries) Regulations 1997.
* **MSN 1754** sets out the instructions regarding safety management of domestic passenger ships of Classes III to VI(A). It describes the objectives of developing a Safety Management System and how to implement it effectively. The **DSM Code**, although not clearly identified as such, is set out in the paragraphs of MSN 1754, which include the following headings: Introduction (paragraphs 1 to 5); Objectives (paragraphs 6 to 9a); Health and safety protection policy (paragraph 10); Responsibilities (paragraphs 11 and 12); Personnel and training (paragraphs 13 and 14); On-board procedures (paragraph 15); Preparation for emergencies (paragraph 16); Reporting of accidents (paragraphs 17 and 18); Maintenance of the ship and equipment (paragraph 19); Certification (paragraphs 20 to 22); Fees (paragraphs 23 and 24); Exemptions (paragraph 25).
* **Paragraph 8** of MSN 1754 provides that safety management must be applied to every passenger ship in domestic trade, and that the **objectives of safety management** are to ensure a simple and cost effective means of:
  * ensuring safety on board;
  * preventing human injury and loss of life;
  * complying with applicable regulations and rules.

* **Paragraph 9** requires each operator to **develop and implement safe practices** which include:
  * a health and safety protection policy;
  * procedures to ensure safe operation of ships in compliance with relevant rules;
  * lines of communication between personnel, ashore and afloat;
  * procedures for reporting accidents; and
  * procedures for responding to emergency situations.
* **Paragraph 9a** provides that the **health and safety protection policy** is required to include environmental protection issues only in so far as they relate to the safety of the ship and the health and safety of persons onboard, and to the safety of other ships and the health and safety of persons on those other ships. Paragraphs 6.2 and 6.3 of MGN 158 refer to legal requirements as respect to the management of garbage and the prevention of oil pollution, and makes recommendations as to the integration of the management of garbage and oil with the health and safety policy.
* **Paragraph 10** provides that the **operator** must ensure that the **policy is implemented**, and that **responsibilities of all personnel are understood**. There must be a **designated link** between the ship and the shore base, to ensure that in the event of an emergency there is immediate communication with the emergency services.
* **Paragraph 11** provides that the **master's responsibility must be laid down** so that there is no misunderstanding, and states that **he has the authority to make decisions regarding the safety of the ship and persons on board**. Assistance must be available ashore from the Company **at all times**.
* The **Company** must, under paragraph 12, nominate an employee to be the **Designated Person**. The Designated Person must have **access to the highest level of management** of that company, and **may** fulfil the requirements of paragraph 7 of MGN 158[3].
* **Paragraph 13** provides that the **operator** must ensure that all persons employed in the operation of the ships have received **appropriate training** for the duties they are required to fulfil and that they have an **understanding** of the relevant regulations and rules. Masters and crew must hold the **appropriate qualifications**.
* **Paragraph 14** provides that **proper instruction in their duties** must be received by personnel before the first occasion of sailing on the ship as a designated crew member, and **as necessary thereafter**. This instruction must be **recorded**.
* **Paragraph 15** provides that there must be **procedures** in place for **key shipboard operations** with regard to **safety**, and that the tasks involved in these procedures must be assigned to **designated personnel**.
* **Paragraph 16** provides that **potential emergency situations** must be **identified**, and **exercises** must be carried out to respond to these emergencies. The exercises must be recorded and where appropriate, must involve the personnel ashore.
* **Paragraph 17** provides that all accidents and near-accidents must be **recorded and reported to the operator**, who must implement corrective action, with the aim of improving safety.
* **Paragraph 18** provides that, in addition, the master must inform the Marine Accident Investigation Branch (**MAIB**) of all **accidents** in accordance with the MS (Accident Reporting and Investigation) Regulations 1999 (see E08k). The **MCA must also be informed** if the accident is such that the validity of the ship's Passenger Certificate (PC) or Domestic Ship Safety Management Certificate (DSSMC) might be affected.
* **Paragraph 19** provides that the **operator must inspect each ship at frequent intervals** to ensure that it is properly maintained and operated in accordance with "the relevant rules". Deficiencies must be corrected, and **records** of inspections kept.
* **Paragraph 20** provides that the **initial audit**, to assess compliance with the Code, must be carried out **at the same time as each ship is surveyed for issue of the Passenger Certificate (PC)**. On satisfactory completion of this audit, a **Domestic Ship Safety Management Certificate (DSSMC)** for each ship, will be issued. The period of validity of this certificate is subject to a **mid-term audit**.
* **Paragraph 21** provides that a **mid- term audit**, when the ship is in service, will be carried out between 3 and 6 months after the issue of the PC, in order to assess whether the safety management system is functioning effectively. If successful, the **DSSMC will be endorsed** to this effect and its period of validity will become the **same as that of the PC**.
* **Paragraph 22** provides that where the **in-service/mid-term audit** is unsuccessful, "normal enforcement procedures" will be followed to ensure that **deficiencies are rectified**.
* **Paragraph 25** provides that **exemptions** from the Code's arrangements will be considered on a **case by case** basis. In accordance with Recommendation 27.40 of Lord Justice Clarke's Inquiry, exemptions from the provisions of the Code will be granted **only** on condition that an **equivalent level of safety** is achieved.
* **MGN 158** provides guidance to owners and operators of "domestic passenger ships" on how to comply with the requirements of the DSM Code as set out in MSN 1754.

---

[3] This states: "The MS and FV (Health and Safety at Work) Regulations specifically require the appointment of one or more competent persons to take responsibility for health and safety. That person/persons should be identified. It is the responsibility of the owner/operator to ensure that the policy is complied with, and that the responsibilities are understood".

C05 The shipowner and the ITF

C05a NATURE AND AIMS OF ITF

* **The International Transport Workers Federation (ITF)** is a London-based democratic federation of worldwide transport workers' trade unions, and includes NUMAST and RMT amongst its members.
* Since 1949 the ITF has been campaigning against **flag-of convenience** (FOC) shipping, the campaign's ultimate objective being the complete elimination of the FOC system from the world's shipping market. David Cockroft, the ITF General Secretary, has promised that no area of the world will be "ITF-safe" in future. The ITF also states that its campaign is designed to secure ITF acceptable agreements for seafarers serving on FOC ships.
* For the purposes of the FOC campaign the ITF Fair Practices Committee lists flags regarded as FOCs (see B01b.2).
* FOC shipowners may sign the **ITF Special Agreement**. This requires owners to employ seafarers on the terms and conditions of the ITF Standard Collective Agreement, and to enter into individual contracts of employment which incorporate the terms of that Agreement. Owners who have signed the ITF Special Agreement will be issued with a **"Blue Certificate"**.
* As well as a monthly magazine, ITF News, and an annual *Seafarers' Bulletin*, ITF produces a pocket book entitled *Message to Seafarers*, regarded as essential for FOC seafarers.
* **Address**: International Transport Workers Federation, 49/60 Borough Road, London SE1 1DS. Tel: 0171-403-2733. Fax: 0171-357-7871. e-mail: mail@itf.org
* **Website**: www.itf.org.uk

C05b ITF ACTION AGAINST FOC SHIPS

* The ITF employs **inspectors** to inspect FOC ships in ports. Typically, when an ITF inspector visits an FOC ship, he will ask to see crew wage accounts, interview crew members, and check living, working and leave arrangements. If these are not in accord with ITF or ILO minimum standards, **boycott action** by affiliated transport union labour in the port (dockers, lock keepers, tugmen, etc.) may be called and the ship may be prevented from proceeding with her operations. Risk of ITF action is highest in **ITF "strongholds"** such as Scandinavia, Australia and New Zealand, and some charter parties prohibit the charterer from ordering the ship to these countries.
* Production of an **ITF "Blue Certificate"** (see C05a) to an ITF inspector should guarantee freedom from anti-FOC action by ITF-affiliated labour unions in ports.
* For notes on **ITF involvement in crew industrial action**, see I06d.2.

C06 Shipowners' and ship managers' organisations

C06a CHAMBER OF SHIPPING

- is the **trade association and employers' association** for British shipowners and shipmanagers.
- **promotes** and protects its members' interests nationally and internationally.
- **represents** British Shipping to Government, Parliament, international organisations, unions and the general public.
- **covers** all issues which have a bearing on British Shipping, from fiscal policy and freedom to trade, to recruitment and training, maritime safety, the environment, navaids and pilotage.
- **represents** 6 different commercial sectors: deep-sea bulk, short-sea bulk, deep-sea liner, ferry, cruise and offshore support.
- has 137 members and associate members, which own or manage 680 merchant ships of 17m dwt, including some managed for foreign owners.
* **Address**: Carthusian Court, 12 Carthusian Street, London EC1M 6EB. Tel. 0171 417 8400. Fax 0171 626 8135. E-mail: postmaster@british-shipping.org
    • **Website**: www.british-shipping.org

C06b INTERNATIONAL CHAMBER OF SHIPPING (ICS)

- is an **international association of national trade associations representing shipowners and operators**.
- has a **membership** comprising **shipowners' associations** in about 30 countries, together representing more than half the world's merchant tonnage.
- **promotes** the interests of shipowners and operators in all matters of shipping policy and ship operations (excluding crew matters, which are the province of its sister organisation, the International Shipping Federation – see C06c.).
- **encourages** high standards of operation and the provision of high quality and efficient shipping services.
- **strives** for a regulatory environment which supports safe shipping operations, protection of the environment and adherence to internationally adopted standards and procedures.
- **promotes** properly considered international regulation of shipping, but opposes unilateral and regional action by governments.
- **presses for** recognition of the commercial realities of shipping and the need for quality to be rewarded by a proper commercial return.
- **promotes** industry guidance on best operating practices (e.g. through publications such as Bridge Procedures Guide and Guide to Helicopter/Ship Operations).
* **Address**: International Chamber of Shipping, Carthusian Court, 12 Carthusian Street, London EC1M 6EZ. Tel +44 20 7417 8844. Fax +44 20 7417 8877. E-mail ics@marisec.org
  • **Website**: www.marisec.org

C06c INTERNATIONAL SHIPPING FEDERATION (ISF)

- is the **international employers' organisation** for shipowners.
- is concerned with **labour affairs and manning and training issues** at international level.
- has a membership comprising **national shipowners' associations** from 30 countries together representing more than half the world's merchant tonnage.
* **Address**: International Shipping Federation, Carthusian Court, 12 Carthusian Street, London EC1M 6EZ. Tel +44 20 7417 8844. Fax +44 20 7417 8877. E-mail isf@marisec.org
* **Website**: www.marisec.org

C06d INTERNATIONAL SHIP MANAGERS' ASSOCIATION (ISMA)

- is an association of ship and crew managers aspiring to a higher quality standard than that demanded by international regulation.
- was formed in 1991 to provide a forum for ship managers as a homogeneous group, to improve standards, and achieve a safer, more environmentally conscious, more reliable and more controllable ship management industry.
- represents ship managers from 16 countries controlling a fleet of more than 2,300 ships. Membership was extended in 1994 to crew managers.
- accepts members who agree to be bound by the **ISMA Code of Shipmanagement Standards** (the "**ISMA Code**") which is claimed to be the most comprehensive quality code for shipping in the world. The cornerstone of ISMA membership is a commitment to establish and maintain a quality assured (QA) management system which meets the requirements of the ISMA Code, and to submit these QA systems to audit by an independent body. The ISMA Code is claimed to exceed the requirements of the ISM Code and incorporates the requirements of ISO 9002 standards.
* It is estimated that **ISMA's membership** represents in excess of 60% of the total world third party managed fleet.
* **Address**: ISMA, Suite 202, Eastlands Court, St Peters Road, Rugby CB21 3QP, UK. E-mail: alan.ward@isma-london.org
* **Website**: www.isma-london.org

C06e INTERNATIONAL ASSOCIATION OF DRY CARGO SHIPOWNERS (INTERCARGO)

- was established in 1980 to **promote and protect the interests of dry bulk shipowners** throughout the world.
- has over 185 members from 34 countries, who own around 1250 large dry bulk carriers totalling about 90m dwt.

- has consultative status with UNCTAD, and with IMO (where it has permanent representation).
- works closely with private sector bodies such as ICS, ISF, Intertanko and BIMCO.
- is the only international association devoted solely to the interests of the dry bulk sector and as such provides both a forum and a focus for that shipping sector.
- has as its current priority a reduction in the number of dry bulk carrier losses and casualties.
- is active in the promotion of free trade and fair competition; international as against unilateral regulation where regulation is necessary; scrapping and market balance; and high standards in business ethics.
- has taken action in support of its members' interests on issues including opposition to the proliferation of surveys by government agencies and others, and legislative proposals in the USA.
* **Address**: International Association of Dry Cargo Shipowners, Second Floor, 4 London Wall Buildings, Blomfield Street, London EC2M 5NT. Tel. +44 (0)20 7638 3989. Fax: +44 (0)20 7638 3943. E-mail: intercargo@compuserve.com
* **Website**: www.intercargo.org

C06f INTERNATIONAL ASSOCIATION OF INDEPENDENT TANKER OWNERS (INTERTANKO)

- **promotes** the interests of owners and managing operators of more than 80% of **independent tanker tonnage** worldwide, i.e. tanker owners other than oil companies and governments.
- has some 300 members and 120 associate members, drawn from 33 nations and between them controlling some 1,900 tankers.
- represents its members at the highest level in governments, IMO and other for a where discussions on policy, technical, safety or environmental matters take place.
- gathers intelligence and gives advice on technical, legal and commercial matters to members.
- publishes **charter parties** and other documents.
- stands "for safe transport, cleaner seas and free competition".
* **Address**: International Association of Independent Tanker Owners, Bogstadveien 27B, P.O. Box 5804 Majorstua, N-0308 Oslo, Norway. Tel: +47 22 12 26 40. Fax: +47 22 12 26 41. E-mail: postmaster@intertanko.com
* **UK address**: International Association of Independent Tanker Owners, The Baltic Exchange, 38 St. Mary Axe, London EC3A 8BH, UK. Tel: +44 (0)207 623 4311. Fax: +44 (0)207 626 7078. E-mail: london@intertanko.com
  * **Website**: www.intertanko.com

C06g BALTIC AND INTERNATIONAL MARITIME CONFERENCE (BIMCO)

- has an international membership of **shipowners, shipbrokers, agents and P&I clubs**.
- acts as a spokesman for the shipping industry.
- helps members **avoid costly business mistakes**.
- **interprets** contract terms; gives opinions on disputes; provides port cost estimates; maintains shipping databases.
- **publishes** approved commercial documents including charter parties (see examples in F04c.2 and F04c.3) and bills of lading, sometimes in conjunction with other bodies, e.g. FONASBA and the UK Chamber of Shipping.
- **publishes BIMCO Bulletin** (an information-packed journal which would be of interest to many shipmasters).
- runs **shipping business courses** and seminars.
- operates **BIMCOM**, an international computer network linking main shipping centres.
* **Address**: BIMCO, 161 Bagsvaerdvej, 2880 Bagsvaerd, Denmark. Tel. +45 44 36 68 00. Fax: +45 44 36 68 68. E-mail: mailbox@bimco.dk
* **Website**: www.bimco.dk

C06h INTERNATIONAL TANKER OWNERS POLLUTION FEDERATION (ITOPF)

- is a non-profit making organisation, funded by the vast majority of the world's shipowners.
- is involved in all aspects of **preparing for and responding to oil spills from tankers**.
- has a staff of 23, of whom 11 are available to respond to spills.

- was established after the *Torrey Canyon* incident to administer the voluntary compensation agreement, TOVALOP, which assured the adequate and timely payment of compensation to those affected by oil spills. TOVALOP came to an end on 20th February 1997. As a result the membership and funding arrangements of ITOPF have now changed.
- now devotes considerable effort to a wide range of **technical services**, of which the most important is responding to oil spills. ITOPF small response team of **technical advisers** have attended on-site at over 400 spills in more than 70 countries and is at constant readiness to assist at marine oil spills anywhere in the world. This service is normally undertaken **on behalf of tanker-owner members and their oil pollution insurers** (normally one of the P&I Clubs) or at the request of **governments or international agencies** such as the International Oil Pollution Compensation Fund.
- also provides **damage assessment services, contingency planning, training and information**.
- maintains an extensive **library** and a number of **databases**, and produces **technical publications and videos**.
* **Address**: ITOPF Ltd, Staple Hall, Stonehouse Court, 87-90 Houndsditch, London EC3A 7AX. Tel: +44 (0)20 7621 1255. Emergency Tel: +44 (0)7626 914112 (24hr). Fax: +44 (0)20 7621 1783. Email: central@itopf.com
* **Website**: www.itopf.com

C06i INTERNATIONAL SUPPORT VESSEL OWNERS ASSOCIATION (ISOA)

- was formed in 1985 to **promote and protect the interests of offshore support vessel operators** in respect of any issue affecting the industry.
- acts as a **representative international entity** co-ordinating and representing the opinions of its members.
- is principally focused on **bringing offshore supply vessel (OSV) operators together** to discuss their mutual problems.
- has the following objects:
  • to communicate to its members on a regular basis matters of importance affecting the OSV industry;
  • to monitor the treatment of the OSV industry by international organisations, governments, authorities or other bodies and assist members in investigating prejudicial treatments and where appropriate take action against such prejudicial treatment;
  • to provide a forum for the discussion of the prevailing standards and market conditions in the offshore industry;
  • to communicate, as appropriate, the views of members to international organisations, governments, the press and other relevant bodies.
* **Address**: International Support Vessel Owners Association, Carthusian Court, 12 Carthusian Street, London EC1M 6EZ. Tel + 44 20 7417 8844. Fax + 44 20 7417 8877. E-mail isoa@marisec.org
* **Website**: www.marisec.org/isoa

Section D

THE SHIP

Section D Contents

D01 Ship registration and identity

D01a INTERNATIONAL LAW ON SHIP REGISTRATION

* Relevant articles of **UNCLOS** (see A02a) are Articles 91, 92 and 94.
* **UNCLOS Article 91 (Nationality of ships)** provides that:
    * Every State must fix the conditions for:
        * the grant of its nationality to ships;
        * the registration of ships in its territory; and
        * the right to fly its flag.
    * Ships have the nationality of the State whose flag they are entitled to fly.
    * There must exist a genuine link between the State and the ship.
    * Every State must issue to ships to which it has granted the right to fly its flag **documents to that effect**.
* **UNCLOS Article 92 (Status of ships)** provides that:
    * Ships must sail under the flag of one State only and, save in exceptional cases expressly provided for in international treaties or in UNCLOS, will be subject to that State's exclusive jurisdiction on the high seas.
    * A ship may not change its flag during a voyage or while in a port of call, save in the case of a real transfer of ownership or change of registry.
    * A ship which sails under the flags of two or more States, using them according to convenience, may not claim any of the nationalities in question with respect to any other State, and may be assimilated to a ship without nationality.
* **UNCLOS Article 94 (Duties of the flag State)** provides (*inter alia*) that:
    * Every State must effectively exercise its jurisdiction and control in administrative, technical and social matters over ships flying its flag.
    * In particular every State must:
    * maintain a **register of ships** containing the names and particulars of ships flying its flag, except those which are excluded from generally accepted international regulations on account of their small size; and
    * assume **jurisdiction under its internal law** over each ship flying its flag and its master, officers and crew in respect of administrative, technical and social matters concerning the ship.
    * Every State must take such measures for ships flying its flag as are necessary to **ensure safety at sea** with regard, *inter alia*, to:
        * the construction, equipment and seaworthiness of ships;
        * the manning of ships, labour conditions and the training of crews, taking into account the applicable international instruments;
        * the use of signals, the maintenance of communications and the prevention of collisions.
    * Such measures must include those necessary to ensure:
        * that each ship, **before registration and thereafter at appropriate intervals, is surveyed** by a qualified surveyor of ships, and
        * **has on board** such charts, nautical publications and navigational equipment and instruments as are appropriate for the safe navigation of the ship.
* The **United Nations Convention on Conditions for Registration of Ships, 1986**, is not yet in force. The convention text can be viewed at: www.admiraltylawguide.com/conven/registration1986.html

D01b PURPOSES AND BENEFITS OF REGISTRATION

* **Registration** of a ship -
    * establishes the ship's **nationality**, **measurements** and **tonnage** for identification purposes;
    * provides **documentary evidence of ownership** (in the register, not on the Certificate of Registry);
    * allows the ship to **operate commercially** (since clearance from ports normally requires production of a Certificate of Registry to prove nationality);
    * grants **recognition as a vessel of the flag State** and enjoyment of the normal **privileges** accorded to vessels of that State, e.g. consular assistance in foreign ports and the protection of the flag State's armed forces;
* A major reason for **Part I** and **Part II registration** (i.e. as a merchant ship, large pleasure vessel or fishing vessel) is to be able to use the vessel as **security for a marine mortgage**. Most finance companies prefer the security of having their mortgage on a ship registered so that their claim against the ship is clear.
* In relation to **flag States**, registration of ships -

- **restricts and controls ownership** of vessels under a flag;
- **facilitates ship purchase, sale and mortgaging** (since proof of title is shown to a buyer or lender by the details on the register, and registration is usually a pre-requisite for mortgaging a ship);
- **brings fee income** (often in US dollars) to many FOC States;
- may have some **prestige value** for some small States with large ship registers;
- may have **strategic importance** (e.g. to an island State which depends on its own ships for carrying imports and exports or wartime supplies).

D01b.1 Additional benefits of "flag of convenience" (FOC) registration

* An **FOC register** (see B01b.2) may offer any or all of the following:
    - freedom to employ **foreign nationals** as master, officers and/or crew;
    - low **taxes** on company earnings;
    - low **registry fees**;
    - low statutory **survey fees**;
    - **limitation of** owner's **liability**;
    - relaxed or non-existent **foreign exchange controls** on owners' earnings;
    - non-restrictive **ownership qualifications** allowing a foreign company or foreign national to register there;
    - freedom to raise a loan by **mortgaging** the ship; and/or
    - benefits from bilateral or multilateral **agreements on trade**, cargo sharing, port entry or taxation.

D01c BRITISH REGISTRY

D01c.1 Registry legislation

* **Legislation** on the **British Register** and **registration of British ships** is contained in:
    - Part II of the **Merchant Shipping Act 1995** (i.e. sections 8 to 23);
    - the **MS (Registration of Ships) Regulations 1993** (SI 1993/3138) as amended by the MS (Registration of Ships) (Amendment) Regulations 1994 (SI 1994/541), the MS (Registration of Ships) (Amendment) Regulations 1998 (SI 1998/2976) and the MS (Registration of Ships, and Tonnage) (Amendment) Regulations 1999 (SI 1999/3206); and
    - in respect of "small ships", the **MS (Small Ships Register) Regulations 1983** (SI 1983/1470).
* The 1993 Regulations were made under the Merchant Shipping (Registration, etc) Act 1993, which is consolidated into Merchant Shipping Act 1995.
* The **MS (Registration of Ships, and Tonnage) (Amendment) Regulations 1999** (SI 1999/3206) make amendments to the 1993 Registration Regulations which mainly concern fishing vessels.

D01c.2 The British Register

- is maintained by the **Registry of Shipping and Seamen** (RSS) (see B05c).
- is in four parts:
    - **Part I** for merchant ships and pleasure vessels;
    - **Part II** for fishing vessels;
    - **Part III** for small ships (under 24m in length); this part is known as the "**Small Ships Register**";
    - **Part IV** for ships which are bareboat chartered.
- is, except for Part III, a **title register** and a **permanent public record** showing:
    - a **description** of every registered ship;
    - all **registered owners** of a ship;
    - all **registered mortgages** against a ship.

- **incorporates** the registers of:
  - the **Crown Dependencies**, i.e. Isle of Man, Guernsey and Jersey; and
  - the **British Overseas Territories**[1] (formerly called British Dependent Territories), i.e. the registers of Anguilla, Bermuda, British Virgin Islands, Cayman Islands, Falkland Islands, Montserrat, St Helena[2], and Turks and Caicos Islands.
- is one of the **Red Ensign Group** of registers, which is a group consisting of the ship registers of the UK, Anguilla, Bermuda, British Virgin Islands, Cayman Islands, Falkland Islands, Gibraltar, Guernsey, St Helena, Isle of Man, Jersey, Montserrat and Turks and Caicos Islands. Although administered individually under the local legislation of their own respective territories, each register is subject to overall control of the UK Department for Transport. The Group meets annually in one of the member countries to exchange views on policies and technical issues relating to regulation, marine safety, pollution prevention and the welfare of seafarers for ships on their registers world-wide and for visiting ships in their waters.
* The **MS (Categorisation of Registries of Relevant British Possessions) Order 2003** (SI 2003/1248), applies to the registration in "relevant British possessions" of ships other than small ships or fishing vessels and establishes two **categories of registry**: Category 1 and Category 2.
* A **Category 1 registry** is a registry that is unrestricted as to the tonnage, type and length of individual ships on its register. The Schedule to the 2003 Order lists Bermuda, Cayman Islands, Gibraltar and the Isle of Man as Category 1 registries.
* A **Category 2 registry** is a registry that is limited as to the tonnage and type of individual ships on its register. Passenger ships, pleasure vessels of more than 150 gross tonnage, or ships which are not passenger ships or pleasure vessels, but are of more than 150 gross tonnage may not be registered on a Category 2 register, but an exception is made for domestic-trading passenger ships, pleasure vessels of less than 400 gross tonnage, and ships of special local importance. The Schedule to the 2003 Order lists Anguilla, British Virgin Islands, Falkland Islands, Guernsey, Jersey, Montserrat, St Helena, and Turks and Caicos Islands as Category 2 registries.
* The **Small Ships Register** (Part III of the Register) is maintained under regulation 3(1) of the **MS (Small Ships Register) Regulations 1983** (SI 1983/1470) for ships of less than 24 metres in overall length and gives cheap, "simple" registration. It does not register title, and mortgages cannot be registered. Ships owned by a company, ships of 24 metres or more in length, fishing vessels and submersible vessels may not be registered on the Small Ships Register. A **Part III certificate**, as issued to a "small ship", is a Certificate of British Registry and should be accepted world-wide.
* A **pleasure vessel** may be registered in the UK with **"full" registration** on Part I, or with **simplified registration** (if less than 24m in length) on Part III. All such vessels may fly the Red Ensign[3].

D01c.3 United Kingdom ships

- are ships registered in (and thus having a port of choice in) the **United Kingdom of Great Britain and Northern Ireland** (i.e. England, Scotland, Wales or Northern Ireland, but not in the Isle of Man and Channel Islands).
- are registered on either **Part I, II, III or IV of the Register** maintained by the RSS at Cardiff.
- are subject, wherever they may be, to **UK merchant shipping legislation**.

D01c.3a Definition of "ship"

* Section 313(1) of the Merchant Shipping Act 1995 provides that, in the Act, unless the context requires otherwise, "**ship**" includes **every description of vessel used in navigation**.

D01c.4 British ships

- include all **United Kingdom ships** (as described in D01c.3).
- include all ships registered in the **Crown Dependencies** (as listed in D01c.2).
- include all ships registered in the **British Overseas Territories** (formerly known as Dependent Territories) (as listed in D01c.2).
- are entitled to fly a **Red Ensign** or the ensign of the Overseas Territory in which they are registered (which in most territories is a Red Ensign defaced with the territory's badge).

---

[1] British Overseas Territories also include British Antarctic Territory, British Indian Ocean Territory, Pitcairn Island, South Georgia and South Sandwich Islands, none of which has a ship register.
[2] Ascension Island and Tristan da Cunha are sub-dependencies of St Helena.
[3] For a definition of "pleasure vessel", see D03l.8.

- **are subject, wherever they may be**, to the merchant shipping legislation of **their own flag State**. For example, Isle of Man legislation applies to an Isle of Man registered ship, Bermuda legislation applies to a Bermuda registered ship, etc.
- **are subject, when in UK ports and waters**, to certain provisions of UK merchant shipping legislation.

D01c.5 Government or Crown ships

- are **UK Government-owned or -controlled ships**, nominally owned by Her Majesty the Queen, e.g. RFA naval auxiliary vessels, SFPA fishery protection vessels, CEFAS fisheries research vessels and RMAS vessels.
- by virtue of **section 308 of the Merchant Shipping Act 1995** are not subject to the Merchant Shipping Acts, including registration legislation, although the Government may by Order in Council make regulations with respect to compliance with certain legislation, e.g. registration legislation, either generally or by any class of Government ship. (Some Government ships are registered, while others are not.)
* The **MS (Ministry of Defence Ships) Order 1991** (SI 1989/1991) makes provision for the **registration** under the Merchant Shipping Acts 1894-1988 of ships belonging to the Secretary of State for Defence and in the service of the Ministry of Defence, and for certain modifications and exceptions in the application of those Acts to such ships. By virtue of section 47 of the Merchant Shipping Act 1988, the Order and the provisions of the Merchant Shipping Acts applied by it (both as modified by that section) apply also to UK-registered ships in the service of the Ministry of Defence by reason of a charter by demise (i.e. a bareboat charter) to the Crown. The Order does not apply to ships forming part of the Royal Navy.
* Similar **Orders making provision for the registration as British ships** of Government ships managed commercially for the MoD and sailing yachts belonging to the Secretary of State for Defence and in the service of the MoD are, respectively, the **MS (Ministry of Defence Commercially Managed Ships) Order 1992** (SI 1992/1293) and the **MS (Ministry of Defence Yachts) Order 1992** (SI 1992/1294).

D01c.6 Entitlement to register

* The former **requirement** of Merchant Shipping Act 1894 for a British ship to be registered is replaced in section 9 of the Merchant Shipping Act 1995 by an **entitlement to register as a British ship**, provided it is owned, to the prescribed extent, by persons qualified to own British ships, and provided certain other requirements of the relevant regulations are met.

D01c.7 Ownership of British ships

* For the purposes of registration, **property in every British ship**, except for "small ships", is divided into **64 shares**. An applicant may be registered as the owner of all, one or some of the shares. Each share may be owned by up to 5 persons or companies as joint owners. Joint owners are considered as one party although all of the names of the joint owners are recorded on the register as owners of that share or shares. (All joint owners or shareholders in a ship must act together if they wish to sell or mortgage the vessel or shares, and all their signatures will be needed by RSS to carry out any action.) Any person qualified to be an owner of a British ship may be registered as the owner of one or more shares. **At least 33 of the 64 shares** must be owned by **persons qualified** to own a British ship. The **balance** of 31 or fewer shares may be owned by **non-qualified persons** such as foreign nationals or companies.
* **Persons qualified to own a British ship on Part I of the Register** include:
  • British citizens or non-UK nationals exercising their right of freedom of movement of workers or right established under Article 48 or 52 of the EEC Treaty or Article 28 or 31 of the EEA Agreement;
  • British Dependent Territories citizens;
  • British Overseas citizens;
  • persons who under the British Nationality Order 1981 are British subjects;
  • persons who under the Hong Kong (British Nationality) Order 1986 are British Nationals (Overseas);
  • companies incorporated in an EEA State (i.e. a country which is a Party to the Agreement on the European Economic Area, known as the EEA Agreement);
  • companies incorporated in any British overseas possession and having their principal place of business in the UK or in any such possession.
  • European Economic Interest Groupings being groupings formed in pursuance of Article I of Council Regulation (EEC) No. 2137/85 and registered in the UK.

* Local authorities which, under section 308 of the Merchant Shipping Act 1995, may register ships as Government ships.
* "Non-UK nationals exercising their right of freedom of movement of workers or right of establishment" means persons who are either:
  * nationals of an EC member State (other than the UK) who are exercising in the UK their rights under Article 48 or Article 52 of the EEC Treaty, as the case may be; or
  * nationals of a State (other than an EC member State) which is a party to the EEA Agreement, who are exercising in the UK their rights under Article 28 or Article 31 of the EEA Agreement, as the case may be.
* Individuals, companies, local authorities and groups who are eligible to register a ship are called "**qualified persons**".

D01c.7a Representative person

* When none of the qualified owners are resident in the UK, a **representative person** must be appointed.
* A representative person may be either:
  * an individual resident in the UK; or
  * a company incorporated in one of the EEA countries with a place of business in the UK.

D01c.7b Managing owner

* If the ship is owned by more than one qualified person (and no representative person has been appointed) one of the qualified owners who lives in the UK must be appointed as **the managing owner**. All RSS correspondence will be sent to that person unless another person, such as an agent, is nominated by the owner to receive correspondence.

D01c.8 Ship's name

* An applicant for registration will be asked to **choose a name** for the ship. **Several names** should be entered on the application form, in order of preference.
* Every ship on Part I and all merchant vessels on Part IV of the Register must have a name that is different from that of any other ship on that part of the Register.
* The RSS may refuse a name which may cause **confusion in an emergency** or one which could be regarded as **offensive**.
* After registry, application for a **change of name** of a ship should be made on the appropriate form, with the appropriate fee, to RSS. It is an **offence** to alter the name marked on a ship until receipt of a Carving and Marking Note showing the approved changes.

D01c.9 Port of choice

* An applicant for registration will be asked to choose the **port of choice**, i.e. the port with which the ship is to be associated. (The actual "**port of registry**" is Cardiff, being the RSS's location and the place where the register on which the ship is entered is kept.) A list of about 80 designated ports of choice in the UK (which are the old UK "ports of registry") is included in Annex 2 of the *Registering British Ships* booklet.
* If, after registry, the port of choice is to be changed, an application for a **change of port of choice** should be made to the RSS on the appropriate form, with the appropriate fee. It is an **offence** to alter the port marked on a ship's stern until receipt of a Carving and Marking Note showing the approved changes.

D01d REGISTRATION PROCEDURE IN THE UK

D01d.1 Application

* Registration was, until the early 1990s, carried out by Registrars of British Ships (who were officers of HM Customs and Excise), at "**ports of registry**" around the UK coast. Registry is now carried out (mainly by post) by the **Registry of Shipping and Seamen** (**RSS**), whose office at **Cardiff** is open to the public on weekdays for counter service.
* A booklet entitled *Registering British Ships in the United Kingdom* is available free of charge from RSS.

* In the case of a ship being "flagged in" to the UK Register, once the owner/manager decides to proceed with UK registration, a **Customer Service Manager** (CSM) will be appointed by RSS. The CSM is a fully qualified surveyor who will be the owner/manager's single point of contact with the RSS and will oversee the smooth transfer to the UK Register.
* **Applications for registry** should be made to RSS well before the required sailing date. Registration will normally take no more than 10 working days from receipt of documents by RSS. Applications must be accompanied by the proper **fee** before being any registration work is completed.
* Information required by RSS to formally register a ship comprises:
    * Application to Register a British Ship;
    * Declaration of Eligibility;
    * Certificate of Survey from classification society;
    * Tonnage Certificate;
    * Certificate of Incorporation (for a company);
    * Evidence of ownership (proof of title) comprising last Bill of Sale;
    * Deletion Certificate from foreign registry (if applicable).
* An **application form** is obtained from RSS by the ship's owner or managing owner, or the owner's agent who is carrying out the registration work, as appropriate. When registering a merchant ship the following details must be entered on the application form:
    * In section 1 (**Details of the ship**): the proposed name of the ship (several names should be entered in order of preference); the port of choice (i.e. the port with which the ship is to be associated: this is selected from an official list in Annex 2 of the Registering British Ships booklet; no physical link with the port is required); the radio call sign, if known (obtained from the Radiocommunications Agency of the Home Office); the IMO number (the Lloyd's Register of Ships serial number preceded by the letters "IMO"), or the Hull Identification Number for a ship which is not listed in Lloyd's Register of Ships; the make and power of engine; the vessel's approximate length (in metres or feet and tenths); the year of build; the type of ship (e.g. bulk carrier); the construction material; the name and address of the builder; the place of build (if different); and the country of build.
    * In section 2 (**Previous registration details**): name of ship (if different from section 1); registration number, port of registration; registered length (m); details of where the ship was registered, with former registration numbers, etc.; whether the ship has any outstanding registered mortgage.
    * In section 4 (**Details of the applicant**): full name and address, etc. stating whether the applicant is the permanent agent of the owner. (All RSS correspondence is sent to the owner or managing owner unless the owner requests it to be sent to a specified person.)
* The application form contains **instructions** to send the form to RSS together with the correct **fee**, the **Declaration of Eligibility**, a copy of any **Certificate of Incorporation** (for each company, if any, amongst the owners), a **Builder's Certificate** and/or **Bills of Sale**. There is also a reminder to the applicant that if the vessel carries a **406MHz EPIRB**, this must be registered with the MCA (see D04b.4).

D01d.2 Evidence of title

* **Evidence of title** on registration must be proved by sending the following documents with the application form:
    * for a new ship, the Builder's Certificate[4];
    * for a ship which is not new, a previous Bill or Bills of Sale showing the ownership of the ship for at least 5 years before the application is made; or
    * if the ship has been registered with full registration at any time within the last 5 years, a Bill or Bills of Sale evidencing all transfers of ownership during the period since it was so registered.
* For a ship which at the time of application is on a **foreign register**, a **certified extract from the register** is required.
* A **Declaration of Eligibility to register a British Ship** is made on a separate form, declaring that a majority interest in the ship is owned by persons qualified to be owners of British ships, and that the ship is otherwise entitled to be registered.
* **The application form is sent to RSS** with the above documents (and those in D01d.1), as well as the company's Certificate of Incorporation (and any certificates of changes of name) and the registration fee as listed in the MS (Fees) Regulations (as amended) in force at the time of application.

---

[4] A **Builder's Certificate** is issued by the shipbuilder to the shipowner following completion, and certifies that the vessel was built for the person whose name and address appears on the certificate. It is required in order to provide evidence of title to the flag State registry when first registering the vessel. The certificate varies in form from one shipbuilder to another. It is not required by UK regulations to be carried on board, and in many cases is kept in the owner's or manager's office.

D01d.3 Transfer of flag survey

* Every ship "flagging in" to the UK Register from another register must have a **"transfer of flag" survey** before it can be registered. MCA's general policy is for this survey to be carried out by an MCA surveyor; however, under certain circumstances, arrangements can be made for this survey to be carried out by a class surveyor on behalf of the MCA.
* The Customer Service Manager will request a copy of all **existing statutory certification** in order that new certificates can be prepared prior to survey.
* If, at survey, the surveyor is satisfied that the vessel **meets international standards of safety and pollution prevention** he will issue **short-term certification** there and then; **full term certification** will follow in due course.

D01d.4 Measurement survey

* Every ship being registered must have a measurement survey to establish her physical characteristics and tonnage under the **MS (Tonnage) Regulations 1997** (SI 1997/1510) for entry on the register. Application for this survey is made to one of six classification societies approved by RSS for measuring ships:
  * **Lloyd's Register of Shipping (LR)**;
  * The British Committee of **Bureau Veritas (BV)**;
  * The British Committee of **Germanischer Lloyd (GL)**;
  * The British Technical Committee of the **American Bureau of Shipping (ABS)**;
  * The British Committee of **Det Norske Veritas (DNV)**; and
  * The British Committee of **Registro Italiano Navale (RINA)**.
* A ship which is being **registered for the first time on the UK register** which has been surveyed and measured for tonnage in the previous 12 months, or which is being re-registered within 12 months of its UK registry ceasing, will not be required to undergo another measurement survey if the owners make a declaration to the RSS that the details have not changed from those previously recorded on the Register. The RSS may, however, require the declaration to be confirmed by an authorised measurer or surveyor.
* Following completion of the measurement survey, the surveyor issues a **Certificate of Survey**[5] certifying the ship's dimensions and tonnage; this is sent to RSS. (The particulars on it are also used for tonnage certification purposes.)

D01d.5 Official number and marking

* When satisfied that the ship is entitled to be registered, etc., RSS issues to the owner the ship's **Official Number** and a **Carving and Marking Note**.
* **Official Numbers of British ships** registered on Part I of the Register, and of Commonwealth ships, are taken from a single series of 6-figure numbers controlled by the RSS. This series is currently used by all Commonwealth countries except India, Sri Lanka, Sierra Leone, Kenya, Malta and Trinidad and Tobago, each of which has its own series. As a general rule the Official Number will not change during the ship's life unless she is sold outside the British Register. **Bareboat chartered ships** on Part IV of the Register generally retain their original national unique number, and only if a ship's primary register does not allocate such numbers will the RSS allocate an Official Number; in the latter case the Official Number will normally be a 4-digit number preceded by the letters "BCS", and only one number will appear on the Certificate of Registry.
* The owner appoints an **Inspector of Marks** (who is normally a surveyor of an authorised classification society) and delivers to him/her the Carving and Marking Note, which bears the **instructions for statutory marking** of the ship.
* A **Carving and Marking Note** (for pleasure vessels of 24 metres and over or merchant ships on Part I and IV of the Register) shows, at the top section of the front: Name of ship; Official Number; Port of choice; Registered tonnage or Net tonnage (as appropriate); and an instruction for the vessel to be marked with:
  * the **official number** and **"appropriate tonnage"**, to be conspicuously carved or marked;
  * the **name**, to be marked on each of its bows and its stern;
  * the **port of choice**, to be marked on the stern.

---

[5] A **Certificate of Survey** is issued by an authorised classification society in respect of a classed ship, or by the MCA in respect of an unclassed ship, in respect of any ship measured for tonnage. It details the measurements of the ship which are required for both registry and tonnage certification purposes. It is sent to the Registry of Shipping and Seamen (RSS) by the measuring authority and a copy is issued to the ship. It is not required by regulations to be carried on board but it may prove to be useful where the Certificate of Registry is lost and details of the ship have to be provided to a proper officer abroad.

* The bottom section of the front of the Carving and Marking Note is for completion by the Inspector of Marks and contains his certification that he has inspected the vessel and that it has been carved and marked in accordance with the instructions.
* The back of the Carving and Marking Note contains the full **instructions for carving and marking**.
* The ship's **official number** and **registered or net tonnage** (as appropriate) must be marked on the main beam of the ship, or if there is no main beam, on a readily accessible visible permanent part of the structure of the ship either by cutting in, centre punching or raised lettering. Alternatively it may be engraved on plates of metal, wood or plastic, secured to the main beam (or if there is no main beam, to a readily accessible visible part of the structure) with rivets, through bolts with the ends clenched, or screws with the slots removed. The official number and registered/net tonnage must be marked as follows:

O.N. 345678   R.T. 30.$\underline{93}$ N.T. 30.$\underline{93}$
                          100   100

* The ship's **name** must be marked on each of its bows, and its name and port of choice must be marked on its stern; the marking must be on a dark ground in white or yellow letters or on a light ground in black letters, the letters being not less than 10 centimetres high and of proportionate breadth. Pleasure vessels, pilot vessels, non-seagoing barges and ships employed solely in river navigation are **exempt** from marking the name on each of the bows.
* When the marks have been made as instructed, the Inspector of Marks certifies the Carving and Marking Note and returns it to the RSS.

D01d.6 Registration

* On receipt of the signed Carving and Marking Note, RSS formally registers the ship on the British Register by completing the computer database entry. The computerised Register entry contains the following details:
  * ship's name and port of choice;
  * details of tonnage and building;
  * particulars of the ship's origin;
  * name and description of the ship's registered owner, and if more than one owner, number of 64th shares owned by each;
  * any mortgages against the vessel;
  * any discharge of a mortgage;
  * any transfer of a mortgage;
  * any alterations and issues of new Certificates of Registry;
  * any transfer of registry from one port to another;
  * any change of ship's name.
* RSS finally issues the owner with a **Certificate of British Registry** printed from the computer file (see D01e).

D01d.7 Alterations of particulars entered on the Register

* If any registered particulars, e.g. tonnage, owner, owner's address, etc., are changed, the changed details must be **registered** with the RSS. A fee is payable for each change.
* When **main dimensions** are altered or where the **propelling machinery** is changed, the ship must be completely re-registered.
* Where **tonnage** is changed, the ship must be re-measured and a new Certificate of Survey sent to the RSS.
* When **ownership** changes the new owner (provided he is qualified to own a British ship) may apply to have the ship re-registered, but this is not always compulsory.
* When changes occur that do not affect tonnage, the owner should notify the RSS who will advise what evidence will be required to be produced, e.g. re-survey, or a declaration by a person with knowledge of the facts.
* After a change is registered, a **new Certificate of Registry** will be issued. This will expire on the day that the original certificate would have expired.
* A **mortgage** remains on the Register until the RSS is notified that it has been discharged, even if the ship and/or shares are sold to another person.
* All **transfers of ownership** must be supported by an approved **Bill of Sale**. A new owner has 30 days to apply to transfer title; failure to do so means a full registration fee, rather than a transfer fee, will be payable.

D01d.8 Removal from the Register

* The Registrar may, subject to service of notices, **terminate a ship's registration** in the following circumstances:
  * on application of the owner;
  * on the ship no longer being eligible to be registered;
  * on the ship being destroyed (by sinking, fire, etc.);
  * if he considers that the condition of the ship as it relates to safety, health and welfare or risk of pollution renders it inappropriate for the ship to remain registered;
  * where a penalty in respect of any of the Merchant Shipping Acts remains unpaid for more than 3 months and no appeal against that penalty is pending;
  * when the owner does not comply with a summons for any contravention in respect of any of the above Acts, and a period of not less than 3 months has elapsed.
* On termination of registration, the owner must **surrender the Certificate of Registry** to RSS for cancellation.

D01d.9 Transfer to another EU register

* **M.1477** (which was cancelled without replacement) contained the text of Council Regulation (EEC) No. 613/91 on the transfer of ships from one register to another within the European Community (EC, now EU). This Regulation is law in the UK.

D01d.10 Renewal of registration

* Between 3 and 6 months before expiry of the 5-year registration period the RSS will issue a **Renewal Notice** to the owner. The owner may apply for renewal at any time after receiving this notice but before expiry of the registration period. Notwithstanding this, an application for renewal may be made prior to the last 3 months of the current registration, but the new Certificate of Registry will not be valid for more than 5 years.
* Application for renewal must be made on the appropriate RSS form accompanied by:
  * a **Declaration of Eligibility**; and
  * a declaration that there have been **no changes to any registered details** of the ship which have not already been notified to the RSS.
* If no application for renewal is made, the RSS notifies each and every mortgagee that the registration has expired.

D01e CERTIFICATE OF BRITISH REGISTRY

* A **Certificate of British Registry** -
  - **establishes** the ship's nationality and tonnages, but does not prove ownership or show mortgages.
  - **is valid** for a maximum of 5 years; if ownership of the ship changes in the 5-year period, a new 5-year certificate will be issued.
  - **contains** the details entered on the Register with the exception of mortgage particulars.
  - **shows on the front** the following details: Name of ship; Official number; Radio call sign; IMO number/HIN; Port; Type of ship; Method of propulsion; Engine make & model; Total engine power (in kW); Length (in metres); Breadth (in metres); Depth (in metres); Gross tonnage; Net tonnage; Registered tonnage; Year of build; Name of builder; Country of build; Date and time of issue of certificate; Date of expiry of certificate; Signature of official signing "For and on behalf of the Registrar General of Shipping and Seamen; badge of the General Register Office of Shipping and Seamen. Note: Figures shown for engine power, dimensions and tonnages are to 2 decimal places.
  - **shows on the back** the following details: Note stating: "For the purposes of registration there are 64 shares in a ship"; Name and address of owner(s); Number of shares (of each owner); Footnote headed "Important information", stating: "A Certificate of Registry is not proof of ownership. Details of registered mortgages are not shown. The Registry must be informed immediately: of any changes to the ship's particulars of ownership; if the vessel is lost. The certificate must be surrendered to the Registry if the ship ceases to be a British registered ship. A duplicate must be obtained if the certificate is lost or becomes illegible. For further information contact the Registry of Shipping and Seamen (address stated)." The address stated on older Certificates will be invalid; for the new RSS address, see B05c.

D01e.1 Status and use of the Certificate of Registry

* **Section 13 of the Merchant Shipping Act 1995** provides that the Certificate of Registry of a British ship will be used only for the lawful navigation of the ship, and will not be subject to detention to secure any private right or claim.
* The **Certificate of Registry** -
    * should always **accompany the ship**, in order to establish her nationality and tonnage when required.
    * is **not a document of title**, and is not to be taken as legal evidence of registered ownership.
    * is probably the **most important document** on the ship.
    * is the **only proof of the vessel's nationality**.
    * should remain in the **master's custody**, even when the ship is chartered or mortgaged (although agents will usually want to take it ashore for production to customs officials for clearance purposes).
    * must be **produced** on every occasion when **clearing outwards** from a UK port, and when entering (and/or clearing) many foreign ports.
* A prudent master will **keep a note of the details** recorded on his ship's Certificate of Registry ; this may make it easier to obtain a duplicate Certificate of Registry in the event that the original is lost by an agent, etc.
* **If the ship is lost**, **sold** to foreigners, **captured** by an enemy or **broken up**, **notice of the circumstances**, together with the **Certificate of Registry** (if existing) must be given immediately to the RSS.

D01e.2 Handing over the Certificate of Registry to a succeeding master

* For notes on the **handing over of ship's documents** to a succeeding master, see D05e.
* Documents handed over should always include the Certificate of Registry. It may be the case, however, that at the time of the hand-over the Certificate is in the custody of the port agent for customs report or clearance purposes, etc.

D01e.3 Loss of Certificate of Registry

* If the Certificate of Registry is **lost or stolen in the UK**, the owner may obtain a **duplicate certificate** from the RSS.
* If the Certificate of Registry is **lost or stolen abroad** (e.g. when an agent fails to return it after taking it ashore for entry or clearance purposes), the master should:
    * make a **declaration** to a Proper Officer that the Certificate of British Registry is lost or stolen, giving names and descriptions of the registered owners;
    * apply to the Proper Officer for a **Provisional Certificate of British Registry**;
    * give the Proper Officer as much information about the ship as possible (e.g. tonnages and measurements from the International Tonnage Certificate 1969 or Certificate of Survey).

D01e.4 Provisional Certificate of British Registry

* Where a ship whose owner intends to register her on the British Register is outside the British Islands, the owner may apply to the RSS for **provisional registration**, or, if the ship is at a port outside the British Islands, the owner may apply to the "appropriate person" (i.e. a Proper Officer, e.g. British Consul) for provisional registration of the ship.
* **Provisional registration** is valid until:
    * expiration of 3 months from the date of issue; or
    * the ship's arrival in the UK; or
    * the termination by the Registrar on request from the owner.
* Where a ship has been provisionally registered once, it cannot be provisionally registered again **within one year** of the date of issue of the certificate except with the consent of the RSS.

D01f BRITISH REGISTRY OF BAREBOAT CHARTER SHIPS

* Section 17 of the Merchant Shipping Act 1995 makes it possible to register as a British ship a foreign-owned merchant or fishing vessel which is **bareboat chartered to a British charterer**[6].
* A "**bareboat charter ship**" is a ship which is registered under the law of a country other than the UK, which is chartered on bareboat charter terms to a charterer who is qualified to own a British ship.
* "**Bareboat charter terms**" means the hiring of a ship for a stipulated period of time on terms which give the charterer possession and control of the ship, including the right to appoint the master and crew.
* The charterer must be one of the qualified persons listed in D01c.6.
* The charterer must apply to the RSS and send:
  * a **Declaration of Eligibility**;
  * a copy of the **bareboat charter party**;
  * the **Certificate of Registry** issued by the responsible authority in the country of **primary registration**; and
  * in the case of a charterer which is a company, its **Certificate of Incorporation**.
* The **same rules** on names, survey or measurement, carving and marking, change of name, etc. apply to bareboat charter ships as to ships on Part I of the Register.
* If none of the charterers is resident in the UK, a **representative person** must be appointed in the UK.
* The registration of a bareboat charter ship will remain in force (unless terminated earlier under regulations) for **5 years or until the end of the bareboat charter period**, whichever is the shorter period.
* Bareboat charter ships become **British ships** for the duration of the bareboat charter period and are entitled to fly the British flag. During this period they are subject to the requirements of the Merchant Shipping Acts.
* The RSS will notify the primary registration authority of the bareboat charter registration under the Red Ensign.
* A **Certificate of British Registry for a Bareboat Chartered Ship** is a buff-coloured form showing **on the front**: Name of ship; Official number; Radio call sign; IMO number/HIN[7]; Port; BCS[8] Number; Country of primary registration; Name on primary register; Type of ship; Method of propulsion; Engine make and model; Total engine power (in kW); Length (in metres); Breadth (in metres); Depth (in metres); Gross tonnage; Net tonnage; Registered tonnage; Year of build; Date and time of issue of certificate; Date of expiry of certificate; Signature of official signing for and on behalf of the Registrar General of Shipping and Seamen; badge of the General Register Office of Shipping and Seamen. Note: Figures shown for engine power, dimensions and tonnages are to 2 decimal places.
* Details shown **on the back** of certificates are: Note stating: "For the purposes of registration there are 64 shares in a ship"; Name and address of owner(s); No. of shares (of each owner); Name and address of the bareboat charterer(s) of the ship; Footnote headed "Important information", stating: "A Certificate of Registry is not proof of ownership. Details of registered mortgages are not shown. The Registry must be informed immediately: of any changes to the ship's particulars of ownership; if the vessel is lost. The certificate must be surrendered to the Registry if the ship ceases to be a British registered ship. A duplicate must be obtained if the certificate is lost or becomes illegible. For further information contact the Registry of Shipping and Seamen, PO Box 165, Cardiff, United Kingdom CF14 5FU. Telephone 029 20747333. Fax: 029 20747877[9]".
* The **MS (Modification of Enactments) (Bareboat Charter Ships) Order 1994** (SI 1994/774) provides that, in relation to bareboat charter ships, references in Merchant Shipping Acts and other enactments to the "owner" (whether of a British, UK or UK registered ship) mean the bareboat charterer.

D01g PROPER COLOURS AND NATIONAL CHARACTER OF BRITISH SHIPS

D01g.1 Proper colours

* **Section 2 of the Merchant Shipping Act 1995** provides that the flag which every British ship, other than Government ships, is entitled to fly is the **Red Ensign** (without any defacement or modification). The following are also **national colours**:
  * any colours allowed to be worn under a **warrant** from Her Majesty or from the Secretary of State (e.g. a Blue Ensign); and

---

[6] Some flag States, such as Bermuda, refer to bareboat charter registry as "demise charter registry", and issue a Certificate of Demise Charter Registry.
[7] **Hull Identification Number**: a coded number marked on small craft in accordance with the International Standards Organisation standard ISO 10087:1995. Schedule1 of The Recreational Craft Regulations 1996 (SI 1996/1353) requires the marking of leisure craft built in the UK with an HIN.
[8] BCS stands for "Bareboat Charter Ship".
[9] The address of the RSS changed in 2002. For the current address and contact details, see B05c.

- in the case of British ships registered in a relevant British possession (i.e. a Crown Dependency or British Overseas Territory), any colours consisting of the **Red Ensign defaced or modified** whose adoption for ships registered in that possession is authorised or confirmed by Order in Council.
* Section 5 of the Merchant Shipping Act 1995 provides that, except in small ships, the Red Ensign or other proper national colours **must be hoisted-**
    - **on a signal** being made to the ship by one of Her Majesty's ships (including any ship under the command of a commissioned naval officer);
    - **on entering or leaving any foreign port**; and
    - in a ship of 50 gross tonnage or more, **on entering or leaving any British port.**

D01g.2 Duty to declare national character of ship

* Section 6 of the Merchant Shipping Act 1995 provides that a customs officer must **not grant a clearance or transire** for any ship until the master has **declared** to him the name of the nation to which he claims the ship belongs (i.e. the flag State). The customs officer must enter that country's name on the clearance or transire (see I07h).

D01g.3 Offences relating to British character of ship

* **Section 3(1) of the Merchant Shipping Act 1995** provides that if the master or owner of a ship which **is not a British ship** does anything, or permits anything to be done, for the purpose of **causing the ship to appear to be a British ship**, then the ship will be liable to **forfeiture** and the master, owner and any charterer will each be guilty of an offence. Exceptions to this are where -
    - the assumption of British nationality has been made to **escape capture** by an enemy or by a foreign warship in the exercise of some belligerent right; or
    - the British registration of the ship has terminated, but **marks** required under British registration regulations are displayed within a **14-day** period from the date of termination.
* If the master or owner of a British ship does anything, or permits anything to be done, for the purpose of **concealing the nationality** of the ship, the ship will be liable to **forfeiture** and the master, owner and any charterer will each be guilty of an offence.

Offence (with offenders shown in bold)	Legislation contravened	Penalties provision and penalties on summary conviction (SC) & conviction on indictment (COI)
The master or owner of a ship which is not a British ship does anything, or permits anything to be done, for the purpose of causing the ship to appear to be a British ship.	Section 3(1), Merchant Shipping Act 1995	Section 3(6). SC: A fine not exceeding £50,000. COI: Max. 2 years imprisonment or a fine or both. Ship liable to forfeiture under section 3(1).
The master or owner of a British ship does anything, or permits anything to be done, for the purpose of concealing the nationality of the ship. (**The master, owner and any charterer**)	Section 3(4), Merchant Shipping Act 1995	Section 3(6). SC: A fine not exceeding £50,000. COI: Max. 2 years imprisonment or a fine or both. Ship liable to forfeiture under section 3(4).
Any distinctive national colours except the red ensign, the Union flag (commonly known as the Union Jack) with a white border, any colours authorised or confirmed under section 2(3)(b), or any colours usually worn by Her Majesty's ships or resembling those of Her Majesty, or the pendant usually carried by Her Majesty's ships or any pendant resembling that pendant, are hoisted on board any British ship without warrant from Her Majesty or from the Secretary of State. (**The master, the owner** [if on board], **and every other person hoisting them**)	Section 4(1), Merchant Shipping Act 1995	Section 4(2). SC: A fine not exceeding the statutory maximum. COI: A fine. Commissioned naval or military officer, officer of customs and excise, or British consular officer may board ship and seize and take away the colours under section 4(3). Colours seized will be forfeited to Her Majesty under section 4(4).

D01h IMO SHIP IDENTIFICATION NUMBER

* **SOLAS regulation XI-1/3** (Ship identification number)[10] applies to all passenger ships of 100gt and upwards and all cargo ships of 300gt and upwards. Every ship must be provided with an identification number which conforms to the IMO Ship Identification Number Scheme adopted by IMO (regulation 3.1). The ship's identification number (the "IMO Number") must be inserted on the certificates and certified copies thereof issued under regulation I/12 or

---

[10] Regulation XI/3 is one of four regulations in **SOLAS Chapter XI-1 (Special measures to enhance maritime safety)**, the others being regulation 1 (Authorization of recognized organizations), regulation 2 (Enhanced surveys) (see D04f.1a) and regulation 4 (Port State control on operational requirements) (see I02c.3l).

regulation I/13 (i.e. the SOLAS "safety certificates") (regulation 3.2). For ships built before 1 January 1996, regulation XI/3 takes effect when a certificate is renewed on or after 1 January 1996 (regulation 3.4).

* Regulation XI-1/3 was modified in December 2002 to require ships' identification numbers to be permanently marked in a visible place either on the ship's hull or superstructure. Passenger ships must carry the marking on a horizontal surface visible from the air. Ships must also be marked with their identification number internally.

* The **IMO Ship Identification Number Scheme** -
    • was introduced as a **voluntary scheme**, recommended in IMO Resolution A.600(15) and intended to enhance maritime **safety** and marine **pollution prevention** and to facilitate the prevention of maritime **fraud**.
    • may be applied for **new or existing ships**, under their flag, engaged on international voyages. Administrations can also assign the "IMO numbers" to ships engaged solely on domestic voyages, and insert the number in national certificates (e.g. a Passenger Certificate).
    • **does not apply to** fishing vessels, non-mechanically propelled ships, pleasure yachts, ships engaged on special service (e.g. lightships, floating radio stations, search and rescue vessels), hopper barges, hydrofoils, hovercraft, floating docks and similar structures, warships, troopships, or wooden ships.

* A ship's **IMO Number** is a 7-digit number, e.g. 8712345, derived from the reference number allocated to the ship when it is first entered in Lloyd's Register's *Register of Ships*. It should not be confused with the ship's **official number**, which is allocated by the flag State register during the registration process.

* The IMO Number is applied to the ship by the flag State Administration under the **IMO Ship Identification Number Scheme**. It is a **permanent identification number** which will remain unchanged upon transfer of flag (whereas the official number assigned by the flag State Administration would cease to be valid upon transfer to another flag State's register).

* The **IMO Number** is assigned by the flag State, for a new ship, **when the ship is registered**, and for an existing ship at **some convenient date** such as during a renewal survey or when new statutory certificates are issued. It should be inserted **on the Certificate of Registry and on all certificates issued under IMO Conventions**. IMO recommend that it is also inserted on **other certificates** such as Suez and Panama Canal Tonnage Certificates. It should preferably be included, according to Resolution A.600(15), in the box headed "Distinctive number or letters" in addition to the call sign.

D01i MMSI AND SELCALL NUMBER

* All digital selective calling (DSC) equipment in the Global Maritime Distress and Safety System (GMDSS) is programmed with a unique nine-digit identification number known as a **Maritime Mobile Service Identity** (**MMSI**). The MMSI is sent automatically with each and every DSC transmission made.

* The first three digits of an MMSI are known as the "Maritime Identification Digits" (**MID**). The MID represents the vessel's country of registration or the country in which the DSC shore station is located. MIDs are allocated on an international basis by the ITU, in much the same way as a callsign prefix.

* **MIDs allocated to different nations** can be viewed at www.itu.int/cgi-bin/htsh/mars/cga_mids.sh

* **MIDs allocated to UK stations** are: 232, 233, 234 and 235.

* **MMSIs allocated to merchant vessels** are normally allocated with three "trailing zeros", while those allocated to recreational craft have two or one trailing zero, and Coast Station MMSI's have two leading zero's. For example, a typical Australian merchant vessel MMSI might be 503001000, where 503 is the Australian MID and 01000 is the individual ship number. A Coast Station MMSI might be 005030001, where 503 is the Australian MID and 0001 is the individual Coast Station number.

* The International Telecommunication Union (ITU) operates an international web-based data base of MMSIs, known as the **Maritime Mobile Access and Retrieval System** (MARS). The **MARS website** is at: www.itu.int/cgi-bin/htsh/mars/ship_search.sh

* The ship's **MMSI** is one of the particulars which, in relation to each EPIRB carried, must be registered under the MS (EPIRB Registration) Regulations 2000 (SI 2000/1850) (see D04b.5). Regulation 2 of the Regulations defines "MMSI" as meaning "Maritime Mobile Service Identity, being a nine-digit identification number made up of the three-digit MID followed by a six-digit identification number".

* **A Selective Calling Number**, commonly known as a "Selcall Number", is a code which, when programmed into a radio receiver, will ensure that the receiver will respond only to calls addressed to it. If a Selcall number is required, it is requested when applying to the Radiocommunications Agency for a Ship Fixed Radio Licence. Selcall numbers allotted will be added to the licence document in addition to the List of Ship Stations published by the ITU.

* For notes on the **Ship Fixed Radio Licence**, see D04m.3a.

D01j CONTINUOUS SYNOPSIS RECORD

* SOLAS regulation XI-1/5 provides that, with effect from 1 July 2004, ships must be issued with a **Continuous Synopsis Record** (CSR) which is intended to provide an on-board record of the history of the ship.
* The CSR will be issued by the **flag State administration** and will contain information such as the name of the ship and of the State whose flag the ship is entitled to fly (the flag State), the date on which the ship was registered with that State, the ship's identification number (i.e. its IMO number), the port at which the ship is registered and the name of the registered owner(s) and their registered address.
* **Any changes** must be recorded in the CSR so as to provide updated and current information together with the history of the changes.

D02 Ship construction standards and ship classification

D02a CONSTRUCTION STANDARDS APPLICABLE TO UK SHIPS

D02a.1 IMO ship construction standards

* **Standards for the construction and equipment of passenger ships (of any tonnage) and cargo ships over 500gt on international voyages** are set out in **SOLAS chapter II-1** (Construction – Structure, subdivision and stability, machinery and electrical installations) and **chapter II-2** (Construction – Fire protection, fire detection and fire extinction).
* **SOLAS chapter II-1** is given effect in the UK -
  * in respect of **passenger ships** by the **MS (Passenger Ship Construction: Ships of Classes I, II and II(A)) Regulations 1998** (SI 1998/2514); and
  * in respect of **cargo ships** by the **MS (Cargo Ship Construction) Regulations 1997** (SI 1997/2367), as amended by the MS (Cargo Ship Construction) (Amendment) Regulations 1999 (SI 1999/643).
* **SOLAS chapter II-2** is given effect in the UK by the **MS (Fire Protection: Large Ships) Regulations 1998** (SI 1998/1012) (see D04l.1).
* **Regulation 3-1 of chapter II-1** provides that in addition to the requirements contained elsewhere in the SOLAS regulations, ships must be **designed, constructed and maintained in compliance with the structural, mechanical and electrical requirements of a classification society** which is recognised by the flag State Administration in accordance with the provisions of regulation XI/1, **or with applicable national standards** of the Administration which provide an equivalent level of safety[11].
* **Standards for the construction and equipment of chemical tankers** are set out in the International Bulk Chemical Code (IBC Code), which is made mandatory by SOLAS regulation VII/10.1 for chemical tankers built on or after 1 July 1986, including those of less than 500gt. The provisions of the IBC Code are implemented in the UK by the **MS (Dangerous or Noxious Liquid Substances Carried in Bulk) Regulations 1994** (SI 1994/2464), as amended by SI 1998/1153 (see D03e.2a).
* **Standards for the construction and equipment of gas carriers** are set out in the International Gas Carrier Code (IGC Code), which is made mandatory by SOLAS regulation VII/13.1 for gas carriers built on or after 1 July 1986, including those of less than 500gt. The provisions of the IGC Code are implemented in the UK by the **MS (Gas Carriers) Regulations 1994** (SI 1994/2464) (see D03d.2a).
* **Standards for the construction and equipment of ships carrying irradiated nuclear fuel (INF) cargo** are set out in the International Code for the Safe Carriage of Packaged Irradiated Nuclear Fuel, Plutonium and High-Level Radioactive Wastes on Board Ships (INF Code), which is made mandatory by SOLAS regulation VII/15.1 ships carrying INF cargo, including those of less than 500gt. The provisions of the INF Code are implemented in the UK by the **MS (Carriage of Packaged Irradiated Nuclear Fuel etc.) (INF Code) Regulations 2000** (SI 2000/3216) (see F07h).
* **Standards for the construction and equipment of high-speed craft** are set out the International Code of Safety for High-Speed Craft. The provisions of the HSC Code are implemented in the UK by the MS (High Speed Craft) Regulations 1996 (SI 1996/3188) (see D03i.2).

---

[11] The vast majority of UK merchant ships are built in accordance with the rules and regulations of a classification society, but some UK ships are unclassed.

D02a.2 EC Directive 94/57/EC

* **European Council Directive 94/57/EC** (see D04d.1) imposes, in Article 14.1, an obligation on every EU Member State to ensure that vessels flying its flag are **constructed and maintained** in accordance with the requirements for hull, machinery and electrical and control installations laid down by a **recognised organisation**.
* The Directive is given effect in the UK by a range of measures including regulations, as listed in D04d.1.

D02b SHIP CLASSIFICATION

* "**Ship classification**" entails inspection of a ship and its components at all stages of construction from design to sea trials, and regular inspection throughout its life to ensure that it is maintained to the required standards of the classification society. It is valuable to insurers, shipbrokers, bankers, shippers and other parties needing reliable information about a vessel's condition.
* **IACS** (see D02c.2) defines "ship classification" as follows: "Ship Classification, as a minimum, is to be regarded as the development and worldwide implementation of published Rules and/or Regulations which will provide for:
  1. the structural strength of (and where necessary the watertight integrity of) all essential parts of the hull and its appendages,
  2. the safety and reliability of the propulsion and steering systems, and those other features and auxiliary systems which have been built into the ship in order to establish and maintain basic conditions on board,
  - thereby enabling the ship to operate in its intended service."
* The **classification process for a new UK ship** typically includes the following steps:
  1. Selection by the shipowner, bareboat charterer or other entity responsible for operating the ship of a classification society authorised by the MCA to perform duties under the MS (Ship Inspection and Survey Organisation) Regulations 1996 (SI 1996/2908) (see D04d.2).
  2. Review by the society's surveyors and engineers of design plans, to verify compliance with the society's rules.
  3. Attendance on-site by the society's surveyors during construction to review the building process and verify that the approved plans are followed, approved material and components are properly installed, good workmanship practices applied, and the society's rules are adhered to. The vessel is said to be built "under survey".
  4. Attendance by the society surveyors at manufacturing plants and fabricating shops to witness testing of materials and components in accordance with the society's rules.
  5. Assignment of an appropriate class, and certification of the vessel to confirm that assignment. Records of the vessel's class status are thereafter maintained by the society[12].
* The **classification process continues** throughout the life of UK ship in the following ways:
  During the vessel's service life, the society's surveyors will conduct periodical surveys to determine that class is being maintained in accordance with the society's rules.
  The society's surveyors will attend during repairs and modifications to make recommendations as appropriate and to determine that the work conforms to the society's rules.
* The American Bureau of Shipping (ABS) describes the **classification process** as consisting of:
  * the **development of rules**, guides, standards and other criteria for the design and construction of marine vessels and structures, for materials, equipment and machinery;
  * the **review of design** and **survey during and after construction** to verify compliance with such rules, guides, standards or other criteria;
  * the **assignment and registration of class** when such compliance has been verified; and
  * the **issuance of a renewable Classification certificate**, with annual endorsements, valid for five years.
  The Rules and standards are developed by Bureau staff and passed upon by committees made up of naval architects, marine engineers, shipbuilders, engine builders, steel makers and by other technical, operating and scientific personnel associated with the worldwide maritime industry. Theoretical research and development, established engineering disciplines, as well as satisfactory service experience are utilized in their development and promulgation. The Bureau and its committees can act only upon such theoretical and practical considerations in developing Rules and standards. For classification, vessels are to comply with both the hull and the machinery requirements of the Rules[13].
* **Classification is not mandatory** for any particular class or type of ship. There is, however, as outlined in D02a.1 and D02a.2, a statutory requirement for UK and other SOLAS Party State ships to be **designed, constructed and maintained in compliance with the structural, mechanical and electrical requirements of a classification society** which is recognised by the flag State Administration in accordance with the provisions of SOLAS regulation XI-1/1, **or with applicable national standards** of the Administration which provide an equivalent level of safety.

---

[12] To establish the **class status** of a ship classed with Lloyd's Register, the **quarterly computer print-out** issued by LR and the Interim Certificates issued on completion of classification surveys should be consulted, in addition to the Certificate of Class.
[13] ABS Rules for Building and Classing Steel Vessels 2001, Part 1: Conditions of Classification, Section 1, paragraph 1.

* **Classification** is in many cases a **contractual requirement** of:
    * hull and machinery underwriters[14];
    * cargo underwriters[15]; and
    * P&I clubs[16],
    - breach of which may render the insurance cover void.
* **Statutory safety certification** under international conventions is **conditional** on a ship's hull structure and essential shipboard engineering systems being satisfactory in all respects. However, the **only recognised authoritative rules** for ensuring this are those of the major classification societies. Compliance with the rules of major classification societies is therefore the only practical basis for essential statutory certification (e.g. Cargo Ship Safety Construction Certificate and Passenger Ship Safety Certificates), and flag States consequently rely to a great extent on class survey information. (See also notes on the MS (Ship Inspection and Survey Organisations) Regulations in D04d.2.)
* A vessel without a valid **Certificate of Class** or **Interim Certificate of Class** is not "in class" and is therefore not **seaworthy** in the eyes of courts. This may have the **knock-on effects** of:
    * breaching the **implied warranty of seaworthiness in the vessel's hull and machinery policy**, rendering the policy void;
    * breaching any **express warranty in the hull and machinery policy** stating that, for example, the vessel will be "LR class and class maintained";
    * breaching the **rules of the owner's P&I club**, rendering the P&I policy void;
    * breaching any similar **warranty of seaworthiness in the cargo insurance policy**, rendering the policy void; and
    * making the **shipowner liable for any loss, damage or delay** to ship or cargo.

D02c CLASSIFICATION SOCIETIES

D02c.1 Nature and functions of classification societies

* An "**international classification society**" may be defined as an independent, non-governmental, non-profit distributing organisation which develops and updates adequate published rules, regulations and standards for the safe design, construction and periodical maintenance of ships which are capable of trading internationally, and implements them on a worldwide basis using its own exclusive staff. Over 50 organisations in the world claim to be classification societies, but few of them fit the definition. (Many of these organisations fail to meet the criteria in the definition, e.g. by employing the services of non-exclusive surveyors.)
* **Leading societies are involved in**:
    * setting **technical standards** for ships;
    * providing **inspection** and assistance to enable the shipping industry to meet these standards;
    * regularly publishing the **survey status of classed ships**, and other vital information, in register books; and
    * providing many **other services** to the industry, such as design advice, bunker fuel and lubricating oil analysis, and quality system accreditation.

D02c.2 International Association of Classification Societies (IACS)

* **IACS** represents the major classification societies shown in the table below.

Society	Letters	Headquarters	Website
American Bureau of Shipping	ABS	Houston, TX, USA	www.eagle.org
Bureau Veritas	BV	Courbevoie, France	www.veristar.com
China Classification Society	CCS	Beijing, China	www.ccs.org.cn
Det Norske Veritas	DNV	Høvik, Norway	www.dnv.com
Germanischer Lloyd	GL	Hamburg, Germany	www.GermanLloyd.org

---

[14] For notes on **Clause 13 – Classification and ISM** of the International Hull Clauses (01/11/02), see G04a.2i. In hull and machinery policies to which the Institute Time Clauses – Hulls (1/10/83) are attached a classification warranty is usually given by owners, e.g.: "Vessel classed LR and class maintained". The warranty may specify a particular society approved by underwriters, but some warranties specify no particular society.
[15] Cargo insurance policies often contain the London **Institute Classification Clause** which provides that the marine transit rates agreed for the insurance apply only to cargoes carried by steel ships classed by either Lloyd's Register, LR, American Bureau of Shipping, Germanischer Lloyd, Nippon Kaiji Kyokai, Det Norske Veritas, Registro Italiano Navale, the Russian Register or the Polish Register.
[16] **Rule 28.4 of Assuranceforeningen Skuld** (Skuld P&I Club) for example, provides that "it shall be a condition precedent of the insurance cover that the entered vessel remains fully classed with a classification society approved by the Association, and that the vessel's classification society is not changed without the Association's prior consent".

Korean Register of Shipping	KR	Taejon, South Korea	www.krs.co.kr
Lloyd's Register of Shipping	LR	London, England	www.lr.org
Nippon Kaiji Kyokai	NK	Tokyo, Japan	www.classnk.or.jp
Registro Italiano Navale	RINA	Genova, Italy	www.rina.org
Russian Maritime Register of Shipping	RS	St Petersburg, Russian Federation	www.rs-head.spb.ru
Hrvatski Registar Brodova (Croatian Register of Shipping)*	CRS	Split, Croatia	www.crs.hr
Indian Register of Shipping*	IRS	Mumbai, India	www.irclass.org

* Associate Member

*   **Full Members** of IACS have, as a minimum, 30 years' experience as a classification society with their own Classification Rules, a classed fleet of not less than 1500 ocean-going vessels of over 100gt with an aggregate total of not less than 8 million gross tonnage, and a professional staff of at least 150 exclusive surveyors and 100 technical specialists, all of whom must be qualified and trained in accordance with IACS Procedures.
*   **Associate Members** of IACS have, as a minimum, 15 years' experience as a classification society with their own Classification Rules, a classed fleet of not less than 750 ocean-going vessels of over 100gt with an aggregate total of not less than 2 million gross tonnage, and a professional staff of at least 75 exclusive surveyors and 50 technical specialists, all of whom must be qualified and trained in accordance with IACS Procedures.
*   **Over 90% of the world's merchant tonnage** is covered by **IACS Members' unified standards for hull structure and essential engineering systems**, which are established, updated, applied and monitored on a continuous basis. To ensure uniform application of high standards, IACS member societies are strictly bound by ISO-based Quality Assurance standards.
*   IACS publishes **Unified Requirements**, which are adopted resolutions on matters directly connected to or covered by specific Rule requirements and practices of individual classification societies and the general philosophy on which the Rules and practices of classification societies are established. Subject to ratification by the governing body of each Member or Associate Member society, Unified Requirements must be incorporated in the Rules and practices of IACS member societies within one year of approval by the IACS Council. The existence of a Unified Requirement on a particular matter does not oblige a member society to issue respective Rules covering that matter. Unified Requirements are minimum requirements; each member society remains free to set more stringent requirements. (For notes on a Unified Requirement relating to anchoring equipment, see D04s.1.)
    *   **Website**: www.iacs.org.uk

D02c.2a Lloyd's Register of Shipping

-   **is a member** of IACS (see D02c.2).
-   **approves** the design, surveys and reports on: hovercraft, non-mercantile shipping, yachts and small craft; amphibious and land and sea and sea bed installations, structures, plant, etc; machinery, apparatus, materials, components, equipment, production methods and processes of all kinds; for the purposes of testing their compliance with plans, specifications, Rules, Codes of Practice, etc., or their fitness for particular requirements.
-   **acts with delegated authority** on behalf of numerous governments in respect of statutory regulations.
-   **provides other technical inspection and advisory services** relating to ships and the maritime industry generally and also in respect of land and sea-based undertakings.
-   **will act**, when authorised on behalf of Governments, in respect of national and international statutory safety and other requirements for passenger and cargo ships.
-   **employs** exclusive surveyors worldwide (whereas some societies use non-exclusive, part-time surveyors).
*   **Website**: www.lr.org

D02c.3 Non-IACS societies

*   More than 50 organisations claim to class ships but most are not IACS members and can not realistically be called classification societies. Many of them are not international in character, being little more than national ship registers which hope to attract shipping (including sub-standard shipping) from other flags. There is no uniformity of rules, or of application of rules, as there is with the IACS member societies.

D02c.4 Class rules and regulations

* Each of the leading classification societies, including all Members and Associate Members of the IACS, publish **rules and regulations for the construction and maintenance of ships** classed by the particular society. Lloyd's Register of Shipping, for example, publishes its *Rules and Regulations for the Classification of Ships* in a 7-volume set comprising the following sections:
  * **Section 1: Regulations;**
  * **Section 2: Rules for the manufacture, testing and certification of materials;**
  * **Section 3: Ship structures** (general) - the basic structural philosophy of hull construction, longitudinal strength, aft end structures, etc.;
  * **Section 4: Ship structures** (ship type) - hull construction requirements for specific ship types, e.g. tugs, ferries, bulk carriers, oil tankers and container ships;
  * **Section 5: Main and auxiliary machinery** - including shaft vibration and alignment, piping systems for oil and chemical tankers, and steering gear;
  * **Section 6: Control, electrical, refrigeration and fire** - automation and control systems, electrical systems, refrigeration systems and fire prevention systems;
  * **Section 7: Other ship types and systems** - highly specialised ships to which the format of the rest of the Rules for Ships cannot easily be applied – e.g. ships with installed process plant, fire-fighting ships, dynamic positioning installed in ships, oil-recovery ships, burning of coal in ships' boilers, positional mooring systems and thruster-assisted positional mooring systems.
* **A classed ship will continue to be "in class"** so long as it is found, in **surveys**, to be maintained in accordance with the society's rules and regulations. Classification is conditional on compliance with the society's requirements for both **hull and machinery**.
* The society may also want to be satisfied that **very small ships** or **ships of a special type** are suitable for the geographical or other limits or conditions of the service contemplated.

D02d CLASS SURVEYS AND DOCUMENTATION

The following notes are based on Lloyd's Register of Shipping's Rules and Regulations for the Classification of Ships (which are broadly similar to the rules of other IACS member societies) and relate chiefly to those aspects of class and class maintenance of importance to the master.

D02d.1 Periodical surveys of existing ships

* Maintenance of class depends on the programme of **periodical hull and machinery surveys** being carried out within stipulated periods. Survey programmes consist chiefly of **special, annual and intermediate surveys**.
* **Special surveys** of the hull are carried out at 5 yearly intervals in order to establish the condition of the hull structure to confirm that the structural integrity is satisfactory in accordance with the classification requirements, and will remain fit for its intended purpose until the next special survey, subject to proper maintenance and operation. Special surveys are also intended to detect possible damages and to establish the extent of any deterioration. Special surveys of machinery are carried out at the same intervals and have corresponding aims. Following satisfactory completion of special surveys (as reported by LR surveyors), a new Certificate of Class is issued by the society.
* **Annual surveys** must be carried out within 3 months before or after each anniversary date of the completion commissioning or special survey in order to confirm that the general condition of the vessel is maintained at a satisfactory level. Following satisfactory completion of an annual survey, the Certificate of Class is endorsed by the LR surveyor.
* **Intermediate surveys** are carried out on all ships instead of either the second or third Annual Survey. Following satisfactory completion of an intermediate survey, the Certificate of Class is endorsed by the LR surveyor.
* **Docking surveys** are carried out by arrangement with the owner. Ships under 15 years old must be examined in drydock twice in any 5 year period; not more than 3 years may elapse between dockings. Ships 15 or more years old must be examined in drydock at 2-yearly intervals with extension to 2.5 years when a suitable high-resistance paint is applied to the underwater portion of the hull.
* **Continuous surveys** of the hull are permitted on all ships other than bulk carriers, combination carriers and oil tankers, which are now subject to enhanced surveys. All hull compartments are to be opened up for survey and testing in rotation with a 5-year interval between examinations of each part.
* **Complete surveys of machinery (CSM)** are carried out every 5 years, with parallel arrangements as for the hull.
* **Chief engineer's examinations of machinery** may be made where the society agrees to some items of the machinery being examined by the ship's chief engineer at ports where the society is not represented, or, where

practicable, at sea. A limited confirmatory survey is carried out at the next port where a society surveyor is available. Where an approved planned maintenance system operates, confirmatory surveys may be held at annual intervals.

* **In-water Surveys** may be accepted in lieu of any one of the two Docking Surveys required every 5 years on ships less than 15 years old and are to provide the information normally obtained from Docking Surveys, so far as practicable. The beam must be greater than 30m (or as agreed), and a suitable high-resistance paint must have been applied to the underwater portion of the hull. (For notes on **statutory provisions relating to in-water surveys**, see D04e.8a.)
* **Inert gas systems** must be surveyed annually. In addition, on ships to which an IGS notation has been assigned, a special survey of the IG plant must be carried out every 5 years.
  * Following satisfactory completion of any periodical survey, the LR surveyor will issue an **Interim Certificate of Class** to the ship and send his survey report to the Committee of LR with his recommendation that class be maintained with new records as shown on the Interim Certificate.

D02d.1a Survey Programme

* Lloyd's Register requires a **Survey Programme** to be prepared by Owners at least 6 months in advance of each survey and submitted to LR for agreement. The Survey Programme is to include the proposals for survey including the means of providing access for **Close-up Survey**, **thickness measurement** and **tank testing**. Detailed requirements for means of access, illumination, etc. are provided in the Rules and Regulations.

D02d.1b Enhanced Survey Programme

* In response to concern over the extraordinarily high rate of **loss of bulk carriers** in the 1980s and 1990s, IACS and IMO introduced more stringent survey requirements for these ships, including a programme of **enhanced surveys**.
* The **Enhanced Survey Programme (ESP) for bulk carriers** was introduced in 1993 as a voluntary measure through IMO resolution A.744(18) and as a mandatory requirement (for bulk carriers classed by IACS member societies) through IACS Unified Requirement Z10.2.
* **Enhanced surveys became mandatory** under international law for bulk carriers under **SOLAS Chapter XII** (Additional safety measures for bulk carriers), which entered into force on 1 July 1999, and for bulk carriers and tankers under **SOLAS Chapter XI-1** (Special measures to enhance maritime safety). For notes on these SOLAS provisions, see D04f.1a.

D02d.2 Damage surveys

* Any **damage, defect or breakdown** which could invalidate the conditions for which a class has been assigned must be **reported** to the society without delay. A **damage survey** may be required. **Damage surveys** are occasional surveys falling outside the periodical survey programme, requested following hull or machinery damage or following discovery of a defect.
* Any **repairs** to hull, equipment and machinery required in order to retain class must be carried out to the satisfaction of the society's surveyors.
* When repairs are made at a place where the services of a LR surveyor are not available, they must be surveyed by a LR surveyor at the **earliest opportunity thereafter**.
* If a ship classed with LR is damaged to such an extent as to necessitate **towage outside port limits**, the owner must **notify LR** at the first opportunity.
* In some cases, depending on the type, location and extent of damage, **permanent repairs may be deferred** following survey to coincide with a planned periodical survey.
* Following satisfactory completion of any recommended repairs, the LR surveyor will issue an **Interim Certificate of Class** to the ship and send his survey report to the Committee of LR with his recommendation that class be maintained.

D02d.3 Certificates of Class

* A **Certificate of Class** is a document issued by a classification society certifying the structural and mechanical fitness of a ship for a particular use or service in accordance with the rules and regulations laid down and made public by that society.
* A valid Certificate of Class may be a requirement of:
  * a Hull and Machinery insurer, for a ship being insured;

- a P&I club, for an entered ship;
- a cargo insurer, for the carrying ship;
- the flag State Administration, for ship registration purposes;
- a port authority or customs administration, for port clearance purposes.

* **Certificates of Class** in respect of **Hull and Machinery** (separately), or **combined certificates**, are issued to builders or owners when reports on completion of a **special survey** have been submitted by a surveyor and approved by the Committee of the society. Separate certificates may be issued in respect of **refrigerating machinery installations** in reefer ships.

* **Certificates of Class Maintenance** in respect of **completed periodical surveys** of hull and machinery are issued to owners on application.

* The ship's "**character of classification symbols**" (e.g. "⊞100A1") and appended **service notation** (e.g. "*United Kingdom coastal service, and to Orkney and Shetland Islands; Ice Class 2*") are recorded on its certificate of class. **Machinery and refrigerating machinery installations** have their own classification symbols, e.g. "⊞LMC" and "⊞RMC".

* The certifying statement on a Lloyd's Register Certificate of Class reads as follows: *"This certificate is issued to the (ship's name, LR number, date of build, port of registry, gross tonnage) to confirm that, having been surveyed by Lloyd's Register Surveyors and reported by them to be in compliance with Lloyd's Register's Rules and Regulations for the Classification of Ships, it has been assigned the class (character of classification symbols and class notation for hull and machinery)"*. The certificate shows the date of assignment of the Special Survey, and the expiry date. The certificate is subject to the terms and conditions on its reverse.

- Where a Certificate of Class is required but the ship is not classed, or is below a certain tonnage (e.g. 500gt), a **Certificate of Seaworthiness** may be acceptable. Certificates of Seaworthiness are issued, chiefly to small ships and craft, by professional surveyors for a variety of purposes, and generally certify that the vessel has been found to be seaworthy for a specified purpose or voyage. Some of the many organisations that offer ship classification services may refer to their "class certificate" as a Certificate of Seaworthiness.

D02d.3a Interim Certificates of Class

* **Class surveyors** of Lloyd's Register of Shipping do not issue Certificates of Class, but endorse them on completion of annual and other surveys. On completion of all survey work at a particular port (including any statutory surveys carried out), and provided that in his opinion the ship is in a fit and efficient condition, a class surveyor will generally issue the master with an **Interim Certificate of Class**, which permits the vessel to proceed on her voyage. The surveyor will send his **survey report and recommendations** to the Committee of Lloyd's Register, which in due course will amend the ship's latest survey details in the class Register Book and may issue a **Certificate of Class**, which may be referred to as a **Certificate of Class Maintenance**.

* Interim certificates of class contain the **surveyor's recommendations for continuance of class**, but in all cases are subject to **confirmation** by the society's Committee (see D02d.4).

- **The surveyor's statement** on a Lloyd's Register Interim Certificate of Class states: *"I have carried out the surveys detailed below. All recommendations made by me have been dealt with to my satisfaction. I am recommending to the Committee of Lloyd's Register of Shipping that class be maintained with new records as follows."*

D02d.3b Conditions of Class

* Where a class surveyor considers that continuance of a ship in class should depend on certain requirements being fulfilled by the shipowner, e.g. the repair at the next dry-docking of certain specified damage, or the inspection or testing of certain specified equipment, or the witnessing of the first loading of a cargo on a new ship, he will list these on the Interim Certificate of Class as "**Conditions of Class Now Imposed**".

* When imposed conditions of class, as listed on an Interim Certificate of Class, have been met to the satisfaction of a class surveyor (e.g. at the next dry-docking or annual survey), these are listed on the next Interim Certificate of Class issued as "**Conditions of Class Deleted**".

* If conditions of class are not complied with, class is liable to be suspended or withdrawn by the society.

* **An example of conditions of class imposed** is shown below.

CONDITIONS OF CLASS NOW IMPOSED	DUE
NO. 4 HOLD DB HOPPER SIDE PLATING FRMS 47 & 49 PORT SIDE TEMPORARILY REPAIRED 03/02. PERMANENT REPAIRS TO BE EFFECTED BY NEXT DRY DOCKING.	07/03
BOTTOM SHELL FRAMES 54, 55 AND 56 PORTSIDE WASTED AND THINNED AT CONNECTION WITH TANK TOP, TO BE PART CROPPED AND RENEWED.	11/02

D02d.3c Ice classes

* Some of the leading classification societies designate a range of **ice classes** for assignment to ships with suitable strengthening and engine output for winter navigation in ice conditions. Where a classed ship meets the strength and power criteria laid down in the society's rules for a particular set of ice conditions, an appropriate ice class will be assigned and shown on the Certificate of Class.
* **General Ice Classes** designated by Lloyd's Register are as follows:
  * **Ice Class AS**. With exception from the engine output requirements in Part 5, Chapter 9,1.3 of LR's Rules, the requirements for Ice Class AS are to be taken as the requirements for Ice Class 1AS. Ice Class AS is not designed for operation in the Northern part of the Baltic in the winter season.
  * **Ice Class A**. With exception from the engine output requirements in Part 5, Chapter 9,1.3 of LR's Rules, the requirements for Ice Class A are to be taken as the requirements for Ice Class 1A. Ice Class A is not designed for operation in the Northern part of the Baltic in the winter season.
* **Baltic ice classes** designated by Lloyd's Register are as follows:
  * **Ice Class 1AS** - for ships intended to navigate in first-year ice conditions equivalent to unbroken level ice with a thickness of 1.0m.
  * **Ice Class 1A** - for ships intended to navigate in first-year ice conditions equivalent to unbroken level ice with a thickness of 0.8m.
  * **Ice Class 1B** - for ships intended to navigate in first-year ice conditions equivalent to unbroken level ice with a thickness of 0.6m.
  * **Ice Class 1C** - for ships intended to navigate in first-year ice conditions equivalent to unbroken level ice with a thickness of 0.4m.
  * **Ice Class 1D** - for ships intended to navigate in light first-year ice conditions in areas other than the Northern Baltic. The standard of strengthening is equivalent to that for Ice Class 1C but only the requirements for strengthening the forward region, the rudder and steering arrangements are applicable.
* Certain ice classes assigned by the classification societies have equivalents in the **Finnish-Swedish Ice Class Designations**. A ship navigating in winter conditions in the Baltic Sea will only be eligible for icebreaker assistance from a Finnish or Swedish government icebreaker subject to assignment of an ice class equivalent to one of the Finnish-Swedish Ice Class Designations.

D02d.4 Class documentation to be carried on board

* Lloyd's Register's *Rules and Regulations for the Classification of Ships* lay down documentation requirements for **bulk carriers** in Part 1, Section 6, **oil tankers** (including ore/oil ships and ore/bulk/oil ships) in Part 1, Section 7, and **chemical tankers** in Part 1, Section 8.
* By way of example, in respect of **bulk carriers**, Part 1, Section 6, paragraph 6.2 requires the Owner to maintain documentation on board as follows:
  * a **survey file** (known as the "**Enhanced Survey Report File**") comprising reports of structural surveys, thickness measurement and executive hull summary in accordance with IMO Resolution A.744(18);
  * **supporting documentation** consisting of:
    * main structural plans of cargo holds and ballast tanks;
    * previous repair history;
    * cargo and ballast history;
    * reports on structural defects/deterioration in general;
    * reports on leakage in bulkheads and piping systems;
    * condition of coatings or corrosion prevention systems, if any;
    * extent of use of inert gas plant and tank cleaning procedures when forming part of approved corrosion control system;
    * information that may help to identify critical areas; and
    * **Survey Programme** as required by 6.3.
* The complete documentation listed above must be readily available for examination by the surveyor and should be used as a **basis for survey**. The documentation should be kept on board for the lifetime of the ship.
* For notes on **Enhanced Survey Programme documentation** required to be carried under the IMO Guidelines, see D04f.1a.

D02d.5 Suspension or withdrawal of class

* When the **society's regulations** as regards surveys on hull, equipment or machinery are **not complied with**, the ship is not entitled to retain class. Class will be **suspended** or **withdrawn**, and a **corresponding notation** will be assigned.
* When it is found, from reported defects in the hull, equipment or machinery, that a ship is **not entitled to retain class** in the Register Book, and the owner **fails to repair such defects** in accordance with the society's requirements, class will be suspended or withdrawn.
* When any society-classed ship **proceeds to sea with less freeboard than that approved by the society**, or when her **freeboard marks are placed higher** than the position assigned or approved by the society, class is liable to be withdrawn or suspended.
* When it is found that a **specialised ship** is being operated in a manner contrary to that agreed at the time of classification, or is being operated in environmental conditions which are more onerous, or in areas other than those agreed by the society, class is liable to be automatically withdrawn or suspended.
* Under regulation 5(2) of the **MS (Ship Inspection and Survey Organisations) Regulations 1996** (SI 1996/2908), an MCA-authorised classification society must not issue certificates to a UK ship **de-classed** or **changing class for safety reasons** before consulting the MCA to determine whether a **full inspection** is necessary. Under regulation 6(3), the society, as a recognised organisation, is required to provide all relevant information to the MCA about changes of class or de-classing of vessels.
* Lloyd's Register's website carries a regularly updated list of **class suspensions and withdrawals**, with reasons given including "overdue surveys", "non-compliance with recommendations and/or conditions of class", "transfer of class", "pending disposition of casualty" and other safety-related and non-safety related reasons.

D03 Ship operational requirements

D03a OPERATIONAL REQUIREMENTS APPLICABLE TO ALL UK SHIP TYPES

D03a.1 ISM Code Regulations

* The **MS (International Safety Management (ISM) Code) Regulations 1998** (SI 1998/1561) -
    - **give effect in the UK to SOLAS chapter IX** (Management for the Safe Operation of Ships) and the **ISM Code** (see C04b), except in relation to ro-ro passenger ferries, in respect of which SOLAS Chapter IX and the ISM Code are given effect by the MS (ISM Code) (Ro-Ro Passenger Ferries) Regulations 1997 (see D03b.1a).
    - **apply to UK ships** wherever they may be, and to other ships while they are in UK waters (regulation 3(1)).
    apply, by virtue of regulation 3(2), to:
        • **passenger ships** of Classes I, II and II(A), from 1 July 1998;
        • **oil tankers**, **chemical tankers**, **gas carriers**, **bulk carriers**, and **cargo high-speed craft**, of 500gt or more and which engage in international voyages, from 1 July 1998; and
        • **other cargo ships**[17] and **mobile offshore drilling units** (MODUs) of 500gt or more which engage in international voyages, from **1 July 2002**.
    - **apply to every company operating a ship** to which the Regulations apply (as above) regulation 3(3).
    - **do not apply to** those companies and ships to which **Council Regulation (EC) No. 3051/95** on the safety management of roll-on/roll-off passenger ferries applies (see D03b.1a) (regulation 3(4)).
    - **provide that every company** must comply with the requirements of the ISM Code as it applies to that company and to any ship owned by it or for which it has responsibility (regulation 4).
    - **provide that the master of every ship** must operate his ship in accordance with the **safety management system** on the basis of which the Safety Management Certificate was issued.
    - **impose obligations on a Company**, including a requirement for the appointment of a **Designated Person**, for **audits** and for the holding of a **Document of Compliance**, as outlined in C04b.3.
        • **impose obligations on each ship operated by the Company**, including a requirement for audits and the holding of a Safety Management Certificate.
    - **are explained** in **MGN 40**.

---

[17] "Cargo ship" in the Regulations means a cargo ship within the meaning of the MS (Cargo Ship Construction) Regulations 1997 (SI 1997/1509), i.e. any mechanically propelled ship which is not a passenger ship, troop ship, pleasure vessel or fishing vessel. Thus the term "cargo ships" includes ships such as survey ships, research ships and other ships which do not carry cargo.

* In the Regulations:
  * "**audit**" means a systematic and independent examination to determine whether the safety management system is suitable to meet the objectives set out in Section 1 of the Code, and, so far as the system has been operated, that the system has been implemented effectively. Such audits must take into account the Guidelines on the Implementation of the ISM Code by Administrations, adopted by IMO pursuant to Assembly Resolution A. 788 (19);
  * "**company**" means the owner of a ship to which the Regulations apply or any other organisation or person such as the manager, or the bareboat charterer, who has assumed the responsibility for the operation of the ship from the owner;
  * "**Document of Compliance**" means the Document of Compliance referred to in SOLAS, Chapter IX, Regulation 4;
  * "**Safety Management Certificate**" means the Safety Management Certificate referred to in SOLAS, Chapter IX, Regulation 4;
  * "**safety management system**" means a structured and documented system enabling company personnel to effectively implement the company safety and environmental protection policy.

D03a.1a Duty to comply with ISM Code (regulation 4)

* **Every company** must comply with the requirements of the ISM Code as it applies to that company and to any ship owned by it or for which it has responsibility.

D03a.1b Duty to hold certificates (regulation 5)

* **No company may operate a ship** unless that company holds a valid **Document of Compliance (DOC)** (regulation 5(1)).
* **No company** may operate a ship unless there is in force in respect of that ship a valid **Safety Management Certificate (SMC)** (regulation 5(2)).
* **No UK ship may be operated** unless the company holds a **DOC** issued or accepted by the MCA, and there is in force in relation to the ship an SMC issued by the MCA (regulation 5(3)).
  * For the purposes of regulation 5 a DOC or SMC is not valid unless it has been **endorsed**, in the circumstances required by the ISM Code, showing, in the case of a **DOC satisfactory annual audits**, or in the case of an **SMC, a satisfactory intermediate audit**.

D03a.1c Duty to carry certificates (regulation 6)

* **Every company** must ensure that a valid **SMC** and a copy of the **DOC** is carried on board each ship to which the Regulations apply.

D03a.1d Duty of master (regulation 7)

* **The master** of every ship must **operate his ship in accordance with the Safety Management System** on the basis of which the SMC was issued.

D03a.1e Designated person (regulation 8)

* **The company must** designate a person who will be responsible for monitoring the safe and efficient operation of each ship with particular regard to the safety and pollution prevention aspects (regulation 8(1)).
* **The designated person must**:
  * take such steps as are necessary to ensure compliance with the company Safety Management System on the basis of which the DOC was issued (regulation 8(2)(a)); and
  * ensure that proper provision is made for each ship to be so manned, equipped and maintained that it is fit to operate in accordance with the Safety Management System (SMS) and with statutory requirements (regulation 8(2)(b)).
* **The company must** ensure that the designated person:
  * is provided with sufficient authority and resources (regulation 8(3)(a)); and
  * has appropriate knowledge and sufficient experience of the operation of ships at sea and in port to enable him to comply with the above requirements (regulation 8(3)(b)).

D03a.1f Issue of Document of Compliance and Safety Management Certificate (regulation 9)

* If the MCA is satisfied that a company operating UK ships complies with the requirements of the ISM Code, the **MCA may** issue the company with a **Document of Compliance (DOC)** valid for not more than **5 years** (regulation 9(1)).
* If the MCA is satisfied that a ship is operated by a company to which it has issued a DOC and that **the company and its shipboard management operate in accordance with the approved SMS**, the **MCA must** issue the ship with a **Safety Management Certificate (SMC)** valid for not more than **5 years** (regulation 9(2)).
* Where a company operating ships registered in more than one country, but **at least one of which is registered in the UK**, complies with the requirements of the ISM Code, the MCA may accept a DOC issued by the government of **one of those countries** to which SOLAS applies, if prior to the issue of the DOC it has agreed to accept it (regulation 9(3)). Conditions for acceptance may include completion of a satisfactory audit of the company by an authorised person.
* Where a **company newly registers a ship in the UK**, the MCA may accept a DOC issued by the government of one of those countries to which SOLAS applies in which ships operated by the company are registered. Conditions for acceptance may include completion of a satisfactory audit by an authorised person (regulation 9(4)).
* If the MCA is satisfied that a UK ship is operated by a company which has a DOC accepted by the MCA under regulation 9(3) or regulation 9(4) and that its shipboard management operates in accordance with a SMS which complies with the ISM Code, the **MCA must** issue in respect of that ship an **SMC** valid for not more than **5 years** (regulation 9(5)).

D03a.1g Interim DOC and SMC (regulation 10)

* **Where a company is newly established**, or the company assumes for the first time the responsibility for operating a **ship type not covered by its DOC**, an **Interim Document of Compliance** may be issued to facilitate implementation of the ISM Code (regulation 10(1)(a)).
* An **Interim DOC**, valid for no more than **12 months**, may be issued to a company following a demonstration that the company has a **safety management system (SMS)** that meets the objectives of section 1.2.3 of the ISM Code (regulation 10(1)(b)).**The company must** demonstrate **plans** to implement a **SMS meeting the full requirements of the ISM Code** within the period of validity of the Interim DOC.
* Under regulation 10(2)(a) an **Interim Safety Management Certificate**, valid for no more than **6 months**, may be issued:
  * in respect of a **new ship on delivery**;
  * when a company takes on the responsibility for the **management of a ship which is new to the company**; or
  * when a ship is **transferred between flag States**.
* The MCA may, if appropriate, **extend** the validity of an Interim SMC for a further **6 months**.
* Regulation 10(2)(b) provides that **an Interim SMC may only be issued** when the MCA is satisfied that:
  * the DOC or Interim DOC is relevant to that ship type;
  * the SMS provided by the company for the ship includes all key elements of the ISM Code and has been assessed in the audit for issuance of the DOC or Interim DOC;
  * the **master and relevant senior officers are familiar with the SMS** and the planned arrangements for its implementation;
  * **instructions** which have been identified as essential to be provided prior to sailing have been given;
  * plans exist for a **company audit of the ship** within the next 3 months; and
  * the relevant **information on the SMS** is given in a **working language or languages** understood by the ship's personnel.

D03a.1h Issue and endorsement of SMC by another government (regulation 11)

* The **MCA may request**, through a proper officer or otherwise, the government of **another SOLAS Convention country** to conduct an **audit of the SMS operated on a UK ship**, and if satisfied that the requirements of the ISM Code are complied with, to **issue the ship with an SMC** or authorise such issue or, where appropriate, **endorse the SMC** in accordance with the requirements of SOLAS after **intermediate audit**.

D03a.1i Issue of certificates on behalf of other governments (regulation 12)

*   The **MCA may**, at the request of the government of another SOLAS Convention country, **audit the SMS of companies and ships registered in that country** and **issue a DOC or SMC or endorse them** in accordance with the requirements of SOLAS after **annual or intermediate audits**.

D03a.1j Annual audit of DOC (regulation 13)

*   The **MCA must** carry out an **annual audit of the SMS of every company** issued by the MCA with a DOC, within 3 months of its anniversary date.

D03a.1k Intermediate audit of SMC (regulation 14)

*   The **MCA must** carry out an **intermediate audit of each ship** to ensure that the conditions for the continued validity of any SMC issued by the MCA are being met, **between the second and third anniversaries of the SMC** and at **such other times as thought fit**.

D03a.1l Renewal of certificates (regulation 15)

*   Before the renewal of any certificate, the MCA must carry out a **renewal audit** of the company or ship during the 6-month period preceding the expiry date of the DOC or SMC as the case may be, to ensure that compliance with the requirements of the ISM Code is maintained.

D03a.1m Powers of audit, inspection, suspension of service and detention (regulation 16)

*   **An audit of the SMS of any company** may be carried out by any **authorised person** (regulation 16(1)(a)). (An "authorised person" means a person authorised by the Secretary State to carry out inspections and audits for the purpose of the Regulations and including **any surveyor of ships** appointed under section 256 of the Merchant Shipping Act 1995.) An authorised person exercising functions under regulation 16 has the powers conferred on an **inspector** by section 259 of the Merchant Shipping Act 1995 (regulation 16(3)). (For notes on powers of inspectors, see B05b.4c.)
*   If an authorised person considers that a company, notwithstanding that it holds a DOC, is unable to operate ships without creating a risk of:
    *   **serious danger to safety of life**; or
    *   **serious damage to property**; or
    *   **serious harm to the environment**,
    *   or that the **company does not hold a DOC**,
    - he may **suspend the operation of ships by the company** until such time as the risk is removed or a DOC is held (regulation 16(1)(b)).
*   Where a service is to be suspended, **notice is to be served** on the company (regulation 16(1)(c)).
*   **Any authorised person may inspect any ship**, and any such inspection may include an **audit of its SMS** (regulation 16(2)(a)).
*   If an authorised person is satisfied that there is a failure to comply with the requirements of regulations 4 or 5, he may detain the ship (regulation 16(2)(b)). A Detention Notice must in this case be served.

D03a.1n Exemption (regulation 17)

*   The MCA may grant **exemptions** from any or all of the provisions of the Regulations for classes of cases or for individual cases on specified terms, and may alter or cancel any exemption granted.

D03a.1o Suspension or cancellation of DOC or SMC (regulations 18 & 19)

*   Regulation 18(1)(a) provides that the MCA may suspend or cancel any DOC or SMC issued by it or at its request under the Regulations where there is reason to believe that:
    *   the certificate was issued on false or erroneous information; or
    *   since any audit required by the Regulations, the management structure of either the company or the ship has changed substantively,
    - or where any audit of the company or a ship has revealed a failure to comply with regulation 4 (see D03a.1a).

* Any DOC or SMC issued by the MCA which has expired or been suspended or cancelled may be required to be surrendered.
* Regulation 18(3) provides that no person may:
    • intentionally alter a DOC or SMC;
    • in connection with any audit conducted under the Regulations, knowingly or recklessly furnish false information;
    • with intent to deceive, use, lend or allow to be used by another, a DOC or SMC;
    • fail to surrender a DOC or SMC required to be surrendered; or
    • in Scotland forge any DOC or SMC.

D03a.1p Defence (regulation 20)

* It will be a defence for a person charged with an offence under the Regulations to show that he took all reasonable precautions and exercised due diligence to avoid the commission of the offence.

D03a.1q MGN 40

* **MGN 40** informs ship operators and crews about the ISM Code and contains:
    • an introduction to the MS (International Safety Management (ISM) Code) Regulations 1998;
    • an introduction to the ISM Code (including, in Annex 1, the full text of IMO Resolution A.741(18) containing the text of the ISM Code itself);
    • a description of ships to which the Code applies and applicable dates;
    • notes on the Voluntary Certification Scheme;
    • in Annex 2, Guidance on Developing a Safety Management System;
    • in Annex 3, Guidance to Companies Operating Multi-Flagged Fleets and Supplementary Guidelines to Administrations;
    • other advice and useful references.

D03a.2 Prevention of Oil Pollution Regulations

* The **MS (Prevention of Oil Pollution) Regulations 1996** (SI 1996/2154) -
    - **give effect** in the UK to **Annex I of MARPOL 73/78**.
    - **apply to**:
        • **all UK ships of any tonnage** (although certain regulations apply to ships of specified tonnages);
        • **non-UK ships** (of any tonnage) while they are within the UK or UK territorial waters; and
        • **Government ships** (of any tonnage) registered in the UK, and UK Government non-registered ships of any tonnage "held for the purposes of HM Government in the UK" (regulation 2(1));
        • **offshore installations**, when engaged in the exploration, exploitation and associated offshore processing of sea bed mineral resources (regulation 32). Both fixed and **mobile installations** must comply with the requirements applicable to ships of 400gt and above other than oil tankers, notwithstanding that they are not proceeding on a voyage, except that they must be equipped as far as practicable with oil filtering equipment and an oil discharge monitoring and control system (as required by regulation 14) and tanks for oil residue (regulation 25(1) and (2)) and must keep a record of all operations involving oil or oily mixture discharges, in an approved form.
    - **do not apply to** warships, naval auxiliaries or other ships owned or operated by a State and being used solely for governmental non-commercial service (regulation 2(2)).
    - **apply in part** to non-tankers which carry bulk oil (regulation 2(4)).
    - **provide for exemptions** to be granted at the discretion of the MCA (regulation 2(3) and 2(5)).
    - **provide for an equivalent fitting, material, appliance or apparatus** to be permitted by the MCA (regulation 3).
    - **are amended by** the **MS (Prevention of Oil Pollution) (Amendment) Regulations 1997** (SI 1997/1910), which increased to **£250,000** the maximum fine on summary conviction for the offence of making an illegal discharge of oil from a ship and to **£255,000** the maximum amount of security an owner or master accused of the offence has to give to secure release of the ship. The Amendment Regulations also correct minor errors in the principal Regulations.
    - **are further amended by** the **MS (Prevention of Oil Pollution) (Amendment) Regulations 2000** (SI 2000/483), which make the **North West European waters area** a special area for the purposes of MARPOL

Annex I, and introduce new requirements specifying the intact stability criteria of tankers of 5,000 tons dwt and above in respect of which building contracts were placed on or after 1 February 1999.

* The Regulations are in **ten Parts** as follows.
* **Part I – General** contains the following regulations: **1**. Citation, commencement, interpretation and revocation; **2**. Application and exemptions; **3**. Equivalents.
* **Part II – Surveys, certificates and oil record book** contains the following regulations: **4**. Surveys before issue of a Certificate; **5**. Annual survey; **6**. Intermediate survey; **7**. Issue and duration of a Certificate; **8**. Responsibilities of owner and master; **9**. Procedure to be adopted when corrective action is necessary; **10**. Oil Record Book.
* **Part III – Requirements for control of operational pollution - control of discharge of oil** contains the following regulations: **11**. General exceptions; **12**. Ships other than oil tankers and machinery space bilges of oil tankers; **13**. Oil tankers; **14**. Oil filtering equipment and oil discharge monitoring and control system; **15**. Retention of oil on board; **16**. Methods for the prevention of oil pollution from ships operating in special areas.
* **Part IV – Requirements for the segregation of cargo** contains the following regulations: **17**. Interpretation of Part IV; **18**. General application; **19**. Protective location of segregated ballast spaces; **20**. Requirements for oil tankers with dedicated clean ballast tanks; **21**. Requirements for crude oil washing. **22**. Existing oil tankers engaged in specific trades; **23**. Existing oil tankers having special ballast arrangements; **24**. Segregation of oil and water ballast and carriage of oil in fore peak tanks; **25**. Tanks for oil residues (sludge); **26**. Pumping, piping and discharge arrangements of oil tankers.
* **Part V – Requirements for minimising oil pollution from oil tankers due to side and bottom damage** contains the following regulations: **27**. Interpretation; **28**. Limitation of size and arrangement of cargo tanks; **29**. Subdivision and stability.
* **Part VA**[18] **– Intact stability of oil tankers of 5,000 tons deadweight and above** contains regulation 29A
* **Part VI –Improved requirements for the design and construction of oil tankers against oil pollution in event of collision or stranding** contains the following regulations: **30**. New oil tankers (Building contracts after 5 July 1993); **31**. Existing oil tankers (Building contracts before 6 July 1993).
* **Part VII – Offshore installations** contains the following regulation: **32**. Requirements for offshore installations.
* **Part VIII – Prevention of pollution arising from an oil pollution accident** contains the following regulation: **33**. Shipboard oil pollution emergency plan.
* **Part IX – Powers to inspect and deny entry, detention and penalties** contains the following regulations: **34**. Power to inspect; **35**. Power to deny entry or detain; **36**. Penalties; **37**. Enforcement and application of fines.
* **Part X – Proceeding for pollution offences committed outside UK waters** contains the following regulations: **38**. Restriction on jurisdiction over offences outside UK limits; **39**. Suspensions of proceedings at flag State request; **40**. Supplementary.
* Regulations in Part II relating to certificates, surveys and Oil Record Books apply to **tankers of 150gt and above** and **non-tankers of 400gt and above**.
* Regulations in Part III relating to control of discharges of oil apply to **tankers and non-tankers of any tonnage**, unless stated otherwise in the regulations.
* For notes on Part II requirements relating to **surveys and certificates** see D04g.
* For notes on Part II requirements relating to **Oil Record Books** see D05b.2.
* For notes on Part III requirements relating to the **control of oil discharges** see H03a.
* For notes on Part VIII requirements relating to **Shipboard Oil Pollution Emergency Plans** (SOPEPs) see D04t.1a.

D03a.3 Load Line Regulations

* The **MS (Load Line) Regulations 1998** (SI 1998/2241) -
    - **replace** section 89 and Schedule 3 of the Merchant Shipping Act 1995, which previously gave effect in the UK to the Load Lines Convention.
    - **revoke** and replace the MS (Load Line) Rules 1968.
    - **are amended by** the MS (Load Line) (Amendment) Regulations 2000 (SI 2000/1335), which incorporate the amendments made to the Load Line Convention by the Protocol of 1988 (i.e. the amendments introducing the Harmonised System of Survey and Certification).
    - as amended, **give effect** in the UK to the provisions of the International Convention on Load Lines, 1966, as modified by the Protocol of 1988.
    - **apply** to UK ships wherever they are and to **non-UK ships** while they are **in UK waters** other than those mentioned below.
    - **do not apply** to warships, ships solely engaged in fishing, pleasure vessels, or ships which do not go to sea.

---

[18] Added by SI 2000/483.

- **do not apply to** ships **under 80 net tons** falling within one of the classes specified in the next paragraph engaged solely in the **coasting trade**, and, subject to regulation 4(3), not carrying cargo. (Under regulation 4(3), a ship listed in the next paragraph will be **excepted** from the provisions of the Regulations while carrying cargo in accordance with the terms, if any, of the ship's Passenger Certificate expressly authorising the carriage of cargo.)

* The **classes of ships under 80nt in the coastal trade** to which the Regulations do not apply are:
   • tugs or salvage ships;
   • hopper barges or dredgers;
   • ships used by or on behalf of –
      ▪ a general or local lighthouse authority for the purpose of the authority's functions as such;
      ▪ a Government department for fishery protection purposes, or a local fisheries committee for the regulation of sea fisheries within its district;
      ▪ a Government department for fishery or scientific research; or
      ▪ the Secretary of State for Defence (i.e. the MoD) for the purpose of ensuring safety in the use of firing ranges or weapons at sea (i.e. "range safety craft") ; and
      ▪ ships in respect of which Passenger Certificates are in force specifying limits beyond which the ship must not ply, and which operate solely within those limits. (These small coastal passenger ships will be excepted from the provisions of the Regulations only while carrying cargo in accordance with the terms, if any, of the ship's Passenger Certificate expressly authorising the carriage of cargo.)

* A number of the **detailed technical requirements and specifications** of the Regulations are contained in **MSN 1752**.

* **Further information on load line legislation** can be found in *Instructions to Surveyors of Load Line Ships*, published by the Stationery Office.

D03a.3a General compliance with Load Line Regulations

* A UK ship to which the Load Line Regulations apply must at all times be in compliance with **regulation 6(3)**, which provides that a ship **may not be so loaded that**:
   • **if the ship is in salt water and has no list**, the appropriate load line on each side of the ship is submerged; or
   • **in any other case** (e.g. where the ship is in dock water or fresh water), the appropriate load line on each side of the ship would be submerged if the ship were in salt water and had no list.

* The requirements of regulation 6(3) **apply in port as well as at sea**, and **the fact that a vessel is not intending to proceed to sea is immaterial**. The only exception to this rule is in respect of a vessel that is to proceed down-river to sea, which may submerge her marks to allow for the consumption of fuel, water, etc. during the river passage.

* Regulation 6(4) provides that a ship may **not proceed to sea** in contravention of regulation 6(3).

* A UK ship to which the Load Line Regulations apply must at all times be in compliance with **regulation 6(3)**.

* For notes on the provisions of the Regulations relating to **surveys and certification**, see D04i.

* For notes on the **requirements of the Regulations to be complied with before proceeding to sea**, see I07b.

D03a.4 Minimum Standards of Safety Communications Regulations

* The **MS (Minimum Standards of Safety Communications) Regulations 1997** (SI 1997/529) -
   - **implement** those provisions in **Council Directive 94/58/EC** on the minimum level of training for seafarers which require means of safe communication among the crew, between the crew and shore-based authorities, and between the crew and passengers on passenger ships in emergency situations.
   - **are amended** by the **MS (Minimum Standards of Safety Communications) (Amendment) Regulations 1999** (SI 1999/1704) to take account of changes made to Council Directive 94/58/EC by **Council Directive 98/35**. (The major amendment was a completely new regulation 5 – Duty to ensure safe communication.)
   - apply (under regulation 3) to:
      • **all UK ships** (of any type and any size); and
      • **non-UK passenger ships** which start or finish a voyage in the UK.
   - **do not apply** to warships, naval auxiliaries, other Crown-owned or Crown-operated ships on governmental non-commercial service, fishing vessels and pleasure vessels.

* In the Regulations **"company"** includes an individual, and in relation to a ship means the owner of the ship or any other organisation or person such as the manager, or the bareboat charterer, who has assumed the responsibility for the operation of the ship from the owner and who, on assuming such responsibility, has agreed to take over all the duties and responsibilities imposed on the company by the Regulations annexed to the STCW Convention (regulation 2(1) as amended).

* Regulation 5(1) provides that **the company and master must** ensure that on **every ship**:

- there are at all times means in place for **effective oral communication related to safety** between all members of the ship's crew, particularly with regard to the correct and timely reception and understanding of messages and instructions (regulation 5(1)(a)); and
- there are **adequate means of communication** between the **ship** and the **shore-based authorities** in the **English** language (regulation 5(1)(b)).
* Regulation 5(2)(a) and 5(2)(b) apply only to **passenger ships** (see D03b.8).
* Regulation 5(3) applies only to UK **oil tankers**, **chemical tankers** and **liquefied gas tankers** (including Government tankers) (see D03c.2c, D03d.2c and D03e.2c).

D03a.5 Navigation bridge visibility

* The **MS (Safety of Navigation) Regulations 2002** (SI 2002/1473) (see H01f.2) –
  - **revoke** and replace the MS (Navigation Bridge Visibility) Regulations 1998 (SI 1998/1419) and the MS (Passenger Ships of Classes IV, V, VI & VI(A) Bridge Visibility) Regulations 1992 (SI 1992/2357).
  - **require compliance** by a ship to which the Regulations apply with **all paragraphs of SOLAS regulation V/22**.
* **SOLAS regulation V/22.1** provides that ships of not less than 45m in length as defined in SOLAS regulation III/3.12, built on or after 1 July 1998, must meet the requirements of paragraphs 1.1 to 1.9 of regulation V/22, which set out the technical requirements relating to visibility aspects of bridge design.
* **SOLAS regulation V/22.2** provides that ships built before 1 July 1998 must, where applicable, meet the requirements of paragraphs 1.1 and 1.2. However, structural alterations or additional equipment need not be required. The regulation is printed, with guidance notes, in the which is published on the MCA website in the "Campaigns and Publications" pages.
* Regulation V/22, together with the MCA's guidance notes in its 2002 SOLAS V publication (see H01f.2a), supersedes M.760.

D03a.6 Ship security requirements of SOLAS and ISPS Code

* SOLAS chapter XI-2 (Special Measures to Enhance Maritime Security) applies (from 1 July 2004), under regulation 2, to the following types of ships engaged on international voyages:
  - passenger ships, including high-speed passenger craft;
  - cargo ships, including high-speed craft, of 500 gross tonnage and upwards; and
  - mobile offshore drilling units.
* SOLAS regulation XI-2/4.2 provides that **ships** (of the above types) must comply with the **relevant requirements of chapter XI-2** and of **Part A of the ISPS Code**, taking into account the **guidance** given in Part B of the ISPS Code. Ships' compliance will be verified and certified as provided for in Part A of the ISPS Code.
* The relevant requirements of chapter XI-2 referred to above include requirements for:
  - a **ship security alert system** (regulation 6) (see D04t.10c); and
  - the ship to keep **records relating to security measures** (regulation 9.2.3) (see D05b.9).
* The relevant requirements of **Part A of the ISPS Code** referred to above include requirements for:
  - the making of a **ship security assessment** (see C03c.8b);
  - ships to operate at a specified **security level** (see D03a.6a);
  - the drawing up of a **Ship Security Plan** (see D04t.10a);
  - the issue, following audit, of an **International Ship Security Certificate** or an **Interim International Ship Security Certificate** (see D04t.10b);
  - **records** to be kept onboard (see D05b.9);
  - the appointment and training of a **ship security officer** (SSO) (see E03d.10);
  - the holding of **ship security training and drills** (see E02d.9); and
  - the completion of a **Declaration of Security** (see I01k.2).

D03a.6a Security levels

* ISPS Code, part A, section 4.1 provides that, subject to the provisions of SOLAS regulations XI-2/3 and XI-2/7, SOLAS Contracting Governments must set **security levels** and provide **guidance** for protection from security incidents. **Higher security levels** indicate greater likelihood of occurrence of a security incident.
* The **setting of the security level** applicable at any time to a **ship at sea** is normally the responsibility of the ship's **flag State Administration**.

* The **setting of the security level** applicable at any time to a **ship arriving at or staying at a port** is the responsibility of the **port State**.
* A **Company** may choose to operate its ships at a specified security level even if international or national regulations do not explicitly require it to do so.
* **Three security levels** are defined in ISPS Code, part A, section 2.1, as follows:
  * **Security level 1** means the level for which minimum appropriate protective security measures must be maintained at all times.
  * **Security level 2** means the level for which appropriate additional protective security measures must be maintained for a period of time as a result of heightened risk of a security incident.
  * **Security level 3** means the level for which further specific protective security measures must be maintained for a limited period of time when a security incident is probable or imminent, although it may not be possible to identify the specific target.
* ISPS Code, part A, section 7.2 provides that **at security level 1**, the following **activities** must be carried out, through appropriate measures, on all ships, taking into account the guidance given in part B of the ISPS Code, in order to identify and take preventive measures against security incidents:
  * ensuring the performance of all ship security duties;
  * controlling access to the ship;
  * controlling the embarkation of persons and their effects;
  * monitoring restricted areas to ensure that only authorized persons have access;
  * monitoring of deck areas and areas surrounding the ship;
  * supervising the handling of cargo and ship's stores; and
  * ensuring that security communication is readily available.
* **At security level 2, additional protective measures**, as specified in the Ship Security Plan, must be implemented for each activity detailed in section 7.2, taking into account the guidance given in part B of the Code.
* **At security level 3, further specific protective measures**, as specified in the Ship Security plan, must be implemented for each activity detailed in section 7.2, taking into account the guidance given in part B of the Code.
* SOLAS Contracting Governments (i.e. flag States and port States), when they set **security level 3**, must issue, as necessary, **appropriate instructions** and must **provide security related information** to the ships and port facilities that may be affected (ISPS Code, part A, section 4.2).
* ISPS Code, part A, section 7.1 provides that a **ship** is required to act upon the **security levels** set by SOLAS Contracting Governments (i.e. flag States and port States).
* ISPS Code, part A, section 7.5 provides that whenever security level 2 or 3 is set by the Administration, the **ship must acknowledge receipt** of the instructions on change of the security level.
* ISPS Code, part A, section 7.9.1 provides that when advising such ships of the applicable security level, a SOLAS **Contracting Government** must, taking into account the guidance given in ISPS Code, part B, also **advise those ships of any security measure** that they should take and, if appropriate, of **measures that have been taken** by the Contracting Government to provide protection against the threat.

D03a.7 Publications applicable to all ship types

* Publications containing **standards of good operational practice** applicable to **all ship types** are shown in the following table.

Document title	Publisher
Bridge Procedures Guide	ICS
Bridge Watchkeeping - A Practical Guide	Nautical Institute
Code of Safe Working Practices for Merchant Seamen	The Stationery Office (tSO)
Code of Safe Working Practices for Merchant Seamen, The	The Stationery Office (tSO)
Drug Trafficking and Drug Abuse: Guidelines for Owners and Masters on Recognition and Detection	ICS
Guide to Helicopter/Ship Operations	ICS
Guidelines on the Application of the IMO International Safety Management (ISM) Code	ICS/ISF
IAMSAR Manual, Volume III	IMO/ICAO
International Shipboard Work Hour Regulations	ISF
Manual on Oil Pollution	IMO
Mariner's Role in Collecting Evidence, The	Nautical Institute
Nautical Institute on Command, The	Nautical Institute
Peril at Sea and Salvage - A Guide for Masters	ICS/OCIMF
Pirates and Armed Robbers: A Master's Guide	ISF
Port State Control: A Guide for Masters	ICS/ISF
Shipmaster's Business Companion, The	Nautical Institute
Shipping and the Environment: A Code of Practice	ICS
Ships Routeing	IMO

D03b OPERATIONAL REQUIREMENTS APPLICABLE TO UK PASSENGER SHIPS AND RO-RO FERRIES

D03b.1 Applicable safety management code and regulations

* **Two safety management codes** are applicable to UK passenger ships. Depending on the statutory class of the ship, a UK passenger ship must comply with either -
  * the **International Safety Management Code (ISM Code)** (which is outlined in C04b); or
  * the **Safety Management Code for Domestic Passenger Ships** (which is outlined in C04c).
* **UK passenger ships of Classes I, II and II(A)** must comply with the **International Safety Management (ISM) Code**, which is given effect in the UK by -
  * the **MS (ISM Code) (Ro-Ro Passenger Ferries) Regulations 1997** (SI 1997/3022) in relation to ro-ro passenger ferries on regular services to or from or within the UK; and
  * the **MS (International Safety Management (ISM) Code) Regulations 1998** (SI 1998/1561) in relation to all other UK ships except passenger ships of Classes III to VI(A).
* **UK passenger ships of Classes III to VI(A)** must comply with the **Safety Management Code for Domestic Passenger Ships**, which is implemented by the **MS (Domestic Passenger Ships) (Safety Management Code) Regulations 2001** (SI 2001/3209).
* **Regulations** implementing the two codes, associated **M Notices**, and chief *Shipmaster's Business Companion* **references**, are summarised in the following table.

Code	UK Regulations giving effect to Code	Ship types to which the Regulations apply	Relevant M Notice	SBC ref.
International Management Code for the Safe Operation of Ships and for Pollution Prevention (ISM Code)	MS (International Safety Management (ISM) Code) Regulations 1998 (SI 1998/1561)	(1) **Passenger ships of Classes I, II and II(A)**; (2) oil tankers, chemical tankers, gas carriers, bulk carriers, and cargo high-speed craft, of 500gt or more and which engage in international voyages; (3) other cargo ships and mobile offshore drilling units (MODUs) of 500gt or more which engage in international voyages, from 1 July 2002 - **other than ro-ro passenger ferries on regular services to or from or within the UK**	MGN 40	C04b (Code) D03a.1 (Regs)
International Management Code for the Safe Operation of Ships and for Pollution Prevention (ISM Code)	MS (ISM Code) (Ro-Ro Passenger Ferries) Regulations 1997 (SI 1997/3022)	Ships to which Council Regulation (EC) No. 3051/95 on the safety management of roll-on/roll-off passenger ferries (ro-ro ferries) applies, i.e. **ro-ro passenger ferries on regular services to or from or within the UK**	MGN 40	C04b (Code) D03b.1a (Regs)
Safety Management Code for Domestic Passenger Ships (DSM Code)	MS (Domestic Passenger Ships) (Safety Management Code) Regulations 2001 (SI 2001/3209)	**Passenger ships of Classes III to VI(A)** - **other than** ships to which Council Regulation (EC) No. 3051/95 on the safety management of roll-on/roll-off passenger ferries (ro-ro ferries) applies, i.e. ro-ro passenger ferries on regular services to or from or within the UK.	MSN 1754 MGN 158	C04c (Code) D03b.1b (Regs)

D03b.1a ISM Code (Ro-Ro Passenger Ferries) Regulations

* The **MS (ISM Code) (Ro-Ro Passenger Ferries) Regulations 1997** (SI 1997/3022) –
  * **came into force** on 20 January 1998 (i.e. 6 months before the ISM Code came into international force).
  * **apply** to any **company** operating at least one ro-ro ferry to or from a port in the UK on a regular service, and to any **ship** operating on such a service (regulation 2(4)).
  * **provide for** the enforcement of **Council Regulation (EC) No. 3051/95 on the safety management of ro-ro passenger ferries**, which implements SOLAS Chapter IX (Management for the Safe Operation of Ships) for all classes of ro-ro passenger ferries on services to and from the UK.
  * **are explained** in **MGN 40**.
* **Regulation 3 (Duty of companies to comply with Article 4.1 of the Council Regulation)** provides that any company which fails to comply with Article 4.1 of the Council Regulation (Duty to comply with the ISM Code) will be guilty of an offence, and liable on summary conviction to a fine not exceeding the statutory maximum, or on conviction on indictment, to imprisonment for a term not exceeding two years, or a fine, or both.
* **Regulation 4** contains the MCA's powers of inspection, suspension of service and detention. Any "authorised person" may **inspect** any ship (including auditing its Safety Management System) and may **audit** the Safety Management System of any company (regulation 4(1)(a)). (An "authorised person" will generally be an MCA surveyor.)

* If an authorised person considers that the Company, notwithstanding that it holds a Document of Compliance, cannot operate a ro-ro ferry on a regular service to or from a port in the UK for reasons of risks of serious danger to safety of life or property, or environment, the **operation of the service** (which includes **all ships** operated by the Company on that service) may be **suspended** (regulation 4(1)(b)).

* If an authorised person is satisfied, on inspecting a ship, that there is a failure to comply with the requirements of the Council Regulation he may **detain** the ship. Any notice of detention must contain the reasons for detention (regulation 4(1)(c)).

* Regulation 5(1) permits the MCA to **suspend or cancel a Document of Compliance or Safety Management Certificate** where there is reason to believe that the certificate or document was issued on false or erroneous information, or since any ISM Code audit the management structure of either the company or the ship has changed substantively.

D03b.1b Domestic Passenger Ships (Safety Management Code) Regulations

* The **MS (Domestic Passenger Ships) (Safety Management Code) Regulations 2001** (SI 2001/3209) -
  - **establish** a common standard for the safe operation of passenger ships employed in the domestic trade.
  - **are the result** of an MCA proposal to develop a **derivative of the ISM Code** for vessels of Classes III to VI(A) (which are not required to comply with the ISM Code). This proposal was subsequently endorsed by the Thames Safety Inquiry Report[19].
  - **apply to** passenger ships, other than ships engaged on international voyages, of Classes III, IV, V, VI and VI(A) (regulation 3(1)). (For a description of these Classes, see D04c.2.)
  - **do not apply** to those companies and ships to which **Council Regulation (EC) No. 3051/95** on the safety management of roll-on/roll-off passenger ferries (ro-ro ferries) applies (i.e. companies and ships to which the ISM Code (Ro-Ro Passenger Ferries) Regulations apply) (regulation 3(2)).
  - permit the granting of **exemptions** by the MCA (regulation 4).
  - **require a Company to comply** with the requirements of the Safety Management Code for Domestic Passenger Ships (DSM Code) as it applies to that company and to any ship owned by it or for which it has operational responsibility (regulation 5).

* A **company must** comply with the requirements of the Safety Management Code for Domestic Passenger Ships as it applies to that company and to any ship owned by it or for which it has operational responsibility (regulation 5). "**Company**" means the owner or any other organisation or person such as the operator, manager, or bareboat charterer, who has assumed the responsibility for the operation of the ship from the owner (regulation 2).

* From the first date on or after 1 November 2001 on which a Passenger Certificate is issued to a ship, the company owning the ship or having operational responsibility for it must hold in relation to that ship a valid **Domestic Ship Safety Management Certificate** (regulation 6(1)).

* Where an authorised person has audited the ship's Safety Management System and is satisfied that the SMS meets the objectives in MSN 1754 and, so far as the SMS is being operated, it is being implemented effectively, the MCA may issue a **Domestic Ship Safety Management Certificate (DSSMC)** which, subject to regulation 6(3) and regulation 9(3), will be valid until the expiry of the ship's Passenger Certificate (regulation 6(2)).

* Under regulation 6(3) a **Domestic Ship Safety Management Certificate will cease to be valid**:
  • if an authorised person has not, within the period between 3 and 6 months after issue of the ship's Domestic Ship Safety Management Certificate, audited the ship's SMS; or
  • if an authorised person who audits the ship's SMS in accordance with regulation 6(3)(a) is not satisfied that it is being implemented effectively.

* Where a Domestic Ship Safety Management Certificate has **ceased to be valid** under regulation 5(3), the MCA may endorse it as valid until the expiry of the ship's Passenger Certificate if an authorised person who audits the SMS after the Certificate has ceased to be valid is satisfied that the SMS is being implemented effectively (regulation 6(4)).

* A company must ensure that a valid **Domestic Ship Safety Management Certificate** held in relation to the ship is carried **on board each ship** owned by it or for which it has operational responsibility (regulation 6(5)).

* The **master** of a ship must operate that ship in accordance with the Safety Management System on the basis of which the Domestic Ship Safety Management Certificate was issued in relation to the ship (regulation 7).

* A **company** must in relation to each ship owned by it or for which it has operational responsibility **designate a person** who will be responsible for monitoring the safe operation of the ship and, so far as it may affect safety, the efficient operation of the ship (regulation 8(1)).

* Under regulation 8(2) the **designated person must**, in particular -

---

[19] The **Thames Safety Inquiry**, conducted by Lord Justice Clarke between September and December 1999, was a response to the *Marchioness/Bowbelle* accident. Recommendation 27.13 of the Report states: "The proposed Safety Management Code for Domestic Passenger Ships should be introduced at the earliest opportunity. If necessary, additional surveys or inspections should be carried out to ensure proper compliance with the Code".

take such steps as are necessary to ensure compliance with the safety management system on the basis of which the Domestic Ship Safety Management Certificate was issued in relation to the ship, and

ensure that proper provision is made for the ship to be adequately manned, equipped and maintained, so that it is fit to operate in accordance with that safety management system and with any enactment relating to safety applicable to the ship.

* The **company** must ensure that a **designated person** is provided with sufficient authority and resources and has appropriate knowledge and sufficient experience of the operation of ships to enable him to comply with his responsibilities as above (regulation 8(3)).

* **MSN 1754** sets out the **statutory instructions** regarding safety management of domestic passenger ships of Classes III to VI(A). It sets out the **objectives** of the Code, **responsibilities** of the master and Designated Person, requirements for **personnel and training**, **onboard procedures**, **preparation for emergencies**, **reporting of accidents**, **maintenance** of the ship and equipment, **certification** requirements, and requirements relating to **fees** and **exemptions**.

* **MGN 158** contains **guidance** to owners and operators of domestic passenger ships on how to comply with the requirements of the DSM Code.

D03b.2 Weighing of Goods Vehicles Regulations

* The **MS (Weighing of Goods Vehicles and other Cargo) Regulations 1988** (SI 1988/1275) apply to any UK ro/ro passenger ship operating as a **Class II or II(A) ship** (regulation 1(4)).

* **Regulation 2** specifies the **requirement for weighing of cargo items, and use of weights for stability calculations**. Subject to certain exceptions, **no qualifying cargo may be loaded** onto a Class II or II(A) ship when sailing between certain ports and destinations (as listed below) unless:
  * the **weight of the cargo has previously been determined** in accordance with the Regulations;
  * **arrangements** at the port in question **to prevent fraud** by changing the composition of the cargo after weighing have been **approved by the MCA**;
  * if weighed outside the port premises, a **certificate of weighing** has been supplied; and
  * there are reliable arrangements in place for the **retention**, within the port premises or on the ship, **of records or documents** showing compliance with the weighing regulations.

* **Qualifying cargo items** are listed in regulation 1(3) as:
  * **goods vehicles** (including their **trailers** where any), of which the weight, including that of the load, water, fuel, tools, etc., or the maximum gross weight, exceeds 7.5 tonnes; and
  * any **other unit of cargo**, other than a bus, if the weight exceeds 7.5 tonnes, unless it forms part of a goods vehicle or trailer.

  Lorries, **trailers**, **semi-trailers** and **combinations** are "qualifying cargo" only if their actual or gross weight is more than 7.5 tonnes.

* The applicable **sailings and destinations** are:
  * sailings from a UK port for a non-UK port;
  * sailings from a port in Great Britain for a port in Northern Ireland, or vice versa;
  * sailings from Scrabster for all destinations;
  * sailings from Stromness for destinations in Shetland or the Scottish mainland;
  * sailings from Aberdeen for all destinations;
  * sailings from Lerwick for destinations in Orkney or the Scottish mainland;
  * sailings from Ullapool for all destinations;
  * sailings from Stornoway for destinations on the Scottish mainland; and
  * sailings from Oban for all destinations.

* The **weights** of qualifying cargo items obtained in compliance with regulation 2(1) must be used for the purposes of any ship stability calculations required to be carried out under the Merchant Shipping Acts (regulation 2(2)). (Breach of this requirement is an offence by the master.)

* **Regulations 3 to 7** deal with the accuracy of weighing machines, and persons qualified to use them, the manner of weighing, the place of weighing, and fraud.

* **M.1393** gives guidance on the application and interpretation of the Regulations.

D03b.3 Code of Practice on the Stowage and Securing of Vehicles on Ro/Ro Ships

* The **Code of Practice on the Stowage and Securing of Vehicles on Ro/Ro Ships** -
    * is the popular title for a **non-statutory code of practice** bearing the title "Roll-on/Roll-off Ships – Stowage and Securing of Vehicles – Code of Practice".
    * is published by the MCA and printed by HMSO (now The Stationery Office) under ISBN 0 11 550995 X.
    * contains **guidance** on the stowage and securing of vehicles and also covers health and safety matters.
    * incorporates IMO Resolutions A.489(XII), A.533(13), A.581(14) and MSC/Circ.385.
* **M.1445** advises that all parties concerned with the operation of ro-ro ships **should** take account of the Code of Practice.

D03b.4 Closing of openings provisions of Passenger Ship Construction Regulations

* The **MS (Passenger Ship Construction: Ships of Classes I, II and II(A)) Regulations 1998** (SI 1998/2514) revoked the MS (Closing of Openings in Enclosed Superstructures and in Bulkheads above the Bulkhead Deck) Regulations 1988 (SI 1988/317) and the MS (Closing of Openings in Enclosed Superstructures and in Bulkheads above the Bulkhead Deck) (Application to Non-UK Ships) Regulations 1988(SI 1988/642)[20] .
* The Regulations impose precise requirements for the **control of cargo and vehicle loading doors** fitted in the hull and enclosed superstructures above the bulkhead deck and for the **supervision of their closing**. They also impose requirements for the **control of watertight and weathertight doors fitted in bulkheads above the bulkhead decks**, as outlined in the following sub-sections.
* **MGN 245** promulgates MAIB recommendations for the **inspection of shell loading doors** on ro-ro ferries. **Records** of such inspections should be retained for at least 12 months.

D03b.4a Means of closing openings in watertight bulkheads and operating sliding watertight doors

* Every door fitted to an opening in a watertight bulkhead must comply with the specifications in either section 3 or 4 of Schedule 4 to MSN 1698, as appropriate (regulation 21(1)).
* In ships built before 1 February 1992, **doors not complying with section 4 of MSN 1698 must be closed before each voyage commences**, and must be kept closed during navigation. The **time of opening** these doors in port and of **closing them before departure** must be entered in the **Official Log Book** (see D05a.4 and D05a.10).

D03b.4b Closure of hull openings, watertight doors and openings in watertight bulkheads

* Under regulation 22(1), the following closing appliances are to be **securely closed before the ship proceeds on any voyage** and are to be **kept closed** until the ship has been secured at a berth or anchorage:
    * **watertight doors** below the margin line fitted in bulkheads which are required to be watertight and which separate cargo spaces;
    * **sidescuttles** below the margin line which can be opened;
    * **deadlights** of any such sidescuttles which (a) will not be accessible while the ship is at sea or (b) which are situated in spaces appropriated for use sometimes for the carriage of cargo and sometimes for use by passengers, while such spaces are being used for the carriage of cargo; and
    * **gangway and cargo loading doors** below the margin line[21].
* No closing appliance listed above is to be considered as securely closed unless it is locked (regulation 22(2)).
* Under regulation 22(3), watertight doors below the bulkhead deck fitted in bulkheads which are required to be watertight, other than those doors in regulation 22(1), must be kept closed while the ship is on any voyage **except** –
    * when opened in accordance with the procedures laid down in **written operational instructions**;
    * when opened for the purpose of **drill** as required by regulation 24; or
    * when any such door is opened on the **express authority of the master for a specific purpose**, for no longer than a specific period of time and on condition that all other watertight doors below the margin line, except those opened in accordance with procedures in written operational instructions, are closed during that period.
* The **operational instructions** referred to above must be kept on board the ship at all times in the custody of the master (regulation 22(4)).

---

[20] These Regulations applied the requirements of the Closing of Openings Regulations to non-UK ro-ro passenger ships while they were in a UK port.
[21] The "**margin line**" means a line at least 76 millimetres below the upper surface of the bulkhead deck at the side of a subdivided ship.

* Any watertight door which may be opened in accordance with the requirements of the **Regulations must be kept clear of obstructions** which might prevent its rapid closure (regulation 24(5)).
* Notwithstanding the requirements of regulation 24, in an **emergency situation** the master may authorise the opening or closing of any watertight door, provided he is satisfied such action is essential for the overall safety of the ship (regulation 24(6)).
* Every **portable plate** closing an opening below the bulkhead deck in any portion of the internal structure of the ship which is required to be watertight **must be fitted in place before the ship proceeds** on any voyage and must be kept in place, except in the case of urgent necessity, until the ship has been secured at a berth or anchorage. In replacing any such plate all reasonable precautions must be taken to ensure that the joints are watertight (regulation 24(7)).
* Both the watertight cover and the automatic non-return valve of a chute or other similar device on the ship with its inboard opening below the margin line **must be kept closed and secured** when the device is not in use (regulation 24(8)).
* For notes on **Official Log Book entries** required in connection with opening and closing of watertight doors, etc., see D05a.4 and D05a.10.

D03b.4c Marking of doors, mechanisms and valves

* In every ship built on or after 25 May 1980 all doors, mechanisms and valves connected with the damage control and watertight integrity of the ship must be **suitably marked** to ensure that they can be properly used to ensure maximum safety (regulation 23).

D03b.4d Drills in closing and inspections of watertight doors, side scuttles, etc.

* All **deadlights** which are accessible, all **watertight doors** to which regulation 22(3) applies[22], all **valves** and **closing mechanisms of scuppers**, and the **devices** referred to in regulation 22(8) (i.e. the watertight cover and the automatic non-return valve of any chute or other similar device on the ship having its inboard opening below the margin line) **must be opened and closed** for the purposes of **drill** at intervals of not more than **7 days** and, if the ship is intended to remain at sea for more than 7 days, **immediately before proceeding to sea** (regulation 24(1)).
* All **watertight doors** fitted in bulkheads required to be watertight which may be opened for the working of the ship in accordance with the requirements of regulation 22(3) **must be opened and closed** for the purpose of **drill** once **every 24 hours** (regulation 24(2)).
* Regulation 24(3) provides that all closing appliances and devices referred to in regulation 22(1), (2) and (8) must be **inspected** by a person appointed by the master for that purpose -
    * **before the ship proceeds** on any voyage; and
    * if the ship is intended to remain at sea for more than 7 days, at intervals of not more than **7 days**, except when they are not accessible.
* Regulation 24(4) provides that the following **closing appliances and mechanisms** must be **inspected** at intervals of not more than **7 days** by a person appointed for that purpose, either generally or on any particular occasion, by the master:
    all watertight doors other than those of the type described in regulation 22(1) (i.e. those below the margin line fitted in bulkheads which are required to be watertight and which separate cargo spaces);
    all mechanisms, indicators and warning devices connected with such doors;
    all valves, the closing of which is necessary to make watertight any compartment below the margin line; and
    all valves, the operation of which is necessary for the efficient operation of damage control cross-connections.
* Suitable **notices and signs** must be provided on, or in the vicinity of, all the closing appliances referred to in the last paragraph to indicate, as necessary, the **procedures for operating** the appliances, the **purpose** of the controls and any **precautions** to be observed (regulation 24(5)).
* For notes on **Official Log Book entries** required in connection with **drills for operation of watertight doors, etc.**, see D05a.4 and D05a.10.

D03b.4e Instructions for the use of watertight doors

* All members of the crew who would have occasion to use any watertight doors must be **instructed** in their safe operation. In addition, **written instructions on the safe operation of the doors**, given in easily understood terms and illustrated wherever possible, must be available to all crew members. These instructions must be based on the **operational instructions** in regulation 22(3) (regulation 25).

---

[22] The watertight doors referred to in regulation 22(3) are those below the bulkhead deck fitted in bulkheads which are required to be watertight, except those which separate cargo spaces.

D03b.4f Closure of main loading doors

* Under regulation 28(1), the following loading doors must be closed and locked before the ship leaves its berth and to be kept closed and locked until it has been secured at its next berth:
  * **gangway and cargo loading doors** fitted in the shell or boundaries of enclosed superstructures;
  * **bow visors**;
  * **weathertight ramps** used instead of doors for closing openings for cargo or vehicle loading;
  * cargo loading **doors in the collision bulkhead**.
* This requirement is subject to the proviso in regulation 28(2) that where a bow visor or a weathertight ramp cannot be opened or closed while the ship is at its berth, it **may be left open while the ship approaches or draws away** from its berth, but **only so far as is necessary to enable the door to be then open or closed**, but subject to the limitation that in no case may such a door be left open when the ship is more than **one ship's length** from the cargo loading or discharging position of its berth.
* The requirement does not apply to **small doors** intended to be used for pilot access, fuelling or other operational matters and not intended to be used by passengers or for loading cargo.

D03b.4g Closure of bulkheads on the ro-ro deck

* All **transverse or longitudinal bulkheads** which are taken into account as effective to **confine seawater accumulated on the ro-ro deck** must be **closed and locked** before the ship leaves the berth, and must remain locked until the ship has been secured at its next berth (regulation 29).
* Notwithstanding the above requirement, **accesses** through such bulkheads may be opened for a period sufficient to allow through passage, on the **express authority of the master** provided that this is required for the essential working of the ship.

D03b.4h Supervision and reporting of closure

* Before the ship proceeds on a voyage an **officer** appointed by the master must **verify that every loading door has been closed and locked**, and **report** the fact to the **master or OOW**. The ship may not proceed on a voyage until the report has been received by the master or OOW (regulation 30).

D03b.4i Closure of watertight and weathertight doors in bulkheads

* **Watertight or weathertight doors above the margin line** (except doors fitted in collision bulkheads to which regulation 28 applies) which are fitted **in bulkheads which are required to be watertight or weathertight** and which separate or form the **boundary of cargo spaces** must be closed and locked before the ship leaves its berth and must be kept closed and locked until the ship has been secured at its next berth (regulation 31).
* **Other watertight or weathertight doors above the margin line** fitted in the shell or in bulkheads which are required to be watertight or weathertight, other than those already mentioned, must be kept closed while the ship is on any voyage except when opened on the express authority of the master.

D03b.4j Opening of doors in an emergency

* Notwithstanding the above requirements, **gangway and cargo loading doors** may be opened in an **emergency** but only when the master considers such opening will not put the safety of the ship at risk (regulation 33).

D03b.4k Official Log Book entries

* For entries concerning watertight doors, etc. in the **Official Log Book Part II – Passenger ships only**, see D05a.10.

D03b.4l List of berths (Berth List)

* Regulation 35(1) requires the owner to ensure that the ship is provided with a **list** (known as the "**Berth List**") of all **loading berths** at which it is intended the ship will load or discharge cargo or vehicles. The Berth List must list separately for each port which the ship is intended to visit to load or discharge cargo or vehicles:
  * the loading berths at which the ship can comply with the requirement of regulation 28(1) without relying on the proviso thereto; and

- where it is intended that the ship will so load or discharge in the manner permitted by the proviso, the loading berths at which it will so load or discharge. (These berths must be listed separately.)
* A **copy** of the Berth List must be sent to the **MCA**.
* No ro-ro passenger ship may, except in an emergency, load or discharge cargo or vehicles through a loading door at any berth which is not listed on the ship's Berth List.

D03b.4m Written instructions

* The **owner** must ensure that the ship is provided with **written instructions**, approved by the Certifying Authority, concerning the doors referred to in the Regulations (regulation 36).

D03b.5 Ro-ro passenger ferry stability standards

D03b.5a SOLAS ro-ro passenger ship stability standards

* The capsize of the ro-ro ferry *Herald of Free Enterprise* in March 1987 brought about improvements in the damaged stability standards applicable to ro-ro passenger ferries under SOLAS chapter II-1. However, the original "SOLAS 90" damaged stability standard was for application only to new ships built after 29 April 1990. Following further amendments to SOLAS, improved damaged stability standards are now applicable to existing ro-ro passenger ships under regulation 8-1 of SOLAS chapter II-1.
* **Regulation 8-1 of SOLAS chapter II-1** provides that ro-ro passenger ships built before I July 1997 must comply with regulation II-1/8 (stability of passenger ships in damaged condition), as amended by resolution MSC.12(56), not later than a date of compliance which is tabulated in the regulation according to the value of the ship's "A/Amax"[23] and which ranges from 1 October 1998 (for ships with an A/Amax of less than 85%) to 1 October 2005 (for ships with an A/Amax of 97.5% or more). In the case of a ro-ro passenger ship carrying 400 persons or more (including crew), regulation 8-2 applies notwithstanding the provisions of regulations 8 and 8-1, and the compliance date is modified so that ships with an A/Amax of 97.5% need not comply with the new standard until 1 October 2010.

D03b.5b Stockholm Agreement

- is the common name for the **Agreement Concerning Specific Stability Requirements for Ro-Ro Passenger Ships Undertaking Regular Scheduled International Voyages Between or To or From Designated Ports in North West Europe and the Baltic Sea.**
- is a **regional agreement** which came into force in April 1997, having been signed at Stockholm in 1996 by 8 European States following the loss in 1994 of the Baltic ferry *Estonia*.
- makes it **mandatory** for ro-ro passenger ships, operating on **scheduled international voyages** to and from ports in a specified area of North West Europe and the Baltic Sea, to be able to meet the **SOLAS 90 survivability standard** with **50cm of water** on the vehicle deck (which is a higher standard than the SOLAS 90 standard). All ro-ro ferries must attain the standard by 31 October 2002.
- is given effect in the UK by the **MS (Ro-Ro Passenger Ship Survivability) Regulations 1997** (SI 1997/647) which apply to all **UK ro-ro passenger ships operating regular scheduled voyages as ships of Classes I, II and II(A)** and to all **non-UK ro-ro passenger ships of these classes** when they are in UK ports. (The UK Regulations thus extend the Stockholm Agreement requirements to **domestic ferries of Class II(A)**.)
- applies to the above Classes of ship between 1 April 1997 and 1 October 2002 in accordance with a timescale based on the **A/Amax** value of the ship.
- is printed in full in **MSN 1673**, Annex 2 of which contains the **Stability Requirements Pertaining to the Agreement.**

---

[23] "**A/Amax**" is the ratio of the ship's attained "A" value to its "Amax" value, expressed as a percentage, e.g. "97.83". "A" is an index of the ship's attained (or existing) degree of survivability. "**Amax**" represents a survivability standard to be attained by the ship by a certain date which will depend on the A/Amax ratio. The higher the A/Amax value, the later the latest compliance date. A/Amax is defined in the annex an IMO document named the Calculation Procedure to assess the survivability characteristics of existing ro-ro passenger ships when using a simplified method based upon resolution A.265(VIII), developed by the IMO Maritime Safety Committee at its 59th session in June 1991 (MSC/Circ.574).

D03b.5c Ro-Ro Passenger Ship Survivability Regulations

* The **MS (Ro-Ro Passenger Ship Survivability) Regulations 1997** (SI 1997/647) -
- **give effect** in the UK to the Stockholm Agreement (see D03b.5b).
- **revoke** the MS (Ro-Ro Passenger Ship Survivability) (No. 2) Regulations 1994, which implemented an earlier International Agreement dated 27th July 1993. The 1993 Agreement has been superseded by the Agreement implemented by these Regulations.
- **apply** the requirements of the **Stockholm Agreement** to all UK ro-ro passenger ships operating on regular scheduled voyages as ships of Classes I, II and II(A) and to all non-UK ships of those Classes when they are in UK waters while proceeding to or from a port in the UK (regulation 4). The requirements are progressively applied to ships from 1 April 1997 to 1 October 2002, in accordance with a timescale based on the A/Amax value for the ship (regulation 6).
- require the **calculation of an A/Amax value** for each ship to be submitted to and approved by the MCA, or to be approved by the Contracting Government to the Agreement whose flag the ship is entitled to fly (regulation 5).
- provide (in regulation 6(2)) that the date for compliance will be as shown in the following table:

Value of A/Amax	Date
Less than 85%	1 April 1997
Less than 90%	31 December 1998
Less than 95%	31 December 1999
Less than 97.5%	31 December 2000
Less than 97.5% or higher	December 2001 but in any case not later than 1 October 2002

- require **every UK ship** to which the Regulations apply which complies with the requirements of the Stockholm Agreement relating to be issued by the MCA with a **certificate** (called **Evidence of Ship Compliance (A/Amax)** but commonly called an "**A/Amax Certificate**") (see D03b.5d) confirming this (regulation 9(1)).provide that a non-UK Contracting Government ship will be deemed to comply with the requirements of the Agreement if the ship has a **certificate** indicating its compliance with those requirements issued by the Government of its flag State (regulation 9(2)).
- require that every ship to which the Regulations apply must **carry on board** the certificate confirming its compliance with the Agreement's requirements (regulation 9(3)).
- provide that the MCA may grant an **exemption** from all or any of the specific stability standards in the Stockholm Agreement to a ro-ro passenger ship which is not normally on a regular scheduled voyage but which is required to undertake a single passage to or from a UK port (regulation 10(1)).
- contain a reference to **MSN 1673** (see D03b.5b).

D03b.5d Evidence of Ship Compliance (A/Amax Compliance Certificate)

- is issued under regulation 9(1) of the MS (Ro-Ro Passenger Ship Survivability) Regulations 1997 (SI 1997/647) by the MCA to a UK ro-ro passenger ship of Classes I, II and II(A) which complies with the requirements of the Stockholm Agreement (see D03b.5b).
- is required to be carried on board under regulation 9(2) of the Regulations.
- **certifies** that the plans and particulars of the ship have been examined and that the **A/Amax value** as defined in the annex to "The Calculation Procedure to Assess the Survivability Characteristics of Existing Ro-Ro Passenger Ships When Using a Simplified Method Based Upon Resolution A.265(VIII)" developed by the IMO Maritime Safety Committee (MSC.Circ.574) is **as stated** on the certificate.
- **shows** the ship's **standard of subdivision** (e.g. one compartment; two compartment); **A/Amax value** (e.g. 100.00 or a lesser figure). ("100.00" indicates full compliance with the specific stability standards of the Agreement.)
- has **no specified period of validity**.

D03b.6 Council Directive 98/18/EC and the Passenger Ships on Domestic Voyages Regulations

D03b.6a Council Directive 98/18/EC

- on Safety Rules and Standards for Passenger Ships **harmonises safety standards on all domestic trading passenger vessels** (i.e. those to which **SOLAS does not ordinarily apply**) operating within EEA waters. The

Directive is an EC response to public concern about major shipping casualties involving passenger ships resulting in massive loss of life, e.g. the *Estonia* sinking.

* The Directive **divides passenger ships into different classes** depending on the range and conditions of the sea areas in which they operate, and **categorises high speed passenger craft** in accordance with the IMO High Speed Craft Code.

* **Directive 98/18/EC applies to**:
  * **new passenger ships** (of any length);
  * **existing passenger ships** (at 17 March 1998) of **24 metres in length and above**; and
  * **high speed passenger craft**,
  - regardless of flag, when engaged on **domestic voyages in or between Member States**.

* **The Directive excludes from application** some categories of ships for which the Rules of the Directive are technically unsuitable or economically unviable.

* **The Directive contains**, in over 100 pages:
  * 16 legal Articles; and,
  * in the annex, **regulations** arranged in four chapters as follows: Chapter I – General Provisions; Chapter II-1 – Construction – Subdivision and Stability, Machinery and Electrical Installations; Chapter II-2 – Fire Protection, Fire Detection and Fire Extinction; and Chapter III – Life-Saving Appliances[24].

* **The Directive includes**, in Articles 10 and 11 respectively, **regulations for surveys and certification** to show compliance with the Directive (see D04f.3).

* **The Directive also includes** procedures to request action at IMO to bring into line the standards for passenger ships on international voyages with the standards of the Directive.

* The Directive is applied through national legislation in each EU member State, the **applicable UK legislation** being the **MS (Passenger Ships on Domestic Voyages) Regulations 2000** (SI 2000/2687) (see D03b.6b).

* **The Directive can be viewed** at http://europa.eu.int/eur-lex/en/consleg/main/1998/en_1998L0018_index.html

D03b.6b Passenger Ships on Domestic Voyages Regulations

* The **MS (Passenger Ships on Domestic Voyages) Regulations 2000** (SI 2000/2687) -
  - **implement** Council Directive 98/18/EC on Safety Rules and Standards for Passenger Ships.
  - **are amended by** the MS (Passenger Ships on Domestic Voyages) (Amendment) Regulations 2003
  - **amend** the Passenger Ship Construction Regulations, the Life Saving Appliances Regulations, the Fire Protection Regulations, the Survey and Certification Regulations, the Radio Installations Regulations and the Navigational Equipment Regulations.
  - **identify** four domestic passenger ship classifications (**Classes A, B, C and D**), as in the Directive. (For definitions of these Classes, see D04c.2b. Classes B, C and D are equivalent to passenger vessel Classes III, VI and VI(A) respectively.)
  - **apply** (under regulations 3 and 4) to:
    * **new** UK and non-UK **passenger ships of Class A, B, C or D** engaged on UK domestic voyages;
    * **existing** UK and non-UK **passenger ships of Class A, B, C or D of 24m or over** in length described in column 1 of the table below, engaged on UK domestic voyages, **from the date specified** in column 2 of the table.

Column 1 Date on which the keel of the ship was laid, or at a similar stage of construction	Column 2 Date from which the Regulations apply
A ship the keel of which was laid, or at a similar stage of construction, before 1 January 1940	1 July 2006
A ship the keel of which was laid, or at a similar stage of construction, on or after 1 January 1940 but before 31 December 1962	1 July 2007
A ship the keel of which was laid, or at a similar stage of construction, on or after 31 December 1962 but before 31 December 1974	1 July 2008
A ship the keel of which was laid, or at a similar stage of construction, on or after 31 December 1974 but before 31 December 1984	1 July 2009
A ship the keel of which was laid, or at a similar stage of construction, on or after 31 December 1984 but before 1 July 1998	1 July 2010

  - **do not apply** to:
    * a ship of war or a troopship;
    * a ship not propelled by mechanical means;

---

[24] At first glance the Directive's chapters and regulations may appear to be copies of parts of SOLAS. Closer inspection reveals many differences, although many of the Directive's regulations require compliance with SOLAS regulations, or parts of them.

- a vessel which is not constructed in steel or equivalent material, and to which the MS (High-Speed Craft) Regulations 1996 do not apply, or which is not a dynamically supported craft for the purposes of the IMO Code of Safety for Dynamically Supported Craft;
- a wooden ship of primitive build;
- an original historical passenger ship designed before 1965, or an individual replica of such a ship built predominately with the original materials;
- a pleasure yacht unless it is or will be crewed and carrying more than 12 passengers for commercial purposes;
- a high-speed passenger craft to which the MS (High-Speed Craft) Regulations 1996 apply, subject to an exception[25]; or
- a vessel exclusively engaged in port waters (i.e. in Category A, B, C or D waters).

* Under regulation 5(1), **the following Regulations will cease to apply** to existing passenger ships of Classes A, B, C or D of 24m or over engaged on domestic voyages on the **date specified in column 2** of the table above (i.e. on the date when the Passenger Ships on Domestic Voyages Regulations apply):
- MS (Passenger Ship Construction: Ships of Classes I, II and II(A)) Regulations 1998 (SI 1998/2514);
- MS (Passenger Ship Construction: Ships of Classes III to VI(A)) Regulations 1998 (SI 1998/2515);
- MS (Life-Saving Appliances for Ships Other Than Ships of Classes III to VI(A)) Regulations 1999 (SI 1999/2721);
- MS (Life-Saving Appliances for Ships of Classes III to VI(A)) Regulations 1999 (SI 1999/2723);
- MS (Fire Protection: Large Ships) Regulations 1998 (SI 1998/1011);
- MS (Fire Protection: Small Ships) Regulations 1998 (SI 1998/1012);
- MS (Navigational Equipment) Regulations 1993 (1993/69); and
- MS (Radio Installations) Regulations 1998 (SI 1998/2070).

* The Schedule to the Regulations contains various amendments to the Regulations listed above.

* **Regulation 6** provides that, from the date of application of the Regulations, a ship to which the Regulations apply must comply with the **safety requirements** specified in **the Directive** in relation to a ship of its Class (i.e. A, B, C or D).

* Regulation 7 permits approval by the MCA of alternative construction, equipment and machinery.

* Regulation 8 permits exemptions of individual ships or classes of ship by the MCA.

* Regulation 10 provides for detention of a ship in breach of the Regulations.

* **MSN 1747**, which comes into force on the same date as the Regulations, augments the Regulations and contains two annexes which set out the **geographical extent of EC sea areas EC/C and EC/D** identified as applicable in waters around the UK, these sea areas being given statutory force by virtue of the Regulations.

D03b.7 Carriage of Cargoes Regulations

* UK passenger ships (including high-speed craft) and UK ro-ro passenger ships, when loaded or intended to be loaded with any cargo, must comply with the **MS (Carriage of Cargoes) Regulations 1999** (SI 1999/336) (see F07g).

D03b.8 Minimum Standards of Safety Communications Regulations

* UK passenger ships must comply with those provisions of the MS (Minimum Standards of Safety Communications) Regulations 1997 (SI 1997/529) which apply to all ships (see D03a.4).

* In addition, under regulation 5(2)(a), the **company** and the **master** of every passenger ship must ensure that, for the purpose of ensuring effective crew performance in safety matters:
- a **working language**, determined by the company or master as appropriate, is **established**, and **recorded** in the ship's Official Log Book (regulation 5(2)(a)(i));
- each **seaman** is required to **understand** and, where appropriate, **give orders and instructions** and **report back** in the working language (regulation 5(2)(a)(ii)); and
- if the working language is not English, all **plans and lists** that must be posted include **translations** into the working language (regulation 5(2)(a)(iii)). (For a list of documents to be displayed on board, see D04w.)

* Regulation 5(2)(b) provides that the company and the master of every passenger ship must ensure that **personnel nominated on muster lists to assist passengers in emergency situations** are readily **identifiable** and have

---

[25] Exclusion of a high-speed passenger craft from the application of the Regulations does not exclude a passenger ship engaged on domestic voyages in sea areas of Class B, C or D when the displacement of that vessel corresponding to the design waterline is less than 500m3 and the maximum speed of that vessel, as defined in paragraph 1.4.30 of the High-Speed Craft Code is less than 20 knots (regulation 4(3)).

communication skills that are sufficient for that purpose, taking into account an appropriate and adequate combination of any of the following criteria:

* the **language** or languages appropriate to the **principal nationalities** of passengers carried on a particular route (regulation 5(2)(b)(i));
* the likelihood that an ability to use **elementary English vocabulary** for basic instructions can provide a means of communicating with a passenger in need of assistance whether or not the passenger and crew member share a common language (regulation 5(2)(b)(ii));
* the possible need to communicate during an emergency by some other means such as by demonstration, or hand signals, or calling attention to the location of instructions, muster stations, life-saving devices or evacuation routes when **verbal communication is impractical** (regulation 5(2)(b)(iii));
* the extent to which complete **safety instructions** have been provided to passengers in their **native language** or languages (regulation 5(2)(b)(iv)); and
* the **languages** in which **emergency announcements** may be broadcast during an emergency or drill to convey critical guidance to passengers and to facilitate crew members in assisting passengers (regulation 5(2)(b)(v)).

D03b.9 Operational limitations

* The **MS (Safety of Navigation) Regulations 2002** (SI 2002/1473) (see H01f.2) require compliance by a ship to which the Regulations apply with **both paragraphs of SOLAS regulation V/30** (which relates to **Operational limitations**).
* **SOLAS regulation V/30.1** provides that regulation V/30 applies to all passenger ships to which SOLAS chapter I applies, i.e. all passenger ships on international voyages.
* **SOLAS regulation V/30.2** provides that a **list of all limitations** on the operation of a passenger ship, including exemptions from any of the regulations of SOLAS chapter V, restrictions in operating areas, weather restrictions, sea state restrictions, restrictions in permissible loads, trim, speed and any other limitations, whether imposed by the Administration or established during the design or the building stages, must be compiled before the passenger ship is put in service. The list, together with any necessary explanations, must be documented in a form **acceptable to the flag State Administration**, and must be **kept on board readily available to the master**. The list must be kept **updated**. If the language used is not English or French, the list must be provided in one of those languages.
* The **Guidance Notes to regulation V/30** in MCA's 2002 SOLAS Chapter V publication states that all UK-registered SOLAS I passenger ships (i.e. those on international voyages) must carry a **document listing the operational limitations**. The document, which is to be **appended to the Passenger Ship Safety Certificate**, must include details of any **exemptions** from the requirements of SOLAS V, **operating restrictions** (speed, weather, sea state or geographical areas), **restrictions on loading or stability conditions** and any **other operational limitations imposed** during the ship's construction or by the MCA. If the ship has no operational limitations the document must be **endorsed** accordingly.
* A sample **Operational Limitations Document**, together with guidance notes on its completion, is contained in Annex 23 of the 2002 SOLAS Chapter V publication. Examples of operational limitations are given.
* For a note on the **relevance of the Operational Limitations Document to seaworthiness**, see H01b.1.

D03c OPERATIONAL REQUIREMENTS APPLICABLE TO UK OIL TANKERS

D03c.1 MARPOL Annex I requirements

* **In relation to their oil installations and control of operational pollution**, UK oil tankers must be equipped, surveyed, certificated and operated in accordance with the provisions of **MARPOL Annex I**, which is implemented in the UK by the **MS (Prevention of Oil Pollution) Regulations 1996** (SI 1996/2154), as amended.

D03c.2 UK legislation applicable to oil tankers

D03c.2a Prevention of Oil Pollution Regulations

* **In relation to operations concerning their cargo and ballast spaces**, UK oil tankers must comply with the **MS (Prevention of Oil Pollution) Regulations 1996** (SI 1996/2154), as amended.

* For notes on oil tanker **equipment, surveys and certification**, see D04g.
* For notes on **Oil Record Books**, see D05b.2.
* For notes on the **discharge provisions** of the Prevention of Oil Pollution Regulations, see H03a.
* For notes on **reporting of pollution incidents at sea**, see H06e.

D03c.2b Dangerous Goods and Marine Pollutants Regulations

* The operation of UK tankers must be in compliance with the **MS (Dangerous Goods and Marine Pollutants) Regulations 1997** (SI 1997/2367) (see F07f.2). For notes on requirements relating to the carriage of **dangerous goods or marine pollutants in bulk** (regulation 20) see F07f.2l. For notes on requirements relating to **documentation** relating to bulk dangerous goods or marine pollutants (regulation 21) see F07f.2m.

D03c.2c Minimum Standards of Safety Communications Regulations

* **UK tankers** must comply with those provisions of the **MS (Minimum Standards of Safety Communications) Regulations 1997** (SI 1997/529) which apply to **all ships** (see D03a.4).
* **In addition**, under **regulation 5(3)**, the company and master of a **UK oil tanker**, chemical tanker or liquefied gas tanker (including Government tankers) must ensure that the **master, officers and ratings** are able to communicate with each other in a **common working language**.

D03c.3 Publications applicable to oil tankers

* **Publications** containing **standards of good operational practice** applicable to **oil tankers** are shown in the following table. For publications applicable to all ship types, see D03a.7.

Document title	Publisher
Clean Seas Guide for Oil Tankers (Retention of Oil Residues on Board)	ICS/OCIMF
Guidance for the Inspection and Maintenance of Double Hull Tanker Structures	IACS
Guidance Manual for Tanker Structures	IACS/Tanker Structure Co-operation Forum
Guidelines on the Enhanced Programme of Inspections During Surveys of Bulk Carriers and Oil Tankers	IMO
Inert Gas Systems	IMO
International Safety Guide for Oil Tankers and Terminals (ISGOTT)	ICS/OCIMF/IAPH
Prevention of Oil Spillages Through Cargo Pumproom Sea Valves	ICS/OCIMF
Safety in Oil Tankers	ICS
Ship to Ship Transfer Guide (Petroleum)	ICS/OCIMF

D03d OPERATIONAL REQUIREMENTS APPLICABLE TO UK LIQUEFIED GAS CARRIERS

D03d.1 Gas carrier codes

* In addition to the standards described in D03a, a **liquefied gas carrier** must operate to the standards of the **relevant gas carrier code**.
* **Three gas carrier codes** have been produced by IMO, as follows:
  * **Code for Existing Ships Carrying Liquefied Gases in Bulk** (the "**GC Code for Existing Ships**" or "**Existing Ships Code**");
  * **Code for the Construction and Equipment of Ships Carrying Liquefied Gases in Bulk** (the "**GC Code**"); and
  * **International Code for the Construction and Equipment of Ships Carrying Liquefied Gases in Bulk** (the "**IGC Code**"); this Code has a **1984 edition** and a **1993 edition**.
* The **applicable Code**, and in the case of the IGC Code the **applicable edition**, depends basically on the date of build of the ship, although the criteria in each Code are somewhat more complex, as shown below.
* The Codes are applicable to gas carriers regardless of size, including those of less than 500gt.
* Where it is proposed that a ship should carry liquid chemicals covered by the Bulk Chemical Codes in addition to substances covered by the Gas Carrier Codes, the ship should also be assessed as a chemical tanker in accordance with the applicable Bulk Chemical Code and certified accordingly.

* When a ship is intended to carry exclusively those substances covered in both Gas Carrier and Bulk Chemical Codes, the requirements of the Bulk Chemical Codes apply.
* The requirements of the Gas Carrier Codes take precedence when the substances proposed to be carried are those covered only in the Gas Carrier Codes along with one or more substances covered in both Gas Carrier and Bulk Chemical Codes.

D03d.1a The GC Code for Existing Ships

* The **Code for Existing Ships Carrying Liquefied Gases in Bulk** (1976 edition) (the "**GC Code for Existing Ships**", also known as the "**Existing Ships Code**") -
  - **applies to** products which are liquefied gases having a vapour pressure exceeding 2.8 kp/cm² absolute at a temperature of 37.8°C, and certain other substances as shown in chapter XIX of the Code, when carried in bulk on board ships regardless of their size (Code, 1.2.1).
  - applies (under 1.2.2 of the Code) subject to 1.2.1 to:
    * gas carriers delivered **on or before 31 October 1976**; and
    * to gas carriers delivered **after 31 October 1976 but prior to the application of the GC Code**.
  - **contains** the following chapters: **I**. General; **II**. Freeboard and stability; **III**. Ship arrangements; **IV**. Cargo containment; **V**. Process pressure vessels and liquid, vapour and pressure piping systems; **VI**. Materials of construction; **VII**. Cargo pressure/temperature control; **VIII**. Cargo tank vent systems; **IX**. Environmental control for cargo containment systems; **X**. Electrical arrangements; **XI**. Fire protection and fire extinction; **XII**. Mechanical ventilation in cargo area; **XIII**. Instrumentation (gauging, gas detection); **XIV**. Personnel protection; **XV**. Filling limits for cargo tanks; **XVI**. Use of cargo as fuel; **XVII**. Special requirements; **XVIII**. Operating requirements; **XIX**. Summary of minimum requirements; **Appendix**. Model form of Certificate of Fitness for the Carriage of Liquefied Gases in Bulk; **Attachment**. Model form of Certificate of Fitness for the Carriage of Liquefied Gases in Bulk (Resolution A.328(IX) modified to include endorsements related to Resolution A.329(IX).
  - **contains** (in paragraph 15.2) requirements for **information to be provided to the master** (see F07i.2).
  - **contains** (in paragraph 17.8) a requirement for a **certificate** relating to **cargo inhibition** (see F07i.2).
  - **contains** (in paragraph 18.1) requirements for **cargo information to be carried** (see F07i.2).
  - was developed to provide international standards for the safe carriage of liquefied gases in bulk by ships which were already in service at 31 October 1976 or otherwise fell outside the scope of the more extensive standards contained in Resolution A.328(IX) and the GC Code.
  - is an **IMO Recommendation only** (under Resolution A.329(IX) and is **not mandatory** under any IMO instrument. (The Code may, however, be applied by flag States to gas carriers of appropriate ages by construction dates.)
* Ships surveyed in accordance with the provisions of section 1.6 of the GC Code for Existing Ships, and found to comply with the Code, should be issued with a **Certificate of Fitness for the Carriage of Liquefied Gases in Bulk** (see D04g.6a).

D03d.1b The GC Code

* The **Gas Carrier Code (GC Code)** -
  - **applies to products** which are liquefied gases having a vapour pressure exceeding 2.8 kp/cm² absolute at a temperature of 37.8°C, and certain other substances as shown in chapter XIX of the Code, when carried in bulk on board ships regardless of their size (GC Code, 1.2.1).
  - **applies** (under 1.2.2 of the Code) **to gas carriers**, other than those ships to which the IGC Code applies -
    * for which the building contract (or contract for a major conversion) is placed after 31 October 1976; or
    * in the absence of a building contract (or a contract for a major conversion), the keel of which is laid or which is at a similar stage of construction (or the conversion of which is begun) after 31 December 1976; or
    * the delivery of which is (or the conversion of which is completed) after 30 June 1980.
  - **contains** the following chapters: **I**. General; **II**. Ship survival capability and cargo tank location; **III**. Ship arrangements; **IV**. Cargo containment; **V**. Process pressure vessels and liquid, vapour and pressure piping systems; **VI**. Materials of construction; **VII**. Cargo pressure/temperature control; **VIII**. Cargo vent systems; **IX**. Environmental control for cargo containment systems; **X**. Electrical arrangements; **XI**. Fire protection and fire extinguishing; **XII**. Mechanical ventilation in cargo area; **XIII**. Instrumentation (gauging, gas detection); **XIV**. Personnel protection; **XV**. Filling limits for cargo tanks; **XVI**. Use of cargo as fuel; **XVII**. Special requirements; **XVIII**. Operating requirements; **XIX**. Summary of minimum requirements; **Appendix**. Model form of Certificate of Fitness for the Carriage of Liquefied Gases in Bulk; **2**. Resolution A.328(IX) – Code for the Construction and Equipment of Ships Carrying Liquefied Gases in Bulk; **3**. Resolution MSC.7(48) –

Recommendation for chemical tankers and gas carriers constructed before 1 July 1986; **4**. Guidelines for the uniform application of the survival requirements of the Bulk Chemical Code and the Gas Carrier Code; **5**. Testing of shore installation cargo hoses – MSC/Circ.220.
- **contains** (in paragraph 15.2) requirements for **information to be provided to the master** (see F07i.2).
- **contains** (in paragraph 17.8) a requirement for a **certificate** relating to **cargo inhibition** (see F07i.2).
- **contains** (in paragraph 18.1) requirements for **cargo information to be carried** (see F07i.2).
* Ships surveyed in accordance with the provisions of section 1.6 of the GC Code, and found to comply with the Code, should be issued with a **Certificate of Fitness for the Carriage of Liquefied Gases in Bulk** (see D04g.6a).

D03d.1c The IGC Code (1983 edition)

* The **International Gas Carrier Code (IGC Code) (1983 edition)** -
- **applies to ships** regardless of their size, including those of less than 500gt, engaged in the carriage of liquefied gases having a vapour pressure exceeding 2.8 bar absolute at a temperature of 37.8°C, and other products as shown in chapter 19 of the Code, when carried in bulk.
- **applies** to gas carriers the keels of which were laid or which were at a stage at which:
  * construction identifiable with the ship began; and
  * assembly of that ship commenced comprising at least 50 tonnes or 1% of the estimated mass of all structural material, whichever is less,
  - on or after 1 July 1986 but before 1 October 1994.
- is **mandatory** under SOLAS chapter VII, regulation 13, which provides that a gas carrier must comply with the requirements of the IGC Code and be surveyed and certified as provided for in the Code, and that the requirements of the Code will be treated as mandatory.
- **contains** the same chapters as the IGC Code 1993 edition (see D03d.1d).
- **contains** (in paragraph 1.5) requirements for **surveys and certification** (see D04g.4).
- **contains** (in paragraph 15.2) requirements for **information to be provided to the master** (see F07i.2).
- **contains** (in paragraph 17.8) a requirement for a **certificate** relating to **cargo inhibition** (see F07i.2).
- **contains** (in paragraph 18.1) requirements for **cargo information to be carried** (see F07i.2).
- **provides** (in paragraph 18.1.3) that a copy of **the Code or national regulations incorporating the provisions of the Code should be on board** every ship covered by the Code[26].
* Ships surveyed in accordance with the provisions of section 1.5 of the IGC Code, and found to comply with the Code, should be issued with an **International Certificate of Fitness for the Carriage of Liquefied Gases in Bulk** (see D04g.6b).

D03d.1d The IGC Code (1993 edition)

* The **International Gas Carrier Code (IGC Code) (1993 edition)** -
- is **mandatory** under SOLAS chapter VII.
- is an **amended** version of the 1983 IGC Code resulting from amendments adopted by the IMO Maritime Safety Committee in December 1992 by resolution MSC.30(61) and which entered into force on 1 July 1994.
- **applies to** ships regardless of their size, including those of less than 500gt, engaged in the carriage of liquefied gases having a vapour pressure exceeding 2.8 bar absolute at a temperature of 37.8°C, and other products as shown in chapter 19 of the Code, when carried in bulk (Chapter 1, paragraph 1.1.1).
- **applies**, unless expressly provided otherwise, to ships the keels of which are laid or which are at a stage at which:
  * construction identifiable with the ship began; and
  * assembly of that ship commenced comprising at least 50 tonnes or 1% of the estimated mass of all structural material, whichever is less,
  - **on or after 1 July 1998** (IGC Code, paragraph 1.1.2, as amended by resolution MSC.32(63)).
- provides that **ships constructed before 1 July 1998** are to comply with resolution MSC.5(48) adopted on 17 June 1983 subject to amendments by resolution MSC.30(61) adopted on 11 December 1992 (Chapter 1, paragraph 1.1.2, as amended by resolution MSC.32(63)).
- **contains** the following chapters: **1**. General; **2**. Ship survival capability and location of cargo tanks; **3**. Ship arrangements; **4**. Cargo containment; **5**. Process pressure vessels and liquid, vapour and pressure piping systems; **6**. Materials of construction; **7**. Cargo pressure/temperature control; **8**. Cargo tank vent systems; **9**. Environmental control; **10**. Electrical installations; **11**. Fire protection and fire extinction; **12**. Mechanical ventilation in the cargo area; **13**. Instrumentation (gauging, gas detection); **14**. Personnel protection; **15**. Filling limits for cargo tanks; **16**. Use of cargo as fuel; **17**. Special requirements; **18**. Operating requirements; **19**.

---

[26] There is no equivalent requirement in the GC Code or the GC Code for Existing Ships for a copy of the Code to be on board.

Summary of minimum requirements; **Appendix**. Model form of International Certificate of Fitness for the Carriage of Liquefied Gases in Bulk; **Resolution MSC.30(61)** – Adoption of amendments to the IGC Code.
- **contains** (in paragraph 1.5) requirements for **surveys and certification** (see D04g.4).
- **contains** (in paragraph 15.2) requirements for **information to be provided to the master** (see F07i.2).
- **contains** (in paragraph 17.8) a requirement for a **certificate** relating to **cargo inhibition** (see F07i.2).
- **contains** (in paragraph 18.1) requirements for **cargo information to be carried** (see F07i.2).
- **provides** (in paragraph 18.1.3) that a copy of **the Code or national regulations incorporating the provisions of the Code should be on board** every ship covered by the Code.
* Ships surveyed in accordance with the provisions of section 1.5 of the IGC Code, and found to comply with the Code, should be issued with an **International Certificate of Fitness for the Carriage of Liquefied Gases in Bulk** (see D04g.6b).

D03d.2 UK legislation applicable to liquefied gas carriers

* In addition to the provisions of the **appropriate gas carrier code** and the statutory provisions applicable to all UK ships (see D03a), the **principal statutory provisions** covering UK gas carriers are:
  * the MS (Gas Carriers) Regulations 1994 (SI 1994/2464);
  * the MS (Dangerous Goods and Marine Pollutants) Regulations 1997 (SI 1997/2367); and
  * the MS (Dangerous or Noxious Liquid Substances in Bulk) Regulations 1996 (SI 1996/3010).
* Regulation 5(3) of the MS (Minimum Standards of Safety Communications) Regulations 1997 (SI 1997/529) also applies to gas carriers (see D03d.2c).

D03d.2a Gas Carriers Regulations

* The **MS (Gas Carriers) Regulations 1994** (SI 1994/2464) apply to "**1986-1994 gas carriers**" and to "**new gas carriers**" (regulation 2(1)).
* "**Gas carrier**" is defined as "a self-propelled cargo ship constructed or adapted and used for the carriage in bulk of any liquefied gas listed in chapter 19 of the IGC Code or any other substance so listed" (regulation 1(1)).
* "1986-1994 gas carriers" are those to which the 1983 edition of the IGC Code applies. "New gas carriers" are those to which the 1993 edition of the IGC Code applies.
* Where a ship is built or adapted to carry one or more of the substances listed both in **Chapter 17 of the IBC Code and in Chapter 19 of the IGC Code** and is not constructed or adapted to carry any substance listed **only** in Chapter 19 of the IGC Code then the Gas Carrier Regulations will not apply to that ship (regulation 2(2)).
* The Regulations apply to all UK 1986-1994 gas carriers and new gas carriers wherever they are, and to non-UK ships of the same description while they are in the UK or UK territorial waters: provided that in the case of a ship registered in a non-SOLAS State the Regulations will not apply by reason of the ship being in the UK or UK territorial waters for reasons of stress of weather or any circumstances which could not have been prevented by the owner, the master or the charterer (if any) (regulation 2(3)).
* **Every ship** to which the Gas Carriers Regulations apply must be constructed, equipped and operated in accordance with the requirements relevant to it of chapter 1, paragraphs 1.1.4.1 to 1.1.4.4 inclusive, and chapters 2 to 19 inclusive, of the **IGC Code** (regulation 3).
* Regulation 4 deals with **survey requirements** (see D04g.4).
* Regulation 5 deals with requirements for the issue of an **International Certificate of Fitness** (see D04g.6b).
* Regulation 6 deals with **maintenance of condition after survey**. (For notes on similar requirements, see D04f.2i).
* Regulation 7 provides that the MCA will, subject to satisfactory trial, etc., allow fittings, materials, appliances, etc. of an **equivalent effectiveness** as that required by the IGC Code.
* Under Regulation 8 the MCA may **exempt** any ship from the requirements of the IGC Code, subject to any specified conditions, and may alter and cancel any exemption.
* Under regulation 9(1), no ship to which the Regulations apply may load or carry in bulk any of the substances listed in Chapter 19 of the IGC Code unless -
  * there is in force in respect of that ship a **valid International Certificate of Fitness** for the Carriage of Liquefied Gases in Bulk covering the substance which the ship is loading or carrying; **or**
  * the **MCA** has given **approval** to its carriage.
* Any MCA **approval** under regulation 9(1) must be in writing and must specify the date on which it takes effect and the conditions (if any) on which it is given (regulation 9(2)).

D03d.2b Dangerous Goods and Marine Pollutants Regulations

* The operation of UK liquefied gas carriers must be in compliance with the **MS (Dangerous Goods and Marine Pollutants) Regulations 1997** (SI 1997/2367) (see F07f.2). **Regulation 20(2)(a)** provides that where **dangerous goods or marine pollutants are handled or carried in bulk** in any ship and are goods listed in Chapter VI of the BCH Code, or in Chapter 17 of the IBC Code, or in **Chapter XIX of the Gas Carrier Code for Existing Ships**, or in **Chapter XIX of the Gas Carrier Code**, or in **Chapter 19 of the IGC Code**, or are classified dangerous goods listed in Appendix B of the Solid Bulk Cargoes Code, they must be **handled** and **carried** in accordance with the requirements of whichever of the codes is appropriate.

D03d.2c Minimum Standards of Safety Communications Regulations

* UK liquefied gas carriers must comply with those provisions of the **MS (Minimum Standards of Safety Communications) Regulations 1997** (SI 1997/529) which apply to all ships (see D03a.4).
* In addition, under regulation 5(3), the company and master of a UK oil tanker, chemical tanker or **liquefied gas tanker** (including Government tankers) must ensure that the **master, officers and ratings** are able to communicate with each other in a **common working language**.

D03d.3 Publications applicable to liquefied gas carriers

* **Publications** containing **standards of good operational practice** applicable to **liquefied gas carriers** are shown in the following table. For publications applicable to all ship types, see D03a.7.

Document title	Publisher
Contingency Planning and Crew Response Guide for Gas Carrier Damage at Sea and in Port Approaches	ICS/OCIMF/SIGTTO
Contingency Planning for the Gas Carrier Alongside and Within Port Limits	ICS/OCIMF/SIGTTO
Safety in Liquefied Gas Tankers	ICS
Ship to Ship Transfer Guide (Liquefied Gases)	ICS/OCIMF/SIGTTO
Tanker Safety Guide (Liquefied Gas)	ICS

D03e OPERATIONAL REQUIREMENTS APPLICABLE TO UK CHEMICAL TANKERS AND OTHER SHIPS CARRYING MARPOL ANNEX II SUBSTANCES

D03e.1 Chemical tanker codes

* In addition to the standards described in D03a, a **chemical tanker** must operate to the standards of the **relevant chemical tanker code**.
* **Two chemical tanker codes** have been produced by IMO, as follows:
  • **Code for the Construction and Equipment of Ships Carrying Dangerous Chemicals in Bulk** (the "BCH Code"); and
  • **International Code for the Construction and Equipment of Ships Carrying Dangerous Chemicals in Bulk** (the "IBC Code").
* The **applicable Code**, and in the case of the IBC Code the **applicable edition**, depends basically on the date of build of the ship, although the criteria in each Code are somewhat more complex, as shown below.
* The Codes are applicable to chemical tankers regardless of size, including those of less than 500gt.
* Where it is proposed that a liquefied gas carrier should carry liquid chemicals covered by the Bulk Chemical Codes in addition to substances covered by the Gas Carrier Codes, the ship should also be assessed as a chemical tanker in accordance with the applicable Bulk Chemical Code and certified accordingly.
* When a liquefied gas carrier is intended to carry exclusively those substances covered in both Gas Carrier and Bulk Chemical Codes, the requirements of the Bulk Chemical Codes apply.

D03e.1a The BCH Code

* The **Code for the Construction and Equipment of Ships Carrying Dangerous Chemicals in Bulk** (the "BCH Code") -

- **applies** (under 1.1 of the Code), for the purposes of MARPOL 73/78, only to chemical tankers as defined in regulation 1(1) of Annex II thereof which are engaged in the carriage of noxious liquid substances falling into category A, B or C and identified as such by an entry of *A*, *B* or *C* in column c of chapter 17 of the IBC Code.
- **applies** (under 1.2.1 of the Code) to bulk cargoes of dangerous and noxious chemical substances, other than petroleum or similar flammable products, as follows:
  * products having significant fire hazards in excess of those of petroleum products and other similar flammable products;
  * products having significant hazards in addition to or other than flammability;
  * products which may present a hazard to the environment, if accidentally released.

* According to paragraph 1.2.1 of the Code, the Code is at present limited to the liquids shown in the summary of minimum requirements in chapter 17 of the IBC Code. Products that have been reviewed and determined not to present safety and pollution hazards to such an extent as to warrant application of the Code are found in chapter 18 of the IBC Code.
* The Code is at present limited to tankships (1.2.2).
* The text of the Code itself makes no reference to the Code being applicable to ships of a particular construction date. However, a **Recommendation for chemical tankers and gas carriers constructed before 1 July 1986**, adopted by Resolution MSC.7(48) on 17 June 1983, resolved that in respect of chemical tankers and gas carriers constructed on or after 1 July 1986, the Bulk Chemical Code and the Gas Carrier Code would be superseded by the IBC Code and IGC Code respectively.
* The Code contains the following **chapters**: **I**. General; **II**. Cargo containment; **III**. Safety equipment and related considerations; **IV**. Special requirements; **V**. Operational requirements; **VA**. Additional measures for the protection of the marine environment; **VI**. Summary of minimum requirements; **VII**. List of chemicals to which the Code does not apply; **VIII**. Transport of liquid chemical wastes. **Appendix**. Model form of Certificate of Fitness for the Carriage of Dangerous Chemicals in Bulk; Decisions of the MSC and MEPC.
* Ships surveyed in accordance with the provisions of section 1.6 of the BCH Code, and found to comply with the Code, should be issued with a **Certificate of Fitness for the Carriage of Dangerous Chemicals in Bulk** (see D04g.5a).

D03e.1b The IBC Code (1998 edition)

* The **International Code for the Construction and Equipment of Ships Carrying Dangerous Chemicals in Bulk** (the "**IBC Code**") **applies** (under 1.1.1 of the Code) to ships regardless of size, including those of less than 500gt, engaged in the carriage of bulk cargoes of dangerous or noxious liquid chemical substances, other than petroleum or similar flammable products, as follows:
  * products having significant fire hazards in excess of those of petroleum products and similar flammable products; and
  * products having significant hazards in addition to or other than flammability.
* Products that have been reviewed and determined not to present safety and pollution hazards to such an extent as to warrant the application of the Code are listed in chapter 18 of the Code.
* Liquids covered by the Code are those having a vapour pressure not exceeding 2.8 bar absolute at a temperature of 37.8°C (1.1.2).
* For the purpose of the 1974 SOLAS Convention, the Code does not apply to ships which are engaged in the carriage of products included in chapter 17 of the Code solely on the basis of their pollution characteristics and identified as such by an entry of "P" only in column *d* (1.1.2A).
* For the purposes of MARPOL 73/78, the Code applies only to chemical tankers, as defined in regulation 1(1) of Annex II thereof, which are engaged in the carriage of noxious liquid substances falling into category A, B or C and identified as such by an entry of "A", "B" or "C" in column *c* (1.1.2B).
* **The IBC Code**
  - **applies**, unless expressly provided otherwise in it, to ships the keels of which were laid or which were at a stage at which:
    * construction identifiable with the ship begins; and
    * assembly commenced comprising at least 50 tonnes or 1% of the estimated mass of all structural material, whichever is less,
    - on or after 1 July 1986.
  - is **mandatory** under SOLAS chapter VII, regulation 10, which provides that a chemical tanker must comply with the requirements of the IBC Code and be surveyed and certified as provided for in the Code, and that the requirements of the Code will be treated as mandatory.
  - **contains** the following chapters: **1**. General; **2**. Ship survival capability and location of cargo tanks; **3**. Ship arrangements; **4**. Cargo containment; **5**. Cargo transfer; **6**. Materials of construction; **7**. Cargo temperature control; **8**. Cargo tank venting and gas-freeing arrangements; **9**. Environmental control; **10**. Electrical

installations; **11**. Fire protection and fire extinction; **12**. Mechanical ventilation in the cargo area; **13**. Instrumentation; **14**. Personnel protection; **15**. Special requirements; **16**. Operational requirements; **16A**. Additional measures for the protection of the marine environment; **17**. Summary of minimum requirements; **18**. List of chemicals to which the Code does not apply; **19**. Requirements for ships engaged in the incineration at sea of liquid chemical waste; **20**. Transport of liquid chemical wastes. **Appendix**. Model form of International Certificate of Fitness for the Carriage of Dangerous Chemicals in Bulk; Relevant decisions of the MSC and MEPC.

- **contains** (in paragraph 1.5) requirements for **surveys and certification** (see D04g.4).
- **contains** (in paragraph 16.2) requirements for **cargo information** to be provided (see F07i.3).
- **provides** (in paragraph 16.2.1) that a **copy of the IBC Code, or national regulations** incorporating the provisions of the Code, should be on board every ship covered by the Code.
- **contains** (in paragraph 16A.2) requirements relating to **conditions of carriage**.
- **contains** (in paragraph 16A.3) requirements for a Procedures and Arrangements Manual (see D04g.3b).
- **contains** (in paragraph 20.5.1) a requirement that in addition to the documentation specified in 16.2, ships engaged in transboundary movement of liquefied chemical wastes should carry on board a **Waste Movement Document** issued by the competent authority of the country of origin.

* Ships surveyed in accordance with the provisions of section 1.5 of the IBC Code, and found to comply with the Code, should be issued with an **International Certificate of Fitness for the Carriage of Dangerous Chemicals in Bulk** (see D04g.5b).

D03e.2 UK legislation applicable to chemical tankers and other ships carrying MARPOL Annex II substances in bulk

D03e.2a Dangerous or Noxious Liquid Substances in Bulk Regulations

* The **MS (Dangerous or Noxious Liquid Substances in Bulk) Regulations 1996** (SI 1996/3010) -
- **give effect** in the UK to Annex II of MARPOL 73/78[27].
- **consolidate and revoke** the IBC Code Regulations, the BCH Code Regulations, the Control of Pollution by Noxious Liquid Substances in Bulk Regulations, and their amendments. The consolidation takes into account the 1992 amendments to the IBC Code, BCH Code and Annex II of MARPOL 1973/78 as set out in MEPC Resolutions, MEPC 55(33), which allow port State control inspection of operational requirements.
- **contain** provisions regulating the **construction**, **equipment** and **operation** of ships carrying in bulk **noxious liquid substances** or **unassessed liquid substances**.
- **are amended** by the MS (Dangerous or Noxious Liquid Substances in Bulk) (Amendment) Regulations **1998** (SI 1998/1153), which raise from £5,000 to £25,000 the penalty on summary conviction for illegal discharges of noxious liquid substances and provide enhanced enforcement powers for the MCA in relation to illegal discharges.

* **Relevant regulations** are numbered as follows: **1**. Citation, commencement and revocation; **2**. Interpretation; **3**. Application; **4**. Construction, equipment and operation; **5**. Discharge of cargo tanks; **6**. Loading and carriage in bulk of dangerous or noxious liquid substances; **7**. Procedures and Arrangements Manual; **8**. Cargo Record Book; **9**. Survey requirements; **10**. Issue of appropriate certificate; **11**. Responsibilities of owner and master; **12**. Equivalents; **13**. Exemptions; **14**. Penalties; **15**. Inspection and detention.

* Regulation 3(1) provides that the Regulations apply to:
- all ships carrying **noxious liquid substances** or **unassessed liquid substances** (as defined below) in bulk;
- all chemical tankers carrying **dangerous substances** (as defined below) in bulk; and
- all oil tankers carrying **pollution hazard substances** (as defined below) in bulk.

* The Regulations apply, under regulation 3(1), to **UK ships** of the above categories, wherever they are. They also apply to **non-UK ships in UK waters** or, in relation to regulation 5 so far as it relates to the discharge or washing of tanks which have carried noxious liquid substances or pollution hazard substances, and subject to regulations 15 and 16 (Restriction on jurisdiction over offences outside UK limits), while they are **in UK controlled waters** (as defined in H01e.1b) or any other waters which are "**sea**" (i.e. outside "categorised waters" as described in D04c.2a). "**Ship**" includes means a vessel of any type whatsoever operating in the marine environment and includes hydrofoil boats, hovercraft, submersibles and floating craft and also fixed or floating platforms except when they are actually engaged in exploration or exploitation of the sea-bed or associated offshore processing of sea-bed mineral resources.

---

[27] At the time of writing the Regulations had not been amended for the requirements of the Harmonised System of Survey and Certification.

* **Regulation 2** defines -
  "**noxious liquid substance**" as a substance listed as such in either MEPC Circular 2/CIRC.1 or a Category A, B, C or D substance (regulation 2(1))[28].
  "**unassessed liquid substance** as a liquid substance which is neither a noxious liquid substance nor a non-polluting substance and is not oil as defined in the Merchant Shipping (Prevention of Oil Pollution) Regulations 1996 (regulation 2(1))[29].
  "**dangerous substance**" as a substance listed in Chapter 17 of the IBC Code having against it in column "d"; an entry "S".
  "**pollution hazard substance**" as a substance listed in Chapter 17 of the IBC Code having against it in column "d"; an entry "P".
* **Regulation 4(1)** provides that every ship carrying in bulk noxious liquid substances or unassessed liquid substances must comply with the provisions of **Schedule 1 of M.1703/NLS 1**.
* Except as provided for in paragraph (3)(b) and (c), **chemical tankers constructed before 1 July 1986** must be constructed, fitted, equipped, arranged and operated in accordance with those requirements of the **BCH Code** (1993 edition) relevant to it (regulation 4(2)).
* **Regulation 4(3)** provides that every ship specified in regulation 4(3)(a), (b) or (c) must be constructed, equipped and operated in accordance with those requirements of the **IBC Code** (1994 edition) relevant to it. These ships are:
  * **chemical tankers built on or after 1 July 1986**;
  * ships **converted to chemical tankers on or after 1 July 1986** (except oil tankers built before that date, or which are converted for the purpose of carrying pollution hazard substances only, or the conversion of which consists only of modifications necessary for compliance with Chapter VA of the BCH Code); and
  * (to the extent that the MCA considers reasonable and practicable) **chemical tankers built before 1 July 1986**, but which undergo **major repairs, alterations and modifications** on or after 1 July 1986.
* **Regulation 4(4)** provides that where a chemical tanker is built or adapted to carry substances listed in Chapter 19 of the IGC Code (whether or not such substances are listed in Chapter 17 of the IBC Code) then, to the extent that the requirements of the IBC and IGC Codes are inconsistent, the requirements of the **IGC Code will prevail**.
* Regulation 2 defines four categories of noxious liquid substance. "**Category A substance**", "**Category B substance**", "**Category C substance**" and "**Category D substance**" mean respectively any substance listed and identified as falling into Category A, B, C, or D in column "c"; in Chapter 17 and Chapter 18 of the IBC Code; and any substance which is provisionally assessed as a Category A, B, C or D substance. A reference to any such substance will include a reference to any mixture containing such substance.
* **Regulation 4(5)** provides that in every **chemical tanker built on or after 1 July 1986** the pumping and piping arrangements serving any tank designated for the carriage of a **Category B substance** or a **Category C substance** must be such that they comply with **Schedule 1 of M.1703/NLS 1**.
* The associated M. Notice, **M.1703/NLS 1**, contains the detailed technical requirements of the Regulations concerning Construction and Equipment, Discharge and Washing of Tanks, and Oil Like Substances. (For notes on NLS discharge requirements at sea, see H03b.)
* **Regulation 5(a)** prohibits the discharge of any noxious liquid substance into the sea, except where permitted by **Schedule 2 of M.1703/NLS 1**.
* **Regulation 5(b)** provides that tanks must be washed, or pre-washed, and the tank washings must be dealt with, as prescribed in **Schedule 2 of M.1703/NLS 1**.
* **Regulation 6** provides that no ship may **load** in bulk, or **carry** in bulk, any dangerous or noxious liquid substances or substances subject to a tripartite agreement unless either:
  there is in force in respect of that ship a valid **INLS Certificate**, a **BCH Code Certificate**, an **IBC Code Certificate** or an **appropriate Certificate** covering the **substance** in question, and the loading and carriage of that substance is in accordance with the **terms of that Certificate**; **or**
  * either the Secretary of State (i.e. the MCA) or the government of a SOLAS or MARPOL party State has given written permission for its carriage, and any conditions subject to which that permission was given are complied with; **or**
  * if the substance is an oil-like substance, an IOPP Certificate or a UKOPP Certificate is in force, suitably endorsed for the substance in question, the loading and carriage of the substance is in accordance with the terms of that certificate, an if of Category C or D it is handled and carried in accordance with **Schedule 3 of M.1703/NLS 1**.
* For notes on the **requirement of regulation 7 to have a Procedures and Arrangements Manual** see D04g.3b.
* For notes on the **requirement of regulation to have a Cargo Record Book**, see D05b.3.

---

[28] Noxious liquid substances carried in bulk and which are categorized as Category A, B, C or D and subject to the provisions of Annex II, are indicated as such in the Pollution Category column of chapters 17 or 18 of the International Bulk Chemical Code.
[29] Liquid substances carried in bulk which are identified as falling outside Categories A, B, C and D and not subject to the provisions of this Annex and indicated as `III' in the Pollution Category column of chapters 17 or 18 of the International Bulk Chemical Code.

* **Regulation 9** prescribes the **survey requirements**, prior to implementation of the Harmonised System of Survey and Certification, for ships carrying noxious liquid substances, and had, at March 2002, not been amended for HSSC arrangements. For notes on **surveys for INLS Certificates** see D04g.3a.
* For notes on the requirements of regulation 10 for the **issue of an appropriate certificate**, see D04g.3.
* For notes on the responsibilities of the owner and master under **regulation 11**, see D04g.3c.
* **Regulation 12** allows for equivalent fittings, materials, appliances or arrangements, subject to approval by the MCA.
* **Regulation 13** permits **conditional exemptions** to be granted by the MCA.
* **Regulation 14** prescribes penalties for breach of the Regulations (see B03b.3f).
* **Regulation 15** permits the inspection and detention, in UK ports, of ships to which the Regulations apply.

D03e.2b Dangerous Goods and Marine Pollutants Regulations

* The operation of UK chemical tankers must be in compliance with the **MS (Dangerous Goods and Marine Pollutants) Regulations 1997** (SI 1997/2367) (see F07f.2). **Regulation 20(2)(a)** provides that where **dangerous goods or marine pollutants are handled or carried in bulk** in any ship and are goods listed in **Chapter VI of the BCH Code**, or in **Chapter 17 of the IBC Code**, or in Chapter XIX of the Gas Carrier Code for Existing Ships, or in Chapter XIX of the Gas Carrier Code, or in Chapter 19 of the IGC **Code**, or are classified dangerous goods listed in Appendix B of the Solid Bulk Cargoes Code, they must be **handled** and **carried** in accordance with the requirements of whichever of the **codes** is appropriate.

D03e.2c Minimum Standards of Safety Communications Regulations

* **UK chemical tankers** must comply with those provisions of the **MS (Minimum Standards of Safety Communications) Regulations 1997** (SI 1997/529) which apply to **all ships** (see D03a.4).
* In addition, under **regulation 5(3)**, the company and master of a **UK oil tanker**, **chemical tanker** or liquefied gas tanker (including Government tankers) must ensure that the **master, officers and ratings** are able to communicate with each other in a **common working language**.

D03e.3 Publications applicable to chemical tankers

* **Publications** containing **standards of good operational practice** applicable to **chemical tankers** are shown in the following table. For publications applicable to all ship types, see D03a.7.

Document title	Publisher
Safety in Chemical Tankers	ICS
Tanker Safety Guide (Chemicals)	ICS

D03f OPERATIONAL REQUIREMENTS APPLICABLE TO UK BULK CARRIERS

D03f.1 Code of Safe Practice for Solid Bulk Cargoes

- is commonly known as the "**BC Code**".
- is **published** by IMO, the latest edition being the **1998** edition.
- **is recommended** to Governments for adoption or for use as the basis for national regulations in pursuance of their obligations under SOLAS chapters VI and VII.
- **is given effect in the UK** (to the extent that the Code covers classified dangerous goods listed in Appendix B) by regulation **20(2)(a)** of the **MS (Dangerous Goods and Marine Pollutants) Regulations 1997** (SI 1997/2367) (see D03e.2b).
- **provides guidance** to Administrations, shipowners, shippers and masters on the standards to be applied in the safe stowage and shipment of **solid bulk cargoes excluding grain** (which is dealt with under separate rules).
- **includes** general advice on the procedures to be followed whenever bulk cargoes are to be shipped, a description of the hazards associated with certain materials, lists of typical materials currently shipped in bulk and details of recommended test procedures to determine various characteristics of solid bulk cargo materials.

- **recommends** (in the Foreword) that **masters** should be encouraged to notify their Administrations of the behaviour of various types of bulk cargoes and, in particular, to report the circumstances of any incidents involving such materials.
- **contains** the following sections:
- • Introduction
- • Section 1 – Definitions
- • Section 2 – General precautions
- • Section 3 – Safety of personnel and ship
- • Section 4 – Assessment of acceptability of consignments for safe shipment
- • Section 5 – Trimming procedures
- • Section 6 – Methods of determining the angle of repose
- • Section 7 – Cargoes which may liquefy
- • Section 8 – Cargoes which may liquefy: test procedures
- • Section 9 – Materials possessing chemical hazards
- • Section 10 – Transport of solid wastes in bulk
- • Section 11 – Stowage factor conversion tables
- • Appendix A – List of bulk materials which may liquefy
- • Appendix B – List of bulk materials possessing chemical hazards
- • Appendix C – List of bulk materials which are neither liable to liquefy (appendix A) nor to possess chemical hazards (appendix B)
- • Appendix D – Laboratory test procedures, associated apparatus and standards
- • Appendix E – Emergency schedules (EmS) for materials listed in appendix B
- • Appendix F – Recommendations for entering enclosed spaces aboard ships
- • Appendix G – Procedures for monitoring of coal cargoes
- • Index of materials
* **MGN 60** draws attention to important changes to the provisions on the carriage of **coal cargoes** in the 1996 amendment of the BC Code.

D03f.2 SOLAS Chapter XII

* **SOLAS chapter XII – Additional Safety Measures for Bulk Carriers** -
  - was **adopted** by IMO in November 1997.
  - is **given effect in the UK** by the **MS (Additional Safety Measures for Bulk Carriers) Regulations 1999** (SI 1999/1644).
  - provides (in regulation XII/2) that **bulk carriers must comply with the requirements of Chapter XII in addition to** the applicable requirements of **other SOLAS chapters**. ("**Bulk carrier**" is defined in regulation IX/1.6 as "a ship which is constructed generally with single deck, top-side tanks and hopper side tanks in cargo spaces, and is intended primarily to carry dry cargo in bulk, and includes such types as ore carriers and combination carriers".)
  - includes regulations as follows: **3**. Implementation schedule; **4**. Damage stability requirements applicable to bulk carriers; **5**. Structural strength of bulk carriers; **6**. Structural and other requirements for bulk carriers; **7**. Survey of the cargo hold structure for bulk carriers; **8**. Information on compliance with the requirements for bulk carriers; **9**. Requirements for bulk carriers not being capable of complying with regulation 4.2 due to the design configuration of their cargo holds; **10**. Solid bulk cargo density declaration; **11**. Loading instrument.
* For notes on the **information and documentation** required under the Additional Safety Measures for Bulk Carriers Regulations see F07i.1.
* The **technical standards for bulk carriers built before 1 July 1999** are laid down in a number of **IMO Resolutions** referred to in the Regulations, while those for new bulk carriers are described in certain Unified Requirements of the International Association of Classification Societies (IACS), as specified in the IMO Recommendation on "Compliance with SOLAS Regulation XII/5".

D03f.3 UK legislation applicable to bulk carriers

D03f.3a Additional Safety Measures for Bulk Carriers Regulations

* The **MS (Additional Safety Measures for Bulk Carriers) Regulations 1999** (SI 1999/1644) -
  - **give effect** in the UK to the provisions of SOLAS Chapter XII.
  - **set** certain minimum standards for the longitudinal strength, buoyancy, stability, damage survivability, strength of double bottoms and transverse bulkheads, loading and survey of certain types of bulk carriers.
  - **apply in addition to** the relevant provisions of the MS (Cargo Ship Construction) Regulations 1997 (SI 1997/1509) as amended by SI 1999/643, and the MS (Carriage of Cargoes) Regulations 1999 (SI 1999/336).
  - **apply to** UK sea-going bulk carriers of 500gt or over, wherever they are, and non-UK sea-going bulk carriers of 500gt or over when in UK waters (but not to a ship flagged under a non-SOLAS country which is only in UK waters by virtue of stress of weather).
  - **contain** similar regulations to SOLAS Chapter XII, and **additional regulations** relating to alternative construction, equipment and machinery (regulation 13), exemptions (regulation 14), penalties (regulation 15) and detention powers (regulation 16).
  - are drawn attention to in **MGN 144**.
* Under regulation 5, bulk carriers built before 1 July 1999 and to which **regulations 6** (Damage stability requirements applicable to bulk carriers) and **8** (Structural and other requirements for bulk carriers constructed before 1 July 1999) apply must comply with regulations 6 and 8 according to an **implementation schedule** which is summarised in the following table.

Age of bulk carrier on 1 July 1999	Date for compliance with regulations 6 and 8
20 years and over	The date of the first intermediate survey or the first periodical survey after 1 July 1999, whichever comes first
15 years and over but less than 20 years	The date of the first periodical survey after 1 July 1999 but not later than 1 July 2002
Less than 15 years	The date of the first periodical survey after the date on which the ship reaches 15 years of age, but not later than the date on which the ship reaches 17 years of age

* **Under regulation 9** a bulk carrier of 150m in length and upwards of single side skin construction, built before 1 July 1999 and 10 years of age or older, **may not carry solid bulk cargoes** having a density of **1780kg/m³ and above** unless it has satisfactorily undergone either a **periodical survey** or a survey of all **cargo holds** to the same extent as required for a periodical survey.
* **Regulation 10(1)** provides that in the case of ships to which regulations 6, 7, 8 and 9, as appropriate, apply (i.e. bulk carriers of 150m or more in length of single side skin construction), the Cargo Loading Manual required under regulation 10(2) of the MS (Carriage of Cargoes) Regulations 1999 (see F07g.1g) must be endorsed by the Certifying Authority to indicate compliance with those regulations.
* For notes on the **information and documentation** required under the Regulations see F07i.1.

D03f.3b Carriage of Cargoes Regulations

* **UK bulk carriers** must comply with the applicable requirements of the **MS (Carriage of Cargoes) Regulations 1999** (SI 1999/336) (see F07g).

D03f.3c Dangerous Goods and Marine Pollutants Regulations

* **Regulation 20(2)(a)** of the **MS (Dangerous Goods and Marine Pollutants) Regulations 1997** (SI 1997/2367) provides that where **dangerous goods or marine pollutants are handled or carried in bulk in any ship** and are goods listed in Chapter VI of the BCH Code, or in Chapter 17 of the IBC Code, or in Chapter XIX of the Gas Carrier Code for Existing Ships, or in Chapter XIX of the Gas Carrier Code, or in Chapter 19 of the IGC Code, or are **classified dangerous goods listed in Appendix B of the Solid Bulk Cargoes Code**, they must be **handled** and **carried** in accordance with the requirements of whichever of the **codes** is appropriate.

D03f.4 Publications applicable to bulk carriers

* Publications containing **standards of good operational practice** applicable to **bulk carriers** are shown in the following table. For publications applicable to **all ship types** see D03a.6.

Document title	Publisher
Bulk Carrier Practice (by Captain J. Isbester)	Nautical Institute
Bulk Carriers - Guidance and Information on Bulk Cargo Loading and Discharging to Reduce the Likelihood of Over-stressing the Hull Structure	IACS
Bulk Carriers - Guidance and information on Bulk Cargo Loading and Discharging to Reduce the Likelihood of Over-Stressing the Hull Structure	IACS
Bulk Carriers – Guidance, InfoBulk Cargo Loading & Discharging	IACS
Bulk Carriers – Handle With Care	IACS
Bulk Carriers: Guidelines for Surveyors, Assessment and Repair of Hull Structure	IACS
Cargo Work (by David House)	Butterworth-Heinemann
Carriage of Cargoes Volume 2: Solid Bulk Cargoes – Instructions for the Guidance of Surveyors (see B05b)	MCA
Code of Practice for the Safe Loading and Unloading of Bulk Carriers (BLU Code)	IMO
Code of Safe Practice for Ships Carrying Timber Deck Cargoes	IMO
Draught Surveys (by W.J. Dibble & P. Mitchell)	Anchorage Press
Guidelines on the Enhanced Programme of Inspections During Surveys of Bulk Carriers and Oil Tankers	IMO
Hatchcover Maintenance and Operation – A Guide to Good Practice (by David Byrne)	Anchorage Press
International Code for the Safe Carriage of Grain in Bulk (International Grain Code)	IMO
Thomas on Stowage: The Properties & Stowage of Cargoes (4th Edition) (by Capt. K. R. Rankin)	Brown, Son & Ferguson

D03g OPERATIONAL REQUIREMENTS APPLICABLE TO UK GENERAL CARGO VESSELS

D03g.1 Legislation applicable to UK general cargo vessels

* UK ships carrying "**general cargo**", e.g. container ships and "break-bulk" cargo vessels -
  - must comply with the **operational requirements applicable to all UK ships**, as outlined in D03a.
  - must, when **loaded or intended to be loaded with any cargo other than bulk cargo**, comply with the general provisions of the **MS (Carriage of Cargoes) Regulations 1999** (SI 1999/336) (see F07g).
  - must, when carrying **any dry cargo in bulk**, comply with the bulk cargo provisions of the **MS (Carriage of Cargoes) Regulations 1999** (SI 1999/336) (see F07g).
  - must, when carrying packaged **dangerous goods or marine pollutants**, comply with the relevant provisions of the **MS (Dangerous Goods and Marine Pollutants) Regulations 1997** (SI 1997/2367) (see F07f.2).
  - must, when carrying any **MARPOL Annex II substance in bulk** (e.g. in a deep tank), comply with the relevant provisions of the **MS (Dangerous or Noxious Liquid Substances in Bulk) Regulations 1996** (SI 1996/3010), as outlined in D03e.2a.

D03g.2 Publications applicable to general cargo vessels

* Publications containing **standards of good operational practice** applicable to **general cargo vessels** are shown in the following table. For publications applicable to all ship types see D03a.6.

Document title	Publisher
Cargo Work (by David House)	Butterworth-Heinemann
Carriage of Cargoes, Volume 1 – The Carriage of Packaged Cargoes and Cargo Units (including Containers and Vehicles) – Instructions for the Guidance of Surveyors (see B05b)	MCA
Carriage of Packaged Dangerous Goods by Sea: Instructions for the Guidance of Surveyors (see B05b)	Department of Transport
Code of Safe Practice for Ships Carrying Timber Deck Cargoes	IMO
Container Top Safety	ICHCA
General Cargo Ships: Guidelines for Surveys, Assessment and Repair of Hull Structure	IACS
Hatchcover Maintenance and Operation – A Guide to Good Practice (by David Byrne)	Anchorage Press
Lashing and Securing of Deck Cargoes (by John R. Knott)	Nautical Institute
Steel – Carriage by Sea (by A. Sparks)	LLP
Thomas on Stowage: The Properties & Stowage of Cargoes (4th Edition) (by Capt. K. R. Rankin)	Brown, Son & Ferguson

* Some excellent **containership cargo carriage information** is available on **P&O Nedlloyd's website** at www.ponl.com

D03h OPERATIONAL REQUIREMENTS APPLICABLE TO UK OFFSHORE VESSELS

* **In addition** to the operational requirements applicable to all UK ships, as outlined in D03a, the following standards apply to offshore vessels.

D03h.1 OSV Code

* **The Code of Safe Practice for the Carriage of Cargoes and Persons by Offshore Supply Vessels** (the "OSV Code") -
  - is a non-mandatory IMO code, adopted under Resolution A.863(20) in November 1997.
  - should be observed by all UK supply vessels[30].
  - contains four sections and three appendices, as follows: 1. General; 2. Port operations; 3. Sea-transport; 4. Operations at the offshore installation; Appendix 1. Examples and types of offshore installation; Appendix 2. Colour code for hoses transferring bulk substances; Appendix 3. Interfacing activities of operators and contractors.
* Section 1 (General) contains paragraphs as follows: 1.1. Definitions; 1.2. Information and documentation; 1.3. Communication; 1.4. Cargo handling and stability.
* Section 2 (Port operations) contains paragraphs as follows: 2.1. Communication; 2.2. Cargo.
* Section 3 (Sea-transport) contains paragraphs as follows: 3.1. General; 3.2. Communication.
* Section 4 (Operations at the offshore installation) contains paragraphs as follows: 4.1. General; 4.2. Mooring requirements; 4.3. Communication; 4.4. Information and documentation; 4.5. Personnel transfer; 4.6. Cargo handling.

D03h.2 Offshore Support Vessel Guidelines

* **Guidelines for the Safe Management and Operation of Offshore Support Vessels** were published jointly in October 1998 by the United Kingdom Offshore Operators' Association (UKOOA) and the UK Chamber of Shipping, replacing The Code of Practice for the Safe Management and Operation of Offshore Support Vessels (the "OSV Code"), and were promulgated in **MGN 42**. **Issue 4 of the Guidelines** is available in CD-ROM format.
* **The Guidelines provide** guidance to operators, owners, logistics companies and especially masters and crews of offshore support vessels (i.e. **supply vessels** and **standby** or **other vessels** involved in offshore supply and anchor-handling activities) and offshore installation managers (OIMs) on avoiding and reducing the hazards and risks which affect offshore support vessels and their crews in their normal operations. For the purpose of the Guidelines, "operators" and "owners" are taken to be the operators or owners of offshore installations. References to "vessel operators" means those persons responsible for the day to day management and operation of the vessel.
* **The Guidelines set out** what is generally regarded in the industry as good practice. This is **not mandatory**, although it does refer, where appropriate, to certain legal requirements of the Merchant Shipping Acts and Health and Safety legislation. Operators/owners and vessel operators should adopt different standards only where this would maintain an equivalent or higher level of safety and would not conflict with relevant legal requirements.
* **Compliance with the Guidelines** will generally be accepted by the MCA as meeting the standards required by the Merchant Shipping Act 1995 and the MS and FV (Health and Safety at Work) Regulations 1997. **Failure to comply** will be regarded as *prima facie* failure to meet those standards.
* With respect to those activities (primarily loading and unloading) to which health and safety legislation administered by the Health and Safety Executive (HSE) applies, adopting the guidance in the Guidelines on good practice will help to meet the legal duties under the Health and Safety at Work etc. Act 1974, and regulations made under it. Although there may be other ways of meeting these legal duties, HSE inspectors will regard the guidance in the Guidelines as meeting the standards necessary for compliance with relevant legislation.
* All offshore installations – fixed and mobile – must produce a site-specific **Offshore Installation Data Card** that is to be made available to all existing vessels; an example is shown in Appendix 7 to the Guidelines. The Guidelines should be read in conjunction with the appropriate Offshore Installation Data Card.
* For notes on Health and Safety Executive (HSE) legislation relating to offshore vessels see B05e.2.

---

[30] MGN 205, paragraph 2. A footnote to the MGN states that the Code is available from the MCA.

D03h.3 IMO Guidelines for the Transport and Handling of Limited Amounts of Hazardous and Noxious Liquid Substances in Bulk on Offshore Support Vessels

* All ships carrying dangerous or noxious liquid substances in bulk, including offshore supply vessels, are subject to the MS (Dangerous or Noxious Liquid Substances in Bulk) Regulations 1996 (SI 1996/3010) as amended (see D03e.2a and H03b.2) and the MS (Dangerous Goods and Marine Pollutants) Regulations 1997 (SI 1997/2367) (see F07f.2). Whereas ships purpose-built for the carriage of MARPOL Annex II substances must also comply with the IMO chemical and gas tanker codes, IMO has agreed that, on certain conditions, **offshore supply vessels** which carry **limited amounts** of these substances do not have to comply in full with the requirements of the IMO Codes in order to meet the requirements of SOLAS and MARPOL. The conditions are that:
  * the **discharge** of category A, B and C noxious liquid substances, or ballast water, tank washings or residues or mixtures containing such substances must be to the offshore **installation** or port **reception facilities**; and
  * the ships comply with the **IMO Guidelines** for the Transport and Handling of Limited Amounts of Hazardous and Noxious Liquid Substances in Bulk on Offshore Support Vessels adopted under resolution A.673(16).
* **M.1458** contains in its annexes the full text of the **Guidelines** and a **General Exemption** from UK regulations in force at the date of publication of the M Notice but which were superseded by the regulations mentioned above.

D03h.4 Standby Vessel Guidelines

* The stationing of an offshore standby vessel or emergency response and recovery vessel (ERRV) at each offshore installation on the UK Continental Shelf meets the requirements of **regulation 17 of the Offshore Installations (Prevention of Fire and Explosion, and Emergency Response) Regulations 1995** (SI 1995/743), which provides that the duty holder (who, in relation to a fixed installation, means the operator, and in relation to a mobile installation, the owner) must ensure that **effective arrangements** are made, which include such arrangements with suitable persons beyond the installation, for:
  * recovery of persons following their evacuation or escape from the installation; and
  * rescue of persons near the installation; and
  * taking such persons to a place of safety.
  - and for the purposes of regulation 17, arrangements will be regarded as being "effective" if they secure a good prospect of those persons being recovered, rescued, and taken to a place of safety. Under regulation 3(2), regulation 17 does not apply in relation to an installation that is in transit to or from a station. An installation is not "in transit to or from a station" while it is being manoeuvred at the station, which means that rescue provision is required during rig mooring operations, etc.
* **Standby vessels** operating on the UK Continental Shelf are regulated (since 1 November 1997) by two voluntary codes of practice drawn up by industry lead bodies:
  * **Guidelines for Survey of Vessels Standing By Offshore Installations**; and
  * **Guidelines for Operation of Vessels Standing By Offshore Installations**.
* The Guidelines are issued jointly by UKOOA, the International Association of Drilling Contractors (IADC) (North Sea Chapter), the British Rig Owners' Association (BROA) and the Standby Ship Operators' Association (SSOA). They provide those with responsibilities for recovery and rescue arrangements with broad guidance on the operational aspects of any vessel standing by an offshore installation when providing arrangements for effective recovery and rescue required by the Offshore Installations (Prevention of Fire and Explosion, and Emergency Response) Regulations 1995 (SI 1995/743) (known as "PFEER"). The Guidelines are not mandatory and operators may adopt different standards in a particular situation where to do so would maintain an equivalent or better level of safety.
* **Guidelines for Survey of Vessels Standing By Offshore Installations** (Joint Industry Guide No.1) contains the following sections:
  * Survey of suitability of SBV
  * Stability
  * Accommodation and survivors' reception
  * SBV equipment
  * Radio and other communications
  * Appendix A – Special medical equipment and stores to be carried by SBV
  * Appendix B – Sample certificate
  * Appendix C – Relevant legal requirements
  * Appendix D – References/Acronyms
* **Guidelines for Operation of Vessels Standing By Offshore Installations** (Joint Industry Guide No.2) contains the following sections:

- Introduction
- Operational standards
- Location and rescue from the water
- Care of casualties
- Transfer of casualties for further treatment
- Evacuation, recovery, rescue and treatment
- Command and control
- Crewing requirements
- Training and crew matters
- Monitoring safety zone
- Appendix A – References/Acronyms.

D03h.5 MODU Code

* **Mobile offshore drilling units** (or "MODUs") should, if their keels were laid or were at a similar stage of construction on or after 1 May 1991, comply with the **Code for the Construction and Equipment of Mobile Offshore Drilling Units**, 1989 (the "**1989 MODU Code**"), which was adopted by IMO Assembly Resolution A.649(16) and superseded the 1979 MODU Code. If constructed before 1 May 1991, MODUs should comply with the **1979 MODU Code**.
* A "**mobile offshore drilling unit**" (or "**MODU**") is defined as a vessel capable of engaging in drilling operations for the exploration or exploitation of resources beneath the sea-bed such as liquid or gaseous hydrocarbons, sulphur or salt (MODU Code, Chapter 1, Paragraph 1.3.1). MODUs include "**surface units**" (such as drill-ships and – barges), "**self-elevating units**" (i.e. jack-up rigs) and "**column-stabilized units**" (i.e. semi-submersible rigs).
* A "**surface unit**" is a unit with a ship- or barge-type displacement hull of single or multiple hull construction intended for operation in the floating condition (MODU Code, Chapter 1, Paragraph 1.3.2).
* A "**self-elevating unit**" is a unit with movable legs capable of raising its hull above the surface of the sea (MODU Code, Chapter 1, Paragraph 1.3.3).
* A "**column-stabilized unit**" is a unit with the main deck connected to the underwater hull or footings by columns or caissons (MODU Code, Chapter 1, Paragraph 1.3.4).
* The coastal State (in which the MODU is operating) may impose additional requirements regarding the operation of industrial systems not dealt with by the MODU Code (MODU Code, Chapter 1, Paragraph 1.2.2).
* A certificate called a **Mobile Offshore Drilling Unit Safety Certificate (1989)** may be issued after an initial or renewal survey to a unit which complies with the requirements of the MODU Code (MODU Code, Chapter 1, Paragraph 1.6.7).

D03h.5a DP Guidelines

* **Dynamically-positioned vessels**, which include (but are not limited to) diving support vessels, drilling vessels, floating production units, accommodation vessels, crane vessels, shuttle tankers, pipelaying vessels and ROV support vessels -
  - are covered by the IMO **Guidelines for Vessels with Dynamic Positioning Systems**[31], which should be implemented under the provisions of the 1989 MODU Code.
  - are covered by the IMCA[32] **Guidelines for the Design & Operation of Dynamically Positioned Vessels**.
* The **MODU Code**, Chapter 4, Paragraph 4.12 provides that dynamic positioning systems used as a sole means of position keeping should provide a level of safety equivalent to that provided for anchoring arrangements.
* Vessels complying with the Guidelines may be issued by the classification society with a **Declaration of Survey** to certify that the ship has been documented, surveyed and tested in accordance with IMO MSC/Circular 645 "Guidelines for Vessels with Dynamic Positioning Systems" and found to comply with the Guidelines for Equipment of the stated class (e.g. "Class III"). Compliance with the operational conditions in the Circular is the responsibility of the owner and is not considered in the survey. In order to maintain a valid Equipment Class, the vessel must be operated, tested and surveyed according to the requirements of the Guidelines. Test results must be recorded and filed together with system documentation, and be available on request by the flag State Administration.
* Following survey by the classification society, and issue of the Declaration of Survey mentioned above, a **Flag State Verification and Acceptance Document** ("**FSVAD**") may be issued by the MCA to a UK dynamically-

---

[31] Disseminated by MSC/Circ.645.

[32] The International Marine Contractors Association (IMCA) is the international trade association representing offshore diving, marine and underwater engineering companies. It was formed in April 1995 from the amalgamation of AODC (the International Association of Offshore Diving Contractors) and DPVOA (the Dynamic Positioning Vessel Owners Association).

positioned vessel to certify that the vessel has been duly documented, surveyed and tested in accordance with the Guidelines for Vessels with Dynamic Positioning Systems and found to comply with the Guidelines. The FSVAD states that the vessel is allowed to operate in DP Equipment Class (as stated, e.g. "III"). The FSVAD is valid until terminated by the MCA, provided that the vessel is operated, tested and surveyed according to the requirements of the Guidelines and the results are properly recorded. Attached to the FSVAD should be a list of the main systems and components covered by the FSVAD, e.g. electrical power system and generating plant, thruster system and the DP control system.

D03h.6 Code of Safety for Diving Systems

- is a **non-mandatory IMO code**, originally adopted in 1983, and adopted in a revised 1995 version by resolution A.831(19).
- was developed to provide a **minimum international standard** for the design, construction, survey and certification of **diving systems on ships and floating structures** engaged in diving operations, in order to enhance safety of divers and associated personnel.
- **should be complied with** by all new diving systems fitted on ships and floating structures.
- **does not include** requirements for diving operations or procedures for control of diving operations.
- sets out (in 1.6) requirements for **survey and certification of diving systems**.
- provides that each diving system should have an **initial survey** before being put into service, a **renewal survey** at intervals not exceeding 5 years, and an **annual survey** within 3 months before or after the anniversary date of the Diving System Safety Certificate.
- provides for the issue, after an initial survey or a renewal survey, of a **Diving System Safety Certificate** for a period not exceeding 5 years. A specimen certificate is contained in the Appendix to the Code.
- provides (in 1.6.12) that **limiting operating parameters**, including vessel's motion and environmental conditions, should be shown in the Diving System Safety Certificate.

D03h.7 Diving Safety Regulations

* The **MS (Diving Safety) Regulations 2002** (SI 2002/1587) -
  - **revoke** and replace the MS (Diving Operations) Regulations 1975 (SI 1975/116) and the MS (Diving Operations) (Amendment) Regulations 1975 (SI 1975/2062).
  - **apply** to a diving project within UK territorial waters which takes place from a craft the master or owner of which is the diving contractor for the project, and to which the Diving at Work Regulations 1997 (SI 1997/2776) or the Diving Operations at Work (Northern Ireland) Regulations 1983 (SI 1983/209) do not apply (regulations 3(1) and 3(3)). (Diving projects covered by regulations 3(1) and 3(3) will mostly involve recreational divers who use a vessel or other floating structure.)
  - **apply** outside UK or other national waters or beyond the UK Continental Shelf, to a diving project launched or operated from a **UK ship**, which relates to an **offshore installation or pipeline**, in relation to which there is a diving contractor (regulation 3(2)(a)).
  - **apply** outside UK or other national waters, to any diving project launched or operated from a UK ship, other than one which relates to an offshore installation or pipeline in relation to which there is a diving contractor (regulation 3(2)(b).
  - **set out duties** of the owner of craft from which diving projects are undertaken (regulation 5), masters of such craft (regulation 6) and diving contractors (regulation 8).
  - require the preparation of a **diving project plan** (regulation 9).
  - require the **appointment of a diving supervisor** (regulation 10) and set out his duties (regulation 11).
  - **confer powers** on the master and diving supervisor to give **directions** (regulation 12).
  - set out requirements for the **competence and fitness of divers** (regulation 13).
  - set out **duties of all persons** taking part in a diving project (regulation 14).
  - set out requirements for a **Certificate of Medical Fitness to Dive** (regulation 15).
  - provide for limited and conditional **exemptions** to be granted by the MCA (regulation 16).
  - require any **diving operations log book** and any **diver's logbook** to be retained for at least 2 years after the last entry (regulation 21).
  - are explained in **MSN 1762**.
* UK regulations covering most commercial diving operations offshore are the **Diving at Work Regulations 1997** (SI 1997/2776), regulation 4 of which provides that every person who to any extent is responsible for, has control over or is engaged in a diving project or whose acts or omissions could adversely affect the health and safety of persons engaged in such a project, must take such measures as it is reasonable for a person in his position to take to ensure

that the Regulations are complied with. (The Regulations impose no duties on a master of any vessel, but do impose duties on the diving contractor.)

D03h.8 Publications applicable to offshore support vessels

* Publications containing **standards of good operational practice** applicable to **offshore support vessels** are shown in the following table. For publications applicable to all ship types see D03a.6.

Document title	Publisher
An Introduction to Marine Drilling	OPL
Handling of Offshore Supply Vessels (by Captain S. Chaudhuri)	Nautical Institute
Operation of Offshore Supply and Anchor Handling Vessels (by Captain P. R. Maudsley)	Nautical Institute
OSV Code: Code of Safe Practice for the Carriage of Persons and Cargoes by Offshore Supply Vessels	IMO

D03i OPERATIONAL REQUIREMENTS APPLICABLE TO UK HIGH SPEED CRAFT AND DYNAMICALLY SUPPORTED CRAFT

D03i.1 HSC Codes

* Because of their special construction and mode of operation, high speed craft (HSC) such as jetfoils, hydrofoils, HSS, SeaCats and similar craft cannot comply with all the requirements of SOLAS that are applicable to conventional ships. IMO therefore developed a special **International Code of Safety for High-Speed Craft** (originally known as the "**HSC Code**"). The original HSC Code was published in 1994, was made mandatory by a new **SOLAS chapter X** and came into force internationally on **1 January 1996**.
* Application of the original HSC Code showed that some parts of it were open to interpretation and that a consistent application of its detailed requirements was necessary. IMO's Maritime Safety Committee therefore agreed to revise the HSC Code. The revised HSC Code, properly called the **International Code of Safety for High-Speed Craft, 2000** but known as the "**2000 HSC Code**", was published in December 2001. To distinguish it from the revised Code, the original HSC Code was then re-named the "**1994 HSC Code**".
* The **1994 HSC Code** applies to high-speed craft engaged in international voyages, the keels were laid on or after **1 January 1996**.
* The **2000 HSC Code** is applicable to high speed craft the keels of which are laid, or which are at a similar stage of construction, on or after **1 July 2002** and is mandatory from that date.

D03i.2 High Speed Craft Regulations

* The **MS (High Speed Craft) Regulations 1996** (SI 1996/3188) -
  - **give effect** in the UK to the **1994 HSC Code**.
  - require high speed craft, constructed after 1 January 1996 (and falling within regulation 3(1)(b) to (e) of the Regulations), to be **constructed, equipped and operated** in accordance with the **HSC Code**.
  - make provisions for **surveys** (regulation 5) and for the issue of **High-Speed Craft Safety Certificates** (regulation 6) and **Permits to Operate** (regulation 7) (see D04v.2).
  - **require compliance with certain rules of classification societies**, thus implementing in part article 14 of Council Directive 94/57/EC on common rules and standards of ship inspection and survey organisations and for the relevant activities of maritime Administrations (regulation 4(2)) (see D04d.1).
  - **amend** a number of other MS regulations so that they cease to apply to high-speed craft (regulation 17).

D03i.3 Mandatory Surveys for Ro-Ro Ferry and High Speed Passenger Craft Regulations

* The **MS (Mandatory Surveys for Ro-Ro Ferry and High Speed Passenger Craft) Regulations 2001** (SI 2001/152) are described in D04f.4.

D03i.4 DSC Code

* The **Code of Safety for Dynamically Supported Craft** (or "**DSC Code**")-
    - forms the Annex to IMO Resolution A.373(X).
    - **applies** (under 1.3.1 of the Code) to craft which:.
        • carry more than 12 passengers but not over 450 passengers with all the passengers seated;
        • do not proceed in the course of their voyage more than 100 nautical miles from the place of refuge; and
        • may be provided with special category spaces intended to carry motor vehicles with fuel in their tanks.
* "**Dynamically supported craft**" -
    - are defined in 1.4.1 as "a craft which is operable on or above water and which has characteristics so different from those of conventional displacement ships, to which the existing International Conventions, particularly the Safety and Load Line Conventions, apply, that alternative measures should be used in order to achieve an equivalent level of safety".
    - **include** craft such as hydrofoil vessels, air cushion vehicles, side wall craft, etc.
    - **are subject to survey and assessment** in accordance with 1.5 of the Code (see D04v.3).
    - should not operate commercially unless certificated in accordance with 1.6 of the Code (see D04v.4).
* For notes on **surveys and certification** required under the DSC Code see D04v.

D03j OPERATIONAL REQUIREMENTS APPLICABLE TO UK SPECIAL PURPOSE SHIPS

* The **Code of Safety for Special Purpose Ships** (the "**SPS Code**") -
    - was developed in recognition of the fact that:
        • specialised types of ships with **unusual design and operational characteristics** may differ from those of conventional merchant ships that are subject to SOLAS;
        • by virtue of the specialised nature of the work undertaken by these ships, **special personnel** are carried, who are neither crew members nor passengers as defined in SOLAS;
        • **certain safety standards, supplementing those of SOLAS**, may be required for special purpose ships.
    - forms the Annex to IMO Resolution A.534(13).
    - **applies** to every new special purpose ship of not less than 500gt. The flag State Administration may also apply the Code as far as reasonable and practicable to special purpose ships of less than 500gt.
    - has been **amended** to include the GMDSS requirements.
* "**Special personnel**" are defined as "all persons who are not passengers or members of the crew or children of under one year of age and who are carried on board in connection with the special purpose of that ship or because of special work being carried out aboard that ship" (1.3.3). Such personnel may include scientific research personnel and technicians. Because special personnel are expected to be able-bodied with a fair knowledge of the layout of the ship and have received some training in safety procedures and the handling of the ship's safety equipment, the special purpose ships on which they are carried need not be considered or treated as passenger ships.
* "**Special purpose ship**" means "a mechanically self-propelled ship which by reason of its function carries on board more than 12 special personnel including passengers" (1.3.4). Special purpose ships to which the Code applies includes the following types:
    • ships engaged in research, expeditions and survey (1.3.4.1);
    • ships for training of marine personnel (1.3.4.2);
    • whale and fish factory ships not engaged in catching (1.3.4.3);
    • ships processing other living resources of the sea, not engaged in catching (1.3.4.4);
    • other ships with design features and modes of operation similar to the above ships which in the opinion of the Adminstration may be referred to this group (1.3.4.5).
* Examples of British ships which meet the above definition include British Antarctic Supply (BAS) polar supply/research vessels[33].
* Every special purpose ship should be subject to the **surveys** as specified for cargo ships, other than tankers, in SOLAS 74/78, which should cover the provisions of the SPS Code (SPS Code, 1.6).

---

[33] The UK has not formally accepted the Special Purpose Ships Code, which means that, strictly speaking, the Code cannot apply to British ships. To avoid problems with port State control inspectors a letter may be carried by a British special purpose ship, issued by the flag State Administration and certifying that, were the Code to be formally accepted, the ship would meet all of its requirements.

* A **Special Purpose Ship Safety Certificate** may be issued after survey in accordance with 1.6 either by the flag State Administration of by any person or organization duly authorized by it (1.7.1). The duration and validity of the certificate should be governed by the respective provisions for cargo ships in SOLAS (1.7.3).

* Exemption is available under 1.4.1 for a special purpose ship engaged on a near-coastal voyage provided that it complies with safety requirements appropriate for the limited area of operation.

* Exemption is available under 1.4.2 for a ship not normally engaged as a special purpose ship which undertakes an exceptional single voyage as a special purpose ship provided it complies with safety requirements adequate for the voyage.

* The Preamble to the Code provides that where a special purpose ship is normally engaged on international voyages as defined in SOLAS it should, in addition to the Special Purpose Ship Safety Certificate, also carry **SOLAS Safety Certificates**, either: (a) for a passenger ship with a SOLAS Exemption Certificate; or (b) for a cargo ship with a SOLAS Exemption Certificate, where necessary, as the Administration deems necessary.

D03k OPERATIONAL REQUIREMENTS APPLICABLE TO UK SAIL TRAINING SHIPS

* **M.1422** states that ships built, equipped, certified and operated in full compliance with the terms of the **Sail Training Vessel Code** will be **exempt** from various statutory requirements which would otherwise have to be met, such as governing the application of load line rules, fire protection standards, carriage of lifesaving appliances and medical stores.

* The Code of Practice for the Construction, Machinery, Stability and Survey of Sail Training Ships between 7 metres and 24 metres in length, also known as the "**Code of Practice for the Safety of Sail Training Ships**" or the "**Sail Training Vessels Code**" -
   - **was published** by the MCA in 1990 and came into effect on 1 January 1991[34].
   - **was superseded** in 1993 by "Code of practice for the construction, machinery, equipment, stability, operation and examination of sailing vessels, of up to 24 metres load line length, in commercial use and which do not carry cargo or more than 12 passengers", more commonly known as the "**Blue Code**". In accordance with section 27.3 of the Blue Code, **sail training ships** previously considered under the Sail Training Vessels Code should now be considered under the Blue Code.

* **Sail training vessels** of less than 24 metres in load line length should now comply with the "**Blue Code**" (see D03l.4).

* **Sail training vessels** of 24 metres in load line length or **over** or (if built before 21 July 1968) of 150 tons gross tonnage or over should comply with the Code of Practice for Safety of Large Commercial Sailing and Motor Vessels (the "**White Code**" or "**Megayacht Code**") (see D03l.7).

* A "**sail training vessel**" is defined in paragraph 2 of the White Code as a sailing vessel which at the time it is being used is being used either:
   • to provide instruction in the principles of responsibility, resourcefulness, loyalty and team endeavour and to advance education in the art of seamanship; or
   • to provide instruction in navigation and seamanship for yachtsmen.

D03l OPERATIONAL REQUIREMENTS APPLICABLE TO UK LICENSED AND CODE CERTIFICATED VESSELS

D03l.1 Licensing of non-regulated pleasure vessels (NRPVs)

* "**Non-regulated pleasure vessels**", or "**NRPVs**" -
   - are vessels of **less than 13.7m** in length which are not operated commercially. Numerous NRPVs are in use in the UK.
   - are **not generally subject** to MCA-administered regulations or Codes of Practice, but are subject to Merchant Shipping law in relation to **navigation**, **collision avoidance** and **pollution prevention**. (A pleasure vessel of 13.7m in length or over is a **Class XII** vessel and as such becomes subject to Merchant Shipping regulations in relation to carriage of life-saving appliances and fire protection.)
   - may be subject to UK **local authority licensing**, and as such may be subject to **bye-laws** relating to the carriage of **life-saving and fire-fighting appliances**.

---

[34] The Code (ISBN No. 0 11 550955 0) is available from HMSO. The Associated Model Stability Information Booklet has ISBN No. 0 11 5509569.

* **Powers** of UK local authorities to licence **small pleasure boats** within their jurisdiction, which do not carry more than 12 passengers, and which stay within 3 miles from land and travel no more than 15 miles from their point of departure, are contained in **section 94 of the Public Health Amendment Act 1907** and in the **Civic Government (Scotland) Act 1982**. Exercise of the powers is optional.

* The areas and conditions of operation under a **Pleasure Boat Licence** may vary between different local authorities. Licensed **commercial vessels** (e.g. boats carrying angling parties, divers, etc.) will mostly be licensed for operation in sheltered waters, e.g. harbours and estuaries, and their area of operation will not normally extend outside of Category D waters (as defined in D04c.2a).

* An "**NRPV Code**" has been developed and is available from I-Force, Tel. 020 8957 5028. Fax. 020 8957 5012.

* The MS (Load Line) (Amendment) Regulations 2000 (SI 2000/1335) removed the exemption from compliance with the Load Line Regulations formerly in place for ships not carrying more than 12 passengers for sport or pleasure on voyages to sea within 3 miles from land and 15 miles from their point of departure, the intention being that such vessels should now comply with the appropriate **Code of Practice**.

* With the introduction on 1 April 2000 of the Code of Practice for the Safety of Small Vessels in Commercial Use for Sport or Pleasure operating from a Nominated Departure Point (NDP) (the "Red Code" or "NDP Code") (see D03l.6), most local authorities began phasing out Pleasure Boat Licences for vessels **which proceed to sea** in favour of the arrangements set out in the Red Code or NDP Code.

* **Charter vessels** engaged in angling, diving or similar **commercial activities** should normally operate under **either** a **local authority licence** or under the **appropriate Code** as detailed below.

D03l.2 UK Codes of Practice applicable to commercial vessels

* When a "pleasure vessel"[35], as defined in D03l.8, is used for chartering, it becomes a "**commercial vessel**" and should, and in certain cases must, be certificated in accordance with the relevant **statutory code of practice** as detailed below. These codes do not apply to "pleasure vessels". They are all administered, and enforced where appropriate, by the MCA.

* The **statutory codes of practice** with which UK vessels, **in commercial use** for various purposes, are required to comply are shown in the following table.

Code title	Popular name	Related SI	Related M Notice	SBC ref.
The Safety of Small Commercial Motor Vessels – A Code of Practice	Yellow Code	1998/2771	-	D03l.3
The Safety of Small Commercial Sailing Vessels – A Code of Practice	Blue Code	1998/2771	-	D03l.4
The Safety of Small Workboats and Pilot Boats – A Code of Practice	Brown Code	1998/1609	MGN 50	D03l.5
The Code of Practice for the Safety of Small Vessels in Commercial Use for Sport or Pleasure operating from a Nominated Departure Point (NDP)	Red Code or NDP Code	-	MIN 77	D03l.6
The Code of Practice for Safety of Large Commercial Sailing and Motor Vessels	White Code or Megayacht Code	1998/2771	-	D03l.7
Code of Practice for Vessels Engaged in Oil Recovery Operations	Black Code	-	M.1663	D04g.11

* A growing **database** of coded vessels is available on the MCA website.

* The MCA intends to **harmonise the Red, Blue, Yellow and Brown Codes** during 2002 for greater convenience and in order to simplify administration.

D03l.3 Code of Practice for the Safety of Small Commercial Motor Vessels (the "Yellow Code")

* The **Safety of Small Commercial Motor Vessels – A Code of Practice** -
- has the **full title** of "Code of practice for the construction, machinery, equipment, stability, operation and examination of motor vessels, of up to 24 metres load line length, in commercial use and which do not carry cargo or more than 12 passengers".
- is commonly known as the "**Yellow Code**" the publication having a yellow cover.
- was **published** in 1993 for The Surveyor General's Organisation of The Department of Transport with ISBN 0-11-551185-7.
- is a **companion Code to** The Safety of Small Commercial Sailing Vessels – A Code of Practice (the "Blue Code"). (Reference to the companion Code is made where a sail assisted motor vessel has a significant sailing rig.)

---

[35] A "**pleasure vessel**" basically means a private vessel used by its owner, or his family or friends, where no money changes hands.

- is an **acceptable Code of Practice for application** in accordance with regulation 5 of the MS (Vessels in Commercial Use for Sport or Pleasure) Regulations 1998 (SI 1998/2771)[36] (see D031.8).
- **may be applied to** (but is **not mandatory** for) any UK commercially operated motor vessel of up to 24 metres load line length[37] (and any such vessel registered or owned in any other country when it operates from a UK port) which -
  - proceeds to sea;
  - does not carry cargo; and
  - does not carry more than 12 passengers[38].

* **Examination and certification** of a vessel in accordance with the Yellow Code means that several Merchant Shipping statutory instruments, listed in Schedule 2 of the MS (Vessels in Commercial Use for Sport or Pleasure) Regulations 1998, will be **disapplied** in respect of that vessel. (For the list of disapplied SIs see D031.8.)

* Compliance with the Code does not obviate the need to comply with **local authority licensing requirements** where applicable (Yellow Code 1.14).

* A vessel may be considered for the issue of a **Small Commercial Vessel Certificate** allowing it to operate in one of the following five areas:
Category 4: up to 20 miles from a safe haven[39], in favourable weather and in daylight;
Category 3: up to 20 miles from a safe haven;
Category 2: up to 60 miles from a safe haven;
Category 1: up to 150 miles from a safe haven;
Category 0: unrestricted service.

* To be issued with a certificate for a particular area of operation a vessel should comply with all the requirements of the Code for that operating area, to the satisfaction of the Certifying Authority.

* **"Certifying Authority"** means either the **MCA** or one of the **organisations authorised by the MCA** to (1) appoint persons for the purpose of examining vessels and issuing and signing Declarations of Examinations, and (2) to issue Small Commercial Vessel Certificates. The organisations authorised by the MCA as **Certifying Authorities are** listed in **MIN 114**. The MCA issues "Yellow Code stickers" to all Certifying Authorities, following the "NDP Code" pattern.

* The **Yellow Code's chief sections and annexes** are: 1. Foreword; 2. Definitions; 3. Application and interpretation; 4. Construction and structural strength; 5. Weathertight integrity; 6. Water freeing arrangements; 7. Machinery; 8. Electrical arrangements; 9. Steering gear; 10. Bilge pumping; 11. Intact stability; 12. Freeboard and freeboard marking; 13. Life-saving appliances; 14. Fire safety; 15. Fire appliances; 16. Radio equipment; 17. Navigation lights, shapes and sound signals; 18. Navigational equipment; 19. Miscellaneous equipment; 20. Anchors and cables; 21. Accommodation; 22. Protection of personnel; 23. Medical stores; 24. Tenders (dinghies); 25. Sailing vessel features; 26. Manning; 27. Compliance procedures, certification, examination and maintenance; 28. Vessels operating under Race Rules; 29. Clean seas; Annex 1. Merchant Shipping Notice M.1194; Annex 2. Life-saving appliances; Annex 3. Open flame gas installations; Annex 4. Fire fighting equipment; Annex 5. Anchors and cables; Annex 6. Medical stores; Annex 7. The manning of small vessels; Annex 8. Handover procedures for bare-boat charter; Annex 9. Skippered charter – safety briefing; Annex 10. Phase-in timetable – existing vessels; Annex 11 – Small Commercial Vessel Certificate.

* A vessel should be **safely manned** (26).

* For vessels other than those on bare-boat charter, the **qualifications of the skipper** (and other crew member(s), where applicable) for operations in the various areas is the subject of a **General Exemption** from relevant Regulations, granted by the MCA. The conditions applicable to the General Exemption and the responsibility of the owner/managing agent for the safe manning of the vessel are given in Annex 7 (26.1).

* A **vessel operating on bare-boat charter as a pleasure vessel** is not subject to the safe manning conditions in Annex 7. The owner/managing agent of a vessel offered for bare-boat charter should ensure that the skipper and crew of the vessel are provided with sufficient information about the vessel and its equipment to enable it to be navigated safely. The owner/managing agent should be satisfied that the bare-boat charter skipper and crew are competent for the intended voyage. Details of **handover procedures** are given in Annex 8 (26.2).

* The skipper of a vessel on skippered charter should ensure that each person on board is briefed on safety in accordance with the requirements given in Annex 9 (26.3).

* Section 27.2 provides that the **owner/managing agent of a vessel to be operated under the Code should**:
  - choose an authorised Certifying Authority and **apply** to them for an **examination**;

---

[36] When the Yellow Code was introduced the relevant Regulations were the MS (Vessels in Commercial Use for Sport or Pleasure) Regulations 1993 (SI 1993/1072). These Regulations were revoked and replaced by the 1998 Regulations.

[37] "Load line length" means either 96% of the total length on a waterline at 85% of the least moulded depth measured from the top of the keel, or the length from the fore side of the stem to the axis of the rudder stock on that waterline, whichever is the greater. In a vessel designed with a rake of keel, the waterline on this length is measured should be parallel to the design waterline.

[38] Such a vessel carrying more than 12 passengers would have to be surveyed and certified as a "passenger ship" of the appropriate class (see D04c.2).

[39] A "safe haven" is defined in the Code as "a harbour or shelter of any kind which affords entry, subject to prudence in the weather conditions prevailing, and protection from the force of weather".

- arrange with the Certifying Authority for the vessel to be **examined** by an **authorised person**[40] and **documented** on the report form for a **Compliance Examination** and **Declaration**[41] as being in compliance with the Code;
- be in receipt of a **Small Commercial Vessel Certificate** for the vessel prior to it entering into service.

* Before a certificate is issued to a vessel of **15 metres or more** in length or carrying **15 or more persons** or operating in area category 0 or 1, the owner/managing agent should be in possession of a **stability information booklet** (27.5.3). Before a certificate is issued to a vessel of **less than 15 metres** in length and carrying **14 or fewer persons** and operating in category 2, 3 or 4, the owner/managing agent should provide the Certifying Authority with **information** necessary to confirm that the vessel's stability meets the standard required by the Code for the permitted area of operation (27.5.4).

* A certificate should be valid for not more than **5 years** (27.5.6).

* Requirements for **compliance examinations** and **annual examinations** are set out in section 27.6. **Compliance examinations** must be made by the Certifying Authority for renewal of a certificate. **Annual examinations** must be made, once in each calendar year, and at intervals of not more than 15 months, by the Certifying Authority in the case of a vessel of 15 metres or more in length or carrying 15 or more persons, and by the owner/managing agent in the case of vessels of less than 15 metres in length and carrying 14 or fewer persons.

* **Details on a Small Commercial Vessel Certificate** include: Name of vessel; name and address of owner/managing agent; official number; port of registry; gross tonnage; maximum number of persons to be carried; length overall; load line length; date of build; unique identification number; certifying statement that the vessel was examined by (name of examiner) of (Certifying Authority) at (place) on (date) and found to be in accordance with the Code (full title printed); statement that the certificate will remain valid until (expiry date) subject to the vessel, its machinery and equipment being efficiently maintained, annual examinations and manning complying with the Code of Practice, and to the conditions (as stated); permitted area of operation; place and date of issue; Certifying Authority; issuing official's name and signature; date of issue.

D03l.4 Code of Practice for the Safety of Small Commercial Sailing Vessels (the "Blue Code")

* The Safety of Small Commercial Sailing Vessels – A Code of Practice –
- has the **full title** of "Code of practice for the construction, machinery, equipment, stability, operation and examination of sailing vessels, of up to 24 metres load line length, in commercial use and which do not carry cargo or more than 12 passengers".
- is commonly known as the "**Blue Code**", the publication having a blue cover.
- was **published** in 1993 by The Surveyor General's Organisation of The Department of Transport with ISBN 0-11-551184-9.
- **succeeds and replaces** "The Safety of Sail Training Ships – A Code of Practice", which was published by the Marine Directorate of the Department of Transport in 1990. **Sail training ships** previously considered under that Code should now be considered under the Blue Code, in accordance with section 27.3 of the Code.
- is a **companion Code to** The Safety of Small Commercial Motor Vessels – A Code of Practice (the "Yellow Code"). (Reference to the companion Code is made where a motor-assisted sailing vessel has a significant motor propulsion installation.)
- is an **acceptable Code of Practice for application** in accordance with regulation 5 of the MS (Vessels in Commercial Use for Sport or Pleasure) Regulations 1998 (SI 1998/2771)[42] (see D03l.8).
- **may be applied to** (but is **not mandatory** for) any UK commercially operated sailing vessel of up to 24 metres load line length[43] (and any such vessel registered or owned in any other country when it operates from a UK port) which –
  - proceeds to sea;
  - does not carry cargo; and
  - does not carry more than 12 passengers[44].

---

[40] An "authorised person" means a person who by reason of relevant professional qualifications, practical experience or expertise is authorised by the Certifying Authority chosen by the owner/managing agent from those listed in the Code to carry out examinations required under section 27 of the Code.

[41] The arrangements, fittings and equipment provided on the vessel are documented on the Declaration.

[42] When the Blue Code was introduced the relevant Regulations were the MS (Vessels in Commercial Use for Sport or Pleasure) Regulations 1993 (SI 1993/1072). These Regulations were revoked and replaced by the 1998 Regulations.

[43] "Load line length" means either 96% of the total length on a waterline at 85% of the least moulded depth measured from the top of the keel, or the length from the fore side of the stem to the axis of the rudder stock on that waterline, whichever is the greater. In a vessel designed with a rake of keel, the waterline on this length is measured should be parallel to the design waterline.

[44] Such a vessel carrying more than 12 passengers would have to be surveyed and certified as a "passenger ship" of the appropriate class (see D04c.2).

* **Examination and certification** of a vessel in accordance with the Blue Code means that several Merchant Shipping statutory instruments, listed in Schedule 2 of the MS (Vessels in Commercial Use for Sport or Pleasure) Regulations 1998, will be **disapplied** in respect of that vessel. (For the list of disapplied SIs see D031.8.)
* Compliance with the Blue Code does not obviate the need to comply with **local authority licensing requirements** where applicable (1.14).
* A vessel may be considered for the issue of a **Small Commercial Vessel Certificate** allowing it to operate in one of the following five areas:
    * **Category 4**: up to 20 miles from a safe haven[45], in favourable weather and in daylight;
    * **Category 3**: up to 20 miles from a safe haven;
    * **Category 2**: up to 60 miles from a safe haven;
    * **Category 1**: up to 150 miles from a safe haven;
    * **Category 0**: unrestricted service.
* To be issued with a certificate for a particular area of operation a vessel should comply with all the requirements of the Code for that operating area, to the satisfaction of the Certifying Authority.
* "**Certifying Authority**" means either the MCA or one of the organisations authorised by the MCA (1) to appoint persons for the purpose of examining vessels and issuing and signing Declarations of Examinations, and (2) to issue Small Commercial Vessel Certificates. The organisations authorised by the MCA as **Certifying Authorities** are listed in **MIN 114**.
* The **Blue Code's chief sections and annexes** are the same as in the Yellow Code (see D031.3) with the sole exception of section 25, which in the Blue Code relates to Storm sails.
* A vessel should be **safely manned** (26). Manning requirements are set out in Annex 7 of the Code.
* For **vessels other than those on bare-boat charter**, the **qualifications of the skipper** (and other crew member(s), where applicable) for operations in the various areas is the subject of a **General Exemption** from relevant Regulations, granted by the MCA. The conditions applicable to the General Exemption and the responsibility of the owner/managing agent for the safe manning of the vessel are given in Annex 7 (26.1).
* A **vessel operating on bare-boat charter as a pleasure vessel** is not subject to the safe manning conditions in Annex 7. The owner/managing agent of a vessel offered for bare-boat charter should ensure that the skipper and crew of the vessel are provided with sufficient information about the vessel and its equipment to enable it to be navigated safely. The owner/managing agent should be satisfied that the bare-boat charter skipper and crew are competent for the intended voyage. Details of **handover procedures** are given in Annex 8 (26.2).
* The skipper of a vessel on skippered charter should ensure that each person on board is briefed on safety in accordance with the requirements given in Annex 9 (26.3).
* Section 27.2 provides that the **owner/managing agent of a vessel to be operated under the Code should**:
    * choose an authorised Certifying Authority and **apply** to them for an **examination**;
    * arrange with the Certifying Authority for the vessel to be **examined** by an **authorised person**[46] and **documented** on the report form for a **Compliance Examination** and **Declaration**[47] as being in compliance with the Code;
    * be in receipt of a **Small Commercial Vessel Certificate** for the vessel prior to it entering into service.
* Before a certificate is issued to a vessel of **15 metres or more** in length or carrying **15 or more persons** or operating in area category 0 or 1, the owner/managing agent should be in possession of a **stability information booklet** (27.5.3). Before a certificate is issued to a vessel of **less than 15 metres** in length and carrying **14 or fewer persons** and operating in category 2, 3 or 4, the owner/managing agent should provide the Certifying Authority with **information** necessary to confirm that the vessel's stability meets the standard required by the Code for the permitted area of operation (27.5.4).
* A certificate should be valid for not more than **5 years** (27.5.6).
* Requirements for **compliance examinations** and **annual examinations** are set out in section 27.6. **Compliance examinations** must be made by the Certifying Authority for renewal of a certificate. **Annual examinations** must be made, once in each calendar year, and at intervals of not more than 15 months, by the Certifying Authority in the case of a vessel of 15 metres or more in length or carrying 15 or more persons, and by the owner/managing agent in the case of vessels of less than 15 metres in length and carrying 14 or fewer persons.
* **Details on a Small Commercial Vessel Certificate** include: Name of vessel; name and address of owner/managing agent; official number; port of registry; gross tonnage; maximum number of persons to be carried; length overall; load line length; date of build; unique identification number; certifying statement that the vessel was examined by (name of examiner) of (Certifying Authority) at (place) on (date) and found to be in accordance with the Code (full

---

[45] A "**safe haven**" is defined in the Code as "a harbour or shelter of any kind which affords entry, subject to prudence in the weather conditions prevailing, and protection from the force of weather".

[46] An "authorised person" means a person who by reason of relevant professional qualifications, practical experience or expertise is authorised by the Certifying Authority chosen by the owner/managing agent from those listed in the Code to carry out examinations required under section 27 of the Code.

[47] The arrangements, fittings and equipment provided on the vessel are documented on the Declaration.

title printed); statement that the certificate will remain valid until (expiry date) subject to the vessel, its machinery and equipment being efficiently maintained, annual examinations and manning complying with the Code of Practice, and to the conditions (as stated); permitted area of operation; place and date of issue; Certifying Authority; issuing official's name and signature; date of issue.

D03l.5 Code of Practice for the Safety of Small Workboats and Pilot Boats (the "Brown Code")

* The Safety of Small Workboats & Pilot Boats – A Code of Practice -
  - has the **full title** of "Code of practice for the construction, machinery, equipment, stability, operation, manning , examination, certification and maintenance of vessels of up to 24 metres load line length which are in commercial use for the carriage of cargo and/or not more than 12 passengers or neither cargo nor passengers".
  - is commonly known as the "**Brown Code**", the publication having a brown cover.
  - was **published** by the Maritime and Coastguard Agency in 1998 with ISBN 0-11-552006-6.
  - is an **acceptable Code of Practice for application** in accordance with regulation 5 or 6 of the MS (Small Workboats and Pilot Boats) Regulations 1998 (SI 1998/1609) (see D03l.5a).
  - **may be applied to** (but is **not mandatory** for) any UK commercially operated vessel of up to 24 metres load line length[48] (and any such vessel registered or owned in any other country when it operates from a UK port) which proceeds to sea –
    * carrying cargo and/or not more than 12 passengers[49]; or
    * providing a service in which neither cargo nor passengers are carried.
  - **is mandatory** for pilot boats[50].
* **Seagoing police boats** should be surveyed and certificated in accordance with the Code of Practice for all Police Craft, published by the General Purposes and Marine Subcommittee of the Association of Chief Police Officers, and which is covered by a General Exemption issued by the MCA on behalf of the Secretary of State.
* **Regulation 5(1) of the Small Workboats and Pilot Boats Regulations** provides that a **workboat** which has been examined and certificated for (voluntary) compliance with the Code need not comply with the Statutory Instruments listed in the Schedule to the Regulations. (A workboat which does not comply with the Code must, however, comply with those SIs.)
* **Regulation 6(1)** of the Regulations provides that the SIs listed in the Schedule to the Regulations do not apply to a **UK pilot boat** (since all UK pilot boats must comply with the Code).
* Until publication of the Code in 1998, **workboats** were exempt from Load Line Regulations as vessels of under 80 tons register (i.e. net tons) engaged solely in the UK coasting trade while not carrying cargo and carrying not more than 12 passengers on a voyage in the course of which they are at no time more than 3 miles from land nor more than 15 miles from their point of departure, unless the point of departure lies within Category A, B, C or D waters when the distance of 15 miles shall be measured from the seaward boundary of such limits". The **exemption has been removed**. (This means that any workboat whose owner chooses not to comply with the Code is not exempt from the Load Line Regulations.)
* Section 3.2 provides that a **vessel other than a dedicated pilot boat**[51] may be considered for the issue of a **Workboat Certificate** allowing it to operate at sea in one of the following areas:
    * **Category 6**: within 3 miles of land and not more than 3 miles radius from either the point of departure to sea or the seaward boundary of protected waters[52];
    * **Category 5**: up to 20 miles from a nominated departure point, in favourable weather and in daylight;
    * **Category 4**: up to 20 miles from a safe haven[53], in favourable weather and in daylight;
    * **Category 3**: up to 20 miles from a safe haven;
    * **Category 2**: up to 60 miles from a safe haven;
    * **Category 1**: up to 150 miles from a safe haven;
    * **Category 0**: unrestricted service.

---

[48] "Load line length" means either 96% of the total length on a waterline at 85% of the least moulded depth measured from the top of the keel, or the length from the fore side of the stem to the axis of the rudder stock on that waterline, whichever is the greater. In a vessel designed with a rake of keel, the waterline on this length is measured should be parallel to the design waterline.
[49] Such a vessel carrying more than 12 passengers would have to be surveyed and certified as a "passenger ship" of the appropriate class (see D04c.2).
[50] Under Regulation 6(2), MS (Small Workboats and Pilot Boats) Regulations 1998.
[51] A "dedicated pilot boat" is defined in the Code as a vessel used, or intended to be used, solely as a pilot boat.
[52] "**Protected waters**" means waters not of Category A, B, C or D, but the location of which are explicitly defined and accepted as protected by the Regional Chief Surveyor of the MCA responsible for the UK coastal area, having regard to the safety of small vessels which operate in those waters.
[53] A "**safe haven**" is defined in the Code as "a harbour or shelter of any kind which affords entry, subject to prudence in the weather conditions prevailing, and protection from the force of weather".

* A **pilot boat** should have a valid **Pilot Boat Certificate** (or a **Pilot Boat endorsement** of a valid Workboat Certificate), allowing it to operate in the area(s) in which it provides a pilotage service, including areas which are not to sea (3.2.2).
* To be issued with a certificate for a particular area of operation a vessel should comply with all the requirements of the Code for that operating area, to the satisfaction of the Certifying Authority (3.3).
* Section 3.7 permits certification by the MCA Regional Chief Surveyor for the vessel's service area in compliance with **alternative safety standards** where full application of the Code would be inappropriate because other safety provisions have been made.
* "Certifying Authority" means either the MCA or one of the organisations authorised by the MCA (1) to appoint persons for the purpose of examining vessels and issuing and signing Declarations of Examinations, and (2) to issue Workboat and Pilot Boat Certificates. The organisations authorised by the MCA as **Certifying Authorities** are listed in **MIN 114**.
* **The Brown Code's chief sections and annexes** are: 1. Foreword; 2. Definitions; 3. Application and interpretation; 4. Construction and structural strength; 5. Weathertight integrity; 6. Water freeing arrangements; 7. Machinery; 8. Electrical arrangements; 9. Steering gear, rudder and propeller systems; 10. Bilge pumping; 11. Intact and damage stability; 12. Freeboard and freeboard marking; 13. Life-saving appliances; 14. Fire safety; 15. Fire appliances; 16. Radio equipment; 17. Navigation lights, shapes and sound signals; 18. Navigational equipment; 19. Miscellaneous equipment; 20. Anchors and cables; 21. Accommodation; 22. Protection of personnel; 23. Medical stores; 24. Tenders (dinghies); 25. Requirements specific to use of vessel; 26. Manning; 27. Compliance procedures, certification, examination and maintenance; 28. Clean seas; Annex 1. The status of persons carried on UK ships; Annex 2. Equivalent safety standards for vessels operating in protected waters and/or a restricted service; Annex 3. Life-saving appliances; Annex 4. Fire test for GRP; Annex 5. Ignitability test for combustible installations; Annex 6. Open flame gas installations; Annex 7. Fire fighting equipment; Annex 8. Power driven vessels – lights, shapes and sound appliances; Annex 9. Anchors and cables; Annex 10. Exposure of personnel to potentially harmful noise; Annex 11. The manning of workboats; Annex 12. Vessels with passengers on board – safety briefing; Annex 13 – Workboat Certificate; Annex 14 – Pilot Boat Certificate; Annex 15. Phasing-in arrangements; Annex 16. List of Certifying Authorities.
* **Section 25** deals with requirements **specific to the use** of a vessel.
* 25.1 deals with **vessels engaged as pilot boats**. A vessel engaged as a pilot boat may be recognised as either a **dedicated pilot boat** (which is certificated as a pilot boat), or a **certificated workboat** which is engaged as a pilot boat from time to time (25.1.1). A pilot boat should always be certificated, even if it does not operate at sea.
* Requirements specific to **dedicated pilot boats** are given in 25.1.2. A dedicated pilot boat should have a **Pilot Boat Certificate**.
* Requirements specific to a **workboat engaged as a pilot boat** are given in 25.1.3. Such a vessel should comply with the Code as it applies to its duties as a workboat and have a **Workboat Certificate** with a **Pilot Boat Endorsement**.
* Requirements for **vessels engaged in towing** are in 25.2.
* Requirements for **vessels carrying cargo** are in 25.3.
* Requirements for **vessels fitted with a deck crane or other lifting device** are in 25.4.
* Requirements for **non-self-propelled vessels** are in 25.5. A Workboat Certificate, valid for no longer than 5 years, may be issued to cover **transit voyages under tow** of an unmanned non-self-propelled vessel or floating object of defined rigid form (25.5.1.1). A Workboat Certificate may also be issued to cover the safety of a non-self-propelled vessel of defined rigid form which is a **working platform** for equipment and/or power producing plant (e.g. a workbarge or pontoon); such a vessel should be assessed for compliance with the parts of the Code which are appropriate to its commercial operation (25.5.1.2).
* A **vessel with jack-up capability** (e.g. a jack-up workbarge) should be equipped and certificated to meet the requirements of the Health and Safety Executive (HSE) when it is jacked up (25.5.1.4).
* Generally, the **freeboard** of workboats and pilot boats **should be assigned** in accordance with the MS (Load Line) Regulations 1998 (25.5.3.1). **Load line marking** should be in accordance with section 12.3 of the Code, but no requirement is made for the marking of draught marks except on **vessels which carry cargo** or a combination of **passengers and cargo** weighing **more than 1000kg**.
* Vessels assigned a freeboard in accordance with 12.2.3 should be marked with a **deck line** and a **freeboard mark** in accordance with the MS (Load Line) Regulations 1998 and have a scale of **draught marks** at the bow and stern on each side. The deck line and freeboard mark should be **red** on a contrasting background. No mark may be applied for fresh water allowance. If the MCA is the Assigning Authority the letters at the sides of the ring should be "**DT**", and in the case of any other Assigning Authority should be "**UK**".
* For vessels other than those referred to in the previous paragraph the marking should be **black** on a light background or white on a dark background.
* **Pilot boat manning** requirements are in 25.1.2. The operational manning of **other Code certificated vessels** should be in accordance with Annex 11.

* Section 27.2 provides that the **owner/managing agent of a vessel to be operated under the Code should**:
  * choose an authorised Certifying Authority and **apply** to them for an **examination**;
  * arrange with the Certifying Authority for the vessel to be **examined** by an **authorised person**[54] and **documented** on the report form for a **Compliance Examination** and **Declaration**[55] as being in compliance with the Code;
  * be in receipt of a **Workboat Certificate** for the vessel prior to it entering into service.
* Before a certificate is issued to a vessel of **less than 15 metres** in length which carry **cargo** or a combination of **passengers and cargo** weighing **more than 1000kg** and all vessels of **15 metres or more** in length, the owner/managing agent should be in possession of an **approved stability information booklet** and **approved damaged stability information** (27.3.1.2).
* Requirements for **compliance examinations** for renewal of a Workboat Certificate are set out in section 27.3.2. Compliance examinations must be carried out by an authorised person from the chosen Certifying Authority.
* Requirements for **annual examinations** are set out in section 27.3.3. Annual examinations must be made, once in each calendar year, within 3 months either side of the anniversary date and at intervals of not more than 15 months, by an authorised person from the Certifying Authority.
* **Section 27.4** deals with the examination and certification of **pilot boats**. The **competent harbour authority** or the **owner/managing agent** should arrange for a **dedicated pilot boat** to be examined by an authorised person at intervals not exceeding **4 years** (27.4.1.1).
* A **Pilot Boat Certificate for a dedicated pilot boat** should normally have a period of validity not exceeding 4 years from the date of examination of the vessel out of the water by an authorised person, and should contain the details shown in Annex 14 of the Code.
* A **Workboat Certificate with a Pilot Boat Endorsement** should normally have a period of validity not exceeding 5 years from the date of examination of the vessel out of the water by an authorised person, and should contain the details shown in Annex 13 of the Code.
* Both a Pilot Boat Certificate and a Workboat Certificate with a Pilot Boat Endorsement should be **displayed** in a prominent position within the vessel, and a **certified copy** should be retained by the competent harbour authority and, where appropriate, by the boat's owner/managing agent (27.4.2.3).
* A dedicated pilot boat should have an **intermediate examination** within 3 months either side of the half-way date of the period of validity of the Pilot Boat Certificate (27.4.3.1). If the examination is satisfactory the certificate should be endorsed by the authorised person (27.4.3.3).
* Procedures where a pilot boat, its machinery or safety equipment are deficient are in 27.4.4.
* 27.4.5 permits **exemptions** to be granted by the MCA from all or any of the Code's requirements.
* A Certifying Authority may **examine** a certified vessel **at any time** (27.6.1).
* **Section 27.6** sets out requirements for **maintaining and operating a vessel**. It is the responsibility of the owner/managing agent to ensure that **at all times** a vessel is **maintained and operated in accordance with the Code**, the **arrangements as documented** in the examination report forms and the **conditions** stated on the Workboat Certificate or Pilot Boat Certificate. The **Certifying Authority must be informed** when the vessel does not continue to comply with these requirements, and if the vessel suffers a **collision**, **grounding**, **fire** or other event which causes **damage** (27.6.3). The owner/managing agent also has a statutory obligation to report accidents to the MAIB (see E08k.1) (27.6.3). The Certifying Authority should be contacted for prior approval of any repairs, changes or modifications affecting the Code's requirements (27.6.4).
* 27.7 deals with validity and cancellation of certificates. When a vessel is found not to have been maintained, equipped or operated in accordance with the Code, arrangements documented in examination reports, the certificate may be cancelled by the Certifying Authority (27.7.2). When a vessel is sold, the certificate is cancelled automatically and the selling owner/managing agent must return it to the Certifying Authority (27.7.3).
* **Details on a Workboat Certificate** include: Name of vessel; name and address of owner/managing agent; official number; port of registry; gross tonnage; maximum number of persons (including crew) to be carried; length overall; load line length (safety length); date of build; hull identification number (HIN); certifying statement that the vessel was examined by (name of examiner) of (Certifying Authority) at (place) on (date) and found to be in accordance with the Code (full title printed); statement that the certificate will remain valid until (expiry date) subject to the vessel, its machinery and equipment being efficiently maintained, annual examinations and manning complying with the Code of Practice, and to the conditions (as stated); date(s) when vessel is to be examined out of the water; permitted area of operation; maximum permissible weight of cargo and passengers which can be carried; place and date of issue; for and on behalf of (Certifying Authority name); issuing official's name and signature; official stamp; date of issue. There is a Record of Annual Examinations. A **Pilot Boat Endorsement** of a Workboat Certificate

---

[54] An **"authorised person"** means a person who by reason of relevant professional qualifications, practical experience or expertise is authorised by the Certifying Authority chosen by the owner/managing agent from those listed in the Code to carry out examinations required under section 27 of the Code.
[55] The arrangements, fittings and equipment provided on the vessel are documented on the Declaration.

states that the vessel has been found satisfactory for use as a pilot boat in (area) with the carriage of not more than (the stated number) of persons (including the crew).

* **Details of a Pilot Boat Certificate** are the same except that there is no reference to the vessel being examined out of the water, nor to maximum permissible weight of cargo and passengers. There is a Record of any Exemptions granted, and a Record of Intermediate Examination.

D03I.5a MS (Small Workboats and Pilot Boats) Regulations

* The MS (Small Workboats and Pilot Boats) Regulations 1998 (SI 1998/1609) -
    - **revoke** the MS (Pilot Boats) Regulations 1991 (SI 1991/65).
    - define "**dedicated pilot boat**" as a vessel used, or intended to be used, solely as a pilot boat.
    - define "**pilot boat**" as a vessel, of whatever size, employed or intended to be employed in pilotage services.
    - define "**small vessel**" as a ship of less than 24 metres in load line length.
    - define "**small workboat**" as a small vessel in commercial use other than for sport or pleasure, including a dedicated pilot boat, **not** being used as:
        * a tug or salvage ship;
        * a ship engaged in the surveying of harbours or the approaches thereto; or
        * a hopper barge or dredger.
* **Regulation 4(1)** provides that, subject to regulation 4(2), the Regulations apply to -
    * UK small workboats, wherever they may be;
    * non-UK small workboats operating from UK ports, whilst in UK waters; and
    * UK pilot boats which do not fall into the definition of "small workboat", wherever they may be.
* Regulation 4(2) provides that **regulation 5** (which applies to **small workboats**) will **not** apply to -
    * dedicated pilot boats, of whatever size; or
    * pilot boats which are not small workboats.
    (Regulation 5 **will**, therefore, apply to workboats which are sometimes used as pilot boats.)
* Part II of the Regulations sets out requirements for small vessels in commercial use.
* **Regulation 5** deals with **small vessels complying with the Code of Practice** (the "Brown Code").
* Subject to provisions of the relevant paragraphs of the Brown Code, the SIs listed in the Schedule to the Regulations (see below) will not apply to any workboat to which regulation 5 applies which has been **examined**, and in respect of which a **Workboat Certificate** has been issued, in accordance with the Code (regulation 5(1)).
* Regulation 5(2) provides that where a vessel has been **examined** and a **certificate** issued in accordance with the Code, it must not proceed or attempt to proceed to sea unless -
    * the **Workboat Certificate** is currently **in force**;
    * the **vessel complies with the requirements of the Code** (including any requirements as to operation, manning and maintenance) and is operated in accordance with any conditions specified in the certificate; and
    * the **Workboat Certificate is displayed** in some conspicuous place on board.
* Where a vessel complies with regulation 5(2), any provision of the Code expressed in the conditional (i.e. where the word "should" is used) becomes a statutory requirement (i.e. for "should" read "must").
* After completion of any survey required by the Code, **no material change** may be made to the vessel, its machinery or equipment without the prior approval of the Certifying Authority (regulation 5(3)).
* **Part III** regulations deal with **requirements for pilot boats**.
* The SIs listed in the Schedule will not apply to UK dedicated pilot boats or to UK pilot boats, not being small workboats (regulation 6(1)).
* Regulation 6(2) provides that a vessel may not be operated as a pilot boat unless -
    * it has been **examined** and a **Pilot Boat Certificate** or a **Workboat Certificate with a Pilot Boat endorsement** has been issued in accordance with the Brown Code;
    * the Certificate is currently in force;
    * the vessel complies with the requirements of the Brown Code (including any requirements as to operation, manning and maintenance) and is operated in accordance with any conditions as specified in the Certificate; and
    * the certificate is displayed in some conspicuous place on board.
* Where a vessel complies with regulation 6(2), any provision of the Code expressed in the conditional (i.e. where the word "should" is used) becomes a statutory requirement (i.e. for "should" read "must").
* After completion of any survey of a boat required by the Code, **no material change** may be made to the boat, its machinery or equipment without the prior approval of the Certifying Authority (regulation 6(3)).
* Regulation 7 permits the MCA to grant an **exemption** to any pilot boat from any or all of the provisions of Part III.
* Regulation 8 permits the carriage of particular pieces of equipment or machinery required by the Code to be of an **equivalent standard**, where approved by the MCA.
* Regulation 9 sets **penalties** for breaches of the Regulations.

* Regulation 10 gives the MCA powers to **detain** a vessel in breach of the Regulations.
* The Schedule to the Regulations contains a list of **SIs** which, under regulations 5(1) and 6(1) are **disapplied** where a vessel complies with the Brown Code. The disapplied SIs and amending SIs are as listed in the following table, which brings the list in the Code up to date for revoked and replaced, and later amending Regulations.

Disapplied regulations	SI year/no.	Amending regulations
MS (Life-Saving Appliances for Ships Other Than Ships of Classes III to VI(A)) Regulations 1999	1999/2721	2000/2558
MS (Survey and Certification) Regulations 1995	1995/1210	1996/2418, 2000/1334
MS (Training and Certification) Regulations 1997	1997/348	1997/1911, 2000/836
MS (Safe Manning, Hours of Work and Watchkeeping) Regulations 1997	1997/1320	1997/1911, 2000/484
MS (Crew Accommodation) Regulations 1997	1997/1508	
MS (Cargo Ship Construction) Regulations 1997	1997/1509	1999/643
MS (Fire Protection: Small Ships) Regulations 1998	1998/1011	1999/992
MS (Fire Protection: Large Ships) Regulations 1998	1998/1012	1999/992
MS (Radio Installations) Regulations 1998	1998/2070	
MS (Load Line) Regulations 1998	1998/2241	2000/1335

D03I.6 Code of Practice for the Safety of Small Vessels in Commercial Use for Sport or Pleasure operating from a Nominated Departure Point (NDP) (the "Red Code" or "NDP Code")

* **The Safety of Small Vessels in Commercial Use for Sport or Pleasure operating from a Nominated Departure Point – A Code of Practice -**
  - has the **full title** of "Code of practice for the construction, machinery, equipment, stability, operation, manning, examination, certification and maintenance of vessels of up to 24 metres load line length which are in commercial use for sport or pleasure; and carry no more than 12 passengers; and do not carry cargo; and operate only in favourable weather and daylight from a Nominated Departure Point".
  - is known by the MCA as the "**Red Code**", the publication having a red cover.
  - is also known as the "**NDP Code**".
  - was **published** in 1999 for the MCA by the Stationery Office with ISBN 0-11-551812-6.
  - **came into effect** on 1 April 2000, when the MS (Vessels in Commercial Use for Sport or Pleasure) (Amendment) Regulations 2000 (SI 2000/482) came into force.
  - is an **acceptable Code of Practice for application** in accordance with the MS (Vessels in Commercial Use for Sport or Pleasure) (Amendment) Regulations 2000 (SI 2000/482) (see D03I.8).
  - **applies to** (but is **not mandatory** for) any UK motor or sailing vessel (either monohull or multihull) of less than 24 metres load line length[56] in commercial use for sport or pleasure around the coast of the UK within the areas defined in 3.2 and the conditions of operation corresponding to the area, provided it does not carry more than 12 passengers[57] and does not carry cargo (3.1.2).
  - **applies to** vessels registered or owned outside the UK, when operating from a UK port (3.1.5).
  - **applies to** vessels operated by proprietary clubs and associations (e.g. angling and diving clubs) (3.1.6).
  - **makes reference** to the Blue Code and Yellow Code, and applies the standards of those Codes to vessels which seek certification to operate in area category 5 (3.1.4).
* The **Red Code's chief sections and annexes** are: 1. Foreword; 2. Definitions; 3. Application and interpretation; 4. Construction and structural strength; 5. Weathertight integrity; 6. Water freeing arrangements; 7. Machinery; 8. Electrical installation; 9. Steering gear; 10. Bilge pumping; 11. Stability; 12. Freeboard; 13. Life-saving appliances; 14. Fire safety; 15. Fire appliances; 16. Radio equipment; 17. Navigation lights, shapes and sound signals; 18. Navigational equipment; 19. Miscellaneous equipment; 20. Anchors and cables; 21. Accommodation; 22. Protection of personnel; 23. Medical stores; 24. Tenders (dinghies); 25. Clean seas; 26. Manning; 27. Certification procedure, compliance examination and maintenance; 28. Vessels operating under Race Rules; Annex 1. Development of the Code; Annex 2. Merchant Shipping Notice M.1194; Annex 3. Phase-in registration; Annex 4. Guidance on the assessment of variations; Annex 5. Shapes and sound signalling equipment; Annex 6. The manning of small vessels; Annex 7. Safety briefing; Annex 8. Small Commercial Vessel Certificate.
* Under 3.2 a vessel may be considered for the issue of a **Small Commercial Vessel Certificate** allowing it to operate within the following areas:
  • **Category 6**: to **sea**, within 3 miles of a nominated departure point(s) and never more than 3 miles from land , in favourable weather and daylight;

---

[56] "Load line length" means either 96% of the total length on a waterline at 85% of the least moulded depth measured from the top of the keel, or the length from the fore side of the stem to the axis of the rudder stock on that waterline, whichever is the greater. In a vessel designed with a rake of keel, the waterline on this length is measured should be parallel to the design waterline.

[57] Such a vessel carrying more than 12 passengers would have to be surveyed and certified as a "passenger ship" of the appropriate class (see D04c.2).

- **Category 5**: to **sea**, within 20 miles from a nominated departure point(s), in favourable weather and daylight.
* Depending on the nature of the vessel and its use, a vessel may be **restricted** to less than the above specified limits. Any restriction should be recorded on the Small Commercial Vessel Certificate.
* Where it is desired to operate a small commercial vessel for sport or pleasure in **areas other than those above,** certification under either the **Yellow Code** (for motor vessels) (see D031.3) or the **Blue Code** (for sailing vessels) (see D031.4) must be obtained.
* **Vessels operating in area category 6** must comply with the standards in Sections 4 to 28 and Annexes 2 to 8 of the Red Code (3.3.1).
* **Motor or sailing vessels operating in area category 5** must comply with the standards for a category 4 vessel in the Yellow Code or Blue Code respectively, although in relation to manning requirements Section 26 and Annex 6 of the Red Code apply, and in respect of compliance procedures, certification, examination and maintenance Section 27 of the Red Code applies (3.3.2).
* Small Commercial Vessel Certificates are valid for not more than **5 years** (3.4.2).
* **Certifying Authorities** are listed in **MIN 114** and include the MCA, certain UK local authorities and harbour commissioners with safety schemes meeting the requirements of the Code and appointed by the MCA, and organisations appointed by them (3.7). Authorised local authorities, or organisations appointed by them, may issue Code certificates for a specified radius of operation of less than 3 miles from a nominated departure point to sea (i.e. Category 6 operation), based on a standard of safety judged by them to be equivalent to that of the Code (3.7.4).
* A vessel certificated under the Red Code must be **prominently marked** with a "suitable annual sticker issued by the Certifying Authority" (3.8). The MCA issues red "**NDP Code stickers**" to all Certifying Authorities.
* **Safe manning requirements** (which do not apply to vessels on bareboat charter or hire) are detailed in Annex 6.
* Standards required to be met in **safety briefings**, to be given to persons on board, are in Annex 7.
* As an **alternative to Code certification**, owners may use Merchant Shipping regulations to obtain Load Line certification, but applying the Code is considered to be easier (1.7).

D031.7 Code of Practice for Safety of Large Commercial Sailing and Motor Vessels (the "White Code" or "Megayacht Code")

* The **Code of Practice for Safety of Large Commercial Sailing and Motor Vessels** -
  - is known in some MCA documents as the "**White Code**", the publication having a partially white cover.
  - is also known in the industry as the "**Megayacht Code**".
  - **embraces** and redefines in one document all the **safety and operational standards and rules** from international conventions (e.g. SOLAS) and UK regulations and which already apply but have rarely been enforced on large, commercially operated yachts.
  - was **published** in 1997 for the MCA by The Stationery Office with ISBN 0-11-551911-4.
  - is a **statutory Code of Practice** developed by the UK and other "Red Ensign Group" flag States (i.e. Bermuda, Cayman Islands, Gibraltar and the Isle of Man) for application to vessels as described below sailing under any of their flags.
  - **applies to** a motor or sailing vessel (either monohull or multihull) of **24 metres in load line length**[58] **or over** or, if built before 21 July 1968, of **150gt or over** and which is in **commercial use** for sport or pleasure and carries **no cargo** and up to **12 passengers**, provided that it is **not** a vessel to which either the International Code of Safety for High Speed Craft (the HSC Code) or the Code of Safety for Dynamically Supported Craft (DSC Code) applies. **Sail training vessels of 24 metres or more** in length are included in this application (3.1.1).
  - **is mandatory** under **regulation 4 of the MS (Vessels in Commercial Use for Sport or Pleasure) Regulations 1998** (SI 1998/2771) (see D031.8) for UK-flagged "large vessels" as defined by those Regulations.
  - will, if complied with, satisfy the requirements of the **MS (Vessels in Commercial Use for Sport or Pleasure) (Amendment) Regulations 2000** (SI 2000/482) (see D031.8) (3.1.2).
* The **White Code's chief sections and annexes** are: 1. Foreword; 2. Definitions; 3. Application and interpretation; 4. Construction and strength; 5. Weathertight integrity; 6. Water freeing arrangements; 7A. Machinery – Vessels of less than 50 metres in length and under 500gt; 7B. Machinery – Vessels of 50 metres in length or over or 500gt or over; 8A. Electrical installations – Vessels of less than 50 metres in length and under 500gt; 8B. Electrical installations - Vessels of 50 metres in length or over or 500gt or over; 9A. Steering gear - Vessels of less than 50 metres in length and under 500gt; 9B. Steering gear - Vessels of 50 metres in length or over or 500gt or over; 10A. Bilge pumping - Vessels of less than 50 metres in length and under 500gt; 10B. Bilge pumping - Vessels of 50 metres in length or over or 500gt or over; 11. Stability; 12. Freeboard; 13. Life-saving appliances; 14. Fire safety; 14A. Structural fire protection - Vessels of less than 50 metres in length and under 500gt; 14B. Structural fire

---

[58] "**Load line length**" means either 96% of the total length on a waterline at 85% of the least moulded depth measured from the top of the keel, or the length from the fore side of the stem to the axis of the rudder stock on that waterline, whichever is the greater. In a vessel designed with a rake of keel, the waterline on this length is measured should be parallel to the design waterline.

protection - Vessels of 50 metres in length or over or 500gt or over; 15A. Fire appliances - Vessels of less than 50 metres in length and under 500gt; 15B. Fire appliances - Vessels of 50 metres in length or over or 500gt or over; 16. Radio; 17. Navigation lights, shapes and sound signals; 18. Navigational equipment and visibility from wheelhouse; 19. Miscellaneous equipment; 20. Anchors and cables and towing arrangements; 21. Accommodation; 22. Protection of personnel; 23. Medical stores; 24. Shore-ship transfer of personnel; 25. Clean seas; 26. Manning; 27. Passengers; 28. Surveys, certification, inspection and maintenance; Annex 1. Categorisation of Red Ensign shipping registers; Annex 2. List of reference documents; Annex 3. Members of the Steering Committee & Working Group responsible for the Code; Annex 4. Open flame gas installations; Annex 5. Manning scale for commercially operated yachts over 24m; Annex 6. List of certificates to be issued; Annex 7. Certificate of Compliance; Annex 8. Small Commercial Medical Fitness.

* **Exemptions** may be granted by the MCA (3.2.2).
* **Manning requirements** are detailed in section 26.
* All seagoing commercial yachts of **24 metres or more** load line length but **less than 3000gt** should carry **qualified deck and engineer officers** as required by **Annex 5** of the Code (26.1.1).
* 26.1.2 and 26.1.3 provide that all seagoing commercial yachts of **more than 3000gt** should carry **qualified deck and engineer officers** as required by the MS (Certification of Deck Officers) Regulations 1985 and MS (Certification of Marine Engineer Officer and Licensing of Marine Engine Operators) Regulations 1985, as amended. These Regulations were revoked and replaced by the **MS (Training and Certification) Regulations 1997** (SI 1997/348), as amended, as described in E02b.1.
* Section 26 also refers to **MGN 14**; this MGN was superseded by **MGN 195**, which details the training and certification requirements for professional yachtsmen serving on vessels over 24 metres in length. It describes the system for harmonising deck officer certification for large commercial sailing and motor vessels in accordance with UK regulations and the principles of STCW 95 and its associated STCW Code. It also contains **deck officer manning scales** for large yachts and sail training vessels. For notes on **MGN 195** see E02c.20.
* Section 26.2 provides that all sea going commercial yachts of 24 metres or more load line length should be **safely manned**, and it is the responsibility of the owner or managing agent to ensure that the master and, where necessary, other members of the crew have, **in addition to** the qualifications required in Annex 5, **recent and relevant experience** of the **type and size of vessel** and of the **type of operation** in which she is engaged.
* Section 26.3 provides that every vessel should carry at least one person holding "an **appropriate radio operator's certificate**" which is suitable for the **radio installation and equipment** on board and reflects the **operating area** of the vessel. Radio personnel training and certification requirements are set out in an MGN forming Part 4 of the MCA's Training and Certification Guidance (see E02c.4).
* Section 26.4 deals with Medical Fitness Certificates and provides in 26.4.1 that officers holding UK certificates of competency must hold an acceptable Medical Fitness Certificate, as described in E06c.2. All other officers are required to produce evidence of medical fitness as described in 26.4.2.
* Section 26.5 provides that all deck officers must, and other crew members are recommended to, hold a **Basic Sea Survival** Course Certificate recognised by the Administration. "Basic Sea Survival" courses are generally known under STCW 95 provisions as **Personal Survival Techniques** courses and form part of Basic Training under STCW 95 (see E02c.6b).
* Section 26.6 provides that all officers must hold a **First Aid At Sea** Certificate acceptable to the Administration. **Elementary First Aid** training is part of STCW 95 Basic Training (see E02c.6b).
* Section 26.7 provides that all officers should hold a **Basic Fire Fighting** Course Certificate acceptable to the Administration. Training in **fire prevention and fire fighting** is part of STCW 95 Basic Training (see E02c.6b).
* **Revalidation** requirements for certificates and licences are set out in 26.8. Certificates must generally be revalidated every 5 years.
* Section 27 relates to **passengers**, and provides a definition of "passenger" which excludes certain categories of person and allows young persons to be carried (e.g. on sail training vessels) as bona-fide members of the crew (see D04f.2a).
* Section 28 deals with **survey, certification, inspection and maintenance**. A table in Annex 6 of the Code shows certificates required to be carried by White Code vessels, but lists certain regulations which have been revoked and replaced since publication. The table below shows the **certificates required by White Code vessels**, the relevant **current regulations** and the **references** in this book to notes on surveys for the certificates listed.

Vessel size	Certificate *Convention*	UK regulations	Survey and certifying organisation	Subjects covered by survey	SBC ref.
Any size	International Tonnage Certificate (1969) *TONNAGE*	SI 1997/1510	Class	Tonnage measurement	D04h.2b
24 metres or more	International Load Line Certificate *LOADLINE*	SI 1998/2241 SI 2000/1335	Class	Freeboard and load lines Intact stability and subdivision	D04i.1d

500gt or more	Cargo Ship Safety Construction Certificate *SOLAS*	SI 1995/1210 SI 1996/2418 SI 2000/1334	Class	Construction	D04f.2k
			MCA (fire protection)	Structural fire protection Means of escape	
500gt or more	Cargo Ship Safety Equipment Certificate *SOLAS*	SI 1995/1210 SI 1996/2418 SI 2000/1334	MCA	Safety equipment (LSA; fire appliances; navigation lights; sounds; signals, etc.)	D04f.2k
300gt or more	Cargo Ship Safety Radio Certificate *SOLAS*	SI 1995/1210 SI 1996/2418 SI 2000/1334	Marconi Marine	Radio equipment	D04f.2k
500gt or more	Safe Manning Document *SOLAS/STCW*	SI 1997/1320 SI 2000/484	MCA	Safe manning	E03b.3

400gt or more	International Oil Pollution Prevention Certificate *MARPOL*	SI 1996/2154 SI 1997/1910 SI 2000/483	MCA: initial survey Other surveys: class	Pollution prevention equipment and arrangements	D04g.2
-	Exemption Certificate *RELEVANT CONVENTION*	Any of the above SIs	MCA	Exemption from relevant provision of Regulations or Convention	D04f.2o
Less than 500gt	Certificate of Compliance -	SI 1998/2771 SI 2000/482	MCA or class	Aspects surveyed under the Code for which other certificates are not required	D03l.7

* **Where a yacht is built to classification society standards** (i.e. built "under class") most of the surveys required to obtain the above certification will be undertaken by class surveyors. Where a yacht is not built under class, or is not to be classed, surveys will still be required to prove compliance with the relevant instruments.
* **Other documents** required to be carried by a White Code vessel include:
  a **stability information booklet** (11.5);
  for a vessel built under class, or classed, a **Certificate of Class** or **Interim Certificate of Class** (see D02d.3).
* All White Code vessels must undergo an "**inclining experiment**" in order to determine the lightship weight, VCG and LCG (11.4).
* **Benefits of compliance** with the White Code include:
  * **legal** operation under any Category 1 or 2 Red Ensign register;
  * avoidance of **detention** by and other problems with **Port State Control** inspectors at non-flag State ports;
  * enhancement of **perceived value** of the vessel in charter and sale and purchase markets;
  * **less likelihood of** owners facing **legal difficulties** following an accident involving the vessel or her crew;
  * compliance with the **warranty of legality** in the insurance policy.
* For notes on **Certificates of Competency** or **Marine Engine Operator Licences** for service as an **engineer officer** on commercially and privately operated **yachts and sail training vessels**, as detailed in Training and Certification Guidance - Part 17 see E02c.17.
* The MCA intends to review the White Code in 2003.
* The White Code is now established as the world-wide standard for the safety of large yachts. In order to support it and to provide a streamlined service to the large yacht industry, the MCA has formed "Ensign", a dedicated large yacht business unit based at Newcastle-upon-Tyne. Manning issues have been retained by the Seafarers Standards Section at MCA Southampton headquarters.

D03l.8 Vessels in Commercial Use for Sport or Pleasure Regulations

* The **MS (Vessels in Commercial Use for Sport or Pleasure) Regulations 1998** (SI 1998/2771) -
  - **revoke** and replace the MS (Vessels in Commercial Use for Sport or Pleasure) Regulations 1993 (SI 1993/1072).
  - **are amended** by the MS (Vessels in Commercial Use for Sport or Pleasure) (Amendment) Regulations 2000 (SI 2000/482) (see footnote to notes on regulation 5, below).
  - **apply** to UK vessels wherever they may be, and to other vessels operating from UK ports whilst in UK waters.
  - **do not apply** to vessels carrying more than 12 passengers[59].
  - **do not apply** to "pleasure vessels" (as defined below).
  - apply to both "**large vessels**" and "**small vessels**" as defined below.

---

[59] A vessel in commercial use for sport or pleasure carrying more than 12 passengers would have to be certified as a "passenger ship" of the appropriate class (see D04c.2).

- **define "small vessel"** as a vessel of less than 24 metres in load line length or, in the case of a vessel the keel of which was laid or which was at a similar stage of construction before 21 July 1968, less than 150 tons[60].
- **define "large vessel"** as a vessel which is not a small vessel. In other words, a "**large vessel**" is a vessel of 24 metres or more in length, or for a vessel the keel of which was laid or which was at a similar stage of construction before 21 July 1968, 150 gross tons or more.
- **define "pleasure vessel"** (in regulation 2) as:
  (a) any vessel which at the time it is being used is:
    (i)
        (aa)   in the case of a vessel wholly owned by an individual or individuals, used only for the sport or pleasure of the owner or the immediate family or friends of the owner; or
        (bb)   in the case of a vessel owned by a body corporate, used only for sport or pleasure and on which the persons on board are employees or officers of the body corporate, or their immediate family or friends; and
    (ii) on a voyage or excursion which is one for which the owner does not receive money for or in connection with operating the vessel or carrying any person, other than as a contribution to the direct expenses of the operation of the vessel incurred during the voyage or excursion; or
  (b) any vessel wholly owned by or on behalf of a members' club formed for the purpose of sport or pleasure which, at the time it is being used, is used only for the sport or pleasure of members of that club or their immediate family, and for the use of which any charges levied are paid into club funds and applied for the general use of the club; and
  (c) in the case of any vessel referred to in paragraphs (a) or (b) above no other payments are made by or on behalf of users of the vessel, other than by the owner.
* In the definition of "pleasure vessel", "immediate family" means, in relation to an individual, the husband or wife of the individual, and a relative of the individual or the individual's husband or wife; and "relative" means brother, sister, ancestor or lineal descendant.
* **Regulation 4** provides that –
  • **"large vessels" must comply** with the provisions of the Code of Practice for Safety of Large Commercial Sailing and Motor Vessels (the "**White Code**" or "**Megayacht Code**"); and
  • any provision of that Code expressed in the conditional tense (i.e. where the word "should" is used) will be a **statutory requirement** (i.e. for "should" in the White Code, read "must").
* **Schedule 1** of the Regulations contains a list of **SIs which are disapplied** where a "large vessel" complies with the White Code. The disapplied SIs and amending SIs are as listed in the following table, which brings the list in the Code up to date for revoked and replaced, and later amending Regulations.

Disapplied regulations	SI year/no.	Amending regulations
MS (Life-Saving Appliances for Ships Other Than Ships of Classes III to VI(A)) Regulations 1999	1999/2721	2000/2558
MS (Means of Access) Regulations 1988	1988/1637	1988/2274
MS (Survey and Certification) Regulations 1995	1995/1210	1996/2418, 2000/1334
MS (Training and Certification) Regulations 1997	1997/348	1997/1911, 2000/836
MS (Safe Manning, Hours of Work and Watchkeeping) Regulations 1997	1997/1320	1997/1911, 2000/484
MS (Crew Accommodation) Regulations 1997	1997/1508	
MS (Cargo Ship Construction) Regulations 1997	1997/1509	1999/643
MS (Fire Protection: Small Ships) Regulations 1998	1998/1011	1999/992
MS (Fire Protection: Large Ships) Regulations 1998	1998/1012	1999/992
MS (Radio Installations) Regulations 1998	1998/2070	
MS (Load Line) Regulations 1998	1998/2241	2000/1335
MS (Safety of Navigation) Regulations 2002	2002/1473	

* **Regulation 5** applies only to "**small vessels**" (as defined above) and provides that the **SIs listed in Schedule 2** of the Regulations **will not apply** to a "small vessel" which has been **examined**, and in respect of which a **certificate** has been issued, in accordance with the provisions of either of the following Codes of Practice:
  • "The Safety of Small Commercial Sailing Vessels – A Code of Practice" (i.e. the "**Blue Code**");
  • "The Safety of Small Commercial Motor Vessels – A Code of Practice" (i.e. the "**Yellow Code**"); or
  • "The Safety of Small Vessels in Commercial Use for Sport or Pleasure operating from a Nominated Departure Point – A Code of Practice" (i.e. the "**Red Code**")[61].
* **Schedule 2** of the Regulations contains a list of Statutory Instruments which are **disapplied** if the "small vessels" to which regulation 5 applies comply with any of the above Codes of Practice. The disapplied SIs and amending SIs are as listed in the following table, which brings the list in the Code up to date for revoked and replaced, and later amending Regulations.

---

[60] "Tons" means gross tons (of 100 cu. ft.) measured under the Tonnage Regulations in force on 20 July 1968, which are now revoked.
[61] The Red Code was added by SI 2000/482.

Disapplied regulations	SI year/no.	Amending regulations
MS (Life-Saving Appliances for Ships Other Than Ships of Classes III to VI(A)) Regulations 1999	1999/2721	2000/2558
MS (Training and Certification) Regulations 1997	1997/348	1997/1911, 2000/836
MS (Crew Accommodation) Regulations 1997	1997/1508	
MS (Fire Protection: Small Ships) Regulations 1998	1998/1011	1999/992
MS (Radio Installations) Regulations 1998	1998/2070	
MS (Load Line) Regulations 1998	1998/2241	2000/1335
MS and FV (Medical Stores) Regulations 1995	1995/1802	1996/2821
MS (Safety of Navigation) Regulations 2002	2002/1473	

* Regulation 5(4) provides that where a small vessel has been **examined** under a Code and a **Small Commercial Vessel Certificate** issued, the vessel may not proceed, or attempt to proceed, to sea unless:
  * the certificate is **in force**;
  * the vessel **complies with the relevant Code of Practice** (including any requirements as to operation, manning and maintenance) (and for this purpose any provision of the Code expressed in the conditional tense (i.e. as "should") will be a statutory requirement); and
  * the **certificate is displayed** in some conspicuous place on board, or, if that is not reasonably practicable, is available for inspection on board.
* **Regulation 5(5)** provides that where a "small vessel" is operating under the phase-in arrangements of a Code of Practice it may not proceed or attempt to proceed to sea unless it meets the **requirements for phase-in** specified in the Code.
* **Regulation 6** provides that **approved equivalent arrangements** may be allowed by the MCA, e.g. for the carriage of **equivalent equipment or machinery**, on a "large vessel" or "small vessel" to which the Regulations apply.
* **Regulation 9** provides that a vessel may be detained for non-compliance with the Regulations under section 284 of the Merchant Shipping Act 1995.
* The 1993 Regulations (which are revoked) amended numerous SIs containing a definition of either "pleasure yacht" or "pleasure craft" and substituted a new definition, "**pleasure vessel**", in their place (see above). The revocation of the 1993 Regulations does not affect those substitutions.

D04 Statutory survey, certification and documentation

D04a UK SHIP CERTIFICATION AND DOCUMENTATION INDEX

Certificate or document	Ship types to which document is applicable	SBC ref.
Accident Log	Ships required to carry a Safety Officer (i.e. sea-going ships in which more than 5 workers are employed)	D05b.4
Anchor Certificates (or Certificates of Inspection – Anchor), Chain Cable Certificates and Chain Cable Accessory Certificates	Ships fitted with anchors and cables	D04s.1
Annual Summary of Admiralty Notices to Mariners	All ships	D04o
Anti-Attack Plan	All ships operating in waters where attacks occur	H04e.5
BCH Code	Chemical tankers built before 1 July 1986	D03e.1a
Berth List	Passenger ships of classes I, II and II(A)	D03b.4l
Bridge movement book	Mechanically propelled ships	D05c.3
Builder's Certificate	All ships	D01d.2
Bulk carrier loading and ballasting booklet	Ships of more than 150m in length specially designed for the carriage of liquids or ore in bulk	D04t.2b
Bunker Declaration	Ships reporting to certain overseas Customs authorities	I01f.4a
California Certificate of Financial Responsibility	Non-tank vessels of 300gt or more operating in California waters	D04t.1c
California oil spill contingency plan	Non-tank vessels of 300gt or more operating in California waters	D04t.1c
Captain's copies (or originals, if carried) of Bills of Lading	Ships carrying cargo under Bill of Lading terms	F07b.2
Cards 1, 2 and 3	Ships with radio-telephone installations	D04m.3b
Cargo book (for HM Customs purposes)	Ships mainly carrying domestic goods coastwise around the UK, not under a Transire	D05b.6 I01f.10
Cargo information	Chemical tankers complying with Chemical Tanker Codes	F07i.3
Cargo information	Gas carriers complying with Gas Carrier Codes	F07i.2
Cargo list (or manifest or stowage plan)	Ships carrying dangerous goods and/or marine pollutants	F07f.2g
Cargo Loading Manual	Ships loading any dry bulk cargo other than grain	F07g.1g

Cargo Record Book (Noxious Liquid Substances)	Ships carrying noxious liquid substances in bulk or unassessed liquid substances in bulk; chemical tankers carrying dangerous substances in bulk; oil tankers carrying pollution hazard substances in bulk	D04g.3b D04x D05b.3 H03b.8 I07c.1
Cargo Securing Manual	Passenger ships and cargo ships carrying cargoes other than solid bulk cargoes, except cargo ships of less than 500gt on non-international (i.e. domestic) voyages	F07g.1b F07g.1c
Cargo Ship Safety Certificate	Cargo ships of 500 gross tonnage or more engaged on international voyages	D04f.2k
Cargo Ship Safety Construction Certificate	Cargo ships of 500 gross tonnage or over engaged on international voyages	D04f.2k
Cargo Ship Safety Equipment Certificate	Cargo ships of 500 gross tonnage or over engaged on international voyages	D04f.2k
Cargo Ship Safety Radio Certificate	Cargo ships of 300 gross tonnage or over engaged on international voyages	D04f.2k
Certificate of Adjustment of Compasses	Ships fitted with magnetic compasses	D04n.2
Certificate of British Registry	Registered ships	D01e
Certificate of British Registry for a Bareboat Chartered Ship	Foreign-owned ships, registered as being on bareboat charter to charterers who are eligible to own British ships	D01f
Certificate of Class (Hull and Machinery)	Classed ships	D02d.3
Certificate of Class (Refrigerating Machinery)	Classed reefer ships; other classed ships with refrigerating machinery (e.g. mainline container ships)	D02d.3
Certificate of Compliance for a Large Charter Yacht	Motor or sailing vessels in commercial use for sport or pleasure of more than 24 metres load line length or (if built before 21 July 1968) of 150gt or more, which do not carry cargo or more than 12 passengers, and which comply with the "Megayacht Code"	D03l.7
Certificate of Entry	Ships entered with a P&I club	G04b.1
Certificate of Financial Responsibility (Water Pollution)	Vessels over 300gt using a place subject to US jurisdiction; vessels using waters of the US Exclusive Economic Zone (EEZ) to trans-ship or lighter oil destined for the USA	G04d.4a H03h.1
Certificate of Fitness for the Carriage of Dangerous Chemicals in Bulk	Chemical tankers built before 1 July 1986	D04g.5a
Certificate of Fitness for the Carriage of Liquefied Gases in Bulk	Liquefied gas carriers built before 1 July 1986	D04g.6a
Certificate of Registration as a Firearms Dealer	Ships on which ammunition is purchased, sold or acquired for clay pigeon shooting (e.g. cruise ships).	D04u
Certificate of Survey	Ships which have been measured for tonnage in the UK	D01d.4
Certificate of Test and Thorough Examination of Derricks Used in Union Purchase	Ships using derricks in union purchase	D04r.2
Certificate of Test and Thorough Examination of Lifting Appliances	Ships fitted with any lifting appliances	D04r.2
Certificate of Test and Thorough Examination of Loose Gear	Ships fitted with any "loose gear"	D04r.2
Certificate of Test and Thorough Examination of Wire Rope	Ships fitted with any wire ropes	D04r.2
Certificates of service and testing of hydrostatic release units	Ships equipped with hydrostatic release units	D04k.2
Certificates of service and testing of inflatable boats	Ships equipped with inflatable boats	D04k.2
Certificates of service and testing of inflatable lifejackets	Ships equipped with inflatable lifejackets	D04k.2
Certificates of service and testing of inflatable liferafts	Ships equipped with inflatable liferafts	D04k.2
Certificates of service and testing of marine escape system	Ships fitted with marine escape system(s)	D04k.2
Chain Cables Certificates (or Certificates of Inspection – Anchor Chain)	Ships fitted with anchors and cables	D04s.1
Charter party (time)	Ships on time charter	F04a.1b F06a
Charter party (voyage)	Ships on voyage charter	F04a.1a F05a
Charts (as necessary for the intended voyage)	Ships of 12 metres or more registered length	D04o
Class survey records	Classed ships	D02d.4
Clearances from last port	Ships on international voyages	I01a.6 I01f.4 I07h.1
Clearances from other EU ports on the same voyage	Ships seeking outwards Customs clearance from UK ports	I07h.1
Closing of Openings Record Book	Passenger ships of Classes III to VI(A)	D05a.10a
Code of Safe Practice for Cargo Stowage and Securing (CSS Code)	Sea-going ships carrying cargo, other than ships engaged in the carriage of grain, if relevant to the cargo and its stowage and securing	F07g.1b
Code of Safe Practice for Ships Carrying Timber Deck Cargoes (TDC Code)	Sea-going ships carrying timber deck cargo	F07g.1b
Code of Safe Practice for Solid Bulk Cargoes (BC Code)	Sea-going ships carrying solid bulk cargo	F07g.1b
Code of Safe Working Practices for Merchant Seamen	All ships	E08c.3
Compass deviation book	Ships fitted with magnetic compasses	D04n.2
Compass deviation card(s) for standard and repeater compasses	Ships fitted with magnetic compasses	D04n.2
Compass test certificate(s)	Ships fitted with magnetic compasses	D04n.2

Continuous Synopsis Record	All ships to which SOLAS chapter XI-1 applies (from 1 July 2004)	D01j
Controlled Drugs Register	Category A vessels as defined in MSN 1726	D04p
Crew Agreement	Ships not exempted from the requirement to have a Crew Agreement	E07a.1 E07c.1
Crew list (for customs, immigration, police, etc.)	Ships on international voyages	I01a.6 I01g.1
Crude Oil Washing Operations and Equipment Manual	Tankers operating with crude oil washing (COW) systems	D04g.1a
Damage control plans and booklets	Sea-going cargo ships of 500 gross tonnage and over, of 100m or over in length	D04t.2e
Dangerous goods list, manifest or stowage plan	Ships carrying dangerous goods and/or marine pollutants in packaged or bulk form	F07f.2g F07f.2m
Deadweight Certificate	Ships in bulk cargo trades	F05a.2
Decision Support System	Ships of Classes I, II and II(A)	E08l.1a
Deck log book	All ships	D05c
Dedicated Clean Ballast Tank Operation Manual	Tankers operating with dedicated clean ballast tanks	D04g.1a
Deratting Certificate	Ships which have been successfully de-ratted	D04q.2 I01e.1g
Deratting Exemption Certificate	Ships which have been inspected and found to be rat-free	D04q.2 I01e.1g
Diving System Safety Certificate	Ships or floating structures fitted with a diving system	D03h.6
Document of Authorization	Ships loaded in accordance with the International Grain Code	F07g.2
Document of Compliance	Ships operated by companies which have been audited as complying with the ISM Code	D03a.1f
Document of Compliance with the Special requirements for Ships Carrying Dangerous Goods	Passenger ships built on/after 1 September 1984; cargo ships of 500gt or over built on/after 1 September 1984; and cargo ships of less than 500gt built on/after 1 February 1992, intending to load dangerous goods; offshore supply vessels operating in or out of the UK, regardless of date of build or voyage definition	F07f.2b
Domestic Ship Safety Management Certificate	Class III, IV, V, VI or VI(A) passenger ships on domestic voyages	D03b.1b
Draught of Water and Freeboard Notice ("FRE 5")	All UK ships proceeding to sea, except on Near Coastal voyages.	I07b.5
Dynamically Supported Craft Construction and Equipment Certificate	High-speed passenger craft complying with the DSC Code as amended	D04v.4
Dynamically Supported Craft Permit to Operate	High-speed passenger craft complying with the DSC Code as amended	D04v.4
Engine room log book	Mechanically propelled ships	D05c
Enhanced Survey Programme survey report file	Bulk carriers and tankers subject to enhanced surveys	D04f.1a
EPIRB registration card(s)	Ships fitted with one or more Cospas-Sarsat 406 MHz or INMARSAT 1.6 GHz band EPIRBs	D04b.5
Evidence of Ship Compliance (A/Amax)	Ro-ro passenger ships of Classes I, II and II(A)	D03b.5d
Exemption Certificate(s)	Ships exempted from any regulation requirement	D04f.2o
Extended protests	Ships whose masters have "noted protest"	I01j.2 I01j.2c
Fire control plans or booklets	Ships to which SOLAS reg.II-2/15.2.4 applies	D04l.3
Fire protection systems maintenance plan	Ships to which SOLAS reg.II-2/14.2.2.2 applies	D04l.3
Fire protection systems maintenance plan (tanker systems and equipment)	Tankers to which SOLAS reg.II-2/14.4 applies	D04l.3
Fire protection systems maintenance plan for low-location lighting	Passenger ships to which SOLAS reg. II-2/14.3 applies	D04l.3
Fire safety operational booklets	Ships to which SOLAS reg.II-2/16.5 applies	D04l.3
Fire training manual	Ships to which SOLAS reg.II-2/15.2.3 applies	D04l.3
Firearms Certificate	Ships carrying a firearm (e.g. for use as a livestock "humane killer" or for clay pigeon shooting)	D04u H01c.2
First Aid Manual	Category C vessels as described in MSN 1726	D04p
Flag State Verification and Acceptance Document	Vessels with dynamic-positioning systems	D03h.5a
Fresh Water Maintenance Log	All ships	E08h.3
Gaming Machine Licence(s)	Ships fitted with gaming machine(s)	D04u
Garbage disposal placards	Ship of 12 metres or more in length overall	D04t.6
Garbage Management Plan	Ships of 400gt or above, ships certified to carry 15 persons or more, and fixed or floating installations	D04t.4
Garbage Record Book	Ships of 400gt or above, ships certified to carry 15 persons or more engaged on voyages to ports or offshore terminals in other MARPOL States, and fixed and floating installations	D04t.5
GMDSS Radio Log	Passenger ships; cargo ships of 300gt or over	D05b.1
Grain Loading Manual	Ships loading grain in bulk	F07g.8a
Helicopter operations manual	SOLAS ships fitted with special facilities for operating helicopters (SOLAS reg.II-2/18.8)	D04l.3
High-Speed Craft Safety Certificate	High speed craft on international voyages	D04v.2
Hours of rest table	Sea-going ships	E03c.1c
Hours of rest records	Sea-going ships	E03c.1e
IBC Code	Chemical tankers built on or after 1 July 1986	D03e.1b

IGC Code	Liquefied gas carriers built on or after 1 July 1986	D03d.1c
Intact stability booklet	Ships to which the Load Line Regulations apply	D04t.2a
Interim Certificate of Class	Classed ships	D02d.3a
Interim Document of Compliance	Ships operated by newly established companies, or companies operating a ship type not covered by their DOC	D03a.1g
Interim Safety Management Certificate	New ships on delivery; ships new to the management of the company; and ships transferred between flag States	D03a.1g
Interim International Ship Security Certificate	Ships without an International Ship Security Certificate: (1) on delivery or prior to entry or re-entry into service; (2) on transfer from one SOLAS flag State to another; (3) on transfer to a SOLAS State flag from a non-SOLAS State flag; or (4) when the Company assumes responsibility for operation of a ship not previously operated by that Company	D04t.10c
International Certificate of Fitness for the Carriage of Dangerous Chemicals in Bulk	Chemical tankers built on or after 1 July 1986	D04g.5b
International Certificate of Fitness for the Carriage of INF Cargo	Ships carrying packaged irradiated nuclear fuel, plutonium and high-level radioactive wastes as cargo	F07h
International Certificate of Fitness for the Carriage of Liquefied Gases in Bulk	Gas carriers built on or after 1 July 1986	D04g.6b
International Code of Signals	Sea-going passenger ships and other ships of 300gt or more	D04o
International Grain Code	Sea-going ships carrying grain	F07g.1b F07g.1h F07g.2
International Load Line Certificate	"Convention size" ships (as above), following implementation of Harmonised System of Survey and Certification	D04i.1d
International Load Line Certificate (1966)	"Convention size" ships, i.e. ships built before 21 July 1968 of not less than 150gt, or ships built on or since 21 July 1968 of not less than 24 metres in length	D04i.1d
International Load Line Exemption Certificate	Ships exempted from the requirements of the MS (Load Line) Regulations 1998 under regulation 5(1) or 5(3)	D04i.1f
International Oil Pollution Prevention (IOPP) Certificate	Oil tankers of 150 gross tonnage and above and other ships of 400 gross tonnage and above engaged on voyages to ports or offshore terminals under the jurisdiction of other MARPOL party States	D04g.2
International Pollution Prevention Certificate for the Carriage of Noxious Liquid Substances in Bulk (NLS Certificate)	Ships carrying in bulk noxious liquid substances or unassessed liquid substances (unless holding a Certificate of Fitness as a chemical tanker)	D04g.3
International Sewage Pollution Prevention Certificate	All ships of 200gt and above, and all other ships certified to carry more than 10 persons (from 27 September 2003)	D04g.8
International Ship Security Certificate	All passenger ships, and all cargo ships of 500gt or over, including high-speed craft and MODUs, engaged on international voyages (from 1 July 2004)	D04t.10b
International Tonnage Certificate (1969)	Ships 24m or more in length	D04h.2b
ITF "Blue Certificate"	Ships covered by an ITF Agreement	C05a
Letters of Protest issued (copies)	Ships from which a Letter of Protest have been sent	I04b
Letters of Protest received	Ships receiving a Letter of Protest	I04b
Light Certificate (last receipted certificate)	Ships which have paid light dues	I07g.3
List of Crew (ALC1(a))	Ships in which non-exempt seamen are engaged	E07b.3 E07c.2
List of Exempt Crew (ALC1(b))	Ships in which exempt seamen are carried	E07b.2a
List of Young Persons (ALC1(c))	Ships on which any persons under 18 are employed as workers	E07c.2d
Lists of Lights	All ships, whether sea-going or not	D04o
Lists of Lights (relevant to the ship's current voyage and operation)	Ships of 12 metres or more registered length, whether sea-going or not	D04o
Lists of Radio Signals	All ships, whether sea-going or not	D04o
Lists of Radio Signals (relevant to the ship's current voyage and operation)	Ships of 12 metres or more registered length, whether sea-going or not	D04o
Load Line Certificate for each additional load line	Ships marked with multiple load lines	D04i.4
Loading or unloading plan	Ships loading or unloading solid bulk cargoes other than grain	F07g.1g
Marine pollutants list, manifest or stowage plan	Ships carrying marine pollutants in packaged or bulk form	F07f.2g F07f.2m
Mariner's Handbook	Sea-going passenger ships and other ships of 300gt or more	D04o
Mate's Receipts (ship's copies)	Ships which have issued Mate's Receipts for goods loaded	F07b.10
Medical or Sick-Bay Log	Ships required to carry an Official Log Book, where records of illnesses and injuries are not kept in the OLB itself	D05b.5 E08j.2
Merchant Shipping Notices, Marine Guidance Notes and Marine Information Notes (relevant to the ship's current voyage and operation)	Ships of 12m or more registered length, whether sea-going or not	D04o B04a.4
Mobile Offshore Drilling Unit Safety Certificate	Mobile offshore drilling units complying with the MODU Code	D03h.4
Muster List Approval document	Ships of Classes I, II, II(A) and III	E08l.1b
Nautical Almanac	Ships of 12m or more registered length, whether sea-going or not	D04o

Nautical publications (as necessary for the current voyage)	Ships of 12 metres or more registered length	D04o
Navigational tables	Ships of 12m or more registered length, whether sea-going or not	D04o
Noise Survey Report	Ships of 1600gt and over	D04t.9
Notice of Readiness (copy)	Ships on voyage charter, which have tendered NOR	F05c.1 F05c.1c
Notices to Mariners (relevant to the ship's current voyage and operation)	Ships of 12 metres or more registered length, whether sea-going or not	D04o
ODMCS Operation Manual	Oil tankers of 150gt and above	D04g.1
ODMCS records	Oil tankers of 150gt and above	D04g.1
Official Log Book - Part 2 (passenger ships) (LOG 2)	Ships of classes I, II and II(A)	D05a.10
Official Log Book (LOG 1)	All ships except lighthouse authority ships, ships less than 25gt and pleasure yachts	D05a.3
Oil Pollution Insurance Certificate (OPIC)	Ships carrying more than 2000 tonnes of persistent oil in bulk as cargo	G04d.1a
Oil Pollution Prevention Certificate for UK Coastal Waters	As for UK Oil Pollution Prevention Certificate	D04g.2
Oil Record Book (Part I) (all ships)	Non-tankers of 400gt and above; tankers of 150gt and above	D05b.2 H03a.9
Oil Record Book (Part II) (oil tankers)	Tankers of 150gt and above	D05b.2 H03a.9
Oil Recovery Certificate	Offshore support vessels adapted for oil recovery operations	D04g.11
Operating and maintenance instructions for navigational aids	All ships of 12m or more registered length (sea-going or not)	D04o
Operating instructions for watertight doors below the bulkhead deck fitted in bulkheads required to be watertight	Passenger ships of classes I, II and II(A)	D03b.4b D03b.4e
Operational Limitations Document	Passenger ships on international voyages	D03b.9 H01b.1
P&I club list of correspondents	Ships entered with a P&I club	G02a.3d
P&I club loss prevention literature	Ships entered with a P&I club	G02a.3b
P&I club rule book(s)	Ships entered with a P&I club	G04b.1
Panama Canal Tonnage Certificate or appropriate document	Ships transiting the Panama Canal	D04h.3
Passenger Certificate(s)	UK passenger ship not engaged on international voyages	D04f.2l D04f.2m D04f.2n
Passenger list or return	Ships arriving at or departing from UK ports with passengers	I01i
Passenger Ship Safety Certificate	Passenger ships engaged on international voyages other than short international voyages (i.e. Class I ships)	D04f.2k D04f.2n
Passenger Ship Safety Certificate for a short international voyage	Passenger ships engaged on short international voyages (i.e. Class II ships)	D04f.2k D04f.2n
PC/UMS Documentation of Total Volume	Ships intending to transit the Panama Canal	D04h.3a
PC/UMS Net Tonnage Certificate	Ships making a second or subsequent Panama Canal transit	D04h.3b
Permit to Operate High-Speed Craft	High-speed craft	D04v.2
Pilot Boat Certificate	Pilot boats of up to 24 metres load line length which comply with the "Brown Code"	D03l.5
Port State Control inspection report	Ships which have been inspected by a Port State Control inspector	I02c.3f
Procedures and Arrangements Manual (P&A Manual)	Ships carrying noxious liquid substances (MARPOL Annex II)	D04g.3b
Protests (or "sea protests") noted	Ships whose masters have "noted protest"	I01j.2
Provisional Certificate of British Registry	Ships outside the British Islands intended for registry; ships outside the UK in which the Certificate of Registry has been lost	D01e.4
Radar shadow sector diagram	Ships fitted with radar	D04n.3
Radio Log Book of appropriate type (e.g. GMDSS Log)	Ships of 300gt and above	D04m.3 D05b.1
Record of Particulars relating to Conditions of Assignment	Ships assigned load lines by an Assigning Authority	D04i.1e
Record of seafarers' daily hours of rest	Sea-going ships	E03c.1e
Register of Lifting Appliances and Cargo Handling Gear	UK ships other than fishing vessels, pleasure craft, offshore installations on or within 500m of their working stations, and ships on which there is, for the time being, no master, crew or watchman	D04r.2 E08f
Register of Young Persons employed on board	Ships exempted from having a Crew Agreement	E05c.1
Safe Manning Document	Every UK ship of 500gt or more	E03b.3
Safety Management Certificate	Ships operated by companies holding an ISM Code Document of Compliance, where the company and shipboard management comply with the Safety Management System	D03a.1f
Safety management manual(s)	Ships to which ISM Code applies	C04b.3
Sailing directions ("pilot books") as necessary for the current voyage	Ships of 12 metres or more registered length	D04o
Schedules of MSN 1726, as relevant to the ship	Ships of Categories A, B, C and D as described in MSN 1726	D04p
Search and Rescue Co-operation Plan	UK passenger ships of all classes wherever they may be, and other passenger ships operating on regular scheduled services while they are within UK waters	D04t.7
Sea waybills	Ships carrying cargo under sea waybill terms	F07b.14

Ship Captain's Medical Guide	Category A or B vessels as defined in MSN 1726	D04p
Ship Fixed Radio Licence	Ships fitted with any radio apparatus	D04m.3a
Ship Sanitation and Hygiene Certificate	Ships in UK ports	D04t.8
Ship Security Plan	All passenger ships, and all cargo ships of 500gt or over, including high-speed craft and MODUs, engaged on international voyages (from 1 July 2004)	D04t.10a
Shipboard Marine Pollution Emergency Plan (SMPEP) (in lieu of separate SOPEP and SMPEP (NLS))	Tankers of 150gt and above carrying noxious liquid substances in bulk	D04t.1b
Shipboard Marine Pollution Emergency Plan for Noxious Liquid Substances (SMPEP (NLS))	Tankers of 150gt and above carrying noxious liquid substances in bulk	D04t.1b
Shipboard Oil Pollution Emergency Plan (SOPEP)	Oil tankers of 150gt and above and non-tankers of 400gt and above	D04t.1a
Shipper's Declaration(s)	Ships loading bulk concentrates or other dry bulk cargo which may liquefy	F07g.1a
Small Commercial Vessel Certificate	Commercially operated motor vessels and sailing vessels of up to 24 metres load line length which do not carry cargo or more than 12 passengers, and which comply with the "Yellow Code" (for motor vessels) or "Blue Code" (for sailing vessels)	D03l.3 D03l.4 D03l.6 D03l.8
Small Commercial Vessel Certificate (SCV1) – Sport or Pleasure Use	Vessels which comply with the Code of Practice for Small Commercial Vessels Operating from a Nominated Departure Point (the "Red Code")	D03l.6
Special Purpose Ships Safety Certificate	Special purpose ships	D03j
Standing instructions to masters (Company's)	All ships	H01a.1
Statement of Compliance with MARPOL Annex IV	Ships equipped with a sewage treatment plant, comminutor and/or holding tank (as applicable) and a discharge pipeline in compliance with MARPOL Annex IV	D04g.8a
Statement of Compliance with the NO$_x$ Technical Code	Ships of 400gt or over built on or after 1 January 2000	D04g.10a
Statement of Facts (ship's copies)	Ships on voyage charter	F05f.1
Steering gear operating instructions	Sea-going ships	D04w
Stevedore damage reports (copies)	Cargo ships	I04c
Stores Declaration	Ships reporting to certain overseas Customs authorities	I01f.4a
Suez Canal Tonnage Certificate	Ships transiting the Suez Canal	D04h.4
Surveyors' certificates (of hold/tank cleanliness, etc.) in connection with cargo, etc.	Ships which have been surveyed by cargo surveyors	I04a
Table of scheduled daily hours of work and rest	Sea-going ships	E03c.1c
Table or curve of residual deviations of each magnetic compass	Ships fitted with magnetic compass(es)	D04n.2
Technical Manual (including Operating Manual, Maintenance Manual and Servicing Schedule)	Dynamically supported craft complying with the DSC Code	D04v.4
Tide tables (relevant to the current voyage and operation)	Ships of 12 metres or more registered length, whether seagoing or not	D04o
Transport Emergency Cards ("Tremcards")	Ships carrying dangerous goods on road trailers	D04u
TV Licence	Ships fitted with television receiver(s)	D04m.3c
Type Approval Certificates for marine equipment	All ships	D04b.2
UK Cargo Ship Safety Construction Certificate	Cargo ship of 500 gross tonnage or over not engaged on international voyages	D04f.2l
UK High Speed Craft Safety Certificate	High speed craft not on international voyages	D04v.2a
UK Load Line Certificate	Ships which are not "Convention-sized" ships ("Convention-sized" ships being ships built before 21 July 1968 of not less than 150gt, and ships built on or since 21 July 1968 of not less than 24 metres in length)	D04i.1d
UK Load Line Exemption Certificate	Ships exempted from the requirements of the MS (Load Line) Regulations 1998 under regulation 5(2)	D04i.1f
UK Oil Pollution Prevention (UKOPP) Certificate	Oil tankers of 150 gross tonnage and above and other ships of 400 gross tonnage and above, not engaged on voyages to ports or offshore terminals under the jurisdiction of other MARPOL party States	D04g.2
Vessel Response Plan (federal)	Vessels entering US waters	D04t.1c
Vessel Response Plan (state)	Vessels entering waters of certain US states	D04t.1c
Voyage Data Recorder Certificate of Compliance	Ships fitted with a VDR	D04b.3
Voyage instructions/letters from owners, managers, operators and/or charterers	Ships on charter	H01a.1 H01a.2
Workboat Certificate	UK vessels of up to 24 metres load line length in commercial use (not for sport or pleasure) and which carry cargo and/or up to 12 passengers or provide a service, and which comply with the "Brown Code"	D03l.5 D03l.5a
Written instructions on the safe operation of watertight doors	Passenger ships of classes I, II and II(A)	D03b.4m

D04b EQUIPMENT APPROVAL AND CERTIFICATION

D04b.1 Marine Equipment Regulations

* The **MS (Marine Equipment) Regulations 1999** (SI 1999/1957) -
  - implement Council Directive 96/98/EC on Marine Equipment ("the **Marine Equipment Directive**")(as amended by Commission Directive 98/85/EC). The Marine Equipment Directive lists, in Annex 1, equipment for which detailed **internationally agreed testing standards** exist, and in Annex 2, equipment for which **no detailed internationally agreed testing standards exist**.
  - provide for **type-approval** of marine equipment of a safety or pollution-prevention nature for use on UK ships.
  - are explained in **MSN 1734** and **MSN 1735**, as amended.
* **Equipment placed on UK ships and listed in MSN 1734** must comply with the applicable international standards specified in MSN 1734 (regulation 6(1)). Equipment will not comply with the applicable international standards unless:
  * it satisfies the **testing standards of the relevant international convention** (SOLAS, MARPOL, etc.) as specified in MSN 1734 (regulation 6(2)(a)); and
  * it has been **manufactured in accordance with the EC conformity-assessment procedure** and the **mark** of conformity, identification, and the last two digits of the year in which the mark was affixed, are on the equipment (regulation 6(2)(b)).
* Notwithstanding the requirement of regulation 6(2)(a) outlined above, equipment manufactured before 1 January 1999 in accordance with type-approval procedures in force in an EC member State before 20 December 1996 may be placed on the market, supplied for use or offered for supply in the UK and **placed on board a ship** the relevant safety certificate of which was issued by or on behalf of that State in accordance with the relevant international convention (regulation 6(3)).
* Exceptions in circumstances of **technical innovation** may be made (regulation 7(1)). Exceptions will be subject to the issue of a restricted or conditional type-approval certificate being issued by the MCA (regulation 7(3)).
* Exceptions to facilitate **testing or evaluation of equipment** may be made subject to the issue of a restricted or conditional type-approval certificate being issued by the MCA (regulation 8(1)).
* When **new ships are transferred to the UK register**, the MCA must inspect, or have inspected, the equipment on board to verify that its condition corresponds to its safety certificates and that it complies with regulation 6 or is equivalent (regulation 9(1)). Where equipment does not comply with regulation 6 but is equivalent, a type-approval certificate must be issued (regulation 9(2)).
* Notwithstanding regulation 6, where **type-approved equipment must be replaced in a port outside the EC** but it is not practicable for reasons of time, delay or cost to replace the equipment with equipment meeting the requirements of regulation 6, **equipment which does not comply** with regulation 6 may be placed on board subject to the conditions in regulation 10(2) being complied with (regulation 10(1)).
* Regulations 11 to 18 specify requirements of the **EC conformity-assessment procedures**. The EC mark of conformity, required under regulation 18(4) to be affixed to the equipment or a data plate, is in the form of a ship's wheel and is shown at Annex C of MSN 1734.
* Regulations 19 to 25 concern **enforcement**. Criminal **offences** are created of:
  * affixing the mark of conformity to equipment otherwise than in conformity with the Regulations, tampering with or altering such a mark or placing on the market, supplying or exposing or offering for supply any equipment which bears a mark affixed otherwise than in conformity with the Regulations or which no longer complies with the applicable international standards (regulation 20);
  * carrying equipment on a ship otherwise than in compliance with regulation 6(1) (regulation 23(1)); and
  * using type-approved equipment otherwise than in compliance with any restriction or condition imposed under the Regulations (regulation 23(2)).

D04b.1a EU Notified Bodies

* Equipment listed in Annex 1 of the EC Directives for which detailed international standards exist ("Annex 1 equipment") must be **type-approved** for use on a UK ship by an "**EU Notified Body**" (originally known as an "EC Notified Body").
* **Annex A to MSN 1734** details all "**Annex 1 equipment**" (i.e. LSA, marine pollution prevention, fire protection, navigation and radio communication equipment) together with the **applicable international instruments**. Annex A is amended by **MSN 1734 Amendment 2**.
* The organisations nominated by the MCA as **EC Notified Bodies** are listed in the Annex to MSN 1734 Amendment 2.
* **Annex 2 to MSN 1734** details the **application procedure** for type approval for EC type-examination.

D04b.1b UK Nominated Bodies

* Equipment listed in Annex 2 of the EC Directives for which **no detailed international standards** yet exist ("Annex 2 equipment") must **be type-approved** for use on a UK ship by one of the "**UK Nominated Bodies**" listed in **MSN 1735 Amendment 2**. Such equipment, which is listed in the **Annex of MSN 1735 Amendment 2**, will continue to be tested, type-approved and certified by Nominated Bodies to standards agreed with the MCA **until international standards are agreed**. The equipment is listed in the Annex to MSN 1735 Amendment 2 under the following headings: Fire appliances; Life-saving appliances; Marine engineering; Equipment required under COLREG 72; Navigation equipment, Marine pollution-prevention; Radio communication equipment; Bulk carrier safety equipment; and Crew accommodation.
* Paragraph 2 of MSN 1735 details the **type approval procedure** to be used by Nominated Bodies.
* **M.1440** contains tables setting out: items required to be type-approved; principal regulation applicable; standard to be met; and grounds for acceptance (e.g. Test Certificate from classification society).

D04b.2 Delegation of Type Approval Regulations

* **Regulation 2(1)(a) of the MS (Delegation of Type Approval) Regulations 1996** (SI 1996/147) enable the MCA to delegate its type approval functions in respect of equipment and arrangements for ships to the organisations specified in **MSN 1734** and **MSN 1735**, as amended. The equipment and arrangements concerned are those required under the SOLAS and COLREG Conventions and Annex I of MARPOL.
* Any **type approval** given under regulation 2 must be **in writing** and must specify the **date** when it is to come into force and the **conditions**, if any, on which it is given (regulation 2(2)).
* **No provision** is made requiring a type approval certificate to be **carried on board** the ship (see D04b.3).

D04b.3 Approval, surveys and performance standards of navigational systems and VDR

* The **MS (Safety of Navigation) Regulations 2002** (SI 2002/1473) (see H01f.2), which give effect in the UK to the revised **SOLAS chapter V** -
  - **revoke** and replace the MS (Navigational Equipment) Regulations 1993 (SI 1993/69), as amended by SIs 1999/1957 and 2000/2687.
  - **require** (in regulation 5) compliance by UK ships, other than those excepted under regulation 4(3), with paragraphs 1, 2, 3, 7 and 8 of **SOLAS regulation V/18** (which relates to **Approval, surveys and performance standards of navigational systems and VDR**).
* The **ships excepted** by regulation 4(3) are ships of less than 150gt engaged on any voyage.
* **SOLAS regulation V/18.1** provides that systems and equipment required to meet the requirements of regulations V/19 and V/20 must be of a **type approved by the flag State Administration**. For notes on the requirements of **regulation V/19**, see D04n.1. For notes on the requirements of **regulation V/20**, see D05b.7.
* **SOLAS regulation V/18.2** provides that systems and equipment, including associated back-up arrangements, where applicable, installed on or after 1 July 2002 to perform the functional requirements of regulations V/19 and V/20 must conform to appropriate **performance standards** not inferior to those adopted by IMO. Footnotes to regulation V/18 list numerous IMO standards for the different items of equipment specified in regulations V/19 and V/20. **Annex 8** to the MCA's 2002 SOLAS V publication deals with Performance standards and type approval. **Annex 9** deals with IMO performance standards for navigational equipment.
* **SOLAS regulation V/18.3** provides that when systems and equipment are replaced or added to on ships constructed before 1 July 2002, such systems and equipment must, as far as is reasonable and practicable, comply with the requirements of regulation V/18.2 above.
* **SOLAS regulation V/18.7** provides that when equipment, for which performance standards have been developed by IMO, is carried on ships in addition to items of equipment required by regulations V/19 and V/20, such equipment will be subject to approval and must, as far as is practicable, comply with performance standards not inferior to those adopted by IMO.
* **SOLAS regulation V/18.8** provides that the voyage data recorder (VDR) system, including all sensors, must be subjected to an annual performance test. The test must be conducted by an approved testing or servicing facility to verify the accuracy, duration and recoverability of the recorded data. In addition, tests and inspections must be conducted to determine the serviceability of all protective enclosures and devices fitted to aid location. A copy of the Certificate of Compliance issued by the testing facility, stating the date of compliance and the applicable performance standards, must be retained on board the ship.

D04b.4 Safety equipment and pollution prevention equipment carried in excess of statutory requirements

* **MGN 79** advises shipowners and masters that safety equipment on board which is in excess of statutory requirements might come to be relied upon in any emergency, and must therefore be **maintained in the same proper condition as statutory equipment**. A similar philosophy applies to **pollution prevention equipment** in excess of statutory requirements.
* Owners and masters are responsible not only for maintaining statutorily required safety and pollution prevention equipment, but also for ensuring that equipment in excess of statutory requirements is **safe**, **suitable** for its intended purpose, **maintained** in good condition and in accordance with the manufacturer's instructions, and (if applicable) comply with any **conditions imposed by a type approval certificate** issued for the equipment.
* Guidelines on this subject are given in the IMO Maritime Safety Committee report MSC XLIII/18 Annex 3 Paragraph 23, which should be adhered to at all times. The report states: "Equipment on board which is expected to be relied on in situations affecting safety or pollution prevention must be in operating condition. If such equipment is inoperative and is in excess of the equipment required by an appropriate Convention and/or the Flag State it should either be repaired, remove or if removal is not practicable, clearly marked as inoperative and secured."

D04b.5 EPIRB Registration Regulations

* The **MS (EPIRB Registration) Regulations 2000** (SI 2000/1850) apply to all UK ships wherever they may be (regulation 3(1)).
* **HM Coastguard** is designated as the competent authority in the UK for the purposes of the Regulations (regulation 4).
* **The owner and the operator** (who is defined as including the **master** and any **charterer**, **manager** or **agent** of the ship) of every UK ship must ensure that **every EPIRB carried** on the ship (whether or not carried in compliance with statutory requirements) is **registered with a competent authority** in a member State of the International Telecommunication Union (ITU), and that the registered particulars are correct (regulation 5(1)). ("**EPIRB**" is defined in regulation 2(2) as "an emergency position indicating radio beacon capable of transmitting a distress alert either through the Cospas-Sarsat satellite service operating in the 406 MHz band or through the INMARSAT geostationary satellites operating in the 1.6 GHz band".) **Particulars to be registered** are listed in regulation 5(2).
* Regulation 5(3) provides that **evidence** that every EPIRB carried on the ship is registered in accordance with regulation 5(1) must be readily available on board for **inspection** at all times by an MCA surveyor. (For this purpose, an **EPIRB registration card** should be carried for each EPIRB on board.)
* Regulation 6 provides that where, in respect of an EPIRB registered with a competent authority, there is any **change** in the particulars registered, the **owner and operator** of the ship to which the particulars relate must, as soon as is reasonably practicable after the change, give **written notice** to the competent authority.
* **MSN 1732** provides guidance on implementation of the Regulations. **MGN 150** provides guidance on registration procedures.
* The **registered particulars** are maintained at the EPIRB Register, HM Coastguard, South Western, Pendennis Point, Castle Drive, Falmouth TR11 4WZ.

D04b.6 Electromagnetic compatibility

* The **MS (Safety of Navigation) Regulations 2002** (SI 2002/1473) (see H01f.2) require compliance by a ship to which the Regulations apply with **paragraphs 2 and 3 of SOLAS regulation V/17**, which relates to **Electromagnetic compatibility**.
* **SOLAS regulation V/17.2** provides that **electrical and electronic equipment must be so installed** that electromagnetic interference does not affect the proper function of navigational systems and equipment.
* **SOLAS regulation V/17.3** provides that **portable electrical and electronic equipment must not be operated** on the bridge if it may affect the proper function of navigational systems and equipment.
* **Statutory electromagnetic compatibility ("EMC") requirements for marine equipment** are laid down in the MS (Marine Equipment) Regulations 1999 (SI 1999/1957) (see D04b.1) and the Electromagnetic Compatibility Regulations 1992 (SI 1992/2372), which respectively implement the Marine Equipment Directive and the Electromagnetic Compatibility Directive.

D04c STATUTORY SHIP CLASSES

D04c.1 Ship classes - general

* The arrangement of the **statutory ship classes** of merchant ship, which are referred to in many Merchant Shipping regulations, is detailed in regulation 3 of the MS (Life-Saving Appliances For Ships Other Than Ships Of Classes III To VI(A)) Regulations 1999 (SI 1999/2721) ("the LSA Regulations") and in regulation 2 of the MS (Fire Protection: Large Ships) Regulations 1998 (SI 1998/1012) ("the Large Ships Regulations"), both as amended by the MS (Passenger Ships on Domestic Voyages) Regulations 2000 (SI 2000/2687). The arrangement is also contained in tabular form in Annex 1 to the MCA's 2002 SOLAS V publication (see H01f.2a).
* The LSA Regulations define certain terms used in the class definitions, as follows:
  * "**Passenger ship**" means a ship carrying more than 12 passengers.
  * "**Cargo ship**" means any ship which is not a passenger ship, pleasure vessel[62] or fishing vessel.
  * "**Tanker**" means a cargo ship constructed or adapted for the carriage in bulk of liquid cargoes of a flammable nature and also means a chemical tanker or gas carrier constructed or adapted to carry cargoes emitting toxic vapours or gases, or cargoes having a flash point not exceeding 60°C (closed cup test).
  * "**Voyage**" includes an excursion.
  * "**International voyage**" means a voyage from a country to which the Convention applies to a port outside that country, or conversely.
  * "**Long international voyage**" means an international voyage which is not a short international voyage.
  * "**Short international voyage**" means an international voyage -
    * in the course of which a ship is not more than 200 miles from a port or place in which the passengers and crew could be placed in safety; and
    * which does not exceed 600 nautical miles in distance between the last port of call in the country in which this voyage begins and the final port of destination.
    (However, for the purposes of this definition, no account will be taken of any deviation by a ship from the intended voyage due solely to the stress of weather or any other circumstances that neither the master nor the owner nor the charterer (if any) of the ship could have prevented or forestalled.)
  * "**Category A, B, C and D waters**" means the waters specified as such in **MSN 1766**, and cognate expressions will be construed accordingly.
  * "**Sea**" does not include any waters specified as Category A, B, C or D.

D04c.2 Classes of passenger ship

* **Passenger ship classes** include:
  * **Classes I to Class VI(A)**, as described in the MS (Life-Saving Appliances for Ships other than Ships of Classes III to VI(A)) Regulations 1999 (SI 1999/2721) (see below); and
  * **Classes A, B, C and D**, as described in the MS (Passenger Ships on Domestic Voyages) Regulations 2000 (SI 2000/2687) (see D04c.2b), and in Annex 1 to the MCA's 2002 SOLAS V publication (see H01f.2a).
* **Classes I to VI(A)** are described in the LSA Regulations as follows.
* **Class I**: Passenger ships engaged on voyages any of which are long international voyages. (This class includes cruise ships, deep-sea cargo ships carrying 13 or more passengers, large naval auxiliaries carrying troops, etc.)
* **Class II**: Passenger ships engaged only on short international voyages. (This class includes, for example, UK - France ferries and UK – Ireland ferries, other than those on Northern Ireland services).
* **Class II(A)**: Passenger ships engaged on voyages other than international voyages, which are not -
  ships of Classes III to VI(A) as defined in the MS (Passenger Ship Construction: Ships of Classes III to VI(A)) Regulations 1998; or
  ships of Class A, B, C or D as defined in the MS (Passenger Ships on Domestic Voyages) Regulations 2000 which are new ships, engaged on domestic voyages, for the purposes of those Regulations.
  (This amended description of Class II(A) is by virtue of regulation 5 of the MS (Passenger Ships on Domestic Voyages) Regulations 2000 (SI 2000/2687) (see D03b.6b).)
* **Class III**: Passenger ships engaged only on voyages in the course of which they are at no time more than 70 miles by sea from their point of departure nor more than 18 miles from the coast of the United Kingdom, and which are at sea only in favourable weather and during restricted periods.
* **Class IV**: Passenger ships engaged only on voyages in Category A, B, C and D waters.

---

[62] For a definition of "**pleasure vessel**", see D03l.8.

* **Class V**: Passenger ships engaged only on voyages in Category A, B and C waters.
* **Class VI**: Passenger ships engaged only on voyages with not more than 250 passengers on board, to sea, or in Category A, B, C and D waters, in all cases in favourable weather and during restricted periods, in the course of which the ships are at no time more than 15 miles, exclusive of any Category A, B, C and D waters, from their point of departure nor more than 3 miles from land.
* **Class VI(A)**: Passenger ships carrying not more than 50 passengers for a distance of not more than 6 miles on voyages to or from isolated communities on the islands or coast of the United Kingdom and which do not proceed for a distance of more than 3 miles from land.

D04c.2a Categorisation of waters

* The categories of waters referred to in the definitions of **Classes IV, V and VI passenger ships** are provided for in the **MS (Categorisation of Waters) Regulations 1992** (SI 1992/2356), which revoked and replaced the MS (Smooth and Partially Smooth Waters) Regulations 1987 (SI 1987/1591). The "smooth waters" listed in the Schedule to the 1987 Regulations were divided by the 1992 Regulations into three Categories: A, B and C, and the "partially smooth waters" became Category D. By virtue of the 1992 Regulations, references in other Merchant Shipping Regulations to "smooth and partially smooth waters" become references to Category A, B, C and D waters.
* **MSN 1776** defines the four categories of waters as stated below and lists the geographical locations of all UK waters designated under Categories A, B, C and D. The categorisations apply specifically to the operation of Class IV and V passenger ships and also determine which waters are **not regarded as "sea"** for the purposes of regulations made, or treated as made, under section 85 of the Merchant Shipping Act 1995. "**Sea**" thus excludes all Category A, B, C and D waters, and a "**seagoing ship**" will be regarded by the MCA as a ship which operates seaward of any categorised waters listed in **MSN 1776**.
* The four categories are defined as follows:
    * **Category A**: Narrow rivers and canals where the depth of water is generally less than 1.5 metres. Example location: Forth and Clyde Canal.
    * **Category B**: Wider rivers and canals where the depth of water is generally more than 1.5 metres or more and where the significant wave height could not be expected to exceed 0.6 metres at any time. Example location: Crinan Canal, from Crinan to Ardrishaig.
    * **Category C**: Tidal rivers and estuaries and large, deep lakes and lochs where the significant wave height could not be expected to exceed 1.2 metres at any time. Example location: Larne, within a line from Larne Pier to the ferry pier on Island Magee.
    * **Category D**: Tidal rivers and estuaries where the significant wave height could not be expected to exceed 2.0 metres at any time. Example location: in winter within a line from Colne Point to Whitstable, and in summer within a line from Clacton Pier to Reculvers, "winter" meaning November to March inclusive and "summer" meaning April to October inclusive.
* "**Categorised waters**", where referred to in MS regulations, means waters of Category A, B, C and D, as defined above. "**Sea**" means waters beyond categorised waters. "**Sea-going**" means going beyond the limits of categorised waters.
* Waters which are **categorised** should not be confused with waters which are **classed** under EC Directive 98/18/EC on Safety Rules and Standards for Domestic Passenger Ships (see D03b.6a).

D04c.2b Classes of passenger ships on UK domestic voyages

* For the purposes of the **MS (Passenger Ships on Domestic Voyages) Regulations 2000** (SI 2000/2687) (which give effect to Council Directive 98/18/EC), passenger ships engaged on domestic voyages in the UK are arranged in classes as follows.
* **Class A**: Ships engaged solely on domestic voyages other than ships of Class B, Class C and Class D.
* **Class B**: Ships engaged solely on domestic voyages in the course of which they are at no time more than 20 miles from the line of the coast where shipwrecked persons can land, corresponding to the medium tide height.
* **Class C**: Ships engaged solely on domestic voyages in sea areas where the probability of significant wave heights exceeding 2.5 metres is less than 10% over a one year period for all year round operation, or over a specific restricted period of the year for operation exclusively in such period, in the course of which they are at no time more than 15 miles from a place of refuge, nor more than 5 miles from the line of the coast where shipwrecked persons can land, corresponding to the medium tide height.
* **Class D**: Ships engaged solely on domestic voyages in sea areas where the probability of significant wave heights exceeding 1.5 metres is less than 10% over a one year period for all year round operation, or over a specific restricted period of the year for operation exclusively in such period, in the course of which they are at no time more

than 6 miles from a place of refuge, nor more than 3 miles from the line of the coast, where shipwrecked persons can land, corresponding to the medium tide height.
* Classes B, C and D are equivalent to Class III, VI and VI(A) passenger ships respectively.
* For the purposes of the above classification of passenger ships on domestic voyages, **sea areas** are classified, and **zones for all year round** and **restricted periodical operation** are designated in accordance with **MSN 1747**.
* "**Domestic voyage**" is defined in Annex 1 to the MCA's 2002 SOLAS V publication (see H01f.2a) as a voyage in sea areas from a port of a member State or EEA State to the same or another port within that member State or EEA State.
    • For notes on **Directive 98/18/EC** and the **Passenger Ships on Domestic Voyages Regulations**, see D03b.6a.

D04c.3 Classes of ships other than passenger ships

* **Class VII**: Ships (other than ships of Classes I, VII(A), VII(T), XI and XII) engaged on voyages any of which are long international voyages. (This class includes most deep-sea merchant ships other than tankers and passenger ships).
* **Class VII(A)**: Ships employed as fish processing or canning factory ships, and ships engaged in the carriage of persons employed in the fish processing or canning industries. (This class includes "klondykers".)
* **Class VII(T)**: Tankers engaged on voyages any of which are long international voyages. (This class includes, for example, ocean-going tankers).
* **Class VIII**: Ships (other than ships of Classes II, VIII(T), IX, XI and XII) engaged only on short international voyages. (This class includes, for example, dry cargo vessels trading between the UK and the near-Continent).
* **Class VIII(A)**: Ships (other than ships of Classes II(A) to VI(A) inclusive, VIII(A)(T), IX, IX(A), IX(A)(T), XI and XII) engaged only on voyages which are not international voyages. (This class includes, for example, UK coastal dry-cargo vessels).
* **Class VIII(T)**: Tankers engaged on voyages any of which are short international voyages. (This class includes, for example, tankers trading between the UK and the near-Continent).
* **Class VIII(A)(T)**: Tankers engaged only on voyages which are not international voyages. (This class includes, for example, UK coastal tankers).
* **Class IX**: Tugs and tenders (other than ships of Classes II, II(A), III, VI and VI(A)) which proceed to sea but are not engaged on long international voyages. (This class includes, for example, UK coastal tugs).
* **Class IX(A)**: Ships (other than ships of Classes IV to VI inclusive) which do not proceed to sea. (This class includes, for example, UK harbour dredgers).
* **Class IX(A)(T)**: Tankers which do not proceed to sea. (This class includes, for example, UK harbour bunker barges).
* **Class XI**: Sailing ships (other than fishing vessels and ships of Class XII) which proceed to sea. (This class includes sea-going sail training vessels).
* **Class XII**: Pleasure vessels of 13.7 metres in length or more. (This class includes large motor and other yachts not used for chartering).
* No **Class X** is listed in regulation 3 of the LSA Regulations; Class X ships are defined in fishing vessel legislation as "fishing boats other than ships of Classes I to VI(A) inclusive".

D04d SHIP INSPECTION AND SURVEY ORGANISATIONS AND APPROVED STANDARDS OF CONSTRUCTION AND MAINTENANCE

D04d.1 Directive 94/57/EC on common rules and standards for ship inspection and survey organisations

* **European Council Directive 94/57/EC** sets criteria for a framework of qualitative and quantitative requirements to be met by classification societies and other private bodies acting on behalf of maritime Administrations of EU Member States. The **aims of the Directive** are to ensure that these organisations are professionally reliable, efficient and able to maintain proper control of compliance with safety and environmental protection standards on the vessels which they either classify under their own rules or certify for statutory requirements on behalf of maritime Administrations[63]. The **text of the Directive** is reproduced in the Annex to **M.1672**.

---

[63] The text of the Directive's preamble states that "….. worldwide a large number of the existing classification societies do not ensure either adequate implementation of the rules or reliability when acting on behalf of national administrations as they do not have adequate structures and experience to be relied upon and to enable them to carry out their duties in a highly professional manner;"

* In the UK Directive 94/57/EC is implemented by:
  - **Formal Agreements with "recognised organisations"** (i.e. certain classification societies) authorised to perform statutory survey and certification work in respect of UK registered ships on behalf of the Secretary of State for Transport;
  - the **MS (Ship Inspection and Survey Organisations) Regulations 1996** (SI 1996/2908);
  - the **MS (Passenger Ship Construction: Ships of Classes I, II and II(A)) Regulations 1998** (SI 1998/2514);
  - the **MS (Passenger Ship Construction: Ships of Classes III to VI(A)) Regulations 1998** (SI 1998/2515);
  - the **MS (Cargo Ship Construction) Regulations 1997** (SI 1997/1509), as amended by SI 1999/643; and
  - the **MS (High Speed Craft) Regulations 1996** (SI 1996/3188).
* **Article 14.1 of the Directive** provides that each EU Member State must ensure that ships flying its flag will be **constructed and maintained** in accordance with the **hull, machinery and electrical and control installation requirements of a recognised organisation**. The obligation on the UK imposed by Article 14.1 is met through **regulation 5(1) of the MS (Ship Inspection and Survey Organisations) Regulations 1996** (see D04d.2), which provides that in performing functions for which they are authorised under the Merchant Shipping Act 1995 and instruments made, or having effect, pursuant to it relating to any UK ship, authorised organisations will ensure that the relevant requirements of one of the approved standards listed in **M.1672** are applied. For a list of those standards, see D04d.2b.

D04d.2 Ship Inspection and Survey Organisations Regulations

* The **MS (Ship Inspection and Survey Organisations) Regulations 1996** (SI 1996/2908) -
  - **implement**, in part, European Council Directive 94/57/EC (see D04d.1).
  - **lay down duties** of authorised organisations and recognised organisations.
  - provide for **withdrawal of recognition** from organisations where the UK is satisfied that the organisation no longer fulfils the criteria set in the Directive for recognition.

D04d.2a Recognised and authorised organisations

* **Regulation 2(1) of the Ship Inspection and Survey Organisations Regulations** defines a "**recognised organisation**" as an organisation recognised by a member State or a State party to the EEA Agreement pursuant to Article 4 of the Council Directive, and defines an "**authorised organisation**" as a recognised organisation authorised by written agreements with the MCA pursuant to Article 3.2, 5 and 6 of the Council Directive to perform duties referred to in Article 3.2(i) and (ii).
* **Regulation 5** sets out two **duties of authorised organisations**, as follows:
  1. In performing functions for which they are authorised under Merchant Shipping Act 1995 and instruments made, or having effect, pursuant to it relating to any UK ship, they must **ensure that the relevant requirements of one of the approved standards listed in M.1672 are applied**.
  2. Without prejudice to any requirements of a statutory instrument as to the issue of certificates, they must **not issue certificates to a UK ship de-classed or changing class for safety reasons before consulting the MCA** to determine whether a full inspection is necessary.
* **Regulation 6** sets out three **duties of recognised organisations**, as follows:
  1. They must consult with each other periodically with a view to maintaining equivalence of their technical standards and the implementation thereof. They must provide the European Commission with periodic reports on fundamental progress in standards.
  2. They must demonstrate willingness to co-operate with port State control administrations when a ship of their class is concerned, in particular, in order to facilitate the rectification of reported deficiencies or other discrepancies.
  3. They must **provide all relevant information to the MCA about changes of class or de-classing of vessels**.

D04d.2b Approved standards

* **M.1672** provides that in respect of **hull, machinery and control installations**, the relevant standard is the **Rules of one of the following classification societies**, applicable to the type and age of the ship:
  - Lloyd's Register of Shipping (LR);
  - Bureau Veritas (BV);
  - Det Norske Veritas (DNV);
  - Germanischer Lloyd (GL);
  - American Bureau of Shipping (ABS);
  - Registro Italiano Navale (RINA),

- these societies being designated by the MCA as **authorised organisations**.
* **M.1672** provides that in respect of **electrical installations**, the approved standard is:
    • the relevant edition of the Regulations for the Electrical and Electronic Equipment of Ships with Recommended Practice for their Implementation, issued by the Institution of Electrical Engineers (IEE), as applicable to the age of the ship; or
    • the equivalent standard of one of the classification societies listed above; or
    • notwithstanding the above, where a ship embodies features of a novel kind, and alternative or equivalent standards are proposed by the authorised organisation, which may involve direct calculations, then such alternative or equivalent standards may be approved provided details have been submitted to the MCA for prior approval.
* **M.1672** provides that any standards must be applied as a consistent whole for each of the elements or installations listed above (hull, machinery, electrical installations, and control installations) as relevant to the regulations for passenger ships, cargo ships or high speed craft, whichever is applicable.
* **There is a requirement** in the two sets of Passenger Ship Construction Regulations, the Cargo Ship Construction Regulations and the High Speed Craft Regulations that with respect to **construction or maintenance** relating to hull, machinery, electrical installations and control installations, **UK ships must comply with the approved standards listed in M.1672** which are relevant to them[64].
* **Amendment No. 1 to M.1672** details a modification to the EC Directive and SOLAS 74 which requires recognised organisations to operate in accordance with the provisions in the Annex to IMO Resolution A.789(19).
* **MSN 1698** contains schedules containing certain standards of construction and stability required under the MS (Passenger Ship Construction: Ships of Classes I to II(A)) Regulations 1998 (SI 1998/2514).
* **MSN 1699** contains schedules containing certain standards of construction and stability required under the MS (Passenger Ship Construction: Ships of Classes III to VI(A)) Regulations 1998 (SI 1998/2515).

D04e HARMONISED SYSTEM OF SURVEY AND CERTIFICATION

D04e.1 Harmonised System of Survey and Certification

- is intended to alleviate the difficulties and extra expense for ship owners and operators who, under the survey provisions of the SOLAS, MARPOL and LOADLINE Conventions, had to **put their ships out of service** at different times for different surveys.
- is a **mandatory system**, but may be implemented on individual ships on different dates.
- was originally adopted by IMO in 1988 at an International Conference on the Harmonised System of Survey and Certification. The Conference adopted Protocols to the SOLAS and Load Lines Conventions to introduce the HSSC. MARPOL 73/78 was amended in 1990 to introduce the HSSC, with a proviso that the amendments would enter into force at the same time as the entry into force date of the 1988 SOLAS Protocol and the 1988 Load Lines Protocol.
- may be implemented by States on or after **3 February 2000**. (Resolution A.745(18) urged earlier adoption by States which had ratified the 1988 SOLAS and Load Lines Protocols.) The **date for introduction of the HSSC** after 3 February 2000 should normally be the **latest expiry date** of certificates issued under the SOLAS, Load Line and MARPOL Conventions, unless **another convenient date**, e.g. the expiry date of the Cargo Ship Safety Construction Certificate, the date of dry-docking or date of repair or renovation, is agreed upon between the shipowner or company and the flag State Administration.
- covers the survey and certification requirements of the following modified or amended instruments:
    • International Convention for the Safety of Life at Sea, 1974 (**SOLAS 74**), as modified by its 1988 Protocol (SOLAS 74/88);
    • International Convention on Load Lines, 1966 (**LLC 1966**), as modified by its 1988 Protocol (LLC 66/88);
    • International Convention for the Prevention of Pollution from Ships, 1973, and the Protocol of 1978 relating thereto (**MARPOL 73/78**), as amended by resolution MEPC.39(29) (MARPOL 73/78/90);
    • International Code for the Construction and Equipment of Ships Carrying Dangerous Chemicals in Bulk (**IBC Code**), as amended by resolutions MEPC.40(29) and MSC.16(58) (IBC Code);
    • International Code for the Construction and Equipment of Ships Carrying Liquefied Gases in Bulk (**IGC Code**), as amended by resolution MSC.17(58); and

---

[64] MS (Passenger Ship Construction: Ships of Classes I, II and II(A)) Regulations 1998, regulation 5; MS (Passenger Ship Construction: Ships of Classes III to VI(A)) Regulations 1998, regulation 5; MS (Cargo Ship Construction) Regulations 1997, regulation 5; and MS (High-Speed Craft) Regulations 1996, regulation 4(2).

- Code for the Construction and Equipment of Ships Carrying Dangerous Chemicals in Bulk (**BCH Code**), as amended by resolutions MEPC.41(29) and MSC.18(58).
- covers the following **certificates**, and **surveys** for issue of those certificates, under SOLAS, MARPOL, the Load Line Convention and the Gas and Chemical Tanker Codes, as follows:
  - Passenger Ship Safety Certificate;
  - Cargo Ship Safety Construction Certificate;
  - Cargo Ship Safety Equipment Certificate;
  - Cargo Ship Safety Radio Certificate;
  - International Oil Pollution Prevention Certificate;
  - International Noxious Liquid Substances Prevention Certificate;
  - International Load Line Certificate;
  - International Certificate of Fitness for the Carriage of Liquefied Gases in Bulk; and
  - International Certificate of Fitness for the Carriage of Dangerous Chemicals in Bulk.
* The harmonised system provides for:
  - A **one-year standard interval between surveys**, based on initial, annual, intermediate, periodical and renewal surveys, as appropriate.
  - A scheme for providing the necessary **flexibility** for the execution of each survey with the provision that:
    - the renewal survey may be completed within 3 months before the expiry date of the existing certificate with no loss of its period of validity;
    - there is a "time window" of 6 months, from 3 months before to 3 months after the anniversary date of the certificate for annual, intermediate and periodical surveys.
  - A maximum period of validity of **5 years** for all certificates for **cargo ships**.
  - A maximum period of validity of **12 months** for the **Passenger Ship Safety Certificate**.
  - A system for the **extension** of certificates limited **to 3 months** to enable a ship to complete its voyage, or **one month** for ships engaged on short voyages[65].
  - The period of validity of the new certificate starting from the expiry of the existing certificate before its extension, when an extension has been granted.
  - A flexible system for the inspection of the **outside of the ship's bottom** on the following conditions:
    - a minimum of two inspections during any 5-year period;
    - the interval between any two such inspections may not exceed 36 months.
  - A provision for a **Cargo Ship Safety Certificate** under SOLAS 74/88, as an alternative to separate Cargo Ship Safety Construction, Cargo Ship Safety Equipment and Cargo Ship Safety Radio Certificates.
  - A flexible system concerning the frequency and the period of validity of certificates, provided that the minimum pattern of surveys is maintained.
* IMO Resolution A.746(18), adopted in 1993, contains **Survey Guidelines** Under The Harmonised System of Survey and Certification.
* The **principal changes** to the survey and certification requirements of SOLAS 74/88 resulting from implementation of the HSSC are as follows:
  1. **Unscheduled inspections** are no longer included and **annual surveys** are mandatory for cargo ships.
  2. Intervals between periodical surveys of equipment covered by the Cargo Ship Safety Equipment Certificate are alternatively at intervals of two and three years instead of two years.
  3. **Intermediate surveys** are required for all ships under the Cargo Ship Safety Construction Certificate.
  4. **Inspections of the outside of the ship's bottom** are required for all cargo ships.
  5. Intermediate surveys for the Cargo Ship Safety Construction Certificate are held within 3 months of either the second or third anniversary date.
  6. All cargo ship certificates may be issued for any period of validity up to **5 years**.
  7. There is a provision for a **Cargo Ship Safety Certificate**.
  8. The **extension** provisions have been reduced from 5 months to **3 months** to enable a ship to complete its voyage and the extension for one month for a period of grace is limited to ships engaged on short voyages.
* With regard to the International Load Line Certificate 66/88, the principal changes to the requirements for survey and certification are the introduction of similar extension provisions as in the previous paragraph and linking of the period of validity of the new certificate to the expiry date of the previous certificate.
* With MARPOL 73/78/90 (IOPPC and INLSC) and the IBC Code 83/90 (COF), the IGC Code 83/90 and the BCH Code 85/90 (COFs), the main changes are the linking of the period of validity of the new certificate to the expiry date of the previous certificate, the holding of the intermediate survey within 3 months of either the second or third anniversary date and the introduction of the same extension provisions as for other certificates[66].

---

[65] Paragraph 15.4 of IMO Resolution A.746(18) defines "short voyage" in this context as a voyage where neither the distance from the port in which the voyage begins and the final port of destination nor the return voyage exceeds 1,000 miles.

[66] Under the pre-harmonisation regulations, a COF could not be extended.

* To determine whether the HSSC has been implemented on a particular ship, the header statement of the relevant certificates should be inspected.
    1. The header statement on any SOLAS Convention certificate or Record of Equipment issued under the HSSC provisions will read: *"Issued under the provisions of the International Convention for the Safety of Life at Sea, 1974 in accordance with Assembly resolution A.883(21) relating to the global implementation of the harmonised system of survey and certification."*
    2. The statement on a Load Line Convention certificate issued under the HSSC provisions will read: *"Issued under the provisions of the International Convention on Load Lines, 1966 in accordance with Assembly resolution A.883(21) relating to the global implementation of the harmonised system of survey and certification."*
    3. The statement on a MARPOL certificate will read: *"Issued under the provisions of the International Convention for the Prevention of Pollution from Ships, 1973, as modified by the Protocol of 1978 relating thereto, and as amended by Resolution MEPC.39(29) (hereinafter referred to as "The Convention)."*
* Similar expiry dates on the relevant certificates is further confirmation of implementation of the HSSC.

D04e.2 Implementation of Harmonised System of Survey and Certification by UK

* In respect of certificates issued under **SOLAS 74**, the Harmonised System of Survey and Certification is applied in the UK by the **MS (Survey and Certification) (Amendment) Regulations 2000** (SI 2000/1334). **MSN 1751** explains the background and requirements of the regulations and defines the seven types of survey under the HSSC.
* In respect of certificates issued under the International Convention on **Load Lines, 1966**, the HSSC is applied in the UK by the **MS (Load Line) (Amendment) Regulations 2000** (SI 2000/1335).
* In general the UK is modelling its instructions for guidance of surveyors on the **Survey Guidelines** under the Harmonised System of Survey and Certification contained in IMO **Resolution A.746(18)**.
* The current certificates on board a particular ship on 8 June 2000 will **remain in force until they expire or until it is decided to implement the HSSC** on that ship.
* The **owner**, in conjunction with the **MCA** and any recognised organisation (e.g. classification society) that issues certificates on its behalf, will then agree a **mutually convenient date** on which to implement the HSSC for the ship. This will normally be the **latest expiry date of certificates** issued under the SOLAS, LOADLINE and MARPOL Conventions. **Alternatively**, a date may be agreed between the shipowner or company to coincide with the expiry date of the **Cargo Ship Safety Construction Certificate** or with the date of **drydocking**, refit or repair.
* In the case where an existing certificate has expired before the introduction of the harmonised system on the ship, a **new certificate** using the form prescribed under the HSSC may be issued after the renewal survey has been carried out. The validity of the new certificate will be limited to the date of the introduction of the harmonised system on that ship.
* On the agreed date, **renewal surveys** leading to the issue of a complete set of new certificates will be carried out and new certificates issued under the harmonised system. The anniversary date common to all certificates should be specified. Renewal surveys carried out within 3 months of the date of the introduction of the harmonised system will be valid and the extent of renewal surveys to be carried out will take account of the date and extent of the previous renewal surveys if carried out recently.
* The survey requirements, periods of validity and extension provisions that form part of the HSSC will then apply to each ship to which the new certificates have been issued.
* **MSN 1751** clarifies and expands the description of the HSSC given in Resolution A.746(18) as follows:
    * The **maximum period of validity** of all certificates except the Passenger Ship Safety Certificate is **5 years**. The Passenger Ship Safety Certificate will be renewed annually. Each full term of 5 years (or one year) will follow directly on from the previous one, unless a ship is laid up or undergoing major repairs. Each certificate will be dated from the expiry date of the previous one.
    * In order to provide the necessary flexibility, the **renewal survey** may be carried out up to **3 months before the expiry** of the existing certificate. The new certificate will be **dated from the expiry date** of the current one, i.e. there will be no loss to its period of validity.
    * A certificate may also be **extended** by a period of up to **3 months to complete a voyage** (or for ships engaged on short voyages, for a period of grace of up to one month) in order that the renewal survey may be carried out. The new certificate will be dated from the expiry date of the old certificate before the extension was granted.
    * **Where a renewal survey has been completed** and a certificate cannot be issued or placed aboard the ship before the expiry date of the existing certificate, the existing certificate may be **endorsed** and will be accepted as the new certificate for a period of up to **5 months** from the expiry date.
    * A certificate (other than a passenger ship certificate) that has been issued initially for a period of **less than 5 years** may be **extended** to the maximum period of 5 years provided that the minimum pattern of surveys is maintained.

- **Every certificate** will be subject to an **annual, intermediate or periodical survey** each year within 3 months of the anniversary date (the day and month of each year corresponding to the date of expiry) as follows:
- The **Passenger Ship Safety Certificate** requires a **renewal survey** each year.
- The **Cargo Ship Safety Radio Certificate** requires a **periodical survey** each year.
- The **International Load Line Certificate** requires an **annual survey** each year.
- The **Cargo Ship Safety Equipment Certificate** requires an **annual survey** each year. On either the second or third year this is replaced by a **periodical survey**.
- The **Cargo Ship Safety Construction Certificate, the International Certificate of Fitness for the Carriage of Liquefied Gases in Bulk**, the **International Certificate of Fitness for the Carriage of Dangerous Chemicals in Bulk**, the **International Oil Pollution Prevention Certificate** and **the International Pollution Prevention Certificate for the Carriage of Noxious Liquid Substances in Bulk** all require **annual surveys** each year. On either the second or third year these are replaced by an **intermediate survey**.
- If an annual, intermediate or periodical survey is completed more than 3 months before the anniversary date, the **anniversary date may be amended** to suit and the expiry date of the certificate brought forward by a corresponding period or, if the expiry date is unchanged, **additional surveys**, as appropriate, carried out so that the **pattern of surveys** remains the same and the maximum intervals between the various types of surveys are not exceeded.
- A new **Cargo Ship Safety Certificate** (**CSSC**), which includes provision for recording all the surveys required for the Cargo Ship Safety Equipment Certificate, Cargo Ship Safety Radio Certificate and Cargo Ship Safety Construction Certificate, may be issued as an **alternative** to the three existing cargo ship safety certificates.

D04e.3 Survey types under the Harmonised System of Survey and Certification

* Resolution A.746(18) defines the **seven types of survey** under the HSSC as follows:
- An **initial survey** is a **complete inspection** before a ship is put into service of all the items relating to a particular certificate to ensure that the relevant requirements are complied with and that these items are satisfactory for the service for which the ship is intended.
- A **periodical survey** is an inspection of (**all**) the items relating to the particular certificate to ensure that they are in a satisfactory condition and fit for the service for which the ship is intended.
- A **renewal survey** is the same as a periodical survey but also leads to the **issue** of a new certificate.
- An **intermediate survey** is an inspection of **specified items** relevant to the particular certificate to ensure that they are in a satisfactory condition and fit for the service for which the ship is intended.
- An **annual survey** is a general inspection of the items relating to the particular certificate to ensure that they have been maintained and remain satisfactory for the service for which the ship is intended.
- An **inspection of the outside of the ship's bottom** is an inspection of the underwater part of the ship and related items to ensure that they are in a satisfactory condition and fit for the service for which the ship is intended.
- An **additional survey** is an inspection, either general or partial according to the circumstances, to be made after a repair resulting from investigations or whenever any important repairs or renewals are made.

* The **scope** of each of these surveys (i.e. the particular items surveyed, inspected and/or tested) depends on whether the ship is a passenger ship or a cargo ship, and is described in **MSN 1751**.

D04e.4 Scope and purpose of passenger ship surveys under the Harmonised System of Survey and Certification

* An **initial survey of a passenger ship** will consist of a complete inspection of the ship's structure, machinery and equipment, including the outside of the ship's bottom and the inside and outside of the boilers, such as to ensure that the arrangements, materials and scantlings of the structure, boilers and other pressure vessels and their appurtenances, main and auxiliary machinery, electrical installation, radio installations including those used in life-saving appliances, fire protection, fire safety systems and appliances, life-saving appliances and arrangements, shipborne navigational equipment, nautical publications, means of embarkation for pilots, lights, shapes, means of making sound and distress signals and other equipment fully comply with the requirements of the relevant regulations, and that the workmanship of all parts of the ship and its equipment is in all respects satisfactory.

* A **renewal survey of a passenger ship** will include an inspection of the structure, boilers and other pressure vessels, machinery and equipment, including the outside of the ship's bottom, such as to ensure that the arrangements, materials and scantlings of the structure, boilers and other pressure vessels and their appurtenances, main and auxiliary machinery, electrical installation, radio installations including those used in life-saving appliances, fire protection, fire safety systems and appliances, life-saving appliances and arrangements, shipborne navigational equipment, nautical publications, means of embarkation for pilots, lights, shapes, means of making sound and distress signals and other equipment is in satisfactory condition and is fit for the service for which it is intended, and fully complies with the requirements of the relevant regulations.

* An **additional survey**, either general or partial, according to the circumstances, will be made following a repair or renewal. The survey will be such as to ensure that the necessary repairs or renewals have been effectively carried out, that the material and workmanship are in all respects satisfactory, and that the ship complies with the provisions of the relevant regulations.

D04e.5 Scope and purpose of cargo ship safety equipment surveys under the Harmonised System of Survey and Certification

* An **initial survey of cargo ship safety equipment** will include an inspection of the fire safety systems and appliances, life-saving appliances and arrangements except radio installations, the shipborne navigational equipment, means of embarkation for pilots and other equipment to which chapters II-1, II-2, III and V of the 1974 SOLAS Convention apply, to ensure that they comply with the provisions of the relevant regulations, and they are in satisfactory condition and are fit for the service for which the ship is intended. In addition the fire control plans, nautical publications, lights, shapes, means of making sound signals and distress signals will also be subject to this survey.
* An **annual survey** will include a **general inspection** of the equipment referred to above to ensure that it has been maintained to conform with the provisions of the relevant regulations to ensure that the ship in all respects will remain fit to proceed to sea without danger to the ship or persons on board and that it remains satisfactory for the service for which the ship is intended.
* A **renewal survey** and a **periodical survey** will include an inspection of (all) the equipment referred to in the initial survey to ensure that it complies with the relevant requirements of the relevant regulations, is in satisfactory condition and is fit for the service for which the ship is intended.

D04e.6 Scope and purpose of cargo ship radio equipment surveys under the Harmonised System of Survey and Certification

* An **initial survey of cargo ship radio equipment** will include a complete inspection of the radio installations of cargo ships, including those used in life-saving appliances, to ensure that they comply with the requirements of the relevant regulations.
* A **renewal survey** and a **periodical survey** will include an inspection of the radio installations of cargo ships, including those used in life-saving appliances, to ensure that they comply with the requirements of the relevant regulations.

D04e.7 Scope and purpose of surveys of cargo ship structure, machinery and equipment under the Harmonised System of Survey and Certification

* An **initial survey** will include a complete inspection of the structure, machinery and equipment, including an inspection of the outside of the ship's bottom, before the ship enters service. The survey will be such as to ensure that the arrangements, materials, scantling and workmanship of the structure, boilers and other pressure vessels, their appurtenances, main and auxiliary machinery including steering gear and associated control systems, electrical installation and other equipment, and in the case of tankers, the pump-rooms, cargo, bunker and ventilation piping systems and associated safety devices comply with the requirements of the relevant regulations, are satisfactory for the service for which the ship is intended and that the required stability information is provided. In the case of tankers such a survey will also include an inspection of the pump-rooms, cargo, bunker and ventilation piping systems and associated safety devices.
* A **renewal survey** will include an inspection of the ship's structure, machinery and equipment such as to ensure that they comply with the requirements of the relevant regulations, are in satisfactory condition and are fit for the service for which they are intended.
* An **intermediate survey** will include an inspection of the structure, boilers and other pressure vessels, machinery and equipment, the steering gear and the associated control systems and electrical installations, and in the case of tankers, the pump-rooms, cargo, bunker and ventilation piping systems and associated safety devices and the testing of insulation resistance of electrical installations in dangerous zones to ensure that they remain satisfactory for the service for which the ship is intended.

* An **annual survey** will include a general inspection of the structure, machinery and equipment referred to above to ensure that they have been maintained to conform with the provisions of the relevant regulations to ensure that the ship in all respects will remain fit to proceed to sea without danger to the ship or persons on board, and that they remain satisfactory for the service for which the ship is intended.

D04e.8 Scope and purpose of inspection of the outside of the ship's bottom under the Harmonised System of Survey and Certification

* The **inspection of the outside of the ship's bottom** is a separate survey.
* For **passenger ships** the inspection is required every year. In the years in which the out-of-water inspection does not take place, an in-water inspection of the ship's bottom will be carried out. As a minimum, two of these surveys in any 5-year period, at intervals not exceeding 36 months, will be conducted with the ship out of the water.
* For **cargo ships** there will be a minimum of two inspections during any 5-year period at intervals not exceeding 36 months. Inspections should normally be carried out with the ship out of the water; however, consideration may be given to alternate inspections being carried out with the ship afloat.

D04e.8a In-water surveys

* Under the rules of leading classification societies, **in-water surveys** (IWS) have for many years been permitted, in the case of certain vessels and under specified conditions, in lieu of one of the two docking surveys normally required in any five-year period (see D02d.1).
* **MGN 217** provides guidance on **statutory in-water survey (IWS) inspection of the ship's bottom** in lieu of inspection out of the water as described in MSN 1751.
* IWS was previously approved by the MCA only for ships of Classes I and VII; proposals for IWS for ships of other classes may now be approved, provided that the guidance in MGN 217 is followed. Specifically, the following types of UK ship may now have IWS:
    • passenger ships which go to sea (i.e. ships of classes I, II, II(A), III, VI and VI(A));
    • other sea-going ships, except tankers and bulk carriers over 15 years of age; and
    • domestic passenger ships which do not go to sea (i.e. ships of classes IV and V), where special arrangements are made.
* In the case of **sea-going passenger ships**, IWS may be carried out each year in which an inspection of the ship's bottom out of the water is not required.
* In the case of **other sea-going ships excluding tankers and bulk carriers**, where two inspections of the ship's bottom are required in any five-year period, one of the two inspections must be carried out with the ship out of the water, while the other may be an IWS. **Dredgers** issued with Load Line Exemption Certificates must continue to be surveyed in dry-dock twice in any five-year period.
* In the case of **domestic passenger ships of Classes IV and V**, the special arrangements in Appendix E of MGN 217 will apply.
* Special consideration must be given before IWS can be considered for **any ship of more than 15 years** of age.
* IWS will not be possible for **tankers and bulk carriers of more than 15 years of age**, to which an Enhanced Survey Programme (ESP) applies.
* Where an IWS is proposed, the owner must make a formal application to the MCA, stating where and when it is to be conducted.

D04f SURVEY AND CERTIFICATION LEGISLATION

D04f.1 Survey and certification requirements of international treaty instruments

* Survey and certification requirements of the chief international maritime treaty instruments are given effect in UK statutory instruments as shown in the following table.

International instrument	UK Regulations containing survey and certification requirements	SBC ref.
SOLAS	MS (Survey and Certification) Regulations 1995 (SI 1995/1210)	D04f.2
MARPOL Annex I	MS (Prevention of Oil Pollution) Regulations 1996 (SI 1996/2154)	D04g.2a
MARPOL Annex II	MS (Dangerous or Noxious Liquid Substances in Bulk) Regulations 1996 (SI 1996/3010)	D04g.3a
LOAD LINE Convention	MS (Load Line) Regulations 1998 (SI 1998/2241)	D04i
TONNAGE Convention	MS (Tonnage) Regulations 1997 (SI 1997/1510)	D04h.2

D04f.1a Enhanced Survey Programme

* For notes on the origins of the **enhanced survey programme**, see D02d.1b.
* **SOLAS chapter XI-1** introduced four **special measures to enhance maritime safety**, one of which is a programme of **enhanced surveys** for bulk carriers and oil tankers. **Regulation XI/2** (Enhanced surveys) provides that **bulk carriers** as defined in regulation IX/1.6[67] and **oil tankers** as defined in regulation II-1/2.12[68] will be subject to an **enhanced programme of inspections** in accordance with the guidelines (see below) adopted by the IMO Assembly by resolution A.744(18), as may be amended.
* **MARPOL 73/78 regulation I/13G** provides that **crude oil tankers of 20,000dwt and above** and **product carriers of 30,000dwt and above** will be subject to the enhanced programme of inspections, the scope and frequency of which will at least comply with IMO guidelines.
* The **IMO guidelines** referred to in the SOLAS and MARPOL provisions are the *Guidelines on the Enhanced Programme of Inspections during Surveys of Bulk Carriers and Oil Tankers*, which were adopted in 1993 by IMO resolution A.744(18) and were subsequently made mandatory under SOLAS regulation XI/2 and MARPOL regulation I/13G. The Guidelines are divided into two annexes:
  * **Annex A**: Guidelines on the enhanced programme of inspections during surveys of **bulk carriers**; and
  * **Annex B**: Guidelines on the enhanced programme of inspections during surveys of **oil tankers**.
* In respect of **bulk carriers**, the Guidelines should apply to surveys of hull structure and piping systems in way of cargo holds, cofferdams, pipe tunnels, void spaces within the cargo length area and all ballast tanks. The surveys should be carried out during the surveys prescribed by SOLAS 74, as amended (Annex A, 1.1.1). The Guidelines contain the extent of examination, thickness measurements and tank testing. The survey should be extended when substantial corrosion and/or structural defects are found and include additional close-up survey when necessary (Annex A, 1.1.2).
* In respect of **tankers**, the Guidelines should apply to all oil tankers of 500gt and above (Annex B, 1.1.1). The Guidelines should apply to surveys of hull structure and piping systems in way of cargo tanks, pump-rooms, cofferdams, pipe tunnels, void spaces within the cargo area and all ballast tanks (Annex B, 1.1.3).
* Enhanced surveys **do not replace other surveys**; the term refers to the **enhancement of the periodical surveys** required under the "ordinary" provisions of SOLAS chapter II-1 and MARPOL 73/78.
* The **scope of enhanced surveys** carried out during periodical inspections is specified in Annex A, 2.1.4, which provides (in respect of bulk carriers) as follows: "All cargo holds, ballast tanks, pipe tunnels, cofferdams and void spaces bounding cargo holds, decks and outer hull should be examined, and this examination should be supplemented by thickness measurements and testing as deemed necessary to ensure that the structural integrity remains effective. The examination should be sufficient to discover substantial corrosion, significant deformation, fractures, damages or other structural deterioration." (In respect of tankers, Annex B, 2.1.4 makes a similar provision, substituting "cargo tanks" for "cargo holds", and adding "pump-rooms" to the spaces to be examined.)
* A "**close-up survey**" is defined in the Guidelines as a survey where the details of structural components are within the close visual inspection range of the surveyor, i.e. preferably within reach of hand.
* "**Substantial corrosion**" is defined as an extent of corrosion such that assessment of corrosion pattern indicates a wastage in excess of 75% of allowable margins, but within acceptable limits.
* **SOLAS regulation XII/7** (Survey of the cargo hold structure of bulk carriers) prohibits a single-skin bulk carrier of 150m in length and upwards, of 10 years of age and over, from carrying solid bulk cargoes with a density of 1,780kg.m^3 and above unless it has satisfactorily undergone either a **periodical survey in accordance with the enhanced programme of inspections** required by regulation XI/2 or a **survey of all cargo holds to the same extent** as required in that regulation.
* **ESP documentation** required to be carried on board under the Guidelines includes:
  * a **survey report file** consisting of:
    * reports of structural surveys;
    * condition evaluation report;
    * thickness measurement reports; and
    * survey planning document.
  * **supporting documentation** including:
    * main structural plans of holds and ballast tanks;
    * previous repair history;
    * cargo and ballast history;

---

[67] SOLAS regulation IX/1.6 defines a **bulk carrier** as a ship which is constructed generally with single deck, top-side tanks and hopper side tanks in cargo spaces, and is intended primarily to carry dry cargo in bulk, and includes such types as ore carriers and combination carriers.
[68] SOLAS regulation II-1/2.12 defines an **oil tanker** as "the oil tanker defined in regulation 1 of Annex I of the Protocol of 1978 relating to MARPOL 73". MARPOL 73/78 regulation I/1 in turn defines **oil tanker** as "a ship constructed or adapted primarily to carry oil in bulk in its cargo spaces and includes combination carriers and any "chemical tanker" as defined in Annex II of the present Convention when it is carrying a cargo or part cargo of oil in bulk".

- inspections by ship's personnel with reference to structural deterioration in general, leakages in bulkheads and piping, and condition of corrosion prevention system, if any.
* The survey report file should also be available in the owner's and flag State Administration offices.

D04f.2 Survey and Certification Regulations

* The **MS (Survey and Certification) Regulations 1995** (SI 1995/1210), as amended -
- give effect to the requirements of the SOLAS Convention (as amended) for surveys and issue of the following certificates:
    • **Cargo Ship Safety Construction Certificate**;
    • **Cargo Ship Safety Equipment Certificate**;
    • **Cargo Ship Safety Radio Certificate**;
    • **Cargo Ship Safety Certificate**; and
    • **Passenger Ship Safety Certificate**.
- contain similar requirements for **UK ships not subject to SOLAS 74**, e.g. ships under 500gt.
- end the requirement for passenger ships on international voyages to be issued with a **Passenger Certificate** in addition to a SOLAS Passenger Ship Safety Certificate.
- provide for **appeals against surveys** by an arbitration procedure described in **M.1613**.
- are amended by:
    • the **MS (Survey and Certification) (Amendment) Regulations 1996** (SI 1996/2418), which provide that the MCA may authorise any person as an appropriate Certifying Authority in relation to radio installations for cargo ships, and make various minor amendments;
    • the **MS (Survey and Certification) (Amendment) Regulations 2000** (SI 2000/1334), which implement the 1988 Protocol to SOLAS 1974, including the Harmonised System of Survey and Certification (HSSC) (see D04e.1), and contain similar requirements for ships not subject to SOLAS 74; and
    • the **MS (Passenger Ships on Domestic Voyages) Regulations 2000** (SI 2000/2687), which implement Council Directive 98/18/EC on Safety Rules and Standards for Passenger Ships (see D03b.6).

D04f.2a Definitions (regulation 1)

* Definitions in regulation 1 which are relevant to this section are as follows.
* "**Appropriate Certifying Authority**" means:
- in relation to passenger ships and safety equipment of cargo ships, the MCA (exercising the functions of "the Secretary of State");
- in relation to cargo ships, except in relation to their radio installations and safety equipment, the MCA or any person authorised by the MCA or any person authorised by the MCA including (if so authorised):
    • Lloyd's Register of Shipping;
    • the British Committee of Bureau Veritas;
    • the British Committee of Det Norske Veritas;
    • the British Committee of Germanischer Lloyd;
    • the British Technical Committee of the American Bureau of Shipping; and
    • the British Committee of Registro Italiano Navale (RINA).
- in relation to radio installations of cargo ships, any person authorised by the Secretary of State (i.e. the MCA or Marconi Marine).
* A "**cargo ship**" means a ship that is not a passenger ship, ship of war, fishing vessel, or pleasure vessel (as defined in D03l.8). (A cargo ship may carry up to 12 passengers.)
* A "**passenger ship**" means a ship carrying more than 12 passengers.
* A "**passenger**" means any person carried on a ship except:
    • a person employed or engaged in any capacity on the business of the ship[69];
    • a person on board the ship either in pursuance of the obligation laid upon the master to carry shipwrecked, distressed or other persons, or by reason of any circumstance that neither the master nor the owner nor the charterer (if any) could have prevented or forestalled; or
    • a child of under one year of age.

---

[69] Section 27 of the Code of Practice for Safety of Large Commercial Sailing and Motor Vessels (the "Megayacht Code") (see D03l.7) explains that "a **person employed or engaged in any capacity on board the vessel on the business of the vessel**" may reasonably include:
1. bona-fide members of the crew over the minimum school-leaving age (about 16 years) who are properly employed on the operation of the vessel;
2. person(s) employed by the owner in connection with business interests and providing a service available to all passengers; and
3. person(s) employed by the owner in relation to social activities on board and providing a service available to all passengers.
The above persons should be included in the Crew Agreement and List of Crew required for the vessel (see E07).

* "**Ro-ro passenger ship**" means a passenger ship provided with cargo or vehicle spaces not normally subdivided in any way and extending to either a substantial length or the entire length of the ship in which vehicles or cargo can be loaded or unloaded in a horizontal direction.
* "**Short international voyage**" means an international voyage in the course of which a ship is not more than 200 miles from a port or place in which the passengers and crew could be placed in safety. Neither the distance between the last port of call in which the voyage begins and the final port of destination nor the return voyage will exceed 600 miles. (The final port of destination is the last port of call in the scheduled voyage at which the ship commences its return voyage to the country in which the voyage began.)
* "**Tanker**" means a cargo ship constructed or adapted for the carriage in bulk of liquid cargoes of a flammable nature. A tanker's age is determined from the year of build as indicated on its Certificate of Registry.

D04f.2b Application and exemption (regulation 2)

* The Regulations apply to **UK ships wherever they may be** and to **other ships while in UK waters**, but not to fishing vessels or pleasure vessels (regulation 2(1)).
* The **MCA may grant exemptions** from all or any of the provisions of the Regulations (as may be specified in the exemption) on such terms, if any, as the MCA may specify. The MCA may, subject to giving reasonable notice, alter or cancel any such exemption (regulation 2(2)).

D04f.2c Validity of certain certificates (regulation 2A)

* Except in special circumstances as determined by the MCA, **a certificate issued before 8 June 2000** by an appropriate Certifying Authority or the government of another country in accordance with regulation 16 will remain valid until it expires in accordance with the provisions of the Survey and Certification Regulations as in force before that date, and will for any other purpose of the Regulations be treated as though it had been issued under the Regulations as amended (regulation 2A(1)).
* Except in special circumstances agreed by the Administration of a SOLAS Convention country, a SOLAS Certificate which was issued, by or on behalf of the government of such a country, before the date on which the 1988 Protocol takes effect as respects that country will remain valid until it expires in accordance with the provisions of that Convention (regulation 2A(2)).

D04f.2d Responsibility for carrying out surveys (regulation 3)

* Except as provided in regulation 3(2), and subject also to regulation 16, **surveys of ships** will be carried out by a surveyor appointed by an appropriate **Certifying Authority** (as defined in regulation 1) (regulation 3(1)).
* **Radio surveys on passenger ships in a UK port** will be carried out by a surveyor appointed by an appropriate **Certifying Authority** (regulation 3(2)(a)(i)). (For notes on the **delegation of radio survey and certification functions**, see D04m.4.)
* **Radio surveys at ports outside the UK** will be carried out, at the option of the shipowner, either by a surveyor appointed by an appropriate **Certifying Authority** for radio surveys, or, if the port is in a country or area where the MCA has appointed a local surveyor, by that **local surveyor**, or else in accordance with regulation 16 (regulation 3(2)(a)(ii)).
* Until 31 October 1996 surveys of radio installations of UK passenger ships in UK ports were carried out by surveyors employed by British Telecom (BT). An amendment to the Survey and Certification Regulations entered into force on that date delegating radio survey work to "an appropriate Certifying Authority", i.e. an organisation to whom a government contract is awarded for the time being. The current holder of the contract for this work is **Marconi Marine**[70]. **MGN 206** details the delegation of radio survey and certification functions.
* Subject to regulation 3(d), **surveys in a UK port or UK territorial waters, of safety equipment of cargo ships** (other than radio-navigational equipment), and **surveys of ro-ro passenger ships**, will be carried out by an MCA surveyor (regulation 3(2)(b)).
* **Surveys of passenger ships other than ro-ro passenger ships** may be carried out in part by a surveyor appointed by another Certifying Authority authorised for that purpose by the MCA (regulation 3(2)(c)).
* **Surveys of radio-navigational equipment** may at the option of the owner be carried out by **Marconi Marine** (regulation 3(2)(d)).

---

[70]The Marine Radio Survey and Inspection Service of **Marconi Marine** is appointed as the exclusive provider of **radio safety survey, Port State Control** and **general inspection** services to the MCA. The service is also the official **Certifying Authority**, issuing Radio Safety Certificates on behalf of the UK Government for all British-registered cargo ships. A team of 38 Radio Surveyors, accredited by the MCA, operate from Regional Offices in 15 ports around the UK coast. The Service also performs radio surveys for classification societies and for flag State Administrations outside the UK. Marconi Marine is the sole UK provider of radio surveys in the UK for Lloyd's Register.

* Surveys of **radio installations** of any UK ship at a **port outside the UK** may be carried out (at the shipowner's option) by:
  - a surveyor of **Marconi Marine**;
  - by the **local surveyor** at a port in a country or area where the MCA has appointed a local surveyor;
  - except on ro-ro passenger ships, by a **government surveyor** of another SOLAS Convention country, on the request of the MCA through the local proper officer.

D04f.2e Survey requirements for passenger ships (regulation 4)

* A **UK passenger ship** (whether **engaged on international voyages or not**) will be subject to the following surveys:
  - before the ship is put in service, a **passenger ship initial survey** as set out in MSN 1751;
  - before the end of every period of 12 months following the issue of the ship's Passenger Ship Safety Certificate, a **passenger ship renewal survey** as set out in MSN 1751;
  - two **inspections of the ship's bottom, out of the water**, to take place within any 5-year period, and at intervals not exceeding 36 months;
  - and
  - after a repair resulting from investigations prescribed in regulation 8(2), or whenever any important repairs or renewals are made, an **additional survey** as set out in MSN 1751.

D04f.2f Surveys of cargo ship safety equipment (regulation 5)

* A **UK cargo ship of 500gt or more engaged on international voyages** will be subject to the following surveys of its life-saving appliances and other equipment:
  before the ship is put in service, a **cargo ship safety equipment initial survey** as set out in MSN 1751;
  at the intervals specified in MSN 1751 which, subject to the provisions of regulation 14(b), (e) and (f) of the Protocol of 1988 to the 1974 SOLAS Convention, will be no more than 5 years, a **cargo ship safety equipment renewal survey** as set out in MSN 1751;
  within 3 months before or after the second or third anniversary date of a Cargo Ship Safety Equipment Certificate first being issued, a **cargo ship safety equipment periodical survey** as set out in MSN 1751;
  within 3 months before or after each anniversary date of the issue of the ship's Cargo Ship Safety Equipment Certificate, other than where a periodical survey is required to be carried out within that period, an **annual survey** as set out in MSN 1751; and
  after a repair resulting from investigations prescribed in regulation 8(2), or whenever any important repairs or renewals are made, an **additional survey** as set out in MSN 1751.

D04f.2g Surveys of cargo ship radio installations (regulation 6)

* A **UK cargo ship of 300 gt or more engaged on international voyages** will be subject to the following surveys of its **radio installations**:
  - before the ship is put in service, a **cargo ship radio installations initial survey** as set out in MSN 1751;
  - at the intervals specified in MSN 1751 which, subject to the provisions of regulation 14(b), (e) and (f) of the Protocol of 1988 to the 1974 SOLAS Convention, will be no more than 5 years, a **cargo ship radio installations renewal survey** as set out in MSN 1751;
  - within 3 months before or after each anniversary date of the issue of the ship's Cargo Ship Safety Radio Certificate, a **cargo ship radio installations periodical survey** as set out in MSN 1751; and
  - after a repair resulting from investigations prescribed in regulation 8(2), or whenever any important repairs or renewals are made, an **additional survey** as set out in MSN 1751.

D04f.2h Surveys of cargo ship structure, machinery and equipment (regulation 7)

* A **UK cargo ship** will be subject to the following surveys of its **structure, machinery and equipment**, other than equipment to which regulations 5 and 6 above apply (i.e. safety equipment and radio installations):
  - before the ship is put in service, a **cargo ship structure etc. initial survey**, including an **inspection of the outside of the ship's bottom**, as set out in MSN 1751;
  - at the intervals specified in MSN 1751 (which subject to regulation 14 of the Protocol of 1988 to the 1974 SOLAS Convention will be no more than 5 years), a **cargo ship structure etc. renewal survey** as set out in MSN 1751;

- within 3 months before or after the second or third anniversary date of a Cargo Ship Safety Construction Certificate being issued, a **cargo ship structure etc. intermediate survey** as set out in MSN 1751;
- within 3 months before or after each anniversary date of the issue of the ship's Cargo Ship Safety Construction Certificate, other than where a cargo ship structure etc. renewal or intermediate survey is required to be carried out within that period, a **cargo ship structure etc. annual survey** as set out in MSN 1751;
- **two inspections of the ship's bottom**, as set out in MSN 1751, to take place, subject to the provision in the footnote[71], within any 5-year period, and at intervals not exceeding 36 months; and
- after a repair resulting from investigations prescribed in regulation 8(2), or whenever any important repairs or renewals are made, an **additional survey** as set out in MSN 1751.

D04f.2i Responsibilities of owner and master (regulation 8)

* The owner and master of every ship to which regulation 8 applies must ensure that:
  - the **condition of the ship and its equipment is maintained** to conform with the provisions of regulations 4 to 7 to ensure that the ship in all respects will remain fit to proceed to sea without danger to the ship or persons on board;
  - after any survey of the ship required by the Survey and Certification Regulations has been completed, **no change is made in the structural arrangements, machinery, equipment and other items covered by the survey**, without the approval of the appropriate Certifying Authority, except by direct replacement; and
  - whenever an accident occurs to a ship or a defect is discovered which affects the safety of the ship or the efficiency or completeness of its life-saving appliances or other equipment:
    - it is **reported at the earliest opportunity** to the appropriate Certifying Authority, or a proper officer; and
    - if a UK ship is in such a case in a port outside the UK it is also **reported to the appropriate authorities of the country** in which the port is situated.
* **MIN 143** (Safety equipment – modifications to vessels which have not been approved by the MCA or by a recognised certifying or competent authority) reminds shipowners that it is an offence for any modification to be made in the structural arrangements, machinery, equipment or other items covered by survey without official sanction of the MCA or the Recognised Organisation to which authority for the relevant survey has been delegated.
* Whenever an **accident or defect** is reported to the Certifying Authority or to a proper officer as required above, the **Certifying Authority or proper officer** must cause **investigations** to be initiated to determine whether or not a survey by a surveyor is necessary and will, if it is found necessary, require such a **survey** to be carried out.

D04f.2j Procedure when a ship, including its structure, machinery and equipment, is deficient (regulation 9)

* Where a surveyor determines -
  - that the **condition of a ship**, including its structure, machinery or equipment, **does not correspond substantially** with the particulars on one or more of the certificates referred to in the Regulations; or
  - is such that **the ship is not fit to go to sea without danger to the ship or the persons on board**,
  - the surveyor must:
  - advise the owner or master of the **corrective action** which in his opinion is required; and
  - **notify the Certifying Authority**.
* If the corrective action is not taken within a period (which must be reasonable) decided by the surveyor or the Certifying Authority, they must, at the end of the period, **notify the MCA**.
* The MCA may, on notification, **suspend the validity of the certificate** after giving notice of suspension to the owner, the surveyor, and the Certifying Authority (who must in turn notify the master).
* This regulation applies only to UK ships and other ships which have been surveyed under the Regulations.

D04f.2k Issue of certificates to UK ships engaged on international or short international voyages (regulation 10)

* On satisfactory completion of a survey or surveys the **MCA** will issue:
  - to a passenger ship engaged on international voyages (other than short international voyages), a **Passenger Ship Safety Certificate**;

---

[71] For the purpose of the provision requiring two inspections of the ship's bottom (in regulation 7(e)), where a **cargo ship structure etc. renewal survey** takes place within 3 months after the end of the 5-year period of validity of a SOLAS Certificate which has been **extended** in accordance with regulation 15(3) or (4), the period of extension of the certificate will be deemed to be within the 5-year period.

- to a passenger ship engaged on short international voyages, **Passenger Ship Safety Certificate for a short international voyage**.
* On satisfactory completion of a survey or surveys the **Certifying Authority** will issue:
  - to a cargo ship of 300gt or more engaged on international voyages, a **Cargo Ship Safety Radio Certificate**;
  - to a cargo ship of 500gt or more engaged on international voyages, a **Cargo Ship Safety Equipment Certificate**;
  - to a cargo ship of 500gt or more engaged on international voyages, a **Cargo Ship Safety Construction Certificate**;
    - in the case of a cargo ship of 500gt or more engaged on international voyages, after an initial or renewal survey in accordance with regulations 5 to 7 and as an alternative to the Cargo Ship Safety Radio Certificate, Cargo Ship Safety Equipment Certificate and Cargo Ship Safety Construction Certificate, a **Cargo Ship Safety Certificate**.

D04f.2l Issue of certificates to UK ships not engaged on international voyages (regulation 11)

* On satisfactory completion of surveys the MCA will issue to a UK passenger ship not engaged on international voyages a **Passenger Certificate** appropriate to its Class.
* On satisfactory completion of surveys the Certifying Authority will issue to a cargo ship of 500gt or more not engaged on international voyages, a **UK Cargo Ship Safety Construction Certificate**.

D04f.2m Form of certificates (regulation 12)

* A **Passenger Certificate** will indicate compliance with the provisions of the Merchant Shipping Acts and state:
  - the **limits** (if any) beyond which the ship is not fit to ply;
  - the **number of passengers** which the ship is fit to carry;
  - any **condition** with which the ship has to comply.
* *A Passenger Ship Safety Certificate, a Cargo Ship Safety Radio Certificate, a Cargo Ship Safety Equipment Certificate, a Cargo Ship Safety Construction Certificate, a Cargo Ship Safety Certificate and an Exemption Certificate must be in the form prescribed by SOLAS 74.*

D04f.2n Duration and validity of certificates (regulation 13)

* Subject to the provisions below concerning extensions, a SOLAS Certificate will be issued from the date of the completion of the relevant survey and will be issued for a period of validity as follows:
  - a **Passenger Ship Safety Certificate** (i.e. for a Class I ship) and a **short international voyage Passenger Ship Safety Certificate** (for a Class II ship) will be issued for a period of validity not exceeding **12 months**; and
  - a **Cargo Ship Safety Construction Certificate**, **Cargo Ship Safety Equipment Certificate**, **Cargo Ship Safety Radio Certificate** or **Cargo Ship Safety Certificate** will be issued for a period of validity not exceeding **5 years** (regulation 13(1)).
* Where a **renewal survey is completed within three months of the expiry** of the relevant certificate, the new certificate may be issued, in the case of a Passenger Ship Safety Certificate, for a period of validity not exceeding 12 months, and in the case of any other certificate, for a period of validity not exceeding 5 years **from the date of expiry of the existing certificate** (regulation 13(2)).
* **Except in special circumstances** as determined by the MCA, where **a renewal survey has been completed after the expiry** of the certificate, the new certificate will be issued, in the case of a Passenger Ship Safety Certificate, for a period of validity not exceeding 12 months, and in the case of any other certificate, for a period of validity not exceeding 5 years, from the date of expiry of the existing certificate (regulation 13(3)).
* Where an **annual, intermediate or periodical survey is completed before the period prescribed** as respects such a survey in regulations 4 to 7 above:
  - the anniversary date shown on the relevant certificate will be amended by endorsement to a date which will not be more than three months later than the date on which the survey was completed;
  - subsequent annual, intermediate or periodical surveys required under regulations 4 to 7 above will be completed at the intervals prescribed by those regulations using the new anniversary date; and
  - the expiry date may remain unchanged provided one or more annual, intermediate or periodical surveys, as appropriate, are carried out so that the maximum intervals between the surveys prescribed by regulations 4 to 7 are not exceeded (regulation 13(4)).
* The **duration of certificates** issued under regulation 11 (i.e. **non-SOLAS UK certificates**) will be as follows:
  - **Passenger Certificate**: not exceeding **12 months**; and

* **United Kingdom Cargo Ship Safety Construction Certificate**: not exceeding **5 years** (regulation 13(5)).
* Under regulation 13(6), a SOLAS Certificate, or a non-SOLAS UK certificate issued under regulation 11, will **cease to be valid**:
    * if its **period of validity has been exceeded** and the certificate has not been extended by the appropriate Certifying Authority in accordance with regulation 15 below or otherwise in accordance with the 1988 Protocol by the government of a country to which the 1974 SOLAS Convention applies; or
    * if the **relevant surveys and inspections have not been completed** within the periods specified under regulations 4 to 7 or otherwise in accordance with the 1988 Protocol by the government of a country to which the 1974 SOLAS Convention applies, and the certificate has either not been extended in accordance with regulation 15 below or otherwise in accordance with the 1988 Protocol by the government of a country to which the 1974 SOLAS Convention applies, or the period of any such extension has expired; or
    * upon **transfer of the ship to the flag of another State**.

D04f.2o Issue and duration of SOLAS Exemption Certificates (regulation 14)

* When an **exemption** is granted to a ship in accordance with the relevant SOLAS regulations, an **Exemption Certificate** will be issued, in addition to any SOLAS certificate issued under regulation 10 (regulation 14(1)).
* An **Exemption Certificate** will be issued for a period of validity no longer than that of the certificate to which it refers (regulation 14(2)).
* An Exemption Certificate will be subject to the **same extension and other provisions** as the certificate to which it refers (regulation 14(3)).
* Where an Exemption Certificate has been issued, a **statement** to that effect must be included on the certificate to which it refers (regulation 14(4)).
* Exemptions may be granted under the provisions of **other Conventions**, and in relation to **non-Convention matters**, under various UK Merchant Shipping regulations. Where **any exemption** from a statutory requirement has been granted, an Exemption Certificate will be issued by the MCA. (Classification societies are not permitted to grant exemptions to UK ships from Convention or statutory provisions.)
* **MGN 218**, which contains the MCA's policy statement on the application of equal safety standards to new and existing vessels, states that a power to grant exemptions should only be exercised where compliance by an existing vessel with a new safety standard would be unreasonable, whether on grounds of practicability or for some other reason, and where the operator of the ship can also satisfy the MCA that an equivalent level of safety is achieved by some means other than strict compliance with the requirements of the regulations.
* **Examples** of cases in which an Exemption Certificate has been issued by the MCA are shown in the following table.

Ship type(s)	Reason for application for exemption	Requirement exempted from	Alternative arrangements
Various types	No need for direction finder since other radio-navigation equipment is provided suitable for use on intended voyages	Fitting of a direction finder (SOLAS reg. V/12(p))	Ship to be provided with GPS SPS or Loran C navigation systems
Class II ferry	No need for pilot ladder since ship has a pilot door in the side shell	Provision of a pilot ladder (SOLAS reg. V/17(c))	Hull side doors to be provided for pilot access

D04f.2p Extensions and other provisions (regulation 15)

* Where a SOLAS Certificate other than a Passenger Ship Safety Certificate has been **issued for less than 5 years** and the surveys required under regulations 5 to 7 have been satisfactorily completed, the Certifying Authority may **extend** the validity of that certificate so that the certificate is valid for a maximum of 5 years (regulation 15(1)).
* Where a **renewal survey** required under regulations 5 to 7 has been satisfactorily **completed before the expiry** of the relevant SOLAS Certificate but the **new certificate cannot be issued or placed on board** the ship before the expiry of the existing certificate, the Certifying Authority may **endorse the existing certificate** as valid for a period not exceeding **5 months** from the expiry date (regulation 15(2)).
* Where a **renewal survey** required under regulations 5 to 7 has **not been satisfactorily completed before the expiry** of the relevant SOLAS Certificate, and at the time of expiry the ship is not in a port in which it is to be surveyed, the Certifying Authority may, where it appears to it proper and reasonable to do so, **extend** the validity of the certificate solely for the purpose of allowing the ship **to complete its voyage to its port of survey** (regulation 15(3)).
* Where **no other extension** has been granted, the Certifying Authority may extend the validity of a SOLAS Certificate of ships used **solely on short international voyages** for a period of no more than **one month** (regulation 15(4)). (This regulation would apply, for example, to Class II passenger ferries, and cargo ships on short international voyages.)

* An extension granted under regulation 15(1) or 15(2), or, except in special circumstances as determined by the MCA, under regulation 15(3) or 15(4) , will be **disregarded** for the purposes of determining the date of expiry of an existing SOLAS Certificate under regulation 13(2) or (3) (regulation 15(5)).

D04f.2q Issue and endorsement of certificates by another government (regulation 16)

* The MCA may request, through a proper officer or otherwise, another SOLAS country's Administration to survey a UK ship (other than a ro-ro passenger ship) and issue or authorise the issue of the certificates in regulation 10.
* A certificate issued in accordance with such a request must contain a statement that it has been so issued and will have the same effect as if it was issued by the MCA.

D04f.2r Ships not registered in the UK and to which SOLAS 74 applies (regulation 17)

* The MCA may, at the request of another SOLAS country's Administration, survey a ship registered in that country and, if satisfied that the requirements of the SOLAS Convention are complied with and that a survey has been satisfactorily completed in accordance with the Survey and Certification Regulations, issue to the ship one or more of the certificates referred to in regulation 10, and, where appropriate, endorse such certificates in accordance with the requirements of SOLAS.
* A certificate issued in accordance with such a request must contain a statement that it has been so issued and will have the same effect as if it was issued by the flag State government and not by the MCA.
* Where a memorandum, issued by or under the authority of the government concerned, is attached to a valid Passenger Ship Safety Certificate or a valid short international voyage Passenger Ship Safety Certificate, in respect of a ship to which SOLAS applies, which modifies the certificate in respect of the persons that may be carried for a particular voyage, the certificate will have effect for the purpose of the voyage as if it was modified in accordance with the memorandum.
* An MCA surveyor may go on board a ship to which SOLAS applies for the purpose of verifying that there is in force a certificate or certificates required by the Survey and Certification Regulations, that the hull, machinery and equipment correspond substantially with the particulars shown on the certificate or certificates and that the provisions of regulation 8 are being complied with.

D04f.2s Other non-UK ships (regulation 18)

* When a survey or surveys of ships which are not UK ships, to meet the requirements of the Survey and Certification Regulations, are completed in accordance with the Regulations:
  * the MCA will issue in the case of a passenger ship not engaged on international voyages, a **Passenger Certificate** appropriate to its Class;
  * the Certifying Authority will issue in the case of a cargo ship of 500gt or more not engaged on international voyages, a **UK Cargo Ship Safety Construction Certificate**.
* These certificates will be subject to the requirements of the Regulations as though they were issued under regulation 11.

D04f.2t Cancellation of a certificate, and offences concerning alteration, forgery, misuse, etc. of certificates (regulation 19)

* The MCA may cancel a certificate issued to a UK ship if it has reason to believe that:
  * the certificate was issued on false or erroneous information;
  * since any survey required by the Regulations, the structure, equipment or machinery has sustained damage or is otherwise deficient.
* The MCA may require that a certificate, issued to a UK ship, which has expired or has been cancelled be surrendered, as directed.
* No person may:
  * intentionally alter a certificate referred to in the Regulations;
  * intentionally make a false certificate referred to in the Regulations;
  * in connection with any survey required by the Regulations, knowingly or recklessly furnish false information;
  * with intent to deceive, use, lend, or allow to be used by another, a certificate referred to in the Regulations;
  * fail to surrender a certificate required to be surrendered under the Regulations;
  * in Scotland, forge any certificate referred to in the Regulations.

D04f.2u Posting up of certificates (regulation 20)

* The owner and **master** of every ship issued with a SOLAS Certificate must ensure that it is **readily available on board for examination** at all times. (The **former requirement** was that SOLAS Certificates had to be **displayed**.)

D04f.2v Prohibition on proceeding to sea without the appropriate documentation (regulation 21)

* **No UK ship may proceed to sea unless** it has been **surveyed** and there is in force the **following certificate(s)**:
  * in the case of a passenger ship engaged on international voyages, a **Passenger Ship Safety Certificate**, or, if the ship is only engaged on short international voyages, a **short international voyage Passenger Ship Safety Certificate**;
  * in the case of a cargo ship of 300gt or more engaged on international voyages, a **Cargo Ship Safety Radio Certificate**;
  * in the case of a cargo ship of 500gt or more engaged on international voyages, a **Cargo Ship Safety Equipment Certificate** and a **Cargo Ship Safety Construction Certificate**.
* In the case of a cargo ship of 500gt or more engaged on international voyages, as an alternative to the Cargo Ship Safety Radio Certificate, Cargo Ship Safety Equipment Certificate and Cargo Ship Safety Construction Certificate, a **Cargo Ship Safety Certificate** may be issued.
* No **ship registered in a country to which the 1974 SOLAS Convention applies** may proceed to sea from a UK port unless there are in force **such Convention certificates that would be required if the ship were a UK ship**. The extension provisions in regulation 15 will apply to such certificates as if the ship were a UK ship and the government of the flag State is substituted for the MCA.
* No cargo ship of 500gt or more not engaged on international voyages may proceed to sea from a UK port unless it has been surveyed and there is in force a **UK Cargo Ship Safety Construction Certificate**, unless there is in force a Cargo Ship Safety Construction Certificate referred to in the Regulations.
* No ship registered in a country to which the 1974 SOLAS Convention does not apply may proceed to sea from a UK port unless the ship carries **documents showing that the ship has been surveyed for compliance** with regulations 4 to 7 **as though it were a UK ship**.
* Where a certificate is issued subject to **conditions**, or specifies **sea areas** in which the ship is certified to operate, the owner and **master** must ensure that all **conditions are complied with**, or, as the case may be, that the ship only **operates in the specified sea areas**.
* The **master** of every ship must **produce to an officer of customs** from whom a clearance is demanded for an international voyage the **certificates or documentation referred to in regulation 21**[72].

D04f.2w Prohibition on proceeding on a voyage or excursion without the appropriate documentation (regulation 22)

* A passenger ship of Class II(A), III, IV, V, VI or VI(A) or A, B, C or D may not proceed on a voyage or excursion unless it has been surveyed and there is in force a **Passenger Certificate** appropriate to the ship's Class and applicable to that voyage or excursion.
* For the purposes of the preceding paragraph, the MCA will recognise a certificate issued in respect of a ship of Class A, B, C or D or equivalent by another EC Member State or an EEA State pursuant to Article 11 of Council Directive 98/18/EC.
* Where a certificate is issued subject to conditions, the ship may not proceed on a voyage or excursion unless all the conditions are complied with.

D04f.2x Limit on the number of passengers on passenger ships (regulation 23)

* The owner and the **master** of a passenger ship must ensure that there is **not on board a greater number of passengers than that stated on the ship's Passenger Ship Safety Certificate or Passenger Certificate**.
* The penalty under regulation 24(5) for breach of this requirement is, on summary conviction, a fine not exceeding **£50,000** or, on conviction on indictment, imprisonment for a maximum of 2 years, or a fine, or both.

---

[72] For notes on procedures for obtaining **outwards clearance** from UK ports, see I07h.2.

D04f.2y Powers to detain, and arbitration (regulations 25 and 26)

* Regulation 25 provides that where a ship does not comply with the Regulations, she is liable to be detained.
* Regulation 26(1) provides that where an owner, or any other person making an application for a survey required by the Regulations, is dissatisfied with the outcome of the survey because the issue of a certificate has been refused or for any other reason, that person may serve notice, within 21 days of the completion of the survey, on the person responsible for issuing the particular certificate under regulation 10 or 11, that their dispute be referred to a single arbitrator appointed by agreement between the parties to be settled by him may be referred to arbitration in certain cases. Other paragraphs of regulation 26 lay down qualifications for arbitrators and their powers. the conduct of the arbitration. The rules for arbitration, as set out in **M.1613**, will apply unless alternative procedures are agreed between the parties before the commencement of the arbitration proceedings.

D04f.3 Survey and certification of passenger ships on domestic voyages under Directive 98/18/EC

* **Council Directive 98/18/EC** applies to passenger ships on domestic voyages in EEA waters. (See D03b.6 for details of the Directive's application, etc. and details of the MS (Passenger Ships on Domestic Voyages) Regulations.) **Articles 10 and 11** contain survey and certification requirements respectively.

D04f.3a Survey requirements of Directive 98/18/EC

* **Article 10 of Council Directive 98/18/EC** provides for surveys as follows.
* Each **new passenger ship** must be subjected by the Administration of the flag State to the surveys specified below:
  * a **survey before the ship is put into service**;
  * a **periodical survey** once every 12 months; and
  * **additional surveys**, as the occasion arises (paragraph 1).
* Each existing passenger ship must be subjected by the Administration of the flag State to the surveys specified below:
  * an **initial survey**, before the ship is put into service on domestic voyages in a host State, or within 12 months after the implementation date of the Directive as established in Article 14(1), for existing ships engaged on domestic voyages in the Member State the flag of which they are entitled to fly;
  * a **periodical survey** once every 12 months; and
  * **additional surveys**, as the occasion arises (paragraph 2).
* Each **high speed passenger craft** having to comply, in accordance with the provisions of Article 6(4), with the requirements of the HSC Code, must be subject by the Administration of the flag State to the surveys required in the High Speed Craft Code. High speed passenger craft, having to comply, in accordance with the provisions of Article 6(4), with the requirements of the DSC Code as amended, must be subject by the Administration of the flag State to the surveys required in the DSC Code. (Paragraph 3)
* The relevant procedures and guidelines for surveys for the Passenger Ship Safety Certificate specified in IMO Assembly Resolution A.746(18) of 4 November 1993 on survey guidelines under the harmonised system of survey and certification, as they are at the time of adoption of this Directive or procedures designed to achieve the same goal, must be followed (paragraph 4).
* The surveys mentioned in paragraphs 1, 2 and 3 must be carried out by the **exclusive surveyors of the flag State Administration** itself, or a **recognised organisation** or of the Member State authorised by the flag State to carry out surveys, with the purpose of ensuring that all applicable requirements of the Directive are complied with (paragraph 5).

D04f.3b Certification requirements of Directive 98/18/EC

* Article 11 of Council Directive 98/18/EC provides for certification as follows.
* All **new and existing passenger ships** must be provided with a **Passenger Ship Safety Certificate** in compliance with the Directive. The certificate must have a format as laid down in Annex II. This certificate will be issued by the flag State Administration after an **initial survey**, as described in Article 10(1)(a) and (2)(a), has been carried out (paragraph 1).
* The Passenger Ship Safety Certificate will be issued for a period not exceeding **12 months**. The validity period may be extended by the flag State Administration for **a period of grace of up to one month** from the date of expiry stated on it. When an extension has been granted, the new period of validity of the certificate starts from the expiry

date of the existing certificate before its extension. A new Passenger Ship Safety Certificate will be issued after a **periodical survey**, as described in Article 10(1)(b) and (2)(b), has been carried out (paragraph 2).

* For **high speed passenger craft** complying with the requirements of the **High Speed Craft Code**, a **High Speed Craft Safety Certificate** and a **Permit to Operate High Speed Craft** will be issued by the flag State Administration, in accordance with the provisions of the High Speed Craft Code.

* For high speed passenger craft complying with the requirements of the **DSC Code as amended**, a **DSC Construction and Equipment Certificate** and a **DSC Permit to Operate** be issued by the flag State Administration, in accordance with the provisions of the DSC Code. Before issuing the Permit to Operate for high speed passenger craft engaged on domestic voyages in a host State, the Administration of the flag State must concur with the host State on any **operational conditions** associated with operation of the craft in that State. Any such conditions must be shown by the flag State Administration on the Permit to Operate (paragraph 3).

* **Exemptions** granted to ships or craft under and in accordance with the provisions of Article 7(3) must be noted on the ship's or the craft's certificate (paragraph 4).

D04f.4 Mandatory Surveys for Ro-Ro Ferry and High Speed Passenger Craft Regulations

* The **MS (Mandatory Surveys for Ro-Ro Ferry and High Speed Passenger Craft) Regulations 2001** (SI 2001/152) -
  - came into force, except for regulation 4(2)(d), on 16 February 2001. (Regulation 4(2)(d) comes into force on 31 January 2003.)
  - implement in the UK **Directive 1999/35/EC** on a system of mandatory surveys for the safe operation of regular ro-ro ferry and high-speed passenger craft services, which applies a specific inspection regime to all ro-ro passenger vessels and high speed craft (HSC) operating ferry services within the European Community (EC) and the European Economic Area (EEA). (The text of the Directive is printed in MGN 171.)
  - **apply to a ro-ro ferry or a high-speed passenger craft** which is operating a **regular service** to or from a port in the UK either on international voyages, or in sea areas covered by Class A as referred to in article 4 of Council Directive 98/18EC on Safety Rules and Standards for Passenger Ships.
  - **require the MCA**:
    * to carry out **verifications** in relation to the **vessel**, including checks of **documentation** and a check for the presence of a **voyage data recorder** (regulation 4);
    * to carry out **verifications** in relation to the **company** operating the vessel, and the **flag State** of the vessel (regulation 5);
    * to carry out an **initial specific survey** before the vessel begins operating on a regular service to or from a United Kingdom port (regulation 6);
    * to carry out **further surveys** every year, or where the circumstances of the vessel change (regulation 8);
    * to issue reports of **Prevention of Operation Notices** preventing a vessel which does not meet the requirements of the Directive from operating, or reports of inspection or Improvement Notices requiring defects to be remedied (regulations 9 to 11);
    * to comply with certain **administrative requirements** (regulation 13); and
    * to operate a **shore-based navigational guidance system** (regulation 14).
  - **require the Chief Inspector of Marine Accidents** to allow substantially interested Member States or EEA States to be involved with a marine accident investigation (regulation 15).
  - **are explained in MGN 171**.
* **MGN 171** explains that the measures will enhance the inspection regime under Directive 95/21/EC on port State control of shipping in EC ports and the Paris Memorandum of Understanding for Port State Control. All ro-ro passenger ships and high-speed passenger craft providing a regular service on international or domestic routes to or from EU ports, irrespective of their country of registration, are affected.
* The **EC Directive** introduces a **system of verification and compliance** whereby ferries are required to be inspected by the host State before being permitted to operate a ferry service. ("Host State" means a Member State to or from whose port a ro-ro ferry or high speed passenger craft is engaged on a regular service.) The **MCA** carry out this work in the UK)
* Vessels on current services must be **inspected by host States within 12 months** of the coming into force of national legislation implementing compliance with this Directive. These inspections will be repeated annually as well as an in-service inspection in between. **Companies** which operate or intend to operate such ferry or craft on regular services will also be required to verify **compliance with the Directive requirements**.
* These measures also introduce a right for a host State to **participate in accident investigation** for any ferry service operating to or from its ports. Currently, if an accident happens to a foreign registered vessel outside the host State's

territorial water, the host State has no right to participate in any investigation, despite the fact that a large number of the passengers on board may be citizens of that State.

* For the purposes of facilitating the investigation into such accidents these measures include the requirement to carry a **voyage data recorder** (**VDR**) on-board each passenger ro-ro vessel and high speed craft with effect as follows:
   • From 16 February 2001 compliance is required for **any new ferry operation**.
   • From 16 February 2001 and before 1 December 2001, compliance is required **for all other ferries currently in service**.
   • From 31 January 2003 VDRs must be fitted to **ro-ro and HSC vessels on domestic voyages** in sea areas covered by **Class A**.

D04f.5 Application for survey or inspection

* **Application for any statutory survey** or inspection of a ship should be made to the MCA on form MSF 5100 (Application for Survey and Inspection of Ships and Fishing Vessels). The completed form and appropriate deposit or fee should be sent to the relevant Marine Office, from whom information on current fees may be obtained. Additional charges will be levied for overtime, surveys abroad, waiting time and abortive time.
* Applicants are reminded on form MSF 5100 that the ship should be prepared ready for survey, and appropriate precautions taken for all areas to be surveyed, including provision of safe means of access for boarding. Surveyors may refuse to continue with surveys if it is not safe for them to do so and may consider charging for any time wasted.

D04g POLLUTION-RELATED EQUIPMENT, SURVEYS AND DOCUMENTATION

D04g.1 Oil pollution-prevention equipment

* The **MS (Prevention of Oil Pollution) Regulations 1996** (SI 1996/2154) –
   - are outlined in D03a.2.
   - prescribe requirements for **oil filtering equipment** and **oil discharge monitoring and control system** (in regulation 14) and arrangements for **retention of oil on board** (regulation 15).
   - define "**filtering equipment**" as "filters or any combination of separators and filters which are designed to produce effluent containing not more than 15 ppm of oil" (regulation 1).
   - define "s**eparating equipment**" as "either separators or filters, or any combination of them, which are designed to produce effluent containing not more than 100 ppm of oil" (regulation 1).
* Regulation 14(1) requires that, subject to regulation 14(3) (which allows for a waiver of the requirements by the MCA), **every ship of 400gt and above but less than 10,000gt** must have **oil filtering equipment**[73] ("**15 ppm equipment**") complying with regulation 14(5). Any such ship carrying **ballast water in its bunker fuel tanks** must also be fitted with an **alarm device** and the **means for automatically stopping the discharge of oily mixture** when the oil content in the effluent exceeds 15 ppm, this equipment to comply with the specifications in regulation 14(6) (regulation 14(1)(a)(i)). The ship must not discharge such ballast water into the sea unless **using that equipment** and a **record of the discharge** is made in the Oil Record Book (regulation 14(1)(a)(ii)). Alternatively, the ship must discharge the ballast water to **reception facilities** (regulation 14(1)(b)).
* Subject to regulation 14(3) (Waiver) and 14(6) (Equipment to be of approved design), **every ship of 10,000gt and above** must be fitted with:
   oil filtering equipment ("15ppm equipment") complying with regulation 14(5) (regulation 14(2)(a)); and
   oil content measuring equipment fitted with a **15 ppm alarm device** and arrangements for **automatically stopping** any discharge of oily mixture when the oil content in the effluent exceeds 15 ppm (regulation 14(2)(b)).
* Regulation 14(3) permits the requirements of regulation 14(1) and (2) outlined above to be **waived** by the MCA where a ship is engaged **exclusively on voyages in special areas** and:
   • is fitted with a **holding tank** with a volume adequate for retaining all oily bilge water (regulation 14(3)(a));
   • all oily bilge water is **retained on board** for discharge to reception facilities (regulation 14(3)(b));
   • adequate **reception facilities** are available in a sufficient number of ports and terminals at which the ship calls (regulation 14(3)(c));

---

[73] Separating equipment (100 ppm equipment) was required to be replaced with filtering equipment by 6th July 1998.

- the IOPP Certificate, when required, is **endorsed** to the effect that the ship is engaged exclusively on voyages within special areas (regulation 14(3)(d)); and
- the relevant entries are recorded in the **Oil Record Book** (regulation 14(3)(e)).

* **Every ship of less than 400gt** must, so far as reasonably practicable, be constructed to ensure that oil or oily mixtures are **retained on board** and discharged to **reception facilities** or, if oil or oily mixtures are to be discharged into the sea, are **discharged in accordance with the requirements of regulation 12** (regulation 14(4)). (For notes on **discharge requirements**, see H03a.3.)

* **Oil filtering equipment, oil content measuring equipment and alarm devices** must be of an **approved design** in accordance with the specifications for such equipment set out in the **IMO Recommendations** on International Performance and Test Specifications for Oily Water Separating Equipment and Oil Content Meters (regulation 14(5) and 14(6)). Arrangements for **automatically stopping** any discharge must be of an **approved design** (regulation 14(6)).

* **Regulation 15** (Retention of oil on board) applies, subject to certain exceptions, to oil tankers of 150gt and above and provides that

- adequate means must be provided for **cleaning cargo tanks** and **transferring dirty ballast residues** and **tank washings** from the cargo tanks into a **slop tank** (regulation 15(2)(a);
- an **oil discharge monitoring and control system (ODMCS)** of an approved design must be fitted (regulation 15(3)(a));
- the ODMCS must have a **recording device** to provide a **continuous record** of the discharge of oil in litres per mile and the total quantity of oil discharged or, in lieu of the total quantity of oil discharged, the oil content and rate of discharge of the effluent, this record to be identifiable as to the time and date and to be kept for **at least 3 years** (regulation 15(3)(b));
- on any **failure** of the ODMCS the discharge must be **stopped** and the failure noted in the **Oil Record Book** (regulation 15(3)(c)). A manually operated alternative system must be provided and may be used in the event of an ODMCS failure. A tanker with a defective ODMCS in the UK or UK territorial waters may be allowed by the MCA to make one ballast voyage before proceeding to a repair port;
- effective **oil/water interface detectors**, of approved design, must be provided (regulation 15(3)(e));
- approved **instruction manuals** on the various components of the **ODMCS** must be provided (regulation 15(3)(f)).

D04g.1a Tanker operational manuals

* MARPOL Annex I requires the carriage by tankers of various **manuals** as follows.

* **Annex I, regulation 13A(4)** provides that **every oil tanker operating with dedicated clean ballast tanks** must be provided with a **Dedicated Clean Ballast Tank Operation Manual** detailing the system and specifying operational procedures and approved by the flag State Administration.

* **Annex I, regulation 13B(5)** provides that **every oil tanker operating with crude oil washing systems** must be provided with a **Crude Oil Washing Operations and Equipment Manual** detailing the system and equipment and specifying operational procedures and approved by the flag State Administration.

* **Annex I, regulation 15(3)(c)** provides that **instructions as to the operation of the oil discharge monitoring and control system** (ODMCS) required to be fitted under regulation 15(3)(a) must be in accordance with an **ODMCS Operational Manual** approved by the flag State Administration. The instructions must cover manual as well as automatic operations.

D04g.2 International and UK Oil Pollution Prevention Certificates

* **Regulation 7 of the MS (Prevention of Oil Pollution) Regulations 1996** (SI 1996/2154) provides that when it is in order to do so, the MCA, or as the case may be, a Certifying Authority, will issue to the ship an appropriate certificate (regulation 7(1)).

* In the case of an oil tanker of 150gt and above and any other ship of 400gt and above engaged on **voyages to ports or offshore terminals under the jurisdiction of other MARPOL party States**, the appropriate certificate is an **International Oil Pollution Prevention Certificate (IOPPC)** (regulation 7(1)(a)).

* In the case of any other oil tanker of 150gt and above and any other ship of 400gt and above (i.e. ships of such sizes **not sailing to ports or terminals in other MARPOL party States**, including ships on **domestic voyages**), the appropriate certificate is a **UK Oil Pollution Prevention Certificate (UKOPPC)** (regulation 7(1)(b))[74].

---

[74] Lloyd's Register issues a certificate (code number 1715) titled "**Oil Pollution Certificate for United Kingdom Coastal Waters**" to ships engaged on UK domestic voyages.

* The MCA may request through a proper officer or otherwise, the Government of a MARPOL Convention country to **survey a UK ship** and, if satisfied that the provisions of MARPOL are complied with, to issue or authorise the **issue of an IOPP Certificate** to the ship (regulation 7(2)). A Certificate so issued must contain a statement that it has been issued in accordance with such a request, and will have the same effect as a Certificate issued under regulation 7(1) (regulation 7(3)). **Reciprocal arrangements** for issue of IOPP Certificates to UK ships in MARPOL party State ports outside the UK are provided for in regulation 7(4).
* **IOPP Certificates** will be in the form prescribed by MARPOL, while **UKOPP Certificates** will be in a form prescribed by the MCA (regulation 7(5)(a)). IOPP and UKOPP Certificates will be valid for a period not exceeding **5 years** from the date of issue (regulation 7(5)(a)).
* An IOPP Certificate or UKOPP Certificate will **cease to be valid** -
    * if without the approval of the MCA or, as the case may be, a Certifying Authority, **significant alteration** has been made to the construction, equipment, systems, fittings, arrangements or material required by the Regulations, other than the direct replacement of such equipment or fittings (regulation 7(6)(a) as amended); or
    * in the case of an IOPP Certificate, if the **intermediate survey is not carried out** within the period specified in regulation 6 (regulation 7(6)(b)); or
    * when the **ship transfers** to the flag of another State (regulation 7(6)(c)).
* The IOPPC or UKOPPC must be **kept on board** and must be **available for inspection** at all reasonable times (regulation 7(7)).

D04g.2a Surveys for IOPP and UKOPP Certificates – pre-harmonisation

* The **MS (Prevention of Oil Pollution) Regulations 1996** provide (in regulation 4(1) and 7(1)), for the formal delegation of **renewal surveys** for and **issue** of resulting IOPP and UKOPP Certificates, to the **Certifying Authorities** (i.e. the six authorised Classification Societies listed below, as well as the MCA).
* The **American Bureau of Shipping**, **Bureau Veritas**, **Det Norske Veritas**, **Germanischer Lloyd**, **Lloyd's Register of Shipping** and **Registro Italiano Navale**, in addition to the **MCA**, are authorised to conduct all annual, intermediate and renewal surveys relating to International and UK Oil Pollution Prevention Certification, and to issue the associated certificates or endorse certificates for annual and intermediate surveys. As a matter of policy, the MCA will not normally attend a vessel to carry out these surveys. If an authorised Certifying Authority surveyor is already onboard carrying out other work, the MCA would expect the survey to be carried out by that surveyor whilst onboard.
* The **MCA** will remain responsible for **initial surveys** and for the issue of the **first IOPP Certificate**, together with surveys of ships that are **not classed** with one of the authorised Certifying Authorities.
* For **foreign vessels changing to the UK Register**, the first survey will be treated as an initial survey. Therefore, applications for all annual, intermediate and renewal surveys should be addressed to the appropriate Certifying Authority. The individual authorisation of Classification Society surveyors by the MCA to undertake surveys on their behalf will no longer be necessary.

D04g.2b Surveys for IOPP Certificates under the Harmonised System of Survey and Certification

* The **Harmonised System of Survey and Certification** (see D04e) came into force on 3 February 2000 and covers survey and certification under MARPOL Annexes I and II.
* **Regulation 4(1) of MARPOL Annex I, as amended** for the Harmonised Survey and Certification requirements[75], provides that every oil tanker of 150gt and above, and every other ship of 400gt and above will be subject to the following surveys:
    * an **initial survey** before the ship is put in service or before the IOPP Certificate is issued for the first time, which will include a complete survey of its structure, equipment, systems, fittings, arrangements and material in so far as the ship is covered by Annex I. This survey will be such as to ensure that the structure, equipment, systems, fittings, arrangements and material fully comply with the applicable requirements of Annex I;
    * a **renewal survey** at intervals specified by the Administration, but not exceeding 5 years, except where regulation 8(2), 8(5), 8(6) or 8(7) of Annex I is applicable. The renewal survey will be such as to ensure that the structure, equipment, systems, fittings, arrangements and material fully comply with applicable requirements of Annex I;
    * an **intermediate survey** within 3 months before or after the second anniversary date or within 3 months before or after the third anniversary date of the IOPP Certificate which will take the place of one of the annual surveys specified in regulation 4(1)(d). The intermediate survey will be such as to ensure that the equipment and

---

[75] At the time of writing, the MCA had not published an M Notice containing the survey and certification requirements in respect of Oil Pollution Prevention Certificates. (Only *SOLAS* surveys and certification are covered in MSN 1751.)

associated pump and piping systems, including oil discharge monitoring and control systems, crude oil washing systems, oily-water separating equipment and oil filtering systems fully comply with the applicable requirements of Annex I and are in good working order. Such intermediate surveys will be endorsed on the IOPP Certificate;

* an **annual survey** within 3 months before or after each anniversary date of the IOPP Certificate, including a general inspection of the structure, equipment, systems, fittings, arrangements and material referred to in the paragraph above covering the initial survey to ensure that they have been maintained in accordance with regulation 4(4) and they remain satisfactory for the service for which the ship is intended. Such annual surveys will be endorsed on the IOPP Certificate;
* an **additional survey**, either general or partial according to the circumstances, will be made after a repair resulting from investigations prescribed in regulation 4(4), or whenever any important repairs or renewals are made. The survey will be such as to ensure that the necessary repairs or renewals have been effectively made, that the material and workmanship of such repairs or renewals are in all respects satisfactory and that the ship complies in all respects with the requirements of Annex I.

D04g.2c Responsibilities of owner and master

* **Regulation 8** of the **MS (Prevention of Oil Pollution) Regulations 1996**, as amended, prescribes **responsibilities of the owner and master**.
* The **owner and master** of every ship must **each ensure** that -
    * the **condition** of the ship and its equipment is **maintained** so as to comply with the relevant provisions of these Regulations (regulation 8(1)(a)); and
    * after any survey of a UK ship required by the Regulations has been completed, **no material change** is made in the structure, equipment, systems, fittings, arrangements or material subject to such survey without the **approval** of the MCA, other than the direct replacement of fittings or equipment (regulation 8(1)(b)).
* Regulation 8(2) provides that whenever an accident occurs to a UK ship or a defect is discovered, either of which affects the integrity of a ship or the efficiency or completeness of its equipment -
    * the **master** or (if the master fails to do so) the **owner** must **report it** at the earliest opportunity to the MCA or a Proper Officer, either of whom may cause **investigations** to be initiated to determine whether a survey by a surveyor is necessary; and
    * if the ship is in a port of a MARPOL Convention country (other than the UK) the **master** or (if the master fails to do so) the owner shall in addition make such a **report** immediately to the **appropriate authorities of the port State**.

D04g.2d Record of Construction and Equipment

* IOPP and UKOPP Certificates must be supplemented by a **Record of Construction and Equipment**, in the case of an IOPPC in the form prescribed by MARPOL, and in the case of a UKOPPC in the form prescribed by the MCA (Prevention of Oil Pollution Regulations, regulation 7(5)(b)).
* The **Record of Construction and Equipment** -
    * must be in the form shown in the Appendices to MARPOL Annex I;
    * is issued as a **Supplement to the IOPP Certificate**, to which it must be permanently attached;
    * lists items included in the IOPP or UKOPP initial survey and will therefore be useful to ships' officers who check survey items before a scheduled survey;
    * records, in the case of a **tanker**: particulars of ship; equipment for the control of oil discharge from machinery space bilges and oil fuel tanks; tanks for oil residues (sludge); standard discharge connection; construction; retention of oil on board; pumping, piping and discharge arrangements; equivalent arrangements for chemical tankers carrying oil; exemption (if any) from Convention requirements; equivalents;
    * records, in the case of a **non-tanker**: particulars of ship; equipment for the control of oil discharge from machinery space bilges and oil fuel tanks; tanks for oil residues (sludge); standard discharge connection; exemption (if any) from Convention requirements; equivalents.

D04g.3 International Pollution Prevention Certificate for the Carriage of Noxious Liquid Substances in Bulk (INLS Certificate)

* **Regulation 10(1)** of the **MS (Dangerous or Noxious Liquid Substances in Bulk) Regulations 1996** (SI 1996/3010) (see D03e.2a) provides that on satisfactory completion of an initial or periodical survey by an **MCA surveyor**, the **MCA** will issue to a ship which complies with the relevant Regulations:

- in the case of a **chemical tanker**:
    - a **Certificate of Fitness for the Carriage of Dangerous Chemicals in Bulk** (in the case of a ship built before 1 July 1986); or
    - an **International Certificate of Fitness for the Carriage of Dangerous Chemicals in Bulk** (in the case of a ship built on or after 1 July 1986); and
- in the case of a ship which is **not a chemical tanker**, an **INLS Certificate**.

* An **INLS Certificate** is required under regulation 10(1) by **any ship carrying in bulk noxious liquid substances or unassessed liquid substances** unless it holds a Certificate of Fitness as a chemical tanker (in which case the COF is **endorsed with the INLS survey details**). Such ships will generally include **oil/products tankers**, **dry cargo ships with deep or dedicated cargo tanks** for the carriage of MARPOL Annex II substances, and **offshore supply vessels** carrying Annex II substances such as zinc bromide brine and sodium silicate solution. **Gas carriers** also require an INLSC if carrying any MARPOL Annex II substance, e.g. in deck tanks.

* An INLS Certificate will be issued for a period not exceeding **5 years** from the date of issue (regulation 10(1)).

* The INLS Certificate will **cease to be valid** if any survey required is not completed within the specified period, or on transfer of the ship to another flag (regulation 10(2)).

* The **INLS Certificate certifies** *inter alia* that the ship is suitable for the carriage in bulk of the noxious liquid substances listed in the certificate, provided that all the relevant operational provisions of Annex II to the Convention are observed. The **list** of noxious liquid substances which the ship is certified to carry is entered by the MCA, together with any **conditions of carriage** (with tank numbers, etc.), as well as a **key** to the conditions of carriage and a **tank plan**.

D04g.3a Surveys for INLS Certificates

* **Regulation 9 of the MS (Dangerous or Noxious Liquid Substances in Bulk) Regulations 1996** prescribes survey requirements prior to implementation of the Harmonised System of Survey and Certification. Surveys include initial, annual, intermediate (within 6 months either way of the half-life), periodical (every 5 years) and additional surveys (after damage repairs, etc.). Initial, intermediate and periodic (renewal) surveys, and any annual survey in the UK are carried out by the MCA. Annual surveys abroad are carried out by MCA-nominated surveyors of LR, BV, DNV, ABS, RINA or GL. **Pre-harmonisation initial survey** guidelines are in **M.1447**.

* Survey requirements of MARPOL Annex II under the Harmonised System of Survey and Certification are similar to those for oil tankers (see D04g.2b).

D04g.3b Procedures and Arrangements Manual

* **Regulation 7(1) of the MS (Dangerous or Noxious Liquid Substances in Bulk) Regulations 1996** provides that every ship carrying noxious liquid substances must have a **Procedures and Arrangements Manual** complying with IMO Standards[76].

* The manual must be **approved**, in the case of a UK ship, by the **MCA** or, in the case of a ship registered in another MARPOL Convention country, by or on behalf of the government of that State (regulation 7(2)).

* The manual must be kept on board the ship in such a place as to be readily **available for inspection** (regulation 7(3)). (It will be examined with the INLS Certificate and Cargo Record Book at surveys.)

* The manual must, in the case of a UK ship, be in **English** and, in the case of any other ship, be in, or include a translation into, English or French (regulation 7(4)).

* For notes on the **Cargo Record Book** required under regulation 8, see D05b.3.

D04g.3c Responsibilities of owner and master

* The responsibilities of the owner and master under regulation 11 of the MS (Dangerous or Noxious Liquid Substances in Bulk) Regulations 1996 are similar to those under regulation 8 of the MS (Prevention of Oil Pollution) Regulations 1996 (see D04g.2c).

---

[76] The Standards for Procedures and Arrangements called for by Annex II of MARPOL 73/78 require that each ship which is certified for the carriage of noxious liquid substances in bulk shall be provided with a Procedures and Arrangements Manual. The standard format for Procedures and Arrangements Manuals are contained in Appendix D to MARPOL Annex II.

D04g.4 Surveys and Certificates of Fitness for UK chemical tankers and gas carriers

* Every UK chemical tanker and every UK gas carrier, of any tonnage, must carry an **appropriate Certificate of Fitness** for the carriage of the particular cargo on board. These certificates are required by the provisions of the various IMO Codes for gas carriers (see D03d.1) and for chemical tankers (see D03e.1).
* **UK chemical tankers** complying with the **BCH Code** must carry a **Certificate of Fitness for the Carriage of Dangerous Chemicals in Bulk** (see D04g.5a).
* **UK chemical tankers** complying with the **IBC Code** (1983 or 1994 edition) must carry an **International Certificate of Fitness for the Carriage of Dangerous Chemicals in Bulk** (see D04g.5b).
* **UK gas carriers** complying with the **GC Code for Existing Ships** or the **GC Code** must carry a **Certificate of Fitness for the Carriage of Liquefied Gases in Bulk** (see D04g.6a).
* **UK gas carriers** complying with the **IGC Code** must carry an International **Certificate of Fitness for the Carriage of Liquefied Gases in Bulk** (see D04g.6b).
* Certificates of Fitness for UK ships are issued only by the **MCA**. Annual surveys carried out abroad are normally made by classification society surveyors appointed by the MCA, in which case applications for survey must be made to the Dangerous Goods Branch, MCA, Southampton.
* Surveys and Certificates of Fitness for gas carriers and chemical tankers are covered by the **Harmonised System for Survey and Certification** (HSSC) (see D04e).
* **Survey guidelines** under the HSSC are contained in the Annex to IMO Resolution A.746(18) (which runs to about 100 pages). Survey requirements for **chemical tankers** are in section 12 of the Annex to the Resolution, while survey requirements for **gas carriers** are in section 13. (Section 13 is reprinted in Annex F to *Survey of Gas Carriers – Instructions for the Guidance of Surveyors*, published by the MCA.)
* **Guidelines for surveys** of chemical tankers prior to implementation of the HSSC are contained in Annex C to *Survey of Chemical Tankers – Instructions for the Guidance of Surveyors*, published by the MCA.

D04g.5 Chemical tanker Certificates of Fitness

* A UK chemical tanker must carry:
  * in the case of a ship complying with the **BCH Code**, a **Certificate of Fitness for the Carriage of Dangerous Chemicals in Bulk**; and
  * in the case of a ship complying with the **IBC Code**, an **International Certificate of Fitness for the Carriage of Dangerous Chemicals in Bulk**.
* Both certificates are valid for a maximum of **5 years**, subject to annual and intermediate surveys.
* *Both certificates may have **Noxious Liquid Substance survey endorsements** as required by Annex II of MARPOL 73/78.*
* For notes on the **codes** applicable to chemical tankers of different construction dates, see D03e.1.

D04g.5a Certificate of Fitness for the Carriage of Dangerous Chemicals in Bulk

* Ships surveyed in accordance with the provisions of section 1.6 of the BCH Code, and found to comply with the Code, should be issued with a **Certificate of Fitness for the Carriage of Dangerous Chemicals in Bulk**.
* **The Certificate shows**: **1**. Name of ship. Port of registry. Official No. Ship type (Code para. 2.2.4). **2**. List of products (continued on signed and dated sheets at annex 1A); conditions of carriage. **3**. Dispensations, equivalents, etc. permitted under 1.7.3 and 2.2.5 of the Code. **4**. Instruction as follows: "Where it is required to load the ship other than in accordance with the above instruction, then the necessary calculations to justify the proposed loading conditions should be submitted to the Department, who may authorise in writing the adoption of the propose loading conditions." **5**. Operational notes (several pages of detailed notes relating to products in product list). **6**. Pollution notes. **7**. General notes. **8**. Strength notes. **9**. Stability notes. **10**. Tank plan. **11**. Appendixes. **12**. Addenda. **13**. Endorsements for annual and intermediate surveys.

D04g.5b International Certificate of Fitness for the Carriage of Dangerous Chemicals in Bulk

* Ships surveyed in accordance with the provisions of section 1.5 of the IBC Code, and found to comply with the Code, should be issued with an **International Certificate of Fitness for the Carriage of Dangerous Chemicals in Bulk**.
* **The Certificate shows** similar details to those on a Certificate of Fitness (see D04g.5a).

D04g.6 Gas carrier Certificates of Fitness

* A UK liquefied gas carrier must carry either:
  * a **Certificate of Fitness for the Carriage of Liquefied Gases in Bulk**, in the case of a ship complying with the GC Code for Existing Ships or the GC Code; or
  * an **International Certificate of Fitness for the Carriage of Dangerous Chemicals in Bulk**, in the case of a ship complying with the IGC Code.
* For notes on the **codes** applicable to gas carriers of different construction dates, see D03d.1.

D04g.6a Certificate of Fitness for the Carriage of Liquefied Gases in Bulk

* Ships surveyed in accordance with the provisions of either section 1.6 of the GC Code for Existing Ships or section 1.6 of the GC Code, and found to comply with the relevant Code, should be issued with a **Certificate of Fitness for the Carriage of Liquefied Gases in Bulk**.
* **The Certificate shows**: **1**. Ship's particulars including: Name of ship, distinctive number or letters, port of registry and ship type (Section 2.5. of the Code). **2**. List of Products with Conditions of Carriage including tank numbers, minimum temperature, maximum pressure, maximum density and numbered tank loading conditions (continued on annexed, signed and dated sheets if necessary). **3**. Endorsements for annual and intermediate surveys, with place and date of survey, and surveyor's signature and official stamp of authority. **4**. Annexed tank loading condition(s) and tank plan.

D04g.6b International Certificate of Fitness for the Carriage of Liquefied Gases in Bulk

* Ships surveyed in accordance with the provisions of section 1.5 of the IGC Code, and found to comply with the Code, should be issued with an **International Certificate of Fitness for the Carriage of Liquefied Gases in Bulk**. For notes on surveys and certification of gas carriers, see D04g.4.
* **The Certificate shows** similar details to those on a Certificate of Fitness (see D04g.6a).

D04g.7 Certificate of Fitness issued under the Guidelines for the Transport and Handling of Limited Amounts of Hazardous and Noxious Liquid Substances in Bulk on Offshore Support Vessels

* IMO has agreed that in the case of offshore supply vessels which carry **limited amounts of certain hazardous and noxious liquid substance**s (NLSs) in bulk, full compliance with the Chemical or Gas Carrier Codes in order to satisfy the requirements of the SOLAS or MARPOL Conventions is unnecessary, provided that:
  * the discharge of Category A, B and C NLSs, or ballast water, tank washings or residues or mixtures containing such substances must be to the offshore installation or to reception facilities in port; and
  * the ships comply with IMO's *Guidelines for the Transport and Handling of Limited Amounts of Hazardous and Noxious Liquid Substances in Bulk on Offshore Support Vessels*, promulgated under Resolution A673(16).
* The Resolution requires the issue of a certificate of fitness, a model form of which is shown in **M.1458**. The certificate indicates the cargoes permitted to be carried and any relevant carriage conditions. It is valid for 5 years, subject to annual survey and has the same force as a Certificate of Fitness to carry Chemicals in Bulk.
* When the vessel is constructed to carry substances having **only a marine pollution hazard** (i.e. **with no "dangerous goods" element**), the **INLS Certificate** required under MARPOL 73/78 Annex II, suitably endorsed, may serve the purposes of the above certificate. (In practice, most OSVs are issued with an INLS Certificate where they carry MARPOL Annex II substances.)
* The MCA states in M.1458 that it has, in the past, issued to OSVs a **general exemption** from certain parts of the MS (Control of Pollution by Noxious Liquid Substances in Bulk) Regulations and the MS (Dangerous Goods and Marine Pollutants) Regulations provided that the ships are surveyed, certificated and operated in accordance with Resolution A673(16).
* "**Limited quantities**" for the purposes of the Guidelines are defined in **M.1458**, which also lists relevant products and defines "**offshore support vessels**" as:
  * vessels which are primarily engaged in the transport of stores, materials and equipment to and from mobile offshore drilling units, fixed and floating platforms and other similar offshore installations; or
  * vessels, including well stimulation vessels, but excluding MODUs, derrick barges, pipelaying barges and floating accommodation units, which are otherwise primarily engaged in supporting the work of offshore installations.

D04g.8 Sewage pollution prevention equipment, surveys and certification

* **MARPOL Annex IV** contains the **Regulations for the Prevention of Pollution by Sewage from Ships**. For notes on various aspects of Annex IV, including ships to which Annex IV applies, see H03d.1.
* **Regulation 3** of Annex IV requires ships to which the Annex applies and which are engaged in voyages to ports or offshore terminals of other Party States to have an **initial survey** and **periodical surveys**. The **initial survey** is to ensure that:
  * any sewage treatment plant meets operational requirements based on IMO standards and test methods;
  * any comminution and disinfection system is type-approved by the flag State Administration;
  * any holding tank is of a capacity adequate for the number of persons on board and the ship's operations, to the satisfaction of the flag State Administration, and has visual means of indicating the amount of the contents; and
  * a pipeline is fitted for the discharge of sewage to a reception facility, and is fitted with an international shore connection.
* **Periodical surveys** are at intervals not exceeding 5 years and are to ensure that the above equipment, fittings and arrangements continue to comply with Annex IV.
* **Regulation 4** requires the issue of an **International Sewage Pollution Prevention Certificate (1973)** ("ISPP Certificate") after survey as required by regulation 3. The Certificate will be issued by the flag State Administration, or by an organisation authorised by the Administration, to any ship engaged on voyages to ports or offshore terminals under the jurisdiction of other Parties to Annex IV. Regulation 5 permits the government of another Party to issue the certificate at the flag State Administration's request. The certificate will be valid for a maximum of **5 years** from the date of issue. **Extensions** will be permitted under regulation 7.
* A **specimen ISPP Certificate** is shown in the Appendix to Annex IV.
* At the time of writing, **no ship sewage pollution prevention legislation** is in force in the UK, although this is expected to be in place by 27 September 2003 when Annex IV enters into force. A number of other maritime States have, however, enacted legislation effectively implementing the requirements of MARPOL Annex IV, and ships in their ports and waters must comply with this legislation. (For notes on the Helsinki Convention, see H03d.2.) Many UK ships are, therefore, already equipped for dealing with sewage to the standards required by Annex IV. Typically, such ships will be issued by a Certifying Authority with a **Statement of Compliance with Annex IV of MARPOL 73/78**.
* **MGN 33** draws attention to hazards that can arise from unsatisfactory designs of sewage systems and from maintenance and operation on board of all sewage systems.
* For notes on **legal sea discharge criteria for ship sewage** under Annex IV, see H03d.2.
* For notes on **disposal of ship sewage in port**, see I06b.

D04g.8a Statement of Compliance with MARPOL Annex IV

* A **Statement of Compliance with Annex IV of the International Convention for the Prevention of Pollution from Ships, 1973 -**
  - is **issued by** an authorised classified society in accordance with IMO Resolution MEPC 2(VI).
  - Certifies that the ship is equipped with a sewage treatment plant, comminutor and/or holding tank (as applicable) and a discharge pipeline in compliance with Regulation 3(1)(a)(i) to (iv) of MARPOL Annex IV.
  - is **valid** for a maximum of 5 years.
  - **shows** a description of the **sewage treatment plant**, including:
    * type of sewage treatment plant (i.e. manufacturer's type name or number);
    * the name of the certifying authority (e.g. United States Coast Guard); and
    * the effluent standards met (e.g. IMO Resolution MEPC 2(VI).
  - **shows** a description of the **comminutor**, including
    * the type;
    * the name of the manufacturer; and
    * the standard of sewage after disinfection.
  - **shows** a description of the **holding tank**, including:
    * the total capacity in cubic metres; and
    * the location.

D04g.9 Garbage pollution prevention equipment, surveys and documentation

* **MARPOL Annex V** contains the **Regulations for the Prevention of Pollution by Garbage from Ships**.
* For notes on various aspects of Annex V see H03e.1.

* Annex V contains **no regulation requiring any special equipment, survey or certificate**.
* **Regulation 9** of Annex V contains requirements for **placards, garbage management plans and record-keeping**.
* For notes on **garbage placards** see D04t.6.
* For notes on **Garbage Management Plans** see D04t.4.
* For notes on **Garbage Record Books** see D04t.5.
* **Regulation 9 permits** flag State Administrations to **waive the requirements for Garbage Record Books** for any ship engaged on voyages of 1 hour or less in duration which is certified to carry 15 persons or more, or fixed or floating platforms while engaged in exploration and exploitation of the sea-bed.
* Requirements for **shipboard incinerators** are contained in Regulation 16 of MARPOL Annex VI (see D04g.10).

D04g.10 Air pollution prevention equipment, surveys and certification

* The **MARPOL Protocol of 1997 adds Annex VI (Regulations for the Prevention of Air Pollution from Ships)** to the MARPOL Convention. For notes on **Annex VI** including requirements relating to control of emissions, see H03f.1. (Deliberate emissions of ozone-depleting substances are banned by regulation 12. Nitrogen oxide (NO_x) emission limits are set in regulation 13 for marine diesel engines with an output of more than 130kW installed in ships, vessels or offshore installations built after 1 January 2000. The sulphur oxide (SO_x) content of fuel oil is restricted in regulation 14.
* **Regulation 5** of Annex VI provides that every ship of 400gt and above and every fixed or floating drilling rig and other platforms will be subject to an **initial survey**, **periodical surveys** at intervals not exceeding 5 years, and at least one **intermediate survey** within 6 months of the mid-point of the validity of the International Air Pollution Certificate. Regulation 5(4) provides that the survey for compliance with regulation 13 must be conducted in accordance with the NO_x Technical Code.
* **Regulation 6** requires the issue, following a survey, of an **International Air Pollution Prevention Certificate (IAPP Certificate)** to any ship of 400gt or above engaged in voyages to ports or offshore terminals under the jurisdiction of other MARPOL Party States, and to platforms and drilling rigs engaged in voyages to waters under the sovereignty or jurisdiction of other Parties to the MARPOL Protocol of 1997. A specimen IAPP Certificate is included in the Appendix to Annex VI. Under regulation 9 the Certificate will be valid for a maximum of **5 years**, with a possible **extension** of up to 5 months to allow the ship to complete a voyage to the survey port. Under regulation 10 the Certificate will be subject to **Port State Control** procedures.
* **Regulation 16** deals with **Shipboard incineration**. Incinerators installed on or after 1 January 2000 must meet the requirements in Appendix IV to Annex VI (regulation 16(2)). Appendix IV provides that incinerators must have an **IMO Type Approval Certificate** which can be obtained if the incinerator is designed and built to an approved standard.
* The **NO_x Technical Code** -
  - **contains** procedures for testing, survey and certification of marine diesel engines to ensure compliance with the emission limits set by the regulations in Annex VI.
  - **contains** provisions which enter into force as mandatory requirements on the same day as Annex VI enters into force, for all Parties to the 1997 MARPOL Protocol.
* **MGN 142** (which is not addressed to masters, but to owners, builders and engine manufacturers) -
  - **contains** information about the Interim Guidelines for the Application of the NO_x Technical Code (MEPC/Circ.344).
  - **contains** interim provisions which the MCA has put into place for ships built on or after 1 January 2000, including arrangements for the issue of **Statements of Compliance with the NO_x Technical Code**, and arrangements for the subsequent issue of **International Air Pollution Prevention (IAPP) Certificates or UK Air Pollution Prevention (UKAPP) Certificates** following the entry into force of Annex VI.
  - **contains** a specimen Statement of Compliance with the NO_x Technical Code.
  - **states** that the MCA will retain responsibility for the initial survey of UK ships when Annex VI enters into force. This will also apply to ships built on or after the date of entry into force and to existing ships which transfer to the UK flag on or after that date.
* **MGN 143** encourages operation of **type-approved incinerators** in compliance with regulation 16 of MARPOL Annex VI, advises of **interim provisions applying to incinerators** on ships built on or after 1 January 2000, pending the entry into force of Annex VI, and contains details of **type-approval certification** for incinerators.

D04g.10a Statement of Compliance with the NO$_x$ Technical Code

* A **Statement of Compliance with the NO$_x$ Technical Code -**
  - **may be issued by** any of the six authorised classified societies (see D04d.2b) (under the authority of the flag State Administration) under the Interim Guidelines for the Application of the NO$_x$ Technical Code (MEPC/Circ.344), subject to satisfactory testing of the engine.
  - **will be issued** in exceptional circumstances by the MCA, subject to satisfactory testing.
  - **will be recognised** by the MCA, if issued by "the recognised certifying authorities", when a ship is subsequently surveyed for the issue of an initial IAPP or UKAPP Certificate.
  - **certifies**:
    * that the marine diesel engine mentioned in the Statement has been surveyed for pre-certification in accordance with the requirements of the Technical Code on Control of Emission of Nitrogen Oxides from Marine Diesel Engines which will become mandatory when Annex VI comes into force; and
    * that the pre-certification survey shows that the engine, its components, adjustable features and technical file, prior to the engine's installation and/or service on board a ship, fully comply with the applicable regulation 13 of MARPOL Annex VI.
  - **shows**:
    * the engine manufacturer;
    * the engine model number;
    * the engine serial number;
    * the test cycle(s);
    * the rated power (kW) and speed (rpm) of the engine; and
    * the engine approval number.
  - **shows in the Supplement**:
    * further particulars of the engine;
    * particulars of the Technical File, as required by chapter 2 of the NO$_x$ Technical Code;
    * Specifications for the On-board NO$_x$ Verification Procedures for the Engine Parameter Survey.
  - **is valid** for the life of the engine, subject to surveys required in accordance with regulation 5 of Annex VI, installed in ships under the authority of this Government.
* The **Technical File** is an essential part of the Statement of Compliance and must always accompany the engine throughout its life and always be available on board a ship.

D04g.10b International and UK Air Pollution Prevention Certificates

* In the event that MARPOL Annex VI comes into force, every ship of 400gt or more engaged on international voyages, and offshore installations engaged on voyages to waters under the sovereignty or jurisdiction of another Party to the 1997 MARPOL Protocol, will have to be surveyed in accordance with regulation 5 of Annex VI (see D04g.10) and issued with a n **International Air Pollution Prevention (IAPP) Certificate** in accordance with regulation 6.
* IAPP Certificates will evidence that engine NO$_x$ emissions comply with the requirements of regulation 13, and will also certify that other Annex VI requirements, relating to ozone-depleting substances, sulphur content of fuels, vapour collection systems and shipboard incinerators, are also met.
* Every UK vessel of 400gt or more and every offshore installation, engaged exclusively on domestic voyages, will be required to be surveyed for and issued with a **UK Air Pollution Prevention (UKAPP) Certificate**.
* Ships built before the date of entry into force of the 1997 MARPOL Protocol must be surveyed for and issued with the relevant certificate no later than the first scheduled dry-docking after its entry into force, and in no case later than 3 years after its entry into force.

D04g.11 Vessels engaged in oil recovery operations

* **M.1663** advises that the MCA has produced a **Code of Practice for Vessels Engaged in Oil Recovery Operations** which provides guidelines for the design, construction, ship's equipment and operation of **offshore support vessels** which may be required to have the capability of handling, storing and transporting oil recovered from a spill in emergency situations. The Code, which is known in the industry as the "Black Code", is available from Stationery Office bookshops.
* The MCA recognises that while adapting an offshore support vessel for oil recovery will make it a "tanker" within the meaning of various Merchant Shipping regulations, these vessels may not be able to meet the usual requirements applicable to tankers.

* When an assessment of the arrangements, including an assessment of the vessel, has been made by the MCA to its satisfaction, an **Oil Recovery Certificate** will be issued, providing a General Exemption from the regulations applicable to tankers, to enable the vessel to operate as a dedicated oil recovery vessel within UK waters. The certificate will remain valid for a period not exceeding 2 years unless previously cancelled.

D04g.12 Pollution liability insurance certification

* For notes on **oil pollution liability insurance and certification** requirements, see G04d.

D04h TONNAGE MEASUREMENT AND CERTIFICATION

D04h.1 International Tonnage Convention, 1969

* **The International Tonnage Convention, 1969** -
  was aimed at achieving a **unified system of tonnage measurement** which would be relatively simple to apply with none of the anomalies existing in the various systems employed previously in Convention countries (such as the UK).
  provides more **meaningful tonnage figures** than those derived from earlier systems.
  does not involve any special tonnage units (such as "tons", "gross tons" or "net tons"), with the consequence that the values obtained are simply a "**gross tonnage**" and a "**net tonnage**" (without units).
  requires that ships of Convention countries are issued with an **International Tonnage Certificate (1969)** certifying their gross and net tonnages as measured under the 1969 system.
  was brought into full effect from the date of build of ships built since July 1982, while older vessels were given a further 12 years, i.e. until 17 July 1994, in which to obtain an International Tonnage Certificate (which required older ships to be re-measured for tonnage)[77].

D04h.1a Gross and net tonnages under the 1969 Convention

* Under the **1969 tonnage measurement system** -
  * every ship is assigned a **gross tonnage** and a **net tonnage**.
  * **single-deck ships**, such as tankers and bulk carriers, had their gross and net tonnages largely unchanged on re-measurement. The most significant effect was in ships such as **ro-ro ferries**, many of which had their tonnages considerably increased.
  * there is no longer any need for such phrases as "tonnage deck", "deducted spaces", "exempted spaces", "alternative tonnage", "modified tonnage" or "tonnage mark", since these are not used in the 1969 Convention.
* **Gross tonnage** -
  * is expressed as a whole number, without any unit, e.g. "Gross tonnage: 8756".
  * is a realistic indication of the **ship's size** based on the moulded volume of the entire ship (hull plus erections and all enclosed spaces) without deductions, exemptions or special allowances.
  * is used mainly in the compilation of statistics.
* **Net tonnage** -
  * is expressed as a whole number, without any unit, e.g. "Net tonnage: 3367".
  * is a general indication of the ship's **earning capacity**, derived from a formula based on the moulded volume of the cargo spaces, the number of passengers carried, the moulded depth of the ship and the summer draught.
  * is used by many authorities as the basis for charging dues, e.g. light dues, port charges and canal dues.
* **Examples of changes in tonnages as a result of re-measurement** are shown in the following table:

	Pride of Kent Ro-ro passenger ferry Built 1980	*British Resolution* VLCC Built 1974	*Queen Elizabeth 2* Passenger/cruise ship Built 1969
Gross tonnage in Lloyd's Register of Ships, 1995-96	20446	130145	70327
Gross tonnage in Lloyd's Register of Ships, 1978-79	7951	133035	67140
Change in gross tonnage on re-measurement	12495 increase	2890 decrease	3187 increase
Net tonnage in Lloyd's Register of Ships, 1995-96	6133	108734	37182
Net tonnage in Lloyd's Register of Ships, 1978-79	3439	108853	37218
Change in net tonnage on re-measurement	2694 increase	119 decrease	36 decrease

---

[77] Older ships which underwent alterations resulting in substantial variation in their existing tonnages had to be re-measured under the 1969 system.

D04h.2 Tonnage Regulations

* The **MS (Tonnage) Regulations 1997** (SI 1997/1510) -
  - **give effect** in the UK to the International Convention on Tonnage Measurement of Ships, 1969.
  - **consolidate**, with amendments, the 1982 MS (Tonnage) Regulations, as amended.
  - re-enact (in Part II) those provisions of the 1982 Regulations relating to the 1969 Tonnage Convention.
  - re-enact (in Part III) those provisions of the 1982 Regulations relating to the calculation of tonnage for pleasure vessels of less than 13.7 metres in length.
  - **simplify the 1982 tonnage requirements for ships of less than 24 metres** in length by adopting a method of tonnage computation, previously restricted to those pleasure vessels of less than 13.7 metres in length, for all ships under 24 metres in length other than fishing vessels.
  - **deal with** the tonnage computation of **segregated ballast oil tankers**, and the use of gross tonnage which has been ascertained under the 1982 Regulations.
  - **enable** the Secretary of State to authorise persons to act as **Certifying Authorities** for the purpose of the Regulations.
* **Definitions** of terms used in the Regulations (including various ship dimensions) are in regulation 2.
* **Part II** (regulations 3 to 12) deals with the ascertainment of tonnage and certification **for UK ships of 24 metres in length and over** contains the following regulations: **3**. Application; **4**. Method of measurement; **5**. Calculation of volumes; **6**. Gross tonnage; **7**. Net tonnage; **8**. Segregated ballast oil tankers; **9**. Issue of certificates; **10**. Cancellation of certificates; **11**. Change of net tonnage necessitating issue of certificate; **12**. Use of gross tonnage ascertained under previous Regulations.
* **Part III** (regulations 13 and 14) deals with the application, ascertainment of tonnage and certification for **UK ships of less than 24 metres** in length, other than fishing vessels.
* **Part IV** (regulation 15) deals with ascertainment of **tonnage and certification of non-UK ships**.
* **Part V** (regulation 16) prescribes **penalties**.

D04h.2a Tonnage measurement

* A ship must be **measured** by a surveyor appointed by a Certifying Authority, i.e. the MCA or an authorised classification society[78] (regulation 4(1)).
* **Gross and net tonnages must be determined** in accordance with regulations 6 and 7, but in the case of novel types of craft with constructional features which render the application of the Regulations unreasonable or impracticable, the gross and net tonnages will be determined as required by the MCA (regulation 4(2)).
* **All measurements** used in the calculations of volumes must be taken and expressed in **metres** to the nearest one hundredth of a metre (regulation 4(3)).
* Gross and net tonnages must be expressed as **whole numbers**, decimals being rounded off downwards (regulation 4(4)).
* All **volumes** included in the calculation of gross and net tonnages will be measured, irrespective of the fitting of insulation or the like, to the inner side of the shell or structural boundary plating in ships constructed of metal, and to the outer surface of the shell or to the inner side of the structural boundary surfaces in ships constructed of any other material (regulation 5(1)). **Volumes of appendages** must be included in the total volume (regulation 5(2)). **Volumes of spaces open to the sea** must be excluded from the total volume (regulation 5(3)).
* **Formulae** for ascertaining gross tonnage and net tonnage are in regulations 6 and 7 respectively.
* Regulation 8 prescribes the **formula for calculating the tonnage of segregated ballast tanks** (SBTs) complying with regulation 13 of MARPOL 73/78 Annex 1 where these are provided in oil tankers. The total tonnage of a tanker's SBTs may be entered on the International Tonnage Certificate (1969).
* In the case of a **passenger ship assigned subdivision load lines** in accordance with the MS (Passenger Ship Construction) Regulations **and load lines** in accordance with the MS (Load Line) Regulations, only one net tonnage will be applied (regulation 11(2)). Where the draught corresponding to the Summer load line differs from that corresponding to the deepest subdivision load line the net tonnage will, subject to regulation 11(3)(a), be that determined in accordance with regulation 7 by applying the draught corresponding to the appropriate assigned load line for the trade in which the ship is engaged.
* Subject to subparagraph (b) below, where **alterations in the values** of V, Vc, d, N1 or N2, as defined in regulations 6 and 7, or changes in the position of the load lines result in a decrease in the net tonnage, a new International Tonnage Certificate (1969) incorporating the decreased net tonnage will not be issued until 12 months have elapsed from the date on which the current certificate was issued (regulation 11(3)(a)).
* Under regulation 11(3)(b) a **new International Tonnage Certificate (1969)** may be issued forthwith when -

---

[78] **Authorised societies** for tonnage measurement purposes are Lloyd's Register of Shipping, the British Committee of Bureau Veritas, the British Committee of Det Norske Veritas, the British Committee of Germanischer Lloyd: the British Committee of Registro Italiano Navale and the British Technical Committee of the American Bureau of Shipping.

- a ship which was registered outside the UK is **re-registered in the UK**;
- a ship **undergoes alterations or modifications of a major character** such as the removal of a superstructure, which requires an alteration of the assigned load line; or
- the ship is a **passenger ship employed in special trades** for carriage of large numbers of special trade passengers, such as the pilgrim trade.

* **Regulation 12** allows ships existing at the date of entry into force of the Regulations (i.e. 11 July 1997) the **continued use of a gross tonnage (gt)** for the purposes of application of the provisions of regulations implementing SOLAS, MARPOL and STCW 95. This has given rise to certain anomalies when applicants for certificates issued under STCW 95 have stated their sea service in GT, as explained in **Part 18 of the Training and Certification Guidance** (see E02c.18).

D04h.2b International Tonnage Certificate (1969)

* If it is in order to do so, the Certifying Authority will issue to the owner an **International Tonnage Certificate (1969)** in the form set out in the Convention (regulation 9). The **official number** of the ship must be included as a distinctive number.

* Where **alterations** are made in the arrangement, construction, capacity, use of spaces, total number of passengers the ship is permitted to carry under the terms of the ship's passenger certificate, assigned load line, or permitted draught such as would cause an increase in the gross or net tonnage, the existing International Tonnage Certificate (1969) will cease to be valid and must be delivered up to and cancelled by the Certifying Authority (regulation 10(1)).

* **When a ship is transferred from the UK Register** the International Tonnage Certificate (1969) will cease to be valid except when the transfer is to the Administration of a State which is a Contracting Government, in which case the certificate may remain in force for a period not exceeding 3 months or until the new Administration issues another International Tonnage Certificate (1969), whichever is the earlier. The Certifying Authority must transmit to the Administration of that Government as soon as possible after the transfer has taken place a copy of the certificate carried by the ship at the time of transfer and a copy of the relevant tonnage calculations (regulation 10(2)).

* When **alterations in the values** of V, Vc, d, N1 or N2 as defined in regulations 6 and 7 result in an increase in the net tonnage a new International Tonnage Certificate (1969) incorporating the increased net tonnage must be issued (regulation 11(1)).

* An **International Tonnage Certificate (1969)** -
- **is issued under** regulation 9 of the MS (Tonnage) Regulations 1997 to all UK ships of 24m length or over, registered or to be registered in the UK under Part II of the Merchant Shipping Act 1995.
- **is issued in the UK by** the MCA, or by Lloyd's Register, Det Norske Veritas, American Bureau of Shipping, Germanischer Lloyd, Bureau Veritas or RINA on the MCA's authorisation, or abroad by any Convention country Administration at the MCA's request. (In practice, it will in most cases be issued by the ship's authorised classification society.)
- **is valid until** any alteration is made in the form or capacity of the ship or it is discovered that the tonnage of the ship has been erroneously computed.
- **is invalidated** when alterations are made in the arrangement, construction, capacity, use of spaces, total number of passengers as allowed by a Passenger Certificate, assigned load lines, or permitted draft such as would increase the gross or net tonnage. The certificate must then be delivered to and cancelled by the Certifying Authority .
- **ceases to be valid** if the ship is transferred from the UK register, except when the transfer is to another Convention Country, in which case it may remain in force for not exceeding 3 months or until the new Administration issues another International Tonnage Certificate (1969), whichever is earlier.
- cannot be issued before a **tonnage measurement survey** is held. If the ship is also being registered or re-registered, the survey is the same measurement survey as that required for British registry. A Certificate of Survey is issued by the surveyor, and this is sent to the Registrar of Ships at the RSS, Cardiff. Application for tonnage measurement survey is made to the relevant classification society and all drawings and plans, etc. must be made available (see D01d).

* **Gross tonnage** and **net tonnage** are printed on the front of the certificate, in whole numbers, e.g.: "Gross tonnage: 13675".

* **On the back** is a list of all spaces included in the tonnage (gross and net). This list includes the name of the space, location and length; list of excluded spaces; number of passengers; moulded draught; date and place of original measurement; date and place of last previous re-measurement; service condition of vessel - includes builder, year built, place built, no. of masts, no. of decks, material, type of stem, type of stern; certifying statement from owner, master or agent that he agrees to the description and measurement set forth herein. A statement certifies that tonnages as shown have been determined in accordance with the International Convention on Tonnage Measurement of Ships 1969.

* **Details shown on the back** are: Main dimensions; Gross Tonnage; Net Tonnage; name, location & length of spaces included in gross tonnage and net tonnage; date & place of original measurement and of last previous re-measurement.
* **Notes** on the back are as follows: **1**. Moulded volume measured for Gross Tonnage. Volume of "earning" spaces measured for Net Tonnage. Volumes of measured spaces, as shown on reverse of certificate, are applied in formulae to obtain Gross Tonnage and Net Tonnage shown on front of certificate. **2**. Ships previously holding Certificate of British Tonnage now have ITC (1969). **3**. New certificate to be issued when alterations in values of V, V_c, d, N, or N_2 as defined in regs. 6 and 7 of Tonnage Regulations, result in an increase in NT. **4**. Certificate of Survey issued following measurement survey, and sent to Registry of Shipping and Seamen, Cardiff.

D04h.3 Panama Canal Tonnage documentation

* **Panama Canal tolls** are charged by the Panama Canal Authority[79] (PCA) and are based on the ship's **PC/UMS net tonnage**. "PC/UMS" is an acronym for "**Panama Canal/Universal Measurement System**", which is an adaptation of the measurement system used under the International Convention on Tonnage Measurement (1969), modified for Panama Canal purposes.
* A ship's **PC/UMS net tonnage** is determined by applying a mathematical formula to her **total volume measurement** as used for obtaining the International Tonnage Certificate (1969) ("ITC69").
* The classification society will, on application of the owner, and following measurement, issue the ship with a certificate named the **PC/UMS Documentation of Total Volume** or similar[80] (see D04h.3a).
* **A vessel intending to transit the Panama Canal** for the first time must, on arrival at the canal entrance, have its total volume verified by the Panama Canal Admeasurer under the rules of the Panama Canal Authority. The **PC/UMS Documentation of Total Volume** and/or a copy of the International Tonnage Certificate (1969) must be presented to the Boarding Official of the Canal Authority. The Authority will then verify the tonnage data on the Documentation of Total Volume and, if satisfactory, will deliver to the ship a **PC/UMS Net Tonnage Certificate** for future transits (see D04h.3b).
* A vessel arriving at the canal for the first time should have ready a **Standard Documentation Folder** containing:
  * General ship information;
  * Copy of the International Tonnage Certificate (1969); and
  * Copy of ITC 69 tonnage computation.
* A blank copy of an "Admeasurement Date Sheet Form" should be obtained by the shipowner from the classification society, completed and sent to the Panama Canal Admeasurement Division prior to the scheduled arrival at the Canal.
* The following **plans** are required by the Panama Canal Admeasurement Division on arrival:
  * General Arrangement plan including profile;
  * Capacity Plan with deadweight scale;
  * Midship Section Plan;
  * Lines Plan (if available and requested).
* The following **additional documents** should also be ready for inspection on first arrival at the Canal:
  International Load Line Certificate (1966);
  Suez Canal Special Tonnage Certificate (if available).

D04h.3a PC/UMS Documentation of Total Volume

* A certificate entitled **PC/UMS Documentation of Total Volume** -
  - **must be obtained** by the owner of a ship which will (at some time) transit the Panama Canal for the first time. A ship will usually carry the document from the time of building, even though she may not transit the canal for some time thereafter.
  - **is issued by the classification society** (or the flag State Administration in the case of an unclassed ship) following measurement under the Authority's Rules for Measurement of Vessels for the Panama Canal.
  - **shows** that, based upon the rules of measurement for the Panama Canal as specified in 35 Code of Federal Regulations section 135 or the International Tonnage Convention of 1969, the vessel has been measured and assigned the total volume in cubic metres as shown.
  - **shows** ship's main particulars; length, breadth, depth, gross tonnage and net tonnage as stated on the International Tonnage Certificate (1969); number of passengers; number of containers above deck; total volume

---

[79] Management of the Panama Canal transferred on 31 December 1999 from the Panama Canal Commission (PCC) to the Autoridad del Canal de Panama (ACP) (known in English as the Panama Canal Authority or "PCA").
[80] The document issued by DNV is entitled "Documentation to be presented to the Panama Canal Commission for the Issuance of PC/UMS Certificate".

in cubic metres based on rules for measurement for the Panama Canal as specified in 35 Code of Federal Regulations section 135[81] or the International Tonnage Convention 1969; PC/UMS Net Tonnage; quantity of bunker fuel for Ballast Rate; K4 factor; K5 factor; place and date of issue. On reverse: details of elements of total volume; details of excluded spaces.

- **certifies** that the vessel has been determined in accordance with the Rules for measurement of Vessels for the Panama Canal, and that the particulars of tonnage contained in the certificate are correct.
- **must be surrendered**, with certain **ship's plans** (as described in D04h.3) on first arrival at the Canal to the Boarding Official of the Panama Canal Authority (PCA).
- will be retained by the Panama Canal Authority following the first transit, after which a permanent certificate (called a **PC/UMS Net Tonnage Certificate**) will be delivered to the vessel on the next subsequent transit (see D04h.3b). The plans will be returned to the vessel via its agent after the Panama Canal net tonnage is verified by the PCA.

D04h.3b PC/UMS Net Tonnage Certificate

* A **PC/UMS Net Tonnage Certificate** -
- has been issued to ships since 1994, replacing the **Panama Canal Tonnage Certificate**.
- **may be issued by the Panama Canal Authority** (ACP) following measurement under the Authority's Rules for Measurement of Vessels for the Panama Canal to ships intending to transit the Panama Canal.
- **certifies** that the ship has been measured in accordance with the Rules for Measurement of Vessels for the Panama Canal, and that the particulars of tonnage contained on the certificate are correct.
- **shows**: Panama Canal Ship Identification Number. Name of ship. Nationality; signal letters; type of power; type of vessel; IMO/Lloyd's Register No.; year built; keel laid; number of passengers; length overall; extreme breadth; ITC(69) length; ITC(69) breadth; ITC(69) depth; ITC(69) Gross Tonnage; ITC(69) Net Tonnage; max. above deck TEU. Statement: 'Based upon a net tonnage of (e.g. '32568') from the Panama Canal Tonnage Certificate issued by the Panama Canal Commission on (date) and an above deck container tonnage of (e.g. '0') this vessel has been assigned the following Tonnages:'; PC Gross (e.g. '40438'); PC Net (e.g. '32568'). Bunker fuel for Ballast Rate limited to: (tonnage, e.g. '2186 MT'). Certifying statement. Issued at Balboa on (date). Signature of Member of Board of Admeasurement.
- **bears the following Notes**: 1. Chapter IV: PC/UMS Net Tonnage Certificate: Article 21: The admeasurement of vessels shall be carried out by the Authority's specialized personnel, or by agents authorized by it. Each transiting vessel shall present to the Authority a complete set of plans and calculation sheets, with the dimensions that served as the basis for obtaining its ITC 69, and a copy of the same. 2. Article 22: The Authority shall deliver to each vessel or its agent, the PC/UMS Net Tonnage Certificate, which shall be maintained aboard as proof that it has been inspected and measured. 3. Article 23: The Authority may correct the PC/UMS Net Tonnage Certificates when a difference in the V of the vessel is found after examining the documents or inspecting the vessel.

D04h.4 Suez Canal Special Tonnage Certificate

* **Suez Canal tolls** are charged by the Suez Canal Authority and are based on the ship's **Suez net tonnage**, as measured under the Authority's Rules (which are called "the Rules adopted by the International Tonnage Commission at Constantinople") and shown on a Suez Canal Special Tonnage Certificate.
- A **Suez Canal Special Tonnage Certificate** -
- **may be issued by** an authorised classification society (or by the MCA in the case of an unclassed ship) following a measurement survey conducted in accordance with the Canal Authority's rules, which are described in the HMSO publication Tonnage Measurement of Ships - Instructions to Surveyors: Measurement of Suez Canal Tonnage. Measurement is based on the old British "Moorsom system" and produces gross and net tonnages. Measurement is usually carried out, and the certificate issued, at building.
- **must be produced** for inspection by the Canal Authority on every arrival at a Suez Canal entrance.
- **certifies** that the ship has been re-measured, and that the tonnage ascertained (as shown) is in accordance with the Rules adopted by the International Tonnage Commission at Constantinople.
- **shows**: ship's main particulars; details of tonnage when passing through the Suez Canal (Gross Register Tonnage, and Net Register Tonnage by actual measurement); Net Register Tonnage by Danube Rule; place and date of issue. On reverse: Deductions from Gross Tonnage; Full dimensions and tonnage of exempted and open spaces; Detailed measurements of machinery spaces; Notes referring to particulars of deducted spaces.
- **is valid** until any change in dimensions used in the tonnage measurements.

---

[81] Details on certificate issued before transfer of Canal administration to PCA.

D04i LOAD LINE SURVEYS AND DOCUMENTATION

D04i.1 Load Line Regulations

* The **MS (Load Line) Regulations 1998** (SI 1998/2241) -
  - contain regulations arranged in parts as follows: **PART 1 – General**. **1**. Citation and commencement. **2**. Interpretation. **3**. Repeals and revocation. **4**. Exemptions. **5**. Exemptions. **6**. General compliance. **PART II – Surveys and Certificates**. **7**. Assignment of freeboards. **8**. Initial and periodical surveys and inspections. **9**. Issue of appropriate certificates. **10**. Duration and extension of certificates. **11**. Cancellation of certificates. **12**. Issue of exemption certificates. **13**. Publication of load line certificates and notification of draughts. **14**. Non-United Kingdom ships. **PART III – Load Lines and Marks**. **15**. Marking. **16**. Deck-line. **17**. Load line mark. **18**. Load lines. **19**. Timber load lines. **20**. Appropriate load line. **21**. Position of load lines. **22**. Method of marking. **23**. Authorisation of removal, etc. of appropriate marks. **24**. Mark of Assigning Authority. **PART IV – Conditions of Assignment**. **25**. Requirements relevant to the assignment of freeboards. **26**. Compliance with conditions of assignment. **27**. Record of particulars. **PART V – Freeboards**. **28**. Types of freeboard. **29**. Determination of freeboards. **30**. Greater than minimum freeboards. **31**. Special position of deck-line: correction of freeboard. **PART VI – Stability**. **32**. Information as to stability of ships. **33**. Information as to loading and ballasting of ships. **PART VII – Equivalents, Penalties and Detention**. **34**. Equivalents. **35**. Penalties. **36**. Offences and penalties in relation to certificates and surveys. **37**. Detention.
  - **are amended by** the MS (Load Line) (Amendment) Regulations 2000 (SI 2000/1335), which incorporate the amendments made to the Load Line Convention by the Protocol of 1988 (i.e. the amendments introducing the Harmonised System of Survey and Certification).
  - **apply** to UK ships wherever they are and to **non-UK ships** while they are in **UK waters** other than those mentioned below.
* For notes on **general compliance with the Regulations** (as required by regulation 6), see D03a.3a.

D04i.1a Assigning authorities

* **Assigning Authorities** authorised by the MCA for classed ships are Lloyd's Register of Shipping (LR), Det Norske Veritas (DNV), Bureau Veritas (BV), American Bureau of Shipping (ABS), Germanischer Lloyd (GL) and Registro Italiano Navale (RINA).
* **In the case of an unclassed ship** (such as a lighthouse tender) the **MCA** will assign freeboards and, where appropriate, issue the Load Line Certificate, in which case the letters alongside the load line disc will be "DT" or "BT".

D04i.1b Assignment of freeboards

* **Regulation 7(1)** provides that before issuing the appropriate certificate to a UK ship the Assigning Authority must **assign freeboards** in accordance with the Regulations. The Assigning Authority must:
  - determine the particulars of the freeboards to be assigned;
  - determine which of the load lines described in Part III (Load Lines and Marks) are to be marked on the sides of the ship in accordance with the requirements of that Part;
  - determine the position where the load lines, the deck-line and the load line mark are to be so marked; and
  - complete a copy of the Record of Particulars relating to the Conditions of Assignment.
* Ships which comply with the highest standard of structural strength required by the Rules of the Assigning Authority and comply in full with the **Conditions of Assignment** may be assigned the **statutory minimum freeboard** allowable under the Load Line Regulations (as tabulated in **MSN 1752**).
* **Regulation 25(1)** provides that, subject to regulation 25(2), every ship to which freeboards are assigned under the Load Line Regulations must comply with the **Conditions of Assignment** applicable to that ship and set out in **Schedule 2 of MSN 1752**. An existing ship, instead of complying with the conditions of assignment referred to in regulation 25(1), may comply with such of the requirements relevant to the assignment of freeboards to ships as were applicable to her under the law in force immediately before 21 July 1968 (regulation 25(2)).
* The **Conditions of Assignment** detailed in Schedule 2 of MSN 1752 are in **five parts**: Part 1: Ships in general; Part 2: Special requirements applicable to type "A" ships; Part 3: Special requirements applicable to certain type "B" ships; Part 4: Special requirements applicable to ships assigned timber freeboards; and Part 5: General.
* **Part 1** – Ships in general – details the requirements for structural strength and stability, superstructure end bulkheads, hatchways: general, hatchways closed by portable covers and secured weathertight by tarpaulins and battening devices, coamings, machinery space openings, miscellaneous openings in freeboard and superstructure decks, ventilators, air pipes, cargo ports and similar openings, scuppers, inlets and discharges, side scuttles, freeing ports and arrangements, and protection of the crew.

* Structure, openings and fittings affecting freeboard, i.e. those items covered by Part 1, are generally designated as being in either "**Position 1**" or "**Position 2**". "**Position 1**" means those positions in which structure, openings or fittings are situated on exposed freeboard and raised quarter decks, and on exposed superstructure decks situated forward of a point located a quarter of the ship's length from the forward perpendicular. "**Position 2**" means those positions in which structure, openings or fittings are situated on exposed superstructure decks situated abaft a quarter of the ship's length from the forward perpendicular. Items in Position 2 are in many cases permitted a lower height than items in Position 1.

D04i.1c Load line surveys

* **Regulation 8(1)**, as amended, provides that a UK ship will be subject to the following **surveys**:
- an **initial survey** before the ship is put into service, which must include a complete inspection of its structure and equipment as required by the Regulations, to ensure that the arrangements, materials and scantlings comply fully with the requirements of the Regulations (regulation 8(1)(a));
- a **renewal survey** at intervals not exceeding 5 years, which is to ensure that the arrangements, materials and scantlings comply fully with the requirements of the Regulations (regulation 8(1)(b));
- an **annual survey**[82] within 3 months either way of each annual anniversary date of the Load Line Certificate, to ensure that no alterations have been made to the hull or superstructures which would affect the basis on which the position of the load line had been assigned and that the fittings and appliances for the protection of openings, the guard rails, the freeing ports and the means of access to crew's quarters are maintained in an effective condition (regulation 8(1)(c)).
* **An initial survey** will generally include:
- a complete and thorough examination of the ship's structure, both internally and externally;
- an examination of all fittings and appliances for the protection of openings giving access to spaces below the freeboard and superstructure decks, the guard rails, the freeing ports and means of access to the crew's quarters;
- an examination of the stability and, where applicable, loading and ballasting information which is required to be supplied to the master of the ship; and
- the determination of all necessary data required for the computation of the freeboard.
- The surveyor will carry out any **tests** as he considers necessary to ascertain the above.
* **Items given particular attention** in the annual survey include:
- hatchways;
- openings in the ship's side below the freeboard deck and in the sides and ends of enclosed superstructures;
- machinery casings, companionways and deckhouses;
- freeing port shutters;
- ventilators and air pipes;
- special fittings for ships marked with timber load lines;
- any departures from recorded conditions of assignment;
- positions of load line marks and deck line.
* The **owner and master must ensure** that after any of the above surveys has been completed, no material alteration is made to the ship, its structure and equipment, without the approval of the Assigning Authority (regulation 8(2)).
* After a satisfactory **annual survey**, the surveyor must **endorse** the International Load Line Certificate, International Load Line Certificate (1966) or, as the case may be, the UK Load Line Certificate (regulation 8(3)).

D04i.1d Appropriate Load Line Certificate

* **Regulation 9(1)**, as amended, provides that, subject to the provisions of regulation 10 (concerning duration and extension of certificates), the Assigning Authority must issue the **appropriate certificate** for a UK ship which has been surveyed and marked in accordance with the Regulations.
* **Under regulation 2** (Interpretation), "**appropriate certificate**" means:
- in the case of a "Convention-size ship", an **International Load Line Certificate** or an **International Load Line Certificate (1966)**; and
- in the case of any other ship, a **UK Load Line Certificate**.
* An **International Load Line Certificate** or an **International Load Line Certificate (1966)** (abbreviated in some documents to "ILLC (1966)") are therefore the appropriate Load Line certificates for a "Convention size" ship, i.e. a ship built before 21 July 1968 of not less than 150gt, or a ship built on or since 21 July 1968 of not less than 24 metres in length.

---

[82] The **annual survey** referred to in the MS (Load Line) Regulations, as amended, was formerly called a "**periodical inspection**".

* "**International Load Line Certificate**" is the name of any Load Line Certificate issued following implementation (in that ship) of the Harmonised System of Survey and Certification[83]. "**International Load Line Certificate (1966)**" is the name of a certificate issued prior to implementation of the Harmonised Survey and Certification.
* A **UK Load Line Certificate** is the appropriate Load Line Certificate for **any ship which is not a "Convention-size" ship**, i.e. a ship built before 21 July 1968 of less than 150gt, or a ship built on or since 21 July 1968 of less than 24 metres in length.
* If the certificate is an **International Load Line Certificate (1966)**, it must be in the form prescribed by the 1966 Load Line Convention (regulation 9(2)).
* The MCA may request, through a proper officer or otherwise, the Government of another Load Line Convention country to survey a UK ship and issue or authorise the issue of an International Load Line Certificate, International Load Line Certificate (1966) or, as the case may be, the UK Load Line Certificate (regulation 9(5)).
* **Regulation 10**, as amended, contains provisions for the duration and extension of certificates under the Harmonised System of Survey and Certification. These duration and extension provisions are similar to those applying to other cargo ship certificates under the HSSC, as described in D04e.1.
* A Load Line Certificate may be **cancelled** under regulation 11 if the MCA is satisfied that:
    * the certificate was issued on **false or erroneous information**;
    * the ship **ceases to comply with the Conditions of Assignment** relating to it;
    * the **structural strength of the ship is reduced** to an extent that the ship is unsafe; or
    * the **information** on the basis of which freeboards were assigned to the ship was **incorrect in a material particular**.
* A Load Line Certificate may also be **cancelled** by the MCA under regulation 11:
    * if the certificate is **not endorsed** in accordance with regulation 8 to show that the ship has been surveyed;
    * if a **new certificate is issued** in respect of the ship; or
    * if the **ship ceases to be a UK ship**.
* Where an appropriate certificate is issued in respect of a UK ship, the owner and **master** must ensure that it is kept **legible** and **posted up** in some conspicuous place on board (regulation 13(1)).
* **An International Load Line Certificate (1966)** contains the following details: Name of ship; official number; port of registry; length; type of ship (type A, B, B modified, etc); freeboards from deck line; positions of load lines; fresh water allowance; position of deck line; diagram of load lines assigned; date of initial survey; date periodical survey due each year; certifying statement; date certificate valid until; place and date of issue; signature of person issuing certificate (e.g. Secretary of classification society) with declaration that he is duly authorised by the UK Government. The certificate states "That the ship has been surveyed and that the freeboards have been assigned and load lines shown have been marked in accordance with the International Convention on Load Lines, 1966."

D04i.1e Record of Conditions of Assignment

* **Regulation 27 of the MS (Load Line) Regulations 1998** provides that **a Record of Particulars Relating to the Conditions of Assignment** must be provided on the ship in a form given in Schedule 3 of MSN 1752. The Record is to be furnished by the Assigning Authority and **kept on board** at all times.
* The title of the document is usually abbreviated to "**Record of Conditions of Assignment**". The MCA form of the document bears the code "FRE 5", and MCA surveyors and examiners will sometimes refer to "the **FRE 5**".
* The Record of Conditions of Assignment **records the characteristics and details of the fittings, appliances and arrangements approved for the ship** and **contains**:
    * ship's name; POR; nationality; ON or call sign; builder; yard number; date of build/conversion; freeboards assigned as a ship of Type ....; classification; date and place of initial survey;
    * sketches of side profile, superstructure deck and freeboard deck (with note stating that a plan of suitable size may be attached instead of sketches) to show disposition of superstructures, trunks, deckhouses, machinery casings, extent of bulwarks, guard rails and wood sheathing on exposed deck, hatchways, gangways and other means of protection for crew, cargo ports, bow and stern doors, side scuttles, scuppers, ventilators, air pipes, companionways and other items that would affect seaworthiness.
    * **tabular reports** of:
        * doorways in superstructures, exposed machinery casings and deckhouses; protected openings in freeboard and superstructure decks;
        * hatchways at Positions 1 and 2 closed by portable covers and secured weathertight by tarpaulins and battening devices;
        * hatchways at Positions 1 and 2 closed by weathertight covers of steel (or other equivalent material) fitted with gaskets and clamping devices;

---

[83] Where the HSSC has been implemented, the expiry date of the ILLC should be the same as that on the SOLAS Certificates and the IOPP Certificate.

- machinery space openings and miscellaneous openings in freeboard and superstructure decks;
- ventilators on freeboard and superstructure decks (i.e. in Position 1 and Position 2);
- air pipes on freeboard and superstructure decks;
- cargo ports and similar openings;
- scuppers, inlets and discharges;
- side scuttles;
- freeing ports;
- protection of crew;
- timber deck cargo fittings; and
- other special features.

* The Record of Conditions of Assignment is checked by the Assigning Authority's surveyor at each annual load line survey. In preparation for a forthcoming survey, it can serve as a useful "mate's checklist" of all items to be checked for condition.

D04i.1f Load Line Exemption Certificate

* **Regulation 5(1) of the Load Line Regulations** provides that **conditional exemption** from the requirements of the Regulations may be granted to:
  - any ship which embodies **features of a novel kind** if the development of those features and their incorporation in ships engaged on international voyages might be seriously impeded if the ship had to comply with all the requirements of the Regulations;
  - any ship plying on **international voyages between near neighbouring ports** if, in the MCA's opinion the **sheltered nature and condition of the voyages** makes it unreasonable or impracticable to apply the Regulations, or the MCA is satisfied that the Government of the other country (or countries) concurs in that opinion.
* Where a UK ship **does not normally ply on international voyages** but is, in exceptional circumstances, required to undertake **a single international voyage**, the MCA may **conditionally exempt** the ship while engaged on that voyage (regulation 5(3)).
* Ships exempted under regulation 5(1) or (3) must be issued with an **International Load Line Exemption Certificate** (regulation 12(1)).
* The MCA may **conditionally exempt** from the Regulations:
  a ship which is **not a Convention-size ship**; or
  any other ship which does not ply on international voyages (regulation 5(2)).
* A **ship exempted under regulation 5(2)** must be issued with a **United Kingdom Load Line Exemption Certificate** (regulation 12(2)).
* Regulation 12(3) provides that, except in so far as the nature or terms of any such exemption require to the contrary:
  - the exempted ship **must be assigned freeboards** in accordance with regulation 7;
  - the ship is to be **subject to surveys** in accordance with regulation 8; and
  - **regulations 9 to 11 will apply** in relation to the Load Line Exemption Certificate as they apply in relation to Load Line Certificates,
  - subject to the substitution, for references in the Regulations, to an Assigning Authority, of references to the Secretary of State (meaning in practice that the **MCA** assumes the usual functions of an Assigning Authority).
* Where a Load Line Exemption Certificate is issued in respect of a UK ship, the owner and **master** must ensure that it is kept legible and **posted up** in some conspicuous place on board (regulation 13(1)).

D04i.2 Subdivision load lines

* **SOLAS chapter II-1, regulation 13** (Assigning, marking and recording of subdivision load lines for passenger ships) provides that in order that the required degree of subdivision will be maintained, **a load line corresponding to the approved subdivision draught** will be assigned and marked on a passenger ship's sides. A ship having spaces specially adapted for the accommodation of passengers and the carriage of cargo alternatively may, if the owners desire, have **one or more additional load lines** assigned and marked to correspond with the subdivision draughts which the Administration may approve for the alternative service conditions.
* **Regulation II-1/13** further provides that:
  - the subdivision load lines assigned and marked must be **recorded in the Passenger Ship Safety Certificate**, and will be distinguished by the notation **C.1** for the principal passenger condition, and **C.2, C.3**, etc., for the alternative conditions;

- the freeboard corresponding to each of these conditions will be measured at the same position and from the same deck line as the freeboards determined in accordance with the International Convention on Load Lines in force;

- the freeboard corresponding to each approved subdivision load line and the conditions of service for which it is approved, will be clearly indicated on the Passenger Ship Safety Certificate;

- in no case will any subdivision load line mark be placed above the deepest load line in salt water as determined by the strength of the ship or the International Convention on Load Lines in force;

- whatever may be the position of the subdivision load line marks, a ship may never be loaded so as to submerge the load line mark appropriate to the season and locality as determined in accordance with the International Convention on Load Lines in force;

- **a ship may never be so loaded that** when it is in salt water the subdivision load line mark appropriate to the particular voyage and condition of service is submerged.

* The SOLAS requirements above are implemented in the UK by **regulation 39 of the MS (Passenger Ship Construction: Ships of Classes I, II and II(A)) Regulations 1998** (SI 1998/2514), which provides that every ship to which the Regulations apply will be marked on its side amidships with the subdivision load lines assigned to it in accordance with **Schedule 5 to MSN 1698**. In respect of **domestic (i.e. non-SOLAS) passenger ships**, equivalent requirements for subdivision load lines are made in regulation 36 of the MS (Passenger Ship Construction: Ships of Classes III to VI(A)) Regulations 1998 (SI 1998/2515), which requires compliance with Schedule 5 to **MSN 1699**.

* **Schedule 5 to MSN 1698** details the marking requirements for subdivision load lines, and provides that they will be identified with the letter "C", and, in ships of Classes I and II, with consecutive numbers beginning from the deepest subdivision load line, which will be marked "**C1**".

* In ships of Class II(A):
  - if there is only one subdivision load line, it will be identified with the letter "**C**"; and
  - if there is more than one subdivision load line, the subdivision load lines will be identified with the letter "**C**" and with consecutive letters beginning from the deepest subdivision load line which will be marked "**CA**".

* **Regulation 7(2) of the MS (Load Line) Regulations 1998** (SI 1998/2241) provides that where a passenger ship is marked with subdivision load lines and the lowest of those lines is lower than the line which is the "appropriate load line" then that subdivision load line is to have effect **as if it is the appropriate load line** for the purposes of the Regulations.

D04i.3 Greater-than-minimum freeboards and "All Seasons" load lines

* **Regulation 30(1) of the MS (Load Line) Regulations 1998** (SI 1998/2241) provides that a freeboard determined in accordance with regulation 29 is the **minimum freeboard** that may be assigned to the ship. (Regulation 29(1) provides that, except where greater than minimum freeboards are assigned, the freeboards assigned to a new ship must be determined in accordance with the provisions of **Schedule 3 in MSN 1752**.)

* Under regulation 30(2)(a), the Assigning Authority may assign **freeboards which exceed the minimum freeboards** by such an amount as it may determine, i.e. "**greater-than-minimum freeboards**". This does not apply to timber freeboards, however, and regulation 30(2)(b) **prohibits the assignment of timber freeboards** to a ship with greater-than-minimum freeboards.

* Under regulation 30(3), **where a greater-than-minimum freeboard is assigned** and the load line appropriate to that freeboard corresponds to, or is lower than, the position at which the lowest of the load lines appropriate to minimum freeboards would be marked then:
  - only load lines appropriate to the greater than minimum **Summer** freeboard and **Fresh Water** freeboard may be marked on the sides of the ship (regulation 30(3)(a));
  - the load line appropriate to the greater than minimum Summer freeboard will be known as the "**All Seasons load line**" and will consist of the **horizontal line intersecting the load line mark** (regulation 30(3)(b));
  - the **vertical line** described in regulation 18 will be **omitted** (regulation 30(3)(c)); and
  - subject to the provisions of regulation 30(3)(c), the **Fresh Water load line** will be as described in regulation 18(1) and be marked accordingly (i.e. it will extend abaft the vertical line, and be marked "F") (regulation 30(3)(d)).

* **Ships to which greater-than-minimum freeboards are commonly assig**ned are those types, e.g. **car carriers, LNG carriers and large container ships**, which, when loaded to capacity, do not attain the maximum draught or minimum freeboard which would be appropriate for a ship of the same physical size and assigned minimum freeboards. The owners of such ships will normally wish to benefit from the cost savings afforded by the **lower net tonnage** achieved by having a smaller moulded draught, as explained below. (Light dues in the UK and some other countries, berth charges in many ports, and certain canal dues are based on net tonnage.)

* The formula for deriving net tonnage is prescribed in regulation 7 of the MS (Tonnage) Regulations 1997 (SI 1997/1510 and contains the factor **4d/3D**, where "**d**" is the moulded draught amidships in metres and "D" is the moulded depth amidships in metres. Regulation 2(1) defines "moulded draught", for ship assigned load lines in accordance with the Load Line Regulations, as "the draught corresponding to the Summer Load Line (other than timber load lines)". Since a ship assigned greater-than-minimum freeboards will have a **smaller Summer draught** than she would have had had she been assigned minimum freeboards, there is a reduction in the value of "d", which results in a **lower net tonnage**.

* An **additional benefit** is that, if the freeboard can be measured from a "virtual deck" of at least one superstructure height below the freeboard deck, then items situated on the freeboard deck (the upper deck in most ships) aft of the forward quarter-length can be considered to be in Position 2 (i.e. as if that deck were a superstructure deck). This allows a reduction in the heights of door sills, hatchway coamings, ventilators, air pipes, etc., and a reduction in scantlings of hatch covers, freeing arrangements, means for protection of crew and windows and side scuttles on the actual freeboard deck, allowing savings in building costs.

D04i.4 Multiple load lines

* **Some tankers and bulk carriers** regularly use cargo terminals at which **maximum deadweight restrictions** are imposed by terminal operators, usually because of loading berth water depth limitations. Whilst it would be a simple matter for ships' officers to refer to hydrostatic data in order to determine the limiting draught for any given maximum deadweight, owners of these ships commonly apply for permission from the flag State Administration to have marked on the ships, for use at such terminals, **additional sets of load lines**, and for the issue of **corresponding Load Line Certificates** for use with the additional load lines.

* Several flag State Administrations, including Bahamas, Liberia, Marshall Islands and Panama, permit the use of multiple load lines and additional Load Line Certificates, subject to their approval of the owner's stated reasons for having them, and subject to certain conditions being complied with. Under some flags the number of sets of additional load lines is limited to five. **Conditions imposed** vary in detail but are in the main similar to those set by the **Bahamas** Administration, which are as follows.

- The ship must comply fully with all requirements appropriate for a ship of maximum deadweight for which minimum freeboards could be assigned.
- There must be no reduction in safety standards when sailing at a reduced deadweight.
- Only one set of load line marks should be on display at any time, and the other sets should be effectively obliterated with paint.
- The master must ensure that, with a class surveyor in attendance, the correct set of marks are displayed together with the corresponding Load Line Certificate, and that the other set of marks are properly obliterated and the other Load Line Certificates are in safekeeping and not on display.
- The master is to make an entry in the Official Log Book on every occasion when the load line marks are changed.
- The master is to ensure that all marks are verified and that their corresponding Load Line Certificates are endorsed at each annual survey of the load line inspection.

* The **Panama** Administration additionally requires that the loading/trim and stability booklet should contain annexes or supplements on the alternate load line conditions.

D04i.5 Timber load lines

* Where a ship is **assigned timber freeboards** in accordance with MSN 1752, is **marked with timber load lines** in accordance with regulation 19(1) of the MS (Load Line) Regulations 1998 (SI 1998/2241), and is **carrying a timber deck cargo in accordance with the special requirements** set out in MSN 1752, she may take advantage of the reduced minimum freeboard permitted to such ships[84].

* **Special requirements applicable to ships assigned timber freeboards** are contained in Part IV of Schedule 2 (Conditions of assignment) of **MSN 1752**. This details requirements for superstructures; double bottom tanks; bulwarks; guard rails and stanchions; siting, distribution and stowage of deck cargo; securing of deck cargo; maximum height of timber deck cargo; access; uprights; stowage of timber deck cargo in relation to superstructures; and securing of timber deck cargo.

* **Requirements for timber freeboards** are contained in Part II of Schedule 4 (Freeboards) of **MSN 1752**. This details requirements for Summer Timber freeboard and Other Timber freeboards.

---

[84] The "block stow" of a timber deck cargo carried as required by the Regulations is assumed to enhance the reserve buoyancy of the ship, thus permitting a reduction in minimum freeboard.

* Regulation 19(1) of the MS (Load Line) Regulations 1998 (SI 1998/2241) sets out the **dimensions, positions and marks of timber load lines**. These must consist of horizontal lines of the dimensions specified in regulation 18(1), extending abaft or forward of a vertical line 25 millimetres in width and marked 540 millimetres abaft the centre of the ring of the load line mark and at right angles to that line. Individual timber load lines must be as follows:
  * the **Summer Timber** load line, which must extend abaft the said vertical line and be marked **LS**;
  * the **Winter Timber** load line, which must extend abaft the vertical line and be marked **LW**;
  * the **Winter North Atlantic Timber** load line, which must extend abaft the vertical line and be marked **LWNA**;
  * the **Tropical Timber** load line, which must extend abaft of the vertical line and be marked **LT**;
  * the **Fresh Water Timber** load line, which must extend forward of the vertical line and be marked **LF**; and
  * the **Tropical Fresh Water Timber** load line, which must extend forward of the vertical line and be marked **LTF**.
* The maximum depth to which a ship may be loaded in relation to a Timber load line is the depth indicated by the upper edge of the appropriate Timber load line (regulation 19(2)).
* Timber freeboards may not be assigned to a ship to which greater than minimum freeboards have been assigned (regulation 30(1)(b)).
* A ship carrying a **timber deck cargo** must comply with the **Carriage of Cargoes Regulations** (see F07g) and must carry a copy of the **IMO Code of Safe Practice for Ships Carrying Timber Deck Cargoes** (TDC Code) (see A03c.5 and F07g.1b).

D04j ISM CODE SHIP AUDITS AND DOCUMENTATION

* For notes on the requirements of **SOLAS Chapter IX** and the **ISM Code**, see C04b. For a table showing the **contents of the revised ISM Code**, see C04b.3. For notes on the **MS (International Safety Management (ISM) Code) Regulations 1998** (SI 1998/1561), see D03a.1.
* Under chapter 13 of the Code, companies and ships are subject to **periodical verification** (which is accomplished by means of **audit**) prior to issue of **certificates** to show compliance with the Code. Regulation 9 of the ISM Code Regulations (see D03a.1f) gives effect in part to Chapter 13 of the Code.
* Chapter 14 of the Code provides for **interim certification** in certain circumstances (see C04b). Regulation 10 of the ISM Code Regulations (see D03a.1g) gives effect to Chapter 14 of the Code.

D04k LIFE-SAVING APPLIANCES: MAINTENANCE, TESTS, INSPECTIONS AND DOCUMENTATION

D04k.1 Life-saving Appliances Regulations

* The requirements for the provision of life-saving appliances (LSA) on UK ships are prescribed in two sets of MS regulations:
  * The **MS (Life-saving Appliances for Passenger Ships of Classes III to VI(A) Regulations 1999** (SI 1999/2723), also known as the "**Small Passenger Ship Regulations**"; and
  * The **MS (Life-Saving Appliances for Ships Other Than Ships of Classes III to VI(A)) Regulations 1999** (SI 1999/2721), also known as the "**Other Ships Regulations**".

D04k.1a "Other Ships Regulations"

* The **MS (Life-Saving Appliances for Ships Other Than Ships of Classes III to VI(A)) Regulations 1999** (SI 1999/2721) (the "**Other Ships Regulations**") -
  - **give effect** in the UK to part of **SOLAS chapter III** (Life-saving appliances and arrangements).
  - **revoke and replace** the MS (Life-Saving Appliances) Regulations 1980 and the MS (Life-Saving Appliances) Regulations 1986, and their amendments.
  - **prescribe** the **numbers of boats, rafts and other LSA items** to be provided in ships of **all Classes except III, IV, V, VI and VI(A)**.
  - **are amended** by the MS (Life-Saving Appliances for Passenger Ships of Classes III to VI(A)) (Amendment) Regulations 2000 (SI 2000/2558), which mainly correct various defects in the principal Regulations[85].

---

[85] As well as correcting some mistaken cross-references and making some clarifications, the 2000 Amendment Regulations make some changes of substance. Substitute regulations are made concerning provision of helicopter pick-up or landing areas on Class I, II and II(A) ships.

- **are amended by** the **MS (Life-Saving Appliances) (Amendment) Regulations 2001** (SI 2001/2642), which implement recommendation 27.38 of the Thames Safety Inquiry Interim Report. (This recommendation included a statement that the life-saving appliances on board *all ships* should comply with the standards required by the MS (Life-Saving Appliances for Passenger Ships of Classes III to VI(A)) Regulations 1999 and associated Merchant Shipping Notices, rather than the 1980 Regulations.) **MGN 176** promulgated the Amendment Regulations.
- **consist of** five Parts, three of which lay down the LSA requirements ships of different ages, as shown in the table below.
- **contain** many provisions requiring the carriage of life-saving appliances complying with the requirements of a particular Schedule, meaning one of the Schedules in either **MSN 1676** or **MSN 1677**, depending on the applicable Part of the Regulations, as shown in the following table[86].

-

Date of construction of ship	Applicable part of Regulations	Applicable MSN
Before 1 July 1986	Part II	MSN 1677
On or after 1 July 1986 but before 1 July 1998	Part III	MSN 1676
On or after 1 July 1998	Part IV	MSN 1676

* **MSN 1676**, which forms an integral part of the Regulations, contains the **technical specifications** of the LSA items prescribed in the Regulations, but does not list the actual provision of appliances (e.g. numbers of boats, rafts, etc. to be carried).

* **Part II** of the Regulations prescribes the LSA requirements for ships **constructed before 1 July 1986**. **Regulations in Part II** are as shown in the following table.

Regulation	Classes of ship covered by the regulation
Regulation 7	Ships of Class I
Regulation 8	Ships of Class II
Regulation 9	Ships of Class II(A) (regulation 9 provides that regulation 8 will apply to Class II(A) ships)
Regulation 10	Ships of Class VII (and, by virtue of regulation 13, Class VIII)
Regulation 11	Ships of Class VII(A)
Regulation 12	Ships of Class VII(T) (and, by virtue of regulation 14, Class VIII(T))
Regulation 15	Ships of Class VIII(A)
Regulation 16	Ships of Class VIII(A)(T)
Regulation 17	Ships of Class IX
Regulation 18	Ships of Class IX(A)
Regulation 19	Ships of Class IX(A)(T)
Regulation 20	Ships of Class XI[87]
Regulation 21	Ships of Class XII

* **MSN 1677** contains 12 schedules which detail the **technical requirements** of the regulations in **Part II**.

* **Part III** of the Regulations prescribes the LSA requirements for ships **constructed on or after 1 July 1986 and before 1 July 1998**. **Regulations in Part III** are as shown in the following table.

Regulation	Classes of ship covered by the regulation
Regulation 42	Ships of Class I
Regulation 43	Ships of Classes II and II(A)
Regulation 44	Ships of Classes VII, VIII, VIII(A) and IX
Regulation 45	Ships of Classes VII(T), VIII(T) and VIII(A)(T)
Regulation 46	Ships of Classes IX(A) and IX(A)(T)
Regulation 47	Ships of Class XI
Regulation 48	Ships of Class XII

* **Part IV** of the Regulations prescribes the LSA requirements for ships **constructed on or after 1 July 1998**. **Regulations in Part IV** are as shown in the following table.

Regulation	Classes of ship covered by the regulation
Regulation 63	Ships of Class I
Regulation 64	Ships of Classes II and II(A)
Regulation 65	Ships of Classes VII, VIII, VIII(A) and IX
Regulation 66	Ships of Classes VII(T), VIII(T) and VIII(A)(T)
Regulation 67	Ships of Classes IX(A) and IX(A)(T)
Regulation 68	Ships of Class XI
Regulation 69	Ships of Class XII

---

[86] The relevant MSN containing the numbered Schedules referred to in a particular Part of the Regulations is generally indicated in a regulation headed 'Interpretation' at the beginning of the Part.
[87] The SI erroneously lists Class IX against Regulation 20.

D04k.1b "Small Passenger Ship Regulations"

* The MS (Life-Saving Appliances for Passenger Ships of Classes III to VI(A)) Regulations 1999 (SI 1999/2723) (which are sometimes known as the "Small Passenger Ship Regulations") -
- **prescribe** the **numbers of boats, rafts and other life-saving appliances** to be provided in ships of **Classes III, IV, V, VI and VI(A).** (Technical specifications of these appliances are found in the LSA Code.)
- **consist** of five Parts, as follows: **Part I.** Preliminary; **Part II.** Ships of Classes III to VI(A); **Part III.** General requirements; **Part IV.** Stowage and handling; **Part V.** Miscellaneous provisions.
- **are amended** by the MS (Life-Saving Appliances) (Amendment) Regulations 2001 (SI 2001/2642) [88].
- **contain** many provisions requiring the carriage of life-saving appliances complying with the requirements of a particular **Schedule**, meaning one of the Schedules in **MSN 1676** as amended by **MSN 1757**.
- **contain**, in regulation 3, the **classification of ships** of Classes III, IV, V, VI and VI(A) (see D04c.2).
- **apply** to ships when operating as passenger ships of **Classes III, IV, V, VI and VI(A)** on voyages, other than international voyages, **wholly or partly within UK waters** (regulation 4(1)).

D04k.2 Operational readiness, maintenance, inspections and servicing of LSA

* **Regulation 84 of the "Other Ships Regulations"** (SI 1999/2721) (referred to below as "OSR") makes the following provisions in respect of ships other than those of Classes III to VI(A). Most of the requirements are mirrored in relation to passenger ships of Classes III to VI(A) by **regulation 11 of the "Small Ships Regulations"** (SI 1999/2723) (referred to below as "SPSR").

* All life-saving appliances must be **in working order** and **ready for immediate use** before any ship commences a voyage and at all times during the voyage (regulation 84(1) OSR; regulation 11(1) SPSR).

* As far as practicable, **maintenance** of life-saving appliances must be carried out in accordance with the **instructions for on-board maintenance**, or in accordance with a **shipboard planned maintenance programme** which includes the requirements of Schedule 14, Part 2 of MSN 1676 (regulation 84(2) OSR; regulation 11(2) SPSR).

* **Falls** used in launching must be turned end for end at intervals of not more than 30 months and must be renewed when necessary due to deterioration or at intervals of not more than 5 years, whichever is earlier. Stainless steel falls, however, need not be renewed within the lifetime recommended by the manufacturer or supplier if, on inspection, there are no signs of mechanical damage or other defects (regulation 84(3)(a) OSR). (Regulation 11(3) SPSR requires only that falls used in launching must be turned end-for-end at "regular intervals".)

* The MCA may accept, **in lieu of "end for ending"**, periodic inspection of falls and their renewal, whenever necessary, due to deterioration, or at intervals of not more than 4 years, whichever one is earlier (regulation 84(3)(b) OSR; no equivalent provision in SPSR.)

* **Spares and repair equipment** must be provided for life-saving appliances and for any of their components which are subject to excessive wear or consumption and which need to be replaced regularly (regulation 84(4) OSR; no equivalent provision in SPSR).

* The following **tests** and **inspections** must be carried out **weekly**:
- all survival craft, rescue boats, inflated boats, Class C boats and launching appliances must be **visually inspected** to ensure that they are ready for use (regulation 84(5)(a) OSR and regulation 11(4)(a) SPSR);
- if practicable all **engines** in lifeboats and other boats must be run ahead and astern (regulation 84(5)(b) OSR; regulation 11(4)(b) SPSR);
- the **general emergency alarm system** must be tested (regulation 84(5)(c) OSR; regulation 11(4)(c) SPSR (where fitted in Class III to VI(A) ships)); and
- any **public address system** fitted must be tested (regulation 84(5)(d) OSR only).

* **Inspection** of the life-saving appliances, including lifeboat equipment, must be carried out **monthly** using the check list referred to in Schedule 14, Part 2 of MSN 1676 (regulation 84(6) OSR). In ships of Classes III to VI(A), the inspection must be carried out using the instructions for on-board maintenance referred to in regulation 11(2) SPSR.

* Every **inflatable liferaft, inflated and rigid inflated rescue boat, inflated boat, inflatable lifejacket** and **hydrostatic release unit** must be **serviced** at a service station accepted by the MCA, at intervals not exceeding **12 months** provided that in any case where this is impracticable, such interval may be **extended** by a period not exceeding 5 months with the consent of the MCA on application to MCA, Southampton (regulation 84(7) OSR).

---

[88] The Amendment Regulations implement various recommendations of Lord Justice Clark's report on the Thames Safety Inquiry. All "small passenger ships" must carry LSA meeting the standards of the principal Regulations, rather than being allowed to continue to use LSA approved in accordance with earlier Regulations. The principal Regulations are amended to permit the granting of exemptions only where LSA meets the standards of the principal Regulations. Under regulation 4 certain Class V ships must carry emergency communications equipment which can make contact with the emergency services for the area in which the ship is operating. (In the case of ships operating on some inland waters, it may be appropriate to contact the police by telephone rather than the coastguard by VHF radio.) Regulation 4 also applies the requirements of regulation 7(6) and (7) to Class V ships operating within Category A and B waters. Regulation 5 provides for ships of Classes IV, V, VI and VI(A) to broadcast emergency alarms over a suitable public address system rather than a general emergency alarm system.

(Following such a service a **Certificate of Service and Testing** should be issued, which should be carried on board until the next service of the item.) In ships of **Classes III to VI(A)**, every inflated boat, inflated rescue boat, rigid inflated rescue boat, inflatable liferaft, open reversible liferaft, inflatable lifejacket and hydrostatic release unit must be serviced at intervals not exceeding 12 months and at a service station approved by the MCA, except disposable hydrostatic release units which have been approved for a service life of 2 years (regulation 11(7) SPSR).

* In addition to or in conjunction with the servicing intervals of **marine evacuation systems** (MES) required by regulation 84(7), each MES must be **deployed** from the ship on rotational basis at **intervals to be agreed** by the MCA which may not be longer than at least once every **6 years** (regulation 84(8) OSR only).

* **Emergency repairs** to inflated rescue boats and inflated boats may be carried out **on board** ship but **permanent** repairs must be effected at an accepted service station, as soon as practicable (regulation 84(9) OSR only).

* **MGN 182** contains guidance on servicing requirements for inflatable liferafts, inflatable boats, rescue boats, fast rescue boats (RIBs), inflatable lifejackets and hydrostatic release units.

D04k.3 Testing of lifeboat and rescue boat launching appliances

* **Regulation 84(10)(a) of the "Other Ships Regulations"** (SI 1999/2721) and **regulation 11(6) of the "Small Passenger Ships Regulations"** (SI 1999/2723) provides that **launching appliances**, including winches and brakes, lifeboat disengaging gears, liferaft automatic release hooks and rescue boat release gears must be serviced and tested at **regular intervals**. At least once every **5 years** the rescue boats and lifeboats must be turned out and lowered when loaded with weights to simulate 1.1 times the total mass of the lifeboat when loaded with its full complement of persons and equipment. During this test the winch brake must be dynamically tested in accordance with **MSN 1676**, Schedule 6, Part 1, paragraph 5.2.2.

* **Regulation 84(1)(b)** of the "Other Ships Regulations" provides that **lifeboat on-load release gear** must be serviced and tested at **regular intervals**. At least once every **5 years** the release gear must be operationally tested under a load of 1.1 times the total mass of the lifeboat when loaded with its full complement of persons and equipment. **M.1655** gives guidance on test procedures. There is no equivalent provision in the Small Passenger Ships Regulations.

D04k.4 LSA Code

* The **International Life-Saving Appliance (LSA) Code** was adopted by the IMO Maritime Safety Committee (MSC) in June 1996 by Resolution MSC.48(66) to provide **international standards** for life-saving appliances required by chapter III of SOLAS 1974. The Code was made **mandatory** under SOLAS by amendments to the Convention adopted by the MSC by Resolution MSC.47(66) and which entered into force on 1 July 1998.

* **Chapters** of the LSA Code are: **I** - General; **II** - Personal life-saving appliances; **III** - Visual signals; **IV** – Survival craft; **V** – Rescue boats; **VI** – Launching and embarkation appliances; **VII** – Other life-saving appliances.

* Each chapter of the Code details the **general requirements and technical specifications** required for the manufacture and operational capability of the relevant appliances; it does not prescribe numbers of the appliances to be carried on any ship (which are matters covered by the relevant Regulations).

D04k.5 Documentation required by Life-Saving Appliances Regulations

D04k.5a LSA documentation required by the "Other Ships Regulations".

* **Regulation 36(1) of the MS (Life-Saving Appliances for Ships Other Than Ships of Classes III to VI(A)) Regulations 1999** (SI 1999/2721) applies to ships of all classes other than those to which the "Small Passenger Ships Regulations" apply, and which carry one or more lifeboats, Class C boats, other boats or liferafts.

* **Regulation 36(2)** provides that all ships (other than those of Classes III to VI(A)) must have:
  * on or in the vicinity of survival craft and their launching controls, **posters or signs** illustrating the **purpose** of controls, the **procedures for operating the appliance** and giving relevant **operating instructions**;
  * in each crew messroom and recreation room or in each crew cabin, a **training manual** complying with the requirements of Schedule 14, Part 1 of MSN 1676;
  * as far as practicable, **instructions** complying with the requirements of Schedule 14, Part 2 of MSN 1676 **for on-board maintenance of LSA**, or (alternatively) a **shipboard planned maintenance programme** which includes the maintenance of LSA.

* Regulation 36(3)(b) provides that in **ships of under 500gt** at least one **training manual** shall be provided appropriate to the life-saving appliances carried and to the type and size of ship on which it is provided.
* Ships of Classes I, II, II(A), VII, VII(A), VII(T), VIII, VIII(T), VIII(A), VIII(A)(T), IX and XI, and ships of Class XII which proceed to sea, must carry on the bridge a copy of the table "**Life-Saving Signals and Rescue Methods, SOLAS No.1**" published by the DfT (regulation 38).

D04k.5b LSA documentation required by the "Small Passenger Ships Regulations"

* **Under the MS (Life-Saving Appliances for Passenger Ships of Classes III to VI(A)) Regulations 1999** (SI 1999/2723) the carriage of the following is required on ships of Classes III, IV, V, VI and VI(A):
  * **posters or signs** on or in the vicinity of lifeboats, liferafts or their launching arrangements to illustrate the purpose of the controls and the procedures for launching and bowsing-in the lifeboats and liferafts (except on ships of Class V operating in Category A waters) (regulation 5(b));
  * a **training manual** (regulation 5(c));
  * **instructions** for on-board maintenance of LSA or a shipboard **planned maintenance programme** which includes the maintenance of LSA (regulation 5(d)); and
  * on the bridge, a copy of the table "**Life-Saving Signals and Rescue Methods, SOLAS No.1**" published by the DfT (regulation 5(10)(e)).

D04l FIRE PROTECTION, EQUIPMENT AND DOCUMENTATION

* Statutory requirements relating to fire protection arrangements and fire-fighting equipment of UK ships are contained in:
  * the **MS (Fire Protection: Large Ships) Regulations 1998** (SI 1998/1012) (also known as the "**Large Ships Regulations**"); and
  * the **MS (Fire Protection: Small Ships) Regulations 1998** (SI 1998/1011) (also known as the "**Small Ships Regulations**").
* These Regulations give effect (in part) in the UK to the requirements of **SOLAS Chapter II-2**.
* The **MS (Fire Protection) (Amendment) Regulations 1999** (SI 1999/992) amend both sets of Regulations to bring into effect the December 1996 amendments to SOLAS Chapter II-2. The main amendment is the mandatory application of internationally agreed tests specified in the IMO publication **Fire Test Procedures Code**. Both the Large Ships Regulations and the Small Ships Regulations are amended so that in respect of domestic (non-SOLAS) shipping there is consistency with the SOLAS requirements.

D04l.1 The Fire Protection: Large Ships Regulations

* The **MS (Fire Protection: Large Ships) Regulations 1998 (SI 1998/1012) apply** (under regulation 7(a)(i), and subject to regulations 7(b), 7(c) and 8(b)) to:
* UK ships of Classes I, II, Class II(A) of 21.34m in length or over, and Classes VII, VII(A), VII(T), VIII, VIII(A), VIII(T), VIII(A)(T), IX, IX(A), IX(A)(T), XI and XII of 500gt or over, wherever they are;
* other such ships while they are within UK waters, when engaged on international voyages;
* other such ships when not engaged on international voyages, while they are in UK national waters; and
* where any requirement of the Regulations relates to ships constructed on or after a certain date, then, to the extent the MCA deems reasonable and practicable, the requirement will also apply in respect of any **major repairs, alterations and modifications** commenced on or after the date to ships constructed before that date.
* **The Regulations do not apply** to fishing vessels, high-speed craft to which the MS (High-Speed Craft) Regulations 1996 apply, non-UK troopships, non-UK ships which are not propelled by mechanical means, or a non-UK ship in the UK or UK territorial waters if she would not have been there but for stress of weather or any other circumstances that neither the master owner or charterer, if any, could have prevented. **The Regulations include** requirements which, in relation to "existing ships" (on the date of entry into force of the Regulations), were previously contained in the MS (Fire Appliances) Regulations 1980 (SI 1980/544), the MS (Passenger Ship Construction) Regulations 1980 (SI 1980/535), the MS (Cargo Ship Construction and Survey) Regulations 1981 (SI 1981/572), the MS (Fire Protection) Regulations 1984 (SI 1984/1218) and the MS (Fire Protection) (Ships built before 25th May 1980) Regulations 1985 (SI 1985/1218), all as amended.
* **The Regulations permit** (under regulation 8(a)) the granting by the MCA of **exemptions** from all or any of the provisions of the Regulations (as may be specified in the Exemption Certificate) for classes of cases or individual cases.

* **The Regulations are in 10 Parts**, as follows: Part **I**. Preliminary (regulations 1 and 2); Part **II**. Fire prevention and fire appliances - Passenger ships (regulations 3 to 15); Part **III**. Fire prevention and fire appliances - Ships other than passenger ships and tankers (regulations 16 to 28); Part **IV**. Fire prevention and fire appliances – Tankers (regulations 29 to 36); Part **V**. Fire prevention and fire Appliances – General (regulations 37 to 50); Part **VI**. Structural fire protection passenger Ships Classes I, II and Class II(A) of 21.34 metres in length or over (regulations 51 to 68); Part **VII**. Structural fire protection - Ships of Classes VII, VII(A), VIII, VIII(A), IX and IX(A); and tankers of Classes VII(T), VIII(T), VIII(A)(T) and IX(A)(T) of 500 tons or over except tankers to which part VIII applies (regulations 69 to 84); Part **VIII**. Structural fire protection –Tankers of Classes VII(T), VIII(T), VIII(A)(T) and IX(A)(T) of 500 tons or over (regulations 85 to 101); Part **IX**. Special requirements for ships carrying dangerous goods (regulations 102 and 103); Part **X**. Equivalents, penalties and detention (regulations 104 to 106).
* Numerous regulations require the fitting of equipment complying with a particular **Schedule** in a Merchant Shipping Notice. The relevant MSNs and Schedules contained in each are as shown in the following table.

M Notice	M Notice title and issue date	Schedules in MSN
MSN 1665	MS (Fire Protection) Regulations 1998: Fire fighting equipment. Mar 1998	Schedule 1: International shore connection Schedule 2: Non-portable foam fire extinguishers Schedule 3: Non-portable carbon dioxide fire extinguishers Schedule 4: Non-portable dry powder fire extinguishers Schedule 5: Breathing apparatus Schedule 6: Portable foam-applicator units Schedule 7: Fire pumps and fire main Schedule 8: Fire extinguishers
MSN 1666	MS (Fire Protection) Regulations 1998: Fixed fire detection, alarm and extinguishing systems. Mar 1998	Schedule 1: Automatic sprinkler, fire detection and fire alarm systems Schedule 2: Fixed pressure water-spraying systems for machinery spaces and cargo pump rooms Schedule 3: Fixed pressure water-spraying systems for cargo spaces Schedule 4: Fixed gas fire-extinguishing systems Schedule 5: Fixed fire detection and fire alarm systems Schedule 6: Sample extraction smoke detection systems Schedule 7: Fixed deck foam systems Schedule 8: Fixed high-expansion foam fire extinguishing systems in machinery spaces Schedule 9: Inert gas systems: standard requirements Schedule 10: Inert gas systems: alternative requirements for chemical tankers
MSN 1667	MS (Fire Protection) Regulations 1998: Passenger ships: Fire integrity of bulkheads, decks and ventilation duct. Mar 1998	Schedule 1: Fire integrity of bulkheads and decks: Ships of Classes I, II and II(A) carrying more than 36 passengers Schedule 2: Fire integrity of bulkheads and decks: Ships of Classes I, II and II(A) carrying not more than 36 passengers Schedule 3: Fire integrity of ventilation ducts: All ships of Classes I, II and II(A)
MSN 1668	MS (Fire Protection) Regulations 1998: Fire integrity of bulkheads, decks and ventilation ducting. Mar 1998	Schedule 1: Fire integrity of bulkheads and decks: Ships of Classes VII, VII(A), VIII, VIII(A), IX and IX(A) of 500 tons and over and tankers of Class VII(T), VIII(T), VIII(A)(T) and IX(A)(T) of 500 tons and over not carrying volatile cargoes Schedule 2: Fire integrity of bulkheads and decks: Tankers of Classes VII(T), VIII(T), VIII(A)(T) and IX(A)(T) of 500 tons and over carrying volatile cargoes Schedule 3: Fire integrity of ventilation ducts
MSN 1669	MS (Fire Protection) Regulations 1998: Special fire safety measures for ships carrying dangerous goods. Mar 1998	Table 1: Application of the requirements to different modes of carriage of dangerous goods in ships and cargo spaces (replaced by Table 1 in the Annex to MSN 1733) Table 2: Application of the requirements to different classes of dangerous goods for ships and cargo spaces carrying solid dangerous goods in bulk (replaced by Table 2 in the Annex to MSN 1733) Table 3: Application of the requirements to different classes of dangerous goods except solid dangerous goods in bulk (replaced by Table 3 in the Annex to MSN 1733)
MSN 1670	MS (Fire Protection) Regulations 1998: Exemptions. Mar 1998	Schedule 1: Conditions for General Exemptions and provisions to be complied with, for ships constructed before 26 May 1965 Schedule 2: Structural fire protection for ships of Classes I, II and II(A) of 21.34m in length or over constructed before 25 May 1980 Schedule 3: Structural fire protection for certain tankers constructed between 25 May 1980 and 1 September 1984 Schedule 4: Structural fire protection for cargo ships of 500 tons or more built between 26 May 1965 and 1 September 1984, other than tankers to which Schedule 3 applies

D04I.2 The Fire Protection: Small Ships Regulations

* The **MS (Fire Protection: Small Ships) Regulations 1998** (SI 1998/1011) consolidate requirements in respect of ships of:
  * Class II(A) of less than 21.34 metres in length;

- Classes III to VI(A); and
- Classes VII to IX, XI and XII of under 500gt.

* The Regulations are in **8 Parts**, as follows: Part **I**. Preliminary (regulations 1 and 2); Part **II**. Fire prevention and fire appliances – Passenger ships (regulations 3 to 16); Part **III**. Fire prevention and fire appliances – Ships other than passenger ships and tankers (regulations 17 to 23); Part **IV**. Fire prevention and fire appliances – Tankers (regulations 24 to 29); Part **V**. Fire prevention and fire appliances – General (regulations 30 to 39); Part **VI**. Structural fire protection – Passenger ships (regulations 40 to 44); Part **VII**. Special requirements for ships carrying dangerous goods (regulation 45); Part **VIII**. Equivalents, exemptions, penalties and detention (regulations 46 to 49).
* Several regulations require the fitting of equipment complying with a particular **Schedule** in a Merchant Shipping Notice (MSN). The **relevant MSNs and Schedules** are as shown in the table in D04l.1.

D04l.3 SOLAS Chapter II-2 operational requirements

* **Amendments to SOLAS Chapter II-2**: Construction – fire protection, detection and equipment, which came into force on 1 July 2002, contain several requirements relating to operational readiness and maintenance, including requirements for the carriage of:
  - **maintenance plans** for fire protection systems and appliances;
  - **fire training manuals**;
  - **fire control plans** or booklets; and
  - **fire safety operational booklets**.
* **SOLAS regulation II-2/14** relates to **operational readiness and maintenance** and provides that maintenance, testing and inspections must be carried out based on IMO guidelines (2.2.1). The **maintenance plan** must be kept on board the ship and must be available for inspection whenever required by the Administration (2.2.2). The maintenance plan must include at least the following fire protection systems and fire-fighting systems and appliances, where installed: fire mains, fire pumps and hydrants, including hoses, nozzles and international shore connections; fixed fire detection and fire alarm systems; fixed fire-extinguishing systems and other fire-extinguishing appliances; automatic sprinkler, fire detection and fire alarm systems; ventilation systems, including fire and smoke dampers, fans and their controls; emergency shutdown of fuel supply; fire doors, including their controls; general emergency alarm systems; emergency escape breathing devices; portable fire extinguishers, including spare charges; and fire-fighter's outfits. The maintenance programme may be computer-based (2.2.4).
* **Ships carrying more than 36 passengers** must, in addition, develop a maintenance plan for low-location lighting and public address systems (regulation II-2/14.3).
* **Tankers** must, in addition, have a maintenance plan for inert gas systems, deck foam systems, fire safety arrangements in cargo pump-rooms, and flammable gas detectors (regulation II-2/14.4).
* **SOLAS regulation II-2/15** deals with **instruction, on-board training and drills**. **Regulation II-2/15.2.3** provides that a **fire training manual** must be provided in each crew mess room and recreation room or in each crew cabin (2.3.1). The training manual must be written in the working language of the ship (2.3.2). The manual, which may comprise several volumes, must contain the instructions and information required in paragraph 2.3.4 in easily understood terms and illustrated wherever possible (2.3.3). Any part of such information may be provided in the form of audio-visual aids in lieu of the manual. 2.3.4 provides that the training manual must explain in detail:
  - general fire safety practice and precautions related to the dangers of smoking, electrical hazards, flammable liquids and similar common shipboard hazards;
  - general instructions on fire-fighting activities and fire-fighting procedures, including procedures for notification of a fire and use of manually operated call points;
  - meanings of the ship's alarms;
  - operation and use of fire-fighting systems and appliances;
  - operation and use of fire doors;
  - operation and use of fire and smoke dampers; and
  - escape systems and appliances.
* **SOLAS regulation II-2/15.2.4** provides that **fire control plans** in the form of **general arrangement plans** must be permanently exhibited for the guidance of the ship's officers, showing clearly **for each deck** the control sections, the various fire sections enclosed by "A" class divisions, the sections enclosed by "B" class divisions together with particulars of the fire detection and fire alarm systems, the sprinkler installation, the fire-extinguishing appliances, means of access to different compartments, decks, etc., and the ventilating system, including particulars of the fan control positions, the position of dampers and identification numbers of the ventilating fans serving each section (2.4.1). **Alternatively**, at the discretion of the Administration, the aforementioned details may be set out in a **booklet**, a copy of which must be supplied to **each officer**, and one copy must at all times be available on board in an accessible position. Plans and booklets must be **kept up to date**; any alterations thereto shall be recorded as soon as practicable. Description in such plans and booklets must be in the language or languages required by the Administration. If the language is neither English nor French, a translation into one of those languages must be included. A **duplicate set of fire control plans or a booklet** containing such plans must be permanently stored in a

prominently marked **weathertight enclosure** outside the deckhouse for the assistance of shore-side fire-fighting personnel (2.4.2). In ships carrying more than 36 passengers, plans and booklets must provide information based on IMO Guidelines adopted under resolution A.756(18).

* **SOLAS regulation II-2/16.4** provides that **fire safety operational booklets** must be provided on board. Regulation II-2/16.5 provides that the booklet must contain the necessary **information and instructions** for the safe operation of the ship and cargo handling operations in relation to fire safety. The booklet must include information concerning the **crew's responsibilities** for the general fire safety of the ship while loading and discharging cargo and while under way. Necessary **fire safety precautions** for handling general cargoes must be explained. For ships carrying dangerous goods and flammable bulk cargoes, the booklet must also provide **reference** to the pertinent fire-fighting and emergency cargo handling instructions contained in the BC Code, the IBC Code, the IGC Code and the IMDG Code, as appropriate. The booklet must be provided in each crew mess room and recreation room or in each crew cabin (5.2.2). The booklet must be written in the working language of the ship (5.2.3) and may be combined with the training manuals required in regulation 15.2.3 (5.2.4).

* In tankers, the fire safety operational booklet must include provisions for preventing **fire spread to the cargo area** due to ignition of flammable vapours and include procedures of **cargo tank gas-purging and/or gas-freeing**.

* **SOLAS regulation II-2/18** contains special fire protection requirements for ships fitted with **special facilities for helicopters**. **Each helicopter facility** must have an **operations manual** including a description and a checklist of safety precautions, procedures and equipment requirements. The manual may be part of the ship's emergency response procedures.

D04m RADIO INSTALLATIONS, SURVEYS AND DOCUMENTATION

D04m.1 Radio Installations Regulations

* The **MS (Radio Installations) Regulations 1998** (SI 1998/2070) -
    - **revoke** and replace, with amendments, the MS (Radio Installations) Regulations 1992.
    - **give effect** to SOLAS Chapter IV including the 1988, 1992 and 1995 "GMDSS Amendments".
    - **apply** (under regulation 3(1)) to:
        * **sea-going UK ships** wherever they are **except** while they are in the Great Lakes of North America and their connecting and tributary waters as far east as the lower exit of the St Lambert Lock at Montreal in the Province of Quebec, Canada[89]; and
        * non-UK seagoing ships while in UK waters.
    - **do not apply** (under regulation 3(2)) to troopships not registered in the UK, ships not propelled by mechanical means, pleasure vessels, fishing vessels, cargo ships of less than 300gt, and craft to which the Merchant Shipping (High-Speed Craft) Regulations 1996 apply.
    - **contain** four Parts and seven Schedules. **Part I** (General) contains provisions dealing with Interpretation (regulation 2), Application (regulation 3), Ships and persons in distress (regulation 4), Equivalents and exemptions (regulation 5) and Performance standards (regulation 6). **Part II** contains the GMDSS ship requirements including the following regulations: 7. Interpretation of Part II; 8. Functional Requirements; 9. Installation, location and control of radio equipment; 10. Installation of a distress panel; 11. Radio equipment to be provided for all sea areas; 12. Additional radio equipment to be provided for area A1 ships; 13. Additional radio equipment to be provided for area A2 ships; 14. Additional radio equipment to be provided for area A3 ships; 15. Additional radio equipment to be provided for area A4 ships; 16. Radio watches; 17. Sources of energy; 18. Serviceability and maintenance requirements; 19. Radio personnel; 20. Radio records. **Part III** contains the requirements for non-GMDSS ships. **Part IV** contains penalty and defence provisions and powers to detain ships. **Schedule 1** details technical requirements for satellite EPIRBs. **Schedule 2** details equipment tests and reserve power checks, Radio log, Equipment tests and battery and reserve power checks, Additional knowledge and training requirements for radiotelephone operators and radio operators, and specimen R/T and W/T Radio logs.

* Ships to which the Regulations apply must, in general, comply with the requirements of Part II of the Regulations, i.e. the **GMDSS ship requirements** (regulation 3).

* Nothing in the Regulations will prohibit any ship, survival craft or person in distress from using **any means at their disposal** to attract attention, make known their position or obtain help (regulation 4).

* **Equivalents and exemptions** are permitted under regulation 5.

* Regulation 6 provides that equipment must conform to **performance standards** adopted by IMO and specified in **MSN 1714** as having been so adopted. It must also be **type-approved** by the MCA.

---

[89] SOLAS Chapter IV does not apply to ships to which SOLAS would otherwise apply while they are being navigated in the Great Lakes of North America and their connecting and tributary waters as far east as the lower exit of the St Lambert Lock at Montreal in the Province of Quebec, Canada.

D04m.2 The GMDSS

* SOLAS 74 was amended in 1988 for the **Global Maritime Distress and Safety System** (GMDSS), which was introduced in a rolling programme that commenced on 1 February 1992 and was completed on **1 February 1999**. **MGN 85** gives guidance on MCA policy for implementation of the GMDSS.
* The **GMDSS applies to** all non-passenger ships of 300gt or over on international voyages, and to all passenger ships (of any tonnage) on international voyages. (National regulations of SOLAS Party States may, as in the case in the UK, extend the application of the GMDSS to cover **vessels on domestic voyages.**)
* Equipment to be carried under GMDSS depends on area of operation and system in use. There are four **GMDSS sea areas**, which are arranged according to range of equipment/system in use as follows.
  * **Area A1** is an area within coverage of at least one VHF coast station in which continuous DSC alerting is available, i.e. approx. 20-30 miles, or line-of-sight, from coasts (but see note below).
  * **Area A2** excludes Area A1 but is within coverage of a shore-based MF coast station operating in the 2-3 MHz band in which continuous DSC alerting is available, i.e. approx. 100 miles
  * **Area A3** excludes Areas A1 and A2 but is within coverage of an INMARSAT geostationary satellite in which continuous alerting is available
  * **Area A4** excludes Areas A1, A2 and A3 but covers the remaining sea areas of the world, i.e. mainly the Polar regions.
* **Admiralty List of Radio Signals, Vol. 5** carries excellent written and diagrammatic descriptions of the GMDSS system, including maps of sea areas[90].
* For statutory requirements relating to **GMDSS equipment and its serviceability and maintenance** see also **M.1617**, **MSN 1690** and **MSN 1714**.

D04m.3 Radio and TV documents to be carried by UK ships

* **GMDSS-fitted ships** must carry the following documents:
  * **Ship Fixed Radio Licence** (see D04m.3a);
  * certificate(s) of the radio operator(s) (see E02b.9 and E02c.4a);
  * **GMDSS Radio Log** (see D05b.1);
  * **ITU List of Callsigns and Numerical Table of Identities of Stations used by the Maritime Mobile and Maritime Mobile-Satellite Services**;
  * **particulars of coast stations and land earth stations** participating in the GMDSS; a list of coast stations and land earth stations with which communications are likely to be established, showing watchkeeping hours rrequencies and charges; and a list of coast stations and land earth stations providing navigational and meteorological warnings and other urgent information for ships;
  * **ITU List of Ship Stations**;
  * **ITU Manual for use by the Maritime Mobile and Maritime Mobile-Satellite Services**; and
  * **Admiralty List of Radio Signals** (ALRS) (see D04m.3d).

D04m.3a Ship Fixed Radio Licence

* A **Ship Radio Licence** issued by the Radiocommunications Agency -
  - **must be obtained** before any radio apparatus may be installed or used on board a UK ship. **Guidance notes** are available on the RA website (see B06a).
  - **covers** the installation or use of marine radio equipment including Mobile Earth Station (MES) equipment, radar, low-powered on-board communications and EPIRBs for use on international marine frequencies.
  - **shows** in Clause 1 of the Validation Document:
    * name of ship;
    * callsign or other identification ("Call Sign");
    * public correspondence category;
    * Maritime Mobile Service Identity ("MMSI"), if any;
    * Selective Calling Number ("Selcall Number"), if any;
    * name and address of Licensee.
  - **shows** in Clause 2 of the Validation Document:
    * name of ship;

---

[90] As shown in ALRS Vol. 5, many coastal States around the world cannot yet obtain A1 status for their inshore sea areas since they do not provide full VHF coverage along the entire coast. Consequently, these waters, which were designed to be A1 sea areas, are having to operate as A2 areas

- type of transmitter equipment;
- transmitter output power;
- classes of emission; and
- frequency bands or assigned frequencies.
- **shows** in the associated Ship Radio Licence Clause Booklet the terms and limitations to which the installation and use of the equipment is subject.
- **permits** - subject to approval of the master - all members of the crew and passengers to install and use radio apparatus for the reception of programmes by sound sent by authorised stations for general reception. (A separate licence is required for the reception of TV programmes and portable "on-board" transceivers).
- **is valid** indefinitely subject to advance payment of an annual renewal fee.
- **may be revoked** by the RA, or have its terms altered at any time by the RA.
- **must be displayed**, where possible, adjacent to the radio equipment.
- **must be kept** in such a way that it can be produced on request for inspection by competent authorities in ports of call.

* A **Ship Radio (VHF) Licence** issued by the Radiocommunications Agency -
covers the installation or use of a marine VHF radio operating in the international marine VHF bands for a particular vessel;
covers radar and EPIRBs;
is required by **small craft**, but not by merchant ships.

D04m.3b Cards 1, 2 and 3

* Regulation 33(6) of the Radio Installations Regulations provides that a **card of instructions** in English giving a clear summary of the **radiotelephone distress, urgency and safety procedures** must be displayed at each radiotelephone operating position. This requirement is usually met in the form of three cards ("Cards 1, 2 and 3"), as follows:
- **Card 1** (Distress transmitting procedures) is for use only when immediate assistance is required and shows an example of an R/T "MAYDAY" call and message.
- **Card 2** (Reception of safety messages) contains a definition of the expressions "MAYDAY", "PAN PAN" and "SECURITÉ".
- **Card 3** (Radiotelephone procedures) is for use in case of language difficulties. It lists the Phonetic Alphabet and shows examples of its use in R/T messages.

D04m.3c TV Licence

* Under the Wireless Telegraphy Act 1949 (c.54), as amended, a ship registered in the UK, the Channel Islands or the Isle of Man must have a **TV Licence** if it receives UK television programme services, i.e. BBC1, BBC2, ITV, Channel 4, Channel 5, satellite, cable or any other satellite service programmes, controlled from within the UK.
* A cruise ship would be eligible for a "**hotel licence**" (details of which are explained on the TV Licensing website).
* Shipowners should obtain TV Licences from: TV Licensing, Barton House, Bristol BS98 1TL, England.
* **TV Licensing website**: www.tv-l.co.uk

D04m.3d Admiralty List of Radio Signals (ALRS)

is published by the UK Hydrographic Office (UKHO) and sold by Admiralty Chart Agents.
provides a comprehensive source of information on all aspects of maritime radio communications.
is published in seven volumes, as shown in the following table.

Vol.	Title	Contents	Revised
1	Coast Radio Stations (NP281) (Parts 1 & 2)	Global marine communications services; coast radio stations; medical advice by radio; radio quarantine reports from ships at sea; pollution reports by radio; ship reporting systems; piracy and armed robbery – reports; alien smuggling – reporting; general radio regulations (extracts from the ITU General Radio Regulations); international telephone/telex codes; numerical list of shore-based MMSI numbers; phonetic alphabet and figure code.	Annually
2	Radio Navigational Aids, Electronic Position Fixing Systems and Radio Time Signals (NP282)	Radiobeacons and radio direction-finding stations; diagrams relating to radiobeacons; radar beacons (racons and ramarks); standard times; legal time; radio time signals; electronic position fixing systems; index of call signs of stations transmitting time signals; index of stations transmitting time signals; index of Morse identification signals of radiobeacons and QTG stations; index of radiobeacons; index of radar beacons; International Morse Code and conventional signals.	Annually

3	Maritime Safety Information (NP283) (Parts 1 & 2)	Radio-facsimile; radio weather services and navigational warnings; glossary of terms used in storm warnings and weather bulletins; ships' weather reports (including list of Port Meteorological Offices); meteorological and oceanographic codes; ice reports; radio navigational warnings; GMDSS; NAVTEX including broadcast area diagrams; global marine meteorological services; tables; general radio regulations; index of radio stations.	Annually
4	Meteorological Observation Stations (NP284)	Meteorological observation stations: introduction and abbreviations; allocations of station numbers; index of geographical sections; diagram of Meteorological Observation Stations Block Numbers; diagram of World Meteorological Organization Regions with Block Numbers; Meteorological observation stations; fixed ship stations; Phonetic Alphabet and Figure Code; International Code of Signals.	-
5	Global Maritime Distress and Safety System (GMDSS) (NP285)	GMDSS; extracts from Rec. ITU-R M.541-8; communications systems for use in the global system; search and rescue radar transponder (SART); equipment carriage requirements – SOLAS; distress communications and false alerts; extracts from the ITU Radio Regulations 1998; the management of VHF; VHF DSC, list of coast stations for Sea Areas A1; MF DSC, list of coast stations for Sea Areas A2 and limits of sea areas diagrams; HF DSC, list of coast stations for Sea Areas A3 and A4; Inmarsat; COSPAS-SARSAT; Maritime Safety Information (MSI) under the GMDSS; SafetyNET; NAVTEX; distress, search and rescue; Appendix 1 – GMDSS Radio Log; index of stations and services; numerical list of shore based MMSI numbers; Phonetic Alphabet and Figure Code; International Code of Signals.	Annually
6	Pilot Services, Vessel Traffic Services and Port Operations (NP286) (Parts 1, 2, 3, 4, 5)	Pilot services, vessel traffic services and port operations: introduction; Stations: service details; table of transmitting frequencies in the 156-174 MHz band; Phonetic Alphabet and Figure Code; index of stations.	Annually
8	Satellite Navigation Systems (NP288)	Satellite Navigation Systems; horizontal datums on charts and satellite-derived positions notes; differential GPS (DGPS); diagrams for beacons transmitting Differential Satellite Position Fixing System Corrections; index of beacons transmitting DGPS Corrections.	Annually

* **For yachtsmen**, UKHO also publishes *Admiralty Maritime Communications* in two volumes covering: UK and the Mediterranean including the Açores and Islas Canarias (NP289); and Caribbean (NP290).

D04m.4 Delegation of radio survey and certification responsibilities

* For notes on **responsibility for carrying out surveys of radio equipment** under the MS (Survey and Certification) Regulations 1995, see D04f.2d.
* For notes on the **scope and purpose of cargo ship radio equipment surveys** required under the **Harmonised System of Survey and Certification**, see D04e.6.
* **Marconi Marine** has been contracted by the MCA to:
  * conduct the survey and certification of radio installations on UK-registered cargo ships in UK ports, and be the first point of contact for surveys carried out abroad;
  * conduct the survey and certification of radio installations on non-UK cargo ships in UK ports at the request of the flag State Administration;
  * conduct the survey of radio installations on UK-registered passenger ships and fishing vessels in UK ports, and be the first point of contact for surveys carried out abroad;
  * perform general inspections of radio installations on any UK-registered ship or fishing vessel in UK ports;
  * assist in Port State Control inspections of foreign ships in UK ports as required by the local Marine Office;
  * conduct the survey of radio installations of stand-by vessels under UK Stand-by Safety Vessel certification procedures.
* **MGN 206** contains details of the delegation of radio survey arrangements[91].
* Radio surveys can be booked on application to: Marconi Communications Ltd, Marconi House, Chelmsford, Essex CM1 1PL. Tel: 01245 275888. Fax: 01245 275500.
* An **initial survey** will be carried out by Marconi Marine regardless of the ship's location.
* A **renewal survey** will be carried out on a ship in the UK by Marconi Marine.
* Where it is impossible to survey a UK-registered cargo ship in a UK port, **application** for radio survey and renewal of a Cargo Ship Radio Certificate may be made through the British Consul or High Commissioner to the local Administration of the port (i.e. local equivalent of the DfT), provided that the port State is a party to SOLAS 74 and its 1978 Protocol (SOLAS 74/78). Where it proves impossible to arrange for survey abroad in this way, **advice** should be sought from the MCA, branch MSAS(A), Tel: 01703 329144. **Special arrangements** are in force for certain areas, e.g. the Persian Gulf and USA.

---

[91] The advice in MGN 206 that only initial surveys and renewal surveys are required for radio equipment takes no account of the periodical surveys required under the Harmonised System of Survey and Certification, as described in MSN 1751 (see D04e.6).

* Applications for survey of **ro-ro passenger ships abroad** should be made to Marconi Marine, and not to the local Consul or High Commissioner.
* After survey of a cargo ship, Marconi Marine will issue a **Cargo Ship Safety Radio Certificate** direct to the owner or his representative. After survey of a passenger ship, Marconi Marine will issue a Declaration of Survey to the MCA, who may use it for issue of the appropriate passenger ship certification. Where a cargo ship has been surveyed abroad by the local Administration, that Administration will issue a Cargo Ship Safety Radio Certificate "at the request of the United Kingdom" (i.e. on behalf of the MCA).
* When it is impossible to arrange for radio survey prior to expiry of the Cargo Ship Safety Radio Certificate, a **request for extension of validity** may be made to MSAS(A), Bay 3/18, Spring Place, 105 Commercial Road, Southampton SO15 1EG, Tel: 01703 329146, Fax: 01703 329161, with:
  * the reason for the request;
  * period of extension requested (which cannot exceed 5 months);
  * confirmation from the master that the radio equipment is in good order;
  * next port of call with expected dates of arrival and sailing; and
  * port where survey is intended, expected date of arrival there, and the organisation by whom the survey is to be carried out.
* Where the MCA cannot be contacted for some reason, application for extension of validity may be made to a British consul or, in a Commonwealth country, British High Commissioner.
* **Marconi Marine surveyors** are prohibited from becoming personally involved in any repairs to equipment under survey. Where Marconi Marine is also the repair contractor, an engineer will be independently assigned by the company. Marconi Marine surveyors undertaking MCA radio surveys are prohibited from any sales activity, and are prohibited from advising on possible sources of supply of radio goods or services in connection with the survey.
* In addition to surveys by MCA-appointed radio surveyors of -Marconi, Marine, a UK ship's radio installations are subject, under the **Wireless Telegraphy Act 1949**, to **inspection by the Radiocommunications Agency (RA)** in order to check whether the conditions imposed by the **Ship Radio Licence** are being met. These inspections are undertaken **randomly** but masters can expect no more than one such inspection per year.
* The competent authorities of any port State may also carry out (**Port State Control**) inspections of a ship's radio installations to ensure compliance with relevant international conventions in force.

D04m.5 Radio equipment tests and checks

* **Regulation 18(7) of the Radio Installations Regulations** provides that in all UK ships to which the Regulations apply a person nominated by the master, who will normally be the person qualified under regulation 19(3), must, while the ship is at sea, carry out the **appropriate tests and checks** specified in Schedule 2 to the Regulations. If any of the radio installations required by the Regulations are not in working order, the nominated person must **inform the master** and **record details of the deficiencies in the Radio Log**.
* The **daily** tests and checks referred to in Schedule 3 are as follows:
  * The proper functioning of the DSC facilities must be tested at least once each day, without radiation of signals, by use of the means provided on the equipment.
  * Batteries providing a source of energy for any part of the radio installations must be tested daily and, where necessary, brought up to the fully charged condition.
* The **weekly** tests and checks referred to in Schedule 3 are as follows:
  * The proper operation of the DSC facilities must be tested at least once a week by means of a test call, when within communication range of a coast station fitted with DSC equipment.
  * Where a ship has been out of communication range of a coast station fitted with DSC equipment for a period of longer than one week, a test call must be made on the first opportunity that the ship is within communication range of such a coast station.
  * Where the reserve source of energy is not a battery (for example, a motor generator), the reserve source of energy must be tested weekly.
* The **monthly** tests and checks referred to in Schedule 3 are as follows:
  * Each EPIRB and satellite EPIRB must be examined at least once a month to determine its capability to operate properly, particularly its ability to float free (where required to do so) in the event of the ship sinking, its security and for signs of damage.
  * Each search and rescue radar transponder must be checked at least once a month for security and signs of damage.
  * Each survival craft two-way VHF equipment must be tested at least once a month on a frequency other than 156.8 MHz (VHF Channel 16).

- A check must be made at least once a month on the security and condition of all batteries providing a source of energy for any part of a radio installation. The battery connections and compartment must also be checked.

D04n NAVIGATIONAL EQUIPMENT

D04n.1 Safety of Navigation Regulations provisions relating to navigational equipment

* The **MS (Safety of Navigation) Regulations 2002** (SI 2002/1473) (see H01f.2), which give effect in the UK to the revised **SOLAS chapter V** -
  - **revoke** and replace the MS (Navigational Equipment) Regulations 1993 (SI 1993/69), as amended by SIs 1999/1957 and 2000/2687.
  - **require** (in regulation 5) compliance by UK ships, other than those excepted under regulation 4(4) as listed below, with **SOLAS regulation V/19** (which relates to **Carriage requirements for shipborne navigational systems and equipment**).
* The ships excepted by regulation 4(4) (i.e. those to which **SOLAS regulation V/19 does not apply** in the UK) are:
  - UK ships of Class V (i.e. passenger ships engaged only on voyages in Category A, B and C waters);
  - UK ships which are neither passenger ships nor sea-going (i.e. ships operating in categorised waters as described in D04c.2a or in other internal waters of the UK);
  - new ships of Class A, B, C or D (as defined in D04c.2b);
  - fishing vessels; and
  - high-speed craft to which the MS (High-Speed Craft) Regulations 1996 (SI 1996/3188) (see D03i.2) apply.
* Regulation 4(3) of the Safety of Navigation Regulations provides that paragraphs 1 to 3 and 7 and 8 of SOLAS regulation V/18 do not apply to ships of less than 150gt on any voyage. (These paragraphs require type approval and the meeting of IMO performance standards for navigational equipment, and an annual performance test for the voyage data recorder (VDR).)
* Regulation 4(5) of the Safety of Navigation Regulations provides that **SOLAS regulation V/19 will cease to apply** on "the relevant date" to **existing ships of Class A, B, C and D, of 24m or more in length**, the "relevant date" meaning the date shown in the table at D03b.6b as the date on which the MS (Passenger Ships on Domestic Voyages) Regulations 2000 apply to the ship.
* **SOLAS regulation V/19** sets out the carriage requirements for "new ships", i.e. ships built on or after 1 July 2002. Requirements are based on tonnage, threshold tonnages being **150gt** and upwards, **300gt** and upwards, **500gt** and upwards, **3000gt** and upwards, **10,000gt** and upwards and **50,000gt** and upwards. The requirements are cumulative, i.e. equipment specified for ships in one tonnage band must be carried by ships in all higher tonnage bands.
* **Existing ships** (i.e. ships built before 1 July 2002) may, under SOLAS regulation V/19.1.2, continue to meet the requirements of SOLAS Chapter V/74, except in respect of **GNSS** (global navigation satellite system) or **terrestrial radionavigation system** (to be fitted by the first survey after 1 July 2002) and **AIS** (see D04n.1a).
* The **Guidance Notes to regulation V/19** in MCA's 2002 SOLAS Chapter V publication include, in **Annex 11**, a table showing **navigational equipment to be carried by all (new) ships** and **equipment to be carried by (new) ships in each tonnage band**. Certain equipment must be carried by all passenger ships of over 150gt or 300gt.
* **IMO performance standards** for navigational equipment are set out in **Annex 9** of the MCA's 2002 SOLAS Chapter V publication. (See also D04b.3.)
* **Equipment manuals** must be provided in accordance with SOLAS regulation V/16 and comply with the IEC requirements specified in Annex 7 to the MCA's 2002 SOLAS Chapter V publication.

D04n.1a Automatic identification systems

* **Regulation V/19.2.4** provides that all ships of 300gt and upwards engaged on international voyages, cargo ships of 500gt and upwards on domestic voyages, and passenger ships of any tonnage must be fitted with an **automatic identification system** (AIS) in accordance with a timetable detailed in the regulation.
* December 2002 modifications to SOLAS chapter V contain a new timetable for the fitting of AIS. Ships, other than passenger ships and tankers, of 300gt and upwards but less than 50,000gt, are required to fit AIS not later than the first safety equipment survey after 1 July 2004 or by 31 December 2004, whichever occurs earlier. Ships fitted with AIS must maintain AIS in operation at all times except where international agreements, rules or standards provide for the protection of navigational information.
* **Annex 17** to the Guidance Notes to regulation V/10 contains the MCA's guidance on AIS as well as IMO Guidelines for the Onboard Operational Use of Shipboard Automatic Identification Systems (AIS) adopted under resolution A.917(22).

D04n.2 Adjustment and repair of compasses

* **Requirements for and guidance on adjustment of compasses**, formerly in MGN 57, is contained in **Annex 13 to the MCA's 2002 SOLAS V publication**.

* **Paragraph 6 of Annex 13** provides that each magnetic compass required to be carried under the MS (Safety of Navigation) Regulations 2002 must be **properly adjusted** and its **table or curve of residual deviations** must be **available at all times**. Magnetic compasses should be adjusted when:
  * they are **first installed**;
  * they **become unreliable**;
  * the ship undergoes **structural repairs or alterations** that could affect its permanent and induced magnetism;
  * electrical or magnetic equipment close to the compass is added, removed or altered; or
  * a period of **two years has elapsed since the last adjustment** and a **record of compass deviations has not been maintained**, or the **recorded deviations are excessive** or when the compass shows **physical defects**.

* Paragraph 11 provides that, in the UK, all adjustments should be made by a **compass adjuster** who holds a **Certificate of Competency as Compass Adjuster** issued by the UK Government.

* Paragraph 12 provides that **if a qualified compass adjuster is unavailable** and the master considers it necessary, then adjustments may be made by a person holding a Certificate of Competency (Deck Officer) Class 1 (Master Mariner). The compass must be **re-adjusted** by a qualified compass adjuster at the next available opportunity.

* Paragraph 12 provides that the date of any adjustment and other details should be noted in the **compass deviation book**. The position of correctors should be recorded in the compass deviation book and on **deviation cards**. **Separate deviation cards** should be prepared for the standard compass and the transmitting magnetic compass repeater by comparing headings.

* Paragraph 14 provides that **repairs** should only be made by a compass manufacturer or other competent person using the proper test facilities. When the work is finished the repairer should supply the owner or master with a **certificate** specifying that the work has been carried out in accordance with the necessary requirements of ISO 2269 for Class A Compass and ISO 10316 for Class B Compass, which are the international standards for magnetic compasses.

* A **compass test certificate** is generally issued by the manufacturer of each magnetic compass and delivered with the compass. Following adjustment by a qualified compass adjuster, a **Certificate of Compass Adjustment** will normally be issued to the ship, showing the adjustments made. (This is not mentioned in Annex 13.)

D04n.3 Documents related to navigational equipment

* Paragraph 1.11 of Annex 20 to the MCA's 2002 SOLAS V publication provides that a ship required by the MS (Safety of Navigation) Regulations 2002 (SI 2002/1437) to be fitted with navigational equipment installations should carry the following **documents**:
  * a **report of survey**, as applicable;
  * a current **Exemption Certificate**, where applicable;
  * **servicing and operating information** in English for each item of navigational equipment;
  * a magnetic compass **deviation card(s)**;
  * records of **compass deviations**; and
  * a record of **radar shadow sectors**[92].

Certificate or document	Relevant ship types	SBC ref.
Certificate of Compass Adjustment	Ships fitted with magnetic compasses	D04n.2
Compass deviation book	Ships fitted with magnetic compasses	D04n.2
Compass test certificate(s)	Ships fitted with magnetic compasses	D04n.2
Compass deviation card(s) for standard and repeater compasses	Ships fitted with magnetic compasses	D04n.2
Radar shadow sector diagram	Ships fitted with radar	D04n.3
International Code of Signals	All passenger ships and all cargo ships of 300gt and over, on international voyages	D04o
Mariners Handbook	Sea-going ships	D04o
Merchant Shipping Notices, Marine Guidance Notes and Marine Information Notes (parts related to ship's voyage and operation)	All ships, whether sea-going or not	D04o
Notices to Mariners	All ships, whether sea-going or not	D04o
Lists of Radio Signals	All ships, whether sea-going or not	D04o
Lists of Lights	All ships, whether sea-going or not	D04o
Sailing Directions	All ships, whether sea-going or not	D04o
Nautical almanac	All ships, whether sea-going or not	D04o

[92] The **angular width and bearing of any shadow sectors** displayed by the radar installation should be determined and **recorded**. The record should be shown on a **diagram adjacent to the radar display** and should be **kept up to date** following any change likely to affect shadow sectors.

Navigational tables	All ships, whether sea-going or not	D04o
Tide tables	All ships, whether sea-going or not	D04o
Operating and maintenance instructions for navigational aids carried by the ship	All ships, whether sea-going or not	D04o

D04o NAUTICAL CHARTS AND NAUTICAL PUBLICATIONS

* The **MS (Safety of Navigation) Regulations 2002** (SI 2002/1473) (see H01f.2) –
  - **revoke** and replace the MS (Carriage of Nautical Publications) Regulations 1998 (SI 1998/2647).
  - **require compliance** by a ship to which the Regulations apply with **SOLAS regulation V/27** (which relates to **Nautical charts and nautical publications**).
* **SOLAS regulation V/27** provides that nautical charts and nautical publications, such as sailing directions, lists of lights, notices to mariners, tide tables and all other nautical publications necessary for the intended voyage, must be **adequate** and **up to date**.
* **Guidance note 1 to regulation 27** in the MCA's 2002 SOLAS V publication (see H01f.2a) advises that **regulation V/27** applies to all (UK) ships other than UK pleasure vessels of less than 150gt.
* **SOLAS regulation V/2.2** defines "nautical chart" or "nautical publication" as a special-purpose map or book, or a specially compiled database from which such a map or book is derived, that is issued officially by or on the authority of a Government, authorized Hydrographic Office or other relevant government institution and is designed to meet the requirements of marine navigation.
* **Nautical chart and publication carriage requirements** are contained in **SOLAS regulation V/19.2.1.4 and 2.1.5**.
* **SOLAS regulation V/19.2.1.4** provides that all ships, irrespective of size, must have **nautical charts and nautical publications** to plan and display the ship's route for the intended voyage and to plot and monitor positions throughout the voyage; an electronic chart display and information system (ECDIS) may be accepted as meeting the chart carriage requirements of this paragraph. See **Guidance note 1**, below.
* **SOLAS regulation V/19.2.1.5** provides that all ships, irrespective of size, must have **back-up arrangements** to meet the functional requirements of subparagraph .4, if this function is partly or fully fulfilled by electronic means. An appropriate folio of paper nautical charts may be used as a back-up arrangement for ECDIS. Other back-up arrangements for ECDIS are acceptable (see appendix 6 to resolution A.817(19), as amended).
* **Annex 3** (Nautical Charts and Publications) to MCA's **2002 SOLAS Chapter V publication** contains **guidance notes**, explained below, which should be read in conjunction with SOLAS **regulations V/19, 21 and 27**.
* **Guidance note 1** advises that SOLAS **regulation V/1.4** allows Administrations to determine to what extent SOLAS regulations V/15 to 28 apply to smaller vessels and fishing vessels, and that the MCA has determined that the **charts and publications carriage requirements** of regulation 19.2.1.4 **do not apply** to:
  UK ships of Class V;
  UK ships which are neither passenger ships nor seagoing;
  new ships of class A, B, C or D;
  fishing vessels; or
  pleasure vessels under 150gt.
* **Guidance note 2** advises small craft users that **regulation V/34** (Safe navigation and avoidance of dangerous situations) is not listed in regulation V/1.4 (see above) and therefore applies to **all ships** on **all voyages** (regulation 1.1). The definition of "ship" in this case includes **small craft**. Operators of small craft which are UK Ships of Class V, UK ships which are neither passenger ships nor seagoing, or new ships of class A, B, C or D should therefore have sufficient charts and published information on board to be able to plan the intended voyage and execute it safely. When the type and structure of such a vessel makes it impracticable to carry charts and publications, the crew should have sufficient knowledge of the area of intended operation and of all local dangers and regulations so that they can complete the intended voyage in safety.
* **Guidance note 3** states that **all ships** other than those listed in Guidance note 1 (see above) must carry:
  1. **Charts**, as defined in SOLAS regulation V/2.2 **or** an electronic chart display and information system (**ECDIS**) using electronic navigational charts or raster navigational charts meeting the requirements of regulation V/19.2.1.4, with the necessary **back-up arrangements** required by regulation V/19.2.1.5. The back-up arrangements may be either **duplication of ECDIS** or a **reduced folio of paper charts**. Advice on determining suitable back-up is given in **MGN 194**.
  2. Such adequate and up-to-date **sailing directions**, **lists of lights**, **notices to mariners**, **tide tables** and other **nautical publications**, as defined in regulation V/2.2 (see above), to meet the requirements of regulation V/19.2.1.4. Nautical publications presented in electronic format are acceptable when issued by or on the authority of an authorised hydrographic office or other relevant government institution.
  3. All sea-going passenger ships, all other ships of 300gt or more, and all other ships required by SOLAS to carry a radio installation, must carry the **IMO International Code of Signals**, as required by regulation V/21.
  * For notes on additional documents to be carried by ships fitted with GMDSS equipment, see D04m.3.

* **Guidance note 4** advises that the charts or ECDIS referred to in regulation V/19.2.1.4 must be of such a scale and contain sufficient detail as clearly to show:
  * all navigational marks which may be used by a ship when navigating the waters covered by the chart;
  * all known dangers affecting those waters; and
  * information concerning any ships' routeing and ship reporting measures applicable to those waters.
* All charts and publications must be of the latest obtainable edition and be kept up-to-date from the latest relevant obtainable notices to mariners and radio navigational warnings.
* **Guidance note 5** advises that the following **publications** are considered by the MCA to satisfy the requirements of SOLAS **regulation V/19.2.1.4**:
  * Annual Summary of Admiralty Notices to Mariners (UKHO);
  * International Code of Signals (published by IMO);
  * Lists of Lights (UKHO);
  * Lists of Radio Signals (UKHO);
  * Mariners' Handbook (UKHO);
  * Merchant Shipping Notices, Marine Guidance Notes and Marine Information Notes (MCA);
  * nautical almanac;
  * navigational tables;
  * Notices to Mariners (UKHO);
  * operating and maintenance instructions for navigational aids carried by the ship.
  * Sailing Directions (UKHO);
  * tidal stream atlases; and
  * tide tables.
* In the case of the above-listed publications, **only those parts** of the publication which are **relevant to the ship's voyage and operation** need be carried.
* Where UKHO is stated as the publisher in the list, any other chart or publication which meets the definition in regulation 2.2 will be acceptable to the MCA.
* **Charts and nautical publications** listed above are liable to be **inspected** in surveys relating to a Passenger Ship Safety Certificate, Cargo Ship Safety Equipment Certificate or Cargo Ship Safety Certificate, in a Port State Control inspection, an ISM Code audit, a general inspection, or in a ship inspection by a P&I club or prospective charterer.
* The requirement to carry Notices to Mariners implies a requirement to carry the latest available Annual Summary of Admiralty Notices to Mariners (NP 247).
* All books and documents published by UKHO are listed in the Catalogue of Admiralty Charts and Publications (NP 131) published by UKHO, whose website is at: www.hydro.gov.uk
* There is **no UK statutory requirement** for a ship to **carry** the following publications, although they may be carried in accordance with company policy, and an ISM auditor might consider their carriage appropriate:
  * Statutory Instruments;
  * IAMSAR Manual;
  * International Maritime Dangerous Goods Code;
  * Ocean Passages of the World;
  * Ships' Routeing;
  * Guide to Port Entry;
  * ISGOTT.

D04o.1 Electronic charts

* **International law on electronic charts** is contained in the **rules of the International Hydrographic Organization** (IHO) and in **SOLAS regulation V/19**.
* An IMO document on electronic charts is available at www.imo.org/Safety/mainframe.asp?topic_id=350
* An IHO document on electronic chart systems and ECDIS is at www.iho.shom.fr/general/ecdis/ecdisnew1.html
* The **Admiralty Guide to Electronic Charting** is available at www.hydro.gov.uk/electronic_charting_guide.html
* Annex 14 of the MCA's 2002 SOLAS V document explains the application of the MS (Safety of Navigation) Regulations 2002 with respect to electronic charts.
* Electronic charts may be carried in accordance with **paragraph 2.1.4 of SOLAS regulation V/19**, which is given effect in the UK by regulation 5 of the MS (Safety of Navigation) Regulations 2002 (SI 2002/1473) (see H01f.2).
* Current requirements and guidance on the use of electronic charts on UK ships is contained in **Annex 14 to the MCA's 2002 SOLAS V publication**. This contains IMO Safety of Navigation Circular SN/Circ.207 (which explains the differences between various official modes of operation of electronic chart systems). The notes in Annex 14, together with the SN Circular, supersede MGN 133.

D04p MEDICAL STORES

* The **MS and FV (Medical Stores) Regulations 1995** (SI 1995/1802), as amended by the MS and FV (Medical Stores) (Amendment) Regulations 1996 (SI 1996/2821).
    - implement part of **EEC Directive 92/29/EEC** on the minimum safety and health requirements for improved medical treatment on board vessels, so far as that Directive relates to the carriage of medicines and other medical stores (regulation 2);
    - **apply to** UK ships and Government ships other than those mentioned below (regulation 3).
    - **do not apply** to ships employed in inland navigation (e.g. lake steamers), pleasure vessels used for commercial purposes and not manned by professional crews, or tugs operating in harbour areas (regulation 3). (Tugs operating beyond harbour areas are not excepted.)
* Under **regulation 4(1)** every ship to which the Regulations apply must carry **medical stores** in accordance with the following table.

Column 1 *Description of ship*	Column 2 *Category of medicines and medical stores*
A sea-going ship (including fishing vessel) with no limitation on length of voyage.	Medical stores as specified in Category A of MSN 1726.
A sea-going ship (including a fishing vessel) making a voyage during which it is not more than 150 nautical miles from the nearest port with adequate medical equipment (or no more than 175 nautical miles from the nearest port with adequate medical equipment provided that in this case it remains continuously within range of helicopter rescue services).	Medical stores as specified in Category B of MSN 1726.
A ship staying very close to shore or with no cabin accommodation other than a wheelhouse.	Medical stores as specified in Category C of MSN 1726.
A sea-going ship carrying a dangerous substance in its cargo, or any residue of a dangerous substance from an earlier cargo.	Medical stores as specified in MSN 1726.
A sea-going ship carrying more than 12 passengers but not a doctor as a member of the crew.	Medical stores as specified in Category D in MSN 1726.

Note: The requirements in entries 4 and 5 above are in addition to those in entry 1, 2 or 3 as appropriate.

* **Category A vessels** are defined in **MSN 1726** as sea-going or sea-fishing vessels with no limitation on length of trips.
* **Category B vessels** are defined as seagoing or sea-fishing vessels making trips of less than 150 nautical miles from the nearest port with adequate medical equipment. This category is extended to seagoing or sea-fishing vessels which make trips of less than 175 nautical miles from the nearest port with adequate medical equipment and which remain continuously within range of helicopter rescue services.
* **Category C vessels** are defined as harbour vessels, boats and craft staying very close to shore or with no cabin accommodation other than a wheelhouse. Lifeboats and liferafts are also required to carry Category C stores. "Very close to shore" is interpreted by the UK as meaning that a vessel operating more than 60 nautical miles out to sea would not be operating very close to shore. Notwithstanding this interpretation, it is for owners and skippers to assess, for the purposes of complying with the Regulations, whether, in respect of voyages in which the vessel goes less than 60 miles out to sea, the vessel is "very close to shore".
* **Schedules to MSN 1726** are as follows:
    * Schedule 1   Requirements for Categories A and B vessels
    * Schedule 2   Requirements for Category C vessels
    * Schedule 3   Additional requirements for passenger ships - Doctor's bag
    * Schedule 4   Requirements for ships carrying dangerous cargoes
    * Schedule 5   Publications
    * Schedule 6   Specifications of disinfectants and insecticides
    * Schedule 7   Precautions against malaria
    * Schedule 8   Guide to the use of medicines
* **MSN 1726** advises that a **checklist of all the medicines and equipment** required by the MSN should be kept on board and **reviewed annually**.
* **Schedule 2** supersedes M.1695 which amended Annex 6 to the two Codes of Practice for the Safety of Small Commercial Motor Vessels and Small Commercial Sailing Vessels (see D031.2).
* Notes to **Schedule 3** state that a **doctor's bag** is required for passenger ships where there is no qualified medical practitioner among the crew and the vessel carries more than 12 passengers. (Class VI and VI(A) vessels are excluded from this requirement.) All the medicines and equipment in the Schedule 3 list should be kept in a doctor's bag or case; the case should be locked and kept in a locked cabinet and the keys held by the master or someone nominated by him. The medicines in this case are only to be used by a qualified medical practitioner, registered general nurse, qualified paramedic or by someone under the direct supervision of a medical practitioner on board the ship. Passenger ships must also carry one **first aid kit** for every 100 persons or fraction of that number that they are

licensed to carry, subject to a maximum of 3 kits, e.g. 250 persons require 3 kits. One kit is to be included in the doctor's bag.

* **Schedule 4** states the requirements for ships transporting dangerous substances. When a UK-registered vessel is carrying a dangerous substance or substances in quantities in excess of those defined in volume 1, section 18 of the IMDG Code, as the whole or part of the cargo, the master must ensure that the correct antidote to the substance (plus the necessary ancillary equipment, e.g. syringes) is carried. The correct antidote can be found in the IMO Medical First Aid Guide for Ships (MFAG), 1994 Edition. The quantities of any medicines to be carried aboard should be based on an estimate of risks, taking into account such factors as the number of crew, length of voyage and risk of accidental exposure[93].

* **Schedule 4** also lists **antidotes to be carried on ferries**. Whether or not a vessel is required to carry Category A or B stores, ferries or similar vessels whose operating arrangements do not allow sufficient forewarning of the nature of any dangerous substances which might be transported on them, must carry at least the antidotes and equipment in the lists shown in the notes to Schedule 4.

* **Schedule 5** lists **publications** to be carried as follows:

Vessel category	Publication
Category A	Controlled Drugs Register Ship Captain's Medical Guide (latest edition)
Category B	Ship Captain's Medical Guide (latest edition)
Category C	First Aid Manual (St John's, Red Cross or St Andrew's) or First Aid instructions, in English on waterproof paper (lifeboats and liferafts only)
All Categories (other than lifeboats and liferafts)	The relevant Schedule(s) of MSN 1726 and any subsequent amendments

* **Schedule 8** includes paragraphs on: (1) general advice about medicines; (2) medicines obtained abroad; (3) medicines obtained by seafarer from a doctor ashore; (4) controlled drugs; (5) obtaining controlled drugs; (6) other drugs and medicines; and (7) storage and security of drugs.

* **MSN 1726** provides three reminders of the **legal responsibilities of the owner and master**, as follows:
  * The **owner** of a vessel is responsible for the **cost** of any medicine and medical equipment including the cost of periodic replacements in order to keep stocks of any required medicines in date and immediately usable.
  * **Section 45 of the Merchant Shipping Act 1995** specifies that if a person, while employed in a UK ship, receives outside the UK any surgical or medical treatment or such dental or optical treatment (including repair or replacement of any appliance) that cannot be postponed without impairing the seafarer's efficiency, the reasonable expenses of this treatment must be paid by the employer(s).
  * Where a **UK ship does not carry a doctor** among the seafarers employed in it, section 53 of the Merchant Shipping Act 1995 holds the **master** responsible for ensuring that **any necessary medical attention** given on board is given either **by him or, under his supervision, by a person appointed by him** for that purpose. The master is also responsible for the **management of the medical supplies** and for ensuring that they are **maintained** in good condition.

* **Regulation 9** provides that **medical stores labelled with expiry dates** must be replaced at the earliest possible date after the expiry date and in any event within 3 months of the expiry date.

* **Medical stores which have passed the expiry date** must, once the replacements have been obtained, or after 3 months (whichever is earlier) be **disposed of** in accordance with the Ship Captain's Medical Guide.

* Following **replenishment of medical stores**, a pharmacist will usually issue a **certificate** stating that he has replenished the medical stores to the standard of the relevant vessel Category. (There is no statutory requirement for such a certificate to be carried.)

* For notes on **The Ship Captain's Medical Guide** see E08j.2a.

D04q DE-RATTING CERTIFICATION

D04q.1 International Health Regulations requirements

* **Article 53 of the International Health Regulations** (see A06a) provides that every ship must be either permanently kept in such a condition that it is free of rodents and the plague vector, or periodically deratted (paragraph 1). A Deratting Certificate or a Deratting Exemption Certificate will be issued only by the health authority for a port approved for that purpose under Article 17 (paragraph 2). Every such certificate will be valid for **six months**, but this period may be **extended by one month** for a ship proceeding to such a port if the **deratting or inspection**, as the case may be, would be facilitated by the operations due to take place there (paragraph 2).

---

[93] Updating of the IMDG Code should be taken into account when preparing the list of medicines to be carried and any associated risk assessment.

Deratting Certificates and Deratting Exemption Certificates must conform with the model specified in Appendix 1 of the International Health Regulations (paragraph 3).

* Paragraph 4 provides that if a valid certificate is not produced, the health authority for a port approved under Article 17, after inquiry or inspection, may proceed in the following manner:
  * If the port has been **designated** under paragraph 2 of Article 17, the health authority may derat the ship or cause the deratting to be done under its direction and control. It shall decide in each case the technique which should be employed to secure the extermination of rodents on the ship. Deratting shall be carried out so as to avoid as far as possible damage to the ship and to any cargo and shall not take longer, than is absolutely necessary. Wherever possible deratting shall be done when the holds are empty. In the case of a ship in ballast, it shall be done before loading. When deratting has been satisfactorily completed, the health authority shall issue a Deratting Certificate.
  * At any port **approved** under Article 17, the health authority may issue a Deratting Exemption Certificate if it is satisfied that the ship is free of rodents[94]. Such a certificate may be issued only if the inspection of the ship has been carried out when the holds are empty or when they contain only ballast or other material, unattractive to rodents, of such a nature or so disposed as to make a thorough inspection of the holds possible. A Deratting Exemption Certificate may be issued for an oil tanker with full holds.
* If the conditions under which a deratting is carried out are such that, in the opinion of the health authority for the port where the operation was performed, a satisfactory result cannot be obtained, the health authority will make a note to that effect on the existing Deratting Certificate (paragraph 5).

D04q.2 Public Health (Ships) Regulations

* **Deratting Exemption Certificates** and **Deratting Certificates** are issued to ships by port health authorities in ports in England or Wales under **regulations 18 and 19 of the Public Health (Ships) Regulations 1979** (SI 1979/1435), which give effect to article 53 of the International Health Regulations, and in Scottish and Northern Ireland ports under equivalent Scotland and Northern Ireland regulations. For notes on the requirements of the Public Health (Ships) Regulations relating to incoming ships, see I01e.1.
* A **Deratting Certificate** –
  - will be issued when **deratting has been completed** to the satisfaction of the authorised officer for a designated approved port (regulation 18(6), Public Health (Ships) Regulations 1979).
  - will be **replaced** by a Deratting Exemption Certificate if, after the ship has been inspected, the authorised officer for an approved port or designated approved port is satisfied that the ship is free from rodents and the plague vector (regulation 18(2)).
  - **is valid** for a maximum of **6 months, extendable by one month** where the ship is proceeding immediately to an approved port or designated approved port (regulation 2(1)).
  - **may be obtained** under equivalent conditions **in any port** with similar status in a country which is a signatory to the **International Health Regulations**.
* A **Deratting Exemption Certificate** –
  - will be issued if, after the ship has been inspected, the authorised officer for an approved port or designated approved port is satisfied that the **ship is free from rodents and the plague vector** (regulation 18(2)).
  - will be **replaced by a Deratting Certificate** following any deratting completed to the satisfaction of the authorised officer for a designated approved port.
  - **is valid** for a maximum of **6 months, extendable by one month** where the ship is proceeding immediately to an approved port or designated approved port (regulation 2(1)).
  - will be issued only if the inspection was done with **the holds empty or containing only ballast or material that is unattractive to rodents** and of such a nature or so disposed as to allow a **thorough inspection**.
  - may be issued to an **oil tanker with full tanks**.
  - **may be obtained** under equivalent conditions in **any port** with similar status in a country which is a signatory to the **International Health Regulations**.
* **On the front page** of a Deratting/Deratting Exemption Certificate issued in a UK port is stated: Certificate name (both names are printed; the inapplicable name is deleted by the issuing officer); port; date; statement as follows: "this Certificate records the inspection and deratting/exemption at this port and on the above date of the ship/inland navigation vessel...(ship's name)...of...(net tonnage)... At the time of the inspection/deratting the holds were laden with........tons of ....cargo. "Recommendations made (in the case of exemption): (here are stated the measures taken for maintaining the ship in such a condition that it is free of rodents and the plague vector, e.g. "vessel maintained in a clean and rodent-free condition throughout".

---

[94] The vast majority of ships normally carry a Deratting Exemption Certificate.

* **On the inside pages** are 9 columns as follows: 1 Compartments; 2 Rat indications; 3 Rat harbours discovered; 4 Rat harbours treated; 5-7 Deratting by fumigation: 5 Space (cubic feet); 6 Quantity used; 7 Rats found dead; 8-9 Deratting by catching, trapping or poisoning: 8 Traps set or poisons put out; 9 Rats caught or killed.
* "**Rat indications**" in column 2 include old or recent evidence of excretia, runs or gnawing.
* "**Quantity used**" in column 6 refers to the weight of sulphur or of cyanide salts or the quantity of HCN acid used.
* The Certificate bears the seal, name, qualification and signature of the Inspector.

D04r LIFTING PLANT INSPECTION, TESTING AND DOCUMENTATION

D04r.1 Lifting plant testing, examination and certification

* The **MS (Hatches and Lifting Plant) Regulations 1988** (SI 1988/1639) apply to UK ships other than fishing vessels, pleasure craft, offshore installations whilst on or within 500 metres of their working stations, and ships on which there is, for the time being, no master or crew or watchman. The Regulations provide that the **employer and master** must -
    * ensure that no **lifting plant** is used after manufacture or installation, or after any repair or modification which is likely to alter the safe working load (SWL) or affect the lifting plant's strength or stability, without first being **tested by a competent person**, except in the case of a rope sling made from rope which has been tested by a competent person and spliced in a safe manner (regulation 7(1));
    * ensure that a **lifting appliance** is not used unless it has been suitably **tested by a competent person** within the preceding **5 years** (regulation 7(2));
    * ensure that any **lifting plant** is not used unless it has been **thoroughly examined by a competent person** at least once in the preceding **12 months** (regulation 8(a) and following a test as required as above (regulation 8(b));
    * ensure that a **certificate or report** in an MCA-approved form is obtained within **28 days** of any test or examination under the Regulations. The certificate or report must be kept in a safe place on board for at least 2 years from receipt or until receipt of the certificate or report of the **next** test or examination (regulation 10(1)).
* Every employer, **master** and any person in carrying out the obligations contained in regulations 6 to 10 (including the obligations above) must take **full account of the principles and guidance** in the Code of Safe Working Practices for Merchant Seamen.
* **Chapter 7 of the Code of Safe Working Practices for Merchant Seamen** relates to **Work Equipment**. Relevant paragraphs in Chapter 7 are: **7.5.** Lifting Plant; **7.6.** Testing and examination of lifting equipment; **7.7.** Marking of lifting equipment; **7.8.** Certificates and reports.
* The master must ensure that a **certificate or report** in the required form (specimens of which are in Annex 7.1) is supplied within 28 days following any **statutory test or examination**. This must be kept in a safe place on board ship for a period of at least **two years** from receipt of the certificate or report of the **next following test** or examination (para.7.8.1).
* Certificates or reports should be kept readily available on board and copies of the latest certificates or reports should be available to any **dock worker** or **shore employer** using the ship's plant (para.7.8.3).
* Reports should be in a form approved by the Secretary of State (i.e. the MCA). Approved forms based on the International Labour Office model are produced by classification societies, and may be varied in style as long as the minimum requirement is met (para.7.8.4).
* A **register of lifting appliances and items of loose gear** should be maintained in a form based on the model recommended by the ILO and shown at Annex 7.2 (para.7.8.5) (see D04r.2).

D04r.2 Register of Lifting Appliances and Cargo Handling Gear

* Certificates or reports kept on board as required by regulation 10(1) of the MS (Hatches and Lifting Appliances) Regulations (see D04r.1) should be kept in the ship's **Register of Lifting Appliances and Cargo handling Gear** which is required to be kept under the provisions of ILO Convention 152 on Occupational Safety and Health (Dock Work), 1979 and ILO Recommendation 160. This may be known as the "chain register".
* The Register of Lifting Appliances and Cargo Handling Gear is known on many ships as the "**Chain Register**"[95].
* The ILO instruments provide that a **register of lifting appliances and items of loose gear** must be kept in a form prescribed by the competent authority[96], account being taken of the model recommended by the International Labour

---

[95] The name "Chain Register" is a relic of the days when the Factories Act required cargo ships to keep a register of the many items of chain working gear normally on board.

Office. (A model register is shown in Annex 7.2 of the Code of Safe Working Practices for Merchant Seamen.) The Register and related certificates must be kept **available to any person authorized by the competent authority**. The **Register and certificates for gear currently aboard the ship** must be preserved for at least **five years after the date of the last entry**.

* Registers in the ILO-recommended form are usually issued by the ship's classification society.

* Registers in the ILO-recommended format contain the following instructions.

Initial Examination and Certification

1.1. Every lifting appliance shall be certified by a competent person before being taken into use for the first time to ensure that it is of good design and construction and of adequate strength for the purpose for which it is intended.

1.2. Before being taken into use for the first time, a competent person shall supervise and witness testing, and shall thoroughly examine every lifting appliance.

1.3. Every item of loose gear shall, before being taken into use for the first time, shall be tested, thoroughly examined and certified by a competent person, in accordance with national law or regulations.

1.4. Upon satisfactory completion of the procedures indicated above, the competent person shall complete and issue the Register of lifting appliances and attach the appropriate certificates. An entry shall be made in part I of the Register.

1.5. A **rigging plan showing the arrangement of lifting appliances** shall be provided. In the case of derricks and derrick cranes, the rigging should show at least the following information.

    (a) the position of guys;

    (b) the resultant force on blocks, guys, wire ropes and booms;

    (c) the position of blocks;

    (d) the identification mark of individual items; and

    (e) arrangements and working range of union purchase;

2. Periodic Examination and Re-testing

2.1. All lifting appliances and every item of loose gear shall be thoroughly examined by a competent person at least once in every twelve months. The particulars of these thorough examinations shall be entered in part I of the Register.

2.2. Re-testing and thorough examination of all lifting appliances and every item of loose gear is to be carried out;

    (a) after any substantial alteration or renewal, or after repair to any stress bearing part, and;

    (b) in the case of lifting appliances, at least once in every five years.

2.3. The re-testing referred to in paragraph 2.2(a) may be omitted provided the part which has been renewed or repaired is subjected by separate test, to the same stress as would be imposed on it if it had been tested in-situ during the testing of the lifting appliance.

2.4. The thorough examinations and tests referred to in paragraph 2.2. are to be entered in part I of the Register.

2.5 No new item of loose gear shall be manufactured of wrought iron. Heat treatment of any existing wrought iron components should be carried out to the satisfaction of the competent person. No heat treatment should be applied to any item of loose gear unless the treatment is in accordance with the manufacturer's instruction; to the satisfaction of the competent person. Any heat treatment and the associated examination are to be recorded by the competent person in part I of the Register.

3. Inspections

3.1. Regular visual inspections of every item of loose gear shall be carried out by a responsible person before use. A record of these regular inspections is to be entered in part II of the Register, but entries need only be made when the inspection has indicated a defect in the item.

4. Certificates

4.1. The certification forms to be used in conjunction with this Register (Form No. 1) are as follows:

- Form No. 2 - Certificate of test and thorough examination of lifting appliance.
- Form No. 2(U) - Certificate of test and thorough examination of derricks used in union purchase.
- Form No. 3 - Certificate of test and thorough examination of loose gear.
- Form No. 4 - Certificate of test and thorough examination of wire rope.

Definitions

- The term "**competent authority**" means a minister, government department, or other authority empowered to issue regulations, orders or other instructions having the force of law.

---

[96] The term "competent authority" means a minister, government department, or other authority empowered to issue regulations, orders or other instructions having the force of law. In the UK this means, in practice, the MCA.

- The term "**competent person**" means a person appointed by the master of the ship or the owner of the gear to be responsible for the performance of inspections and who has sufficient knowledge and experience to undertake such inspections.
- The term "**responsible person**" means a person appointed by the master of the ship or the owner of the gear to be responsible for the performance of inspections and has sufficient knowledge and experience to undertake such inspections.
- The term "**thorough examination**" means a detailed visual examination by a competent person, supplemented if necessary by other suitable means or measures in order to arrive at a reliable conclusion as to the safety of the lifting appliance or item of loose gear examined.
- The term "**lifting appliance**" covers all stationary or mobile cargo handling appliances used on board ship for suspending, raising or lowering loads or moving them from one position to another while suspended or supported.
- The term "**loose gear**" covers any gear by means of which a load can be attached to a lifting appliance, but which does not form an integral part of the appliance or load.

* **Regulation 17 of the Docks Regulations 1988** (SI 1988/1655) (see E08f) provides that where the Regulations apply, the **master** of a ship must supply a copy of the latest **certificate or report of examination of lifting plant** to any employer or self-employed person hiring or using the plant.

D04s ANCHORING EQUIPMENT AND DOCUMENTATION

D04s.1 Anchoring equipment requirements

* Statutory requirements for anchor-handling equipment, anchors and chain cables are contained in the:
  - **MS (Passenger Ship Construction: Ships of Classes I, II and II(A)) Regulations 1998** (SI 1998/2514), regulation 81;
  - **MS (Passenger Ship Construction: Ships of Classes III to VI(A)) Regulations 1998** (SI 1998/2515), regulation 64; and
  - **MS (Cargo Ship Construction) Regulations 1997** (SI 1997/1509)[97], regulation 53.
* The above three regulations, each of which is similarly worded, require that every ship (to which the respective regulations apply) be provided with **anchor-handling equipment**, **together with such anchors and chain cables** as are **sufficient** in number, weight and strength, having regard to the size of the ship. This equipment must be **tested** and **certificated** to the satisfaction of the Certifying Authority. The **Certifying Authority** may be the Secretary of State (whose functions are exercised by the MCA) or any person authorised by the Secretary of State, which in practice means the **six classification societies**[98] authorised by the MCA (see D04f.1) or the **Ministry of Defence**. For the majority of ships the Certifying Authority is, in practice, the ship's classification society.
* **Detailed requirements for anchoring equipment for ships of different sizes** are contained in Part A of the **Unified Requirements** of the International Association of Classification Societies (IACS), which can be viewed on the IACS website (see D02c.2)[99].
* Each of the six authorised classification societies sets its own requirements for the **manufacture, testing and certification** of mooring and anchoring equipment provided on ships classed, or intended to be classed, by the society. The requirements of **Lloyd's Register of Shipping** (LR), for example, are in Chapter 10 (Equipment for Mooring and Anchoring) of Part 2 (Rules for the Manufacture, Testing and Certification of Materials) of LR's *Rules and Regulations for the Classification of Ships*. Chapter 10 has sections as follows: 1. Anchors; 2. Stud link chain cables for ships; 3. Stud link mooring chain cables; 4. Studless mooring chain cables; 5. Short link chain cables; 6. Steel wire ropes; and 7. Fibre ropes. Each of these sections prescribes test certification to be issued for the relevant item.
* Tests are conducted at a testing establishment approved by the classification society. **Certificates of test** are supplied as outlined in D04s.2.

---

[97] The MS (Anchors and Chain Cables) Rules 1970 (SI 1970/1453), which prescribed more detailed requirements for anchoring equipment, were revoked by the MS (Cargo Ship Construction) Regulations 1997.

[98] Lloyd's Register, American Bureau of Shipping, Bureau Veritas, Det Norske Veritas, Germanisher Lloyd and Registro Italiano Navale.

[99] Table 1 in Part A of the Unified Requirements, when entered with an Equipment Number which is obtained from a formula based on the Summer displacement and windage of the ship, gives the number of stockless bower anchors to be fitted, the mass per anchor, and the diameter of the stud link chain cable to be fitted to bower anchors.

D04s.2 Anchor, chain cable and chain cable accessory certificates

* Each anchor, chain cable and chain cable accessory supplied to a ship will, under the Certifying Authority's rules, be accompanied by a **test certificate** showing the results of tests carried out at the approved testing establishment.
* All certificates should be signed on behalf of the Certifying Authority and will generally show: a serial number; name of Certifying Authority; mark of Certifying Authority; name of testing establishment; mark of testing establishment (if any); name of Supervisor of Tests. Also shown are:
  * on an **Anchor Certificate**: type of anchor; weight (excluding stock) in kilogrammes; weight of stock in kilogrammes; length of shank in millimetres; length of arm in millimetres; diameter of trend in millimetres; proof load applied in tonnes;
  * on a **Chain Cable Certificate**: type of cable; grade; diameter in millimetres; total length in metres; total weight in kilogrammes; length of link in millimetres; breadth of link in millimetres; tensile breaking load applied in tonnes; tensile proof load applied in tonnes; number and types of accessories included;
  * on a **Chain Cable Accessory Certificate**: type of accessory; quantity; total weight in kilogrammes; tensile breaking load applied in tonnes; tensile proof load applied in tonnes.

D04t MISCELLANEOUS STATUTORY DOCUMENTATION

D04t.1 Shipboard Emergency Plans

D04t.1a Shipboard Oil Pollution Emergency Plan (SOPEP)

* **Regulation 33 of the MS (Prevention of Oil Pollution) Regulations 1996** (SI 1996/2154) provides for the carriage of a **shipboard oil pollution plan**, commonly known as a "**SOPEP**".
* Every oil tanker of 150gt and above and every ship (not being an oil tanker) of 400gt and above must carry on board an approved shipboard oil pollution emergency plan (regulation 33(1)).
* The plan must be in accordance with the IMO Guidelines for the Development of Shipboard Oil Pollution Emergency Plans and must include at least:
  * the procedure to be followed by the master or other persons having charge of the ship to report an oil pollution incident as required by the MS (Reporting Requirements for Ships Carrying Dangerous or Polluting Goods) Regulations 1995;
  * the list of persons (including national and local authorities) to be contacted in the event of an oil pollution incident;
  * a detailed description of the action to be taken immediately by persons on board to reduce or control the discharge of oil following an incident; and
  * the procedures and point of contact on the ship for co-ordinating shipboard action with national and local authorities in combating the pollution (regulation 33(2).
* The MCA takes the view that SOPEPs should be simple documents which make use of summarising flow charts or checklists to guide the master through the various actions and decisions required in responding to an incident.
* To accomplish its purpose the plan must be realistic, practical and easy to use. SOPEPs should be drawn up in conformity with the IMO Guidelines and submitted for approval by the shipowner to the MCA Marine Office normally dealt with.
* The validity of a ship's IOPP or UKOPP Certificate depends on the carriage of a SOPEP.
* Failure to carry a SOPEP may also cause difficulties in Port State Control inspections or at port clearance.
* **MGN 231** draws attention to international requirements for shipboard pollution emergency plans effective from 1 January 2003, and outlines MCA's policy and arrangements regarding approval of plans.

D04t.1b Shipboard Marine Pollution Emergency Plan for Noxious Liquid Substances (SMPEP)

* **1999 Amendments to MARPOL Annex II**, and which entered into force on 1 January 2001, include a new **regulation 16**, which provides that every tanker of 150gt and above which is certified to carry noxious liquid substances in bulk must carry a **Shipboard Marine Pollution Emergency Plan for Noxious Liquid Substances** (known as an "**SMPEP (NLS)**") not later than 1 January 2003.
* **MGN 231**, which explains the requirement for an SMPEP, advises that in respect of oil tankers which must also have an SMPEP (NLS), the SMPEP (NLS) may be combined with the SOPEP, the combined plan being called the **Shipboard Marine Pollution Emergency Plan (SMPEP)**.

* An SMPEP (NLS) or SMPEP must be in accordance with the **IMO Guidelines** for the Development of Shipboard Marine Pollution Emergency Plans for Oil and/or Noxious Liquid Substances, MEPC Resolution 85(44), details of which are given in **MGN 231**.
* The validity of a ship's COF or INLSC Certificate will depend on the carriage of an SMPEP (NLS) or SMPEP.
* Failure to carry an SMPEP (NLS) or SMPEP may also cause difficulties in Port State Control inspections or at port clearance.

D04t.1c Federal and State Vessel Response Plans (VRPs)

* **United States federal law** requires the owner of every vessel (of any tonnage) carrying oil as cargo in US waters to submit for **federal** government approval a **Vessel Response Plan** (**VRP**) in respect of that vessel. The US Coast Guard operates the approval scheme and maintains a **VRP web page** at www.uscg.mil/vrp
* In addition to the federal law requirement, the **state law** of several US states requires the owner of any tanker entering state waters to submit a **state VRP**. (Some states use another name for the state VRP, such as "**Vessel Contingency Plan**" or "**Spill Prevention and Control Contingency Plan**".) According to the US Coast Guard, the VRP submitted to meet federal requirements will also meet state planning requirements in **Alaska**, **Washington**, **Oregon** and/or **California**.
* Details of federal and state VRP requirements should be obtained from the **P&I club** with which the ship is entered before commencing any voyage to the USA, and the requisite plans drawn up with the club's guidance. In most cases, these plans will differ from the SOPEP required by MARPOL 73/78.
* **California legislation** prohibits any non-tank vessel (defined as a vessel that is not designed to carry oil as cargo) of 300gt or more from operating in the marine waters of California (i.e. within 3 miles from the shore) unless her owner or operator has prepared and submitted to the California Office of Spill Prevention and Response (OSPR) an **oil spill contingency plan** which names (*inter alia*) a "qualified individual", a spill management team and response organisations. The owner or operator must have obtained a **California Certificate of Financial Responsibility** from OSPR on demonstrating the ability to pay at least $300 million to cover damages caused by a spill. The owner or operator will normally be able to obtain the COFR from the California authorities on production of their P&I Certificate of Entry.

D04t.2 Stability, loading and ballasting information

* **Stability information** must be provided on board under the provisions of:
  * **regulation 32 of the MS (Load Line) Regulations 1998** (SI 1998/2241) (see D04t.2a);
  * **regulation 16 of the MS (Cargo Ship Construction) Regulations 1997** (SI 1997/1509) (see D04t.2c);
  * **regulation 38 of the MS (Passenger Ship Construction: Ships of Classes I, II and II(A)) Regulations 1998** (SI 1998/2514) (see D04t.2d); and
  * **regulation 31 of the MS (Passenger Ship Construction: Ships of Classes III to VI(A)) Regulations 1998** (SI 1998/2515) (see D04t.2d).
* Loading and ballasting information must be provided in the case of certain ships carrying liquids or ore in bulk under the provisions of regulation 33(1) of the **MS (Load Line) Regulations 1998** (SI 1998/2241) (see D04t.2b).

D04t.2a Intact stability booklet and inclining test

* **Regulation 32(1) of the MS (Load Line) Regulations 1998** (SI 1998/2241) provides that the owner of every ship to which the Regulations apply (see D03a.3) must provide, for the guidance of the master, **information relating to the stability of the ship** in accordance with the Regulation. The information must be in the form of a book which must be kept on the ship at all times in the master's custody. (This book is sometimes referred to as the **intact stability booklet**.)
* In the case of a UK ship the (intact) stability information must include all matters specified in Schedule 6 in **MSN 1752** [100], and must be in the form required by that Schedule (regulation 32(1)). The information must also be in accordance with the requirements of regulation 32(3), (4) and (5) (as outlined in D04t.2b).
* Before the stability information is given to the master of any of the ship types listed in regulation 32(5) [101], it must be **approved** either by the MCA or the Assigning Authority which assigned freeboards to the ship. In the case of any other ship, the information must be approved by the MCA (regulation 32(5)).

---

[100] MSN 1752 replaced MSN 1701. Schedule 6 lists 12 items of "Information as to Stability" required to be in the intact stability booklet.

[101] The ships listed in regulation 32(5) (i.e. those for which the inclining test may be carried out in the presence of an Assigning Authority surveyor) are: oil tankers over 100 metres in length; bulk carriers, or ore carriers, over 150 metres in length; single deck bulk carriers over 100 metres in length but not exceeding 150 metres in length; single deck dry cargo ships over 100 metres in length; purpose-built container ships over 125 metres in length; column-stabilised mobile offshore drilling units; and column-stabilised mobile offshore support units.

* Subject to regulation 32(4), the intact stability information must be based on the determination of stability taken from an **inclining test** carried out in the presence of a surveyor appointed by the MCA or, for ships listed in regulation 32(5), the Assigning Authority (regulation 32(3)). This information is to be **amended** whenever any alterations are made to the ship or changes occur to it which will materially affect the information and, if necessary, the ship must be **re-inclined**.
* Regulation 32(4) provides that the **inclining test may be dispensed with** if –
  * in the case of any ship basic stability data is available from the inclining test of a sister ship and it is known that reliable stability information can be obtained from such data; and
  * in the case of a ship specially designed for the carriage of liquids or ore in bulk, or of any class of such ships, the information available in respect of similar ships shows that the ship's proportions and arrangements will ensure more than sufficient stability in all probable loading conditions.

D04t.2b Bulk carrier loading and ballasting booklet

* Regulation 33(1) of the Load Line Regulations provides that the owner of **any ship of more than 150 metres in length specially designed for the carriage of liquids or ore in bulk** must provide, for the guidance of the master, information relating to the **loading and ballasting** of the ship. (This information is normally provided in a booklet known as a **bulk carrier loading and ballasting booklet**.)
* The loading and ballasting information must indicate the maximum stresses permissible for the ship and specify the manner in which the ship must be loaded and ballasted to avoid the creation of unacceptable stresses in its structure (regulation 33(2)).
* Before the loading and ballasting information is given to the master of any of the ship types listed in regulation 32(5), it must be approved either by the MCA or the Assigning Authority which assigned freeboards to the ship. In the case of any other ship, the information must be approved by the MCA (regulation 33(3)).

D04t.2c Stability information required by Cargo Ship Construction Regulations

* **Regulation 16 of the MS (Cargo Ship Construction) Regulations 1997** (SI 1997/1509) applies to every cargo ship of 100 metres or over in sub-division length built on or after 1 February 1992, except any ship complying with:
  * MARPOL Annex I, regulation 25 (which concerns **subdivision and damage stability of new oil tankers**);
  * the International Code for the Construction and Equipment of Ships Carrying Dangerous Chemicals in Bulk;
  * the International Code for the Construction and Equipment of Ships Carrying Liquefied Gases in Bulk;
  * the Code for the Construction and Equipment of Ships Carrying Dangerous Chemicals in Bulk;
  * the Code for the Construction and Equipment of Ships Carrying Liquefied Gases in Bulk;
  * the Guidelines for the Design and Construction of Offshore Supply Vessels;
  * the Code for the Safety of Special Purpose Ships;
  * the damage stability requirements of regulation 27 of the International Load Line Convention 1966 (as modified); and
  * enactments of the Merchant Shipping Act 1995 or SIs implementing MARPOL 73/78 or the Codes listed above.
* **Regulation 16** provides that the master of every **sea-going UK cargo ship of 500 gross tonnage or over**, wherever it is, and **every sea-going non-UK cargo ship of 500 gross tonnage or over while in UK waters**, other than high-speed craft to which the MS (High Speed Craft) Regulations 1996 apply, must be supplied with such reliable information as is necessary to enable him **by rapid and simple means to determine the stability** of the ship under various conditions of service. The information must include:
  1. **one** of the following:
       a **curve of minimum operational GM versus draught** assuring compliance with the applicable intact stability requirements of Schedule 4, Part I of the MS (Load Lines) Rules 1968 or with the attained subdivision index of the ship, whichever is the more onerous condition or, where curves representing the requirements cross, the part of each curve which represents the more onerous requirement; **or**
       a (corresponding) curve of the **maximum allowable vertical centre of gravity (KG) versus draught**; **or**
       a **tabular or equivalent presentation of either** of these curves; **and**
  2. **instructions** concerning the operation of **cross-flooding arrangements**; **and**
  3. **all other data** and means of presentation necessary to assist the crew to **maintain stability after damage**.
* The above information, before being supplied to the master, must be **approved** by the Assigning Authority.

D04t.2d Stability information required by Passenger Ship Construction Regulations

* **Regulation 38(1) of the MS (Passenger Ship Construction: Ships of Classes I, II and II(A)) Regulations 1998** (SI 1998/2514) provides that every ship of Class I, II or II(A) on her completion must be **inclined** and the **elements**

of her stability determined. The master must be supplied by the owner with **approved information** relating to the stability of the ship in accordance with the provisions of regulation 38.

* Every ship of Class I, II or II(A) must have a **lightweight survey** carried out within each period of **5 years** to verify any changes in lightship displacement and longitudinal centre of gravity. Such periods must commence on the date of issue of a Passenger Ship Safety Certificate or Passenger Certificate or from a previous inclining or lightweight survey, whichever date is the earliest (regulation 38(2)). The ship must be **re-inclined** whenever, in comparison with the ship's approved stability information derived from the previous inclining experiment, a **deviation** from the lightship displacement exceeding 2 per cent or a deviation of the longitudinal centre of gravity exceeding 1 per cent of the ship's length is found or anticipated. **Every inclining or lightweight survey** made for the purpose of regulation 38(2) must be carried out in the presence of a **nominated surveyor**. The interval between lightweight surveys of any such ship may be extended for a period of not more than one year if, on the production of relevant information about the ship, it can be shown that the lightweight survey is not necessary at the required interval.

* An **approved report** of each inclining or lightweight survey carried out in accordance with regulation 38(2) and of the **calculation** therefrom of the lightship condition must be placed on board for the use of the master (regulation 38(3)).

* Where elements of a ship's stability have been found to have changed following any inclining or lightweight survey carried out in accordance with the requirements of paragraph (2) the master must be supplied with **amended approved stability information** (regulation 38(4)).

* Where any alterations are made to a ship so as materially to affect the stability information supplied to the master, **amended stability information** must be provided, and the ship must be **re-inclined** (regulation 38(5)).

* **Regulation 31 of the MS (Passenger Ship Construction: Ships of Classes III to VI(A)) Regulations 1998** (SI 1998/2515) provides that **every subdivided ship** of Classes III, IV, V, VI or VI(A) on completion must be **inclined** and the **elements of her stability** determined. Every other ship (i.e. every non-subdivided ship of those classes) must undergo the **heeling test or buoyancy test** specified in Sections 3 and 4 (respectively) of Schedule 2 in MSN 1699. The master must be supplied by the owner with **approved information** relating to the stability of the ship in accordance with the following provisions of regulation 31.

* Regulation 31(2) provides that in each period of five years, every subdivided ship must have a **lightweight survey** to verify any changes in lightship displacement and longitudinal centre of gravity. Every other ship must undergo the **heeling test or buoyancy test** specified in Sections 3 and 4 (respectively) of Schedule 2 in MSN 1699, to verify any changes in the heeling or buoyancy characteristics. The 5-year periods commence either on the date of issue of the Passenger Certificate or from a previous inclining or lightweight survey, whichever is earliest.

* The ship must be **re-inclined** whenever, in comparison with the ship's approved stability information derived from the previous inclining experiment, a deviation from the lightship displacement exceeding 2 per cent or a deviation of the longitudinal centre of gravity exceeding 1 per cent of the ship's length is found or anticipated. Every inclining or lightweight survey or tests made for this purpose or for the purpose of regulation 32 must be carried out in the presence of a **nominated surveyor**. The interval between the lightweight surveys or tests may be **extended** for a period of not more than one year if, on the production of relevant information about the ship, it can be shown that the lightweight survey or test is not necessary at the required interval.

* An **approved report** of each inclining or lightweight survey or test carried out in accordance with this regulation and of the calculation therefrom of the lightship condition, or heeling or buoyancy particulars, as applicable, must be placed on board for the use of the master (regulation 32(3)).

* Where **elements of a ship's stability** have been found to have **changed** following any inclining or lightweight survey or test carried out in accordance with the requirements of paragraph (3), the master must be supplied with **amended approved stability information** (regulation 32(4)).

* Where any **alterations** are made to a ship so as materially to affect the stability information supplied to the master, amended stability information must be provided and the ship must be **re-inclined** (regulation 32(5)).

* For subdivided ships, stability information provided pursuant to regulations 32(1), (3), (4) and (5) must be furnished in the form of a book (the **stability information book**) which must be kept on board the ship at all times in the custody of the master. The information must include particulars appropriate to the ship and must be in a **form acceptable to the certifying authority** (regulation 32(6)).

* **Ships required to comply with the heeling test or buoyancy test** specified in Sections 3 and 4 of Schedule 2 in MSN 1699 must be furnished with **stability information** in the form of a **written record setting out the principal particulars** (regulation 32(7)).

D04t.2e Damage control plans and booklets

* **Regulation 16 of the MS (Cargo Ship Construction) Regulations 1997** applies to **all cargo ships** (including tankers) of 100 metres in length or over, of any age. **Regulation 16(5)** provides that there must be, permanently exhibited or readily available on the navigating bridge for the guidance of the officer in charge of the ship, **plans** showing clearly for each deck and hold:

* the boundaries of the watertight compartments;
* the openings therein;
* the means of closure and position of any controls thereof; and
* the arrangements for the correction of any list due to flooding.

* In addition to the damage control plans, **booklets** containing the same information must be made available by the owners for the use of the officers of the ship.

* Part V of the MS (Cargo Ship Construction) Regulations 1997 relates to damage control in dry cargo ships. **Regulation 20** details the requirements for **dry cargo ships constructed on or after 1 February 1992**. There must be **permanently exhibited or readily available** on the navigating bridge, for the guidance of the officer in charge of the ship, **a plan** showing clearly for each deck and hold, the boundaries of the watertight compartments, the openings therein with the means of closure and position of any controls thereof, and the arrangements for the correction of any list due to flooding; in addition, **booklets** containing this information must be made available to the ship's officers (regulation 20(1)).

* The **booklets** required by regulation 20(1) must contain **general precautions** being a listing of equipment, conditions and operational procedures, considered by the Certifying Authority to be necessary to maintain watertight integrity under normal ship operations (regulation 20(3)). Booklets must also contain **specific precautions** being a listing of elements (such as closures, security of cargo, sounding of alarms), considered by the Certifying Authority to be vital to the survival of the ship and its crew (regulation 20(4)).

* **Indicators** must be provided on the navigating bridge for all **sliding doors and hinged doors in watertight bulkheads** to show whether these doors are open or closed. In addition, shell doors and other openings which, in the opinion of the Certifying Authority, could lead to major flooding if left open or not properly secured, must also be provided with such indicators (regulation 20(2)).

* **Regulation 47 of the MS (Passenger Ship Construction: Ships of Classes I, II and II(A)) Regulations 1998** (SI 1998/2514) provides that there must be **permanently exhibited** in the ship, for the information of the officer in charge, **plans** showing clearly for each level the boundaries of the watertight compartments, the openings therein, the means of closing such openings and the position of the controls and the arrangements for the correction of any list due to flooding. In addition, **booklets** containing such information must be made available by the owner for the use of the ship's officers. These requirements also apply, by virtue of **regulation 38 of the MS (Passenger Ship Construction: Ships of Classes III to VI(A)) Regulations 1998** (SI 1998/2515), to every **subdivided ship** of Classes III to VI(A).

D04t.3 Safe Manning Document

* For notes on the **Safe Manning Document**, see E03b.3.

D04t.4 Garbage Management Plan

* **Regulation 10 of the MS (Prevention of Pollution by Garbage) Regulations 1998** (SI 1998/1377) gives effect to a 1995 Amendment to MARPOL 73/78 requiring ships to carry a **Garbage Management Plan**. This requirement applies to every ship of 400gt or above, every ship certified to carry 15 persons or more, and every fixed or floating installation.

* Any ship or installation to which regulation 10 applies must carry a **Garbage Management Plan** (regulation 10(2)). The plan must provide written procedures for collecting, storing, processing and disposing of garbage, including the use of the equipment on board (regulation 10(2)(a)). It must also designate the person in charge of carrying out the plan (regulation 10(2)(b)). The plan must be in accordance with IMO Guidelines (regulation 10(2)(c)) and be written in the crew's working language (regulation 10(2)(d)). The crew of a ship required to carry a Garbage Management Plan must follow the plan (regulation 10(3)).

* Under regulation 12(2) an MCA inspector may investigate any operation regulated by the Regulations if he has clear grounds for believing that the master or crew are not familiar with the ship's on-board procedures for preventing pollution by garbage. If the inspector is satisfied that either the master or crew are not familiar with the ship's on-board procedures for preventing pollution by garbage he must take such steps as he considers necessary, including detaining the ship, to ensure she does not sail until the situation has been brought into accordance with the requirements of the Regulations (regulation 12(3)).

* Each Garbage Management Plan will be individual to a particular ship, since the trading area and ship type will vary the garbage management policy.

* Garbage Management Plans are liable to be inspected by flag State and port State control inspectors.

* The International Chamber of Shipping (ICS) publishes a model Garbage Management Plan for use of shipping companies.

D04t.5 Garbage Record Book

* **Regulation 11 of the MS (Prevention of Pollution by Garbage) Regulations 1998** (SI 1998/1377) gives effect to a 1995 Amendment to Annex V of MARPOL 73/78 requiring ships and installations to carry a **Garbage Record Book (GRB)**. This requirement took effect from 1 July 1998 and applies to every ship of 400gt or above, every ship certified to carry 15 persons or more which is engaged on voyages to ports or offshore terminals under the jurisdiction of a Party to the MARPOL Convention other than its flag State, and every fixed and floating installation.
* "Garbage" is defined in regulation 2 as "all kinds of victual, domestic and operational wastes excluding fresh fish and parts thereof, generated during the normal operation of the ship and liable to be disposed of continuously or periodically except sewage originating from ships". (See definition in MSN 1720, below.)
* Any ship or installation to which regulation 11 applies must carry a **Garbage Record Book**, whether as part of the ship's Official Log Book or otherwise, in the form specified in MSN 1720.
* The **officer in charge of a discharge operation, or incineration**, must make and sign an entry in the Garbage Record Book in respect of the **discharge or completed incineration** on the date it took place. "Discharges" includes discharges at sea, to shore reception facilities, or to other ships.
* Entries in the Garbage Record Book must include:
  the **date and time** of the discharge or incineration;
  position of ship or installation at time of discharge or incineration;
  description of, and estimated amount of, garbage discharged or incinerated.
* If a **discharge, escape or accidental loss** occurs, an entry must be made in the Garbage Record Book of its circumstances and reasons.
* Any entries made in the Garbage Record Book must:
  * in the case of a UK ship, or an installation of any flag, be in **English** and, if different, the **working language of the crew**;
  * in the case of a non-UK ship, be in an official language of the flag State and in English or French. (In the case of a discrepancy between the different language entries, those in the official language of the flag State will prevail).
* **Each completed page** of the Garbage Record Book must be signed by the **master** or the installation manager as appropriate.
* The **Garbage Record Book** must:
  * be **kept on board** the ship or installation and in such a place as to be available for inspection in a reasonable time;
    * be preserved by the ship's or installation's owner for **two years after the final entry** in it.
* The MCA may **waive** the requirement for a Garbage Record Book to be kept in respect of:
  * any ship certified to carry 15 persons or more engaged on a voyage of one hour or less in duration; or
  * any fixed or floating installation.
* **MSN 1720 –**
  explains the requirements to keep a Garbage Record Book.

  defines "**garbage**" as "all kinds of victual, domestic and operational wastes excluding fresh fish and parts thereof, generated during the normal operation of the ship and liable to be disposed of continuously or periodically, except those substances which are defined or listed in other annexes to MARPOL 73/78 (such as oil, sewage or noxious liquid substances)". (The part of this definition after the word "periodically" differs from that in regulation 2 of the Garbage Regulations.)

  states that garbage is to be grouped into the following **categories for the purposes of entries in the Garbage Record Book**:
  * Plastics;
  * Floating dunnage, lining, or packing material;
  * Ground-down paper products, rags, glass, metal, bottles, crockery, etc.;
  * Paper products, rags, glass, metal, bottles, crockery, etc.
  * Food waste;
  * Incinerator ash.
  - lists the **entries to be made in the Garbage Record Book** on the following occasions:
    * when garbage is discharged into the sea;
    * when garbage is discharged to reception facilities ashore or to other ships;
    * when garbage is incinerated; and
    * when there is an accidental of other exceptional discharge of garbage.
  states that the master should obtain from the operator of port reception facilities, or from the master of the ship receiving the garbage, a **receipt or certificate specifying the estimated amount of garbage transferred**. The receipts or certificates must be kept on board the ship with the Garbage Record Book for 2 years.

states that the **amount of garbage before and after processing on board** should be estimated in cubic metres, if possible separately according to category. It is recognised that the accuracy of estimating amounts of garbage is left to interpretation. Volume estimates will differ before and after processing. Some processing procedures may not allow for a usable estimate of volume, e.g. the continuous processing of food waste. Such factors should be taken into account when making and interpreting entries in a record. Shipboard procedures adopted in accordance with IMO recommended guidance for the handling, storage and processing of garbage may on some vessels (e.g. ferries) give rise to plastics not being segregated and therefore an estimate of their quantity being impossible. Also, weight measurement, rather than volumetric measurement, may be a more appropriate way of estimating and recording amounts of processed garbage. Such variations will continue to be acceptable according to MSN 1720.

contains an **example of the required format** for recording garbage discharges.

* For notes on inspection of Garbage Record Books and garbage-related operations, see I06c.7.

D04t.6 Garbage disposal placards

* **Regulation 9 of the MS (Prevention of Pollution by Garbage) Regulations 1998** (SI 1998/1377) gives effect to an Amendment to Annex V of MARPOL 73/78 and requires every ship of 12 metres or more in length overall to display placards notifying crew and passengers, if any, of the disposal requirements of regulations 4 to 7 of the Garbage Regulations (see H03e).

* In the case of a UK ship, the information on the placards must be in English and, if different, the working language of the crew (regulation 9(2)).

* In the case of a non-UK ship, the information on the placards must be in the official language of the flag State, and, where the ship is engaged on voyages to ports or offshore terminals under the jurisdiction of another MARPOL signatory State, in English or French (regulation 9(3)).

* Every fixed or floating installation must display placards notifying all persons on board of the disposal requirements of regulation 7. The information must be written in English and, if different, in the working language of the crew (regulation 9(4)).

D04t.7 Search and Rescue Co-operation Plan

* The **MS (Safety of Navigation) Regulations 2002** (SI 2002/1473) (see H01f.2) –
- **revoke** and replace the MS (Co-operation with Search and Rescue Services) Regulations 1998 (SI 1998/1692).
- **require (in regulation 5) compliance** by a ship to which the Regulations apply with **paragraph 3 of SOLAS regulation V/7** (which relates to **Search and rescue services**).

* **SOLAS regulation V/7.3** provides that passenger ships to which SOLAS chapter I applies (i.e. all passenger ships engaged on international voyages) must have on board a plan for co-operation with appropriate search and rescue services in the event of an emergency. The plan must be developed in co-operation between the ship, the company as defined in regulation IX/1, and the search and rescue services. The plan must include provisions for periodic exercises to be undertaken to test its effectiveness. The plan must be based on the guidelines developed by IMO (i.e. IMO Guidelines for Preparing Plans for Co-operation between Search and Rescue Services and Passenger Ships (MSC Circ.1000)).

* **Guidance note 5 to regulation V/7 in MCA's 2002 SOLAS Chapter V publication** states that **all UK passenger ships** (i.e. including UK passenger ships on domestic voyages) are required to comply with the requirements of SOLAS V/7.3.

* Full details of the requirements for SAR Co-operation Plans on UK passenger ships are contained in **MSN 1761**, which contains **Guidelines for developing plans** in accordance with SOLAS V/7.3. (MSN 1761 is not superseded by the MCA's 2002 SOLAS Chapter V publication.)

* For notes on **search and rescue operations**, see H04b.12.

D04t.8 Ship Sanitation and Hygiene Certificate

* A **Ship Sanitation and Hygiene Certificate** may be issued to a ship in a UK port by a port health authority to record an inspection of the ship in accordance with article 14 of the Internatiornal Health Regulations, section 79 of the Environmental Protection Act 1990, provisions contained in the Public Health (Ships) Regulations, and compliance with recommendations in the WHO *Guide to Ship Sanitation*. An equivalent certificate may be issued by the health authorities in a non-UK port under article 14 of the International Health Regulations and relevant national legislation.

* **Details shown** on a typical certificate issued in the UK include: Vessel name; port of registry; Net Tonnage; Deratting/Exemption Certificate port of issue and date; Date of inspection and signature and stamp of inspector (e.g. "Manchester Port Health Authority" or "Aberdeen City Council"); Record of Inspection covering: 1. Potable water; 2. Waste disposal; 3. Accommodation; 4. Swimming pools; 5. Food sanitation. Details of unsatisfactory conditions or practices to be remedied are listed (including Ref. No.; location; defect; action required). The certificate is usually signed and issued by an Environmental Health Officer of the issuing health authority.

D04t.9 Noise Survey Report

* A **Noise Survey Report** may be issued to a ship under section 4.3 of the **Code on Noise Levels on Board Ships** and IMO Resolution A.468(XII), paragraph 4.3.
* Paragraph 1.3 of Code provides that:
  * the Code applies to new ships of 1600gt and over;
  * the provisions relating to potentially hazardous noise levels contained in the Code should also apply to existing ships of 1600gt and over, as far as reasonable and practicable, to the satisfaction of the Administration; and
  * the Code should apply to new ships of less than 1600gt, as far as reasonable and possible, to the satisfaction of the Administration.
* Paragraph 2.1 of the Code provides that on completion of the construction of the ship, or as soon as practicable thereafter, **measurement of noise levels** in all spaces specified in Chapter 4 should take place under the operating conditions specified in 2.2 and 2.3 and should be suitably recorded as required by 4.3.
* Paragraph 4.3.4 of Code states: "Where a ship does not comply with Chapter 4 (Maximum Acceptable Sound Pressure Levels) and where the use of ear protectors is required, a **copy of the noise survey report** should be carried on board".
* A model format for a Noise Survey Report is set out in Appendix 1 to the Code.
* The **purposes** of the Noise Survey Report is to report the results of a **noise survey** in accordance with the Code on Noise Levels on Board Ships. **2**. Purposes of the Code are to limit noise levels and to reduce exposure to noise, in order to: (1) provide for safe working conditions by giving consideration to the need for speech communication and for hearing audible alarms, and to an environment where clear-headed decisions can be made in control stations, navigation and radio spaces and manned machinery spaces; (2) protect the seafarer from excessive noise levels which may give rise to a noise-induced hearing loss; and (3) provide the seafarer with an acceptable degree of comfort in rest, recreation and other spaces and also provide conditions for recuperation from the effects of exposure to high noise levels.
* **Details shown** in the report (as recommended in 4.3.3 of Code) include: **1**. Hull number, name of ship, gross tonnage, main dimensions and ship type. **2**. Leading particulars of ship's machinery. **3**. Builder's and owner's names. **4**. Date and time of measurements. **5**. Type of voyage, meteorological conditions, sea state and ship's position during measurements. **6**. Under-keel clearance during measurements. **7**. Main operating conditions including those items on the main machinery line which were operating and the operating condition. **8**. Names and addresses of those carrying out the measurements. **9**. Make, type and serial number of instrumentation used. **10**. Details and date of instrument calibration. **11**. List of main noise abatement measures applied on board. **12**. Other particulars of interest, including exceptions to the standard laid down in the Code.

D04t.10 Ship Security equipment, verifications and documentation

* The International Ship and Port Facility Security Code (**ISPS Code**) (see A03c.5), which is in force from 1 July 2004, applies to every passenger ship and every cargo ship of 500gt or over, including high-speed craft and MODUs, when engaged on international voyages. Under the provisions of the ISPS Code, those ships will be required to carry a **Ship Security Plan** (**SSP**) (see D04t.10a), be equipped with a **ship security alert system** (see D04t.10b) and be issued with an **International Ship Security Certificate** (ISSC) or an **Interim ISSC** (see D04t.10c).

D04t.10a Ship Security Plan

* ISPS Code, part A, section 9 contains requirements for **Ship Security Plans** (SSPs).
* **Ship Security Plan** is defined as "a plan developed to ensure the application of measures on board the ship designed to protect persons on board, cargo, cargo transport units, ship's stores or the ship from the risks of a security incident" (Section 9.1).
* Each ship must carry on board a **Ship Security Plan** approved by the flag State Administration. The plan must make provisions for the **three security levels** as defined in this Part (Section 9.2).

* The flag State Administration may entrust the **review and approval** of Ship Security Plans, or of amendments to a previously approved plan, to a **Recognized Security Organization** (RSO), **provided** the RSO has not been involved in either the preparation of the ship security assessment or of the Ship Security Plan, or of the amendments, under review (Section 9.3). For notes on RSOs, see B02c.1.
* Submission of Ship Security Plans, or a plan amendment, for approval must be accompanied by the **security assessment** on which the plan or amendment was based (Section 9.4).
* Section 9.5 provides that such a **Ship Security Plan** must be developed, taking into account the guidance given in Part B of the ISPS Code and must be written in the working language or languages of the ship. The **plan must consist, at least, of**:
    * measures designed to prevent weapons, dangerous substances and devices intended for use against people, ships or ports and the carriage of which is not authorized from being taken on board the ship;
    * identification of restricted areas and measures for the prevention of unauthorized access to the ship and to restricted areas on board;
    * procedures for responding to security threats or breaches of security, including provisions for maintaining critical operations of the ship or ship/port interface;
    * procedures for responding to any security instructions Contracting Governments may give at security level 3;
    * procedures for evacuation in case of security threats or breaches of security;
    * security related duties assigned to shipboard personnel;
    * procedures for auditing the security activities;
    * procedures for training, drills and exercises associated with the plan;
    * procedures for interfacing with port facility security activities;
    * procedures for the periodic review of the plan and for updating;
    * procedures for reporting security incidents;
    * identification of the ship security officer;
    * identification of the company security officer including 24-hour contact details;
    * procedures and schedule for inspection, testing, calibration, and maintenance of any security equipment on board;
    * identification of the locations where the ship security alert system activation points are fitted;
    * procedures, instructions and guidance on the use of the ship security alert system, including the testing, activation, deactivation and resetting, and to limit false alerts.
* **Personnel conducting internal audits** of the security activities specified in the plan or evaluating its implementation must be independent of the activities being audited unless this is impracticable due to the size and the nature of the Company or the ship (Section 9.6).
* The flag State Administration must determine what **changes** to an approved **Ship Security Plan** or to any security **equipment** specified in an approved plan **must not be implemented** unless the relevant amendments to the Plan are approved by the Administration. Any such changes must be at least as effective as those measures prescribed in Chapter XI-2 of SOLAS and Part A of the ISPS Code. The nature of the changes to the Ship Security Plan or the security equipment that have been specifically approved by the flag State Administration must be **documented** in a manner that clearly indicates such approval. This **approval** must be available on board and must be presented together with the International Ship Security Certificate (or the Interim ISSC). If these changes are temporary, once the original approved measures or equipment are **reinstated**, this documentation no longer needs to be retained by the ship (section 9.7).
* The plan may be kept in an **electronic format**; if so, it must be protected by means to prevent it from being deleted, destroyed or overwritten (section 9.8).
* The plan must be **protected** from unauthorized access or disclosure (section 9.9).
* Ship Security Plans are **not generally subject to inspection by officers of a port State**. However, if there are **clear grounds** for believing that the ship is in violation of the requirements of Chapter XI-2 of SOLAS or of the ISPS Code, **limited access** to the specific sections of the plan relating to the non-compliance is allowed, but **only with the consent of the Flag State Administration or the master of the ship** (section 9.10).

D04t.10b Ship security verifications

* ISPS Code, part A, section 19 contains requirements relating to **verifications**.
* Each ship to which part A of the Code applies (see D03a.6) will be subject to the following **verifications**:
    * an **initial verification** before the ship is put in service or before the International Ship Security Certificate (ISSC) or Interim ISSC is issued for the first time. This verification will include a **complete verification** of the ship's **security system** and any associated **security equipment** covered by the relevant provisions of chapter XI-2, part A of the Code and the approved Ship Security Plan. This verification will ensure that the security system and any associated security equipment of the ship fully complies with the applicable requirements of

chapter XI-2 and part A of the Code, is in satisfactory condition and fit for the service for which the ship is intended;

- a **renewal verification** at intervals specified by the flag State Administration, but not exceeding 5 years, except where section 19.3.1 or 19.3.4 is applicable. The purposes of this verification are the same as those of the initial verification;
- at least one **intermediate verification**. If **only one** intermediate verification is carried out it must take place between the second and third anniversary date of the ISSC or Interim ISSC. The intermediate verification will include **inspection** of the security system and any associated security equipment of the ship to ensure that it remains satisfactory for the service for which the ship is intended. Such intermediate verification must be endorsed on the certificate;
- any **additional verifications** as determined by the flag State Administration.

* Verifications of ships must be carried out by officers of the **flag State Administration**. The Administration may, however, entrust the verifications to a **Recognized Security Organization** referred to in regulation XI-2/1 (19.1.2).

* In every case, the Administration concerned must fully guarantee the completeness and efficiency of the verification and must undertake to ensure the necessary arrangements to satisfy this obligation (19.1.3).

* The **security system and any associated security equipment** of the ship after verification **must be maintained** to conform with the provisions of regulations XI-2/4.2 and XI-2/6, part A of the Code and the approved Ship Security Plan. After any verification under section 19.1.1 has been completed, **no changes** may be made in the **security system** and in any associated **security equipment** or the approved **Ship Security Plan** without the sanction of the flag State Administration (19.1.5).

D04t.10c International Ship Security Certificate (ISSC) and Interim ISSC

* ISPS Code, part A, section 19 contains provisions relating to **certification for ships**. Section 19.2 relates to **Issue or endorsement of certificate**. Section 19.3 relates to **Duration and validity of certificate**. Section 19.4 relates to **Interim certification**.

* An **International Ship Security Certificate** (ISSC) must be issued after an initial or renewal verification in accordance with the provisions of section 19.1 (section 19.2.1). The ISSC must be **issued or endorsed either by the flag State Administration or by a Recognized Security Organization** (RSO) acting on behalf of the flag State Administration (section 19.2.2). Verification and issue of the ISSC may be by or on behalf of **another SOLAS Contracting Government** at the request of the flag State Administration (section 19.2.3).

* An ISSC will be issued for a period specified by the flag State Administration which may not exceed **5 years** (section 19.3.1).

* When the **renewal verification is completed within 3 months before the expiry date** of the existing ISSC, the new ISSC will be valid from the date of completion of the renewal verification to a date not exceeding 5 years from the date of expiry of the existing ISSC (section 19.3.2).

* When the **renewal verification is completed after the expiry date of the existing ISSC**, the new ISSC will be valid from the date of completion of the renewal verification to a date not exceeding 5 years from the date of expiry of the existing ISSC (section 19.3.2.1).

* When the **renewal verification is completed more than 3 months before the expiry date** of the existing ISSC, the new ISSC will be valid from the date of completion of the renewal verification to a date not exceeding 5 years from the date of completion of the renewal verification (section 19.3.2.2).

* If a **certificate is issued for a period of less than 5 years**, the flag State Administration may **extend** the validity of the certificate beyond the expiry date to the maximum period specified in section 19.3.1 (i.e. 5 years), provided that the verifications referred to in section 19.1.1 applicable when an ISSC is issued for a period of 5 years are carried out as appropriate (section 19.3.3).

* If a renewal verification has been completed but a **new ISSC cannot be issued or placed on board the ship before the expiry date** of the existing ISSC, the flag State Administration or RSO acting on behalf of the flag State Administration may endorse the existing ISSC, which must then be accepted as valid for a further period which may not exceed 5 months from the expiry date (section 19.3.4).

* Section 19.4.1 provides that, for the purposes of:

- a **ship without a certificate, on delivery** or **prior to its entry or re-entry into service**;
- **transfer of a ship** from the **flag of one SOLAS Contracting Government to another**;
- **transfer of a ship** to the **flag of a SOLAS Contracting Government from a non-SOLAS State**; or
- when a **Company assumes the responsibility for the operation of a ship** not previously operated by that Company;

- until the ISSC is issued, the flag State Administration may cause an **Interim International Ship Security Certificate** (IISSC) to be issued.

* Section 19.4.2 provides that an **Interim International Ship Security Certificate** will only be issued when the flag State Administration, or RSO on behalf of the flag State Administration, has verified that:

- the **ship security assessment** required by this part of the Code has been completed;
- a copy of the **Ship Security Plan** is provided on board, has been submitted for review and approval, and is being implemented on the ship;
- the ship is provided with a **ship security alert system**, if required;
- the **company security officer** (CSO) has fulfilled various obligations set out in section 19.4.2.4;
- arrangements have been made for carrying out the required **verifications** under section 19.1.1.1;
- the **master**, the **ship security officer** (SSO) and **other ship's personnel with specific security duties** are **familiar** with their duties and responsibilities under the ISPS Code; and with the relevant provisions of the Ship Security Plan; and have been provided with such **information** in the **working language** of the ship's personnel or languages understood by them; and
- the **ship security officer** (SSO) meets the requirements of part A of the ISPS Code.

* An IISSC may be issued by the Administration or by an RSO authorized to act on its behalf (section 19.4.3).
* An IISSC will be valid for **6 months, or until the ISSC is issued**, whichever comes first, and **may not be extended** (section 19.4.4).
* No SOLAS Contracting Government may cause a subsequent, consecutive IISSC to be issued to a ship if, in the judgement of the flag State Administration or the RSO, one of the purposes of the ship or a Company in requesting such IISSC is to avoid full compliance with chapter XI-2 and part of the ISPS Code beyond the period of the initial IISSC as specified in section 19.4.4 (section 19.4.5).
* For the purposes of regulation XI-2/9, SOLAS Contracting Governments may, prior to accepting an IISSC as a valid certificate, ensure that the requirements of sections 19.4.2.4 to 19.4.2.6 have been met (section 19.4.6).

D04t.10d Ship security alert system

* SOLAS regulation XI-2/6.1 provides that all ships must be provided with a **ship security alert system**, as follows:
  - ships constructed on or after 1 July 2004;
  - passenger ships, including high-speed passenger craft, constructed before 1 July 2004, not later than the first survey of the radio installation after 1 July 2004;
  - oil tankers, chemical tankers, gas carriers, bulk carriers and cargo high speed craft, of 500 gross tonnage and upwards constructed before 1 July 2004, not later than the first survey of the radio installation after 1 July 2004; and other cargo ships of 500 gross tonnage and upward and mobile offshore drilling units constructed before 1 July 2004, not later than the first survey of the radio installation after 1 July 2006.
* Regulation XI-2/6.2 provides that the ship security alert system, when activated, must:
  - initiate and transmit a **ship-to-shore security alert** to a competent authority designated by the flag State Administration, which in these circumstances may include the Company, identifying the ship, its location and indicating that the security of the ship is under threat or it has been compromised;
  - **not send** the ship security alert to any other ships;
  - **not raise any alarm** on-board the ship; and
  - **continue the ship security alert** until deactivated and/or reset.
* Regulation XI-2/6.3 provides that the ship security alert system must:
  - be capable of being **activated from the navigation bridge** and in **at least one other location**; and
  - conform to **performance standards** not inferior to those adopted by IMO.
* Regulation XI-2/6.4 provides that the ship security alert system activation points must be designed so as to **prevent the inadvertent initiation** of the ship security alert.
* Regulation XI-2/6.5 provides that the requirement for a ship security alert system may be complied with by **using the radio installation** fitted for compliance with the requirements of chapter IV, provided all requirements of this regulation are complied with.
* Regulation XI-2/6.6 provides that when a flag State Administration receives notification of a ship security alert, that Administration must immediately notify the State(s) in the vicinity of which the ship is presently operating.
* Regulation XI-2/6.7 provides that when a SOLAS Contracting Government receives notification of a ship security alert from a ship which is not entitled to fly its flag, that Contracting Government must immediately notify the relevant Administration and, if appropriate, the State(s) in the vicinity of which the ship is presently operating.

D04u ADDITIONAL PASSENGER SHIP AND RO-RO FERRY DOCUMENTATION

* In addition to relevant certificates and documents detailed in D04c, D04g, D04h and D04i, UK ro-ro ferries may require:

- a **Berth List** detailing all ports and berths at which it is intended to load/discharge cargo or vehicles (see D03b.4l);
- an **Evidence of Ship Compliance document** ("A/Amax Compliance Certificate") certifying compliance with the requirements of the Stockholm Agreement (see D03b.5b, D03b.5c and D03b.5d);
- a **Muster List Approval document** issued by the MCA (see E08l.1b);
- a **Firearms Certificate**, required under the Firearms Acts when carrying a weapon and ammunition - in the case of ro-ro ferries for the humane killing of livestock, and in the case of a cruise ship for use in clay pigeon shooting[102] (see H01c.2);
- a **Gaming Machine Licence** for any gaming machine (i.e. "slot machine") on board;
- a **Certificate of Service and Testing** for any Marine Escape System (MES) fitted;
- **Transport Emergency cards** (known as "**Tremcards**"), which under the ADR Road Transport Regulations must accompany all loads of chemicals travelling by road vehicle[103].

D04v HIGH-SPEED CRAFT AND DYNAMICALLY SUPPORTED CRAFT SURVEYS AND DOCUMENTATION

D04v.1 Survey and maintenance of condition of high-speed craft

* For notes on the **operating standards applicable to high-speed craft** see D03i.
* **Regulation 5(1) of the MS (High Speed Craft) Regulations 1996** (SI 1996/3188) provides that every high-speed craft will be **subject to surveys** in accordance with paragraph 1.5 of Chapter 1 of the High-Speed Craft Code.
* Paragraph 1.5.1 of Chapter 1 of the HSC Code provides that each craft should be subject to:
  - an **initial survey** before the craft is put into service or before the Certificate is issued for the first time;
  - a **renewal survey** at intervals specified by the flag State Administration but not exceeding 5 years except where 1.8.5 or 1.8.10 is applicable;
  - a **periodical survey** within 3 months before or after each anniversary date of the Certificate; and
  - an **additional survey** as the occasion arises.
* For notes relating to 1.8.5 and 1.8.10 of the HSC Code, see D04v.2a.
* Regulation 5(2) of the MS (High Speed Craft) Regulations 1996 provides that the **condition** of every high-speed craft and its equipment **must be maintained after survey** pursuant to section 1.7 of Chapter 1 of the High-Speed Craft Code.
* 1.7 of the HSC Code sets out the requirements for maintenance of conditions after survey. After any survey required by 1.5 has been completed, **no change** should be made to the structure, fittings, arrangements and materials covered by the survey without the sanction of the flag State Administration (1.7.2).
* **Accidents or defects** affecting safety or the efficiency or completeness of structure, fittings, arrangements and materials must be reported to the flag State Administration or the responsible nominated surveyor or recognised organisation, who must investigate to determine whether (an additional) survey is necessary, as required by 1.5. Where the craft is in an area under the jurisdiction of another Government, the person in charge or the owner should **also report** immediately to the appropriate authorities of the port State (1.7.3).

D04v.2 Documents required by high-speed craft

* The High Speed Craft Regulations require that UK high-speed craft and non-UK high-speed craft operating to or from UK ports or in UK waters must carry:
  - an appropriate **High-Speed Craft Safety Certificate** (regulation 6(1)); and
  - a **Permit to Operate** (regulation 7(1)).
* Where a Safety Certificate or a Permit to Operate is issued subject to conditions required by an Administration, the owner and master of a high-speed craft must ensure that all conditions are complied with throughout the voyage.
* The master of every high-speed craft must produce to a customs officer, from whom clearance is demanded for an international voyage, the **appropriate HSC Safety Certificate and Permit to Operate** as specified below.
* The **owner and master of a passenger high-speed craft** must ensure that no more passengers are on board than are stated on the craft's Permit to Operate.

---

[102] Where ammunition is sold to passengers, a separate **Certificate of Registration as a Firearms Dealer** is required to allow the sale of ammunition. Both documents are obtained in the UK from the regional Police headquarters.

[103] A "**Tremcard**" (Transport Emergency Card) contains details of the load, the dangers the load poses, first aid requirements, and action to be taken by the emergency services as well as a contact telephone number for specialist advice, written in a standard format.

* The **MCA may grant exemptions** from all or any provisions of the HSC Regulations.

D04v.2a Documents required by UK high-speed craft

* Regulation 6(1) of the High Speed Craft Regulations provides that where a survey of a **UK high-speed craft** is satisfactorily completed, the MCA will issue:
  - in the case of a **UK high-speed craft on international voyages**, a **High-Speed Craft Safety Certificate** (**HSCSC**) in accordance with section 1.8 of chapter 1 of the HSC Code;
  - in the case of a **UK high-speed craft not on international voyages**, a **UK High-Speed Craft Safety Certificate** (**UKHSCSC**).
* The **period of validity** of these certificates will be as specified in section 1.8 of chapter 1 of the HSC Code. 1.8.4 of the Code provides that the period of validity should not exceed 5 years. Under **1.8.5**, where the renewal survey is completed within 3 months before the expiry date of the existing Certificate, the new Certificate should be valid from the date of completion of the renewal survey to a date not more than 5 years from the date of expiry of the existing Certificate.
* **1.8.10** provides for an **extension of not more than one month** to be granted by the flag State Administration to allow a craft which is not at the renewal survey place when her Certificate expires to proceed to the survey place. An extension will not allow a craft to leave the survey place without a new Certificate. The new Certificate will expire not later than 5 years from the date of expiry of the existing Certificate before the extension was granted.
* A **UKHSCSC** will have the same period of validity as a HSCSC (regulation 6(2)).
* **Regulation 7(1) of the High Speed Craft Regulations** provides that where a UK high-speed craft meets the requirements of Paragraphs 1.2.2 to 1.2.11 of the HSC Code, the MCA will issue to the owner, after consultation with the Administration of another country where the high-speed craft is intended to operate, a **Permit to Operate**. This will include any **operational conditions** requested by the Administration of another country where the high-speed craft is intended to operate, and will be **approved** by that country's Administration (regulation 7(2)).
* The MCA may request the government of **another SOLAS 74 convention country** to survey a UK high-speed craft and issue, or authorise the issue of, a HSCSC and/or a Permit to Operate (regulation 8(1)).
* Under regulation 11 a HSCSC or Permit to Operate issued to a UK high-speed craft may be **cancelled** where the MCA has reason to believe that:
  - the certificate or permit was issued on **false or erroneous information**;
  - since any survey required by the HSC Regulations, the structure, equipment or machinery of the high-speed craft has sustained **damage** or is otherwise **deficient**; or
  - there has been **non-compliance with the conditions** of the permit such that the safety of the craft or life were imperilled.
* Under regulation 12(1) no UK high-speed craft may proceed to sea or otherwise on a voyage unless it has been **surveyed** and there are in force the appropriate **Certificate and Permit** as set out above.

D04v.2b Documents required by non-UK high-speed craft

* The MCA may, at the request of another SOLAS 74 convention country, survey a non-UK high-speed craft and issue a **High Speed Craft Safety Certificate** and/or a **Permit to Operate**.
* **Permits to Operate** of non-UK high-speed craft intended to operate to or from the UK on international voyages, will contain **operational conditions** requested by the MCA and will be **approved** by the MCA.
* In the case of a non-UK high-speed craft intended to operate on non-international voyages (i.e. UK domestic voyages), the MCA may, where surveys meet the requirements of the HSC Code, issue a **UK High Speed Craft Safety Certificate**.
* Where a Permit to Operate has been **issued by the flag State**, the MCA may **request** the inclusion of operational conditions and will approve the Permit; without such approval, the Permit will not be valid. Where a Permit to Operate issued by the flag State is not in force, the MCA may issue a Permit to Operate.
* No non-UK high-speed craft may proceed to sea from the UK on an international voyage, or otherwise on a non-international voyage, unless the **appropriate certificate and permit** are in force as if the high-speed craft were a UK high-speed craft, and the permit contains any operational conditions required by the MCA.

D04v.3 Survey of dynamically supported craft

* For a **definition** of "dynamically supported craft" and notes on the **operating standards** applicable to dynamically supported craft see D03i.4.
* **Survey and approvals** of dynamically supported craft are provided for in 1.5 of the DSC Code, as outlined below.

* 1.5.1 of the DSC Code provides that a dynamically supported craft -
  - must have an **initial assessment** in accordance with 1.5.1(a) before the Certificate in 1.6 (see D04v.3) is issued for the first time.
  - must have **periodical surveys** in accordance with 1.5.1(b) at intervals specified by the flag State Administration, but not exceeding one year.
  - must **have intermediate inspections** in accordance with 1.5.1(c) at intervals specified by the flag State Administration.
* **No change** should be made (following survey) that would affect the structural integrity, change the functional operation of a system, or change the arrangement of materials covered by the survey, without the sanction of the flag State Administration, except the direct replacement of such equipment and fittings for the purpose of renewal, repair or maintenance (1.5.2).
* **Surveys** should be carried out by competent persons duly authorised by the flag State Administration (1.5.3).

D04v.4 Documents required by UK dynamically supported craft

* 1.6.1 of the DSC Code provides that a dynamically supported craft **should not operate commercially** unless:
  • a **Dynamically Supported Craft Construction and Equipment Certificate** has been issued following survey as in 1.5.1, and is valid (1.6.1(a)); and
  • a **Dynamically Supported Craft Permit to Operate** has been issued if the flag State Administration is satisfied that all other requirements of the Code have been met (1.6.1(b)).
* Both certificates should remain in force for not more than **one year** provided that the terms of issue are complied with (1.6.2).
* A **specimen DSC Construction and Equipment Certificate** is shown in Annex I of the DSC Code.
* **Exemption** by the flag State Administration from any of the provisions of the Code is permitted under 1.7.3 if the application of the provision would seriously impede research into the development of such craft engaged on international voyages provided that equivalent safety is achieved.
* 1.8.1 provides that the flag State Administration should ensure that the craft is provided with adequate information and guidance in the form of a Technical Manual to enable the craft to be operated and maintained safely. The Technical Manual should consist of an Operating Manual, Maintenance Manual and Servicing Schedule. Contents required to be contained in the Operating Manual are set out in 1.8.2 of the Code.

D04w DOCUMENTS AND INFORMATION TO BE DISPLAYED ON BOARD

* The following documents and items of information are required to be displayed on board:
  • compass deviation curve[104] (see D04n.2);
  • damage control plans (either exhibited or readily available on the navigating bridge) (see D04t.2e);
  • Employer's Liability Insurance Certificate (where there is no personal injury P&I cover) (see C03c.4);
  • garbage disposal placards (see D04t.6);
  • International Load Line Certificate (1969) or International Load Line Exemption Certificate (see D04i.1d);
  • manoeuvring information (see below);
  • muster list (see E08l.1b);
  • Passenger Certificate, if any (see D04f.2l and F08a.1);
  • posters or signs showing operating instructions on or in the vicinity of survival craft and their launching controls (see D04k.5a and D04k.5b);
  • R/T operating instruction cards 1, 2 and 3 (see Appendix G to Annual Notice to Mariners No. 4 and D04m.3b);
  • radar shadow sector diagram (see D04n.3);
  • Ship Radio Licence and disc (affixed to wheelhouse window) (see D04m.3a);
  • "SOLAS 1" poster (see D04k.5a and below);
  • steering gear change-over operating instructions (see below and I07i.4);
  • table of scheduled hours of rest (see E03c.1c).
* **Regulation 5 of the MS (Safety of Navigation) Regulations 2002** (SI 2002/1473) (see H01f.2) requires compliance by UK ships with **SOLAS regulation V/29**, which provides that an **illustrated table describing the life-saving signals** must be readily available to the officer of the watch of every ship to which chapter V applies. The signals must be used by ships or persons in distress when communicating with life-saving stations, maritime rescue units and aircraft engaged in search and rescue operations. The life-saving signals referred to are shown on the "**SOLAS No.1**" poster displayed on the navigation bridge in accordance with the LSA Regulations (see D04k.5), are described

---

[104] Although the deviation curve is normally displayed, the statutory requirement is only that it must be *available* at all times (see D04n.2).

in the International Aeronautical and Maritime Search and Rescue (IAMSAR) Manual Volume III (Mobile Facilities), and are illustrated in the International Code of Signals.

* **Regulation 5 of the Safety of Navigation) Regulations** also requires compliance by UK ships with **paragraph 3.1 of SOLAS regulation V/26**, which provides that simple **operating instructions**, with a block diagram showing the **change-over procedures** for **remote steering gear control systems** and **steering gear power units** must be permanently displayed on the navigation bridge and in the steering (gear) compartment. For detailed notes on the requirements of regulation V/26, see I07i.4.
* **Manoeuvring information**, as described by **MGN 201**, is recommended by the MCA to be displayed, in accordance with IMO Resolution A.601(15) (see I01b.8a). Manoeuvring information consists of:
    * a **pilot card** (for providing pilots with relevant information about the ship);
    * a **wheelhouse poster** (containing general particulars and detailed information about the manoeuvring characteristics of the ship); and
    * a **manoeuvring booklet** (containing comprehensive details about the ship's manoeuvring characteristics and other relevant data).
* Examples of a **pilot card and wheelhouse poster**, and a list of **recommended information** to be included in the **manoeuvring booklet** are included in the appendices to MGN 201.
* Under regulation 20 of the MS (Survey and Certification) Regulations 1995 (SI 1995/1210), as amended, **SOLAS certificates** must be **readily available** on board for examination at all times, but are not required to be posted up (see D04f.2u).

D04x SPARE OFFICIAL DOCUMENTS

* It may be beneficial to carry on board **spare copies** of the official documents listed below.
    * Cargo Record Book (Noxious Liquid Substances) if appropriate (see D05b.3);
    * Certificate of Discharge forms (see E07b.4c);
    * Certificates of quality of a seaman's work (see E07b.4c);
    * Crew Agreement and List of Crew (ALC) documents (see E07);
    * Engine Watch Rating certificates (see E02b.8);
    * Garbage Record Book (see D04t.5);
    * Hazardous cargo check lists (ships carrying dangerous/polluting cargoes) (see I01a.7b);
    * Incident Report Forms (IRF) (see E08k.1g);
    * Navigational Watch Rating certificates (see E02b.8);
    * Official Log Book(s) (see D05a);
    * Oil Record Book(s) (see D05b.2);
    * Radio Log (see D05b.1);
    * RBD/1 forms (see E14b.3);
    * Sea service testimonials ("watchkeeping certificates") (see E02c.1f);
    * Steering certificates (see E02d.4).

D05 Ship's records

D05a OFFICIAL LOG BOOK

D05a.1 Requirement to keep an Official Log Book

* **Section 77(1) of the Merchant Shipping Act 1995** provides that, except as provided by the Official Log Books Regulations, an Official Log Book in a form approved by the MCA must be kept in every UK ship. (See D05a.2 for ships not required to keep an Official Log Book). Only one Official Log Book may be kept to cover all the crew.
* If a person intentionally destroys or mutilates or renders illegible any entry in an official log book he will be liable on summary conviction to a fine not exceeding level 4 on the standard scale (section 77(6)).

D05a.2 Official Log Books Regulations

* The **MS (Official Log Books) Regulations 1981** (SI 1981/569) -
  - provide that the **requirement to keep an Official Log Book** does not apply to a ship belonging to a general lighthouse authority, a ship of less than 25 gross tons or a pleasure yacht (regulation 2).
  - **specify rules for**: the making of specified entries (regulation 3); the manner of making, signing and witnessing of entries (regulation 4); the making of annexes to the Official Log Book (regulation 6); the time for making entries (regulation 7); the amendment and cancellation of entries (regulation 8); the production of the Official Log Book (regulation 9); and the delivery of the Official Log Book (regulation 10).
  - **are amended by the MS (Property of Deceased Seamen and Official Log Books) (Amendment) Regulations 1983** (SI 1983/1801); these Regulations revoked the MS (Property of Deceased Seamen) Regulations 1972, which made provision in respect of certain property and wages of specified deceased seamen, and removed the requirement for certain entries required by paragraph 36 of the Schedule to be made.
  - **are amended by the MS (Official Log Books) (Amendment) Regulations 1985** (SI 1985/1828). These Regulations revoked the MS (Disciplinary Offences) Regulations 1972, which required certain entries to be made when a seaman was charged with a disciplinary offence under those Regulations. (These entries were required by paragraph 39 of the Schedule).
  - **are amended by the MS (Official Log Books) (Amendment) Regulations 1991** (SI 1991/2145). Amendments made by these Regulations take account of changes made to other regulations in implementing the recommendations of the formal investigation into the loss of the ro-ro passenger ferry *Herald of Free Enterprise*. The main amendments consist of: (1) the addition at regulation 9(1) of MCA surveyors to the list of persons authorised to demand production of the Official Log Book; (2) the insertion at Part IV of the Regulations of a specific reference to passenger ships, together with a new requirement for masters to enter the times of closing and opening the shell and bulkhead doors in accordance with the MS (Closing of Openings in Enclosed Superstructures and in Bulkheads above the Bulkhead Deck) Regulations[105]; (3) a new requirement at Part IV to record draughts, trim and vertical distances in accordance with the Passenger Ship Regulations 1980 and 1984. Other changes include a new regulation 6A to make it an offence to make a false entry in the Official Log Book, and provision for indefinite crew agreements in addition to fixed term crew agreements.
  - **are amended by the MS (Official Log Books for Merchant Ships and Fishing Vessels) (Amendment) Regulations 1997** (SI 1997/1511), which remove the requirement to make certain entries relating to the discharge of seamen outside the UK, Conveyance Orders and reductions in the scale of provisions or water (i.e. paragraphs 17, 19 and 33 of the Schedule).

D05a.3 Official Log Book (LOG 1)

is produced by the MCA in large and small versions as follows: **LOG 1(L)** (76 pages), and **LOG 1(S)** (45 pages). (**LOG 2** is an additional Official Log Book for passenger ships (see D05a.10). The following notes in this section refer to LOG 1.)

is **obtainable** from any MCA Marine Office in the UK or from Proper Officers (e.g. British Consuls) abroad. (An Official Log Book is usually collected together with a radio log and the necessary documents for engagement of a crew.

remains in force, where there is a **running agreement** or **indefinite agreement**, from the time of opening the Crew Agreement until the expiry of **6 months after making the first entries** in the Official Log Book.must be **delivered** on closure to the MCA (via the proper officer if abroad). Where a ship has more than one crew agreement in force (e.g. where ratings hired through an overseas manning agency are on a separate agreement), the time for delivery is the time of closure of the officers' agreement.

remains in force, where there is a **voyage agreement**, from the time of opening the Crew Agreement until the time when **the last person has been discharged** (i.e. on closure of the Crew Agreement).

must be produced by the master, if demanded, to the RSS, a superintendent, a proper officer, a surveyor or customs officer (regulation 9).

has (when new) a **paper outer cover** on which is printed **A Guide for Masters About Keeping Official Log Books**. Since the paper cover may easily become detached from the Official Log Book, it may be prudent to remove it when new for safe-keeping. The Guide is not comprehensive and a warning is printed that it should not be regarded as interpreting any Act of Parliament or Statutory Instrument. Every master should (it advises) first obtain a copy of the current MS (Official Log Books) Regulations and relevant amendments which are available from bookshops which stock Government Publications.

---

[105] Since revoked by the MS (Passenger Ship Construction) Regulations 1998.

has a **brown card inner cover**, on the outside front of which the master who opens the Official Log Book should complete the relevant boxes with the ship's, registered owner's and his own details. Subsequent masters should add their details, and details of their qualifications, to the list of masters.

contains a number of "**special pages**" for specified entries, as shown in the table below, and a "**narrative section**" consisting of several lined, blank pages at the back, for making any entry for which there is no special page.

is available only from old stock bearing printed references to various repealed Acts and revoked SIs.

* *The following list shows the "special pages" in the large edition, LOG 1(L), and entries required. References to repealed or revoked legislation, printed on the pages, have not been included in the list.*

Pages	Entries
1	Front cover (Ship's particulars; masters' particulars; owner's/manager's name and address; dates and places of opening and closing of Official Log Book, etc.).
2-7	Record of **seamen employed** in the ship. (Number in crew list; name; capacity employed in; narrative entry.)
8-9	Returns and entries of **births** and **deaths** in the Official Log Book.
10-14	Record of **musters, boat drills and fire drills, training** of crew, and **inspections** of life-saving appliances and fire appliances.
15-17	Record of test drills and inspections of the ship's **steering gear**. (Date; time; place; nature of inspection, etc; date; signature.)
18	Record of tests and inspections of **pilot hoists**. (Date; time; place; nature of tests, etc.; date; signature.)
19-23	Record of **inspections of crew accommodation** carried out under the MS (Crew Accommodation) Regulations.
24-28	Record of **inspections of food and water** provided for the crew. (Date; inspector; result; date of entry; signature.)
29	Positions of the **deck line and load lines**.
30-39	**Dates of departure** from **and arrival** at each dock, wharf, harbour or other place – with **draught of water and freeboard** upon every occasion of the ship proceeding to sea.
40-76	Official log (narrative pages). (Date and hour of occurrence; place of occurrence or situation by lat. and long. at sea; date of entry; fine imposed, if any; entries made under the Official Log Book Regulations

D05a.4 Entries required in Official Log Book

* **Regulation 3 of the Official Log Books Regulations** provides that, subject to the provisions of the Merchant Shipping Acts and regulations made thereunder, entries of particulars specified in the **Schedule** to the Regulations must be made in the Official Log Book of any ship not exempted from the requirement to have one.
* **The Schedule** to the Regulations is in **four parts**, each of which applies to different categories of ships, and lists 47 entries, several of which are now deleted by the various amending statutory instruments, i.e. SIs 1983/1801, 1985/1828, 1991/2145 and 1997/1511.
* **Part I** contains entries **Nos. 1 to 38**, and applies to **every ship**. Entries 17, 19, 23, 27 and 33 have been deleted.
* **Part II** contains entries **Nos. 39 to 42**, which related to ships to which the MS (Disciplinary Offences) Regulations 1972 applied. Those Regulations were revoked by SI 1985/1828, which deleted the whole of Part II.
* **Part III** contains entries **Nos. 43 and 44** which relate to ships, excluding ships of Class I, II, II(A) and IV, in respect of which a Load Line Certificate has been issued and which are not exempted by the Official Log Books Regulations from having an Official Log Book.
* **Part IV** contains entries **Nos. 45 to 47** which relate to passenger ships. Entries Nos. 45 and 46 relate to all passenger ships, while entry No. 47 relates to all ships of Class I, II, II(A) and IV.
* Entries currently required by existing legislation are summarised in the following table. Entries required to be made by the **master in person** are shown in bold type. Note that the table shows only **statutory entries**, and excludes the various non-statutory entries which it would be appropriate to make in the Official Log Book.

Para	Entry	Where recorded	Signatory	Witness
1	**Ship's name**, port of registry, official number and gross or register tonnage	Front cover	Master	None required
2	Name and address of **registered owner** or registered managing owner or ship's husband or manager	Front cover	Master	None required
3	**Master's name and certificate number**	Front cover	Master	None required
4	**Delivery to succeeding master of documents** relating to the ship or crew	Narrative section	Master in person and former master in person	None required
5	Date & place of **opening of Official Log Book**	Front cover	Master	None required
6	Date & place of **closing of Official Log Book**	Front cover	Master	None required
7	Date and hour of **departures for sea and arrivals from sea**	Special page and annexed Additional Freeboard Sheet (AFS) forms	Master in person	An officer
8	Notification of proper officer when **sailing short-handed (deck officer)** (but see E03d.6)	Narrative section	Master	None required

9	Notification of proper officer when **sailing short-handed (engineer officer)** (but see E03d.6)	Narrative section	Master	None required
10	**LSA or fire-fighting musters, drills or training** held; lowering or launching of survival craft; examinations of LSA or equipment	Special page	Master	Any crew member
11	**Reasons for not holding** or only part-holding any **musters, drill, training or inspection**	Special (musters) page	Master	Any crew member
12	**Casualties** as follows: loss of life or major injury to anyone on board; person is lost from ship or ship's boat; ship is lost or presumed lost; ship is abandoned; ship is materially damaged; ship strands; ship is in collision; ship is disabled; ship causes material damage (description of casualty; place or position)	Narrative section	Master	Any crew member
13	**Distress signals or messages** that a vessel, aircraft or person is in distress at sea, observed or received	Narrative section (or annexed radio log)	Master	Any crew member
14	**Reasons for not going to assistance** of persons in distress, where master is unable, or considers it unreasonable or unnecessary	Narrative section (or annexed radio log)	Master in person	Any crew member
15	In a **seaman's wages dispute**: • record of identity of superintendent or proper officer; • statement of the dispute; acceptance of the dispute; decision or referral	Narrative section Narrative section	Master Superintendent or proper officer	Any crew member None required
16	Record of every **seaman discharged** from ship (i.e. whether on Crew Agreement or not), with place, date and time of discharge	Narrative section	Person in whose presence seaman is discharged; or if seaman is not present: master	Any crew member
17	**Deleted** by SI 1997/1511	-	-	-
18	Where a **seaman is left behind outside UK** or is taken to a country outside UK after shipwreck, or a person engaged outside UK is left behind in UK: • name of seaman; • date and place where left behind; • reason (if known) for leaving behind; • informing of proper officer	Narrative section	Proper officer (if practicable) or master in person	If master is signatory) any crew member
19	**Deleted** by SI 1997/1511	-	-	-
20	Where a **seaman left behind leaves any property** (including money) behind: • list of property left; • list of property sold	Narrative section	Master	Any crew member
21	Weekly **crew accommodation inspections**: • date and time; • names and ranks of inspectors; • details of any non-compliance with regulations	Special page	Master	Any crew member
22	Weekly **inspections of provisions and water**, with results of inspection	Special page	Persons making inspection	None required
23	**Deleted** by SI 1991/2145	-	-	-
24	Testing and inspection by crew of **rigging of pilot hoist and load test**	Special page	Master	None required
25	**Steering gear drills**, checks and tests by crew under Regulations (see I07i.4)	Special page (plus annexed sheets if required)	Master	Any officer
26	**Complaints** by 3 or more seamen about food and water: • names of seamen making the complaint; • the complaint (specifying provisions or water complained of and whether of bad quality, etc.) • action taken by master; • whether seamen state their dissatisfaction with action taken, and whether they claim to complain to a superintendent or proper officer; • arrangement made for seamen to complain to superintendent or proper officer, where they claim to do so; • investigation of the complaint	Narrative section	Master Superintendent or proper officer	One of the seamen making complaint None
27	Deleted by SI 1991/2145	-	-	-

28	Where it appears to the master that an **officer may be unfit to discharge his duties** due to incompetence or misconduct or any other reason, or may have been seriously **negligent**, or may have **failed to give assistance and information after a collision** – • name of officer; grade and number of certificate; • details of the event or other related entry; • any statement made to master by officer which the officer wishes to be recorded • statement that the above entries have been read over to the officer by the master, or reasons for not reading them over to him	Narrative section	Master in person	Another officer
29	**Re-ratings** (including promotion) of any seaman, including effective date	Narrative section	Master	Any crew member
30	Where a seaman is alleged to have committed a **"dismissal" breach** of a code of conduct promulgated by the employer - nature of the allegation; name of person against whom allegation is made; statement that master has read allegation to seaman; statement that master has advised seaman of right to be accompanied by a friend to advise/speak for him; statement of whether seaman admits allegation or denies it; any statement made by seaman, or by his friend, in answer to allegation; a record that master has given a formal warning; a record that master has given a written reprimand; a record that master has formally warned seaman that he will be dismissed at first opportunity or at end of voyage; a record that seaman has been given, and has acknowledged receipt of, copy of all entries in OLB	Narrative section	Master	Another crew member
31	Where a **seaman is convicted** by a legal tribunal of any offence committed in the ship during a voyage, a record of the conviction and the punishment.	Narrative section	Master	Any crew member
32	Where, in the master's opinion, consideration should be given to **prosecution** of any person (i.e. crew or non-crew) in respect of any conduct in the ship – • the event • the name of the person • any statement made to the master by the person which the person wishes to be recorded • a record that the other entries have been read over to the person	Narrative section	Master in person	Another crew member

33	Deleted by SI 1997/1511	-	-	-
34	**Births** in the ship or a ship's boat: Date of birth; Position of ship if at sea, or place if not; Name and surname of child; Sex of child; Name and surname of father; Father's usual address; Father's nationality; Father's occupation; Mother's name and surname; Mother's maiden surname and name at marriage, if different; Mother's usual address; Mother's nationality; Record of the making of a Return, identifying the person to whom made	Special page	Master in person	Mother of the child

35	**Deaths** in the ship or a ship's boat, or loss of a person from the ship or a ship's boat, or death of a person employed in the ship outside the UK:			
	date of death or loss; position or place at time of death; name and surname of deceased; sex of deceased; date of birth, or age; maiden surname in case of a married woman; occupation of deceased; usual address of deceased; nationality;	Special page	Master in person	Any crew member
	cause of death or loss;	Special page	Ship's doctor (if carried)	Any crew member
	if death was not due to natural causes, the circumstances of death or loss; if deceased was lost from ship or boat, the steps taken to rescue him; record of the making of a Return, identifying the person to whom made; notification of the death to deceased's next of kin, with their name and address	Special page	Master in person	Any crew member
36	Where a **seaman dies** while or after being employed in the ship: whether he left any **property** (including money) on board; a list of each item of the property	Narrative section	Master in person	Any crew member
37	Where an **inquiry** into the cause of death is required under section 271 Merchant Shipping Act 1995 (see B05e.7) -			
	• name of deceased and reference to relevant OLB entry no. 35;	Narrative section	Master	None required
	• name of superintendent or proper officer holding inquiry, if held, and date and place of inquiry; or	Narrative section	Superintendent or proper officer	None required
	• where an **inquiry was not held**, at the next port of call after the death where there was a superintendent or proper officer, a record of the facts	Narrative section	Master	None required
38	**Illnesses** and **injuries** of persons employed in ship:			
	• circumstances of injury;	Narrative section (or annexed medical log)	Master	Any crew member
	• nature of illness or injury, or symptoms;	Narrative section (or annexed medical log)	Ship's doctor, or master where no doctor is carried	Any crew member
	• treatment adopted;			
	• progress of illness or injury.			
39	**Deleted** by SI 1985/1828	-	-	-
40	**Deleted** by SI 1985/1828	-	-	-
41	**Deleted** by SI 1985/1828	-	-	-
42	**Deleted** by SI 1985/1828	-	-	-
43	Assigned **freeboards**; positions of **deck line** and **load lines** (from Load Line Certificate); maximum Summer **draught** (on even keel) (entry not required in ships of Class I, II, II(A) or IV)	Special page	Master	None required
44	Forward and aft **departure draughts**; port and starboard departure **freeboards**; departure **mean freeboard** Additional entries to be made when ship is at maximum Summer load line when ready to sail: • water density when draughts were taken; • dock or river water freeboard allowance, if any; • weight of fuel, water and stores required for consumption on passage to sea (entry not required in near coastal ships); • mean salt water draught and freeboard (These entries are not required in ships of Class I, II, II(A) or IV)	Special page plus annexed Additional Freeboard Sheet (AFS) forms	Master	Any officer

45	In passenger ships only: • times of last **closing of watertight doors** and appliances before sailing, and times of next opening; • times of opening and closing of any watertight door at sea; • whether portable plates are in place on departure, and times of any removal and replacement when at sea; • drills and inspections, and whether appliances to which drills and inspections relate are in good working order	LOG 2	Master	Any officer
46	In passenger ships only: • times of last **closing of watertight and weathertight doors**, and times of next opening; • times of opening and closing of any watertight or weathertight door	LOG 2	Master	Any officer
47	In ships of Class I, II, II(A) and IV only: • **draughts, trim and vertical distances**; • result of calculation of **GM**.	AFS/RO/89 (sheets annexed to OLB)	Master	Any officer

* Regulation 5(2)(a)(i) of the **MS (Minimum Standards of Safety Communications) Regulations 1997** (SI 1997/529) provides that the **company and the master of every passenger ship** must ensure that, for the purpose of ensuring effective crew performance in safety matters a **working language**, determined by the company or master as appropriate, is **established**, and recorded in the ship's **Official Log Book**. The entry should be made in the narrative section.
* **Regulation 17(5) of the MS and FV (Health and Safety at Work) Regulations 1997** (SI 1997/2962) provides that the appointment of the following persons must be recorded:
  * the appointment by the employer under regulation 14(1) of **competent person(s) for protective and preventive services**;
  * the appointment by the Company under regulation 15(2) of the ship's **safety officer**;
  * the appointment of any **safety representative** elected under regulation 17(1); and
  * the appointment of any of the above persons onto a **safety committee**.
* *The appropriate place for making the above records on board ship is the narrative section of the Official Log Book or, in the case of a ship with no Official Log Book, the deck log book.*

D05a.5 Making, signing and witnessing Official Log Book entries

* Each entry must be made **as soon as practicable after the occurrence** to which it relates or, if amending or cancelling an existing entry, as soon as practicable after the person intending to sign it becomes aware of the facts giving rise to the amendment or cancellation.
* The **person required to make each entry** is specified in column 2 of the Schedule to the Official Log Book Regulations. (See "Signatory" column in table above.)
* Each entry must be **signed** by the specified person, and where required, **witnessed** by the person specified in column 3 in the Schedule. (See "Witness" column in table above.)
* Entries required to be signed by the master may, unless "**the master in person**" is specified in the Schedule, be signed by an officer authorised by master for that purpose. Only duly certificated officers may be authorised by the master to act in his stead.
* Each entry must be **dated**.
* The **master** commits an offence if an entry is not made, signed and witnessed in accordance with the Regulations and the Schedule.

D05a.6 Amending or cancelling Official Log Book entries

* Entries should not be amended or cancelled except in the following manner. If an entry appears inaccurate or incomplete, the current master or the person making the entry must make and sign a **further entry** referring to the entry and amending or cancelling it. For example, where the wrong seaman's name has been written in an entry, the further entry could state: "In previous line, for 'A. Smith' read 'J. Brown'".

D05a.7 Annexes to Official Log Book

* If any entry cannot be contained in the Official Log Book by reason of its length or for any other reason, it may be contained in a **separate document** annexed to the Official Log Book. An annex to the Official Log Book need not be physically attached to it, but an **entry** should be made in the main part of the Official Log Book recording the **existence of an annex**. Every annexed document should be given and be referred to by a **reference number**, e.g. "Annex No. 01").
* Entries in any such annexed document will be regarded as made in the Official Log Book and must therefore be signed and treated as if they had been made in the Official Log Book itself.
* **Examples** of documents commonly annexed to Official Log Books are Additional Freeboard Sheets and accident and medical logs (see D05b.5).
* It may be more appropriate to make any lengthy narrative report of an **accident** as an annexed document rather than as a full entry in the narrative pages of the Official Log Book.

D05a.8 Official Log Book entries relating to freeboard, draught and dock allowance (ships other than ro-ro passenger ferries)

* Details of **positions of the deck line and load lines** and the **maximum summer draught in millimetres** should be copied from the Load Line Certificate onto page 29 of the Official Log Book. These particulars are not required on sludge carriers, dredgers, hopper barges, tugs or tenders on voyages of not more than 600 nautical miles keeping within 200 nautical miles of a port or place where personnel could be placed in safety and carrying no more than 12 passengers, if any.
* Details of **draughts, freeboard and dock allowance** must be recorded on pages 30-31 (the "**freeboard sheet**") before the ship leaves any dock, wharf, harbour, or other place to proceed to sea.
* **Actual freeboard amidships on each side** is to be measured from upper edge of the deck line to the surface of the water when the ship is loaded and ready to leave. "Actual mean freeboard" is the mean of the actual freeboards, port and starboard, measured in this way.
* If **converting freeboards** from Imperial to metric units, or vice-versa, 25.4 mm = 1 inch is to be used.
* No entries are needed in **columns 8 to 14** inclusive when the actual mean freeboard (as stated in col. 7) is not less than the appropriate SW freeboard shown on the Load Line Certificate (i.e. when no DWA is applicable).
* In **Near Coastal ships**, columns 9 to 15 inclusive on the freeboard sheet need not be filled in. These columns concern allowances, mean draught and freeboard in SW after calculating allowances, and the date and time of posting the FRE.13 form, which is not required in Near Coastal ships.
* If **additional freeboard sheets** are required, **Form AFS** (Additional Freeboard Sheet) must be used and annexed to the Official Log Book. In ro-ro ferries **Form AFS/RO/89** (Additional Freeboard and Stability Sheet) must be used in place of the freeboard sheet printed in the Official Log Book (see D05a.9).

D05a.9 Official Log Book entries relating to freeboard, draught and dock allowance (ro-ro passenger ferries)

* **M.1391** gives guidance on the recording of draughts, freeboard and stability required by the MS (Loading and Stability Assessment of Ro-Ro Passenger Ships) Regulations 1989, which are revoked by the MS (Passenger Ship Construction: Ships of Classes I, II and II(A)) Regulations 1998.
* The MCA produces a special Additional Freeboard Sheet (**Form AFS/RO/89**) for the use of ro-ro passenger ferries only. Sheets of this form can be attached as an **annex** to one Official Log Book in order to provide the required record of the many departures a ferry will normally make during the currency of a Crew Agreement.
* As well as date, hour and places of departure and arrival, and forward and aft draughts, AFS/RO/89 contains details of:
  * departure trim;
  * distance from the waterline to the "C" mark;
  * displacement from observed draughts and from calculations, and the difference between the two figures;
  * maximum KG or minimum GM or maximum permitted deadweight moment calculated KG or GM or deadweight moment;
  * reference number of loading condition representing actual condition (Class IV ships only);
  * signatures of master and an officer to attest "ship in satisfactory condition of loading".

D05a.10 Official Log Book (Part II - Passenger ships only) (LOG 2)

* **Regulation 26 of the MS (Passenger Ship Construction: Ships of Classes I, II and II(A)) Regulations 1998** (SI 1998/2514) requires entries to be made in the Official Log Book recording the following:
  * the times of the last **closing**, before the ship proceeds on any voyage, of the watertight doors and other closing appliances referred to in regulation 22(1) and of the next **opening** of such doors and closing appliances;
  * the times of the **opening** and **closing** of any watertight door under regulation 22(3)(c) (see D03b.4b);
  * the times when all portable plates referred to in regulation 22(7) are **fitted in place** and the times of any **removal and replacement** of such plates while the ship is on any voyage (see D03b.4b);
  * the occasions on which **drills** are held and **inspections** made in compliance with the Regulations and whether or not the closing appliances and devices to which any such drill or inspection relates are in **good working order** when the drill or inspection takes place; and
  * the occasions when the valves referred to in regulation 15(4) are **operated**.
* The **Official Log Book (Part II – Passenger Ships Only) (LOG 2)** -
  - is the appropriate Official Log Book for making the above entries, which correspond to **entries numbers 45 and 46** in the Schedule to the Official Log Books Regulations.
  - has a **blue card cover**, with the following boxes for completion by the master: name of ship; port of registry; official number; gross tonnage; net tonnage; name of masters and numbers of certificates of competency; date and place at which log book was opened; date and place at which log book was closed.
  - **contains** four A3-size pages with headings as follows:
    * Practices of Opening and Closing Watertight Doors, etc. (pages 1 and 2);
    * Time of Opening and Closing Watertight Doors, etc. (page 3);
    * Inspection of Watertight Doors and Valves (page 4).

D05a.10a Closing of Openings Record Book for small passenger ships

* **Regulation 20 of the MS (Passenger Ship Construction: Ships of Classes III to VI(A)) Regulations 1998** (SI 1998/2515) provides that entries must be made in **a book** retained on board to record the following:
  * the times of the last **closing**, before the ship proceeds on any voyage, of the closing appliances referred to in regulation 16(1) and of the next **opening** of such closing appliances;
  * the times when the **portable plates** referred to in regulation 16(3) are **fitted in place** and the times of any removal and replacement of such plates whilst the ship is on any voyage; and
  * the occasions on which **drills** are held and inspections made in compliance with these Regulations and whether or not the closing appliances and devices to which any such drill or inspection relates are in good working order when the drill or inspection takes place.

D05b OTHER STATUTORY LOGS AND RECORDS

D05b.1 GMDSS Radio Log

* **Regulation 20(1) of the MS (Radio Installations) Regulations 1998** (SI 1998/2070) (see D04m.1) provides that a record (i.e. the **GMDSS Radio Log**) must be kept of the matters specified in **Schedule 3** to the Regulations, i.e., as they occur:
  a summary of communications relating to distress, urgency and safety traffic and the time such communications occurred;
  a record of important incidents connected with the radio service and the time such incidents occurred; and
  where appropriate, the position of the ship at least once a day and the time at which the ship was in that position.
* The **master** must **inspect and sign each day's entries** in the GMDSS Radio Log (regulation 20(2)).
* The GMDSS Radio Log must be **available for inspection** by officers authorised by the MCA (e.g. a radio surveyor or a ship surveyor) to make such inspection (regulation 20(3)).
* Regulation 20(4) provides that regulation 9 of the MS (Official Log Books) Regulations 1981 will apply to the GMDSS Radio Log as it applies to the Official Log Book. The effect is that the **GMDSS Radio Log must be produced** by the master, if demanded, to the RSS, a superintendent, a proper officer, a surveyor or customs officer (regulation 9).
* The **MCA's guidance** on the retention of records, in the 2002 SOLAS V publication (see H01f.2a) advises that the GMDSS log book should be retained on board until completed, then dispatched to MCA Southampton Marine Office.

* A **specimen page** of the GMDSS Radio Log is shown in **MGN 51**.
* The **Radio Log Book (GMDSS)** (ISBN 0-11-551634-4), is produced by MCA and is available from the Stationery Office (TSO) Publication Centre, TSO Bookshops and TSO Accredited Agents. It incorporates instructions for completion.

D05b.2 Oil Record Books

* **Regulation 10 of the MS (Prevention of Oil Pollution) Regulations 1996** (SI 1996/2154) provides that every UK **non-tanker of 400gt and above** and every UK **tanker of 150gt and above** must have an **Oil Record Book (Part 1) Machinery Space Operations (All Ships)** (ISBN 0 11 551605 0, available from Government Bookshops).
* Every UK oil tanker of 150gt and above must also have an Oil Record Book (Part 2) Cargo/Ballast Operations (Oil Tankers) (ISBN 0 11 551605 9, available from Government Bookshops).
* The Oil Record Book must be in the form prescribed in the MARPOL Convention.
* In the event of a discharge of oil or oily mixture as referred to in **regulation 11 (General Exceptions)** or in the event of an accidental or other exceptional discharge of oil **not excepted by regulation 11**, a statement must be made in the Oil Record Book of the circumstances of, and the reasons for, the discharge.
* The Oil Record Book must be completed on **each occasion**, on a **tank-to-tank basis** if appropriate, when any of the operations listed below takes place.
* Any Oil Record Book entry required to be made must be **fully recorded without delay** so that all entries appropriate to that operation are completed.
* **Each completed operation** must be signed by the **officer(s) in charge of the operations** concerned.
* **Each completed page** of the Oil Record Book must be signed by the **master**.
* The Oil Record Book must be kept in such a place as to be **readily available for inspection** at all reasonable times and, except in the case of unmanned ships under tow, must be **kept on board**.
* The Oil Record Book must be **preserved for a period of 3 years after the last entry** has been made.
* The MCA or a person authorised by the Certifying Authority may inspect the Oil Record Book whilst the ship is in a port or offshore terminal and may take a **copy of any entry** in the Oil Record Book and may require the ship's master to certify that the **copy is a true copy** of the entry. Any such copy will be **admissible in any judicial proceedings** as evidence of the facts stated in the entry.
* The inspection of an Oil Record Book and the taking of a certified copy by the MCA or authorised person must be performed as expeditiously as possible without causing the ship to be unduly delayed.

D05b.2a Entries in the Oil Record Book (Part I) (Machinery Space Operations)

* **Entries required** under regulation 10(2)(a) are as follows:
  * ballasting or cleaning of oil fuel tanks;
  * discharging ballast or cleaning water from oil fuel tanks;
  * disposal of oily residues (sludge);
  * discharging overboard bilge water which has accumulated in machinery spaces;
* A **note** in the Oil Record Book advises that masters should obtain from the operator of the reception facilities, which include barges and tank trucks, a **receipt or certificate** detailing the quantity of tank washings, dirty ballast, residues or oily mixtures transferred, together with the time and date of the transfer. This receipt or certificate, if attached to the Oil Record Book, may aid the master of the ship in clarifying that his ship was not involved in an alleged oil pollution incident. The receipt or certificate should be kept together with the Oil Record Book. See also **M.1197**.

D05b.2b Entries in the Oil Record Book (Part 2) Cargo/Ballast Operations (Oil Tankers)

* Entries required under regulation 10(2)(b) are as follows:
  * loading oil cargo;
  * internal transfer of oil cargo during voyage;
  * unloading oil cargo;
  * ballasting cargo tanks and dedicated clean ballast tanks;
  * cleaning cargo tanks including crude oil washing;
  * discharging ballast except from segregated ballast tanks;
  * discharging water from slop tanks;
  * closing, after the discharge of the contents of slop tanks, all valves or similar devices opened to permit such
  * operations;

- closing those valves necessary for the isolation of dedicated clean ballast tanks from cargo and stripping lines after slop tank discharge operations; and
- disposing of residues.

D05b.3 Cargo Record Book (Noxious Liquid Substances)

* **Regulation 9(1) of MARPOL Annex II** provides that every ship to which Annex II applies will be provided with a Cargo Record Book, whether as part of the ship's official log book or otherwise, in the form specified in appendix IV to Annex II.
* **Regulation 8(1) of the MS (Dangerous or Noxious Liquid Substances in Bulk) Regulations 1996** (SI 1996/3010) provides that every ship carrying noxious liquid substances will be provided with a Cargo Record Book in the form specified in MARPOL Annex II.
* **Regulation 8(2) of the MS (Dangerous or Noxious Liquid Substances in Bulk) Regulations 1996** provides that whenever any of the following operations takes place in respect of any noxious liquid substance a record of the operation must be made in relation to each tank affected by the operation:
  - loading of cargo;
  - internal transfer of cargo;
  - unloading of cargo;
  - cleaning of cargo tanks;
  - ballasting of cargo tanks;
  - discharge of ballast from cargo tanks;
  - disposal of residues to reception facilities;
  - discharge of residues into the sea in accordance with Schedule 2 to M.1703/NLS1;
  - removal of residues by ventilation.
* When any **emergency discharge** of a kind referred to in Schedule 2 to M.1703/NLS1 is made of a noxious liquid substances or a mixture containing such a substance, an entry must be made **without delay** in the Cargo Record Book stating the circumstances of and reason for the discharge (regulation 8(3)).
* Entries must be in English in a UK ship, and in other ships in the official language of the flag State, but where that language is neither English or French, the entries are to be in either English or French (regulation 8(4)).
* Each entry must be **signed by the officer(s) in charge of the operation** and **each page must be signed by the master** (regulation 8(4)).
* The Cargo Record Book must be kept **readily available for inspection**. Except in unmanned ships under tow, it must be **on board** the ship (regulation 8(5)).
* The Cargo Record Book must be **retained on board the ship for 3 years after the last entry** has been made (regulation 8(5)).

D05b.4 Accident log

* Regulation 16 of the **MS and FV (Health and Safety at Work) Regulations 1997** (SI 1997/2962) provides that it will be the **safety officer's duty to use his best endeavours to maintain a record of every accident** involving death, major or serious injury and every dangerous occurrence[106], and make it available to any elected safety representative, to the master and to any person duly authorised by the MCA.
* The **safety officer's duty** to maintain an accident log is separate and distinct from the **master's duty** under the Official Log Books Regulations to record injuries (see D05b.5). Some of the accidents which a safety officer is required to record will inevitably result in injuries which the master is also required to record, but others may not.

D05b.5 Medical records

* Regulation 3 of the **MS (Official Log Books) Regulations 1981** (SI 1981/569) (see D05a) requires a record (entry No. 38) to be made in the Official Log Book of any case of **illness or injury**, including:
  the **circumstances** of the injury;
  the **nature** of the illness or injury, or the symptoms;
  the **treatment** adopted (i.e. given); and
  the **progress** of the illness or injury.

---

[106] For notes on former "**dangerous occurrences**", see E08k.1c.

* Under regulation 6 a **medical log book** may be used as an annex to the Official Log Book, provided that all the required components of entry No. 38 are made in it.
* **Where a medical log book is used**, a record should be made in the narrative section of the Official Log Book to the effect that all entries concerning illnesses and injuries during the currency of the Official Log Book are made in a separate medical log. When more than one medical log has been used they should each be **numbered** and recorded as **separate annexes**. (For notes on **annexes** to the Official Log Book see D05a.7.)
* Apart from being a statutory duty, the proper recording of illnesses and injuries in the Official Log Book or medical log book will assist the owner's **P&I club** in dealing with claims. It may also be useful evidence for a master who, perhaps several months later, is required to respond to enquiries in connection with a seaman's allegations against himself or his company.
* For notes on **action in cases of personal injury or illness**, see E08j.2.

D05b.6 Cargo book for UK coastal trading vessels

* For notes on the **cargo book required under HM Customs rules** to be kept by ships mainly carrying domestic goods between UK ports, see I01f.10.

D05b.7 Voyage data recorder

* The **MS (Safety of Navigation) Regulations 2002** (SI 2002/1473) (see H01f.2) require compliance by a ship to which the Regulations apply with **paragraph 1 of SOLAS regulation V/20**, which relates to **Voyage data recorders**.
* **SOLAS regulation V/20.1** provides that, to assist in casualty investigations, ships on international voyages, subject to the provisions of regulation V/20.1.4, must be fitted with a voyage data recorder (VDR) in accordance with the following timetable:
  * passenger ships built on or after 1 July 2002: when built;
  * ro-ro passenger ships built before 1 July 2002: not later than the first survey on or after 1 July 2002;
  * passenger ships, other than ro-ro passenger ships, built before 1 July 2002: not later than the first survey on or after 1 July 2004; and
  * ships, other than passenger ships, of 3,000gt and upwards built on or after 1 July 2002: when built.
* Administrations may **exempt** ships, other than ro-ro passenger ships, built before 1 July 2002, from being fitted with a VDR where it can be demonstrated that interfacing a VDR with the existing equipment on the ship is unreasonable and impracticable (regulation V/20.2).
* **Annex 10 to the MCA's 2002 SOLAS Chapter V publication** (see H01f.2a) contains **MCA Guidance for VDRs**, **IMO Guidelines** on Voyage Data Recorder – Ownership and Recovery, and **EU requirements** for VDRs on passenger ships on domestic voyages.
* **SOLAS regulation V/18.8** provides that the voyage data recorder (VDR) system, including all sensors, must be subjected to an **annual performance test**. The test must be conducted by an approved testing or servicing facility to verify the accuracy, duration and recoverability of the recorded data. In addition, **tests and inspections** must be conducted to determine the serviceability of all protective enclosures and devices fitted to aid location. A copy of the **Certificate of Compliance** issued by the testing facility, stating the date of compliance and the applicable performance standards, must be retained on board the ship. For notes on **performance standards**, see D04b.3.
* **Annex 20 to the MCA's 2002 SOLAS Chapter V publication** contains MCA guidance on **inspection and survey of VDRs**. Paragraph 13 of Annex 20 states that, as well as annually testing the VDR, the surveyor will check that the mandatory **Performance Check Certificate** is in date and that **mandatory routine maintenance** has been completed and is entered in the ship's **planned maintenance log**.

D05b.8 Records of navigational activities

* The **MS (Safety of Navigation) Regulations 2002** (SI 2002/1473) (see H01f.2) require compliance by a ship to which the Regulations apply with **all paragraphs of SOLAS regulation V/28**, which relates to **Records of navigational activities**.
* **SOLAS regulation V/28** provides that all ships on international voyages must keep on board a **record of navigational activities and incidents which are of importance to safety of navigation**. This record must contain sufficient detail to restore a **complete record of the voyage**, taking into account the recommendations adopted by IMO in resolution A.916(22) - Guidelines for the recording of events relating to navigation. If this information is not

recorded in the "ship's log book" (i.e. the deck log), it must be maintained in **another form approved** by the flag State Administration.

* **Annex 22 to the MCA's 2002 SOLAS V publication** contains the **IMO Guidelines for the Recording of Events Related to Navigation** which form the Annex to resolution A.916(22), the main points of which are as follows.
* **In addition to national requirements**, it is recommended that the events and items shown in the following table, as appropriate, be *among* those recorded:

Time	Details to be recorded
Before commencing the voyage	Details of all data relating to the general condition of the ship, e.g. manning and provisioning, cargo aboard, draught, result of stability/stress checks when conducted, inspections of controls, steering gear and navigational and radio-communication equipment.
During the voyage	Details related to the voyage, e.g. courses steered and distances sailed, position fixings, weather and sea conditions, changes to the voyage plan, details of pilots' embarkation/disembarkation, entry into areas covered by, and compliance with, routeing schemes or reporting systems.
On special events	Details on special events, e.g. death and injuries among crew and passengers, malfunctions of shipboard equipment and aids to navigation, potentially hazardous situations, emergencies and distress messages received.
When the ship is at anchor or in a port	Details on operational or administrative matters and details related to the safety and security of the ship.

* **Methods of recording should be permanent** and may be handwritten, electronic or mechanical.
* In general, information on the events and items specified in the table above, which are adequately recorded in a **special-purpose log**, need not be duplicated in the ship's log book. (For example, details of crew or passenger injuries may be recorded in an accident log.)
* In order to be able to restore a complete record of the voyage, **records should be maintained as follows**:
  * each page of the ship's log book (i.e. the deck log) should have a **page number** printed on it;
  * hand-written records requiring correction should not be erased or removed but should be crossed out (with a single line) and re-written;
  * times used in automatic and permanent recording facilities should be synchronised by using a common clock;
  * **electronically or mechanically input records** should be **protected** by means to prevent them from being deleted, destroyed or overwritten;
  * **records should be kept**, irrespective of the method of recording, **for at least one year**, or such longer period as **the flag State Administration requires**.
* **Guidance note 3 to the MCA's 2002 SOLAS V document** advises that (in accordance with the IMO Guidelines) **all bridge orders requiring changes in direction or speed of the main propulsion unit** must be recorded. In addition other **key navigational events** should be recorded including changes of course, passing of waypoints, weather and sea conditions, incidents and events including pilot embarkation/disembarkation, tugs, hazardous occurrences and accidents.
* **Guidance note 4** advises that **time-marked electronic or mechanical records** are acceptable, including those from echo sounders, course recorders, engine telegraphs and NAVTEX receivers.
* **Guidance note 5** states that **it must be possible to reconstruct the ship's track** throughout the voyage. The IMO Guidelines state that **navigational records** (whether paper, electronic or mechanical) should be **retained on board** for a period not less than **12 months**. The MCA's interpretation of this requirement is that records retained for 12 months should provide **sufficient detail to reconstruct any voyage during that period**. The MCA recognises that it is impractical to retain voyage details on paper charts for longer than the duration of the voyage. Therefore **sufficient details** of waypoints, courses, times of alteration of course and or speed and other relevant details must be entered in the log book (i.e. the deck log) and courses and positions on all navigational charts should be retained until the voyage is completed. This information should be saved electronically when ECDIS is used to fulfil the requirements of SOLAS regulation V/19.2.1.4.
* The MCA's guidance notes include **guidance on the retention and preservation of records** of navigational activities, based on the requirements of investigation authorities (e.g. MAIB) in following up an accident. The following table summarises the guidance.

Form of record	Preservation guidelines
Paper navigational charts	Provided that sufficient information relating to the ship's position, course and speed has been recorded elsewhere to enable an accurate reconstruction of her passage, there is no requirement to retain this information on paper charts. Following a navigational accident or incident however, the paper charts in use must be retained, and the information shown must not be altered or erased.
ECDIS	Record of previous 12 hours and of the voyage track to be preserved following a navigational accident or incident.
ECS/AIS/ARPA	Voyage recording information to be preserved for as long as the system in use allows; it should not be manually deleted. Following a navigational accident or incident, every effort should be made to preserve and copy the recorded voyage data.

Bridge deck log	To contain sufficient navigational information to reconstruct a voyage including: • the recording of position at regular intervals; • alterations of course and speed; • weather and sea conditions; • precautions taken in restricted visibility or heavy seas; • significant navigational events. To be retained either onboard or ashore for at least 7 years.
Engine movement record book (bell book)	To be retained for the duration of the voyage and preserved following a navigational accident or incident.
Automatic engine/ propeller pitch/ bow thruster movement record	To be retained for the duration of the voyage and preserved following a navigational accident or incident.
Automatic course record	To be retained for the duration of the voyage and preserved following a navigational accident or incident.
NAVTEX messages	To be retained for the duration of the voyage and preserved following a navigational accident or incident.
Passage plan	To be preserved following a navigational accident or incident.
Echo sounder trace	To be preserved following a navigational accident or incident.
GMDSS Log Book	To be retained onboard until completed, then dispatched to MCA Southampton Marine Office.
Chart correction log	To be preserved following a navigational accident or incident.
Pre-sailing check lists	To be retained for duration of the passage.
VDR	To be retained in accordance with IMO Guidelines. (See MCA's 2002 SOLAS V publication, Annex 10.)

*   For notes on the **preservation of evidence** in compliance with the MS (Accident Reporting and Investigation) Regulations 1999 (SI 1999/2567), see E08k.1j.

D05b.9 Ship security records

*   SOLAS regulation XI-2/9.2.3 provides that **ships** to which SOLAS chapter XI-2 applies (see D03a.6) must keep **records** of the information referred to in regulation XI-2/9.2.1 (as listed below) for the **last 10 calls at port facilities**. (A "**port facility**" is defined as a location, as determined by the Contracting Government or by the Designated Authority, where the ship/port interface takes place. This includes areas such as anchorages, waiting berths and approaches from seaward, as appropriate.)
*   The **information** of which records must be kept under SOLAS regulation XI-2/9.2.1 includes:
    •   a record that the ship possesses a **valid International Ship Security Certificate** (or Interim ISSC) and the name of its issuing authority;
    •   a record of the **security level** at which the ship is **currently** operating;
    •   a record of the **security level** at which the ship operated in any **previous port** where it has conducted a ship/port interface within the timeframe specified in paragraph 2.3;
    •   a record of any **special or additional security measures** that were taken by the ship in any **previous port** where it has conducted a ship/port interface within the timeframe specified in paragraph 2.3;
    •   a record that the **appropriate ship security procedures** were maintained during any ship to ship activity within the timeframe specified in paragraph 2.3; or
    •   a record of **other practical security related information** (but not details of the Ship Security Plan), taking into account the guidance given in part B of the ISPS Code.
*   SOLAS regulation XI-2/9.2.1 provides that for the purpose of chapter XI-2, a SOLAS Contracting Government may require that **ships intending to enter its ports provide the above information** to officers duly authorized by that Government to ensure compliance with chapter XI-2 **prior to entry into port** with the aim of avoiding the need to impose control measures or steps. If requested by the SOLAS Contracting Government, the ship or the Company must **provide confirmation**, acceptable to that Government, of the information.
*   SOLAS regulation XI-2/9.2.3 provides that the ship must keep **records** of the information referred to in regulation XI-2/9.2.1 **for the last 10 calls** at port facilities.
*   ISPS Code, part A, section 10 provides that **records** of the following **activities** addressed in the Ship Security Plan must be kept on board for at least the minimum period specified by the flag State Administration, bearing in mind the provisions of regulation XI-2/9.2.3 (outlined above):
    •   training, drills and exercises;
    •   security threats and security incidents;
    •   breaches of security;
    •   changes in security level;
    •   communications relating to the direct security of the ship such as specific threats to the ship or to port facilities the ship is, or has been;
    •   internal audits and reviews of security activities;
    •   periodic review of the ship security assessment;

- periodic review of the ship security plan;
- implementation of any amendments to the plan; and
- maintenance, calibration and testing of security equipment, if any including testing of the ship security alert system.

* The above records must be kept in the **working language or languages** of the ship. If the language or languages used are not English, French or Spanish, a translation into one of these languages must be included. The records may be kept in an **electronic format**; in such a case, they must be **protected** by procedures aimed at preventing their unauthorised deletion, destruction or amendment. The records must be **protected** from unauthorised access or disclosure.

D05c DECK AND ENGINE ROOM LOGS

D05c.1 General rules for making log entries

* All entries should be made **neatly**, **carefully** and **precisely**, and only after **due consideration**.

* **Alterations** and **interlineations** (i.e. adding entries between written lines) should be avoided.

* A **faithful and accurate** account of the voyage should be given.

* In addition to the usual entries about course, speed, weather, etc., entries should be made regarding:
- switching navigation lights on and off;
- changing from automatic to hand steering and vice-versa;
- making routine and emergency hand signals, and
- displaying special signals such as "not under command" or "constrained by draught".

* **Exaggerated entries** of weather conditions or other circumstances should never be made. If a judge, arbitrator or investigator believes, or has good reason to suspect, that a statement is false or exaggerated, he may suspect all other statements, even though these may have been made honestly and accurately.

* Besides routine particulars of the navigation of the vessel, entries should be made of all **extraordinary happenings** and of all **matters affecting the owner's interests**, particularly in circumstances where **claims** by or against the ship are likely to arise, where matters are **likely to be disputed** or where log entries may be needed in **support of protests** made and/or extended by the master.

* In particular where the circumstances require it, **all relevant facts** should be logged relating to the following:
- adjustments of cargo space ventilation;
- loss or damage to the ship or cargo from any cause whatsoever;
- strandings and groundings;
- collisions with other vessels or fixed objects (with particulars of apparent damage);
- machinery breakdowns;
- searches of ship for drugs, stowaways or contraband;
- rendering or receipt of salvage services;
- times of commencing, suspending and completion of loading, discharging and bunkering;
- investigation of unusual or unexpected soundings;
- attention to moorings and clearing of hawse;
- passing through oil slicks;
- delays in preliminary voyage to loading port;
- times of arrival, berthing and serving and receipt of notice of readiness;
- particulars of delays in loading or discharging;
- quantity of cargo loaded or discharged each day;
- time of signing bills of lading on completion of loading.

D05c.2 Fair copies of log books

* The "**mate's log**", kept in ships of some companies, is a fair copy of the deck "**scrap log**". It should be written up daily and signed at the foot of each page by the chief mate, who should take care to see that the statements it contains are strictly accurate. The master should examine the log periodically (preferably daily) and also sign each page.

* If a pencil is used to write up the scrap log it should be an indelible one, whilst the mate's log should be written in ink.

* Where a mate's log is not required, the scrap log should be kept in ink and should be signed daily by the master and the chief officer after careful scrutiny of the entries.
* Should any collision or other incident give rise to **litigation or inquiry**, it will be the scrap log that will be of most interest to the court and which will come under the closest investigation, for the reason that it will (or *should*) have been **written up immediately after the described events** have occurred.
* The practice of writing up log books from information jotted on scraps of paper which are afterwards thrown away is a bad one. If the **original record** cannot be produced in court, it may very well prejudice the master's or owner's case.

D05c.3 Bridge books and movement books

- may be useful when **entering or leaving port** or when navigating in **pilotage waters**, where it is impracticable to make contemporaneous log entries.
- should record **engine movements, changes of course, signals made,** etc.
- should be used to write up the deck and engine room log book **as soon as possible after manoeuvres** are complete.
- should not be used before **synchronising** bridge and engine room clocks before manoeuvring commences.
- should be **preserved** so that the evidence contained in them will be available for production if and when required.

D05c.3a Recording of main engine movements

* **M.1104** (which was superseded by the MCA's SOLAS V 2002 document) stated that, with certain exceptions, all bridge orders requiring **changes in direction or speed of the main propulsion unit** must be recorded[107]. Automatic recording devices or hand-written **movement books** will comply with this requirement. Movement records are not required, however, in:
  * vessels of less than 150kW registered power;
  * vessels with unidirectional main propulsion machinery driving controllable pitch propellers, while on bridge control; or
  * vessels whose engines are directly controlled from remote control units on the bridge while under remote control.
* Records are required on a vessel with a controllable pitch propeller when the main propulsion machinery is in "manual control" mode.

D05c.4 Data print-outs

* Print-outs which should be retained at least until the end of the current voyage, and include:
  * data logger sheets;
  * engine room printouts;
  * echo sounder and course recorder graphs;
  * NAVTEX messages;
  * GMDSS messages.

D05c.5 Sounding book

* **Soundings** should be made, either manually or by other means, on a twice-daily or daily basis whether a tank is believed to be empty or partially full, and whether tanks have been pumped or not.
* **Sounding records** should be preserved for the duration of the voyage, and at least until cargo is discharged.

---

[107] This was a requirement of the MS (Certification and Watchkeeping) Regulations 1982 (SI 1982/1699), which were revoked by the MS (Safe Manning, Hours of Work and Watchkeeping) Regulations 1997 (SI 1997/1320).

D05d USE OF DOCUMENTS IN LEGAL PROCEEDINGS

D05d.1 Admissibility in evidence and inspection of certain documents

* **Section 287 of the Merchant Shipping Act 1995** provides that the following documents will be admissible in evidence and, when in the custody of the Registrar of Shipping and Seamen, will be open to public inspection:
    * documents purporting to be **submissions to or decisions by superintendents or proper officers** under section 33;
    * the **Official Log Book** of any ship kept under section 77 and any document purporting to be a copy of an Official Log Book entry and certified as such by the master;
    * **Crew Agreements**; **Lists of Crew** made under section 78;
    * **returns or reports of births and deaths** under section 108; and
    * **documents transmitted to the RSS** under section 298 by superintendents and customs officers.
* A **Certificate of Competency** issued under section 47 will also be admissible in evidence.
* Section 288 of the Merchant Shipping Act 1995 provides that **where a document is admissible in evidence** under the Act, it will:
    * be admissible in evidence in any court or before any person having by law or consent of parties authority to receive evidence; and
    * subject to all just exceptions, be evidence (or in Scotland sufficient evidence) of the matters stated in the document.
* A **copy of, or extract from, any admissible document** will also be admissible if it is certified as a true copy or extract.
* Forgery of the seal, stamp or signature on any admissible document (or copy document) will render the forger liable to the statutory maximum fine on summary conviction and, on conviction on indictment, to 7 years' max. imprisonment.
* In the Admiralty Court, and in arbitrators' hearings, great value is placed on documents created prior to, or at the time of a casualty, including rough or "scrap" bridge logs, bell or movement books, working charts, satellite navigator logs, port or cargo logs, sounding books, course records, engine movement records, and radar plots.
* The Official Log Book, the rough log, the deck or mate's log and the engine room log are the most important of the above logs.
* The risk of losing litigation can be decreased by the proper use and handling of documents. Courts and arbitrators are not impressed by **untidy logs**, or by **fair or official logs written after an event**. Entries in logs of any kind should be made neatly in ink and errors should never be erased. In logs other than the Official Log Book, or annexes thereto, if a mistake is made when making an entry, a single line should be drawn through the erroneous entry, initialled by the writer, with the amendment following it. For notes on **amending Official Log Book entries** see D05a.6.
* Under section 289 of the Merchant Shipping Act 1995, copies or other reproductions of statutory documents (e.g. Official Log Books) which have been sent to the RSS, but which have been destroyed, may be admissible in evidence and open for public inspection.

D05d.2 Legal professional privilege

* **"Privilege"** is a special right or immunity in connection with legal proceedings, conferred upon a person by virtue of his rank or office. **Private privileges** include the privilege against self-incrimination, **privilege attaching to "without prejudice" documents** in the course of litigation, and **legal professional privilege**.
* The **doctrine of legal professional privilege** protects confidential communications between lawyers and their clients and between lawyers and third parties with a view to advising their clients. A **privileged communication** between parties to a confidential relationship, such as a solicitor and his client, may not be used in evidence without the consent of the party to whom the privilege is given.
* If an accident occurs which is likely to give rise to litigation, reports sent to owners or their agents will normally have to be produced to the other party. Many of these "post-casualty documents" can, with foresight, attract legal privilege and therefore in subsequent English litigation need not be shown to the other party.
* **In order not to lose the right of legal professional privilege**, documents should only be created after a casualty following consultation with the owner's or master's lawyers, as the case may be. These documents include **master's reports** sent by fax, telex or mail, and **protests**. None of these will be privileged unless they have been prepared by, or at the request of, the owner's or master's lawyer for the **sole purpose of subsequent litigation**.
* Documents which are not solely for the purpose of litigation can be prepared under the guidance of the lawyer so that when disclosed to the other party they will not create unnecessary litigation risks.
* **Statements** taken by the owner's or master's lawyer from the master and other witnesses are also privileged.

* Following a casualty, e.g. a collision, the master may make notes in his personal notebook. Masters should remember, however, that if these notes are used by the owner's or P&I club's lawyers, the **entire contents** of the notebook may be required to be disclosed to the lawyers acting for the "other side".
* For notes on provisions of section 259 of the Merchant Shipping Act 1995 with respect to **production of privileged documents**, see B05b.4c.

D05d.2a "Without prejudice"

- is an abbreviation of "Without prejudice to the matter in question", and is a legal term used in letters and other documents to enable two parties to negotiate the settlement of a claim without implying any admission of liability.
* When, for example, a lawyer acting for a P&I club writes on behalf of a shipowner member to the lawyer representing a cargo claimant offering a compromise, he may want to guard against giving the impression that he is making an admission of liability, and by using the expression "without prejudice" he indicates that what he is offering is without prejudice to the matter in dispute.
* Letters and other documents bearing the heading "Without prejudice" cannot be mentioned in evidence in a court action or arbitration without the consent of both parties.

D05d.3 Evidence required by P&I clubs

* **P&I clubs stress the importance of the submission of evidence** of various kinds whenever the possibility of a claim against the member arises. **Documents required** will vary with the type of incident, but generally include:
    * **log books** including Official Log Book, deck log, engine log, engine movement or bell books, Oil Record Book, Cargo Record Books, sounding book, cargo gear certificates/chain register;
    * **contemporaraneous notes** such as rough note books and scrap logs;
    * **master's reports** to company superintendents, etc.;
    * **photographs** (e.g. of damage) and **video recordings** (e.g. of the vessel in boisterous weather);
    * **accident report forms** (company's and IRF);
    * **data print-outs** from various bridge and engine room recording instruments;
    * **letters of protest**;
    * **protests** (or "sea protests") noted before a notary public, consul, etc.;
    * **statements to lawyers** approved by the owner's P&I club.
* In all cases where the master is considering taking a **statement** from a witness, it is advisable to first consult the P&I club. In some cases, the statement may have to be disclosed to the opposing party's lawyers and to a court. (See notes on **privilege** in D05d.2.)
* P&I clubs advise their members to have a **camera**, loaded and ready for use, on board each ship. **Photographs** should be taken carefully so as to avoid showing defects that could be used by the opposing party's lawyers in their favour.

D05d.3a Evidence required for defence against allegations of non-cargoworthiness or unpreparedness for cargo operations

- includes:
    * **maintenance records** of cargo-handling equipment (e.g. chain register);
    * **maintenance records** of other deck equipment (e.g. planned maintenance records of hatchcover rubber replacement, checks of hatch closing and locking devices, ventilators, smoke detectors, lights, etc.);
    * sounding books;
    * logged **records of hold or tank cleaning**, painting, etc.;
    * logged **records of tests** (e.g. scupper tests, hose tests of hatch covers, etc.);
    * **hold inspection reports** (e.g. noting damage to ladders, spar ceiling, etc.) and evidence of repairs to defects;
    * copies of **hold/tank clean and pre-load survey reports**;
    * **documents of authorisation to load cargoes** (e.g. for dangerous goods and grain);
    * **records of pre-cooling** of reefer compartments.

D05d.3b Evidence required when on passage (to defend cargo damage claims)

- includes:
    * course and weather records (as routinely entered in deck log book, including sea temperatures);
    * detailed accounts of unusual weather conditions (e.g. violent weather or extreme air temperatures, etc.);

- bilge sounding records;
- bunker sounding records;
- bilge pumping records (either manual or automatic) and other entries required in oil record books;
- records of air and sea temperatures, air humidity and cargo ventilation;
- inert gas operations;
- records of checks of hatches, watertight doors, etc.
- fire patrol records;
- safety equipment check records;
- temperatures of fuel oil in tanks under holds/tanks containing sensitive cargoes;
- reefer compartment temperatures and gas measurements.

D05d.3c Evidence required from cargo-handling operations

- includes:
  - weather records;
  - times of opening and closing hatches;
  - times of starting and stopping loading/discharging/trimming operations;
  - bilge sounding records;
  - ballast loading and discharging records;
  - records of cargo securing operations;
  - cargo temperatures;
  - copies of stability calculations;
  - loading plans and stowage plans.

D05d.3d Evidence required when the vessel causes or sustains damage

- includes:
  items in D05d.3; and
  statements from witnesses including deck and engineer officers, ratings, pilot, tugmasters, linesmen (if possible);
  radar plots;
  charts in use (unchanged);
  chart correction records;
  navigational publications in use (and records of correction);
  letters of protest received;
  illustrations of damage (either photos, videos or sketches);
  letters received (e.g. holding the vessel liable);
  copies or logs of communications with other stations (e.g. shore stations, VTS);
  detailed records of tide, current, sea, wind and visibility conditions.

D05d.3e Evidence required following a personal injury

- includes:
  - copies of **accident reports** (including detailed report sent to MAIB and report to company);
  - record of any **first aid and medical treatment** given, including details of **providers**;
  - record of **movement of patient** from scene of accident to place(s) of treatment, including details of handlers;
  - **statement** from injured person, if possible;
  - **statements** from witnesses;
  - surveyors' reports;
  - **illustrations** (photos, videos or sketches) of accident scene and any relevant equipment (but not showing anything adverse to owner's interests);
  - relevant **log book entries**;
  - **records** of ballasting, tank cleaning, cargo loading or other operations relevant to the accident;
  - copy of ship's **safety officer's report** of accident;
  - **retained items of relevant equipment** where possible (e.g. defective shackles, broken wires, etc.);
* Where witnesses may be "hostile" to the interests of the owner, or may become unreliable as time passes, their **statements** should be taken **immediately after the incident**, while memories are clear. The injured person should be asked for a statement at this stage, if possible.

D05d.3f Evidence of ship security measures

- includes:
  - records of **pre-arrival searches** for drugs and stowaways;
  - records of **locking of spaces** (e.g. holds and storerooms) and of minimising usable entrances;
  - records of **gangway and security watch-keeping**;
  - records of **security and fire patrols**;
  - records of **posting of notices prohibiting unauthorised boarding**;
  - records of **checks of extra precautions** taken in ports of known security risk (e.g. in Algeria).
* For notes on **ship security records** required to be kept under SOLAS regulation XI-2/9, see D05b.9.

D05e HANDING OVER DOCUMENTS

* Section 81(1) of the Merchant Shipping Act 1995 provides that if a person ceases to be the master of a UK ship during a voyage, he must **deliver to his successor** the documents relating to the ship or its crew which are in his custody.
* The off-going (i.e. superseded) master should:
  - **hand over** all documents, monies, etc., and command of the ship;
  - make an entry in the narrative section of the **Official Log Book** recording **delivery** of these items to his successor;
  - sign and date the Official Log Book entry;
  - have the Official Log Book entry jointly signed by the superseding (i.e. new) master.
* In cases **where the superseded master has already left the ship**, the new master should enter a statement in the Official Log Book of the reasons why a personal hand-over was not possible, and have an officer witness his signature.
* **Documents** handed over may include all or some of the documents listed in D05e.1 and D05e.2. The lists are not exhaustive. For a full list of ships' certificates and documents, see D04a.
* For notes on **handing over command to a successor**, see E04c.2. For notes on **taking over command in normal circumstances**, see E04c.1

D05e.1 General documents

1. Anchors and Chain Cables Certificates.
2. Berth List (UK ro-ro ferries).
3. Bulk carrier booklet.
4. Cargo book (for UK coastal ships/UK Customs & Excise).
5. Cargo Record Book (NLS).
6. Cargo Securing Manual.
7. Cargo Ship Safety Certificate (in lieu of 8, 9 and 10).
8. Cargo Ship Safety Construction Certificate.
9. Cargo Ship Safety Equipment Certificate.
10. Cargo Ship Safety Radio Certificate.
11. Certificate of Financial Responsibility (Water Pollution) (ships trading to USA).
12. Certificate of Fitness for Offshore Support Vessels.
13. Certificate of Registry (or Provisional Certificate of Registry).
14. Certificate(s) of Class or Interim Certificate of Class.
15. Certificates of service and testing of inflatable liferafts, marine escape systems, inflatable boats, hydrostatic release units, lifejackets, etc..
16. Class survey records.
17. Code of Safe Working Practices for Merchant Seamen.
18. Compass error book.
19. Compass test certificates.
20. Continuous synopsis record.
21. Damage control booklet.
22. Decision Support System (passenger ships).
23. Deratting Exemption Certificate or Deratting Certificate.
24. Diving System Safety Certificate.

25. Document of Compliance with the Special requirements for Ships Carrying Dangerous Goods.
26. Dynamically Supported Craft Construction and Equipment Certificate.
27. Dynamically Supported Craft Permit to Operate.
28. Enhanced Survey Report file.
29. Exemption Certificate(s) (SOLAS).
30. Extensions to certificates.
31. Firearms Certificate.
32. Gaming Machine Licence(s).
33. Garbage Management Plan.
34. Garbage Record Book.
35. High-Speed Craft Safety Certificate.
36. Intact stability booklet.
37. International Certificate of Fitness (or Certificate of Fitness) for the Carriage of Dangerous Chemicals in Bulk.
38. International Certificate of Fitness for the Carriage of INF Cargo.
39. International Certificate of Fitness (or Certificate of Fitness) for the Carriage of Liquefied Gases in Bulk.
40. International Code of Signals.
41. International Load Line Certificate (ILLC 1966) or International Load Line Exemption Certificate.
42. International Oil Pollution Prevention (IOPP) Certificate or UKOPP Certificate.
43. International Sewage Pollution Prevention Certificate (from 27 September 2003).
44. International Ship Security Certificate (from 1 July 2004).
45. International Tonnage Certificate (1969).
46. ISM Document of Compliance.
47. ISM Safety Management Certificate.
48. ISM Safety Management System documents.
49. ITF "Blue Certificate".
50. Letter(s) of Compliance issued re- defective/deficient equipment, etc.
51. Lifting appliances test/examination certificates (in "Chain Register" file).
52. List of Operational Limitations (passenger ships).
53. Mobile Offshore Drilling Unit Safety Certificate.
54. Muster List Approval document.
55. Nautical publications.
56. Noise Survey report.
57. Official Log Book - Part 2 (passenger ships).
58. Official Log Book.
59. Oil Pollution Insurance Certificate (OPIC).
60. Oil Record Book (Part I) (all ships).
61. Oil Record Book (Part II) (oil tankers).
62. P&I club Certificate of Entry.
63. P&I club handbook and list of correspondents.
64. Panama Canal Tonnage Certificate or appropriate document.
65. Passenger Ship Safety Certificate or Passenger Certificate.
66. Permit to Operate High-Speed Craft.
67. Procedures and Arrangements Manual (P&A Manual).
68. Registration cards for EPIRBs and SARTs.
69. Safe Manning Document.
70. Search and Rescue Co-operation Plan (passenger ships).
71. Ship Radio Licence.
72. Ship Security Plan.
73. Shipboard Marine Pollution Emergency Plan for Noxious Liquid Substances (SMPEP).
74. Shipboard Oil Pollution Emergency Plan (SOPEP).
75. Special Purpose Ships Safety Certificate.
76. Suez Canal Tonnage Certificate.
77. TV Licence.
78. Vessel Response Plans for US or other waters, as required.

D05e.2 Documents relating to the current voyage

1. Accounts of Seamen's Wages forms (ASW, ASW2).
2. Apprentices' indentures.

3. Captain's copies (or originals, if carried) of Bills of Lading.
4. Cargo manifest.
5. Cash book.
6. Certificate(s) of test of solid bulk cargoes.
7. Certificates of competency (STCW 95) for masters, officers and ratings.
8. Charter party.
9. Charts.
10. Clearance from last port.
11. Crew Agreement and List(s) of Crew.
12. Crew list (for customs, immigration, police, etc.).
13. Dangerous goods list, manifest or stowage plan.
14. Disbursements sheets and vouchers.
15. Discharge books (if in master's custody).
16. Document of Authorization for the Carriage of Grain.
17. Grain Loading Certificate.
18. Hand-over notes for new master.
19. Hours of work schedule and related documents.
20. Income Tax Schedules and tables.
21. Letters of protest issued (copies).
22. Letters of protest received.
23. Marine pollutants list, manifest or stowage plan.
24. Master's bond book.
25. Monthly accounts, cash books, etc.
26. National Insurance Schedules and tables.
27. Passenger list.
28. Portage bill forms.
29. Protests (or "sea protests") noted, and extended protests.
30. Radio Log Books.
31. Sea waybills.
32. Ship security records for the last 10 voyages.
33. Ship's copies of Mate's Receipts or Shipping Notes.
34. Shipper's declaration for cargoes of coal, etc.
35. Stores lists (for customs).
36. Surveyors' certificates (of hold/tank cleanliness, etc.) in connection with cargo, etc.
37. TREM cards for dangerous goods.
38. Voyage instructions/letters from owners, managers, operators and/or charterers.

D06 Ship sale and purchase

Masters and officers present during the transfer of ownership of a vessel may find the following notes useful.

D06a NORWEGIAN SALEFORM

* **Second hand ship purchase deals** are normally made through specialist **sale and purchase brokers**, Sellers and Buyers having separate brokers.
* **Sellers** will send to Buyers' brokers particulars sheets containing details of flag, year built and builders, gross and net tonnage, cubic capacity, deadweight on loaded draft, dimensions, bunkers, water ballast, engines, boilers, winches, derricks, deck plan, tween decks, average speed, consumption, passengers, number of bulkheads, holds, hatchways and dimensions, class and survey details and remarks.
* **Norwegian Saleform** (NSF) is the usual standard agreement form used. Main features of this of relevance to shipmasters are as follows:
  • Buyers pay a 10% **deposit** within an agreed number of banking days from the agreement date.
  • Buyers may inspect **classification records** and declare whether these are accepted or not within an agreed time. Sellers arrange for **inspection** at an agreed place. Buyers must inspect without undue delay to the vessel and must inspect afloat without opening up, at their expense. Deck and E/R logs must be available for Buyers' inspection.

- If vessel is accepted after afloat inspection, the **purchase becomes definite** except for other possible "subjects", on condition that Sellers receive notice from Buyers within 48 hours of completion of inspection. If acceptance of vessel and class records is not received by then, the deposit is released and the contract is null and void.
- **Delivery** is at an agreed place and time when the vessel can be **drydocked**. Sellers keep Buyers posted on the vessel's itinerary and estimated time/place of drydocking. If vessel becomes a total loss or CTL before delivery, the deposit is released and the contract becomes null and void.
- **Drydocking** is arranged by Sellers so that their Classification Society can inspect the bottom and other underwater parts (rudder, propeller, etc.) below Summer Load Line. If anything below the SLL is found broken, damaged or defective so as to affect clean Certificate of Class, the defects must be made good at Sellers' expense to the satisfaction of a Classification Society nominated by Buyers.
- If required by Buyers or the Classification Society, Sellers must arrange for the **tailshaft** to be drawn while in drydock. If the tailshaft is found defective so as to affect clean Certificate of Class, it must be renewed or made good at Sellers' expense, to the Classification Society's unqualified satisfaction. Buyers' representative has the right to be present in drydock without interfering with the Class Surveyor's decisions.
- **Sellers must deliver** everything belonging to the ship, whether on board or ashore. Spares belonging to the vessel at the time of inspection, except for spares on order, then become Buyers' property. Sellers need not replace spares used before delivery, but spares fitted before delivery become Buyers' property. Sellers may replace own house crockery, etc. with unmarked items.
- **Bunkers, unused lubricating oil, stores and provisions** are bought by Buyers at the current market price at port and date of delivery of the vessel.
- **Purchase money** (free of bank charges) is paid on delivery of the vessel, but not later than 3 banking days after the vessel is ready for delivery and written or telexed notice is given to Buyers by Sellers.
- Sellers must give Buyers a legal **Bill of Sale** free from encumbrances and maritime liens and debts, attested by a Notary and legalised by Buyers' country's consul with a certificate confirming that the vessel is free from registered encumbrances.
- **Until delivery**, the vessel and everything on her is at **Sellers' risk** and expense, but subject to conditions of the contract, the vessel must be delivered and taken over as she was at the time of inspection, fair wear and tear excepted.
- The vessel must be delivered with her **present class free of recommendations**. Sellers must notify the Classification Society of any matters coming to their notice prior to delivery which, if the Society were told, could result in imposition of a recommendation re- class.
- On delivery, Sellers must arrange for **deletion of the vessel from their flag State Register** and give Buyers a Certificate of Deletion.
- Buyers must change the vessel's **name and funnel markings** on delivery.
- **Sellers must hand over** all Classification Certificates, plans, etc. on board, and forward all other technical documentation to Buyers. Sellers may keep the log books, but Buyers may make copies.
- **Sellers warrant** the vessel **free of encumbrances, maritime liens and debts** at the time of delivery, and indemnify the Buyers against consequences of claims arising before delivery.
- The **sale is legally carried out** by execution of the Bill of Sale, which must be executed under seal in English law and may have to be signed before a Notary and bear the visa of the Buyers' consul. The Bill of Sale is handed over against a letter releasing the Deposit and a Banker's Draft for the balance of the price. Extra payment for bunkers, stores, etc. is made at the same time.
- The **time for delivery** is normally noon since insurance runs from then.
- New Owner's broker ensures he has **insurance and ship's documents**.
- The broker may be asked to **register** the vessel in the Owner's name.

Section E

THE MASTER AND CREW

Section E Contents

Section E Contents

E01 Legislation relating to seafarers

E01a INTERNATIONAL TREATY PROVISIONS RELATING TO SEAFARERS

E01a.1 STCW 95 and the STCW Code

* The **International Convention on Standards of Training, Certification and Watchkeeping for Seafarers, 1978** (**STCW 78**) was extensively revised in July 1995. The revised version is known as **STCW 95** and entered into force on 1 February 1997 under IMO's "tacit acceptance" procedures.

* **Important amendments to chapter 1 (General Provisions) in STCW 95** include:
  * enhanced procedures concerning exercise of **Port State Control**;
  * a requirement for Parties to establish **procedures for investigating acts** by persons to whom they have issued certificates that **endanger safety or the environment**;
  * recognition of **technical innovations**, such as different working practices and the use of **simulators** for training purposes. Simulators will become mandatory for training in the use of radar and ARPA. Parties must ensure that training, certification and other procedures are continuously monitored by means of a **quality-assurance system**;
  * the inclusion of **medical standards** (in regulation 9). Certificates must be issued showing that levels of fitness have been met, particularly regarding eyesight and hearing;
  * a requirement for every master, officer and radio operator, at **intervals of not more than 5 years**, to meet the **fitness standards** prescribed in regulation 9 and the levels of **professional competence** contained in section A-I/11 of the STCW Code;
  * a reference (in regulation 14) to the **ISM Code**. The regulation details further company responsibilities for manning, certification, etc.

* The remaining chapters contain regulations concerning **specific departments and ranks**. Chapter II, for example, deals with the master and deck department and chapter III with the engine department.

* Special requirements have been introduced in chapter V concerning training and qualifications of personnel on board **ro-ro passenger ships**. Crews must undergo training in technical aspects and also in **crowd management and human behaviour**.

* Regulations concerning the **functional approach to training** are introduced in chapter VII.

* Parties could, until 1 February 2002, continue to issue, recognise and endorse certificates which applied before that date in respect of seafarers who began training or seagoing service before 1 August 1998.

* STCW 95 incorporates the **STCW Code**, to which many technical regulations of the Convention have been transferred. A major benefit of the Code is that future amendments will be easy to introduce, since there is no need to call a full IMO Conference to update a Code. Generally speaking, the revised Convention contains general, basic requirements that are enlarged and explained in the STCW Code.

* **Part A of the STCW Code** is **mandatory** and contains, for example, **tables of minimum standards** required of seafarers. **Part B** is only **recommended** and contains **guidance and advice** intended to help with implementation of the revised Convention.

* For each STCW Convention regulation (as contained in the amended annex to the Convention) there is a related mandatory section in Part A of the STCW Code and a related guidance section in Part B. For example, on the matter of revalidation of certificates:
  * **Regulation I/11** is entitled *Revalidation of certificates*;
  * **Section A-I/3** is entitled *Revalidation of certificates*;
  * **Section B-I/3** is entitled *Guidance regarding the revalidation of certificates*;

* **STCW 95 is implemented** in the UK by:
  * the **MS (Training and Certification) Regulations 1997** (SI 1997/348) (see E02b.1); and
  * the **MS (Safe Manning, Hours of Work and Watchkeeping) Regulations 1997** (SI 1997/1320) (see E03b.1).

E01a.1a The White List

* Under regulation 7 of chapter 1 (General Provisions) of STCW 95, Parties must provide detailed information to IMO concerning administrative procedures taken to ensure compliance with the Convention, education and training courses, certification procedures and other factors relevant to implementation. This information is used by IMO's Maritime Safety Committee to identify complying Parties. Other Parties will then be able to accept certificates issued by these Parties. (No proof of compliance was required under STCW 78.) Countries assessed by IMO to be properly implementing STCW 95 are placed on a so-called "**White List**" (properly called the **List of Confirmed Parties**) published by IMO on its website.
* To gain a place on the White List, countries must report details to the IMO Secretary-General of national laws, training requirements, standards and systems in place, and ensure that all of those elements meet the revised STCW 95 requirements and can pass the scrutiny of persons with a detailed knowledge of those requirements.
* A position on the White List entitles other parties to the STCW Convention to accept, in principle, that certificates issued by or on behalf of the parties on the list are in compliance with STCW 95.
* A flag State party that is on the White List may, as a matter of policy, elect **not to accept** for service on its ships seafarers holding certificates issued by non- White List countries. If it does accept such seafarers, they are required, since 1 February 2002, to have an endorsement, issued by the flag State, to show that their certificate is recognised by the flag State.
* At 31 December 2002 the White List comprised **109 IMO Member States**.

E01a.2 SOLAS regulation V/14

* **SOLAS chapter V (Safety of navigation)**, unless otherwise expressly provided in that chapter, applies to all ships on all voyages, except ships of war and ships solely navigating the Great Lakes of North America and their connecting and tributary waters as far east as the lower exit of the St Lambert Lock at Montreal. **Regulation V/14** lays down requirements for **safe manning**, **Safe Manning Documents**, and **the working language of crew on passenger ships**, as detailed below.
* Contracting Governments (i.e. SOLAS Party States) undertake to maintain or, if necessary, adopt measures for the purpose of ensuring that, from the point of view of safety of life at sea, all ships flying their flags will **be sufficiently and efficiently manned**[1] (regulation V/14.1.
* Every ship to which SOLAS chapter I (General provisions) applies[2] must be provided with an **appropriate Minimum Safe Manning Document** or equivalent issued by the flag State Administration as evidence of the minimum safe manning considered necessary to comply with regulation V/14.1 (regulation V/14.2).
* **On all ships**, to ensure effective crew performance in safety matters, a **working language** must be established and recorded in the ship's log book[3]. The Company, as defined in SOLAS regulation IX/1 (see C04b.3) or the master, as appropriate, must determine the working language. Each seafarer must be required to understand, and, where appropriate, give orders and instructions and to report back in that language. If the working language is not an official language of the flag State, all plans and lists required to be posted must include a translation into the working language (regulation V/14.3).
  * **On ships to which SOLAS chapter I applies**, **English** must be used on the bridge as the working language for bridge-to-bridge and bridge-to-shore communications as well as for communications on board between the pilot and bridge watchkeeping personnel[4], unless those directly involved in the communication speak a common language other than English.

E01a.3 ILO Conventions

* A number of International Labour Organization (ILO) Conventions concern aspects of the health, safety and welfare of seafarers, as well as manning and certification. For a list of **ILO's maritime conventions**, see A04c.
* A draft agreement to provide security for seafarers in cases of abandonment, death or personal injury was drawn up in January 2001 by a joint IMO/ILO ad hoc expert working group. Under the proposals, owners would have contractual and statutory responsibilities to cover such elements as outstanding wages, medical care and repatriation

---

[1] Reference should be made to the Principles of Safe Manning adopted by IMO by Resolution A.890(21) and to MSC/Circ.242 on single-handed voyages.
[2] SOLAS chapter I applies to all ships on international voyages, except (by virtue of regulation 3) ships of war and troopships, cargo ships of less than 500 gross tonnage, ships not propelled by mechanical means, wooden ships of primitive build, pleasure yachts not engaged in trade, and fishing vessels.
[3] The appropriate log book in which to make the record of the working language in a UK ship is the Official Log Book (narrative section).
[4] The IMO Standard Marine Communication Phrases (SMCPs) contained in MSC/Circ.794, as amended, may be used in this respect (see H06b.5).

following abandonment. An associated draft resolution proposed procedures intended to provide effective insurance cover to ensure that seafarers and their dependants receive full and prompt payment of compensation for death and personal injury.

E01b UK LEGISLATION RELATING TO SEAFARERS

E01b.1 Merchant Shipping Act 1995 provisions relating to masters and seamen

* **Part III of the Merchant Shipping Act 1995** contains the following sections which relate to **masters and seamen**: **24**. Application of this Part (i.e. Part III); **25**. Crew agreements; **26**. Regulations relating to Crew Agreements; **27**. Discharge of seamen; **28**. Seamen left behind abroad otherwise than on discharge; **29**. Discharge of seamen when ship ceases to be registered in United Kingdom; **30**. Payment of seamen's wages; **31**. Account of seamen's wages; **32**. Regulations relating to wages and accounts; **33**. Power of superintendent or proper officer to decide disputes about wages; **34**. Restriction on assignment of and charge upon wages; **35**. Power of court to award interest on wages due otherwise than under Crew Agreement; **36**. Allotment notes; **37**. Right of person named in allotment to sue in own name; **38**. Right, or loss of right, to wages in certain circumstances; **39**. Protection of certain rights and remedies; **40**. Claims against seamen's wages for maintenance, etc. of dependents; **41**. Remedies of master for remuneration, disbursements and liabilities; **42**. Obligation of shipowners as to seaworthiness; **43**. Crew accommodation; **44**. Complaints about provisions or water; **45**. Expenses of medical and other treatment during voyage; **46**. Application of sections 47 to 51; **47**. Manning; **48**. Power to exempt from manning requirements; **49**. Prohibition of going to sea undermanned; **50**. Production of certificates and other documents of qualification; **51**. Crew's knowledge of English; **52**. Unqualified persons going to sea as qualified officers or seamen; **53**. Medical treatment on board ship; **54**. Special certificates of competence; **55**. Young persons; **56**. Financial assistance for training; **57**. Uniform; **58**. Conduct endangering ships, structures or individuals; **59**. Concerted disobedience and neglect of duty; **60**. Breaches by seamen of codes of conduct; **61**. Inquiry into fitness or conduct of officer; **62**. Disqualification of holder of certificate other than officer's; **63**. Inquiry into fitness or conduct of seaman other than officer; **64**. Re-hearing of and appeal from inquiries; **65**. Rules as to inquiries and appeals; **66**. Failure to deliver cancelled or suspended certificate; **67**. Power to restore certificate; **68**. Power to summon witness to inquiry into fitness or conduct of officer or other seaman; **69**. Procedure where inquiry into fitness or conduct of officer or other seaman is held by sheriff; **70**. Civil liability for absence without leave; **71**. Civil liability for smuggling; **72**. Civil liability for fines imposed under immigration laws; **73**. Relief and return of seamen etc. left behind and shipwrecked; **74**. Limit of employer's liability under section 73; **75**. Recovery of expenses incurred for relief and return, etc.; **76**. Financial assistance in respect of crew relief costs; **77**. Official log books; **78**. Lists of crew; **79**. British seamen's cards; **80**. Discharge books; **81**. Handing over of documents by master; **82**. Maintenance of Merchant Navy Reserve; **83**. Supplementary provisions as respects the Reserve; **84**. Interpretation.

E01b.2 Secondary legislation relating to seafarers

* **UK statutory instruments** relating to seafarers, and principal references in this book, are shown in the table below.

Subject	Principal regulations	Amending SIs	SBC ref.
Accommodation	MS (Crew Accommodation) Regulations 1997 (SI 1997/1508)	-	E08g.1
Allotments	MS (Seamen's Allotments) Regulations 1972 (SI 1972/1698)	-	E09c
Crew agreements, engagement and discharge	MS (Crew Agreements, Lists of Crew and Discharge of Seamen) Regulations 1991 (SI 1991/2144)	-	E07b.1
Health and safety at work	MS & FV (Health and Safety at Work) Regulations 1997 (SI 1997/2962)	SI 1998/2411 SI 2001/54	E08b.2
Hours of work	MS (Hours of Work) Regulations 2002 (SI 2002/2125)	-	E03c.1
Medical fitness requirements	MS (Medical Examination) Regulations 1983 (SI 1983/808)	SI 1985/512 SI 1990/1985	E06c.2
Property of deceased seamen	MS (Property of Deceased Seamen and Official Log Book) (Amendment) Regulations 1983 (SI 1983/1801)	-	E14c
Protective clothing and equipment	MS (Personal Protective Equipment) Regulations 1999 (SI 1999/2205)	-	E08e.6
Provisions and water	MS (Provisions and Water) Regulations 1989 (SI 1989/102)	-	E08h.1
Safe manning, hours of work & watchkeeping	MS (Safe Manning, Hours of Work and Watchkeeping) Regulations 1997 (SI 1997/1320)	1997/1911 2000/484	E03b
Seamen's documents (Discharge Book, British Seaman's Card)	MS (Seamen's Documents) Regulations 1987 (SI 1987/408)	1995/1900	E06a.2
Training and certification (post-STCW 95)	MS (Training and Certification) Regulations 1997 (SI 1997/348)	1997/1911 2000/836	E02b.1

| Wages | MS (Seamen's Wages and Accounts) Regulations 1972 (SI 1972/1700) | SI 1978/1757 SI 1985/340 SI 1994/791 SI 1999/3360 | E09b.2 |
| Young persons, employment of | MS and FV (Health and Safety at Work) (Employment of Young Persons) Regulations 1995 (SI 1995/972) | - | E05c.1 |

E02 Training and certification

E02a LEGISLATION RELATING TO SEAFARERS' TRAINING AND CERTIFICATION

* **Section 47(1)(a) of the Merchant Shipping Act 1995** enables Regulations to be made requiring ships to carry such number of qualified officers of any description, qualified doctors and qualified cooks and such number of other seamen or qualified seamen of any description as may be specified in the Regulations.
* **Section 47(1)(b)** enables Regulations to be made prescribing or specifying standards of competence to be attained and other conditions to be satisfied by officers and other seamen of any description in order to be qualified.
* **Secondary UK legislation** relating to **seafarers' training and certification** is shown in the table below.

Subject	Principal regulations	Amending SIs	SBC ref.
Certificate of Competency as AB	MS (Certificate of Competency as AB) Regulations 1970 (SI 1970/294)	-	E02d.2
Certification of Ships' Cooks	MS (Certification of Ships' Cooks) Regulations 1970 (SI 1981/1076)	-	E02d.3
Disqualification of Holder of Seaman's Certificates	MS (Disqualification of Holder of Seaman's Certificates) Regulations 1997 (SI 1997/346)	-	E02d.8
Masters' Licences and Hours, Manning and Training (Local Passenger Vessels)	MS (Local Passenger Vessels) (Masters' Licences and Hours, Manning and Training) Regulations 1993 (SI 1993/1213)	-	E02d.1
Training and Certification	MS (Training and Certification) Regulations 1997 (SI 1997/348)	1997/1911 2000/836	E02b.1

E02b TRAINING AND CERTIFICATION REGULATIONS

E02b.1 Training and Certification Regulations

* The MS (Training and Certification) Regulations 1997 (SI 1997/348) -
    - are the **principal regulations** relating to training and certification in accordance with STCW 95 criteria
    - **give effect** in the UK to some of the requirements of the International Convention on Standards of Training, Certification and Watchkeeping 1978 as amended in 1995 (STCW 95) and its associated STCW Code.
    - set out a **certification structure** for UK merchant ship personnel reflecting the requirements of STCW 95.
    - specify the **conditions to be satisfied for the issue of certificates** of competency and endorsements to those certificates, for service **in UK ships**.
    - **revoke** (by regulation 1(2)) the MS (Tankers - Officers and Ratings) Regulations 1984 (SI 1984/94); the MS (Engine Room Watch Ratings) Regulations 1984 (SI 1984/95); the MS (Navigation Watch Ratings) Regulations 1984 (SI 1984/96); the MS (Certificates of Proficiency in Survival Craft) Regulations 1984 (SI 1984/97); the MS (Certification of Deck Officers) Regulations 1985 (SI 1985/1306); the MS (Certification of Marine Engineer Officers and Licensing of Marine Engine Operators) Regulations 1986 (SI 1986/1935); the MS (Certification of Deck and Marine Engineer Officers and Licensing of Marine Engine Operators) (Amendment) Regulations 1987 (SI 1987/884); the MS (Certification of Deck Officers and Marine Engineer Officers) (Amendment) Regulations 1991 (SI 1991/1819); and the MS (Certification of Deck and Marine Engineer Officers) (Amendment) Regulations 1995 (SI 1995/1429).
    - are in three parts: **Part I: Preliminary** (regulations 1 and 2); **Part II: Ships** (regulations 3 to 21) and **Part III: Hovercraft** (regulations 22 to 24). The notes in this section concern only Parts I and II.
    - provide for the recognition by the MCA of certificates of other countries which are parties to STCW 95 (regulation 5).
    - provide that persons wishing to hold certificates issued under the Regulations must satisfy the **appropriate training and competency requirements** specified in Part A of the STCW Code annexed to STCW 95, and that they must also satisfy any other requirements specified by the MCA (regulations 7, 8 and 9).

- provide for minimum training and qualification requirements for **seamen working on tankers** (regulation 10) and ro-ro passenger ships (regulation 11).
- provide for minimum training and qualification requirements for **personnel serving on passenger ships other than ro-ro passenger ships and high speed craft**, where such ships are engaged on international voyages (regulation 11A).
- provide for minimum requirements for the **training of personnel on high speed craft** constructed after 1 January 1996 which are "ships" (regulation 12).
- are explained in detail in a series of Training and Certification Marine Guidance Notes issued by the MCA (see E02c).

* Notwithstanding the revocations made by regulation 1(2) (as detailed above), certificates and licences granted, endorsements made and standards of competency already met, pursuant to the revoked regulations, and as specified in MSN 1692, were treated as **equivalent** to certificates and licences granted, endorsements made and standards of competency referred to in the new regulations, as provided in MSN 1692, as amended, and accordingly remained of full validity (subject to revalidation requirements) **until 1 February 2002** (regulation 1(3)).
* Interpretations of terms used in the Regulations are in regulation 2.
* For notes on the **Training and Certification Regulations**, see E02b.1. For notes on **Training and Certification Guidance**, see E02c.

E02b.2 Amendments to Training and Certification Regulations

* The MS (Training and Certification) Regulations 1997 -
  - **are amended** by the MS (Training, Certification and Safe Manning) (Amendment) Regulations 1997 (SI 1997/1911), which correct deficiencies in the principal Training and Certification Regulations and in the MS (Safe Manning, Hours of Work and Watchkeeping) Regulations 1997.
  - **are further amended** by the MS (Training and Certification) (Amendment) Regulations 2000 (SI 2000/836), which implement amendments to STCW 95 as follows:
    • masters, officers, ratings and other personnel on ro-ro passenger ships no longer need to undertake 5-yearly refresher training if they can prove they have achieved the required standard of competence within the previous 5 years (regulation 2(3)); and
    • training and qualification requirements are introduced for masters, officers, ratings and other personnel on passenger ships (other than ro-ro passenger ships and high speed craft) engaged on international voyages, so that they are now similar to those for such personnel on ro-ro passenger ships (regulation 2(2) and (4)).

E02b.3 Application of regulations (regulation 3)

* Part II of the Regulations applies to masters and seamen employed in sea-going ships registered in the UK other than:
  • fishing vessels; or
  • pleasure craft which are less than 80gt or under 24 metres in length.

E02b.4 Qualification as an officer (regulation 4)

* A person is **qualified as an officer** if he holds a certificate of competency, or certificate of equivalent competency, or a certificate treated as equivalent pursuant to the (now-revoked) Certification Regulations (as listed in E02b.1), in one of the following capacities: master; chief mate; officer in charge of a navigational watch; chief engineer officer; second engineer officer; officer in charge of an engineering watch; or radio operator.

E02b.5 Recognition of certificates (regulation 5)

* The **MCA may recognise a certificate** issued by or under the authority of another Party to STCW 95 to a master, officer or radio operator if satisfied that the requirements of STCW 95 concerning standards of competence, the issue and endorsement of certificates and record keeping are fully complied with, and that prompt notification will be given to the MCA of any significant change in the arrangements for training and certification provided in compliance with STCW 95 (regulation 5(1)). Certificates must be **endorsed** by the MCA to attest recognition (regulation 5(2)). The **endorsement** will be in the form of a separate document entitled "**Certificate of Equivalent Competency**" (regulation 5(3)).

* Where, under regulation 5(1), the MCA has recognised the standard of competence required for the issue of a certificate by another Party to STCW 95 as being in part the standard to be attained for officers qualified for the purposes of the (UK) Training and Certification Regulations, any conditions specified by the MCA must be limited to:
  * **aptitude tests** for the purpose of assessing the applicant's ability to pursue the profession of officer on UK ships, in the light of subjects and training and related assessment procedures, which differ substantially from those covered by the applicant's certificate issued by that State; or
  * in the case of applicants who are nationals of a member State of the European Economic Area (EEA) (at the applicant's option) an **adaptation period** not exceeding 3 years, as specified by the MCA (regulation 5(4)).

E02b.6 Revalidation of certificates (regulation 6)

* The certificate of a master or other officer issued with a certificate under regulation 4 or 5 (i.e. a Certificate of Competency or Certificate of Equivalent Competency) and radio operator certificates (including GMDSS certificates) issued under regulation 16 of the MS (Radio Installation) Regulations 1998 will not be valid for sea-going service unless **revalidated** at intervals not exceeding 5 years to establish continued professional competence in accordance with STCW Code section A-I/11 (regulation 6(1) and (2)).
* Every master and officer must, for continued sea-going service **on chemical tankers, liquefied gas tankers or oil tankers**, successfully complete **approved refresher training** at intervals specified by the MCA (regulation 6(3)).

E02b.7 Appropriate certificates (regulation 7)

* Any officer serving in the capacity shown in column 1 of the table below must hold an appropriate certificate for that capacity. A person will only be entitled to be issued with such a certificate if he complies with the criteria in the Regulations annexed to STCW 95, as shown in column 2, and any other requirements specified by the MCA.

Column 1	*Column 2*
Master and deck department	**Regulation annexed to STCW 95**
Officer in charge of a navigational watch on any ship on voyages not limited to near-coastal voyages[5].	II/1.2
Master and chief mate on a ship of 3000gt or more	II/2.2
Master and chief mate on a ship of less than 3000gt.	II/2.4
Officer in charge of a navigational watch on a ship of less than 500gt engaged on near-coastal voyages.	II/3.4
Master on a ship of less than 500gt engaged on near-coastal voyages.	II/3.6

Column 1	*Column 2*
Engine department	**Regulation annexed to STCW 95**
Officer in charge of an engineering watch in a manned engine room, or designated duty engineer officer in a periodically unmanned engine room, on a ship powered by main propulsion machinery of 750 kW propulsion power or more.	III/1.2
Chief engineer officer or second engineer officer on a ship powered by main propulsion machinery of 3000 kW propulsion power or more.	III/2.2
Chief engineer officer or second engineer officer on a ship powered by main propulsion machinery of between 750 and 3000 kW propulsion power.	III/2.2

E02b.8 Ratings and holders of other qualifications (regulation 8)

* Every **rating** forming part of a navigational watch on a ship of 500gt or more, other than ratings under training and ratings whose duties while on watch are of an unskilled nature, must hold a certificate issued under paragraph 8(1)(a) of the Training and Certification Regulations (i.e. a **Navigational Watch Rating Certificate**) (regulation 8(1)(a)). No person will be entitled to be issued with such a certificate unless he complies with the criteria in STCW 95 regulation II/4.2 (regulation 8(1)(b)).
* Every rating forming part of an engine room watch or designated to perform duties in a periodically unmanned engine room on a ship powered by main propulsion machinery of 750 kW propulsion power or more, other than ratings under training and ratings whose duties are of an unskilled nature, must hold a certificate issued under paragraph 8(2)(a) of the Regulations (i.e. an **Engine Watch Rating Certificate**) (regulation 8(2)(a)). No person will be entitled to be issued with such a certificate unless he complies with the criteria in STCW 95 regulation II/4.2 (regulation 8(2)(b)).

---

[5] For the definition of the UK near-coastal area, see E02c.1.

* Any person designated to perform watchkeeping duties in a manned or periodically unmanned engine room on a ship powered by main propulsion machinery of 350 kW power or more, but less than 750 kW, must hold one of the engineering certificates of competency referred to in the table above or hold a **Marine Engine Operator's Licence** issued in compliance with criteria specified by the MCA (regulation 8(3)).

E02b.9 Radiocommunication and radio personnel on GMDSS ships (regulation 9)

* No person may be granted a certificate under **regulation 19 of the MS (Radio Installations) Regulations 1998**[6] unless he is **at least 18** and has completed **approved education and training** and meets the standard of competence specified in the **STCW Code section A-IV/2**.
* For notes on **radio personnel certification requirements**, see E02c.4a. For **GMDSS operator carriage requirements** see E03d.3.

E02b.10 Training and qualifications of masters, officers and ratings on tankers (regulation 10)

* Officers and ratings assigned specific duties and responsibilities related to cargo or cargo equipment on tankers must have completed an **approved shore-based advanced fire-fighting course** in addition to the training required by STCW Code section A-VI/1, and must have completed:
  • at least **3 months' approved seagoing service** on tankers in order to acquire adequate knowledge of safe operational practices; or
  • an **approved tanker familiarisation course** covering at least the syllabus given in section A-V/1 of the STCW Code (regulation 10(1)).
* Regulation 10(2) permits the 3 months' approved seagoing service to be reduced to not less than one month if:
  • the tanker on which the approved seagoing service is performed is of less than 3000gt; and
  • the duration of each voyage on the above-mentioned tanker does not exceed 72 hours; and
  • the operational characteristics of the tanker and the number of voyages and loading and discharging operations completed during the period allow the same level of knowledge and experience to be acquired as would have been acquired in the 3 months' (min.) approved seagoing service on a larger tanker performing longer voyages.
* Masters, chief engineers, chief mates, second engineers and any person with immediate responsibility for loading, discharging and care in transit or handling of cargo on tankers must, in addition to meeting the above requirements for completion of approved seagoing service or a tanker familiarisation course:
  • have experience appropriate to their duties on the type of tanker on which they serve; and
  • have completed an approved specialised training programme which at least covers the subjects set out in STCW Code section A-V/1 appropriate to their duties on the tanker on which they serve (regulation 10(3)).
* An appropriate certificate will be issued to masters and officers who are qualified in accordance with the above requirements, or their existing certificate will be endorsed. Every rating who is similarly qualified must be certificated (regulation 10(4)).

E02b.11 Training and qualifications of masters, officers, ratings and other personnel on ro-ro passenger ships (regulation 11)

* Regulation 11 applies to masters, officers, ratings and other personnel serving on ro-ro passenger ships (regulation 11(1)).
* Prior to being assigned shipboard duties on ro-ro passenger ships, seafarers must have completed the training required by paragraphs (4) to (8) of regulation 11 (as detailed below), in accordance with their capacity, duties and responsibilities (regulation 11(2)).
* Seafarers who are required to be trained in accordance with regulation 11(4), (7) and (8) must, at intervals not exceeding 5 years, undertake appropriate refresher training or alternatively must provide evidence of having achieved the required standard of competence within the previous 5 years (regulation 11(3)). "The required standard of competence" means the standard of competence ensured by:
  • training in **crowd management** as required by regulation 11(4);
  • training in **passenger safety, cargo safety and hull integrity** as required by regulation 11(7); and

---

[6] The Training and Certification Regulations actually state 'regulation 16 of the MS (Radio Installation) Regulations 1992'. The 1992 Regulations were revoked and replaced by the MS (Radio Installations) Regulations 1998 (SI 1998/2070), in which regulation 19 is the relevant regulation.

- approved training in **crisis management and human behaviour** as required by regulation 11(8).

* Masters, officers and other personnel designated on muster lists to assist passengers in emergency situations must have completed **training in crowd management** as specified in the STCW Code, section A-V/2, paragraph 1 (regulation 11(4)).

* Masters, officers and other personnel assigned specific duties and responsibilities on ro-ro passenger ships must have completed the **familiarisation training** specified in the STCW Code, section A-V/2, paragraph 2 (regulation 11(5)).

* Personnel providing direct service to passengers in passenger spaces on ro-ro passenger ships must have completed the **safety training** specified in the STCW Code, section A-V/2, paragraph 3 (regulation 11(6)).

* Masters, chief mates, chief engineer officers, second engineer officers and every person assigned immediate responsibility for embarking and disembarking passengers, loading, discharging or securing cargo, or closing of hull openings on ro-ro passenger ships must have completed **approved training in passenger safety, cargo safety and hull integrity** as specified in the STCW Code, section A-V/2, paragraph 4 (regulation 11(7)).

* Masters, chief mates, chief engineer officers, second engineer officers and any person having responsibility for the safety of passengers in emergency situations on ro-ro passenger ships must have completed **approved training in crisis management** as specified in the STCW Code, section A-V/2, paragraph 5 (regulation 11(8)).

* Any person providing the above training must issue **documentary evidence** to every person successfully completing such training (regulation 11(9)).

E02b.11a Training and qualifications of masters, officers, ratings and other personnel on passenger ships other than ro-ro passenger ships and high speed craft on international voyages (regulation 11A)

* Regulation 11A (which was added to the Regulations by virtue of SI 2000/836) applies to masters, officers, ratings and other personnel on passenger ships other than ro-ro passenger ships and high speed craft, on international voyages (regulation 11A(1)).

* Before being assigned shipboard duties on passenger ships, seafarers must have completed the training required by regulation 11A, paragraphs (4) to (8) in accordance with their capacity, duties and responsibilities (regulation 11A(2)).

* Seafarers who are required to be trained in accordance with regulation 11A(4), (7) and (8) must, at intervals not exceeding 5 years, undertake appropriate refresher training or alternatively must provide evidence of having achieved the required standard of competence within the previous 5 years (regulation 11A(3)). "The required standard of competence" means the standard of competence ensured by the training referred to in regulation 11A(4), (7) and (8), as detailed below.

* Personnel designated on muster lists to assist passengers in emergency situations on passenger ships must have completed the **crowd management training** in the STCW Code, section A-V/3, paragraph 1 (regulation 11A(4)).

* Masters, officers and other personnel assigned specific duties and responsibilities on passenger ships must have completed the **familiarization training** in the STCW Code, section A-V/3, paragraph 2 (regulation 11A(5)).

* Personnel providing a direct service to passengers in passenger spaces on passenger ships must have completed the **safety training** in the STCW Code, section A-V/3, paragraph 3 (regulation 11A(6)).

* Masters, chief mates, and every person assigned immediate responsibility for embarking and disembarking passengers must have completed the **approved training in passenger safety** in the STCW Code, section A-V/3, paragraph 4 (regulation 11A(7)).

* Masters, chief mates, chief engineer officers, second engineer officers and any person with responsibility for the safety of passengers in emergency situations on passenger ships must have completed the **approved training in crisis management and human behaviour** in the STCW Code, section A-V/3, paragraph 5 (regulation 11A(8)).

* Any person providing training referred to in regulation 11A must issue **documentary evidence** to every person successfully completing such training (regulation 11A(9)).

E02b.12 Training and qualifications of masters, officers, ratings and other personnel on high speed craft (regulation 12)

* Regulation 12 applies to masters, officers, ratings and other personnel serving on high speed craft which are ships constructed on or after 1 January 1996 (regulation 12(1)).

* Before being assigned shipboard duties on high speed craft, masters, officers, ratings and other personnel must have completed the training specified in **MSN 1740** (regulation 12(2)).

* The person providing the above training must issue **documentary evidence** to every person successfully completing the training. For masters and officers with an operational role, the evidence must be a certificate in the form specified in MSN 1740 and must be endorsed as specified in that MSN (regulation 12(3)).
* See also **MGN 95**, **MSN 1740**, **MGN 26** and **MGN 97**.

E02b.13 Familiarisation, basic safety training and instruction for all seafarers (regulation 13)

* All seamen[7] must receive **familiarisation and basic safety training or instruction** in accordance with STCW Code section A-VI/1, and must meet the appropriate standard of competence specified therein.
* STCW Code section A-VI/1 provides that seafarers, before being assigned to any shipboard duties -
  * must receive **appropriate basic training or instructions** in:
    * **personal survival techniques**;
    * **fire prevention and fire fighting**;
    * **elementary first aid**; and
    * **personal safety and social responsibilities**.
  * must be required to **produce evidence of having achieved the required standard of competence** to undertake the tasks, duties and responsibilities listed in column 1 of Tables A-VI/1-1, A-VI/1-2, A-VI/1-3 and A-VI/1-4 within the previous five years through:
    * demonstration of competence in accordance with the methods and criteria for evaluating competence in columns 3 and 4 of those tables; and
    * examination or continuous assessment as part of an approved training programme in the subjects listed in column 2 of those tables.
* The tables mentioned above show specifications for minimum standards of competence as follows:
  * Table A-VI/1-1: Personal Survival Techniques;
  * Table A-VI/1-2: Fire Prevention and Fire Fighting;
  * Table A-VI/1-3: Elementary First Aid; and
  * Table A-VI/1-4: Personal Safety and Social Responsibilities.

E02b.14 Certificates of proficiency in survival craft, rescue boats and fast rescue boats (regulation 14)

* Every person designated to launch or take charge of **survival craft or rescue boats** other than fast rescue boats must have a **certificate of proficiency** in such craft; no person will be granted such a certificate unless he meets the criteria specified in STCW regulation VI/2.1 (regulation 14(1)).
* Every person designated to launch or take charge of a **fast rescue boat** must have a certificate of proficiency in such boats; no person will be granted such a certificate unless he meets the criteria specified in STCW regulation VI/2.2 (regulation 14(2)).
* In regulation 14, "fast rescue boat" means a rescue boat which is not less than 6 metres but not more than 8.5 metres long, and is capable of manoeuvring for at least 4 hours at a speed of at least 20 knots in calm water with a suitably qualified crew of at least 3 persons, and at least 8 knots with a full complement of persons and equipment (regulation 14(3)). "survival craft" and "rescue boat" have the same meanings as in the LSA Regulations.

E02b.15 Training in advanced fire-fighting (regulation 15)

* Seamen designated to control fire-fighting operations must have successfully completed advanced training in fighting fire with particular emphasis on organisation, tactics and command as specified in STCW Code section A-VI/3 and must meet the standard of competence specified therein (regulation 15(1)).
* Where advanced fire-fighting training is not included in the qualifications for the certificate to be issued, a special certificate or documentary evidence, as appropriate, must be issued indicating attendance on an advanced fire-fighting course (regulation 15(2)).

---

[7] "Seamen" is not defined in the Regulations, but is assumed to mean, for the purposes of the Regulations, all seafarers, including masters.

E02b.16 Training in first aid and medical care (regulation 16)

* Seamen designated to **provide medical first aid** on board must meet the standard of competence specified in STCW Code section A-VI/4, paragraphs 1 to 3 (regulation 16(1)).
* Seamen designated to **take charge of medical care** on board ship must meet the standard of competence in medical care on board ships specified in STCW Code section A-VI/4, paragraphs 4 to 6 (regulation 16(2)).
* Where training in medical first aid or medical care is not included in the qualifications for the certificate to be issued, a special certificate or documentary evidence, as appropriate, must be issued indicating that the holder has attended a course of training in medical first aid or medical care (regulation 16(3)).

E02b.17 Form, validity, record and surrender of certificates (regulation 17)

* Certificates and endorsements issued by the MCA will remain valid for sea-going service only so long as the holder can comply with the standards and conditions as to **medical fitness** and **professional competency** to act in the appropriate capacity specified by the MCA (regulation 17(2)).
* A **record of all certificates and endorsements** issued under the Regulations, or have expired or been revalidated, suspended, cancelled, or reported lost or destroyed, and any alteration of or any other matters affecting any such certificates or endorsements, shall be kept by the Registrar General of Shipping and Seamen (**RSS**) (regulation 17(3)).
* Where a **certificate holder is issued with a higher certificate**, he must surrender the lower certificate to the MCA for cancellation (regulation 17(4)).
* Where a **certificate holder is convicted of an offence** under section 47(5) of the Merchant Shipping Act 1995 (making a false statement to gain a certificate), or where the MCA's **conditions for the issue of a certificate or endorsement have not been complied with**, the holder must deliver the certificate to the MCA for cancellation (regulation 17(5)).

E02b.18 Refusal of certificates, and appeals against refusal (regulation 18)

* Notwithstanding that an applicant for a Certificate of Competency or Certificate of Equivalent Competency complies with the standards or fulfils the conditions of the Regulations, the MCA may refuse to issue a certificate unless they are satisfied that the applicant is a fit person to be the holder of the certificate and to act in the capacity to which it relates (regulation 18(1)).
* Where the MCA intends to refuse the issue or revalidation of a certificate, written notice must be given to the applicant, who will have the right, before a date which will be specified in the notice, to have the application reviewed at an inquiry (regulation 18(2)).

E02b.19 Loss of certificates (regulation 19)

* If a person entitled to a certificate loses or is deprived of a certificate already issued to him, and the MCA is satisfied that the loss was without the holder's fault, a certificated copy must be issued. Where the MCA is not satisfied that there was no personal fault, they may issue a certificated copy (regulation 19).

E02b.20 Endorsement of UK certificates (regulation 20)

* A certificate issued by the MCA must be endorsed in accordance with the STCW Convention if the MCA is satisfied that the holder complies with the requirements of regulation 7, 9 or 10.

E02b.21 Designated authority (regulation 21)

* For the purposes of certain EEC Council Directives on systems for the recognition of educational awards on completion of officers' professional education and training, the Secretary of State for Transport (whose powers in this regard are exercised by the MCA) is the designated authority for the recognition of professional education and training of officers.

E02c TRAINING AND CERTIFICATION GUIDANCE

* A 21-part series of M Notices issued by the MCA gives guidance on application of the Training and Certification Regulations and consists of the notices shown in the following table[8].

Part	Subject	Current MGN	Issue date	SBC reference
1	Certificates of competency – General requirements for certification and medical fitness	MGN 91	Apr 2000	E02c.1
2	Certificates of competency – Deck department	MGN 92	Apr 2000	E02c.2
3	Certificates of competency – Engine department	MGN 93	Apr 2000	E02c.3
4	Certificates of competency – Radio personnel	MGN 214	May 2002	E02c.4
5	Special training requirements for personnel on certain types of ship	MGN 95	Apr 2000	E02c.5
6	Emergency, occupational safety, medical care and survival functions	MGN 96	Apr 2000	E02c.6
7	Alternative certification – dual certification	MGN 7	Apr 2000	E02c.7
8	Education and training schemes	MGN 8	Apr 2000	E02c.8
9	Procedure for the issue and revalidation of certificates of competency, marine engine operator licences and tanker endorsements	MGN 9	Apr 2000	E02c.9
10	Ratings	MGN 97	Apr 2000	E02c.10
11	Conduct of MCA oral examinations	MGN 69	Apr 2000	E02c.11
12	Safety training for concessionaires working on passenger ships	MGN 120	Apr 2000	E02c.12
13	Use of fishing vessel certificates of competency in standby, seismic survey and oceanographic research vessels – revised arrangements	MGN 121	Apr 2000	E02c.13
14	STCW 95 application to certificates of service	MGN 116	Apr 2000	E02c.14
15	Certification of inshore tug personnel	MGN 209	Apr 2002	E02c.15
16	Certification of personnel serving on inshore craft (other than tankers of 500gt or over, all tugs and all passenger ships)	MIN 123	Nov 2000	E02c.16
17	Certificates of competency or marine engine operator licences for service as an engineer officer on commercially and privately operated yachts and sail training vessels.	MGN 156	Feb 2001	E02c.17
18	STCW 95 certificates of competency – conversion of tonnage limitations - GRT to gt	MGN 164	Jan 2001	E02c.18
19	Certificates of Equivalent Competency	MGN 221	Mar 2003	E02c.19
20	Certificates of Equivalent Competency for fishing vessels	MGN 220	Mar 2003	-
21	Deck officer certificates of competency for service on commercially and privately operated yachts and sail training vessels	MGN 195	Feb 2002	E02c.20

* The parts listed above contain a great deal of information which is not possible to reproduce in full in this text; only those details considered to be of concern to shipmasters are therefore covered in the following sections. Details, such as medical fitness requirements, which are repeated in different parts are only covered under the principal part. For full details, readers should consult the relevant MGN.

* See also **MSN 1692** as amended.

E02c.1 Training and Certification Guidance - Part 1: Certificates of competency - General requirements for certification and medical fitness

* **Training and Certification Guidance Part 1** is contained in **MGN 91** and gives an introduction to the requirements of STCW 95 and revised general guidance on the requirements for the certification of officers and ratings in both the deck and engine departments. It also describes the sight testing and the medical standards which apply to candidates for certification.

* STCW 95 prescribes mandatory minimum requirements for certification of deck and engineer officers and watch ratings including requirements relating to age, medical fitness, seagoing service and standards of competence. To satisfy these requirements, candidates for UK certificates of competency must:
   • meet certain medical standards (including eyesight);
   • satisfactorily complete the minimum period of seagoing service;
   • reach the required vocational and academic standard;
   • undertake ancillary technical training; and
   • in the case of officer candidates, on completion of programmes of education and training approved by the MCA, pass an oral examination conducted by an MCA examiner.

Information on these requirements is detailed in various parts of the Training and Certification Guidance series.

* For notes on the provisions of STCW 95 and the STCW Code concerning "**near-coastal voyages**", see E03d.2. The **UK Near-Coastal Area** is defined in paragraph 2.4 of MSN 1692 as being "within 150 miles from a safe haven in

---

[8] Since first publication of the series, several Parts have been revised and re-issued with new MGN numbers which are non-consecutive.

the UK or 30 miles from a safe haven in Eire"[9]. A diagram indicating the UK Near-Coastal area is shown in Appendix 1 of MSN 1692. The area beyond the Near-Coastal Area is not defined in regulations or in MSN 1692 but is referred to in UK Safe Manning Documents as the "**Unlimited**" area and in UK Crew Agreements as the "**Unlimited Trading**" area.

* For the purposes of Training and Certification Guidance Part 1, "**seagoing**" means any voyage beyond Category C and D waters, which are defined in **MSN 1776**.

E02c.1a Certificates of Competency (paragraph 2.0)

* Part 1, paragraph 2 of the Training and Certification Guidance outlines the certificate structures for deck and engine departments. More detailed guidance is given in Part 2 (see E02c.2) and 3 (see E02c.3).
* All **certificates may be limited** by the MCA for service on specific **ship types**, **engine types**, or **trades** as appropriate.
* Every certificate will be issued in the form required by STCW 95 regulation I/2.

E02c.1b Dual certification (paragraph 2.3)

* Part 1 outlines dual certification arrangements, which are described in more detail in Training and Certification Guidance Part 7 (see E02c.7).

E02c.1c Procedure for obtaining a Certificate of Competency (paragraph 3.0)

* There are two routes to gaining the necessary skills and underpinning knowledge required for the issue of a certificate of competency:
  * the vocational qualification (VQ) route; and
  * a route based on traditional examinations.
* Both routes are detailed in Training and Certification Guidance Part 8 (see E02c.8).

E02c.1d Extra Master and Extra First Class Engineer Certificates (paragraph 4.0)

* The **Extra Master** and **Extra First Class Engineer** certificates were created for the benefit of those candidates who wished to demonstrate that they had professional qualifications superior to the standard certificates of competency required for service at sea as master and chief engineer respectively. These certificates are outside any internationally recognised certification structure. Since the number of candidates for examination leading to the issue of these certificates dropped very substantially over recent years, the MCA withdrew these examinations and ceased issuing the certificates from 1 August 1998.

E02c.1e Competency and training (paragraph 5.0)

* Certificates of competency are obtainable only by assessment and examination consisting of practical, written and oral components. Details of examination arrangements for these components are given in Training and Certification Guidance Parts 8, 9 and 11 (see E02c.8, E02c.9 and E02c.11 respectively).
* Candidates will be assessed by the MCA to ensure they meet the standards of competence required by STCW 95. The STCW Code details the levels of knowledge, understanding and proficiency and the methods which may be used to determine candidates' competence to undertake different functions associated with different levels of responsibility.
* STCW 95 defines seven **functions** as follows:
  * Navigation;
  * Cargo handling and stowage;
  * Control and operation of the ship and care for persons on board;
  * Marine engineering;
  * Electrical, electronic and control engineering;
  * Maintenance and repair; and
  * Radiocommunications;
  - at the following **levels of responsibility**:
    1. Management - (master, chief mate, chief engineer, second engineer);

---

[9] This definition coincides with one of the more extensive operating areas used in the MCA's Codes of Practice for small commercial craft (see D03l) for determining manning and competency requirements relative to ship type, size, power and distance from a "safe haven".

2. Operational - (watchkeeping officers); and

3. Support - (watch ratings and other ratings with safety and pollution prevention responsibilities).

* **Management level** means the level or responsibility associated with: serving as master, chief mate, chief engineer officer or second engineer officer on board a seagoing ship, and ensuring that all functions within the designated area of responsibility are properly performed (STCW Code, Section A-I/1.1.2).

* **Operational level** means the level or responsibility associated with: serving as officer in charge of a navigational watch or engineering watch or as designated duty engineer for periodically unmanned machinery spaces or as radio officer on board a seagoing ship, and maintaining direct control over the performance of all functions within the designated area of responsibility in accordance with proper procedures and under the direction of an individual serving in the management level for that area of responsibility (STCW Code, Section A-I/1.1.3).

* **Support level** means the level of responsibility associated with performing assigned tasks, duties and responsibilities on board a seagoing ship under the direction of an individual serving in the operational or management level (STCW Code, Section A-I/1.1.4).

E02c.1f Sea service requirements: general provisions (paragraph 6.1)

* The minimum amount of service acceptable for each grade of certificate of competency is given in Training and Certification Guidance Part 2 for deck officers and Part 3 for engineer officers (see E02c.2 and E02c.3 respectively).

* Unless candidates can prove the full amount of sea-service claimed, they will not normally be considered for assessment or examination. In a case where a candidate completes assessment or passes an examination prior to having completed the required sea-service, he or she will not be issued with a certificate until the required sea-service has been completed. At least 6 months of the qualifying sea-service must have been performed within the 5 years preceding the application.

* Applicants for certificates other than first certificates (i.e. regulation II/1, II/3, or III/1) must produce **certificates of watchkeeping service** signed by the Master or Chief Engineer of the ships in which the service has been performed. In the case of service as Master or Chief Engineer, the certificate must be signed by a responsible official of the company concerned. The certificates of watchkeeping service may incorporate the **testimonials** referred to in E02c.1j. (The specimen forms at Appendixes 1B and 1D of Training and Certification Guidance Part 1 may be used as a guide for this purpose.)

* Any applicant for a certificate of competency who has followed an approved Vocational Training (VQ) programme of on-board training must produce a **Training Record Book** or **Training Portfolio** completed in accordance with the recommendations of the Merchant Navy Training Board (MNTB).

* Applicants for a first certificate of competency as deck officer not undertaking approved VQ training must produce, as a minimum, **evidence of participation in shipboard drills, exercises and training**. This may be documented in appropriate testimonials or in a Personal Training and Service Record Book published by the International Shipping Federation (ISF).

* Applicants for a first certificate of competency as engineer officer not undertaking approved VQ training must obtain an approved **Personal Training and Service Record Book** published by the ISF, and record as fully as possible the work they have done on board ships. All entries must be verified by the Chief Engineer and/or other appropriate officers wherever possible.

E02c.1g Verification of service (paragraph 6.2)

* Entries in a Discharge Book or Certificates of Discharge supported by testimonials will be treated as evidence of sea service.

* Where there are doubts about the sea service claimed or it cannot be verified as above, it will only be accepted upon written confirmation by some responsible person having personal knowledge of the facts to be established.

E02c.1h Calculation of service (paragraph 6.3)

• Sea service entered in official documents as detailed above will be reckoned by the calendar month, i.e. the time included between any given day in any month and the preceding day of the following month, both inclusive. The number of complete months from the start of the period, ascertained in this way, should be worked at first, after which the number of odd days should be counted. The day on which the Crew Agreement began, as well as that on which it ended, should both be included, all leave of absence excluded and all odd days added together and reckoned at 30 days to the month.

E02c.1i Testimonials required (paragraph 6.4)

* All applicants for first and subsequent certificates of competency must produce **testimonials** covering character, standards of behaviour including sobriety, experience and ability on board ship and good conduct at sea, for at least the last 12 months of sea service preceding the date of application.
* For applicants for certificates other than the first watchkeeping certificate, testimonials may be incorporated in the watchkeeping service certificates referred to in paragraph 6.1 (see E02c.1f).
* For applicants for a first watchkeeping certificate of competency, the testimonials may be incorporated in a loose-leaf format into the Record Book or Training Portfolio for those following MNTB approved training programmes. In other cases, the specimen forms at Appendix 1A and 1C of Training and Certification Guidance Part 1 may be used as a guide.
* Unless there are exceptional circumstances, the required testimonials must be signed by the Master or Chief Engineer of the ships in which qualifying sea service has been performed. In the case of service as Master or Chief Engineer, the testimonials must be signed by a responsible official of the company concerned.

E02c.1j Unsatisfactory conduct (paragraph 6.5)

* Candidates or potential candidates who, after having signed crew agreements have neglected to join their vessels, or who, after having joined have left their ships other than upon discharge, or who have committed misconduct on board, will be required when applying for a Notice of Eligibility to produce satisfactory proof of two years' subsequent service with good conduct at sea, unless the MCA, after investigation, should see fit to reduce this period.

E02c.1k Medical Fitness Certificates: general provisions (paragraph 7.0)

* All candidates for and holders of STCW 95 certificates of competency issued in the UK must also hold a valid **Medical Fitness Certificate**, irrespective of the size of ship on which they are working or on which they intend to work.
* The **standards of medical fitness** are set out in **MSN 1765**, which superseded MSN 1746 and MSN 1760.
* Any seafarer, whose certificate expires whilst in a location where a medical examination in accordance with the Regulations cannot be arranged, may continue to be employed without a valid Medical Fitness Certificate for not more than three months from the date on which the certificate expired (regulation 4(2), MS (Medical Examination) Regulations 2002).
* Guidance on **medical fitness standards relating to pregnancy** is contained in **MGN 112**.

E02c.1l Medical Fitness Certificates acceptable for a Certificate of Competency (paragraph 7.0)

* Certificates acceptable to the MCA as a Medical Fitness Certificate for service on a UK ship are:
  * a certificate (commonly known as **ENG 1**) issued by an approved medical practitioner in accordance with the MS (Medical Examination) Regulations 2002 (see E06c.2); or
  * an appropriate **Medical Fitness Certificate** issued by any of the countries listed in Appendix 2 to Training and Certification Guidance Part 1.
* In each case the certificate is only valid if it is within the period of validity stated on it, (see below).
* Application for a Medical Fitness Certificate should be made directly to an approved medical practitioner who is entitled to require payment of a prescribed maximum fee. **MSN 1777** contains a list of **approved medical practitioners**.
* If the approved medical practitioner considers that the seafarer meets the UK medical standards, a **Medical Fitness Certificate (ENG 1)** will be issued. This may be restricted to such capacity of sea service (e.g. catering department) or geographical area (e.g. excluding service in tropical areas) as the medical practitioner thinks appropriate. The period of validity will be entered on the certificate, subject to the seafarer's age, as specified in regulation 8 of the **MS (Medical Examination) Regulations 2002** (SI 2002/2055) (see E06c.2), i.e.:
  * under 18 years: valid for 1 year;
  * 18 years or more: valid for 2 years,
  * and **not for the periods stated in MGN 91** in respect of seafarers of 18 years of age or over[10].
* If the seafarer's health (or type of work) demands it, an approved medical practitioner can issue a certificate valid for a shorter period. The Medical Fitness Certificate should be retained by the seafarer.

---

[10] The MS (Medical Examination) Regulations 2002 came into force on 1 September 2002, amending the periods of validity of Medical Fitness Certificates shown in MGN 91.

* If the approved medical practitioner refuses to issue a certificate or issues a certificate containing a restriction on sea service or geographical area, he must also give the seafarer a notice of failure to meet the medical standards and right of appeal form (currently numbered ENG 3).
* Provisions concerning review of a valid Medical Fitness Certificate, and appeals, are contained in Training and Certification Guidance Part 1.

E02c.1m Eyesight standards (paragraph 7.7)

* An **ENG 1** includes confirmation that eyesight standards have been met. However for deck candidates, if the ENG 1 is more than 2 years old, a separate sight test (a seafarer vision test) will be required for the issue of a first certificate of competency. Details of the required standards and test arrangements for the seafarer vision test are in **MSN 1765**.

E02c.1n Appendixes

* **Appendixes 1A, IB, 1C and 1D** to Training and Certification Guidance Part 1 show examples of Sea Service Testimonial forms for Deck Cadet/Rating, Deck Officer, Engineer Cadet/Rating and Engineer Officer respectively.
* **Appendix 2** is a list of overseas countries whose Medical Fitness Certificates, if issued in accordance with STCW 95 requirements, will be accepted by the MCA as evidence of medical fitness, provided that they meet the validity requirements in paragraph 7.4.2 (see E02c.1l).
* **Appendix 3** is a list of MCA Marine Offices.

E02c.2 Training and Certification Guidance - Part 2: Certificates of competency – deck department

* **Training and Certification Guidance Part 2** is contained in **MGN 92** and gives revised information and guidance regarding the certification structure and requirements for deck officers and navigation watch ratings. It is additional to the general guidance given in Part 1. MGN 92 supersedes MGN 2 and should be read in conjunction with **M.1328** and **MSN 1692**, as amended.
* Candidates for UK certificates of competency have to meet certain medical standards (including eyesight); satisfactorily complete the minimum period of seagoing service; reach the required vocational and academic standard; undertake ancillary technical training, and in the case of officer candidates, on completion of programmes of education and training approved by the MCA, pass an oral examination conducted by an MCA examiner.
* A pass in each part of every examination i.e. written MCA oral and, where appropriate, signals, will remain valid for a period of **3 years**. Passes in Higher National Diplomas (HND), Ordinary National Diploma examinations and Certificates of Achievement will remain valid for certification purposes for **7 years**.

E02c.2a Deck department certificate structure (paragraph 2.0)

* The Training and Certification Regulations provide for the certification of masters and deck department personnel involved in bridge watchkeeping and navigational duties as shown in Table 1 below. Additional flexibility is provided by further limitations and restrictions on certification for specific ship types or trades, as appropriate.

Table 1: Deck officer certificates of competency

Capacity	Area Limitation	Tonnage Limitation	STCW 95 Regulation
OOW	Near-coastal	Less than 500gt	II/3
	None	None	II/1
Chief mate	Near-coastal	Less than 3,000gt	II/2
	Near-coastal	None	II/2
	None	Less than 3,000gt	II/2
	None	None	II/2
Master	Near-coastal	Less than 500gt	II/3
	Near-coastal	Less than 3,000gt local domestic passenger vessels	II/3
	Near-coastal	None	II/2
	None	Less than 3,000gt	II/2
	None	None	II/2
Navigational watch rating	None	None	II/4

* There are **two routes**[11] to gaining the necessary skills and underpinning knowledge required for the issue of a certificate of competency: the **Vocational Qualification (VQ) route** and a **route based on traditional examinations**. Full details are given in Training and Certification Guidance **Part 8** (see E02c.8).
* Further information on the various requirements for progression to each level of certification is shown in a flowchart (see Table 2 in MGN 92).

E02c.2b Approved sea service (paragraph 3.0)

* STCW 95 defines "**seagoing service**" as time spent on board a ship, relevant to the issue of a certificate or other qualification. The period of sea service required for certification varies with the level of certification and the training programme followed. The minimum requirements for the issue of a deck officer certificate of competency are shown in the tables below.

Table 2: Deck officers - sea service requirements for certificates of competency

Unlimited trading area; unlimited ship size

Capacity	VQ Level in Marine Vessel Operations	Min. age	Sea service required	
			VQ route	Examination route
OOW unlimited (II/1)	VQ Level 3	18	36 months* (reduced to 12 months* if following an MNTB approved course of VQ training)	36 months*
Chief Mate unlimited (II/2)	VQ Level 4	-	12 months' watchkeeping service whilst holding a II/1 certificate	18 months' watchkeeping service whilst holding a II/1 certificate
Master unlimited (II/2)	VQ Level 4 plus additional units	-	36 months' watchkeeping service whilst holding a II/1 certificate, including at least 12 months whilst holding a Chief Mate unlimited II/2 certificate or 24 months' watchkeeping service whilst holding a II/1 certificate, including at least 12 months whilst holding a Chief Mate unlimited II/2 certificate and sailing as Chief Mate	36 months' watchkeeping service whilst holding a II/1 certificate, including at least 18 months whilst holding a Chief Mate unlimited II/2 certificate

Unlimited trading area; ships less than 3,000 gross tonnage

Capacity	VQ Level in Marine Vessel Operations	Min. age	Sea service required	
			VQ route	Examination route
OOW unlimited (II/1)	VQ Level 3	18	36 months* (reduced to 12 months* if following an MNTB approved course of VQ training)	36 months*
Chief Mate unlimited (II/2)	-	-	6 months' watchkeeping service whilst holding a II/1 certificate	
Master (II/2)	VQ Level 4	-	36 months' watchkeeping service whilst holding a II/1 certificate, including at least 12 months whilst holding a Chief Mate unlimited II/2 certificate or 24 months' watchkeeping service whilst holding a II/1 certificate, including at least 12 months whilst holding a Chief Mate unlimited II/2 certificate and sailing as Chief Mate	

Near-coastal trading area; ships less than 500 gross tonnage

Capacity	VQ Level in Marine Vessel Operations	Min. age	Sea service required	
			VQ route	Examination route
OOW (II/3)	VQ Level 3 near-coastal units	18	36 months* (reduced to 12 months* if following an MNTB approved course of VQ training)	36 months*
Master (II/3)	-	20	12 months as OOW holding a II/3 or II/1 certificate	

Near-coastal trading area; ships less than 3,000 gross tonnage

Capacity	VQ Level in Marine Vessel Operations	Min. age	Sea service required	
			VQ route	Examination route
OOW unlimited (II/1)	VQ Level 3	18	36 months* (reduced to 12 months* if following an MNTB approved course of VQ training)	36 months*
Chief Mate (II/2)	-	-	Nil	

---

[11] Paragraph 2.2 of MGN 92 states that there are three routes, but this conflicts with statements in other Parts and is misleading.

Near-coastal trading area; unlimited ship size

Capacity	VQ Level in Marine Vessel Operations	Min. age	Sea service required	
			VQ route	Examination route
OOW unlimited (II/1)	VQ Level 3	18	36 months* (reduced to 12 months* if following an MNTB approved course of VQ training)	36 months*
Chief Mate (II/2)	VQ Level 4 near-coastal units	-	12 months' watchkeeping service whilst holding a II/1 certificate	18 months' watchkeeping service whilst holding a II/1 certificate
Master unlimited (II/2)	VQ Level 4 plus additional units	-	24 months' watchkeeping service including at least 12 months watchkeeping service whilst holding a Chief Mate (more than 3,000gt near-coastal) II/2 certificate or Chief Mate (unlimited) II/2 certificate	36 months' watchkeeping service including at least 18 months' watchkeeping service whilst holding a Chief Mate (more than 3,000gt near-coastal) II/2 certificate or Chief Mate (unlimited) II/2 certificate

Domestic passenger vessels operating in the near-coastal area within a nominated area

Capacity	VQ Level in Marine Vessel Operations	Min. age	Sea service required	
			VQ route	Examination route
OOW (II/3)	VQ Level 3	18	36 months* (reduced to 12 months* if following an MNTB approved course of VQ training)	36 months*
Master (II/3)	-	20	12 months' watchkeeping service in the operating area whilst holding an OOW II/3 certificate is required before this certificate will be issued	

* 6 months of the last 12 months' sea service must have been whilst engaged in bridge watchkeeping.

E02c.2c General requirements for qualifying sea service (paragraph 3.2)

* The qualifying service specified for any particular deck officer certificate of competency must be performed in the deck department and is reckoned from the date of engagement to the date of discharge. At least 6 months of the qualifying service must have been performed within the 5 years preceding the application. Sea service should normally be performed on merchant ships of at least 24 metres in length or not less than 80gt proceeding to sea. Other sea service may be accepted in lieu of a limited amount of service in specialised ships (see paragraph 3.7 of Training and Certification Guidance Part 2) or a limitation may be imposed on the certificate of competency.
* Candidates for certification as officer of the navigational watch (OOW) must produce a statement from their employers, or the master(s) under whom they have served, that at least 6 of the last 12 months of their sea service have been spent on navigational watchkeeping duties under the supervision of a certificated officer. These duties may include keeping a look-out on the bridge or acting as helmsman but should not generally exceed 2 months out of the required 6 months. Where watchkeeping service is required for other certificates, candidates must provide proof of having served as watchkeeping officer for not less than 8 hours out of every 24 hours service claimed.
* Trainee deck officers must produce evidence that an approved training programme (details in Training and Certification Guidance Part 8) has been followed, and that all service while on board ship was performed in a satisfactory manner. Not more than 2 months of that service may have been spent standing-by a new vessel during the final stages of construction, in dry dock, or undergoing engine repairs. Candidates who fail to produce satisfactory evidence that they have followed a training programme approved by the MCA may be required to complete an additional period of sea service before being considered eligible for a certificate of competency. Other candidates may claim sea service reduction for attendance on approved training programmes or in recognition of higher academic achievements (see paragraph 3.6.3 of Training and Certification Guidance Part 2).
* The sea service requirements for candidates for deck officer II/1 certificates of competency as OOW who are not following approved cadet training programmes, such as ratings, Royal Navy officers, holders of Fishing Vessel certificates of competency, certificated engineer officers and radio officers, may be varied as detailed in Training and Certification Guidance Part 1.

E02c.2c Verification of service (paragraph 3.3)

* Requirements detailed in E02c.1h apply.

E02c.2d Calculation of service (paragraph 3.4)

* Requirements detailed in E02c.1i apply.

E02c.2e Testimonials required (paragraph 3.5)

* Requirements detailed in E02c.1j apply.

E02c.2f Service in specialised ships (paragraph 3.7)

* Service in the specialised ships listed in Tables 3 and 4 below will be counted towards the qualifying sea service required for a certificate of competency, subject to the conditions stated.
* Candidates taking advantage of the sea service reductions in Table 4, will have their certificates of competency restricted to service in tugs until the full sea service requirements have been met.

Table 3: Sea service allowances for service in specialised ships

Type of service or vessel	Rate applicable	Conditions
Ministry of Defence vessels at sea e.g. RN, RMAS, RAF, Range vessels	1	At least 3 months' service on merchant ships also required
cable ships; sail training vessels; fishery protection vessels; research and survey vessels; salvage vessels; navaid tenders; stand-by vessels; cruising pilot vessels; seagoing ferries, MOUs on passage	1 OR 1.5 (of actual steaming time)	Sea-service counted in full towards unlimited certificate provided at least 2/3 of time on board spent at sea; OR if less than 2/3 of time on board is spent at sea
Standing by new construction in final stages; or vessels in dry dock or undergoing engine repairs	1	Maximum of 2 months for trainee deck officers and a maximum of 3 months for other personnel
Service in fishing vessels more than 16.5m outside near-coastal area	1	At least 6 months' service on merchant ships also required
FPSOs; MOUs on station	0.5	Counted at half rate towards a max of 50% total sea or w/k service required. NOT applicable for approved cadet training programmes

Key: RN = Royal Navy; RMAS = Royal Maritime Auxiliary Service; RAF = Royal Air Force; MOU = Mobile Offshore Unit; FPSO = Floating Production Storage & Offloading; w/k = Watchkeeping

Table 4: Sea-service allowances for service in tugs

Type of service	Rate Applicable	Conditions
Seagoing	1	Counted at full rate towards 100% sea or w/k service required
Service in Category D* waters	¾	Counted at three quarter rate towards a maximum of 75% of total sea or w/k service required
Service in Category C* waters	½	Counted at half rate towards a maximum of 50% sea as w/k service required

*As defined in MSN 1776

* Where candidates have other types or combinations of sea service not included in the above tables, details of service together with documentary evidence should be submitted for consideration to the Chief Examiner, Seafarer Standards Branch, MCA, Spring Place, Southampton SO15 1EG.

E02c.2g Ancillary Training (paragraph 6.0)

* Ancillary training in safety and technical subjects is also required for the issue of a certificate of competency, as summarised in Table 5 below.
* Although under the VQ system this training may be subsumed in VQ units, a certificate for each ancillary course unit must be obtained by the candidate from the training provider.

Table 5: Ancillary training and other requirements for deck department certification

Additional training requirements	STCW 95 Regulation				STCW Code ref.
	II/1	II/2	II/3	II/4	
Personal Survival Techniques	✔		✔	✔	A-VI/1-1
Fire Prevention and Fire Fighting	✔		✔	✔	A-VI/1-2
Elementary First Aid	✔		✔	✔	A-VI/1-3
Personal Safety and Social Responsibility	✔		✔	✔	A-VI/1-4
Proficiency in Survival Craft and Rescue Boats	✔		✔		A-VI/2*
Advanced Fire Fighting	✔		✔		A-VI/3
Medical First Aid	✔		✔		A-VI/4-1
Medical Care		✔			A-VI/4-2**
Radar and ARPA Simulator Training – Operational level	✔		✔		A-II/1
Radar and ARPA Simulator Training – Management level		✔			A-II/2
Efficient Deck Hand (EDH)	✔		✔		
GMDSS (GOC)	✔				A-IV/2
Restricted Operator Certificate (ROC)			✔		A-IV/2
Other requirements:					
Medical Fitness (including sight)	✔	✔	✔	✔	

* Required for all seafarers in charge of lifesaving equipment

** Required before taking up position as master or chief mate and by any other person on board designated as being in charge of medical care. In order to serve on a UK flag ship as master and/or person in charge of medical care, it will be necessary to have undertaken the approved medical care training within the previous five years or, if such training was taken earlier, to have at least undertaken an approved refresher course within the previous five years.

* Ancillary training certificates issued by overseas Administrations in accordance with STCW/ILO, as listed at Appendix A of Training and Certification Guidance Part 2, and reproduced in Table 6 below, will be accepted by the MCA towards UK certificates of competency.

Table 6: Acceptance of overseas short training programmes for issue of UK certificates of competency

Training	Any STCW signatory
Basic Training: Personal Survival Techniques	✔
Basic Training: Fire Precautions & Fire-Fighting	✔
Basic Training: Elementary First-Aid (not equivalent to First Aid at Sea)	✔
Basic Training: Personal Safety & Social Responsibility	✔
Navigational or Engine-Room Watchrating certificate	✔
Efficient Deck Hand (EDH) (ILO)	✔
AB Certificate (ILO)	✔
Certificate of Proficiency in Survival Craft and Rescue Boats (CPSC & RB) (replaces existing CPSC, which itself replaced the Lifeboatman Certificate)	✔ 1
CPSC & RB for Fast Rescue Boats	-
Advanced Fire-Fighting	✔ 2
Medical First-Aid (replaces existing First Aid at Sea)	✔ 3
Proficiency in Medical Care (replaces existing Ship Captain's Medical Training)	-
Global Maritime Distress and Safety System (GMDSS) – General Operators Certificate	✔ 4
Radar-ARPA Simulator Training (operational level)	✔ 3
Radar-ARPA Simulator Training (management level)	-
Tanker Familiarisation Training	✔ 5
Specialised Tanker Training (oil/chemical/gas) (for Tanker Endorsements)	-
Medical Fitness Certificate	✔ 6

1 Not when a requirement for the issue of a UK certificate of competency, but acceptable for engineer revalidation under STCW 95 if from a UK-recognised Administration as listed below.
2 Not when a requirement for the issue of a UK certificate of competency.
3 Only when higher UK training in the same field is being undertaken.
4 Only CEPT countries (and others with whom UK has bilateral agreements as listed below).
5 Ratings only (and officers when training for higher certificates of competency is being undertaken)
6 Only those countries specified in the relevant Merchant Shipping Notice (see MGN 91 Appendix 2)

* UK-recognised Administrations referred to in Note 1 in the table are: Australia, Belgium, Canada, Denmark, Faroe Islands, Finland, France, Germany, Hong Kong, India, Ireland, Italy, Malta, Netherlands, New Zealand, Norway, Pakistan, Poland, Portugal, Singapore, Spain, South Africa, Sweden, Ukraine and USA. At the date of publication of MGN 92 (April 2000), Croatia, Greece, Iceland and the Philippines were likely to be recognised in the near future.
* At the date of publication of MGN 92 GMDSS certificates from the following countries were accepted by the MCA: Australia; Canada; Greece; New Zealand; South Africa; Hong Kong (if issued under UK sovereignty); CEPT countries as follows: Croatia; Czech Republic; Denmark; Finland; Germany; Hungary; Iceland; Ireland; Liechtenstein; Netherlands; Norway; Philippines[12]; Poland; Portugal; Romania; Sweden; Switzerland; Turkey; United Kingdom. (A GMDSS General Operators Certificate which is not from one of the UK-recognised Administrations listed will be acceptable as equivalent to a GMDSS Restricted Operators Certificate for the purpose of revalidation only, even though the UK does not otherwise recognise these GMDSS certificates.)

E02c.3 Training and Certification Guidance - Part 3: Certificates of competency – engine department

* **Training and Certification Guidance Part 3** is contained in **MGN 93** which gives revised information and guidance regarding the certification structure and requirements for engineer officers and engine-room watch ratings, and is additional to the general guidance given in Part 1. Information on the requirements for Marine Engine Operator Licences is also included in Part 3.
* Candidates for certificates of competency must:
    * meet certain medical standards (including eyesight) detailed in Training and Certification Guidance Part 1;
    * satisfactorily complete the minimum period of seagoing service;
    * reach the required vocational and academic standard;

[12] Philippines GMDSS accepted with certificates issued by the national authorities and with diplomas from: Norwegian Training Centre, Manila; Consolidated Training Systems Inc, Manila, (former Consolidated Maritime Resources Foundation Inc); Philippine Transmarine Carriers Inc, Manila.

- undertake ancillary technical training; and
- in the case of officer candidates, on completion of programmes of education and training approved by the MCA, must pass an oral examination conducted by an MCA examiner.

* Examinations are divided into academic and professional subjects as described in Training and Certification Guidance Part 8. The professional subject examinations and the MCA oral examination MUST be passed within a 3-year period prior to the date of issue of a certificate of competency. Successes in the academic written examinations remain valid indefinitely.

* For details of acceptance of overseas short training programmes for issue of UK certificates of competency, see the table in E02c.2g.

E02c.3a Engine department certificate structure (paragraph 2.0)

* The Training and Certification Regulations provide for the following certification for chief engineers and engine department personnel involved in watchkeeping and associated engine-room duties. Additional flexibility is provided by further limitations and restrictions on certification for specific ship types, propulsion systems, or trade as appropriate.

* Engineer officers serving on ships of less than 750 kW are not required to hold certificates of competency.

* Engine department certificates of competency are shown in the following table.

Capacity	Propulsive Power Limitation	STCW 95 Regulation
OOW	Unlimited	III/1
Second engineer	Less than 3,000kW	III/3 *
	Unlimited	III/2
Chief engineer	Less than 3,000kW	III/3 **
	Unlimited	III/2
Engine-room watch rating	Unlimited	III/4

*This certificate will be endorsed for service in vessels up to 6,000kW in the near-coastal area

**This certificate may be endorsed, if required, for service in vessels up to 6,000kW in the near-coastal area for those with not less than 36 months' sea-service

* **Engineer officers on ships of below 750 kW** are not required to hold certificates of competency. However, Marine Engine Operator Licences (MEOL) and Senior Marine Engine Operator Licences (SMEOL) for ships of between 350 and 750 kW are available, although these do not carry an STCW 95 endorsement.

* For details on **routes** to gaining the necessary skills and underpinning knowledge required for the issue of a certificate of competency, see E02c.8.

* Engineer officers serving on vessels with **gas turbine propulsion** may hold motor, steam or combined certificates of competency. (Some additional training related to the gas turbine machinery on a particular vessel will also be required for specified senior engineer officers).

* Further information on the various requirements for progression to each level of certification is shown in flowchart form in Tables 2a and 2b in Training and Certification Guidance Part 3.

E02c.3b Approved sea service (paragraph 3.0)

* STCW 95 defines seagoing service as time spent on board a ship, relevant to the issue of a certificate or other qualification. The period of sea service required for certification varies with the level of certification and the training programme followed.

* A summary of qualifying sea service requirements for those following the VQ route to engineer officer certificates of competency is given in Table 1 below.

Table 1: Qualifying sea service requirements for certificates of competency by the VQ route

STCW 95 Reg. III/1 OOW	Minimum watchkeeping on main propulsion machinery or UMS duties (on ships of 350kW or more)	Total minimum sea service
Motor (M)	4 months on motor ships	6 months
Steam (S)	4 months on steam ships	6 months
Combined Steam and Motor (S & M)	8 months (4 steam and 4 motor)	8 months

STCW 95 Reg. III/3 2nd Engineer ships less than 3,000 kW	Minimum watchkeeping on main propulsion machinery or UMS duties (on ships of 350kW or more)	Total minimum sea service (with III/1 certificate)
Motor (M)	9 months on motor ships	12 months
Steam (S)	9 months on steam ships	12 months
Combined (S & M)	18 months (9 steam and 9 motor)	18 months

STCW 95 Reg. III/2 2nd Engineer Unlimited	Minimum watchkeeping on main propulsion machinery or UMS duties (on ships of 750kW or more)	Total minimum sea service (with III/1 certificate)
Motor (M)	9 months on motor ships	12 months
Steam (S)	9 months on steam ships	12 months
Combined (S & M)	18 months (9 steam and 9 motor)	18 months

STCW 95 Reg. III/3 Chief Engineer ships less than 3,000 kW	Minimum sea service while qualified to serve as III/3 2nd Engineer (on ships of 350kW or more)	Total minimum sea service
Motor (M)	12 months (9 months of which in charge of watch or UMS duties on motor ships)	30 months
Steam (S)	12 months (9 months of which in charge of watch or UMS duties on steam ships)	30 months
Combined (S & M)	18 months (9 steam and 9 motor in charge of watch or UMS duties)	30 months

STCW 95 Reg. III/2 Chief Engineer Unlimited	Minimum sea service while qualified to serve as III/2 2nd Engineer (on ships of 1,500kW or more)	Total minimum sea service
Motor (M)	12 months (9 months of which in charge of watch or UMS duties on motor ships of 3,000 kW or more)	36 months
Steam (S)	12 months (9 months of which in charge of watch or UMS duties on steam ships of 3,000 kW or more)	36 months
Combined (S & M)	18 months (9 steam and 9 motor in charge of watch or UMS duties on ships of 3,000kW or more)	36 months

* A summary of qualifying sea service requirements for those following the examination route to engineer officer certificates of competency is shown in Table 2 below.

Table 2: Qualifying sea service requirements for certificates of competency by the examination route

STCW 95 Reg. III/1 OOW	Minimum sea service on main propulsion machinery or UMS duties (on ships of 350kW or more)	Total minimum sea service
Motor (M)	6 months (4 months of which on watchkeeping or UMS duties on motor ships)	6 months
Steam (S)	6 months (4 months of which on watchkeeping or UMS duties on steam ships)	6 months
Combined (S & M)	8 months (4 steam and 4 motor on watchkeeping or UMS duties)	8 months

STCW 95 Reg. III/2 2nd Engineer Unlimited	Minimum sea service while qualified to serve as III/1 OOW (on ships of 750kW or more)	Total minimum sea service
Motor (M)	18 months (9 months of which in charge of watch or UMS duties on motor ships)	24 months
Steam (S)	18 months (9 months of which in charge of watch or UMS duties on steam ships)	24 months
Combined (S & M)	18 months (9 steam and 9 motor in charge of watch or UMS duties)	26 months

STCW 95 Reg. III/2 Chief Engineer Unlimited	Minimum sea service while qualified to serve as III/2 2nd Engineer (on ships of 1,500kW or more)	Total minimum sea service
Motor (M)	18 months (9 months of which in charge of watch or UMS duties on motor ships of 3,000 kW or more)	42 months
Steam (S)	18 months (9 months of which in charge of watch or UMS duties on steam ships of 3,000 kW or more)	42 months
Combined (S & M)	18 months (9 steam and 9 motor in charge of watch or UMS duties on ships of 3,000kW or more)	44 months

E02c.3c General requirements for qualifying sea service (paragraph 3.4)

* Except where there are particular limitations or where relaxations are specifically allowed, qualifying sea service means service under crew agreement as engineer officer on regular watch, on Unmanned Machinery Spaces (UMS) duties, or on day work and is reckoned from the date of engagement to the date of discharge. At least 6 months of qualifying sea service must have been performed within the 5 years preceding the application.

E02c.3d Sporadic use of main propelling machinery (paragraph 3.5)

* Service performed in ships where for considerable periods the main propelling machinery is not used, is reckoned as one and a half times the number of days actually spent under way, but in no case can it exceed the time served under a crew agreement. In such cases the testimonials produced in accordance with Training and Certification Guidance Part 1 must state the number of days actually spent under way with the main propelling machinery in full use.

E02c.3e Auxiliary machinery (paragraph 3.6)

*   Watchkeeping service on auxiliary machinery will be counted in full towards the overall minimum sea service required. However, such service will not be accepted as counting towards the minimum required to be spent watchkeeping on main propelling machinery.

E02c.3f Day work (paragraph 3.7)

*   Engineering work carried out at sea, other than that performed on regular watch, will be counted in full towards the overall minimum sea service required. However, such service will not be accepted as counting towards the minimum required to be spent in watchkeeping on main propelling machinery.

E02c.3g Sheltered water service (paragraph 3.8)

*   Service in ships operating on lakes or rivers, or within category C and D waters as specified in **MSN 1776** (or any subsequent Notice), may be accepted at half rate. However, an unrestricted certificate of competency will not be issued on the basis of sheltered water service only. Three months' sea service will be required before this restriction is lifted.

E02c.3h Offshore service (paragraph 3.9)

*   Service in self-propelled offshore units where the unit is undertaking sea-going passages or well shifts or when it is engaged in maintaining a fixed station by continuous use of the main propelling machinery, will be accepted at full rate.
*   Service in self-propelled offshore units where the unit is fixed on station in either the drilling or service mode will be accepted at full rate. Such service will be accepted, up to a maximum of half the minimum required watchkeeping service, as counting towards the minimum required to be spent in watchkeeping or UMS duties on main propelling machinery.
*   Service in an offshore unit which is not self-propelled but is termed a ship under the Merchant Shipping Act 1995 will be accepted at half rate. However, such service will not be accepted as counting towards the minimum required to be spent in watchkeeping or UMS duties on main propelling machinery.

E02c.3i Royal Navy personnel (paragraph 3.10)

*   Sea service performed in Royal Navy ships will be assessed as if it had been performed in merchant ships. Service performed whilst holding a Royal Navy Marine Engineer Officer of the Watch Certificate will be assessed as if it had been performed whilst in possession of a certificate as watchkeeping officer issued in accordance with regulation III/1 of STCW 95; however, this does not entitle the holder to be issued with such a certificate unless all other requirements are met. Royal Navy candidates for a Second Engineer certificate issued in accordance with regulation III/2 or III/3 of STCW 95 must perform at least 3 months' merchant vessel familiarisation sea service in the engine department.

E02c.3j Fishing vessel personnel (paragraph 3.11)

*   Sea service performed on fishing vessels will be assessed on its merits.

E02c.3k Verification of service (paragraph 3.12)

*   Requirements in E02c.1h apply.

E02c.3l Calculation of service (paragraph 3.13)

*   Requirements detailed in E02c.1i apply.

E02c.3m Testimonials required (paragraph 3.14)

* Requirements detailed in E02c.1j apply.

E02c.3n Reduction in sea service (paragraph 3.15)

* The amount of qualifying sea service for certificates of competency may be reduced as follows:
    * Engineer Officer of Watch: A candidate who has satisfactorily completed MCA approved education and training may be granted reduction of equal length and the same description (motor or steam) as the sea service carried out during the training, provided that his or her on-board Training Record book has been completed to the satisfaction of the MCA.
    * Engineer Officer of the Watch Endorsement: An engineer officer who wishes to serve as engineer officer in charge of a watch on vessels of a different machinery type to that specified in his chief engineer certificate, will be granted a full remission of the sea service required for OOW but must pass the qualifying OOW oral examination for the type of machinery for which the endorsement is required.
    * Chief Engineer Combined: A reduction of three months from either of the nine month periods specified in Table 2 above will be granted to an officer who has spent at least six months of either period whilst holding a chief engineer certificate of competency.

E02c.3o Marine Engine Operator Licence (MEOL) (paragraph 4.0)

* The Training and Certification Regulations provide for the licensing of personnel serving on ships having a registered power of 350kW or more and less than 750kW.
* A Marine Engine Operator Licence (MEOL) may be obtained by both deck and engine-room personnel who qualify by oral examination. The application procedure and MCA oral examination syllabus is given in Training and Certification Guidance Parts 9 and 11.
* In order to be able to meet the entry requirements, applicants for examination should have satisfactorily completed: the short training programmes listed in Table 4 below; and either:
    * 24 months' sea-service in ships of not less than 200kW registered power and training in basic engineering skills to the satisfaction of the MCA; or
    * 2 years shore employment with an engineering background acceptable to the MCA and 3 months' qualifying sea service as a trainee marine engine operator in ships of not less than 200kW registered power; or
    * an approved structured training programme.
* Sea service or other industrial training completed before the age of sixteen will not be accepted.
* Sea service and training may be performed in a dual purpose capacity provided such service is confirmed by appropriate testimonials stating the type of main propelling machinery and the nature of the duties performed. The MCA will be prepared to accept satisfactory completion of a structured training programme which provides sea service, basic engineering skills training and qualifying sea service as a trainee engine operator within a 24 month period.

E02c.3p Senior Marine Engine Operator Licence (SMEOL) (paragraph 5.0)

* Any applicant for a SMEOL is required to have 6 months' qualifying sea service as a Marine Engine Operator on ships of not less than 200 kW registered power, whilst holding an MEOL, before examination for the SMEOL.
* The application procedure and MCA oral examination syllabus are given in Training and Certification Guidance Parts 9 and 11.

E02c.3q Engine-Room Watch Ratings (paragraph 6.0)

* STCW 95 requirements for engine-room watch ratings are laid down in STCW 95 regulation III/4. Details of the training standard required are in STCW Code section A-III/4. Details of procedures relating to the certification of ratings are in Training and Certification Guidance Part 10.
* Owners of UK ships may apply for authorisation to issue UK watch rating certificates on behalf of MCA.

E02c.3r Ancillary training (paragraph 7.0)

* Ancillary training in safety and technical subjects is also required for the issue of a certificate of competency and is summarised below in Table 3. Although under the VQ system this training may be subsumed in VQ units, a certificate for each separate ancillary course unit must be obtained by the candidate from the training provider. Other

ancillary training is also required for service on certain types of ships and is detailed in Training and Certification Guidance Part 5.

Table 3: Ancillary training and other requirements for engine department certification

Additional training requirements	STCW 95 Regulation				MEOL	SMEOL	STCW Code ref.
	III/1	III/2	III/3	III/4			
Personal Survival Techniques	✔			✔	✔		A-VI/1-1
Fire Prevention and Fire Fighting	✔			✔	✔		A-VI/1-2
Elementary First Aid	✔			✔	✔		A-VI/1-3
Personal Safety and Social Responsibility	✔			✔	✔		A-VI/1-4
Advanced Fire Fighting	✔				✔		A-VI/3
Proficiency in Survival Craft and Rescue Boats	✔				✔		A-VI/2 para 1-4
Medical First Aid	✔				✔		A-VI/4 para 1-3
Other requirements:							
Medical Fitness	✔	✔	✔	✔	✔	✔	

Note: Evidence of successful completion of training at an MCA approved centre is required for all ancillary training listed above.

* **Ancillary training certificates issued by overseas Administrations** in accordance with STCW/ILO (as listed at Appendix A to Training and Certification Guidance Part 3 and reproduced in E02c.2g, Table 6) will be accepted by the MCA towards UK certificates of competency.

E02c.4 Training and Certification Guidance - Part 4: Certificates of competency – Radio personnel

* **Training and Certification Guidance Part 4** is contained in **MGN 214** and gives revised information and guidance regarding certification of and requirements for radio personnel. It is additional to the general guidance given in Part 1. MGN 214 supersedes MGN 94 and should be read in conjunction with MSN 1692, as amended.
* Regulation 9 of the Training and Certification Regulations prescribes the mandatory minimum requirements for certification of radio personnel appointed for distress and safety radiocommunication purposes in accordance with regulation 19 of the MS (Radio Installations) Regulations 1998 (SI 1998/2070) (see E02b.9). The Radio Installations Regulations implement SOLAS chapter IV in the UK.

E02c.4a Certification requirements (paragraph 2.0)

* All radio personnel serving on UK ships, in accordance with the Radio Installations Regulations, must reach the required vocational and academic standards as specified in STCW Code A-IV/2 and hold one of the following suitably endorsed radio certificates of competency:
  * a Restricted Operator's Certificate (ROC); or
  * a General Operator's Certificate (GOC).
* In addition, all radio personnel and electro-technical officers (ETOs) must undertake some **ancillary training** as specified in STCW Code A-VI and listed in paragraph 3.2 of Training and Certification Guidance Part 4 (see E02c.4b).
* In accordance with STCW 95regulation IV/1, **every officer in charge of a navigational watch** must be in possession of an **appropriate radio operator's certificate**, i.e. at least an ROC. For operation outside Sea Area A1, as defined in SOLAS chapter IV, every vessel is required to carry at least one GOC holder.
* A UK GOC or ROC is obtained following examination by the MCA-appointed examination body, the Association of Marine Electronics and Radio Colleges (AMERC). Further information on the examinations is available from: AMERC, National Administration Centre, PO Box 4, Ambleside, Cumbria LA22 0BE. Phone: 015394 440218. Fax: 015394 440219. For notes on **AMERC** see B06b.1.

E02c.4b STCW 95 endorsement (paragraph 3.0)

* In order to comply with STCW 95 requirements, all GOC and ROC certificates must be endorsed by the MCA.
* An application for an STCW 95 endorsement must include the following:
  * the original GOC or ROC;
  * a valid Medical Fitness Certificate; and
  * evidence that the ancillary training requirements listed below have been met.

Ancillary training for radio personnel

Ancillary training requirements	STCW 95 regulation VI/1	STCW Code Ref.
Personal Survival Techniques	✔	A-VI/1-1
Fire Prevention and Fire Fighting	✔	A-VI/1-2
Elementary First Aid	✔	A-VI/1-3
Personal Safety and Social Responsibility	✔	A-VI/1-4

* Holders of deck and engineer certificates of competency will not be required to produce evidence of the ancillary requirements listed above by virtue of the training undertaken to obtain their certificates of competency.
* Electro-technical officers (ETOs) must hold a valid Medical Fitness Certificate and evidence that the ancillary training requirements listed above have been met.

E02c.4c Revalidation (paragraph 4.0)

* To qualify for seagoing service, an endorsement given for a UK GOC or ROC must be revalidated by the MCA at intervals not exceeding 5 years, in accordance with STCW 95 regulation I/11.
* Applications for revalidation should be sent to the MCA Seafarer Standards Branch, together with the following:
  * the original GOC or ROC;
  * proof of service performing functions appropriate to the certificate held, for a period of at least one year in total during the previous 5 years; and
  * a valid Medical Fitness Certificate.

E02c.4d Training for maintenance of GMDSS installations (paragraph 5.0)

* To ensure the availability of radio equipment as required by SOLAS chapter IV, regulation 18 of the Radio Installations Regulations and MSN 1692 make provision for the use of "at-sea electronic maintenance capability". The person designated to perform at-sea electronic maintenance must hold an appropriate certificate as specified by the International Telecommunications Union (ITU) Radio Regulations, and as referred to in STCW Code B-I/IV, or alternatively, have equivalent at-sea electronic maintenance qualifications. Further information and details on suitable training courses may be obtained from AMERC. (For notes on **AMERC**, including its website address, see B06b.1.)

E02c.5 Training and Certification Guidance - Part 5: Special training requirements for personnel on certain types of ship

* **Training and Certification Guidance Part 5** is contained in **MGN 95** and gives revised information and guidance regarding the mandatory minimum requirements for the training and qualification of officers and ratings on tankers, ro-ro passenger ships, other passenger ships and high speed craft. MGN 95 supersedes MGN 5 and should be read in conjunction with **M.1015**, **MSN 1692**, as amended, **MSN 1740** and **MGN 26** (or subsequent amendments).

E02c.5a Tanker familiarisation training (paragraph 2.0)

* Ratings assigned specific duties and responsibilities related to cargo or cargo equipment (e.g. pumpman) and all officers on tankers must have completed:
  * at least 3 months' seagoing service on tankers in order to acquire adequate knowledge of safe operational practices; or
  * an MCA-approved tanker familiarisation training programme covering the syllabus in STCW Code section A-V/1, paragraphs 2 to 7; or
  * at least 30 days' service under the supervision of qualified officers on a tanker of less than 3000gt engaged on voyages not exceeding 72 hours.
* In addition to the above, ratings must undertake the advanced fire fighting training programme specified in STCW Code section A-VI/3.
* A specimen Tanker Familiarisation Certificate for issue to seafarers who do not hold UK Discharge Books is shown in Annex 1 of Training and Certification Guidance Part 5.

E02c.5b Specialised oil, gas and chemical tanker training (paragraph 3.0)

* In addition to the requirements in E02c.5a, masters, chief engineer officers, chief mates, second engineer officers and any person, such as a cargo officer or cargo engineer officer, with immediate responsibility for loading, discharging and care in transit or handling of cargo in an **oil tanker**, must have completed:

- an MCA-approved specialised oil tanker training programme covering the syllabus in STCW Code section A-V/1, paragraphs 8 to 14; and
- at least 3 months' sea service on an oil tanker.

* In addition to the requirements in E02c.5a, masters, chief engineer officers, chief mates, second engineer officers and any person, such as a cargo officer or cargo engineer officer, with immediate responsibility for loading, discharging and care in transit or handling of cargo in a **chemical tanker** must have completed:
  - an MCA-approved specialised chemical tanker training programme covering the syllabus in STCW Code section A-V/1, paragraphs 15 to 21; and
  - at least 3 months' sea service on a chemical tanker.
* In addition to the requirements in E02c.5a, masters, chief engineer officers, chief mates, second engineer officers and any person, such as a cargo officer or cargo engineer officer, with immediate responsibility for loading, discharging and care in transit or handling of cargo in a **liquefied gas tanker** (LPG & LNG) must have completed:
  - an MCA-approved specialised liquefied (gas tanker training programme covering the syllabus in STCW Code section A-V/1, paragraphs 22 to 34; and
  - at least 3 months' sea service on a liquefied gas tanker.
* Where endorsements for service on a second or third type of tanker are sought, the requirement for 3 months' sea service on the specific type of tanker may be substituted by successful completion of 28 days approved shipboard training, involving at least one loading and one discharging operation.
* Candidates for a first tanker endorsement serving on tankers of less than 3000gt engaged on voyages not exceeding 72 hours may, as an alternative to Tanker Familiarisation Training and Specialised Tanker Training detailed above, complete:
  - an MCA-approved specialised tanker training programme appropriate to the type of tanker, i.e. oil , chemical or liquefied gas; and
  - a period of 28 days' MCA-approved shipboard training on that type of tanker, involving at least 4 loading and 4 discharging operations.

E02c.5c Tanker endorsements (paragraph 4.0)

* Officers meeting the Specialised Tanker Training requirements detailed above should have their certificates of competency, certificates of equivalent competency or certificates of service (until 31.1.2002) endorsed by the MCA for service on the appropriate type of tanker(s).
* Officers who hold non-UK certificates of competency may obtain tanker endorsements (as separate documents) if they undertake a UK approved relevant tanker training programme and produce evidence of required sea service on tankers. (The issue of such endorsements will not imply recognition by the UK of these officers' certificates of competency.)
* Ratings and officers meeting the requirements of Tanker Familiarisation Training only, should submit the evidence to an MCA Marine Office where their discharge books will be appropriately endorsed. Those not in possession of a UK discharge book may be issued with a Tanker Familiarisation Certificate as per the specimen shown at Annex 1 in Training and Certification Guidance Part 5.
* The requirements for Tanker Familiarisation Training and Specialised Tanker Training must be completed within the 5-year period prior to the date of application for an endorsement or Tanker Familiarisation certificate.

E02c.5d Revalidation of tanker endorsements (paragraph 4.5)

* In addition to the general requirements for revalidation of a certificate of competency (detailed in Training and Certification Guidance Part 9), a tanker endorsement will be revalidated provided the holder can provide evidence of the following service in the preceding 5 years:
  - at least 3 months, which need not be continuous, on any type of tanker; or
  - at least 6 months on a storage tanker, barge or terminal engaged in operations involving loading or discharging of tankers.
* If this evidence cannot be provided, the tanker (or dangerous cargo) endorsement will be withdrawn. Before it can be re-issued, the applicant will be required to complete:
  - the relevant specialised tanker training programme as described in paragraph 3 above; or
  - 14 days supervised ship-board training in a supernumerary capacity in the relevant type of tanker.

E02c.5e Ro-ro passenger ships: introduction (paragraph 5.0)

* Whilst the STCW 95 requirements regarding training of personnel on seagoing ro-ro passenger ships and other passenger ships apply only to personnel on ships on international voyages, the Training and Certification Regulations apply the STCW 95 requirements to all UK seagoing ro-ro passenger ships irrespective of type and area of voyage.

* STCW 95 introduced special training requirements for seafarers on seagoing ro-ro passenger ships on 1 February 1997. Amendments to STCW 95 regulation V/2 relating to approved **crisis management and human behaviour training** entered into force on 1 January 1999. All these training requirements are described below.

E02c.5f Ro-ro passenger ships: general training requirements (paragraph 6.0)

* Prior to being assigned shipboard duties, masters, officers, ratings and other personnel with responsibility for guidance of passengers in an emergency on a ro-ro passenger ship, must undertake **appropriate training** (which does not require MCA approval), as follows:
    * all personnel providing a direct service to passengers, including those working in shops, bars and restaurants, must be able to **communicate effectively** between themselves and with passengers during an emergency, as detailed in STCW Code section A-V/2, paragraph 3, and be able to **demonstrate the correct donning of lifejackets**;
    * all personnel designated on muster lists to assist passengers in an emergency, must complete **crowd management training** as described in STCW Code section A-V/2, paragraph 1. This essentially practical training can readily be provided on board ship and can be kept up to date through regular drills. This will enable the STCW 95 requirement for refresher training at 5-yearly intervals to be met;
    * all personnel with responsibilities related to loading ro-ro cargo and securing for sea must be **sufficiently familiar** with the design and operational limitations affecting ro-ro passenger ships and the tasks detailed in STCW Code section A-V/2, paragraph 2.
* The practical elements of training required could be undertaken on board under supervision. An element of formal instruction is also considered appropriate to ensure attainment of the abilities necessary to meet all of the requirements specified in the paragraph.
* In line with the responsibilities of companies required by STCW 95, and provisions in the International Safety Management (ISM) Code, records should be maintained and documentary evidence provided to any person meeting the appropriate standard, indicating the date the standards were met.

E02c.5g Ro-ro passenger ships: approved training requirements (paragraph 7.0)

* Prior to being assigned shipboard duties, masters, chief engineer officers, chief mates, second engineer officers and persons having immediate responsibility on ro-ro passenger ships for:
    * embarking and disembarking passengers;
    * loading, discharging or securing of cargo; and
    * closing hull openings,
    - must successfully complete MCA-approved **training in passenger safety, cargo safety and hull integrity** specified in STCW Code section A-V/2, paragraph 4, which extends the knowledge required for those with responsibilities related to loading ro-ro cargo and securing for sea, and includes more detailed training in the specialist requirements applying to ro-ro passenger ships.
* Masters, chief mates, chief engineer officers, second engineers officers and any person having responsibility for the safety of passengers in emergency situations on board ro-ro passenger ships shall have completed MCA-approved **training in crisis management and human behaviour** as specified in STCW Code section A-V/2, paragraph 5, which extends the crowd management training and safety training required in section A-V/2 paragraphs 1 and 3. (This training requirement came into force on 1 January 1999.)
* The training referred to above may be carried out in-house or in conjunction with external training providers. The training referred to above and the crowd management training referred to in paragraph 6 must be undertaken once every 5 years; evidence must alternatively be produced of having achieved the required standard by way of initial training followed by at least 3 months' service in every five years in the relevant type of ships.
* Training and Certification Guidance Part 12 gives detailed guidance on the safety training requirements for concessionaires working on passenger ships.

E02c.5h Passenger ships other than ro-ro ships: introduction (paragraph 8.0)

* STCW 95 regulation V/3 relating to the minimum requirements for the training and qualifications of personnel on passenger ships other than ro-ro passenger ships engaged on international voyages entered into force on 1 January 1999. The requirements of regulation V/3 are described below.

E02c.5i Passenger ships other than ro-ro ships: general training requirements (paragraph 9.0)

* Prior to being assigned shipboard duties, masters, officers, ratings and other personnel with responsibility for guidance of passengers in an emergency on passenger ships other than ro-ro passenger ships engaged on international voyages must undertake **appropriate training** (which does not require MCA approval), as follows:
  * all personnel providing a direct service to passengers, including those working in shops, bars and restaurants, must be able to **communicate effectively between themselves and with passengers during an emergency**, as detailed in STCW Code section A-V/3, paragraph 3, and be able to **demonstrate the correct donning of lifejackets**;
  * all personnel designated on muster lists to assist passengers in an emergency, must complete **crowd management training** as described in STCW Code section A-V/3, paragraph 1. This essentially practical training can readily be provided on board ship and can be kept up to date through regular duties. This will enable the STCW 95 requirement for refresher training at 5 yearly intervals to be met;
  * all personnel assigned specific duties and responsibilities on board (such as those related to design and operational limitations of the ship) must be **sufficiently familiar** with the special nature of passenger ships and the tasks detailed in STCW Code section A-V/3, paragraph 2. The practical elements of training required could be undertaken on board under supervision.
* In line with the responsibilities of companies required by STCW 95 and provisions in the ISM Code, documentary evidence should be provided to any person meeting the appropriate standard, indicating the date that the standards were met. Records should be maintained and be made available on request to any authorised person.

E02c.5j Passenger ships other than ro-ro ships: approved training requirements (paragraph 10.0)

* Masters, chief mates and all persons assigned immediate responsibility for embarking and disembarking passengers must complete MCA-**approved training in passenger safety** as specified in STCW Code section A-V/3, paragraph 4, which extends the knowledge required by personnel assigned specific duties and responsibilities on board as detailed in paragraph 9.
* Masters, chief mates, chief engineer officers, second engineer officers and all persons having responsibility for the safety of passengers in emergency situations on board passenger ships must complete MCA-**approved training in crisis management and human behaviour** as specified in STCW Code section A-V/3, paragraph 5, which extends the crowd management and safety training detailed in paragraph 9.
* The training referred to above may be carried out in-house or in conjunction with external training providers. The training referred to above, as well as the crowd management training referred to in paragraph 9, must be undertaken once every 5 years; evidence must alternatively be produced of having achieved the required standard by way of initial training followed by at least 3 months' service in every 5 years in the relevant type of ships.

E02c.5k Passenger ships other than ro-ro ships: use of common certificates (paragraph 11.0)

* The training requirements for ro-ro passenger ships, being more comprehensive than for non ro-ro passenger ships, will be acceptable for service on non ro-ro passenger ships, subject to completion of ship-specific training.

E02c.5l High speed craft training requirements (paragraph 12.0)

* High speed craft training requirements are detailed in **MSN 1740** and **MGN 26** but are summarised in Training and Certification Guidance Part 5, to which the following notes relate.
* In addition to a valid certificate of competency and the applicable requirements of paragraphs 5 – 11 of Part 5, the master and all officers with an operational role serving on high speed craft (HSC) must hold a valid **Type Rating Certificate** (TRC) complying with the requirements of chapter 18.3 of the International Code of Safety for High Speed Craft (HSC Code). HSC operators are responsible for ensuring that **appropriate approved training** is given to personnel so that they may qualify for the issue of a TRC.
* Type Rating Certificates are issued by the approved organisations providing the training, but must be endorsed by the MCA and require revalidation at intervals of not more that 2 years. The approved training required by the HSC Code includes knowledge of the craft's propulsion and control systems, handling characteristics, communication and navigation procedures, intact stability, and survivability of the craft.
* **Engineer** officers serving on HSC with gas turbine propulsion may hold either motor, steam or combined certificates of competency. In addition, senior engineer officers specified in the vessel's Safe Manning Document

must hold a certificate attesting to the completion of an **approved gas turbine training programme** for the machinery on their vessel.
* **Ratings** serving on HSC must be trained to meet the requirements of the HSC Code, chapter 18.3.3, paragraphs 6 to 12. These include knowledge of the location and use of all items listed in the training manual, e.g. escape routes, life-saving appliances, fire protection and fire-extinguishing appliances and cargo securing systems. This training can be included in training meeting the requirements of paragraphs 5 and 6 of Training and Certification Guidance Part 5.

E02c.5m Application procedure (paragraph 13.0)

* Requests for MCA approval of training programmes required under Training and Certification Guidance Part 5 by companies or training organisations should be addressed to the Surveyor in Charge of the local MCA Marine Office.
* Applications for Tanker Endorsements (using form MSF 4210) and endorsement of Type Rating Certificates should be sent to the MCA Seafarer Standards Branch. Forms are available from any MCA Marine Office.

E02c.6 Training and Certification Guidance - Part 6: Emergency, occupational safety, medical care and survival functions

* **Training and Certification Guidance Part 6** is in **MGN 96** and gives revised information and guidance on the mandatory basic and further safety training and certification requirements of STCW 95 for masters, officers, ratings and other persons employed on ships who have emergency, occupational safety, medical care and survival functions. MGN 96 supersedes MGN 6 and should be read in conjunction with **M.1494** and **MSN 1692**, as amended.
* Detailed information on training standards is in STCW 95 regulation VI and the STCW Code section A-VI.
* Candidates successfully completing any of the MCA-approved training programmes described below, should be issued by the training provider with a certificate in the format shown in Annex 1 of Training and Certification Guidance Part 6. (Records relating to the issue of these certificates should be maintained by the training provider.)
* A specimen Certificate for Specialised Marine Training is shown in Annex 1 of Training and Certification Guidance Part 6.

E02c.6a Familiarisation training (paragraph 2.0)

* **Before being assigned to shipboard duties**, all persons employed or engaged on a seagoing ship other than passengers, including stewards, shop staff, hairdressers and entertainers, must:
  * undertake **approved familiarisation training in personal survival techniques**; or
  * **be given sufficient information and instruction** to ensure that they can carry out the tasks listed in STCW Code section A-VI/1, paragraphs 1.1 to 1.7.
* A **record** should be retained on board to show that this instruction has been given.

E02c.6b Basic training (paragraph 3.0)

* All seafarers with less than 6 months' sea-service prior to 1 August 1998 or who have been assigned **designated safety or pollution prevention duties** in the operation of the ship must successfully complete **those elements of approved basic training appropriate to their duties and functions**.
* The four **elements of basic training** are:
  * **personal survival techniques** (STCW Code - Table A-VI/1-1);
  * **fire prevention and fire fighting** (STCW Code - Table A-VI/1-2);
  * **elementary first aid** (STCW Code - Table A-VI/1-3);
  * **personal safety and social responsibilities** (STCW Code - Table A-VI/1-4).

E02c.6c Proficiency in Survival Craft and Rescue Boats (PSC & RB) (other than Fast Rescue Boats) (paragraph 4.0)

* All candidates for certificates of competency, AB certificates and any other persons required to take charge of survival craft must prove **proficiency in survival craft and rescue boat operations**.
* Candidates must:
  * be at least 18 years old;
  * have received **approved or recognised training in Personal Survival Techniques** within the preceding 5 years;
  * have performed **at least 6 months' sea-service**; and

- have successfully completed an MCA-**approved or recognised training programme** meeting the standards in STCW Code A-VI/2-1.
* In certain circumstances the MCA may permit companies to place persons practised in the handling and operation of liferafts in charge of liferafts in lieu of persons qualified as above. (Applications should be made to the MCA's Chief Examiner.)

E02c.6d Fast rescue boat (FRB) training (paragraph 5.0)

* Persons involved in the operation of fast rescue boats must, in addition to the (PSC & RB) training above, have successfully completed an MCA-**approved training programme** meeting the standards laid down in STCW Code section A-VI/2-2.

E02c.6e Advanced Fire Fighting

* All candidates for certificates of competency, any other seafarer designated to control fire fighting operations and any ratings on tankers, assigned specific duties and responsibilities related to cargo or cargo equipment, must receive **specialist training in advanced fire fighting techniques**. Candidates must have performed at least 6 months' sea service and have successfully completed an MCA-approved training programme meeting the standards laid down in STCW Code section A-VI/3.

E02c.6f Medical training (paragraph 7.0)

* Proficiency in **Medical First Aid**: All candidates for certificates of competency and all seafarers designated to provide medical first aid must have successfully completed an MCA-**approved training programme** meeting the standards laid down in STCW Code A-VI/4-1.
* Proficiency in **Medical Care**: All candidates for master and chief mate certification under STCW Regulation II/2, and any person designated to take charge of medical care on board ship must, in addition to the above medical first aid training, have successfully completed an MCA-**approved medical care training programme** meeting the standards laid down in STCW Code A-VI/4-2 within the preceding 5 years.
* Validity and Refresher Training: The master and any other person in charge of medical care on a UK flag vessel will be required to undertake **refresher training in Proficiency in Medical Care** every 5 years.
* Suitability qualified health care professionals (i.e. doctor, nurse or paramedic) will be exempted from the above requirements.

E02c.6g Marine evacuation system (MES) training

* Masters, officers and ratings with designated duties on the deployment of **marine evacuation systems (MES)** must be trained in accordance with the requirements of SOLAS regulation III/19.3.3.8. Documentary evidence to this effect should be issued by the training provider.[13]

E02c.6h Transitional arrangements

* The following table sets out the existing MCA-approved training which was considered as meeting the STCW 95 requirements during the transitional period until 31 January 2002.

Para. ref. in Part 6 of Training & Certification Guidance	MCA-approved training required for STCW 95 certification	Training undertaken prior to 31.1.2002 acceptable for STCW 95 certification*
3.1.1	Personal Survival Techniques	Basic Sea Survival
3.1.2	Fire Prevention & Fire Fighting	Basic or Advanced Fire Fighting
3.1.3	Elementary First Aid	First Aid At Sea
4.1	Proficiency in Survival Craft & Rescue Boats (PSCRB)	Proficiency in Survival Craft (or equivalent)
6.1	Training in Advanced Fire Fighting	Advanced Fire Fighting (4 day)
7.1	Proficiency in Medical First Aid	First Aid at Sea
7.2	Proficiency in Medical Care	Ship Captain's Medical

* Other training may be acceptable at the discretion of the MCA.

---

[13] SOLAS regulation III/19 paragraph 3.3.8 requires that if a ship is fitted with MES, drills must include exercising of the procedures required for the deployment of such a system up to the point immediately preceding actual deployment. This aspect of drills must be augmented by regular instruction using the on-board training aids required by regulation III/35.4. Every MES party member must also, as far as practicable, be further trained by participation in a full deployment of a similar MES into water, either on board ship or ashore, at intervals not exceeding 2 years, but in no case longer than 3 years; this training can be associated with the deployments required by regulation III/20.8.2.

E02c.7 Training and Certification Guidance - Part 7: Alternative certification – dual certification

* **Training and Certification Guidance Part 7** is in **MGN 7**.
* STCW 95 Chapter VII (Alternative Certification) allows for officers to be issued with a **single certificate** of competency **combining deck, engineering and radio competencies** subsequent to approved education, training and assessment.
* The UK, whilst approving training schemes for officers who wish to combine deck and engineering training, has decided for the time being not to issue certificates of competency under STCW 95 Chapter VII (regulation VII). Officers successfully participating in combined deck and engineering training programmes ("dual schemes") will be granted separate deck officer and engineer officer certificates of competency issued in accordance with STCW 95 Chapters II and III (regulations II and III) as set out in Training and Certification Guidance Parts 2 and 3 respectively.

E02c.8 Training and Certification Guidance - Part 8: Education and training schemes

* **Training and Certification Guidance Part 8** is contained in **MGN 8** and gives information and guidance on the education and training schemes available to seafarers wishing to obtain Merchant Navy certificates of competency by either the vocational qualification (VQ) or traditional written examination routes.
* Since September 1997, all new entrant deck and engineer officer cadets have been enrolled on approved training programmes which achieve the standards of competence laid down in the STCW Code by the attainment of a Vocational Qualification (VQ) based on continuous assessment of knowledge and performance.
* Existing seafarers (at 1 September 1997) and others not enrolled on approved cadet training programmes are, for the time being, able to meet the required standards for certain certificates by following either a VQ route (described in paragraphs 4 - 7 of Training and Certification Guidance Part 8) or a non-VQ route based on traditional written examinations and assessment (described in paragraphs 8 - 11 of Part 8).
* Both routes involve an MCA oral examination, details of which are given in Training and Certification Guidance Part 11.
* Since the VQ route includes **on-board training** whilst completing the necessary sea service, closely monitored and supervised by certificated officers and documented in a **Record Book or Portfolio**, masters and other officers may find Training and Certification Guidance Part 8 helpful in understanding the VQ system's structure and requirements.
* **M.1634** introduced the concept of VQs for Merchant Navy certificates and may also be of interest.

E02c.9 Training and Certification Guidance - Part 9: Procedure for the issue and revalidation of Certificates of Competency, Marine Engine Operator Licences and tanker endorsements

* **Training and Certification Guidance Part 9** is contained in **MGN 9** and gives information and guidance on the requirements and procedures for the issue and revalidation of STCW 95 certificates of competency, Marine Engine Operator Licences and tanker endorsements.
* Certificates and Marine Engine Operator Licences issued under STCW 78 were valid, subject to revalidation requirements, until 31 January 2002. The guidance in Part 9 relates to certificates of competency, tanker endorsements and revalidation procedures under STCW 95, and Marine Engine Operator Licences issued under the MS (Training and Certification) Regulations 1997.

E02c.9a Issue of certificates of competency and Marine Engine Operator Licences: application requirements (paragraph 2.0)

* A **first certificate of competency or Marine Engine Operator Licence** will only be issued after the following have been satisfactorily completed:
  * demonstration of the required standard of medical fitness, by passing a medical examination/seafarer's vision test;
  * basic training requirements;
  * approved training programmes and assessments;
  * appropriate watchkeeping and/or sea service; and
  * an MCA oral examination.

* After obtaining a first certificate of competency a candidate may progress to the next level of certification by:
  * accumulating further qualifying sea service;
  * undertaking further education, training and assessment;
  * confirming continuing medical fitness; and
  * passing the MCA oral examination for the appropriate level.

E02c.9b Medical fitness requirements (paragraph 2.0)

* **Training and Certification Guidance Part 1** gives further details of medical fitness requirements (see E02c.1k and E02c.1l).
* A Medical Fitness Certificate issued to a **deck candidate** must confirm the candidate's fitness for lookout duties. If the medical certificate is more than two years old when the candidate becomes eligible for the issue of a first certificate of competency, a seafarer's **vision test report** issued within the previous two years will also be required.

E02c.9c Basic training (paragraph 4.0)

* All seafarers with less than 6 months' sea service before 1 August 1998, employed or engaged in any capacity on board ship as part of the ship's complement, and having **designated safety or pollution prevention duties** in the operation of the ship, must receive **appropriate basic training** as described in Training and Certification Guidance Part 6 (see E02c.6b).
* However, since all candidates for a first Certificate of Competency or Marine Engine Operator Licence must receive **more advanced training** in each of the first three items of basic training listed in E02c.6b, they will only be required to produce **evidence of training in Personal Safety and Social Responsibilities**, if appropriate, when submitting their application. The more advanced training referred to is:
  * proficiency in survival craft and rescue boats (PSC & RB);
  * training in advanced fire-fighting; and
  * proficiency in medical first aid.
* Alternatives which will be considered as meeting the STCW 95 requirements are shown in the table in E02c.6h.
* Other training may be acceptable at the discretion of the MCA.

E02c.9d Approved training programmes (paragraph 5.0)

* See Training and Certification Guidance Part 8 and E02c.8.

E02c.9e Watchkeeping and sea service (paragraph 6.0)

* For sea service requirements for **traditional examination candidates** see Training and Certification Guidance Part 8.
* For sea service requirements for **deck VQ candidates** see Training and Certification Guidance Part 2 and E02c.2.
* For sea service requirements for **engineer VQ candidates** see Training and Certification Guidance Part 3 and E02c.3.
* For sea service requirements for **Marine Engine Operator Licences candidates** see Training and Certification Guidance Part 3 and E02c.3.

E02c.9f Applications for MCA oral examinations (paragraph 7.0)

* Candidates for MCA oral examinations must apply to the MCA for a **Notice of Eligibility** (NOE), which will permit entry to an oral examination at an MCA Marine Office of the candidate's choice.
* Applications should be made on forms which may be obtained from nautical colleges in the UK, from the MCA's Seafarer Standards Branch, or from any MCA Marine Office. Completed application forms, with supporting documents and the appropriate fee, should be sent to the Seafarer Standards Branch. The supporting documents must be original. Any candidate failing to submit all the required documents will have their application returned without being processed. 28 days should be allowed for processing.
* Paragraphs 7.2 and 7.3 in Part 9 describe the different application procedures which must be followed, depending on whether the candidate is following the VQ route or the written examination route respectively. Paragraph 7.4 describes the application procedure for Marine Engine Operator Licences.

E02c.9g Issue of certificates of competency and Marine Engine Operator Licences[14] (paragraph 8.0)

* Notices of Eligibility issued to candidates who have fulfilled all the requirements for the issue of a certificate of competency, apart from passing the oral examination, will bear a red endorsement to this effect.
* Candidates who pass the oral examination and who hold a Notice of Eligibility bearing the red endorsement will be asked to surrender any existing certificate of competency to the examiner, who will make the necessary arrangements with the Seafarer Standards Branch for the new certificate to be issued.
* Candidates who pass the oral examinations, but whose Notice of Eligibility does not bear a red endorsement, will have the Notice returned for their retention. When they have fulfilled all the remaining requirements for the issue of a certificate of competency, they should return the Notice, together with the outstanding documentation and any existing certificate of competency, to the Seafarer Standards Branch of the MCA for the issue of their new certificate of competency.

E02c.9h Requirements for revalidation of certificates of competency (paragraph 10.0)

* Every master, officer and radio operator holding a certificate of competency issued or recognised under STCW 78 or STCW 95 who wishes to serve at sea must revalidate the certificate at intervals not exceeding 5 years. Revalidation of Watch Rating Certificates is not required.
* All candidates for revalidation must:
  * meet the **medical fitness requirements** of the MS (Medical Examination) Regulations 1983 (as amended) and produce a valid **medical fitness certificate** (see Training and Certification Guidance Part 1 for further details);
  * for service in the **deck** department, have served as a master or deck officer in seagoing ships of any flag (other than fishing vessels) of more than 80gt or 24 metres in length, for at least 12 months (which need not be continuous) during the preceding 5 years;
  * for service in the **engine** department, have served as an engineer officer on sea-going ships (other than fishing vessels), of at least 350kW registered power, of any flag for at least 12 months (which need not be continuous) during the preceding 5 years;
  * for service as a **radio operator**, have served as a radio operator or an officer on sea-going ships of any flag for at least 12 months (which need not be continuous) during the preceding 5 years.
* **Deck officers not meeting the relevant requirements** above may serve on ships, other than fishing vessels, in a supernumerary capacity for 3 months before applying for revalidation of the certificate. During this period officers are expected to update their professional knowledge. Officers who have served at sea in vessels as described above for at least 3 months in a deck officer capacity immediately prior to the expiry of their certificate may, within 3 months after the expiry date, also apply for revalidation. Alternatively, they can satisfactorily complete an **approved shore-based updating course**.
* **Engineer officers not meeting the relevant requirements** above may serve on ships, other than fishing vessels, of 350kW or more registered power, in a supernumerary capacity for 3 months before applying for revalidation of the certificate. During this period officers are expected to update their professional knowledge. Officers who have served at sea in an engineering capacity, in vessels described above, for at least 3 months immediately prior to the expiry of their certificate may also apply for revalidation within 3 months after the expiry date.
* Deck and engineer officers who do not meet the revalidation criteria above may, **alternatively** sail in a lower rank than that for which they are certificated, for 3 months before applying for revalidation of their certificate. In order to do this they must first contact an MCA Marine Office and apply on form MSF 4258 for a revalidation oral examination by an MCA examiner. Successful candidates, who must present a valid Medical Fitness Certificate to the examiner, will be issued with a **Certificate of Dispensation**, which may be presented to interested parties as confirmation of their eligibility for service at a lower rank. Those who wish to restrict their service to a certain type of vessel may elect to be examined only on that type of vessel, in which case the Certificate of Dispensation will indicate any such limitation.
* In addition to the above options, STCW 95 provides for the acceptance of a master's or officer's continued proficiency by virtue of his having performed functions relating to the duties appropriate to the class or grade of certificate held which are considered to be at least equivalent to the sea service required for revalidation. A list of occupations which will be favourably considered is given in Part 9 and reproduced below. It is not exhaustive and applications from certificate holders engaged in other occupations may also be considered. Applications for revalidation may be made by certificate holders who have been engaged in the listed occupations for at least two and a half of the preceding five years.
  * marine pilots;
  * MCA surveyors;

---

[14] The procedure for the issue of Tanker Endorsements is detailed in paragraph 9 of T&C Guidance Part 9.

- marine college lecturers;
- technical, engineering and marine superintendents or ship repair managers;
- harbour masters;
- hydrographic surveyors; and
- classification society marine surveyors.

* Applicants for revalidation of STCW 78 certificates and Marine Engine Operator Licences to STCW 95 criteria must provide details and evidence of the following, in addition to the relevant requirements described in the preceding paragraphs above:

- **deck officers**:
  - a GMDSS General Operator's Certificate (GOC) or Restricted Operator's Certificate (ROC) approved by the MCA; and
  - evidence of attending MCA-approved training programmes on Radar Observer, Radar simulator and ARPA simulator; (not required for holders of Class 1 certificates of competency); or
  - for holders of Deck Officer Class 5, 4 or 3 or 2nd Mate (FG) certificates of competency, evidence of attending an MCA-approved training programme on Electronic Navigation Systems (ENS), Navigation Control (NCC), or Navigation, Radar and ARPA simulator (operational level); (not required for holders of Class 1 certificates of competency); or
  - for holders of Master (HT), Mate (HT), First Mate (FG), Deck Officer Class 2 certificates of competency or lower certificates with command endorsements, evidence of attending an MCA-approved training programme on NCC or Navigation, Radar and ARPA simulator (Operational or Management level) (not required for holders of Class 1 certificates of competency).

- **engineer officers**:
  - a First Aid at Sea certificate or Medical First Aid certificate;
  - a Lifeboatman certificate, or a Certificate of Proficiency in Survival Craft (CPSC), a Certificate of Proficiency in Survival Craft and Rescue Boats other than Fast Rescue Boats (PSC & RB), or an MCA-approved onboard survival craft training programme;
  - for holders of newly issued Class 2, 3, or 4 certificates of competency, a minimum of 6 months' sea service whilst in possession of the certificate being revalidated. This does not apply to those who have qualified for a chief engineer's service endorsement.

- **Marine Engine Operator Licences**:
  - a First Aid at Sea certificate, a Medical First Aid certificate or Offshore Petroleum Industry Training Organisation (OPITO) basic Medical Aid certificate; and
  - a Lifeboatman certificate, or a Certificate of Proficiency in Survival Craft (CPSC) or a Certificate of Proficiency in Survival Craft and Rescue Boats other than Fast Rescue Boats (PSC & RB).

* When STCW 78 certificates of competency and engine operator licences which are limited for service by trading area, tonnage or power are revalidated to STCW 95 criteria, the STCW 95 certificate will bear the same limitations as the STCW 78 certificate. MSN 1692 gives further details.

* In addition to the arrangements described in the preceding paragraph, **holders of deck officer certificates of competency Class 2, First Mate Foreign Going or Master Home Trade** who have completed a minimum of two years' watchkeeping service as the officer in charge of a navigational watch or one year's watchkeeping service as chief mate whilst holding one of the above certificates, and who hold a valid Ship Captain's Medical or Medical Care certificate, will have the following **endorsements** added to their STCW 95 certificate:

> "Master 3,000gt (unlimited area) *and*
> Master – any vessel in near-coastal waters"

E02c.9i Requirements for revalidation of tanker endorsements (paragraph 11.0)

* See Training and Certification Guidance Part 5, paragraph 4.5, and E02c.5d.
* The application procedure for revalidation of tanker endorsements is described in Part 9, paragraph 12.0.

E02c.9j Annexes to Part 9

* Part 9 has six annexes as follows:
- Annex 1: Documents to be submitted in support of applications for MCA oral examinations - VQ route;
- Annex 2: Documents to be submitted in support of applications for MCA oral examinations - written examination route;
- Annex 3: Documents to be submitted in support of applications for MCA oral examinations - Marine Engine Operator Licences;
- Annex 4: Specimen report of tanker service from master/chief engineer;

- Annex 5: Specimen report of 14 days' supervised shipboard tanker training; and
- Annex 6: Addresses of MCA Marine Offices where oral examinations are held.

E02c.10 Training and Certification Guidance - Part 10: Ratings

* **Training and Certification Guidance Part 10** is contained in **MGN 97** and gives revised information and guidance regarding the grading and training requirements for ratings employed on different types of merchant ship. MGN 97 supersedes MGN 10 and should be read in conjunction with MSN 1692, as amended, and MSN 1740 or subsequent amendments.

* The three international instruments regulating the training and certification of ratings are the **ILO Able Seaman Convention 1946**; **STCW 95** and its associated STCW Code; and **SOLAS**. These Conventions specify certain training and experience requirements for all seafarers and further requirements for those who have designated safety and pollution prevention duties on board. The UK is a party to all three Conventions, and all ratings serving on UK ships must be properly trained, with appropriate certification, in accordance with their requirements.

* Those seafarers who were serving as Category 1 or Category 2 seamen on or before 1 August 1998 could continue in this capacity until 31 January 2002, by which date they had to have obtained an STCW 95 Watch Rating Certificate.

* The term "seafarer", where used in Training and Certification Guidance Part 10, does *not* include hairdressers, entertainers, shop assistants or other staff employed by concessionaires on ro-ro ferries or passenger vessels; requirements for these personnel are covered in Training and Certification Guidance Part 12.

E02c.10a Mandatory requirements (paragraph 2.0)

* For **medical fitness** requirements see E02c.1, Training and Certification Guidance Part 1 and MSN 1765.
* For **familiarisation training** requirements see E02c.6a.
* For **basic training** requirements see E02c.6b.
* The shipowner or operator must ensure that all seafarers are able to **communicate in the common working language** determined for the ship. (See also D03b.8.)

E02c.10b Grading of seafarers (paragraph 3.0)

* **Seafarers are graded** according to their training, qualifications and experience. The MS (Safe Manning, Hours of Work and Watchkeeping) Regulations 1997 require shipowners to ensure that their manning arrangements provide a good balance of experience and skill within the crew as a whole. The grading of seafarers described in the following subsections is designed by the MCA to assist in achieving this aim.

E02c.10c Trainee Rating (deck or engine departments) (paragraph 3.2)

* **Trainee Ratings** must be at least 16 years of age, be medically fit and have undertaken **Personal Survival Techniques training** and **familiarisation training** before being assigned to duties.
* However, young persons sponsored by Job Centres in the UK, who are not employed as part of the normal crew and do not accumulate more than one month's service in total on board the vessel, are not required to undertake the training in Personal Survival Techniques.

E02c.10d Deck department (paragraph 3.3)

* **Deck Rating Grade 2**: To qualify for this grading, a seafarer must be at least 17 years old and should have either: successfully completed the four elements of **basic training** (see E02c.6b); or
  - have completed, prior to 1 August 1998, acceptable **survival and fire-fighting training and more than 6 months' sea-service**, and have obtained a **Navigational Watch Rating Certificate** after meeting the requirements of STCW Code A-II/4 (see E02c.10i); or
  - be the holder of an **Efficient Deck Hand (EDH) certificate** (in which case the seafarer must obtain a Watch Rating Certificate within one month of joining the vessel); or
  - be the holder of a **VQ2 in Marine Vessel Operation** (in which case the seafarer must obtain a Watch Rating Certificate within one month of joining the vessel).
* **Deck Rating Grade 1**: To qualify for this grading, a seafarer must either:
  - hold an **AB certificate**; or

- have completed **36 months' sea service** in total, of which at least 12 months must have been served in the deck compartment, and have met the requirements for **Deck Rating Grade 2**.

E02c.10e AB Certificate (paragraph 3.4)

* To qualify for the issue of a **Certificate of Competency as AB**, a seafarer must have:
  - attained the age of **18**;
  - obtained a **Watch Rating Certificate** (see E02c.10i);
  - obtained an **EDH certificate** (see E02c.10f) or a **VQ2 in Marine Vessel Operation** (see E02c.8);
  - obtained a Certificate of Proficiency in Survival Craft and Rescue Boats (**CPSCRB**) or a Certificate of Proficiency in Survival Craft (**CPSC**) or a **Lifeboatman** certificate;
  - produced proof of **medical fitness** (see E06c.2) and
  - completed at least **24 months' sea-service in the deck department**, or **36 months as a General Purpose (GP) rating** of which at least 12 months was on deck duties.
* Sea-service performed in a deck capacity on sea-going fishing vessels of more than 16.5m in registered length, Royal Naval ships or mobile offshore units (MOUs) will be counted in full but at least 6 months' sea-service on merchant ships will be required for certification as an AB seaman.
* Seafarers with MOU sea service unable to complete the required 6 months on merchant ships will be issued with an AB Certificate suitably endorsed with a limitation for use on MOUs. This limitation will be removed at an MCA Marine Office on completion of 6 months' sea service on merchant ships.
* An AB Certificate may be obtained from any MCA Marine Office on completion of an application form and on production of supporting evidence to confirm that all the relevant conditions listed above have been met. A prescribed fee will be charged for this service.
* For notes on the MS (Certificates of Competency as A.B.) Regulations 1970 (SI 1970/294) see E02d.2.

E02c.10f Efficient Deck Hand (EDH) Certificate (paragraph 3.5)

* EDH is the qualifying examination for Able Seaman (AB) and Deck Rating certification. The EDH exam can be attempted after a seafarer has:
  - attained the age of **17**;
  - served at least **12 months in the deck department of sea-going merchant ships**; and
  - obtained a **Navigational Watch Rating Certificate or a Steering Certificate**.
* Service in the deck department in high speed craft (HSC), tugs, dredgers, standby vessels, survey vessels, RN ships and fishing vessels of more than 16.5m registered length is also acceptable. Service in MOUs will be counted if serving as part of the deck crew.
* 6 months' service in the deck department in HSC will be accepted in place of the 12 months' service specified above, towards the issue of an EDH limited to HSC. This limitation may be removed on completion of 12 months' sea service.
* The syllabus for EDH training and certification is in Annex 1 of Training and Certification Guidance Part 10.
* Training providers must obtain approval from the MCA both to conduct EDH courses and for individual examiners. Approved training providers will issue EDH Certificates on behalf of the MCA and must maintain full records of all certificates issued. Annex 2 of Training and Certification Guidance Part 10 shows a specimen EDH Certificate; any EDH certificate issued must be in the format shown.
* Holders of a level 2 VQ in Marine Vessel Operations may obtain an EDH certificate without further examination.

E02c.10g Engine department (paragraph 3.6)

* **Engine-Room Rating**: To qualify for this grading, a seafarer must be at least 17 years old and have:
  - obtained an Engine-Room Watch Rating Certificate after meeting the requirements of STCW Code A-III/4, as described in paragraphs 4.1 to 4.5 below; and have either
  - successfully completed the four elements of the basic training (see E02c.6b); or
  - completed prior to 1 August 1998 acceptable survival and fire-fighting training and more than 6 months' sea service.

E02c.10h General Purpose (GP) Ratings (paragraph 3.7)

* **GP ratings** are those who have been trained in both deck and engine-room duties. They may be employed in either department according to the needs and requirements of the company.

* **GP Ratings Grade 2** are those who hold a Navigational Watch Rating Certificate as well as an Engine-room Watch Rating Certificate. They can be employed where the ship's Safe Manning Document stipulates the requirements for Deck or GP Rating Grade 2 or Engine-Room Rating.
* **GP Ratings Grade 1** are those who meet the requirements for Deck Rating Grade 1 and hold an Engine-room Watch Rating Certificate. They can be employed where the Safe Manning Document stipulates the requirements for Deck Rating Grade 1 or 2, Engine-Room or GP Rating.

E02c.10i Watch Rating Certificates (paragraph 4.0)

* UK companies which are in full compliance with the ISM Code may apply to the MCA Seafarer Standards Branch for approval to issue Watch Rating Certificates on its behalf.
* Watch Rating Certificates issued must be in the approved format shown in the specimen certificate in Annex 3 of Training and Certification Guidance Part 10.
* In their application, companies must demonstrate that they have adequate arrangements for training and assessing watchkeeping ratings and an acceptable quality control system. They will also be required to provide details of any **special training** they may propose to give to meet the requirement of Part 10, paragraph 4.3.2. Any approved special training may be undertaken either ashore or on board and may form part of a pre-sea training programme.
* MCA approval will be subject to periodic review and evaluation and may be withdrawn if the MCA's requirements are not met.
* Once a company has been approved by MCA, it may issue approved Watch Rating Certificates in the approved format shown at Annex 3 to Training and Certification Guidance Part 10 to any rating who, in accordance with STCW 95 requirements:
  * is not less than **17** years old;
  * has completed either at least **6 months' approved sea-going service in the relevant department** or has completed **special training and at least 2 months' approved sea going service**; and has either:
    * successfully completed all 4 elements of the basic training (see E02c.6b); or
    * has completed, prior to 1 August 1998, acceptable survival and fire-fighting training and more than 6 months' sea-service; or
    * has an EDH certificate or a Level 2 VQ in Marine Vessel Operations (Deck); **and**
  * has been **assessed by a responsible officer** of the ship appointed by the company, and has been found to have **met the requirements and performance standards** specified in STCW Code A-II/4 or A-III/4 for deck and engine-room ratings respectively[15].
* A copy of each Watch Rating Certificate issued must be forwarded for registration to the Seafarer Standards Branch, MCA as soon as possible after issue of the original to the rating. The company must maintain full records of all certificates issued to enable questions on validity to be answered and checks to be made.
* **Companies approved by the MCA** for the issue of Watch Rating Certificates should have ensured, by 1 February 2002, that **ratings** holding STCW 78 Watch Rating Certificates (EXN 87 and 88) are issued with STCW 95 certificates, following the procedure outlined above.

E02c.10j Additional Training Requirements (paragraph 5.0)

* Additional STCW 95 training requirements for ratings serving on certain types of ship are detailed in Training and Certification Guidance Part 5.

E02c.11 Training and Certification Guidance - Part 11: Conduct of MCA oral examinations

* **Training and Certification Guidance Part 11** is contained in **MGN 69**. It provides information and guidance concerning the conduct of MCA oral examinations and sets out the oral examination syllabuses for STCW 95 certificates of competency.
* The MCA oral examination is aimed at ensuring the candidate's ability to undertake the duties appropriate to the officer of the watch (OOW), chief mate, master, second engineer or chief engineer. Oral examinations are part of the procedure for the attainment of all MCA certificates of competency, and all candidates must demonstrate an adequate knowledge of the English language.
* The examination syllabuses are divided into topics. Each topic contains a group of tasks, duties and responsibilities considered necessary for ship operation, safety of life at sea or protection of the marine environment. As indicated in the preamble to each examination syllabus, the examination will be conducted from a particular perspective, and this

---

[15] This implies that the responsible officer should have access to a copy of the relevant table(s) from the STCW Code.

will be based upon the level of responsibility assumed, i.e. either management level (master, chief engineer, chief mate or second engineer) or operational level (officer in charge of a navigational or engineering watch).
* Appendix A details the oral examination syllabuses (A to E) for the various grades of STCW 95 deck department certificates. At the date of publication of MGN 69, syllabuses F–H were still being developed.
* Appendix B details the oral examination syllabuses for the various grades of STCW 95 engine department certificates.
* Appendix C lists addresses of MCA Marine Offices where oral examinations are held.

E02c.12 Training and Certification Guidance - Part 12: Safety training for concessionaires working on passenger ships

* **Part 12** of the Training and Certification Guidance is contained in **MGN 120** and gives information and guidance regarding the training requirements for concessionaires working on passenger vessels and the responsibility of companies to ensure they are met.
* **Concessionaires** may be defined as personnel providing direct services to passengers, such as franchise caterers, hairdressers, entertainers and sales staff. They are neither seafarers nor crew for the purposes of qualifications or certification, and are not assigned specific safety and pollution prevention duties. It must be recognised that while they may be considered as concessionaires by the employing company, they are looked on as crew by passengers who may need assistance in an emergency situation.
* Both the ISM Code and STCW 95 require that all personnel, including concessionaires, on board sea-going vessels must receive training to cope with emergency situations.
* Training and Certification Guidance Part 12 establishes the minimum mandatory training for concessionaires required by the Training and Certification Regulations and how it may be achieved. In addition it places a responsibility on companies to ensure all personnel can act effectively in emergency situations.

E02c.12a General (paragraph 2.0)

* The Training and Certification Regulations establish the mandatory minimum requirements for **familiarisation training** as required by the ISM Code, for all personnel including concessionaires (see E02c.12b).
* The Regulations also establish mandatory minimum requirements for training of all personnel, including concessionaires, designated on muster lists to **assist passengers in emergency situations** and **providing direct services** on passenger ships (see E02c.12c and E02c.12d).
* It is the responsibility of the company to ensure effective actions by all personnel in emergency situations.
* Since concessionaires are not assigned specific safety and pollution prevention duties, they are **not required to undertake basic training** as set out in STCW 95 regulation V1/1 (described in Training and Certification Guidance Part 6) (see E02c.6b). However, this may be undertaken on a **voluntary** basis.

E02c.12b Requirements for familiarisation training (paragraph 3.0)

* The minimum requirements for **familiarisation training** are that concessionaires must be able to:
  1. communicate with other persons on board on elementary safety matters and understand safety information symbols, signs and alarms;
  2. know what to do if:
     * a person falls overboard;
     * fire or smoke is detected;
     * the fire or abandon ship alarm is sounded;
  3. identify assembly and embarkation stations and emergency escape routes;
  4. locate and don lifejackets;
  5. raise the alarm and have a basic knowledge of the use and types of portable fire extinguishers;
  6. take immediate action upon encountering an accident or other medical emergency, before seeking further medical assistance on board; and
  7. close and open the fire, weathertight and watertight doors fitted in the particular ship, other than those for hull openings.

E02c.12c Requirements for crowd management training for concessionaires designated on muster lists to assist passengers in emergency situations (paragraph 4.0)

* The Regulations set out the requirements for crowd management training for all personnel designated on muster lists to assist passengers in emergency situations. In order to meet these requirements, concessionaires must receive training which includes, but is not necessarily limited to the following:
  1. awareness of life-saving appliances and control plans, including:
     * knowledge of muster lists and emergency instructions;
     * knowledge of emergency exits; and
     * restrictions on the use of elevators;
  2. the ability to assist passengers en route to muster and embarkation stations, including:
     * the ability to give clear reassuring orders;
     * the control of passengers in corridors, staircases and passageways;
     * maintaining escape routes clear of obstructions;
     * methods available for evacuation of disabled persons and persons needing special assistance; and
     * search of accommodation spaces;
  3. mustering procedures, including:
     * the importance of keeping order;
     * the ability to use procedures for reducing and avoiding panic;
     * the ability to use, where appropriate, passenger lists for evacuation counts; and
     * the ability to ensure that the passengers are suitably clothed and have donned their lifejackets correctly.

E02c.12d Requirements for safety training for concessionaires providing a direct service to passengers in passenger spaces (paragraph 5.0)

* The Training and Certification Regulations set out the requirements for safety training for all personnel, including concessionaires, providing a direct service to passengers in passenger spaces. In order to meet these requirements concessionaires must have the ability to:
  1. communicate with passengers in an emergency, taking into account:
     * the language or languages appropriate to the principal nationalities of the passengers
     * carried on a particular route;
     * the use of elementary English vocabulary for basic instructions for communicating with a
     * passenger in need of assistance;
     * the possible need to communicate during an emergency by some means, other than oral,
     * for example by hand signals or calling attention to the location of instructions, assembly
     * stations, life saving appliances or evacuation routes;
     * the extent to which complete safety instructions have been provided to passengers in their
     * native language(s); and
     * the languages in which emergency announcements are broadcast in an emergency in order
     * to give critical guidance to passengers and help crew in assisting passengers.
  2. demonstrate to passengers the use of personal life saving appliances.

E02c.12e Records (paragraph 6.0)

* Companies should maintain records of all training given and attendance at drills and provide documentary evidence, if requested by the MCA or other authorised body.
* Concessionaires may also be requested by MCA surveyors to demonstrate their knowledge.

E02c.13 Training and Certification Guidance - Part 13: Use of fishing vessel certificates of competency in standby, seismic survey and oceanographic research vessels – revised arrangements

* The **MS (Training and Certification) Regulations 1997** replace the MS (Certification of Deck Officers) Regulations 1985 and the MS (Certification of Marine Engineer Officers and Licensing of Marine Engine Operators) Regulations 1986, as amended. The earlier regulations allowed for the employment of officers holding fishing vessel certificates of competency in standby, seismic survey and oceanographic research vessels.

* Following full implementation of STCW 95 on 1st February 2002, **holders of fishing vessel certificates of competency** are no longer permitted to work on standby, seismic survey and oceanographic research vessels.
* **Training and Certification Guidance Part 13** is contained in **MGN 121** and gives details of how holders of fishing certificates of competency can obtain STCW 95 Merchant Navy certificates of competency for use in these vessels.
* It has been decided by the MCA, in consultation with the offshore industry, that where officers satisfy the criteria in Part 13, they will be issued with a restricted STCW 95 certificate of competency to allow for continued employment in standby, seismic survey or oceanographic research vessels.
* Part 13 contains the requirements for all applicants, additional requirements for deck officers other than master, additional requirements for master, application procedure, a table showing limitations and capacities endorsed on STCW 95 certificates, the MCA oral examination syllabus for Certificate of Service holders applying for STCW 95 Certificates of Competency, and other relevant information.

E02c.14 Training and Certification Guidance - Part 14: STCW 95 application to certificates of service

* **Training and Certification Guidance Part 14** is contained in **MGN 116** and provides information for Certificate of Service holders who wished to continue employment at sea after the final date for implementation of STCW 95 on 1 February 2002. (**Certificates of service** have not been valid for sea-going service since 31 January 2002.)
* In order to obtain an STCW 95 certificate of competency, holders of valid certificates of service had to comply with the criteria laid down in Part 14.
* Successful candidates retain the existing tonnage, power and area limitations endorsed upon their old Certificate of Service. In the case of deck officers, the tonnage limitation of 1,600 GRT will be increased to 3,000gt.

E02c.15 Training and Certification Guidance - Part 15: Certification of inshore tug personnel

* **Training and Certification Guidance Part 15** is contained in **MGN 209** and gives details of the certification system devised for the UK towage industry that enables uncertificated personnel, not previously required to hold STCW certificates of competency, to obtain a qualification complying with the requirements of STCW 95, prior to the full implementation of STCW 95 on 1 February 2002. The qualification system described in Part 15 is intended to enable tug personnel employed in the UK inshore towage industry to obtain a restricted STCW 95 certificate of competency to enable them to continue in their normal employment following full implementation of STCW 95 on 1 February 2002.
* The certificates for inshore tug personnel are:
  * **Master (Inshore Tugs)** – Reg. II/3 (tugs less than 500gt, limited to 30 miles from a safe haven);
  * **Watchkeeper (Inshore Tugs)** – Reg. II/3 (tugs less than 500gt, limited to 30 miles from a safe haven);
  * **Engineer (Inshore Tugs)** – Reg. III/2 (tugs less than 6,000kW, limited to 30 miles from a safe haven); and
  * **Engine Room Watchkeeper (Inshore Tugs)** – Reg. III/1 (tugs less than 6,000kW, limited to 30 miles from a safe haven).
* "**Safe haven**" means a harbour or shelter of any kind which affords safe entry and/or protection from the force of weather.
* **Part 15 includes** details of the British Tugowners Association (BTA) Apprenticeship Training Scheme and VQ Training Scheme; tug service requirements; ancillary training requirements; medical standards; proof of tug service; application procedure; Inshore Tugs Master and Deck Officer Testimonial form specimen (Annex A); Inshore Tugs Engineer Officer Testimonial form specimen (Annex B); addresses of MCA Marine Offices (Annex C); deck oral examination syllabuses for Master (Inshore Tugs) STCW Reg. III/2 (Annex D); deck oral examination syllabuses for Watchkeeper (Inshore Tugs) STCW Reg. II/2 (Annex E); engineer oral examination syllabus for Engineer Officer (Inshore Tugs) STCW Reg. III/2 (Annex F); engineer oral examination syllabus for Engine Room Watchkeeper (Inshore Tugs) STCW Reg. III/1 (Annex G).

E02c.16 Training and Certification Guidance - Part 16: Certification of personnel serving on inshore craft (other than tankers of 500gt or over, all tugs and all passenger ships)

* **Training and Certification Guidance Part 16** was in **MGN 126** (which expired on 31 January 2002) and gave details of the certification system devised for UK inshore craft over 24m in length, under 3000gt, and under 6000kW propulsion power, limited to operation between ports in and within 30 miles from a safe haven in the UK or Ireland (excluding tankers of 500gt or over, all tugs* and all passenger ships). This scheme was intended solely for personnel, exempted from the certification requirements under the **general exemptions** for specified areas described in MSN 1727, who needed to obtain STCW 95 certification before STCW 95 came fully into force on 1 February 2002. For current requirements, see **MIN 123**.

E02c.17 Training and Certification Guidance - Part 17: Certificates of competency or Marine Engine Operator Licences for service as an engineer officer on commercially and privately operated yachts and sail training vessels

* **Training and Certification Guidance Part 17** is contained in **MGN 156** and describes a system for harmonising "large yacht" (sometimes called "**megayacht**") **engine department certification** with the requirements of STCW 95. Part 17 gives details of a certification system for **engineer officers and other engine personnel** serving on:
  * **yachts or sail training vessels** of 24m or more loadline length which are in **commercial use** for sport or pleasure and which do not carry cargo and do not carry more than 12 passengers, covered by the MCA's Code of Practice for Safety of Large Commercial Sailing and Motor Vessels (known as the "White Code" by the MCA but also widely known as the "Megayacht Code"); and
  * **privately operated yachts** of over 24m or more loadline length which are used for sport or pleasure and which do not carry cargo and do not carry more than 12 passengers.
* The **certification system**, which came into effect on 1 September 2000, comprises a series of training modules, ancillary training, yacht service, and (for certain qualifications) an MCA oral examination. Success leads to the issue of a Marine Engine Operator's Licence (Yacht) or STCW 95 Engineer Officer (Yacht) certificates of competency.
* **Part 17 includes**: details of the certification system; the criteria for certification; details of training modules; ancillary training requirements; manning scales for motor or sailing yachts (Annex A); testimonial pro-forma (Annex B); addresses of MCA Marine Offices and oral examination centres (Annex C); training module syllabuses (Annex D); addresses of Scottish Qualification Authority (SQA) written examination centres (Annex E); and oral examination syllabuses (Annex F)
* The MCA's **Code of Practice for Safety of Large Commercial Sailing & Motor Vessels**, published in 1997, requires that **engineering personnel** serving on yachts and sail training vessels of less than 3,000gt should be qualified in accordance with the MS (Training and Certification) Regulations 1997. However, since the introduction of STCW 95, it has become apparent that some engineering personnel serving on yachts of this type may be unable to meet the full UK requirements as set out in the MS (Training and Certification) Regulations 1997.
* In order to meet the STCW 95 requirements and address the needs of professional seafarers serving on yachts and sail training vessels of less than 3,000gt and under 9,000 kW propulsion power, as well as privately operated yachts of a similar size not covered by the Code, the MCA, in consultation with the "large yacht" industry, sail training organisations and UK maritime colleges, developed an **alternative route to the gaining of engineer certification** specifically limited to service in this sector of industry. This route makes use of a series of **training modules** which include tuition, written examinations and ancillary training, and these, in conjunction with suitable engineering practical training and yacht service, permit entry to an MCA oral examination. Success in the MCA **oral examination** leads to the issue of either **a STCW 95 Certificate of Competency** limited to service on yachts and sail training vessels, or a **Marine Engine Operator Licence** limited to service on yachts and sail training vessels. No MCA oral examination or written examination is required for candidates taking the Approved Engine Course certificate.
* The qualifications available through this route are:
  * **MCA Approved Engine Course Certificate** (**AEC**) as required by the Code. These certificates are issued directly by MCA-approved Training Providers (details available from the MCA's Seafarer Standards Branch);
  * **Marine Engine Operator Licence (Yacht)** (**MEOL(Y)**). These licences are issued by the MCA after the candidate has satisfied the criteria set out in Part 17 paragraph 6.2 and has undertaken the approved education and training described in Annex D;
  * **Chief Engineer Reg. III/3** certificate of competency, referred to as "Yacht 4" or "Y4";
  * **Chief Engineer Reg. III/2** certificate of competency (Chief Engineer "service Endorsement"), referred to as "Yacht 3" or "Y3";

* **Chief Engineer Reg. III/2** certificate of competency, referred to as "Yacht 2" or "Y2"; and
* **Chief Engineer Reg. III/2** certificate of competency ("Large Yacht Endorsement"), referred to as "Yacht 1" or "Y1".

* These qualifications, except the AEC and MEOL, will be issued in accordance with the requirements of STCW 95. The AEC and MEOL are not STCW certificates.

* The certificates of competency listed above will be annotated before issue with capacities (Chief Engineer, Second Engineer or OOW Engineering) and tonnage and power limitations as set out in Part 17 paragraph 1.7.

* **Manning scales for engineering personnel** to be carried on UK motor or sailing yachts are set out in Annex A of Part 17.

* For notes on the **Megayacht Code** see D03l.7.

E02c.18 Training and Certification Guidance - Part 18: STCW 95 certificates of competency – conversion of GRT to gt

* **Training and Certification Guidance Part 18** is contained in **MGN 164** and gives guidance on the conversion of certification tonnage limitations measured in **gross registered tons (GRT)** to **gross tonnage (gt)**, for the purposes of STCW 95 certification.

* Under the **MS (Tonnage) Regulations 1982** (SI 1982/841) ships were measured **in gross registered tons (GRT)**. When the **MS (Tonnage) Regulations 1997** (SI 1997/1510) entered into force, revoking the 1982 Regulations, new ships were required to be measured only in **gross tonnage (gt)**. However, under regulation 12 of the 1997 Regulations, **existing ships** were additionally permitted the continuing use of a **gross tonnage (GT), ascertained in accordance with the 1982 Regulations,** for the purpose of application of SOLAS, MARPOL and STCW 95 provisions.

* Under STCW 95, deck officer certificates of competency are limited to service on vessels measured in **gross tonnage (gt)**.

* Holders of pre- STCW 95 certificates with a **GRT tonnage limitation** have had this stated in **gt** when applying for STCW 95 certificates. (This is in accordance with the MS (Training and Certification) Regulations 1997 and the STCW 1978/1995 equivalency tables in MSN 1692.) However, this has raised **anomalies** in that holders of some pre- STCW 95 certificates find that the **GRT tonnage limitations** of their pre- STCW 95 certificates do not allow them to serve in ships of a similar physical size when measured in **gt**.

* **Tankers**, when re-measured for gross tonnage under the 1997 Regulations, do not attract the same numerical increase in tonnage as other vessel types, and limitations will not be increased on STCW 95 certificates for service on ships on which a tanker endorsement is required.

* Following publication of Part 18 in January 2001, holders of pre- STCW 95 certificates of competency will have their GRT limitations **converted** by the MCA as follows:

Pre- STCW 95 tonnage limitation	STCW 95 tonnage limitation
5,000GRT	5,000GRT or 15,000gt *
10,000GRT	10,000GRT or 20,000gt**

* limited to 5,000gt on tankers
** limited to 10,000gt on tankers

* Holders of STCW 95 certificates already issued who consider they have been disadvantaged by the level conversion from GRT to gt, are advised in Part 18 that they may apply for a **replacement certificate** with the revised gt limitations. Applicants should send an application form, together with their current certificate, two passport sized photographs and a replacement fee to the Seafarer Standards Branch, MCA (from whom application forms can be obtained).

E02c.19 Training and Certification Guidance - Part 19: Certificates of Equivalent Competency

* **Training and Certification Guidance Part 19** is contained in **MGN 221** which superseded MGN 179 and describes the requirements and procedures for issue of **Certificates of Equivalent Competency (CECs)**, which enable officers holding STCW 95 certificates issued by certain countries other than the UK to serve as officers in UK ships.

* For notes on regulation 5 of the MS (Training and Certification) Regulations 1997, which permits recognition by the MCA of non-UK certificates and permits the granting of UK **Certificates of Equivalent Competency (CECs)**, see E02b.5.

* Administrations whose Certificates of Competency are recognised by the MCA for **service in any position** on UK ships (including **master**, **mate** and **chief engineer**) are listed at Annex 1 of Part 19. (In UK "**strategic ships**" the position of **master** is restricted to nationals of certain countries, as outlined in E03d.1a. Annex 3 of Part 19 sets out the current provisions.)
* **CECs will be issued**, on application to the MCA, to officers holding STCW Certificates of Competency issued by other Administrations where the MCA is satisfied that there are no substantial differences between the standard applying to the UK's certificates and that applying to the other country's certificates (paragraph 2.3).
* **CECs carry identical rights and obligations** to those applying to Certificates of Competency. A CEC **remains valid** only as long as the original STCW 95 Certificate of Competency remains valid, and requires **revalidation** at intervals of not more than 5 years (paragraph 2.3).
* The underlying **non-UK STCW Certificate of Competency must be carried at all times with the CEC** and must be made **available for inspection** by authorised persons (paragraph 2.3).
* For the purposes of compliance with the MS (Training and Certification) Regulations and with Safe Manning Documents, CECs may be treated by employers as equivalent to Certificates of Competency (paragraph 2.4).
* Paragraph 3 explains that where the MCA identifies a difference in the standard of education and training represented by an applicant's STCW Certificate of Competency, it will assess the applicants in the subject areas where it detects a shortcoming. The main areas where a difference might exist and which would need to be assessed are:
  * standards of competency;
  * use of the English language; and
  * knowledge of UK legal and administrative processes ("UKLAP").
* No CEC will be issued until the **standards of technical competency** of an applicant's country are determined by the MCA to be equivalent to those of the UK (paragraph 3.3).
* **English Language** requirements are dealt with in paragraph 3.5.
* **UK Legal and Administrative Processes** (**UKLAP**) requirements are set out in paragraphs 3.8 to 3.14.
* **Medical fitness** requirements are dealt with in paragraph 3.15.
* **Application procedures and documentation** requirements are set out in paragraph 4.
* Provisions relating to **company-based assessments** are set out in paragraph 5.
* Where there is an urgent need to ensure that a ship is able to sail under the UK flag with appropriately certificated crew, and in order to minimise the risk of officers being without documentation during a Port State Control Inspection, special provisions may apply, as set out in paragraph 5.1.
* **Temporary CECs** may be issued for up to 6 months at a time in circumstances as detailed in paragraph 6.
* Only companies meeting the MCA standards for "flagging-in" to the UK register may carry a full complement of officers serving an adaptation period, at or below the rank specified on their Certificate of Competency.
* Original Certificates of Competency will have to be duly **revalidated** before a revalidated UK CEC can be issued. The revalidation application procedure is explained in Part 19.
* UK immigration rules require that CEC applicants who are not nationals of EEA countries may need to hold a **work permit** if they are intending to work on a ship which operates solely within UK territorial waters.
* **Annex 1** lists countries whose Certificates of Competency have been evaluated by the MCA for the purposes of comparing standards of competency with those of the UK. This list will be updated by Marine Information Note (MIN).
* **Annex 2** lists countries whose medical and sight test certificates are accepted by the UK towards a Merchant Navy Certificate of Equivalent Competency.
* **Annex 3** details the special manning requirements applying to UK "strategic ships".
* **Annex 4** sets out the requirements relating to evidence of knowledge of the English language.
* **Annex 5** contains recommended criteria for company-based English assessments for Certificates of Equivalent Competency.
* **Annex 6** details the knowledge required for a UKLAP oral assessment: Grade 1 for Master, including a list of suggested reading.
* **Annex 7** details the knowledge required for a UKLAP assessment: Grade 2 for Chief Officer, Chief Engineer and 2nd Engineer, including a list of suggested reading.
* **Annex 8** contains details concerning oral examination of holders of US Coast Guard Certificates of Competency.
* **Annex 9** lists fees relating to Certificates of Equivalent Competency.

E02c.20 Training and Certification Guidance - Part 21: Deck officer Certificates of Competency for service on commercially and privately operated yachts and sail training vessels

* **Training and Certification Guidance Part 21** is contained in **MGN 195** and describes the system for harmonising deck officer certification for large commercial sailing and motor vessels in accordance with UK regulations and the principles of STCW 95 and the STCW Code. It provides details of the certification system for deck officers and personnel serving in:
  * yachts and sail training vessels of 24m and over in loadline length which are in commercial use for sport or pleasure and which do not carry cargo nor more than 12 passengers, and which are subject to the Code of Practice for Safety of Large Commercial Sailing and Motor Vessels (known as the "Megayacht Code" or "White Code"); and
  * privately-owned yachts of 24m and over in loadline length used for sport or pleasure and which do not carry cargo nor more than 12 passengers.
* **Masters and deck officers** serving in UK-registered private or commercially-operated yachts and sail training vessels of 24m or more in loadline length and of less than 3000gt **must be qualified** in accordance with either the MS (Training and Certification) Regulations 1997 or the Code of Practice for Safety of Large Commercial Sailing and Motor Vessels. In consultation with the yachting industry, sail training organisations and nautical colleges, the MCA has devised a route to gaining appropriate certification which is **limited** to service in the professional large yacht sector of the industry. Candidates meeting the requirements will be issued with an STCW Certificate of Competency **limited to service on yachts and sail training vessels**, as shown in the following table.

Capacity	Limitations
Officer of the Watch (Yacht) – STCW reg. II/1	Commercially and privately operated yachts and sail training vessels less than 3000gt. Unlimited area.
Chief Mate (Yacht) – STCW reg. II/2	Commercially and privately operated yachts and sail training vessels less than 3000gt. Unlimited area.
Master 500gt (Yacht) - STCW reg. II/2	Commercially and privately operated yachts and sail training vessels less than 500gt. Unlimited area.
Master (Yacht) - STCW reg. II/2	Commercially and privately operated yachts and sail training vessels less than 3000gt. Unlimited area.

* **Eligibility** requirements are set out in paragraph 4.
* **Medical standards** are laid down in paragraph 5.
* **Entry and examination** requirements are set out in paragraph 6.
* **Revalidation** requirements are set out in paragraph 8.
* The **examination application procedure** is explained in paragraph 9.
* All training assessment and examinations must be taken at an **MCA-approved training institution**, notes on which are in paragraph 10.
* **Annex A** contains **manning scales for deck officers** to be carried in motor or sailing yachts and sail training vessels. The manning scales enter into force on 1 August 2003.
* **Annex B** shows a **testimonial** pro-forma.
* **Annex C** lists addresses of MCA Marine Offices where **oral examinations** are held.
* **Annex D** lists addresses of **examination centres** for MCA Yacht Deck written examinations.
* **Annexes E to N** contain notes on the **training modules** and **outline syllabuses** for the various grades of Yacht Certificate of Competency.
* For notes on the Code of Practice for Safety of Large Commercial Sailing and Motor Vessels, see D031.7.

E02d MISCELLANEOUS PROVISIONS CONCERNING TRAINING AND CERTIFICATION

E02d.1 Local Passenger Vessels (Masters' Licences and Hours, Manning and Training) Regulations

* The **MS (Local Passenger Vessels) (Masters' Licences and Hours, Manning and Training) Regulations 1993** (SI 1993/1213) -
  - **were made** in response to the 1990 MAIB report on the "Marchioness" river boat disaster.

- **impose** requirements in relation to "**local passenger vessels**", i.e., broadly, UK ships which carry more than 12 passengers and operate only in Category A, B, C or D waters (see D04c.2a) or, if at sea, not more than 3 miles from land[16].
- **contain** regulations in four Parts as follows: PART I – GENERAL: **1**. Citation and commencement; **2**. Interpretation; **3**. Application. PART II – MASTERS' LICENCES: **4**. Masters to be qualified. **5**. Licence applications, standards and conditions; **6**. Grades and area restrictions of licences; **7**. Continuing validity; **8**. Record and surrender of licences; **9**. Loss of licences. PART III – MASTERS' HOURS OF WORK: **10**. Interpretation for Part III; **11**. Application of Part III; **12**. The working hours code; **13**. Contravention of regulation 12. PART IV – MANNING AND TRAINING: **14**. Additional crew; **15**. Training in emergency procedures; **16**. Power to detain.

* Part II (Master's licences) applies to:
  • every UK passenger ship of Class IV, V, VI or VI(A) (as defined in D04c.2); and
  • every non-UK passenger ship of one of the above Classes which carries passengers between places in the UK or on a voyage which begins and ends at the same place in the UK and on which the ship calls at no place outside the UK.
* **Parts III and IV (Masters' hours of work, and Manning and training) apply to** every UK vessel which is a passenger ship of a class mentioned in the previous paragraph.
* **Regulation 4** provides that a vessel to which Part II applies must carry **in command** a person qualified with a valid **Boatmaster's Licence** issued by the MCA and of an appropriate grade for the waters and the number of passengers.
* **Regulation 5** contains provisions relating to Boatmaster's Licence applications, standards and conditions. The requirements are fully explained in **M.1525**. Annex 1 of M.1525 contains the syllabus requirements, while Annex 2 details additional short course certificates required.
* **Regulation 6** provides for the issue of **Boatmaster's Licences of Grades 1, 2 and 3**, the grade required depending on the waters in which the vessel operates and the number of passengers carried, as shown in the following table.

Waters	Number of passengers	Minimum grade of Boatmaster's Licence
Category A	13 or more	3
Category B	13 to 100	3
	over 100	2
Category C	13 or more	2
Category D	13 to 100	2
	over 100	1
Sea	13 to 100	2
	101 to 250	1 (See note)

Note: The holder of a Boatmaster's Licence is not allowed to carry more than 250 passengers to sea on any vessel.

* **Regulation 6(3)** provides that a licence of any grade will be subject to **restriction** as to the area or areas in which a vessel may be navigated under the command of the holder, all restrictions to be stated on the licence. (In some cases, licences are restricted solely to canals.)
* **Regulation 7** provides that a Boatmaster's Licence will remain valid only so long as the holder complies with the standards of competence and the conditions (including medical fitness conditions) specified in regulation 5.
* **Regulation 8** provides for **records** and **copies of licences** to be kept by the RSS.
* **Regulation 9** allows a copy of a **lost Boatmaster's Licence** to be issued.
* **Regulation 12(1)** provides that a **master** must, so far as is reasonably practicable, ensure that he is **properly rested** when first going on duty on any working day. Subject to any exemption by the MCA, the **working day** of a master must not exceed 16 hours (regulation 12(2)). Subject to any exemption by the MCA, a master may not con a vessel or vessels for aggregate periods of more than **10 hours** in any working day (regulation 12(3)). The **maximum period of continuous work** (which includes breaks of less than 30 minutes) is limited to **6 hours**, after which a period of at least **30 minutes' rest** must be taken (regulation 12(4)). A **daily rest period** of at least **8 hours** must be taken between two working days (regulation 12(5)). **Exemption** from the hours of work provisions may be applied for under regulation 12(6). Penalties for breaches of the hours of work provisions are laid down in regulation 13.
* **Regulation 14** requires the owner to submit for approval by the MCA his **proposals for manning with additional crew members**. The MCA will give any **approval in writing**.
* **Regulation 15** provides that the **owner** must establish **emergency procedures** to be observed by the master and other crew members, in particular the action to be taken by crew other than the master to **assist passengers**, and the arrangements for ensuring that the master and crew members receive **on-board training** in such procedures.
* **Regulation 16** provides for the detention of vessels contravening Part IV.
* **M.1525** explains the operation of the Regulations.
* Since the introduction of Boatmaster's Licences, **Boatman's Licences** have not been issued.

---

[16] A vessel operating more than 3 miles from land, and carrying more than 12 passengers, would have to be certificated and manned as a sea-going passenger vessel of the appropriate class (see D04c.2).

E02d.2 Certificate of Competency as AB Regulations

* The MS (Certificate of Competency as AB) Regulations 1970 (SI 1970/294) -
    - prescribe the requirements for the grant to seamen of Certificates of Competency as AB (or "AB Certificates").
    - contain, in regulation 4, the eligibility requirements for a person to take the AB examination, which have been superseded by the requirements under STCW 95, as detailed in Part 10 of the MCA's Training and Certification Guidance (see E02c.10).
    - contain, in Schedule 1, the AB examination syllabus.
* For notes on provisions of Part 10 of the Training and Certification Guidance relating to AB Certificates, see E02c.10e.

E02d.3 Certification of Ships' Cooks Regulations

* The MS (Certification of Ships' Cooks) Regulations 1970 (SI 1981/1076) -
    - prescribe requirements for the qualification and certification of ships' cooks.
    - permit the MCA to specify that certificates issued by countries outside the UK may be treated as equivalent to certificates of competency under the Regulations.
* **M.1482** details the qualifying requirements for ships' cooks. There is no exemption from the Ships' Cook examination on any grounds.
* For the provisions of the Regulations relating to the **carriage of a certificated ship's cook**, see E03d.5.

E02d.4 Steering Certificate

* The entry requirements for UK Efficient Deck Hand (EDH) certificate examinations are set out in Annex 1 of Training & Certification Guidance Part 10, which is contained in **MGN 97**. Paragraph 1.1.3 states that candidates must hold either:
    • a **Navigational Watch Rating Certificate**; or
    • a **steering certificate**; or
    • **proof** of having obtained **sufficient experience**.
* No detailed requirements are laid down for steering certificates. However, a steering certificate usually shows that, apart from periods of instruction, the seaman has taken turns at the wheel in steering ships (other than fishing boats) of 100gt or more, or sailing ships of 40gt or more, for periods totalling at least 10 hours. Masters are requested (on older certificates) to certify the time spent at the wheel by seamen who will require a steering certificate and to ensure that certificates are issued to them.
* Under regulation 5(1)(a) of the MS (Certificate of Competency as AB) Regulations 1970 (SI 1970/294) one of the requirements for a person to be eligible to take the qualifying examination for an AB Certificate is that he has, "otherwise than for the purpose of receiving instruction therein, taken turns at the wheel in steering a major ship, not being a fishing boat, for periods totalling not less than 10 hours". A "major ship" is defined in regulation 2 as a ship having in the case of a sailing ship a gross tonnage of 40 tons or more and in the case of any other ship a gross tonnage of 100 tons or more".

E02d.5 DP training certification

* There is no statutory requirement for dynamic positioning (DP) training in the UK, and no M Notice specific to DP training is in force. However, M.1292 (Training and qualifications of masters and officers of vessels controlled by DP systems) (which was superseded by MGN 5, which in turn was superseded by MGN 95[17]) stated that the Department of Transport recommends the **Nautical Institute training programme** which culminates in the award of a DP Operator's Certificate. Officers with more than 12 months' DP watchkeeping experience can undertake a special 2-day advanced simulator course in emergency procedures to qualify for a certificate. Details can be obtained from The Registrar, The Nautical Institute, 202 Lambeth Road, London SE1 7LQ. Tel: 0171 928 1351. Fax: 0171 401 2817. E-mail: sec@nautinst.org
* **DP training** is offered by various nautical training organisations in the UK, most of which advertise in *Seaways* and/or the NUMAST *Telegraph*.

---

[17] MGN 95 makes no specific reference to DP training and qualifications.

E02d.6 Shiphandling training

* **M.1015** contains recommendations for the training of masters and chief mates of large ships with unusual handling and manoeuvring characteristics in shiphandling.

E02d.7 False statements to obtain qualification

* **Section 47(5) of the Merchant Shipping Act 1995** provides that if a person makes a statement which he knows to be **false**, or recklessly makes a statement which is false in a material particular for the purpose of obtaining for himself or another person a document which may be issued under Merchant Shipping regulations, he will be liable on summary conviction to a fine not exceeding level 5 on the standard scale.

E02d.8 Disqualification of holder of seaman's certificates

Home
* Under **section 62(1) of the Merchant Shipping Act 1995**, where it appears to the MCA that a person who is the holder of a certificate other than an officer's[18] is unfit to be the holder of such a certificate, whether by reason of incompetence or misconduct or for any other reason, the MCA may give him notice in writing that he is considering the suspension or cancellation of the certificate.
* The **MS (Disqualification of Holder of Seaman's Certificates) Regulations 1997** (SI 1997/346) prescribe the procedure to be followed with respect to the making and consideration of representations where the MCA is considering suspending or cancelling a certificate issued to a seaman (other than an officer) pursuant to **section 47 and 54** of the Merchant Shipping Act 1995.
* The form of the notice to be served on the certificate holder stating that the Secretary of State is considering suspending or cancelling his certificate is prescribed (regulation 3(1)).
* The certificate holder may give notice of his intention to make written or oral representations to the Secretary of State within six weeks of receipt of the notice (regulation 4(1)).
* The representations, whether written or oral, must be made within ten weeks of the receipt of the notice (regulation 4(4)).
* After considering any representations the Secretary of State must inform the certificate holder concerned of his decision in writing (regulation 5(2)).
* Schedules 1 and 2 of the Regulations are specimens of a Notice of Intention to Suspend or Cancel a Certificate and a Notice of Decision Concerning Suspension or Cancellation of Certificate, respectively.

E02d.9 Ship security training and drills

* ISPS Code, part A, section 13 contains requirements for **ship security training and drills**.
* The **company security officer** (CSO) and **appropriate shore-based personnel** must have **knowledge** and have received **training**, taking into account the guidance given in part B of the ISPS Code. ISPS Code, part B, section 13 details the training required for company security officers and "appropriate shore-based personnel".
* The **ship security officer** (SSO) must have **knowledge** and have received **training**, taking into account the guidance given in part B of the Code (section 13.2). ISPS Code, part B, section 13 details the training required for ship security officers.
* **Shipboard personnel having specific security duties and responsibilities** must **understand** their responsibilities for ship security as described in the Ship Security Plan (see D04t.10a) and must have sufficient **knowledge** and **ability** to perform their assigned duties, taking into account the guidance given in Part B of the ISPS Code (section 13.3). ISPS Code, part B, section 13 details the training required for shipboard personnel having specific security duties and responsibilities.
* To ensure the effective implementation of the Ship Security Plan, **drills** must be carried out at **appropriate intervals** taking into account the ship type, ship personnel changes, port facilities to be visited and other relevant circumstances, taking into account guidance given in part B of the ISPS Code (section 13.4).
* The **company security officer** must ensure the effective co-ordination and implementation of Ship Security Plans by **participating in exercises** at appropriate intervals, taking into account the guidance given in part B of the ISPS Code (section 13.5).
* ISPS Code, part A, section 13.5 advises that the **objective of drills and exercises** is to ensure that shipboard personnel are **proficient in all assigned security duties at all security levels** and the identification of any **security related deficiencies** which need to be addressed.

---

[18] For example, a ship's cook's or AB's certificate.

* ISPS Code, part A, section 13.6 advises that to ensure the effective implementation of the provisions of the Ship Security Plan, **drills** should be conducted **at least once every three months**. In addition, in cases where more than 25% of the ship's personnel has been changed, at any one time, with personnel who have not previously participated in any drill on that ship within the last 3 months, a drill should be conducted **within one week** of the personnel change. These drills should test **individual elements of the plan** such as those security threats listed in paragraph 8.9, i.e.:
  * damage to, or destruction of, the ship or of a port facility, e.g. by explosive devices, arson, sabotage or vandalism;
  * hijacking or seizure of the ship or of persons on board;
  * tampering with cargo, essential ship equipment or systems or ship's stores;
  * unauthorized access or use, including presence of stowaways;
  * smuggling weapons or equipment, including weapons of mass destruction;
  * use of the ship to carry those intending to cause a security incident and/or their equipment;
  * use of the ship itself as a weapon or as a means to cause damage or destruction;
  * attacks from seaward whilst at berth or at anchor; and
  * attacks whilst at sea.
* ISPS Code, part A, section 10.1 provides that **records of training** must be kept on board for at least the minimum period specified by the flag State Administration, bearing in mind the provisions of SOLAS regulation XI-2/9.2.3, which requires ships to keep records for the last 10 calls at port facilities.

E03 Safe manning, hours of work and watchkeeping

E03a LEGISLATION RELATING TO SAFE MANNING, HOURS OF WORK AND WATCHKEEPING

E03a.1 Primary legislation relating to safe manning, hours of work and watchkeeping

* **Section 47(1)(a) of the Merchant Shipping Act 1995** enables regulations to be made requiring ships to carry such number of qualified officers of any description, qualified doctors and qualified cooks and such number of other seamen or qualified seamen of any description as may be specified in the regulations.
* **Section 47(2)** provides that the Secretary of State must not exercise his power to make regulations requiring ships to carry seamen other than doctors and cooks except to the extent that it appears to him necessary or expedient in the interests of safety.
* **Under section 48(1) of the Merchant Shipping Act 1995** the MCA may **exempt any ship or description of ship** from manning requirements. Exemptions may be confined to a particular period or to one or more particular voyages (section 48(2)).

E03a.2 Secondary legislation relating to safe manning, hours of work and watchkeeping

* **Principal regulations relating to safe manning and watchkeeping** and applicable to the majority of seagoing vessels are the **MS (Safe Manning, Hours of Work and Watchkeeping) Regulations 1997** (SI 1997/1320), which are amended by SIs 1997/1911, 2000/484 and 2002/2125 (see E03b). Provisions in these regulations relating to hours of work have been removed by virtue of SI 2002/2125 (see below).
* **Principal regulations relating to hours of work** applicable to the majority of seagoing vessels are the MS (Hours of Work) Regulations 2002 (SI 2002/2125) (see E03c.1), which removed the hours of work provisions from the Safe Manning Regulations.
* Regulations relating to "local passenger vessels", i.e. broadly, UK ships which carry no more than 12 passengers and which operate only in Category A, B, C or D waters or, if at sea, not more than 3 miles from land, are the **MS (Local Passenger Vessels) (Master's Licences and Hours, Manning and Training) Regulations 1993** (SI 1993/1213) (see E02d.1).

E03b SAFE MANNING, HOURS OF WORK AND WATCHKEEPING REGULATIONS

E03b.1 Safe Manning Regulations: introduction

* The **MS (Safe Manning, Hours of Work and Watchkeeping) Regulations 1997** (SI 1997/1320) -
  - are the **principal regulations** relating to safe manning, hours of work and watchkeeping in accordance with STCW 95 criteria.
  - **give effect** in the UK to some of the requirements of the International Convention on Standards of Training, Certification and Watchkeeping 1978 as amended in 1995 (STCW 95) and its associated STCW Code.
  - **apply to sea-going UK ships** wherever they are, and sea-going non-UK ships in UK waters.
  - **do not apply to** fishing vessels, pleasure craft of less than 80gt or under 24 metres in length, and commercially operated small vessels complying with a Code of Practice (regulation 3).
  - **revoke**:
    • the MS (Certification and Watchkeeping) Regulations 1982 (SI 1982/1699);
    • the MS (Safe Manning Document) Regulations 1992 (SI 1992/1564); and
    • the MS (Hours of Work) Regulations 1995 (SI 1995/157).
  - are **amended** by:
    • the **MS (Training, Certification and Safe Manning) (Amendment) Regulations 1997** (SI 1997/1911), which apply the principal Regulations to pleasure vessels over 24 metres and 80gt); and
    • the **MS (Safe Manning, Hours of Work and Watchkeeping) (Amendment) Regulations 2000** (SI 2000/484), which require owners and others responsible for the operation of ships to ensure that not only seamen but masters hold appropriate Certificates of Competency or Equivalent Competency, and have had the special training in the Training and Certification Regulations; they must also ensure that documentation and data relevant to masters, as well as that relevant to seamen, is maintained and readily available for inspection; and
    • the **MS (Hours of Work) Regulations 2002** (SI 2002/2125) (see E03c.1), which removed the provisions (originally in regulations 6 to 10) relating to hours of work.
* In the Regulations "**company**" includes an individual, and in relation to a ship means the owner or any other organisation or person such as the manager, or the bareboat charterer, who has assumed responsibility for the ship's operation from the owner and who has agreed to take over all the duties and responsibilities imposed on the company by the Regulations annexed to the STCW Convention.
* **Regulation 15** contains the MCA's **powers of inspection of non-UK ships** for the purposes of verifying that all seamen serving on board who are required to be certificated hold valid appropriate certificates, and assessing the ability of the the master and seamen in the ship to maintain the watchkeeping standards required by the Regulations where there are grounds for believing that the standards are not being maintained.
* **Regulation 16** provides for the possible **detention** of a UK ship for any contravention of the Regulations, and of non-UK ships for certain contraventions.
* **Regulation 17** contains penalty provisions. **Regulation 18** permits the granting of exemptions by the MCA.

E03b.2 Responsibilities of companies, masters and others (regulation 4)

* Regulation 4 of the MS (Safe Manning, Hours of Work and Watchkeeping) Regulations 1997 applies **only to UK ships**.
* **Every company** must ensure under regulation 4(1) that:
  • every seaman assigned to any of its ships holds an **appropriate certificate** in respect of any function he is to perform on that ship (regulation 4(2)(a));
  • every seaman on any of its ships has had **training** specified in the Training and Certification Regulations in respect of any function he is to perform on that ship (regulation 4(2)(b)); and
  • **documentation and data** relevant to all seamen employed in its ships (related to experience, training, medical fitness and competency for assigned duties inter alia) are maintained and readily available for inspection (regulation 4(2)(c)).
* Nothing in regulation 4(2)(a), (b) or (c) prohibits the allocation of tasks for training under supervision or in case of *force majeure* (regulation 4(3)).
* The **company** must provide **written instructions** to the master of each of its ships setting out the **policies and procedures** to be followed to ensure that all seamen who are **newly employed** in the ship are given a **reasonable**

opportunity to become familiar with the ship's equipment, operating procedures and other arrangements needed for the proper performance of their duties, **before being assigned to those duties** (regulation 4(4)).
* The **policies and procedures** referred to in regulation 4(4) must, under regulation 4(5), include:
  * allocation of a **reasonable period of time to become acquainted** with the specific equipment the seaman will be using or operating, as well as **ship-specific watchkeeping, safety, environmental protection and emergency procedures and arrangements** which the seaman needs to know to perform the assigned duties properly; and
  * **designation of a knowledgeable crew member** who will be responsible for ensuring that an opportunity is provided to each newly-employed seaman to receive essential information in a language which the seaman understands.
* Regulation 4(6) makes it the **duty of any master and any member of a crew designated** with an obligation under regulation 4(4) to carry out that obligation.

E03b.3 Safe Manning Document (regulation 5)

* **Regulation 5(1)** of the MS (Safe Manning, Hours of Work and Watchkeeping) Regulations 1997 provides that it is the duty of the **company** to ensure that for **every UK ship of 500gt or more**:
  * a **Safe Manning Document** (SMD) is in force (regulation 5(1)(a));
  * the Safe Manning Document is **kept on board** the ship at all times (regulation 5(1)(b)); and
  * the **manning of the ship is maintained at all times** to at least the levels specified in the Safe Manning Document (regulation 5(1)(c)).
* The **master** must ensure that the **ship does not proceed to sea without a valid Safe Manning Document** and that the ship's **manning complies with the Safe Manning Document** (regulation 5(2)).
* The **company** must, under regulation 5(3):
  * submit to the MCA **proposals** as to the number and grades of personnel **it considers should be carried** when safely manned on intended voyages (regulation 5(3)(a));
  * take account of any **guidance from the MCA** when preparing proposals (regulation 5(3)(b)); and
  * **inform the MCA** after the issue of a Safe Manning Document of any **relevant changes of circumstances** (e.g. voyages, duties, etc.) (regulation 5(3)(c)).
* **MIN 115** was issued in December 2001 to remind holders of **Safe Manning Certificates** issued under the MS (Safe Manning Document) Regulations 1992 (SI 1992/1564), and before the MS (Safe Manning, Hours of Work and Watchkeeping Regulations) 1997 came into force, that those Certificates would no longer be valid after 1 February 2002 and must be replaced before that date by Safe Manning Documents as described in the Notice[19][20]
* **MSN 1682**, which has been superseded by MSN 1767, detailed the requirements of and gave guidance on application of the Regulations. **Section 1** of MSN 1682 (on safe manning) was superseded by the **Guidance Notes to SOLAS regulation V/6** (Principles of Safe Manning) in the MCA's **2002 SOLAS V publication** and IMO Resolution A.890(21). **Sections 2 and 3** of MSN 1682 were superseded by Sections 2 and 3 of MSN 1767, respectively concerning safe manning and watchkeeping.
* **Section 2 of MSN 1767**, which concerns **safe manning**, contains paragraphs as follows: 12. Introduction; 13. Responsibilities of owners and operators: general principles; 14. Establishing safe manning requirements; 15. Guidance on appropriate manning levels; 16. Nationality restrictions; 17. Consultation on safe manning levels; 18. Safe Manning Document; 19. Application for Safe Manning Document; and 20. Approval of a Safe Manning Document by the MCA. **Tables** in Annex C show guidance on appropriate manning levels in respect of deck officers and engineer officers.

E03b.3a Principles of safe manning

* The **MCA will consider a ship to be safely manned** if the crew includes sufficient officers and ratings with appropriate **skills and experience** to ensure that Principles of Safe Manning can be followed. These Principles, which are contained in the Annex to IMO resolution A.890(21), should be consulted by companies and others when determining safe manning levels.
* The Annex to **resolution A.890(21)**, which is printed in Annex 6 to the MCA's 2002 SOLAS V publication, contains the following principles:
  1. the capability to:

---

[19] MIN 115 refers in paragraph 2 to "Regulation 5(4) of the Merchant Shipping (Safe Manning Document) Regulations 1997", which regulations do not exist. It should have stated "Regulation 5(4) of the Merchant Shipping (Safe Manning, Hours of Work and Watchkeeping) Regulations 1997".
[20] Under regulation 5(4) a Safe Manning Document issued under the 1992 Regulations continued to be valid (if circumstances had not changed) until 1 February 2002. (The "Provisions for sailing short-handed" printed on its reverse side were not valid, however, in view of the revocation of the Regulations under which they were made.)

- • maintain **safe navigational, engineering and radio watches** in accordance with regulation VIII/2 of the 1978 STCW Convention, as amended, and also maintain general surveillance of the ship;
- • **moor and unmoor** the ship safely;
- • manage the **safety functions** of the ship when employed in a **stationary or near-stationary mode** at sea;
- • perform operations, as appropriate, for the **prevention of damage to the environment**;
- • maintain the **safety arrangements and the cleanliness of all accessible spaces** to minimise the risk of fire;
- • provide for **medical care** on board ship;
- • ensure **safe carriage of cargo** during transit; and
- • inspect and maintain, as appropriate, the **structural integrity** of the ship.

2. the ability to:

- • operate all **watertight closing arrangements** and maintain them in effective condition, and also deploy a competent **damage control party**;
- • operate all on-board **fire-fighting and emergency equipment and life-saving appliances**, carry out such maintenance of this equipment as is required to be done at sea, and **muster and disembark** all persons on board; and
- • operate the **main propulsion and auxiliary machinery** and maintain them in a safe condition to enable the ship to overcome the foreseeable perils of the voyage.

* **Guidelines** for the application of Principles of Safe Manning are contained in Annex 6 to the MCA's 2002 SOLAS V publication.

E03b.3b Establishing safe manning requirements

* All ships must be **sufficiently and efficiently manned** for their safe operation, having regard to the nature of their **work** and their **location**. This means that an anchor-handling supply vessel, for example, may need a larger crew when operating in the North Sea than in other, less hostile waters, and that when engaged in anchor-handling work she will need more hands than when engaged in "straight supply" operations.

* **General principles** to be applied by owners and operators are described in **paragraph 13** of MSN 1767. **Paragraph 14** details **specific factors** to be taken into account in determining the safe manning level, and includes all factors listed in the IMO Principles of Safe Manning.

E03b.3c Guidance on appropriate manning levels

* **Annex C of MSN 1767** contains guidance tables showing **appropriate manning levels**, as follows.

Trading area	Size of ship (gt)	Number of certificated deck officers to be carried			
		STCW Reg. II/2 - Master	STCW Reg. II/2 – Chief Mate	STCW Reg. II/I - OOW	STCW Reg. II/3 - OOW
Unlimited	3000 or more	1	1	2	-
Unlimited	500 or more but less than 3000	1	1	1	-
Unlimited	Less than 500	1	-	2(a)	-
Near-coastal	3000 or more	1	1	1	-
Near-coastal	500 or more but less than 3000	1	1	1(b)	-
Near-coastal	Less than 500	-	-	-	2(c)

In the table above:
(a)   May be 1 if the master keeps watch.
(b)   Need not be carried if the master keeps watch.
(c)   One of these II/3 certificates must have an endorsement for the capacity of master.

Trading area	Registered power (kW)	Engineer Officers requirements			
		Chief Engineer	Second Engineer	Engineer OOW	Total
Unlimited	3000 or more	C/E III/2 Unlimited	2/E III/2 Unlimited	1 x III/1	3
Unlimited	750 or more but less than 3000	C/E III/3 <3000kW	2/E III/3 <3000kW	1 x III/1	3
Unlimited	350 or more but less than 750	2/E III/3 <3000kW	MEOL (a)	-	2
Near-coastal	6000 or more	C/E III/2 Unlimited	2/E III/2 Unlimited	-	2
Near-coastal	3000 or more but less than 6000	C/E III/2 <6000 kW NC	2/E III/2 <6000 kW NC	-	2
Near-coastal	750 or more but less than 3000	C/E III/3 <3000 kW NC	2/E III/3 <3000 kW NC	-	2
Near-coastal	350 or more but less than 750	SMEOL	-	-	1

The table above assumes that the ship is classed for UMS.
In the table above:
(a)   The holder may serve in a dual capacity, deck and engine room, provided that the ship is not a tanker and the deck service is not as an essential watchkeeper or master.

Notes:
(i)   All engine room watch ratings must hold Watch Rating Certificates (STCW III/4 certification) issued by MCA-approved companies, except on vessels of less than 750kW.
(ii)   The manning levels are subject to meeting the requirements of section 1 of MSN 1767.
(iii)   The following factors will be considered in varying the requirements in the above table:
   • Restriction of the vessel's area of operation;
   • The trading pattern of the vessel;
   • The complexity of the machinery spaces;
   • The vessel not operating under UMS conditions;
   • Technical complexity of the machinery including its control and monitoring systems;
   • Redundancy of the essential machinery;
   • The maintenance regime employed in the upkeep of the machinery and its control systems;
   • The level and availability of technical shore support.

E03b.3d Grades of seafarer listed in Safe Manning Documents

* Seafarers are graded according to their training, qualifications and experience. The Safe Manning, Hours of Work and Watchkeeping Regulations require owners to ensure that their manning arrangements provide a good balance of **experience** and **skill** within the crew as a whole. Various grades of seafarer are listed in paragraph 3 of MGN 97 to assist in achieving that aim[21].

* **MGN 97** lists the following grades of rating:
   • **Trainee Rating (Deck or Engine Department)** (paragraph 3.2);
   • **Deck Rating Grade 2** (paragraph 3.3.1);
   • **Deck Rating Grade 1** (paragraph 3.3.2);
   • **AB Certificate** (paragraph 3.4);
   • **Efficient Deck Hand** (paragraph 3.5);
   • **Engine-Room Rating** (paragraph 3.6.1);
   • **GP Rating Grade 2** (paragraph 3.7.2);
   • **GP Rating Grade 1** (paragraph 3.7.3).

* For notes on requirements for service as a **Trainee Rating (Deck or Engine Department)**, see E02c.10c.
* For notes on requirements for service as a **Deck Rating Grade 2**, see E02c.10d.
* For notes on requirements for service as a **Deck Rating Grade 1**, see E02c.10d.
* For notes on requirements to gain an **AB Certificate**, see E02c.10e.
* For notes on requirements to gain an **EDH Certificate**, see E02c.10f.
* For notes on requirements for service as a **Engine-Room Rating**, see E02c.10g.
* For notes on requirements for service as a **GP Rating Grade 1 or 2**, see E02c.10h.
* For notes on requirements to gain **Watch Rating Certificates**, see E02c.10i.

* **Personnel listed in standard STCW 95 Safe Manning Documents** issued by the MCA are categorised by the following grades:
   • Master;
   • Chief Mate;
   • OOW (Deck);
   • Deck Rating Grade 1;
   • Deck Rating Grade 2;
   • Chief Engineer;
   • 2nd Engineer;
   • OOW (Engine);
   • Engine Rating Grade 1;
   • Engine Rating Grade 2;
   • Doctor;
   • Cook;
   • Other.

E03b.4 Watchkeeping arrangements (regulation 11)

* **Regulation 11** of the MS (Safe Manning, Hours of Work and Watchkeeping) Regulations 1997 provides that the **master** of any ship must ensure that the **watchkeeping arrangements** for the ship are at all times **adequate for**

---

[21] The grades of rating shown in Safe Manning Documents issued by the MCA vary slightly from the gradings shown in MGN 97.

maintaining safe navigational and engineering watches having regard to chapter VIII of section A of the STCW Code (Standards regarding watchkeeping).

* The master must give **directions** to the deck watchkeeping officers responsible for navigating the ship safely during their periods of duty, in accordance with Part 3-1 of section A VIII/2 of the STCW Code and any requirements of the MCA.

* The **chief engineer** of any ship must ensure that the **engineering watchkeeping arrangements** for the ship are at all times **adequate for maintaining a safe watch**, in accordance with Part 3-2of section A VIII/2 of the STCW Code, and when deciding the composition of the watch the chief engineer must observe the principles set out in Part 3-2 of that section and any requirements of the MCA.

* For notes on **watchkeeping arrangements in port** (which are the subject of regulation 12) and watchkeeping arrangements in port for ships carrying hazardous cargo (which are the subject of regulation 13), see I05h.

* **Section 3 of MSN 1767** contains guidance on watchkeeping.

E03c HOURS OF WORK REGULATIONS

E03c.1 Hours of Work Regulations

* The **MS (Hours of Work) Regulations 2002** (SI 2002/2125) -
  - **came into force** on 7 September 2002.
  - **implement** the majority of the provisions of Council Directive 1999/63/EC concerning the European Working Time Agreement (see E03c.2) and Directive 1999/95/EC concerning the enforcement of provisions in respect of seafarers' hours of work on board ships calling at Community ports.
  - **revoke and replace** the hours of work provisions contained in regulations 6 to 10 of the MS (Safe Manning, Hours of Work and Watchkeeping) Regulations 1997 (SI 1997/1320) (see E03b.1).
  - **contain** regulations and schedules numbered as follows: 1. Citation and commencement; 2. Interpretation; 3. Application; 4. General duty of company, person employing a seafarer, master; 5. Minimum hours of rest; 6. Minimum hours of rest: further provision; 7. Posting-up of table; 8. Exception for emergencies; 9. Records; 10; Working at night; 11. Power to require information; 12. Entitlement to annual leave; 13. Entitlements under other provisions; 14. Inspection and detention of a United Kingdom ship; 15. Inspections of ships of other member States; 16. Rectification of deficiencies; 17. Enforcement of detention; 18. Arbitration and compensation; 19. Release of information; 20. Penalties; 21.Miscellaneous amendments; Schedule 1. Workforce agreements; Schedule 2. Miscellaneous amendments.
  - **apply** to **sea-going UK ships** other than fishing vessels, pleasure vessels, offshore installations while on their working stations and tugs which ordinarily do not go beyond category A, B, C or D waters, wherever they may be (regulation 3). Regulations 15 and 16 apply to such sea-going ships of other EU member States when they are in UK ports or waters.
  - **do not apply** to any seafarer who is subject to any requirement contained in the Working Time Regulations 1998 (SI 1998/1833), as amended by SIs 1999/3432, 1999/3372 and 2001/3256.
  - **permit** the detention of UK ships where there is a breach of regulations 4, 7 and 9.

* **Section 1 of MSN 1767** contains detailed requirements relating to hours of work. Paragraph 2.2.2 states that the Regulations will not be taken (by the MCA) to apply to those whose normal place of work is ashore but who are working on a seagoing ship on a temporary or short term basis, e.g. fitters, guest lecturers and entertainers, research scientists, riding crews, trainees and volunteers on sail training ships who are not carrying out safety-critical roles, provided such workers are covered by the requirements of the Working Time Regulations 1998 (SI 1998/1833).

E03c.1a General duty of company, person employing a seafarer, master (regulation 4)

* Subject to regulation 8, it is the duty of a **company**, an **employer** of a seafarer and a **master** of a ship to ensure that a seafarer is provided with **at least the minimum hours of rest**.

E03c.1b Minimum hours of rest (regulations 5 and 6)

* Regulation 5(1) provides that, subject to regulation 6, the **minimum hours of rest** must be not less than:
  * **10 hours** in any **24-hour period**; and
  * **77 hours** in any **7-day period**.
* Subject to regulation 6, **hours of rest may be divided** into no more than **two periods**, one of which shall be at least **6 hours** in length, and the interval between consecutive such periods shall not exceed 14 hours (regulation 5(2)).

* Musters, fire-fighting drills and lifeboat drills prescribed by the MS (Musters, Training and Decision Support Systems) Regulations 1999 (see E08l.1) must be conducted in a manner which minimises the disturbance of rest periods and does not induce fatigue (regulation 5(3)).
* A seafarer who is on call on board ship shall have an **adequate compensatory rest period** if his normal period of rest is disturbed by call-outs to work (regulation 5(4)).
* Nothing in regulation 5 will restrict the operation of regulation 6 of the MS and FV (Health and Safety at Work) (Employment of Young Persons) Regulations 1998 (see E03c.4 and E05c.1) (regulation 5(5)).
* Regulation 6(1) permits the MCA to authorise a **collective agreement or workforce agreement** permitting exceptions to the limits in regulations 5(1) and (2). Such exceptions may take account of more frequent or longer leave periods, or the granting of compensatory leave for watchkeeping seafarers or seafarers working on board ship on short voyages (regulation 6(2)).

E03c.1c Posting-up of table of scheduled hours of work and rest (regulation 7)

* The **master** of a ship, or a **person authorised** by the master, must ensure that a **table of scheduled hours of rest** complying with regulation 7(2) is **posted-up in a prominent and easily accessible place** in the ship (regulation 7(1)). The table must contain the information specified in **MSN 1767**, must be in the format specified in MSN 1767 (or in a format substantially like it), and must be in **English** and in the **working language** of the ship if that is not English (regulation 7(2)).
* Paragraph 5 of **MSN 1767** contains detailed requirements relating to the **posting up of the table of duties** and a specimen **table of shipboard working arrangements** is shown in Annex A(i) of the MSN. This table shows, for each seafarer:
  * position/rank;
  * scheduled daily work hours at sea;
  * scheduled daily work hours in port;
  * comments; and
  * total daily rest hours.

E03c.1d Exception for emergencies (regulation 8)

* The master of a ship may require a seafarer to work **any hours of work necessary for the immediate safety of the ship, persons on board ship or cargo** or for the purpose of **giving assistance to another ship or to a person in distress** at sea (regulation 8(1)).
* For the purposes of regulation 8(1), the master may **suspend** the hours of rest scheduled in the table under regulation 7 and require a seafarer to perform any hours of work necessary until the normal situation has been restored (regulation 8(2)).
* As soon as practicable after the normal situation has been restored the master must ensure that any **seafarer who has performed work in hours of rest** scheduled in the table under regulation 7 is provided with an **adequate rest period** (regulation 8(3)).

E03c.1e Records of daily hours of rest (regulation 9)

* A **record of a seafarer's daily hours of rest** must be maintained by the master or a person authorised by the master (regulation 9(1)). The procedures for keeping such records (including the intervals at which the information is to be recorded) and the format of such records must comply with the requirements specified in **MSN 1767** (regulation 9(2)). A record must be in English and in the working language of the ship if that is not English (regulation 9(3)).
* The record kept under regulation 9(1) must be **endorsed** by the master or a person authorised by the master, and by the seafarer in question, and a **copy** of the record as endorsed must be given to the seafarer by the master or the person authorised by the master (regulation 9(4)).
* The company and the master must ensure that a **copy of the Hours of Work Regulations** (including any relevant Merchant Shipping Notices) and **any collective agreements or workforce agreements** relevant to the ship which are authorised under regulation 6 are **carried at all times** on board the ship in an easily accessible place (regulation 9(5)).
* Regulation 9(6) provides that "the relevant inspector" must **examine and endorse**, at appropriate intervals, records kept under regulation 9(1). A "relevant inspector" is a person mentioned in paragraphs (a), (b) or (c) of section 258(1) of the Merchant Shipping Act 1995, who will, in practice, be an MCA surveyor of ships. Regulation 14(1) provides powers for a relevant inspector to inspect any UK ship and detain the ship if he is satisfied that there has been a failure to comply in relation to that ship with any of the requirements of regulations 4, 7 and 9.
* Paragraph 7 of **MSN 1767** gives detailed **requirements relating to records**, and a **specimen record of hours of rest** is shown at Annex B(i) of the MSN.

E03c.1f Working at night (regulation 10)

* Subject to regulation 10(2), **no seafarer under the age of 18 may work at night** (regulation 10(1)). "Night" means a period the duration of which is not less than nine consecutive hours and which includes the period between midnight and 5 a.m. (local time) (regulation 10(3)).
* Regulation 10(2) provides that a seafarer of the age of 16 or 17 may work at night if the work forms part of an established programme of training the effectiveness of which would be impaired by the prohibition in regulation 10(1).

E03c.1g Entitlement to annual leave (regulation 12)

* A seafarer is entitled to **paid annual leave of at least four weeks**, or a proportion of four weeks in respect of a period of employment of less than one year (regulation 12(1)).
* Leave to which a seafarer is entitled under regulation 12 may be taken in instalments (regulation 12 (2)(a) but may not be replaced by a payment in lieu, except where the seafarer's employment is terminated (regulation 12(2)(b)).

E03c.1h Entitlements under other provisions (regulation 13)

* Where during any period a seafarer is entitled to hours of rest or annual leave both under a provision of the MS (Hours of Work) Regulations and under a separate provision (including a provision of his contract), **he may not exercise the two rights separately**, but may, in taking hours of rest or annual leave during that period, take advantage of whichever right is, in any particular respect, the more favourable.

E03c.2 European Working Time Agreement

* **Council Directive 1999/63/EC** of 21 June 1999 concerning the Agreement on the organisation of working time of seafarers concluded by the European Community Shipowners' Association (ECSA) and the Federation of Transport Workers' Unions in the European Union (FST) is known as the **Maritime Working Time Directive**, and contains in its Annex the **European Agreement on the organisation of working time of seafarers**, commonly known as the "**European Working Time Agreement**".
* Under the European Working Time Agreement, the **limits on hours of work or rest are**, at the discretion of the adopting Member State[22], either:
  * **maximum hours of work** which shall not exceed:
    * 14 hours in any 24-hour period; and
    * 72 hours in any 7-day period; or
  * **minimum hours of rest** which shall not be less than:
    * 10 hours in any 24-hour period; and
    * 77 hours in any 7-day period.
* **Hours of rest** may be divided into no more than two periods, one of which must be at least 6 hours in length and the interval between consecutive periods of rest must not exceed 14 hours.
* The majority of the provisions of the above Directives are implemented by the MS (Hours of Work) Regulations 2002 (SI 2002/2125) (see E03c.1).
* **MGN 211** reminds owners and operators of their responsibility for ensuring that masters and crews are adequately rested to perform their duties safely. It is relevant to seafarers on both seagoing and non-seagoing ships and follows up a specific recommendation of the *Marchioness* Formal Investigation. It also draws attention to Guidance on Fatigue Mitigation and Management issued by IMO. MGN 211 refers to the Maritime Working Time Directive, outlined above, and two other Directives: Directive 1999/95/EC on the enforcement of working time restrictions on ships, and Directive 93/104/EC as amended by Directive 2000/34/EC.

E03c.3 ILO Convention 180

* **ILO Convention (No.180) concerning Seafarers' Hours of Work and the Manning of Ships, 1996**, was adopted on 22 October 1996, was ratified by the UK in December 2001 and came into force on 8 August 2002.
* Article 5 of the Convention imposes **limits on hours of work or rest** that are the same as those in the European Working Time Agreement (see E03c.2).

---

[22] The UK has chosen the **minimum hours of rest** option and applied this in the Hours of Work Regulations (see E03c.1).

* The requirements of Convention 180 are reflected in Directive 1999/63/EC, which is applied by Directive 1999/95/EC.

E03c.4 Rest periods of young persons

* **Regulation 6** of the **MS and FV (Health and Safety at Work) (Employment of Young Persons) Regulations 1998** (SI 1998/2411) (see E05c.1) provides that where a **young person** (i.e. a person under the age of 18, but see definition in E05c.1) is engaged as a worker on any ship, he must be provided with:
  * a rest period of at least 12 consecutive hours in every 24-hour period; and
  * a rest period of at least 2 days, which must be consecutive if possible, in every week.
* Where a young person's daily working time is more than four and a half hours, he must be provided with a rest break of at least 30 minutes, which must be consecutive if possible.
* Time spent on training by a young person, whether under a theoretical or practical or combined theoretical and practical work training scheme, is to be counted as working time.
* Where a young person is engaged as a worker by more than one employer, working days and working hours are to be cumulative.
* The minimum daily rest period of at least 12 hours in every 24-hour period may be interrupted in the case of activities involving periods of work that are split up over the day or of short duration.
* The minimum weekly rest period of at least 2 days –
  * may be interrupted in the case of activities involving periods of work that are split up over the day or of short duration; and
  * may be reduced to a period which is not less than 36 hours where this is justified by **technical or organisational reasons**.
* Where the hours of work of a young person are subject to a schedule of duties complying with regulation 9 of the MS (Safe Manning, Hours of Work and Watchkeeping) Regulations 1997 (which provision is now removed from the Regulations – see E03c.1), the minimum rest periods stated above do not apply, provided that -
  * the young persons are allowed compensatory rest time; and
  * measures are taken to ensure that there is no risk to their health and safety, by reason of their hours of work.
* Where the preceding paragraph above does not apply, young persons may be permitted to work during their weekly rest periods, provided that –
  - such hours are provided for in a relevant agreement;
  - they are allowed compensatory rest time; and
  - measures are taken to ensure that there is no risk to their health and safety.
* The Company (i.e. shipowner or other organisation, e.g. manager or charterer, assuming operational responsibility from the owner) must ensure that the duties placed on the employer or other person in control of the matter are complied with.
* **Guidance** on application of the Regulations is in **MGN 88**.

E03c.5 Hours of work and manning on domestic passenger ships

* The statutory provisions relating to the **hours of work of the master of a domestic passenger ship** (and minimum manning levels of such ships) are contained in the **MS (Local Passenger Vessels) (Master's Licences and Hours, Manning and Training) Regulations 1993** (SI 1993/1213). The Regulations apply only to the master of the ship.
* For notes on the Regulations, see E02d.1.

E03d MISCELLANEOUS PROVISIONS CONCERING MANNING

E03d.1 Nationality and language of master and crew

E03d.1a Officer Nationality Regulations

* The **MS (Officer Nationality) Regulations 1995** (SI 1995/1427) replace the nationality restrictions in section 5 of the Aliens Restriction (Amendment) Act, 1919 (which is now repealed), under which no alien could act as master, chief officer or chief engineer of a merchant ship registered in the UK except in the case of a ship or boat employed habitually in voyages between ports outside the UK.

* **Regulation 3** provides that the **master** of every "**strategic ship**" must be:
  * a **Commonwealth** citizen; or
  * an **EEA** national; or
  * a national of a State (other than an EEA State) which is a member of **NATO**.
* A "**strategic ship**" is defined in regulation 2 as:
  * a British registered fishing vessel of 24 metres or more in length; or
  * a UK ship of 500gt or more which is a cruise ship, a product tanker, or a ro-ro ship[23].

E03d.1b Nationality of ratings

* There are **no statutory restrictions on the nationality of ratings** on UK ships, provided that they hold the certificates required under or recognised by UK regulations.
* For notes on training and certification requirements relating to ratings, see Part 10 of the Training and Certification Guidance and related notes in E02c.10.

E03d.1c Crew's knowledge of English

* **Under section 51(1) of the Merchant Shipping Act 1995**, where in the opinion of a superintendent or proper officer the crew of a sea-going UK ship consists of or includes persons who **may not understand orders** given to them in the course of their duty because of their **insufficient knowledge of English** and the absence of adequate arrangements for transmitting the orders in a language of which they have sufficient knowledge, then:
  * if the superintendent or proper officer **has informed the master** of that opinion, the ship must not go to sea; and
  * if the ship is in the UK, it may be **detained**.
* The **MS (Minimum Standards of Safety Communications) Regulations 1997** (SI 1997/529) make various requirements relating to **language used on board** and in **ship-to-shore communications** (see D03a.4).

E03d.2 Trading areas under STCW 95

* **STCW regulation I/3** contains **Principles governing near-coastal voyages**. "**Near-coastal voyages**" means "voyages in the vicinity of a Party as defined by that Party" (STCW regulation I/1.13). It is thus for each Party to the Convention, so long as they communicate their definitions to IMO in accordance with regulation I/7. Section A-I/3, which has the same title as regulation I/3, contains no mandatory provisions. Section B-I/3 contains **Guidance regarding near-coastal voyages** and contains a list of factors that should be taken account of by Parties defining "near-coastal voyages". An STCW Party which includes voyages off another Party's coast within the limits of its "near-coastal voyage" definition may enter into a bilateral agreement with the (other) Party concerned. It is not intended that ships engaged on near-coastal voyages should extend their voyages world-wide, under the excuse that they are navigating constantly within limits of designated near-coastal voyages of neighbouring Parties.
* Trading areas specified in UK Safe Manning Documents in force from 1 February 2002 are "**Unlimited**" and "**Near-coastal**". For a definition of the **UK Near-Coastal area**, see E02c.1. The area beyond the UK "Near-Coastal" area is the "**Unlimited**" area (see also E02c.1).

E03d.3 Radio personnel on GMDSS ships

* **Part II of the MS (Radio Installations) Regulations 1998** (SI 1998/2070), regulation 19, contains the requirements for **radio personnel in GMDSS ships** (i.e. ships fitted with GMDSS equipment).
* **Every GMDSS ship** must carry a person or persons qualified for distress and safety radio communication purposes as specified in paragraph (3) or (4) (as appropriate) of regulation 19. Such person or persons must be holders of certificates specified in the ITU Radio Regulations as appropriate (regulation 19(1)).
* In the case of **GMDSS passenger ships**, at least one person as mentioned in regulation 19(1) must be assigned by the master to perform **only radio communication duties during distress incidents** (regulation 19(2)(a)). In the

---

[23] Annex 3 of MGN 179 (which deals with Certificates of Equivalent Competency) defines "strategic vessels" rather differently (and inaccurately) as "(a) fishing vessels over 24 metres in length; (b) other British ships of 500 GT or more which are passenger ships with a Class 1 passenger vessel certificate certified to carry more than 200 passengers; (c) ro-ro vessels, i.e. ships provided with cargo or vehicle spaces in which cargo or vehicles can be loaded and unloaded in a horizontal direction; or (d) product tankers, i.e. namely oil tankers constructed for the carriage of petroleum products in bulk or chemical tankers constructed for the carriage in bulk of any liquid chemical".

case of **all other GMDSS ships**, one person as mentioned in regulation 19(1) must be designated by the master **to have primary responsibility for radio communications** during distress incidents (regulation 19(2)(b)).

* On **area A1 ships** the person qualified as mentioned in regulation 19(1) above must hold at least a **GMDSS restricted operator's certificate** issued in accordance with subsection D of Section IIIA of Article 55 of the Radio Regulations (regulation 19(3)).
* On **area A2, area A3 and area A4 ships** the person qualified as mentioned in regulation 19(1) above must hold at least a **GMDSS general operator's certificate** issued in accordance with sub-section C of Section IIIA of Article 55 of the Radio Regulations, or equivalent (regulation 19(4)).

E03d.4 Ships' Doctors Regulations

* The **MS (Ships' Doctors) Regulations 1995** (SI 1995/1803) implement Council Directive 92/29/EEC on the minimum safety and health requirements for improved medical treatment on board vessels, so far as that Directive requires the carriage of doctors.
* **Under regulation 3** where a UK ship with **more than 100 persons**[24] on board, is engaged on an **international voyage of more than 3 days** or is on a voyage during which the ship is **more than one and a half days' sailing time from a port with "adequate medical equipment"**, the owner must ensure that the ship carries a qualified doctor. "Qualified doctor" is defined in regulation 2(1) as a fully registered person within the meaning of section 55 of the Medical Act 1983 (c.54).
* **M.1627** advises that there is no longer any provision for the granting of exemptions from any requirement of the Regulations.

E03d.5 Certification of Ships' Cooks Regulations

* The **MS (Certification of Ships' Cooks) Regulations 1981** (SI 1981/1076) -
  - require **UK ships of 1,000gt or over**, other than pleasure craft or fishing vessels, which go to sea beyond the Near Continental trading area[25] and which carry a crew, the majority of whom are **domiciled in the UK**, to carry a **qualified and certificated ship's cook** (regulation 2).
  - prescribe the requirements for **qualification and certification as a ship's cook** (see E02d.3 and **M.1482**).

E03d.6 Sailing short-handed

* **Regulation 17 of the MS (Certification of Deck Officers) Regulations 1985** (which were revoked by the MS (Training and Certification) Regulations 1997) set out the **exceptional provisions** whereby a ship could proceed to sea with one qualified deck officer less than the number prescribed by the Regulations. Similar provisions were contained in regulation 19 to permit sailing when short of one qualified marine engineer officer or one licensed marine engine operator.
* The MS (Safe Manning, Hours of Work and Watchkeeping) Regulations 1997 contain **no equivalent provision permitting sailing short-handed**. Regulation 5(2) provides that the **master** must ensure that the **ship does not proceed to sea without a valid Safe Manning Document** and that the ship's **manning complies with the Safe Manning Document** (see E03b.3). Only where the conditions endorsed on a Safe Manning Document permit any reduction in manning at specified times (e.g. in the possible case of a dynamically-positioned vessel on her working location in DP mode), may there be any reduction from the minimum personnel numbers stated on the face of the Safe Manning Document.
* For notes on the **effect of a crew member's death on safe manning** of a ship, see E14e.

E03d.7 Prohibition of going to sea undermanned

* Subject to any exemption granted by the MCA under section 48, it is an offence under section 49 of the Merchant Shipping Act 1995 for a sea-going UK ship to go to sea or attempt to go to sea without carrying such officers and other seamen as it is required to carry under section 47, and the owner or master will be liable to a penalty. If the ship is in the UK it may be detained.

---

[24] Under Merchant Shipping Act 1894 the criterion was "a foreign-going ship with **100 persons or more** on board".

[25] No longer recognised under STCW 95, and replaced by the "Near Coastal Area" (see E02c.1 and E03d.2).

* Undermanning is also reason by virtue of which, under section 98 the Merchant Shipping Act 1995 a ship may be rendered "**dangerously unsafe**" (see I02d).

E03d.8 Non-statutory manning

* Safe Manning Documents issued by the MCA show only those grades of seafarer required to be carried in the interests of **safety** (see E03b.3d). In addition to the requirement for these personnel, there may be a contractual agreement made between employers and seafarers' organisations for the carriage of additional ranks or ratings, e.g. pursers, chefs, shop and bank staff, especially in passenger ships. Where the relevant agreements are incorporated by reference into the Crew Agreement, there is a **contractual obligation on** the master and owner to ensure that these persons are, in fact, carried on board.

E03d.9 Unqualified persons going to sea as qualified officers or ratings

* If a person goes to sea as a qualified officer or seaman of any description **without being such a qualified officer or seaman** he will be liable on summary conviction to a fine of the statutory maximum, or on conviction on indictment, to a fine (section 52 Merchant Shipping Act 1995)[26].
* The validity of any document issued by the MCA or the RSS (e.g. UK Certificates of Competency, Certificates of Equivalent Competency and Discharge Books) may be checked with the RSS.

E03d.10 Ship security officer

* ISPS Code, part A, section 12 provides that -
   1. A **ship security officer** (SSO) must be designated on each ship and must be identified in the Ship Security Plan.
   2. The ship security officer must have **knowledge** and have received **training** in all aspects of security involving the ship.
   3. The **duties and responsibilities** of the ship security officer include, but are not limited to:
      * undertaking regular **security inspections** of the ship to ensure that appropriate security measures are maintained;
      * **maintaining and supervising** the implementation of the **Ship Security Plan**, including any amendments to the plan;
      * **co-ordinating** the security aspects of handling cargo and ship's stores with other shipboard personnel and with port facility security officers;
      * **proposing** modifications to the Ship Security Plan;
      * **reporting** to the company security officer (CSO) any deficiencies and non-conformities identified during internal audits, periodic reviews, security inspections and verifications of compliance and implementing any corrective actions;
      * enhancing **security awareness and vigilance** on board;
      * ensuring that adequate **security training** has been provided to shipboard personnel;
      * **reporting all security incidents** to the company security officer ;
      * **co-ordinating implementation** of the Ship Security Plan with the company security officer and the port facility security officer (PFSO);
      * ensuring that **security equipment** is properly operated, tested, calibrated and maintained, if any; and
      * **completing the Declaration of Security** on behalf of the ship.
* **Ship security officer** is defined in the ISPS Code, part A, section 2, as "the person on board the ship, accountable to the master, designated by the Company as responsible for the security of the ship, including implementation and maintenance of the Ship Security Plan and for liaison with the company security officer and port facility security officers".
* ISPS Code, part A, section 6.2 provides that the Company must ensure that the company security officer , the master and the ship security officer are given the **necessary support to fulfil their duties and responsibilities** in accordance with Chapter XI-2 of SOLAS and Part A of the ISPS Code.

---

[26] M.1067, which has been withdrawn, told of a seaman who, in the early 1980s, was convicted at Liverpool Magistrates Court, under section 16 of the Theft Act 1968, of fraudulently obtaining employment. He had claimed to be the holder of a Certificate of Competency as Master (Foreign Going) when, in fact, his only qualification was as Efficient Deck Hand. He had gained employment as master of two British vessels and attempted to gain employment on a third. One of these vessels stranded and his employment on the other "caused extreme financial difficulties for the owners". He was also known to have sailed as chief officer on at least two foreign vessels, one of which was a 130,000GRT tanker.

* ISPS Code, part A, section 13 provides that the **ship security officer** must have **knowledge** and have received **training**, taking into account the guidance given in part B of the ISPS Code (section 13.2).
* ISPS Code, part B, section 4 provides that the **company security officer or the ship security officer** should **liaise** at the earliest opportunity with the **port facility security officer** of the port facility the ship is intended to visit **to establish the security level** applying for that ship at the port facility (section 4.11).
* For notes on the **Ship Security Plan**, see D04t.10a.
* For notes on the **company security officer**, see C03c.8a.
* For notes on the **port facility security officer**, see I01k.1.

E04 The master

E04a DEFINITION OF SHIPMASTER, MASTER AND SEAMAN

* A "**shipmaster**" has been defined by the Nautical Institute[27] as "the captain of a merchant ship qualified by the appropriate certificate of competency who is appointed by the shipowner. He has the responsibility to efficiently prosecute the voyage and an overriding responsibility to ensure the safety of his passengers, crew, ship and cargo with the duty generally to save and preserve life at sea. In the event of his death or incapacity command descends to the second-in-command who is the senior deck officer and then through the other deck officers in order of rank".
* **Section 313(1) of the Merchant Shipping Act 1995** provides that, in the Act, unless the context otherwise requires, the term "**master**" includes every person (except a pilot) having command or charge of a ship, and provides that the term "**seaman**" includes every person (except masters and pilots) employed or engaged in any capacity on board any ship. In the application and interpretation of UK merchant shipping legislation, the legal distinction in section 313 between "master" and "seaman" is important.

E04b MASTER'S CONTRACT OF EMPLOYMENT

* The **master's contract of employment** may be contained in:
  * his **company service contract**, if any;
  * his **joining instructions**;
  * **pre-voyage interviews** or **briefings** from superintendents, personnel officers, managers, Designated Person, etc. (whether face-to-face or over the telephone);
  * **company's standing instructions** to masters; and
  * the **traditional practice** (or custom) of masters in the company.
* The master's contract of employment is thus quite **separate and different** from the contract made by the employer with the "seamen" (i.e. crew members, including officers), as expressed in the terms of the Crew Agreement document (on form ALC1(d) in a UK ship). Under the MS (Crew Agreements, Lists of Crew and Discharge of Seamen) Regulations (see E07b) the master is not a "seaman" for the purposes of Part I and therefore **should not "sign on" on the ALC1(a)** along with those seamen who are party to the Crew Agreement.
* A master who signs the ALC1(d) as the **employer's representative** and also "signs on" on the ALC1(a) as a "**seaman who is party to the agreement**" has signed both sides of a contract of employment. However, his exclusion from the term "seaman" (as defined in E04a) may mean that that contract will be void due to mistake.
* **Regulation 4 of part I of the MS (Crew Agreements, Lists of Crew and Discharge of Seamen) Regulations 1991** (SI 1991/2144) lists the categories of **seamen** to whom the requirements of section 1 of the Merchant Shipping Act 1970 relating to Crew Agreements will not apply. Masters are not amongst the categories listed, since they are not in any case "seamen" in terms of that Act.
* When joining ship, the **new master** should enter his particulars on **ALC1(b)** (including certificate and endorsement details at the foot of the page) along with personnel who are exempt from signing a Crew Agreement.

---

[27] The definition is listed in a Nautical Institute Council report prepared by the Nautical Institute Command Working Group and reprinted in Chapter 1 of *The Nautical Institute on Command – A Practical Guide*.

E04c TAKING OVER AND HANDING OVER COMMAND

E04c.1 Taking over command in normal circumstances

* A prudent master, **on arriving at his ship**, should:
  * have ready a **check list** of "things to do on joining";
  * note (from the quayside) the **condition of the visible exterior of the vessel**, including draught marks, load line, etc.;
  * note the **standard of rigging and maintenance of the accommodation ladder** or gangway, and its accessories[28];
  * note (on the way to the master's quarters) the **standard of maintenance of decks** and visible **life-saving appliances** and **fire-fighting equipment**;
  * **take delivery** from the off-going master of all **official documents** and sight same[29];
  * **make an Official Log Book entry** (entry number 4) (if not already made by the off-going master) recording **delivery of the documents** relating to the ship and its crew, and sign it jointly with the off-going master (see D05a.4);
  * **enter his name, certificate of competency type and number** in the boxes on the front cover of the Official Log Book (entry number 3);
  * **add his reference number** in the List of Crew (e.g. "E02"), name and capacity in which employed to the Record of Seamen Employed in the Ship inside the front cover of the OLB;
  * **enter his particulars on the List of Crew** form ALC1(b) (see E07c.2a)[30];
  * obtain the **combination number of the ship's safe** and all associated **keys** from the off-going master;
  * count all **monies** and sight all **accounts** and related documents[31] in the master's custody;
  * sight all **owners', managers', classification and P&I documentation** in the master's custody;
* **Before sailing**, the new master should:
  * receive **familiarisation training** in accordance with STCW 95 and MS (Training and Certification) Regulations[32] (see E02c.6a);
  * sight his personal **lifejacket** and ensure that he knows how to quickly don it in an emergency;
  * inspect the **muster list** and ensure that it is updated (see E08l.1b);
  * read the relevant clauses of the **charter party** or **bill of lading** (see F05 or F06, and F07b);
  * note any owner's or charterer's **voyage instructions** and/or side letters or addenda to the charter party;
  * consult the chief engineer on the **condition of the machinery** and the bunker **fuel** and lubricating oil situation, ensuring that any "safety surplus" of fuel required by the charter party to be carried is on board in addition to normal passage requirements;
  * consult the chief officer on the situation with **cargo**, **stability**, **ballast**, **fresh water**, **stores**, **maintenance of ship**, etc.;
  * examine the **passage plan**, if already made, for the next leg of the voyage, and consult appropriate officer;
  * check that all **required charts and nautical publications** are on board;
  * check that all **crew** are on board as required by the Safe Manning Document (see E03b.3);
  * check the ISM documentation for **outstanding non-conformities** (which may have a time limit for action) (see C04b.3);
  * read and, if necessary, write **standing orders**;
  * satisfy himself that he has personally exercised **due diligence in ensuring that the vessel is seaworthy** at the start of the voyage (see H01b.1);
  * make a **full inspection** of the ship as soon as practicable and, if possible, before taking the ship to sea.

E04c.2 Handing over command to a successor

* **Before relinquishing command** and leaving his ship, the master should:
  * ensure that he has signed each completed page of the **Oil Record Book(s)** (see D05b.2);

---

[28] The standard of the rigging and maintenance of a ship's accommodation ladder or gangway may give a first hint as to the general standard of operation of the ship.

[29] A check list of ship's documents should be kept on board. In the absence of a check list, see the list at D04a.

[30] The employer must be informed within 3 days of any change in the List of Crew (see E07b.3d).

[31] "Related documents" includes miscellaneous pieces of paper bearing obscure (but perhaps important) notes, e.g. "Cook - $32.50" , which may indicate a debt to the company or the master.

[32] Familiarisation training must be received by **all persons employed or engaged** on a seagoing ship other than passengers, etc.

- bring his **accounts** with owners or managers up to date (see E09d);
- count all **ship's money** in the master's custody;
- write **hand-over notes** for the succeeding master (see D05e.2);
- have all **documents** relating to the ship, crew, cargo, etc. in order for handing over to the succeeding master (see D05e);
- **make the hand-over in person**, if possible, to the succeeding master;
- make an entry in the narrative section of the Official Log Book (entry number 4) recording that he has **delivered to his successor the documents** relating to the ship or its crew which are in his custody, and sign this entry jointly with the succeeding master.

E04c.3 Succession to command in emergency

* The master's proper successor to command in emergency is the **senior surviving deck officer**.
* Should the appointed master be incapacitated or die whilst the ship is at sea, the next-in-command is legally entitled to take the ship to her **next port of call**; he does not have to make for the nearest port in order for another master to join unless so instructed by the owner or manager.
* Whether the temporary master (e.g. the former chief officer) may legally command the vessel on departure from a port of call will depend on:
    - whether he has the appropriate **STCW 95 master's qualification** required for the size and operating area of the vessel (see E02b.7);
    - whether the **safe manning provisions** of the Regulations will be complied with. The Safe Manning Document, including any attached conditions, should be checked and its requirements adhered to whenever the ship goes to sea (see E03b.3).
* A temporary master may be **confirmed** in his position by the employer. Written confirmation should, in this case, be obtained and retained for production to officials in ports (see E04d).

E04d PROOF OF APPOINTMENT AS MASTER

* The name of the first master of a British ship is no longer entered on the ship's Certificate of British Registry, and succeeding masters are no longer required to have their names endorsed on the back of the Certificate by a Registrar of British Ships.
* In order to avoid possible problems with immigration, port State and other officials, particularly at overseas ports, it would be prudent for a shipmaster joining a vessel to carry a **letter of appointment** to the command of the vessel, written on the company's notepaper and signed by a senior company official.
* In the **absence of a letter of appointment**, the details in the Official Log Book should suffice as proof of the master's position, and he should take the **Official Log Book** and his **passport** with him when visiting any British consul, port State official or notary public.

E04e MASTER'S LEGAL RELATIONSHIP WITH HIS EMPLOYER

* Like the rest of the crew, the master is a **servant of the employer**.
* The master is also the **employer's representative** on board.
* In certain circumstances the master is also the **agent of the employer**, and may act as such on his behalf.

E04e.1 Master as employer's servant

* As his employer's servant, the master must carry out the **employer's lawful instructions**, but is not bound to comply with any **unlawful** instructions, e.g. steaming (on the instructions of the owners) at an unsafe speed in fog in order to make a tide or particular arrival time, or discharging illegal quantities of pollutants into the sea.

E04e.2 Master as employer's representative

* The master may act as the **employer's representative** in various situations, e.g. when supervising the **engagement of crew**, or when **receiving gifts** from shippers, charterers, shipbuilders, etc. (Such gifts should always be given by the master to an appropriate company official; a receipt may be requested if desired.)
* Legally, the master may simultaneously have the capacity of an **agent**.

E04e.3 Master as employer's agent

* An "**agent**" is a person having express or implied authority to represent, or act on behalf of, another person (i.e. the principal) with the object of bringing the principal into legal relations with third parties.
* "**Agency**" is the relationship between the principal and his agent and is usually created by express provisions contained in the contract between them. For notes on the **law of agency**, see B03d.
* An agent has **implied authority** to do whatever is necessary for the performance of his contract. However, his authority cannot exceed that of his principal, i.e. if he acts beyond the limits of his authority, his principal will generally not be bound by any contract the agent makes.
* **In the absence of express instructions**, an agent must act according to **custom**. If there is no custom, he must exercise **proper discretion**.
* A shipmaster is the "**special agent**" of his employer whenever he deals with a third party on the employer's behalf (see B03d.3). As such, the master may only act **within the limit of his authority**. While a shipmaster had a great deal of authority before the days of fast communications and could often act as a **general agent** and carry out **all the normal business** of his owners, (e.g. making binding contracts for the carriage of goods and employment of crew, etc.), modern communications nowadays enable shipowners to **restrict the authority of their masters** to that of a "special agent".
* As a **special agent**, the master may only act **within his instructions**, whether these are express (i.e. oral or written) or implied into his contract (e.g. by the normal practice of the company's masters). E.g. the master may be required to sign bills of lading on behalf of the owner, and may have to enter into contracts on the owner's behalf, e.g. for the supply of stores or bunkers or pilotage services. (Generally, however, he will no longer have the power of a general agent to pledge the ship to raise money - termed "bottomry", as masters once did.)
* The master has authority, as an agent of the owners or managers, to **purchase stores and equipment reasonably necessary for the safe prosecution of the voyage**, and may charge the owners or managers for such purchases. The master will be **liable personally**, however, for the cost of any goods purchased **unreasonably or unnecessarily**.
* The owners are bound by every contract entered into by the master when acting as their agent **within the limit of his authority**. A third party with whom the master deals on behalf of the owners is **entitled to assume** that the master has his owners' authority as their agent.
* In cases of **general average** and, in certain circumstances, **salvage**, the master's authority is still sacrosanct (see B03d.3b and H05e.1).
* On the face of it, the master will always be responsible for **contracts made in his own name** and should ensure that it is clear to a contractor when he is acting **on behalf of another party**, e.g. his employer or a charterer. If, for example, the master fails to qualify his signature on a bill of lading with the words "as Agent for (Owners or Charterers, as the case may be)", the cargo owners may proceed against the **master in person**, although they will normally choose to proceed against his **principal** (i.e. the carrier or shipowner).
* With respect to the limits of his authority, a **prudent master** will:
  * always ensure that he has **authority to sign** documents;
  * always **qualify his signature**: "for and on behalf of ...…............. (Owner)" where the owner is concerned;
  * always **qualify his signature**: "for and on behalf of ...…........... (Charterer) as Agent only" where a charterer is concerned (e.g. when signing for bunker fuel received for a time charterer's account);
  * always **retain copies of any documents signed** as protection against later alteration of their originals; and
  * **never sign blank papers**.

E04f MASTER'S LEGAL RELATIONSHIP WITH THE CARGO OWNER

E04f.1 The master as bailee

* When cargo is delivered to a ship for carriage, the carrier becomes the **bailee** of the cargo owner and the master, as the carrier's servant, assumes the duties of a bailee.

* "**Bailment**" is the transfer goods by one person (a **bailor**) to another (a **bailee**) for a particular purpose, e.g. delivery of goods by a shipper to a carrier (for carriage by sea, etc.), delivery of goods to a freight forwarder (for forwarding to a carrier). In bailment there is a transfer of *possession* but not of *title*, i.e. the bailor remains the owner of the goods until title is passed to another person. The bailee is responsible for the safekeeping of the goods and must, when the purpose for which the goods are bailed has been fulfilled, either return them or deliver them as the bailor instructs. While there does not have to be a contract between bailor and bailee, there must be intention to create a bailment relationship, and most bailments are on contract terms (e.g. a carrier's terms and conditions). A contract for the carriage of goods by sea is, at the same time, a **contract of bailment**.
* Whenever a bill of lading is issued, the contract of carriage becomes a **contract of bailment**. Ownership of the goods remains with the bailor, who has the right to demand their return or give directions as to their delivery, etc. However, this right is qualified by any **lien** that the bailee has over the goods, e.g. a **carrier's lien** for unpaid freight.
* The master of a loaded cargo ship is, as a servant of the bailee, responsible for the care and proper delivery in good condition of his goods. The master has **no title** (i.e. legal right to ownership) in the goods. He may, however, have cause to **dispose** of the goods as an **agent of necessity** (see B03d.3b).

E04f.2 The master as agent of necessity

* For notes on the general law of **agency of necessity**, see B03d.3b.
* As an **agent of necessity**, the **master** of a vessel in peril:
  * will have **implied powers to act** in best interests of all owners of property in his care;
  * may take **special emergency measures to preserve the property in peril** or minimise any loss due to damage already suffered;
  * may **make a General Average sacrifice or expenditure**, e.g. have goods landed, transshipped, reconditioned or even sold, **without liability for misappropriation**;
  * may **deviate from the contract route** (although he would have to show very good reason for doing so);
  * may **enter into a salvage agreement** which may oblige the property owner to contribute to the salvor's award.
* Where property is owned by more than one owner (e.g. as in the case of a loaded general cargo ship), the master is the agent of necessity in respect of each of property owner.
* **Examples** of maritime situations where agency of necessity may arise are:
  * where a **salvage agreement must be urgently made by a master** (on behalf of the owners of cargo, cargo containers and freight at risk, as well as the shipowners) but there is insufficient time to contact the cargo owners for their instructions;
  * where a **carrier**, who has goods in his possession which are starting to deteriorate, and who is unable to contact the owner, takes action to preserve the goods; and
  * (perhaps) where a **shipmaster** of a vessel loading in a port which comes under military or terrorist attack, makes an **emergency departure** from the port to preserve cargo from destruction or capture.

E04g MASTER'S RESPONSIBILITIES

E04g.1 Master's chief responsibilities

* Chief amongst a shipmaster's numerous responsibilities are:
  * the preservation of the **safety** of the crew, any passengers and the ship;
  * the safeguarding of the **marine environment**;
  * to act as if ship and cargo were his own **uninsured property**;
  * the prosecution of the voyage with the **minimum of delay and expense**;
  * to always act in the **best interests of the shipowner**;
  * to carry out all that is **usual and necessary for the employment** of the vessel;
  * to **obey the owner's instructions** (except where they would mean breaching the law); and
  * to **exercise care of the goods** entrusted to him and see that everything necessary is done to preserve them from harm during the voyage (e.g. ensuring proper ventilation, bilges are pumped, temperatures monitored and controlled, etc.).

E04g.2 ISM Code requirement for definition of master's responsibilities

* See E04h.2.

E04g.3 Master's responsibility for safety and maintenance of ship

* The master's overriding responsibility is for the **safety** of his ship and all persons sailing in the ship.
* The master of every vessel (of any type or size, in any trade and in any situation) is responsible at all times for the **safety** of his vessel. He has the authority to decide whether any operation affecting his vessel should proceed or terminate. He should question any instructions from any other source which may create a hazard to his vessel or crew.
* The master has an implied duty to maintain the **seaworthiness and good condition** of his vessel as far as he can do so with the means at his disposal.

E04g.4 Master's responsibility for occupational health, safety and welfare of crew

* The master has responsibility for the **occupational health, safety and welfare** of the crew whilst on board ship. He must observe all flag State and port State health and safety legislation, including those duties placed on the employer.
* Where no doctor is carried in the crew, the master is responsible for giving necessary **medical attention** to crew and others on board.

E04g.5 Master's responsibility for cadets and apprentices

* The master is responsible for seeing that any cadets or apprentices carried are fully informed as to their duties and the duties of a junior watchkeeping officer.
* Cadets and apprentices should not be used as "cheap labour" or as substitutes for crew required for the safe and efficient manning of the vessel.
* Under the Vocational Qualification (VQ) system of training which has come into effect nationwide in the UK (as NSVQ or SVQ), masters and senior officers may be expected to become **Ship's Assessors** and participate in the assessment and record-keeping procedures required by the MNTB.
* The **rest periods of young persons** (under 18) are longer than those of other crew members and are prescribed in the MS and FV (Health and Safety at Work) (Employment of Young Persons) Regulations 1998 (SI 1998/2411) (see E05c.1).

E04g.6 Master's responsibility for cargo

* The master is the **bailee** of the cargo (see E04f.1). As such he is the custodian or "warehouseman" of the goods on board and is responsible for their **safe carriage** to their discharge port or place.

E04g.7 Master's responsibility for passengers

* At common law, the master is responsible for the **safety of passengers** and may be **personally liable** where this is compromised. However, many companies now include a **Himalaya Clause** in their standard contract terms so as to protect their employees from legal action (see F07b.9a).
* For notes on various matters relating to the **carriage of passengers**, see I07f.

E04h MASTER'S AUTHORITY

E04h.1 Common law position

* In common law the master is the **supreme authority** on board his vessel. This is the case even where the shipowner, charterer or employer is on board.

E04h.2 ISM Code requirement for statement of master's responsibility and authority

* **ISM Code, paragraph 5** (Master's Responsibility and Authority) provides as follows:
  "**5.1** The **Company should clearly define and document the master's responsibility** with regard to:
     .1   implementing the safety and environmental-protection policy of the Company;
     .2   motivating the crew in the observation of that policy;
     .3   issuing appropriate orders and instructions in a clear and simple manner;
     .4   verifying that specified requirements are observed; and
     .5   reviewing the SMS (Safety Management System) and reporting its deficiencies to the shore-based management.
  5.2 The Company should ensure that the SMS operating on board the ship contains a **clear statement emphasising the master's authority**. The Company should establish in the SMS that the master has the overriding authority and the responsibility to make decisions with respect to safety and pollution and to request the Company's assistance as may be necessary."

E04h.3 Keeping order in passenger ships

* For notes on the **master's power to exclude drunken passengers** from certain passenger ships, see F08c.2.

E04h.4 Master's power of restraint

* The master of any UK ship may cause **any person on board** the ship to be put **under restraint** if and for so long as it appears to him necessary and expedient in the interest of **safety** or for the preservation of **good order or discipline** on board the ship (section 105, Merchant Shipping Act 1995).
* In order to avoid an action for **false imprisonment**, especially since the passing of the Human Rights Act 1998, the power under section 105 must be exercised with caution. False imprisonment has been defined as "the unlawful imposition of constraint on another's freedom of movement from a particular place" and is both a tort and a crime. For notes on **tort law**, see B03e.

E04h.5 Master's discretion

* See H01a.11.

E04h.6 Production of certificates and other documents of qualification to master

* Under section 50 of the Merchant Shipping Act 1995 persons engaged to serve in sea-going UK ships must, on demand, produce certain **documents** to the master (see E06d).

E04h.7 Master's authority and responsibility with respect to ship security

* ISPS Code, part A, section 6.1 provides that the Ship Security Plan must contain a **clear statement emphasizing the master's authority**. The **Company** must establish in the Ship Security Plan that the master has the **overriding authority** and **responsibility to make decisions** with respect to the security of the ship and to request the **assistance of the Company** or of any SOLAS Contracting Government as may be necessary.

E04i MASTER'S LIABILITIES

E04i.1 Criminal liabilities of shipmasters

* The volume of UK merchant shipping legislation has, especially in the last 100 years or so, grown enormously, and in parallel the number of shipping-related criminal offences which it is possible for a shipmaster to commit has become alarmingly large. (If possible offences under foreign port State and coastal State legislation could be ascertained and added, the list would become almost infinite.) It is most unlikely, then, that any other category of

employee bears so great a weight of potential criminal liability as does the master of an internationally-trading UK merchant ship[33].

* While the **maximum fine on summary conviction in a UK court** is currently £250,000 (see B03b.3d), the penalty on conviction on indictment in a UK court is in many cases an unspecified (i.e. unlimited) fine, often with an accompanying jail sentence of up to 2 years. For similar offences in **foreign jurisdictions** the penalty on a shipmaster or seaman may be more severe than the UK penalties.
* **Penalties of up to £250,000 on summary conviction** are designed primarily for imposing on a shipowner and not on the master, but where the shipowner cannot be prosecuted, perhaps because of legal problems surrounding the identity of the shipowner, the master may well be an "easy target" for prosecution. It is unlikely, however, that given the moderate financial means of most shipmasters, any court would see fit to impose such a massive fine as might be imposed on a shipowner.
* The MCA website (see B05b.6) contains **prosecutions** pages in the "News" section. Case and penalty details are given.

E04i.2 Civil liabilities of shipmasters

* Shipmasters are subject, during the course of their duties, to **civil liabilities**.
* Where the master has breached his contractual obligations to the shipowner, manager or employer (as the case may be) he may be **sued in contract**, rendering him liable for damages.
* Where the master **exceeds his authority or acts without authority**, causing the owner to suffer loss or damage, he may also render himself liable to civil action for recovery of damages.
* A shipmaster may also be **liable in tort** for a variety of civil wrongs claimed to have been done to third parties, an example being the successful suing by a passenger of the master of the P&O liner *Himalaya* in *Adler v. Dixon* (1954). As a result of the judgement in that case, many shipowners now insert a "**Himalaya Clause**" into their contracts of carriage or passage, in order to protect their servants and contractors from liability for wrongs committed during the course of their duties.
* For more detailed notes on the Adler v. Dixon case and **Himalaya Clauses**, see F07b.9a. For notes on **tort law**, see B03e.

E04j MASTER'S DISMISSAL

* The master's employer has an employer's usual right to terminate the master's contract, and thus to remove the master from command, for any reason at any time, subject to contractual terms providing for a period of notice.
* For **serious misconduct** of the master, dismissal may be summary, i.e. without notice.
* A **court** may also remove a master from command.
* Where a court has ordered the suspension of a master's certificate of competency, the employer would be obliged to dismiss the master from command of the vessel.
* The master may otherwise be protected by UK employment legislation in the same way as other employees of the shipowner or manager (see E05).

E04k MASTER'S LIEN

* **Section 41 of the Merchant Shipping Act 1995** provides that the master of a ship will have the **same lien** for his remuneration, and all disbursements or liabilities properly made or incurred by him on account of the ship, as a seaman has for his wages (see E09b.1c).
* For notes on **maritime liens**, see B03g.3. To exercise his lien (e.g. where a master is unable to obtain his proper remuneration), a master should consult a firm of shipping lawyers. If the master is a NUMAST member, the Legal Department of NUMAST should be able to advise on the proper procedure.

---

[33] Where the master is liable to a criminal penalty, the shipowner is also usually liable. Many Merchant Shipping regulations and other legislation contains obligations applicable only to the owner, so in fact it is the owner who bears the greatest weight of legislation of all.

E05 Employment law

E05a UK EMPLOYMENT LAW

* **UK employment law** covers such matters as categories of worker, contracts of employment, equal pay, maternity and parental leave, sick pay and sickness absence, discrimination, union organisation, industrial action, dismissal, redundancy, and business transfers. It comprises a vast body of complex and constantly developing statute and case law which is the field of specialist employment lawyers and law books. With the exception of a few topics of direct concern to seafarers, such as crew agreements, the employment of young persons, the different types of dismissal, and employment tribunals, the subject of employment law is beyond the scope of this book.
* Shipmasters and others interested in employment law can obtain a great deal of useful legal guidance from the following websites:
  * the **Department of Trade and Industry** website at www.dti.gov.uk/er/regs.htm
  * the **TUC** website at www.tuc.org.uk/law/index.cfm
  * the **Advisory, Conciliation and Arbitration Service (ACAS)** website at www.acas.org.uk
  * the **Transport Salaried Staffs' Association** website at www.tssa.org.uk
* The **Labour Research Department** (78 Blackfriars Road, London SE1 8HF, tel. 020 7928 3649) publishes a useful UK employment law booklet entitled *Law at Work*.

E05b SEAFARERS' CONTRACTS OF EMPLOYMENT

* Seafarers in UK ships are employed under various forms of contract, chiefly including:
  * a **crew agreement**. This is the basic written contract of employment for all seafarers other than those exempted by the MCA.
  * a **company service contract** (CSC). This is supplemented by a Crew Agreement when the seafarer is signed on; dismissal occurs in this case when the CSC is terminated, not on the seafarer's discharge from the Crew Agreement.
  * a **master's contract**. The position of masters not serving under a CSC is less clear, since a master, not being a "seaman" under Crew Agreement regulations, is exempt from the requirement to sign a Crew Agreement. The master's contract terms may be contained in his letter of appointment, in company standing orders, in oral or written instructions from superintendents, managers, etc.
  * a **training agreement** for cadets and rating-to-officer trainees. This is supplemented by the Crew Agreement when signed on. The training agreement is usually a fixed-term contract giving entitlement to the same protection against unfair dismissal as other seafarers have. A special feature of these contracts, which expire automatically after the fixed term, is that where the fixed period exceeds one year, a statement may be included saying that failure to offer further employment at the end of the fixed term will not give rise to a remedy for unfair dismissal.
* A clause in an employment contract should specify the governing **law and jurisdiction**. The contract of a seafarer serving in a UK ship may be subject to the law and jurisdiction of some other state, e.g. Isle of Man, Bahamas or Guernsey, and different arrangements may apply to different sections of the crew[34]. Where the employment contract is not UK-based, it is an "offshore contract" and the seafarer will not have the employment rights and other benefits conferred by UK law, including the right to make a claim of unfair dismissal to a UK employment tribunal (see E05e).

E05c EMPLOYMENT OF YOUNG PERSONS IN UK SHIPS

* **Section 55 of the Merchant Shipping Act 1995** provides that a person under school-leaving age[35] shall not be employed in any UK ship except as permitted by the MS (Employment of Young Persons) Regulations (SI 1995/972). Those Regulations have been revoked and replaced by the **MS and FV (Health and Safety at Work) (Employment of Young Persons) Regulations 1998** (SI 1998/2411) (see E05c.1).

---

[34] It may be the case, for example, that in a UK-flagged cruise ship, the deck and engineer officers are employed by a UK company on UK-based contracts and are engaged on "BSF" crew agreement terms. The ratings may simultaneously be employed by a Cyprus-based ship management company on Cyprus contracts and be engaged on an NFD crew agreement, while the hotel staff may be employed by a Hong Kong company on Hong Kong contracts and also be engaged on an NFD crew agreement.

[35] Normal school-leaving age in the UK is 16, but there various exceptions are allowed.

* For notes on the statutory **rest periods** of young persons, see E03c.4.
* For notes on the **procedure for engagement** of a young person, see E07d.4.

E05c.1 Employment of Young Persons Regulations

* The **MS and FV (Health and Safety at Work) (Employment of Young Persons) Regulations 1998** (SI 1998/2411) –
    - **revoke** the MS (Employment of Young Persons) Regulations 1995 (SI 1995/972).
    - **give effect** as respects shipping activities in the UK both to **Council Directive 94/33/EC** on the protection of young people at work and in part to the **Merchant Shipping (Minimum Standards) Convention 1976** (ILO Convention 147).
    - **apply** to all activities of young persons (as defined below) engaged as workers on UK ships, wherever they are.
    - **apply to** all UK ships (regulation 3(1)), and ships which are not UK ships when in United Kingdom waters are subject to regulations covering inspection and detention (regulations 3(2) and 14-16).
    - **do not apply** if the Health and Safety (Young Persons) Regulations 1997 (S.I. 1997/135) or the Health and Safety (Young Persons) Regulations (Northern Ireland) 1997 (S.R. 1997 No. 387) cover the matter (regulation 3(3)(a)), or if the work carried out is exceptional in various respects and equivalent compensatory rest time will be allowed in the next 3 weeks (regulation 3(3)(b)).
    - **contain** the following **regulations**: **1**. Citation, commencement and revocations; **2**. Interpretation; **3**. Application and exemption; **4**. Persons on whom duties are imposed; **5**. Additional general duties; **6**. Rest periods for young persons; **7**. Health assessment; **8**. Young persons' medical certificates; **9**. Record of young persons; **10**. Penalties; **11**. Offences by body corporate and partnerships; **12**. Onus of proving what is reasonably practicable; **13**. Inspection and detention of a United Kingdom ship; **14**. Inspection, detention and other measures in respect of ships registered outside the United Kingdom; **15**. Enforcement of detention; **16**. Compensation; **17**. Miscellaneous amendments.
    - **contain** a **Schedule** related to regulation 5 listing Non-exhaustive list of agents, process and work.
* "**Young person**" means, in relation to employment on a **sea-going UK ship**, any person who is of the age of 16 or 17, and in relation to employment on a **UK ship which is not a sea-going ship**, any person who is under the age of 18 and, in Great Britain is over school-leaving age for the purposes of section 55 of the Merchant Shipping Act 1995 or, in Northern Ireland, is over compulsory school age within the meaning in Article 46 of the Education and Libraries (Northern Ireland) Order 1986. (The definition in the Employment of Young Persons Regulations was modified by paragraph 4 of Schedule 2 to the MS (Hours of Work) Regulations 2002 (SI 2002/2125) (see E03c.1).
* An obligation is placed on the employer to comply with the requirements of the Regulations as well as on any person specifically named in the provision. There is facility to extend the employer's duty to another person if the employer is not in control of the particular matter because he does not have responsibility for the operation of ship (regulation 4(1) and (2)).
* In addition to general duties required by the MS and FV (Health and Safety at Work) Regulations 1997 (SI 1997/2962) the employer must take **appropriate measures** to protect young persons at work (regulation 5(1)). This includes making an **assessment** of the risks to their health and safety in accordance with the provision of this regulation (regulation 5(2) and (5) and the Schedule). He must **inform young persons of identified risks and protective measures** (regulation 5(3)), and shall ensure that they are not engaged in certain specified work (regulation 5(4)). Where the assessment shows the young person's safety or health is at risk, or the young person will be regularly required to **work at night**, **free health monitoring** must be provided (regulation 7).
* The employer must provide the young person with **specific minimum daily and weekly rest periods**, and the Company (owner) is required to ensure that the employer meets that obligation (regulation 6).
* Except in specific circumstances, no young person may be employed on ship without an **appropriate medical certificate** (regulation 8).
* There must be included in every Crew Agreement a list of the young persons who are **engaged as workers** on the ship, together with particulars of their dates of birth (regulation 9(1)). (This is normally made on MCA form ALC1(c) (see E07c.2d).)
* There must be included in every Crew Agreement a short summary of the provisions of the Employment of Young Persons Regulations (regulation 9(2)). In a ship with no Crew Agreement, the master must, if young persons are engaged as workers on board, keep a **register** of them with particulars of their dates of birth and dates on which they were engaged (regulation 9(3)).
* Guidance on application of the Regulations is in **MGN 88**.
* For provisions of regulation 6 relating to **rest periods** of young persons, see E03c.4.

E05d DISMISSAL

E05d.1 When and how dismissal can occur

* "**Dismissal**" is termination by the employer of the employee's contract of employment. An employer usually dismisses an employee by giving him the at least the minimum period of notice specified in the contract, but in certain circumstances (e.g. for gross misconduct) may dismiss the employee without notice.
* Statute law on unfair dismissal is contained in **Part X of the Employment Rights Act 1996** (ERA 1996). Under section 94 an employee has the **right not to be unfairly dismissed** by his employer.
* Section 95 of the ERA 1996 provides that **an employee is dismissed if**:
    * the contract under which he is employed is terminated by the employer (whether with or without notice)[36];
    * he is employed under a **contract for a fixed term** and that **term expires without being renewed** under the same contract; or
    * the **employee terminates the contract** under which he is employed (with or without notice) in circumstances in which he is entitled to terminate it without notice by reason of the **employer's conduct** (called "**constructive dismissal**" – see E05d.4c).

E05d.2 Fair dismissal

* "**Fair dismissal**" means dismissal for a **fair reason** and in a **fair manner**. The law on unfair dismissal does no more than give employees a legal right to be treated in a way in which a fair and reasonable employer would treat them anyway.
* For an employer to dismiss an employer **fairly** he must:
    * have a **valid reason** for doing so[37]; and
    * **act reasonably** in treating that reason as a sufficient reason for dismissing the employee[38].
* The second of the above conditions does not apply in cases where the dismissal is **unquestionably unfair**.
* The five **potentially fair reasons for dismissal** are:
    * **capability**;
    * **conduct**;
    * **redundancy**;
    * **statutory requirement**; and
    * "**some other substantial reason**".
* **Capability** is defined by section 98(3) of the ERA 96 as "skill, aptitude, health or any other physical or mental quality".
* **Conduct** (or, more properly, **misconduct**) can only amount to a fair reason for dismissal if the alleged misconduct was such as to significantly interfere with the employer's business or destroy the employment relationship. It will usually fall into one of the following categories:
    * disobeying reasonable orders;
    * damaging the employer's business; or
    * committing a criminal offence.
    Breaches of paragraph 9 of the Merchant Navy Code of Conduct (which may simultaneously fall into two or all three of the above categories) may be fair reasons for dismissal in certain circumstances. For example, an officer who falls asleep on watch, allowing his ship to run aground, may be prosecuted and found guilty of a breach of section 58 of the Merchant Shipping Act 1995, and his dismissal will be fair if for that reason.
* **Redundancy** is a fair reason for dismissal providing the reason for selection for redundancy is also fair. It would not be fair to select a seafarer for redundancy because he was a trade union activist.
* "**Statutory requirement**" may be a fair reason for dismissal where it would be illegal to continue to employ the employee. Section 98(2)(d) of the ERA 96 provides that where an employee who is dismissed could not continue to work in the position which he held without contravention (either on his part or that of his employer) of a duty or restriction imposed by or under an enactment, the dismissal will be for a fair reason. Suspension or cancellation of

---

[36] "The contract", in relation to a seafarer serving under a company service contract, means that contract, and in relation to a seafarer serving only under a Crew Agreement, means that agreement.
[37] In the case of a seafarer on a Crew Agreement incorporating the MN Code of Conduct, a "valid reason" would be any proven breach of paragraph 9 of the Code.
[38] Compliance with the procedures for dismissal in the MN Code of Conduct will ensure that the employer has acted "reasonably" in dismissing a seaman.

an officer's Certificate of Competency would, for example, leave his employer no alternative but to dismiss him from his employment on board ship.

* **"Some other substantial reason"** has been described by employers as a "catch all" potentially fair reason for dismissal. The dismissal of a temporary replacement employee on the return to work of a woman who had been on maternity leave may be deemed fair, provided the temporary employee had been warned of the temporary nature of the job.

E05d.3 Fair dismissal procedures

* Employees (including crew members) should be **made aware** of the circumstances that could lead to their dismissal. The **Merchant Navy Code of Conduct** (or alternative approved company code of conduct), **Crew Agreement**, **company service contract terms** and **company standing orders** will cover most situations. These documents should be made **available** to seafarers at the time of their engagement.
* If possible, problems arising on board should be **resolved** before reaching the formal dismissal proceedings stage.
* The following procedure should be adopted in cases involving **lack of capability due to inadequate performance**:
  1. Make **informal constructive remarks** to the seafarer.
  2. Give the seafarer the **opportunity to reply** to any criticisms of him.
  3. Give the seafarer **further training**.
  4. Have skilled crew members **supervise** the seafarer.
  5. **Assess** the seafarer's **subsequent performance**.
  6. If no improvement results, give the seafarer a **formal warning in writing** to the effect that if there is no future improvement, dismissal may or will probably follow.
  7. **Continue** supervision and assessment.
  8. If still no improvement, the employer should offer an **alternative job** and give the seafarer **time to consider** the offer, or, if there is no alternative job available, **dismiss** the seafarer.
  9. **Record each step** above in the seafarer's file.
* Where **performance is very poor** or the potential **consequences** of the incompetence are very serious (e.g. they pose a threat to the vessel or persons on board), it may not be necessary to follow all the steps listed. The **employer must be able to show**, however, that **effective training and supervision** were provided and that issue of a formal warning would have had no appreciable effect on the seafarer's performance. Even then, the seafarer should have an **opportunity to explain** why his performance was below standard before dismissal takes place.
* In cases of **lack of capability due to ill health of a company service contract seafarer**, the **company** should deal with the dismissal.
* Where a medical report indicates that the seafarer is **fit, but he refuses to work**, it may be better to treat the case as one of **misconduct**.
* If a seafarer is to be **signed off sick abroad**, he should be given clear advice as to the **arrangements** made for his **maintenance, repatriation and payment after discharge**, if necessary after consultation with the company.
* If a seafarer shows symptoms of **alcoholism**, the company's **personnel and medical departments** should be advised as soon as possible. Unless drunkenness leads to breaches of the MN Code of Conduct, **disciplinary measures should not be invoked** except where treatment is refused or satisfactory work performance is not subsequently maintained.
* Where a seafarer can be shown to have **fraudulently misrepresented his qualifications or experience**, summary dismissal is justified. The MCA should be advised as soon as possible, and full and complete records should be sent to the Seafarers Standards Branch of the MCA at Southampton.
* **ACAS** has a **Code of Practice on Disciplinary Practice and Procedures in Employment** which gives employers practical advice on how to deal with disciplinary matters in a way which is fair and can be seen to be fair by their employees. Compliance with the **Code of Conduct for the Merchant Navy** will normally have the **same effect** as compliance with the ACAS Code.

E05d.4 Wrongful, unfair and constructive dismissal

* Employees may have:
  * a common law right to claim **wrongful dismissal**; and
  * a statutory right to claim **unfair dismissal**.

E05d.4a Wrongful dismissal

* "**Wrongful dismissal**" may arise when there is a **breach of the contract of employment by the employer**. A contract of employment can normally be terminated either **summarily** (for good cause) or by **giving notice** (as expressed in the contract). Normally, therefore, **wrongful dismissal** will mean either:
* summary dismissal where the employee's **conduct does not justify summary dismissal**; or
* dismissal where the **employer has not given the notice required** by the contract of employment.
* In most cases, wrongful dismissal occurs in the latter event.
* An employee who has been wrongfully dismissed has a **common law right to sue his employer for damages** which, if awarded, are not limited by statute, although they will not normally exceed the amount of wages which would have been earned had proper notice been given.
* Wrongful dismissal cases must be brought before a **court**, not an employment tribunal.

E05d.4b Unfair dismissal

* "**Unfair dismissal**" occurs when an employee is dismissed but:
    * the employer has **no valid reason** for dismissing the employee; and/or
    * the **employer does not act reasonably** in treating that reason as a sufficient reason for dismissing the employee.
* Unfair dismissal cases are heard by **employment tribunals** (see E05e), not courts of law.
* Certain reasons for dismissal, such as for union membership, are always considered by a tribunal to be unfair.
* Certain categories of worker, including employees whose work is outside Great Britain, have no right to claim unfair dismissal to a tribunal in the UK.

E05d.4c Constructive dismissal

* "**Constructive dismissal**" is a form of unfair dismissal. An employment tribunal may determine that an employee was **constructively dismissed** when he or she resigns because of certain conduct by the employer.
* The **employer's action** must be such that it can be regarded as a **substantial breach of the terms of the contract** of employment such that the employer **no longer intends to be bound** by that contract. Examples of such situations are:
    * when **pay or conditions are reduced** without the employee's agreement;
    * when the employee is **arbitrarily reduced in rank**;
    * when there is **discrimination against the employee**;
    * when **higher performance** is demanded from the employee than from other employees;
    * when the employee's **contractual or agreed rights are denied**;
    * when the employee's **authority is consistently undermined**;
    * when there is **deliberate unfair treatment**;
    * when the employee is **unreasonably required to do other work** than his own;
    * when the **employee is publicly berated** with marked discourtesy;
    * when the employee is **denigrated to others**;
    * where the employer **attempts to force a seafarer to sign off** a Crew Agreement or terminate his company service contract.
* It is usually very difficult for employees to succeed in constructive dismissal cases.

E05e EMPLOYMENT TRIBUNALS

E05e.1 Taking a complaint to an employment tribunal

* **Employment tribunals**[39] are judicial bodies established by Parliament at various cities and towns throughout the UK to resolve disputes over employment rights. They sit in public and can compel the attendance of witnesses.

---

[39] "Industrial tribunals" have been renamed employment tribunals since 1 August 1998, when Part I of the Employment Rights (Dispute Resolution) Act 1998 came into force. This Act amended the law relating to dismissal procedures and other alternative methods of resolving disputes about employment rights.

* In most cases **application** must be made within **three months** beginning with the date on which the employment ended, or in some cases when the matter being complained about happened. Applications may be in writing or on line, and guidance notes are available in writing and on line.
* An employment tribunal consists of a **chairman**, who is a barrister or solicitor appointed in England or Wales by the Lord Chancellor or in Scotland by the Lord President of the Court of Session, and **two lay members** appointed by the Secretary of State for Trade and Industry from persons with experience in dealing with work-related problems, each having an equal voice in any decision.
* A **pre-hearing review** of the case may be conducted by the full tribunal, or by the chairman sitting alone. If it appears that the case has little prospect of success, or is frivolous, vexatious or otherwise unreasonable, either party may be ordered to pay a **deposit** as a condition of continuing to proceed with, or defend the case. If the complaint is not settled or withdrawn at an early stage, it proceeds to a **full hearing** by the tribunal.
* Many applicants and respondents put their own cases although some choose to have a **representative** who may be a lawyer, trade union official, representative of an employers' organization, or simply a friend or colleague.
* Tribunal hearings are generally completed in **one day**. Decisions may be by majority vote but in practice are nearly all **unanimous**.
* **Employment Tribunals website**: www.employmenttribunals.gov.uk
* **Addresses** of employment tribunals can be found in Yellow Pages and on the website.

E05e.2 Remedies available to an employment tribunal

* If the tribunal's decision is that the dismissal was either for an **unfair reason** or for a fair reason but made in an **unfair manner**, it may order either:
  * **reinstatement**;
  * **re-engagement**; or
  * an award of **compensation**.
* **Reinstatement** can only apply where the employee agrees. He must be treated in all respects as if he had not been dismissed, but is entitled to arrears of pay, benefits accrued during the period of dismissal and all rights and privileges including seniority and pension rights.
* **Re-engagement** can only apply where the employee agrees where it is neither possible nor feasible to order reinstatement. An order is made that the complainant is engaged by the employer or by the successor of the employer or by an associated employer, in a position comparable to that from which the employee was dismissed.
* An award of **compensation** will normally be made where:
  * the employee indicates that he no longer wants to return to work for his previous employer; or
  * the tribunal decides that reinstatement or re-engagement is impracticable; or
  * the employer fails to comply with an order for re-engagement or reinstatement.

E06 Seafarers' documents

* For notes on **Certificates of Competency** and **Certificates of Equivalent Competency**, see E02.

E06a BRITISH SEAMEN'S CARDS AND DISCHARGE BOOKS

E06a.1 Primary legislation relating to British Seamen's Cards and Discharge Books

* For notes on section 50(1) of the Merchant Shipping Act 1995 concerning **production of seamen's documents**, see E06d.
* **Section 79 of the Merchant Shipping Act 1995** enables regulations to be made concerning British Seamen's Cards. Section 79(3) provides that in Part III of the Act "British seamen" means persons who are not aliens within the meaning of the British Nationality Act 1981 and are employed, or ordinarily employed, as masters or seamen. Section 79(4) sets the penalty where a person makes a false statement in order to obtain for himself or another person a British Seamen's Card.
* **Section 80 of the Merchant Shipping Act 1995** enables regulations to be made relating to Discharge Books. Section 80(4) sets a penalty where a person who obtains employment as a seaman on board a UK ship and does so

when he is disentitled to a Discharge Book, or employs as such a seaman a person who he knows or has reason to suspect is disentitled.

E06a.2 Seamen's Documents Regulations

* The **MS (Seamen's Documents) Regulations 1987** (SI 1987/408) -
  - **revoke** the MS (Seamen's Documents) Regulations 1972, as amended.
  - **are amended** by the **MS (Seamen's Documents) (Amendment) Regulations 1995** (SI 1995/1900), which remove the requirement for a seaman's National Insurance number to be entered on his application form.
  - **are further amended** by the **MS (Seamen's Documents) (Amendment) Regulations 1999** (SI 1999/3281), which allow the issue of Diischarge Books to persons who are British Citizens within the meaning of the British Nationality Act 1981 and who have the right of abode within the UK who are or have been employed in non-UK ships. The Regulations also make minor amendments to the principal Regulations to omit references to the Merchant Navy Establishment Administration and to up-date the list of countries specified in Schedule 4. **MGN 134** explains the amendments.
  - **are in** three parts. **Part I** provisions relate to **British Seamen's Cards** (see E06a.2a); **Part II** provisions relate to **Discharge Books** (see E06a.2b); **Part III** provisions relate to both **British Seamen's Cards and Discharge Books** (see E06a.2c).

E06a.2a Provisions relating to British Seamen's Cards

* Regulations 2, 3 and 4 relate to **applications** for British Seaman's Cards. Subject to the provisions of regulation 3, a British seaman to whom regulation 2 applies and who does not already hold a British Seaman's Card may apply for a British Seaman's Card (regulation 2(1) and (2)). Regulation 2 applies to any British seaman employed or ordinarily employed in a ship other than in the following types of employment:
  * employment in a fishing vessel;
  * employment in a ship belonging to a General Lighthouse Authority;
  * except in the case of a person who is a cadet, employment on terms under which he receives no wages or only nominal wages; and
  * in the case of a person who is not a citizen of the UK and colonies or a British protected person, employment in a ship registered otherwise than in the UK, the Channel Islands, the Isle of Man or any colony, protectorate or protected State.
* Regulation 3 excludes certain categories of person from **eligibility** for a British Seaman's Card, as follows:
  * a person who is not a British citizen, a British Dependent Territories citizen or a British Overseas citizen, a British protected person or a British subject without citizenship, and who holds a seaman's identity document issued to him by or under the authority of:
    * the Government of a country specified in schedule 3 to the British Nationality Act 1981; or of
    * any territory or trust territory under the protection of or administered by such government; or of
    * the Republic of Ireland, and of which he has not ceased to be regarded as the holder by that government;
  * a person who holds a seaman's identity document which has been issued to him by the government of any colony, protectorate, or protected State and of which he has not ceased to be regarded as the holder by that government;
  * a person in the employment of the Crown who is employed, but not ordinarily employed, as a master or seaman; and
  * a member of the naval, military or air forces of the Crown or of any service administered by the Defence Council.
* Regulation 4 provides that a person applying for a British Seaman's Card must make an **application** in accordance with regulation 29 and unless it has been lost or destroyed, surrender to the Registrar General of Shipping and Seamen or an MCA superintendent any British Seaman's Card or British Seaman's Identity Card[40] previously held by him.
* A British Seaman's Card must be issued (by the RSS on behalf of the Secretary of State) to a person having the right of abode in the UK if the applicant satisfies the conditions of regulation 2(2) and has paid the prescribed fee. In any other case, a British Seaman's Card may be issued (regulation 5).
* Regulation 6 deals with the book **form and contents** of British Seaman's Cards. Schedule 2 contains a list of required contents.

---

[40] British Seaman's Identity Cards were issued under the British Seamen's Identity Cards Order 1942 (S.R. & O. 1942/2681)

* A British Seaman's Card will be **valid for 10 years** from the date of issue provided that if at the end of that period the holder is not present in the UK, his British Seaman's Card will remain valid until he first returns to the UK or the expiry of a further 12 months from the date of expiry, whichever is sooner (regulation 7).
* Regulation 8 concerns British Seaman's Cards issued under the revoked Merchant Shipping (Seamen's Documents) Regulations 1972 and which are no longer valid.
* When his British Seaman's Card is lost, destroyed, defaced or required to be surrendered, a person ceases to be regarded as the **holder** of a British Seaman's Card (regulation 9).
* Regulation 10(1) requires the holder of a British Seaman's Card to **produce it** to the Registrar General of Shipping and Seamen, an MCA superintendent, a proper officer, his employer, or the master of his ship, on demand or within such period as the person requiring its production may allow.
* The holder of a British Seaman's Card must **surrender** it to the Registrar General of Shipping and Seamen or an MCA Marine Officer superintendent forthwith upon his ceasing to be a British seaman or upon the card being defaced, and on demand, after he has ceased to have the right of abode in the UK (regulation 11(1)).
* A person who comes into possession of a British Seaman's Card of which he is not the holder must immediately deliver it to the Registrar General of Shipping and Seamen or an MCA Marine Officer superintendent (regulation 12(1)).
* **Schedule 2** (which relates to regulation 6) lists the particulars to be recorded in a British Seaman's Card, which include a statement that the document is a seafarer's identity document for the purpose of International Labour Organisation Convention Number 108.

E06a.2b Provisions relating to Discharge Books

* Subject to other provisions of the Regulations, a person must **apply for a Discharge Book within 7 days** of satisfying the conditions of regulation 15(2) (regulation 15(1)). The **conditions** of regulation 15(2) referred to in regulation 15(1) are that the person -
  * **is not exempted** from the requirements of section 1 Merchant Shipping Act 1970 (which related to Crew Agreements) (i.e. is not exempted from signing a Crew Agreement); and either -
    * **is employed as a seaman in a UK ship** (other than in a fishing vessel or in a ship exempted from having a Crew Agreement); or
    * is a citizen of the UK and overseas territories who has been **discharged abroad after being employed as a seaman in a UK ship** and has arrived in the UK within 6 months of being discharged, unless, at the time he arrived, he did not intend to take such employment; and
  * is not (already) the holder of a UK Discharge Book; and
  * has not been required by the MCA, under regulation 27(1), to surrender a UK Discharge Book.
* Regulation 16(1) provides that **regulation 15 does not apply** to a person if he already holds a document -
  * containing substantially the same information as a Discharge Book; and
  * which has been issued to him by or under the authority of the government of a country specified in Schedule 4 to the Regulations[41]; and
  * of which he has not ceased to be regarded as the holder by that government.
* **Regulation 15 does not apply** to a person in the employment of the Crown who is not ordinarily employed as a master or seaman (regulation 16(2)).
* A person applying for a Discharge Book must apply in accordance with regulation 29 and unless it has been lost or destroyed, produce to the Registrar General of Shipping and Seamen or an MCA Marine Office superintendent the latest Discharge Book or Seaman's Record Book if any, previously held by him (regulation 17(1)).
* Under regulation 18(1) the **MCA must issue a Discharge Book** to a person who is required to apply and who has paid the prescribed **fee**; the particulars in the Discharge Book must be those in Schedule 3.
* A Discharge Book **may be issued** under 18(2) (as amended by SI 1999/3281) by the MCA to a person who is not required to apply but who is, or has been employed in a UK ship or, if the person is a British citizen, in a non-UK ship, and in respect of employment in a non-UK ship is otherwise unable, for whatever reason, to obtain a document containing substantially the same information as a Discharge Book or acceptable to the ship's flag State, and has paid the prescribed fee (regulation 18(2)).
* Regulation 19 sets out requirements for the **form and content** of Discharge Books. A Discharge Book must be in book form and must provide for the recording of the following particulars. Regulation 20 authorises certain persons to enter the particulars required under regulation 19. Those persons are shown in the right hand column of the table

---

[41] The countries listed in Schedule 4, as amended by SI 1999/3281, are: Bangladesh, Barbados, Canada, Falkland Islands, Fiji, Ghana, Guyana, Hong Kong, India, Republic of Ireland, Isle of Man, Jamaica, Kenya, Kiribati, Malaysia, Malta, Mauritius, Nigeria, Pakistan, Papua New Guinea, Saint Lucia, Seychelles, Sierra Leone, Singapore, South Africa, Sri Lanka, Tanzania, Tonga, Trinidad and Tobago, Tuvalu, Western Samoa, Zambia

Particulars in Discharge Book (regulation 19)	Persons authorised to enter particulars (regulation 20)
Particulars (except paragraph 4) as specified in Schedule 3 to the Regulations, i.e.: 1. Name and address of the person applying for the document; 2. His home address; 3. The date and place of his birth; 4. (not required) 5. His nationality; 6. The colour of his eyes; 7. His distinguishing marks (if any); 8. His height; 9. The number of his discharge book (if any); 10. The grade, number and date of issue of any certificate of competency held by him; 11. (NI No. omitted by SI 1995/1900). 12. The name, relationship and address of his next of kin; 13. Merchant Navy Officer's Pension Fund (MNOPF)/Merchant Navy Ratings Pension Fund (MNRPF) number; 14. Union membership number (if any) (para. (a))	A superintendent; the RSS; a proper officer

The master of the ship in which the holder is employed, or the holder himself, may enter Paragraphs 2 and 12 (home address and name, relationship and address of next of kin) |
Name of each ship registered in the UK in which he is employed, its port of registry, official number and gross or register tonnage, the capacity in which he is employed in the ship, the date on which and the place at which he begins to be so employed, and the description of each voyage and the date and place of his discharge (para. (b)(i))	A superintendent; the RSS; a proper officer; the master of the ship in which the holder is employed or a ship's officer authorised by the master
The same details as above in respect of employment in any other vessel (para. (b)(ii))	The master of the ship in which the holder is employed or a ship's officer authorised by the master
Dates of any Merchant Navy Training Board training courses he attends for instruction in survival at sea and the certificates or other qualifications (if any) obtained (para. (c)(i))	A superintendent; the RSS; the principal of the training establishment attended or the instructor in charge of the holder's training
Dates and nature of any other training courses (including pre-sea training courses) he attends and the certificates or other qualifications (if any) obtained (para. (c)(ii))	A superintendent; the RSS; the principal, or his approved deputy, of the MCA-approved training establishment attended
Income tax code, the year to which it applies and the date on which it becomes effective (para. (d))	A superintendent; the RSS; the master of the ship in which the holder is employed; the seaman's employer
Inoculation and vaccination certificates (para. (e))	A superintendent; the RSS; a proper officer
Records of tests of his eyesight except where these formed part of a statutory medical examination (para. (f))	A superintendent; the RSS
Record of certificates issued under the MS (Medical Examination) Regulations 1983 (para. (g))	A superintendent; the RSS

* Under regulation 21 an MCA superintendent, a proper officer or the Registrar General of Shipping and Seamen may at any time **correct any entry** in a Discharge Book.
* Under regulation 22(1) the holder of a Discharge Book must **produce** it on demand at any time to a superintendent, a proper officer, the Registrar General of Shipping and Seamen, his employer, the master of the ship in which he is employed, and to any other person authorised by regulation 20 to make an entry in it, for the purpose of making that entry.
* Under regulation 22(3) a person to whom a Discharge Book is produced must **return it to the holder** as soon as practicable after the entry has been made or after any inspection of it[42].
* Under regulation **23**(1) any person having possession of a Discharge Book must, after he becomes aware that the **holder has died**, has been **discharged** from any ship, or has been **left behind** in any country, deliver it to a superintendent or proper officer or to the Registrar General of Shipping and Seamen as soon as practicable.
* Under regulation **24** when his Discharge Book is lost, destroyed or defaced, or the space provided in it for entries except those referred to in Schedule 3 is filled up, a person must, within 7 days of satisfying the conditions specified in regulation 15(2), apply for a new Discharge Book.
* Schedule 3, which relates to regulations 18, 19 and 29, lists the particulars to be furnished in applications for seamen's documents. Item 11 in the list (National Insurance number) was omitted by the MS (Seaman's Documents) (Amendment) Regulations 1995 (SI 1995/1900).

E06a.2c Provisions relating to both British Seamen's Cards and Discharge Books

* In Part III of the Regulations "seaman's document" means a British Seaman's Card or a Discharge Book, and references to the holder of a seaman's document must be construed accordingly (regulation 25).
* Under regulation 26(1) if it appears to the holder that any entry in a seaman's document is not correct, he must forthwith inform the Registrar General of Shipping and Seamen or a superintendent.
* Under regulation 27(1) if it appears to a superintendent, a proper officer, a police officer or the Registrar General of Shipping and Seamen that the holder of a seaman's document was not entitled to apply for it, or that the person in possession of a seaman's document is not the legal holder, the person (including the holder) in possession of the document must, on demand made by a superintendent, a proper officer, a police officer, or the Registrar General of Shipping and Seamen, as the case may be, surrender it.

---

[42] The practice of some masters of retaining Discharge Books during the voyage has no statutory basis and is actually a contravention of regulation 22(3).

* Under regulation 28(1) no person other than a person authorised by regulation 5, 8, 18, 20 or 21 may make any mark or entry upon, or erase, cancel or alter any mark or entry made upon or otherwise deface or destroy a seaman's document.

* Under regulation 29 an application for the issue of a seaman's document or for the endorsement of a British Seaman's Card under regulation 8 must be made in writing to the Registrar General of Shipping and Seamen or an MCA superintendent.

E06b PASSPORTS, VISAS AND WORK PERMITS

E06b.1 UK passport

* A UK passport -
  - is evidence of the holder's identity and nationality and is therefore a very valuable document when abroad;
  - is issued by the UK Passport Agency;
  - is machine readable (new passports only) so as to reduce delay at airports, etc.;
  - must be signed by the holder;
  - will share a common format with the passports of other member States of the EU if the holder is a UK national for EU purposes, i.e.:
    • a British citizen;
    • a British subject with the right of abode in the UK; or
    • a British Dependent Territories citizen by virtue of a connection with Gibraltar;
  - will not have references to the European Community on the front cover and inside if the holder has any other form of nationality.
* Machine-readable passports must be completely renewed when any detail (e.g. the holder's address) changes.
* In some countries the law requires the holder to carry his passport at all times as a form of identity.
* A foreign authority or organisation may occasionally need to hold a passport temporarily, e.g. during a ship's stay or to enable a seaman left behind to be registered with the police, where the local law requires this.
* In case of any problem concerning a UK passport, the master should immediately contact the nearest British Consul.
* A seafarer travelling abroad should ensure that his/her passport will be valid for the voyage.
* Some countries have an immigration requirement for a passport to remain valid for a minimum period beyond the date of entry to the country.
* **UK Passport Agency website**: www.ukpa.gov.uk

E06b.2 Visas

- are required by many countries to be obtained by foreign passport holders before arrival in the country.
- must normally be obtained on the instructions of the seafarer's employer, before travelling to join a ship.
* For information on the visa requirements of a particular country, the embassy or a consulate of the country should be contacted.
* A UK Passport holder's national status is shown on the personal details page of the passport. If this is any of the following, the holder may, in certain countries, need a visa that is not required by British Citizens.
• British Dependent Territories Citizen;
• British Overseas Citizen;
• British Subject;
• British Nationals Overseas; or
• British Protected Person.
* A **nonimmigrant visa** is required by anyone seeking to enter the **United States** for a temporary period who is not eligible to travel visa-free under the Visa Waiver Program. It is important to note that the validity period of a visa relates only to the time in which the holder may travel to the United States and apply for admission at a port of entry. It does not guarantee entry into the United States. The officer of the Immigration and Naturalization Service at the port of entry determines a person's eligibility for admission.
* **US Embassy London Visa Services website**: www.usembassy.org.uk/cons_web/visa/visaindex.htm
* **UK Foreign and Commonwealth Office Visa website**: http://visa.fco.gov.uk/

E06b.3 Work permits

* Where a national of one country intends to work in another country or on a ship belonging to another country, he will generally need a **work permit** issued by that country. This applies to **UK nationals working in non-UK ships**, and to some **non-UK nationals working in UK ships**. Work permits are often restricted to persons who are **sponsored by an employer**, and must be obtained **before** entering the country.
* In the UK a "**work permit**" is a document issued by Work Permits (UK)[43] that allows a person to work in the UK for a particular employer.
* Under the Immigration Act 1971 anyone wishing to work in the UK must generally have the approval of Work Permits (UK). If they are not in possession of a **work permit** and a **valid passport** when they arrive, the Immigration Officer may refuse them entry.
* Paragraph 9.1 of MGN 179 (Certificates of Equivalent Competency) states that CEC applicants who are not nationals of EEA countries should note that they might need to have a work permit if they are intending to work on a ship which operates solely within UK territorial waters.
* **UK Government website** containing work permit information: www.ind.homeoffice.gov.uk
* **UK work permit information** can also be found at www.workpermit.co.uk/uk/employee.htm

E06c VACCINATION AND MEDICAL FITNESS DOCUMENTS

E06c.1 International Vaccination Certificate

* **Regulation 9(3) of The Public Health (Ships) Regulations 1979** (SI 1979/1435) provides that on arrival of any ship which during its voyage has been in a foreign port other than an excepted port the authorised officer, or at any port where their employment for this purpose is sanctioned by the Commissioners of Customs and Excise, a customs officer, may, and if so required by the Secretary of State must, require any person on board or disembarking from the ship to produce a valid **International Vaccination Certificate**.
* The International Health Regulations (1969) (see A06a) currently provide that a certificate of vaccination against **yellow fever** is the only certificate that should be required for international travel[44]. However, vaccination against yellow fever is strongly recommended by WHO to all travellers who intend to go to places other than the major cities in the countries where the disease occurs in man or is assumed to be present in primates.

E06c.2 Medical Fitness Certificate

* The **MS (Medical Examination) Regulations 2002** (SI 2002/2055) -
  - **revoke** the MS (Medical Examination) Regulations 1983 (SI 1983/808), the MS (Medical Examination) (Amendment) Regulations 1985 (SI 1985/512) and the MS (Medical Examination) (Amendment) Regulations 1990 (SI 1990/1985).
  - **apply** to sea-going UK ships of any tonnage wherever they may be, other than fishing vessels, pleasure vessels, and offshore installations on their working stations (regulation 3(1)).
  - **prohibit** the employment of a seafarer in a ship to which the Regulations apply unless he holds a valid Medical Fitness Certificate (regulation 4(1)).
  - **permit** a seafarer to continue to be employed for a period of three months without a valid Medical Fitness Certificate if the validity of his Medical Fitness Certificate expires while he is in a location where medical examination in accordance with the Regulations is impracticable (regulation 4(2)).
  - **prohibit** the employment of a seafarer in a ship in a capacity or in a geographical area precluded by any restriction in the seafarer's Medical Fitness Certificate (regulation 4(3)).
* **Arrangements** for provision of seafarer medical examinations are explained in **MGN 219**.
* Any Medical Fitness Certificate issued to a seafarer by an approved medical practitioner in respect of a medical examination conducted before 1 September 2002 (the date on which the Regulations came into force) will be deemed to be **equivalent** to a Medical Fitness Certificate issued under regulation 7 (regulation 5(1)). Any such certificate will remain valid for the period specified in it, notwithstanding the maximum periods specified in regulation 8 (regulation 5(2)).
* Any **Medical Fitness Certificate** issued to a seafarer by an approved authority under the laws of **another country or territory outside the UK**, as specified in **MSN 1765**, will be deemed to be **equivalent** to a Medical Fitness

---

[43] Work Permits (UK) is the Home Office department responsible for issuing work permits. It was formerly part of the Department for Education and Employment (DfEE) and was known as the Overseas Labour Service (OLS).

[44] The requirements of some countries are, however, in excess of the International Health Regulations.

Certificate issued under regulation 7 (regulation 6(1)). Any such certificate will remain in force for the period specified in it, notwithstanding the maximum periods specified in regulation 8 (regulation 6(2)).

* **Every application for a Medical Fitness Certificate** must, on payment of the prescribed fee, be **considered** by an approved medical practitioner (regulation 7(1)).
* If, after **examination** of the applicant, the practitioner considers that the applicant is **fit**, having regard to the **medical standards** specified in **MSN 1765**, he must issue the applicant with a **Medical Fitness Certificate** in an approved form (regulation 7(2)). The certificate may be **restricted** to such capacity of sea service or geographical areas as the practitioner considers appropriate (regulation 7(3)).
* The seafarer's employer at the time an application for a Medical Fitness Certificate is made under regulation 7(1) must ensure that the application is at **no cost to the seafarer** (regulation 7(4)).
* Under regulation 8, the approved medical practitioner must specify on the Medical Fitness Certificate its **period of validity**, from the date of the medical examination, subject to the following maximum periods:
  * in respect of applicants **under 18** years of age, **one year**;
  * in respect of applicants of **18 years of age or over, two years**[45].
* **Regulation 9(1)** provides that if an approved medical practitioner has **reasonable grounds** for believing that:
  - there has been a **significant change in the medical fitness** of a seafarer during the period of validity of his Medical Fitness Certificate; or
  - when the Medical Fitness Certificate was issued, the practitioner, **had he been in possession of full details of the seafarer's condition**, could not reasonably have considered that he was fit, having regard to the medical standards referred to in regulation 7; or
  - the Medical Fitness Certificate was **not issued in accordance with the Regulations**,
  he may:
  * **suspend** the validity of the certificate until the seafarer has undergone a **further medical examination**;
  * **suspend** the certificate for such period as he considers the seafarer **will remain unfit** to go to sea; or
  * **cancel** the certificate if he considers that the seafarer is **likely to remain permanently unfit** to go to sea,
  and must **notify the seafarer** accordingly.
* The approved medical practitioner may require that a **Medical Fitness Certificate which has been suspended or cancelled** under regulation 9(1) be **surrendered** as he directs (regulation 9(2)).
* **Regulation 10** provides for a **review** of the matter by a single medical referee appointed by the MCA where a seafarer is aggrieved by a refusal to issue him with a Medical Fitness Certificate, or any restriction imposed on a Certificate, or the cancellation or suspension for more than 3 months of a Certificate.
* Where an approved medical practitioner has certified that a **seafarer engaged on watchkeeping duties** is suffering from **health problems** which the practitioner considers are due to the fact that the seafarer performs **night work**, and it is possible for the employer to transfer the seafarer to day work to which the seafarer is suited, the **employer must transfer the seafarer** accordingly (regulation 11).
* **Regulation 13** permits a "relevant inspector" to **inspect any UK ship** to which the Regulations apply and to **detain the ship** if he is satisfied that any seafarer is unable to produce a Medical Fitness Certificate as required by the Regulations.
* For notes on **requirements relating to medical fitness and certification** in Part 1 of the MCA's Training and Certification Guidance, see E02c.11 and E02c.1m.

E06d CARRIAGE AND PRODUCTION OF DOCUMENTS BY SEAFARERS

* Under **section 50(1) of the Merchant Shipping Act 1995** (Production of certificates and other documents of qualification), any person serving or engaged to serve in any ship to which section 50 applies (i.e. ships which are sea-going ships) and holding any certificate or other document which is evidence that he is qualified for the purposes of section 47 must on demand produce it to any superintendent, surveyor of ships or proper officer and (if he is not himself the master) to the master of the ship.
* **Regulation 14 of the MS (Safe Manning, Hours of Work and Watchkeeping) Regulations 1997** (SI 1997/1320) provides that without prejudice to regulation 4 (which concerns responsibilities of companies, masters and others), the **company and the master** must ensure that there are **carried at all times on board ship all original certificates and other documents** issued pursuant to the STCW Convention indicating the qualification of **any member of the crew** to perform functions which they are required to perform aboard ship in the course of their designated duties.
* The requirement of regulation 14 (above) should be construed in the light of the **guidance for port State control officers in MSC/Circ.1030**, issued by IMO on 29 May 2002, which can be summarised as follows:

---

[45] MGN 91, which contains Part 1 of the MCA's Training and Certification Guidance (see E02c.1), specifies periods of validity which, for seafarers of 18 years of age or over, are no longer correct.

1. The Maritime Safety Committee noted that some port State control officers were requiring **documentary evidence of successful completion of short-course training** meeting the requirements in (STCW 95) regulations VI/1, VI/2, VI/3 and VI/4 from seafarers holding certificates of competency issued under (STCW 95) regulations II/1, II/2, II/3, III/1, III/2, III/3 and VII/2 even though the Convention includes this training as a pre-requisite for the issue of these certificates of competency.

2. The Committee agreed that **certificates of competency** issued in compliance with regulations II/1, II/2, II/3, III/1, III/2, III/3 and VII/2 **also included the following competency requirements** of chapter VI: **proficiency in survival craft and rescue boats other than fast rescue boats** (regulation VI/2, paragraph 1), training in **advanced fire fighting** (regulation VI/3), and **medical first aid** (regulation VI/4, paragraph 1).

3. The Committee further agreed that it was therefore **not necessary for the holders of certificates of competency to carry additional documentary evidence** in respect of those **competences of chapter VI** listed in paragraph 2 above.

E07 Engagement and discharge of crew

E07a LEGISLATION RELATING TO ENGAGEMENT AND DISCHARGE

E07a.1 Primary legislation relating to engagement and discharge

* **Section 24 of the Merchant Shipping Act 1995** provides that, with certain exceptions which do not directly concern engagement and discharge, Part III applies only to ships which are **sea-going ships** and **masters and seamen employed in sea-going ships**. It does not apply, therefore, to ships operating in categorised waters, or their crews (see D04c.2a).

* Under **section 25** an **agreement in writing** must be made between each person employed as a seaman in a UK ship and the persons employing him and must be signed both by him and by or on behalf of them (section 25(1)). Except in the case of multiple ship agreements, Crew Agreements must be **contained in one document**, although there may be more than one Crew Agreement[46] covering the persons employed in a ship (section 25(2)). The provisions and form of a Crew Agreement must be **approved** by the MCA (section 25(3)). A Crew Agreement must be **carried in the ship to which it relates** whenever the ship goes to sea (section 25(4)). Exemption regulations may be made and **exemptions** may be granted (section 25(5)). Where an exemption has been granted, the ship must carry a **document evidencing the exemption** (section 25(6)).

* **Sections 26, 27 and 28** provide the **enabling powers** under which any new legislation relating to Crew Agreements, etc. may be made. **Section 26** enables various regulations relating to Crew Agreements to be made. **Section 27** enables various regulations concerning discharge of seamen to be made. **Section 28** enables regulations made under section 27 (if any) to be applied where a seaman employed in a UK ship is left behind outside the UK otherwise than on being discharged.

* **Section 29** provides that where a **UK ship ceases to be registered** (i.e. registered in the UK), any seaman employed in the ship must be discharged from the ship **unless** he consents in writing to continue his employment in the ship; and, in relation to his wages, sections 30 to 33 will apply as if the ship had remained a UK ship. For notes on discharge procedure where the ship is leaving the UK Register, see E07d.10.

* **Section 55(1)** provides that a person under school-leaving age must not be employed in any UK ship except as permitted by regulations made under section 55. Section 55(2) contains enabling powers for the making of regulations prescribing circumstances in which young persons may be employed on UK ships.

* **Section 78(1)** provides that except as provided by regulations made under section 78, the master of every UK ship must **make and maintain a list of the crew** containing such particulars as are required by the regulations. Section 78(2) provides enabling powers to make regulations relating to Lists of Crew.

* **Section 84** contains **definitions** used in the interpretation of Part III.

* **Secondary legislation** on Crew Agreements and engagement and discharge procedures is chiefly in **the MS (Crew Agreements, Lists of Crew and Discharge of Seamen) Regulations 1991** (SI 1991/2144).

---

[46] Some cruise ships have separate agreements for officers, ratings and hotel staff, each group often having a different employer in a different country. The agreements may include both BSF and NFD agreements, e.g. BSF for senior officers and hotel personnel, and NFD for others. All documents must be contained in one ALC1 outer cover.

E07a.2 Secondary legislation relating to engagement and discharge

* **Principal regulations** are the **MS (Crew Agreements, Lists of Crew and Discharge of Seamen) Regulations 1991** (SI 1991/2144) (see E07b).
* Other SIs relating to engagement and discharge include:
    * the **MS and FV (Health and Safety at Work) (Employment of Young Persons) Regulations 1998** (SI 1998/2411) (see E05c.1);
    * the **MS (Seamen's Documents) Regulations 1987** (SI 1987/408) (see E06a.2);
    * the **MS (Safe Manning, Hours of Work and Watchkeeping) Regulations 1997** (SI 1997/1320) as amended by SIs 1997/1911 and 2000/484 (see E03b).
* Relevant M Notices include **MGN 111**, **MGN 123** and **MGN 148**. In the case of **pleasure yachts** with crew agreements, **MGN 149** is relevant.

E07b CREW AGREEMENTS REGULATIONS

E07b.1 Crew Agreements Regulations - introduction

* The **MS (Crew Agreements, Lists of Crew and Discharge of Seamen) Regulations 1991** (SI 1991/2144) -
    - **were made** under provisions of the Merchant Shipping Act 1970.
    - **revoke**, and re-enact with amendments, the MS (Crew Agreements, Lists of Crew and Discharge of Seamen) Regulations 1972 as amended. **2**. The amendments principally end certain requirements of the 1972 Regulations, i.e.
        * the requirement to notify superintendents of the intention to open a Crew Agreement;
        * the requirement to deliver a copy of the Crew Agreement to a superintendent or proper officer;
        * the requirement to notify superintendents and proper officers of crew changes;
        * the requirement to notify superintendents and proper officers of the intention to discharge seafarers unless a wages dispute is pending.
    - provide, in addition to fixed term Crew Agreements, for **indefinite Crew Agreements**.
    - **contain** the following regulations: **1**. Citation, commencement and revocation. **2**. Interpretation. PART I - ENGAGEMENT OF SEAMEN. **3**. Interpretation of Part I. **4**. Exemptions from requirements of section 1 (Crew Agreements). **5**. Carrying of copy of Crew Agreement in ships. **6**. Delivery of copy of Crew Agreement. **7**. Display of Crew Agreement. **8**. Supply and production of copy documents. **9**. Production of documents to officers of Customs and Excise, and a superintendent, and Registrar General of Shipping and Seamen. **10**. Offences under Part I. PART II – LISTS OF CREW. **11**. Interpretation of Part II. **12**. Exemptions from the requirements of section 69 of the Act (Lists of Crew). **13**. List of crew contained in Crew Agreement. **14**. Particulars to be specified in List of Crew. **15, 16** and **17**. Copies of List of Crew. **18**. Delivery of List of Crew to Registrar-General. **19**. Duration of List of Crew. **20**. Delivery of List of Crew. **21**. Production of Lists of Crew. **22**. Offences under Part II. PART III – DISCHARGE OF SEAMEN. **23**. Notice of discharge. **24**. Discharge. **25**. Procedure on discharge. **26**. Offences under Part III.
* In Part II of the Regulations (Lists of Crew), "**seaman**" includes the master of a ship (see E07c.2a). The **master is not a "seaman"** for the purposes of Part I, and **is not engaged on a Crew Agreement** (see E04b).

E07b.2 Provisions relating to Crew Agreements (Part I)

E07b.2a Exemptions from provisions relating to Crew Agreements (regulation 4)

* Under regulation 4(1) the provisions relating to Crew Agreements do not apply to the following descriptions of ships and voyages:
    * ships owned by General Lighthouse Authorities;
    * ships of less than 80 net tonnage on coastal voyages (e.g. small inter-island UK ferries);
    * pleasure yachts on coastal voyages, or on other voyages if no more than 4 crew are paid; and
    * ships on coastal trials voyages.
* Under regulation 4(2) the provisions relating to Crew Agreements do not apply to a person solely employed in work directly related to:
    * the **exploration** of the seabed or sub-soil or the **exploitation** of their natural resources;
    * the storage of **gas** in or under the seabed or the recovery of gas so stored;

- the laying, inspection, testing, repair, alteration, renewal or removal of any submarine telegraph **cable**; or
- **pipeline works** as defined in section 26(2) of the Petroleum and Submarine Pipe-Lines Act 1975 including the assembling, inspection, testing, maintaining, adjusting, repairing, altering, renewing, changing the position of, or dismantling a pipe-line or length of pipe-line; or
- the **provision of goods, personal services or entertainment** on board; and who is not employed by the owner or the person employing the master of the ship and is not engaged in the navigation of the ship in the deck, engine room, radio, medical or catering department of that ship and who has been given a written statement by his employer specifying the nature of the employment, the remuneration, the intervals at which the remuneration is to be paid and the length of notice which he is required to give and entitled to receive to determine his employment; and any terms or conditions of his employment relating to sick pay, hours of work (including any terms and conditions relating to normal working hours), pensions and entitlement to holidays;

* Under regulation 4(2) the provisions relating to Crew Agreements do not apply to a member of the **naval, military or air forces** of the Crown or of **any service administered by the Defence Council**, when acting as such a member[47].

* **Exempted personnel** as listed above must be entered on a List of Crew, the appropriate List of Crew being form ALC1(b) - List of Crew exempted from the requirement to sign a Crew Agreement.

* **Exempted ships** are not required to have a Crew Agreement but must carry:
  - an **Exemption Certificate** issued by the MCA; and
  - a **List of Crew Exempted from the Requirement to Sign a Crew Agreement** (i.e. form **ALC1(b)** inside an outer cover, **ALC(EX.1)**).

E07b.2b Carrying of copy of Multiple Ship Crew Agreement (regulation 5)

* Under regulation 5(1) a ship required to carry a Crew Agreement may, in the case of an Agreement which relates to both that and other ships (i.e. a "multiple ship agreement") and which is kept at an address ashore in the UK, comply with that requirement by carrying a copy of the Agreement certified as required by regulation 5(2).

* A copy of a multiple ship Crew Agreement carried in a ship in accordance with regulation 5(1) must bear a **certificate** signed by the master certifying that it is a **true copy of the Crew Agreement** and specifying the **address** in the UK at which the Crew Agreement is kept and the name of the person by whom it is so kept.

* For **general notes on multiple ship agreements**, see E07c.1g.

E07b.2c Delivery of Crew Agreement (regulation 6)

* Regulation 6 provides that the employer must, within **three days** of the date when the last person remaining employed under the Crew Agreement ceases to be employed under that agreement, or, if it is not practicable within that period, as soon as practicable thereafter, deliver the Crew Agreement to a superintendent or proper officer for the place where the ship was when that person ceased to be so employed. (In practice the master usually sends the agreement on behalf of the employer.)

* **If the Crew Agreement covers an indefinite period** (i.e. it is an "indefinite Crew Agreement") the employer must deliver the Crew Agreement within seven days of it being opened to a superintendent or proper officer for the place where the ship was when the agreement was opened. (In practice the master should send a copy.)

E07b.2d Display of copy of Crew Agreement (regulation 7)

* Under regulation 7 the **master** of a ship must arrange that **a copy** of any Crew Agreement relating to the ship, **or an extract** containing the terms of the agreement applicable to all seamen employed under it, and to each description of seamen so employed, **is posted in some conspicuous place** on board where it **can be read by the persons employed** under the crew agreement. The document must be kept so posted and legible so long as any seaman is employed in the ship under the Crew Agreement.

E07b.2e Supply of copy of documents (regulation 8)

* Under regulation 8, the **employer or the master** must, **on demand on a seaman**, and within a reasonable time:
  - arrange to be **supplied** to him a **copy of the Crew Agreement** under which he is employed **or such extracts therefrom** as are necessary to show the terms on which he is employed; and
  - arrange to be **made available** to him a copy of **any document referred to**[48] in the Agreement.

---

[47] Examples of the many services administered by the Defence Council are the Royal Fleet Auxiliary and the UK Hydrographic Office.
[48] Documents referred to in the standard terms of a BSF Agreement include the Code of Conduct for the Merchant Navy and the NMB Conditions in force at 30 September 1990. Documents that may be referred to in an additional clause may include, for example, the company's Drug and Alcohol

E07b.2f Production of Crew Agreements and exemption certificates to officials (regulation 9)

* Under regulation 9 the **master** must, **on demand by a UK Customs and Excise officer, an MCA superintendent or the Registrar General of Shipping and Seamen** produce:
  * **any Crew Agreement**, or the **copy of any Crew Agreement** carried in the ship under regulation 5; and
  * **any certificate evidencing an exemption** from the statutory requirements relating to Crew Agreements with respect to the ship or to any person in it (as referred to in E07b.2a).

E07b.3 Provisions relating to Lists of Crew (Part II)

E07b.3a Exceptions from requirements relating to Lists of Crew (regulation 12)

* Under regulation 12 the statutory duty to make and maintain a List of Crew does not apply in relation to a pleasure yacht which is -
  * engaged on a coastal voyage; or
  * engaged on a non-coastal voyage, provided that not more than 4 members of the crew receive wages for their employment.

E07b.3b List of Crew contained in Crew Agreement (regulation 13)

* Regulation 13 provides that a List of Crew may be contained in the same document as a Crew Agreement relating to one ship only and any particulars entered in the Crew Agreement shall be treated as forming part of the particulars entered in the list.

E07b.3c Particulars to be specified in List of Crew (regulation 14)

* Regulation 14(1) sets out the **particulars** which must be contained in a List of Crew, which are:
  * the name of the ship, its port of registry and official number;
  * the name of the owner of the ship and his address and of any other person registered as manager or ship's husband and
  * the number of any Exemption Certificate (in relation to Crew Agreements) granted by the MCA to the ship or any person in it ; and
  * subject to regulation 14(4), with respect to every seaman on board, whether or not he is employed under a Crew Agreement:
    * his name and address;
    * the number of his current discharge book (if any) or the date and place of his birth;
    * the name of the ship in which he was last employed, and, if he was discharged from that ship more than 12 months before he became employed in the ship to which the List of Crew relates, the year in which he was so discharged;
    * the capacity in which he is employed in the ship;
    * the grade (including any command, service or other endorsement) and number of any certificate of competency or of service held by him;
    * the date on which he went on board the ship to commence his employment in it;
    * the date on and place at which he left the ship and, if he left on discharge, the reason for his discharge;
    * if he is left behind otherwise than on discharge, the date and place of and the reason (if known to the master) for this being done; and
    * the name and relationship of his next of kin and the address of his next of kin, if different from that of the seaman.
* A List of Crew of a ship belonging to a **General Lighthouse Authority**[49] need contain only the ship's name, port of registry and official number and, in respect of each seaman, his name, address, date and place of joining, date and place of leaving, and if he left on discharge, the reason for his discharge (regulation 14(2)).

Policy and agreements made with seafarers' trades unions. In an NFD Agreement the MN Code of Conduct or another (approved) code of conduct may be incorporated into the Agreement by reference.

[49] The General Lighthouse Authorities are Trinity House (in respect of England and Wales), the Northern Lighthouse Board (in respect of Scotland and the Isle of Man) and the Commissioners of Irish Lights (in respect of Ireland and Northern Ireland).

* So long as the remaining particulars listed above are contained in the Crew Agreement, a **List of Crew which relates to seamen employed under a Crew Agreement** need contain only the ship's name, port of registry and official number and, in respect of each seaman, his name, address, number of his current discharge book (if any) or date and place of his birth, capacity in which he is employed, date and place of joining, date and place of leaving, and if he left on discharge, the reason for his discharge (regulation 14(3)).
* Lists of Crew relating to members of the **naval, military or air forces of the Crown or of any service administered by the Defence Council** (when the members are acting as such) need contain only a seaman's name, address, date and place of joining, date and place of leaving, and if he left on discharge, the reason for his discharge (regulation 14(4)).

E07b.3d Copies of List of Crew (regulations 15, 16 and 17)

* Under regulation 15(1) a copy of every List of Crew (including all changes in it notified to the owner) must be maintained by the owner of the ship at an address in the UK.
* The master must, as soon as practicable and in any event within 3 days of any change being made in the List of Crew, notify the change to the owner of the ship (regulation 15(2)).
* In regulation 15 the "owner of the ship" means the person registered as managing owner, ship's husband or manager, or if there is no such person, the owner of the ship (regulation 15(3)).
* Under regulation 16 when any person (e.g. the owner or manager) having in his possession the copy of a List of Crew has reason to believe that the ship to which it relates has been lost or abandoned, he must immediately deliver the copy of the list to an MCA superintendent.
* Under regulation 17 a person (e.g. the owner or manager) having in his possession a copy of a List of Crew must produce it on demand to an MCA superintendent.

E07b.3e Delivery of List of Crew on demand of RSS (regulation 18)

* Under regulation 18 the **owner** must, within 28 days of any demand by the Registrar General of Shipping and Seamen, deliver a list of the crew on board the ship at a date specified by the Registrar General of Shipping and Seamen. In practice the demand would be made by the RSS, Cardiff, in circumstances where, for example, a ship was overdue and it was necessary to know the details of the personnel on board.

E07b.3f Duration of List of Crew (regulation 19)

* Regulation 19 provides that, except in the case where a Crew Agreement for the ship covers an indefinite period, a List of Crew will remain in force -
  * if any person is employed in the ship under a Crew Agreement, until all the persons employed under that agreement in that ship have been discharged (regulation 19(a));
  * in the case of a ship engaged on coastal voyages for port authorities, whose crew are returned to shore within each period of 24 hours, for 12 months after the first entry relating to a seaman is made on the list (regulation 19(b)); and
  * in any other case, until the ship first calls at a port more than 6 months after the first entry relating to a seaman is made in the list (regulation 19(c)).

E07b.3g Delivery of Lists of Crew no longer in force (regulation 20)

* Regulation 20(1) provides that the **master** must, within 3 days after a List of Crew (other than one relating to a ship of less than 25gt or to a ship belonging to a General Lighthouse Authority) has ceased to be in force or, if it is not practicable within that period, as soon as practicable thereafter, deliver the list to an MCA superintendent or proper officer for the place where the ship is when the List of Crew ceases to be in force.
* Regulation 20(2) provides that where the Crew Agreement covers an indefinite period the **owner** must deliver a list **every six months** after the Crew Agreement is opened, showing all changes that have occurred since the list was last submitted, to the superintendent at a port in the UK where the ship was when the six month period expired, or, if the ship was out of the UK at that time, to the Registrar General of Shipping and Seamen, within seven days of the expiry of each period of six months.

E07b.3h Production of Lists of Crew (regulation 21)

* Under regulation 21 a master must, on demand, produce to the Registrar General of Shipping and Seamen (including the RSS), a superintendent or proper officer, a surveyor of ships in the course of any inspection of the ship or an officer of Customs and Excise the List of Crew required to be maintained in the ship.

E07b.4 Provisions relating to discharge of seamen (Part III)

E07b.4a Notice of Discharge (regulation 23)

* Regulation 23(1) provides that in the event of any **dispute** about a seaman's wages, and that dispute is at the time of discharge to be submitted to a superintendent or proper officer, then subject to regulation 24 the master must, not less than 48 hours before the seaman is discharged or, if it is not practicable within that period, as soon as practicable thereafter, give a **Notice of Discharge in writing** to a superintendent or proper officer for the place where the seaman is to be discharged.
* A Notice of Discharge must contain the name of the ship, its port of registry and official number; the place, date and time of the seaman's discharge; and the capacity in which the seaman is employed in the ship (regulation 23(2)).
* If a Notice of Discharge relates to more than one seaman, it must also state, the number of seamen being discharged (regulation 23(3)).

E07b.4b Discharge (regulation 24)

* Regulation 24 provides that a **Notice of Discharge is not required** in respect of a seaman discharged if the seaman is to be discharged from a **ship exempted** from the requirements relating to Crew Agreements by regulation 4(1) or if the **seaman is exempted** from signing a Crew Agreement under regulation 4(2).

E07b.4c Procedure on discharge (regulation 25)

* Regulation 25(1)(a) provides that **where a seaman is present** when he is discharged, the **master**, or one of the ship's officers authorised by him in that behalf, must, before the seaman is discharged -
    - if the seaman produces his **discharge book** to him, record in it the ship's name, port of registry, gross or net tonnage and official number, the description of the voyage (e.g. "Unlimited Trading" or "Near Coastal Area"), the capacity in which the seaman has been employed in the ship, the date on which he began to be so employed and the date and place of his discharge (regulation 25(a)(i)); or
    - if the seaman does not produce his discharge book to him, give him a **Certificate of Discharge** containing the same particulars (regulation 25(a)(ii). (**MGN 123** contains a specimen Certificate of Discharge which can be photocopied if necessary.)
* Regulation 25(1)(b) provides that the **master** must ensure that the seaman is discharged in the presence of the master himself, the seaman's employer or a person authorised in that behalf by the master or employer.
* Regulation 25(1)(c) provides that the **person in whose presence the seaman is being discharged** must:
    * make and sign an **entry in the Official Log Book** recording the **place, date and time** of the seaman's discharge; and
    * make and sign an **entry in the Crew Agreement** or, if there is a List of Crew separate from a Crew Agreement, in the **List of Crew**, recording the **place and date of, and the reason** for, the seaman's discharge.
* Under regulation 25(1)(d) the **seaman** must sign the entry in the Crew Agreement and List of Crew.
* Regulation 25(2) provides that where a **seaman is not present** when he is discharged, the master, or a person authorised in that behalf by the master, must make the entries referred to in regulation 25(1)(c).
* Regulation 25(3) provides that all entries in the official log book required under the preceding paragraphs of this regulation must, in addition to being signed by the person making the entry, be **signed** also by a **member of the crew**.
* Regulation 25(4) provides that **if a seaman so requests**, within a period of 6 months from the date of his discharge from or his leaving the ship, the master, or one of the ship's officers authorised by him in that behalf, must give him a **certificate** (which must be separate from any other document) either as to the **quality of his work** or indicating whether he has fully **discharged his obligations** under his contract of employment. (This applies in respect of seamen who are discharged from a Crew Agreement and other personnel who are signed off ALC1(b).)

E07c GENERAL INFORMATION ON CREW AGREEMENTS AND LISTS OF CREW

E07c.1 General information relating to Crew Agreements

* A **Crew Agreement** -
    - is a **contract** made between the **employer** (not the master) and **each seaman** whose name appears on a List of Crew incorporated into the Crew Agreement document.
    - must be in **writing**.
    - must be **approved** by the MCA.
    - must be **signed** by both parties, although the **master** or other authorised person may sign it as an **agent** of the employer.
    - must be **carried** in the ship to which it is related when at sea.
* All individual agreements with the crew must be contained in an ALC1 document. ("ALC" stands for Agreement and List of Crew.) In ships with large crews, such as cruise ships, different sections of the crew are commonly engaged on Crew Agreements made with different employers; all these Agreements must be contained in the ALC1.
* A Crew Agreement should be opened, and seamen engaged, by the **master**, or a **person authorised** by him, or the **employer**; there is no statutory requirement in the Crew Agreements Regulations as to who should engage seamen. The person opening the agreement should sign the foot of the terms and conditions on ALC1(d).
* For notes on **provisions of the Crew Agreements Regulations**, see E07b.

E07c.1a The master as employer's agent for Crew Agreement purposes

* In some shipping companies, e.g. ferry companies, shore office personnel may organise and supervise the engagement of crew; in most companies the master is expected to do this himself. Where the master prepares the Crew Agreement documents and signs the foot of form ALC1(d) (terms of the agreement), he does so acting as the **employer's representative**.
* In common law, the master's agreement with his employer is considered to be contained in his personal contract, in verbal agreements, in his letter of appointment, in company standing orders to masters, etc. (see E04b). For these reasons, and since the master represents the employer for crew engagement purposes (see E04e.3), he should not sign the Crew Agreement.

E07c.1b Approved Crew Agreements

* The **provisions** and **form** of all Crew Agreements must be **approved by the MCA** ("form" meaning the size, shape, layout and provision for information in the agreement, as distinct from its contractual clauses).
* In consultation with the UK shipping industry, the MCA has produced a set of **standard Crew Agreements** for merchant ships, i.e.:
    * Form **ALC(BSF)1(d) – Contractual clauses** - for ships formerly operating under National Maritime Board (NMB) conditions. ("BSF" stands for British Shipping Federation.) Employers who were previously bound by the old NMB agreements may wish to use this agreement, which adopts all NMB agreements in force at 30 September 1990, when the NMB ceased to exist.
    * Form **ALC(NFD)1(d) – Contractual clauses** - a "minimum agreement" for other merchant ships (i.e. "non-federated" ships – hence "NFD"). This form has fewer standard terms than the BSF agreement, and does not incorporate the Merchant Navy Code of Conduct (although an employer may add a conduct-related clause with MCA approval).
* The **latest versions of the standard Crew Agreements** have been amended for the trading areas provided for by STCW 95, and also recognise that many UK ships no longer operate from the UK. They are available as paper documents from MCA Marine Offices in the UK and from proper officers abroad, and in **downloadable** form on the MCA website (see B05b.5). They are also printed in Annex 2 to **MGN 148**.
* Employers may produce their own copies of Crew Agreements, Lists of Crew and the List of Young Persons, provided that they replicate exactly the information on the MCA's standard documents or have been submitted to and approved by the MCA.
* **Contractual provisions** must be contained in all approved Crew Agreements to cover:
    * the persons between whom agreement is made;
    * the description of the voyage or voyages to which the agreement relates, and their geographical limits and/or the duration of the employment;
    * the capacity in which each seafarer is to be employed;

- the seafarer's pay, hours, leave and subsistence, which may be dealt with wholly or in part by incorporation of provisions of industrial agreements between the employer and the relevant trades unions (e.g. NUMAST and RMT) or the old NMB Agreements which were current on 30 September 1990;
- other rights and duties of the parties to the agreement;
- the terms under which either party may give notice to terminate the agreement; and
- the circumstances in which, notwithstanding the notice provisions, the agreement may be terminated by either party.

Provisions covering these items are in all standard Crew Agreements, i.e. ALC1(d)(BSF) and ALC1(d)(NFD).

* The provisions included in the standard Crew Agreement forms ALC1(d)(BSF) and ALC1(d)(NFD) cover the above items, and will be regarded by the MCA as approved provisions.
* Clauses dealing with the **duration and scope of the voyage and the rate of wages** require the insertion of further particulars. These should be inserted by the employer or the master on the employer's behalf, and are subject to the limitations in voyage clauses in fixed term crew agreements (see E07c.1d). Subject to those limitations the standard documents may be used without seeking prior approval from the MCA.
* An **outer protective cover** must be provided on the front of which provision should be made for the following information to be recorded:
  - name of ship, port of choice and official number;
  - description of the ship (e.g. passenger, tanker, ferry, general cargo, bulk cargo);
  - net tonnage);
  - name and address of registered owner or manager;
  - dates and places of commencement and (if appropriate) termination of the agreement.
* Provision should be made on the inside of the outer cover for entries by superintendents and proper officers.
* The **contractual provisions** should be enclosed in and attached to the outer cover.

E07c.1c Non-standard or modified Crew Agreements

* Employers who wish to use agreements **other than the standard forms** or who wish to use **modified versions of the standard forms** must submit them to MCA at Southampton for approval not less than 14 days before use. Such agreements will only be approved if:
  - the agreement complies with ILO Convention 22 (Seamen's Articles of Agreement);
  - the employment terms do not conflict with the general law of the UK, or place the UK in breach of her international obligations (e.g. under ILO Convention 87 (Freedom of Association and Protection of the Right to Organise).
* Where the terms of an existing Crew Agreement terms are to be modified after agreement between the employer and a seafarers' organisation, the employer must notify the change to the MCA.

E07c.1d Limitation on voyage clauses in fixed-term Crew Agreements

* Following implementation in the UK of the requirements of STCW 95, the **trading limits** for UK certificate holders have changed so that there are now only two trading areas for sea-going ships: **Near-Coastal** and **Unlimited Trading**. For a definition of the UK's Near-Coastal Area, see E02c.1.
* The MCA's **revised standard agreements** take account of the changes arising from STCW 95 and also recognise that many UK registered ships no longer operate to and from UK ports.
* **Approved durations** for Crew Agreements are:
  - **6 months** for a **running agreement** for vessels engaged in **frequent short voyages**, e.g. cross-channel ferries, unless the vessel has a small crew and a low staff turnover, in which case the agreement may be extended to 12 months;
  - **12 months** for any **other running agreement**;
  - **24 months** or first call at a port for a **voyage agreement**.
* These periods are subject to any **additional period** provided for in associated approved notice clauses.
* **Approved voyage clauses** (and **notice periods**) are open for agreement between the parties in fixed-term Crew Agreements.
* The **geographical limitations of a voyage clause** should be clearly stated when the clause is completed and used.

E07c.1e Running Agreements

* **Running agreements** -
  - are Crew Agreements for use in ships which are kept continuously manned for sea, so that one agreement "runs" up against another.are used in the majority of UK deep-sea and short-sea vessels.

- can be opened and closed at sea or in port. (It is not unusual to "change articles" at sea when on a running agreement.)
- may be for a maximum duration of **6 months** for vessels engaged in frequent short voyages, e.g. cross-channel ferries, unless the vessel has a small crew and a low staff turnover, in which case the agreement may be extended to 12 months.
- may be for a maximum duration of **12 months** in any other ship.

E07c.1f Voyage Agreements

* **Voyage agreements -**
  - are Crew Agreements used in ships which may not be continuously manned for sea, and where there may be an interval between the discharge of one "voyage crew" and the engagement of another[50].
  - are appropriate for a ship making occasional or "one off" voyages.
  - may only be opened or closed in port.
* A "**run agreement**" is a voyage agreement for a single voyage from one place to another, such as a delivery voyage or a scrapping voyage. A suitable standard voyage clause for insertion in a run agreement is produced by the MCA and is printed in MGN 148.

E07c.1g Multiple Agreements

* **Multiple agreements -**
  - are Crew Agreements **relating to more than one ship** and are used where several ships (e.g. ferries) run between the same ports and need to have crews who are willing to be employed on any of the company's ships operating from that port during the currency of the Agreement[51].
  - may be voyage or running agreements, but are more likely to be running agreements.
  - must be approved by the MCA.
  - are in the same form and contain the same provisions as ordinary standard agreements, except that the **name of each ship** to which they are related is entered on the **outer cover**. The original Agreement is kept at a place ashore, and each ship carries a copy of that Agreement. Each copy Agreement must be **certified** by the ship's master as a true copy and specify the **address** where the original is kept and the name of the person keeping it.
* For notes on statutory requirements relating to **carriage of a copy of a Multiple Ship Crew Agreement**, see E07b.2b.

E07c.1h Indefinite Agreements

- **are** Crew Agreements which **run without limit of time**, i.e. they remain open continuously so long as the ship is manned.
- **are permitted** under ILO Convention No.22 (Seamen's Articles of Agreement).
- **are permitted** by the MCA in **approved cases**.
- **must be specially requested** by the owner through MCA Southampton, marine office superintendents or British Consuls abroad.
- have **no special standard form of document**, i.e. the ordinary ALC documents are used.
- **are restricted** to ships trading in the Near Coastal Area, in order to protect employers from possible high repatriation costs (since a seaman may give notice at any time, irrespective of the location of the ship). In practice they are used mainly by ferry operators.
* In vessels which have an Indefinite Agreement there will be no need to "change articles" after 6 or 12 months. There is, however, a requirement for the owner to **deliver a list to the MCA every 6 months** showing all crew changes made in the last 6 months.
* Within 7 days of opening an indefinite agreement, the employer (or the master on his behalf) must deliver the agreement (meaning a copy) to an MCA superintendent or a proper officer.
* **In addition to the contractual provisions** contained in a standard agreement, **Indefinite Agreements must state**:
  • the intervals at which wages are to be paid;
  • the method of calculating leave entitlement;
  • the maximum period that a seaman can be required to remain on board between leave periods (in many cases a copy of the duty rosters will be sufficient);

---

[50] A voyage agreement was the traditional form of crew agreement under which, until the 1970s, the "deep sea crew" of a foreign-going UK ship would complete the overseas voyage, following which the discharge and loading period "on the coast" of the UK and near-Continent would be spent on Home Trade articles with a relief crew. The deep-sea crew would then rejoin and sign on a foreign-going voyage agreement.
[51] A seafarer may, for example, arrive for his duty shift to find that, following a breakdown, another ship has replaced the expected ship. He is contracted to work on any of the named ships.

- the notice required from each party to terminate a seaman's employment under the agreement which should not be less favourable than the provisions of section 49 Employment Protection (Consolidation) Act 1978 except in the following cases:
  - by mutual consent;
  - if medical evidence indicates that a seaman is incapable of continuing to perform his duties by reason of illness or injury;
  - if, in the opinion of the master, the continued employment of the seaman would be likely to endanger the ship or any person on board;
  - if a seaman, having been notified of the time the vessel is due to sail, is absent without leave at the time fixed for sailing and the vessel proceeds to sea without him or if substitutes have been engaged. Substitutes shall not, however, be engaged on a Crew Agreement more than 2 hours before the time fixed for sailing.
  - if the master is satisfied that an appropriate breach of the appropriate Code of Conduct for the time being in force has occurred.

E07c.1i Voyage clauses in Crew Agreements

* The geographical limits of the crew's employment should be clearly stated when the voyage clause is completed, e.g. "within the limits of 75° north latitude and 60° south latitude".
* Taking crew outside the geographical limits of the Crew Agreement, except for purposes of distress response or other *force majeure*, will amount to a breach of contract by the employer. Charter party terms may therefore be restricted by the terms of the Crew Agreement.

E07c.1j Breach of the Crew Agreement

* Breach of the Crew Agreement is a matter of contract law, i.e. **civil law** (see B03a.4), and may result in **dismissal** and/or a **civil action for damages** brought by the employer. The act constituting the breach of the Crew Agreement (e.g. assault, or possession of drugs) may, at the same time, be a **criminal offence** and may be dealt with accordingly; this may necessitate the master requesting police assistance from the port State or coastal State authorities. (For notes on civil and criminal consequences of a wrong, see B03b.6.)
* Crew Agreements contain a **Notice Clause** listing breaches for which the Agreement may be terminated by the master. Clause (iii) of a standard NFD agreement, for example, provides that in relation to an individual seaman the agreement may be terminated:
  - if a seaman is absent without leave at a time fixed for sailing; or
  - if, in the opinion of the master, the continued employment of the seaman would be likely to endanger the vessel or any person on board.
* Where any **code of conduct** is expressly incorporated into the Crew Agreement, the procedures in that code should be rigidly followed by the master in dealing with any breach of the Crew Agreement (see E10b).

E07c.1k Crew not required to sign off on leaving vessel

* Where **MCA approval** has been obtained, it is unnecessary for seamen working on **one-on/one-off** or similar rotas (e.g. 2 weeks on/2 weeks off or 2 weeks on/3 weeks off), and who are on **continuous pay** throughout, to sign off before each leave period, provided that they **expect to rejoin** after their leave and **before the expiry** of the Crew Agreement.
* If, under these arrangements, a **seaman fails to rejoin**, he should be **discharged in his absence** (following the procedure in E07d.7) and **re-engaged** if and when he rejoins. The same action should be taken if he is sent to another ship of the same fleet; a seaman cannot be on two Crew Agreements at once. His **Discharge Book** should be completed and **sent** to him.

E07c.2 General information relating to Lists of Crew

* For provisions of the Crew Agreements Regulations relating to **Lists of Crew**, see E07b.3.
* Two forms of List of Crew are in use in UK ships:
  - **ALC1(a)** - List of Crew and Signatures of Seamen who are Parties to the Crew Agreement; and
  - **ALC1(b)** - List of Crew Relating to Seamen Exempted under section 1(5) of Merchant Shipping Act 1970 from the Requirement to sign a Crew Agreement.

* **ALC1(a)** is both a record of the details of the employed crew, and a list of their signatures as parties to the Crew Agreement. When a seaman signs the ALC1(a) he is agreeing to the terms of the Crew Agreement (ALC1(d)), which he should be shown, and is signing a contract of employment.
* **ALC1(b)** is a record of all persons on board, including the master and all "exempted" personnel, other than those crew members who signed the ALC1(a), any pilot engaged and on board, and any passengers. For a definition of "passenger", see D04f.2a.
* **MGN 111** advises masters of their obligations to maintain a copy of every List of Crew at an address in the UK and to update the list within 3 days of any crew changes occurring.

E07c.2a Master's particulars in Lists of Crew

* Since, for List of Crew purposes, the master is defined as a "seaman" (see E07b.1) his details must be entered in a List of Crew. The proper list for the master's details is the **ALC1(b)** (see E07c.2). See also E04b.

E07c.2b Particulars entered in Lists of Crew

* Particulars entered in form **ALC1(a)** (revision 2/98) **when engaging seamen** are as follows.
  * **At top of page**: Reference number; Name of seaman (block letters); Discharge Book number (if any) or date and place of birth; Name of ship in which last employed (and year of discharge if more than 12 months before commencing this employment); Address of seaman; Name and relationship of next of kin and address, if different from seaman's; Date of commencement of employment on board; Signature of seaman on engagement.
  * **At foot of page**: Reference number (as at top of page); Capacity in which employed; Number of Certificate of Competency (stating "None" if none held); Full description of Certificate of Competency and/or Service, including all endorsements (e.g. restrictions, Dangerous Cargo Endorsements, etc.),
* Particulars entered in form **ALC1(b)** (revision 2/98) **when exempt seamen join the ship** are as follows: Reference number, with prefix "E"; Number of Certificate of Exemption; Name of seaman (block letters); Discharge Book number (if any) or date and place of birth; Name of ship in which last employed (and year of discharge if more than 12 months before commencing this employment); Address of seaman; Name and relationship of next of kin and address, if different from seaman's; Capacity in which employed; Grade and number of Certificate of Competency; Date of commencement of employment on board.
* Particulars entered in form **ALC1(a)** (revision 2/98) **when seamen are discharged** are (in the grey spaces at the top of the page): If discharged, the reason for discharge; Date and place of leaving the ship; Signature of seaman on discharge or if not discharged, the reason for being left behind, if known; Signature of person before whom the seaman is discharged.
* Particulars entered in form **ALC1(b)** (revision 2/98) **when exempt seamen leave the ship** are (in the grey spaces at the top of the page): Date and place of leaving the ship; Signature of seaman on discharge or if not discharged, the reason for being left behind, if known; Signature of person before whom the seaman is discharged.

E07c.2c Rates of pay in Lists of Crew

* The entry for each seaman in the List of Crew of seamen who are parties to the Crew Agreement must indicate his/her **rate of pay at the time of engagement**. Form ALC1(a) has a special column for this entry; if more convenient, however, a **company pay scale** from which the rate can be determined may be annexed to the Crew Agreement.
* Entries such as "As Agreed" or "Salary" are not acceptable.

E07c.2d List of Young Persons (ALC1(c))

* Section 2 of the MS (International Labour Conventions) Act 1925.provides that a **list of young persons** must be included in every Crew Agreement.
* The MCA document for use in Crew Agreements is form **ALC1(c) – List of Young Persons**. This is normally supplied in the pack containing all other Crew Agreement documents.
* **ALC1(c)** -
  - is not a List of Crew as such, but an **extract** of details from any List of Crew (ALC1(a) or ALC1(b)) containing details showing that a person who works on board is under 18 years of age at the time of his engagement or his joining the ship.
  - contains a short summary of the provisions of **section 55 of the Merchant Shipping Act 1995** (see E05c) and the MS and FV (Health and Safety at Work) (Employment of Young Persons) Regulations 1998 (see E05c.1).

- contains **columns** for the following details to be entered: Reference number in List of Crew; Surname and other names in full; Date of birth; Place of birth; and Capacity.
- must be completed **in addition** to the entry of the seaman's details on the appropriate List of Crew (ALC1(a) or ALC1(b)) and not instead of it.
- must, whenever a young person joins during the voyage, be **completed** with his/her details.
- must be **delivered** with the other Crew Agreement documents on closure of the Crew Agreement.

* Regulation 9(3) of the MS and FV (Health and Safety at Work) (Employment of Young Persons) Regulations 1998 (see E05c.1) provides that in a ship with no Crew Agreement, the master must, if young persons are engaged as workers on board, keep a **register** of them with particulars of their dates of birth and dates on which they were engaged.

E07d ENGAGEMENT AND DISCHARGE PROCEDURES

E07d.1 Opening the first Crew Agreement, List of Crew and Official Log Book of a UK ship

1. **Ascertain** from the employer the **type of crew agreement** to be opened, i.e. whether a **running** agreement (**12 months** or **6 months**), **voyage** agreement or **indefinite** agreement, and whether on **BSF** or **NFD** terms, or is **non-standard** or **modified** in any way.
2. If intending to use a **non-standard** or **modified** agreement, or an **indefinite** agreement, verify from the employer that **MCA approval** of the agreement and any additional clauses has been obtained. (Approval should have been obtained at least **14 days** before use.)
3. **Obtain a pack of the necessary documents** from any MCA Marine Office in the UK or from a proper officer (e.g. British consulate) outside the UK. In the pack should be:
   - **ALC1** (outer cover) with **ALC1(a)**, **ALC1(b)**, **ALC1(c)**, **ALC1(d)** and **ALC6** sheets;
   - a set of gummed **paper clauses**;
   - at least one **Official Log Book** (LOG 1) (large or small edition, as required);
   - at least one **Radio Log Book** of the appropriate type (e.g. GMDSS Log Book); and
   - for a **passenger ship** of Classes I, II or II(A) only, at least one **Official Log Book Part II** – Passenger ships only (LOG 2).
4. **Obtain** from the employer any approved **additional clauses** to be added to the standard agreement, e.g. incorporating agreements made with trade unions, company's Drug and Alcohol Policy, company's Rules of Conduct, etc.
5. **Ensure** that any **documents referred to** in the standard or additional clauses on ALC1(d), e.g. the Merchant Navy Code of Conduct or company's Drug and Alcohol Policy, will be **available for inspection** by any seaman at the time of his engagement.
6. **Ensure** that it will be possible to provide, on the request of any seaman, a **personal copy** of the Crew Agreement terms (i.e. a copy of the fully completed ALC1(d)). A photocopy will suffice.
7. **Complete** the front cover details on the ALC1 and Official Log Book. The ship's gross and net tonnages should be ascertained from the International Tonnage Certificate. The name and address of the registered owner and the engine power in kiloWatts should be obtained from the Certificate of Registry.
8. **Copy the ship's load line and freeboard details** from the Load Line Certificate into the special page in the Official Log Book (LOG 1).
9. **Select two copies** of ALC1(d)(BSF) or (NFD), as appropriate. (After completion with the details and clauses described below, one will go into the ALC1 outer cover and the other onto the ALC6 for posting up.) **Enter the employer's name and address** on the dotted line at the top of both copies of ALC1(d).
10. **In the case of a BSF agreement**, insert the appropriate **Voyage and Notice Clauses** (clauses ii and iii) in the reserved space on both copies of the ALC1(d)(BSF). (NFD agreements contain standard, printed Voyage and Notice Clauses.)
11. **In the Voyage Clause** (clause ii) on both copies of ALC1(d), enter the **geographical limits** of the voyage, e.g. "75°N" and "60°S" or other details as appropriate.
12. **In the Notice Clause** (clause iii) on both copies of ALC1(d), enter the **notice period required** (e.g. "72 hours").
13. **Affix** or insert in the appropriate spaces on both copies of the ALC1(d) any MCA-approved **additional clauses** required by the employer.
14. **Sign both copies of ALC1(d)** on behalf of the employer.

15. **Attach** the second copy of ALC1(d), completed as above, and with any additional clauses attached, to the **ALC6**. Although this must later be posted up in the crew accommodation, it may be a good idea to display it outside the master's office when seamen are waiting to sign on, so that they can read their terms of service.

16. **Enter own (i.e. master's) particulars** on the ALC1(b). Copy the reference number (e.g. "E01") to the crew list pages inside the front cover of the Official Log Book and enter own name and capacity.

17. **Engage seamen** on ALC1(a) as described in E07d.2.

18. **Enter details of exempt seamen** on ALC1(b) as described in E07d.3.

19. **Extract details** of any person employed on board who is under the age of 18 and insert on ALC1(c) (see E07c.2d).

20. **Assemble** the ALC1 document pages by stapling ALC1(a), ALC1(b), ALC1(c) and ALC1(d) sheets to the spine of the outer cover. Do not attach ALC6.

21. **Make an entry** in the narrative section of the Official Log Book recording the opening of a Crew Agreement and List of Crew. (This entry does not need to be witnessed.)

22. **Send** a copy of the List of Crew documents (ALC1(a) and ALC1(b)) to the **employer** within 3 days (see E07b.3d).

23. **In the case of an indefinite agreement** (only), send a copy of the ALC1(d), fully completed and including any additional clauses, to any MCA superintendent in the UK or proper officer abroad (see E07b.2c).

24. **Post up ALC6** in some conspicuous place in the crew accommodation (see E07b.2d).

E07d.2 Procedure for engaging non-exempt crew (i.e. seamen who are party to a Crew Agreement)

1. Prepare all necessary documents as in E07d.1 and announce a **time** for "signing on". Crew members may be signed on in **any order**, regardless of rank.

2. A seaman may be engaged by the **master**, a **person authorised by him** (e.g. a purser), or the **employer** (e.g. a person from the personnel office ashore).

3. Ask the **first seaman** who will be a party to the Crew Agreement for his **seaman's documents**.

4. Check the seaman's **Medical Fitness Certificate** for **validity and acceptability** under UK regulations. The certificate should be an **ENG.1** or a non-UK **equivalent certificate** issued by an MCA-approved country, as listed in Appendix 2 to Training and Certification Guidance Part 1 (see E02c.11) and in **MSN 1765**.

5. Check the seaman's **Certificate of Competency** for **validity under STCW 95** provisions, for any **revalidation endorsement,** for any **other endorsement** (e.g. Dangerous Cargo Endorsement) and for any restrictions. Certificates of Competency of **deck officers** must be valid for the ship's **trading area** (i.e. "Near Coastal" or "Unrestricted") and the ship's **gross tonnage** (gt). Certificates of Competency of **engineer officers** must be valid for the ship's **engine power** (in kW, as entered on the front of the Official Log Book).

6. In the case of a deck or engineer officer holding a non-UK Certificate of Competency, **check his UK Certificate of Equivalent Competency** for validity and authenticity, including any revalidation.

7. If necessary, **verify** the validity and/or authenticity of **suspect certificates** with the **employer**, who may in turn need to check with the MCA or the issuing authority. MCA may be able to confirm details with the Administration of the issuing State, but cannot guarantee to do so in all cases. The RSS has no facilities for checking validity of foreign certificates.

8. **Show each seaman** the terms of the ALC1(d), which is the contract to which he will be bound if he "signs on".

9. **Show each seaman**, on request, any document mentioned in the ALC1(d) or additional clauses (e.g. the MN Code of Conduct, or the company's Drug and Alcohol Policy).

10. Ensure that a **table of scheduled hours of rest** is posted-up in a prominent and easily accessible place in the ship as required by regulation 7 of the **MS (Hours of Work) Regulations 2002** (see E03c.1c).

11. **Allocate the first seaman** the reference number "01" (or, where the crew numbers more than 100, "001" or some appropriate other number) and write his details against this in the **white spaces of ALC1(a)**.

12. **Write** the details of the seaman's **Certificate of Competency, Certificate of Equivalent Competency** and **endorsements** at the foot of ALC1(a). Where he has no certificate, write "None".

13. Have the seaman insert his **signature in the top white space** on the ALC1(a), right hand column.

14. Give the seaman, on request, his **personal copy of the Crew Agreement terms** (ALC1(d)).

15. **Repeat steps 11 to 13** for all other seamen being engaged.

16. When all seamen have been engaged, **note each seaman under 18** years of age, and copy their particulars onto **ALC1(c)** (see E07c.2d). (Note also the special hours of work and rest for young persons detailed on ALC1(c).)

17. **Copy the reference number, name and capacity** of every seaman engaged into the crew list spaces inside the front cover of the Official Log Book (LOG 1).

18. **Make an entry** in the narrative section of the Official Log Book recording the engagement of the crew.

19. **Send** a copy of the List of Crew documents (ALC1(a) and ALC1(b)) to the **employer** within 3 days (see E07b.3d).

20. **Make a Crew List** for port officials' purposes.

21. Ensure that every crew member joining receives **familiarisation training** before being assigned duties (see E02b.13).

E07d.3 Procedure where an exempted person joins ship

1. **Enter** details of each exempted person joining ship (e.g. accompanying wives and children, supercargo, shore repair gang, company superintendents) in white spaces on **ALC1(b)**. Allocate each person an "E"-prefixed reference number, e.g. "E02". (The master will normally have reference number "E01".)
2. **Copy the reference number, name and capacity** of every exempted person into the "Record of seamen employed in the ship" inside the front cover of the Official Log Book (LOG 1).
3. **Notify** the shipowner or manager within 3 days of the change in the List of Crew.
4. **Amend** the Crew List maintained for port officials' purposes.
5. Ensure that every person joining (including every concessionaire and every "supernumerary") receives **familiarisation training** before being assigned duties (see E02b.13).

E07d.4 Procedure where a "young person" joins ship

1. Where any **person listed on either ALC1(a) or ALC1(b) is under the age of 18** on the date of joining ship (which can be ascertained from the date of birth in the seaman's document or passport), copy their reference number, name, date and place of birth and capacity to form **ALC1(c)** (see E07c.2d).
2. Ensure that the young seaman's Head of Department is familiar with the **special rest period provisions** applicable to young persons, as shown on ALC1(c) (see E07c.2d).
3. When a **young person listed on ALC1(c) reaches the age of 18** while in employment on board, his or her details should **not be deleted** from the ALC1(c).

E07d.5 Opening a List of Crew on a ship which is not required to have a Crew Agreement

1. For details of **ships and voyages in which a Crew Agreement is not required**, see E07b.2a.
2. **Obtain** the necessary documents from an MCA Marine Office, as in E07d.1. Documents required are an outer cover (**ALC(EX)1**), form **ALC1(b)** and, in case any seamen are under 18, **ALC1(c)**. Forms ALC1, ALC1(a) and ALC1(d) are not required. **No additional clauses** will be necessary, since there is no ALC1(d).
3. **Enter** details of each crew member joining ship in white spaces on **ALC1(b)**, allocating "E"-prefixed reference numbers, e.g. "E02". (The master will normally have reference number "E01".)
4. **Add** details of **certificates and endorsements** at foot of ALC1(b).
5. **Identify any person under 18** listed on ALC1(b) and copy particulars to ALC1(c) (see E07c.2d)
6. **Attach** ALC1(b) and 1(c) to the spine of outer cover **ALC(EX)1**.
7. **Send** a copy of the **ALC1(b)** to the shipowner or manager within **3 days** (see E07b.3d).
8. **Copy the reference number, names and capacity** of every person listed on ALC1(b) into the "Record of seamen employed in the ship" inside the front cover of the Official Log Book (LOG 1).
9. **Make a Crew List** for port officials' purposes.
10. Ensure that every person joining receives **familiarisation training** before being assigned duties (see E02b.13).

E07d.6 Discharging a seaman from the Crew Agreement, where he is present at his discharge

1. "**Discharge**" means discharge from the Crew Agreement contract. Seamen who are *not* party to a Crew Agreement are not actually "discharged" (since there are no contractual obligations to discharge them from), and simply "sign off" the List of Crew (ALC1(b)).
2. In some cases a seaman who is to be discharged may not be present at his discharge, e.g. where he has been taken to hospital and he is discharged in his absence; see procedure in E07d.7. The following procedure should be used to discharge a seaman where he **is present** at his discharge (i.e. he is able to "sign off" in person).
3. In the case of any **seaman claiming his discharge**, ensure that he has **given notice** in accordance with the **Notice Clause** in the Crew Agreement. (In most cases the company will have notified the master of the names of seamen to be discharged.)

4. **Notify** the **employer** and port **agent** of the intention to discharge the seaman, so that travel, immigration and customs arrangements can be made.
5. **In the case of a seaman paid** wages and/or overtime in cash on board, make up his **cash** and **account of wages** (see E09b), ensuring that the seaman has **settled any account** on board, e.g. a bar account.
6. A seaman may sign off before the **master**, a **person authorised by him** (e.g. a purser), or the **employer** (e.g. a person from the personnel office ashore).
7. **In the seaman's Discharge Book** (or foreign equivalent), if he produces it, record his service details and return the book to him. Details to be recorded in a UK Discharge Book are: ship's name; port of registry/choice; gross tonnage or net tonnage; official number; description of voyage; capacity in which seaman was employed; dates of commencing employment and of discharge.
8. **If the seaman does not produce a Discharge Book** (or foreign equivalent), make out a **Certificate of Discharge** recording his service on board, and deliver it to him (see E07b.4c). **MGN 123** contains a specimen Certificate of Discharge which can be photocopied if necessary.
9. Complete the **discharge details** in the shaded spaces in **ALC1(a)**, i.e. the reason for discharge and the date and place of leaving the ship.
10. **Seaman enters his signature** in the upper shaded space of the right hand column in ALC1(a).
11. **Person before whom the seaman is discharged** enters his **signature** in the lower shaded space of the right hand column in ALC1(a).
12. **If the seaman requests**, give him a Certificate as to the quality of his work or that he has fully discharged his obligations under his contract (see E07b.4c). This must be given to him within 6 months of his discharge. MCA form DIS.4 should be used if available.
13. If the seaman is being discharged because of his **dismissal following disciplinary procedures**, give him a copy of all **Official Log Book entries** relating to the disciplinary proceedings (see E10b.7).
14. **Permit the seaman to leave** the vessel only after receiving port **health, customs and immigration clearance** from the relevant official(s).
15. **Make an entry** in the narrative section of the **Official Log Book** recording the place, date and time of the seaman's discharge, quoting the seaman's reference number on ALC1(a).
16. **Notify the employer** within 3 days of the change in the List of Crew.
17. **Amend** the Crew List maintained for port officials' purposes.

E07d.6a "Signing off" from the List of Crew a seaman who is exempt from signing a Crew Agreement

1. Seamen who are not party to a Crew Agreement are not discharged, but simply "sign off" the List of Crew (ALC1(b)). The following procedure applies where, for example, concessionaire personnel on a cruise ship are leaving the ship, or where shipyard personnel have completed their work on board.
2. **Notify** the **employer** and port **agent** of the intention to sign personnel off, so that travel, immigration and customs arrangements can be made.
3. **In the seaman's Discharge Book** (or foreign equivalent), if he produces it, record his service details and return the book to him. Details to be recorded in a UK Discharge Book are: ship's name; port of registry/choice; gross tonnage or net tonnage; official number; description of voyage; capacity in which seaman was employed; dates of commencing employment and of discharge.
4. **If the seaman does not produce a Discharge Book** (or foreign equivalent), make out a **Certificate of Discharge** recording his service on board, and deliver it to him. **MGN 123** contains a specimen Certificate of Discharge which can be photocopied if necessary.
5. In ALC1(b), complete the **date and place of leaving the ship**.
6. **Seaman enters his signature** in the upper shaded space of the right hand column in ALC1(b).
7. **Person before whom the seaman is discharged** enters his **signature** in the lower shaded space of the right hand column in ALC1(b).
8. **If the seaman requests**, give him a Certificate as to the quality of his work or that he has fully discharged his obligations under his contract (see E07b.4c). This must be given to him within 6 months of his leaving the ship. MCA form DIS.4 should be used if available.
9. **Permit the seaman to leave** the vessel only after receiving port **health, customs and immigration clearance** from the relevant official(s).
10. **Make an entry** in the narrative section of the **Official Log Book** recording the place, date and time of the seaman's discharge, quoting the seaman's reference number on ALC1(b).
11. **Notify the employer** within 3 days of the change in the List of Crew.
12. **Amend** the Crew List maintained for port officials' purposes.

E07d.7 Discharging a seaman from the Crew Agreement, where he is not present at his discharge

1. Where a seaman is **not present at his discharge** (i.e. he is unable to "sign off" the List of Crew in person), the **master**, a **person authorised by him** (e.g. a purser), or the **employer** (e.g. a person from the personnel office ashore) should make the relevant entries in his absence as described below.
2. If **outside the UK** and the **seaman is being left behind** in the country, **notify a proper officer** (e.g. the nearest British consul) and **record his notification** in the Official Log Book narrative section.
3. **In the seaman's Discharge Book** (or foreign equivalent), if he available, record his service details as in E07d.6. If his Discharge Book is not available, complete a **Certificate of Discharge**. The Discharge Book, if available, or the Certificate of Discharge should be sent to the seaman if his whereabouts are known, since they may help to facilitate his eventual repatriation.
4. Complete the **discharge details** in the shaded spaces in **ALC1(a)**, i.e. the reason for discharge and the date and place of leaving the ship.
5. In the space in the right hand column of ALC1(a) where the seaman would normally sign off, had he been present, enter the **reason for his absence or being left behind**, e.g. "AWOL" or "Hospitalised".
6. **The person making the entries** should enter his **signature** in the lower shaded space of the right hand column in ALC1(a).
7. **Make an entry** in the narrative section of the **Official Log Book** recording the place, date and time of the seaman's discharge, quoting the seaman's reference number on ALC1(a).
8. **Notify the employer** within 3 days of the change in the List of Crew.
9. **Amend** the Crew List maintained for port officials' purposes.

E07d.8 "Changing articles" when on a Running Agreement

1. **At the expiry of the Running Agreement** (as indicated by reference to the date of commencement on the front cover of the ALC1 and the period, i.e. 12 months or 6 months) copy the details from the front cover of the expiring ALC1 to the front cover of a new ALC1 outer cover.
2. **On the expiring ALC1** outer cover, enter the date and place of termination (i.e. present port or place, or "At sea").
3. **Prepare new copies** of forms ALC1(a), (b), (c) and (d) and ALC6 as described in E07d.1.
4. **Copy** the details from the front cover of the current Official Log Book[52] to the front cover of a new Official Log Book.
5. **Copy load line and freeboard details** from the special page in the expiring Official Log Book to the same page in the new Official Log Book.
6. **Discharge seamen** from the expiring Crew Agreement following procedure in E07d.6.
7. **Engage seamen** on the new Crew Agreement following procedure in E07d.2.
8. **Proceed with exempt persons and young persons** as in E07d.3 and E07d.4 respectively.
9. **Take down expired ALC6** and **post up new ALC6**.
10. **Make an entry** in the narrative section of the new Official Log Book recording the closure of the expired Crew Agreement and the opening of the new one.
11. **Where a seaman declines to sign the new Crew Agreement**, make arrangements for his replacement and repatriation.
*   Some masters insist that crew members **sign on the new Crew Agreement** before signing off the expiring one. For notes on the (lack of) **legality of this practice**, see B03c.3.

E07d.9 Closing a Crew Agreement and List of Crew

1. **Discharge each seaman** from the Crew Agreement as in E07d.6 and **sign off** each persons listed on ALC1(b) as in E07d.6a.
2. Enter the **date and place of termination** of the Agreement and List of Crew on the front of ALC1.
3. Make an entry in the narrative section of the Official Log Book recording the closure of the Crew Agreement and List of Crew.
4. Enter the date and place of closing of the Official Log Book(s) on the front cover.
5. Remove form ALC6 from the place where it was posted up.
6. Send to a Marine Office superintendent in the UK or a proper officer abroad, the following documents:
    *   the **Official Log Book** (plus any **annexes**);

---

[52] On a passenger ship of Classes I, II or II(A), the Supplementary Official Log Book (LOG 2) must be changed as well as LOG 1 and the Radio Log.

- the **ALC** document (containing ALC1(a), (b), (c) and (d)); and
- the original pages of the **Radio Log**(s)

- within 3 days of the last person employed on the Crew Agreement signing off, or as soon as possible.

7. **If the ship has been lost or abandoned**, the **employer** must immediately deliver a copy of the List of Crew to a Marine Office superintendent.

E07d.10 Procedure when the ship is leaving the UK Register

1. Close the Crew Agreement and List of Crew as in E07d.9. (Crew members accepting any offer of employment under the new flag will have to sign a new Crew Agreement or List of Crew as provided for by regulations of the new flag State Administration.)
2. Send documents to Marine Office superintendent or proper officer as in E07d.9.
3. Section 29 of the Merchant Shipping Act 1995 provides that where a UK ship ceases to be registered (i.e. registered in the UK), any seaman employed in the ship must be discharged from the ship unless he consents in writing to continue his employment in the ship; and, in relation to his wages, sections 30 to 33 (see E09b.1) will apply as if the ship had remained a UK ship.

E08a LEGISLATION RELATING TO SEAFARERS' HEALTH, SAFETY AND WELFARE

* **International Labour Organization (ILO) Conventions** form the chief sources of **international law** on seafarers' health, safety and welfare. For a list of the chief maritime ILO Conventions, see A04c.
* Whereas new ILO instruments are relatively rare, the number of **EC Directives** relating to workers' health and safety matters is steadily increasing. (For examples, see E08b.2, E08b.2h and E08e.7.)
* **Primary UK legislation** relating to seafarers' health, safety and welfare is contained in the sections of the **Merchant Shipping Act 1995** shown in the following table.

Section	Section title	SBC reference
43	Crew accommodation	E08g.1
44	Complaints about provisions or water	E08h.4, E11b, E11c
45	Expenses of medical and other treatment during voyage	E08j.3
53	Medical treatment on board ship	E08j.1

* **Secondary legislation** relating to seafarers' health, safety and welfare is summarised in the following table.

Subject	Principal regulations	Amending SIs	SBC ref.
Accident reporting and investigation	MS (Accident Reporting and Investigation) Regulations 1999 (SI 2000/2567)	-	E08k.1
Accommodation	MS (Crew Accommodation) Regulations 1997 (SI 1997/1508)	-	E08g.1
Code of Safe Working Practices for Merchant Seamen	MS (Code of Safe Working Practices for Merchant Seamen) Regulations 1998 (SI 1998/1838)	-	E08c.3
Entry into dangerous spaces	MS (Entry into Dangerous Spaces) Regulations 1988 (SI 1988/1638)	-	E08e.3
Guarding of machinery and safety of electrical equipment	MS (Guarding of Machinery and Safety of Electrical Equipment) Regulations 1988 (SI 1988/1636)	-	E08e.1
Hatches and lifting plant	MS (Hatches and Lifting Plant) Regulations 1988 (SI 1988/1639)	-	E08e.4
Health and safety at work	MS & FV (Health and Safety at Work) Regulations 1997 (SI 1997/2962)	SI 2001/54	E08b.2
Hours of work	MS (Hours of Work) Regulations 2002 (SI 2002/2125)	-	E03c.1
Manual handling operations	MS and FV (Manual Handling Operations) Regulations 1998 (SI 1998/2857)	-	E08e.8
Means of Access	MS (Means of Access) Regulations 1988 (SI 1988/1637)	-	E08e.2
Medical fitness requirements	MS (Medical Examination) Regulations 1983 (SI 1983/808)	SI 1985/512 SI 1990/1985	E06c.2
Personal protective equipment	MS and FV (Personal Protective Equipment) Regulations 1999 (SI 1999/2205)	-	E08e.6
Provisions and water	MS (Provisions and Water) Regulations 1989 (SI 1989/102)	-	E08h.1
Safe movement on board ship	MS (Safe Movement on Board Ship) Regulations 1988 (SI 1988/1641)	-	E08e.5
Safety signs and signals	MS and FV (Safety Signs and Signals) Regulations 2001 (SI 2001/3444)	-	E08e.7
Suspension from work on maternity grounds	Suspension from Work on Maternity Grounds (Merchant Ships and Fishing Vessels) Order 1998 (SI 1998/587)	-	E08b.2h

E08 Crew health, safety and welfare

E08a LEGISLATION RELATING TO SEAFARERS' HEALTH, SAFETY AND WELFARE

* **International Labour Organization (ILO) Conventions** form the chief sources of **international law** on seafarers' health, safety and welfare. For a list of the chief maritime ILO Conventions, see A04c.
* Whereas new ILO instruments are relatively rare, the number of **EC Directives** relating to workers' health and safety matters is steadily increasing. (For examples, see E08b.2, E08b.2h and E08e.7.)
* **Primary UK legislation** relating to seafarers' health, safety and welfare is contained in the sections of the **Merchant Shipping Act 1995** shown in the following table.

Section	Section title	SBC reference
43	Crew accommodation	E08g.1
44	Complaints about provisions or water	E08h.4, E11b, E11c
45	Expenses of medical and other treatment during voyage	E08j.3
53	Medical treatment on board ship	E08j.1

* **Secondary legislation** relating to seafarers' health, safety and welfare is summarised in the following table.

Subject	Principal regulations	Amending SIs	SBC ref.
Accident reporting and investigation	MS (Accident Reporting and Investigation) Regulations 1999 (SI 2000/2567)	-	E08k.1
Accommodation	MS (Crew Accommodation) Regulations 1997 (SI 1997/1508)	-	E08g.1
Code of Safe Working Practices for Merchant Seamen	MS (Code of Safe Working Practices for Merchant Seamen) Regulations 1998 (SI 1998/1838)	-	E08c.3
Entry into dangerous spaces	MS (Entry into Dangerous Spaces) Regulations 1988 (SI 1988/1638)	-	E08e.3
Guarding of machinery and safety of electrical equipment	MS (Guarding of Machinery and Safety of Electrical Equipment) Regulations 1988 (SI 1988/1636)	-	E08e.1
Hatches and lifting plant	MS (Hatches and Lifting Plant) Regulations 1988 (SI 1988/1639)	-	E08e.4
Health and safety at work	MS & FV (Health and Safety at Work) Regulations 1997 (SI 1997/2962)	SI 2001/54	E08b.2
Hours of work	MS (Hours of Work) Regulations 2002 (SI 2002/2125)	-	E03c.1
Manual handling operations	MS and FV (Manual Handling Operations) Regulations 1998 (SI 1998/2857)	-	E08e.8
Means of Access	MS (Means of Access) Regulations 1988 (SI 1988/1637)	-	E08e.2
Medical fitness requirements	MS (Medical Examination) Regulations 1983 (SI 1983/808)	SI 1985/512 SI 1990/1985	E06c.2
Personal protective equipment	MS and FV (Personal Protective Equipment) Regulations 1999 (SI 1999/2205)	-	E08e.6
Provisions and water	MS (Provisions and Water) Regulations 1989 (SI 1989/102)	-	E08h.1
Safe movement on board ship	MS (Safe Movement on Board Ship) Regulations 1988 (SI 1988/1641)	-	E08e.5
Safety signs and signals	MS and FV (Safety Signs and Signals) Regulations 2001 (SI 2001/3444)	-	E08e.7
Suspension from work on maternity grounds	Suspension from Work on Maternity Grounds (Merchant Ships and Fishing Vessels) Order 1998 (SI 1998/587)	-	E08b.2h

E08b HEALTH AND SAFETY AT WORK

E08b.1 The Health and Safety at Work etc. Act 1974

* The **Health and Safety at Work etc. Act 1974** ("**HSW Act**"), as amended -
  - is the **chief piece of health and safety legislation** in Great Britain. (Equivalent NI legislation[53] covers Northern Ireland.)
  - is an "**enabling Act**", i.e. it enables Government ministers to make regulations to cover most working situations, and does not contain a great deal of detailed regulations itself.
  - **applies** to most workplaces in Great Britain, including shops, schools and colleges, factories, hospitals, etc.

---

[53] The Northern Ireland equivalent legislation is the Health and Safety at Work (Northern Ireland) Order 1978 (NI 9), which is enforced in Northern Ireland by the Health and Safety Executive for Northern Ireland.

- **applies**, by virtue of extension legislation, to **offshore installations** on the UK Continental Shelf (see E08b.1a).
- **applies to ships** whilst in ports and territorial waters in Great Britain (i.e. Scotland, England and Wales).
- **does not apply to UK ships outside UK waters** (but equivalent Merchant Shipping regulations, i.e. the MS (Health and Safety at Work) Regulations **1997** (SI 1997/2962) apply to UK ships anywhere).
- **covers everyone** who is affected by work activity.
- places the burden of **legal responsibility** for health and safety at work mostly on the **employer**.
- is **enforced** by the Health and Safety Executive (HSE) (see B05e).

* Under the Act an **employer** –
  - must ensure as far as reasonably practicable the **health, safety and welfare** at work of all his employees;
  - must **maintain plant and systems of work** in a condition that **protects** the employees;
  - must **prepare, revise and bring to the notice** of the employees a **written statement of general policy regarding the health and safety at work** of the employees, and the organisation and arrangements for carrying out this policy;
  - must provide employees with **information, instruction, training and supervision**.
* **Enforcement** of the requirements of the HSW Act is the responsibility of inspectors employed by the Health and Safety Executive (HSE).
* Where a **breach of the law** is observed, inspectors may, under section 21, issue an **Improvement Notice** requiring the breach to be **remedied** by a specific date. There is a right of appeal to an employment tribunal against an Improvement Notice, and meanwhile work may continue.
* Where activities are seen to be "involving a risk of serious personal injury", whether a breach of the law is observed or not, a **Prohibition Notice** may be served by an inspector under section 22. In this case the activities must cease immediately or by a stated date, and only after they cease is there a right of appeal to an employment tribunal. The inspectors may prosecute for non-compliance. For detailed notes on **Improvement Notices and Prohibition Notices**, see E08b.4.
* HSE inspectors may go on board UK and other ships in British ports and territorial waters to enforce the Act.

E08b.1a Application of HSWA to offshore installations and vessels

* **Article 3(1) of The Health and Safety at Work etc. Act 1974 (Application Outside Great Britain) Order 2001** (SI 2001/2127) provides that the **prescribed provisions of the HSW Act** (i.e. sections 1 to 59 and 80 to 82) will apply to and in relation to the premises and activities outside Great Britain which are so specified, as those provisions apply within Great Britain. (The reference to "premises and activities" does not include an aircraft which is airborne.)
* **Article 4(1)** provides that the prescribed provisions of the 1974 Act will apply within the **UK territorial sea** or a **designated area** to and in relation to:
  * **any offshore installation** and **any activity on it**;
  * **any activity in connection with an offshore installation**, or any **activity which is immediately preparatory thereto**, whether carried on **from the installation** itself, **in or from a vessel** or **in any other manner, other than**:
    - transporting, towing or navigating the installation; and
    - any activity in or from a vessel being used as a stand-by vessel.
* "Designated area" in article 3(1) means any area designated by an Order under section 1(7) of the Continental Shelf Act 1964 (c.29).
* Under article 4(2)(b), "**offshore installation**" includes a structure which is, or is to be, or has been, used while standing or stationed in water -
  * for the exploitation, or exploration with a view to exploitation, of mineral resources by means of a well;
  * for the storage of gas in or under the shore or bed of any water or the recovery of gas so stored;
  * for the conveyance of things by means of a pipe; or
  * mainly for the provision of accommodation for persons who work on or from a structure falling within any of the provisions of article 4(2).
* Article 4(3)(d) excludes from the definition of "offshore installation" a mobile structure which has been taken out of use and is not yet being moved with a view to its being used for any of the purposes specified in article 4(2)(b).
* **Article 8(1)** provides that, subject to article 8(2), the prescribed provisions of the 1974 Act will apply within the **UK territorial sea** to and in relation to:
  * the construction, reconstruction, alteration, repair, maintenance, cleaning, use, operation, demolition and dismantling of any building, energy structure or other structure, not being in any case a vessel, or any preparation for such activity;
  * the transfer of people or goods between a vessel or aircraft and a structure (including a building) mentioned in the previous line (above);
  * the loading, unloading, fuelling or provisioning of a vessel;

- a diving project;
- the construction, reconstruction, finishing, refitting, repair, maintenance, cleaning or breaking up of a vessel except when carried out by the master or any officer or member of the crew of that vessel;
- the maintaining on a station of a vessel which would be an offshore installation were it not a structure to which article 4(3)(d) applies;
- the operation of a cable for transmitting electricity from an energy structure to Great Britain;
- the transfer of people or goods between a vessel or aircraft and a structure mentioned in the last line but one (above).

* **Article 8 does not apply** to a case where article 4, 5, 6 or 7 applies, or to non-UK vessels on passage through the UK territorial sea.

E08b.2 Health and Safety at Work Regulations

* The **MS and FV (Health and Safety at Work) Regulations 1997** (SI 1997/2962) -
- give effect to:
  - **Council Directive 89/391/EEC** on the introduction of measures to encourage improvements in the safety and health of workers at work (OJ No. L 183, 29.6.89, p. 1);
  - **Council Directive 91/383/EEC** supplementing the measures to encourage improvements in the safety and health at work of workers with a fixed-duration employment relationship or a temporary employment relationship (OJ No. L206 29.7.91 p. 19), and
  - **Council Directive 92/85/EEC** on the introduction of measures to encourage improvements in the safety and health at work of pregnant workers and workers who have recently given birth or are breast-feeding (OJ No. L. 348 28.11.92, p. 1).
- **revoke** and replace the MS (Health and Safety: General Duties) Regulations 1984 (SI 1984/408), and the MS (Safety Officials and Reporting of Accidents and Dangerous Occurrences) Regulations 1982 (SI 1982/987) (regulation 1).
- define "**Company**", in relation to a ship to which the Regulations apply, as "the owner of the ship or any other organisation or person such as the manager, or bareboat charterer, who has assumed the responsibility for operation of the ship from the owner" (regulation 2(2)).
- apply to all activities of workers on UK ships except when:
  - the activity of a worker is on a public service vessel[54] or a vessel engaged in search and rescue (regulation 3(1)(a)); and
  - characteristics of that activity inevitably conflict with a provision of these Regulations (regulation 3(1)(b)), - and in such a case the employer has a duty so far as is reasonably practicable to ensure the health and safety of the worker when performing that activity.
- are amended by the **MS and FV (Health and Safety at Work) (Amendment) Regulations 2001** (SI 2001/54), which re-draw the dividing line between the legislative responsibilities of the HSE and the MCA (see B05d) and implement the recommendations of the Thames Safety Inquiry (see below), as explained in **MGN 175**.
* Regulations 1, 2, 3, 28, 29 and 30 apply to **non-UK ships in UK waters** (regulation 3(2)).
* An obligation is placed on the **employer** to comply with the requirements of the Regulations as well as on **any person specifically named** in the provision. There is facility to **extend the employer's duty to another person** if the employer is not in control of the particular matter because he does not have responsibility for the operation of the ship (regulation 4(1) and (2)).
* The **MS and FV (Health and Safety at Work) (Amendment) Regulations 2001** (SI 2001/54) make two amendments to the principal Regulations to implement recommendations made by Lord Justice Clarke in his Interim Report on the **Thames Safety Inquiry** (Cm. 4530), published in December 1999. The effect of the first amendment is to apply Merchant Shipping health and safety legislation to **non-seagoing ships**, thereby allowing effective enforcement by the MCA. The second aligns the general duties of employers under the Merchant Shipping legislation (see E08b.2a) with those under the Health and Safety at Work Act 1974.

E08b.2a General duties of employer (regulation 5)

* **Regulation 5(1)** provides that the **employer must ensure the health and safety of workers and other persons** so far as is reasonably practicable, having regard to the following principles:

---

[54] **"Public service vessel"** is defined in regulation 2 as "any vessel operated by or on behalf of a public body while it is carrying out the authorised functions of that body".

- the avoidance of risks, which among other things include the combating of risks at source and the replacement of dangerous practices, substances or equipment by non-dangerous or less dangerous practices, substances or equipment (regulation 5(1)(a));
- the evaluation of unavoidable risks, and the taking of action to reduce them (regulation 5(1)(b));
- adoption of work patterns and procedures which take account of the capacity of the individual, especially in respect of the design of the workplace and the choice of work equipment, with a view in particular to alleviating monotonous work and to reducing any consequent adverse effect on workers' health and safety (regulation 5(1)(c));
- adaptation of procedures to take account of new technology and other changes in working practices, equipment, the working environment and any other factors which may affect health and safety (regulation 5(1)(d));
- adoption of a coherent approach to management of the vessel or undertaking, taking account of health and safety at every level of the organisation (regulation 5(1)(e));
- giving collective protective measures priority over individual protective measures (regulation 5(1)(f)); and
- the provision of appropriate and relevant information and instruction for workers (regulation 5(1)(g)).
* Without prejudice to the generality of these duties, the **matters to which those duties extend** will include, in particular:
  - provision and maintenance of **plant, machinery and equipment and systems of work** that are, so far as is reasonably practicable, **safe and without risk to health** (regulation 5(2)(a));
  - arrangements for ensuring, so far as is reasonably practicable, **safety and absence of risk to health** in connection with the **use, handling, stowage and transport of articles and substances** (regulation 5(2)(b));
  - such arrangements as are appropriate, having regard to the nature of, and the substances used in, the activities and the size of the operation, for the effective **planning, organisation, control, monitoring and review of preventative and protective measures** (regulation 5(2)(c));
  - provision of such **information, instruction, training and supervision** as is necessary to ensure the health and safety of workers and that of other persons aboard ship who may be affected by their acts or omissions (regulation 5(2)(d));
  - maintenance of all places of work in the ship in a condition that is, so far as is reasonably practicable, **safe and without risk to health** (regulation 5(2)(e));
  - arrangements to ensure, so far as is reasonably practicable, that no person has access to any area of the ship to which it is necessary to restrict access on grounds of health and safety unless the individual concerned has received adequate and appropriate health and safety instruction (regulation 5(2)(f));
  - provision and maintenance of an environment for persons aboard ship that is, so far as is reasonably practicable, safe and without risk to health (regulation 5(2)(g)); and
  - collaboration with any other persons covered by regulation 4 (Persons on whom duties are imposed) to protect, so far as is reasonably practicable, the health and safety of all authorised persons aboard the ship or engaged in loading or unloading activities in relation to that ship (regulation 5(2)(h)).

E08b.2b Health and safety policy (regulation 6)

* Regulation 6(1) provides that, subject to regulation 6(2), a **written statement** must be prepared and, as often as may be appropriate, **revised**, of:
  - the **employer's general policy with respect to health and safety;** and
  - the **organisation and arrangements for the time being in force for carrying out that policy**. This statement and any revisions to it must be brought to the notice of the workers.
* The written statement will **not** apply where **five or fewer workers in aggregate** are employed by the same employer, or by associated employers[55], in a UK ship (regulation 6(2)).

E08b.2c Risk assessment (regulation 7)

* A **suitable and sufficient risk assessment** must be made of the risks of the health and safety of workers arising in the normal course of their activities or duties, for the purpose of identifying:
  - groups of workers at particular risk in the performance of their duties; and
  - the measures to be taken to comply with the employer's duties under the Regulations (regulation 7(1)).
* Any **significant findings** of the risk assessment, and any revision of it, must be **brought to the notice** of the workers (regulation 7(1)).
* The risk assessment must extend to the risks to the health and safety of other persons on board ship in so far as they may be affected by the acts and omissions of the employer (regulation 7(2)).

---

[55] For the meaning of "associated employers", see section 231 of the Employment Rights Act 1996.

* The **risk assessment must be reviewed** if there is reason to suspect that it is no longer valid, or if there has been a significant change in the matters to which it relates, and where such a review identifies a need for a change in procedures or practices, the changes must be made (regulation 7(3)).
* Every employer and every self-employed person on board ship must **inform the Company** of any **relevant risks to health and safety** arising out of or in connection with the conduct of his own undertaking (regulation 7(4)).
* **Measures** must be taken, and if necessary **protective equipment supplied**, to ensure an improvement in the health and safety of workers and other persons in respect of those **risks identified** (regulation 7(5)).
* **Workers must be informed** of the measures taken for their protection (regulation 7(6)).
* Chapter 1 of the Code of Safe Working Practices for Merchant Seamen (1998 edition) explains in detail the **principles and practice of risk assessment**. Guidance on the **main elements of risk assessment**, based on British Standard 8800, is given in Annex 1.1 to Chapter 1. Annex 1.2 is an example **worksheet** for making an **initial assessment** of those risks which require further consideration, while Annex 1.3 is an example **worksheet** for a **detailed assessment** of those risks. Company risk assessment worksheets may differ in format.
* **Annex 1 to MGN 20** contains a similar explanation of the principles and practice of risk assessment to that in the CSWP.

E08b.2d Capabilities and training (regulation 12)

* **In entrusting tasks to workers**, account must be taken of their **capabilities** as regards health and safety (regulation 12(1)).
* Workers must be provided with **adequate and appropriate health and safety training and instruction**:
  * **before** being assigned to shipboard duties (regulation 12(2)(a));
  * on being **exposed to new or increased risks** because of:
    * being transferred or given a change in responsibilities (regulation 12(2)(b)(i));
    * the introduction of new equipment or a change to equipment already in use (regulation 12(2)(b)(ii));
    * the introduction of new technology (regulation 12(2)(b)(iii)); or
    * the introduction of new shipboard practices, a new system of work or a change to a system of work already in use (regulation 12(2)(b)(iv)).
* The training referred to above must:
  * be **repeated** periodically where appropriate (regulation 12(3)(a));
  * be **adapted** to take account of any new or changed risks to the health or safety of the workers concerned (regulation 12(3)(b)); and
  * take place **during the working hours** of the worker concerned (regulation 12(3)(c)).
* Every person carrying on the activity of an employment agency whose employee is to carry out work on a ship to which the Regulations apply must be provided by the Company with **information** on:
  * any **special occupational qualifications required** by workers to carry out their work safely (regulation 12(4)(a));
  * any **specific features of the jobs** to be filled by those workers (in so far as those features are likely to affect their health and safety) (regulation 12(4)(b)); and
  * any **health surveillance** required to be provided to workers under these or other relevant regulations (regulation 12(4)(c)),
  - and the **employment agency** concerned must ensure that the information provided is given to the relevant workers.

E08b.2e Consultation with workers (regulation 20)

* Regulation 20(1) provides that **workers or their elected representatives must be consulted in advance** and in good time on all matters relating to their health and safety, and in particular on –
  * the arrangements for **appointing a competent person** under regulation 14 to provide protective and preventive services for the undertaking; (see E08d.2);
  * the findings of the **risk assessment** (see E08b.2c);
  * arrangements for **health and safety training** under regulation 12 (see E08b.2d); and
  * the introduction of **new technology** (see E08b.2a).
* Under regulation 20(2) employers must allow workers or their elected representatives to make representations about health and safety, and must implement any agreed measures as soon as may be reasonable and practicable.
* Under regulation 20(3), workers or their elected representatives must be given **access** by the employer and, where applicable by the Company, to **any relevant information** about:
  * **health and safety matters** from inspection agencies and health and safety authorities; and
  * every **accident** involving death, major or serious injury, and every dangerous occurrence.

* Under regulation 20(4), elected representatives must be given **adequate time off work** without loss of pay in order to exercise their rights and functions under regulation 20, and must be provided with adequate training.
* Under regulation 20(5), workers or their elected representatives must not be **placed at a disadvantage** (whether economic or otherwise) because of their activities under regulation 20.

E08b.2f General duties of workers (regulation 21)

* Regulation 21(1) provides that it will be the **duty of every worker on a ship** to which the Regulations apply –
  * to **take reasonable care** for the health and safety of **himself** and of **any other person** aboard ship who may be affected by his acts or omissions; and
  * as regards any duty or requirement imposed on the Company, his employer or any other person by the Regulations and the Health and Safety at Work Act or any regulation or rule made under it, with regard to health and safety, to **co-operate with that person** so far as is necessary to enable that duty or requirement to be performed or complied with.
* Under regulation 21(2), **no worker may** –
  * use any machinery, equipment, dangerous substance, transport equipment, means of production or safety device provided by his employer or the Company other than in accordance with any relevant **training or instructions** which have been received or provided by the employer or the Company in compliance with the Regulations; or
  * **disconnect, change or remove or otherwise interfere** with any safety device provided by the employer or the Company.
* Under regulation 21(3), every worker must immediately **inform the master or the safety officer** or another competent person appointed under regulation 14(1) of any matter which may reasonably be considered to represent a **deficiency** in the Company's protection arrangements for the health and safety of any persons on board the ship.
* Under regulation 21(4), every worker must immediately **inform his employer, the safety officer or other competent person** –
  * of any work situation which he reasonably considers to represent a **serious and immediate danger** to health and safety; and
  * of any matter which he reasonably considers to represent a **deficiency** in the employer's protection arrangements for health and safety.

E08b.2g Prohibitions, penalties, inspections and detentions

* Regulation 22 provides that **no charge** in respect of anything done or provided in pursuance of any specific requirement of the Regulations may be levied or permitted to be levied on any worker.
* Under regulation 23 it is an offence for any person to **intentionally or recklessly interfere** with or **misuse** anything provided in the interests of health and safety aboard a UK ship in pursuance of the Regulations or the Health and Safety at Work Act or any regulation or rule made thereunder.
* Regulation 27 provides that a relevant inspector (see B05b.3e) may **inspect any UK ship** and if he is satisfied that there has been a failure to comply with the requirements of the Regulations may **detain the ship** until the health and safety of all workers and other persons on board is secured. Regulation 28 contains similar powers in respect of non-UK ships which are in UK ports in the normal course of business, and provides that where the ship does not conform to the standards required of UK ships, a **report** will be sent to the flag State government with a copy to the ILO.

E08b.2h Suspension from work on maternity grounds

* Regulations 8(3) and 9(2) of the Health and Safety at Work Regulations 1997 require that in certain circumstances **new or expectant mothers** must be **suspended** from work for health and safety reasons.
* Under section 66 of the Employment Rights Act 1996, an employee is "**suspended on maternity grounds**" if she is suspended under a provision specified in an Order made by the Secretary of State. The **Suspension from Work on Maternity Grounds (Merchant Shipping and Fishing Vessels) Order 1998** (SI 1998/587) specifies regulations 8(3) and 9(2) of the Health and Safety at Work Regulations, so that suspension under those provisions constitutes "**suspension on maternity grounds**". In this way, certain Articles of Council Directive 92/85/EEC on the introduction of measures to encourage improvements in the safety and health of pregnant workers and workers who have recently given birth and are breastfeeding are given similar effect in the UK in relation to women employed at sea as they have in relation to women employed on land.
* Sections 67 and 68 of the Employment Rights Act 1996 provide that before an employee is suspended from work on maternity grounds she has the right to be offered alternative work, and if she is suspended she has the right to be paid during the period of suspension.

* **MGN 112** contains guidance for employers and seafarers on Health and Safety legislation for the **protection of new and expectant mothers at work**, and **medical fitness standards** as they relate to **pregnancy**.

E08b.3 Protection against noise on board ships

* **UK statutory requirements** relating to protection against noise on board ships are contained in:
  * regulation 75 of the MS (Passenger Ship Construction: Ships of Classes I, II and II(A)) Regulations 1998 (SI 1998/2514);
  * regulation 62 of the MS (Passenger Ship Construction: Ships of Classes III to VI(A)) Regulations 1998 (SI 1998/2515); and
  * regulation 40 of the MS (Cargo Ship Construction) Regulations 1997 (SI 1997/1509).
* **Both** of the above-mentioned regulations relating to **passenger ships** provide that:
  * **measures must be taken** to reduce noise levels in machinery spaces as far as is reasonable and practicable;
  * on completion of a ship, **noise levels in machinery spaces must be measured** when the largest number of machines that operate simultaneously in service are working at their normal service loads; measurements taken during **sea trials** at the maximum ahead service speed of the ship can be used to provide the necessary information;
  * the **equipment and procedures** for measuring and recording noise levels in machinery spaces must be generally in accordance with the provisions of the HMSO publication **Code of Practice for Noise Levels in Ships** (see E08b.3a);
  * **noise levels in machinery spaces must not exceed 110dB(A)** provided that the **MCA may**, under such conditions as may be specified, **permit higher noise levels** having regard to the size of ship and the type of machinery installed;
  * any **machinery space** in which the noise level **exceeds 90dB(A) and which is required to be manned** must be provided with a designated **refuge from noise**;
  * every **entrance to a machinery space** in which the noise level exceeds 85dB(A) must be provided with a **warning notice** comprising a symbol complying with British Standards Institution specification number BS 5378: 1980 and supplementary sign stating "High Noise Levels. Use Ear Protectors". Sufficient ear protectors must be provided for use in such spaces.
* Regulation 40 of the **Cargo Ship Construction Regulations** provides that:
  * in every ship, **measures must be taken** to reduce noise levels in machinery spaces as far as is reasonable and practicable;
  * on completion of a ship, **noise levels in machinery spaces must be measured** and a **record** of the measurements taken must be **retained on the ship**;
  * noise levels and their measurement must be in accordance with the provisions of **Schedule 8 in MSN 1671** (which contains broadly similar provisions to those contained in the Passenger Ship Construction Regulations).
* **MSN 1731** contains (in Annex I) a table of **Standards of Personal Protective Equipment** which lists equipment to be provided for various work activities. When entering or working in a space with machinery or equipment where the noise level exceeds 85dB(A), the equipment to be provided is "hearing protection complying with section 10 and appendix 3 of the Code of Practice for Noise Levels in Ships published by the Department of Transport (1990)" (see E08b.3a). (Section 10 relates to Ear protection; Appendix 3 relates to Ear protectors.)

E08b.3a Code of Practice for Noise Levels in Ships

- is a **UK** Department of Transport publication, first published in 1978 under ISBN 0 11 550950 X.
- was last revised in **1990**.
- **deals** with:
  * the measurement of noise levels;
  * recommendations for acceptable maximum noise levels for all spaces to which persons normally have access;
  * the means of protecting the seafarer from the risk of noise-induced hearing loss under conditions where at the present time it is not technically feasible to limit the noise to a level that is not potentially harmful;
  * noise abatement measures generally acceptable on board ships.
- **applies** to new ships (except private pleasure craft and fishing vessels) of 500gt and over, with some exceptions for vessels on short trips, daywork, or where crew do not normally sleep aboard, etc.
- **should also be applied** to new ships of less than 500gt where reasonable and practicable.
- **takes account** of **some** of the provisions of the IMO publication **Noise on Board Ships** (see E08b.3b) and other technical developments.

- takes the form of **recommendations**, although the provision of hearing protection complying with the Code may, where noise levels exceed limits specified in regulations or in MSN 1731, may be a statutory requirement.
- provides for a **noise survey** to be carried out on new ships (section 6) and contains a format for presentation of ship noise survey results in a **noise survey report** (appendix 1).
- provides (in paragraph 9.11) that **if noise levels become the cause of complaint**, noise measurement in the relevant spaces should be undertaken by the owners, e.g. the chief engineer (or other senior officer) with the ship in service. If the complaint is found to be reasonable after assessment of the results, the owner should endeavour to reduce the noise to the level recommended in section 7 as appropriate to the space concerned.
* **Compliance with the Code** should help to meet the employer's obligation under regulation 5(2)(e) of the MS (Health and Safety at Work) Regulations 1997 (SI 1997/2962) to maintain all places of work in the ship in a condition that is, so far as is reasonably practicable, **safe and without risk to health**. (Failure to comply with the Code is not an offence in itself.)
* **M.1415** explains the application of the Code.

E08b.3b IMO publication "Noise on Board Ships"

- **was published** in 1982 with sales number 814 82.05.E and ISBN 92-801-1134-5.
- **contains** the **Code on Noise Levels on Board Ships**, adopted under IMO resolution A.468(XII), and "Recommendation on methods for measuring noise levels at listening posts", adopted under resolution A.343(IX).
- **was developed** to stimulate and promote noise control at a national level within the framework of **internationally agreed guidelines**.
- **applies** (under paragraph 1.3 of Code) to new ships of 1600gt and over. The Code's provisions relating to potentially hazardous noise levels should also apply to existing ships of 1600gt and over, as far as reasonable and practicable, to the satisfaction of the Administration. The Code should apply to new ships of less than 1600gt, as far as reasonable and possible, to the satisfaction of the Administration.
- **provides** (in paragraph 4.3) for the issue of a **Noise Survey Report** (see D04t.9) following a **noise survey**.
- is, in part, taken account of by the 1990 edition of the UK Department of Transport publication **Code of Practice for Noise Levels in Ships** (see E08b.3a).

E08b.4 Improvement Notices and Prohibition Notices

* **Sections 261(1) and 262(1) Merchant Shipping Act 1995** confer powers on inspectors appointed under section 256(6) to issue **Improvement Notices and Prohibition Notices** to persons in breach of their statutory duties under the Merchant Shipping Acts (see B05b.4f and B05b.4g). These powers, which are normally exercised by MCA surveyors acting as "inspectors", are similar to those given by sections 21 and 22 of the Health and Safety at Work Act to HSE inspectors in Great Britain or on installations on the UK Continental Shelf, but may, in relation to a UK ship, be exercised anywhere.
* An **Improvement Notice** -
    - **may be served** by an inspector under **section 261(1) of the Merchant Shipping Act 1995**. The Notice will be served by an **MCA surveyor** or an **HSE inspector**, depending on the location of the ship and the work activity being carried out (see B05f).
    - **gives notice** that, in the opinion of the named inspector, in respect of the named ship, the recipient is either **contravening** or **has contravened** the provisions listed.
    - **must specify** the **relevant provisions** contravened.
    - **must state** the **reasons for the inspector's opinion**.
    - **states** that the inspector requires the recipient to **remedy** the listed contraventions, or, as the case may be, the matter occasioning them, by a **specified date** and in the **manner specified in the attached schedule** which forms part of the notice.
    - **could be served**, for example, on the master of a ship in port where the accommodation ladder is not properly rigged. In this case, the necessary measures required to bring the rigging of the ladder into compliance with the MS (Means of Access) Regulations would be specified on the schedule to the Notice.
* A **Prohibition Notice** -
    - **may be served** by an inspector under **section 262(1) of the Merchant Shipping Act 1995**. The Notice will be served by an **MCA surveyor** or an **HSE inspector**, depending on the location of the ship and the work activity being carried out (see B05f).
    - **gives notice** that, in the opinion of the named inspector, the stated **activities**, which are being carried out or are likely to be carried out by or under the control of the recipient, aboard the named ship, **involve, or will involve a risk or imminent risk of serious personal injury or serious pollution of navigable waters**, as the case may

be, and that the inspector is further of the opinion that the said matters involve **contraventions** of the listed statutory provisions.

- **must specify** the **relevant provisions** contravened.
- **must state** the **reasons for the inspector's opinion**.
- **states** that the **inspector directs** that the stated activities **shall not be carried out** by the recipient or under his control either **immediately or after a specified date and time**.
- **could be served**, for example, on the master of a ship in which certain operations involving dangerous equipment are being carried on.

* Improvement Notices and Prohibition Notices may include **directions as to the method of compliance**; these will be written on the reverse side of the notice.

* **Receipt** of a Prohibition or Improvement Notice could involve an owner in much difficulty and expense, but **contravention of a Notice's directions is a criminal offence**.

* For notes on the **powers of an inspector** see B05b.3e. For notes on the **power to serve Improvement Notices** see B05b.4f. For notes on the **power to serve Prohibition Notices** see B05b.4g.

E08c CODE OF SAFE WORKING PRACTICES

E08c.1 Code of Safe Working Practices for Merchant Seamen

- is a Maritime and Coastguard Agency publication, sold in the UK by The Stationery Office and its accredited agents.
- **must,** under the MS (Code of Safe Working Practices for Merchant Seamen) Regulations 1998 (SI 1998/1838) (see E08c.3), be carried on **all UK ships on which workers are employed**.
- was published in its latest edition in **1998** in loose-leaf form, so that additional and replacement pages may be added, and superseded pages removed. Amendments are promulgated by Marine Information Note. Amendment 02 was promulgated by **MIN 121**. Amendment 03 was promulgated by **MIN 132**.
- has a **special page numbering system** which is explained inside the front cover so that revisions can easily be made.
- is arranged in **sections** which deal with broad areas of concern. The **Introduction** gives the **regulatory framework** for health and safety on board ships and overall safety responsibilities under that framework. **Section 1** is largely concerned with the **safety management** and the **statutory duties** underlying the advice in the remainder of the Code. **Section 2** begins with a chapter setting out the areas that should be covered in **introducing a new recruit** to the safety procedures on board. It goes on to explain what individuals can do to improve their personal health and safety. **Section 3** is concerned with various **working practices common to all ships**. **Section 4** covers safety for **specialist ship operators**.
- contains **chapters** in each section as shown in the following table.

Section	Chapt	Subject	Related Statutory Instrument
Section 1: Safety Responsibilities/Shipboard Management	1	Risk assessment	MS & FV (Health & Safety at Work) Regulations 1997 (SI 1997/2962)
	2	Health surveillance	MS & FV (Health & Safety at Work) Regulations 1997 (SI 1997/2962)
	3	Safety officials	MS & FV (Health & Safety at Work) Regulations 1997 (SI 1997/2962)
	4	Personal protective equipment	MS (Personal Protective Equipment) Regulations 1999 (SI 1999/2205)
	5	Safety signs	MS & FV (Safety Signs and Signals) Regulations 2001 (SI 2001/3444)
	6	Means of access and safe movement	MS (Means of Access) Regulations 1988 (SI 1988/1637); MS (Safe Movement on Board Ship) Regulations 1988 (SI 1988/1641)
	7	Work equipment	MS & FV (Health & Safety at Work) Regulations 1997 (SI 1997/2962); MS (Guarding of Machinery and Safety of Electrical Equipment) Regulations 1988 (SI 1988/1636); MS (Hatches and Lifting Plant) Regulations 1988 (SI 1988/1639)
Section 2: Personal Health and Safety	8	Safety induction	MS (Training and Certification) Regulations 1997 (SI 1997/348); MS (Prevention of Pollution by Garbage) Regulations 1998 (SI 1998/1377); All SIs governing occupational health and safety
	9	Fire precautions	-
	10	Emergency procedures	MS (Musters, Training and Decision Support Systems) Regulations 1999 (SI 1999/2722)
	11	Security on board	-
	12	Living on board	-
	13	Safe movement	MS (Safe Movement on Board Ship) Regulations 1988 (SI 1988/1641)
	14	Food preparation and handling	-

Section 3: Work Activities	15	Safe systems of work	MS & FV (Health & Safety at Work) Regulations 1997 (SI 1997/2962)
	16	Permit to work systems	MS & FV (Health & Safety at Work) Regulations 1997 (SI 1997/2962)
	17	Entering enclosed or confined spaces	MS (Entry Into Dangerous Spaces) Regulations 1988 (SI 1988/1638)
	18	Boarding arrangements	MS (Means of Access) Regulations 1988 (SI 1988/1637)
	19	Manual handling	MS & FV (Manual Handling Operations) Regulations 1998 (SI 1998/2857)
	20	Use of work equipment	-
	21	Lifting plant	MS (Hatches and Lifting Plant) Regulations 1988 (SI 1988/1639)
	22	Maintenance	-
	23	Hot work	-
	24	Painting	-
	25	Anchoring, mooring and towing operations	-
	26	Hatch covers and access lids	MS (Hatches and Lifting Plant) Regulations 1988 (SI 1988/1639)
	27	Hazardous substances	MS (Dangerous Goods and Marine Pollutants) Regulations 1997 (SI 1997/2367); MS (Carriage of Cargoes) Regulations 1999 (SI 1999/336)
	28	Use of safety signs	MS & FV (Safety Signs and Signals) Regulations 2001 (SI 2001/3444)
Section 4: Specialist Ships	29	Dry cargo ships	MS (Carriage of Cargoes) Regulations 1999 (SI 1999/336); MS (Load Line) Regulations 1998 (SI 1998/2241); MS (Dangerous or Noxious Liquid Substances in Bulk) Regulations 1996 (SI 1996/3010)
	30	Tankers and other ships carrying bulk liquid cargoes	MS (Training and Certification) Regulations 1997 (SI 1997/348); MS (Entry Into Dangerous Spaces) Regulations 1988 (SI 1988/1638); MS (Gas Carriers) Regulations 1994 (SI 1994/2464); MS (Dangerous or Noxious Liquid Substances in Bulk) Regulations 1996 (SI 1996/3010)
	31	Ships serving offshore gas and oil installations	MS (Hatches and Lifting Plant) Regulations 1988 (SI 1988/1639); MS (Dangerous Goods and Marine Pollutants) Regulations 1997 (SI 1997/2367)
	32	Ro-ro ferries	MS (Fire Protection: Small Ships) Regulations 1998 (SI 1998/1011); MS (Fire Protection: Large Ships) Regulations 1998 (SI 1998.1012); MS (Fire Protection) (Amendment) Regulations 1999 (SI 1999/992)
	33	Port towage industry	-

E08c.2 Legal significance of Code of Safe Working Practices

* An **industrial code of practice** is a **simple and flexible extension of the law**. It generally specifies technical and other legal requirements in **more detail** or in a **more liberal style** than is practicable or desirable in regulations.
* Compliance with the provisions of a code of practice, where relevant, would normally be considered to constitute **satisfactory compliance with the requirements of a relevant statute**.
* Failure to observe any provision of a code of practice will not in itself render a person liable to criminal or civil proceedings; a person cannot be prosecuted for breaching a provision of a code of practice.
* Where in **criminal proceedings in the UK** a person is alleged to have contravened a statutory requirement or prohibition, the court is required to **admit in evidence** any provisions of a code of practice which appear to the court to be **relevant**. (In a prosecution of an officer for an alleged breach of the MS (Entry into Dangerous Spaces) Regulations, for example, the requirements of Chapter 17 of the Code of Safe Working Practices for Merchant Seamen) would be relevant.)
* Where a court considers that the code's provisions **are relevant** to matters which must be proved to establish a contravention of a statutory provision, **evidence of failure to observe the code's provisions will generally be proof of contravention of the statutory provision**.
* Certain MS Regulations (e.g. the Hatches and Lifting Plant Regulations, Means of Access Regulations and various other health and safety-related SIs) require **full account** to be taken of the **principles and guidance** of the corresponding chapters of the Code of Safe Working Practices for Merchant Seamen. Failure to take full account of the Code's provisions, where this is required, may therefore result in a conviction for a breach of the Regulations.
* When a **Prohibition Notice** or **Improvement Notice** is issued in respect of operations on or in connection with a ship and includes **directions** specifying remedial measures, those directions may be framed **by reference to the Code of Safe Working Practices**. To the extent to which a Notice is framed by the Code, the **Code becomes part of the Notice** and has **legal effect** accordingly. (An Improvement Notice may, **for example**, require the rigging of the accommodation ladder to be improved in compliance with Chapter 18.)

* The **ISM Code** states that the Company's **Safety Management System** should ensure that **applicable codes**, guidelines and standards recommended by the flag State Administration are taken into account. The Code of Safe Working Practices is one such code, and an ISM audit may consider how, or whether, the Code's guidance has been implemented on board.
* The ISM Code requires that the "safety management objectives of the Company should, *inter alia* ..... establish safeguards against all identified risks.....". The Code of Safe Working Practices will assist the Company in **identifying risks** and **establishing safe practices** to safeguard against them.
* The ISM Code requires the Company to "define and document the responsibility, authority and interrelation of all personnel who manage, perform and verify work relating to and affecting safety and pollution prevention". The Code of Safe Working Practices gives **advice on the roles of those with particular safety responsibilities**, and highlights **work areas** where specific responsibilities should be allocated to a "competent person".

E08c.3 Code of Safe Working Practices Regulations

* The **MS (Code of Safe Working Practices for Merchant Seamen) Regulations 1998** (SI 1998/1838) -
  - **revoke** the MS (Code of Safe Working Practices) Regulations 1980 (SI 1980/686).
  - **apply to all UK ships** except fishing vessels and pleasure vessels (regulation 3).
  - define "**worker**" as "any person employed by an employer under a contract of employment including trainees or apprentices other than trainees who are training on a sail training vessel".
  - **provide** (in regulation 4) that a **certain number of copies** must be carried on board, as stated below.
* **On a ship in which 5 or fewer workers are employed**, at least **one copy** must be on board, in the custody of the **master**. It must be readily **accessible and available** to workers (regulation 4(1)).
* **On a ship in which between 5 and 20 workers are employed**, a "**suitable number**" of copies must be carried (regulation 4(2)). On these ships:
  * **one** copy must be kept by the **master**,
  * **one** copy must be kept by the **safety officer**,
  * **one** copy must be provided for **each safety representative**, where elected;
  * **one or more** copies must be kept in a place **readily accessible** to other workers; and
  * **nobody** is required to keep more than one copy;
* **On a ship in which more than 20 workers are employed**, a "**suitable number**" of copies must be carried (regulation 4(3)). On these ships:
  * **one** copy must be kept by the **master**;
  * **one** copy must be kept by the **chief officer**;
  * **one** copy must be kept by the **chief engineer**;
  * **one** copy must be kept by either the **purser or the catering officer**;
  * **one** copy must be kept by the **safety officer**;
  * **one** copy must be kept by **each safety representative**, where elected; and in addition,
  * a **number of copies** which is **adequate for the number of workers employed**, taking account of the nature of their duties, must be **readily available** and kept in a place or places **readily accessible** to them;
  * nobody is required to hold more than one copy.
* Where, as the case may be, **no safety officer or safety representative is appointed** for the ship, any requirement in regulation 4 for a safety officer or safety representative to keep a copy of the Code will not apply, and in either case the number of copies which the Company is required by regulation 4 to ensure are carried may also be reduced, as long as the total number will not be less than a suitable number (regulation 4(4)).
* It is an offence for any person to **remove** a copy of the Code, carried in compliance with the Regulations, without the consent of the Company or the master (regulation 4(5)).

E08d SAFETY OFFICIALS

E08d.1 Part IV of Health and Safety at Work Regulations

* **Part IV of the MS and FV (Health and Safety at Work) Regulations 1997** (SI 1997/2962) relates to "special responsibility for health and safety and consultation with workers", and contains regulations numbered as follows: **14.** Protective and preventive services; **15.** Appointment of safety officers; **16.** Duties of safety officers; **17.** Election of safety representatives and safety committees; **18.** Powers of safety representatives and safety committees; **19.** Duties of the Company and master; **20.** Consultation with workers.

E08d.2 Protective and preventive services

* **Regulation 14(1) of the Health and Safety at Work Regulations** provides that one or more **"competent persons"** must be appointed by the employer in order to provide such **protective and preventive services** for the undertaking as are necessary to enable him to comply with the requirements of the Regulations[56].

* **"Competent person"** is defined in regulation 2(1) as "a person who has sufficient training and experience or knowledge and other qualities, to enable him properly to undertake the duty imposed under the relevant provision in these Regulations". A modified form of the definition applies in the case of a safety officer (see E08d.3).

* Where there is **no competent person available** within the undertaking, the employer must employ an **external person** who is a competent person (regulation 14(2)). (A company may in this case bring in a safety **consultant**, etc.) If he is a competent person, the employer may appoint **himself** for this duty (regulation 14(3)).

* The **number of persons appointed** must be sufficient in number to carry out the requirements of the Regulations, and the appropriate persons must have the necessary time, resources and means to carry out their duties (regulation 14(4)).

* The **appointment of a competent person** appointed under regulation 14(1) must be **recorded in writing** (regulation 17(5)).

E08d.3 Safety officer

* **Regulations 15** (Appointment of safety officer), **16** (Duties of safety officers), **17** (Election of safety representatives and safety committees) and **18** (Powers of safety of representatives and safety committees) **apply to sea-going ships in which more than 5 workers are employed**, except fishing vessels.

* Regulation 15(1) provides that regulation 15 and regulations 16 to 18 apply to **sea-going ships in which more than 5 workers are employed**.

* **Regulation 15(2)** provides that in every ship to which regulation 15 applies, the Company must appoint a **competent person** as safety officer. **"Competent person"**, in the case of a safety officer, is defined in regulation 2(1) as "a person who has sufficient training and experience or knowledge and other qualities, to enable him properly to undertake the duty imposed under the relevant provision in these Regulations, and who has in addition a minimum of **two years' consecutive sea service** since attaining the age of 18, which, in the case of a safety officer on board a **tanker**, shall include at least **six months' service** in such a ship".

* The **appointment of a safety officer** under regulation 15(2) must be **recorded in writing** (regulation 17(5)). The appropriate place for making such a record is the narrative section of the Official Log Book, or in the case of a ship with no Official Log Book, the deck log book.

* The MCA may grant **conditional exemptions** from the requirement to have a safety officer, or to appoint one, for classes of cases or individual cases.

* **Regulation 16(1)** provides that it will be the **safety officer's duty to use his best endeavours to**:
  * **improve** the standard of safety consciousness among the crew and ensure that the provisions of the Code of Safe Working Practices and safety instructions, rules and guidance for the ship relating to health and safety are complied with;
  * **investigate**, so far as is reasonably practicable,
    * **every accident** involving death, major or serious injury and every dangerous occurrence as defined in the MS (Accident Reporting and Investigation) Regulations 1994 (which are now superseded by the MS (Accident Reporting and Investigation) Regulations 1999);
    * all **potential hazards** to health and safety; and
    * all **reasonable complaints** by workers about health and safety,
    - and **make recommendations** to the master to prevent their recurrence or to remove any hazard, provided that the duty to investigate will not extend to accidents arising from a casualty to the ship;
  * **ensure** that health and safety inspections of each accessible part of the ship are carried out at least once every 3 months, and more frequently if there have been substantial changes in the conditions of work;
  * **make representations** and, where appropriate, **recommendations** to the master about any deficiency in the ship in respect of:
    * any legislative requirement relating to health and safety;
    * any relevant Merchant Shipping Notice; or
    * any provision of the Code of Safe Working Practices,
    - and also **suggest** whether those representations and recommendations should be passed by the master on to the employer or other person who has control of the matter;

---

[56] The appointment of one or more Company or fleet safety superintendents or safety officers may meet this requirement.

- **maintain a record** of every accident involving death, major or serious injury and every dangerous occurrence, and make it available to any elected Safety Representative, to the master and to any person duly authorised by the MCA;
- **stop** any work which he observes in progress and reasonably believes may cause a serious accident, and immediately inform the master or the master's deputy (who will decide when work can safely be resumed).

* The safety officer is not required to carry out any of the above duties at a time when **emergency action** to safeguard life or the ship is being taken (regulation 16(2)).
* The Code of Safe Working Practices advises that because the safety officer investigates all accidents, **he should not be in charge of medical treatment**, and he should avoid direct involvement with any treatment. He should instead concentrate on establishing the facts of the case and should:
  - record the names (and addresses if shore personnel are involved) of all those in the vicinity;
  - note and mark the positions of the injured and details of clothing, equipment and tools likely to have been in use; and
  - take possession of portable items which might be relevant to the investigation. Sketches and photographs should be used if possible.
* The safety officer should try to determine **how and why the accident occurred** and **must assist the master** in reporting the accident on an **IRF form**.

E08d.4 Safety representatives

* In every sea-going ship in which more than 5 workers are employed, other than fishing vessels, and where there is no existing arrangement under the Safety Representatives and Safety Committee Regulations 1977 (SI 1977/500), the Company must make **rules for the election and appointment of safety representatives** (regulation 17(1)).
* In every election for a safety representative the candidate receiving the most votes will be elected, provided that no safety representative may be appointed who has less than 2 years' consecutive sea service since attaining the age of 18, which in the case of a safety representative on board a **tanker** must include at least 6 months' tanker service (regulation 17(2)).
* Under regulation 17(3), the **appointment** of a safety representative will **terminate** –
  - on that person ceasing to be employed in the ship; or
  - from the date on which that person resigns from that position or on which another duly elected person is elected in his place.
* The **MCA strongly recommends** officers and ratings to elect safety representatives, but their election and appointment is **not a statutory requirement**. (It may, however, be a company contractual requirement).
* If the crew (including the master) numbers from **6 to 15**, one safety representative should be jointly elected by the officers and ratings.
* If the crew numbers **more than 16**, one safety representative should be elected by the officers and one by the crew.
* If there are **more than 30 ratings**, one safety representative should be elected by the officers and three by the ratings (one each from the deck, engine and catering departments, GP ratings being included as deck ratings).
* The **appointment of a safety representative** under regulation 17(1) must be **recorded in writing** (regulation 17(5)). The appropriate place for making such a record is the narrative section of the Official Log Book, or in the case of a ship with no Official Log Book, the deck log book.
* A safety representative has the following **powers** under regulation 18:
  - to **participate**, subject to the concurrence of the safety officer, in any investigation or inspection made by the safety officer under regulation 16;
  - to **make similar investigations or inspections** to the safety officer's, whether or not already made by the safety officer (in which case the master or his deputy must be notified);
  - to **make representations** to the employer on potential hazards and dangerous occurrences at the workplace which affect, or could affect, workers on the ship;
  - to **make representations** to the master and the employer on general matters affecting the health and safety of workers on the ship and, in particular, on such matters as those on which the employer carries out consultation under regulation 20;
  - to **request the safety officer** to carry out any occupational health and safety inspection they consider necessary and to report the findings to them.
* **A safety representative should** develop a good relationship with the safety officer and should work with the safety officer to raise the safety standard on board.

E08d.5 Safety committee

* In all ships where a safety representative is elected, the Company must **appoint a safety committee** which must include the **master** as chairman, the **safety officer** and **every safety representative**, and may also include any other **person appointed under regulation 14(1)** (i.e. competent persons appointed to provide protective and preventive services) (regulation 17(4)).

* The **appointment of any competent person, safety officer or safety representative onto a safety committee** must be **recorded in writing** (regulation 17(5)). The appropriate place for making such a record is the narrative section of the Official Log Book, or in the case of a ship with no Official Log Book, the deck log book.

* A safety committee has the same **powers** under regulation 18 as safety representatives (see E08d.4).

* The **secretary** of the safety committee should preferably not be one of the safety officials, as they need to concentrate on the discussion.

* Also on the committee may be any **other persons necessary for the proper conduct of business**, e.g. heads of department, but the committee should be kept compact to maintain interest and for its proper functioning.

* **Frequency of meetings** should be about every 4 to 6 weeks or as required by circumstances.

* Meetings should include: (1) circulation of the agenda; (2) minutes of the last meeting; (3) "any other business" (the discussion); and (4) an announcement of the date/time/place of the next meeting.

* **Duties of a safety committee** are:
  * to use its best endeavours to **ensure the CSWP is complied with**;
  * to **improve** the standard of safety consciousness among the crew;
  * to **make representations and recommendations** on the crew's behalf on occupational health and safety matters;
  * to **inspect** the safety officer's records;
  * to **ensure the observance** of the employer's occupational health and safety policies and make recommendations for their improvement;
  * to **consider and take appropriate action** concerning any occupational health and safety matters, accident reports, M Notices and other occupational health and safety publications issued by government or safety organisations, etc. and any new occupational health and safety legislation;
  * to **keep a record** of meetings and any representations, replies or action resulting therefrom.

E08d.6 Duties of Company and master

* Under regulation 19(1) of the Health and Safety at Work Regulations the **Company** and the **master** must, in co-ordination with the **employer, facilitate the work** of any person appointed to provide protective and preventive services, any safety officer appointed and any safety representative appointed in carrying out their health and safety functions, and **in particular** to:
  * **provide** for their use a copy of the **Code of Safe Working Practices for Merchant Seamen** (where appropriate), and access to any necessary **information, documents** and **similar material** including relevant **legislation** and **Merchant Shipping Notices**;
  * **provide** them with relevant **information** about –
    * the **risks** and **measures for protection** identified under regulation 7;
    * **factors** known, or suspected, by them to **affect the health and safety** of the workers on the ship;
    * **arrangements** for **fire-fighting, first aid** and other **emergency procedures**.
  * **ensure** that those persons have the necessary **resources** and **means** to carry out their functions and duties;
  * **allow** any of those persons such **absence from ship duties** without loss of pay as may be necessary to enable them to fulfil their functions, or to undertake any necessary training in health and safety matters;
  * **receive** at any reasonable time, **representations** about health and safety from the safety officer, safety representatives or the safety committee, **discuss** their representations with them and **implement** any agreed measures as soon as may be reasonable and practicable.

* Under regulation 19(2), where no safety officer is appointed under regulation 15, the **Company** must maintain a **record of every accident** involving death, major or serious injury, and every dangerous occurrence and make it **available** on request to any worker and any person duly authorised by the Secretary of State (e.g. MAIB inspectors, MCA surveyors and proper officers).

E08e OCCUPATIONAL HEALTH AND SAFETY

* **In addition to** the -
  * MS (Safe Manning, Hours of Work and Watchkeeping) Regulations 1997 (SI 1997/1320);
  * MS and FV (Health and Safety at Work) Regulations 1997 (SI 1997/2962);
  * MS and FV (Health and Safety at Work) (Employment of Young Persons) Regulations 1998 (SI 1998/2411);
  * MS and FV (Manual Handling Operations) Regulations 1998 (SI 1998/2857);
  * MS (Code of Safe Working Practices for Merchant Seamen) Regulations 1998 (SI 1998/1838);
  - occupational health and safety secondary legislation applicable to UK ships wherever they may be is contained in the following SIs:
  * MS (Guarding of Machinery and Safety of Electrical Equipment) Regulations 1988 (SI 1988/1636);
  * MS (Means of Access) Regulations 1988 (SI 1988/1637);
  * MS (Entry Into Dangerous Spaces) Regulations 1988 (SI 1988/1638);
  * MS (Hatches and Lifting Plant) Regulations 1988 (SI 1988/1639);
  * MS (Safe Movement on Board Ship) Regulations 1988 (SI 1988/1641);
  * MS (Personal Protective Equipment) Regulations 1999 (SI 1999/2205); and
  * MS and FV (Safety Signs and Signals) Regulations 2001 (SI 2001/3444).
* In the 1988 SIs:
  * "**master**" includes any person in charge of a vessel during the master's absence except a watchman;
  * "**offshore installation**" means any offshore installation within the meaning of section 1 of the Mineral Workings (Offshore Installations) Act 1971;
  * where an offence is committed by one person due to an act or neglect of another person, the **other person may be charged** with and convicted of the offence, whether proceedings are taken against the first person or not; and
  * an authorised **MCA or HSE inspector may inspect any UK ship and may detain the** ship until the health and safety of all persons on board is secured (but must not detain or delay ship unreasonably).

E08e.1 Guarding of Machinery Regulations

* The **MS (Guarding of Machinery and Safety of Electrical Equipment) Regulations 1988** (SI 1988/1636) -
  - **apply**, except for regulation 8, to UK ships (regulation 2(1)(a)).
  - **apply**, except regulation 7, to non-UK ships in a UK port (regulation 2(1)(b)).
  - **do not apply** to fishing vessels, pleasure craft, offshore installations on or within 500 metres of their working stations, or ships on which there is no master or crew or watchman for the time being (regulation 2(2)).
  - provide for the granting of **exemptions** under regulation 2(3).
  - provide in regulation 7 for the **inspection** of any UK ship by the MCA and for **detention** of the ship if found not to be complying with the Regulations.

E08e.1a Definitions

* Machinery is "**securely guarded**" for the purposes of the Regulations if protected by a properly installed guard or device of design and construction which prevents foreseeable contact between a person or thing worn or held by a person and any dangerous part of the machinery (regulation 1(3)).

E08e.1b Master's duties

* The **master must** -
  - ensure that every dangerous part of the ship's machinery is **securely guarded** unless of such construction or so positioned or otherwise safeguarded as to be as safe to anyone on board as if it were securely guarded (regulation 3(1)).
  - ensure that all **guards and other devices** provided under the regulations are of **substantial construction** and **properly maintained** and (subject to the provisos in regulation 3(2)) are **kept in position** whilst the parts to be guarded are in motion (regulation 3(3)).
  - ensure that there is a **means for taking prompt action to stop** any machinery and for **cutting off the power** in an emergency (regulation 3(4)).
  - ensure that all ship's **electrical equipment and installations** are so constructed, installed, operated and maintained that the ship and all persons are protected against electrical hazards (regulation 4).
* Under regulation 3(2) it will be a **defence** for a person charged with a contravention of regulation 3(1) to show it was **necessary** for the dangerous part of machinery to be in motion whilst not securely guarded to ensure the safety of the

ship or for an examination and any adjustment, lubrication or test shown by that examination to be immediately required provided that:

- exposure of the dangerous part was the minimum necessary;
- exposure was authorised by a responsible ship's officer or other responsible person;
- the examination was carried out only by a competent person;
- any person who was required to be close to the machinery had, so far as was reasonably practicable, an area which was of adequate size, properly illuminated and clear of obstructions and loose material in which to work;
- any person operating or close to machinery had been instructed as necessary in the safe systems of work for that machinery and in the dangers arising from and precautions to be observed while the machinery was operating;
- a conspicuous notice warning of the danger was exhibited on or close to the machinery.

E08e.1c Employer's duties

*   The duties imposed by the Regulations on the master are also imposed on his **employer**.

E08e.2 Means of Access Regulations

*   The **MS (Means of Access) Regulations 1988** (SI 1988/1637) -
    -   **apply**, except for regulation 14, to UK ships (regulation 3(1)(a)).
    -   **apply**, except regulations 5, 6, 7(c) and 13, to non-UK ships in a UK port (regulation 3(1)(b)).
    -   **do not apply** to fishing vessels, pleasure craft, offshore installations on or within 500 metres of their working stations, or ships on which there is no master or crew or watchman for the time being (regulation 3(2)).
    -   provide for the granting of **exemptions** under regulation 3(3).
    -   provide in regulation 13 for the **inspection** of any UK ship by the MCA and for **detention** of the ship if found not to be complying with the Regulations.

E08e.2a Definitions (regulation 2)

*   "**Access**" means, in the Regulations, embarking on or disembarking from a ship.
*   "**Portable ladder**" does not include a rope ladder.

E08e.2b Master's duties

*   The master must –
    -   ensure that a safe means of access exists between the ship and any quay, pontoon or similar structure or a ship alongside (regulation 4(1)).
    -   ensure that equipment required under regulation 4(1) is promptly positioned after the ship has been made fast and remains in position while the ship is made fast (regulation 4(1)(a)).
    -   ensure that access equipment which is in use is properly rigged, secured, deployed and is safe to use and is adjusted when necessary to maintain safe access (regulation 4(1)(b)).
    -   ensure that access equipment and the immediate approaches thereto are properly illuminated (regulation 4(1)(c)).
    -   ensure that any access equipment used and any safety net is of good construction, sound material, adequate strength for its purpose, free from patent defect and properly maintained (regulation 4(1)(d)).
    -   ensure that access necessary between ship and shore when the ship is not secured alongside is provided in a safe manner (regulation 4(2)). (This refers to boats, etc.)
    -   take full account, in carrying out the obligations of the Regulations, of the principles and guidance in the Code of Safe Working Practices (regulation 4(3)).
    -   ensure that a portable ladder is used only for access to the ship where no safer means of access is reasonably practicable (regulation 7(a)).
    -   ensure that a rope ladder is used only for access between a ship with high freeboard and a ship with low freeboard or between a ship and boat if no safer means of access is reasonably practicable (regulation 7(b)).
    -   ensure that any rope ladder used for access to a ship complies with the specifications of the Code of Safe Working Practices relating to rope ladders (regulation 7(c)).
    -   ensure that a life-buoy with self-activating light and separate safety line attached to a quoit or similar device is ready for use at the point of access aboard the ship (regulation 8).
    -   ensure that an adequate number of safety nets is carried on board or is otherwise readily available (regulation 9(1)).

- ensure that when access equipment is in use and there is a risk of a person falling from it or from the ship or quay immediately adjacent to the equipment, a safety net is rigged (regulation 9(2)).
* The various requirements of regulation 7, as outlined above, do not affect those of the MS (Pilot Transfer Arrangements) Regulations (regulation 7).

E08e.2c Employer's duties

* The master's **employer must** -
  - comply with the **same obligations** as the master.
  - also ensure that a **gangway** is carried in every ship of 30 metres or more registered length, appropriate to the deck layout, size, shape and maximum freeboard, complying with the specifications of the Code of Safe Working Practices relating to gangways (regulation 5).
  - also ensure that an **accommodation ladder** is carried in a ship of 120 metres or more registered length, appropriate to deck layout, size, shape and maximum freeboard, complying with the specifications of the Code of Safe Working Practices relating to gangways (regulation 6).

E08e.2d Duties of any person boarding or leaving the ship

* When access equipment is provided in accordance with the Regulations, **any person boarding or leaving the ship** must **use the equipment** except in emergencies (regulation 10).

E08e.3 Entry into Dangerous Spaces Regulations

* The **MS (Entry into Dangerous Spaces) Regulations 1988** (SI 1988/1638) -
  - **apply**, except regulation 11, to UK ships (regulation 3(1)(a)).
  - **apply**, except regulations 6 and 10, to non-UK ships in a UK port (regulation 3(1)(b)).
  - **do not apply** to fishing vessels, pleasure craft, offshore installations on or within 500 metres of their working stations, or ships on which there is no master or crew or watchman for the time being (regulation 3(2)).
  - **do not** provide for the granting of **exemptions**.
  - provide in regulation 10 for the **inspection** of any UK ship by the MCA and for **detention** of the ship if found not to be complying with the Regulations.

E08e.3a Definitions

* A "**dangerous space**" means any enclosed or confined space in which it is foreseeable that the atmosphere may at some stage contain toxic or flammable gases or vapours, or be deficient in oxygen, to the extent that it may endanger the life or health of any person entering that space.

E08e.3b Master's duties

* The **master must** -
  - except when necessary for entry, ensure that all **entrances to unattended dangerous spaces** are either kept closed or otherwise secured against entry (regulation 4).
  - ensure that all **procedures** for ensuring safe entry and working in dangerous spaces are observed on board (regulation 5(1)(ii)).
  - **take full account** of the principles and guidance contained in the Code of Safe Working Practices relating to entry into dangerous spaces (regulation 5(3)).
  - ensure that in any tanker of 500gt or over, and in any other ship of 1000gt and over, **drills simulating the rescue of a crew member** from a dangerous space are held at intervals not exceeding 2 months, and that a record of such drills is entered in the Official Log Book (regulation 6).
  - ensure that the oxygen meter and any other testing device required by regulation 7 is maintained in good working order and, where applicable, regularly serviced and calibrated to the maker's recommendations (regulation 7).

E08e.3c Employer's duties

*   The **master's employer must** -
    -   ensure that **procedures** for ensuring safe entry and working in dangerous spaces are **clearly laid down** (regulation 5(1)(ii).
    -   ensure that each ship where entry into a dangerous space may be necessary carries or has available an **oxygen meter** and such **other testing device as appropriate to the hazard** likely to be encountered in any dangerous space (regulation 7).

E08e.3d Duties of any person

*   Any person entering a dangerous space must **take full account** of the principles and guidance in the Code of Safe Working Practices (regulation 5(3)).

E08e.3e Prohibitions on any person

*   No person may **enter or be in a dangerous space** except in accordance with the procedures laid down by the employer under regulation 5(1) (regulation 5(2)).

E08e.4 Hatches and Lifting Plant Regulations

*   The **MS (Hatches and Lifting Plant) Regulations 1988** (SI 1988/1639) -
    -   **apply**, except for regulation 14, to UK ships anywhere (regulation 3(1)(a)).
    -   **apply**, except for regulation 13, to non-UK ships when in a UK port (regulation 3(1)(b)).
    -   **do not apply** to fishing vessels, pleasure craft, offshore installations on or within 500 metres of their working stations, or ships on which there is no master or crew or watchman for the time being (regulation 3(2)).
    -   provide for the granting of **exemptions** under regulation 3(3).
    -   provide in regulation 13 for the **inspection** of any UK ship by the MCA and for **detention** of the ship if found not to be complying with the Regulations.

E08e.4a Definitions

*   In the Regulations "**competent person**" means a person over 18 with the knowledge and experience required for the performance of thorough examinations and tests of ships' lifting plant.
*   "**Hatch covering**" includes hatch covers, beams and attached fixtures and fittings.
*   "**Lifting appliance**" means any ship's stationary or mobile appliance (and every part thereof except vehicle coupling arrangements) used on board for suspending, raising or lowering loads or moving them from one position to another while suspended, and includes ship's lift trucks and similar vehicles. It does not include survival craft or rescue boat launch and recovery appliances, pilot hoists, pipes or gangways or screw, belt, bucket or other conveyors used for the continuous movement of cargo or people, but does include the lifting appliances used to raise or lower these appliances.

E08e.4b Master's duties in relation to hatches (regulation 4)

*   The **master must** -
    -   in carrying out obligations under regulation 4, **take full account** of the principles and guidance in the **Code of Safe Working Practices** (regulation 4(1)).
    -   ensure that any **hatch covering** used is of sound construction and material, of adequate strength for its purpose, free from patent defect and properly maintained (regulation 4(2)).
    -   ensure that a **hatch covering is not used unless** it can be removed and replaced, whether manually or with mechanical power, without endangering any person (regulation 4(3)(a)).
    -   ensure that **information** showing the correct replacement position is clearly marked, except insofar as hatch coverings are interchangeable or incapable of being incorrectly replaced (regulation 4(3)(b)).
    -   ensure that a **hatch is not used unless** the hatch covering has been completely removed, or if not completely removed, is properly secured (regulation 4(4)).

E08e.4c Master's duties in relation to lifting plant (regulations 5 to 10)

* The master must -
  - in carrying out obligations under regulations 6 to 10, **take full account** of the principles and guidance in the Code of Safe Working Practices (regulation 5).
  - ensure that any **lifting plant** is of good design, of sound construction and material, of adequate strength for its purpose, free from patent defect, properly installed or assembled and properly maintained (regulation 6(1)).
  - ensure that any **pallet or similar piece of equipment** for supporting loads **or lifting attachment** which forms an integral part of the load or one-trip sling or pre-slung cargo sling is not used unless it is of sound construction, of adequate strength for the purpose for which it is used and free from patent defect (regulation 6(2)).
  - ensure that lifting plant is not used except in a **safe and proper manner** (regulation 6(3)).
  - ensure that except for the purpose of carrying out a test under regulation 7, the lifting plant is **not loaded in excess of its safe working load** (regulation 6(4)).
  - ensure that no lifting plant is used after manufacture or installation, or after repair or modification which is likely to alter the safe working load or affect the lifting plant's strength or stability, without first being **tested by a competent person**, except in the case of a rope sling made from rope which has been tested by a competent person and spliced in a safe manner (regulation 7(1)).
  - ensure that a lifting appliance is not used unless it has been **suitably tested by a competent person** within the preceding 5 years (regulation 7(2)).
  - ensure that any lifting plant is not used unless it has been **thoroughly examined by a competent person** at least once in the preceding 12 months, and also following a test in accordance with regulation 7 (regulation 8).
  - ensure that each lifting appliance is **clearly and legibly marked** with its safe working load and a means of identification (regulation 9(1)).
  - ensure that any **crane carried whose safe working load varies** with the operating radius is fitted with an accurate **indicator**, clearly visible to the driver, showing the radius of the load-lifting attachment at any time and the safe working load corresponding to that radius (regulation 9(2)).
  - ensure that each item of lifting gear is clearly and legibly marked with its safe working load and a means of identification, except where not reasonably practicable, but in such a case a safe working load must be readily ascertainable by any user (regulation 9(3)).
  - ensure that **each item of lifting gear which weighs a significant proportion** of the safe working load of any lifting appliance with which it is intended to be used is, in addition to the requirement above, clearly **marked** with its weight (regulation 9(4)).
  - except in relation to non-UK ships, ensure that a **certificate or report** in an MCA-approved form is obtained within 28 days of any test under regulation 7 or examination under regulation 8 and is kept in a safe place on board for at least 2 years from receipt or until receipt of the certificate or report of the next test or examination (regulation 10(1)). For notes on the **Register of Lifting Appliances** see D04r.2.

E08e.4d Employer's duties

* The duties imposed by the Regulations on the master are also imposed on his **employer**.

E08e.4e Duties of other persons

* Every person carrying out obligations under regulation 4 (Hatches) must **take full account** of the principles and guidance in the Code of Safe Working Practices (regulation 4(1)).
* Every person carrying out obligations under regulations 6 to 10 (Lifting Plant) must **take full account** of the principles and guidance in the Code of Safe Working Practices (regulation 5).

E08e.4f Prohibitions on any person

* Except in the event of an emergency endangering health or safety, no person may **operate a power-operated hatch covering** or a ship's **ramp** or a **retractable car-deck** unless **authorised** by a responsible officer (regulation 4(5)).
* No person may **operate any lifting plant** unless he is **trained** and **competent** to do so and has been **authorised** by a responsible ship's officer (regulation 6(5)).

E08e.5 Safe Movement on Board Ship Regulations

* The **MS (Safe Movement on Board Ship) Regulations 1988** (SI 1988/1641) -
  - **apply**, except for regulation 15, to UK ships anywhere (regulation 3(1)(a)).
  - **apply**, except for regulation 14, to non-UK ships when in a UK port (regulation 3(1)(b)).
  - **do not apply** to fishing vessels, pleasure craft, offshore installations on or within 500 metres of their working stations, or ships on which there is no master or crew or watchman for the time being (regulation 3(2)).
  - provide for the granting of **exemptions** under regulation 3(3).
  - provide in regulation 14 for the **inspection** of any UK ship by the MCA and for **detention** of the ship if found not to be complying with the Regulations.

E08e.5a Master's duties

* The **master must** -
  - ensure that **safe means of access is provided and maintained** to any place on the ship where a person may be expected to go (regulation 4(1)).
  - take full account in carrying out the obligation of regulation 4(1) of the principles and guidance in the Code of Safe Working Practices (regulation 4(2)).
  - ensure that all **deck surfaces** used for transit about the ship, and all **passageways, walkways and stairs**, are **properly maintained** and kept **free from materials and substances** liable to cause a person to slip or fall (regulation 5).
  - ensure that those areas of the ship being used for **loading or unloading** of cargo or for other **work processes** or for **transit** are adequately and **properly illuminated** (regulation 6).
  - ensure that any **opening, open hatchway or dangerous edge** into, through, or over which a person may fall is fitted with **secure guards or fencing** of adequate design and construction, kept in a good state of repair (regulation 8(1)). The requirement of regulation 8(1) **does not apply** where any opening affords a permanent means of transit about the ship, to the side of the opening used for access, or where guards or fencing is not reasonably practicable given the nature of the work process involved (regulation 8(2)).
  - ensure that all **ship's ladders** are of good construction and sound material, of adequate strength for their purpose, free from patent defect and properly maintained (regulation 9).
  - ensure that no **ship's powered vehicle or powered mobile lifting appliance** is driven in the course of a work process except by a **competent and authorised person** (regulation 10(a)).
  - ensure that **danger** from use or movement of all **ship's powered vehicles and mobile lifting appliances** is so far as is reasonably practicable prevented (regulation 10(b)).
  - ensure that all **ship's vehicles and mobile lifting appliances** are **properly maintained** (regulation 10(c)).
* **Regulation 7**, which required the employer and master to ensure that any permanent safety signs used on board the ship for the purpose of giving health or safety information or instruction comply with BS 5378 part I or with any equivalent standard, was revoked by the MS and FV (Safety Signs and Signals) Regulations 2001 (see E08e.7).

E08e.5b Employer's duties

* The duties imposed by the Regulations on the master are also imposed on his **employer**.

E08e.5c Owner's duties

* The **owner must** ensure that in a **new ship**, **hold access ladders** comply with requirements specified in the Code of Safe Working Practices in relation to such ladders (regulation 11).

E08e.6 Personal Protective Equipment Regulations

* The **MS (Personal Protective Equipment) Regulations 1999** (SI 1999/2205) -
  - **revoke** the MS (Protective Clothing and Equipment) Regulations 1985 (SI 1985/1664).
  - are explained in **MSN 1731**.
  - define "**personal protective equipment**" as all clothing and equipment designed to be worn or held by the worker for protection against one or more hazards likely to endanger his health or safety at work, and any addition or accessory designed for this purpose, with the exception of:
    * ordinary working clothes and uniforms which are not specifically designed to protect the health and safety of the worker;

- equipment provided for the purposes of fire-fighting or lifesaving;
  - personal protective equipment worn or used by the military, the police and other public order agencies;
  - personal protective equipment required for road transport;
  - sports equipment;
  - self-defence or deterrent equipment; or
  - portable devices for detecting and signalling risk and nuisances.
- define "**worker**" as any person employed by an employer under a contract of employment, including trainees or apprentices.
- **apply to all activities of workers** on UK ships **except** when the activity of a worker -
  - is on a public service vessel or a vessel engaged in search and rescue; and
  - characteristics of that activity inevitably conflict with a provision of these Regulations (in which case there is a duty on the employer so far as is reasonably practicable to ensure the health and safety of the worker when performing that activity).
- **apply certain requirements** (in regulations 2, 3(1) and (3), 15, 16 and 17) to non- UK ships which are in UK waters.
- **do not apply** to or in relation to the activities of a worker which are covered by the Personal Protective Equipment at Work Regulations 1992 (SI 1992/2966) or the Personal Protective Equipment at Work Regulations (Northern Ireland) 1993 (SR 1993/20).
* Regulation 4 provides that where a person on whom a duty is imposed by any provision of the Regulations does not have control of the matter to which the regulation relates because he does not have responsibility for the operation of the ship, then any duty imposed by that regulation shall also extend to any person who has control of that matter.

E08e.6a General rule (Regulation 5)

* Regulation 5 makes the following general rule: **personal protective equipment must be used** when risks cannot be avoided or reduced to an acceptable level by means of systems of work that are safe and without risk to health or by means of collective protection or by other means which are in use equally or more effective.

E08e.6b Employer's duties (Regulation 6)

* Regulation 6 provides that the employer must ensure that the personal protective equipment required to be used under regulation 5 is actually **provided**, and that the equipment is **suitable**, i.e. in relation to any work activity described in **MSN 1731**, it is of the **kind** and to the **standard** specified in the MSN, in relation to that work activity.
* Regulation 6 also provides that the personal protective equipment must be:
  - **appropriate** for the risks to which the worker is exposed, to the task which he is performing and to the existing conditions at the work place, without itself leading to any increased risk;
  - correctly **fitting** the worker, or capable of being **adjusted** to fit;
  - taking into account **ergonomic requirements** and the worker's **state of health**; and
  - **compatible** with any other equipment the worker has to use at the same time, so that it continues to be effective against the risk.
* Personal protective equipment must be provided **free of charge** to the worker except that where use of the equipment is not exclusive to the work place, workers may be required to **contribute** towards the cost of personal protective equipment.

E08e.6c Assessment of personal protective equipment (Regulation 7)

* Regulation 7 provides that before personal protective equipment is provided, the employer must ensure that an **assessment** is made to identify:
  - those **circumstances** where risk to the health and safety of individual workers at work cannot be avoided or reduced by other means;
  - the **characteristics required** of personal protective equipment in order to provide protection to workers from that risk; in accordance with the findings of the assessment, equipment which complies with the characteristics identified and meets the standards in MSN 1731 must be provided.
* The assessment must be **reviewed** to take account of any changes to the factors on which it was based.

E08e.6d Storage, issue and maintenance (Regulation 8)

* Regulation 8 provides that, subject to the proviso in the next paragraph, the employer must ensure that personal protective equipment is provided to a worker for his **individual use**.

* The proviso is that equipment may be provided **for the use of more than one person** if it is:
  * **adjustable** to fit all sizes,
  * easily **accessible** and kept in clearly marked places, and
  * **maintained** in a hygienic condition and repaired, decontaminated and replaced as necessary, so that it will not create any health or hygiene problems.
* The employer must ensure that appropriate **instructions** for the proper use and maintenance of any personal protective equipment provided under regulation 6 are readily available to any worker required to use that equipment, and shall be comprehensible to him.
* The employer must ensure that personal protective equipment provided is properly **stored** and **maintained**, having due regard to any recommendations made by the manufacturers, so that it can immediately be used when required to be used in accordance with regulation 5.
* In the case of **respiratory protective equipment**, which provides protection against dust (either nuisance or toxic), toxic gases or atmospheres or lack of oxygen, the employer must ensure that the equipment is **inspected and checked** that it is in satisfactory working order before and after use, or in other cases, **regularly inspected** in accordance with the manufacturer's instructions or the guidance in the Code of Safe Working Practices for Merchant Seamen, and, where appropriate, **checked** that it is in satisfactory working order.

E08e.6e Training and instruction (Regulation 9)

* Regulation 9 provides that the employer must ensure that workers are provided with adequate and appropriate **information, training and instruction**, which may include the organisation of **demonstrations** in the wearing of personal protective equipment, in respect of-
  * the risks against which the personal protective equipment is designed to provide protection;
  * the circumstances in which it shall be used; and
  * the correct use, maintenance and storage of the equipment.
* The information, training and instruction provided is not "adequate and appropriate" unless it is **comprehensible** to the persons to whom it is provided.

E08e.6f Use of personal protective equipment (Regulation 10)

* Regulation 10 provides that the employer must take all reasonably practicable steps to ensure that any personal protective equipment provided to workers is **used as instructed**.
* Every worker must:
  * use any personal protective equipment provided to him; and
  * follow any training in the use of the personal protective equipment which has been received by him and the instructions respecting that use.

E08e.7 Safety Signs and Signals Regulations

* The **MS (Safety Signs and Signals) Regulations 2001** (SI 2001/3444) -
  - **implement** Council Directive 92/58/EEC on the minimum requirements for the provision of safety and/or health signs at work.
  - **apply** to **all activities of workers on UK ships** wherever they may be except when the worker is on a public service vessel[57] or a vessel engaged in search and rescue and characteristics of the activity inevitably conflict with a provision of the Regulations (in which case there is a duty on the employer so far as is reasonably practicable to ensure the health and safety of the worker when performing that activity) (regulation 3(1)).
  - **revoke** regulation 7 of the MS (Safe Movement on Board Ship) Regulations 1988 (see E08e.5a).
* **Regulation 5** relates to **provision and maintenance of safety signs** and **applies if** the risk assessment made under regulation 7(1) of the MS & FV (Health and Safety at Work) Regulations 1997 (see E08b.2c) indicates that the employer, having adopted all appropriate techniques for collective protection, and measures, methods or procedures used in the organisation of work, **cannot avoid or adequately reduce risks** to workers except by the provision of **appropriate safety signs** to warn or instruct, or both, of the nature of those risks and the measures to be taken to protect against them.
* Where regulation 5 applies, the **employer** must, under regulation 5(2):
  * **ensure** that there is **in place** an **appropriate safety sign** in accordance with the requirements set out in Annexes I to VII of Council Directive 92/58/EEC (regulation 5(2)(a));

[57] A "**public service vessel**" means any vessel operated by and on behalf of a public body while it is carrying out the authorised functions of the body.

- subject to regulation 5(5), in accordance with the requirements of Annexes I, VIII and IX of the Directive, **ensure**, so far as is reasonably practicable, that any **appropriate hand signal or verbal communication** described in those Parts **is used** (regulation 5(2)(b));
- and
- **maintain any appropriate safety sign** (other than a hand signal or verbal communication) which he is required to ensure is in place (regulation 5(2)(c)).

* For the purposes of regulation 5(1), risks may only be treated as having been "adequately reduced" if, having adopted the appropriate techniques, measures, methods or procedures referred to in regulation 5(1), there is **no longer a significant risk of harm** having regard to the magnitude and nature of the risks arising from the work concerned (regulation 5(3)).

* Without prejudice to regulation 5(1), regulation 5(2)(a) and (b) will also apply in relation to **fire safety signs** where they are required under any Act or SI (regulation 5(4)).

* For the purposes of regulation 5(2)(b), the **appropriate hand signal** described in the documents specified in the Schedule to the Regulations may be an alternative to the corresponding hand signal described in paragraph 3 of Annex IX of the Directive (regulation 5(5)). The documents specified in the Schedule are:
- BS 7121: 1989 Code of Practice for Safe Use of Cranes; and
- Annex 21.1 of the MCA Code of Safe Working Practices for Merchant Seamen (as amended).

* Where it is appropriate to provide safety signs in accordance with regulation 5(1) because at a place of work there is a risk to the health and safety of any worker in connection with the **presence or movement of traffic**, the appropriate safety sign required under regulation 5(2) will be in accordance with the requirements prescribed in the Traffic Signs Regulations and General Directions 1994 (SI 1994/1519), whether or not that instrument applies to the place of work (regulation 5(6)).

* Regulation 6(1) provides that the employer must ensure that **comprehensible and relevant information** on the **measures to be taken in connection with safety signs** is provided to each worker.

* Regulation 6(2) provides that the employer must ensure that each worker **receives suitable and sufficient instruction and training** in the **meaning of safety signs** and **the measures to be taken in connection with safety signs**.

* **Chapters 5 and 28 of the Code of Safe Working Practices for Merchant Seamen** also relate to safety signs and signals.

* **MSN 1763** explains the application of the Regulations and contains the text of the Annexes to Council Directive 92/58/EEC, with graphics of the range of signs that may be used.

E08e.8 Manual Handling Operations Regulations

* The **MS (Manual Handling Operations) Regulations 1998** (SI 1998/2857) -
- **give effect** as regards shipping activities in the UK to the Council Directive 90/269/EEC on the minimum health and safety requirements for manual handling where there is a risk, particularly of back injury, to workers.
- **apply** to all UK ships except public service vessels and vessels engaged in search and rescue.
- **do not apply** if the Manual Handling Operations Regulations 1992 (SI 1992/2793) or the Manual Handling Operations Regulations (Northern Ireland) 1992 (SR 1992/535) cover the matter.

* Under regulation 5 the **employer must avoid**, so far as is reasonably practicable, the **need** for any manual handling of a load which would involve a health and safety risk to a worker, but **if avoidance is not reasonably practicable the employer must**:
- carry out an assessment (i.e. a **risk assessment**) having regard to specified factors and consider specified questions in relation to those factors;
- take appropriate steps to **reduce the risk of injury** to workers to the lowest level that is reasonably practicable;
- take steps to **provide the worker with precise information** on the **weight** and **centre of gravity** where it is practicable to do so; and
- provide workers who will be involved in a manual handling operation with **proper training and information**.

* **MGN 90** contains guidance on implementation of the Regulations and contains, in its Annex, examples of the factors for consideration when making an assessment of manual handling operations or providing instruction for workers as required by regulation 5(2)(a).

* Under regulation 4 the **employer's obligations** under regulation 5 as outlined above can be **extended to another person** if the employer is not in control of the matter because he does not have responsibility for the operation of the ship.

* Regulation 6 imposes an **obligation on every worker** to **make full use of any system of work** provided by the employer to reduce the risk to the lowest level that is reasonably practicable.

E08f DOCKS REGULATIONS

* Health and safety law affecting ships in ports underwent a radical change in the late 1980s. The **Docks Regulations 1934**, which had operated under the Factory Act 1961, were repealed. Provisions relating to matters such as hatches and lifting plant and means of access, formerly contained in the Docks Regulations, were made the subjects of a range of new Merchant Shipping health and safety statutory instruments (see E08e.1, E08e.2, E08e.3, E08e.4 and E08e.5). The **Docks Regulations 1988** were introduced.
* **The Docks Regulations 1988** (SI 1988/1655) -
  - **apply in Great Britain** (but not in Northern Ireland, where separate, but similar, legislation applies); and
  - apply in cases **where shore-based workers are involved in any dock operation** (as defined in the Regulations) carried out in any dock operation carried out within British territorial waters, which extend to 12 miles beyond baselines by virtue of the Territorial Sea Act 1987.
  - are **enforced by** the Health and Safety Executive (HSE).
* Under regulation 4, **no duty imposed by the Regulations will be placed on the master or crew of a ship** or any **person employing them** in relation to:
  • plant which **remains on board** the ship; and
  • any dock operation carried out **on the ship solely by the ship's master or crew**.
* Where any **ship's plant**, e.g. a fork lift truck, **does not remain on board the ship**, the Regulations will apply.
* Where any **dock operation** (as defined below) is **carried out by the ship's crew in conjunction with shore labour**, the Regulations will apply. This could include, for example:
  • mooring and unmooring;
  • bunkering;
  • loading potable water;
  • loading and discharging goods, vehicles and passengers.
* "**Dock operation**" means:
  • the loading or unloading of goods from a ship at dock premises;
  • the embarking or disembarking of passengers on or from a ship at dock premises;
  • any activity incidental to the above activities which takes place on dock premises, including any of the following activities if they are so incidental and take place on dock premises:
  • the fuelling and provisioning of a ship;
  • the mooring of a ship;
  • the storing, sorting, inspecting, checking, weighing or handling of goods;
  • the movement of goods, passengers or vehicles;
  • the use of welfare amenities in relation to the carrying out of the above activities;
  • attending dock premises for the purposes of the above activities; or
  • the embarking or disembarking on or from a ship of its crew at dock premises.
* **Where the Regulations apply**, the **master of a ship** must -
  - ensure that **suitable and adequate lighting** is provided (regulation 6). (These requirements will be met for access between ship and shore by compliance with the MS (Means of Access) Regulations and for areas on the ship with the MS (Safe Movement on Board Ship) Regulations.
  - ensure that **safe means of access** to all parts of the vessel are provided and properly maintained (regulation 7). (These requirements will be met for access between ship and shore or between ship and ship by compliance with the MS (Means of Access) Regulations and for access to areas on the ship with the MS (Safe Movement on Board Ship) Regulations.
  - ensure that **no portable ladders** are used for access to the ship, holds or stacks of cargo or containers on board, except where no safer means of access is practicable (regulation 7) . Where ladders are used they must be securely fixed, be of adequate strength and project at least 1 metre above the access point.
  - ensure that there is **adequate fencing** around any place where a person might fall more than 2 metres (regulation 7).
  - ensure that **lifting gear** is used in a safe and proper manner (regulation 13).
  - ensure that **lifting gear and equipment** is properly marked with its safe working load (regulation 16).
  • supply a copy of the latest **certificate or report of examination of lifting plant** to any employer or self-employed person hiring or using the plant (regulation 17). (This means that the **Register of Lifting Appliances**, or "Chain Register" (see D04r.2) must be available for inspectors.)

E08g CREW ACCOMMODATION

E08g.1 Crew Accommodation Regulations

* **Section 43 of the Merchant Shipping Act 1995** enables regulations with respect to crew accommodation to be made.
* The **MS (Crew Accommodation) Regulations 1997** (SI 1997/1508) -
  - **contain** regulations relating to: divisions between crew accommodation and other parts of the ship (regulation 5); interior bulkheads (regulation 6); overhead decks (regulation 7); floor decks (regulation 8); access and escape arrangements (regulation 9); pipes in crew accommodation spaces (regulation 10); awnings (regulation 11); heating (regulation 12); lighting (regulation 13); ventilation (regulation 14); sidescuttles and windows (regulation 15); drainage (regulation 16); interior finishes (regulation 17); marking (regulation 18); sleeping rooms (regulation 19); beds (regulation 20); furniture and fittings in sleeping rooms (regulation 21); mess rooms (regulation 22); furniture and fittings in mess rooms (regulation 23); recreation spaces (regulation 24); offices (regulation 25); sanitary accommodation (regulation 26); supply of drinking water and fresh water (regulation 27); facilities for washing and drying clothes and for hanging oilskins and working clothes (regulation 28); galleys (regulation 29); dry provision store rooms (regulation 30); cold store rooms and refrigerating equipment (regulation 31); hospitals (regulation 32); medical cabinet (regulation 33); protection from mosquitoes (regulation 34); and maintenance and inspection of crew accommodation (regulation 35).
* Under regulation 36, floor coverings, sidescuttles and windows, vacuum discharge pipe systems, thermostatic mixing valves and plant used to produce drinking water and/or fresh water must be of an approved type, but **exemptions** from approval requirements may be granted under regulation 37.
* The Schedule to the Regulations contains the illuminance values of electric lighting in spaces referred to in regulation 13(7).
* Subject to regulation 32(23), no part of the crew accommodation may be shared with passengers or used by or for the benefit of passengers.
* Regulation 32(23) provides that in passenger ships, one hospital may be provided to serve both crew and passengers, subject to separate male and female sanitary arrangements being provided.)

E08g.2 Maintenance of crew accommodation

* Crew accommodation must be maintained in a **clean and habitable condition** and all equipment and installations required by the Regulations must be maintained in good working order (regulation 35(1)).
* Every part of the crew accommodation, except store rooms, must be kept **free from stores and other property** not belonging to or provided for the use of persons for whom that part of the accommodation is appropriated, and in particular **no cargo** may be kept in any part of the crew accommodation (regulation 35(2)).

E08g.3 Inspections of crew accommodation

* The **master** or an officer appointed by him for the purpose, accompanied by **at least one other crew member**, must **inspect every part of the crew accommodation** at intervals not exceeding **7 days** (regulation 35(3)).
* Regulation 35(4) provides that the master must cause an entry to be made (on the special page) in the Official Log Book recording:
  * the time and date of the inspection;
  * the names and ranks of the inspectors; and
  * particulars of any respect in which the accommodation or any part of it was found by either inspector not to comply with the Regulations.

E08g.4 Obligations of crew members in relation to accommodation

* **Clause x(j) of the standard BSF Crew Agreement** incorporates a clause providing that **each seaman agrees** -
  - to **keep his quarters clean** and **tidy** and **in readiness for inspection** by the master or officer deputed by him.
  - at a time when a seaman finally leaves a ship at the termination of his employment under the Agreement, to leave his quarters in a **clean** and **orderly condition** to the satisfaction of the master (or his authorised deputy).

When he is ready to leave the ship, the master (or his authorised deputy) shall, **on request** made by the seaman, issue to the seaman a **certificate** that the quarters are clean.

E08h PROVISIONS AND WATER

E08h.1 Provisions and Water Regulations

* The **MS (Provisions and Water) Regulations 1989** (SI 1989/102) -
    - **give effect** in the UK to **ILO Convention No. 68** concerning food and catering for crews on board ships;
    - **apply**, except for regulation 9, to **sea-going UK ships** except those listed below (regulation 3(1)(a)).
    - **do not apply** to ships under 24 metres long, pleasure craft, submersible craft or offshore installations whilst on or within 500 metres of their working stations (regulation 3(2)).
    - provide for **exemptions** to be granted by the MCA (regulation 3(3)).
    - impose (in regulation 4) a **duty on the employer and the master** of every ship to ensure that provisions and water are provided on their ship which:
        • are **suitable** in respect of quantity, nutritive value, quality and variety having regard to the size of the crew and the character and nature of the voyage (regulation 4(a));
        • **do not contain** anything which is likely to cause sickness or injury to health or which renders any provision or water unpalatable (regulation 4(b)); and
        • are otherwise fit for consumption (regulation 4(c)).
    - require **weekly inspections** of provisions and water (regulation 5).
    - provide for the **inspection of any ship** to which the Regulations apply by a person duly authorised by the **MCA** (regulation 8). Where there has been a breach of the Regulations, he may **detain** the ship until the health and safety of all employees and other persons aboard ship is secured.
    - provide for the **inspection of any non-UK ship** which is in a UK port on her normal business or operations by a person duly authorised by the MCA (regulation 9). If he is satisfied that the ship does not conform to the standards required of UK ships, he may:
        • **send a report** to the flag State government and a copy to the Director General of the ILO (regulation 9(1)(a));
        • where conditions on board are clearly hazardous to safety or health, **take such measures as are necessary to rectify those conditions**, and **detain** the ship (regulation 9(1)(b)).
* Where the inspector takes neither of the above measures, he must **notify** the nearest maritime, consular or diplomatic representative of the flag State (regulation 9(2)).
* Despite the practice of some masters of UK ships of attaching a Weekly Scale of Provisions and Water to the Crew Agreement document and of posting this on the ALC6, there has been **no statutory scale** since the current Provisions and Water Regulations came into force in 1989.

E08h.2 Guidelines for food hygiene

* **MGN 61** -
    - provides practical advice on the **fundamental rules of food hygiene** consistent with the catering and meat industry in general. The key points it makes are that (1) bacterial contamination is the most serious risk to food safety; (2) food hygiene principles must be adhered to regardless of the age, size and type of vessel; and (3) food handlers should receive appropriate education and training in the principles and practice of food hygiene.
    - advises that food should comply with the **Food Safety Act** and respective **regulations** or **other EU standards** and **ILO Convention No. 68**.
    - advises that owners should consider the **special needs of mariners** whose **religion**, **special dietary requirements**, or **customary dietary practices** necessitate the observance of certain rules or requirements with regard to some foods or with the way the food is prepared.
    - advises that ship operators should ensure that all **food handlers receive appropriate education and training** in the principles and practice of food hygiene and associated health and safety issues and that they **maintain acceptable standards** to secure the health and well-being of ships' crews by: (1) protecting food from risk of contamination, including harmful bacteria, poisons and foreign bodies; (2) preventing any bacteria present multiplying to an extent which would cause illness or early spoilage of the food; and (3) destroying any harmful bacteria in the food by thorough cooking.

- has **sections** covering: Bacterial food contamination (paragraph 2); Personal hygiene (paragraph 3); Fitness to work (paragraph 4); Segregation of raw and cooked foods (paragraph 5); Temperature control (paragraph 6); Cleaning procedures (paragraph 7); Pests (paragraph 8); Stock control (paragraph 9); Ventilation in galleys (paragraph 10); Sanitary facilities (paragraph 11); Potable water (paragraph 12); Health and safety issues (paragraph 13); Education and training for food handlers (paragraph 14); Crew information (paragraph 15); and Advice (paragraph 16). Annex 1 lists Ten Tips for Food Safety. Annex 2 details the statutory framework.
* **Chapter 14 of the Code of Safe Working Practices for Merchant Seamen** (Food preparation and handling) gives guidance on standards expected of catering hygiene.
* The MCA's **Food and Hygiene Inspector** visits UK ports to provide guidance to surveyors making ship inspections.

E08h.2 Inspections of provisions and water

* **Regulation 5 of the Provisions and Water Regulations** provides that it is the **duty of the master** to ensure that he, or a person authorised by him, together with a **member of the crew employed in catering** on the ship, inspects not less than **once a week** provisions and water for the purpose of checking whether they still comply with sub-paragraphs (a) to (c) of regulation 4, i.e. that they:
  * are **suitable** in respect of quantity, nutritive value, quality and variety having regard to the size of the crew and the character and nature of the voyage;
  * **do not contain** anything which is likely to cause sickness or injury to health or which renders any provision or water unpalatable; and
  * are otherwise **fit for consumption**.
* The **results of the inspections** must be recorded in the Official Log Book.

E08h.3 Domestic fresh water

* The **MS (Crew Accommodation) Regulations 1997** (SI 1997/1508) provide that -
  - **cold drinking water** for purposes of drinking, cooking and dish washing must be laid on to taps in galleys, bars and pantries, and in the case of any mess room provided for members of the crew for whom no pantry is provided, to a tap in that mess room (regulation 27(1));
  - the **tanks** from which drinking water and the fresh water laid on to wash basins, baths and showers is supplied and any plant installed on board ship from which drinking water and/or fresh water is produced must be of a **capacity to ensure an adequate supply of such water at all times** for all members of the crew, provided that as a minimum the tanks will be sufficient to provide **at least 2 days' supply** of such water (regulation 27(2));
  - the drinking water and fresh water storage tanks, any manholes leading into them and all pipes and other parts of the distribution systems for drinking and fresh water must be so arranged and constructed as to allow **efficient maintenance and prevent any risk of contamination** (regulation 27(3));
  - where drinking water and/or fresh water is produced by plant on board, the water so produced must be **treated** by suitable **automatic means of disinfection** (regulation 27(4));
  - in every ship of 1,000 tons or over a cooling tank or other **suitable means of cooling a supply of drinking water** must be provided, and the water so cooled must be laid on so that it is **readily available to the crew** (regulation 27(5));
  - in ships of 1,000 tons or over any primary pumping necessary for the supply of drinking water and/or fresh water in the crew accommodation must be by mechanical power, but **alternative pumping arrangements** must be provided to supply drinking water and/or fresh water in the event of a breakdown of the primary pumping system. When an enclosed pressurized system is employed, the pumps provided for the alternative pumping system must be power operated and all pumps required for primary and alternative pumping must be fitted with automatic controls (regulation 27(6)).
* **M.1214** contains **Recommendations to prevent contamination** of ships' fresh water storage and distribution systems and contains sections as follows:
  * **Fresh water loading and supply arrangements** (freshwater obtained from shore mains supply or water barge; routine treatment of fresh water; fresh water from low pressure evaporator or reverse osmosis plant);
  * **Storage tank arrangements** (storage tanks and delivery system intended for drinking or washing water; siting of tanks; construction; coatings);
  * **Distribution systems** (water treatment, filters, mineralisers, softeners, etc.; freshwater distribution pumps; calorifiers, pressure tanks, etc.; piping; overall design of freshwater systems; fittings and accessories);
  * **Maintenance** (fresh water storage tanks; distribution system; hoses; chlorination; corrosion and scale inhibitors)

* **Further recommendations** (new ships; existing ships; all ships).
* **M.1401** updates M.1214, adding electro-silver ionisation systems as an acceptable method for automatic disinfecting of fresh water produced on board UK ships, subject to conditions contained in the Notice.
* **MGN 61** advises that **potable water should be bright, clear, virtually colourless and should bubble** when shaken. This does not however guarantee that the water is safe. There is a tendency to assume that little or no action is needed to protect the purity of the water, particularly when using quayside facilities regularly. Although the water may come from the same source as that supplied to the general public in their homes, there is a vast difference to the operation of supplying and storing the water, exposing it to a much higher risk of contamination. It is therefore essential that control measures are taken to minimise the risk of contamination according to that provided in the Ship Captain's Medical Guide. A **Fresh Water Maintenance Log** detailing all aspects of treatment and maintenance carried out should be kept and include a record of the following routine treatments as well as replacing filters or other elements of water making plants.
* Dedicated **fresh water hoses** should be superchlorinated at 100ppm for a contact of one hour at intervals of not longer than 6 months.
* All **fresh water taken from shore should be chlorinated on loading** to ensure a residual free chlorine content of 0.2ppm, unless an automatic chlorination unit is used. Concentration levels should be checked.
* **Chlorine tests of taps and shower outlets** should be carried out at monthly intervals.
* **Storage tanks should be opened up, emptied, ventilated and inspected at intervals not exceeding 12 months** for inspection and maintenance. **Tanks should be thoroughly cleaned, recoated as necessary and flushed out**.
* It is also recommended that **water be tested for bacterial and chemical contamination every 3 months**. The local Port Health Authority can arrange to **take samples and have them analysed**.

E08h.4 Complaints about provisions or water

* **Article 8 of ILO Convention No. 68 and section 44 of the Merchant Shipping Act 1995** allow for a special inspection of the ship following a complaint from at least three of the crew about food and water supplies. For notes on **the statutory right of seamen to complain about provisions or water** see E11b.
* For notes on **appropriate action in response to complaints** see E11c.

E08i HOURS OF WORK

* For notes on the **MS (Hours of Work) Regulations 2002** (SI 2002/2125), see E03c.1
* For notes on the **European Working Time Agreement**, see E03c.2.

E08j MEDICAL ATTENTION

E08j.1 Master's statutory duty relating to medical attention

* **Section 53 of the Merchant Shipping Act 1995** provides that where a **UK ship does not carry a doctor** among the seamen employed in it, the **master** must make arrangements for securing that any medical attention on board the ship is given either **by him** or **under his supervision** by a **person appointed by him**.
* By implication, in a vessel in which **there is a doctor** amongst the crew, the **doctor** is responsible for any medical attention given on board.

E08j.2 Action in cases of personal injury or illness

* The following notes assume that the ship is at **sea, or in a port with no medical facilities**.
* **Actions in case of personal injury** should be:
  1. For casualties resulting from **non-toxic hazards**, give **first aid treatment** as described in the **Ship Captain's Medical Guide (SCMG) Chapter 1**.
  2. For casualties resulting from **toxic hazards** give first aid treatment as described in the **SCMG, Chapter 2** and the **Medical First Aid Guide for Use in Accidents involving Dangerous Goods** ("MFAG").
  3. Take the casualty to the ship's hospital or his cabin for **further treatment** for wounds and other injuries as per **SCMG, Chapter 4**.
  4. If necessary, **obtain radio medical advice** (see H04c.3).

5. If on-board treatment is insufficient, make for a position where the seaman may be landed for **treatment ashore** (see H01d and H04c.4).

*   **Actions in case of illness** should be:

1. **Diagnose illness** as described in the **Ship Captain's Medical Guide - Introduction** (page 3), and list **symptoms**. The Introduction recommends use of the check list for Radio Medical Advice on page 210 (section A) as a guideline. In case of severe abdominal pain see the chart on page 130; in case of chest pain see the chart on page 138.

2. Having listed all symptoms and findings, and the patient's temperature, pulse and respiration rate, **consult the relevant section of the SCMG**, and follow the **treatment** recommended. A bulleted list in the Introduction (page 3) may assist.

3. Carefully **monitor and record** the patient's progress.

4. Where unable to make a diagnosis, or if the patient's condition worsens, see Radio Medical Advice (see

*   **In all cases**, all actions taken and treatment given should be **recorded** in the Official Log Book (see D05a), if necessary using annexed sheets, or in the medical or sick bay log (see requirement for **entry No.38** in D05a.4).

*   **In port with medical facilities**, the ill or injured person should be landed to the appropriate medical facility if insufficient treatment cannot be given on board. Arrangements should be made through the agent as outlined in H04c.

*   For notes on **illness, injury and deaths at sea**, see H04c.

E08j.2a Ship Captain's Medical Guide

-   is required to be carried on certain vessels under regulation 4(1) of the MS and FV (Medical Stores) Regulations 1995 (SI 1995/1802). For notes on the Regulations and their requirements relating to medical stores, see D04p. The Guide should be kept in the ship's **medical cabinet**.

-   must be carried on **Category A vessels** as defined in MSN 1726, i.e. seagoing vessels with no limitation on length of trips.

-   must be carried on **Category B vessels** as defined in MSN 1726, i.e. seagoing vessels making trips of less than 150 nautical miles from the nearest port with adequate medical equipment. This category is extended to seagoing vessels which make trips of less than 175 nautical miles from the nearest port with adequate medical equipment and which remain continuously within range of helicopter rescue services.

-   can be **downloaded** in full from: www.mcga.gov.uk/publications/medical/index.htm

-   **contains** a preface and introduction, and the following chapters: 1. First aid; 2. Toxic hazards of chemicals including poisoning; 3. General nursing; 4. Care of the injured; 5. Causes and prevention of disease; 6. Communicable diseases; 6.1. Sexually transmitted diseases; 7. Other diseases and medical problems; 8. Diseases of fishermen; 9. Female disorders and pregnancy; 10. Childbirth; 11. Survivors; 12. The dying and the dead; 13. External assistance. Annexes are: I. Anatomy and physiology; II. Anatomical drawings. There is an index.

-   is primarily intended for use on ships not carrying a doctor.

-   has **three functions**, as follows: 1. To enable a master to diagnose and treat injured and sick seafarers; 2. To serve as a text book for Medical First Aid and Proficiency in Medical Care courses; 3. To help masters give some training to crew.

-   is currently in its 22nd (1998) edition and is published by The Stationery Office under ISBN 0 11 551658 1.

-   can be downloaded (in full) from the MCA website at: www.mcga.gov.uk/publications/medical/index.htm

*   All crew members should be encouraged to learn the immediate life-saving measures described in the first part of Chapter I.

E08j.2b Medical records

*   For notes on **medical records required under the MS (Official Log Books) Regulations 1981** see D05b.5.

E08j.3 Employer's liability for expenses of medical and other treatment

*   **Section 45 of the Merchant Shipping Act 1995** provides that if a person, while **employed in a UK ship**, receives **outside the UK** -

-   any **surgical** or **medical treatment** or

-   such **dental** or **optical treatment** (including the repair or replacement of any appliance) as cannot be postponed without impairing efficiency,

-   the **reasonable expenses** of the treatment must be borne by the **employer**[58].

---

[58] Most shipowners are insured against their liability for medical expenses through their P&I club policy.

E08k ACCIDENT REPORTING, INVESTIGATION AND RECORDING

E08k.1 Accident Reporting and Investigation Regulations

* The **MS (Accident Reporting and Investigation) Regulations 1999** (SI 1999/2567) -
  - are the regulations forming (with Part XI of Merchant Shipping Act 1995) the framework around which the **Marine Accident Investigation Branch (MAIB) operates**.
  - **revoke** the MS (Accident Reporting and Investigation) Regulations 1994 (SI 1994/2013).
  - contain a **new, broader, definition of "accident"** which includes some of those events previously known as "dangerous occurrences".
  - contain a **new definition of "serious injury"** which no longer applies only to people employed or carried in a UK ship.
  - update various regulations with reference to modern methods of communication, and accordingly **reduce statutory accident reporting times**.
  - remove the concept of an "**Inspector's Inquiry**" and the reference to summary reports. All reports of investigations will be made publicly available in such a manner as the Chief Inspector of Marine Accidents sees fit, subject to certain safeguards with respect to national security.
  - **apply** under regulation 3(1) to accidents involving or occurring on board:
    * **any UK ship**, except that regulation 5 (Duty to report accidents) does not apply to pleasure vessels; and
    * any **non-UK ship in the UK or UK territorial waters**, except that regulation 5 and regulation 7 (Preservation of evidence) do not apply to such a ship unless she is within the defined limits of a UK port or is employed in carrying passengers to or from a UK port.
  - **apply** under regulation 3(2) to "serious injuries" and "hazardous incidents" as they apply to "accidents". However, under regulation 3(2)(a), regulations 5 and 7 do not apply to hazardous incidents (which removes any duty to report, and any duty to preserve evidence in relation to a hazardous incident), and regulations 5(1) and 5(3)(a) do not apply to serious injuries (making serious injuries reportable within 14 days rather than 24 hours, and removing the requirement for the master to provide the Chief Inspector of Marine Accidents with any report other than the one required within 14 days by regulation 5(3)(b)).
* Regulation **4** sets out the **purpose of investigation**. Regulation **5** contains the **duty to report accidents and serious injuries**. Regulation **6** provides for the ordering of an investigation by the Chief Inspector of Marine Accidents. Regulation **7** requires the **preservation of evidence** which may be pertinent to an accident (see E08k.1j). Regulation **8** prescribes the **conduct of investigations**. Regulation **9** makes rules concerning the **disclosure of records** relating to an investigation. Regulation **10** requires the Chief Inspector to publish certain **reports**. Regulation **11** permits the Chief Inspector to make **recommendations** at any time. Regulation **12** allows an investigation to be re-opened in certain circumstances (see B05e.1). Regulation **13** provides for a time extension for making representations to the Chief Inspector by persons whose reputations may be adversely affected by the publication of his report. Regulation 14 sets penalties for breaches of the Regulations.
* Guidance on the operation of the Regulations is in **MGN 115** (Accident reporting and investigation).
* For notes on the **MAIB** see B05d.

E08k.1a Accidents

* **Under regulation 2(1)**, for the purposes of the Regulations and of section 267 Merchant Shipping Act 1995 (which relates to Investigation of marine accidents), "**accident**" means any contingency caused by an event on board a ship or involving a ship whereby:
  * there is **loss of life or major injury** to any person on board (regulation 2(1)(a));
  * any **person is lost or falls overboard** from a ship or ship's boat (regulation 2(1)(a);
  * a ship causes any **loss of life**, **major injury** or **material damage** (regulation 2(1)(b)(i));
  * a **ship is lost** or is presumed to be lost (regulation 2(1)(b)(ii));
  * a ship is **abandoned** (regulation 2(1)(b)(iii));
  * a ship is **materially damaged** by fire, explosion, weather or other cause (regulation 2(1)(b)(iv));
  * a ship **grounds** (regulation 2(1)(b)(v));
  * a ship is in **collision** (regulation 2(1)(b)(vi));
  * a ship is **disabled** (regulation 2(1)(b)(vii));
  * a ship causes **serious harm to the environment** (regulation 2(1)(b)(viii));
  * there is a **collapse or bursting** of any pressure vessel, pipeline or valve (regulation 2(1)(c)(i));
  * there is a **collapse or failure** of any lifting equipment, access equipment, hatch-cover, staging or boatswain's chair or any associated load-bearing parts (regulation 2(1)(c)(ii));

- there is a **collapse of cargo**, **unintended movement of cargo or ballast** sufficient to cause a **list**, or **loss of cargo overboard** (regulation 2(1)(c)(iii));
- there is a **snagging of fishing gear** which results in the vessel heeling to a dangerous angle (regulation 2(1)(c)(iv));
- there is a contact by a person with **loose asbestos fibre** except when full protective clothing is worn (regulation 2(1)(c)(v)); or
- there is an **escape of any harmful substance** or agent (regulation 2(1)(c)(vi));
- **if** the occurrence, taking into account its circumstances, **might have been liable to cause serious injury or to cause damage to the health** of any person.

* The incidents listed in regulation 2(1)(c) were mostly reportable under the 1994 Regulations as "**dangerous occurrences**" (see E08k.1c)

E08k.1b Major and serious injuries

* Regulation 2(2) defines "**major injury**" as:
- any fracture, except to the fingers, thumbs or toes (regulation 2(2)(a));
- any loss of a limb or part of a limb (regulation 2(2)(b));
- dislocation of the shoulder, hip, knee or spine (regulation 2(2)(c));
- loss of sight (whether temporary or permanent) (regulation 2(2)(d));
- penetrating injury to the eye (regulation 2(2)(e)); or
- any other injury leading to hypothermia or unconsciousness, requiring resuscitation or requiring admittance to hospital or similar for more than 24 hours or, if at sea, requiring confinement to bed for more than 24 hours (regulation 2(2)(f)).

* A "**major injury to any person on board**" and a "**major injury caused by a ship**" are defined as "accidents" under regulation 2(1) and are therefore **reportable as accidents** under regulation 5(1).

* Regulation 2(2) defines a "**serious injury**" as **any injury, except a major injury**, to a person employed or carried in a ship which occurs on board or during access which results in **incapacity for more than three consecutive days** excluding the day of the accident, or as a result of which the **person concerned is put ashore and the ship sails** without that person, **unless** the incapacity is known or advised to be of three consecutive days or less, excluding the day of the accident. "Incapacity" is defined as inability to undertake the full range of activities normally undertaken.

* The **reason for distinguishing between major and serious injuries** is to avoid setting a requirement for urgent reporting when it is not really needed. Whereas a "major injury", which is included in the definition of an "accident", must be reported relatively quickly, a "serious injury" must be reported under regulation 5(3)(b) within 14 days (see E08k.1h).

E08k.1c Former "dangerous occurrences"

* Most of those incidents which were required under the 1994 Regulations to be reported as "dangerous occurrences" are reportable under the 1999 Regulations as "accidents" under regulation 2(1) (see E08k.1a). The descriptions of some of the events formerly defined as "dangerous occurrences" are changed in the 1999 Regulations, while others (e.g. "any fire or explosion" and "the parting of a tow-rope") are not included at all. (A fire or an explosion is now reportable as an "accident", but only where it has materially damaged the ship.)

E08k.1d Duty to report an accident

* **Regulation 5(1)** provides that, subject to regulation 5(2), (3) and (4), when an **accident** occurs the **master** must send a **report to the Chief Inspector of Marine Accidents** by the **quickest means available** and within **24 hours**. (In practice the report may be addressed to the MAIB.)

* Reports must, as far as practicable and possible, include the **information** listed in E08k.1e (regulation 5(1)).

* **Where a ship is lost or presumed lost or abandoned**, the report must be sent to the MAIB by the owner, the master, or a senior surviving officer **as soon as practicable** and by the quickest means available (e.g. telephone, fax, telex or e-mail.) (regulation 5(2)).

* The master must, so far as reasonably practicable, ensure that the **circumstances of every accident are examined** and must, on request, provide the MAIB with an **additional report** (regulation 5(3)). (The examination should be carried out by the ship's safety officer, if any, and recorded in his accident log and in the Official Log Book.)

* Regulation 5(4) provides that the **requirement to report to MAIB does not apply to**:
- an accident where the person killed or injured is a **stevedore or shore-based worker** and the accident occurs in a UK port; or

- to an accident which occurs in a **UK shipyard** (see E08k.1k).

(In these cases the accident must be reported to the **Health and Safety Executive** (HSE).)
* For **MAIB contact details** see E08k.1f.

E08k.1e Information needed in accident reports

* Regulation 5(1) provides that accident reports sent to the MAIB (in accordance with regulation 5(1) as outlined in E08k.1d) must, so far as is practicable and possible, include the following **details**:
  - name of ship and IMO number, official number or fishing vessel number;
  - name and address of owners;
  - name of the master, skipper or person in charge;
  - date and time of the accident;
  - where from and where bound;
  - latitude and longitude or geographical position in which the accident occurred;
  - part of ship where the accident occurred, if on board;
  - weather conditions;
  - name and port of registry of any other ship involved;
  - number of people killed or injured, together with their names, addresses and gender; and
  - brief details of the accident, including, where known, the sequence of events leading to the accident, extent of damage and whether accident caused pollution or hazard to navigation.

E08k.1f MAIB address and contact numbers for sending of reports

* **MAIB address**: Marine Accident Investigation Branch, First Floor, Carlton House, Carlton Place, Southampton SO15 2DZ
* **Telephone** (office hours): 023 8039 5500
* **Telephone** (24 hours): 023 8023 2527
* **Fax**: 023 8023 2459
* **Telex**: 477917 MAIB SO G
* **e-mail**: maib@dft.gsi.gov.uk
* **MAIB website**: www.maib.dft.gov.uk

E08k.1g Incident Report Form (IRF)

- was introduced to facilitate reporting under the Accident Reporting and Investigation Regulations.
- **replaced** forms ARF1 and WRE1 under which "shipping casualties" were formerly reported.
- can be used to **amplify the initial report** of any accident.
- can also be used to **report serious injuries**. If completed and sent within the time allowed, its submission will suffice without a separate initial report.
- **is obtainable** in hard copy from the MAIB, from MCA Marine Offices.
- **can be downloaded** from the MAIB website.
- **should be sent** after completion to the MAIB at the address in E08k.1f.
* One IRF should be used for each incident.
* Completing and signing an IRF does not constitute an admission of liability of any kind.
* **Section A** is for the date and time of the incident and identity of the vessel. **Section B** is for the voyage details, location of the incident and type of incident (fatal injury, non-fatal injury, vessel lost or abandoned, vessel damaged, or other). **Section C** is for details (i.e. position and age only) of the person(s) injured or killed. **Section D** is for a brief description of the events leading to the incident. **Section E** is for statements of how the incident is thought to have happened, whether any action been recommended as a result (and if so, what?), whether any action been taken (and if so, what?). **Section F** is for the signature and name of either the master or the owner's representative, and the ship's safety officer's signature and name. **Section G** contains the following statement: "If the incident involved a reportable personal accident or was a dangerous occurrence[59] and there is an elected Safety Representative on board the vessel, he must be shown the completed report and allowed to write in this section any comments which he may wish to make. If the injured persons are represented by different Safety Representatives, each may make additional comments if desired in the space below but in any event, they should all sign the form."

---

[59] No longer applicable (see E08k.1c).

E08k.1h Duty to examine and report the circumstances of an accident or serious injury

* Regulation 5(3) provides that the **master must**, so far as us reasonably practicable, ensure that the **circumstances of every accident are examined**. The Regulations make no mention of a safety officer, but where a shipboard safety officer has been appointed, the accident investigation should be made by him and logged by him in the accident log which he is required to keep (see D05b.4). For notes on the **ship's safety officer's statutory duty to investigate accidents** under regulation 16 of the MS and FV (Health and Safety at Work Regulations) 1997, see E08d.3.
* Regulation 5(3)(a) provides that, except in the case of a serious injury, the master must, on request, provide the MAIB with a **report**, in addition to any initial report made under regulation 5(1) or (2), **giving the findings of the examination** and stating any **measures taken or proposed to prevent a recurrence**.
* In the event of a **serious injury**, the master must, under regulation 5(3)(b), and whether a request has been made or not, provide the MAIB with a **report within 14 days** giving the findings of the examination and stating any measures taken or proposed to prevent a recurrence. This report could be made on an IRF form (see E08k.1g).

E08k.1i MAIB investigation

* Regulation 6(1) provides that any accident may be **investigated** by the MAIB. Where a report of an accident or serious injury has been received under regulation 5, the MAIB will notify the master of any decision to investigate within 28 days of receipt of the report or information. Before deciding whether or not to investigate an accident, the MAIB may require **further information** to be obtained; under regulation 6(2) the master or owner and any other relevant person or corporate body **must provide this information** to the best of their ability and knowledge.
* Under regulation 6(7) any initial decision not to investigate may later be reversed by the MAIB.
* Regulation 4 explains that the **fundamental purpose** of investigating an accident is to determine its **circumstances** and **causes** with the aim of improving the safety of life at sea and the avoidance of future accidents. It is not the purpose to apportion liability, nor, except so far as is necessary to achieve its fundamental purpose, to apportion blame.

E08k.1j Preservation of evidence

* Regulation 7(1) provides that the **master, owner and any other relevant person or corporate body must**, so far as is practicable, ensure that all charts, log books, voyage data and other records, electronic and magnetic recording and video tapes and all documents which might reasonably be considered pertinent to an accident reportable under regulation 5, are **kept** and that **no alteration** is made to recordings or entries in them, and that any equipment which might reasonably be considered pertinent to the investigation of the accident must be left **undisturbed** as far as practicable until:
    * notification is received from the Chief Inspector that **no investigation** is to take place; or
    * **unless** notified of a decision to investigate, **28 days after receipt by the MAIB of an initial report** of an accident or serious injury, or of additional information obtained under regulation 6(2); or
    * the Chief Inspector or the inspector carrying out an investigation indicates that he **no longer requires them**.
* For notes on the requirements of the MS (Safety of Navigation) Regulations 2002 (SI 2002/1473) relating to **records of navigational activities** and the **retention and preservation of records of navigational activities**, based on the requirements of accident investigation authorities, see D05b.8.

E08k.1k Accidents to stevedores and shore-based workers in UK ports, and accidents in UK shipyards

* Regulation 5(4) provides that regulation 5 (Duty to report accidents and serious injuries) does not apply -
    * to an accident when the person killed or injured is a **stevedore or shore-based worker** and the accident occurs in a **UK port**; or
    * to an accident which occurs in a **UK shipyard**.
* Accidents occurring in a UK port where the person killed or injured is a stevedore or shore-based worker should be reported by the person's employer to the **Health and Safety Executive (HSE)**.
* Any accident occurring in a shipyard in the UK (whether to a ship-based or shore-based person) should be reported to the **HSE by the shipyard operator**.
* Accidents as defined in regulation 2(1) occurring in **ports and shipyards outside the UK** should be reported to the MAIB in accordance with regulation 5.
* For notes on **stevedore accidents and accidents to other persons in port**, see I05b.3.

E08k.1l Unspecified hazardous incidents

* A "**hazardous incident**" is defined in regulation 2(2) as any event, other than an accident, associated with the operation of a ship which involves circumstances indicating that an accident nearly occurred.
* Although there is **no statutory requirement** to report "unspecified hazardous incidents", owners and masters are strongly urged by the MAIB to report them voluntarily, since useful lessons can be learned.
* **Examples** of unspecified hazardous incidents are:
    * navigational or engineering incidents causing hazard;
    * failure of procedures in any aspect of shipboard operations; and
    * human failures.
* An example in the first of the above categories would be the failure of an automatic pilot causing the vessel to alter her course. If this occurred without a collision resulting, it may be reported as an "unspecified hazardous incident". If a collision resulted, then an "accident" as defined in regulation 2(1) must be reported under regulation 5(1) of the Accident Reporting and Investigation Regulations.
* The **critical question** in deciding whether or not to report is: **Did the incident have the potential to lead to an accident?**
* Reports of unspecified hazardous incidents should be **sent to the MAIB**, and form **IRF** may be used.
* The MAIB recognises that for various reasons there may be some reluctance to report incidents. So far as is possible, a report would be treated in confidentiality if the sender wishes, in which case he should send an accompanying letter requesting confidentiality and giving his name and address (required both to authenticate the report and so that clarification can be sought on any point in the report). The letter will be returned to the sender and no record of his name or personal details will be kept. No copy will be made. The MAIB cannot, however, go beyond the law, or ignore evidence of serious breach of the law (in which case the MCA would be notified), but subject to this, any action in following a report of an unspecified hazardous incident which has been submitted in confidence will not identify its source.
* **As an alternative** to reporting unspecified hazardous incidents to the MAIB, masters may wish to report to the **International Marine Accident Reporting Scheme** ("**MARS**"), operated by the Nautical Institute (see H06f.8).

E08k.2 Official Log Book entries relating to accidents

* **Paragraph 12 of the Schedule to the MS (Official Log Books) Regulations 1981** (SI 1981/569), as amended by SI 1991/2145, requires an entry, signed by the master and a member of the crew, to be made in the Official Log Book where any of the following accidents has occurred:
    * there is loss of life or major injury to any person on board, or any person is lost from, a ship or ship's boat; or
    * a ship is lost or presumed to be lost, or is abandoned or materially damaged; or
    * a ship strands or is in collision; or
    * a ship is disabled; or
    * any material damage is caused by a ship.
* The entry should be made in the narrative section of the Official Log Book and must include:
    * a description of the casualty; and
    * the place where it occurred or the position of the ship when it occurred.
* **Paragraph 38** of the Schedule requires an entry to be made in the Official Log Book where a person employed in the ship **falls ill or is injured**. The entry must include:
    * a record of the circumstances of the injury (signed by the master and witnessed by a member of the crew); and
    * a record of the nature of the illness or injury or the symptoms thereof, the treatment adopted and the progress of the illness or injury (signed by the ship's doctor, or if there is no doctor, the master, and witnessed by a member of the crew).
* A full entry should also be made in the **deck log** or, if appropriate, the **engine room log**; this could be used in an MAIB Investigation or Formal Investigation. Only facts should be stated, and no amendments or deletions should be made.

E08l MUSTERS, TRAINING AND DECISION SUPPORT SYSTEMS

E08l.1 Musters, Training and Decision Support Systems Regulations

* The **MS (Musters, Training and Decision Support Systems) Regulations 1999** (SI 1999/2722) -
    * **revoke and replace** the MS (Musters and Training) Regulations 1986 (SI 1986/1071) and the MS (Musters and Training) (Amendment) Regulations 1993 (SI 1993/3231).

- **apply**, unless otherwise stated, to all sea-going UK ships wherever they are, and to other sea-going ships while in UK waters.
- **do not apply** to fishing vessels, ships of Classes VI and VI(A), pleasure vessels, non-UK cargo ships of less than 500gt, non-UK ships not propelled by mechanical means, and craft to which the MS (High-Speed Craft) Regulations 1996 apply.
- **are explained** in detail in **MGN 71**.

E08I.1a Decision support systems (Regulation 4)

* **Regulation 4** (which gives effect to **SOLAS regulation III/29**) applies to any ship of Class I, II or II(A) and provides that on every ship of these Classes a **decision support system for emergency management** must be provided on the navigation bridge. Ships built before 1 July 1997 need not comply until the ship's first periodical survey after 1 July 1999.
* The decision support system must, as a minimum, consist of a **printed emergency plan in English** and, if different, in the **working language of the crew**, in respect of **each Class** in which the ship operates.
* The emergency plan or plans provided must identify **all foreseeable emergency situations** including, but not limited to:
  * fire;
  * **damage to the ship**;
  * **pollution** caused or likely to be caused by the ship;
  * **unlawful acts** threatening the safety of the ship and the security of its passengers and crew;
  * serious **accidents or injuries** to the crew or passengers;
  * serious **cargo-related accidents**; and
  * being required to provide **emergency assistance** to another ship.
* The emergency plan or plans provided must establish **emergency procedures** for each emergency situation identified.
* The emergency plan or plans provided must provide decision support to the master for handling **any combination of the emergency situations** identified.
* The emergency plan or plans provided must have a **uniform structure** and be **clear** and **easy to understand** in accordance with MGN 71.
* The emergency plan or plans provided must, where applicable, use the **actual loading condition** as calculated for the ship's voyage stability for damage control purposes.
* In addition to the printed emergency plan or plans required to be carried as the decision support system the ship may carry a **computer-based decision support system** on the navigation bridge and in any other safety control centre. Such a system may, however, only be carried if it provides all the information contained in the emergency plan or plans, including the emergency procedures, and any associated checklists, referred to above, and is able to present a list of recommended actions to be carried out in any foreseeable emergency situation.

E08I.1b Muster list and emergency instructions (Regulation 5)

* **Regulation 5** applies to:
  * any ship of Class I, II, II(A), III, VII, VII(T), VIII or VIII(T); and
  * any ship of Class IX or XI engaged on international voyages.
* The **master** of a ship to which regulation 5 applies must:
  * before the ship proceeds to sea, **prepare a muster list**;
  * **maintain the muster list** for the duration of the voyage for which it was prepared; and
  * **revise the muster list**, or prepare a new list, if any change takes place in the crew which necessitates an alteration to the muster list.
* The muster list of any ship of Class I, II, II(A) and III must be in a **format approved by the MCA**. (MCA will normally issue a **Muster List Approval letter** which should be carried on the ship at all times.)
* The **muster list must specify**:
  * the general emergency alarm signal;
  * the action to be taken by crew and passengers when the general emergency alarm signal is sounded;
  * how the abandon ship order will be given;
  * other emergency signals and action to be taken by the crew hearing them;
  * on ro-ro passenger ships and on passenger ships built before 1st July 1998, the location of assembly stations and the procedures for locating and rescuing passengers trapped in their cabins; and
  * on ships of Classes I, II, II(A) and III except those referred to in the previous bulleted line above, the location of muster stations and the procedures for locating and rescuing passengers trapped in their cabins.

* The **muster list must show the duties** assigned to the different members of the crew, including duties as respects:
    * closing of watertight doors, fire doors, valves, scuppers, sidescuttles, portholes and other similar openings;
    * equipping of survival craft and other LSA;
    * preparation and launching of survival craft;
    * general preparations of other LSA;
    * muster of passengers (if any);
    * use of communication equipment;
    * manning of fire parties assigned to deal with fires; and
    * special duties assigned in respect of the use of fire-fighting equipment and installations (e.g. B/A parties);
* The **muster list must also show the duties** assigned to crew members **in connection with passengers** in case of emergency, including:
    * warning the passengers;
    * seeing that passengers are suitably clad and have donned their lifejackets correctly;
    * mustering passengers at assembly or muster stations as appropriate;
    * keeping order in passageways and stairways and generally controlling the movements of passengers; and
    * ensuring that a supply of blankets (where carried) is taken to survival craft.
* The **muster list must also specify** which **officers** are assigned to ensure that **the LSA and fire appliances are maintained in good condition** and are ready for immediate use, and the **substitutes for key persons** who may become disabled (e.g. the master, chief officer and chief engineer), taking into account that different emergencies may call for different actions.
* The **master** must ensure that:
    * **copies of the muster list are exhibited** in conspicuous places throughout the ship including the navigation bridge, engine room and crew accommodation spaces;
    * **clear instructions** to be followed in the event of an emergency are **provided** for every person on board; and
    * **illustrations and instructions** in English and in any other appropriate languages are **posted** in passenger cabins and **conspicuously displayed** at assembly or muster stations (as appropriate) and other passenger spaces to inform passengers of their assembly or muster station (as appropriate), the essential actions they must take in an emergency, and the method of donning lifejackets.
* **M.1579** details the **minimum training requirements** for personnel nominated on muster lists to assist passengers in emergency situations.

E08I.1c General emergency alarm signal (Regulation 6)

* The **general emergency alarm signal** for summoning passengers and crew to assembly or muster stations and initiating the actions specified in the muster list must consist of **at least seven short blasts followed by one long blast**, made:
    * on all ships, on the ship's whistle or siren; and
    * on all ships of Classes I, II, II(A) and III, and of Classes VII, VII(T), VIII, VIII(T) and IX of at least 45.7metres in length, on an electrically operated bell or klaxon or other equivalent electrically operated warning system.
* The general emergency alarm signal must be:
    * capable of **operation from the navigation bridge** and, except for the ship's whistle, also from **other strategic points**; and
    * audible throughout all the **accommodation and normal crew spaces**.
* Once activated, the general emergency alarm signal must continue to sound until it is **manually turned off** or is temporarily **interrupted by a message** on the public address system.

E08I.1d Public address systems (Regulation 7)

* Every ship must have a **public address (PA) system** consisting of a **loudspeaker installation** enabling the broadcast of messages into all spaces where crew members or passengers, or both, are normally present and to all assembly or muster stations (as appropriate).
* The PA system must:
    * provide for the broadcast of messages from the bridge and other strategic points;
    * be installed with regard to acoustically marginal conditions;
    * not require any action by the addressee in order to be audible; and
    * be protected against any unauthorised use.

E08I.1e Practice crew drills (Regulation 8)

* **Regulation 8** applies to:
  * any ship of Class I, II, II(A), III, VII, VII(T), VIII, VIII(T), VIII(A), VIII(A)(T) or IX ; and
  * any ship of Class XI engaged on an international voyage.
* On any ship to which regulation 8 applies, each crew member must participate in **at least one abandon ship drill and one fire drill every month**.
* Without prejudice to the above requirement for participation in drills, in any ship of **Class I, II, II(A) or III**, an abandon ship drill and fire drill must take place **weekly**. (Note that in ships of other Classes there is no such requirement.)
* If **more than 25%** of a ship's crew have not participated in abandon ship drills and fire drills on that ship in the **previous month**, an abandon ship drill and a fire drill must take place **within 24 hours of the ship leaving a port**, unless this is impracticable (in which case **other suitable arrangements** must be made).
* Where a ship is **entering service** for the first time, or is **re-entering service** after a major modification, or where an entirely new crew has been engaged, an **abandon ship drill and a fire drill** must take place **before the ship sails**.
* **Drill and instruction procedures** are detailed in MGN 71.
* Regulation 5(3) of the MS (Hours of Work) Regulations 2002 (SI 2002/2125) provides that musters, fire-fighting drills and lifeboat drills prescribed by the MS (Musters, Training and Decision Support Systems) Regulations 1999 must be conducted in a manner which **minimises the disturbance of rest periods and does not induce fatigue** (see E03c.1b).

E08I.1f Practice passenger musters and safety briefings (Regulation 9)

* For notes on the **MS (Emergency Information for Passengers) Regulations 1990** (SI 1990/660), see I07f.3.

E08I.1g Abandon ship drills (Regulation 10)

* **Each abandon ship drill** required by the Regulations must include:
  * summoning passengers and crew to assembly or muster stations (as appropriate) with the general emergency alarm signal followed by drill announcement on the PA system or other equivalent communication system and ensuring that they are made aware of the abandon ship order specified in the muster list;
  * reporting to stations and preparing for the duties in the muster list;
  * checking that passengers and crew are suitably dressed;
  * checking that lifejackets are correctly donned;
  * where practicable, lowering of at least one lifeboat after any necessary preparation for launching;
  * starting and operating each lifeboat engine;
  * operation of davits used for launching liferafts;
  * a mock search and rescue of passengers trapped in their staterooms; and
  * instruction in the use of radio life-saving appliances.
* **Different lifeboats** must, as far as practicable, be lowered at successive drills.
* An abandon ship drill must, as far as practicable, be conducted **as if there were an actual emergency**.
* **Each lifeboat** must be launched with its assigned operating crew aboard and manoeuvred in the water at least once every 3 months during an abandon ship drill. If the berthing arrangements in port and trading patterns of a ship operating on short international voyages make launching on one side impracticable, then launching of boats on that side will not be required, but all boats on that side must be lowered at least once every 3 months and launched at least annually.
* Where carried, **rescue boats** other than lifeboats doubling as rescue boats must, as far as practicable, be launched each month with their assigned crew aboard and manoeuvred in the water. In any event this must be done at least once every 3 months.
* A **free-fall lifeboat** should be launched at least once every 3 months, but where free-fall launching is impracticable the lifeboat may be lowered into the water provided that the boat is free-fall launched with the assigned operating crew aboard, and manoeuvred in the water, at least once every 6 months. If it is impracticable to free-fall launch a lifeboat within a 6 month period, the MCA, on the owner's application, may approve an extension of the period to 12 months. Such approval will be on the condition that the lifeboat will be subjected to simulated launchings at intervals not exceeding 6 months.
* On a ship fitted with a **marine evacuation system (MES)**, statutory drills must include exercising of the procedures required for the deployment of the MES up to the point immediately preceding its actual deployment. The **drill must be augmented** by:
  * regular instruction of the crew using on-board LSA training aids; and

- training of each MES party member, as far as practicable, by participation in a full deployment of a similar MES into the water, either on board a ship or ashore, at intervals not exceeding 2 years, or, if this is impracticable, not exceeding 3 years.

* If lifeboat and rescue boat launching drills are carried out with the **ship making headway or anchored or moored in a tideway or current**, such drills must, because of the dangers involved, be practised in sheltered waters only under the supervision of an officer experienced in such drills, and in accordance with the guidance specified in MSN 1722.

* **Emergency lighting** for mustering and abandonment must be tested at each abandon ship drill.

E08I.1h Fire drills (Regulation 11)

* **Each fire drill** required by the Regulations must include:
  - **reporting** to stations and **preparing** for duties specified in the muster list;
  - starting of a **fire pump** using:
    - in ships of Class II(A) of 21.34m in length or less, Class III or Class VII, VII(T), VIII(T), VIII(A), IX or XI of 500gt or less, at least **one jet** of water;
    - in all other ships, at least **two jets** of water,
    - in order to demonstrate that the system is in proper working order;
  - checking **firemen's outfits** and **personal rescue equipment**;
  - checking the relevant **communications equipment**;
  - checking the operation of **watertight doors**, **fire doors**, **fire dampers** and the main inlets and outlets of any **ventilation systems** in the drill area; and
  - checking the necessary arrangements for subsequent **abandonment** of the ship.

* Any **equipment used** during a fire drill must immediately be brought back to its **fully operational condition** at the end of the drill and have any **faults or defects** discovered during the drill remedied as soon as possible thereafter.

* A fire drill must, as far as practicable, be conducted as if there were an **actual emergency**.

E08I.1i On-board training and instructions (Regulation 12)

* **Regulation 12** applies to any ship of Class I, II, II(A), III, VII, VII(T), VIII, VIII(T), VIII(A), VIII(A)(T) or IX, and to any ship of Class XI on an international voyage.

* **On-board training** in the use of the ship's LSA, including survival craft equipment and fire extinguishing appliances, must be given to each crew member a.s.a.p. and in any event within 2 weeks of the crew member joining ship. However, if the crew member is on a regularly scheduled rotating assignment (e.g. month on, month off), this training must be given within 2 weeks of his first joining ship.

* **Instructions** in the use of the ship's LSA, in sea survival, and in the use of the ship's fire extinguishing appliances must be given at the same interval as statutory drills.

* **Individual instruction** may cover different parts of the ship's LSA system and FEA, but **all the ship's LSA and fire extinguishing appliances must be covered within any 2 month period**.

* Each member of the crew must be given **instructions** including, but not necessarily limited to:
  - operation and use of the ship's inflatable liferafts;
  - problems of hypothermia, first-aid treatment for hypothermia and other appropriate first-aid procedures;
  - special instructions necessary for use of the ship's LSA in severe weather and sea conditions; and
  - operation and use of fire-extinguishing appliances.

* **On-board training in the use of davit-launched liferafts** must take place at intervals of not more than 4 months on ships fitted with them. Whenever practicable this training must include the inflation and lowering of a liferaft. The liferaft used for this purpose may be a special training raft which is not part of the LSA, but must be conspicuously marked as such.

* Every member of the crew with **assigned emergency duties** in respect of a voyage must be familiar with those duties **before the voyage begins**.

E08I.1j Records of musters, drills and on-board training (Regulation 13)

* The **master** (or an officer authorised by the master) must record in the **Official Log Book**:
  - each occasion when a **muster, abandon ship drill, fire drill, drill of other LSA or on-board training is held** pursuant to the Regulations, including the date on which the muster, drill or training was held, details of the training and type of drill held, and date on which the lifeboats, rescue boats and davit-launched liferafts (as applicable) are lowered or launched; and

- each occasion when a **full muster, drill or training session is not held** as required by the Regulations, including the circumstances which made the full muster, drill or training session impracticable, and the extent of any muster, drill or training session held.

E09 Financial business and law

E09a LEGISLATION RELATING TO SEAFARERS' WAGES, ACCOUNTS AND ALLOTMENTS

* **Primary UK legislation** on seafarers' wages, accounts and allotments is contained in Part III of the Merchant Shipping Act 1995, sections 30 to 41, which deal with the matter shown in the following table.

Section	Section title	SBC reference
30	Payment of seamen's wages	E09b.1a
31	Account of seamen's wages	E09b.1b
32	Regulations relating to wages and accounts	E09b.1b
33	Power of superintendent or proper officer to decide disputes about wages	E09b.1c
34	Restriction on assignment of and charge upon wages	E09b.1c
35	Power of court to award interest on wages due otherwise than under crew agreement	E09b.1c
36	Allotment notes	E09c.1
37	Right of person named in allotment to sue in own name	E09c.1
38	Right, or loss of right, to wages in certain circumstances	E09b.1c
39	Protection of certain rights and remedies	E09b.1c
40	Claims against seamen's wages for maintenance, etc. of dependents	E09b.1c
41	Remedies of master for remuneration, disbursements and liabilities	E09b.1c

* **Secondary UK legislation** relating to **seafarers' wages, accounts and allotments** is shown in the following table.

Subject	Principal regulations	Amending SIs	SBC ref.
Seamen's wages and accounts	MS (Seamen's Wages and Accounts) Regulations 1972 (SI 1972/1700)	1978/1757 1985/340 1994/791 1999/3360	E09b.2
Seamen's allotments	MS (Seamen's Allotments) Regulations 1972 (SI 1972/1698)	-	E09c.2
Deductions from wages	MS (Seamen's Wages) (Contributions) Regulations 1972 (SI 1972/1699)		E09b.2c

E09b WAGES AND ACCOUNTS

E09b.1 Provisions of Merchant Shipping Act 1995 relating to Wages and Accounts

* **Section 30** of the Merchant Shipping Act 1995 deals with the **payment of seamen's wages**.

E09b.1a Provisions relating to payment of wages

* **Section 30(1)** provides that where a seaman employed under a Crew Agreement relating to a UK ship leaves the ship on being **discharged** from it then, except as provided by or under Part III of the Act or any other enactment, the wages due to the seaman under the Agreement must either:
  - be paid to him **in full** at the time when he leaves the ship (i.e. at his discharge); or
  - be paid **in accordance with section 30(4) and 30(5)** (as outlined below).
* If the **amount** shown in an Account of Wages (i.e. Form ASW1) delivered to a seaman under section 31(1) is **replaced by an increased amount** shown in a further account (i.e. an amended account, on Form ASW2), the balance must be paid within 7 days of final discharge (section 30(2)).
* If the **amount shown in the account exceeds £50** and it is impracticable to pay all of it on discharge, **not less than £50 or a quarter** of the amount shown, whichever is greater, must be paid on discharge and the **balance paid within 7 days** of discharge (section 30(2)).

* If any amount payable under section 31(1) or 31(2) is **not paid at the proper time**, as above, the seaman will be entitled to wages for the **next 56 days** at the rate at which he was last payable under the Crew Agreement, and any amount payable **after that period** will carry **interest at 20%** per annum (section 30(3)).

* **Section 30(4)** provides that where the Crew Agreement provides for the seaman's basic wages to be payable up-to-date at specified intervals not exceeding one month, and for any additional amounts of wages to be payable within the pay cycle following that to which they relate, **any amount of wages due** to the seaman under the Agreement must (subject to section 30(5)) be paid to him not later than the date on which they next payment of his basic wages following the time of discharge would have fallen due if his employment under the agreement had continued.

* **Section 30(5)** provides that if it is not practicable, in the case of any amount due to a seaman by way of wages **additional to his basic wages**, to pay that amount by the date mentioned in section 30(4), that amount must be paid to him not later than what would have been the last day of the pay cycle immediately following that date if his employment under the Crew Agreement had continued.

* If any amount payable under section 30(4) or 30(5) is not paid at the proper time, it will carry **interest** at the rate of 20 per cent per annum (section 30(6)).

* The entitlements in sections 30(3) and 30(6) will not apply if the failure to pay the wages at the proper time was due to a **mistake** or a **reasonable dispute** as to liability or to the **act or default of the seaman**, or to any other cause, provided it is not due to the wrongful act or default of the person liable to pay the wages, or of his servants (section 30(7)).

* Where a seaman is employed on a **multi-ship agreement**, any reference to the **time of discharge** will have effect as if substituted by the **time of termination of employment** under the agreement (section 30(8)).

* Where a seaman is discharged from a UK ship outside the UK under section 29 (i.e. where the ship ceases to be registered) but returns to the UK under arrangements made by the persons who employed him, the preceding provisions of section 30 will have effect, in relation to wages due to him under the ship's Crew Agreement, as if references in 30(1) to (4) to the **time of discharge** specified the **time of his return to the UK**, and section 30(8) were omitted (section 30(9)).

* Section 30(10) provides that, for the purposes of section 30, any amount of wages will, **if not paid to a seaman in cash**, be taken to have been paid to him -
  * on the date when a cheque, or a money or postal order issued by the Post Office for that amount was **despatched** by the recorded delivery service to the seaman's last known address; or
  * on the date when any account kept by the seaman with a bank or other institution was credited with that amount.

E09b.1b Provisions relating to accounts of seamen's wages

* **Section 31(1)** provides that, subject to sections 31(4) and 31(5) and to regulations made under section 32 or 73, the **master** of every UK ship must deliver to **every seaman** employed in the ship under a Crew Agreement an **account of the wages due to him** under that crew agreement and of the **deductions** subject to which the wages are payable.

* The account of wages must indicate that the amounts in it are subject to any **later adjustment** that may be found necessary and must be delivered **not later than 24 hours before the time of discharge** or, if the seaman is discharged without notice or at less than 24 hours' notice, at the time of discharge (section 31(2)).

* If the amounts stated in the account of wages require **adjustment**, the persons who employed the seaman must deliver to him a **further account** stating the adjusted amounts; and that account must be delivered not later than the **time at which the balance of his wages is payable** to the seaman (section 31(3)).

* **Section 31(4)** provides that where section 30(4) or 30(5) applies to the payment of any amount of wages due to a seaman under a Crew Agreement -
  * the persons who employed the seaman must deliver to him an **account of the wages** payable to him under the relevant subsection and of the **deductions** subject to which the wages are payable; and
  * any such account must be so **delivered** at the time when the wages are paid to him; and
  * sections 31(1), 31(2) and 31(3) will not apply; and
  * section 30(10) will apply for the purposes of section 31(4) as it applies for the purposes of section 30.

* **Where a seaman is employed under a crew agreement relating to more than one ship**, any account which under the preceding provisions of section 31 would be required to be delivered to him by the master must instead be delivered to him by the persons employing him and must be so delivered on or before the termination of his employment under the crew agreement (section 31(5)).

* **Section 32** enables new regulations relating to wages and accounts to be made.

E09b.1c Other provisions relating to wages

* **Section 33(1)** provides that any **dispute** relating to the amount payable to a seaman employed under a Crew Agreement may be submitted by the parties to a superintendent or proper officer for decision. The superintendent or

proper officer will not be bound to accept the submission or, if he has accepted it, to decide the dispute, if he is of the opinion that the dispute, whether by reason of the amount involved or any other reason, ought not to be decided by him. **Section 33(2)** provides that the **decision of a superintendent or proper officer** under section 33 will be **final**.

* **Section 34** makes various provisions relating to attachment of wages, etc. which are not likely to be of concern to a shipmaster.

* **Section 35** provides that in any **proceedings by the master** of a ship or a **person employed in a ship otherwise than under a Crew Agreement** for the recovery of any sum due to him as wages **the court**, unless it appears to it that the delay in paying the sum was due to -
  * a mistake;
  * a reasonable dispute as to liability;
  * the act or default of the person claiming the amount; or
  * any other cause, not being the wrongful act or default of the persons liable to make the payment or their servants or agents,
  - may order them to pay, in addition to the sum due, interest on it at the rate of 20 per cent per annum, or such lower rate as the court may specify, for the period beginning seven days after the sum became due and ending when the sum is paid.

* **Section 38(1) of the Merchant Shipping Act 1995** provides that **where a UK ship is wrecked or lost** a seaman whose employment in the ship is thereby terminated before the date contemplated in the Crew Agreement will, subject to the other provisions of section 38, be entitled to wages at the rate payable under the Crew Agreement at the date of the wreck or loss for every day on which he is unemployed in the **two months following that date**.

* **Section 38(2)** provides that **where a UK ship is sold** while outside the UK or **ceases to be a UK ship** and a seaman's employment in the ship is thereby terminated before the date contemplated in the Crew Agreement, then, unless it is otherwise provided in the Agreement, he will, subject to the following provisions of section 38, be **entitled to wages** at the rate payable under the Crew Agreement at the date on which his employment is terminated for **every day on which he is unemployed in the two months** following that date.

* **Section 38(3)** provides that a seaman will not be entitled to wages by virtue of section 38(1) or 38(2) for a day on which he was unemployed, if it is shown -
  * that his **unemployment was not due to** the wreck or loss of the ship or, as the case may be, the termination of his employment on the sale of the ship or its ceasing to be a UK ship (section 38(3)(a)); or
  * that he was **able to obtain suitable employment** for that day but **unreasonably refused or failed** to take it (section 38(3)(b)).

* Section 38 applies to a **master** as it does to a seaman (section 38(4)).

* **Section 39(1)** provides that a **seaman's lien**, his **remedies for the recovery of his wages**, **his right to wages in case of the wreck or loss of his ship**, and **any right he may have or obtain in the nature of salvage** will **not be capable of being renounced by any agreement**. Section 39(1) does not affect such of the terms of any agreement made with the seamen belonging to a ship which, in accordance with the agreement, is to be employed on **salvage service**, as provide for the remuneration to be paid to them for salvage services rendered by the ship (section 39(2)).

* **Section 40** deals with claims against seaman's wages for maintenance, etc. of dependants.

* **Section 41** provides that the master of a ship will have the **same lien** for his remuneration, and all disbursements or liabilities properly made or incurred by him on account of the ship, as a seaman has for his wages.

E09b.2 Seamen's Wages and Accounts Regulations

* The **MS (Seamen's Wages and Accounts) Regulations 1972** (SI 1972/1700) –
  - were made under the Merchant Shipping Act 1970 and came into force on 1 January 1973[60].
  - are amended by SIs 1978/1757, 1985/340, 1994/791 and 1999/3360.
  - apply to seamen employed under crew agreements, as defined in section 1(2) of the Merchant Shipping Act 1970, in UK-registered ships other than fishing vessels.
  - deal with the **manner of payment** of wages and the **form and contents of accounts of wages**.
  - specify the **deductions** which are authorised to be made from a seaman's wages and the **conditions** which are to be observed before deductions relating to breaches of the crew agreement may be made.

* **Regulations** are as follows: **1**. Citation, commencement and interpretation; **2**. Manner in which wages are to be paid; **3**. Accounts of seamen's wages; **4**. to **8**. Deductions from wages; **Schedule**: Accounts of Seamen's Wages.

---

[60] When the Regulations were made, wages for ratings and officers were commonly paid in cash on board ship, at discharge, by the master on the employer's behalf. It was routine , especially "on the coast", to have to make up Accounts of Wages using Income Tax and National Insurance Codes and Schedules.

* **Regulation 3** provides that the Account of Wages required to be delivered to a seaman must contain the particulars prescribed in the Schedule and must indicate which amounts (if any) are estimated amounts[61].

E09b.2a Manner of payment (regulation 2)

* **Regulation 2(1)** provides that, subject to regulation 2(2), the **wages** due to a seaman under a Crew Agreement must be paid **in cash**. However, regulation 2(2) provides that if the seaman has agreed, the whole or part of the wages due to him may be paid by means of a **cheque**, **money order** or directly to a **bank or giro account**.

E09b.2b Account of Seaman's Wages (regulation 3)

* **Regulation 3(1)** provides that the account of wages required to be delivered to a seaman must contain the **particulars specified in the Schedule** to the Regulations and must indicate which amounts (if any) are **estimated amounts**.
* **Regulation 3(2)** provides that a **further account of wages** required to be delivered (under section 31(3)) must -
  * contain the same particulars as in an account of wages, adjusted in such manner as the circumstances may require;
  * indicate which amounts are adjusted amounts;
  * state the amount of wages already paid to the seaman; and
  * state the balance remaining to be paid.
* The **Schedule** to the Regulations contains a list of particulars to be shown in the Account of Wages to be delivered to a seaman under section 8(1) and (4) of the 1970 Act.

E09b.2c Deductions from wages (regulations 4 to 8)

* **Regulation 4(1) authorises the deductions** specified in regulation 5 to be made from the wages due to a seaman under a Crew Agreement.
* **Regulation 4(2)** provides that the **deductions** authorised by regulation 4 -
  * will be **without prejudice to any dispute** relating to the amount payable to a seaman under the Crew Agreement and, subject to the provisions of the Act, to the rights and obligations, whether of the employer or of the seaman, under the agreement or otherwise (regulation 4(2)(b)); and
  * will be in addition to any deduction authorised by any provision of the Act (except section 9) or of any other enactment.
* The **deductions** referred to in regulation 4(1) are listed in **regulation 5**, and are:
  * deductions of **amounts payable by the seaman to his employer** in respect of canteen bills, goods supplied, radio or telephone calls, postage expenses, cash advances and allotments (regulation 5(a));
  * **contributions** by the seaman to a **fund** (e.g. charities and pension funds) or in respect of **membership** of a body declared by regulations under section 11(3) of the Act[62] to be a fund or body to which section 11 applies;
  * subject to regulations 6, 7 and 8, a deduction of an amount being the **actual expense or pecuniary loss** incurred or sustained by the employer in consequence of the seaman's **absence or absences without leave**, where the employer is satisfied on reasonable grounds that such absence or loss was caused by **a breach or breaches of the seaman's obligations under the Crew Agreement** (regulation 5(c));
  * subject to regulations 6 and 8 and to any additional limitations imposed by the Crew Agreement, a deduction of an amount being the **actual expense or pecuniary loss** incurred or sustained by the employer, where the employer is satisfied on reasonable grounds that the expense or loss was caused by a breach or breaches of the seaman's obligations under the Crew Agreement not falling within regulation 5(c) (regulation 5(d));
  * subject to regulation 8, in cases where a seaman is employed under an approved Crew Agreement to which the **NMB Agreement on Disciplinary Procedure** applies and which requires him to comply with the **Code of Conduct**, has been dismissed from the ship because he has committed one of the breaches of the Code specified in paragraph 9 thereof, a contribution by the seaman to his **repatriation expenses**, incurred by the employer, of an amount provided for in the crew agreement (regulation 5(e)).
* **Regulation 6** provides that the **amount which may be deducted** from a seaman's wages in respect of **any number** of breaches of his obligations under the crew agreement -

---

[61] An estimated amount often had to be entered on an Account of Seaman's Wages where, for example, the seaman being "paid off" was leaving earlier than the rest of the crew, and the master had not finalised the wages accounts (including overtime, etc.).
[62] The MS (Seamen's Wages) (Contributions) Regulations 1972 (SI 1972/1699) were made under section 11(3) of Merchant Shipping Act 1970 and declare (in regulation 2) that section 11 of the Act applies to contributions to any pension fund, any charity, any trade union and any "friendly society" (i.e. a society registered under the Friendly Societies Act 1896).

-     by virtue of regulation 5(c) must not exceed £100[63] (regulation 6(a)); and
-     by virtue of regulation 5(d) must not exceed £300 (regulation 6(b)).
* **Regulation 7** provides that **no deduction** may be made by virtue of regulation 5(c) if the seaman satisfies the master:
  * that his absence was due to an **accident or mistake** or some other **cause beyond his control**; **and**
  * that he took all **reasonable precautions** to avoid being absent.
* A deduction may not be made by virtue of regulation 5(c), (d) or (e) unless regulations 8(2) or 8(3) have been complied with (regulation 8(1)).
* **Under regulation 8(2)**, where it is possible for him to give a **notice of deduction** complying with regulation 8(4) not less than 24 hours before the seaman's wages fall due to be paid, the employer or the **master** on his behalf must give the seaman:
  * a **notice of deduction** complying with regulation 8(4); and
  * the **opportunity to make representations** about the deduction to the employer or the master.
* **Under regulation 8(3)**, where it is not possible to give **notice of deduction** complying with regulation 8(4), the employer or the master must give the seaman:
  * if it is possible to do so before the seaman's wages fall due to be paid, give the seaman a notice of deduction complying with regulation 8(4) and an opportunity to make representations about the deduction to the employer or to the master; or
  * if the seaman has not been given such notice and opportunity, send to the seaman by registered post at his last address a notice of deduction complying with regulation 8(4).
* **Regulation 8(4)** provides that a notice of deduction must state that the employer is satisfied on reasonable grounds that there has been a breach or breaches, as the case may be, of the seaman's obligations under the Crew Agreement and that, subject to the provisions of regulations 4 to 7, the deduction specified in the notice appears to the employer to be authorised to be made from the wages due to the seaman under the Crew Agreement; and such notice shall also:
  * **identify** each provision of the Crew Agreement of which the employer is satisfied on reasonable grounds that there has been a breach and in respect of which he intends to make a deduction.
  * **state** the grounds upon which the employer is satisfied that each such breach has taken place;
  * **specify**, with sufficient particulars to show how it is calculated, the amount of the actual expense or pecuniary loss incurred or sustained by the employer in respect of each such breach or, if the total amount of such expense or loss in respect of which a deduction is made under regulation 5(c), (d) or (e) (or all or any of them as the case may be) exceeds the maximum which may be deducted under the appropriate paragraph or paragraphs, with sufficient particulars to show that such maximum is exceeded.
* The imposition of **shipboard fines** is no longer permitted in UK ships (see E10b.11).

E09b.3 NMB agreement on absence from duty

* An NMB agreement on Absence from Duty in force on 30 September 1990 (and therefore incorporated in any BSF Crew Agreement) stated that "in accordance with the terms of the Crew Agreement, a seafarer who absents himself from duty without leave, refuses or neglects to work, or is incapable of work through illness or injury caused by own wilful act or default, will receive no wages during hours of such absence."

E09c ALLOTMENTS

E09c.1 Provisions of Merchant Shipping Act 1995 relating to allotments

* **Section 36(1) of the Merchant Shipping Act 1995** provides that, subject to the provisions of section 36, a seaman may, by means of an **allotment note** issued in accordance with Merchant Shipping regulations, **allot to any person or persons** part of the wages to which he will become entitled in the course of his employment in a UK ship or ships.
* A seaman's right to make an allotment is subject to any **limitations** as may be imposed by regulations (section 36(2)).
* **Section 37(1)** provides that a person to whom any part of a seaman's wages has been allotted by an allotment note issued in accordance with regulations made under section 36 will have the right to **recover that part in his own**

---

[63] This amount has been amended from its original £50 to £200 (by SI 1985/340), to £300 (by SI 1994/791) and (by SI 1999/3360) back down to £100, to bring it into line with section 70(3)(b) of Merchant Shipping Act 1995 (see E10g.2). **MGN 136** promulgated the reduction.

name and for that purpose shall have the same remedies as the seaman has for the recovery of his wages. (This refers to a **maritime lien**.)

* **Section 37(2)** provides that in any proceedings brought by a person named in such an allotment note as the person to whom any part of a seaman's wages has been allotted **it will be presumed**, unless the contrary is shown, that the **seaman is entitled to the wages specified** in the note and that the allotment has not been varied or cancelled.

E09c.2 Seamen's Allotments Regulations

* The **MS (Seamen's Allotments) Regulations 1972** (SI 1972/1698) set out:
  * the circumstances in which a seaman may make an allotment (regulation 2);
  * certain limitations on the issue of allotment notes (regulation 3);
  * the times and intervals of payments under allotment notes (regulation 4); and
  * the form of allotment notes (regulation 5).
* **Regulation 2** provides that a seaman employed under a Crew Agreement relating to one or more ships who -
  * is not exempted from signing a Crew Agreement; or
  * is employed in a ship which is not exempted from having a Crew Agreement,
  - may at any time while so employed allot part of his wages to any persons by means of an **allotment note**.
* For the purpose of determining the amount which can be allotted, wages are taken as the rate stipulated in the Crew Agreement without any addition or deductions whatsoever (regulation 3(2)(a)).
* Unless the employer or master agrees otherwise, no seaman may allot more than half of his wages (regulation 3(1)(a)) or allot that part of his wages to more than two persons (regulation 3(1)(b)).
* Unless the employer or master agrees otherwise, the **first allotment** is payable not less than **1 month** from the date on which the allotment note is issued and **subsequent sums** become payable at regular intervals of not less than one month reckoned from the date when the first sum is payable (regulation 4(a)).
* Unless the employer or master agrees otherwise, no sum can be paid under an allotment note before the seaman has earned any of the wages allotted by it (regulation 4(b)).
* Allotment notes must be in the form prescribed by the Schedule to the Regulations (regulation 5). Allotment Notes are printed on Form ASW3, obtainable from MCA Marine Offices.
* The statement on Form ASW3 reads: "I, (name of seaman), employed in (name of ship, port of registry and official number) require you (name of employer) to pay to (names and addresses of persons to whom the allotment is made) the sum of (amount of each payment) on (date of first payment) and at intervals of (intervals at which payments are to be made) thereafter until (number of payments) payments have been made or until the agreement under which I am now employed is terminated or until 7 days after I have given notice in writing of revocation of this allotment note to you or to the master of my ship, whichever shall be the earlier."
* **An NMB agreement** on allotments, dated 1 December 1964, provides as follows: "It is agreed that any member of the crew, if he so desires, and the state of his indebtedness to the ship permits, shall be granted an allotment note payable at weekly, twice monthly, or monthly intervals. A second allotment payable once monthly may be made direct to a bank. The total amount allotted shall not exceed 90 per cent of his wages after allowance for statutory deductions (Income Tax, Pension Fund and National Insurance Contributions). Where this agreement is incorporated into the Crew Agreement, it will prevail."

E09d MASTER'S ACCOUNT WITH OWNERS

E09d.1 Portage bill

* A "**portage bill**" is an analysis of a crew's wages for one voyage, sometimes used on a ship in which the master is responsible for paying **wages in cash**. It is made up by the master at the end of the voyage and shows all payments to crew such as gross wages, overtime and leave pay, and all deductions from crew such as income tax, allotments, cash advances, postage, radio bills, canteen purchases, etc.
* The portage bill provides the master with a summary of all items entered on individual wages account sheets or slips, and also lists the amounts which will be entered in the owner's account current with master (see E09d.2).
* The portage bill and the **owner's account current with master** (or "owner's portage bill") are often drawn up on opposite sides of the same sheet, in which case the complete document may be known (improperly) as the "portage bill".

E09d.2 Owner's Account Current with Master

- may be required from a master at the end of the voyage, or when handing over to a successor, or monthly.
- shows all transactions made by the master on the owner's behalf during the voyage, including all **cash received by the ship and all cash paid out from the ship**. Payments from the ship are **debited from** the owners, while all sums received are **credited to** the owners.
- is compiled from **sources** such as the portage bill, the cash book, the radio account, the steward's account and all receipts or vouchers supporting miscellaneous disbursements.

E09d.3 Double-entry bookkeeping method

* The account sheet is laid out like any company's **profit and loss account**, i.e. divided into left and right columns.
* The left columns, headed "Debit" or "**Dr.**", record payments made by the master on the owner's behalf.
* The right columns, headed "Credit" or "**Cr.**", record the sums received by the master on the owner's behalf.
* The **totals of the two columns must always be the same**, but to ensure this it will be necessary for a **balance** to be inserted on one side or the other.
* The balance will be **due the master** if payments from the ship exceed receipts by the ship, and **due the owner** if receipts by the ship exceed payments from the ship.

E09d.4 Example

* On 29 September a master joined a newbuilding and was handed £500 by the agent. The ship incurred no expenditure before the end of the month, so this sum remained onboard at 30 September. On 30 September, therefore, the balance sheet would show:

Dr.		Cr.	
Balance due owners	£500.00	Cash from agent	£500.00
	£500.00		£500.00

* The cash received from agents is recorded as a Credit entry because it is really the owners who have indirectly advanced their own cash to the ship.
* If the account was closed before any further transactions were made, the £500 balance due owners (i.e. money remaining on board) would be carried forward to the next accounting sheet, but would appear on the Credit side as balance due owners b/f.
* Now suppose that on 3rd October, after joining as above, the master paid joining expenses of £35 to the Chief Officer, and paid a shipchandler £20 cash for galley stores bought:

Dr.		Cr.	
C/O's joining expenses	£35.00	Cash from agent	£500.00
Stores	£20.00		
Balance due owners	£445.00		
	£500.00		£500.00

The owners have effectively paid out £55, so the balance due owners is reduced by £55.
* Next, suppose that on 4th October the agent gives the master $400.00 at $2.00 = £1, which converts to £200 Sterling. This increases the cash onboard, and therefore also increases the balance due owners:

Dr.		Cr.	
C/O's joining expenses	£35.00	Cash from agent	£500.00
Stores	£20.00	Cash from agent	£200.00
Balance due owners	£645.00		
	£700.00		£700.00

* **Crew wages** If the crew are paid off in cash at the end of the voyage, the gross wages and all deductions should appear in a portage bill, from which the entries for the account current can be readily transferred. Suppose the following sums are due the crew:

Gross wages	*£1200.00*
Overtime	*£300.00*
Leave pay	*£500.00*

Ignore deductions for the moment.
* These sums are all to be paid out by the master on the owners' behalf, so they are Debit items. Because the total debits exceeds the amount of cash on board, a balance due master is created, in this case required to pay off the crew.

Dr.		Cr.	
C/O's joining expenses	£35.00	Cash from agent	£500.00
Stores	£20.00	Cash from agent	£200.00
Crew wages	£1200.00	Balance due master to pay off crew £1355.00	
Overtime	£300.00		
Leave pay	£500.00		
	£2055.00		£2055.00

* The £1355 required to pay off the crew will have to be ordered from the agent.
* **Deductions from wages** Ashore, the normal practice is for employers to pay Income Tax and National Insurance direct to the Collector of Taxes on behalf of their employees (i.e. by owners' cheque). On ships, these statutory deductions should be made by the master from gross wages together with non-statutory deductions for pension fund contributions, union dues, allotments, etc. where these are remitted by owners on the crew's behalf. All sums deducted by the master from gross wages must then be credited to the owners. This will reduce the balance due master or increase the balance due owners.
* Suppose in the above example the following payments were due:

Allotments	*£150.00*	*Crew postage*	*£15.00*
Income Tax	*£50.00*	*Crew radio messages*	*£5.00*
Crew NI	*£30.00*	*Canteen stores*	*£20.00*

* The account current should now appear as follows:

Dr.		Cr.	
C/O's joining expenses	£35.00	Cash from agent	£500.00
Stores	£20.00	Cash from agent	£200.00
Crew wages	£1200.00	Allotments	£150.00
Overtime	£300.00	Income Tax	£50.00
Leave pay	£500.00	Crew NI	£30.00
		Crew postage	£15.00
		Crew radio	£5.00
		Canteen stores	£20.00
		Balance due master to pay off crew £1085.00	
	£2055.00		£2055.00

* The master now requires only £1085.00 to pay off the crew.
* The following list of items and explanations of how they should be dealt with should be sufficient to cover most situations. Note that the only items appearing in the account current are items in which owners have an interest. E.g. if cash advances (or "subs") are given out to the crew on the voyage, but are deducted from wages before these are paid at the end of the voyage, the owners will not be interested in them. These "internal" deductions are therefore omitted from the account. Likewise, if the master personally remits any deducted income tax, National Insurance or pension contributions to the authorities, the owners will not be interested in these items and they may be omitted from the account.

E09d.4a DEBIT items

* These may be thought of as payments made by the master on behalf of the owners.
* **Crew's wages** are gross wages if they are not stated as having any deductions or additions. Wages are payments from the ship, and should therefore be entered as a Debit item. In the absence of any statement to the contrary, assume that "crew's wages" include master's wages.
* **Overtime** is an addition to gross wages and is also paid by the master, therefore enter as a Debit item.
* **Leave pay and subsistence** are added to gross wages, therefore enter as Debit items.
* **Port disbursements** are sums paid out in port for various reasons on the owners' behalf, therefore enter as Debit items. Examples are fees for noting protest, taxi fares to agents office, etc. It is unnecessary to give details of all disbursements as it would be normal for a separate detailed Disbursements Sheet to be sent to the owners with all relevant vouchers attached.

* **Crew's and master's expenses joining ship** are refunded to individuals in cash by the master on the owners' behalf, therefore enter as Debit items. Assume that the crew have been instructed to claim travelling expenses from the master.
* **Master's incidental expenses** may be claimed either as a fixed allowance to cover official entertainments and other expenses, or the actual amount spent may be reclaimed from ship's funds, depending on company policy.

E09d.4b CREDIT items

* These can be thought of as all sums received by the master on the owners' behalf.
* **All deductions from gross wages** made by the master but which must be remitted by the owners to authorities (e.g. Income Tax and crew's share of NI and MNOPF contributions) should be entered as Credit items (i.e. credited to the owners). Remember, however, that if the master personally remits these to the authorities, they should also be shown as Debit items. In that case, they would appear on both sides of the account, and could therefore alternatively be omitted from the account altogether.
* **Allotments** are paid directly by the owners on behalf of individual crew members. Therefore deduct the amounts from wages and enter as a Credit item.
* **Advance notes** may be thought of as allotments to crew members, rather than to their families. If the expression advances on joining is used in a question, it should be assumed that an advance note was given. The crew member would exchange the note for cash on joining the ship, so the sum would be owed to the owners and should be entered as a Credit item.
* **Cash drawn from agents** can be considered as a loan or "sub" to the ship from the owners, therefore credit the owners regardless of how cash was subsequently disbursed.
* **Steward's account, "Bar Account", "Slops", "Tobacco & Postage", etc.** are all Credit items. In the absence of any statement to the contrary, assume that the bond is an "owners' bond", and that the owners are therefore due the proceeds of all bond sales. (If the bond was a "master's bond", the proceeds could be omitted from the account current as they would be of no interest to the owners.) If owners pay the crew's postage, this will of course be a Debit item.
* **Officers' pension fund contributions** are entered on the Credit side as owners generally nowadays remit the officers' as well as their own share of pension contributions direct to the appropriate fund. On older question sheets it is sometimes stated that master pays MNOPF. In this case, enter the officers' contribution first as a Credit item (i.e. deducted from wages), then enter both the owners' and officers' contributions as Debit items (i.e. paid out on the owners' behalf from the ship to the pension fund).
* **Seamen's union contributions** are, like officers' contributions, entered as Credit items. Assume that the owners remit union dues collected to RMT or the appropriate union on behalf of the ratings while the ship is abroad. Therefore, deduct the dues from wages and credit the owners. (Where the master remits dues personally to unions, proceed as with officers' contributions, however.)
* **Crew's radio messages** are entered as Credit item.

E09d.4c "PROBLEM" items

* **Cash advances** from the master are "internal" affairs. The sums are paid from money already on the ship and are repaid before the crew member is paid off. Owners do not have any interest in these sums, so they can be omitted from the account current. They are often included in exam questions as "red herrings", though!
* **Advance freight payable at loading port in accordance with C/P terms** Pre-paid freight would normally be collected by owners' agents at the loading port and remitted to owners through a bank. But if it is mentioned in a question, assume that the master collects the net amount after the agreed interest and insurance charges have been deducted. The proper method of including it in the account current is to enter the gross amount of the advance freight (before deductions) as a Credit item, and to enter the interest and insurance charges as Debit items, bearing in mind that it is the gross amount of the advance freight which is subject to both charges.
* **Freight, or balance of freight, due under C/P at discharge port** Likewise, owners' agents usually collect freight at the discharge port. But if freight is to be paid to the master, it should be included in the account current. Some C/Ps make provision for sufficient of the freight to meet ship's disbursements (or a specified amount) to be paid in cash, with the remainder "in good and approved bills of exchange (B/Es) on London". Any freight B/Es given to the master should be remitted to the owners without delay, i.e. in effect, paid out by the ship to the owners. Therefore, first enter the gross amount of freight collected (cash plus B/Es) as a Credit item, then enter the amount of freight B/Es sent to owners as a Debit item.
* **National Insurance contributions**: Three cases arise:
  1. If NI contributions are stated as being "paid by owners' cheque", simply enter the crew's contributions recovered from wages as a Credit item.

2. If NI contributions are stated as being "paid by master" (i.e. remitted by the master to the Collector of Taxes), enter the combined amount of employers' and employees' contributions on the Debit side. Then enter the crew's contributions, which have been deducted from wages, on the Credit side. (The same effect is achieved if the crew's share is ignored on both sides and only the owners' share is shown as a Debit from the account.)

3. If it is not stated how NI is paid, assume that a remittance is made by one party or the other, make the appropriate entry and state assumptions made.

* **Income Tax**: Three cases arise:
1. If stated as being "paid by owners' cheque" (from the office), then assuming that the appropriate deductions have been made from wages, enter the amount deducted on the Credit side.
2. If stated as being "paid by the master" (i.e. remitted direct to the Collector of Taxes), it is of no interest to the owners, so omit it from the account current altogether.
3. If it is not stated how income tax is paid, assume one way or other, calculate accordingly and state assumptions made.

* **Cash advances on voyage**: Two cases arise:
1. If "subs" were issued by the master but repaid by means of a deduction from gross wages, they are of no interest to the owners and can be omitted from the account current. (In the absence of any indication to the contrary, always assume that this is the case.)
2. If some or all of the cash drawn from agents has been used for crew advances, enter this on the Credit side under the heading of "cash from agents".

E09d.4d To balance the account

* If the sum of the Credit items listed in a question exceeds the sum of the Debit items, the difference - i.e. the "**balance**" - will be **due the owners**. This figure, with the statement balance due owners, should therefore be entered on the Debit side. Then, when both sides are totalled, the bottom line on each side will show the same total, i.e. the account will balance.

* The "debt" to the owners can be discharged either by transferring the balance to the master's personal account, or by carrying it forward to the beginning of the next month or voyage. (In the latter case, the master would begin the next voyage account with the entry balance due owners from previous voyage account on the credit side.

* If the sum of the Debit items exceeds the sum of the Credit items, the difference (i.e. the balance) will be in favour of the master. This figure with the statement balance due master or, where wages are due to be paid, cash required to pay off crew, as appropriate, should be shown on the Credit side.

E09d.5 Worked example

* From the following information, the master of a ship must draw up an Owner's Account Current with Master, stating the balance due and to whom it is due. Income tax is paid by owners' cheque.

Crew's wages	£15225.78	Income tax	£3252.68
Leave pay	£892.43	Cash from agents	£1400.00
Subsistence	£99.40	NI (crew)	£906.72
Overtime	£286.82	MNOPF (officers)	£384.42
Allotments	£7319.00	Disbursements	£972.24
Cash bar sales	£421.78	Crew's postage	£48.73
Radio messages	£73.45		

* The account should appear as follows:

Dr.		Cr.	
Crew's wages	£15225.78	Allotments	£7319.00
Leave pay	£892.43	Cash bar sales	£421.78
Subsistence	£99.40	Radio messages	£73.45
Overtime	£286.82	Postage	£48.73
Disbursements	£972.24	Income tax	£3252.68
		NI (crew)	£906.72
		MNOPF (officers)	£384.42
		Cash from agents	£1400.00
		Balance due master	£3669.89
	£17476.67		£17476.67

* The **balance due the master** is £3669.89.

E09e NATIONAL CURRENCIES

This section may prove useful to masters of ships calling at foreign ports.

Territory	Currency	Territory	Currency
Afghanistan	Afghani	Ecuador	Sucre
Albania	Lek	Egypt	Pound
Algeria	Dinar	El Salvador	Colon & US Dollar
Andorra	Euro	Equatorial Guinea	Franc CFA
Angola	Kwanza	Eritrea	Ethiopian Birr
Anguilla	East Caribbean Dollar	Estonia	Kroon
Antigua & Barbuda	E Caribbean Dollar	Ethiopia	Birr
Argentina	Peso	Falkland Islands	Falklands Pound
Armenia	Dram	Faroe Islands	Danish Krone
Aruba	Aruban Guilder/Florin	Fiji	Fiji Dollar
Australia	Australian Dollar	Finland	Euro
Austria	Euro	France	Euro
Azerbaijan	Manat	French Guinea	French Franc
Azores	Escudo	French Polynesia	French Franc
Bahamas	Bahamian Dollar	Gabon	Franc CFA
Bahrain	Bahrain Dinar	Gambia, The	Dalasi
Balearic Islands	Spanish Peseta	Georgia	Lari
Bangladesh	Taka	Germany	Euro
Barbados	Barbados Dollar	Ghana	Cedi
Belarus	Rouble	Gibraltar	Gibraltar Pound
Belgium	Euro	Greece	Euro
Belize	Belize Dollar	Greenland	Danish Krone
Benin	Franc CFA	Grenada	East Caribbean Dollar
Bermuda	Bermuda Dollar	Guadaloupe	French Franc
Bhutan	Ngultrum	Guam	US Dollar
Bolivia	Boliviano	Guatamala	Quetzal
Bonaire	Neth. Antilles Guilder/Florin	Guiana	French Franc
Bosnia-Herzegovina	Dinar	Guinea	Franc
Botswana	Pula	Guinea-Bissau	Peso
Brazil	Real	Guyana	Dollar
Brunei	Brunei Dollar	Haiti	Gourde
Bulgaria	Lev	Hawaii	US Dollar
Burkina	Franc CFA	Honduras	Lempira
Burundi	Franc	Hong Kong	Hong Kong Dollar
Cambodia	Riel	Hungary	Forint
Cameroon	Franc CFA	Iceland	Krona
Canada	Canadian Dollar	India	Rupee
Canary Islands	Spanish Peseta	Indonesia	Rupiah
Cape Verde	Escudo	Iran	Rial
Cayman Islands	Cayman Island Dollar	Iraq	Dinar
Central African Republic	Franc CFA	Ireland, Republic of	Euro
Chad	Franc CFA	Isle of Man	Pound Sterling
Channel Islands	Pound Sterling	Israel	Shekel
Chile	Peso	Italy	Euro
China	Yuan	Ivory Coast	Franc CFA
Cocos (Keeling) Islands	Australian Dollar	Jamaica	Jamaican Dollar
Colombia	Peso	Japan	Yen
Comoros	Franc	Jordan	Dinar
Congo	Franc CFA	Kazakhstan	Tenge
Cook Islands	New Zealand Dollar	Kenya	Shilling
Costa Rica	Colon	Kiribati	Australian Dollar
Croatia	Kuna	Korea, North	Won
Cuba	Peso	Korea, South	Won
Curacao	Neth. Antilles Guilder/Florin	Kuwait	Dinar
Cyprus	Pound	Kyrgyzstan	Som
Czech Republic	Koruna	Laos	Kip
Denmark	Krone	Latvia	Lat
Djibouti	Franc	Lebanon	Pound
Dominica	East Caribbean Dollar	Lesotho	Loti
Dominican Republic	Peso	Liberia	Liberian Dollar
East Timor	US Dollar	Libya	Dinar

Territory	Currency	Territory	Currency
Liechtenstein	Swiss Franc	Seychelles	Rupee
Lithuania	Litas	Sierra Leone	Leone
Luxembourg	Euro	Singapore	Dollar
Macau	Pataca	Slovakia	Koruna
Macedonia	Denar	Slovenia	Tolar
Madagascar	Franc	Solomon Islands	Solomon Islands Dollar
Madeira	Escudo	Somalia	Shilling
Malawi	Kwacha	South Africa	Rand
Malaysia	Ringgit	Spain	Euro
Maldives	Rufiyaa	Sri Lanka	Rupee
Mali	Franc CFA	St Bathelemy	French Franc
Malta	Lira	St Croix	US Dollar
Mariana Islands	US Dollar	St Eustasius	Neth. Antilles Guilder/Florin
Marshall Islands	US Dollar	St Helena and Dependencies	St Helena Pound
Martinique	French Franc	St John	US Dollar
Mauritania	Ouguiya	St Kitts and Nevis	East Caribbean Dollar
Mauritius	Rupee	St Lucia	East Caribbean Dollar
Mexico	Peso	St Maarten	Neth. Antilles Guilder/Florin
Micronesia	US Dollar	St Martin	French Franc
Moldova	Leu	St Thomas	US Dollar
Monaco	Euro	St Vincent & The Grenadines	East Caribbean Dollar
Mongolia	Tughrik	Sudan	Pound
Montserrat	East Caribbean Dollar	Suriname	Guilder
Morocco	Dirham	Swaziland	Lilangeni
Mozambique	Metical	Sweden	Krona
Myanmar (Burma)	Kyat	Switzerland	Franc
Namibia	Rand	Syria	Pound
Nauru	Australian Dollar	Tahiti	French Franc
Nepal	Rupee	Taiwan	Taiwan Dollar
Netherlands	Euro	Tajikistan (Tadzhikistan)	Rouble
Netherlands Antilles	Neth. Antilles Guilder/Florin	Tanzania	Shilling
New Caledonia	Franc CFP	Thailand	Baht
New Zealand	Dollar	Togo	Franc CFA
Nicaragua	Cordoba	Tokelau	New Zealand Dollar
Niger	Franc CFA	Tonga	Pa'anga
Nigeria	Naira	Trinidad & Tobago	Trinidad & Tobago Dollar
Norway	Krone	Tunisia	Dinar
Oman	Rial	Turkey	Turkish Lira
Pakistan	Rupee	Turkmenistan	Manat
Palau (Belau)	US Dollar	Tuvalu	Australian Dollar
Panama	Balboa	Uganda	Shilling
Papua New Guinea	Kina	Ukraine	Hryvna
Paraguay	Guarani	United Arab Emirates	Dirham
Peru	Neuvo Sol	United Kingdom	Pound Sterling
Philippines	Peso	United States	US Dollar
Pitcairn Islands	New Zealand Dollar	Uruguay	Peso
Poland	Zloty	Uzbekistan	Sum
Portugal	Euro	Vanuatu	Vatu
Puerto Rico	US Dollar	Vatican City	Euro
Qatar	Riyal	Venezuela	Bolivar
Reunion	French Franc	Vietnam	Dong
Romania	Leu	Virgin Islands (US)	US Dollar
Russian Federation	Rouble	Wallis and Futuna	French Franc
Rwanda	Franc	Western Sahara	Moroccan Dirham
Saba	Neth. Antilles Guilder/Florin	Western Samoa	Tala
Saint Pierre & Miquelon	French Franc	Yemen, North	Riyal
Samoa	Tala	Yemen, South	Dinar
San Marino	Euro	Yugoslavia	Dinar
Sao Tome and Principe	Dobra	Zaire	Congolese Franc
Saudi Arabia	Riyal	Zambia	Kwacha
Senegal	Franc CFA	Zimbabwe	Dollar

E10 Seafarers' conduct and discipline

E10a LEGISLATION RELATING TO SEAFARERS' CONDUCT AND DISCIPLINE

* **Primary legislation** on **seafarers' conduct and discipline** is contained in Part III of the Merchant Shipping Act 1995, sections 58 to 72, which deal with the matter shown in the following table.

Section	Section title	SBC reference
58	Conduct endangering ships, structures or individuals	E10d.1
59	Concerted disobedience and neglect of duty	E10d.2, E12a.1
60	Breaches by seamen of codes of conduct	-
61	Inquiry into fitness or conduct of officer	B07c, B07e
62	Disqualification of holder of certificate other than officer's	B07d, B07e, E02d.8
63	Inquiry into fitness or conduct of seaman other than officer	B07d
64	Re-hearing of and appeal from inquiries	-
65	Rules as to inquiries and appeals	-
66	Failure to deliver cancelled or suspended certificate	-
67	Power to restore certificate	-
68	Power to summon witness to inquiry into fitness or conduct of officer or other seaman	-
69	Procedure where inquiry into fitness or conduct of officer or other seaman is held by sheriff	-
70	Civil liability for absence without leave	E10g.1
71	Civil liability for smuggling	E10g.2
72	Civil liability for fines imposed under immigration laws	E10g.3

E10b MERCHANT NAVY CODE OF CONDUCT

E10b.1 2001 edition of MN Code of Conduct

* The **Code of Conduct for the Merchant Navy** -
  - contains **basic rules of reasonable behaviour** expected of officers and ratings.
  - has been agreed between **NUMAST**, **RMT** and the **Chamber of Shipping**.
  - is **approved** by the MCA.
  - has been effective in its revised edition since 1 June 2001.
  - is **incorporated by express reference into every BSF Crew Agreement** which has been opened in a UK ship by virtue of Clause (x)(g) of the contractual clauses (ALC1(d)), which provides that "It is agreed that each seaman agrees to comply with the Code of Conduct for the Merchant Navy for the time being in force".
  - may be used in an **NFD Crew Agreement**, if expressly incorporated by means of an **additional clause** inserted after clause (vi). Non-federated companies may alternatively choose to use a **modified MN Code of Conduct** or even a **different code of conduct**, or their own **company rules of conduct**; any non-standard provisions must, however, be **approved by the MCA** before being incorporated into a Crew Agreement, and should not conflict with UK employment law.
  - contains **paragraphs** as follows: Introductory (paragraphs 1 to 4); Conduct in emergencies (paragraph 5); Conduct in situations other than emergencies (paragraphs 6 and 7); Dealing with breaches of the code (paragraph 8); Serious or "dismissal" breaches (paragraph 9); Procedure for dealing with "lesser" breaches (paragraph 10); "Lesser" or "non-dismissal" breaches (paragraph 11); Procedures for dealing with breaches of the Code (paragraph 12); Dismissals (paragraphs 13 to 16).
* **Master's standing orders** relating to conduct should not conflict with the MN Code of Conduct.

E10b.2 Conduct in emergencies (paragraph 5)

* In **emergency** and other situations when safety of the ship or any person on board is at risk, the master, officers and petty officers are entitled to expect immediate and unquestioning obedience of orders, without exception.
* Failure to comply is a serious "dismissal" breach and may also warrant prosecution under section 58 of the Merchant Shipping Act 1995 (Conduct endangering ships, structures or individuals) (see E10d.1).

E10b.3 General rules for everyday conduct (paragraph 7)

* Paragraph 7 sets out some basic rules covering:
    * **punctuality**, e.g. when joining vessel, returning from shore leave, reporting for watchkeeping duty and all other work;
    * **drugs**: unlawful possession renders a seafarer liable to dismissal as well as possible legal proceedings and exclusion from the industry;
    * **drinking**: there should be strictly enforced ship's rules about bringing alcoholic drink on board. Bar rules should be strictly adhered to;
    * bringing **unauthorised persons** on board;
    * **offensive weapons**: these should not be brought on board;
    * **smoking** in prohibited areas and use of **naked lights** or **unapproved electric torches**;
    * **duties**: crew members are entitled to be told what their duties are and to whom they are responsible. Within the scope of their duties, reasonable commands and instructions must be obeyed;
    * **treatment of accommodation**;
    * **behaviour towards others**: anti-social behaviour, e.g. excessive drinking, causing excessive noise, abusive language, aggressive attitudes and offensive personal habits. Some behaviour may be a safety hazard as well as a nuisance to others.

E10b.4 Paragraph 11 ("non-dismissal") breaches

* Paragraph 11 or "non-dismissal" breaches are:
    * paragraph 9 breaches (see E10b.6), but not justifying dismissal in the particular case (paragraph 11a);
    * minor acts of negligence, neglect of duty, disobedience and assault (paragraph 11b);
    * unsatisfactory work performance (paragraph 11c);
    * poor time keeping (paragraph 11d);
    * stopping work before the authorised time (paragraph 11e);
    * failure to report to work without satisfactory reason (paragraph 11f);
    * absence from the place of duty or from the ship without leave (paragraph 11g); and
    * offensive or disorderly behaviour (paragraph 11h).
* Some companies **add breaches** related to special trading patterns, etc. Any added clauses must be agreed with seafarers' trades unions and approved by the MCA.

E10b.5 Procedure for dealing with a paragraph 11 breach (paragraph 12)

* A paragraph 11 breach may be dealt with by:
    * an **informal warning** administered at an appropriate level lower than that of master (e.g. a petty officer such as the bosun, or a junior officer). If the petty officer or officer is satisfied that no further action is called for, or that the breach, although proved, calls only for an informal warning, he should give such a warning and the matter should be regarded as closed. No formal records should be kept. If the master is informed, the matter should not be recorded in the Official Log Book.
    * a **formal warning** by the Head of Department (e.g. the mate or chief engineer), recorded on a company disciplinary document if desired, but not in the Official Log Book.
* Where a breach is more serious (but not listed under paragraph 9), or is a repetition of a paragraph 11 breach, a **Head of Department's formal warning** should be given and, if required, recorded on a **company disciplinary document**, but not in the Official Log Book.
* Alternatively the matter may be referred to the master, in which case it must be **recorded** in the Official Log Book.
* When a formal warning is given, either by the Head of Department or by the master, the seafarer should be advised of the likely consequences of a further breach.

E10b.6 Paragraph 9 ("dismissal") breaches

* The very serious or "dismissal" breaches are:
    * assault (paragraph 9a);
    * wilful damage to the ship or any property on board (paragraph 9b);

- theft, or possession of stolen property (paragraph 9c);
- possession of offensive weapons (paragraph 9d);
- persistent or wilful failure to perform duty (paragraph 9e);
- unlawful possession or distribution of drugs (paragraph 9f);
- conduct endangering the ship or persons on board (paragraph 9g) (see also E10d.1);
- combination with others to impede the progress of the voyage or the navigation of the ship (paragraph 9h);
- disobedience of orders relating to the safety of the ship or of any person on board (paragraph 9i);
- being asleep on duty or failing to remain on duty if this prejudiced the safety of the ship or any person on board (paragraph 9j);
- incapacity through drink or drugs to carry out duty to the prejudice of safety of the ship or of any person on board (paragraph 9k);
- to smoke, use a naked light or unapproved electric torch in any part of a ship carrying dangerous cargo or stores where smoking or the use of naked lights or unapproved torches is prohibited (paragraph 9l);
- intimidation, coercion and/or interference with the work of other employees (paragraph 9m);
- behaviour seriously detracting from the safe and/or efficient working of the ship (paragraph 9n);
- conduct of a sexual nature, or other conduct based on sex affecting the dignity of women and men at work which is unwanted, unreasonable and offensive to the recipient (paragraph 9o);
- behaviour seriously detracting from the social well-being of any other person on board (paragraph 9p);
- causing or allowing unauthorised persons to be on board whilst at sea (paragraph 9q);
- repeated commissions of breaches listed in paragraph 11 after warnings have been given in accordance with the procedures in paragraph 10 (paragraph 9r).
* If any of the above breaches is proved to have been committed to the master's reasonable satisfaction, dismissal from the ship, either immediately or at the end of the voyage, will be appropriate in addition to any legal action called for.

E10b.7 Procedure for dealing with a paragraph 9 ("dismissal") breach

* The procedure for dealing with an alleged serious breach of the Code of Conduct is somewhat similar to the procedure in summary proceedings in a magistrate's or sheriff court (see B03b.1a), with the master adopting the roles of the magistrate or sheriff as well as clerk of the court. The following table shows a comparison of some of the aspects of court and shipboard procedures.

Court procedure	Shipboard procedure
Accused appears before magistrate(s) or sheriff	Seafarer appears before master
Charge is read out by clerk of court: accused is charged with a particular offence (e.g. breach of a particular Regulation or section of an Act)	Charge is read out by master: accused seafarer is charged with a particular breach of the Code of Conduct
Accused is asked how he pleads to charge	Accused seafarer is asked whether he admits or denies the breach
If accused pleads "guilty", magistrate passes appropriate sentence after consideration of the facts; no trial is necessary	If accused seafarer admits the breach, master passes appropriate sanction after consideration of facts; no hearing is necessary
If accused pleads "not guilty", case must be tried, with evidence heard for the prosecution and for the defence	If accused seafarer denies the breach, hearing is necessary, with evidence heard against and for the seafarer
Accused may have a lawyer to represent him	Accused seafarer may have a friend to speak on his behalf
Witnesses may be called	Witnesses may be called
Evidence presented may be cross-examined by lawyers	Accused (or friend) may question witnesses on their evidence
All evidence is recorded and considered by magistrate	All evidence is recorded (in Official Log Book) and considered by master
Magistrate decides matters of facts and law	Master decides matters of fact and law (i.e. procedure)
Accused is formally told whether he has been found guilty as charged or not	Accused seafarer is formally told whether he has been found to have committed the alleged breach or not
Magistrate passes appropriate sentence, limited by law	Master imposes appropriate sanction, limited by the Code of Conduct

* The master should deal with any alleged serious breach referred to him **as soon as possible**.
* Cases referred to the master may include **repeated commissions of minor (paragraph 11) breaches, or serious (paragraph 9) breaches**.
* Every serious breach should be dealt with by the **master in person**.
* A serious breach need not always result in dismissal; an oral warning or a written reprimand may be given.
* The master should always **inform the seafarer of the alleged breach** and give him the opportunity to:
  - **admit or deny** the allegation;
  - **be accompanied throughout** the hearing by a friend who may advise him and speak on his behalf;
  - **call any witnesses** he chooses;

- **question the witnesses** on their evidence; and
- **make any statement** he wishes in answer to the alleged breach, including comments on evidence produced against him.

* After careful and thorough **investigation**, and having **considered all the evidence**, the master should **orally inform the seafarer whether or not he finds that the seafarer committed the alleged breach**.

* If the master finds the seafarer **did commit the breach**, he should **impose a sanction** which he considers **reasonable** in all the circumstances, taking into account his **record** on the ship and any **other relevant factors**.

* The **range of sanctions** the master may impose are:
- a **formal (oral) warning** from the master, **recorded** in the Official Log Book;
- a **written reprimand** from the master, **recorded** in the Official Log Book; or
- **dismissal from the ship**, either immediately (if in a UK or overseas port), or at the next port. If the master decides that the continued presence of the seafarer on board would be detrimental to the efficient and safe running of the ship or to the maintenance of harmonious personal relations on board, the master may arrange for dismissal of the seafarer at the next port of call for repatriation to the UK.

* If **dismissal** is the master's chosen sanction it is vital that he **follows the correct procedure** which is, in every case:
- having a **disciplinary hearing** before the master, **properly conducted** in accordance with the procedure in the **Code** and with the principles of **natural justice**;
- making a **formally-announced finding** that the seafarer has committed a serious breach of the Code listed in paragraph 9;
- **dismissal** of the seafarer from the ship (after completion of usual **discharge formalities** as in E07d.6).

* **Whichever sanction the master imposes**, an Official Log Book entry should be made in the narrative section recording full **details of the breach** and the **action taken by the master** in response to it.

* The **seafarer must be given a copy of every Official Log Book entry** relating to his case. He should **acknowledge receipt** by signing another Official Log Book entry made by the master. If he **refuses** to sign this entry, a **further appropriate entry** should be made to that effect; this entry should be signed by the master and witnessed by another person who was present.

E10b.8 Examples of written warnings and reprimands, and records to be made

E10b.8a Formal warning by Head of Department

```
m.v. "Thistle Brae"
RECORD OF FORMAL WARNING BY HEAD OF DEPARTMENT
Department: Deck            No. TSC.01/96
Name: I. Hardman    Rank/rating: GP1   Dis. Book No.: R 790530  Ref. No.: 72 was
today advised that he had been found to be in breach of paragraph 11(b) of the
Code of Conduct for the Merchant Navy, in that at 1205 hours on 2 January 2003
he refused to comply with an order from Bosun A. Splicer to return to work.
Hardman was formally warned as to his future conduct.

(Signed) H. Tait, C/O (H.o.D)
(Signed) A. Splicer, Bosun (Supervisor)
I acknowledge receipt of this formal warning.
(Signed) I. Hardman
Date: 2 January 2003
```

E10b.8b Master's Official Log Book entry made on the reporting to him of an alleged breach of the Code of Conduct

```
0900, 3 January 2003. At sea. Chief Officer H. Tait reported that I. Hardman,
GP1, Ref. No. 72, had appeared to have committed a breach of paragraph 9(a) of
the Code of Conduct in that at 1005 hours he had struck Bosun A. Splicer and had
been referred to me for this allegation to be investigated.

(Signed) B. Careful, Master
(Signed) H. Tait, C/O
```

E10b.8c Formal warning by master

```
m.v. "Thistle Brae"
RECORD OF FORMAL WARNING BY MASTER
Department: Deck              No. 001/96
Name: I. Hardman     Rank/rating: GP1   Dis. Book No.: R 790530  Ref. No.: 72 was
today advised that he had been found to be in breach of paragraph 9(a) of the
Code of Conduct for the Merchant Navy, in that at 1005 hours on 3 January 2003
he had struck Bosun A. Splicer.
Hardman was formally warned that if his future behaviour did not comply with the
Code of Conduct for the Merchant Navy he would be liable to be dismissed from
the vessel.
(Signed) B. Careful, Master
(Signed) H. Tait, C/O (H.o.D)
I acknowledge receipt of this formal warning.
(Signed) I. Hardman
Date: 3 January 2003
```

E10b.8d Written reprimand

```
m.v. "Thistle Brae"
WRITTEN REPRIMAND
Department: Deck              No. 002
Name: I. Hardman     Rank/rating: GP1   Dis. Book No.: R 790530  Ref. No.: 72 was
today advised that he had been found to be in breach of paragraph 9(e) of the
Code of Conduct for the Merchant Navy, in that at 1405 hours on 4 January 2003
he had wilfully refused an order from Bosun A. Splicer.
Hardman is hereby reprimanded in writing and formally warned that any further
breach of the Code of Conduct for  the Merchant Navy will lead to his
dismissal.
 (Signed) B. Careful, Master
(Signed) H. Tait, C/O (H.o.D.)
I acknowledge receipt of this written reprimand.
(Signed) B. Hardman
Date: 4 January 2003
```

E10b.8e Master's Official Log Book entry made when dismissal may be appropriate

```
1900 hrs, 5 January 2003. At sea. A disciplinary hearing was held into an
allegation reported by Chief Officer W.
Tait that I. Hardman, GP1, Dis. Book No. R 790530, Ref. No. 72, had committed a
breach of paragraph 9(a) of the Code of Conduct in that at 0710 hrs today he had
struck Bosun A. Splicer.
This allegation was read by me to Hardman, who was advised of his right to be
accompanied by a friend who may advise him and speak on his behalf. Hardman
declined to exercise this right. He admitted striking the Bosun but claimed that
the Bosun had been harassing him unfairly. (See written statement in Annex No. 3
to Official Log Book.)
Chief Officer H. Tait reported that at 0712 the Bosun had shown him a cut lip
and alleged that Hardman had hit him in the crew's mess. On interviewing Hardman
immediately thereafter he had admitted hitting the Bosun but said that "the
b..…….. had been asking for it all trip". (See written statement in Annex No. 3
to Official Log Book.)
Bosun A. Splicer said that at 0710 he had found that Hardman still had not
started work. Upon being ordered to do so, Hardman had struck him on the jaw. It
was true that he had had cause to warn Hardman on a number of occasions but he
```

had persistently been late starting work and was reluctant to obey orders.
(Written statement in Annex No. 3 to Official Log Book.)
Hardman was advised that he had been found to be in breach of paragraph 9(a) of
the Code of Conduct for the Merchant Navy in that he had assaulted Bosun Splicer
at 0710 on 5th January 2003.
Chief Officer H. Tait reported that Hardman had previously been given a formal
warning as to his conduct on 2 January 2003.
Hardman was accordingly ....(enter appropriate sanction as follows)
1. formally warned as to his future conduct and notified that his warning would
   be recorded in the Official Log Book (see Record of Formal Warning by Master
   No. 001, annexed). In reply to this he made no comment. He was given a copy
   of the log book entries and of the Record of Formal Warning by Master No. 001
   and acknowledged their receipt.
2. given a written reprimand and severely warned as to his future conduct. On
   being notified that this written reprimand (see Written Reprimand No. 002 in
   Annex No. 3 to Official Log Book) would be recorded in the Official Log Book,
   he said "it's all a frame-up" and refused to sign acknowledging its receipt
   or accept a copy of the Official Log Book entries.
3. advised that he would be discharged from the ship (immediately/at the next
   convenient port of call/at the end of the voyage); and that the case would be
   reported to the employing company for appropriate action to be taken in
   accordance with the Code of Conduct for the Merchant Navy and recorded in the
   Official Log Book. He made no comment. He was given a copy of the log book
   entries relating to this incident, and acknowledged receipt of them.
(Signed) B. Careful, Master
(Signed) H. Tait, C/O

E10b.8f Additional Official Log Book entry by master (in person) where prosecution is advised

Hardman was further warned that the company may bring the details of this
incident to the attention of the (MCA/police) with a view to prosecution upon
his return to the United Kingdom.

E10b.9 Importance of correct procedures in dismissal cases

* Following the dismissal by the master of a seafarer for a paragraph 9 breach, the **employer** will decide whether or not to terminate the seafarer's company service contract, if any, or otherwise not to re-engage him. Dismissal will be easier, and the success of any claim of unfair dismissal taken by the seaman to an Employment Tribunal less likely, if the correct action has been taken by the master, officers and petty officers involved in the shipboard disciplinary case. The master's role is critical. It is imperative that the master follows the prescribed procedures precisely and accurately and comprehensively **records in the Official Log Book** all steps of the procedures and all evidence given, with written **statements** appended to the Official Log Book.
* Useful information is given in the Chamber of Shipping publication **Master's Guide to the Shipboard Disciplinary Procedures**.
* The master should ensure that Heads of Department and other officers and petty officers (e.g. the bosun and senior engine room and catering department ratings) are entirely **familiar with the proper procedures**.
* If the master dismisses a seafarer from the ship, the company or the seafarer's employer will, **within 5 working days** of the dismissal if in the UK, or within 5 working days of arrival in the UK if the seafarer is dismissed abroad, convene **a hearing ashore** to review the circumstances of the dismissal and decide whether dismissal should be **confirmed** or, in the case of a permanent employee, whether the **contract of employment should be terminated**.
* If requested by the seafarer, an **official of his union or a fellow employee** will be invited to be present at the hearing.
* The seafarer will be **advised in writing** of the **outcome** of the hearing. Where dismissal is confirmed or the contract is terminated he will be advised of the **time limits** (normally 14 days) within which any **appeal** against the dismissal should be lodged. Any such appeal will normally be to a **higher level of authority** within the company.
* These procedures may be amended in accordance with local circumstances should this be agreed to by the company and the relevant seafarers' union.

* Nothing in the Code of Conduct shall be read as negating any seafarer's right to bring a **claim of unfair dismissal** before an Employment Tribunal in the UK as provided for in the Employment Rights Act 1996.

E10b.10 Deductions from wages for breaches of Crew Agreement

* For details of **deductions authorised** under regulation 4(1) of the MS (Seamen's Wages and Accounts) Regulations 1972 to be made from wages where there has been a breach of the Crew Agreement, see E09b.2c.

E10b.11 Shipboard fines

* The **Merchant Shipping Act 1979 (Commencement No. 9) Order 1985** came into operation on 31 December 1985, repealing certain sections of the Merchant Shipping Act 1970 and related legislation, part of which were the **MS (Disciplinary Offences) Regulations 1972**. Since then the **levying by the master of shipboard fines** in respect of offences by seafarers has been illegal (see **M.1198**).

E10c DRUG AND ALCOHOL ABUSE BY CREW MEMBERS

* Following the entry into force of US legislation requiring random and other drug testing on all US flag vessels and for post-accident testing on all vessels in US waters, OCIMF published its **Guidelines for the Control of Drugs and Alcohol Onboard Ships** in 1990. These were adopted by the oil majors, who required personnel on independently-owned, chartered-in tonnage to be subject to a company Drug and Alcohol Policy that either met or exceeded OCIMF Guidelines[64].
* **Drug and alcohol testing** has since spread to other sectors of the shipping industry and it is now a common condition of service for crew members (including masters) to agree, usually in a written undertaking, to comply with company policy requirements for D&A testing. These will usually require submission to random or scheduled testing, at times specified in an instruction to the master by the employer. Testing is normally carried out by analysis of urine samples, taken in accordance with company written instructions. The samples are usually forwarded to the company's designated laboratory via a rigorously monitored chain of custody. The **master's own test** is usually supervised by the chief engineer.
* A company may reserve the right to **search personal belongings** of crew members who have signed the D&A undertaking, where reasonable cause exists to believe that the manufacture, distribution, use or possession of drug or drug paraphernalia is occurring contrary to its D&A policy.
* **Possession or distribution of drugs by any person**, including a passenger as well as a seafarer or other category of person on board a UK ship is a breach of UK criminal law.
* **Possession or distribution of drugs by a seafarer** who has signed a Crew Agreement on a UK ship, as well as being a breach of UK criminal law, is a breach of paragraph 9 of the Merchant Navy Code of Conduct (see E10b), where this is incorporated into the Crew Agreement, and is likely to be a breach of any other code or rules of conduct incorporated by reference into the Crew Agreement.

E10d CRIMINAL LIABILITY OF SEAFARERS

* Whether bound by the Merchant Navy Code of Conduct or not, seafarers (of any nationality) are subject to the **general law of the UK** whilst on board a UK ship.
* For certain offences **prejudicial to the safety** of the ship or those on board, there is a liability to **prosecution** under the Merchant Shipping Acts (see E10d.1 and E10d.2).

---

[64] A **Drug and Alcohol Policy Clause** is commonly inserted in a tanker charter party under which the owner warrants that (1) a policy on drug and alcohol abuse is applicable to the vessel and meets or exceeds the standards in the Oil Companies International Marine Forum (OCIMF) Guidelines for the Control of Drugs and Alcohol Onboard Ship, (2) the policy will remain in effect during the term of the charter, and (3) the owner will exercise due diligence to ensure that the policy is complied with.

E10d.1 Conduct endangering ships, structures or individuals

* The following applies under **section 58(1) of the Merchant Shipping Act 1995** to:
  * the **master** of or any seaman employed in a UK ship, or
  * the **master** of or any seaman employed in a non-UK ship which is in a port in the UK or within UK waters while proceeding to or from a UK port.
* Under section 58(2), if one of these persons, while **on board his ship or in its immediate vicinity** -
  * does any act which causes or is likely to cause -
    * the **loss** or **destruction** of or **serious damage** to **his ship** or its machinery, navigational equipment or safety equipment; or
    * the **loss** or **destruction** of or **serious damage** to any **other ship or any structure**; or
    * the **death** of or **serious injury** to any person;
  * or **omits to do anything** required -
    * to **preserve his ship** or its machinery, navigational equipment or safety equipment from being lost, destroyed or seriously damaged; or
    * to **preserve any person** on board his ship from death or serious injury; or
    * to **prevent his ship from causing** the loss or destruction of or serious damage to any other ship or any structure, or the death of or serious injury to any person not on board his ship -
  - and either of the conditions mentioned below is satisfied with respect to that act or omission, he shall (subject to defences mentioned below) be guilty of an **offence**.
* The **conditions** referred to above are (under section 58(3)):
  * that the act or omission was **deliberate** or amounted to a **breach or neglect of duty**;
  * that the master or seaman in question was under the influence of **drink or a drug** at the time of the act or omission.
* Possible **defences** in respect of the above offences are (under section 58(6)):
  * where the act or omission alleged against the accused constituted a breach or neglect of duty, that the accused took **all reasonable steps** to discharge that duty;
  * that at the time of the act or omission alleged against the accused he was **under the influence of a drug taken by him for medical purposes** and either that he took it on medical advice and complied with any directions given as part of that advice or that he had no reason to believe that the drug might have the influence it had.
* Under section 58(4) a person as defined in section 58(1) also commits an **offence** if he -
  * **discharges any of his duties**, or performs any other **function** in relation to the operation of the ship or its machinery or equipment, **in such a manner as to cause**, or to be likely to cause, any such **loss, destruction, death or injury** as mentioned above, or
  * **fails to discharge any of his duties**, or to perform any such **function**, properly or to such an extent as to cause, or to be likely to cause, any of those things.
  A **defence** in this case will be that the accused took all reasonable precautions and exercised all due diligence to avoid committing the offence.
* In proceedings for all the offences mentioned above, it will, under section 58(6)(d), be a defence that the person -
  * could have avoided committing the offence only by disobeying a lawful command, or
  * that in all the circumstances the loss, destruction, damage, death or injury in question, or (as the case may be) the likelihood of its being caused, either could not reasonably have been foreseen by the accused or could not reasonably have been avoided by him.
* **Regulation 8 of the MS (Dangerous Goods and Marine Pollutants) Regulations 1997** (SI 1997/2367) provides that in connection with the handling, stowage and carriage of dangerous goods in a UK ship, no person may **intentionally or recklessly interfere with or misuse** anything provided on, or **disobey instructions** displayed on, the ship in the interests of health or safety in pursuance of the Merchant Shipping Act 1995 or any regulation or rule made thereunder (regulation 8(1)).
* **Regulation 9** provides that in any proceedings for an offence under regulation 5 or 6 consisting of a failure to comply with a duty or requirement to do something so far as is reasonably practicable, it shall be for the accused to prove that it was not reasonably practicable to do more than was in fact done to satisfy the duty or requirement.

E10d.2 Concerted disobedience, neglect of duty, or impeding the voyage or navigation

* An offence is committed under **section 59 of the Merchant Shipping Act 1995** if a seaman employed in a UK ship combines with other seamen employed in that ship -

- to disobey lawful commands which are required to be obeyed at a time while the ship is at sea (i.e. at any time when it is not securely moored in a safe berth);
- to neglect any duty which is required to be discharged at such a time; or
- to impede, at such a time, the progress of a voyage or the navigation of the ship.
* For the purposes of section 59 a ship will be treated as being "at sea" at any time when it is not securely moored in a safe berth (whether in the UK or elsewhere).

E10e OFFENCES COMMITTED BY BRITISH SEAFARERS OUTSIDE THE UK

* For notes on the **jurisdiction of UK courts in case of offences** by British (and non-British) citizens on board ships, see B03b.2g.
* For notes Merchant Shipping Act 1995 provisions relating to **offences committed by British masters and seamen**, see B03b.2h.
* The **port State or coastal State has criminal jurisdiction** for all offences committed by seafarers and other persons on UK and other ships in its **national waters**, i.e. in its **internal waters** and in its **territorial sea**. (For notes on **zones of coastal State jurisdiction**, see H01e.1. For notes on **coastal State law**, see I01a.2.) Thus, where a seafarer in a UK ship which is exercising its right of innocent passage through the coastal State's territorial sea has committed, for example, a serious assault and the matter is brought to the attention of the coastal State authorities (e.g. by the master), the coastal State's law enforcement agencies have the right to intervene and remove the seafarer from the ship and deal with him under the coastal State's laws. A case of minor assault in the same ship should be dealt with under disciplinary procedures incorporated into the crew agreement, such as the Merchant Navy Code of Conduct (see E10b).
* Any serious offence under UK law committed by a person on a UK ship anchored or berthed in a foreign port will probably also be an offence under the port State's laws, and may similarly be dealt with by the port State's law enforcement agencies and courts.
* Where a **seafarer is arrested** by a foreign port State or coastal State, the **agent** (if any) should be notified and the **P&I club correspondent** contacted for advice. A suitable entry should be made in the **Official Log Book**. For notes on procedure where the seafarer is **left behind**, see I05f.

E10f OFFENCES RELATING TO MERCHANT NAVY UNIFORM

* It is an offence under **section 57(1) of the Merchant Shipping Act 1995** if any person, not being entitled to wear the Merchant Navy (MN) uniform, wears that uniform or any part thereof, or any dress (i.e. clothing) having the appearance or bearing any of the distinctive marks of that uniform. (This does not apply under section 57(3) to persons wearing MN uniform in stage plays, etc. as long as the uniform is not worn in such a manner or under such circumstances as to bring it into contempt.)
* It is an offence under section 58(4) if any person entitled to wear MN uniform when aboard ship in port or on shore appears dressed **partly in uniform and partly not in uniform** under such circumstances as to be **likely to bring contempt** on the uniform.
* It is also an offence under section 58(4) if a person, being entitled to wear the uniform appropriate to a particular rank or position, wears the uniform appropriate to **some higher rank or position**.

E10g CIVIL LIABILITIES OF SEAFARERS

E10g.1 Civil liabilities

* Under the Merchant Shipping Act 1995 there are three cases in which a seaman employed in a UK ship may be **liable for damages to his employer** in a civil court action in the UK. These civil liabilities are in respect of:
  - absence without leave;
  - smuggling; or
  - breach of immigration laws.
* These civil liabilities exist whether the ship operates under a BSF or an NFD Crew Agreement.

E10g.2 Civil liability for absence without leave

* Under **section 70 of the Merchant Shipping Act 1995** a seaman employed in a UK ship may be liable for damages for being **absent from his ship** at a time when he is required by his contract of employment to be on board.
* If he proves that his absence was due to an accident, mistake or some cause beyond his control and that he took all reasonable precautions to avoid being absent, his absence will not be treated as a breach of contract.
* Where the seaman is held to be liable, his liability will be:
  * £10 where no special damages are claimed;
  * maximum £100 if special damages[65] are claimed.

E10g.3 Civil liability for smuggling

* Under **section 71 of the Merchant Shipping Act 1995** if a seaman employed in a UK ship is found in civil proceedings before a court in the UK to have committed an act of smuggling, **whether in or outside the UK**, he will be liable to make good **any loss or expense** that the act has caused to any other person (e.g. the employer).

E10g.4 Civil liability for fines imposed under immigration laws

* **Section 72 of the Merchant Shipping Act 1995** provides that the provision below applies where a UK ship has been in the national or territorial waters of any country outside the UK, and a seaman employed in the ship has been absent without leave and present in that country in contravention of the local national law.
* If, as a result, the employer has incurred a fine, this will be treated as being attributable to the seaman's absence without leave.
* Subject to the provisions of section 70 (see E10g.2), the employer's fine may be recovered from the seaman as special damages for breach of contract (or, in Scotland, as damages in respect of specific expense incurred or loss sustained). (Note: special damages are damages which can be specifically proved or quantified, as opposed to presumed.)
* If, by reason of the contravention, a fine is incurred under those laws by any other person, the amount of the fine, or £100 (whichever is the greater) may be recovered from the seaman.

E11 Complaints by crew members

E11a LEGISLATION RELATING TO COMPLAINTS BY CREW MEMBERS

* **Article 8 of ILO Convention 68** allows for a special inspection of a ship following a written complaint about the food and water supplies made by a certain proportion of the crew.
* **Primary UK legislation** relating to **complaints by crew members** is contained in section 44 of the Merchant Shipping Act 1995 (see E11b)[66].
* There is no secondary UK legislation relating to complaints by crew members.
* The **Code of Practice for Noise Levels in Ships** contains a recommendation where **noise levels** are the cause of complaint (see E08b.3a).

E11b COMPLAINTS ABOUT PROVISIONS OR WATER

* If three or more seamen employed in a UK ship consider that the provisions or water provided for the seamen are not in accordance with safety regulations containing requirements as to the provisions and water to be provided on

---

[65] **Special damages** are awarded for losses that are not presumed and must therefore be specifically proved, whereas **general damages** are awarded for losses which the court presumes will have followed as a natural consequence of the wrongful act, e.g. a damaged reputation following an act of libel against the plaintiff.

[66] Under section 23 of the Merchant Shipping Act 1970 a seaman had a statutory right to complain to the master if he considered that he had cause to complain about the master; or any other seaman employed in the ship; or about the conditions on board the ship. Section 23 was repealed by Merchant Shipping Act 1988 and no replacement provision was included in the Merchant Shipping Act 1995.

ships (whether because of **bad quality, unfitness for use or deficiency in quantity**) they may **complain to the master**, who **must investigate** the complaint (section 44(1)).

* If the seamen are dissatisfied with the actions taken by the master as a result of his investigation or by his failure to take any action, they **may state their dissatisfaction to him** and may claim to complain to an MCA superintendent or a proper officer (section 44(2)).
* The **superintendent or proper officer must investigate** the complaint, and **may examine** the provisions and water, or **cause them to be examined** (section 44(3)).
* If the master is **notified in writing** by the superintendent or proper officer that any provisions or water are unfit for use or not of regulation quality, he **must replace them within a reasonable time**.
* For notes on statutory requirements relating to the supply of **domestic fresh water**, see E08h.3.

E11c MASTER'S ACTION IN RESPONSE TO COMPLAINTS

* **When three or more seamen complain about provisions or water**, the master should, as soon as possible, make an entry in the Official Log Book (narrative section) of the names of the seamen making the complaint, and the nature of and reason(s) for their complaint.
* In compliance with section 44 of the Merchant Shipping Act 1995, the master should, as soon as reasonable and practicable, **investigate** the complaint and take **appropriate action**, if necessary, to remedy it. (Complaints are more likely to be made in the evening than at other times, and it may not be practicable to take immediate action.) Where action taken involves treatment of domestic fresh water, guidance in relevant Merchant Shipping Notices, referred to in E08h.3, should be followed.
* For notes on the requirements of the **MS (Provisions and Water) Regulations 1989** (SI 1989/102) see E08h.1.
* Chapter 14 of the Code of Safe Working Practices relates to food preparation and handling; there is no chapter specific to domestic fresh water.
* A **further entry** should be made in the Official Log Book detailing the master's response to the complaint.
* **If the seamen are dissatisfied with the master's action** in response to their complaint, a further entry should be made in the Official Log Book and arrangements made to facilitate the seamen's complaining to an MCA superintendent of proper officer (e.g. a British consul) as soon as practicable.
* **Where a complaint is made about some other matter**, consideration should be given as to whether to record it in the Official Log Book, even though no legislation requires this. It may be prudent to record any complaint that is not of an obviously frivolous or vexatious nature, especially where it relates to the **safety** of the ship or the safety or **social well-being** of any person on board. Where a complaint is of a matter included in paragraphs 9 or 11 of the Merchant Navy Code of Conduct, or any other code or rules of conduct applicable on board, the complaint should be recorded in the Official Log Book and the matter investigated according to the procedure outlined in E10b.

E12 Industrial action by crew members

E12a CREW STRIKE ACTION

E12a.1 Legislation on crew strike action

* **Section 42(2) of the Merchant Shipping Act 1970** provided that notwithstanding anything in any agreement, a seaman employed in a UK-registered ship could terminate his employment in the ship by leaving the ship in contemplation or furtherance of a trade dispute after giving the master at least 48 hours' notice of his intention to do so, and could not be compelled (unless the notice was withdrawn) to go to sea in the 48 hours following the giving of the notice. Such notice was of no effect, however, unless at the time it was given the ship was in the UK and securely moored in a safe berth. This provision was, however, repealed by section 57(5) and Schedule 7 of the Merchant Shipping Act 1988, for which no direct replacement legislation was incorporated into the Merchant Shipping Act 1995.
* **The relevant current legislation on strike action** by seamen in UK ships now appears to be **section 59 of the Merchant Shipping Act 1995** (see E10d.2), which makes it illegal for seamen[67] in sea-going UK ships (i.e. those operating outside waters of Categories A, B, C or D) to combine with other seamen to disobey lawful commands or

---

[67] For the purposes of this section the term "seamen" excludes masters.

neglect any duty or impede the progress of the voyage **at a time while the ship is at sea**. ("At sea", for the purposes of section 59 means at any time when the ship is not securely moored in a safe berth (in the UK or elsewhere.)

* **General UK statute law relating to industrial action** is contained in various Acts of Parliament and is beyond the scope of this book. Good sources of information on industrial action (and other employment matters) are the following websites:
  * www.emplaw.co.uk/free/index.htm – Notes on UK employment law;
  * www.emplaw.co.uk/topinfo/portal.htm#4 - employment law "super-portal";
  * http://dtiinfo1.dti.gov.uk/er – Department of Trade and Industry employment rights information, including useful downloadable leaflets.
* For notes on **strike action in port**, see I05d.1. For notes on **ITF involvement in strike action**, see I05d.2.

E12a.2 NUMAST advice to members concerning industrial action

* The notes below are extracts from NUMAST's Standing Policy.

E12a.2a When members of other unions are on strike

* When members of other unions are on strike, NUMAST members should not carry out any duty which is normally carried out by members of the strikers" union and should not take any action which would tend to exacerbate the situation, so making a solution of the problem more difficult.
* In carrying out their own responsibilities, under legislation and their own contracts of employment, members should ensure that a full crew of properly trained and qualified persons is on board and all other safety requirements are met before taking any ship to sea. There should not be any attempt by members to break the strike by sailing ships with gaps in the crew complement or with any unsafe condition.
* In carrying out this standing policy, members should take whatever steps are necessary to ensure the safety of any person on board and try to ensure, consistent with not provoking incidents, that the ship and her equipment are available in a seaworthy state to continue the voyage as soon as a settlement of the dispute has been achieved.
* In taking steps to ensure their own comfort, members should maintain a low profile and, if necessary, seek the co-operation of the local strike convener, in order to maintain a relationship which will facilitate a speedy return to normality.

E12a.2b Disciplining of striking seafarers

* If an entry is to be made in the Official Log Book naming individual seafarers who are on strike, NUMAST members should not participate in the making of the entries either by way of writing the entries or of witnessing an entry, other than an entry in the following form:
  "This day the normal working of the ship was disrupted by reason of members of the crew being on strike in furtherance of a trade dispute."

E12a.2c Pickets

* Violence and lasting bitterness can easily occur when any person endeavours to cross a picket line. Should a member need to cross a picket line to reach his temporary home on board a ship, the leader of the pickets should be approached in a non-aggressive manner, with a request to permit passage to the member's living quarters. Should such an approach fail, members should contact the nearest NUMAST office, giving the name of the union concerned and the location of the pickets.

E12a.2d Particular situations

* For the protection of members against unfair pressure from individual personnel managers, members may receive instructions rather than advice from the general secretary in particular situations.

E12a.2e Local difficulties

* Situations not covered in this standing policy should be handled with the usual discretion and tact expected of officers, if possible in consultation with the nearest local official of NUMAST.

E12a.2f Shipmasters

* It is in the interests of all concerned that shipmasters should not participate in any strike by officers either as part of the strike or as strike-breaker. The shipmaster must maintain his or her statutory and contractual position and all members of NUMAST must ensure in their conduct of any strike that company managers or agents or local police or military are not given any excuse to overrule or displace the shipmaster. In this way, any dispute between officers and management has a chance of being concluded without the danger of subsequent post-strike disruption of shipboard relationships and perhaps even safety arrangements.
* Shipmasters abiding by this standing policy will be fully supported by the Union's council.

E12a.2g Doctors and medical staff

* Doctors and medical staff should particularly note the requirements of this policy upon members to take whatever steps are necessary to ensure the safety of any person on board. This implies using their skills to assist any person needing medical attention, whether or not that person is part of the ship's crew.

E13 Relief and repatriation of seafarers

*For notes on **deserters**, see I05e. For notes on **leaving a seaman behind**, see I05f.*

E13a LEGISLATION RELATING TO RELIEF AND REPATRIATION

* **Primary legislation** is contained in **Part III of the Merchant Shipping Act 1995, sections 73 to 76. Section 73** relates to the **relief and repatriation** of seamen, etc. left behind and shipwrecked (see E13b). **Section 74** relates to the **limit on the employer's liability** under section 73 (see E13b). **Section 75** relates to the **recovery of expenses** incurred for relief and return, etc. **Section 76** relates to **financial assistance** for crew relief costs.
* **Secondary legislation** is contained in the **MS (Repatriation) Regulations 1979** (SI 1979/97) (see E13c).

E13b EMPLOYER'S LIABILITY FOR SEAMEN'S RELIEF AND REPATRIATION: PRIMARY LEGISLATION

* Under **section 73(1) of the Merchant Shipping Act 1995**, where a person employed as a seaman in a UK ship is **left behind in any other country**, or is taken to such a country on being **shipwrecked**, or where a person who became employed as a seaman in a UK ship under an agreement entered into outside the UK is **left behind in the UK**, the **persons who last employed him as a seaman** must make such **provision for his return and for his relief and maintenance** until his return and such other provisions as may be required by Merchant Shipping regulations (i.e. the **MS (Repatriation) Regulations 1979** (SI 1979/97) (see E13c)).
* The provisions to be made by the employer under section 73(1) **may include** the payment of expenses of the burial or cremation of a seaman who dies before he can be returned (section 73(2)).
* Section 73(3) enables the making of regulations providing for the manner in which any wages due and any property left behind or taken to any country (e.g. following a shipwreck) are dealt with. Sections 73(4), (5) and (6) also contain enabling powers.
* The provisions of section 73 also apply to the **master** (section 73(8)) and to a person left behind on being discharged when a **ship ceases to be a UK ship**, whether or not at the time he is left behind the ship is still a UK ship (section 73(7)).
* **Section 74** provides that where a person left behind or taken to any country as mentioned in section 73(1) **remains there after the end of a period of three months**, the persons who last employed him as a seaman **will not be liable** under section 73 to make provision for his return or for any matter arising after the end of that period, **unless** they have before the end of that period been under an obligation imposed on them by regulations made under section 73 to make provision with respect to him[68].

---

[68] The above provision may apply, for example, in a case where a British seaman goes absent without leave in another country for period of more than three months, after which he asks his former ship's agent or a British consul for repatriation.

E13c REPATRIATION REGULATIONS

E13c.1 Repatriation Regulations

* The **MS (Repatriation) Regulations 1979** (SI 1979/97) -
    - **apply** to any seaman employed in a UK registered ship who is **left behind** in any place or country outside the UK or is **taken to** any place or country outside the UK on being shipwrecked (regulation 2(1)(a)).
    - **apply** to any seaman who became so employed under an **agreement entered into outside the UK** and who is left behind in the UK or is taken to the UK on being shipwrecked (regulation 2(1)(b)).
    - **contain** regulations numbered as follows: **1**. Citation, commencement and interpretation; **2**. Application; **3**. Return and relief of seamen left behind or shipwrecked; **4 and 5**. Other provisions relating to seamen left behind and shipwrecked seamen; **6**. Place of return; **7**. Provision for a seaman's return, relief and maintenance by superintendents and proper officers; **8, 9 and 10**. Conveyance orders and directions; **11**. Wages of seamen, employed in ships, who are left behind; **12, 13 and 14**. Wages of seamen, employed in fishing vessels, who are left behind; **15**. Other records and accounts; **16**. Property of seamen left behind and of shipwrecked seamen; **17**. Official Log Book entries.
* **Regulations 11 to 14 also apply** to any seaman who became employed in a UK registered ship under an agreement entered into in the UK and who **leaves his ship in the UK otherwise than on being discharged** (regulation 2(2)) (e.g. where the seaman deserts his ship in the UK).

E13c.1a Obligation to return seaman

* **Regulation 3(1)** provides that the **employer** must, if his obligation to return a seaman has arisen under regulation 3(2):
    • as soon as practicable after the seaman is left behind or is brought ashore after shipwreck, make such **provision** as is necessary for his return to a place ascertained under regulation 6 (regulation 3(1)(a)); and
    • from the time when the seaman is left behind or brought ashore after the shipwreck and until he is returned or until the employer's obligation to return him ceases in accordance with regulation 3(3) of this, make such provision for the seaman's **food and lodging** and such **other relief and maintenance as may be necessary** having regard to the **personal circumstances** of the seaman and any **requirement special to him** (regulation 3(1)(b)).
* The employer will not, however, be under any obligation to return or make provision for any seaman who is **absent for a period of more than three months** from the date when he was left behind, if during that period , the employer did not know and could not reasonably have known of the seaman's whereabouts (regulation 3(1)).
* **Regulation 3(2)** provides that the **obligation to return** a seaman under regulation 3(1)(a) **will arise**:
    • as soon as the seaman is **available for return**; or
    • as soon as the seaman **informs** his employer, his employer's agent, a superintendent or a proper officer of his whereabouts and **asks** to be returned by his employer: or
    • if the seaman is **unable** by reason of **illness, incapacity or other cause beyond his control** so to inform any of the persons mentioned above, as soon as one of those persons obtains from his **confirmation** that he wishes to be returned to his employer.
* **Regulation 3(3)** provides that the **obligation** to return a seaman under regulation 3(1)(a) **will cease** if the seaman:
    • being fit and able to undertake employment in a ship, fails to comply with **reasonable request** made of him by his employer that he should enter into an **agreement for employment in any ship** (including any such ship as is mentioned in regulation 8(1)(a)) in which he is, in accordance with the provision made by his employer, to be carried in the course of his return; or
    • without reasonable cause, **fails to comply with any other reasonable arrangement** made for him by his employer in relation to the provision for his return; or
    • **informs** his employer in writing that he **does not wish to be returned** by him.
* **Regulation 3(4)** provides that in deciding whether the seaman is to be returned by land, sea or air (or by which combination of any of those means), his employer shall have regard to all the circumstances including the personal circumstances of the seaman and of any requirement special to him.
* **Regulation 3(5)** provides that without prejudice to the generality of regulation 3(1)(b), the provision for relief and maintenance to be made in accordance with that paragraph must include:
    • clothing;
    • toilet and other personal necessaries;
    • surgical or medical treatment and such dental or optical treatment (including the repair or replacement of any appliance) a cannot be postponed without impairing efficiency;

- in cases where the seaman is not entitled to legal aid, or legal aid is insufficient, reasonable costs for the defence of a seaman in ant criminal proceedings in respect of any act or omission within the scope of his employment, being proceedings where neither the employer not the employer's agent is a party to the prosecution; and
- sufficient money to meet ant minor ancillary expenses necessarily incurred or likely to be so incurred by the seaman for his relief and maintenance.
* **Regulation 3(6)** provides that the provisions to be made by an employer must include:
    - the repayment of **expenses incurred in bringing a shipwrecked seaman ashore** and **maintaining him** until he is brought ashore; and
    - the payment of the **expenses of the burial or cremation** of a seaman who dies before he can be returned to a place ascertained under regulation 6.

E13c.1b Notification of superintendent or proper officer of seaman left behind

* **Regulation 4(1)** provides that the **employer** of a seaman to whom the Regulations apply must, within 48 hours after the seaman is left behind or it has come to his notice that the seaman has been brought ashore after being shipwrecked (as the case may be), or if it is not practicable within the time, as soon as practicable thereafter, make provision to ensure that the **MCA superintendent** or the **proper officer** for the place where the seaman is left behind or brought ashore is **informed** of the particulars specified in regulation 4(2), which are:
    - the name of the seaman;
    - his home address as stated in the list of crew;
    - the name and address of his next of kin as stated in the list of crew;
    - in the case of a seaman left behind:
        - the name of the ship form which he was left behind;
        - the date on which he was left behind;
        - the place where he was left behind and, if known to the employer, the present whereabouts of the seaman;
        - the reason why (if known to the employer) for his being left behind; and
        - the name and address of the employer and the name and address of the employer's agent, if any, at or nearest to the place where the seaman was left behind;
    - in the case of the shipwrecked seaman:
        - the name of the ship from which he was shipwrecked;
        - the dates on which he was shipwrecked and on which he was brought ashore;
        - the place where he was brought ashore and (if known to the employer) the name and address of the person by whom he was brought ashore and the present whereabouts of the seaman; and
        - the name and address of the employer and the name and address of the employer's agent, if any, at or nearest to the place where the seaman was brought ashore.

E13c.1c Official Log Book entries

* **Regulation 4(3)** provides that the **master** must make entries, in relation to any seaman left behind, recording:
    - both in the **Official Log Book** and in the **List of Crew**, the **date** on which and the **place** at which the seaman was left behind and the **reason** (if known to the master) for leaving the seaman behind; and
    - in the **Official Log Book**, any provision which he has made on the employer's behalf to ensure that the superintendent or proper officer is **informed** as required by regulation 4(1) (e.g. an instruction of the ship's agent to inform the British Consul).
* **Regulation 9(1)** provides that the **master** must make entries in the Official Log Book recording the particulars of any conveyance order made under regulation 8 (see E13c.1e), and of any related directions given to him by a superintendent or proper officer.
* For notes on entries required under **regulation 16(3)(b)** relating to property of seamen left behind, see E13c.1g.
* **Regulation 17** provides that all entries in the Official Log Book required to be made by the master under regulations 4(3), 9 and 16(3)(b) must be signed by the master and by a member of the crew.

E13c.1d Miscellaneous requirements relating to repatriation of seamen

* **Regulation 5(1)** requires the employer to keep the superintendent or proper officer informed of the arrangements made for meeting his obligations under regulation 3.
* **Regulation 6(a)** provides that a seaman who is to be returned under the Regulations and who is resident in the UK must be returned either to his home or to the place at which the Merchant Navy Establishment Administration Office at which he is registered is situated, whichever is nearer. Since the closure of MNEA (or "Pool") offices in the early

1990s, a seaman should always be returned to his home, or (under regulation 6(c)) to any other place which may be agreed between the seaman and his employer.

* **Regulation 6(b)** provides that a seaman who is not resident in the UK must be returned to the place in the country in which he is resident, being:
  * if he joined the ship from which he was left behind or shipwrecked in that country, the place where he joined the ship (regulation 6(b)(i); or
  * if he did not join the ship in that country, the place in that country where he was engaged to join the ship (regulation 6(b)(ii); or
  * (under regulation 6(c)) to any other place which may be agreed between the seaman and his employer.
* **Regulation 7** imposes on superintendents and proper officers obligations to make provision for relief and return of seamen where the employer has failed to meet his obligations under regulation 3.

E13c.1e Conveyance Orders

* **Regulation 8** makes provision for the issue by superintendents or proper officers of **Conveyance Orders** where an obligation to return a seaman has arisen under regulation 3 or 7. For notes on requirements for related Official Log Book entries, see E13c.1c.)
* Regulation 10 contains provisions for payment of the master of a ship in which a person is conveyed under regulation 8.

E13c.1f Wages of a seaman left behind

* **Regulation 11(1)** provides that unless a seaman left behind was discharged in the normal way and received his wages on his discharge, any **wages due under a Crew Agreement** must be paid by the employer, or by the **master** acting on the employer's behalf, within 28 days of the seaman's arrival at his place of return. An Account of Wages (ASW) must be delivered at the same time. When the employer's obligation to return the seaman ceases, the wages must be paid within 28 days of the obligation ceasing. If the employer does not know the seaman's whereabouts, an Account of Wages and a notice that the wages may be obtained on application to the employer must be sent to the seaman's last known address.
* **Regulation 14** provides that where the wages cannot be paid to a seaman in accordance with regulation 11 and the seaman is not known to be dead, then the wages must be paid and accounts delivered to the next-of-kin named in the List of Crew as soon as practicable after the expiry of 4 months from the time of payment specified in regulation 11.

E13c.1g Property of seamen left behind and of shipwrecked seamen

* Subject to regulation 16(2), regulation 16 applies to any property (including money) left on board a ship by a seaman to whom the Repatriation Regulations apply. Regulation 16(2) provides that in the case of any property left on board by a seaman who has been shipwrecked, regulation 16 will have no effect if the ship is lost, and if the ship is not lost but as a result of the shipwreck, no person is master of the ship, the relevant master's duties will instead be imposed on the employer.
* **Under regulation 16(3)** the master must **take charge of the seaman's property** (including money) (regulation 16(3)(a) and **enter a list of it in the Official Log Book** (regulation 16(3)(b)).
* **Under regulation 16(4)** the master may at any time:
  * **sell** any part of the property if of a perishable or deteriorating nature (the proceeds of sale then forming part of the property); and
  * **destroy** or otherwise **dispose of** any part which, in his opinion, endangers or is likely to endanger the health or safety of any person on board.
* A **description** must, under regulation 16(3)(b)(ii), be entered in the Official Log Book of **each article sold** and the sum received; and, under regulation 16(3)(b)(iii), **each article destroyed or disposed of** and the **name** of any person to whom disposal was made.
* **Under regulation 16(5)** the master must, when directed by the employer, **have the property delivered to the employer** at an address in the country to which the seaman is to be returned. The **employer** must deliver the property **to the seaman at his last known address**, or if wages are payable to a next-of-kin named in the List of Crew, to that next-of-kin at his or her address as in the List of Crew. Costs are to be borne by the person to whom they were delivered.
* **If the seaman requests**, the master must have the property delivered at the address named by him, and the costs are to be borne by the seaman (regulation 16(6)).

* **Under regulation 16(7)** the master must, when delivering property to a seaman or a next-of-kin, deliver also a **record of the property** delivered. If any property has been **sold**, this must include a description of each article sold and the sum received for it, and if any property has been **destroyed or disposed of**, a description of each article.
* The **seaman's discharge book** should be returned with his property.

E14 Births and deaths in ships

E14a LEGISLATION RELATING TO BIRTHS AND DEATHS IN SHIPS

E14a.1 Primary legislation relating to births and deaths in ships

* **Section 108 of the Merchant Shipping Act 1995** (Returns of births and deaths in ships, etc.) enables regulations to be made in relation to births and deaths.

E14a.2 Secondary legislation relating to births and deaths in ships

* **Statutory instruments** containing provisions relating to deaths of persons in ships or deaths of seamen include:
  * the **MS (Official Log Books) Regulations 1981** (SI 1981/569), which require a record to be made of a death of a person on a UK ship or the death ashore of a UK seafarer;
  * the **MS (Returns of Births and Deaths) Regulations 1979** (SI 1979/1577), which require a return of death to be made;
  * the **MS (Property of Deceased Seamen and Official Log Book) (Amendment) Regulations 1983** (SI 1983/1801) which amend the requirements of the Official Log Book Regulations relating to property left behind by a seaman who died during or after employment in the ship.

E14b RETURNS OF BIRTHS AND DEATHS

E14b.1 Requirement to make a return of birth

* Regulation 2 of the **MS (Returns of Births and Deaths) Regulations 1979** (SI 1979/1577) provides that where a **child is born in a ship** registered in the UK, the master of the ship must make a **return of the birth** in accordance with regulations 5 and 6 (see E14b.3).

E14b.2 Requirement to make a return of death

* **Regulation 3 of the MS (Returns of Births and Deaths) Regulations 1979** (SI 1979/1577) provides that where **any person** (i.e. a crew member, passenger, stevedore, or any other person) **dies in** a UK registered ship, or any **person employed** in a UK registered ship **dies outside the UK**[69], the **master** must:
  * **make a return of the death** in accordance with regulations 5 and 6 (see E14b.3); and
  * as soon as practicable, but not more than **3 days** after the death, **notify the death** to such person (if any) as the deceased may have named to him as **next of kin**[70].
* Where a citizen of the UK or British Overseas Territories is born or dies in a **ship not registered in the UK**, and the **ship calls at a UK port** during or at the end of the voyage in which the birth or death occurs, the master must make a return of the birth or death in accordance with regulations 5 and 6 (regulation 4).

---

[69] This includes, for example, a crew member or "concessionaire" who dies whilst ashore, or whilst visiting another ship, or whilst in a boat.
[70] The name and relationship of the next of kin of a person employed in the ship, together with their address if different from the seaman's address, should be entered in the third column of the List of Crew (ALC1(a) or ALC1(b)).

E14b.3 Returns of births and deaths

* **Regulation 5(1) of the MS (Returns of Births and Deaths) Regulations 1979** (SI 1979/1577) provides that any return of a birth or of a death required to be made under regulation 2 or 3 must be made by the **master** of the ship **as soon as practicable** after, but within **6 months** after, the birth or death.
* In the case of a **birth or a death occurring in the ship**, the return must be made to an **MCA superintendent** or the **proper officer** for the place where the ship is at the time of the birth or death, or at the next place of call (regulation 5(1)(a)).
* In the case of a **death which does not occur in the ship**, the return must be made to an **MCA superintendent** or the **proper officer** for the place where the ship is when the master first becomes aware of the death or at the next place of call (regulation 5(1)(b)).
* A **return of a birth or of a death** required under regulation 4 (see E14b.2) must be made by the master to an **MCA superintendent** for the **first UK port of call** after the birth or death, before the ship leaves that port (regulation 5(2)).
* **Regulation 6** provides that a **return of a birth or death** must be **in writing**, must be **signed by the master** of the ship as "informant", and must **contain**:
  * in the case of a **birth**, the particulars specified in **Schedule 1** to the Regulations; or
  * in the case of a **death**, the particulars specified in **Schedule 2** to the Regulations,
  - or so many of those particulars as the master may reasonably be able to obtain, having regard to the circumstances of the birth and the death.
* **Returns of births and deaths** should be made on form **RBD/1**, copies of which may be obtained from MCA Marine Offices and British consulates. The particulars required on an RBD/1 fulfil the requirements of regulation 6 and are similar to those required on the special pages (pages 8 and 9) for recording births and deaths in the Official Log Book (LOG 1).
* **The death of a seaman** or a person on a UK ship outside the UK cannot be officially registered in the UK until the RBD/1 is received by the RSS, Cardiff from the superintendent or proper officer and, where required, an inquiry has been held.
* An RBD/1 should be completed as above **where a person has been lost overboard and has not been found**, even though he may, in fact, be alive.
* **Where the master has died**, the senior surviving officer should make the return of death.
* **M.1074** (Deaths on UK Ships), which is now withdrawn, gave guidance on the identification of Proper Officers abroad. (For the address of the RSS, see B05c.)
* **Regulation 12 extends** the provisions of the regulations (except regulations 4 and 10(1)(a) and (b)) to **unregistered sea-going British ships** owned by a person resident in, or body corporate having a principal place of business in the UK, and to **masters and seamen employed in them**.

E14c PROPERTY OF DECEASED SEAMEN

* The **MS (Property of Deceased Seamen & Official Log Book) (Amendment) Regulations 1983** (SI 1983/1801) -
  - **revoke** the MS (Property of Deceased Seamen) Regulations 1972 (SI 1972/1697).
  - **amend** the MS (Official Log Books) Regulations 1981 (SI 1981/569) by deletion of the requirement for all details in the entry (**Entry No. 36**) relating to the property of a deceased seaman other than the requirement to record whether the seaman left any property (including money) on board the ship, and by adding a requirement for a record of each item of the property, both entries to be made by the master in person and witnessed by a member of the crew.
* **The personal effects of a seaman who dies while or after being employed in the ship** should be tallied (i.e. checked and listed) by two officers and sent, accompanied by one copy of the tally sheet, to the deceased seaman's next-of-kin, if necessary via the owner or agent's office.
* **One copy of the tally** of property should be annexed to the Official Log Book and an entry should be made in the narrative section recording the existence of the annex.

E14d OFFICIAL LOG BOOK ENTRIES RELATING TO BIRTHS AND DEATHS

* **In relation to a birth**, regulation 3 of the MS (Official Log Books) Regulations 1981 (SI 1981/569) requires a record to be made as detailed in **paragraph 34** of the Schedule to the regulations, (see D05a.4). These entries should be made on the special pages in the Official Log Book (LOG 1) (pages 8 and 9).

* **In relation to a death**, the following entries are required by regulation 3 of the Official Log Books Regulations:
  * To record the **occurrence of the death**: **Entry No. 35**. This entry should be made on the special pages (pages 8 and 9) in the Official Log Book (LOG 1) (pages 8 and 9), where a summary of the statutory requirements relating to entries can be found. Part of the note on page 9 states: "When completing form RBD 1, or making entries in the Log Book as to "cause of death", terms such as "suicide" or "missing" should be avoided and more specific terms such as "gunshot wound to the head" or "lost at sea believed killed or drowned" used instead. If the master is in any doubt about the completion of the forms required to be submitted by him or about any entries in the Official Log Book he should get in touch with the appropriate superintendent or proper officer."
  * To record any **property left behind** by a deceased seaman: **Entry No. 36**.
  * To record any **inquiry** held, or not held, into the cause of death, as appropriate: **Entry No. 37**.
  * To record any **illness or injury** that caused the death: **Entry No. 38**.
* Where the death is caused by a **casualty** to the vessel (e.g. a fire), the requirement to record the casualty itself (**Entry No. 12**) should not be neglected.

E14e EFFECT OF A CREW MEMBER'S DEATH ON SAFE MANNING

* Where the vessel is at sea when a crew member dies, the death will not jeopardise the validity of the Safe Manning Document until the next departure for sea from a port or place.
* STCW 95 provisions **do not permit sailing short-handed**. (For notes on **sailing short-handed**, see E03d.6. For notes on the **prohibition of going to sea undermanned**, see E03d.7.)
* **Where the deceased person was listed on the Safe Manning Document** as one of the persons essential to the safe manning of the vessel, it will not normally be possible to make the next departure for sea until a **replacement** is engaged.
* Where the deceased person was **not** one of the persons listed on the Safe Manning Document, there is no statutory prohibition on departing for sea without engagement of a replacement. Any conditions specified in the Safe Manning Document should, however, always be checked, since in passenger ships, for example, certain numbers of catering staff and others may be stipulated as being required when specified numbers of passengers are on board.
* **Where it is essential to make a replacement** for the deceased person, and a person amongst the present crew can be promoted, having regard to the required standards of training and certification for the position:
  * A **record of the promotion** should be made in the narrative section of the Official Log Book.
  * The **promoted person should be discharged** in the usual manner (see E07d.6) from his previous position and **engaged** in the usual manner (see E07d.2) in his new position on the crew agreement.
* The above notes also apply where a crew member is **left behind**.

E14f SUMMARY OF PROCEDURE FOLLOWING A DEATH ON BOARD

1. **Consult the Ship Captain's Medical Guide, Chapter 12** (The Dying and the Dead) for guidance. As well as sections on **Care of the dying** and **Signs of death**, Chapter 12 contains sections on **Cause of death, Procedure after death** and **Disposal of the body**.
2. **Establish the cause of death**, if possible. See page 206 of the Ship Captain's Medical Guide for guidance. If a doctor is available, have the cause of death certified by the doctor.
3. Obtain **witness statements** from relevant personnel as soon as possible after the occurrence of the death. Statements should be available for any MCA superintendent or proper officer who may come on board in connection with the death.
4. **Inform** the ship owner or manager as soon as possible.
5. **Check the Safe Manning Document** to ascertain whether a replacement for the deceased seafarer needs to be obtained before the vessel proceeds to sea (see E03d.6). If a replacement is necessary, advise the ship owner or manager as soon as possible.
6. If the vessel is in or nearing a port, **inform the agent**, requesting him to **inform the relevant authorities** of the port State (e.g. port health authority, police and customs).
7. **Inform the next-of-kin** as soon as possible and in any case within **3 days**. (This will probably be done by the owner or manager, but it remains the **master's statutory obligation** under the Returns of Births and Deaths Regulations (see E14b.2).)
8. **Inform the P&I club correspondent**. He will be able to advise on local formalities and procedure for repatriation of the body, if this will be required.

9. If the death was or may have been accidental, have the ship's **safety officer** make his statutory **investigation**, report and accident log entry (see E08d.3). (The safety officer's accident log entry does not meet the statutory requirement for the master to make an Official Log Book entry.)

10. **Preserve the body** if at all possible, in conformity with the advice on page 206 of the Ship Captain's Medical Guide. The usual and preferred procedure is to preserve the body by **chilling**. Where the body cannot be preserved, any burial at sea should be in conformity with the advice on page 207 of the Ship Captain's Medical Guide, and only with the express permission of the deceased person's next-of-kin.

11. If the death was, in the opinion of the safety officer, caused by an **accident** as defined in E08k.1a, **inform the MAIB** within 24 hours following the procedure in E08k. Supplement the initial report to the MAIB with a completed **IRF** form and **narrative report** when time permits.

12. **Make appropriate entries** in the Official Log Book (see E14d and D05a.4).

13. **Obtain**, from a superintendent or proper officer, form **RBD/1** (Return of Births and Deaths). Complete this with the same details as in the special pages of the Official Log Book and send the form as soon as possible to the superintendent or proper officer. (Until the RBD/1 is received by the RSS in Cardiff, the death cannot be registered in the person's home district, if in the UK.)

14. If the deceased person was employed on board (i.e. he/she was on a List of Crew), complete the **grey spaces** of the appropriate **List of Crew** (ALC1(a) or (b)) and have the entries witnessed (see E07d.7).

15. If the deceased person had a **Discharge Book**, record the period service on board in the normal manner, entering "DECEASED" in the "date of discharge" space.

16. Amend the **Crew List** and **all copies** maintained for the purposes of port officials.

17. **If the deceased person was paid in cash on board and was due wages or overtime**, make up the accounts, complete an Account of Seaman's Wages form (ASW2) and send it to the owner for forwarding to the next-of-kin with the other property (see E09b.2b). If the person was paid from the **shore office**, the office will probably require details of overtime and other payments due, and of any sums to be deducted (e.g. radio account).

18. **Have** two officers **tally and pack the deceased's personal property**. Pack one copy of the tally sheet with the property and attach one to the Official Log Book as an annex. Make a record in the narrative section of the Official Log Book recording the existence of the annex and the list of property (see E14c).

19. Where the ship is outside the UK and the body of a deceased seafarer is to be **repatriated or buried** locally, consult with the **proper officer**, the **agent** and the **P&I club correspondent** about the procedure. It is vital that the deceased person's **next of kin are consulted** and kept fully informed; the master should ensure that the shore office staff are doing this if he cannot communicate personally with next of kin.

Section F

THE SHIP'S EMPLOYMENT

Section F Contents

F01 Modes of ship employment

F01a EMPLOYMENT IN THE LINER TRADES

* As a **liner**, either in a passenger trade or a cargo trade, a ship is operated on one or more **fixed routes**, with **advertised**[1], **scheduled sailings**.
* True **passenger liners** operating on ocean services were mostly displaced in the 1960s by jet airliners. Today, very few long-haul passenger liners remain[2], and most passenger ships now operate as cruise ships. For notes on **employment as a passenger vessel**, see F01c.
* A **liner cargo vessel** will accept any suitable cargo if space permits. Most liners are **container ships**, **ro/ros** or **multi-purpose (ro-ro/lo-lo) vessels**.
* The **ship's operator** may be the owners or bareboat charterers or time charterers (in which case they may be referred to in chartering documents as "**disponent owners**" or "**time-chartered owners**").
* A liner vessel's operator is normally the "**performing carrier**" (known as the "**ocean carrier**" in the USA). The carrier's customers are **shippers**[3], who may include **freight forwarders** (see F03a.1) and **non-vessel-operating carriers** (NVOCs) (see F07a.2a).
* A carrier may issue a **booking note** when a cargo booking is made, and will usually issue a **bill of lading** (see F07b) or a **sea waybill** (see F07b.14), depending on the shipper's requirements, as a form of receipt to the shipper of each consignment of goods, and as evidence of the contract of carriage. The carrier will usually employ **liner agents** and/or **loading brokers** in order to canvass for and book his cargoes. The carrier may be a member of a liner **conference**, **consortium**, **alliance** or similar arrangement, or may be a **non-conference operator**.

F01b EMPLOYMENT IN THE CHARTER MARKETS

* Where a ship is employed in the **charter markets** (sometimes known as the "tramp trades"), the owner generally intends that she will be "**fixed**" by **shipbrokers** on a succession of charters. The ship may be employed in the **voyage charter market** (also called the "**spot market**") or in the **time charter market**, and in both cases may be **sub-chartered** by the "**head charterer**" to another charterer (see F04a.1e). The ship may simultaneously be employed under a **contract of affreightment** (see F04a.3). As a "tramp", the ship will not normally operate on a fixed route to an advertised schedule, except when time-chartered to a liner operator. Most ships employed in the charter markets are dry bulk carriers, tankers, combination carriers (e.g. OBOs), or reefer vessels, although there is also a charter market for container ships and for vessels of various special purpose types (see F04a.1d).
* A chartered ship's **charterers** may be **time charterers** or **voyage charterers**, and will normally employ the services of a **shipbroker** to **fix** the ship (see F04b.1). The charterers may in some cases be the legal **carrier** (see F07a), in which case they may order the ship to issue bills of lading on their behalf to shippers of goods loaded. The charterers may be carrying their own goods in an "in house" shipment, or the goods of another party. In other cases the charterers may only be hired to fix the ship and load the cargo.

F01b.1 Dry bulk carrier market categories

* For charter marketing purposes, dry bulk carriers are categorised by owners, charterers and brokers, and in market reports, as outlined below.
    * **Handysize** bulk carriers are vessels in the range 10,000-29,999 dwt.
    * **Handymax** bulk carriers are vessels in the range 30,000-49,999 dwt.
    * **Panamax** bulk carriers are vessels in the range 50,000-79,999 dwt.
    * **Capesize** bulk carriers are vessels of 80,000 dwt or more.
* A good example of a **dry bulk shipping market report** can be seen on the website of E.A.Gibson Shipbrokers Ltd: www.eagibson.co.uk

---

[1] Liner cargo services from and to the UK are advertised in **Lloyd's Loading List**, published by the Informa Group.
[2] RMS *St Helena* is an example of a true passenger liner.
[3] A "**shipper**" may be defined as any person who, whether as principal or agent for another, consigns goods for carriage by sea.

F01b.2 Tanker market categories

* For charter marketing purposes, tankers are categorised (by owners, charterers and brokers, and in market reports) as outlined below.
  * **Handysize** tankers are vessels in the range 27,000-36,999 dwt.
  * **Handymax** tankers are vessels in the range 37,000-49,999 dwt.
  * **Panamax** tankers are vessels in the range 50,000-74,999 dwt.
* The London Tanker Brokers' Panel determine market rates under a freight billing system called "Average Freight Rate Assessment" or "**AFRA**". This allows an assessment to be made of a freight scale for tankers of various sizes, categorised as shown in the following table.

Tanker dwt	Category	Notes
Under 16,500	Coastal, Small, Harbour and Lake tankers	Some brokers refer to tankers of 10,000-49,999 dwt as "Handysize". SSY regard "Small" as 10,000-26,999 dwt.
16,500-24,999	General Purpose	
25,000-49,999	Medium Range	
50,000-79,999	Large Range 1 (MR1)	SSY regard "Panamax" as 50,000-74,999 dwt.
80,000-159,999	Large Range 2 (LR2)	Vessels in this category of less than 100,000 dwt are divided into "dirty" and "clean" groups, "dirty" vessels carrying "black" cargoes such as crude oil, heavy fuel oils, asphalt, etc. and clean vessels carrying refined "white" products.
160,000-319,999	Very Large Crude Carrier (VLCC)	Some brokers consider VLCCs to start at 200,000 dwt.
320,000 and above	Ultra Large Crude Carrier (ULCC)	

* **Aframax** tankers are vessels large enough to carry "Aframax"-size cargoes of between 80,000 tonnes and 119,000 tonnes. The average size of Aframax cargoes varies from one world region to another, resulting in different tanker market practitioners quoting different sizes for an "Aframax" tanker[4].
* A **Suezmax** tanker is a vessel of such a size (around 150,000-200,000 dwt, depending on dimensions and draught) that she can sail through the Suez Canal when fully loaded. Some brokers categorise "Suezmax" tankers as vessels in the range 120,000-199,999 dwt.

F01c EMPLOYMENT AS A PASSENGER VESSEL

* **Passenger liners** operating on trans-ocean routes were mostly displaced in the 1960s by jet airliners. A large passenger ship today is therefore more likely to operate as a **cruise ship**. The ship is likely to be operated by her owner, or apparent owner. In view of the high cost of new cruise ships, the real owner may be one or more banks or finance houses, while the ship is leased or bareboat chartered to the cruise line[5]. Small passenger ships may be operated as ferries or excursion vessels.
* A cruise ship may occasionally be **chartered** on voyage or time terms to a holiday operator, or to another cruise line to meet extra demand or replace and out-of-service vessel, or to a club, society, etc. for a special voyage.
* The contract between the operator and each passenger is a **contract of passage**, which on international voyages may be subject to the terms of the **Athens Convention** (see F08a.2).

F01d EMPLOYMENT AS A SPECIAL SERVICE VESSEL

* The vessel is employed for a **special purpose**, e.g. oilfield supply and/or anchor-handling, carriage of heavy lifts, towage, surveying, salvage, polar supply/research, dredging, wind turbine installation, etc.
* The vessel may be operated by her owner, or may be hired under a time charter (as in the case of most offshore support vessels) or under a voyage charter.
* If on charter, the vessel will usually be employed in a specialised charter market, e.g. the heavy lift market, the anchor-handling supply vessel market or seismic survey vessel market, etc. If the vessel is an offshore support vessel, the charterers are likely to be an oilfield operator or a drilling contractor.
* In many cases, mostly where the vessel is time-chartered, a **charterer's representative** will sail in the vessel; this is commonly the case where the vessel is engaged in sophisticated operations such as offshore drilling or diving support. In highly specialised, technical operations such as these, a team of technical personnel (e.g. divers and dive

---

[4] "K" Line, for example, classifies "Aframax" as between 80,000dwt and 120,000dwt. Brokers Simpson Spence and Young (SSY), on the other hand, quote 75,000-119,999dwt. Another broker, Drewry, states in its website (on 13 July 2002): "Until recent years, when a new range - 80-119,999 dwt was adopted, the size range 60-99,999 was most commonly used to describe an Aframax tanker."
[5] The registered owners of P&O's well known cruise ship *Canberra* were, in fact, Abbey National March Leasing.

support personnel on a DSV) may work from the vessel, in effect using her as a work platform. (For notes on the engagement and discharge of such personnel, see E07.)

F02 Contractual relationships

F02a CONTRACTUAL RELATIONSHIPS RELATED TO THE SHIP'S EMPLOYMENT

* In connection with the ship's employment, **contractual relationships** will exist between:
    * the ship's **owner** and any **ship manager** employed (embodied in a ship management contract);
    * the ship's **owner**, **manager** or **operator** and any **charterers** (charter party);
    * the **head charterer** and any **sub-charterer** (charter party);
    * the ship's **owner**, **manager** or **operator** and a **shipbroker** who fixes the ship's employment;
    * the **buyer** and **seller** of each consignment of goods carried on board (sale of goods contract);
    * an **exporter** and any **freight forwarder** hired to arrange for the delivery of goods;
    * the legal **carrier** and each **shipper** of goods on board (contract of carriage);
    * the ship's **owner**, **manager** or **operator** and each **port agent** appointed by him;
    * the ship's **owner, manager or operator** and various other parties whose services are used during a voyage such as **chandlers**, **equipment suppliers**, **repairers**, **tugowners**, **pilotage authorities**, **port authorities**, **stevedoring companies**, etc. (contract for services);
    * a **shipowner** and each **passenger** (contract of passage).
* Clearly, a detailed examination of all these legal relationships is beyond the scope of this book. The following notes will therefore be confined to:
    * the contract between the **cargo seller and buyer** (see F03);
    * the contract between the **shipowner and charterer: general** (see F04);
    * the contract between the **shipowner and charterer: voyage charter** (see F05);
    * the contract between the **shipowner and charterer: time charter** (see F06);
    * the contract between the **shipowner and the cargo owner** (see F07); and
    * the contract between the **shipowner and passengers** (see F08).

F03 Contract between cargo seller and buyer

* The **contract of sale** between the seller and the buyer of the goods is separate from the **contract of carriage** which one party or the other, or a third party (such as a freight forwarder), will make with the carrier.
* Certain aspects of the sale of goods contract are important for a shipmaster to understand, as outlined in the following notes.

F03a SALE OF GOODS CONTRACTS

* Goods are most often carried by sea as a result of a **sales contract** (or **sale of goods contract**) made between the seller and buyer. The **contract of carriage**, which is separate, comes about as a result of this sales contract.
* UK sales are subject to the provisions of the Sale of Goods Act 1979, as amended. This Act sets out an unpaid seller's rights, one of which (in section 44) is the right of **stoppage in transit** (see F03d).
* Contracts for the sale of goods usually include provisions covering three important points:
    * the time or circumstances of the **passing of title** (i.e. ownership) of the goods from seller to buyer;
    * the time when **payment** becomes due; and
    * the time when the **risk** (of loss or damage) passes from seller to buyer.
    These points are normally addressed in international sale of goods contracts by incorporation of one of a set of mutually-agreed standard trade terms named **INCOTERMS** (see F03b).

F03a.1 Parties involved in sea transportation of goods

* **The transport of goods by sea from seller to buyer** usually involves several parties whose roles may be unclear to those on board ship. The following notes are intended to outline the **basic functions of the most prominent players** forming links in the transport chain.
* The **seller** and the **buyer** are the parties contracting with each other for the delivery of the goods. The seller may be the producer or manufacturer of the goods, or may be a party acting as the producer/manufacturer's agent. Both parties agree on the **trade terms** (see F03b) which will influence the type and terms of shipping documents (e.g. bill of lading or sea waybill).
* As far as the shipowner is concerned, the **shipper** is the party who contracts for the carriage of the goods by sea and delivers the goods into his care, whether this party is the seller or an agent of the seller. The seller, however, may be employing the services of a **freight forwarder** to perform the various functions involved in exporting the goods, and it may be the freight forwarder who contracts for carriage of the goods with the shipowner, making the freight forwarder the legal shipper. Another possibility is that a certain amount of cargo space on board the ship has been contracted to a **non-vessel owning carrier** (NVOC) (see F07a.2a), and the seller or his agent has contracted with the NVOC to transport the goods; in that case, the NVOC will be the legal shipper in the contract with the shipowner. Whoever the shipper is in law, however, the document evidencing receipt of the goods by the carrier (e.g. a bill of lading or sea waybill) will be issued by the carrier to that party, and that party will be giving employment to the ship. In some countries, including the USA, the shipper may be called the **consignor**.
* A **freight forwarder** is a transport intermediary, operating in the liner trades, who arranges the export of another party's goods (by land, sea or air) and "forwards" the goods into the care of the sea carrier. Freight forwarders can advise on routeing, can arrange carriage with a carrier (booking space, paying freight, etc.), can prepare or assist in preparting customs documents, can make customs entry (clearance) of goods, can arrange packaging and warehousing of goods before shipment, can arrange goods transit insurance, and can in many cases arrange "groupage" or "consolidation", meaning the more cost-effective shipment in one transport unit of several small parcels sent by different shippers, where they are all destined for the same delivery port or place)[6].
* A **carrier** is a party who contracts with a shipper for the transport of goods by sea. In the liner trades, where **non-vessel owning carriers** offer shipping services (see above and F07a.2a), the carrier with whom the seller or the seller's agent makes his carriage contract is not necessarily the carrier actually *performing* the sea carriage. Furthermore, where a ship is chartered and is being operated commercially by the charterer (such as a time charterer), the identity of the legal carrier may depend on the information stated on the bill of lading or sea waybill (see F07b.6).
* The **consignee** is the party to whom the goods are consigned or sent by the shipper. The consignee may be the buyer of the goods, or a party acting as import agent for the buyer.
* The **receiver** is the party who takes receipt of the goods from the sea carrier at the port or place of delivery. Some consignees will take direct delivery of goods from carriers, but many consignees in the liner trades employ an agent such as a freight forwarder to act as a "clearing agent" in the customs and other formalities of importing the goods, and for transportation of goods to their ultimate destination. When loss or damage to goods is discovered on discharge, it is often the receiver who notifies the carrier.
* The **notify party** (a term found in most bills of lading and sea waybills) is the party who must be informed by the carrier of the ship's arrival, so that collection of the goods can be arranged. The notify party may be the consignee or a receiver.
* **Banks** will form links in the transport document chain when payment for the goods is being made by means of a Letter of Credit. For notes on the **documentary credit system**, see F03c. For notes on the **bill of lading in the documentary credit system**, see F07b.3.
* Depending on the trade terms, either the seller or the buyer will usually take out goods transit insurance with a **cargo insurer**. For notes on **cargo insurance**, see G04c.

F03b INTERNATIONAL TRADE TERMS (INCOTERMS)

* It is important for the seller and buyer of goods, as well as their bankers, cargo insurers and the various carriers who may be involved in the total journey to know precisely when the right to **ownership** and **risk** of loss or damage passes from seller to buyer, so that the respective obligations, rights and liabilities of each party can be determined and disputes avoided. The obligations of the seller and buyer with respect to delivery of the goods and the division of functions, costs and risks related to the delivery should be contained in **trade terms** incorporated in the contract of sale.

---

[6] Freight forwarders and liner carriers offering a "groupage" service advertise an "LCL" service, meaning "Less-than-Container Load". The alternative, where one shipper's consignment can fill one transport unit, is "FCL", meaning "Full Container Load".

* **Misinterpretation of trade terms** and uncertainties may result where there are different trading practices in the respective countries of the buyer and seller which are not known to each other. The trade term "FOB", for example, has a different meaning to a merchant in the USA than to a UK merchant. **Language differences** between buyer and seller, or lack of a common language, may also cause misinterpretation of contract terms.
* **INCOTERMS is a set of rules**, published by the International Chamber of Commerce, for the **uniform interpretation** of the most commonly used **trade terms** used in international trade contracts. The main purpose of INCOTERMS is to clearly set out the obligations of the seller and buyer with respect to the delivery of the goods and the division of functions, costs and risks associated with delivery. By the use of INCOTERMS misinterpretations or uncertainties described above may be avoided or reduced.
* INCOTERMS are published in various languages used by the chief trading nations. The latest edition is INCOTERMS 2000. A sales contract should contain an express reference to the edition used.
* **Thirteen INCOTERMS** are defined, which can be arranged in four groups: E, F, C and D according to the seller's basic obligations, as follows:
  * Group E – where the goods are to be made available to the buyer at the seller's premises;
  * Group F – where the seller and buyer must deliver the goods to a carrier appointed by the buyer;
  * Group C – where the seller must contract for the carriage of the goods without bearing the risk of loss of or damage to the goods or additional costs following shipment; and
  * Group D – where the seller has to bear all costs and risks required to bring the goods to their destination.
* INCOTERMS can be further grouped into two basic categories: terms **suitable for use in contracts involving water transport**, and terms suitable for **all transport modes**. The table below combines the two groupings.

Group	Term type	Terms suitable for sea transport only	Terms suitable for all transport modes
E	Departure term		EXW (Ex Works)
F	Shipment term, main carriage unpaid	FAS (Free Alongside Ship) FOB (Free On Board)	FCA (Free Carrier)
C	Shipment term, main carriage paid	CFR (Cost and Freight) CIF (Cost, Insurance and Freight)	CPT (Carriage Paid To) CIP (Carriage and Insurance Paid To)
D	Delivery term	DES (Delivered Ex Ship) DEQ (Delivered Ex Quay)	DAF (Delivered At Frontier) DDU (Delivered Duty Unpaid) DDP (Delivered Duty Paid)

* In the first three groups the **risk** of loss or damage during transportation is the **buyer's**, while in the fourth group the **seller bears all risks** up to the point of delivery.
* Of the INCOTERMS which are suitable for water transport, **FOB** and **CIF** are the most commonly used terms.
* An outline meaning of each INCOTERM is shown in the following table.

EXW	Ex Works (named place)	Seller to place goods at disposal of buyer at seller's premises or another named place, not cleared for export and not loaded onto any collecting vehicle. Title and risk pass to buyer at seller's door.
FCA	Free Carrier (named place)	Seller to deliver goods, cleared for export, to carrier nominated by buyer at named place. Title and risk pass to buyer on delivery to carrier.
FAS	Free Alongside Ship (named port of shipment)	Seller to place goods, cleared for export, alongside vessel at named port of shipment. Title and risk pass to buyer alongside ship.
FOB	Free On Board (named port of shipment)	Seller delivers goods, cleared for export, when they pass ship's rail at named loading port. Title and risk pass to buyer as goods pass ship's rail.
CFR	Cost and Freight (named port of destination)	Seller delivers goods when they pass ship's rail at named loading port and must pay costs and freight necessary to bring goods to named port of destination. Buyer bears all additional costs and risks after goods have been delivered over ship's rail at loading port. Title and risk pass to buyer when goods delivered on board ship.
CIF	Cost, Insurance and Freight (named port of destination)	Seller's obligations same as under CFR with addition that seller must obtain insurance against buyer's risk of loss/damage during sea carriage. Title and risk pass to buyer when goods delivered on board ship.
CPT	Carriage Paid To (named place of destination)	Seller delivers goods to nominated carrier and pays cost of carriage to named destination. Buyer bears all additional costs and risks after goods delivered to carrier. Title, risk and insurance cost pass to buyer when goods delivered to carrier.
CIP	Carriage and Insurance Paid To (named place of destination)	Obligations same as under CPT with addition that seller procures insurance against buyer's risk of loss/damage to goods during carriage. Title and risk pass to buyer when goods delivered to carrier.
DAF	Delivered at Frontier (named place)	Seller to place goods at disposal of buyer on arriving means of transport, not unloaded, cleared for export but uncleared for import, at named border point. Title, risk and responsibility for import clearance pass to buyer when delivered to named border point by seller.
DES	Delivered Ex Ship (named of destination)	Seller delivers when goods are placed at buyer's disposal on board ship, not cleared for import, at named port of destination. Title, risk and responsibility for vessel discharge and import clearance pass to buyer when seller delivers goods on ship at destination port.
DEQ	Delivered Ex Quay (named port of destination)	Seller delivers when goods are placed at disposal of buyer, not cleared for import, on quay at named port of destination. Title and risk pass to buyer when delivered on board ship at destination point by seller who delivers goods on dock at destination point cleared for import.

DDU	Delivered Duty Unpaid (named place of destination)	Seller must deliver the goods to the buyer, not cleared for import, and not unloaded, at the named place of destination. Title, risk and responsibility of import clearance pass to buyer when seller delivers goods to named destination point. Buyer is obligated for import clearance.
DDP	Delivered Duty Paid (named place of destination)	Seller must deliver goods to buyer, cleared for import, and not unloaded, at named place of destination. Title and risk pass to buyer when seller delivers goods to named destination point cleared for import.

* From the top (EXW) to the bottom (DDP) in the table, the seller gathers more responsibility and the point of transfer of property (i.e. the right of ownership) in the transport chain moves from the seller's premises towards the buyer's premises.
* The two INCOTERMS most commonly used in sales contracts involving sea transportation are FOB and CIF, which are explained in more detail below.

F03b.1 FOB

- means **Free On Board** (named port of shipment), e.g. *"FOB Newcastle NSW"*.
* The **seller** must supply the goods and documents stated in the contract of sale. He must load the goods on board the vessel named by the buyer at the named port of shipment on the date or within the period stipulated. He must bear all costs and risks of the goods until they have passed the ship's rail at the named port of shipment, including export charges and taxes. He must also pay for packing where necessary. **Risk** passes when the goods pass the ship's rail. The **seller** must notify the buyer when the goods have been loaded. The **seller** must give sufficient information to the buyer for him to arrange insurance; if the seller fails to give enough information, the risk stays with him.
* The **buyer** must charter a ship or reserve the necessary space on a ship and notify the seller of the ship's name, loading berth and loading dates. The **buyer** must bear all costs, including insurance (which he must arrange) and freight, from the time the goods cross the ship's rail at the loading port, from when he is liable to pay the contract price. (Freight is normally collectable by the carrier from the buyer at the discharge port.) The **buyer** must also pay the seller for providing the required documents, e.g. bills of lading and certificate of origin.
* **FOB is advantageous** when the cargo is of a type (e.g. oil) and size that the buyer wishes to charter a particular vessel, or where foreign currency restrictions compel an importer to use FOB (e.g. where governments want importers to use national flag vessels). It is mainly used for bulk sales contracts. With respect to the bill of lading, **title** in the goods does not pass to the buyer until shipment. The FOB contract is **based on the loading port**, so the buyer is free after loading to re-sell the goods, even while they are on the vessel. The **FOB invoice price** is lower than the CIF price.
* **Variants of FOB** are: FOB Stowed, FOB UK Port, FOB With Services (e.g. arranging shipping space). Passing of property may be delayed with variants.

F03b.2 CIF

- means **Cost, Insurance and Freight** (paid to a named place), e.g. CIF London.
- is a contract based on the **discharge port**.
* The **seller** must pay all costs including marine insurance and freight to carry the goods to the named destination, but risk passes from the seller to the buyer when the goods cross the ship's rail at the loading port. The **seller** must supply the goods and make a contract (at his own expense) for carriage of the goods to the agreed port of destination, paying freight and charges for loading/unloading. He must arrange (at his own expense) a marine insurance policy covering the goods against the risks of carriage for the CIF price plus 10%. Any war risks insurance required by the buyer must be arranged by the **seller** but charged to the buyer. (The cost of providing these services are included in the invoice price for the goods.)
* The **seller** must provide the buyer with **clean, negotiable bills of lading** (dated for the agreed period of loading), an **invoice** and an **insurance policy or certificate of insurance**. The bills of lading must be a full set of **negotiable "order" marine bills** so that delivery can be made to the order of the buyer or his agreed representative. (This enables the bills of lading to be passed to a bank in the documentary credit system, enabling the seller to obtain early payment.) If the bill of lading contains a reference to a charter party, the **seller** must also provide a copy of the charter party. The **seller** must tender all the documents to the buyer, his agent or his bank.
* The **buyer** must accept the documents when tendered by the seller, and must pay the agreed contract price. Property passes on transfer to the buyer of the documents. The **buyer** bears all costs and charges excluding freight, marine insurance and unloading costs unless included in the freight when collected by the carrier. The **buyer** must also pay for war risks insurance if he requires it. He must effectively bear all risks of the goods from passing the ship's rail at the port of shipment. (He is protected by the insurance arranged by the seller.)

* As freight is paid by the seller, the bill of lading is normally marked "FREIGHT PRE-PAID", but the **master** should ensure that freight has been paid before signing the bills of lading.

* The **buyer** bears the risks during the voyage, but **title** in the goods only passes when the documents are taken up by the buyer. When the **buyer** has received the documents he must pay for the goods; he cannot demand receipt of the goods first.

* The **purpose of a CIF contract** is not so much the sale of goods as the sale of documents relating to the goods, so as to enable the negotiability of the bill of lading. CIF is therefore widely used where the documentary credit system is used.

* The **advantage of CIF to the buyer** is in making the seller wholly responsible for arranging the shipment. The **seller** is protected against loss or damage before payment by the insurance policy. The **seller** can also retain title in the goods beyond the time of shipment and as security against payment by the buyer, so it is easier for the seller to obtain credit at his bank. Once the buyer receives the documents and pays, he can secure credit or resell the goods. However, the goods will cost more on CIF terms than on FOB terms.

* In view of the advantages in CIF for normal international sales, in which the banks' **documentary credit system** requires the transfer of title through the passing of documents (including the set of bills of lading and a certificate of insurance), the vast majority of international seaborne cargo shipments are CIF.

F03c DOCUMENTARY CREDIT SYSTEM

- is a **money transfer system** commonly used in overseas trade to enable sellers to obtain early payment, i.e. soon after shipment of the goods.
- relies heavily on **documents**, which are carefully checked by the banks involved before they make payment.
- operates with the **procedure** in the following example, which assumes a Seller in the UK and a Buyer in New Zealand.
    1. Seller and Buyer conclude their **sales contract**, specifying payment by documentary credit.
    2. Buyer instructs his bank in NZ to open a **Credit** in favour of Seller.
    3. Buyer's NZ bank verifies Buyer's credit-worthiness and issues a **Letter of Credit** (LOC) containing terms of the Credit (i.e. stringent requirements regarding use of CIF terms, documents, time of loading, etc. Buyer's bank sends LOC to Seller's bank.
    4. Seller's bank checks LOC requirements, then sends LOC to Seller.
    5. Seller despatches goods, assembles documents required by LOC (usually invoice, insurance certificate, **full set of "clean on board" bills of lading** made "to order" which are obtained once goods are shipped). Seller presents all shipping documents to his bank and asks for his payment.
    6. Seller's bank checks documents against LOC requirements. If they comply (including "clean" bills of lading), Seller's bank pays Seller and sends documents to Buyer's bank.
    7. Buyer's bank checks documents against LOC. If they comply, Buyer's bank releases documents to Buyer against payment, then reimburses Seller's bank.
    8. Buyer receives documents, enabling him to obtain release of goods from ship.

* For notes on the **bill of lading in the documentary credit system**, see F07b.3.

* A **problem** will arise when a bank is instructed by the Letter of Credit to pay only on production of a full set of "clean on board" bills of lading, whereas the bills of lading have been **claused** in respect of some defect or shortage (see F07b.5a).

F03d STOPPAGE IN TRANSIT

* Section 44 of the **Sale of Goods Act 1979** provides a seller with a statutory right to have the goods stopped while still in transit to the buyer after it has become known that the buyer is insolvent and has failed to pay for the goods.

* Three conditions must exist to enable this right to be exercised:
- the purchaser must be **insolvent**;
- the seller must be **unpaid**; and
- the goods must have left the seller's possession but must not yet have come into the buyer's **possession**.

* It makes no difference whether or not the property has passed to the buyer (i.e. the legal title in the goods). While the goods are on board the carrying ship, they are still in the seller's **constructive possession**, and he may exercise his right of stoppage. However, once the goods are physically delivered to the buyer (or his agent), the right is lost.

* The seller must give the ship **written instructions** (e.g. by telex or fax) which should be retained by the master as evidence. The carrier is then obliged to return the goods to the port of shipment, the seller being liable for the back-freight and other expenses.

F04 Contract between shipowner and charterer: general

F04a CHARTERS

F04a.1 Nature of charters

* A "**charter**" is a contract for the hire of a vessel, aircraft, bus, etc. for a specified journey or an agreed period of time.
* In a maritime context, **charters** include:
    • **contracts for carriage** of specified quantities of cargo in specified vessels between specified ports (i.e. **voyage charters**); and
    • **contracts for hire** of specified vessels, including:
        ▪ **time charters**; and
        ▪ **bareboat charters** (also known as "**demise charters**").

F04a.1a Nature of a voyage charter

* A **voyage charter** -
    - is a contract for the **carriage** by a named vessel of a **specified quantity of cargo** between **named ports or places**.
    - may be thought of as equivalent to the **hire of a taxi** for a single journey, or for a series of several consecutive journeys in the case of a **consecutive voyage charter**.
* The **shipowner** basically agrees that he will **present** the named vessel for loading at the agreed place within an agreed period of time and, following loading (responsibility for which will be as agreed between the parties), will **carry** the cargo to the agreed place, where he will **deliver** the cargo.
* The **charterer**, who may be the cargo owner or may be chartering for the account of another party such as the shipper or the receiver, agrees to **provide** for loading, within the agreed period of time, the agreed quantity of the agreed commodity, to **pay** the agreed amount of **freight**, and to **take delivery** of the cargo at the destination place.
* In effect the charterers hire the **cargo capacity** of the vessel, and not the entire vessel, and to this extent a voyage charter agreement can be considered as the maritime equivalent of a taxi hire agreement. (Control of the ship's operations remains with the shipowner.)
* In some trades, e.g. chemical tankers, several cargo parcels carried on one voyage may have been fixed with several **different charterers**.
* The **shipowner** must provide the master and crew, act as carrier and pay all running and voyage costs, unless the charter party specifically provides otherwise. (For notes on **running costs and voyage costs**, see C02a.)
* For detailed notes on **voyage charters**, see F05.

F04a.1b Nature of a time charter

* A **time charter** -
    - is a contract for the **hire** of a **named vessel** for a **specified period of time**.
    - may be thought of as equivalent to the **hire of a chauffeur-driven car** (the ship's crew being "the chauffeur").
* The charterers agree to **hire** from the shipowner a named vessel, of specified technical characteristics, for an **agreed period of time**, for the charterer's purposes subject to agreed restrictions. The **hire period** may be the duration of one voyage (a "**trip charter**") or anything up to several years ("**period charter**").
* The **shipowner** is responsible for vessel's **running expenses**, i.e. manning, repairs and maintenance, stores, master's and crew's wages, hull and machinery insurance, etc. He operates the vessel technically, but not commercially. The owners bear no cargo-handling expenses and do not normally appoint stevedores.
* The charterers are responsible for the commercial employment of the vessel, bunker fuel purchase and insurance, port and canal dues (including pilotage, towage, linesmen, etc.), and all loading/stowing/trimming/discharging arrangements and costs. They direct the ship's **commercial operations**, but not her daily running and maintenance. The charterers normally appoint stevedores and nominate agents.
* There may be an agreement between the parties for an **extra payment** (of perhaps several hundred US$) to be made by the charterers each time the ship's crew sweep and/or wash down the holds of a dry cargo ship.
* A **Directions and Logs Clause** requires the charterers to provide the master with all instructions and sailing directions, and the master and chief engineer to keep full and correct logs accessible to the charterers or their agents, so that they can monitor the vessel's efficiency. **Stevedoring damage notification forms**, and **log extracts** (or "**abstracts**") will usually be required to be sent to the charterers.

* Time charterers are normally allowed to fly their own **house flag** and, at their own expense, paint their own **colours** on the funnel and/or sides.
* For detailed notes on **time charters**, see F06.

F04a.1c Nature of a bareboat charter and lease arrangement

* A **bareboat charter** (sometimes called a **charter by demise** or **demise charter**, particularly by lawyers) –
  - is a contract for the **hire** of a vessel for an agreed period during which the charterers acquire most of the rights of the owners.
  - may be thought of as the marine equivalent of a **long-term vehicle lease** contract.
  - is most usually on the **BARECON 89** charter party form.
  - is used by owners such as **banks** and **finance houses** who are not prepared to operate or manage ships themselves.
  - is often hinged to a **management agreement**. (e.g. where an oil company bareboat charters a tanker from an independent tanker owner but agrees that the owners will manage the ship on the oil company's behalf during the charter period).
  - may be hinged to a **purchase option** after expiry of the charter or during the hire period. (Hire payments may include instalments of the purchase price, and transfer of ownership may follow the final instalment. Many permutations are possible.)
* In essence the vessel owners put the vessel (without any crew) at the complete disposal of the charterers and pay the capital costs, but (usually) no other costs. The charterers have commercial and technical responsibility for the vessel, and pay all costs except capital costs.
* The "**BARECON A**" form, under which the owners bear responsibility for insurance premiums, was designed by BIMCO for short-period chartering (e.g. the summer hire of a passenger vessel).
* The "**BARECON B**" form was designed as a long-period, financial type of contract, mainly for newbuildings although it can be modified for second-hand tonnage. The charterers are responsible for insurance premiums.
* "**BARECON 89**" is an amalgamation of the "BARECON A" and "B" forms designed to reflect the growing use of bareboat charter registration. Part I contains the familiar BIMCO-style boxed details. Part II contains the standard clauses. Part III contains provisions applicable to newbuilding vessels. Part IV contains a hire-purchase agreement. Part V contains provisions to apply for vessels registered in a bareboat charter registry.
* A **lease** arrangement is a means of financing the acquisition of a vessel that utilises a bareboat charter party as the vehicle for the loan repayment agreement. It is used as an alternative to a traditional **ship mortgaging** arrangement. The "sharing" of tax benefits available to the owner and charterer is sometimes the main purpose of a lease arrangement. In a typical lease arrangement, the **lessee** or borrower already owns a vessel or has contracted a newbuilding from a shipyard. On entering into the lease agreement, ownership of the vessel is formally transferred to the **lessor** or lender, who then becomes the registered owner. The lessor then charters the vessel to the borrower on the terms of a bareboat charter party. The lessor retains ownership of the vessel for a (usually) lengthy period, following which ownership may pass to the lessee/charterer. The charter hire payments cover the instalments of a loan that represents the finance required to acquire the vessel. The lender's tax benefits, which stem from ownership of the vessel, are passed on to the lessee/charterer by way of reduced charter hire payments. A vast set of financial documents is required in addition to the bareboat charter party. Some of the terms of the bareboat charter party are designed to protect the lessor/charterer against the risks and liabilities normally associated with ownership of a vessel.

F04a.1d Charters for special purposes

* A **special service vessel**, such as a heavy lift ship, could be chartered on a general purpose charter party form, e.g. "GENCON", suitably adapted by the parties, but this would necessitate a large number of amendments and rider clauses. It would therefore be preferable to charter the vessel on a form specific to the type of operation concerned, e.g. BIMCO's "HEAVYCON" form - the standard transportation contract for heavy and voluminous cargoes.
* "SLOTHIRE" is a BIMCO form on which a **slot charterer** hires a number of container bays on a containership's sailings, but not the entire cargo capacity. For notes on NVOCs (who may be users of "SLOTHIRE") see F07a.2a.
* "TOWCON" is an international ocean towage agreement for a lump sum, used in the professional towage industry. "TOWHIRE" is an ocean towage agreement for a daily hire rate.

F04a.1e Sub-charters

* It is common for the terms of both time and voyage charters to permit the charterers to **sub-let** the vessel in whole or in part, on condition that the **head charterer** remains responsible to the shipowner for the performance of the original charter. It would be possible, therefore, for a vessel to be:

1. **owned** by a bank or finance house;
2. **leased or bareboat chartered** to Company A;
3. **time-chartered** from Company A by Company B;
4. **voyage-chartered** from Company B by Company C;
5. **employed** by Company C in its own liner service, or even **sub-chartered** from Company C by Company D.
* Any reference in a charter party to a "**disponent owner**" refers to the time or bareboat charterer of a sub-let vessel, who assumes, in relation to the sub-charterer, the responsibilities of a real owner.

F04a.2 Road vehicle hire contracts compared to ship charter agreements

* The following comparative tables may help to clarify the basic obligations of parties to vessel charters.

Vehicle lease agreement	Bareboat charter agreement
Agreement for hire	Agreement for hire
Of specified vehicle (e.g. Jaguar XJS)	Of specified vessel (e.g. m.v. "Carrymuch")
For agreed duration (e.g. 12 months)	For agreed duration (e.g. 10 years)
Commencing at agreed time and place	Commencing at agreed time and place
Ending at agreed time and place	Ending at agreed time and place
Vehicle owner to pay capital costs (e.g. to car maker)	Vessel owner to pay capital costs (e.g. to shipbuilder)
Hirer to pay all other costs during hire period	Charterers to pay all other costs during hire period
Hire payments to be made at specified intervals in advance (e.g. monthly)	Hire payments to be made at specified intervals in advance (e.g. monthly)

Chauffeur-driven car hire agreement	Time charter agreement
Agreement for hire	Agreement for hire
Of specified vehicle (e.g. Rolls-Royce Silver Cloud)	Of specified vessel (e.g. m.v. "Carrymuch")
For specified purposes (e.g. wedding)	For specified purposes (e.g. to carry any non-excluded cargoes)
For agreed duration (e.g. 24 hours)	For agreed duration (e.g. 12 months)
Commencing at agreed time and place	Commencing at agreed time and place
Ending at agreed time and place	Ending at agreed time and place
Vehicle owner to pay all running costs (e.g. maintenance, MOT tests, road tax, insurance, chauffeur's wages)	Vessel owner to pay all running costs (e.g. maintenance, surveys, lubricating oil, crew wages)
Hirer to pay all journey costs during hire period (e.g. fuel, bridge tolls, parking fees)	Charterers to pay all voyage costs during hire period (e.g. bunker fuel, canal and port dues, loading and discharge costs)
Hire payments to be made at specified intervals in advance (e.g. monthly)	Hire payments to be made at specified intervals in advance (e.g. monthly)

Taxi hire agreement	Voyage charter agreement
Agreement for carriage	Agreement for carriage
Of specified "load" (e.g. one person plus luggage)	Of specified cargo (e.g. 20,000mt coal in bulk)
Car to "pick up" at agreed time (e.g. 7.30 a.m.)	Ship to be presented at loading port between agreed dates (e.g. 2/6 May)
Load to be carried from agreed "pick-up" point (e.g. 20 Station Road, Brighton)	Cargo to be carried from agreed loading port (e.g. "Singapore")
To agreed "drop-off" point (e.g. Gatwick Airport)	To agreed discharge port (e.g. "Rotterdam")
No agreed journey duration	No agreed voyage duration
Vehicle owner to pay all running and journey costs	Vessel owner to pay all running and voyage costs, with exception of loading and discharge costs where terms are "free in and out" (FIO)
Hire charge to be paid on completion of journey	Freight to be paid on completion of voyage (before delivery of cargo)

F04a.3 Contracts of affreightment

* In modern shipping parlance, a **contract of affreightment** (often abbreviated to "**COA**") -
  * is essentially a contract to satisfy a long-term need for transport, most often for iron ore and coal in bulk.
  * is an agreement between a charterer and a shipowner, disponent owner or carrier for the carriage of a **specified** (and often large) **quantity of specified goods** between **specified places**, **over a specified** (and usually long) **period** of time, by **vessels of a type and size stipulated by the charterer**, but which are **nominated by the owners**. (In a charter for consecutive voyages, by contrast, the carrying ship is named.) The vessels may be chartered. The goods to be carried and the total period are clearly defined, but the **shipment dates** may be approximate, often giving an even spread of shipments over the period (which may, for example, be 12 months). A stated **minimum quantity** must usually be loaded each voyage, with a "**more-or-less**" **margin** at the option of either the charterers (**MOLCO**) or the owners (**MOLOO**).

- may be based on a standard charter party as the main COA document, with a number of rider clauses added, or on a main COA document (such as BIMCO's VOLCOA form) supplemented by separate voyage charter parties relating to each voyage made under the COA.
- may be used by an operator who has no fleet of his own and who charters ships in for each voyage.
- is the type of contract on which a very large ore carrier or Capesize bulk carrier is likely to be employed under[7].

* In summary:
  - the owners agree to transport an agreed volume of cargo over a specified period;
  - the charterers nominate cargoes and loading dates;
  - the owners nominate suitable vessels.
* **Note**: The term "contract of affreightment" is also commonly used in maritime law textbooks for what (in view of the modern usage of COAs as described above) might be better termed a "**contract of carriage by sea**".

F04b FIXING OF SHIPS ON CHARTER

F04b.1 Shipbrokers

* Ships are normally "**fixed**" on charters arranged between the shipowner and charterer by **shipbrokers** acting as negotiators for the two parties. Shipbrokers include:
  - **owners' brokers**, who find and arrange employment for their principals' ships;
  - **charterers' brokers** (or "chartering brokers") who find ships to carry out their principals' requirements;
  - **tanker brokers**, who arrange oil cargo fixtures in the specialist tanker market;
  - **liner brokers** and liner agents, who find cargoes for liner owners and operators;
  - **coasting brokers**, who work in the short sea market and often combine the functions of owners' and charterers' brokers;
  - **ships' agents**, who are employed by shipowners and charterers to service their vessels' needs in ports; and
  - **sale and purchase brokers**, who buy and sell ships and can, if required, arrange newbuilding contracts for their principals.
* Many shipbrokers are self-employed, while others work in large firms active in several of the above disciplines.
* The **chief stages in the fixing process** include:
  1. Circulation by the charterers' broker of "**cargo orders**", outlining charterers' forthcoming cargo transportation requirements.
  2. Circulation by the owners' broker of "**position lists**" or "tonnage lists", detailing expected "open" dates and positions of available ships.
  3. Study of **market reports** by brokers.
  4. **Negotiations on main terms** between brokers on behalf of their respective principals, with offers and counter-offers by either side; if main terms cannot be resolved, there is little or no point in negotiating further details.
  5. **Negotiations "on subjects"**, e.g. "subject stem", "subject receiver's approval", etc., where the main terms have been agreed, but final agreement is subject to various secondary conditions being agreed.
  6. **Fixture**, i.e. the full and final agreement, with all "subjects" removed[8].
* Following fixture is a "**post-fixture**" or follow-up period during which the broker may undertake various administrative functions on behalf of his principal, such as (in some cases) collection of freight or hire.
* Shipbrokers are remunerated by **commission**, called "**brokerage**", payable by the shipowner to each broker involved in arranging a contract. In voyage or time charters the brokerage payable is stipulated in a **Brokerage Clause** and is normally 1.25% of the shipowner's gross receipts from hire, freight, deadfreight and demurrage, payable to each broker involved. (It is not uncommon to see a total brokerage figure of 3.75% or 5% in a charter party.)
* The **professional body for shipbrokers** world-wide is the London-based **Institute of Chartered Shipbrokers**, whose motto is "Our Word, Our Bond". The Institute sets and monitors professional standards for shipbrokers through annual examinations. Its **TutorShip** correspondence courses enable shipbroking students (including serving mariners) to study for the Institute's annual exams (from which qualified mariners are usually granted some exemptions).
* **Institute of Chartered Shipbrokers address**: 3 St Helen's Place, London EC3A 6EJ. Tel. 020 7628 5559. Fax. 020 7628 5445. TutorShip e-mail: tutorship@ics.org.uk
* **Institute of Chartered Shipbrokers website**: www.ics.org.uk

---

[7] These vessels, which may be on long-term time charters, are unlikely to trade on the "spot market" since they are usually employed in dedicated trades.
[8] In English law there is binding agreement only once this stage is reached, whereas in US law there may be binding agreement once main terms are agreed.

F04b.2 The Baltic Exchange

* **London** is the hub of the international shipbroking community, and many individual brokers and broking firms are members of the **Baltic Exchange**, which is a **self-regulated shipbroking marketplace**. The activities of its members, who are mostly **shipowners**, **cargo interests** and **shipbrokers**, include the **matching of bulk ships and bulk cargoes**, and the **sale and purchase** of ships. Baltic Exchange members undertake to abide by a **strict code of business practice**, enshrined in the famous Baltic motto "**Our Word Our Bond**".
* The **Baltic's membership** includes **shipbrokers** of all types as well as **non-trading individuals** such as maritime lawyers, insurers, financiers, classification societies and consultants who wish to mix with key players in the bulk-shipping market and take advantage of the Baltic's facilities. Many operators in the **dry and wet bulk trades** are members of the Baltic, particularly **international commodity traders** in grain, oils, seeds and fats.
* **Market information** in various forms published by the Baltic Exchange is internationally recognised and serves as "barometers" of the cost of transporting dry and wet cargoes. Brokers working at the Baltic collect market data from a number of major broking houses around the world, from which five **daily indices** are built up and published:
  * Baltic Panamax Index (BPI);
  * Baltic Capesize Index (BCI);
  * Baltic Handymax Index (BHMI);
  * Baltic Tanker Dirty Index;
  * Baltic Tanker Clean Index;

  The indices are built up from specifically defined international bulk routes for the particular trades and ship sizes. The three "dry" indices (BPI, BCI and BHMI) are combined to produce the **Baltic Dry Index**.
* About half of the world's **sale and purchase** of ships is estimated to be dealt with through firms represented at the Baltic Exchange. Altogether, this international business generates around $2½ billion a year in freight commissions which comprise 5% of the UK's total **invisible earnings**. In addition, tens of billions of dollars in **chartering costs** go through London's banking system.
* **Website**: www.balticexchange.co.uk

F04b.3 Chartering abbreviations

The table below, while not exhaustive, includes many terms commonly used by shipbrokers and others involved in ship chartering, mainly to save time and effort in communications. Shipmasters may come across many of the acronyms and abbreviations in documents relating to charters, e.g. in telexed voyage orders and market reports.

Term	Meaning	Term	Meaning
AA	always afloat	GSP	good and safe port
ABT	about	HAT	highest astronomical tide
AG	Arabian Gulf	HSS	heavy grain, sorghums, soyabeans
APS	arrival pilot station	HWOST	high water, ordinary spring tides
B	ballast	IWL	Institute Warranty Limits
B/Ls or Bs/L	bills of lading	K	knots
BB	below bridges; ballast bonus	L	laden
BBB	before breaking bulk	L/C	letter of credit
BENDS	both ends (load and discharge ports)	LAT	lowest astronomical tide
BWAD	brackish water arrival draft	LCL	less than container load
C/P	charter party	Liner terms	carrier arranges/pays for cargo-handling at load and discharge ports as well as carriage
CD	customary despatch	LO/LO	lift-on/lift-off
CFR	cost and freight	LT	long ton (1LT = 2240lb = 1.016MT)
CHOPT	charterers' option	LWOST	low water, ordinary spring tides
CIF	cost, insurance and freight	MHWN	mean high water neaps
COA	contract of affreightment	MHWS	mean high water springs
COMBO	combination port	Min/max	minimum/maximum (i.e. exact quantity)
CONT	Continent	MLWN	mean low water neaps
COP	custom of port	MLWS	mean low water springs
CQD	customary quick despatch	MOL	more or less
CVS	consecutive voyages	MOLCO	more or less at charterers' option
DELY	delivery	MOLOO	more or less at owners' option
DFD	demurrage/free despatch	MT	metric tonne (1 MT = 1000kg = 0.9842LT)
DHD	demurrage/half despatch	NAABSA	not always afloat but safe aground
DLRS	US dollars	Nett terms	cargo-handling is arranged/paid for by charterers or shipper
DOP	dropping outward pilot	NOR	Notice of Readiness
DWAT	deadweight all told	NVOC(C)	non-vessel-owning (common) carrier
DWCC	deadweight cargo capacity	PCT	percent

ECSA	East Coast South America	PPT	prompt (cargo or ship available promptly)
EIU	even if used	RO/RO	roll-on/roll-off
ETA	estimated/expected time of arrival	ROB	remaining on board
ETC	estimated/expected time of commencement/completion	SA	safe anchorage
ETD	estimated/expected time of departure	SATPMSHEX	Saturday afternoons, Sundays & holidays excluded
ETS	estimated/expected time of sailing	SB	safe berth
FAC	fast as can	SC	scale
FAS	free alongside	SCALE LOAD	load rate according to C/P scale
FCL	full container load	SHEX	Sundays and holidays excluded
FDESP	free of despatch	SHINC	Sundays and holidays included
FEAST	Far East	Sous palan	under hook (i.e. barge cargo)
FHEX	Fridays and holidays excepted	SP	safe port
FHINC	Fridays and holidays included	Spot	cargo or ship available immediately
FILO	free in, liner out	Stem	readiness of cargo
FIO	free in and out	SWAD	salt water arrival draft
FIOS	free in, out and stowed	SWL	safe working load
FIOSPT	free in, out and spout-trimmed	T/C	time charter
FIOST	free in, out, stowed and trimmed	TIP	taking inward pilot
FIOT	free in, out and trimmed	USNH	US East Coast north of Cape Hatteras
FIT	free in and trimmed	W/M	weight or measure
FLT	full liner terms	WCCON	whether customs cleared or not
FOB	free on board	WIBON	whether in berth or not
FOQ	free on quay	WIFPON	whether in free pratique or not
FOW	free on wharf	WIPON	whether in port or not
FP	free pratique	WP	weather permitting
FWAD	fresh water arrival draft	WW	weather working
Gross terms	carrier arranges/pays for cargo-handling, but laytime will probably apply	WWReady	when and where ready
GSB	good and safe berth		

F04c CHARTER PARTY FORMS

F04c.1 Nature of a charter party

* A **charter party** (commonly abbreviated to "C/P") -
    - is a document containing the **written terms** of a charter agreement between a shipowner and a charterer, who are usually respectively referred to in the text in the plural, i.e. as "Owners" and "Charterers".
    - defines the **obligations**, **rights** and **liabilities** of the shipowner and charterer.
    - is usually drawn up by the **broker** representing the charterers following negotiation and agreement of terms between both parties.
    - is usually based on a particular edition of a recognised **standard form** (e.g. GENCON, BALTIME, NYPE).
    - is sometimes based on a specified charter party already performed by another vessel at an earlier date, in order to save effort and time in negotiating many of the terms.
    - usually comprises a set of **standard clauses** on a printed form, with additional typed **rider clauses** appended if the standard clauses fail to cover all aspects of the parties' agreement. Where there is a conflict between standard and rider terms, the rider clauses override the standard clauses.
    - may have many **amendments** to the standard clauses, as agreed by the parties. Generally, the more amendments there are, the more scope for legal disputes, and it is preferable to have as few amendments as possible.
    - may be in a modern "boxed" layout, with plain wording of clauses (as with BIMCO-designed forms), or in a more traditional style with (sometimes) rather archaic wording.
    - may contain **annexes** dealing with special arrangements (as with CRUISEVOY, which has five annexes).
    - may have sensitive clauses in an **addendum** and/or **side letter**. Side letters are legally not so important as addenda.
    - should be **signed** by a broker representing each party to the contract, unless their principals sign instead.
    - should ideally be **balanced** so that it does not favour one party to the disadvantage of the other. (Some charter parties, such as SUGAR CHARTER 1999, are sometimes accused of being biased.)
* Numerous **charter party forms** are in use for different trades and purposes. The use of an "off-the-shelf" form which has been carefully drafted, amended and improved over the years to avoid legal pitfalls is generally preferred by brokers and shipping practitioners to creating a totally new document for an individual charter.
* Many forms have more than one **edition**, having been amended and improved over the years. Brokers may still use an older version, however, in preference to a newer version that has not gained their confidence.

* Modern charter party forms drafted by **BIMCO**[9] generally have boxed layouts, whereas older forms are in "conventional" layout. In a BIMCO boxed layout form, **variable information** is contained in boxes in **Part I**, while **standard terms** are contained in printed terms in **Part II**. Legally, the contract is generally contained in the Part I details, and in any other variable details in rider clauses, etc.

F04c.2 Voyage charter party forms

* **Examples of voyage charter party forms** used in various trades are as follows:

Codename	Trade	Remarks
AFRICANPHOS	Moroccan phosphates	Charterers' form.
AMWELSH	Coal	Americanized Welsh coal C/P. Widely used.
ASBATANKVOY	Tanker	American form.
AUSTWHEAT	Australian wheat	Australian Wheat Board form.
BEEPEEVOY	Tanker	BP form, used by many companies.
CHEMTANKVOY	Chemicals	BIMCO form. Boxed layout.
CRUISEVOY	Cruising	BIMCO form for cruise ship charter
C"ORE"7	Iron ore	Full name: Mediterranean Iron Ore C/P.
FERTIVOY	Fertilisers	Unknown origin.
GENCON	General purpose	BIMCO form. 1922, 1976 and 1994 revisions.
GRAINVOY	Grain	BIMCO form.
INTERTANKVOY	Tanker	Intertanko form, used by independent owners.
NORGRAIN	North American grain	American form.
NUBALTWOOD	Timber	Used in Baltic trade.
OREVOY	Iron ore	BIMCO form with boxed layout.
PANSTONE	Stone (UK/Eire and N Continent trade)	BIMCO form last amended 1995 but retaining traditional layout.
SHELLVOY	Tanker	Shell form, used by many companies. Various editions.

F04c.3 Time charter party forms

* **Examples of time charter party forms** in use are as follows:

Codename	Trade	Remarks
ASBATIME	Dry cargo tramp or liner	American form.
BALTIME	Dry cargo tramp or liner	BIMCO form. Boxed layout. Popular in short sea trades.
BEEPEESUPPLYTIME	Offshore service	BP form.
BEEPEETIME	Tanker	Widely used BP form with various versions.
GENTIME 1999	Dry cargo tramp or container	Designed to replace BALTIME 1939 and LINERTIME, and as an alternative to NYPE.
INTERTANKTIME	Tanker	Intertanko form. Used by independent owners.
LINERTIME	Dry cargo liner	BIMCO form. Boxed layout.
NEW YORK PRODUCE EXCHANGE (NYPE)	Dry cargo tramp or liner	Most commonly used time C/P form. 1946 version more popular than 1993 version.
SHELL VESSEL TIME	Offshore service	Shell form. 1986 revision of SHELL SUPPLY.
SHELLTIME	Tanker	Shell form, but widely used. Various versions.
SUPPLYTIME	Offshore supply	BIMCO form.
TEXACOTIME	Tanker	Texaco form. Various versions.

---

[9] The Baltic and International Maritime Council. For notes on **BIMCO**, see C06g.

F05 Contract between shipowner and charterer: voyage charter

F05a VOYAGE CHARTER AGREEMENTS

F05a.1 Voyage charter party clauses

* A **general purpose dry cargo voyage charter party** will usually incorporate clauses covering the **basic provisions** tabulated below.
* The provisions may be expressed in different charter parties by clauses bearing different names, or by numbered clauses with no names.

Name of clause	Matters covered in clause	SBC ref.
Preamble	Identity of parties; identity of vessel; warranty of seaworthiness; present position of vessel; expected date of readiness to load; obligation to proceed to loading port or place; identity of and safety of loading port or place; amount and nature of cargo to be loaded; obligation to proceed to and identity of discharge port or place; obligation to deliver cargo.	F05a.2
Owners' Responsibility	Responsibility of the owners for loss of or damage to goods or delay in delivery of goods; exclusion of owner's liability for loss of or damage to goods or delay in delivery of goods.	F05a.3
Deviation	Liberty of vessel to call at ports in any order; liberty of vessel to tow and assist vessels; liberty of vessel to deviate for purpose of saving life or property or other purposes.	F05a.4
Freight	Rate and amount of payment of freight.	F05a.5
Loading/Discharging Costs	Responsibility for costs of loading and/or discharging of cargo.	F05a.6
Laytime	Duration of laytime allowed; exceptions to laytime; commencement of laytime; time and manner of tendering of notice of readiness.	F05a.7, F05c.1c
Demurrage	Duration of demurrage period allowed; whether demurrage allowed at loading and/or discharge ports.	F05a.8
Lien	Whether the owners are to have a lien on cargo for freight, deadfreight, demurrage and/or damages for detention; whether the charterers are to be responsible for freight and demurrage, etc. incurred at the discharge port.	F05a.9
Bills of Lading	Master's obligation to sign bills of lading.	F05a.10
Laydays and Cancelling	Laydays; cancelling date; conditions under which charterers have option to cancel charter; charterers' obligation to declare intention to exercise option to cancel, if applicable.	F05a.11
General Average	Rules under which any General Average is to be settled; obligation of cargo owners to pay cargo's share of General Average expenses.	F05a.12
Agency	Owner's (or charterer's) obligation to appoint agents at loading and discharge ports.	F05a.13
Brokerage	Amount of brokerage commission due and party or parties to whom payable.	F05a.14
Strikes	Allocation of responsibility for consequences of strikes or lock-outs preventing fulfilment of obligations.	F05a.15
War Risks	Liberty of owner to cancel charter in event of outbreak of war; liberty of master to sail from loading port before completion of loading in event of outbreak of war.	F05a.16
Ice	Liberties of master in event of inaccessibility of, or threat of trapping at, loading and/or discharge ports due to ice.	F05a.17
Clause Paramount	Identity of liability regime applying to bills of lading issued.	F05a.18
New Jason Clause	Protection of owner against US lawsuits where General Average is to be adjusted in accordance with US law.	F05a.19
Both To Blame Collision Clause	Protection of owner against US law in collision cases.	F05a.20
Law and Arbitration	Jurisdiction to which any dispute will be referred; place of any arbitration; appointment of arbitrators.	F05a.21

* **Rider clauses**, as agreed between the parties, will generally be appended to the standard clauses (see F04c.1).

F05a.2 Preamble

* The **Preamble** -
    - identifies the **parties** to the contract (usually referred to as "Owners" and "Charterers").
    - identifies the chartered **vessel**.
    - contains the owners' **warranty of seaworthiness** in respect of the vessel (see F05a.2a).
    - states the **present position** of the vessel, i.e. her position at the time the agreement was made, e.g. "*now trading*", or "*ETA King's Lynn 30th Oct. pm tide/last cargo stone*".
    - states the **expected date of readiness to load** or **ETA** at the loading port.

- contains the obligation for the vessel to **proceed to the loading port or place**, which is usually required to be a "**safe port**" or "**safe berth**" (see F05a.2b).
- specifies the **quantity and nature of the cargo** to be loaded, including any **margin** allowed (e.g. "*5% more or less*"), and the party having the option, if any.
- contains the obligation on the vessel to **proceed to the discharge port or pl**ace.
- contains the obligation to **deliver the cargo** at the discharge port or place.
* **The vessel -**
  - must have the **deadweight cargo capacity** ("DWCC") or **deadweight all told** ("DWAT") required by the charterer[10].
  - must be of the required **dimensions** (e.g. Panamax, Suezmax, etc.) for the charterer's purposes.
  - must have the required number of **holds and hatches**, of the required sizes, for the charterer's purposes.
  - may be required by the charterers to be in a certain **class** (e.g. "*highest class Lloyd's Register*").
  - must, in common law, be **seaworthy** (sometimes described in charter parties as "*tight, staunch and strong, and in every way fitted for the voyage*") when provided for the charterer's use, and at each stage of loading. (Although this is an implied common law obligation and does not have to be stated in writing, many charter parties nevertheless contain an express **warranty of seaworthiness**.)

F05a.2a Warranty of seaworthiness

* Unless a contract of carriage by sea has an express provision concerning seaworthiness, the absolute (common law) obligation, known as the **warranty of seaworthiness**, is implied in the contract.
* In a charter party the absolute warranty of seaworthiness is usually moderated, however, to an undertaking that the shipowner or carrier will only **exercise due diligence** to make the vessel seaworthy before sailing.
* For a shipowner or carrier to exercise **due diligence** he must:
  1. make a reasonable and careful **inspection** and perform **maintenance** of the vessel in accordance with the custom of the trade; and
  2. do this **before the commencement** of the voyage.
* **Exercising due diligence** to ensure that a vessel is seaworthy would therefore mean, for example, ensuring that:
  - class surveys and statutory safety construction, equipment and loadline surveys are carried out and passed in accordance with current requirements (i.e. the vessel is **technically seaworthy**);
  - the **cargo spaces are fit** for the reception and carriage of the cargo and that the cargo is properly loaded and stowed taking into account the expected perils of the voyage (the vessel is "cargoworthy");
  - the vessel is properly **equipped and supplied** for the expected duration of the voyage in terms of sufficient competent crew, navigational equipment and supplies, stores, provisions and spares, bunker fuel, fresh water, etc. ("fittedness for the voyage").

F05a.2b Safe ports and berths

* An important contractual provision in virtually all time and voyage charter parties is that the vessel may be sent only to **safe ports and berths**. This requirement will often be expressed in the preamble to the terms of a modern charter party rather than in a separate clause.
* Charterers usually give an absolute warranty that ports to which they will send the vessel will be "good and safe", but in some charter parties the charterer's warranty is one of "due diligence" only. If charterers breach their warranty, the master has a right to refuse to enter, or refuse to stay at, the port in question.
* **The legal definition of "a safe port"** is contained within the following legal opinion[11]: "A port will not be safe unless, in the relevant period of time the particular ship can reach it, use it and return from it without, in the absence of some abnormal occurrence, being exposed to danger which cannot be avoided by good navigation and seamanship." For **examples of practical conditions which may make a port "unsafe"** within the meaning of this definition, see I01d.1.
* **Requirements for a port to be considered a "safe port"** are as follows:
  1. There must be **safe access** to the port and it must be free from permanent obstruction. However safe a port may be in other respects, it is not "safe" if the vessel cannot reach it without serious risk of damage by ice, etc. A temporary obstruction, e.g. neap tides, does not, however, make a port unsafe.
  2. It must be a port where the vessel **can lie safely afloat** at all states of the tide, unless it is customary and safe to load and/or discharge aground or there is special agreement to do so. Whereas the standard terms may require the vessel to "proceed to the loading port or place stated or as near thereto as she may safely get and lie always afloat", the terms will often be amended to permit a short-sea vessel to lie "**safe aground**".

---

[10] A **Deadweight Certificate**, usually provided by the ship's builder, may be required where the owners guarantee the vessel's deadweight to a charterer.
[11] The opinion was given by Lord Justice Sellers in his 1958 judgement of the "*Eastern City*" case.

3. There must be **adequate facilities for trade**, including a safe shore landing of goods, proper wharves, warehouses and other establishments for dealing with the kind of cargo contemplated.
4. It must be a **politically safe** port, free from any state of war or embargo.
5. The ship, having reached the port (and discharged her cargo), must be **able to leave safely**, e.g. without having to lower or cut her masts to pass under a bridge.

* Unless there is specific agreement to the contrary, the **master is always entitled to refuse to enter** a port which his vessel cannot safely reach (due to lack of sufficient water depth) without first lightening in a roadstead or other port, even if it is a customary method of discharge at the port.
* A **safe berth** must be safe in the same respects as a "safe port". The master's duty is normally to ascertain whether the berth is safe and to refuse to go to an unsafe berth even if ordered to do so. Damage done to the ship or quay at an unsafe berth is usually the shipowner's liability, not the charterer's (although courts have held the reverse).
* **If the charterers order the vessel to an unsafe port or berth**, they will usually be in breach of contract. For notes on the master's **action on being ordered to an unsafe port or berth** see I01d.3.

F05a.3 Owners' Responsibility Clause

- is a BIMCO clause that states the conditions under which the owners **will be responsible** for loss, damage or delay of the goods, to the exclusion of all other causes.
- replaces the traditional form of **Exceptions Clause** that often employs archaic language (see F07a.8).
* Owners will usually accept liability only where the loss, damage or delay has been caused by the improper or negligent stowage of the goods (unless the stowage is performed by shippers or charterers or their stevedores or servants), or by personal want of due diligence on the part of the owners or their manager to make the vessel in all respects seaworthy and to secure that she is properly manned, equipped and supplied, or by the personal act or default of the owners or their manager.

F05a.4 Deviation Clause

- is a standard protecting clause giving the vessel the liberty to call at any port or ports in any order, for any purpose, to sail with or without pilots, to tow and/or assist vessels in all situations, and also to deviate for the purpose of saving life and/or property. See also F07a.5.
* A **P&I Bunker Deviation Clause** is a form of deviation clause recommended by the P&I clubs which allows the vessel to deviate off the contract route in order to load bunker fuel without breaching the contract. Bunkers are often cheapest at ports near oil producing centres, and the shipowners may wish to take advantage of the vessel's proximity to such a port so as to have sufficient bunkers on board for a future voyage (e.g. the ballast voyage following discharge of the present cargo).

F05a.5 Freight Clause

- specifies the **freight rate**, how freight will be calculated, when it must be paid, and the arrangements for payment. Details of bank accounts may be in a separate document annexed to the charter party.
- **"Freight"** -
- is the remuneration payable by the charterers to the owners for the performance of the contract.. It may be called **charter party freight** in the contract.
- is normally payable in **US dollars** in the deep-sea trades, but may be payable in local currency in short-sea trades.
- must be paid, under common law, and in the absence of any term to the contrary, on **delivery** of the cargo to the consignee or his receiver at the agreed destination.
- is normally payable in accordance with the terms of a **Freight Clause** which stipulates the amount of freight, the time for payment and the method of payment.
- is often payable under charter party terms **partially in advance**, e.g. on loading, or on the issue of bills of lading.
- may depend in amount on the **intaken weight** of cargo, or (less commonly) on the outturn weight, the cargo volume, cargo value, or on some other stipulated basis.
- is not payable unless the **entire cargo reaches the agreed destination**, even if not the carrier's fault, e.g. if the voyage is abandoned after a General Average act. (The owners usually protect themselves by insuring against possible **loss of freight**, so that in a case of General Average the loss of freight insurers become a party to the "common maritime adventure").
- is not payable where the owners have breached the contract. When cargo is delivered damaged, however, full freight is normally payable and a separate claim is presented by the cargo owners for the damage.

- if payable in advance, is collected by the agent at the loading port before issue of **bills of lading** marked "FREIGHT PAID" or "FREIGHT PRE-PAID".
- if payable on delivery of the goods, is collected from the consignee or his receiver by the port agent on the **first presentation of an original bill of lading**.
- is not payable on delivery if the goods have lost their "specie", i.e. changed their physical nature.
- may be of the following kinds: ordinary or **charter party freight** (described above); **lumpsum freight**; **bill of lading freight**; **advance** or **pre-paid freight**; pro-rata freight; or **ad valorem freight**.

F05a.5a Bill of lading freight

- is freight calculated on **shipped or intaken weights**, as stated in a bill of lading.
- is used in trades where intaken and outturn weights are likely to differ, e.g. where:
  - oil evaporates during the voyage;
  - there is "clingage";
  - there is sedimentation;
  - logs loaded from the water dry out on the voyage;
  - ice melts on timber after loading;
  - grabs cannot discharge all of a cargo.
- is the usual type of freight stipulated in tanker charter parties.
- may be payable in advance or at destination.
- may be payable, where outstanding, by any endorsee of a bill of lading.

F05a.5b Lumpsum freight

- is a fixed sum payable irrespective of the amount of cargo carried, the owners usually guaranteeing a specified cargo capacity for the charterer's use.
- is useful in "mixed cargo" charters where cargoes are of varying densities.
- is more common in the **tanker trades** than in dry cargo trades.

F05a.5c Advance or pre-paid freight

- is often demanded by carriers of dry cargoes, and is the usual type of freight in the **liner trades**.
- may be the total freight or an agreed proportion of it, payable in advance at the loading port, the balance being payable on delivery of the cargo.
- is deemed to be **earned as the cargo is loaded**.
- is not refundable if the vessel and cargo are lost (albeit that the owners may be liable for damages to the charterer).
- is commonly required where cargo is shipped under a negotiable bill of lading, as buyers of goods covered by a bill of lading often require a "freight paid" bill of lading.
- is not often seen in tanker charter parties, since tanker charterers are usually in a stronger bargaining position than dry cargo charterers, and tanker owners would have problems in storing large quantities of oil when exercising their lien for unpaid freight.

F05a.5d Pro-rata freight

- is payable in common law where only **part of the voyage has been completed**, e.g. when the voyage is abandoned following an outbreak of war or an accident, and the cargo is discharged at an intermediate port, or if the vessel had to leave port because of the onset of ice.
- is not "freight" in the normal sense, but the shipowner's **compensation** for carrying the goods at least part-way to their destination.

F05a.5e *Ad valorem* freight

- is freight charged at a rate stated as a **percentage of the value of a shipment**, usually of high-value goods, e.g. bullion.
- is not normally used in voyage charter parties, generally being confined to **liner shipments**. An *ad valorem* bill of lading is one on which the value of the cargo is recorded and under which the carrier waives his right to limit his liability to the goods owner under the package limitation provisions in the contract, usually in return for the higher *ad valorem* freight.
* P&I clubs do not normally cover owners for liabilities in connection with high-value cargoes, and owners must usually make other insurance arrangements.

F05a.5f Back freight

- is freight paid by a shipper for the **return carriage of goods not delivered** to or not accepted by their receiver or consignee.
- is normally not mentioned in charter party terms.
* If the non-delivery or non-acceptance was the vessel's fault (e.g. due to over-carrying), no back-freight will be payable.

F05a.5g Deadfreight

- is not genuine freight, but owners' **compensation for lost freight**, payable by the charterers on a quantity of cargo short-shipped, i.e. a quantity which he agreed, but failed, to load. E.g., if the charter party agreement was that the charterers would load 60,000 tonnes of wheat, but he loaded only 50,000 tonnes, the shipowner will claim deadfreight on 10,000 tonnes at the agreed rate of freight. (Some shipowners place **deadfreight claim forms** on board, on which the master quantifies the amount short-shipped.)
* For notes on procedure where **charterers cannot provide the agreed cargo quantity**, see F05c.4d.

F05a.5h Worldscale

- is the **code name** for the "**New Worldwide Tanker Nominal Freight Scale**", published by the Worldscale Association (London) Limited and the Worldscale Association (NYC) Inc., which are controlled by panels of leading tanker brokers in London and New York City respectively.
* Because an oil cargo may be bought and sold many times whilst aboard a tanker at sea, the cargo owner requires great flexibility in his choice of discharge options. If tanker fixtures were priced in the same way as dry cargo fixtures the shipowner would have to calculate a different freight rate for each discharge port that the charterers may opt for. Worldscale avoids this problem in that it provides a set of nominal rates designed to provide roughly the same daily income irrespective of the place of discharge.
* **Worldscale is a schedule of nominal tanker freight rates** used as a standard of reference by means of which **rates for all voyages and market levels** in the crude and oil products tanker trades can be readily compared and judged. This is aimed at making the business of fixing tankers simpler, quicker and more flexible.
* Worldscale is based on an **average vessel with average costs earning an average rate**. It works on the basis that, using the **realistic costs of operating an imaginary standard tanker** of "average" size on an "average" 15,000-mile round voyage, the **break-even freight rate** for that ship on that route can be calculated. This "**Worldscale Flat**" rate is calculated in US dollars per metric ton of cargo carried on a standard loaded voyage between a loading port and a discharge port with a ballasted return voyage. The standard vessel is of 75,000 dwt with an average service speed of 14.5 knots and consumption of 55 m.t. of 380 CSt fuel per day while steaming, plus 100m.t. per round voyage for other purposes and an additional 5 m.t. in each port in the voyage. Port time allowed is 4 days for the voyage. The fixed hire element (on the assumption that the ship is time-chartered) is $12,000 per day. Bunker prices are assessed annually by the Worldscale Associations and are based, as are port charges, on the previous year's average. Average exchange rates for the previous September are used. The total of the voyage costs divided by the cargo tonnage will give the Worldscale Flat rate, or "W100" for that voyage.
* From the Worldscale Flat rate for the average voyage, the Associations calculate the rate for **about 60,000 other key tanker routes** and list these "scale rates" daily in a Schedule made available to subscribers[12]. Steaming distance, Suez and Panama Canal transit dues, port charges, bunker price differences between ports and various other factors mean that, in order for the ship to break even, some routes will require a higher freight rate than others. Rates are listed by port of discharge (or ports of discharge in the case of multi-port discharges). For example, for a voyage to Rotterdam and Wilhemshaven from Mina al Fahal (via Suez) the Schedule will list the distance as 12002 miles and may, on a given day, list a Worldscale Flat rate of USD11.08, while for the same voyage via the Cape (21642 miles) it might list USD17.37. These published Worldscale Flat rates are used as a **basis for tanker chartering negotiations** between tanker owners and charterers.
* It is customary in the tanker trades to express market freight levels as a **percentage of the published Worldscale rates**, a method known as "**points of scale**". Thus "Worldscale 100" or "W100" means 100 points of 100% of the published rate - in other words, the published rate itself, or "Worldscale flat". "Worldscale 243" means 243 points **or 243 per cent of the published rate** and "Worldscale 31.5" means 31.5 points or 31.5% of the published rate.
* Economies of scale dictate that, in order to break even on a voyage, a large tanker carrying a large quantity of oil will require a lower freight rate per tonne than a smaller tanker lifting a smaller cargo. A VLCC might therefore be quoted at W41 while a 50,000-tonner may require well over W100 or even more than W200.

---

[12] The annual fee entitles a subscriber to the Schedule, notices of amendments and the right to request rates for any voyage not shown in the Schedule.

* The freight rate actually negotiated in a fixture, using the Worldscale Flat rate as a basis for negotiation, is called the "**Worldscale Freight Rate**". This negotiated rate will depend on the strength of the market and will be quoted in market reports in Worldscale points in the way outlined above.
* An extract from a tanker market report in a shipping journal might, for example, show the following:
  * **Persian Gulf to Singapore** – *Biggar Mariner*, **255,000t, W39.5, July 20. (Lanark Oil)** - and
  * **Libya to Sarroch** – *Symington*, **43,000t, W175, July 6. (ClydePet)**
    - meaning (in the first case) the tanker *Biggar Mariner* has been fixed to the charterers Lanark Oil to load 255,000 tonnes in the Persian Gulf on July 20 for a round voyage to Singapore at a freight rate of 39.5% (or 39 points) of the published Worldscale rate;
    - and (in the second case) the *Symington* has been fixed to the charterers ClydePet to load 43,000 tonnes in Libya on July 6 for a round voyage to Sarroch at a freight rate of 175% (or 175 points) of the published Worldscale rate.

F05a.6 Loading and Discharging Costs Clause

- allocates responsibility for the costs of bringing cargo alongside and loading, stowage, any required trimming, and discharging.
* In the **dry bulk trades** it is normal for the charterers to make arrangements for bringing cargo forward and for payment of all loading and discharging costs, in which case the terms are known as "**free in an out**" (**FIO**).
* Where the owners are responsible for the cargo handling costs, terms are "**liner terms**", sometimes called "**gross terms**".
* Standard terms may contain clauses covering both Liner and FIO arrangements, the inappropriate one to be deleted.
* An agreement may provide for a combination of the above, such as "Free in/Liner out".

F05a.7 Laytime Clause

- states the period of time allowed for loading and for discharging. The clause may provide for **separate laytime** for loading and discharging or for **total laytime**.
- states the conditions under which Notice of Readiness (see F05c.1c) may be tendered.
* For a **definition of laytime** and more detailed notes on the **use of laytime**, see F05c.1.

F05a.8 Demurrage Clause

- states the **maximum period of time allowed on demurrage** and the **rate** at which demurrage will be calculated.
* For a **definition of demurrage** and more detailed notes on demurrage, see F05c.2.
* The clause is often combined with a provision covering payment of despatch money (see F05c.3).

F05a.9 Lien Clause

- gives owners a lien on the cargo for specified debts, which generally include freight but may also include demurrage, deadfreight and damages for detention (or any of these).
* For notes on the **carrier's lien on cargo**, see F05e.2. For notes on liens in general, see B03g.

F05a.10 Bills of Lading Clause

- requires the master or owner's agent to sign bills of lading, sometimes "*at such rate of freight as presented, without prejudice to this charter party*".
- may require the owners to give agents written authority to sign bills of lading.
* For notes on **bills of lading**, see F05b.

F05a.11 Cancelling Clause

- gives the charterers an **option to cancel the charter party** if the vessel is not ready to load on the cancelling date indicated in the charter party.

- may contain an **obligation on owners to inform the charterers of any delay** to the ship's arrival, and an **obligation on the charterers to declare whether he will exercise this option** or not (which could save the owners a considerable amount of steaming uselessly towards a port where the ship is no longer required). The master of a delayed ship should consult his owners and inspect the charter party for any such clause.

F05a.12 General Average Clause

- identifies the **Rules** under which any General Average will be settled, e.g. "*York-Antwerp Rules 1994 and any subsequent modification thereof*".
- states the **obligation of cargo owners to pay cargo's share** of General Average expenses, even where these are necessitated through neglect or default of the owners' servants.
- may be combined with the **New Jason Clause**, which will apply if General Average is to be adjusted in accordance with US law.

F05a.13 Agency Clause

* Unless there is an agreement to the contrary, port agents are normally selected, appointed and have their fees paid by the shipowner. Where the charter party terms are **free in and out** (f.i.o.), the charterers are responsible for loading and discharge costs, and he will often reserve the right to nominate port agents at "both ends", i.e. at loading and discharge ports. In such cases the "charterer's agent" should not neglect the ship's (i.e. owner's) business in favour of the charterer's business, even though there may be a long-standing relationship between agent and charterer and the agent may hesitate to take any action that may prejudice this relationship.
* Where such a conflict of interest cannot otherwise be resolved, the shipowner may appoint a **protecting agent** (sometimes called a **husbandry agent**) to protect his own interests, although this will mean paying two agency fees.
* For notes on the **appointment and duties of a ship's agent**, see I01h.

F05a.14 Brokerage Clause

- specifies the amount of any **brokerage commission** due, and the party to whom it is payable.
* For additional notes on **brokerage** and **Brokerage Clauses**, see F04b.1.

F05a.15 Strikes Clause

- allocates responsibility for the consequences of workers' stoppages that prevent fulfilment of the parties' obligations under the charter party.
* Different strikes clauses feature in different charter party forms, e.g. the General Strike Clause and Centrocon Strikes Clause. Some clauses refer only to strikes, some to strikes and lock-outs, and others including all forms of industrial action.

F05a.16 War Risks Clause

- sets out the rights of the owners and the vessel's master should the vessel find herself in a war zone.
* Various forms of War Risks Clause are in existence, the best known of which is probably "Voywar". "Voywar 1950" is in the standard terms of the GENCON 1976 charter party, while "Voywar 1993" is in the GENCON 1994 form.

F05a.17 Ice Clause

- should be included in the charter party terms where there is any possibility of the vessel being sent to a port which is ice-bound on her arrival, or where the onset of ice may cause the master to decide to leave the port before cargo operations are complete. Some charter parties, e.g. OREVOY, are notorious, however, for the absence of an ice clause.
* BIMCO recommends insertion of a suitable ice clause in charter parties and bills of lading to protect the owners' interests if a vessel is to trade to an ice-affected area.

* Several versions of Ice Clause exist, each setting out the master's and owners' rights in the circumstances. In the owners' interests, the preferred clauses are "Nordice 1947" and the "General Ice Clause".
* Any **bill of lading** issued under the terms of a charter party should include the **same ice clause** as in the charter party.

F05a.18 Clause Paramount

* A **Clause Paramount** (sometimes named "General Paramount Clause") incorporates into the contract of carriage one of three international conventions setting out minimum terms and conditions out of which the carrier cannot contract, i.e. the **Hague Rules**, the **Hague-Visby Rules** or the **Hamburg Rules**. It is inserted in any charter party under which a **bill of lading** is required to be issued, and is also found in various forms in liner and charter party bills of lading.
* Most maritime States have incorporated one or other of the three conventions into their national law. (The Hague-Visby Rules are the Schedule to the UK's Carriage of Goods by Sea Act 1971.) In such cases the relevant rules are usually automatically incorporated in contracts for carriage from that country (see F07c).
* Where the sea carriage is from a country which compulsorily applies none of the three conventions, the parties to the contract may still agree to be bound voluntarily by the rules of one of them so as to simplify the resolution of disputes; in this case the contract should have a Clause Paramount to identify the applicable rules.
* An example of a simple Clause Paramount is: *"The Hague Rules as Amended by the Brussels Protocol 1968 shall apply to this Charter party and to any Bills of Lading issued hereunder. The Charterers shall procure that all Bills of Lading issued under this Charter party shall contain a clause to include these rules."*

F05a.19 New Jason Clause (or Amended Jason Clause)

- is required to protect owners against the possibility of **US lawsuits**.
* Under US common law, a shipowner cannot claim General Average contributions from cargo where there has been faulty navigation or management of the ship. The owners will therefore seek to exonerate himself from liability for loss from these causes. However, the Harter Act 1893 made it illegal to insert any clause in a bill of lading exonerating the ship from liability for loss caused through negligence, improper stowage, etc. Even so, a clause was commonly inserted in bills of lading giving owners the right to claim General Average contributions from cargo.
* Validity of the clause was tested in a 1904 court case concerning the s.s. *Jason*, and in 1911 after lengthy litigation, the clause's validity was upheld by the court. It has since been extended to include salvage, and is now called the New (or Amended) Jason Clause and commonly inserted in bills of lading and charter parties.

F05a.20 Both to Blame Collision Clause

* Under the Hague and Hague-Visby Rules **collision**, as a "peril of the sea", is an excepted peril, allowing the carrier to avoid cargo loss or damage claims arising out of a collision with another ship. Normally an owner of collision-damaged cargo must therefore claim on his cargo insurance policy.
* Under the law of the USA and certain other countries which have not ratified the Collision Convention 1910, a merchant whose cargo has been damaged in a collision may claim the full amount against the owners of the non-carrying ship and thereby circumvent the Hague or Hague-Visby Rules. The non-carrying ship's owners may then recover from the owners of the carrying ship a proportion of the claim equivalent to their percentage of the blame for the collision. In collision cases where US law is applied, the defence of "excepted peril" is lost.
* The **Both to Blame Collision Clause** is designed to enable a carrier to preserve the collision defence and get round the US law. Under the clause, the cargo owner agrees to indemnify the carrying ship against any liability to the non-carrying ship in the event of collision.
* Validity of the clause was tested in the US Supreme Court in 1952 in a case involving a bill of lading, but was held to be invalid. There is a possibility that in the future another court may decide that the clause is valid when included in a bill of lading issued under a charter party containing the same clause. It is therefore usually still included in bills of lading and some charter parties on the advice of P&I clubs.
* **Example**: Ships A and B collide in American waters. Ship A is the cargo-carrying ship, ship B the non-carrying ship. Ship A is held by a US court to be 60% to blame for the collision, and ship B 40% to blame. Shipper A loses $1000 worth of cargo damaged on ship A, but cannot claim against the owners, who are protected by their bill of lading terms (incorporating the Hague-Visby Rules). Shipper S is allowed to claim the entire $1000 from the owners of the non-carrying ship B. But Ship B is only 40% to blame, so her owners can claim $600 back from the owners of

ship A. The net effect is that the owners of ship A, while in no way contractually liable to shipper S, must pay 60% of S's loss.

F05a.21 Law and Arbitration Clause

- identifies the **law** or jurisdiction which is to govern the agreement e.g. "English law". (English civil courts such as the Commercial Court will hear disputes between two non-British parties where their agreement provided for dispute resolution in England.)
- may contain paragraphs providing for a **choice of jurisdictions**, e.g. US law or English law.
- provides that any disputes arising from the charter or bill of lading issued under it will be referred to **arbitration** (rather than to litigation).
- may contain rules for the appointment of arbitrators.
* For notes on **arbitration**, see B03i.1.

F05b THE PRELIMINARY VOYAGE, LAYDAYS AND CANCELLING DATE

F05b.1 Laydays and the cancelling date

* **Laydays** -
    - refers to a period of specified days (e.g. "Jan 8/15") during which owners must present the vessel for loading.
    - should not be confused with *laytime*, which is the period allowed to the charterers for loading and/or discharging without payment additional to the freight. (Some textbooks confuse the two terms.)
* For notes on laydays under time charters, see F06b.2.
* The **cancelling date** -
    - is the **final layday** and the date beyond which, if the chartered vessel has not been presented for loading, the charterers may reject her and cancel the charter.
    - will usually be found in a **Cancelling Clause**, which provides that the charterers will not be entitled to cancel the charter before the stated cancelling date, even when it is obvious that the vessel cannot arrive at the loading port by this date.
* Together, **laydays/cancelling** or, as it is often called, the **"laycan"** is the period within which the vessel must be presented at the agreed port or place. If the vessel arrives before the first day of the period, the charterers do not have to accept her until commencement of the agreed laydays. If she arrives after the final layday, the charterers are entitled to reject the vessel and cancel the charter.
* The charterers cannot be made to declare whether they intend to cancel or not before the vessel arrives at the loading port. Even after the cancelling date has passed, owners can still not compel the charterers to declare whether or not they will load the vessel (and in practice the charterers will often stay silent, hoping to make a new contract with owners). To avoid delay to the vessel in awaiting the charterer's decision on cancellation, some charter parties have an extension to the Cancelling Clause compelling the charterers to declare within a specified time whether or not they elect to cancel after being informed of the vessel's late arrival.
* In charter parties and related documents the laycan will usually be written as (for example) "10/20 May", meaning 10 May is the **first layday** while 20 May is the **cancelling date**.

F05b.2 Preliminary voyage to the loading port

* When a voyage charter party is signed, the vessel is usually stated to be at a certain place or position, or at sea. If the charter party usually specifies an ETA or a laydays/cancelling range (which is usually the case), the vessel is obliged to proceed from that place or position no later than the date on which it would normally be necessary to sail in order to reach the load port on or about the estimated date of arrival.
* Where the charter party requires the vessel to "....proceed with all convenient speed...." to the loading port or place, she must proceed with **all reasonable speed**.
* Provided the owners despatches the vessel on this **"preliminary voyage"** at the appropriate time, they will be protected by the Exceptions Clause or Owners' Responsibility Clause in the charter party in the event that the vessel is unable, due to an excepted peril, to reach the loading port by the cancelling date.
* If, however, the vessel does not depart at the appropriate time, the owners will be liable for the late arrival even though the delay was due to an excepted peril, i.e. one named in the Exceptions Clause.

* If the owners use time in hand before the stipulated loading date for an intermediate charter, and the vessel is late as a result, they will not be protected by an Exceptions Clause or Owners' Responsibility Clause and will be in breach of contract.
* For notes on **procedure when delayed on a preliminary voyage**, see H06f.1.

F05c AT THE LOADING PORT

For notes on other business in port, see Section I - In Port

F05c.1 Laytime

- is **defined** in Voyage Charter party Laytime Interpretation Rules 1993 (see F05f.2) as "the period of time agreed between the parties during which the owners will make and keep the vessel available for loading or discharging without payment additional to the freight". The words "*without payment additional to the freight*" are important.
- is **time allowed to the charterers for cargo operations without additional payment**.
- should, in the interests of the owners, commence as soon as practicable.
- may be **separate** for load and discharge ports, or **reversible** (or **"all purposes"**); the master should check the charter party.
- may be of **three types** with respect to the method of determining the duration:
  • **definite** laytime;
  • **calculable** laytime; or
  • **indefinite** laytime.
- if **definite** will be stated in the charter party as a specified period of time, e.g. "6 (six) days...." or ".....48 running hours". In the oil tanker trades, 72 running hours is the industry norm.
- if **calculable** must be determined by making a computation from information in the charter party, e.g. where a cargo weighing 20,000 tons is to be loaded at a rate of 10,000 tons per day, the laytime will be 2.00 days.
- if **indefinite** the charter party may state that the cargo is to be loaded with **"customary despatch"** or **"customary quick despatch"** or **"as fast as the vessel can receive"**.
- can only start to count against the charterers after **three conditions** have been fulfilled:
  1. the vessel has become an **"arrived ship"** within the terms of the charter party;
  2. the vessel is **in all respects ready** to load/discharge; and
  3. **notice of readiness** has been served on the charterers or their agent (or, in a few cases, such as under the SHELLVOY 4 charter party, has been *received* by the charterers or their agent) in accordance with the charter party.
- normally runs until completion of loading (or discharging). However, some charter parties provide that if, after completion of loading, there is a delay of one hour or more for the charterer's purposes (e.g. testing of samples, preparation of documentation), time will be deemed to run until termination of the delay.
* Masters should obtain from their owners or managers a copy of **Voyage Charter party Laytime Interpretation Rules 1993**, which explain all the usual terms associated with the calculation of laytime, demurrage and despatch.

F05c.1a "Arrived ship"

* To determine whether the vessel has become an **"arrived ship"** within the charter party terms the master will need to know whether the charter party is a **"port charter party"** or a **"berth charter party"**. Which of the parties bears the **risk of delay** following arrival of the vessel will depend on which of the two types the charter party is.
* The **agreed voyage** is defined by the **places** named in the charter party for loading and discharging. These will either be **ports** (e.g. ".....shall proceed to Rotterdam, and there load....") or **berths** (e.g. ".....shall proceed to one safe berth Rotterdam (Vaalhaven), and there load.....").
* If a **port** is defined as the place for loading (e.g. "Rotterdam"), without stipulating a particular berth, the charter party is a **port charter party**.
* The **characteristics of a port charter party** are:
  • the contractual destination is a **named port** (as opposed to a named berth within a port);
  • in order to qualify as having **arrived** at the named port and therefore be entitled to give notice of readiness to load (or discharge) the following two conditions must be satisfied:
    1. if the vessel cannot immediately proceed to a berth, she has reached a **position within the port where waiting ships usually lie**; and
    2. she is at the **immediate and effective disposal of the charterer**.
* It is not necessary for the vessel to be on her loading berth to be an "arrived ship" under a port charter party. All delays in berthing will be for the charterer's account, and this is the more favourable charter party for owners.

* **Examples of port charter parties** are ASBATANKVOY, EXXONVOY and BEEPEEVOY.
* **If a particular berth is defined** as the loading place, the charter party is a "**berth charter party**".
* The **characteristics of a berth charter party** are:
  * the contractual destination is a berth designated by the charterers within a named port;
  * in order to qualify as an arrived ship, and therefore be entitled to give notice of readiness to load (or discharge) the vessel must have reached the berth and be ready to begin to load (or discharge).
* An example of a **berth charter party** is MULTIFORM.
* To protect themselves, and convert a berth charter party into a port charter party, the owners will often:
  - insert a "**Waiting for Berth**" **clause** (e.g. BIMCO's recommended "Waitberth" clause); or
  - insert a **protecting phrase** in the Laytime Clause to make it clear that time can count as laytime once the vessel is at the customary waiting place. These phrases include "whether in berth or not", "whether in port or not", "whether customs cleared or not" and "whether in free pratique or not", and may be inserted in full or as abbreviations as follows:

Abbreviation	Meaning
w.i.p.o.n. or WIPON	whether in port or not
w.i.b.o.n. or WIBON	whether in berth or not
w.c.c.o.n. or WCCON	whether customs cleared or not
w.i.f.p.o.n. or WIFPON	whether in free pratique or not

F05c.1b "In all respects ready to load"

- means the vessel is **seaworthy and in every way fit** to carry the particular cargo on the voyage contemplated by the charterer. The vessel must be **fully at the charterer's disposal**, i.e. with derricks or cranes ready for operation, holds or tanks cleaned, prepared and surveyed, free pratique and customs clearance granted, etc. - unless the charter party allows otherwise, which it may do by the inclusion of a protecting phrase as outlined above.
* At common law the duty to provide a seaworthy ship on presentation was **absolute**, i.e. no exceptions were allowed. However, most modern charter party forms have reduced the absolute obligation to a duty of "**exercising due diligence**", i.e. doing everything which a prudent shipowner can reasonably do to make the vessel seaworthy without actually guaranteeing her seaworthiness.

F05c.1c Notice of readiness

- is a notice to the charterer, shipper, receiver or other person **as required by the charter party** that the vessel has arrived at the port or berth, as the case may be, and is **ready to load or discharge**.
- may be (and is often) given by the **ship's agent** on the master's behalf. (In many cases the Notice of Readiness is sent by the ship's agent to an agent of the charterer.)
- must be given before **laytime** can commence.
- must be given **within the "laycan" period**.
- must be given in accordance with the procedure in the **Notice Clause** or **Laytime Clause** in the charter party.
- is often required to be given during **office hours** from Monday to Saturday.
- need only be given **at the first of two or more load ports**, unless the charter party provides otherwise.
- may (in common law) be oral, but for practical purposes (and because nearly all charter parties require it) should be given **in writing**. Notice of Readiness may be tendered by delivery of a printed form or letter, or by telex, fax or cable, unless the charter party provides otherwise. Charterers', owners' and agents' Notice of Readiness forms are often pre-printed for masters to complete, but where necessary the master should write his own notice. (See example below.)
- must be addressed **to the charterers or their agent** (although delivery may be made through the owners' agent).
- should be sent **in duplicate** with a request that the second copy, with the time and date of acceptance completed, should be returned for the master's retention.
* If receipt of Notice of Readiness is not acknowledged on the first day notice is tendered, **daily attempts** to have it accepted should be made.
* The charter party will normally state that laytime will commence a certain number of hours after Notice of Readiness is given or accepted; the waiting period is usually termed "notice time" or "turn time". If such a period is not specified, laytime will commence as soon as Notice of Readiness is given.
* It is important to the shipowner or time charterer that Notice of Readiness is tendered **as soon as the possible**. A few minutes' delay in tendering on a Saturday morning could mean that laytime will not commence until Tuesday morning, even though cargo work starts earlier.

* A Court of Appeal decision[13] in 2002 established that under a voyage charterparty which requires a Notice of Readiness (NOR) to be served, laytime can commence even when no **valid notice** has been served, where the following all apply:
  1. a NOR in the required form is served on charterers or receivers prior to the vessel's arrival;
  2. the vessel subsequently arrives and is, or is expected to be, ready to discharge, to the knowledge of the charterers; and
  3. discharge commences to the order of the charterers or receivers without either having given any indication of rejection or reservation about the NOR already served, or any indication that a further NOR is required before laytime commences.

  In these circumstances, charterers can be deemed to have waived their right to rely on the invalidity of the original NOR as from the time of commencement of cargo operations, and laytime will commence in accordance with the charterparty as if a valid NOR had been served at that moment.

* An **example** of a Notice of Readiness is as follows:

```
                          NOTICE OF READINESS
                                           m.v. "Hudson Bay"
                                           At Rotterdam
                                           15th September 2003

         Messrs. EuroNed Transport BV
         P.O. Box 1493
         Rotterdam

         Dear Sirs

         Please be advised that the above-named vessel, under my command, arrived within
         Rotterdam port limits at 0625 hours Local Time on 15th September 2003 and is now in
         every respect ready to commence discharge in accordance with all terms, conditions and
         exceptions
         as per the charter party dated Hamburg, 17th July 2003.

         Cargo: 149,252 longtons iron ore.

         Kindly sign and return the enclosed copy, acknowledging receipt
         of this notice of readiness.

         Yours faithfully
         (Signed)
         John McNab
         Master

         Notice tendered at 0900 hours Local Time on 15th September 2003.
         Notice received at .... hours Local Time on ....................
         ........................for EuroNed Transport BV.
```

F05c.2 Demurrage

* If cargo operations are completed after expiry of the laytime, there is a breach of contract for which the charterers would be technically liable for damages. Owners and charterers will often find themselves in this situation, and to avoid the expense and unpleasantness of legal proceedings, liquidated damages, termed **demurrage**, normally become payable by the charterers to the owners for each day, or part of a day, that the ship is detained beyond the time of expiry of laytime.

* **Demurrage is defined** in the Voyage Charter Party Laytime Interpretation Rules 1993 as "an agreed amount payable to the owners in respect of delay to the vessel beyond the laytime, for which the owners are not responsible. Demurrage shall not be subject to laytime exceptions."

* Demurrage will only be payable if provided for in a clause in the charter party, e.g. a **Demurrage Clause** or **Demurrage/Despatch Money Clause**. The **demurrage rate**, which is normally quoted in US Dollars, will normally be a daily rate that will at least cover the owners' costs of keeping the ship in the port.

* Demurrage is normally paid **per running day**, i.e. without exclusion of any Sundays, holidays, or bad weather, strikes, etc., occurring during the detention period - hence the well-known expression **"once on demurrage, always on demurrage"**.

* Some charter parties, e.g. GENCON, provide for a specified **maximum number of days** allowed on demurrage, which if exceeded will allow the shipowner to claim for his actual losses caused by the delay, i.e. **damages for**

---

[13] Flacker Shipping Ltd v. Glencore Grain Ltd *(The "Happy Day")*

detention, which, if awarded by an arbitrator or court, will normally be more punitive than demurrage. An owner would have a claim for damages for detention where, for example, an extended delay in port on one charter prevented him from taking up a second charter on which his ship had been fixed on the assumption that she would be available.

F05c.3 Despatch

* If cargo operations are completed before expiry of the laytime, a monetary reward, termed **despatch** or **despatch money**, is normally payable by the owners to the charterer.
* **Despatch money** or **despatch** is defined as an agreed amount payable by the owners if the vessel completes loading or discharging before the laytime has expired.
* Despatch will **only be payable** if provided for in a charter party clause (e.g. a **Demurrage/Despatch Money Clause**). Some charterparties stipulate "free dispatch", meaning that the owners will not pay any dispatch money if time is saved.
* The **daily despatch rate**, which is normally quoted in US Dollars, is traditionally **half the agreed demurrage rate**, the reasoning being that while early completion of cargo may give the owners an opportunity to complete the voyage early and fix the vessel on another charter, the charterers may also benefit from early berthing of the next due vessel.
* If despatch is payable **for all time saved**, the laytime exclusions (for weather stoppages, etc.) are not taken into account after the completion of cargo. If despatch is payable only for **working time saved**, laytime exclusions must be taken into account. For definitions of these despatch variations in Voyage Charter Party Laytime Interpretation Rules, see F05f.2.

F05c.4 Charter-related and other problems at the loading port

F05c.4a Tankers' slops

* Most tanker charter parties provide that **slops** will be dealt with as the charterers direct. In practice the charterers have **two options**:
  1. to **load on top**, which is only practicable if the slops are compatible with the loaded cargo. The charterers will pay freight on the slops but are entitled to demand that they are discharged with the cargo at the destination port. The charterers effectively buy the slops at the cost of the freight; or
  2. to **keep the slops segregated from the loaded cargo**, either by arranging for slops to be discharged to shore before loading, or keeping slops on board, but segregated, and paying **freight** on them plus the **deadfreight** incurred as a result of a full cargo no longer being carried to the discharge port.
* If the charter party gives the charterers the option of dealing with slops as they decide, but the vessel arrives at the loading port with **more slops than can be carried (segregated) along with the full contemplated cargo**, the owners may be in **breach of contract**.
* For notes on the **MS (Port Waste Reception Facilities) Regulations 1997**, which require harbour and terminal operators in the UK to provide adequate reception facilities, see I06c.1.
* For notes on procedure where there is any **inadequacy of waste reception facilities**, see I06c.3.

F05c.4b If charterers repeatedly reject the vessel on grounds of unclean holds or tanks

* Most charter parties have clauses dealing with cleaning of compartments before loading. Some charter parties give the master sole authority to decide when the vessel is sufficiently clean for loading to commence, while others require the vessel to be cleaned "to the satisfaction of the Charterer's Inspector", which may lead to the charterers repeatedly rejecting the vessel and asking for more cleaning to be done before acceptance. The charterers must be able to show that such rejections and requests were **reasonable**.
* Unless the charter party provides otherwise, the **master** has final responsibility for deciding when cargo compartments are sufficiently clean for loading. If personally satisfied that compartments are clean enough for the intended cargo, the master should:
  * act reasonably;
  * bear in mind that he is acting in the interests of both the owners and the charterer;
  * politely and firmly point out to the surveyor that the responsibility outlined above is the master's;
  * point out that the cost of any further cleaning will be for the charterer's account; and
  * note protest.

* If ordered to leave the loading berth before acceptance, the master should not agree to do so unless so instructed by the owners/disponent owners, or unless there is a clause in the charter party giving the charterers the right to order the vessel off the berth, in which case the order should come from the charterers to the master via the owners.

F05c.4c If charterers cannot provide a cargo on arrival

* The master should **tender notice of readiness** in accordance with the charter party, and **inform the shipowner**.
* The charterers are not in breach of contract until the agreed laytime has expired.
* The vessel should **"sit out" the laytime**, the period of which should be computed from the charter party. If no cargo has been provided by the time of expiry of laytime, the master should **note protest**, stating that the owners' obligations under the charter party have been met, and **await instructions**.

F05c.4d If charterers cannot provide the agreed cargo quantity

* It is customary in the bulk trades for the charter party to allow for the actual weight intaken to be **more or less** (**MOL**) than the proposed weight by a margin of perhaps 10%, in either the charterer's option (**MOLCO**) or the owners' option (**MOLOO**).
* If the weight loaded is less than the agreed margin, the charterers will be in breach of contract and liable for **deadfreight**. The owners will be entitled to take reasonable steps to find other cargo to fill the unused space.
* In such a case the master should send a **letter of protest to the charterer**, **contact the owners**, and **note protest**. A **deadfreight claim form** may have to completed by the master, for submission to the charterer.

F05d ON THE LOADED (OR "CHARTERED") VOYAGE

* The vessel must normally proceed to the destination port or place with **"due despatch"** (but sometimes **"utmost despatch"**) and always **without deviation** from the contracted voyage, which includes ports of loading and discharge (and their rotation), dates of loading and discharge where stipulated, voyage route and other agreed elements.
* **If the vessel deviates** in any respect (e.g. by discharging at a port other than that originally agreed, unless with the charterer's consent, or in the wrong rotation of ports) there is a serious breach of contract and the owners will not be able to rely on any of the exceptions in the contract. The owners will be reduced to the status of **"common carrier"** and will be have no protection against liability for loss of or damage to the goods carried other than the "common law exceptions" (see F07a.1a). The owners would also have to prove that the loss/damage would inevitably have occurred even if the contract had not been breached; this applies whether the loss/damage occurred before, during or after the deviation. For further notes on **deviation**, see F07a.5.

F05e AT THE DISCHARGE PORT

F05e.1 Outturn problems

* Problems may arise over the **outturn** of cargo, i.e. discrepancies between the loaded (or "bill of lading") quantity and the discharged quantity. The carrier is obliged to deliver the cargo in the same quantity and condition as when loaded and has a *prima facie* case to answer if any loss or damage occurs during the voyage. The carrier must then be able to show that he is exempt from liability under one or more of the **exceptions** in the contract of carriage. If he cannot prove that the loss/damage was covered by one of the exceptions in the contract, he will be liable for the loss/damage.
* If the carrier can prove exemption from liability, however, the cost of the loss/damage will lie with the **party bearing the risk** in the cargo (e.g. the consignee), subject to possible **recovery** from the seller or the cargo insurer. In order to provide the necessary proof, the carrier will require full **documentary evidence** from the ship.

F05e.2 Carrier's lien on cargo

* In common law, a carrier may exercise a **possessory lien** on any part of the cargo in respect of which **freight** is owing at the destination, and also for money which has been spent in **protecting the cargo** (e.g. where reefer goods have been warehoused by the shipowner while a damaged reefer vessel has been drydocked). A common law lien is not allowed on unpaid deadfreight or demurrage. However, carriers often insist on the insertion in the contract of carriage of a **Lien Clause** giving themselves a **contractual lien** on the cargo for deadfreight and demurrage, and sometimes also for damages for detention. A contractual lien for anything other than freight must be clearly **expressed** in the contract terms.

* The carrier's lien is exercised by the shipowner's port agent or by the master as agent of the shipowner; it is **not the master's lien**.
* Once **delivery** of the goods is made, the lien is lost. (For this reason most dry cargo charter party forms require freight to be paid on or at some time before delivery.)
* To preserve his lien, the carrier must retain **actual or constructive possession** of the goods on which freight is due. The cargo on which the lien is exercised should therefore be discharged into a warehouse under the exclusive control of the carrier's agent who should be given instructions to release the goods only after surrender of an original bill of lading and payment of freight.
* If freight is still not paid after a certain period of time, local law may allow the goods to then be **sold** to pay freight, storage charges, customs duty, etc.
* Many bills of lading have a clause (such as a "London Clause") giving the master the right to discharge cargo immediately on arrival and without notice to receivers.
* For notes on the carrier's possessory lien for **General Average contributions**, see I02i.3.

F05e.2a Cesser and Lien Clause

* Where the charterers are not the owners of the goods but is acting only as an agent or broker for the loading of another party's goods, he will probably be anxious to ensure that his liability for the cargo ceases once it is loaded. This is usually expressed in a **Cesser Clause** stating that "...charterers' liability will cease on shipment of cargo and payment of freight, deadfreight and demurrage", i.e. sums incurred at the loading port. The shipowner, however, will not want to find himself without a remedy for any breach of contract or damage done to his vessel after the charterer's liability has ceased, and will want legal recourse against another party, who will usually be the receiver of the goods. Therefore, if a **Cesser Clause** is incorporated in the charter party, a **Lien Clause** will also be included giving the owners the right to retain possession of the goods at the discharge port until outstanding debts are paid. The two clauses are often combined in a **Cesser and Lien Clause**. The relief given to the charterers from their obligations only operates to the extent that outstanding sums can be recovered at the discharge port. The owners must proceed against the receiver first, but the charterers will remain liable for sums which cannot be recovered from the receiver.

F05e.2 Pumping Clause

* Tanker charter parties often contain a clause under which the owner warrants that the vessel will discharge her full cargo within 24 hours, or will maintain a specified manifold pressure (e.g. 188 psi), provided that the shore facility is capable of receiving at the stated rate.
* The clause further provides that if the vessel fails to comply with the stated warranty, the charterer will have the right to order the vessel to be withdrawn from the berth at the owner's time and expense until such time as the berth again becomes available for discharging the balance of cargo remaining on board.

F05e.3 Cargo Retention Clause

* Tanker charter parties often contain a clause making the owner bear the risks of any difference between the cargo quantity stated in the bill of lading and the actual quantity discharged, where less.
* Such a clause will usually provide that if any cargo remains onboard on completion of discharge, the charterer will have the right to deduct from freight an amount equal to the value of the cargo alleged to remain on board plus the amount of freight due on that quantity of cargo, provided that the volume of cargo remaining onboard is "pumpable" as determined by an independent surveyor. The meaning of the word "pumpable" has been the subject of numerous legal disputes.

F05e.4 If the consignee fails to take delivery of cargo

* When market conditions are poor, a consignee faced with having to take delivery of goods damaged during a voyage may prefer to **reject the goods** on the grounds that the damage is so extensive that it amounts to a total loss. However, whether his goods are damaged or not, it is the consignee's duty to:
  * take delivery of his goods;

- mitigate his loss; and
- make his claim against the carrier.
* The consignee should be persuaded by the agent to take delivery for these reasons.

F05f LAYTIME CALCULATIONS

F05f.1 Purpose, stages in calculations, etc.

* The purpose of laytime calculations is to determine whether on completion of loading or discharge operations despatch is payable to the charterers or demurrage is due to the owners.
* The port agent is normally responsible for calculating the sum due and rendering accounts, but the master should also keep a tally of laytime used as he may be required to confirm the agent's figures. The master should also be aware, at any given moment, of whether laytime has commenced, is still running, is interrupted or has expired.
* Laytime calculations are recorded on a **laytime statement**.
* There are seven stages in a laytime calculation:
    1. **Read** relevant clauses in the charter party.
    2. Obtain **Statement of Facts** from agent.
    3. Determine **duration** of laytime allowed.
    4. Establish time of **commencement** of laytime.
    5. Allow for **interruptions** to laytime as per the charter party.
    6. Establish time of **expiry** of laytime.
    7. **Calculate** despatch or demurrage payable.
* The **Statement of Facts** is an extract from the port operations log kept by the charterer's agent, and contains times of all relevant events, including:
    - arrival of ship;
    - tendering of Notice of Readiness;
    - commencement of laytime;
    - commencement of cargo operations;
    - periods of suspension of laytime, with reason in each case (so that risk of stoppage can be apportioned);
    - termination of cargo operations;
    - termination of laytime.
* The Statement of Facts should be approved by all parties involved (master, stevedore, agent, etc.), and will normally be presented by the agent to the master for his signature and return; the master should retain a copy. It is important before signing to compare the times stated with those recorded on board the ship, since the charterer's agent may have obtained inaccurate times from his terminal supervisor, or may, for example, have recorded a period of rain in the vicinity of his office that did not affect the ship for the same period. For a ship on a demurrage rate of USD24,000 per day, 6 minutes of time on demurrage is worth USD100; it is therefore important that all times are accurately recorded.
* The Statement of Facts is used by the agent in drafting up the Laytime Statement, from which any amount of demurrage or despatch money payable will be calculated.
* The **duration** of the laytime allowed depends on whether the laytime is:
    - **definite**, e.g. "2 running days";
    - **calculable**, e.g. where there is a given tonnage of cargo and a given rate of loading or discharging; or
    - **indefinite**, e.g. on "FAC" ("fast as can") terms - which are unusual.
* Where calculable, the allowed laytime for the operation involved (loading or discharging) should be calculated to the nearest minute.
* **Interpretation** of the contract laytime terms should be in accordance with the law governing the contract (which is determined from the Jurisdiction Clause), or, if expressly provided for, the internationally recognised **Voyage Charter party Laytime Interpretation Rules 1993**. As a result of court rulings, definitions of certain laytime expressions under English law differ from those given in the Laytime Interpretation Rules.

F05f.2 Voyage Charter party Laytime Interpretation Rules 1993

* The following Rules, which were issued jointly by BIMCO, CMI, FONASBA and INTERCARGO, replace the Charter party Laytime Definitions 1980.

* The interpretation of words and phrases used in a charter party, as set out below, and the corresponding initials if customarily used, **shall apply when expressly incorporated** in the charter party, wholly or partly, save only to the extent that they are inconsistent with any express provision of it.

* When the word **"charter party"** is used, it shall be understood to extend to any form of contract of carriage or affreightment including contracts evidenced by bills of lading.

1. **"Port"** shall mean an area within which vessels load or discharge cargo whether at berths, anchorages, buoys or the like, and shall also include the usual places where vessels wait for their turn or are ordered or obliged to wait for their turn no matter the distance from that area. If the word "PORT" is not used, but the port is (or is to be) identified by its name, this definition shall still apply.

2. **"Berth"** shall mean the specific place within a port where the vessel is to load or discharge. If the word "berth" is not used, but the specific place is (or is to be) identified by its name, this definition shall still apply.

3. **"Reachable on arrival"** or "Always accessible" shall mean that the charterers undertake that an available loading or discharging berth be provided to the vessel on her arrival at the port which she can reach safely without delay in the absence of an abnormal occurrence.

4. **"Laytime"** shall mean the period of time agreed between the parties during which the owners will make and keep the vessel available for loading or discharging without payment additional to the freight.

5. **"Per hatch per day"** shall mean that the laytime is to be calculated by dividing (A), the quantity of cargo, by (B), the result of multiplying the agreed daily rate per hatch by the number of the vessel's hatches. Thus:

$$\text{Laytime} = \frac{\text{Quantity of cargo}}{\text{Daily Rate x Number of Hatches}} = \text{Days}$$

Each pair of parallel twin hatches shall count as one hatch. Nevertheless, a hatch that is capable of being worked by two gangs simultaneously shall be counted as two hatches.

6. **"Per working hatch per day"** (WHD) or **"Per workable hatch per day"** (WHD) shall mean that the laytime is to be calculated by dividing (A), the quantity of cargo in the hold with the largest quantity, by (B), the result of multiplying the agreed daily rate per working or workable hatch by the number of hatches serving that hold. Thus:

$$\text{Laytime} = \frac{\text{Largest quantity in one hold}}{\text{Daily Rate per Hatch x Number of Hatch serving that Hold}} = \text{Days}$$

Each pair of parallel twin hatches shall count as one hatch. Nevertheless, a hatch that is capable of being worked by two gangs simultaneously shall be counted as two hatches.

7. **"Day"** shall mean a period of 24 consecutive hours running from 0000 hours to 2400 hours. Any part of a day shall be counted pro rata.

8. **"Clear days"** shall mean consecutive days commencing at 0000 hours on the day following that on which a notice is given and ending at 2400 hours on the last of the number of days stipulated.

9. **"Holiday"** shall mean a day other than the normal weekly day(s) of rest, or part thereof, when by local law or practice the relevant work during what would otherwise be ordinary working hours is not normally carried out.

10. **"Working days"** (WD) shall mean days not expressly excluded from laytime.

11. **"Running days"** or **"Consecutive days"** shall mean days which follow one immediately after the other.

12. **"Weather working day"** (WWD) or **"Weather working day of 24 hours"** or **"Weather working day of 24 consecutive hours"** shall mean a working day of 24 consecutive hours except for any time when weather prevents the loading or discharging of the vessel, or would have prevented it, had work been in progress.

13. **"Weather permitting"** (WP) shall mean that any time when weather prevents the loading or discharging of the vessel shall not count as laytime.

14. **"Excepted"** or **"excluded"** shall mean that the days specified do not count as laytime even if loading or discharging is carried out on them.

15. **"Unless sooner commenced"** shall mean that if laytime has not commenced but loading or discharging is carried out, time used shall count against laytime.

16. **"Unless used"** (UU) shall mean that if laytime has commenced but loading or discharging is carried out during periods excepted from it, such time shall count.

17. **"To average laytime"** shall mean that separate calculations are to be made for loading and discharging and that any time saved in one operation is to be set off against any excess time used in the other.

18. **"Reversible laytime"** shall mean an option given to the charterers to add together the time allowed for loading and discharging. Where the option is exercised the effect is the same as a total time being specified to cover both operations.

19. **"Notice of Readiness"** (NOR) shall mean the notice to charterer, shipper, receiver or other person as required by the charter party that the vessel has arrived at the port or berth, as the case may be, and is ready to load or discharge.

20. **"In writing"** shall mean any visibly expressed form of reproducing words; the medium of transmission shall include electronic communications such as radio communications and telecommunications.

21. **"Time lost waiting for berth to count as loading or discharging time"** or **"as laytime"** shall mean that if no loading or discharging berth is available and the vessel is unable to tender notice of readiness at the waiting-place

then any time lost to the vessel shall count as if laytime were running, or as time on demurrage if laytime has expired. Such time shall cease to count once the berth becomes available. When the vessel reaches a place where she is able to tender notice of readiness laytime or time on demurrage shall resume after such tender and, in respect of laytime, on expiry of any notice time provided in the charter party.

22. **"Whether in berth or not"** (WIBON) or **"berth or no berth"** shall mean that if no loading or discharging berth is available on her arrival the vessel, on reaching any usual waiting place at or off the port, shall be entitled to tender notice of readiness from it and laytime shall commence in accordance with the charter party. Laytime or time on demurrage shall cease to count once the berth becomes available and shall resume when the vessel is ready to load or discharge at the berth.

23. **"Vessel being in free pratique"** and/or **"having been entered at the Custom House"** shall mean that the completion of these formalities shall not be a condition precedent to tendering notice of readiness, but any time lost by reason of delay in the vessel's completion of either of these formalities shall not count as laytime or time on demurrage.

24. **"Demurrage"** shall mean an agreed amount payable to the owners in respect of delay to the vessel beyond the laytime, for which the owners are not responsible. Demurrage shall not be subject to laytime exceptions.

25. **"Despatch money"** or **"despatch"** shall mean an agreed amount payable by the owners if the vessel completes loading or discharging before the laytime has expired.

26. **"Despatch on (all) working time saved"** (WTS) or **"on (all) laytime saved"** shall mean that despatch money shall be payable for the time from the completion of loading or discharging to the expiry of the laytime excluding any periods excepted from the laytime.

27. **"Despatch on (all) time saved"** (ATS) shall mean that despatch money shall be payable for the time from the completion of loading or discharging to the expiry of the laytime including periods excepted from the laytime.

28. **"Strike"** shall mean a concerted industrial action by workmen causing a complete stoppage of their work which directly interferes with the working of the vessel. Refusal to work overtime, go-slow or working to rule and comparable actions not causing a complete stoppage shall not be considered a strike. A strike shall be understood to exclude its consequences when it has ended, such as congestion in the port or effects upon the means of transportation bringing or taking the cargo to or from the port.

F05f.3 Laytime calculation procedure

* Layout of the laytime statement should be in some acceptable style. Several formats are in use in the industry including a BIMCO recommended format and various charterers' house styles, each slightly different but containing the same essentials, which are columns as follows:

Day	Date	Time or Hours worked	Remarks	Laytime used	Time saved or time on demurrage

* Space should be left at the foot for despatch/demurrage calculations. The "bottom line" is usually the amount, in US Dollars, of **despatch** or **demurrage** due and the **party** to whom the payment is due.
* **Commencement of laytime** must be ascertained from a very careful inspection of the wording of the charter party Laytime Clause. If no definite time is ascertainable, it should be assumed that it starts to count from commencement of loading/discharging.
* **Interruptions** to cargo work mentioned on the Statement of Facts (e.g. rain, winch breakdowns, etc.) may only be allowed against laytime strictly in accordance with the charter party provisions and the Charter party Laytime Definitions. A work stoppage due to rain will mean a suspension of laytime if the charter party stipulates weather working days of 24 hours for example, but not if the charter party stipulates working days.
* Enter **important dates and times** (e.g. of arrival, of tendering and acceptance of notice, and of start and completion of cargo operations, at the top of the form.
* Enter each day and date from the date when laytime starts to count or from the start of cargo operations, whichever is sooner. (Laytime may commence before the vessel starts cargo work, or cargo work may start first.) Make an entry for each subsequent day until expiry of laytime. The expiry date will not be known at first as laytime may be interrupted for various reasons, but each period of laytime should be recorded and the expiry date and time calculated in due course.
* Calculate the **laytime allowed** (if calculable).
* Enter the **hours actually worked** each day.
* Enter **remarks** referring to the day's events, e.g. "laytime as per charter party", "0600-0800: rain prevented work", "public holiday - excepted as per charter party", etc..
* Enter the **laytime allowed** for each day. There is no "cumulative laytime" column, but a note of the cumulative laytime used should be made elsewhere. As the **laytime used** accumulates, the **laytime still available** will reduce. As it reduces, the day, date and time of **laytime expiry** will become apparent.

* Enter the **laytime actually used** each day.
* **Laytime expires** when the allowed laytime has all been used. If cargo operations have not been completed by the time of expiry, the vessel will go **on demurrage** until completion of cargo operations. The period between laytime expiry and completion of cargo must therefore be timed and the **demurrage due** from the charterers calculated in accordance with the charter party **Demurrage Clause**. If cargo operations are completed before laytime expiry, **despatch** will be payable to the charterers at the rate agreed in the charter party (which will usually be half the demurrage rate). The time between cargo completion and laytime expiry must in that case be noted and the aamount of **despatch due** calculated.
* When all laytime has expired check that the "laytime allowed" column figures add up to the actual laytime allowed and enter the figure at the foot of the sheet.
* Enter the date and time of **completion of cargo operations**.
* Compare the **laytime expiry date/time** with the **cargo completion date/time** to determine the **time saved or time on demurrage**.
* Calculate the **sum due the owners or charterer**, as the case may be.
* **Sign and date** the laytime statement, and hand to the agent, retaining a copy on board.

F06 Contract between shipowner and charterer: time charter

F06a TIME CHARTER AGREEMENTS

F06a.1 Time charter party clauses

* A general purpose dry cargo time charter party will usually incorporate clauses covering at least the **basic provisions** tabulated below.
* The provisions may be covered in different charter parties by clauses bearing different names, or by numbered clauses without names.

Clause name	Matters covered by clause	SBC ref.
Preamble	Identity of parties; identity and technical specifications of vessel; present position of vessel.	F06a.2
Period/ Port of Delivery/ Time of Delivery	Period of hire; place and time of delivery to charterers.	F06a.3
Trade	Legality of vessel's employment; legality of cargoes carried; safety of ports used; prohibition of cargoes injurious to ship.	F06a.4
Owners to Provide	Owners' obligation to pay for specified items.	F06a.5
Charterers to Provide	Charterers' obligation to pay for specified items.	F06a.6
Bunkers	Charterers' obligation to buy bunkers remaining on board at delivery port; owners' obligation to buy bunkers r.o.b. at redelivery port; minimum quantity of bunkers to be on board at redelivery.	F06a.7
Hire	Charterers' obligation to pay hire at the specified rate at the specified intervals until redelivery; owners' right to withdraw vessel for default on hire payments.	F06a.8
Redelivery	Charterers' obligation to re-deliver vessel in same condition as when delivered (fair wear and tear excepted); redelivery place, date and time; giving of notice of redelivery by charterers; provisions where vessel is on a voyage at agreed redelivery time.	F06a.9
Cargo Space	Agreement that entire carrying capacity of vessel will be at charterers' disposal.	F06a.10
Master	Master's speedy prosecution of voyages; master's and crew's assistance to charterer; master's obedience of charterers' orders relating to vessel's employment, agency, etc.; charterers' indemnification of owners against consequences of owners' servants signing bills of lading or other documents, or complying with charterers' orders, etc.; exclusion of owners' liability for cargo claims; owners' agreement to investigate charterers' complaints about crew.	F06a.11
Directions and Logs	Charterers' obligation to provide master with voyage instructions and information; obligation of master and engineers to make voyage logs available to charterers and their agents.	F06a.12
Suspension of Hire, etc.	Suspension of hire payment for duration of any "downtime" of vessel in specified circumstances; charterers' responsibility for loss of time in specified circumstances.	F06a.13
Cleaning Boilers	Owners' obligation to clean boilers with vessel in service, if possible; charterers' obligation to allow boiler cleaning time where necessary; suspension of hire when boiler cleaning time extends beyond specified time.	F06a.14

Responsibility and Exemption	Conditions under which owners will be responsible for delay in delivery, delay during the charter, or loss or damage to cargo; owners' exclusion of responsibility in all other circumstances; charterers' responsibility for loss or damage to vessel or owners caused by improper or negligent loading, bunkering or other acts on their or their servants' part.	F06a.15
Advances	Charterers' obligation to advance necessary funds to master for ordinary disbursements at any port; deduction of advances from hire.	F06a.16
Excluded Ports	Prohibition on charterers from ordering vessel to a place where disease is prevalent or which would be beyond the agreed limits of the Crew Agreement, or to any ice-bound place.	F06a.17
Loss of Vessel	Cessation of hire from date of loss of vessel.	F06a.18
Overtime	Owners' obligation to make vessel available for work 24h per day if required; charterers' obligation to reimburse owners for crew overtime.	F06a.19
Lien	Owners' lien for claims under the charter on cargoes, sub-freights and bill of lading freight.	F06a.20
Salvage	Equal sharing of salvage money after deduction of master's and crew's proportions and other expenses.	F06a.21
Sublet	Charterers' option to sublet vessel; original charterers' responsibility for due performance of charter.	F06a.22
War	Prohibition on charterers from using vessel in war zones or for carriage of goods which will expose her to risks of capture, etc.; charterers' responsibility to pay any war risks premiums, hire for time lost due to warlike operations and increased costs due to war zone operations; liberty of vessel to comply with flag State orders during war; cancellation of charter by either party, and redelivery of vessel, if flag State becomes involved in war.	F06a.23
Cancelling	Charterers' option of cancelling charter if vessel is not delivered by agreed date; charterers' obligation to declare intention to cancel.	F06a.24
Arbitration	Reference of disputes to arbitration in London or other agreed place; nomination of arbitrators by parties; umpire's decision where arbitrators disagree.	F06a.25
General Average	Rules under which any General Average is to be settled; non-contribution of hire to General Average.	F06a.26
Commission	Amount of (brokerage) commission to be paid by owners, and party to whom payable.	F06a.27

F06a.2 Preamble

- identifies the **parties** to the contract (usually referred to as "Owners" and "Charterers").
- identifies the chartered **vessel** and specifies her **technical characteristics**.
- states the vessel's **present position**, i.e. her position at the time the agreement was made, e.g. *"now trading"*, or *"ETA King's Lynn 30th Oct. pm tide/last cargo stone"*.

F06a.2a The vessel

* Time charter parties normally include a **statement of general particulars** about the vessel including classification, dimensions, tonnages (gt, NT, dwt), constant weight, draughts, grain/bale cubic capacity of holds/tanks, dimensions, speeds (laden/in ballast), consumptions of FO and DO (laden/in ballast/in port working/idle), type of engines, fuel used, call sign, etc. For special ship types other specialist information will be required, e.g. lane and ramp details of a ro/ro ship. General arrangement and capacity **plans** may also be required by the charterer. Tanker time charter parties require technical details such as **drawings** of the cargo manifold, pumping arrangement and ventilation system, pump characteristic curves, etc. to be submitted for approval of the charterer.
* **Speed** and **fuel consumption** are vitally important to the charterers for determining whether the vessel is performing the contract efficiently and whether he is entitled to claim for any alleged under-performance. (This is a frequent subject of dispute, since modern bunker prices fluctuate greatly.)
* The declared **constant weight** (a fixed tonnage allowed for water, stores, provisions, spares, etc.) is important to the charterers in their cargo planning.
* At common law, the vessel provided by the owners must be **seaworthy** for the purposes of the contract at the time of the contract's making. Thereafter, the owners usually agree only to **exercise due diligence** to make the vessel seaworthy for each voyage during the charter period.
* A time charter party usually contains an undertaking by the owners to **maintain** the vessel in good condition throughout the charter period, and the owners may be required to keep the vessel in the condition she was stated to be in when the contract was made, e.g. to "LR class 100A1 or equivalent". Some time charter parties require the owners to "exercise due diligence to make the vessel tight, staunch, strong, in good order and condition, and in every way fit for the service, both before, at and throughout the time charter period, taking whatever steps are necessary to so maintain the vessel, even if the cause of repairs and/or additional maintenance result from a cause for which owners are not directly responsible".

* A **Suspension of Hire Clause** will provide for hire payments to be suspended if the vessel is out of service for more than a specified minimum period due to drydocking, maintenance, machinery breakdown, lack of crew, damage, etc. A **Cleaning Boilers Clause** will also limit the time out of service before hire is suspended.
* A **Cargo Space Clause** provides that the whole **"reach and burthen"** of the vessel, including lawful deck capacity, is to be at the charterer's disposal, excluding crew accommodation and space for equipment, provisions and stores.

F06a.3 Period/Port of Delivery/Time of delivery

- specifies the period of hire, the port or place of delivery, and the date and time of delivery.
* The **place, time and conditions of delivery and redelivery** of the vessel are key points in a time charter agreement, since the amount of the owners' and charterers' income may hinge upon them, and disputes can easily arise in cases of misunderstanding. The charter party's provisions covering these matters should be carefully noted and adhered to by the master.
* For notes on **delivery**, see F06b.

F06a.4 Trade

- specifies any restrictions on the employment of the ship.
* For notes on **employment of the vessel**, see F06c.1.

F06a.5 Owners to Provide

- obliges owners to provide crew's provisions and wages, insurance on the vessel, deck and engine-room stores.
- obliges owners to maintain the vessel's condition.
- states other obligations of the owners.
* For notes on **owners' responsibility for costs**, see C02a and F04a.2.

F06a.6 Charterers to Provide

- obliges charterers to provide fuel and pay for port charges, pilotage, tugs, canal, dock and other dues, agencies and commissions.
- obliges charterers to pay for loading, trimming, stowage, surveys, discharging, slings, etc.
* For notes on the **charterer's responsibility for costs**, see C02a and F04a.2.

F06a.7 Bunkers

- obliges charterers to buy the bunkers remaining on board at the port of delivery.
- obliges the owners to buy the bunkers remaining on board at the port of redelivery.
- specifies the minimum quantity of bunkers to remain on board at redelivery.
* For notes on **bunkers on delivery**, see F06b.4. For notes on **bunkers on redelivery**, see F06d.4.

F06a.8 Hire

- specifies the charterers' obligation to pay hire at the specified rate until redelivery, in cash in advance in the specified currency.
- specifies the owners' right to withdraw the vessel for default on hire payments.
* For notes on **hire**, see F06c.2.

F06a.9 Redelivery

- specifies charterers' obligation to redeliver the vessel in the same condition as when delivered, fair wear and tear excepted.

- specifies the place and date of redelivery.
- obliges charterers to give notice of redelivery.
- specifies the requirements where the vessel is on an uncompleted voyage at the agreed redelivery time.
* For notes on **redelivery**, see F06d.

F06a.10 Cargo Space

- provides that the whole "reach and burden" of the vessel (i.e. her lawful cargo-carrying capacity), including her lawful deck capacity, are to be at the charterers' disposal, reserving the proper space for the crew, gear and stores, etc.

F06a.11 Master

- obliges the master to prosecute voyages with the "utmost despatch", and render "customary assistance" to the charterers with the crew.
- provides that the master will be under the charterers' orders as regards employment of the ship, agency, etc.
- provides that charterers will indemnify the owners against the consequences or liabilities arising from the master, officers or agents signing bills of lading or other documents, or otherwise complying with such orders, or for irregularities in papers or for overcarrying goods.
- provides that the owners will bear no responsibility for shortage, mixture, marks, number of packages, etc. or for damage or claims caused by bad stowage or otherwise.
- obliges the owners to promptly investigate charterers' complaints about the master, officers or engineers, and if necessary change personnel.

F06a.12 Directions and Logs

- obliges charterers to give the master all instructions and sailing directions relevant to the voyage.
- obliges the master and engineers to keep logs accessible to charterers or their agents.

F06a.13 Suspension of Hire etc.

- provides that no hire will be paid for any time in excess of the stated number of hours if the vessel goes out of service due to drydocking, shortage of crew or stores, machinery breakdown, hull damage, etc., and that any advance hire will be adjusted accordingly.
- Obliges charterers to be responsible for any time lost when the vessel is driven into port or anchorage through stress of weather, or trading to shallow harbours with bars, or having an accident to cargo, or for detention of the vessel, etc., even if contributed to by the negligence of owners' servants.

F06a.14 Cleaning Boilers

- obliges the owners to have any boiler cleaning done with the vessel in service if possible.
- obliges charterers to allow the owners boiler cleaning time where it is impossible to have cleaning done with the vessel in service.
- states that hire will be suspended for the duration of any boiler cleaning in excess of a specified time (e.g. 48 hours).

F06a.15 Responsibility and Exemption

- states that the owners will only be responsible for delay in delivery or delay during the charter and for loss or damage to goods on board if caused by want of due diligence on their or their manager's part in making the vessel seaworthy and fitted for the voyage or any other personal act or omission of the owners or their manager.

- states that the owners will not be responsible in any other case nor for damage or delay, even if due to the neglect or default of their servants.
- states that the owners will not be liable for loss or damage arising from strikes, etc. (including by the master, officers or crew).
- Makes charterers responsible for loss or damage caused to the vessel or to the owners by goods being loaded contrary to the terms of the charter party or by improper or careless bunkering or loading, stowage or discharging or any other improper or negligent act on their or their servants' part.

F06a.16 Advances

- obliges charterers (or their agents) to advance the master the necessary funds for "ordinary disbursements" for the vessel's account at any port, with annual interest at the rate specified.
* Advances are normally deducted from the next hire payment.

F06a.17 Excluded Ports

- prohibits the charterers from ordering the vessel to any place where fever or epidemics are prevalent, or to which the master, officers or crew are not obliged by law to follow the vessel (i.e. locations outwith the limits imposed by the Voyage Clause in the Crew Agreement).
- prohibits the charterers from ordering the vessel to any ice-bound place where navigation is dangerous, and not to oblige the vessel to force ice.
- permits the master to sail from any ice-bound place to a "convenient open place" to await charterers' instructions.
- provides that the cost of delay due to unforeseen detention in ice-bound ports will be for charterers' account.

F06a.18 Loss of Vessel

- provides that hire payment will cease from the date the vessel is lost.
- States that if the date of loss is not ascertainable, half hire is to be paid from the date on which the vessel last reported until the calculated date of arrival at the destination, and any advance hire to be adjusted accordingly.

F06a.19 Overtime

- obliges the owners to make the vessel available for working 24 hours a day if required.
- provides that charterers will refund officers' and crew's overtime paid by the owners. This refers to overtime worked for charterers' purposes, e.g. on cargo hold cleaning, as opposed to ship's maintenance, etc.

F06a.20 Lien

- provides that for all claims under the charter, the owners will have a lien on all cargoes and sub-freights belonging to time charterers, and on any bill of lading freight.
- provides that charterers will have a lien on the vessel for all moneys paid in advance and not earned.
* For notes on **liens**, see B03g.

F06a.21 Salvage

- provides that all salvage money earned by the ship is to be equally shared by the owners and charterers after deduction of the master's and crew's proportions and all legal and other expenses including hire paid for time lost during the salvage operations, damage repairs and fuel consumed.

F06a.22 Sublet

- gives charterers the option of subletting the vessel to a time or voyage sub-charterer.
* If the charterers exercise their option to sublet, the original charterers (the "head charterers") remain responsible to the owners for the due performance of the charter. (The present charter could, in fact, be a sub-charter and not the head charter.)

F06a.23 War

- prohibits the charterers from using the vessel in war zones or for carrying goods which will expose her to risks of capture, etc.
- obliges charterers to pay for any war risk premiums incurred.
- obliges charterers to pay hire for any time lost due to warlike operations, including time lost due to injury of or action of crew.
- obliges charterers to pay for any increased costs (e.g. for insurance, wages, stores or provisions) due to war zone operations.
- gives the vessel liberty to comply with any orders or directions given by her flag State government.
- gives both owners and charterers the right to cancel the charter if the ship's flag State becomes involved in hostilities, in which case the vessel is to be redelivered at the destination or a safe port after discharge.
- provides that anything done or not done under the War Clause will not be considered a deviation from the contract.

F06a.24 Cancelling

- provides that charterers have the option of **cancelling** the charter if the vessel is not delivered by the date stated.
- provides that if the vessel cannot be delivered by the cancelling date, the charterers, if required, must declare within a stated period of receiving notice thereof whether they will cancel or take delivery.
* A time charterer has a similar right to cancel as that of a voyage charterer. For notes on **cancelling a voyage charter**, see F05b.1.

F06a.25 Arbitration

- provides that disputes will be referred to **arbitration in London** or some other named place.
- specifies the arrangements for the **nomination of arbitrators**. A common agreement is that one arbitrator will be nominated by the owners and one by charterers; if they cannot agree, an umpire's decision will be final and binding.
* For notes on **arbitration**, see B03i.1.

F06a.26 General Average

- specifies the rules under which any General Average is to be settled, the usual rules being the York-Antwerp Rules 1994.
- may provide that hire will not contribute to the General Average.
* For notes on **General Average** and the **York-Antwerp Rules**, see G06.

F06a.27 Commission

- specifies the amount of any **brokerage commission** due, and the party to whom it is payable.
* For additional notes on **brokerage** and **Brokerage Clauses**, see F04b.1.

F06b DELIVERY

F06b.1 Delivery conditions

* A time-chartered vessel goes "**on hire**" when she is **delivered** to the charterers at the agreed place and time, is fully at the charterer's disposal and is in a fit condition for the employment contemplated.
* Acceptance of delivery may be contingent on the passing of a **condition survey** carried out by the charterer's surveyors, particularly where the charterers are an oil company and the vessel is over a certain age. In addition, in almost every case, an **on-hire survey** or **delivery survey** will be required.

F06b.2 Time of delivery

* Delivery will either be "**spot**" (i.e. immediate) or between stated **laydays** for presentation of the vessel. If the vessel is not presented by the final layday (i.e. the "**cancelling date**"), the charterers have the option of cancelling the charter.
* If the vessel cannot be delivered by the cancelling date, the charterers may be required by the charter party terms to **declare** within a stated period after receiving notice of the delay whether they will cancel or take delivery.
* **When the vessel is delayed on a positioning/delivery voyage**, the master should adopt the same procedure as in similar circumstances on a preliminary voyage under a voyage charter (see H06f.1), i.e. he should continue with all despatch to the agreed delivery place, checking the charter party for a Cancelling Clause or any instructions and keeping the charterers and the owners informed.

F06b.3 Place of delivery

* One of a number of types of delivery arrangement may be agreed in a time charter party:
  * The ship may be delivered **at the final discharge port** under her previous employment. Unless she also loads at that port, she may have to make a ballast passage to a loading port; the ballast passage costs would be for the time charterer's account.
  * Even where the vessel has already left her final discharge port under her previous employment, the parties may agree to **commence the hire retrospectively** at that port.
  * The vessel may be delivered **on arrival at a loading port**, the owners having paid the costs of any ballast passage to that port. (In this case they would ensure that the rate of hire compensated them for those costs.)
  * The hire may commence **at the time when the vessel passes a particular geographic position** during her passage between the final discharge port under the previous employment and the first loading port under the new time charter, or at some particular time during that voyage, such as 72 hours before arrival at the loading port. This is a compromise between other arrangements.
  * The vessel may deliver **at a loading port following a ballast voyage**, the costs of which are paid by the charterers to the owners as a "**ballast bonus**".
* **Delivery** will be made either when the ship is in a named **geographical location** (e.g. "*passing Cape Passero*" or "*passing The Skaw*") or at a specified **event** (e.g. "*taking inbound pilot New York*" or "*t.i.p. New York*", or "*dropping outward pilot Hong Kong*" or "*d.o.p. Hong Kong*"). Time charters often commence with a ballast voyage to a loading port, so that "*dropping outward pilot......*" at the last discharging port is frequently agreed as the place for delivery.

F06b.4 Bunkers on delivery

* A **Bunker Clause** will usually require a certain quantity of fuel to be on board at delivery, with approximately the same quantity to be on board at redelivery, and in any case enough to reach the next bunkering port.
* The charter party will provide for cash settlement of the balance, so that in effect the charterers buy all bunkers remaining on board at delivery from the owners and sells bunkers r.o.b. at redelivery back to the owners.

F06b.5 On-hire survey and Delivery Certificate

* There will usually be an agreement that there will be an **on-hire survey** or **delivery survey** to establish:
  * **bunkers remaining on board** (r.o.b.), in order to determine the quantity the charterers will have to pay the owners for;
  * the **general condition of the vessel**; and
  * that **tanks or holds are fit** for the carriage of the contemplated cargoes.
* Holds of a dry cargo vessel must be dry and swept clean, etc., and tanks for oil or chemicals must pass survey and be certified fit.
* The surveyor will note any **existing damage** in holds/tanks, etc.
* The on-hire survey is usually to be carried out by **jointly-approved surveyors**, paid for 50/50 by the owners and the charterer. Time spent on the survey is normally at the owners' risk, i.e. the vessel is not on-hire until passing of the survey.
* A **Delivery Certificate** should be issued by the surveyor to confirm the date and time of hand-over, bunkers r.o.b. (and perhaps boiler water r.o.b.), and the condition of holds or tanks. The certificate should be attached to the **survey report** and is a vital document for the assessment of hire payments due and the commencement of various charterer's liabilities.
* The on-hire survey should not be confused with the **condition survey** that may be required by a prospective charterer, particularly where this is an oil company or in the case of older tonnage.

F06c DURING THE HIRE PERIOD

F06c.1 Employment of the vessel

* A time charter party usually incorporates a clause defining the ship's permitted **employment** or **trade limits**.
* Typically, the charterers may employ the vessel only in **lawful trades**, carrying **lawful merchandise**, using only "**good and safe ports or berths**" and sometimes **safe anchorages** where the vessel can lie **always safely afloat** within the agreed **trading limits**, which will be specified, e.g. "United Kingdom/Continent/Mediterranean excluding Syria/Libya/Israel/lebanon excluding Scandinavia/including Morocco excluding Irish Sea trading".
* The charter party should always be checked for **trade limits**. Some countries, areas and ports (e.g. Israel, Persian/Arabian Gulf, Cuba, Vietnam, Kampuchea, North Korea, Lebanon, Angola, Namibia, Syria, Libya, Somalia, Ethiopia and South Africa) may be excluded from the permitted trading area. "**Worldwide within Institute Warranty Limits**" is a common term describing agreed trading areas (the "Institute" being the Institute of London Underwriters). "Institute Warranty Limits" is sometimes abbreviated as "IWLs".
* **Guarantees** may be required from owners that the vessel has not traded to certain countries since a particular date (e.g. Cuba or North Vietnam since 1961, nor Israel), since the discovery of a past visit to a particular country may cause problems for the ship in another country.
* The charter party should be checked for **cargo exclusions**. At common law, the charterers are under an implied obligation not to load any **dangerous cargoes**, but most charter parties state that the charterers may load certain dangerous goods if various statutes and regulations (e.g. the IMDG Code) are complied with. Usually, the vessel will be allowed by her owner to carry any "lawful merchandise" with the exception of certain **excluded commodities** which may be injurious to the ship, e.g. "bulk asphalt, pitch or tar, livestock, logs, acids, scrap, sulphur, petroleum coke, explosives, fishmeal and nuclear materials".
* **Lightening** at sea is not normally allowed without permission of underwriters (since this is usually outside terms of the Hull and Machinery policy).
* As outlined in F04a.1b, the charterers are responsible for the vessel's commercial **employment** and direct her commercial operations, e.g. by giving instructions as to the sailing itinerary and cargo to be loaded. Until the decision by the House of Lords in the *Hill Harmony* case (see H01a.2), it was widely understood by shipowners and masters that "employment" matters did not extend to voyage routeing. Following the House of Lords' decision, which explained that "employment" *did* extend to strategic voyage routeing (although *not* to tactical navigational decisions on encountering hazards), a new **Performance of Voyages Clause** has been drafted for use in time charter parties with the aim of restoring the master's discretion in these matters. The clause, which adds to Clause 8 of the NYPE time charter party some newly-drafted words (shown in bold print below), may help to protect the owner's position by supporting the master's decisions as to the voyage route, as long as those decisions are made in good faith. The clause reads as follows: "*The Master shall perform the voyages with due despatch, and shall render all customary assistance with the Vessel's crew and equipment. The Master shall be conversant with the English language and (although appointed by the Owners) shall be under the orders and directions of the charterers as*

*regards employment and agency **but the Master shall have the right to reject charterers' orders and/or directions
as to the employment of the vessel where, in his sole discretion, he considers that these may compromise the
safety and/or seaworthiness of the vessel, such right of the Master to be exercised in good faith;** and the
charterers shall perform all cargo handling, including but not limited to loading, stowing, trimming, lashing,
securing, dunnaging, unlashing, discharging, and tallying, at their risk and expense, under the supervision of the
Master".*

F06c.2 Hire

* **Hire**, or charterhire -
  - is the owners' remuneration, payable by the charterer.
  - is usually payable in **US Dollars** every **15 days** ("semi-monthly") or **30 days** ("monthly") **in advance**.
  - may be payable as an **agreed sum** (e.g. $10,000) **per day** or as a **sum per Summer deadweight tonne** (e.g. $7.50 per sdwt) **per calendar month**.
  - is usually paid after deduction of **brokerage** and **commission**.
* Charterers' claims for **under-performance**, etc. must usually be negotiated with the owners and deducted from the following month's hire.

F06c.3 The master

* Although he is a servant of the the owners, the master is always under the time charterer's orders as far as the **employment** of the vessel and **agency** matters are concerned. He must accordingly prosecute the voyage with **utmost despatch** and give the charterers "customary and reasonable assistance" with the crew and ship's equipment.
* The charter party may require the owners to investigate **complaints** by the charterers regarding the master or officers, and replace them if requested.
* For related notes on **charterers' instructions**, see H01a.2.

F06c.4 Liability as carrier

* When cargo is shipped, the shipper may be given a **mate's receipt** (or equivalent document) as acknowledgement. The information in a mate's receipt forms the basis of a bill of lading, which in many non-liner trades is prepared by the shipper.
* The bill of lading functions as a **receipt**, as a **document of title** (if appropriately worded) and as **evidence of a contract** of carriage. Although a time charterer is a "disponent owner", the contract of carriage evidenced by a bill of lading, if a bill is issued to a shipper, is between the real shipowner and the shipper. If the ship fails to deliver the goods described in the bill of lading, the owners (and not the charterer) will therefore be liable to the owners of the goods.
* Whether or not time charter hire has been paid, the shipowner must deliver the goods to the final holder of the bill of lading and **frauds** occasionally occur where a time charterer was the original cargo owner but sells the cargo to a consignee, fails to pay the next hire payment due, and disappears. In these cases the shipowner is (usually) still legally obliged to deliver the cargo to the holder of the bill of lading, but receives nothing for carrying the goods.
* If a **time-chartered ship** issues a bill of lading using her **owner's own "house" bill of lading form** and without mention of the fact that the vessel is time-chartered (e.g. in a statement that "all terms and conditions of carriage are in the relevant charter party dated....."), the contract of carriage may be deemed to be **between the shipowner and the shipper**.
* If the charterers insist on the issue of their own **(charterers')** bill of lading forms, the contract of carriage will normally be between the charterers **and the shipper**; in this case the terms on the bill of lading should make the identity of the carrier clear.
* Where there is any doubt as to the identity of the legal carrier, it is safer for a shipmaster to assume that even where his vessel is time-chartered, the **shipowner will be the carrier** under the contract evidenced by bill of lading, and to take care with documentation accordingly.
* The **Master Clause**, which may appear in some charter parties as an **Employment and Indemnity Clause**, transfers from the owners to the charterers the **freedom of choice as to the way the vessel is employed** under the charter, but in return the **charterers agree to indemnify the owners** for the consequences of the master complying with the charterer's orders. The charterers may only give the master orders regarding **employment** of the vessel, and

not regarding navigation, safety, etc. (If the master did obey the charterer's orders regarding navigation, and loss or damage occurred, the owners would be liable, with no recourse from the charterer.) For related notes on **charterers' instructions**, see H01a.2.

* The charter party may provide for a **supercargo** to be carried in order to protect the charterer's interests during the voyage (e.g. with respect to care of the cargo, discharge, etc.). Since the supercargo's **meals** will normally be paid for by the charterer, the master should keep **records of meals provided**.

F06c.5 Agents

* Since time charterers require their cargo operations in each port to be overseen by reliable port agents, particularly in specialised trades, the charterers will normally reserve the right to **nominate** agents, although these "charterers' agents" will usually be appointed and have their fees paid by the owners. (The owners will therefore be the principal in the legal relationship.)
* As well as expediting cargo operations, charterer's agents should attend to the ship's (i.e. owner's) business, e.g. crew reliefs and repatriation, subs, etc., and a **Disbursements Clause** may provide that they will be paid for this work by a commission on the actual cost of the disbursements.
* As in a voyage charter on free in and out terms (see F05a.6), a **protecting agent** may be appointed by the owners where there is any conflict of interest between owner's and charterer's requirements.
* Since the master is normally under the charterer's orders regarding employment and **agency** (see F06a.11 and F06c.3), charterer's agents have the right to sign bills of lading on behalf of the master, although the master will usually be required to sign a form or letter authorising them to do this. For an example of an **agent's authorisation to sign bills of lading**, see I01h.3a.

F06c.6 Maintenance and other off-hire provisions

* A **Drydock Clause** may provide for the vessel to be made available to the owners, free of cargo, after a stated period of notice for cleaning, painting, survey, routine repairs and maintenance. During this period she will be off-hire.
* The charter party will normally provide in a **Suspension of Hire Clause** (or equivalent) that in the event of drydocking or other measures to maintain the efficiency of the vessel, or lack of crew or owner's stores, or machinery breakdowns, hull damage or other accident either hindering or preventing the working of the vessel, and continuing for more than a specified number of hours, no hire will be paid for time in which the vessel was not at the immediate disposal of the charterer. Hire paid in advance will be adjusted accordingly.
* **If deviating for the owners' purposes**, e.g. for landing a sick seaman, repairs, collecting stores, etc., the vessel will be off-hire from the moment of the deviation until she is ready to resume service in a position no less favourable to the charterer. A deduction from hire will be calculated on the basis of fuel used in the deviation, including fuel oil and diesel oil at the port deviated to.
* **If deviating for the charterer's purposes**, e.g. stress of weather, the vessel will remain on hire.

F06d REDELIVERY

F06d.1 Redelivery conditions

* A time-chartered vessel goes "**off hire**" when she is **redelivered** to her owner.
* A **Redelivery Clause** will normally be found in a time charter party.
* Under most time charter parties the vessel must be in the **same good order** at redelivery as when delivered (fair wear and tear excepted). An **off-hire survey** is required to determine the extent of any damage done during the period of hire. The charterers will normally be liable for the cost of repairs.
* The vessel may be redelivered "**clean**" or "**dirty**". If the charterers are given the option of redelivering the vessel "dirty", a sum in compensation to the owners will be provided for in the charter party.

F06d.2 Time of redelivery

* It may be agreed that redelivery will be between certain stated hours, e.g. 0900-1800 (or 1400 on Saturday) - and not on a Sunday or holiday. The charterers may be required to give the owners not less than 10 days notice.
* A time charterer may want to **delay redelivery** when freight rates are high, while the owners may be content with a late redelivery when freight rates are low, if the hire negotiated was better than the equivalent freight rate.
* **Redelivery** must be made between **agreed dates** and may occur at a named **geographical location** or at a specified **event**, as with delivery, or there may be an agreed **range** of ports or places, perhaps not north or south of a specified latitude, etc., within which the charterers may redeliver the vessel.

F06d.3 Place of redelivery

* **The place and time for redelivery** of the ship to the owner will be specified in the charter party, and various types of arrangement may be made, as for delivery (see F06b).
* Redelivery at an ice-free port or place, or a port chosen from a range of ports within stated geographical limits, may be provided for.

F06d.4 Bunkers on redelivery

* See notes on the **Bunker Clause** at F06b.4.

F06d.5 Off-hire survey and Redelivery Certificate

* The charterers must normally re-deliver the vessel in the "*same good order as when delivered to the charterer, fair wear and tear excepted......*" In the event of redelivery not being in the same good order and condition, the charterers would be liable for the cost of repairs. If the charterers are given the option of redelivering the vessel "dirty", a sum in compensation to the owners will be provided for.
* The **off-hire survey** will normally be carried out by an independent surveyor to ascertain the extent of damage done during the charter, bunkers r.o.b., etc.. The Redelivery Clause may provide that **repairs** necessary to make the vessel seaworthy must be done immediately on redelivery, and any other repairs at a more convenient time, e.g. at the next drydocking.
* The off-hire survey is similar in scope to the on-hire survey (see F06b.5). Bunkers r.o.b. are measured so that they can be "bought back" by the owners. The condition of the vessel and her cargo spaces is examined for damage attributable to charterer's operations. A **Redelivery Certificate** should be issued to the master.
* It is normal to have on-hire and off-hire surveys carried out by independent surveyors to ascertain the extent of damage done during the charter. A **Redelivery Clause** may provide that repairs necessary to make the vessel seaworthy are done immediately on redelivery, and any other repairs at a more convenient time, e.g. at the next drydocking.

F07 Contract between shipowner and cargo owner

F07a THE CARRIER

* A **carrier** is a party who agrees to carry, on a business basis, goods or persons from one place to another. Most shipowners have the legal status of carrier.
* The law recognizes two kinds of carrier: the **common carrier** and the **private carrier**.

F07a.1 Common carriers

- advertise themselves as being ready to carry goods or passengers, within their usual trading area, for anyone wanting to employ their services.

- are subject to the **common law obligations** (see below).
- are **strictly liable for any loss of or damage** to the goods they carry, so that effectively they are the insurer of the goods whilst in their care.
* See also notes on **NVOCs** at F07a.2a.

F07a.1a Common law exceptions from liability

* Recognising the special nature of the perils facing a carrier by sea, the English courts have reduced the strict liability of a common carrier to the following **six common law exceptions** from liability:
  * **act of God**, i.e. some unforeseen and unpreventable natural event, e.g. lightning or earthquake;
  * **act of Queen's enemies**, i.e. a State or people with whom the carrier is at war during the carriage of the goods (but excluding robbers, rioters and pirates);
  * **inherent vice in the goods**, i.e. a natural tendency of a commodity to deteriorate without human negligence, e.g. fruit and fish deteriorating, liquids fermenting, loss of weight in hides due to evaporation, severe pitting of steel plates not due to atmospheric rusting. A carrier will not be liable for ordinary wear and tear in transit, ordinary loss or deterioration in quality or quantity such as evaporation, but he will be liable if he aggravates any loss or damage due to inherent vice through a breach of contract, e.g. by not protecting steel plates from the weather. Difficulty is often experienced in deciding whether deterioration in perishable goods is due to inherent vice or to bad ventilation or stowage (for which the ship would be liable);
  * **negligence of the consignor**, e.g. insufficient or defective packing of goods inside containers or cases;
  * fraud of the owner or consignor of the goods, e.g. where the shipper makes an untrue statement to the carrier as to their nature or value, or their threat to safety as well as (for sea carriers only);
  * **jettison or other proper General Average sacrifice**, i.e. when cargo is intentionally and properly destroyed or damaged during the voyage in order to preserve the ship and other cargo from a danger threatening the entire "adventure".
* A sea carrier will not, however, be protected by the common law exceptions when the true cause of the loss or damage to the goods was:
  * his **negligence**, e.g. in not taking reasonable steps to protect cargo from loss or damage;
  * his vessel was **unseaworthy** at the start of the voyage; or
  * the loss or damage occurred while the vessel was unjustifiably **deviating** from the contract.

F07a.2 Private carriers

- make a **special contract** with their customers excluding or restricting their strict liability, i.e. **contracting out of the common law obligations** by stating their **special terms of carriage**. Although the law allows any carrier to do this the Unfair Contract Terms Act 1977 applies to the terms incorporated into his contract and provides that any exclusion of liability must be **reasonable**.
* The terms under which a private carrier contracts out of his common law obligations must be **clearly stated** if they are to protect him in law. (Most carriers print their terms on their bills of lading or other contract of carriage documents.)
* If a court holds that his contract terms were unreasonable or unfair, a private carrier may find himself reverting to the position of a **common carrier**.
* As a private carrier, a carrier becomes a **bailee** of the goods carried; as such he is only liable for damage or the consequences of delay occurring through his negligence.
* Most shipowners make themselves private carriers.

F07a.2a NVOCs and NVOCCs

* A **non- vessel owning carrier** or **non- vessel operating carrier** (**NVOC**) operates a shipping service (usually in the liner/general cargo trades) without owning or operating his own vessel, instead buying a volume of cargo space on vessels owned or operated by one or more shipowners with whom he contracts as a "shipper", and then selling that space to individual merchants.
* The NVOC issues **his own bill of lading** to each shipper with whom he contracts.
* In relation to the merchant, the NVOC is the contractual **carrier**. In relation to the owner/operator of the carrying ship, the NVOC is a **shipper**, and will be issued with a bill of lading like any ordinary shipper.
* Essentially, an NVOC is a freight forwarder in all but name. (Many freight forwarders and cargo consolidators advertise as **NVOCs** or **NVOCCs**.)

* An NVOC may, for example, hire a number of "slots" from a mainline containership owner on a charter party such as "SLOTHIRE", securing the total space hired at a lower rate than the carrier's usual tariff rate. The NVOC then "sells" his space to the merchants at a slightly lower rate than the normal tariff rate that they would have to pay to the shipowner as individual shippers. In that way, the NVOC makes a profit.
* The expression "**NVOCC**" means **non-vessel operating common carrier**. It has legal definition **only in the USA**, where a party contracting as an NVOCC has to file his status with the Federal Maritime Commission (FMC) and carries the usual heavy legal burden of any common carrier (see F07a.1). Many forwarders outside the USA also advertise as an "NVOCC" when, in fact, they would they would certainly not want to be held accountable as a common carrier. The US legal definition of NVOCC is "….a common Carrier that does not operate the vessel by which ocean transportation is provided, and is a shipper in its relationship with the Ocean Common Carrier" (the Ocean Common Carrier being the shipowner).

F07a.3 Common law obligations of carriers

* All carriers of goods or passengers by sea (both common and private) are subject to the **three common law obligations**, which are that:
  * The carrier must provide a vessel which is **seaworthy** for the purpose of the contract at the time it is made.
  * The carrier must **not deviate** from the contract, geographically or otherwise, without justification.
  * The carrier must ensure his vessel will be ready to load the cargo and proceed on the voyage with **reasonable despatch**.
* These obligations are **implied conditions** and need not, therefore, be expressed in the contract. Even so, they are often expressed in the printed conditions of carriage on bills of lading, etc.

F07a.4 Seaworthiness

* The obligation to provide a seaworthy vessel is **absolute**, i.e. there are no exceptions from the rule. At the time the contract is made the vessel must be fit to encounter the "ordinary perils of the sea" (e.g. bad weather) and other incidental risks to which she will be exposed on the voyage. However, the common law recognises that owners cannot guarantee their vessels' seaworthiness once they have left port, so the obligation is only imposed at the start of the voyage, i.e. when the vessel leaves the berth either under her own power or under tow.
* Seaworthiness has three aspects:
  * **technical seaworthiness**, relating to the vessel's design, condition of her hull and machinery, and her stability, etc.;
  * **"cargoworthiness"**, relating to her suitability for the intended cargo and the condition of her cargo spaces; and
  * **fittedness for the intended voyage**, relating to her equipment (including charts), manning, bunkering and stores for the voyage.
* The ship may be held to be unseaworthy, therefore, if she sails without:
  * statutory certificates in force;
  * certificate (or interim certificate) of class in force;
  * holds properly fitted for the cargo (e.g. ventilation system working, dunnage, fire-fighting agent);
  * cargo properly stowed or secured;
  * a properly qualified master or officers;
  * appropriate (and corrected) charts for the voyage; or
  * sufficient bunkers for the voyage.
* Under the **doctrine of stages**, seaworthiness at each stage of the voyage, e.g. in dock, in a river, in an estuary, must be considered separately.

F07a.5 Deviation

* **Deviation** in the context of carriage of goods law (and insurance law, including P&I club rules) is **not restricted to geographical deviations**, but includes **any departure from a contractually agreed provision relating to the voyage**, e.g. in respect of:
  * any **departure from the customary route** for vessels in the trade which are not authorised by the shipper or charterer;
  * any non-agreed **change in ports of loading and/or discharge**;
  * any **change in the rotation of ports** not authorised by the shipper or charterer;

- any non-agreed change in the **cargo** offered for loading;
- any **unreasonable delay** in the voyage due to ship's operations;
- any **short loading** (unless the fault of shipper or charterer);
- any non-agreed change in the **stowage place** (i.e. on deck or underdeck);
- any **transshipment of cargo** not authorised by the shipper or charterer;
- any unauthorised **on-carriage of cargo** in another vessel;
- any deviation from proper carriage conditions (e.g. temperature or pressure to be maintained); or
- any unauthorised **storage of cargo**.

* The **carriage of cargo on deck**, for example, which is not customarily carried on deck and is not clearly stated on the face of the bill of lading to be carried on deck, will usually be regarded by the courts as tantamount to a deviation. (See also notes on **carriage of deck cargo** at F07e.)
* The general rule in common law is that the ship must not leave the route contemplated in the contract without **justification**. The route must be the **shortest safe geographical route**, unless varied by usual custom of the trade.
* Deviations usually regarded in common law as lawful or "**justifiable**" are:
  - a deviation made **to save life**, e.g. responding to a Mayday;
  - a deviation made **to avoid imminent danger**, e.g. a TRS;
  - a deviation **due to the default of the charterer**, e.g. where the master found the discharge port nominated by the charterer unsafe;
  - an involuntary deviation **due to force majeure** beyond the control of either party to the contract, e.g. where a channel is blocked; or
  - a deviation made **to save property**, e.g. for salvage purposes.
* Examples of **unjustifiable or unreasonable deviations** include:
  - taking a route which is not the custom of the trade, e.g. for purely private reasons;
  - putting in to an intermediate port or place for stores or provisions which were not essential to the safe completion of the voyage;
  - calling at an intermediate port to replenish bunkers for a future voyage when there is no provision in the current contract of carriage permitting this. (The P&I Bunker Deviation clause (see F05a.4) is designed to protect an owner who wishes to take advantage of cheap bunkers available at off-route ports.)
* Charter parties and bills of lading usually incorporate a **Deviation Clause** (see F05a.4) appearing to give the vessel the right to deviate almost anywhere, but courts interpret this clause strictly.
* Under Article 4 of the Hague Rules and Article IV of the Hague-Visby Rules, **any deviation in saving or attempting to save life or property at sea** or **any reasonable deviation** will not be deemed to be an infringement or breach of the Rules or from the contract of carriage, and the carrier will not be liable for any loss or damage resulting therefrom.
* Where a shipowner knows his vessel is going to deviate from the contracted voyage in any respect, his **P&I club** will normally advise that he immediately **contacts the club**, which will decide whether the deviation can be covered under the club rules. Minor deviations may be covered, but where the club considers the deviation flagrant they will probably not cover it and will advise the member to obtain special deviation/shipowner's liability (SOL) insurance on the market.
* Where the master is unable to prevent a contractual deviation, he should **record the facts** fully in the official log book and immediately contact his owners and, if in port, the **P&I club correspondent** (see G02a.3d).

F07a.6 Reasonable dispatch

* The carrier must carry out the voyage **without undue delay**. The vessel must be ready to load and commence the voyage either within a time stated in the contract or within a reasonable time if not stated.

F07a.7 Summary of the common law rules applying to carriers

* **3 common law obligations** (as to seaworthiness, deviation, reasonable despatch) are basic obligations of all carriers.
* **6 common law exceptions** (act of God, Queen's enemies, inherent vice, defective packing, fraud, jettison/general average) protect the carrier from liability, unless he is negligent, if his vessel was unseaworthy at the start of the voyage, or if there was a serious deviation from the contract (e.g. cargo taken to a non-agreed port, etc.).

F07a.8 Exceptions clauses used by private carriers

- exclude or limit the carrier's strict liability.
- extend the list of "excepted perils" beyond the six common law exceptions.

* The **effectiveness of exceptions clauses** is severely restricted by UK statutes, including the Carriage of Goods by Sea Act 1971, the Merchant Shipping Act 1995 and the Unfair Contract Terms Act 1977 (which provides that there can be no exclusion of liability for death or personal injury). Under **section 186(1) of the Merchant Shipping Act 1995**, for example, the owner of a UK ship will not be liable[14] for any loss or damage where:
  - any property on board ship is lost or damaged through **fire** on board; or
  - any **gold, silver, watches, jewels or precious stones** on board are lost or damaged through theft, robbery or other dishonest conduct and their nature and value were not at the time of shipment declared by their owner or shipper to the owner or master in the bill of lading or otherwise in writing.

* Exceptions commonly inserted by carriers in older forms of contract document include:
  - **Restraints of rulers, princes and peoples**, i.e. forcible interference with the business of the ship by a constituted authority on the high seas or in port or other places. It includes frustration of the voyage due to embargo or blockade, and refusal to allow the ship to load or discharge. Arrest of the ship is only included if this is not due to normal legal proceedings such as for recovery of port dues.
  - **Piracy**. Pirates are bandits of the high seas plundering for personal gain. Seizure of the ship by passengers is also piracy.
  - **Robbers and thieves**, i.e. persons from outside the ship taking violent action to seize goods. It normally excludes theft by persons carried on the vessel, such as passengers and crew.
  - **Barratry**, i.e. any wrongful act on the part of the master or crew to the owner's or charterer's detriment, e.g. theft of cargo, and delaying the voyage.
  - **Fire**. Under section 186(1) of the Merchant Shipping Act 1995 the owner of a UK ship will not be liable for any loss of or damage to property caused by fire on board[15].
  - **Inherent vice** (explained above).
  - **Jettison**, including jettison rendered necessary by a "peril of the seas" and jettison necessary due to the neglect of the master or crew, provided the vessel was initially seaworthy and the goods were not being carried in a manner contrary to the contract terms (e.g. unlawfully stowed on deck).
  - **Act, neglect or default of the master**, which applies to the ship's navigation, but not to improper stowage, bad preparation of the holds, poor ventilation, etc. The shipowner would therefore not be responsible for damage done to goods if the master or an officer ran the ship aground, provided that the owner had hired apparently competent and properly qualified officers.
  - **Explosions, bursting of boilers, breakages of shafts and latent defects**. A latent defect is one not apparent to the eye, or discoverable by "such an examination as a reasonably careful man skilled in the matter would make". The owner is only protected from liability if there is no negligence on the part of her crew.

* As an alternative to an Exceptions Clause stating what the owners/carrier will *not* be liable for, some modern charter parties, such as "GENCON", have an **Owners' Responsibility Clause** stating what the carrier *will* accept responsibility for (see F05a.3).

F07b BILLS OF LADING AND RELATED DOCUMENTS

F07b.1 Outline of bill of lading functions

* A **bill of lading** -
  - is a **receipt** for goods either received (before shipment) or shipped on board (see F07b.5).
  - is good **evidence of the existence and terms of a contract** between the shipper and carrier (see F07b.6). (A contract of carriage may exist without issue of a bill of lading, however.) A bill of lading is not a true contract, since it is usually signed by only one of the parties.
  - is a **document of title**, signifying that the holder has the **legal right to possession** of the goods it describes (see F07b.7). (The right to possession should not be confused with the **right to ownership**, which will usually be determined by the terms of the sales contract.)

---

[14] Under Article 4 of the Convention on Limitation of Liability for Maritime Claims 1976, a person liable will not be entitled to limit his liability if it is proved that the loss resulted from his personal act or omission, committed with the intent to cause such loss, or recklessly and with knowledge that such loss would probably result.

[15] Under section 186(3), section 186 does not exclude the liability of any person for any loss or damage resulting from a personal act or omission committed with intent to cause such loss, or recklessly and with knowledge that such loss would probably result.

- may, depending on how it is made out, be **negotiable**, i.e. transferable to a third party so as to effect transfer of title to the goods it describes.
* For a better understanding of the main functions of a bill of lading it is useful to know the **basic documentary procedures** used in tramp and liner shipping operations, as outlined below.

F07b.2 Dry cargo tramp shipping procedure

* The following procedure is the traditional, basic shipping practice followed in many parts of the world and in many trades other than modern liner operations. An understanding of it should help when attempting to understand the roles of bills of lading and related documents.
    1. Exporter/shipper makes a goods **sales contract** with an overseas buyer/consignee.
    2. Carrying ship is **voyage chartered**, proceeds to loading port, arrives on berth.
    3. **Shipping note** containing details of goods (as stated by shipper) is presented to chief mate or master.
    4. **Goods are loaded** (i.e. shipped) on board. Break bulk goods (i.e. bagged, baled, crated, etc., goods) are **tallied** on board by ship's tally clerk; if in bulk, ship **ascertains in-taken cargo weight or quantity** by some means.
    5. Chief mate compares ship's tally or in-taken cargo tonnage with details on shipping note and issues a **mate's receipt** from ship's triplicate book. Mate's receipt contains accurate and truthful details of quantity and condition of goods, i.e. their "**apparent order and condition**", with references to any shortage, damage, etc. One or more copies are given to shipper's representative; ship retains one copy in book. (In practice the port agent may issue mate's receipts for the carrier.)
    6. Shipper obtains a full set of **blank bills of lading** (e.g. "CONGENBILL" forms) from carrier or printer and types in details of shipped goods exactly as stated on mate's receipt. Set most often comprises **3 originals**, but sometimes fewer and very occasionally more, with several **copies** (marked "COPY – NON-NEGOTIABLE") for various parties and purposes (often including one marked "CAPTAIN'S COPY").
    7. **Shipper tenders all original bills for signing** by or on behalf of the carrier, i.e. by carrier's head office, port agent or ship's master.
    8. Person authorised to sign carefully **checks details** inserted by shipper to see that they correspond to those in ship's copy of mate's receipt, stamps/writes any required **endorsements**, then **signs** all original bills in set.
    9. Full **set of signed original bills is issued** to shipper, together with copies as required. (Mate's receipt, as issued by ship, may be demanded by carrier before issue of bills of lading.) Master retains one copy of bill of lading on board as "**captain's copy**".
    10. **Ship sails** from loading port.
    11. Shipper sends full set of bills of lading to **consignee** (usually in exchange for payment for goods, but as agreed in sales contract). At least one bill should be posted in a later post than others, in case all are lost/stolen.
    12. Ship **arrives** at discharge port.
    13. Consignee, or **receiver** acting as consignee's agent (e.g. haulage contractor), proves his identity to port agent and presents **one original** bill of lading, duly endorsed to him. **Freight**, demurrage or other charges owed to carrier are paid to agent.
    14. Agent stamps presented bill of lading "ACCOMPLISHED"; all other original bills of lading in set are now legally **void**. Agent issues **delivery order** to consignee or receiver to enable collection of goods from quay, warehouse, tank, ship, etc.
    15. **Delivery order is presented** to warehouseman, ship, etc. Goods are released into possession of consignee or receiver and become legally **delivered**.
* The above is a simplification of the procedure in modern shipping operations. The **documentary credit system** (see F03c) is often used to facilitate early payment of the seller by the buyer, and this complicates the journey of the bills of lading, since the original bills must be transferred to specified **banks** as security for their credit advances, made out in such a way that each bank involved has a good legal title in the goods represented by the bill of lading (see F07b.3).

F07b.3 The bill of lading in the documentary credit system

* For notes on the documentary credit system see F03c.
* The following outlines the basic process relating to the **bill of lading** where a Letter of Credit is used, i.e. in the "documentary credit system". Assume that the **seller/shipper** is "UK Exporter" and **buyer/consignee** is "NZ Importer".
    1. **UK Exporter and NZ Importer** conclude **sales contract** specifying CIF terms (see F03b.2) and **payment by documentary credit** (to allow early payment of UK Exporter).
    2. **NZ Importer** instructs his bank in NZ to **open a Credit** in favour of UK Exporter.

3. **NZ bank** verifies NZ Importer's credit-worthiness and **issues Letter of Credit** (LOC) containing terms of the Credit (stringent requirements re-documents, time of loading, etc.). NZ bank sends LOC to UK Exporter's bank in UK.
4. **UK bank** checks terms of LOC, sends it to UK Exporter.
5. **UK Exporter** despatches goods, assembles documents required by LOC (usually invoice, insurance certificate, full set of "clean" "on board" bills of lading, which it obtains once goods are shipped).
6. **UK Exporter** presents all documents to UK bank, asks for payment.
7. **UK bank** checks documents against LOC; if they comply (including "clean" bills of lading, with loading port and date as specified in LOC), pays UK Exporter and sends documents to NZ Importer's bank.
8. **NZ bank** checks documents against LOC; if they comply, releases documents to NZ Importer against payment, and reimburses UK bank.
9. **NZ Importer** receives all documents from bank and presents one bill of lading to carrier's port agent to obtain release of goods from ship (as described under "tramp shipping procedure" in F07b.2).

* A major problem arises when the bank is instructed in the Letter of Credit to pay on production of a full set of "**clean on board**" bills of lading, but the bills of lading have been **claused** in respect of defective or short goods. Other Letter of Credit problems include **incorrect ship's name, loading or discharge port,** or **loading date** outside the range of dates allowed by the LOC. Banks will refuse payment if any details on the bill of lading do not match the requirements of the LOC.

F07b.4 Liner shipping procedure

* In modern liner shipping, documentary procedures have been simplified where possible, and many of the liner companies now have their own computerised bill of lading issuing systems. Shippers require rapid issue of bills of lading and an invoice by the carrier as soon as goods are packed into a container, and to facilitate this the carrier needs accurate shipping documentation from the shipper.
* The system used by most liner operators ("carriers") is basically as in the following notes. Assume the carrier is "Linerco", the exporter is "UK Shipper" and the consignee is "NZ Importer". The exporter has a small consignment of goods which he will send to Linerco's inland container freight station for consolidation in an LCL (Less than Container Load) container. No freight forwarder is hired by the exporter.
1. **UK Shipper** in Glasgow, Scotland contacts Linerco and makes a telephone **booking** for carriage of cargo consignment from Coatbridge (container base near Glasgow) to NZ.
2. **Linerco** confirms booking and sends UK Shipper an **Export Cargo Shipping Instruction** (ECSI) form, on which UK Shipper provides information about the goods and their route to final destination, any transport requirements, customs information, who is to receive what documents and allocation of costs. UK Shipper returns ECSI to Linerco, who enter details in computer system.
3. **UK Shipper sends goods** to Linerco's depot at Coatbridge container base along with a 6-part **Standard Shipping Note** (SSN), which is the receiving document for UK ports and container bases, containing necessary information for handling of the goods (see F07b.11). If goods are dangerous goods or marine pollutants, a Dangerous Goods/Marine Pollutants Note with Container Vehicle Packing Certificate is used instead of the SSN (see F07f.2c).
4. On receipt of goods and a "clean" Standard Shipping Note or Dangerous Goods Note, Linerco issues a "**received" bill of lading** to UK Shipper (see F07b.5).
5. **Linerco fills LCL container** destined for NZ with goods of UK Shipper and other NZ-bound consignments, then transports container by rail to loading port in south of England. ("**LCL**" means "Less than Container Load".)
6. **Linerco-owned or chartered ship** arrives at loading port and loads **FCL and LCL containers**. ("**FCL**" means "Full Container Load", i.e. a container filled with one exporter's goods.)
7. On payment of advance **freight** by UK Shipper, Linerco issues set of "**shipped" bills of lading** to replace "received" bill.
8. UK Shipper sends to his **bank** all original bills of lading and other documents in accordance with **Letter of Credit instructions**, in order to receive payment of invoice price.
9. Procedure thereafter is as with tramp shipping (see F07b.2).

F07b.5 The bill of lading as a receipt for goods

* The bill of lading's prime function is as a **receipt** issued for:
    * **goods received for shipment** either by a carrier or a freight forwarder, etc. pending shipment on a vessel; or
    * **goods shipped** on board the carrying vessel,

- depending on the wording or endorsements on the bill.
* A bill of lading states the **quantity and apparent order and condition of the goods when received** into the carrier's care and is normally printed with wording such as "Received in good order and condition unless otherwise stated..." or "shipped in good order and condition unless otherwise stated....". If this statement is not true, appropriate remarks should be made on the face of the bill of lading. Any shortage or damage to the goods occurring before acceptance by the carrier should therefore be stated on the face of the bill of lading.
* If there is no **clausing** of the bill of lading showing a **defective condition or quantity** of the goods on receipt by the carrier, the consignee may reasonably expect to receive his goods in good order and condition. Any loss or damage found on delivery will be assumed to be caused by the carrier's negligence unless he can prove it to be attributable to one of the excepted perils listed in his contract of carriage (e.g. Act of God, inherent vice, etc.).
* Where a mate's receipt is issued, the bill of lading's description of the quantity/condition of the goods is copied from the description in the mate's receipt. It is most important, therefore, that the mate's receipt states the **actual quantity/condition** of the goods at the time of loading where this is other than "in good order or condition" or differs in quantity from that stated in the shipping note.

F07b.5a The problem of the clean bill of lading

* A **clean bill of lading** is a bill of lading bearing no superimposed clauses stating a defective condition or shortage of the goods. It states that the goods have been received "in apparent good order and condition...", without further remarks as to their condition.
* A **dirty bill of lading**, also known as a "claused" or "foul" bill, is one claused with remarks such as "torn bags", "rusty drums", "three (3) more c/s in dispute - if on board to be delivered", etc.
* A full set of "clean on board bills of lading" is normally demanded as a condition of a bank's **letter of credit**, and if not issued will prevent early payment of the exporter by the bank. Pressure may therefore be exerted by a shipper for clean bills to be issued, even where these would not be justified by the actual condition or quantity of the goods.
* A **Letter of Indemnity** (or "back letter") may be offered by the shipper, promising to indemnify the master or carrier against any loss or liability as a consequence of signing a clean bill of lading. However, acceptance of a Letter of Indemnity of this type in return for clean bills makes the master a party to an act of deception or fraud on banks, consignee/buyer, and insurers, since it is an attempt to obtain payment for goods knowing them to be unsound. There may be personal criminal liability for fraud on the part of the carrier and the master, and a heavy financial liability on the shipowner. This type of Letter of Indemnity has no legal standing in English law and cannot be sued on if the shipper goes back on his promise of indemnity.
* A master should consult his owners and their P&I club's **correspondent** if he is in any doubt, but should **never accept a Letter of Indemnity of this sort** without the written orders of his owners.

F07b.5b The bill of lading in the hands of a third party

* At common law, a bill of lading is only **prima facie** *evidence* as to the quantity, weight and condition of goods shipped, i.e. if a bill is signed for a greater quantity of cargo than is actually shipped, it may be possible, provided the bill is not endorsed to a third party, for the carrier to refute the statements on it. Once the bill is endorsed to a third party, however, it becomes **conclusive evidence** of the shipment, i.e. the carrier will be bound by the bill of lading's terms and conditions, whether the goods were shipped or not. (Since liner bills of lading are usually made out in a shore office and not on board, it is quite possible for bills to be issued for cargo that was not shipped for some reason.)
* **Section 4 of the Carriage of Goods by Sea Act 1992** underlines the common law position in the UK by providing that: "A bill of lading which (a) represents goods to have been shipped on board a vessel or to have been received for shipment on board a vessel; and (b) has been signed by the master of the vessel or by a person who was not the master but had the express, implied or apparent authority of the carrier to sign bills of lading, shall, in favour of a person who has become the lawful holder of the bill, be **conclusive evidence** against the carrier of the shipment of the goods or, as the case may be, of their receipt for shipment. every bill of lading in the hands of a consignee or indorsee for valuable consideration becomes conclusive evidence of the shipment as against the master or person signing the bill of lading, notwithstanding that such goods or part of them may not have been shipped."
* A **Conclusive Evidence Clause** is inserted in some bills of lading stating that the contents of the bill will be conclusive evidence against the contracting parties. It is very important, therefore, for the master to ensure, before signing a bill containing such a clause, that an accurate tally has been made of the goods received on board. (If there has been **fraud** on the part of the shipper, however, the clause will not be binding on the carrier.)

F07b.5c The bill of lading as a receipt for freight

* If the bill of lading is endorsed with words such as "FREIGHT PAID or "FREIGHT PREPAID", then once it is signed it becomes *prima facie* a **receipt for the freight**.
* If the freight has not actually been paid, but the receipted bill of lading is endorsed to a third party, the carrier will probably lose his right to recover the freight, i.e. the statement becomes **conclusive evidence** that freight has been paid. It is important, therefore, to **verify** before signing such a bill of lading that freight has in fact been paid. (In practice the agent will normally do this.)

F07b.6 The bill of lading as evidence of a contract

* The conditions on which goods are accepted for shipment constitute the terms of the contract of carriage between the shipper and the carrier, except when the shipper is also a charterer. Three cases arise:
    * where there is no charter party;
    * where there is a charter party and the charterer is also the shipper; and
    * where there is a charter party but the charterer is not the shipper.
* **Where there is no charter party**, e.g. where containerised cargo is loaded on a container vessel in the shipowner's own liner service, the shipowner is the legal carrier and issues to the shipper its own bill of lading containing the company's terms and conditions of carriage. (Some liner operators issue a **booking note** containing their contract terms which, when signed by both parties, becomes the contract of carriage.)
* **Where there is a charter party and the charterer is also the shipper**. The charterer is shipper of his own goods. The contract of carriage in this case is contained in the **charter party**. If the charter party requires the ship to issue a bill of lading on shipment of the cargo, the charterer is in effect issuing himself with a bill of lading. Therefore the bill of lading serves only as a receipt for the goods shipped and as a document of title should the charterer/shipper decide to sell the cargo by endorsement and transfer of the bill of lading. Because it does not contain the contract terms, the bill of lading in this case will usually be a "short form" bill, bearing only a few important printed clauses such as a Clause Paramount, Both-to-Blame Collision Clause and New Jason Clause. Since the bill of lading may be transferred to a third party, there should be a statement that "all terms and conditions of the Charter party (dated as shown) are deemed to be contained herein." Any terms on the bill of lading must be consistent with those in the charter party unless there is an express provision to the contrary in the charter party.
* **Where the charterer is not the shipper**, e.g. where a carrier is time-chartering a vessel and operating her in his own liner services. The **contract of hire** between the carrier and the shipowner is contained in the time charter party. The **contract of carriage** between the carrier and a shipper is evidenced by the **bill of lading** issued to the shipper. If the bill of lading contains **no reference** to the existence of a charter party, the shipper's contract of carriage will be with the shipowner. But if bill of lading contains **a reference** to a charter party, the shipper's contract will be with the time charterer.

F07b.7 The bill of lading as a document of title

* "**Title**", in the context of carriage of goods, means **the right to possession**, as distinct from the right to **ownership**.
* A "**document of title**" is a document embodying the undertaking of a person holding goods (who is called a "**bailee**") to hold the goods for whoever is the current holder of the document and to deliver them to that person in exchange for the document[16].
* **Possession of an original bill of lading** is equivalent in law to the **right to possession of the goods** described in the bill, i.e. it gives **title** or "constructive possession" to the goods it represents. In other words, an original bill of lading, being a "bearer document", is good evidence that its holder is the rightful possessor of the goods. This enables any holder to obtain delivery of the goods at the discharge port by production of an original bill of lading.
* **Title to the goods may be transferred** after shipment to a third party, such as a bank under a Letter of Credit arrangement, by "**negotiation**" (i.e. transfer) of the full set of original bills of lading by the shipper, subject to the bills being made out in a way that permits this in law. A bill of lading made out so as to enable its negotiation is a "**negotiable document of title**". Bills which are not made out in a way that permits negotiation are termed "non-negotiable", and are often endorsed to clearly indicate this.

---

[16] According to one American commercial glossary, the term "document of title" includes a bill of lading, dock warrant, dock receipt, warehouse receipt, order for the delivery of goods, and any other document that in the regular course of business or financing is treated as adequate evidence that the person in possession of it is entitled to receive, hold, and dispose of the document and the goods it covers.

* **To make the original bills of lading negotiable** they must either be made out with the words "**to order**" in the space allocated for the consignee's name, or "**to (XYZ CONSIGNEE LTD.) or his order**" in the same space, which allows the original consignee to transfer title to a third party, such as another buyer of the goods, if required.
* **Transfer of title** from the shipper may be made by any one of three methods, as follows:
    * By means of a "**blank endorsement**", whereby the shipper stamps the back of each original bill with his company's stamp and adds his signature, but without inserting any transferee's name, before passing the set of bills to the transferee. A blank-endorsed "order" bill of lading (i.e. one made out "to order") is a bearer document, like a postal order or a cheque made out to "Cash", and the carrier must deliver the goods to whoever presents any one of the originals (unless he has reason to suspect fraud). Like a bearer cheque, a blank-endorsed bill of lading is a dangerous document but due to the requirements of banks which are asked by international traders to advance money against documents it is commonly used.
    * By "**specific endorsement**" on the back of the bill of lading, e.g. "deliver to ABC Receivers Ltd", with the stamp and signature of the shipper. The person to whom title is thus transferred may be termed the "**endorsee**".
    * By **attaching authorised delivery instructions** on the shipper's stationery, e.g. a Delivery Order from the shipper to the consignee.
* Once a bill of lading has been negotiated, the endorsee or transferee becomes subject to the same liabilities and has the same rights against the carrier as if the contract of carriage had originally been made with the endorsee. This means that if freight or demurrage is payable before delivery of the cargo, the endorsee may be liable for the payment. To protect the endorsee the contract terms must be clear and unambiguous, and where some term in the original contract is not included in the bill of lading terms, it will not be binding on the endorsee.
* The **reason for making out a set of original bills of lading** is that, if a single bill of lading were to be lost, the consignment of goods would have to be warehoused, a duplicate obtained (which would cause delay), or an indemnity given to the carrier, before the goods could be released. Since this would be time-consuming and costly, bills of lading are normally issued in sets of two or more "originals", the most common number of originals being three[17].
* It is **unwise to enclose a full set of bills of lading in one envelope**, because of the danger of all the bills being lost together. Banks will therefore split a set into two envelopes, one being posted immediately and the second being held for 2, 3 or 4 days and then posted, to avoid the possibility of both envelopes being in transit in the same bag.
* Several non-negotiable, "**copy**" **bills of lading** will normally be made for filing and other purposes, and one of them is usually marked "CAPTAIN'S COPY" and travels on the ship in the master's custody.

F07b.8 Types of bill of lading

* Bill of lading forms are produced in many styles by shipping companies, shippers, charterers, freight forwarders and organisations such as BIMCO. Several types are used for different purposes.
* A "**long-form**" **bill of lading** has spaces or boxes on its front for typed details and numerous printed conditions of carriage on its back. Most liner shipping companies print their own long-form bills of lading with their company conditions of carriage on the back.
* A "**short form**" **bill of lading** has only a few standard terms printed on it, avoiding the need for shippers to hold stocks of bills of lading for every carrier they use, so that they can prepare the bill of lading with the required details before presentation for signature. A short form bill of lading made out for cargo loaded aboard a voyage-chartered ship will usually indicate that the terms and conditions of the relevant charter party are deemed to be incorporated in the bill of lading. This allows any party to whom the bill of lading is transferred to see where the contract of carriage actually is.
* A "**direct**" **bill of lading** is issued when the goods are for carriage from one port to another. Transshipment is not anticipated although there may be a clause giving the carrier liberty to transship (in which case the goods may lie at the merchant's risk whilst in the transshipment port). This type of bill of lading has printed clauses on the reverse and is used in liner services.
* A "**combined transport**" **bill of lading** covers carriage from door-to-door by several modes of transport, which is common in many liner services. The "combined transport operator" (CTO) takes responsibility for the goods throughout the entire journey and issues the CT bill of lading at its start.
* A "**through**" **bill of lading** is issued when the carriage will involve both sea and other transport modes, but different carriers will be involved at each stage, e.g. a railway company, a shipping company, a road haulier. The bill of lading is issued by the sea carrier but he states on it that he only accepts responsibility for the goods during the sea passage.

---

[17] In the short sea trades, where cargo is likely to arrive long before the bill of lading if sent by courier or post, one original is sometimes issued, for carriage on the ship with the goods it represents. In other unusual cases, two, four or five original bills may be issued.

* A **"received for shipment" bill of lading** or "received" bill of lading is issued for goods received at a freight depot or some other place before loading on the ship. This type of bill of lading may be issued by a freight forwarder and covers the goods while they are in his care. When the goods are eventually shipped the "received" bill of lading must be replaced by a "shipped" bill of lading.
* A **"shipped" bill of lading** or "on board" bill of lading is one that is issued by the carrier after the goods are loaded on the carrying ship.
* A **"straight" bill of lading** is an American term for a non-negotiable bill of lading.

F07b.9 Contents of bills of lading

* **Long form bills of lading**, as issued by carriers operating liner services, typically contain about 30 printed and numbered clauses. The majority of clauses are common to the bills of most major carriers, although the wording may differ. Additional clauses are added by carriers to address the special features of their particular trades.
* A long form liner bill of lading will usually, when issued, contain the following details:
  * a **reference number**;
  * name and address of the **shipper** or his agent;
  * name and address of the **consignee**, or **"to order", or "to the order of (consignee's name inserted)"**;
  * name and address of any **notify party** (e.g. a receiver taking delivery of the goods for the consignee);
  * **ports of loading and discharge**;
  * name of the carrying **vessel**;
  * any leading **marks** for identification of the goods (as stated by the shipper);
  * the **number and kind of packages** or pieces (as stated by the shipper);
  * **description of the goods** (as stated by the shipper);
  * **gross weight or measurement** (as stated by the shipper);
  * the **order and condition of the goods** if not in "apparent good order and condition" on receipt;
  * the place where **freight** is payable, if freight has not been paid;
  * the **number of original bills of lading** forming the "set" (so that the consignee or any transferee, such as a bank, can determine whether all original documents in the set have been delivered, in case of fraud or mistake);
  * the **date of receipt** of the goods for shipment or, on a "shipped" bill of lading, the **date of shipment**;
  * the place and date of **issue**;
  * the **signature** of the carrier, master or carrier's agent; and
  * the carrier's standard **terms and conditions** (on the back).
* **P&O Nedlloyd's bill of lading** includes clauses numbered and named as follows: **1**. Definitions; **2**. Carrier's tariff; **3**. Warranty; **4**. Sub-contracting and indemnity; **5**. Carrier's responsibility – port-to-port shipment; **6**. Carrier's responsibility – combined transport; **7**. Sundry liability provisions; **8**. Shipper-packed containers; **9**. Inspection of goods; **10**. Carriage affected by condition of goods; **11**. Description of goods; **12**. Shipper's/merchant's responsibilities; **13**. Freight; **14**. Lien; **15**. Optional stowage and deck cargo; **16**. Live animals; **17**. Methods and routes of carriage; **18**. Matters affecting performance; **19**. Dangerous goods; **20**. Notification and delivery; **21**. FCL multiple bills of lading; **22**. General average and salvage; **23**. Variations of the contract; **24**. Law and jurisdiction; **25**. Validity; **26**. Limitation of liability; **27**. USA clause paramount.
* **A charter party bill of lading** will usually contain a clause to the effect that all **terms and conditions of the charter party** identified in the bill of lading are incorporated in the bill.
* The **"CONGENBILL" charter party bill of lading** (1994 edition) includes clauses numbered and named as follows: 1. Unnamed (see below); 2. General Paramount Clause; 3. General Average; 4. New Jason Clause; 5. Both-to-Blame Collision Clause.
* "CONGENBILL" Clause 1 states as follows: "All terms and conditions, liberties and exceptions of the Charter Party, dated as overleaf, are herewith incorporated. The Carrier shall in no case be responsible for loss of or damage to cargo arisen prior to loading and after discharging."
* The carrier's **exceptions from liability** are contained in the Hague or Hague-Visby Rules, which are normally applied to the contract by the Clause Paramount.
* Stamped or hand-written clauses, e.g. "CLEAN ON BOARD" and "FREIGHT PREPAID", may be endorsed on a bill of lading, and will override any printed clauses. A bill of lading that has been surrendered at the discharge port may be endorsed by the carrier's agent with the word "ACCOMPLISHED".

F07b.9a Himalaya Clause

* A **Himalaya Clause** is a clause, found in some bills of lading (and in other forms of contract, including the terms of a passenger ticket), that **extends to specified third parties**, such as servants and agents of the carrier, and

independent contractors (e.g. stevedores and terminal operators) employed by the carrier, the **benefit of the carrier's bill of lading exemptions, limitations, defences and immunities**.

* The name of the clause is derived from the Court of Appeal decision in *Adler v. Dickson* (1954) (*The Himalaya*) in which the master and bosun of the P&O liner *Himalaya* were successfully sued in tort by a passenger who had been injured in falling from an improperly positioned gangway. P&O's passenger ticket contained an exclusion clause, freeing the carrier from any liability for death or injury, howsoever caused, and limiting the amount recoverable from the carrier, and the passenger therefore sought to make up the balance by **suing in tort individual servants of the carrier**, including the master and bosun. The Court of Appeal held that, despite the carrier's exemptions, she could do so. Since that judgement, many carriers have, therefore, inserted in their contracts a "Himalaya Clause" (or a clause with another name but a similar effect) to protect their employees, contractors and agents. In some jurisdictions, however, these clauses are ineffective.
* For notes on the **law of torts**, see B03e. For notes on **civil liabilities of shipmasters**, see E04i.2.

F07b.10 Mate's receipts and tallies

* A **mate's receipt** -
    - is a receipt, issued and signed by the carrying ship's chief mate (or the ship's agent on his behalf), for goods received on board.
    - may be encountered in virtually any conventional trade (general cargo, dry bulk or tanker), but has been replaced in the liner trades (i.e. container and ro-ro shipping) by a more modern document, the **Standard Shipping Note** (see F07b.11).
    - is the document on which the details entered on the bill of lading are based; the information on both mate's receipt and bill of lading should therefore be identical. The mate's receipt should not be copied directly from the shipping note presented when the goods are brought alongside, but should be compiled from a ship's tally or measurement and show the actual quantity and condition of the goods as received.
    - should, when the condition or quantity of the cargo justifies it, be **endorsed** with remarks such as "torn bags", "stained bales", "rusty drums", etc.
    - should, **where the ship's and shipper's tallies disagree**, be made out for the smaller figure, with the clause "X more (drums) in dispute; if onboard to be delivered", "X" being the difference between the tallies.
    - will normally be on the shipowner's form, in a triplicate pad or book kept on board. The **original** should be given to the person delivering the goods to the ship, a **copy** should go to the agent, and a **second copy** should be retained in the pad on the ship for comparing with bills of lading before signature, and for use in compiling the cargo plan.
    - is **not a document of title** to the goods shipped and does not pass any title by its endorsement or transfer.
* In ports and trades where mate's receipts are used, the shipper must usually present the signed mate's receipt to the agent in order to be issue with the signed set of original bills of lading before the vessel sails.

F07b.11 Standard Shipping Note (SSN)

- is a **shipping document** widely used in the **UK liner trades** to accompany a consignment of goods from their place of origin (e.g. a factory) to the place of loading (e.g. an inland container depot) or the port of shipment. The SITPRO form of SSN is most commonly used; this is a 6-part set compiled by the shipper or freight forwarder. A copy is retained by each party handling the goods until they are finally on board, when a **"shipped" bill of lading** is issued after matching the details on the documents (see F07b.4).
- **replaces** a mate's receipt in trades where it is used.
- gives full **details** of the exporter, customs status, carrier's booking number, consignee, freight forwarder, international carrier, vessel, port of discharge, shipping marks, number and type of packages, description of the goods, special stowage requirements, gross weight, cubic measurement of goods, container ID number, seal number, container/vehicle size and type (e.g. 40ft open top), tare weight and shipper preparing the note.
- enables all receiving parties to have clear, accurate and precise information on how the goods should be handled and the applicable Customs procedures.
- **should not be used where the consignment is classified as hazardous** (in which case a Dangerous Goods/Marine Pollutant Note should be provided by the shipper).

F07b.12 Signing bills of lading

* Where a shipmaster has to sign and issue original bills of lading, great care must be taken to see that all potential contractual pitfalls are covered. In such cases it would be advisable to consult the P&I club correspondent beforehand.
* **"Shipped" bills of lading** are signed on behalf of the carrier by or for the master of the carrying ship. A full set of original bills will be signed, then returned (via the agent) to the shipper. **Freight** may be payable before signing bills, depending on the carrier's terms.
* Where a mate's receipt was issued to the shipper on shipment of cargo, this may be required to be surrendered in exchange for the "shipped" bills of lading.
* The master or his authorised deputy should always check the following when signing a bill of lading:
    1. that the goods have actually been **shipped** (which may be determined from the ship's copy of any mate's receipt issued; this should be identical to the original mate's receipt issued to the shipper, which should be presented by the shipper when requesting his bills of lading);
    2. that the **date of shipment** is correct, i.e. as stated on the mate's receipt or standard shipping note;
    3. that the bill of lading is not marked "freight paid" or "freight prepaid" if not true;
    4. that any **clausing** of the corresponding mate's receipt is also contained in the bill of lading;
    5. that reference is made to the **charter party** where one exists;
    6. that any **charter party terms** do not conflict with the bill of lading terms; and
    7. that the **number of original bills** in the set is stated.
* **Every original** in the set must be **signed**.

F07b.12a Agents' authority to sign bills of lading

* See I01h.3a.

F07b.13 Delivery of the goods

* The carrier, carrier's agent or master is legally obliged to deliver the goods to the **first person presenting a signed original bill of lading** at the discharge port, together with proof of his **identity** and proof that **freight** and any other **charges** due have been paid. (A negotiable bill of lading is effectively, therefore, **a cloakroom ticket for cargo**: whoever has the bill of lading can collect the cargo.)
* Once the goods are released to a receiver (i.e. legally delivered), any carrier's **lien** for unpaid freight, etc. will be lost.
* If the bill of lading has been transferred by the original consignee, the **endorsements** on it should be checked before delivery.
* If the presented bill of lading appears to be in order, the master or the agent should sign it and date it (known as "**sighting the bill**"). It is then said to be "**accomplished**" and is usually stamped "ACCOMPLISHED". The goods can then be released to the receiver. A **delivery order** may be issued by the agent to the receiver (see F07b.2).
* Delivery may be (and in practice is often) made without presentation of a bill of lading, but only when certain precautions have been taken (see F07b.16l).

F07b.14 Sea waybills

* A **sea waybill** -
    - is a **receipt for goods shipped** on board.
    - is good **evidence of the existence and terms of a contract** between the shipper and carrier, but is not a contract itself.
    - **identifies the person to whom delivery of the goods is to be made** by the carrier in accordance with the contract of carriage. In contrast with a bill of lading, a sea waybill **always bears the consignee's name** (and usually also his address) in the appropriate box on its face.
    - is **non-negotiable**. Sea waybills usually (but do not always) bear the words "NON-NEGOTIABLE" on their face. The conditions of carriage may also bear a statement such as: "This Waybill is not a bill of lading and no bill of lading will be issued", or "This Waybill, which is not a document of title to the cargo....".
    - is **not a document of title**. For a definition of "document of title", see F07b.7. Rightful possession of a sea waybill does not give the right to possession of the goods described in it.
    - may be a **receipt for freight**, if endorsed to indicate that freight has been paid.

- may contain the full **conditions of carriage**, which will usually be similar to the carrier's bill of lading conditions. (Liner waybills tend to have the full terms on their reverse, whereas other waybills, such as gas tank waybills, do not.)
- **may be subject to** the Hague Rules or Hague-Visby Rules, and if so may contain a Clause Paramount.

* The **Carriage of Goods by Sea Act 1992** contains a definition of a sea waybill in section 1(3) which provides that:
    (a) "References in this Act to a **sea waybill** are references to any document which is not a bill of lading but -
        is such a receipt for goods as contains or evidences a contract for the carriage of goods by sea; and
    (b) identifies the person to whom delivery of the goods is to be made by the carrier in accordance with that contract".

* **A sea waybill can (and should) be used** when it is clear that a **negotiable document of title will not be required**, i.e. when -
    • **the goods will not sold** to a third party (i.e. a new consignee) while in transit; or
    • **credit will not be raised on the security of the goods**, e.g. on a bank's documentary credit terms.
    If these are not possibilities, and the shipper and buyer are well-established trading partners, the use of a sea waybill is appropriate and is encouraged by BIMCO.

* The **benefits of using sea waybills** instead of bills of lading are that -
    - they **can be carried on board** the carrying vessel, since they do not need to be produced by the receiving party in order to claim delivery of the goods. This means that the documents will arrive at the discharge port with the goods, overcoming the problems of postal delay, theft in transit, etc., and the non-availability of bills of lading on arrival of the ship. (Postal and administrative delays are especially troublesome in the short-sea trades where voyages are short and turn-round times fast.) A "ship's bag" containing the sea waybills, manifest, dangerous goods documentation, etc. will usually be brought on board by the loading port agent for handing by the master to the discharge port agent.
    - they are **not subject to any documentary formalities** other than a reasonable check by the carrier or his agent of the identity of the person claiming delivery of the goods.
    - because they are not documents of title, they are **less likely to be used fraudulently**. Money cannot be raised against a sea waybill as it can against negotiable original bill of lading.

* **Sea waybills are issued** by the carrier using a similar procedure as for issuing bills of lading.
* **If the sea waybill is not carried on the ship** it must be **sent** by the shipper (by mail, courier, etc.) to the consignee and **produced** by him or his agent (e.g. his receiver) to the carrier or his agent at the discharge port, in order to claim delivery of the goods.
* The carrier or his agent must still exercise due care in ensuring that **delivery is made to the proper party**, by making a reasonable **check of his identity**. In event of misdelivery, no responsibility is normally accepted unless due to fault or neglect on the part of the carrier.
* A substantial proportion of international liner trade consignments is now shipped under sea waybills, normally in circumstances where the goods are not the subject of a sale contract and where the shipper retains the right to nominate the identity of the receiver.

F07b.15 Bolero System

* The **Bolero System**, the "shop front" of which is the **bolero.net** website, is a technological environment, owned by the world's logistics and banking communities, in which paper bills of lading and other trade documentation are replaced by **electronic messages** sent via the Internet. Bolero is designed for all parties in the trade process: importers, exporters, freight forwarders, port authorities, inspection agencies, carriers, ship's agents, customs agencies and financial institutions.
* The Bolero technological environment is supported by a legal framework based on a Bolero Rule Book which establishes a contractually binding set of rules which all users of the Bolero System are required to sign.
* The backbone of the Bolero System is the Core Messaging Platform, which enables users to exchange electronic trade documents via the Internet. The system is secure, is underpinned by a unique legal structure, and is maintained by a trusted third party. All messages between users are validated. All messages are acknowledged, and notifications are provided as requested. Additional messages determine whether the recipient accepts or refuses the stated offer. Another major feature is the Title Registry application, which allows for the ownership of goods to be exchanged online.
* **Website**: www.bolero.net

F07b.16 Bill of lading-related problems

F07b.16a If damaged or otherwise defective cargo is presented for loading

* Where shippers offer damaged or defective goods for shipment, i.e. cargo which is not in the "apparent good order and condition" as stated in the printed terms on most bills of lading, the master's duty is either:
* to **reject the goods** (with the advice/assistance of an independent cargo surveyor where necessary); or
* to **accept** the goods for carriage on **condition** that he will issue a **claused bill of lading** stating the nature of the deficiency.
* The master is entitled, as the carrier's agent, to enter remarks on the bill of lading as to the apparent order and condition of the goods.
* Since some remarks may not be effective in protecting the carrier against claims by third parties, the master should contact the owner's P&I club correspondent before making any remarks of which he is uncertain; certain remarks may have adverse consequences for the shipper when he presents a "shipped" bill of lading to his bank in compliance with the terms of a Letter of Credit. For notes on the problem of the clean bill of lading, see F07b.5a.
* Where the damaged or defective cargo is **steel** in any form, the P&I club correspondent should always be consulted before any remarks are made on the bill of lading.
* **Where rusty steel is shipped**[18], as is often the case, claims will inevitably arise. The master is fully justified in clausing a bill of lading relating to a steel cargo on which rust is apparent. However, to simply write "rusty" on the bills of lading is not recommended by the P&I clubs, since it may not be effective in protecting the carrier's position and it may have adverse consequences for the shipper when he presents the bills of lading to his bank and demands payment for the goods.
* The P&I clubs advise that remarks on the **degree** of rusting, e.g. "extremely rusty" or "superficially rusty" **should never be made**.
* **In every case where steel is being loaded and rust is apparent**, the master should contact the P&I club correspondent before making any remarks on the bill of lading. Certain clauses will be recommended by the club, while the use of others will not be approved of.

F07b.16b If master is asked to sign "clean" bills of lading when these are not justified

* For notes on the problem of the clean bill of lading, see F07b.5a.

F07b.16c If ship and shore loading figures differ

* Where the ship's cargo quantity measurements show less cargo loaded than the quantity stated by the shipper, the master should generally enter the **ship's figures** on the face of the bill of lading.
* Some shipowners require their masters to endorse a bill of lading which does not provide space for the ship's figures in the following terms: "Vessel's measurements are stated below and this Bill of Lading only acknowledges the shipment of the weight or quantity given in the vessel's measurements on completion of loading".
* Where the shipper refuses to accept such an endorsement the master should write a Letter of Protest to the shipper, pointing out the discrepancy in the figures and stating that the bill of lading will be signed under protest. A copy of the Letter of Protest should be stapled to each negotiable copy of the bill of lading (i.e. each bill of lading in the set of "originals").
* If the ship's measurements show **more** cargo loaded than advised by the shipper, the **shipper's figures** should be entered on the bill of lading. No Letter of Protest will be necessary.

F07b.16d If a charterer's bill of lading has to be used

* Where a charter party requires the master to sign bills of lading as presented by the charterer, the master should first **verify** that the bills of lading incorporate the terms of the Hague or Hague-Visby Rules. (This will generally be stated in the Clause Paramount or Paramount Clause.)
* P&I clubs usually restrict cover to contracts incorporating terms at least as favourable as those given by the Hague Rules or Hague-Visby Rules. **Where there is no reference** in the charterer's bill of lading to the incorporation of these Rules, the P&I club correspondent should be contacted.
* **Where the master is required to sign "clean" bills of lading as presented by the charterer**, "clean" has been held by a court to mean only that the bill of lading should not be claused to the effect that demurrage was due at the

---

[18] Masters of vessels carrying **steel cargoes** should obtain *Steel – Carriage by Sea*, by A.Sparks, MNI, published in 1995 by LLP.

loading port, without affecting the master's right to clause the bill of lading as to the apparent order and condition of the goods where necessary.

* **Where a contractual lien for demurrage is given** by the charter party terms, and demurrage is due at the loading port but not paid, the master should **clause the bill of lading to that effect** so that the lien can be exercised if necessary at the discharge port.

F07b.16e If the number of original bills of lading shown on the face of the bill is not the same as the number of negotiable bills of lading

* The **number of original bills of lading** in the set should, before signing, be entered in a space provided on the face of each bill. (In addition to these "originals", there may be several other "non-negotiable copy" bills, each of which should be clearly marked as such.)
* Where the master is asked to sign bills of lading and the number of "original" bills presented for signature is not the same as the number indicated on the face of the bill, the master should:
    * attempt to ascertain the reason for the discrepancy;
    * call the P&I club correspondent;
    * refuse to sign the bills until the correct number is inserted.

F07b.16f If two or more sets of bills of lading are requested by the shipper

* **Two or more sets of original bills of lading** may have to be issued in the following circumstances:
    * where cargo is shipped by more than one shipper (e.g. at multiple loading ports);
    * where cargo is consigned to more than one consignee; or
    * where more than one type, grade or specification of cargo is shipped by one shipper.
* **In the tanker trades** it may happen that two or more consignments of cargo, shipped by different shippers, are intentionally loaded into one tank, so that it becomes impossible to determine the respective shippers' quantities on completion of loading. In such cases the master should **endorse and sign separate bills of lading** to the effect that the shipments are part cargoes, or are part of a bulk cargo.
* Where multiple consignments are loaded, but **only one total figure** is given, the master should **consult the shipper** as to the apportionment of quantities on the bills of lading for each consignment. Where no instructions are obtainable, the **total quantity loaded should generally be divided** between the bills of lading in proportion to the original split of the nominated consignments. For example, where the consignments were nominated as 40,000 tons consigned to Party A and 60,000 tons to Party B, but only 99,400 tons are loaded, the apportionment on the bills of lading should be 39,760 tons and 59,640 tons respectively.

F07b.16g If a bill of lading presented for signing is written in an incomprehensible foreign language or alphabet

* Bills of lading are, in some countries (e.g. Libya), presented for signing in a foreign language or alphabet which may not be known to the master. In such case the master should arrange for the bill of lading to be **translated** by an independent third party (i.e. someone other than an agent of either the carrier or charterer). If in doubt, the P&I club correspondent or British consul should be asked whom to employ.
* If a translator cannot be found, the master should make out his **own bill of lading** in English (using another bill of lading form as a model), and issue this to the shipper for completion of the shipment details before signing. Only appropriate clauses should be incorporated.

F07b.16h If the master is asked to sign blank or partially completed bills of lading

* Except where the Early Departure Procedure is being properly used in the tanker trades (see F07b.16i), blank or partially-completed bills of lading should **never** be signed and issued by the master, for obvious reasons.
* In all cases where the master is asked to sign blank or partially-completed bills of lading, the P&I club correspondent should be advised.

F07b.16i If Early Departure Procedure is used

* Some oil terminals and tanker companies use an **"Early Departure Procedure"** ("EDP") to allow tankers to sail on completion of cargo operations without having to wait for cargo figures to be prepared and documents produced. The practice is more commonly used when the ship's time is at a premium, but at other times is discouraged.
* In the EDP system:

1. **Bills of lading are prepared before completion of loading**, but without any loaded cargo quantity as advised by the shipper.
2. The agent presents the bills of lading for the master's signature before completion of loading.
3. The master **returns the originals** of the bills of lading to the agent **but retains the non-negotiable "captain's copies"** together with **"copy" bills for consignees**, and other completed cargo documents.
4. The master writes any necessary **Letter of Protest** regarding the order or condition of the cargo, and allows any investigation to be completed before departure.
5. After departure of the ship, the **agent communicates the shipper's final loading figures** to the master as soon as they are available.
6. If the master agrees the communicated figures, he **enters them on his "captain's copies"** of the bill of lading and on the **consignee's copies**, while the **agent completes the original bills of lading** and signs them on behalf of the master.
7. **If the master does not agree with the shipper's figures** he informs the agent, who writes a **Letter of Protest** to the shipper on the master's behalf and completes and signs the bills of lading under protest.
8. The **agent releases all original documents** to the shipper, who sends them to the consignee.

* At some ports the practice may be to present bills of lading to the master for signature either blank or only partially-completed, but the master should **never sign such documents**, and should instead call the P&I club correspondent.
* Agents should be authorised to sign bills of lading on behalf of the master **only after the master has been made aware** of, and has **agreed** to, any **details (including loading figures) to be entered**.

F07b.16j If bills of lading have to be re-issued or amended

* The master may be asked to re-issue or amend a previously issued bill of lading. He should never agree to this without the **consent of the P&I club correspondent**.
* The P&I club correspondent will normally ensure that before a second set is issued, all bills of lading in the first set are **returned and cancelled or destroyed**. (The number of original bills returned should, of course, tally with the number of originals issued, as stated on the face of each bill.)
* **Each bill of lading in the new set** should be claused as follows:

```
This is a replacement Bill of Lading issued at.................... on the ...... day of ..................... (month/year)
on cancellation of an original Bill issued at .................. on the ...... day of .....................(month/year) to
show (reason for re-issuing bills of lading).
```

F07b.16k If the master is asked to pre-date or post-date bills of lading

* Under the terms of a Letter of Credit, payment to the seller of the goods will normally depend on the goods being shipped on a particular date, or between particular dates, and banks will generally refuse to pay the seller if the actual date of loading does not correspond with the date stipulated in the Letter of Credit. Cases therefore arise where the incorrect loading date is inserted in bills of lading in an attempt to evade a delay in obtaining payment.
* A "shipped" bill of lading should always be dated for **the actual date of loading**, or the **date of completion** of loading. Although the master may be requested to sign pre-dated or post-dated bills of lading, he should **never do so**.

F07b.16l If delivery of cargo is requested without presentation of the relevant bill of lading

* **In the tanker trades**, cargoes are commonly bought and sold many times during a voyage, causing delays in the arrival of the bills of lading, and the problem commonly arises that the cargo arrives at the discharge port before a copy of an original bill of lading can be produced.
* In other cases, the bill of lading may be missing for a variety of reasons. The receiver may claim that the bills have been lost, stolen or delayed. In such cases, there is there is the possibility of **misdelivery** and a serious risk of fraud.
* If the master negligently delivers cargo to the wrong party without first requiring production of an original bill of lading, the carrier will be held wholly liable for the consequences and will receive no backing from his P&I club or sympathy from the courts. Wrongful delivery may even result in the **arrest** and **sale of the ship** to recover the cargo's value for the rightful owner.
* If it is likely that the bill of lading has merely been **delayed**, the goods may be delivered - with the shipowner's and the P&I club's agreement - after the receiver signs an acceptable **Letter of Indemnity**. An "acceptable" Letter of Indemnity is one that:
  * promises to indemnify the shipowner against all consequences and liabilities of delivery to the wrong person;
  * is phrased in terms acceptable to the owner's P&I club; and
  * is countersigned by a first class bank or cargo insurance underwriter, i.e. one able to meet any claim.

* Some P&I clubs print the text of their standard Letter of Indemnity in their club handbook or rulebook, which should be carried on board. This does not imply, however, that the club will always give cover for claims arising under such Letters of Indemnity. (See also G04b.2.)
* If an acceptable Letter of Indemnity cannot be offered, the cargo should not be delivered.

F07b.16m If cargo delivery is requested against presentation of an original bill of lading carried on board

* In some cases an original bill of lading may be sent to the consignee on board the carrying vessel.
* The master **should issue a receipt** to the shipper or his representative (e.g. the freight forwarder).
* The master **should not accept** for carriage original bills of lading made out **"to order"**, or where there is **no named destination** or where the **destination is qualified**, e.g. "Lands End for orders/intention Le Havre".
* The master **should not accept** original bills of lading for carriage if the shipper refuses to sign the receipt, or if no party is named as receiver in the bill of lading.
* The master **should not discharge** against an original bill of lading carried on board if the discharge port is different from the destination shown in the bill of lading. In this case he should consult the owner and the P&I club correspondent.
* On arrival at the discharge port the master **should hand the bill of lading to the party named** in the receipt, if his identity can be confirmed.

F07b.16n If two parties present "original" bills of lading

* The master should immediately contact the P&I Club correspondent.
* The bills of lading may be left with a court of law to settle the dispute. In the meantime, the goods should be **landed** to a warehouse/tank, etc., where they should be held until the dispute has been settled and freight and charges have been paid.

F07b.16o If goods are unclaimed at the discharge port

* The master is not obliged to deliver goods to a receiver until one original bill of lading is presented, but neither is he obliged to retain unclaimed goods on board.
* At common law, if goods are not claimed within a reasonable time, the master may **land** and **warehouse** them. The master has a duty to do this, in fact, rather than detain his ship in port beyond her laytime and make the charterer liable for demurrage. The warehouseman becomes a common agent of both carrier and consignee and should be instructed to release the goods only on payment of all outstanding charges (e.g. freight and demurrage). **Warehousing expenses** will be for account of the receiver of the goods.
* If the goods remain unclaimed, they may usually be **sold** by the carrier after a reasonable time (depending on local law) and after advertising for the consignee in the national press.
* Carriers often insert a clause known as a **London Clause** in their bills of lading giving them the right to land goods on arrival; this clause overrides the common law position.

F07c RULES GOVERNING CARRIER'S OBLIGATIONS AND LIABILITY

F07c.1 International conventions applicable to contracts of carriage

* Three sets of rules are in use in the international transport industry which contain "minimum" terms and conditions and, where a bill of lading is issued, set out:
  * the carrier's obligations;
  * the carrier's exceptions from liability;
  * the extent of the carrier's liability to the shipper;
  * the shipper's responsibilities; and
  * the amounts recoverable from the carrier in case of loss of or damage to the goods while in the carrier's care.
* These sets of rules are:
  * the **Hague Rules**, which have been adopted by the majority of trading countries;
  * the **Hague-Visby Rules**, adopted by the UK and nearly 30 other countries; and
  * the **Hamburg Rules**, adopted by relatively few countries (and not favoured by shipowners since they are less to their advantage than the other rules).

* In most cases, where a set of rules is adopted by a particular State, the rules are incorporated by law into the domestic legislation of the State. (For notes on the UK's adoption of the Hague-Visby Rules, see notes on the Carriage of Goods by Sea Act 1971 in F07c.3)
* Some States have not adopted any of the above rules into their national law but have made domestic legislation which adopts the **principles** of one or more sets of rules.
* Some States have not, for one reason or another, adopted any of the sets of rules, leaving it open to the carrier, in the absence of any domestic legislation in the port State, to decide which set of rules, if any, will be incorporated into the contract of carriage. A shipmaster can determine which set of rules applies to the contract of carriage in this situation by inspecting the **Clause Paramount** in the charter party and/or bill of lading relating to the particular carriage or voyage.

F07c.2 Hague-Visby Rules (HVRs)

- are properly called the **Hague Rules as Amended by the Brussels Protocol 1968**.
- apply to every bill of lading or any similar document of title relating to the carriage of goods **between ports in two different States** if:
  • the bill of lading or document is issued in a contracting State; or
  • the carriage is from a port in a contracting State; or
  • the contract contained in or evidenced by the bill of lading provides that the Hague-Visby Rules or the legislation of any State giving effect to them (e.g. the UK's Carriage of Goods by Sea Act 1971) are to govern the contract.
* Under Article V, the **Rules will not be applicable to charter-parties**, but **if bills of lading are issued in the case of a ship under a charter-party, they must comply** with the Rules.
* Many States, such as the UK, have legislation incorporating the Hague-Visby Rules into national law. Where no such national law applies, the Hague-Visby Rules may still apply to the carriage by agreement of the contracting parties. (See Clause Paramount in bill of lading, waybill or charter party.)
* **Article II** provides that, subject to the provisions of Article VI, **under every contract of carriage of goods by sea**, the **carrier**, in relation to the loading, handling, stowage, carriage, custody, care and discharge of such goods, will be subject to the **responsibilities** and **liabilities**, and entitled to the **rights** and **immunities**, set out in the Rules.
* "**Goods**" is defined in Article I as including goods, wares, merchandise, and articles of every kind whatsoever except live animals and cargo which by the contract of carriage is stated as being carried on deck and is so carried.

F07c.2a Carrier's responsibilities under the Hague-Visby Rules

* The carrier has three basic obligations:
  • to ensure the vessel's **seaworthiness**;
  • to **care for the cargo**; and
  • to issue a **bill of lading** where the shipper requests one.

F07c.2b Obligation in respect of seaworthiness

* Article III paragraph 1 provides that the carrier must, before and at the beginning of the voyage (i.e. up to the moment of sailing), exercise due diligence to:
  • make the ship seaworthy;
  • properly man, equip and supply the ship; and
  • make the holds, refrigerating and cool chambers, and all other parts of the ship in which goods are carried, fit and safe for their reception, carriage and preservation.
* "**Exercising due diligence**" means taking all reasonable precautions to see that the vessel is fit for the voyage contemplated. The carrier is not obliged to give an absolute guarantee of seaworthiness. The carrier may delegate his duty to exercise due diligence (e.g. to surveyors or repairers) but he will be responsible if his servants or contractors, etc. fail to exercise due diligence in carrying out their work.
* "**Seaworthy**" in this context means that the hull must be in sound condition, the vessel must be mechanically sound, equipped with charts, etc., and crewed by a properly trained crew. She need only be seaworthy at the commencement of the voyage, which usually means when she leaves the berth, whether under her own motive power or with the aid of tugs.
* If a cargo owner can show that his loss was caused by a failure of the carrier to exercise due diligence to make the vessel seaworthy, the carrier will not be able to rely on any other clauses in the Rules which reduce his liability (i.e. the exceptions from liability).

* **The holds** must be fit and safe for the reception, carriage and preservation of the cargo and, in particular, the hatch covers must be tight and there must be no instability of the vessel through improper stowage. It has been held that the neglect to protect a water pipe in a hold from frost which could have been expected at the time of year showed lack of due diligence to make the vessel seaworthy.

F07c.2c Carrier's obligation in respect of the cargo

* Article III paragraph 2 provides that, subject to the provisions of Article IV, the carrier must "**properly and carefully** load, handle, stow, carry, keep, care for and discharge any goods carried". Unlike seaworthiness, this duty extends **throughout the voyage** and implies a greater degree of care than exercising "due diligence". The courts do not expect perfection from the carrier, but it has been held that stowage was improper where -
    * contamination of other goods occurred;
    * there was inadequate or no ventilation;
    * dry cargo was damaged by liquid goods; and
    * vehicles were secured only by their own brakes.
* The carrier must have a proper system for looking after the cargo when stowed. He has a duty to use all reasonable means to ascertain the nature and characteristics of the cargo and to care for it accordingly, although the shipper should give special instructions where special care is required. (Where water in tractor radiators froze, it was held that the carrier should have been told of the risks.)

F07c.2d Obligation to issue a bill of lading

* Article III paragraph 3 provides that after receiving the goods into his charge, the carrier, the master or the carrier's agent must, if the shipper demands, **issue a bill of lading** to the shipper showing, amongst other things:
    * all leading marks for identification of the goods, as stated by the shipper before loading (in his shipping note), provided these are visible on the goods or their coverings;
    * either the number of packages or pieces, or the quantity, or weight, as stated by the shipper (in his shipping note); and
    * the apparent order and condition of the goods.
* The carrier, master or agent need not insert any inaccurate statements on the bill of lading or give any details which he cannot reasonably check. (Hence the practice for statements to be made such as "**said to weigh....**" and "**shipper's load and count**".)
* Any bill of lading thus issued will be *prima facie* evidence of receipt of the goods by the carrier as described, but proof to the contrary will not be admissible if the bill of lading is transferred to a third party acting in good faith (Article III paragraph 4).
* Any bill of lading issued after loading must be a "shipped" bill of lading if the shipper demands, provided he surrenders any previously issued document of title (e.g. a "received" bill of lading issued when the goods arrived at a warehouse or depot before shipment) (Article III paragraph 7).

F07c.2e Carrier's rights and immunities

- concern:
    * the carrier's **exceptions from liability**;
    * the carrier's right to **deviate**; and
    * the carrier's rights in respect of **dangerous goods**.
* Article IV paragraph 2 grants **seventeen exceptions from liability** to the carrier (compared with six under English common law). Neither the carrier or ship will be responsible for loss or damage arising or resulting from:
    * act, neglect or default of the master, mariner, pilot, or the servants of the carrier in the navigation or management of the ship;
    * fire, unless caused by actual fault or privity of the carrier;
    * perils, dangers and accidents of the sea or other navigable waters;
    * act of God;
    * act of war;
    * act of public enemies;
    * arrest or restraint of princes, rulers or people, or seizure under legal process;
    * quarantine regulations;
    * act or omission of the shipper or owner of the goods, his agent or representatives;
    * strikes, lockouts, stoppage or restraint of labour;

- riots and civil commotions;
- saving or attempting to safe life or property at sea;
- wastage in bulk or weight or any other loss or damage arising from inherent defect, quality or vice of the goods;
- insufficiency of packing;
- insufficiency or inadequacy of marks;
- latent defects not discoverable by due diligence;
- any other cause arising without the actual fault or privity of the carrier, or without the fault or neglect of the agents or servants of the carrier (but the burden of proof will be on the carrier to show that his fault or privity or the fault or neglect of his agents or servants did not contribute to the loss or damage).

* Article IV paragraph 4 provides that any **deviation** in saving or attempting to save life or property at sea, or any reasonable deviation, will not be an infringement or breach of the Hague-Visby Rules or of the contract of carriage, and the carrier will therefore not be liable for any resulting loss or damage.
* Article IV paragraph 6 provides that **goods of an inflammable, explosive or dangerous nature**, if not properly marked, or if shipped without the knowledge or consent of the carrier, may be landed, destroyed, jettisoned or rendered innocuous at any time before discharge. Such goods, even when shipped with the carrier's knowledge and consent, may be dealt with in this way without liability to the carrier, should they become dangerous.

F07c.2f General Average under the Hague-Visby Rules

* Under Article V, nothing in the Rules may be held to prevent the insertion in a bill of lading of any lawful provision regarding General Average. (Most bills of lading have a clause making the merchant or shipper aware that he may become liable for a contribution in General Average.)

F07c.2g Exclusion of deck cargo and live animals from Hague-Visby Rules cover

* **Article I(c)** excludes from the items defined as "goods" **live animals** and cargo which by the contract of carriage is **stated as being carried on deck and is so carried**. Live animals are excluded from cover **at all times**. Cargo which is carried on deck without being stated as such in the contract will, therefore, be subject to the Rules, as will cargo which is stated as being carried on deck but which is, in fact, carried below deck.
* Where the carrier's terms and conditions of carriage incorporate the Hague-Visby Rules, then in the absence of any term expressly providing to the contrary those terms will not cover live animals or deck cargo. A shipper of live animals or deck cargo should therefore make a **special contract** with the carrier, and should specifically state "FOR DECK CARRIAGE" on his shipping note. See also F07e.2.

F07c.2h Carriage of dangerous goods under Hague-Visby Rules

* See F07f.4.

F07c.3 Carriage of Goods by Sea Act 1971 (COGSA 71)

- is a UK act **to make the Hague-Visby Rules apply to the carriage of goods in certain circumstances**.
- **contains** sections as follows: 1. Application of Hague Rules as amended; 2. Contracting States, etc.; 3. Absolute warranty of seaworthiness not to be implied in contracts to which Rules apply; 4. Application of Act to British possessions, etc.; 5. Extension of application of Rules to carriage from ports in British possessions, etc.; 6. Supplemental.
- **contains** one Schedule: The Hague Rules as amended by the Brussels Protocol 1968 (i.e. the Hague-Visby Rules).
- **provides**, in section 1(2), that the **Hague-Visby Rules will have the force of law in the UK**.
- **provides**, in section 1(3), that the **Hague-Visby Rules will apply to the carriage of goods by sea where the port of shipment is a port in the UK**, whether or not the carriage is between ports in two different States. This means that **UK coastal cargo shipped under bill of lading terms** is covered by the Hague-Visby Rules, whereas Article X of the Hague-Visby Rules (where they apply by agreement alone) states that the Hague-Visby Rules apply only to a bill of lading covering carriage between ports in two different countries.
* Many other maritime States have enacted a Carriage of Goods by Sea Act or other legislation similar in purpose to COGSA 71, which will apply in certain situations (usually where goods are loaded in ports of the State), but the provisions of each statute may differ. The **US COGSA**, for example, applies to inward as well as outward cargoes at US ports.
* **COGSA 71** makes the Hague-Visby Rules apply to the following documents:

- any **bill of lading** if the contract contained in or evidenced by it expressly provides (e.g. in a Clause Paramount) that the Hague-Visby Rules will govern the contract;
- any **receipt which is a non-negotiable document**, marked as such (e.g. a **sea waybill**), if the contract contained in or evidenced by it is a contract for the carriage of goods by sea expressly providing that the Hague-Visby Rules are to govern the contract as if the receipt were a bill of lading. (Most sea waybills do this.)

* Although COGSA 71 applies to all **shipments from UK ports** (coastwise or overseas), it does not cover shipments into UK ports (unlike the US COGSA).

* COGSA 71 applies only to the **seaborne part of the carriage** (although the bill of lading may have been issued to cover a multi-modal operation, e.g. a Combined Transport Operation; in that case, "warehouse-to-warehouse" insurance would be arranged to cover the other modes of transport).

F07c.3a Carrier's obligation of seaworthiness under COGSA 71

* COGSA 71 states, in section 3, that where the Act applies, there may not be implied in any contract of carriage of goods by sea to which the Hague-Visby Rules apply under the Act any **absolute undertaking** (i.e. a guarantee) by the carrier **to provide a seaworthy ship**. However, the carrier still has the clear obligation to exercise, before and at the beginning of the voyage, **due diligence** to make the ship seaworthy, properly man, equip and supply her, and make her holds, refrigerating and cool chambers, and all other parts of the ship in which goods are carried, fit and safe for their reception, carriage and preservation.

F07c.3b COGSA 71 provisions relating to live animals and deck cargo

* Although the Hague-Visby Rules, as they stand alone, **do not apply** to live animals or to deck cargo which is stated on the bill of lading as being carried on deck and is so carried, **COGSA 71 reverses this** in section 1(7) by stating that the **Rules will apply as if they did not exclude** deck cargo and live animals.

F07c.4 Hague Rules

* In respect of obligations imposed on the master of the carrying ship, the Hague Rules may be considered to be the same as the Hague-Visby Rules.

F07c.5 Hamburg Rules

- are properly called the **United Nations Convention on the Carriage of Goods by Sea 1978**,
- were drafted under the auspices of the UN agency UNCITRAL and introduced in 1992 in response to shippers' complaints that the Hague and Hague-Visby Rules were unfavourably weighted in favour of the carrier.

* The Hamburg Rules are supported by very few States with any significant maritime trade.
- The **main features** of the Hamburg Rules of interest to a shipmaster are:
- The carrier is liable from the time he accepts the goods at the port of loading until he delivers them at the port of discharge. (Under the other rules the carrier is liable from "tackle to tackle".)
- The carrier is liable for loss, damage or delay to the goods occurring whilst in his charge unless he proves that "he, his servants or agents took all measures that could reasonably be required to avoid the occurrence and its consequences".
- The Hamburg Rules do not give the carrier so many **exceptions from liability** as the Hague and Hague-Visby Rules. In particular, the carrier is not exonerated from liability arising from **negligence in navigation** or **management of the ship**.
- The Hamburg Rules govern both **inward and outward bills of lading**, whereas the Hague and Hague-Visby Rules govern only outward bills of lading.
- The Hamburg Rules cover **live animals**, unlike the Hague and Hague-Visby Rules, but the carrier is not liable for loss, damage or delay in delivery resulting from any special risks inherent in their carriage.
- The carrier can only carry **cargo on deck** if there is a custom of the trade to do so or by an agreement with the shipper. If such an agreement exists the carrier must insert a statement to this effect on the bill of lading. Where goods are carried on deck without a custom of the trade or an agreement with the shipper, the carrier is liable for loss, damage or delay.

F07c.6 P&I club cover for liabilities under rules

* The contracts of carriage of most shipowner-carriers incorporate either the Hague or Hague-Visby Rules, and which give entitlement to the benefits of the defences contained in those rules. Provided such a contract is used, then even where a court with proper jurisdiction refuses to recognise the defences under the rules, the shipowner's liabilities will be covered by his P&I club. However, where he uses a contract incorporating terms less favourable than those of the Hague Rules or Hague-Visby Rules (such as the terms in the Hamburg Rules) the club will normally refuse to cover liabilities arising under the contract. Masters should therefore ensure, especially where the Hamburg Rules are mentioned in the contract terms as applying, that the owners' P&I club approves of their incorporation.

F07d CARRIAGE OF GOODS BY SEA ACT 1992 (COGSA 92)

- **repeals the Bill of Lading Act 1855** and makes major changes to the law regarding who has the **right to sue the carrier** and who the **carrier can sue** for freight, demurrage, etc. Because of uncertainties and anomalies about the wording of the Bill of Lading Act 1855, much legal time and expense had been incurred before the passing of COGSA 92 over the question of who had the right to sue under a bill of lading.
- applies to any **bill of lading**, **sea waybill** and **ships' delivery order**.
- contains **powers** to enable regulations to be made for the application of the Act to **electronic documents**.
* **Section 3 of COGSA 92** lays down guidelines establishing when liabilities under a bill of lading, sea waybill or ship's delivery order will be transferred to a party who is **not an original party** to the contract of carriage (i.e. an endorsee or transferee). The party who takes or demands delivery of the goods to which a bill of lading, sea waybill or ship's delivery order relate becomes subject to the same liabilities as the original shipper.
* If delivery is demanded before the bill of lading is transferred (e.g. under a Letter of Indemnity), then once the bill of lading is transferred the holder will become subject to the same liabilities (i.e. the obligation to pay freight, port charges, demurrage. etc.) as the previous holder.
* Liabilities are not imposed on third parties who take up shipping documents with **no intention of demanding delivery or making a claim** under the contract of carriage, e.g. banks taking up the documents as security.
* The case of *Grant v. Norway* (1851) involved a master who had signed a bill of lading for 12 bales of wool which were not in fact shipped. It was held that the carrier was not liable to the receivers since the master did not have authority to sign the bill of lading for goods which had not actually been shipped. Section 4 of COGSA 92 overturns that decision. A bill of lading which represents that goods **have been shipped** on board or received for shipment will be **conclusive evidence** of such shipment against the carrier in the hands of a lawful holder of the bill of lading, provided that the bill of lading was signed by the master or a person with the authority of the master. This rule will not apply, however, if the bill of lading has not been transferred (e.g. where cargo is delivered against a Letter of Indemnity where a bill of lading has not arrived).
* **Section 4 (Representations in bills of lading)** provides that a properly signed bill of lading representing goods to have been shipped or received for shipment will, in favour of a person who has become the lawful holder (i.e. a transferee), be **conclusive evidence against the carrier** of the shipment of the goods or, as the case may be, of their receipt for shipment.
* The **chief consequences** of the Act for **carriers** are that:
  • the number of **claims made in tort** is likely to be substantially reduced since it is much clearer as to who has the right to claim under the bill of lading; and
  • the **carrier's rights of claim** or counter-claim against cargo receivers, in addition to the original shippers, are now free from uncertainty.

F07e CARRIAGE OF DECK CARGO

F07e.1 Deck cargo and the common law

* **At common law**, the proper place for the stowage of cargo is below deck, since deck cargo is exposed to greater risks (of water damage, loss overboard, lightning, frost, etc.) than under-deck cargo.
* **Unlawful carriage on deck** is usually regarded by courts as being an unjustifiable **deviation** and is penalised severely. Where a carrier stows goods on deck without **express agreement** of the shipper, he is breaching his contractual duty. If the wrongly-stowed deck cargo is lost overboard or damaged on passage, the carrier will not be able to rely on any of the exceptions from liability in the contract of carriage, since they can only be relied on whilst

he is performing (i.e. not deviating from) the contract (see F07a.1 and F07a.5). A court may "set the contract aside", making the carrier revert to common carrier status. As such, the carrier would then be liable for the cargo claim unless he could prove the loss or damage to have been caused by one of the six common law exceptions (see F07a.1a).

F07e.2 Deck cargo and the Hague-Visby Rules

* For notes on Article I(c) of the Hague-Visby Rules, which excludes from the items defined as "goods" **live animals** and cargo which by the contract of carriage is **stated as being carried on deck and is so carried**, see F07c.2g.
* Unless the contract contained in the bill of lading, charter party or sea waybill expressly provides otherwise, goods stated in the contract of carriage as being carried on deck and which are, in fact, stowed on deck **will not be protected by the Hague-Visby Rules**. (Where the UK Carriage of Goods by Sea Act 1971 applies, however, this will not be the case – see F07c.3).
* In view of the exclusion of coverage of deck cargo, where the Hague-Visby Rules are incorporated into a contract of carriage (e.g. by insertion of a Clause Paramount in a charter party or bill of lading), a shipper of deck cargo must make a **separate contract** with the carrier. The carrier, not being bound by any special rules covering deck cargo, is then free to insert in his "on deck" bill of lading any exceptions from liability he wishes. This generally means that the deck cargo will be **carried on deck "at shipper's risk"**, i.e. without liability to the carrier for any loss or damage, however caused. Many carriers' bill of lading forms contain an express clause underlining this position.
* Where goods are, with the shipper's agreement, stowed on deck, the carrier (or the master or agent on his behalf) should issue a bill of lading expressly recording the fact that the goods are carried on deck (e.g. by a "STOWED ON DECK" endorsement on the face of the bill) so that there is no doubt as to the special risks of the carriage. Any innocent transferee or endorsee of the bill of lading acting in good faith (e.g. a bank or third party buyer) will then know the risks attaching to the goods. (It would be unfair to transfer a bill of lading relating to deck cargo without declaring to the transferee that the goods are on deck and may therefore be damaged.)
* Cargo which is carried on deck without being expressly stated as such in the bill of lading or waybill will be subject to the Rules, as will cargo which is stated as being carried on deck but which is, in fact, carried below deck.

F07e.3 P&I Clubs' advice regarding deck cargoes

* Where there is an agreement between the carrier and a shipper or owner of goods (or their agents) to carry goods under deck, but the goods are stowed on deck, the deck carriage will be a **fundamental breach of contract** similar in gravity to an unlawful deviation. The consequences will probably be that the carrier will have no defences to a claim for loss or damage, and he will not be indemnified by his P&I club.
* P&I clubs recommend their members who regularly or **occasionally carry cargo on deck** to cover the deck cargo by an **"on deck" bill of lading** expressly recording the deck stowage. They also recommend the inclusion in the bill of lading of a **clause disclaiming liability** for loss or damage, howsoever caused. A statement such as "CARRIED ON DECK WITHOUT LIABILITY TO THE CARRIER" fulfils both these functions.
* Even when there is no agreement concerning under-deck stowage, it may well be a fundamental breach of the contract of carriage to stow cargo on deck which:
  * **is not suitable** for on-deck carriage; or
  * is stowed in an **unsuitable position** on deck.
* Some types of goods should **never be stowed on deck**. Other types of goods are **unsuitable** for deck carriage if they are not packed in such a way as to protect them from sea water damage.
* The **place of stowage** on deck is also important. For example, an open-top container should not be stowed in an exposed tier at the forward end of the ship but could, in appropriate circumstances, be safely carried in a lower tier further aft. Unprotected vehicles and boats, etc. should not be carried outboard on the forepart of the upper deck, especially if their window glass is not specially protected.
* The P&I clubs warn carriers that it is most important that, where their bills of lading are not claused for "on deck" carriage, they should incorporate a suitable **liberty clause permitting on-deck stowage at the carrier's option**. Such a liberty clause is recommended even when the custom of the trade permits on-deck stowage, e.g. when closed containers are carried on purpose-built container ships. The purpose of these clauses (which are nevertheless ineffective in a few jurisdictions which do not follow the generally accepted principles of maritime law) is to ensure that the carrier has a **contractual right** to stow cargo on deck at his option. Liberty clauses must always be **used reasonably**, however, and should not be used to justify deck stowage for cargo which is unsuitable for deck stowage.

F07e.4 Containerised deck cargo

* The courts generally regard the carriage on deck of **goods in closed containers on purpose-built containerships** as being equivalent to under-deck carriage of goods, and container line bills of lading generally give the carrier the **option** of stowing the cargo either on or under deck without notification of the shipper.
* Goods in containers stowed on deck on a vessel which is not a purpose-built container ship should, however, be treated like non-containerised deck cargo, and a proper **liberty clause** should be inserted in the bill of lading as mentioned in F07e.3.

F07e.5 Deck cargo and general average

* For notes on the principles and application of general average, see G06.

F07e.5a Where deck cargo is jettisoned in a general average act

* **Rule I - Jettison of Deck Cargo - of the York-Antwerp Rules 1994** provides that: "No jettison of deck cargo shall be made good as general average unless such cargo is carried in accordance with the recognised custom of the trade." This means that where there is a general average act (e.g. of jettisoning cargo to save the ship, other cargo, etc.) but the jettisoned cargo is not of a type **customarily carried on deck** (i.e. not timber, logs, containers on a purpose-built container ship, etc.) the cargo owner will have no claim under the York-Antwerp Rules to a general average contribution from the other parties to the adventure.
* Where the jettisoned deck cargo was being carried in accordance with the recognised custom of the trade, however, as in the case of containers on a purpose-built container ship or logs on a purpose-built log carrier, the cargo owner will have a claim to general average contributions from the other parties to the adventure. He will also have a claim if the cargo had been carried on deck with the **consent** of all the other parties to the adventure.

F07e.5b Where jettisoned cargo had been wrongfully stowed on deck

* **Where jettisoned deck cargo had been stowed on deck without the shipper's consent or knowledge**, the shipowner, apart from being liable for breach of contract, will be totally liable to the goods owner.

F07e.5c Where deck cargo has been saved by a general average act

* Where deck cargo is saved by a General Average act (e.g. by the refloating of a grounded ship), the owner of the deck cargo is liable to make a General Average contribution along with the other parties to the adventure who have benefited by the General Average act. Carriers usually underline this in an express statement in their bills of lading.

F07e.6 Timber deck cargo

* For notes on **statutory requirements for the assignment of timber freeboards and load lines, and the carriage of timber deck cargoes**, see D04i.5.
* Under regulation 5 of the MS (Carriage of Cargoes) Regulations 1999 (SI 1999/336) (see F07g), a ship carrying a timber deck cargo must carry a copy of the **IMO Code of Safe Practice for Ships Carrying Timber Deck Cargoes** (see A03c.5 and F07g.1b).

F07f CARRIAGE OF DANGEROUS GOODS AND MARINE POLLUTANTS

F07f.1 MARPOL Annex III

- **contains** the **Regulations for the Prevention of Pollution by Harmful Substances Carried by Sea in Packaged Form**.
- **came into force** on 1 July 1992 and had (at May 2002) 101 **Contracting States** (which include the UK), representing 81.46% of world tonnage.

- **requires** (in regulation 1) Governments of MARPOL Party States to supplement the provisions of the Annex by issuing **detailed requirements** on the subjects covered by the various regulations, for preventing or minimizing pollution of the marine environment by harmful substances.
- **contains regulations** relating to **packaging** (regulation 2), **marking and labelling** (regulation 3), **documentation** (regulation 4), **stowage** (regulation 5), **quantity limitations** (regulation 6) and **exceptions** (regulation 7), none of which makes detailed requirements (these being contained in the IMDG Code).
- **includes** in an Appendix "Guidelines for the Identification of Harmful Substances in Packaged Form".
- **makes no provision** for any "special areas".
- **is given effect in the UK** by the MS (Dangerous Goods and Marine Pollutants) Regulations 1997 (SI 1997/2367) (see F07f.2).

F07f.2 Dangerous Goods and Marine Pollutants Regulations

* The **MS (Dangerous Goods and Marine Pollutants) Regulations 1997** (SI 1997/2367) -
  - give effect in the UK to **Annex III of MARPOL** 73/78, **Chapter VII (Dangerous Goods) of SOLAS** 74/78 and **EC Council Directive No. 93/75/EEC**.
  - **define** (in regulation 2) "**dangerous goods**" as "goods classified in the IMDG Code or in any other IMO publication referred to in these Regulations as dangerous for carriage by sea, and any other substance or article which the shipper has reasonable cause to believe might meet the criteria for such classification". The expression **also includes** "residues in empty receptacles, empty tanks or cargo holds previously used for carrying dangerous goods unless cleaned, dried, purged, gas freed or ventilated as appropriate or, in the case of radioactive materials, have been both cleaned and adequately closed; and goods labelled, marked or declared as dangerous goods. dangerous goods do not include ship's equipment or stores".
  - **define** a "**marine pollutant**" as a substance classified as such in the IMDG Code, or as a noxious liquid substance in the IBC Code, and any other substance, material or article that the shipper has reasonable cause to believe might meet the criteria for such classification.
  - **apply** (under regulation 5) to **all UK ships anywhere**, and other ships in UK waters, carrying:
    • **dangerous goods in bulk or packaged** form; or
    • **marine pollutants in packaged** form.
  - contain **general provisions** in **Part I**, including regulations relating to **interpretations** (regulation 2), **exemptions** (regulation 4), **application** (regulation 5), **general duties of operators and employers** (regulation 6), **general duties of employees aboard ship** (regulation 7), **misconduct endangering a UK ship or persons aboard** (regulation 8), and **onus of proving what is reasonably practicable** (regulation 9).
  - contain in **Part II** provisions for the **carriage of packaged goods** including regulations relating to **Declaration** (regulation 10), **Preparation of goods for transport** (regulation 11), **Container or Vehicle Packing Certificates** (regulation 12), **Documentation by electronic data processing or electronic data interchange** (regulation 13), **List, manifest or stowage plan** (regulation 14), **Marking and labelling** (regulation 15), **Stowage on board ship** (regulations 16 and 17), **Cargo securing documentation** (regulation 18) and **Operational requirements** (regulation 19).
  - contain in **Part III** two regulations: **Carriage of Dangerous Goods or Marine Pollutants in Bulk** (regulation 20) and **Documentation** (regulation 21).
  - contain in **Part IV** one regulation relating to **Spaces for carriage of packaged goods and dangerous goods in solid form in bulk** (regulation 22).
  - contain in **Part V** provisions relating to **Enforcement** including regulations on **Power to detain** (regulation 23), **Penalties** (regulation 24) and **Offences due to fault of another person** (regulation 25).
  - refer to certain **codes**, e.g. the Bulk Cargoes Code, BCH Code, Gas Carrier Code, Gas Carrier Code for Existing Ships, IBC Code, IGC Code, IMDG Code and to IMO Recommendations. Where the Regulations require carriage to be in accordance with a Code or Recommendation, and the MCA specify in MSN 1705 or MSN 1706 conditions in relation to the carriage, the **Code or Recommendations must also be complied with**.
  - provide that the **general duties of operators and employers of persons aboard a ship and every shipmaster** include ensuring, as far as reasonably practicable, that nothing in the manner in which dangerous goods are handled, stowed or carried is such as might create a **significant risk to the health or safety** of any person.
  - provide in regulation 6 that matters to which the **duty of the operator and employer** extend include:
    • provision and maintenance of **ship's structure**, **fittings** and **equipment** for the handling, stowage and carriage of dangerous goods; and
    • provision of such **information**, **instruction**, **training** and **supervision** to all employees in connection with the handling, stowage and carriage of dangerous goods in the ship.
  - provide in regulation 7 that **general duties of employees aboard ship** are to take reasonable care for the health and safety of themselves and of others who may be affected by their acts or omissions in connection with the

handling, stowage and carriage of dangerous goods in the ship, and to co-operate with the shipowner or employer in carrying out their statutory duties under the Merchant Shipping Act 1995 and the Regulations.
- are explained in part in **MGN 37**.
- provide in regulation 8 that in connection with the handling, stowage or carriage of dangerous goods, it is an **offence** to intentionally or recklessly interfere with or misuse anything provided on board under merchant shipping legislation in the interests of health, safety or welfare. The onus of proving what is "reasonably practicable" is on the accused, if charged with an offence of failing to comply with something "so far as is reasonably practicable".
- incorporate certain MSNs (which should be read in conjunction with the Regulations), e.g. **MSN 1705** and **MSN 1706**.
* Where a ship fails to comply with the Regulations, she is liable to be **detained** (regulation 23).

F07f.2a Documents required before loading packaged goods

* **Documents required before loading packaged dangerous goods or marine pollutants** include:
  • a **Document of Compliance with the special requirements for ships carrying dangerous goods** as required by regulation 22 (see F07f.2b); and
  • a **Dangerous Goods Declaration** or **Marine Pollutants Declaration** (as appropriate) as required by regulation 10 incorporating a **Packing Certificate** as required by regulation 12 (see F07f.2e).

F07f.2b Document of Compliance (regulation 22)

* **Regulation 22** applies to:
  • passenger ships built on or after 1 September 1984;
  • cargo ships of 500gt or over built on or after 1 September 1984; and
  • cargo ships of less than 500gt built on or after 1 February 1992.
* Regulation 22(2) provides that no packaged goods or solid dangerous goods in bulk may be taken on board or accepted for carriage on any ship to which regulation 22 applies unless the **spaces** in which they are to be carried or are carried, as the case may be, comply with the provisions of **regulation 54 of Chapter II-2 of SOLAS**, whether or not the ship is engaged on international voyages. (Chapter II-2 of SOLAS deals with Construction - Fire protection, fire detection and fire extinction. Regulation II-2/54 concerns **Special requirements for ships carrying dangerous goods** and contains requirements relating to **water supplies, sources of ignition, detection system, ventilation, bilge pumping, personnel protection, portable fire extinguishers, insulation of machinery spaces** and **water spray system**. Regulation II-2/54.3 provides that the flag State Administration must provide the ship with an "appropriate document" as evidence of compliance of construction and equipment with the requirements of regulation 54.)
* Regulation 22(3) provides that in the case of ships to which regulation 22 applies engaged on international voyages, no packaged goods or solid dangerous goods in bulk may be taken on board or carried unless the ship has on board a **Document of Compliance** issued by or on behalf of the MCA or the competent authority of the flag State.
* Regulation 22(4) provides that any **operator or master** who accepts for carriage, or carries, packaged goods or dangerous goods in solid form in bulk:
  • on a ship in which the spaces in which they are to be or are carried in do not comply as required by regulation 22(2); or
  • in the case of a ship engaged on international voyages, on a ship which does not have on board a Document of Compliance as required by regulation 22(3),
  - will be guilty of an **offence** punishable on summary conviction by a fine not exceeding the statutory maximum or, on conviction on indictment, to imprisonment for up to 2 years, or an unlimited fine, or both.
* A Document of Compliance issued by the MCA is **valid for a maximum of 5 years** and certifies:
  • that the construction and equipment of the ship was found to comply with the provisions of regulation II-2/54 of SOLAS 74, as amended, and
  • that the ship is suitable for the carriage of those classes of dangerous goods as specified in the appended Schedules to the certificate, subject to any provisions of the IMDG Code and the Code of Safe Practice for Solid Bulk Cargoes (BC Code) for the individual substances also being complied with.
* **Schedule 1** of a Document of Compliance contains a small **plan** of the ship's stowage spaces and a **table** showing the Classes of dangerous goods suitable for stowage in each category of space. **Schedule 2** lists the **special requirements**, as required by the Fire Protection Regulations in force when the certificate was issued, for the ship to carry dangerous goods.

* Older Documents of Compliance, issued between 1984 and 1998, certify compliance with regulation 143 of the MS (Fire Protection) Regulations 1984 (SI 1984/1218), which Regulations have been revoked and replaced by the MS (Fire Protection: Large Ships) Regulations 1998 (SI 1998/1012).
* New Documents of Compliance certify compliance with regulation **103** of the MS (Fire Protection: Large Ships) Regulations 1998, which contains broadly the same provisions as regulation 143 of the 1984 Regulations. The technical requirements of regulation 103 are contained in **MSN 1669**, as amended by **MSN 1733**.
* **MGN 36** explains the requirement for a Document of Compliance and includes a specimen copy.

F07f.2c Dangerous Goods/Marine Pollutants Declaration (regulation 10)

* **No packaged dangerous goods** may be **offered for carriage** or **taken aboard** any ship unless a **dangerous goods declaration or marine pollutants declaration** (or a combined declaration) has been given to the master or operator (regulation 10(1)).
* The **declaration** must accurately identify the date the document was prepared and the name, status and company or organisation of the signatory (regulation 10(2)).
* No packaged goods may be offered for carriage or taken on board unless the master or operator has been provided with a **document** showing the following details:
  * the proper shipping name;
  * the class and division where applicable;
  * the UN Numbers where allocated by the IMDG Code;
  * where relevant the packaging or packing group;
  * the number and kind of packages;
  * the total quantity of dangerous goods or net explosive mass of the contents;
  * the words MARINE POLLUTANT where appropriate; and
  * any other information required by the IMDG Code (regulation 10(3)).
* This document (which is usually known as a "**Dangerous Goods Note**") must be combined with the dangerous goods declaration, marine pollutants declaration or combined dangerous goods/marine pollutants **declaration** as the case may be (regulation 10(4)). A correctly completed **SITPRO**[19] **Dangerous Goods Note** will fulfil these requirements.
* Where the goods are delivered direct to the ship or its agent, the **shipper** must deliver the declaration to the operator or master (regulation 10(5)).
* In consigning the goods for carriage by sea, the **shipper** must make proper provision to ensure the onward delivery of the required declaration and document to the ship or its agent (regulation 10(6)).
* Where the goods are not sent direct to the ship or agent, but are sent to another person (e.g a freight forwarder) for onward delivery or for consolidation (groupage) with other goods or cargoes for eventual delivery, responsibility for delivering the declaration and document is on the **forwarder** and **each person** responsible for onward transfer and delivery. This responsibility does not, however, extend to persons solely engaged in loading of the goods onto the ship or moving the goods (regulation 10(7)). These requirements are without prejudice to the duties of the shipper in regulations 11 and 12 (regulation 10(8)).
* An **offence** is committed under regulation 10(9) if a shipper, forwarder or other person:
  * fails to provide the operator or master with a declaration; or
  * provides a declaration which he knows to be false or recklessly makes a declaration which is false in a material particular.
* An **offence** is committed by the operator or master under regulation 10(10) if he accepts for carriage or takes or receives on board any packaged goods without a document and declaration where these are required by the Regulations.

F07f.2d Preparation of goods for transport (regulation 11)

* The **shipper must not offer** packaged goods for carriage unless:
  * all the **conditions** relating to their declaration, classification, marking, packaging, labelling, placarding and prior notification to competent authority or consignee, as specified in the IMDG Code, have been **complied with**; and
  * in the case of **goods in a portable tank or tank container or vehicle** the goods have been properly and safely **prepared for carriage by sea** and **comply with applicable tank requirements** in accordance with the IMDG Code.

---

[19] **SITPRO** (The Simpler Trade Procedures Board) is the UK's national trade facilitation agency. As part of its mission to simplify the international trading process, it promotes the adoption of user-friendly shipping documents such as the SITPRO Dangerous Goods Note. A specimen of the SITPRO DG Note was contained in MGN 100, but is not shown in its replacement, MGN 159.

* An operator or **master** must not accept for carriage or take or receive on board any packaged goods where he has reasonable cause to suspect that the **shipper has not complied** with the above requirements.
* In preparing any goods for shipment the **shipper must identify and classify any dangerous goods or marine pollutants** in order to ensure that the proper transport precautions and preparations can be made.

F07f.2e Goods packed in containers or vehicles (regulation 12)

* Regulation 12(1)(a) provides that **where packaged goods are to be packed or shipped in or on a cargo transport unit**, the person responsible for packing such goods therein must ensure that the stowage, segregation and securing of the goods is adequate and **in accordance with the IMDG Code**.
* Regulation 12(2) provides that regulation 12 **does not apply** in relation to goods packaged within a portable tank, road tank vehicle, rail tank wagon or tank container.
* **Where packaged goods are to be packed or shipped in or on a cargo transport unit**, the **person responsible for packing the goods** in the unit must provide the operator or master or shipper or forwarder with a signed **Packing Certificate** complying with the requirements of the IMDG Code, indicating the cargo transport unit, identification number or numbers and identifying the place and date of the operation, the name of the person responsible for the packing and his status, and company or organisation. This regulation does not apply to goods packaged in a portable tank, road tank vehicle, rail tank wagon or tank container (regulation 12(1)(b)).
* The **Packing Certificate** is a declaration that:
  * the goods are, if required, **properly packaged** and have been **securely packed** and **adequately braced** for the intended voyage;
  * that the **container or vehicle** was **clean**, **dry** and appeared **fit to receive** the goods;
  * that **no incompatible substances** have been packed except where permitted by the DG Regulations;
  * that where **packages or receptacles** have been packed into a container or vehicle they are in a **sound condition**; and
  * that the **labelling** or other appropriate **marking** on the packages and on the container or vehicle complies with the DG Regulations.
* The **shipper or forwarder** commits an offence if he fails to provide the operator or master of the ship with a signed Packing Certificate (regulation 12(3)(b)).
* An **operator or master** must not accept on any ship any cargo transport unit with packaged dangerous goods in it without a signed Packing Certificate (regulation 12(4)).
* A Packing Certificate is an integral part of a SITPRO Dangerous Goods Note. The Packing Certificate and the dangerous goods declaration **must each be signed** for a shipment of packaged dangerous goods or marine pollutants.

F07f.2f Documentation by electronic data processing or electronic data interchange (regulation 13)

* **A dangerous goods declaration, marine pollutants declaration, any accompanying documentation** required by regulations 10 and 12 and a **Packing Certificate** may be provided directly to the master or operator in the form of a **paper document** or by **electronic data processing** (EDP) or **electronic data interchange** (EDI) methods.

F07f.2g List, manifest or stowage plan (regulation 14)

* The **master** of any ship carrying packaged goods (i.e. dangerous goods or marine pollutants) must ensure that a **special list, manifest or stowage plan** is carried in the ship (regulation 14(1)). This document must set out details, obtained from the shipping documents submitted by the shipper, of the packaged goods on board including:
  * the correct technical name of the goods;
  * their classification in accordance with the IMDG Code;
  * their mass or volume; and
  * details of the stowage location in the ship.
* The information may be in one **combined document** relating to both dangerous goods and marine pollutants, or in **separate lists** (regulation 14(2)). Combined lists must show clearly which goods are dangerous goods and which are marine pollutants.
* The **master** must also carry in the ship any additional special documents where required by the IMDG Code for the carriage of packaged dangerous goods (regulation 14(3)).
* Any **list, manifest or stowage plan** and any **additional special documents** required for the acceptance of goods for carriage in the ship must be **kept on board and available for reference or inspection** until the goods have been discharged (regulation 14(4)).

F07f.2h Marking or labelling (regulation 15)

* Packaged dangerous goods or marine pollutants may not be taken on any ship for carriage in that ship unless they are marked, labelled and placarded, and display a fumigation warning sign, as appropriate, as specified in the IMDG Code. The **shipper** commits an offence if this requirement is breached.
* An **operator or master** is guilty of an offence if he accepts dangerous goods or marine pollutants on board in any packaged which is not marked, labelled, placarded or displaying a fumigation warning sign as required.

F07f.2i Stowage on board ship (regulations 16 and 17)

* Packaged goods must not be accepted on board if their stowage is prohibited by the IMDG Code (regulation 16).
* Packaged goods must not be accepted on board unless any necessary additional safety equipment is provided in accordance with the IMDG Code (regulation 16).
* Packaged goods must be adequately stowed, segregated and secured in accordance with the IMDG Code (regulation 16).
* Where the vessel carries a **Cargo Securing Manual** in compliance with regulation 18, **cargo transport units**, including containers, must be loaded, stowed and secured throughout any voyage **in accordance with that manual** (regulation 17).

F07f.2j Cargo securing documentation (regulation 18)

* No **packaged goods** may be carried on:
  * any ship on an international voyage;
  * any passenger ship on a domestic voyage; and
  * any cargo ship of 500gt and above on a domestic voyage -
  - without carrying a **Cargo Securing Manual** conforming to the standard in IMO circular MSC/Circ.745 and approved by or on behalf of the flag State Administration.
* For notes on the **Cargo Securing Manual** see F07g.1b and F07g.1c.

F07f.2k Operational requirements (regulation 19)

* The operator and master must ensure that all employees are familiar with the essential actions to be taken in an emergency involving any packaged goods carried on the ship.

F07f.2l Carriage of dangerous goods or marine pollutants in bulk (regulation 20)

* **Dangerous goods or marine pollutants must not be handled or carried in bulk** in any ship if the operator has any cause to believe that they may not be handled or carried **safely** in the ship.
* Without prejudice to the above requirement:
  * where the dangerous goods or marine pollutants are goods listed in Chapter VI of the BCH Code, or in Chapter 17 of the IBC Code, or in Chapter XIX of the Gas Carrier Code for Existing Ships, or in Chapter XIX of the Gas Carrier Code, or are classified dangerous goods listed in Appendix B of the Solid Bulk Cargoes Code, they must be handled and carried in accordance with the requirements of the appropriate code; or
  * where the dangerous goods or marine pollutants consist of a liquid chemical or a liquefied gas which is not listed in the codes mentioned above, they must be handled and carried in accordance with **written approval** given by the MCA specifying the date on which it takes effect and the conditions (if any) on which it is given.
* Where there is any breach of the above requirements, the operator and the master will each be guilty of an **offence** (regulation 20(3)).

F07f.2m Documentation relating to bulk dangerous goods or marine pollutants (regulation 21)

* The shipper of any **bulk dangerous goods or marine pollutants** must give the **operator or master written notification** of the nature of the goods, specifying:
  * their correct technical name;
  * their UN number, if any;
  * for any solid bulk dangerous goods, the classification as listed in the IMDG Code; and
  * for liquid dangerous goods with a flashpoint below 60°C (closed cup), the flashpoint.

* The shipper of any bulk dangerous goods or marine pollutants commits an offence if he fails to provide the operator or master with a written notification, or provides a notification which is **false** in a material particular.

* The **master** of a ship carrying any bulk dangerous goods or marine pollutants must ensure that a **specific list, manifest or stowage plan** is carried in the ship for the current voyage. This document must set out the details, obtained from the shipping documents submitted by the shipper, of the dangerous goods or marine pollutants carried including:
  * the correct technical name of the goods;
  * their mass or volume;
  * where the dangerous goods are shown in Appendix B of the Bulk Cargoes Code, the classification as shown in the IMDG Code; and
  * the stowage location in the ship.

* The master must also carry in the ship any **additional special documents** (e.g. a bulk coal **Declaration by Shipper**, a **Certificate of Test of Solid Bulk Cargo**, a **Certificate of Fitness**, etc.) where required for dangerous goods or marine pollutants by the **Bulk Cargoes Code**, the **BCH Code**, the **IBC Code**, the **IGC Code** or the **Gas Carrier Code**.

* The **list, manifest or stowage plan** and any additional special documents must be **kept available** for reference or inspection on board until the goods have been discharged.

* The **MS (Reporting Requirements for Ships Carrying Dangerous or Polluting Goods) Regulations 1995** (SI 1995/2498) require the operator and master to arrange, before the ship departs from a port, for a **copy of the list, manifest or stowage plan** to be kept on shore. It is the duty of the operator to retain it there until the goods are discharged from the ship or for 6 months from loading, whichever is the shorter period.

* The **operator** must furnish the list, manifest or stowage plan on demand:
  * where the port of departure is in the UK, to any person or authority designated for this purpose by the MCA; or
  * where the port of departure is not in the UK, to the port State.

F07f.2n Spaces for carriage of packaged goods and solid bulk dangerous goods (regulation 22)

* Regulation 22 applies only to -
  * passenger ships constructed on or after 1 September 1984;
  * cargo ships of 500gt or over, constructed on or after 1 September 1984; and
  * cargo ships of less than 500gt constructed on or after 1 February 1992,
  - and provides that no packaged goods or solid bulk dangerous goods may be loaded or accepted for carriage in the ship unless their **stowage spaces** comply with the requirements of **regulation 54 of Chapter II-2** of SOLAS **whether the ship is engaged on international voyages or not**.

* In the case of ships engaged **on international voyages**, no packaged goods or solid bulk dangerous goods may be loaded or carried unless the ship has on board a **Document of Compliance** issued by or on behalf of the MCA or the competent authority of the State in which the ship is registered. For notes on the Document of Compliance, see F07f.2b.

F07f.3 The International Maritime Dangerous Goods (IMDG) Code

* The **International Maritime Dangerous Goods (IMDG) Code** -
  - was **adopted** by IMO resolution A.716(17) and **published** in 1965.
  - was **recommended** to governments for adoption or for use as the basis for national regulations in pursuance of obligations under SOLAS regulation VII/1.4 and MARPOL Annex III regulation 1(3).
  - **contains** basic principles; detailed requirements for individual substances, materials and articles; and a number of recommendations for good operational practice including advice on terminology, packing, labelling, stowage, segregation and handling, and emergency response action.
  - **does not include** all details of procedures for packing of dangerous goods or actions to take in the event of an emergency or accident involving personnel who handle goods at sea; these aspects are covered by the publications associated with the IMDG Code and which are included in the **Supplement**.

* The **2000 edition** was published in reformatted (A4 softback, 2-volume) form as **Amendment 30**, which came into force on 1 January 2001 with a 12-month implementation period until 31 December 2001, during which period the old "traditional format" 4-volume edition could be used. 30 contained editorial inaccuracies that caused difficulties for users; IMO therefore published a set of errata and corrigenda and made these available to purchasers of the Code. The 2000 edition (Amendment 30) was promulgated by the MCA in MSN 1755.

* The **2002 edition** was published in A4 softback, 2-volume form as **Amendment 31-02**. It is no longer recommendatory, the **majority of the Code being mandatory from 1 January 2004** under Amendments to SOLAS chapter VII (Carriage of Dangerous Goods) adopted in May 2002. The 2002 edition consists of two A4 paperback volumes.
* The provisions of the following parts of the 2002 edition remain recommendatory after 1 January 2004:
  * chapter 1.3 (Training);
  * chapter 2.1 (Explosives, Introductory Notes 1 to 4 only);
  * chapter 2.3, section 2.3.3 (Determination of flashpoint only);
  * chapter 3.2 (columns 15 and 17 of the Dangerous Goods List only);
  * chapter 3.5 (Transport schedule for Class 7 radioactive material only);
  * chapter 5.4, section 5.4.5 (Multimodal dangerous goods form), insofar as layout of the form is concerned;
  * chapter 7.3 (Special requirements in the event of an incident and fire precautions involving dangerous goods only).

  Where a provision in the above chapters is recommendatory and not mandatory, the word "should" is used in the text instead of "shall".
* The two-volume Code is divided into **seven parts**.
* **Volume 1** contains the following Parts:
  * Part 1: general provisions, definitions, training;
  * Part 2: classification;
  * Part 4: packing and tank provisions;
  * Part 5: consignment procedures;
  * Part 6: construction and testing of packagings, intermediate bulk containers (IBCs), large packagings, portable tanks and road tank vehicles; and
  * Part 7: provisions concerning transport operations.
* **Volume 2** contains:
  * Part 3: Dangerous Goods List and limited quantities exceptions;
  * Appendix A: List of generic and N.O.S. (not otherwise specified) proper shipping names;
  * Appendix B: Glossary of terms; and
  * Index.
* The **Supplement** is published separately by IMO and contains the following texts related to the IMDG Code:
  * Emergency Response Procedures for Ships Carrying Dangerous Goods (The EmS Guide);
  * Medical First Aid Guide for use in Accidents Involving Dangerous Goods;
  * Reporting Procedures;
  * IMO/ILO/UN ECE Guidelines for Packing Cargo Transport Units;
  * International Code for the Safe Carriage of Packaged Irradiated Nuclear Fuel, Plutonium and High-Level Radioactive Wastes on board Ships (INF Code);
  * Recommendations on the Safe Use of Pesticides;
  * Appendix: Resolutions and Circulars referred to in the IMDG Code and Supplement.
* The **BC Code**, included in the Supplement to the pre-2000 edition of the Code, is now published separately.

F07f.3a Dangerous goods classes

* The following **classes and divisions** are listed in the **IMDG Code 2002 edition**:
  Class 1: Explosives
  > Division 1.1: substances and articles which have a mass explosion hazard
  > Division 1.2: substances and articles which have a projection hazard but not a mass explosion hazard
  > Division 1.3: substances and articles which have a fire hazard and either a minor blast hazard or a minor projection hazard or both, but not a mass explosion hazard
  > Division 1.4: substances and articles which present no significant hazard
  > Division 1.5: very insensitive substances which have a mass explosion hazard
  > Division 1.6: extremely insensitive articles which do not have a mass explosion hazard

  Class 2: Gases
  > Class 2.1: flammable gases
  > Class 2.2: non-flammable, non-toxic gases
  > Class 2.3: toxic gases

  Class 3: Flammable liquids
  Class 4: Flammable solids; substances liable to spontaneous combustion; substances which, in contact with water, emit flammable gases
  > Class 4.1: flammable solids, self-reactive substances and desensitized explosives

Class 4.2: substances liable to spontaneous combustion
Class 4.3: substances which, in contact with water, emit flammable gases
Class 5: Oxidising substances and organic peroxides
Class 5.1: oxidising substances
Class 5.2: organic peroxides
Class 6: Toxic and infectious substances
Class 6.1: toxic substances
Class 6.2: infectious substances
Class 7: Radioactive material
Class 8: Corrosive substances
Class 9: Miscellaneous dangerous substances and articles
* The numerical order of the classes and divisions is not that of the degree of danger.

F07f.3b Compliance with IMDG Code by offshore supply vessels

* Offshore supply vessels (OSVs) are required to carry a variety of dangerous goods including those in packaged form; however, their design does not facilitate easy compliance with the IMDG Code. Furthermore, it has been noted that the backloading process often gives lead to incorrectly stowed and labelled dangerous goods.
* **MGN 205**, which replaced MGN 140, outlines the required standard of compliance with the requirements of the IMDG Code and SOLAS Chapter VII for offshore support vessels (OSVs) utilising only weather deck stowage and goods stowed in offshore containers.
* MGN 205 provides that the SOLAS Convention and provisions of the IMDG Code in force at any time will apply, except as given below. IMO Resolution A.863(20) - **Code of Practice for the Carriage of Cargoes and Persons by Offshore Supply Vessels** should be observed.
* **OSVs of 500gt and over built after 1 September 1984**, and **OSVs under 500gt built after 1 February 1992, carrying dangerous goods**, must comply with SOLAS regulation II-2/54 regardless of whether the vessel is engaged on international voyages or not.
* From 1st January 2001 all OSVs operating in or out of the UK, regardless of date of build or voyage definition, are required to carry a **Document of Compliance**.
* It is known that the particular construction and design features of OSVs do not make for easy compliance with SOLAS 74 Chapter II-2/54. However, **full compliance is required with regulations 54.2.6 and 52.2.7**. The MCA will accept demonstrable **equivalence**. (The onus is on the operator of the vessel to demonstrate such equivalence.) Some aspects that can be considered are:
  * 2.1.2 Amount and throw of water/ foam from fixed monitors/hydrants; and
  * Suitable means to provide effective boundary cooling in lieu of A60 boundaries where required in sub paragraph 2.8.
* Dangerous goods must be carried in closed offshore containers.
* Containers should be built to the standards specified in MSC.Circ. 860 or DNVC 2.7-1 or BS EN 12079 or BS 7072.
* Each container should only carry dangerous goods of a single class.
* Where the IMDG Code specifies the standard of segregation between containers of incompatible goods to be "Away from" and "separated from" each other, such containers may be stowed adjacent to each other. Where the segregation standard is "separated by a complete compartment or hold from", such containers should be separated by at least one standard container, either empty or containing non-hazardous goods but not foodstuffs. This relaxation does not apply to goods of Class 1, Class 6.2 or Class 7
* The inherent OSV design means goods are generally only transported on deck. If design is such that an under deck space is utilised, then full compliance with the IMDG Code is required and paragraph 4 of this note does not apply.
* The general stowage requirements given in Chapter 14 of the Introduction to the IMDG Code will apply in all cases.
* It is recommended that containers be placarded on the top surfaces in addition to the sides in order to assist the Master and crew in the event of an emergency.
* There have been cases where back-loaded cargoes of dangerous goods have not been delivered and documented in accordance with the regulations. It is the responsibility of the shipper/packer to ensure that **back-loaded goods** are delivered to the vessel in accordance with the requirements of the IMDG Code. That means correctly **declared, stored, labelled, and placarded** with the **correct documentation**. Consideration must also be given to the order of back-loading to ensure that the requirements given in paragraph 6 can be complied with. In this case the **shipper** is the Offshore Installation Manager. Any incidents of incorrectly delivered or documented back-loads identified will be pursued rigorously with a view to prosecution.
* **OSVs must comply** with the requirements of the MS (Reporting Requirements for Ships Carrying Dangerous or Polluting Goods) Regulations 1995 (SI 1995/2498), as amended.

F07f.4 Carriage of dangerous goods under the Hague-Visby Rules

* Under Article IV(6) of the Hague-Visby Rules, any **inflammable, explosive or dangerous goods** which have been shipped without the consent of the carrier, master or agent, may at any time before discharge -
  * be **landed** at any place;
  * be **destroyed**; or
  * be **rendered innocuous** by the carrier,
  - without compensation, and the shipper of the goods will be liable for all damages and expenses directly or indirectly arising out of or resulting from the shipment.
* If any such goods, legally shipped with the knowledge and consent of the carrier, master or agent, become a danger to the ship or other cargo, they may similarly be **landed** at any place, **destroyed** or **rendered innocuous** by the carrier **without liability** on the part of the carrier except to General Average, if any.

F07f.5 Notification requirements of the Reporting Requirements Regulations

* For notes on the **requirements of regulation 5(1) of MS (Reporting Requirements for Ships Carrying Dangerous or Polluting Goods) Regulations 1995** (SI 1995/2498), as amended by SI 1999/2121, to make **hazardous cargo notifications prior to sailing** in various circumstances, see I07d.
* Without prejudice to the requirements of regulation 5(1), the **shipper** must give **prior notification of each shipment of radioactive materials** as classified in the IMDG Code for Class 7 goods in accordance with the requirements of that Code in accordance with the requirements in the IMDG Code for Class 7 goods (regulation 5(2)).

F07g CARRIAGE OF CARGOES REGULATIONS

F07g.1 Carriage of Cargoes Regulations

* The **MS (Carriage of Cargoes) Regulations 1999** (SI 1999/336) -
  - **consolidate and revoke** the MS (Carriage of Cargoes) Regulations 1997 (SI 1997/19) and the MS (Carriage of Cargoes) (Amendment) Regulations 1997 (SI 1997/2366). The principal change from the revoked regulations is that the **master and terminal representative must agree a loading plan** before bulk cargoes are loaded. The plan must be adhered to, and the **master may stop loading** if the permissible limits are or might be breached. The 1997 Regulations revoked the MS (Grain) Regulations 1985 (SI 1985/1217).
  - **implement** chapter VI of SOLAS 74, as amended.
  - **apply to all sea-going UK ships** (including passenger ships and high-speed craft) wherever they may be and to sea-going **non-UK ships while in the UK or UK territorial waters**, when loaded or intended to be loaded with **any cargo** as defined in the regulation 2. "Cargo" is defined in regulation 2 as any cargo which, owing to its particular hazard to ships or persons on board, may require special precautions, **with the exception of liquids carried in bulk and gases carried in bulk**. (The Regulations do not, therefore, apply to oil, gas and chemical tankers or ships carrying noxious liquid substances in bulk.)
  - are subject to any requirements contained in the MS (Dangerous Goods and Marine Pollutants) Regulations 1997 (the "DG Regulations") in respect of the carriage of dangerous goods and marine pollutants as defined in those Regulations. Where any requirement in the DG Regulations regulates an aspect of carriage provided for in the Carriage of Cargoes Regulations, the DG Regulations shall apply to that extent, and not the Carriage of Cargoes Regulations.
  - are explained in **MGN 107**.
  - are in **5 parts** which contain **regulations as follows: PART I** - GENERAL: **1**. Citation, commencement and revocation; **2**. Interpretation; **3**. Application. **PART II** - GENERAL PROVISIONS: **4**. Cargo information; **5**. Carriage of documentation; **6**. Stowage and securing; **7**. Oxygen analysis and gas detection equipment; **8**. The use of pesticides in ships. **PART III** - SPECIAL PROVISIONS FOR BULK CARGOES OTHER THAN GRAIN: **9**. Acceptability for loading; **10**. Loading, unloading and stowage of bulk cargo. **PART IV** - REQUIREMENTS FOR CARGO SHIPS CARRYING GRAIN: **11**. International Grain Code. **PART V** – ENFORCEMENT: **12**. Power to detain; **13**. Penalties and defences; **14**. Offences due to the fault of another person; **15**. Equivalents and exemptions.

F07g.1a Cargo information (regulation 4)

*   **Regulation 4(1)** provides that the **shipper** must provide such **information to the operator or master** sufficiently **in advance of loading** to enable them to ensure that:
    *   the different commodities to be carried are compatible with each other or suitably separated;
    *   the cargo is suitable for the ship;
    *   the ship is suitable for the cargo; and
    *   the cargo can be safely stowed and secured on board the ship and transported under all expected conditions during the intended voyage.
*   The **cargo information must include**:
    *   in the case of **general cargo**, and cargo carried in cargo units, a general description of the cargo, the gross mass of the cargo or cargo units, and any relevant special properties of the cargo;
    *   in the case of **bulk cargoes**, information on the **stowage factor** of the cargo, the **trimming procedures**, the **likelihood of shifting** including **angle of repose**, if applicable, and any other relevant **special properties**. In the case of a **concentrate or other cargo which may liquefy**, additional information in the form of a **certificate** indicating the **moisture content** of the cargo and its **transportable moisture limit (TML)** (this certificate is sometimes known as a **Shipper's Declaration**);
    *   in the case of **bulk cargoes which are not classified** in accordance with SOLAS regulation VII/2, but have chemical properties that may create a potential hazard, information on the chemical properties in addition to the information (specified above) required by other bulk cargo.
*   The cargo information must be confirmed **in writing** and by appropriate **shipping documents** (e.g. shipping instructions, loading plan, etc.) prior to loading the cargo on the ship (regulation 4(2)).
*   In preparing cargo units (e.g. wheeled cargo, containers, pallets, tanks, etc.) for carriage by ships, the **shipper** or **forwarder**, as the case may be, must ensure that the gross mass of the units is in accordance with the gross mass declared on the shipping documents (regulation 4(3)).
*   Where the shipper does not deliver the cargo to the ship or its agent he must provide the forwarder with such cargo information, and the **forwarder** must then provide the operator or master with the appropriate cargo information (regulation 4(4)).
*   If a shipper or forwarder fails to provide appropriate cargo information as required by regulation 4, or provides cargo information which he knows to be false or recklessly furnishes cargo information which is false, he will be guilty of an **offence** (regulation 4(5)).
*   If an **owner or master** accepts for carriage, or takes or receives on board any cargo for which appropriate cargo information as required by regulation 4 has not been provided, he will be guilty of an offence (regulation 4(7)).
*   An MCA-recommended **form** for presentation of cargo information is contained in Appendix 2 to The Carriage of Cargoes, Volume 2 – Instructions for the Guidance of Surveyors (1999). The form is not applicable if the cargo to be loaded requires a declaration under SOLAS regulation VII/5, MARPOL Annex III regulation 4, or the IMDG Code, General Introduction, section 9.
*   Ships carrying **dangerous goods or marine pollutants** must, in addition, carry a dangerous goods or marine pollutants **list, manifest or stowage plan** (see F07f.2g).
*   Prior to loading a solid bulk cargo on a sea-going bulk carrier of 500gt or over, the shipper is required to make a **Solid Bulk Cargo Density Declaration** (see F07i.1).

F07g.1b Carriage of documentation (regulation 5)

*   The owner and master of every ship to which the Regulations apply, other than a ship engaged in the carriage of grain, must ensure that "**appropriate documentation**" relevant to the **cargo and its stowage and securing**, which should specify in particular the **precautions necessary for the safe carriage** of that cargo by sea, is carried on board (regulation 5(1)).
*   Under regulation 5(2) the documentation referred to above **may consist** of one or more of the following codes of safe practice:
    *   the IMO **Code of Safe Practice for Cargo Stowage and Securing (CSS Code)** 1992 edition, as amended in 1994 and 1995;
    *   the IMO **Code of Safe Practice for Ships Carrying Timber Deck Cargoes (TDC Code)** 1992 edition; and
    *   the IMO **Code of Safe Practice for Solid Bulk Cargoes (BC Code)**, 1991 edition, as amended in 1996.
*   The owner and master of **every ship carrying grain** to which the Regulations apply must ensure that the **International Grain Code is carried on board**, and will be guilty of an **offence** for any breach of this requirement (regulation 5(3)). For notes on the **requirements of the International Grain Code**, see F07g.2.
*   All **passenger ships and cargo ships carrying cargoes other than solid bulk cargoes**, except cargo ships of less than 500gt on non-international (i.e. domestic) voyages, must carry a **Cargo Securing Manual** (regulation 5(4)). "Cargo Securing Manual" means a manual drawn up to the standard in IMO circular MSC/Circ.745 and approved, in

the case of UK ships, by the MCA, or in the case of non-UK ships, by or on behalf of the flag State[20] (regulation 2(1)). **MGN 146** gives guidance on the preparation and format of the Cargo Securing Manual.

F07g.1c Stowage and securing (regulation 6)

* The **owner and master** must ensure that:
  * cargo and cargo units carried on or under deck are **loaded, stowed and secured** so as to prevent as far as practicable, throughout the voyage, damage or hazard to the ship and the persons on board, and loss of cargo overboard;
  * appropriate precautions are taken during loading and transport of **heavy cargoes or cargoes with abnormal physical dimensions** to ensure that no structural damage to the ship occurs and to maintain adequate stability throughout the voyage;
  * appropriate precautions are taken during loading and transport of **cargo units on board ro-ro ships**, especially with regard to the securing arrangements on board such ships and on the cargo units and with regard to the strength of the securing points and lashings;
  * cargo on ships required to carry a **Cargo Securing Manual** (see F07g.1b) is stowed and secured throughout the voyage in accordance with the Cargo Securing Manual; and
  * cargo on board all ships having **ro-ro cargo spaces and required to carry a Cargo Securing Manual** is stowed and secured in accordance with the Cargo Securing Manual before the ship leaves the berth.
* Where **packaged goods** have been packed into or onto a cargo unit, the **shipper or forwarder** of the goods must ensure that:
  * the cargo is packed and secured so as to prevent, throughout any voyage, damage or hazard to the ship and the person on board; and
  * if the cargo unit is a container, it is not loaded to more than the maximum gross weight indicated on the Safety Approval Plate attached to the container in accordance with the IMO International Convention for Safe Containers (CSC 1972).

F07g.1d Oxygen analysis and gas detection equipment (regulation 7)

* In the case of a ship transporting or accepting for transport a bulk cargo which is liable to emit a toxic or flammable gas, or cause oxygen depletion in the cargo hold, an appropriate **instrument for measuring the concentration of gas or oxygen in the air** must be provided together with detailed instructions for its use. The instrument must be of a type approved by a Certifying Authority, and the crew must be trained in its use.
* The **owner** of a ship which transports, or the **master** who accepts for carriage, such a bulk cargo without ensuring that the above requirements are complied with, will be guilty of an **offence**.

F07g.1e Use of pesticides in ships (regulation 8)

* Where pesticides are used in cargo spaces, they must be used in accordance with **MSN 1718**, which provides that:
  * **where pesticides are used** in the cargo spaces of ships prior to, during or following a voyage, the IMO publication *Recommendations on the Safe Use of Pesticides in Ships*, where relevant thereto, must be complied with;
  * the use of pesticides includes the fumigation of cargo spaces and of cargo, in port, or in transit, and any part of the ship so affected as a consequence of their application or use, as referred to in the IMO Guidelines;
  * fumigation which is to continue during a voyage must only be carried out with the agreement of the ship's master;
  * the master may choose to permit in-transit fumigation only after first referring to the requirements of the flag State Administration;
  * the proposed in-transit fumigation process must be acceptable to the Administration of the next port of call or destination;
  * whether approval of proposed in-transit fumigation has been received from the flag State and port State Administrations or not, prior to the arrival of the vessel and in general not less than 24 hours in advance, the master must inform the port authorities of the port of destination and of ports of call that a fumigation in transit is being carried out.
* Other advice on fumigation is contained in **MSN 1718** and in **MGN 86**.

---

[20] IMO publishes Guidelines for the Preparation of the Cargo Securing Manual (1997 edition).

F07g.1f Bulk cargoes other than grain: acceptability for loading (regulation 9)

* **Regulation 9** applies to ships loading **bulk cargoes other than grain**.
* **Prior to loading a bulk cargo other than grain** the master must be in possession of **stability information**, as required by regulation 32 of the MS (Load Line) Regulations 1998 (SI 1998/2241), containing comprehensive information on the ship's stability and on the distribution of cargo and ballast for the standard loading conditions. (See D04t.5) The owner must ensure that the master is provided with this information.
* The master must not accept for loading **concentrates or other cargoes which may liquefy** unless either:
  * the moisture content of the cargo indicated in the Moisture Content Certificate or Shipper's Declaration specified in F07g.1a is less than its TML; or
  * if the moisture content is above that limit, appropriate safety arrangements are made to the satisfaction of the Certifying Authority to ensure adequate stability in the case of cargo shifting, and the ship has adequate structural integrity.
* Prior to loading a **bulk cargo which is not classified** in accordance with regulation VII/2 of the SOLAS Convention, but has chemical properties that may create a potential hazard, appropriate special precautions for its safe carriage must be taken.
* The **master must not accept cargo for loading unless**:
  * he has in his possession the **appropriate information** as specified above;
  * he is **satisfied by calculations** that the proposed loading arrangements would ensure sufficient stability in accordance with the ship's stability information provided under the MS (Load Line) Regulations 1998;
  * the **appropriate special precautions**, where required by this regulation, **have been taken**.
* A **master** who accepts cargo for loading in breach of the above requirements will be guilty of an **offence**.

F07g.1g Bulk cargoes other than grain: loading, unloading and stowage (regulation10)

* **Regulation 10** applies to ships loading **bulk cargoes other than grain**.
* In regulation 10 "**terminal representative**" means an individual who represents the terminal or other facility where the ship is loading or unloading and who has responsibility for operations conducted by that terminal or facility with regard to the particular ship.
* **Regulation 10(2)** provides that to enable the master to prevent excessive stresses in the ship's structure, it will be the duty of the **owner** to ensure the ship has a **Cargo Loading Manual**, which must be written in a language with which the ship's officers responsible for cargo operations are familiar[21]. If this language is not English, the ship must **also** have a manual in English. The manual may consist of one or more **booklets** and must, as a minimum, include:
  * stability data, to the extent required by regulation 32 of the Merchant Shipping (Load Line) Regulations 1998;
  * ballasting and deballasting rates and capacities;
  * maximum allowable load per unit surface area of the tank top plating;
  * maximum allowable load per hold;
  * general loading and unloading instructions with regard to the strength of the ship's structure including any limitations on the most adverse operating conditions during loading, unloading, ballasting operations and the voyage;
  * any special restrictions such as limitations on the most adverse operating conditions imposed by the Administration or organization recognised by it, if applicable; and
  * where strength calculations are required, maximum permissible forces and moments on the ship's hull during loading, unloading and the voyage.
* Under **regulation 10(3)**, before a solid bulk cargo is loaded or unloaded, the **master** and the **terminal representative** (who is defined in regulation 10(1)(a) as "an individual who represents the terminal or other facility where the ship is loading or unloading and who has responsibility for operations conducted by that terminal or facility with regard to the particular ship") must agree on a **plan** (i.e. a "**loading plan**" or "**unloading plan**") which:
* will ensure that the permissible forces and moments on the ship are not exceeded during loading or unloading, and
* will include the sequence, quantity and rate of loading or unloading,
  - taking into consideration the intended speed of loading or unloading, intended number of pours and the deballasting or ballasting capability of the ship. The plan and any subsequent amendments to it must be lodged with the appropriate authority of the **port State**[22].

---

[21] Regulation 10(1) of the MS (Additional Safety Measures for Bulk Carriers) Regulations 1999 (SI 1999/1644) requires that the Cargo Loading Manual of a bulk carrier of 150m or more in length, of single side skin construction, must be endorsed by the Certifying Authority to indicate that regulations 6, 7, 8 and 9, as appropriate, of those Regulations are complied with. (For notes on the Additional Safety Measures for Bulk Carriers Regulations see also D03f.2 and D03f.3a.)

[22] Regulation 10(1)(b) provides that for the purposes of paragraphs (3) and (7) of regulation 10, the "appropriate authority of **a port**" in the United Kingdom will be the harbour authority of that port, and that if a terminal in the port is not operated by the harbour authority, then the operator of the

* The master must ensure that bulk cargoes are **loaded and trimmed reasonably level**, as necessary, to the boundaries of the cargo space so as to minimise the risk of shifting and to ensure that **adequate stability will be maintained** throughout the voyage (regulation 10(4)).
* Under regulation 10(5), the **master** must ensure that:
  * **when bulk cargoes are carried in 'tween-decks**, the hatchways of such 'tween-decks are closed in those cases where the loading information indicates an unacceptable level of stress of the bottom structure if the hatchways are left open (regulation 10(5)(a));
  * the **cargo is trimmed reasonably level** and either extends from side to side or is secured by additional longitudinal divisions of sufficient strength (regulation 10(5)(b)); and
  * the **safe load-carrying capacity of the 'tween-decks is observed** to ensure that the deck -structure is not overloaded (regulation 10(5)(c)).
* The **master and terminal representative** must ensure that loading and unloading operations are conducted **in accordance with the agreed loading or unloading plan** (regulation 10(6)).
* If during loading or unloading any of the above-mentioned limits of the ship (e.g. maximum allowable load per hold) are exceeded or are likely to become so if the loading or unloading continues, the **master has the right** to suspend operations, and if he does so he **must notify** accordingly the appropriate authority of the port State with which the plan has been lodged (regulation 10(7)(a)). (For the meaning of "appropriate authority", see above.) In this event both the master and the terminal representative must ensure that corrective action is taken (regulation 10(7)(b)).
* When unloading cargo, the master and terminal representative must ensure that the **unloading method does not damage the ship's structure** (regulation 10(7)(c)).
* The **master** must ensure that ship's personnel continuously **monitor cargo operations** (regulation 10(8)(a)).
* Where possible, the ship's **draught must be checked regularly** during loading or unloading to confirm the tonnage figures supplied (regulation 10(8)(b)).
* Each **draught and tonnage observation** must be recorded in a **cargo log book** (regulation 10(8)(c)).
* If **significant deviations** from the agreed loading or unloading plan are detected, cargo or ballast operations or both must be **adjusted** to ensure that the deviations are corrected (regulation 10(8)(d)).

F07g.1h Bulk grain cargoes: International Grain Code (regulation 11)

* A ship **carrying grain** must comply with the requirements of the **International Grain Code** (see F07g.2) (regulation 11(1). Without prejudice to this requirement, or any other requirement of the Carriage of Cargoes Regulations, the operator and master must ensure that:
  * a ship **loading grain** complies with the International Grain Code (regulation 11(2)(a)); and
  * the ship has on board a **Document of Authorisation** as required by International Grain Code (regulation 11(2)(b)).
* In the case of a UK ship, the Document of Authorisation must be issued by the **Certifying Authority** (regulation 11(2)(b)).
* Except when the ship may be in distress, the **owner and master** may not permit a ship loaded with grain in bulk outside the UK **to enter any port in the UK so laden**, unless the ship has **been loaded in accordance with the International Grain Code** (regulation 11(3)).
* Regulation 11(4) provides that **no person** may order the commencement of loading of grain into a ship in the UK unless he is satisfied that:
  * the ship has on board a **Document of Authorisation**; or
  * the **master has demonstrated** to the satisfaction of the Certifying Authority that the ship, in its proposed loading condition, **will comply** with the appropriate requirements of the International Grain Code and has obtained a **document to this effect** signed by a surveyor of a Certifying Authority.
* For notes on the statutory requirement to carry the International Grain Code, see F07g.2.
* For notes on additional grain cargo-related documentation that may be required, see F07i.4.

F07g.2 International Grain Code requirements

* **SOLAS regulation VI/9.1 (Requirements for cargo ships carrying grain)** provides that a cargo ship carrying grain must hold a **Document of Authorization** as required by the International Grain Code, and for the purposes of regulation 9, the requirements of the Code should be treated as **mandatory. A ship without a Document of**

---

terminal will be the appropriate authority. However, regulation 10(3) and 10(7) do not specify the "appropriate authority of a **port**", but the appropriate authority of the **port State**. It is assumed that regulation 10(3) and 10(7) were meant to have referred to the "appropriate authority of a port".

Authorization must not load grain until the master satisfies the flag State Administration, or the SOLAS Contracting Government of the port of loading on behalf of the Administration, that the ship will comply with the requirements of the International Grain Code in its proposed loaded condition (regulation 9.2). (See below for a related provision in A.9.1 of the Code.)

* The International Code for the Safe Carriage of Grain in Bulk -
  - is commonly called the "International Grain Code".
  - was adopted by the IMO Maritime Safety Committee by resolution MSC.23(59).
  - applies to ships regardless of size, including those of less than 500gt, engaged in the carriage of grain in bulk, to which part C of chapter VI of the 1974 SOLAS Convention, as amended, applies (A 1.1).
  - defines "grain" as including wheat, maize (corn), oats, rye, barley, rice, pulses, seeds and processed forms thereof, whose behaviour is similar to that of grain in its natural state (A 2.1).
* A **Document of Authorization** must be issued by or on behalf of the flag State Administration for every ship loaded in accordance with the Code, and must be accepted as evidence that the ship is capable of complying with the Code (A 3.1).
* The Document of Authorization must accompany or be incorporated into the **Grain Loading Manual** provided to enable the master to meet the requirements of A 7 (A 3.2). The Manual must meet the requirements of A 6.3 (A 3.2).
* The Document of Authorization, grain loading stability data and associated plans may be in the **official language** or languages of the issuing country. If the language used is neither English nor French, the text must include a translation into either English or French.
* A **copy of the Document of Authorization**, **grain loading stability data** and **associated plans** must be placed on board so that the master, if required, may produce them for inspection by the SOLAS Contracting Government at the loading port (A 3.4).
* A 3.5 repeats, with small changes, the wording of SOLAS regulation VI/9.2 (as above).
* The flag State Administration, or a SOLAS Contracting Government on its behalf, may **exempt** individual ships or classes of ship from particular requirements of the Code if it considers that the sheltered nature and conditions of the voyage are such as to render their application unreasonable or unnecessary.
* **Information** in printed booklet form (i.e. a **Grain Loading Manual**) must be provided to enable the master to ensure that the ship complies with the Code when carrying grain in bulk on an international voyage (A 6.1). Information to be in the booklet is listed in A 6.2 and A 6.3. The information in A 6.2 must be acceptable to the flag State Administration (or a Contracting Government on its behalf), while the information in A 6.3 must be approved by that body.
* **A ship not having on board a Document of Authorisation** issued in accordance with A 3 of the Code may be permitted to load bulk grain subject to certain conditions, one of which is that the **total weight of the bulk grain** does not exceed **one third of the ship's deadweight** (A 9.1).

F07g.3 BLU Code provisions

* The **Code of Practice for the Safe Loading and Unloading of Bulk Carriers** -
  - is a non-mandatory IMO code, adopted in November 1997 under Resolution A.862(20).
  - provides guidance to owners and masters of bulk carriers, charterers, terminal operators and other parties concerned for the safe handling, loading and unloading of solid bulk cargoes. The recommendations in the Code are subject to terminal and port requirements, or national regulations.
  - primarily covers the safety of ships loading and unloading solid bulk cargoes, excluding grain, and reflects current issues, best practices and legislative requirements. Broader safety and pollution issues, such as those covered by the SOLAS, MARPOL and Load Line Conventions, are not specifically included in the Code.
  - is linked to, but is not mandatory under, regulation VI/7 (Loading, unloading and stowage of bulk cargoes) of SOLAS 74, as amended by resolution MSC.47(66).
  - contains sections and appendices as follows: Section **1**. Definitions; Section **2**. Suitability of ships and terminals; Section **3**. Procedures between ship and shore prior to the ship's arrival; Section **4**. Procedures between ship and terminal prior to cargo handling; Section **5**. Cargo loading and handling of ballast; Section **6**. Unloading cargo and handling of ballast; Appendix **1**. Recommended contents of port and terminal information books; Appendix **2**. Loading or unloading plan; Appendix **3**. Ship/shore safety checklist; Appendix **4**. Guidelines for completing the ship/shore safety checklist; Appendix **5**. Form for cargo information.
* The **requirements of individual terminals and port authorities** should be published in terminal and port information books. The type of information which should be given in these books is listed in Appendix 1 of the BLU Code. Such a book should be given to the master of any bulk carrier arriving at a loading or unloading port or terminal.

F07h CARRIAGE OF PACKAGED IRRADIATED NUCLEAR FUEL ETC. (INF CODE) REGULATIONS

* The **MS (Carriage of Packaged Irradiated Nuclear Fuel etc.) (INF Code) Regulations 2000** (SI 2000/3216) -
    - **implement** in the UK 1999 amendments to chapter VII (Carriage of Dangerous Goods) of SOLAS 74, the purpose of which amendments is to give effect to the International Code for the Safe Carriage of Packaged Irradiated Nuclear Fuel, Plutonium and High-Level Radioactive Wastes on Board Ships (INF Code).
    - **apply to** all ships, regardless of size, engaged in the carriage of packaged irradiated nuclear fuel, plutonium and high-level radioactive wastes.
    - **define "INF cargo"** as "packaged irradiated nuclear fuel, plutonium and high-level radioactive wastes carried as cargo".
    - **define "packaged"** as "contained in packagings complying with the requirements of Class 7 of the IMDG Code, Schedules 10, 11, 12, 13 or 14".
    - **define "irradiated nuclear fuel"** as "material containing uranium, thorium or plutonium isotopes which has been used to maintain a self-sustaining nuclear chain reaction".
    - **define "plutonium"** as "the resultant mixture of isotopes of that material extracted from the reprocessing of irradiated nuclear fuel".
    - define "**high-level radiactive wastes**" as "liquid wastes resulting from the operation of the first stage extraction system or the concentrated wastes from subsequent extraction stages, in a facility for reprocessing irradiated nuclear fuel, or solids into which such liquid wastes have been converted".
    - require ships to hold a valid **International Certificate of Fitness**, which is issued to UK ships by the MCA, certifying that they have been constructed to certain standards including such matters as strength and stability, fire protection, cargo securement and temperature control,
* Every ship to which the Regulations apply must be constructed, equipped, inspected and surveyed in accordance with the requirements of the **INF Code** (regulation 4(1)).
* The operator and **master** must ensure that a ship carrying INF cargo **complies with the requirements of the INF Code** (regulation 4(2)).
* The MCA must, on the application of the operator of a UK-registered ship, if satisfied that the ship complies with the requirements of the INF Code, issue a **Certificate of Fitness** certifying compliance with the INF Code (regulation 4(3)). (This certificate is the **International Certificate of Fitness for the Carriage of INF Cargo**, as provided for by the INF Code.)
* An operator or master **must not accept INF cargo** for carriage in a ship which has not been issued with a Certificate of Fitness by the MCA, as mentioned in regulation 4(3), or in the case of a non-UK ship by the flag State Administration (regulation 5).

F07i OTHER CARGO INFORMATION AND DOCUMENTATION

* In addition to documents required by the Dangerous Goods Regulations and Carriage of Cargoes Regulations as described in F07f and F07g, ships carrying cargoes may be required to carry the documents detailed in the following sections.

F07i.1 Cargo information and documentation required under Additional Safety Measures for Bulk Carriers Regulations

* **Regulation 10(1) of the MS (Additional Safety Measures for Bulk Carriers) Regulations 1999** (SI 1999/1644) provides that in the case of ships to which **regulations 6, 7, 8 and 9** (as appropriate) apply, the **Cargo Loading Manual** required by regulation 10(2) of the MS (Carriage of Cargoes) Regulations 1999 (see F07g.1g) must be **endorsed** by the Certifying Authority to indicate that regulations 6, 7, 8 and 9 (as appropriate) are complied with.
* The **ships referred to** in regulation 10(1) (i.e. those to which regulations 6, 7, 8 and 9 apply) are:
    * in regulation 6: bulk carriers of 150m in length and upwards of single side skin construction, designed to carry solid bulk cargoes with a density of 1000 kg/m3 and above, constructed on or after 1 July 1999; bulk carriers of 150m in length and upwards of single side skin construction, carrying solid bulk cargoes with a density of 1780 kg/m3 and above, constructed before 1 July 1999;
    * in regulation 7: bulk carriers of 150m in length and upwards of single side skin construction, constructed on or after 1 July 1999, and designed to carry solid bulk cargoes with a density of 1000 kg/m3 and above;

* in regulation 8: bulk carriers of 150m in length and upwards of single side skin construction, constructed before 1 July 1999, and carrying solid bulk cargoes with a density of 1780 kg/m3 and above;
* in regulation 9: bulk carriers of 150m in length and upwards of single side skin construction, constructed before 1 July 1999, of 10 years of age or over, carrying solid bulk cargoes with a density of 1780 kg/m3 and above.

* Under **regulation 10(2)** any **restrictions** imposed under **regulation 8** on the carriage of solid bulk cargoes with a density of 1780 kg/m3 and above must be **identified and recorded in the Cargo Loading Manual**.
* **Regulation 11(1)** provides that **prior to loading solid bulk cargo on a bulk carrier**, the shipper must declare the density of the cargo, in addition to **providing the cargo information** required by regulation 4(1) of the MS (Carriage of Cargoes) Regulations 1999 (as outlined in F07g.1a). (The shipper's declaration may be referred to as a **Solid Bulk Cargo Density Declaration**.)
* **Regulation 11(2)** provides that for bulk carriers of 150m in length and upwards of single side skin construction constructed before 1 July 1999, any cargo carried on or after the implementation date specified in regulation 5 and declared to have a **density within the range 1250 kg/m^3 to 1780 kg/m^3** must have its **density verified** by an accredited testing organisation unless such bulk carriers comply with all the relevant requirements of the Regulations applicable to the carriage of solid bulk cargoes having a density of 1780 kg/m3 and above.

F07i.2 Information and documentation relating to liquefied gas cargoes

* The various **Gas Carrier Codes** (which are described in D03d.1) -
  - **contain** (in paragraph 15.2) requirements for **information to be provided to the master**.
  - **contain** (in paragraph 17.8) a requirement for a **certificate** relating to **cargo inhibition**.
  - **contain** (in paragraph 18.1.1) requirements for **cargo information to be on board**.
* **15.2 (Information to be provided to the master)** provides: The **maximum allowable loading limits for each cargo tank** should be indicated **for each product** which may be carried, for each loading temperature which may be applied and for the applicable maximum reference temperature, on a **list** to be approved by the Administration. **Pressures** at which the pressure relief valves, including those valves required by 8.3 of the Code, have been set should also be stated on the list. A **copy of the list should be permanently kept on board by the master**.
* **17.8 (Inhibition)** provides: Care should be taken that the cargo is sufficiently inhibited to prevent polymerization at all times during the voyage. Ships should be provided with a certificate from the manufacturer stating:
  - .1 name and amount of inhibitor added;
  - .2 date inhibitor was added and the normally expected duration of its effectiveness;
  - .3 any temperature limitations affecting the inhibitor; and
  - .4 the action to be taken should the length of the voyage exceed the effective lifetime of the inhibitors.
* **18.1.2** provides that products required to be inhibited should be **refused** if the certificate required by 17.8 is **not supplied**.
* **18.1 (Cargo information)** provides: Information should be on board and available to all concerned, giving the necessary date for the safe carriage of cargo. Such information should include for each product carried:
  - .1 a full description of the physical and chemical properties necessary for the safe containment of the cargo;
  - .2 action to be taken in the event of spills and leaks;
  - .3 counter-measures against accidental personal contact;
  - .4 fire-fighting procedures and fire-fighting media;
  - .5 procedures for cargo transfer, gas-freeing, ballasting, tank cleaning and changing cargoes;
  - .6 special equipment needed for the safe handling of the particular cargo;
  - .7 minimum allowable inner hull steel temperatures; and
  - .8 emergency procedures.

F07i.3 Information and documentation relating to bulk chemical cargoes

* Regulation 7(1) of the **MS (Dangerous or Noxious Liquid Substances in Bulk) Regulations 1996** (SI 1996/3010) provides that every ship carrying noxious liquid substances must be provided with a **Procedures and Arrangements Manual** (see D04g.3b).
* Regulation 8(1) provides that every ship carrying noxious liquid substances must be provided with a **Cargo Record Book** (see D05b.3).
* The various **Chemical Tanker Codes** (which are described in D03e.1) -
  - **contain** (in paragraph 2.2.5) a requirement for the master to be provided with a **loading and stability information booklet**.
  - **contain** (in paragraph 8.2.6) a requirement for the master to be provided with **information about loading rates**.

-   **contain** (in paragraph 16.2) a requirement for **cargo information to be on board**.
*   **In 2.2 (Freeboard and intact stability), paragraph 2.2.5** provides that the master of the ship should be supplied with a loading and stability information booklet. This booklet should contain details of typical service and ballast conditions, provisions for evaluating other conditions of loading and a summary of the ship's survival capabilities. In addition, the booklet should contain sufficient information to enable the master to load and operate the ship in a safe and seaworthy manner.
*   **In 8.2 (Cargo-tank venting), paragraph 8.2.6** provides that the master should be provided with the maximum permissible loading and unloading rates for each tank or group of tanks consistent with the design of the venting systems.
*   **Paragraph 15.1 and 15.5.11** provide that, in respect of cargoes of acetone cyanohydrin and lactonitrile solution (80% or less), and hyrogen peroxide solutions, a **certificate of stabilization** should be provided by the manufacturer, and kept on board, specifying:
    *   the name and amount of stabilizer added;
    *   the date on which the stabilizer was added and its duration of effectiveness;
    *   any temperature limitations qualifying the stabilizer's effective lifetime; and
    *   the action to be taken should the length of voyage exceed the effective lifetime of the stabilizer.
*   **Paragraph 15.13.3** provides that, in respect of cargoes protected by additives, a **certificate of protection** should be provided by the manufacturer, and kept on board, specifying:
    *   the name and amount of additives present;
    *   whether the additive is oxygen-dependent;
    *   the date on which additive was put in the product and its duration of effectiveness;
    *   any temperature limitations qualifying the additives' effective lifetime; and
    *   the action to be taken should the length of voyage exceed the effective lifetime of the additives.
*   **In 16.2 (Cargo information), paragraph 16.2.1** provides that a copy of the Code, or national regulations incorporating the provisions of the Code, should be on board every ship covered by the Code.
*   **Paragraph 16.2.2** provides that any cargo offered for bulk shipment should be indicated in the shipping documents by the **correct technical name**. Where the cargo is a **mixture**, an **analysis** indicating the dangerous components contributing significantly to the total hazard of the product should be provided, or a complete analysis if this is available. Such an analysis should be certified by the manufacturer or by an independent expert acceptable to the flag State Administration.
*   **Paragraph 16.2.3** provides that information should be on board, and available to all concerned, giving the necessary data for the safe carriage of the cargo. Such information should include a cargo stowage plan, to be kept in an accessible place, indicating all cargo on board, including (for) each dangerous chemical carried:
    *   a full description of the physical and chemical properties, including reactivity, necessary for the safe containment of the cargo;
    *   action to be taken in the event of spills or leaks;
    *   countermeasures against accidental personal contact;
    *   fire-fighting procedures and fire-fighting media;
    *   procedures for cargo transfer, tank cleaning, gas-freeing and ballasting;
    *   for those cargoes required to be stabilised or inhibited in accordance with 15.1, 15.5.11 or 15.13.3, the cargo should be refused if the certificate required by these paragraphs is not supplied.

F07i.4 Additional grain cargo documentation

*   In addition to the grain cargo documentation described in F07g.1h, a ship loading or carrying grain may be required by port or port State regulations, or charterer's instructions, to carry any or all of the following documents.
*   A **Ship Inspection Report/certificate and Treatment Order**, or a document with a similar title, will usually be issued following inspection of cargo holds by a government-authorised surveyor before loading grain. Most grain-exporting countries have regulations requiring the holds of grain-loading ships to be inspected, and loading will not usually be permitted until the surveyor has issued the certificate, which states that the ship's holds will not contaminate or otherwise affect the grain. There will usually be a nil tolerance for certain species of insect and fumigation may be required where any live pests are discovered.
*   A **Paint Compliance Certificate** may be issued by a chemical research laboratory to confirm that the paint used on a newly-painted hold in which it is intended to load grain (or other foodstuffs) is not in contravention of the port State's foodstuffs regulations. It may be demanded from the ship by the shipper before loading commences.
*   A **Fumigation Certificate** is issued by a responsible authority, such as the port State's agricultural Administration, and gives details of fumigation carried out, including spaces covered, fumigants and concentrations used, etc. It is likely to be required where a **treatment order** has been issued after a hold inspection.

* A **Certificate of Loading (Bulk Grain)** is issued in a US port by the National Cargo Bureau to certify that a bulk grain cargo has been loaded in accordance with US Coast Guard Regulations.

F07i.5 Hazardous bulk cargo documentation

* A **Shipper's Declaration** is required under the IMO Code of Safe Practice for Solid Bulk Cargoes (BC Code) to be made by the shipper of a hazardous solid bulk cargo, e.g. coal, for the guidance of the master. It outlines the cargo's characteristics, including (for coal):
  * transportable moisture limit (TML);
  * estimated stowage factor (SF);
  * angle of repose;
  * contractual sizing;
  * contractual sulphur content;
  * IMO category for ocean transportation purposes.
* The Shipper's Declaration also lists any **special precautions** required and states where **emergency procedures** may be found, e.g. in the Coal section of the BC Code, and reproduces relevant extracts. See also F07g.1a.
* A **Master's Response Sheet** may be issued by a shipper to the master after loading a hazardous bulk cargo in an effort to obtain information on the behaviour of the cargo during the voyage, where this **behaviour does not correspond to that stated on the Shipper's Declaration**.
* For notes on **documentation for dangerous goods in bulk**, see F07f.2m.

F07i.6 Pre-loading documentation

* An **export permit** may be required by the carrier from the shipper before loading certain goods, e.g. arms and works of art, under the exporting port State's legislation. It may be required where the goods are destined for a country which is subject to a legal embargo, e.g. a UN embargo.
* A **certificate of origin** is often a requirement under the terms of a Letter of Credit, and is therefore demanded by banks involved in documentary credit transactions. It is usually issued by a chamber of commerce in the country of origin to attest to the true source of the goods.
* A **certificate of quality** may be required under the terms of a contract of sale of goods.
* A **certificate of readiness to load** is issued by the loading port State authorities in respect of a cargo which is subject to special loading requirements, such as grain, concentrates and timber on deck, to certify that the intended loading compartments have been inspected and that the requirements of the relevant regulations or approved practice have been complied with. It may contain special requirements of the port State authorities as to loading.

F07i.7 Post-loading documentation

* A **cargo stowage plan**, **cargo plan** or **hold distribution plan** may be produced by shore loading staff or by ship's staff. When sent ahead of the vessel to the agent at the port of discharge enables stevedores to plan the discharge operation.
* A **hatch sealing certificate** may be issued by specialist hatch-sealing operatives after compartments have been sealed to prevent unauthorised entry after following loading or fumigation
* A **certificate of fitness to proceed to sea** may be issued by a marine Administration at a loading port State to certify that insofar as the stowage of the cargo conforms to the appropriate regulations or approved practice, the vessel is fit to proceed to sea. It may be required to obtain **outwards clearance** from a customs officer. It should not be confused with a **certificate of seaworthiness**.

F07i.8 Post-discharging documentation

* An **empty hold (or empty tank) certificate** may be issued to the master by the discharging stevedores' representative to confirm that holds or tanks which should have been completely discharged of cargo are, in fact, empty. It may be useful in countering claims of short-landing.
* **Ship's delivery orders** (SDOs) may be issued by the shipowner to cargo receivers where a bulk cargo, portions of which are consigned to different consignees, is carried under a single bill of lading. A ship's delivery order is defined in section 1 of the Carriage of Goods by Sea Act 1992 as "any document which is neither a bill of lading nor

a sea waybill but contains an undertaking which (a) is given under or for the purposes of a contract for the carriage by sea of the goods to which the document relates, or of goods which include those goods; and (b) is an undertaking by the carrier to a person identified in the document to deliver the goods to which the document relates to that person". Instead of the shipowner's agent at the discharge port accepting surrender of an original bill of lading and issuing a new bill to each receiver, he issues a ship's delivery order to each receiver in exchange for the bill, on payment of any freight and charges due. In the ship's delivery order the shipowner undertakes to deliver to the named consignee the quantity of cargo intended for him. The ship's delivery order is, therefore, a document of title.

F07i.9 Pre-departure hazardous cargo notifications

* For notes on the requirements of regulation 5(1) of MS (Reporting Requirements for Ships Carrying Dangerous or Polluting Goods) Regulations 1995 (SI 1995/2498), as amended by SI 1999/2121, to make hazardous cargo notifications prior to sailing under various circumstances, see I07d.

F08 Contract between shipowner and passengers

F08a CONTRACT OF PASSAGE

F08a.1 Definition of "passenger"

* **M.1194** (The status of persons carried in UK ships) (which has been cancelled without replacement) stated that the **legal definition of a passenger** is given in section 26 of the MS (Safety Convention) Act 1949, which provides as follows: "In Part III of the Merchant Shipping Act 1894, in the MS (Safety and Load Lines Conventions) Act 1932, and in the MS (Safety Conventions) Act 1949, the expression "passenger" means any person carried in a ship except:
   • a person employed or engaged in any capacity on board the ship on the business of the ship;
   • a person on board the ship either in pursuance of the obligations laid upon the master to carry shipwrecked, distressed or other persons, or by reason of any circumstance that neither the master nor the owner nor the charterer (if any) could have prevented or forestalled; and
   • a child under one year of age".
* During an appeal case in the High Court in 1983, the legal status of persons on board a UK ship came under close scrutiny, in particular the distinction between "**persons engaged on the business of the ship**" and "**passenger**". The Department of Transport, after carefully considering the Court's judgement, held the view that the only persons who can be considered as being "lawfully engaged on the business of the ship" are those over the minimum school leaving age (about 16 years) who:
   • have a contractually binding agreement to serve on the ship in some defined capacity and which could include carrying out such duties under training; or
   • are duly signed-on members of the crew.
* For the purposes of the rule of certain P&I clubs on Crew Claims (sometimes called the "Seaman Rule"), the expression "**seaman**" includes "any person.....engaged or employed in any capacity in connection with the business of any entered ship as part of such ship's complement....and includes **any relative of a seaman**....whom an owner has agreed to maintain or carry on board an entered ship....and includes **any person engaged under articles of agreement for nominal pay**." However, the UK Merchant Shipping Acts provide that a person carried on a ship must be either a *bona fide* **crew member or a passenger**, in order to prevent owners from getting round the passenger safety legislation. Thus in the UK there is now no such person as a "su**pernumerary**"[23].
* The MCA recommends that whenever the carriage of passengers is contemplated on any ship, the contents of **M.913** (The carriage of passengers in ships and motor vessels, including those plying on inland rivers, canals, estuaries and lakes) should be carefully studied. M.913 advises that no ship carrying passengers to, from or between any places in the UK may ply or proceed to sea or on any voyage or excursion with more than 12 passengers on board unless it holds a **valid Passenger Certificate** issued by the MCA after survey. A ship holding a Passenger Certificate must not carry passengers in excess of the number specified on the certificate. **A copy of the Passenger Certificate must**

---

[23] The literal meaning of "supernumerary" is a person or thing that is in excess of the regular, necessary, or usual number.

be posted up in a conspicuous place on board the ship. M.913 further warns masters of the **consequences of carrying more passengers than are allowed** by the Passenger Certificate, and advises owners and masters of ships intending to carry passengers to acquaint themselves with the relevant legal provisions not only for their own interests, but also to ensure that proper precautions are taken for the safety of their passengers and crew.

F08a.2 Athens Convention

- is properly called the **Convention Relating to the Carriage of Passengers and their Luggage by Sea, 1974**.
- was also known as the **Passengers and Luggage (PAL) Convention**.
- was adopted in 1974, was originally given effect in the UK by Merchant Shipping Act 1979, and came into force internationally in 1987.
- has three **Protocols**, of 1976, 1990 and 2000, of which only the 1976 Protocol is in force.
- **is incorporated into UK law** by section 183 of the Merchant Shipping Act 1995, the text of the Convention forming Schedule 6 of the Act.
- applies to the **international carriage of passengers by sea** in certain circumstances.
- establishes the **carrier's liability** for death or injury to passengers, or for loss or damage to their luggage.
- was extended in the UK by the MS (Carriage of Passengers and Their Luggage by Sea (Domestic Carriage) Order 1987 (SI 1987/670) to cover carriage of **domestic (i.e. non-international) passengers** and their luggage.
- defines "**carrier**" as "a person by or on behalf of whom a contract of carriage has been concluded, whether the carriage is actually performed by him or by a performing carrier".
- defines "**performing carrier**" as "a person other than the carrier, being the owner, charterer or operator of a ship, who actually performs the whole or a part of the carriage".
- defines a "**contract of carriage**" as a contract made by or on behalf of a carrier for the carriage by sea of a passenger or of a passenger and his luggage, as the case may be.
- defines a "**ship**" only as a seagoing vessel, excluding an aircushion vehicle.
- defines "**passenger**" as "any person carried in a ship (a) under a contract of carriage, or (b) who, with the consent of the carrier is accompanying a vehicle or live animals which are covered by a contract for the carriage of goods not governed by this Convention".
- defines "**luggage**" as any article or vehicle carried by the carrier under a contract of carriage, excluding: (a) articles and vehicles carried under a charter party, bill of lading or other contract primarily concerned with the carriage of goods, and (b) live animals.
- defines "**cabin luggage**" as "luggage which the passenger has in his cabin or is otherwise in his possession, custody or control". (In most circumstances "cabin luggage" includes luggage which the passenger has in or on his vehicle.)
- defines "**loss of or damage to luggage**" as including pecuniary loss resulting from the luggage not having been re-delivered to the passenger within a reasonable time after the arrival of the ship on which the luggage has been or should have been carried, but does not include delays resulting from labour disputes.
- defines "**carriage**" as covering the following periods:
  - **with regard to the passenger and his cabin luggage**, the period during which the passenger and/or his cabin luggage are on board the ship or in the course of disembarkation, and the period during which the passenger and his cabin luggage are transported by water from land to the ship or vice-versa, if the cost of such transport is included in the fare or if the vessel used for this purpose of auxiliary transport has been put at the disposal of the passenger by the carrier. However, with regard to the passenger, carriage does not include the period during which he is in a marine terminal or station or on a quay or in or on any other port installation;
  - **with regard to cabin luggage**, also the period during which the passenger is in a marine terminal or station or on a quay or in or on any other port installation if that luggage has been taken over by the carrier or his servant or agent and has not been re-delivered to the passenger;
  - **with regard to other luggage which is not cabin luggage**, the period from the time of its taking over by the carrier or his servant or agent on shore or on board until the time of its re-delivery by the carrier or his servant or agent;
  - defines "**international carriage**" as "any carriage in which, according to the contract of carriage, the place of departure and the place of destination are situated in two different States, or in a single State if, according to the contract of carriage or the scheduled itinerary, there is an intermediate port of call in another State".

F08a.2a Application

* **Article 2**, paragraph 1 provides that the Convention will apply to any carriage if:
  - it is international carriage and the contract of carriage is made in the UK; or

- it is international carriage and, under the contract of carriage, a place in the UK is the place of departure or destination; or
- under the contract of carriage, the places of departure and destination are in the area consisting of the United Kingdom, the Channel Islands and the Isle of Man and there is no intermediate port of call outside the area.

* Notwithstanding paragraph 1 of Article 2, the Convention will not apply when the carriage is subject, under any other international convention concerning the carriage of passengers or luggage by another mode of transport, to a civil liability regime under the provisions of such convention, in so far as those provisions have mandatory application to carriage by sea.

F08a.2a Carrier's liability

* **Article 3** provides that the carrier will be liable for the damage suffered as a result of the **death** of or **personal injury** to a passenger and the **loss of or damage to luggage** if the incident which caused the damage so suffered occurred in the course of the carriage and was **due to the fault or neglect of the carrier or his servants or agents** acting within the scope of their employment. The **burden** of proving that the incident which caused the loss or damage occurred in the course of the carriage, and the extent of the loss or damage, will lie with the **claimant**.

* **Fault or neglect of the carrier** or of his servants or agents acting within the scope of their employment **will be presumed**, unless the contrary is proved, if the **death of or personal injury** to the passenger or the loss or damage to **cabin luggage** arose from or in connection with the shipwreck, collision, stranding, explosion or fire, or defect in the ship. In respect of loss of or damage to **other luggage**, such fault or neglect will be presumed, unless the contrary is proved, **irrespective of the nature of the incident** which caused the loss or damage. In all other cases the **burden** of proving fault or neglect will lie with the claimant.

F08a.3 Obligations of carrier of passengers

* The English **common law duties** of a carrier of passengers under a contract of passage are to take the passengers to the agreed destination -
  - with **due care**;
  - within a **reasonable time**; and
  - with **reasonable speed**.

* **No absolute warranty of seaworthiness** is implied into a contract of passage, but the carrier must use all reasonable care to provide a **safe ship**, **properly equipped and manned**, and **carefully navigated**.

* The carrier will be liable to the passenger for death, injury or loss of passage due to **negligent navigation**. Even where the carrier has disclaimed liability for injury "howsoever caused", he may still be liable if he has not brought the exclusion to the passenger's attention in sufficient time **before embarkation**.

* The carrier will be liable for any injury occurring through the means of transit being improper, whether arising through the negligence of his own servants or other parties who help to provide the means of transit.

* A passenger with a valid complaint against a carrier may attempt to avoid the exclusions in the contract of passage by suing in tort the actual wrongdoer(s) or tortfeasor(s), who may, for example, be the master and/or a member of the crew, where they can be identified (although in most cases this will not be financially worth the passenger's while). Following the success of a passenger-plaintiff against the master and bosun of the P&O liner *Himalaya* in 1954, a Himalaya Clause should be incorporated in the terms and conditions of the passenger ticket in order to protect the master, crew and other servants and contractors of the carrier. For other notes on the Himalaya Clause, see E04i.2, F07b.9a and I05b.2.

* For notes on **vicarious liability of employers**, see B03e.5.

F08b RESTRICTIONS ON PASSENGER NUMBERS

* The **maximum number of passengers permitted to be carried in a passenger ship** is specified in the ship's Passenger Certificate or Passenger Ship Safety Certificate, depending on which certificate is in force. ("**Passenger ship**" means a ship carrying more than 12 passengers – see D04c.1.)

* The **maximum number of passengers permitted to be carried in a cargo ship is twelve,** subject to sufficient **lifesaving appliances** being provided for all persons on board, as certified in the Cargo Ship Safety Equipment Certificate or Cargo Ship Safety Certificate, depending on which certificate is in force. ("Cargo ship" means any ship which is not a passenger ship, pleasure vessel or fishing vessel – see D04c.1).

* Masters may occasionally be asked to carry shore personnel (e.g. owners' or charterers' office staff) when manouevring in port, etc. (i.e. when the vessel is not "at sea" and is not, therefore, in apparent breach of regulations.) In view of the possibility of having to use lifesaving appliances as a result of an accident at such a time, the **number of persons actually on board** when means of direct access to the shore are not provided should never be greater than the number of persons for which the ship is provided with lifesaving appliances.

F08c KEEPING ORDER IN PASSENGER SHIPS

F08c.1 Offences in connection with passenger ships

* **Section 101 of the Merchant Shipping Act 1995** provides that a person commits an **offence** if, in a ship for which there is in force a Passenger Ship Safety Certificate or Passenger Certificate, he does any of the following things:
   - if, being **drunk or disorderly**, he has been on that account refused admission to the ship by the owner or any person in his employment, and, after having his fare (if paid) returned or tendered to him, nevertheless **persists in attempting to enter the ship**;
   - if, being **drunk or disorderly** on board the ship, he is requested by the owner or any person in his employment to leave the ship at any place in the UK at which he can conveniently do so, and, after having his fare (if paid) returned or tendered to him, **does not comply with the request**;
   - if, on board the ship, after warning by the master or other officer, he molests or continues to **molest** any passenger;
   - if, after having been refused admission to the ship by the owner or any person in his employment on account of the ship being full, and having had his fare (if paid) returned or tendered to him, he nevertheless **persists in attempting to enter the ship**;
   - if, having gone on board the ship at any place, and after being requested, on account of the **ship being full**, by the owner or any person in his employment to leave the ship before it has left that place, and having had his fare (if paid) returned or tendered to him, he **does not comply** with that request;
   - if, on arriving in the ship at a point to which he has paid his fare, he **knowingly or intentionally refuses or neglects to leave the ship**;
   - if, on board the ship he **fails**, when requested by the master or other officer, either **to pay his fare or show his ticket**, if any.
* A person commits an **offence** under section 101 if, on board any ship with a Passenger Ship Safety Certificate or Passenger Certificate, he intentionally does or causes to be done anything in such a manner as to –
   - **obstruct or damage** any part of the machinery or equipment of the ship; or
   - **obstruct, impede or molest the crew**, or any of them, in the navigation or management of the ship, or otherwise in the execution of their duty on or about the ship.
* The **master or other officer of any ship with a PSSC or PC**, and all persons called by him to his assistance, may, without any warrant, **detain** any person who commits an offence listed above and whose name and address are unknown to the master or officer, and deliver that person to a police constable.

F08c.2 Master's power to exclude drunken passengers

* **Section 102 of the Merchant Shipping Act 1995** applies to a ship (whether a UK ship or not) carrying more than 12 passengers and employed in carrying passengers between places in the Limited European Trading Area, and provides that the master of any ship to which this section applies may refuse to receive on board any person who by reason of drunkenness or otherwise is in such a state, or misconducts himself in such a manner, as to cause annoyance or injury to passengers on board, and if any such person is on board, may put him on shore at any convenient place.
* A person so refused admittance or put ashore will not be entitled to the return of any fare he has paid.

Section G

INSURANCE AND CLAIMS

Section G Contents

G01 Marine insurance cover requirements of owners, shippers, etc.

G01a MARINE INSURANCE COVER AND BUYERS

G01a.1 Insurance cover of ship owners and managers

* A **shipowner or ship manager** (acting on behalf of the owner) may require marine insurance cover against:
  - actual or constructive **total loss** of his ship's hull, machinery and equipment (**H&M cover**);
  - accidental (particular average) **damage** to his ship's hull, machinery and equipment (**H&M cover**);
  - liability to owners of other vessels (or their cargoes) with which his ship collides (**collision liability**);
  - liability for **general average charges**;
  - liability for **salvage charges**;
  - liability for damage done by his ship to a **third party's property**;
  - liability for **other third party risks**, e.g. cargo claims, personal injuries, pollution, wreck removal costs, etc. (called "**P&I risks**");
  - liability for **oil pollution claims**;
  - loss of earnings due to **strikes**;
  - loss of earnings due to operation of **war risks**;
  - loss of **freight**;
  - loss of **charter hire** (e.g. when vessel goes "off-hire" after sustaining damage);
  - **increased value**, **disbursements** and **excess liabilities** (an additional source of recovery over and above the hull and machinery insured value in case of total loss); and
  - **employer's liability** to workers.
* A shipowner may need to take out other **special insurances** on an emergency basis in certain circumstances. When his vessel deviates from its contracted voyage in some respect, for example, **shipowners' liability insurance** (SOL) may be needed to protect the owner against the extra risks he incurs if he loses his defences to liability under the Hague or Hague-Visby Rules.
* There is **no UK statutory requirement** for ships or goods to be insured. However, without insurance cover, shipowners and owners of goods would have to protect themselves by self-insuring[1].
* For notes on certain risks not covered by the shipowner's H&M policy, see G04b.1.
* **IMO Guidelines on Shipowners' Responsibilities in Respect of Maritime Claims**, adopted by resolution A.898(21) in November 1999 and explained in **MGN 135**, recommend owners of all seagoing ships of 300gt and over (and encourages owners of smaller ships) to ensure that liability for relevant claims up to the limits set under Articles 6 and 7 of the Limitation Convention or any lower limit which the shipowner may invoke, is covered by insurance. The Guidelines recommend shipowners to ensure that their ships have on board a **certificate** issued by the insurer; an appropriately worded P&I Club **Certificate of Entry** will meet this recommendation (see G04b.1).

G01a.2 Insurance cover of sellers or buyers of goods for shipment

* A **seller or buyer of goods for shipment** may require insurance cover against:
  - loss of or damage to his **goods in transit**;
  - loss of earnings due to **strikes**;
  - loss of earnings due to operation of **war risks**;
  - liability for **general average charges**;
  - liability for **salvage charges**.
* The **party** obliged to obtain the insurance cover will depend on the terms of the **sales contract** (see F03a and F03b).

---

[1] A few major shipowners carry all or part of their own hull and machinery insurance. Alfred Holt & Co. were well known for self-insuring their Blue Funnel Line ships.

G01a.3 Insurance cover of time and voyage charterers

* A **time charterer or voyage charterer** may require insurance cover against:
- **legal costs and expenses** arising from disputes concerning, for example, hire, freight, deadfreight and passage money, general and particular average, demurrage or despatch, detention, breach of charter party, bill of lading etc., the proper loading etc. of cargo, quality of bunkers supplied.
- **liability** for:
  - loss of or damage to the **vessel**;
  - loss of or damage to **cargo**;
  - **oil pollution** other than that arising from a tanker in US territorial waters
  - loss of or damage to **third party property**;
  - **death** or **personal injury claims**;
  - **fines**;
  - damage to **fixed property** (e.g. wharf or dock);
  - **wreck clearance** costs;
  - proportion of **general average or salvage charges** not covered by any other insurance;
- **liability** arising from **breach** of or **deviation** under a **bill of lading** (e.g.cargo carried on deck against underdeck bills of lading);
- physical **loss of charterer's bunkers**;
- loss of **freight** at risk;
- **oil pollution** arising from a **tanker in US territorial waters**; and
- **stowaway costs**.

G02 UK marine insurance providers and related bodies

G02a UK MARINE INSURANCE PROVIDERS

* The **London marine insurance market** -
- is the largest insurance market in the world covering marine risks.
- comprises:
  - **Lloyd's** (the Lloyd's market); and
  - **companies** represented at the **International Underwriting Association** (IUA) (sometimes referred to as the "**Companies market**");
* **P&I clubs** (properly called **protection and indemnity associations**), of which several are based in the UK, also provide marine insurance.

G02a.1 Lloyd's

- is also known as **Lloyd's of London**.
- is an **insurance market** situated at One Lime Street, in the City of London.
- **should not be confused with Lloyd's Register of Shipping**, which is a separate organisation with different (but related) functions (see D02c.2a and D02c.1).
- is not a company, but a **society** of individual and corporate members with uniform practices and procedures, regulated by strict rules.
- provides **facilities** for the transaction of insurance business.
- is involved in four areas of business: **marine** (forming 18% of Lloyd's business in 2001), non-marine (59%), aviation (7%) and motor (16%). Approximately 13% of the world's marine business is placed at Lloyd's, risks ranging from yachts to ULCCs and their cargoes. The **liability risks** of most of the world's ocean going ships are reinsured at Lloyd's under the International Group of P&I Clubs' Excess of Loss Contract (see G07b).
- had a **market capacity** of $16,484 million (£11,063 million) in 2001.
* **Members of Lloyd's** provide the capital which supports the risks underwritten at Lloyd's. They are either wealthy **individual members** (called "**names**"), who trade with unlimited liability, or **corporate members** who trade with limited or unlimited liability. In 2001 there were 2,852 individual members and 854 corporate members[2].

---

[2] In January 2002 a plan was put forward at Lloyd's to replace the market's three years-in-arrears accounting regime with a yearly system and to end, by January 2005, unlimited liability for "names".

* **Syndicates** are groups of Lloyd's members who band themselves into joint ventures. Each syndicate has a professional **underwriter** and support staff, working from a "box" (an open-plan desk/office) in the Lloyd's Building. In 2001 there were 108 trading syndicates. A **corporate syndicate** is a syndicate with a single corporate member.
* **Underwriters** (or "underwriting members") are insurance professionals who, on behalf of their syndicates, assess risks involved in insuring and charge premiums accordingly. At their boxes they deal directly with brokers who bring them slips containing information on risks to be insured.
* **Managing agents** supervise the syndicates, employ the underwriters and provide administrative back-up.
* **Members' agents** advise individual members of Lloyd's on their underwriting commitments and provide a link between them and their syndicates. Licensed **Lloyd's advisers** perform a similar function on behalf of corporate members.
* **Lloyd's brokers** are the intermediaries between the general public and the Lloyd's market who supply business to the Lloyd's market. They give advice to their principals (the **"assureds"**) on premiums and policy types, and buy insurance from underwriters after face-to-face negotiations with underwriters. They may also place business with insurance companies. 126 large and small firms were authorised as brokers at Lloyd's in 2001.
* The **Committee of Lloyd's** is elected by members and exercises control over the election and conduct of underwriting members.
* **Website**: www.lloydsoflondon.co.uk

G02a.1a Lloyd's associated bodies and activities

* **Bodies associated with Lloyd's** include:
  * a network of **Lloyd's Agents** throughout the world (see G02b.1); and
  * **Lloyd's Casualty Reporting Service**, operated by Lloyd's Marine Intelligence Unit (part of the Informa Group) at Colchester, Essex, which collects and disseminates shipping information (e.g. casualty reports and shipping movements from Lloyd's Agents) and informs salvors, Lloyd's Salvage Arbitration Branch and other interested parties of casualties.
* Lloyd's produces standard shipping agreements including **Lloyd's Open Form of Salvage Contract** (LOF) (see H05d.1, H05d.2 and H05d.3) and **Lloyd's Average Bond** (see I02i.3).
* The daily insurance and shipping journal *Lloyd's List*, long regarded as the daily journal of the London marine insurance markets, is no longer published by Lloyd's, but by the Informa Group, which now also publishes the freight forwarders' weekly guide *Lloyd's Loading List*.

G02a.2 International Underwriting Association (IUA)

- succeeded the **Institute of London Underwriters** (ILU) in 1998 as the world's largest representational organisation for international **commercial insurers and reinsurers**.
- has a membership of over 100 companies, including virtually every large and medium-sized international company in the insurance industry.
- transacts about 50% of all marine, aviation and transport underwriting business in the London market.
* A marine policy on a high-value ship or cargo is commonly underwritten at both the Lloyd's market and the IUA "Companies market", the underwriter for each participating IUA company "writing a line" in the same manner as particpating Lloyd's underwriters (see G04a).
* **Website**: www.iua.co.uk

G02a.3 P&I Clubs

- are properly called "**protection and indemnity associations**". ("Protection" in the title originally referred to shipowners' protection from the one fourth of collision liability that, traditionally, London hull and machinery insurers did not cover, while "indemnity" referred to the club's indemnity, or compensation, for liability to cargo under a contract of carriage.)
- are associations of member shipowners and charterers, owned and controlled by the insured shipowner or charterer members, for the purpose, basically, of **mutual insurance against third party liabilities** which arise in connection with the operation of ships.
- include the 13 members of the International Group of P&I Clubs (and their 4 associate clubs) (see G02a.3a), and a number of small independent clubs. There are also some P&I facilities in the commercial insurance market. The Charterers P&I Club offers cover for time and voyage charterers.

- mostly offer two principal types of cover: **Protection and Indemnity** (called "**P&I**"), and **Freight, Demurrage and Defence** (called "**FD&D**") (see G04b.1).
- retain representatives called **correspondents** in many ports, as well as reliable lawyers and surveyors.
- issue books containing **club rules** and **lists of correspondents**, and in some cases **master's handbooks**, which are very useful to a master seeking advice and assistance when in any kind of trouble on board ship, e.g. in a pollution incident, a casualty, when under arrest, when under pressure to sign "clean" bills of lading, etc.
- disseminate **loss prevention information** in circulars, bulletins, booklets, videos, etc., aimed at keeping members' premiums down.
- produce **standard forms** of letters of indemnity and protest.
* For notes on **cover available from P&I clubs**, see G04b.1. For notes on **P&I claims**, see G07b.

G02a.3a The International Group of P&I Clubs

- is an association of 13 leading P&I clubs and their associates (i.e. a "club of Clubs").
- exists to provide a **forum** for discussion of legal and technical issues affecting the member clubs, to provide a **mutual reinsurance scheme** for the member clubs through the International Group Pool and Excess Loss Reinsurance contracts, and to **monitor the transfer of business** between member clubs under the terms of the International Group Agreement.
- includes the following clubs:

Association title	Familiar name	Website
American Steamship Owners Mutual Protection and Indemnity Association, Inc.	The American Club	www.americanclub.com
Assuranceforeningen Gard (Gjensidig)	Gard	www.gard.no
Assuranceforeningen Skuld (Gjensidig)	Skuld	www.skuld.com
The Britannia Steam Ship Insurance Association Ltd	The Britannia	www.britanniapandi.com
The Japan Ship Owners' Mutual Protection and Indemnity Association	The Japan Club	www.piclub.or.jp
The London Steam-Ship Owners' Mutual Insurance Association Ltd	The London Club	www.lsso.com
The North of England Protecting and Indemnity Association Ltd	The North of England Club	www.nepia.com
The Shipowners' Mutual Protection and Indemnity Association (Luxembourg)	The Shipowners Club	www.shipownersclub.com
The Standard Steamship Owners' Protection and Indemnity Association Ltd	The Standard Club	www.standard-club.com
The Standard Steamship Owners' Protection & Indemnity Association (Bermuda) Ltd	Standard Bermuda	www.standard-club.com
The Standard Steamship Owners Protection and Indemnity Association (London) Ltd	Standard London	www.standard-club.com
The Steamship Mutual Underwriting Association Ltd	Steamship	www.simsl.com
The Steamship Mutual Underwriting Association (Bermuda) Ltd	Steamship Bermuda	www.simsl.com
The Steamship Mutual Underwriting Association (Europe) Ltd	Steamship London	www.simsl.com
Sveriges Angfartygs Assurans Forening	The Swedish Club	www.swedishclub.com
The United Kingdom Mutual Steam Ship Assurance Association (Bermuda) Ltd	The UK Club	www.ukpandi.com
The West of England Ship Owners Mutual Insurance Association (Luxembourg)	The West of England Club	www.westpandi.com

* With the exception of Gard and Skuld (which are Norwegian), and the American, Japanese and Swedish Clubs, all of the above clubs are British in origin, and most are managed from London offices.
* The member clubs of the International Group together insure about 90% of the world's merchant tonnage.

G02a.3b P&I club control and management

* P&I clubs -
    - are **controlled** by boards of directors representing the shipowner members. Large claims are examined and approved by the directors at regular meetings before payment is made.
    - are **managed** by firms of insurance experts, maritime lawyers and mariners.
    - operate on a **non-profit-making** basis.
* In some clubs, members' entered ships may be subjected to random **ship inspections** concentrating on the management of the vessel. If failed, a more intensive **condition survey** by independent surveyors may be called by the club's managers. An owner who fails to keep his vessel in the condition required by the club's rules may be expelled from the club.
* Managers generally strive to keep the "calls" on members at a minimum, e.g. through **loss prevention** methods such as **information bulletins**, **handbooks** and **videos** aimed at owners and ships' officers. (These should be on board entered ships, and not kept in owners' and managers' offices.)
* Whereas market marine insurers only entertain a claim covered by a peril insured against, P&I clubs assume the conduct of **any matter** likely to give rise to a claim against a member. The shipowner, instead of having to "sue and labour" to minimise the claim against the insurer (see G04a.2e), consults his club managers or, if his vessel is overseas, the nearest correspondent of the club.

G02a.3c P&I underwriting

* Whereas with hull and machinery insurance the cost of the insurance (the premium) is fixed at the start of the period of insurance, a P&I club member will not know exactly how much his insurance will cost for at least a year, and perhaps not for four or five years.
* Each P&I club sets a **premium rating** for an individual owner reflecting the risks against which he requires cover, his fleet's ship types, ages, gross tonnage, trades, flags, crew nationality, exposure to risks, and other factors including the member's **claims record** and the likelihood of large claims in the coming year.
* The member is advised of his **total estimated call** for the next 12 months; this comprises an **advance call** and a **supplementary call**. **Advance calls** are levied on all members at the start of the P&I year, which is February 20[3]. Later in the year, if claims have been heavier than expected, the managers will ask members for a **supplementary call** to "balance the books". Clubs aim to be accurate in their predictions of future claims so as not to burden owners with supplementary calls. **Refunds** are made when income (calls + investments) exceeds outgoings (claims + expenses).
* For notes on **P&I claims**, see G07b.

G02a.3d P&I club correspondents

* P&I clubs retain **correspondents** at numerous ports worldwide. In some countries the correspondent may be a firm of insurance specialists acting for more than one club, or alternatively a shipbroking or insurance company only occasionally handling P&I business. In the USA a correspondent is often a law firm with maritime law practitioners.
* In all cases **correspondents**:
    - are, for legal reasons, **representatives**, and not agents of the club;
    - will attend members' vessels when so requested by the master or agent in order to protect a member's interests;
    - are generally well acquainted with the club's rules and policy, etc.
    - will **report** any occurrence likely to result in a claim on the club to the club's managers, but will generally be able to anticipate the managers' reply and instructions.
    - may, pending instructions, **appoint surveyors** to inspect damage, etc.
    - may be instructed by the club to offer a **Letter of Undertaking** in cases of possible liability (see I01d.4). In most cases, e.g. where there has been pollution following a bunkering accident, or jetty damage caused by a ship, this will avert the need for a **bond** to be posted to avoid arrest.
* Most clubs provide each entered ship with a **list of correspondents** for the use of the master. In the absence of such a list on board, the port agent should be able to furnish the name of the nearest correspondent of most clubs.

G02b INSURANCE-RELATED ORGANISATIONS

G02b.1 Lloyd's Agents

- are established in numerous **ports** world-wide, in some cases as Lloyd's Sub-Agents[4];
- exist basically to **protect the interests of Lloyd's underwriters** and act in their interests;
- **collect and transmit information** of likely interest to the Lloyd's market and insurers worldwide;
- are usually **well-established firms** in the port or place, such as a shipping agency, general merchant, etc.;
- have a very thorough knowledge of local facilities and customs;
- have **duties** including:
    * **keeping Lloyd's informed** of the latest information regarding movements of ships and cargoes, strikes, port congestion, bad weather and all other matters of special interest to underwriters.
    * **appointing surveyors** to survey damage to vessels and cargoes on behalf of underwriters;
    * **issuing certificates of sea damage** (which should be signed by the appointed surveyor as "surveyor to Lloyd's Agent"; and
    * **rendering assistance to masters** in cases of wreck, damage to ship or cargo, and difficulties arising in connection with payment of port disbursements.
* The **Notice of Claim and Tenders Clause** in the Institute Time Clauses - Hulls (1/10/83) requires that in any circumstances that may result in a claim on underwriters relating to ship, cargo, bunkers, etc., the nearest Lloyd's

---

[3] February 20 was the earliest date on which sailing vessels would depart for the Baltic from ports on the north-east coast of England following their winter lay-up, and by tradition was – and still is - the date from which insurance was required.

[4] In 2001 there were over 400 main Lloyd's Agents and over 500 Lloyd's Sub-Agents. About 250 Agents had authority to adjust and settle claims arising under Lloyd's certificates of insurance.

Agent must be informed if the vessel is abroad. There is no requirement to notify Lloyd's Agent in Clause 46 – Notice of Claims – in the International Hull Clauses (01/11/02) (see G04a.2r).

* Lloyd's Certificates of Insurance covering consignments of goods often bear the clause: "In the event of loss or damage which may result in a claim under this insurance immediate notice should be given to the **Lloyd's Agents** at the port or place where the loss or damage is discovered, in order that he may examine the goods and issue a survey report".
* With the increasing scope and complexities of insurance, some Lloyd's Agents have moved into other fields including aviation and non-marine surveys and investigations. Much of the routine work of Lloyd's Agents relates to cargo loss or damage, but there is a wide range of other cargo- and/or hull-related survey activity carried out by Lloyd's Agents, including draft surveys, bunker surveys, ship damage and collision surveys, on-and-off-hire condition surveys, pre-shipments surveys and cargo out-turn surveys.
* For notes on the **role of Lloyd's Agents in hull claims**, see G07a.
* For notes on the **role of Lloyd's Agents in cargo claims**, see G07c.

G02b.2 The Salvage Association

- is an **association of shipping surveyors**, renowned for its **integrity** and **impartiality**, with headquarters in London and offices in several major ports worldwide.
- **investigates shipping casualties** in which underwriters have an interest, and will act likewise for other principals, e.g. shipowners, P&I clubs, average adjusters, solicitors, government departments, merchants and manufacturers. Once instructed, the SA will investigate the circumstances of a casualty or cargo damage, determine the cause and extent of any damage, and provide the owners and underwriters with information and recommendations for the protection and preservation of the interests of all parties.
- conducts **pre-risk surveys** and **condition surveys** (generally known as **warranty surveys**) which are basically pre-voyage inspections (e.g. of a heavy lift ship deck cargo, or of a damaged vessel to be towed to a repair port) to ensure that all proper arrangements have been made to minimise risk of accident on a voyage, and issues **warranty certificates** stating, for example, *"warranted approval of tug, tow, towage and stowage arrangements by S.A. and all recommendations complied with"*. The **SA's warranty** will usually make insurance easier to obtain from underwriters.
- can assist in the **negotiation** of ship repair contracts, checking cargo in congested port areas or cargo stranded ashore, and survey and approval of lay-up sites and arrangements.
- is also heavily involved in **offshore oil industry** work, and in **non-marine** industries such as nuclear power and aviation.
* The services offered by the SA can be summarised under two broad headings: **casualty management** and **risk management**. **Casualty management (cargo)** encompasses: damage surveys, investigation of cause, casualty co-ordination, general average surveys, third party liability surveys, advice on underwater location and recovery, hull or machinery surveys, advice on damage limitation and mitigation of loss, and speed and angle of blow surveys. **Casualty management (hull)** encompasses: damage surveys, speed and angle of blow surveys, advice on repairs and costs, preparation of repair specifications, negotiation of repair accounts, advice on salvage operations and wreck removal, casualty investigation, casualty co-ordination, damage engineering, third party liability surveys, and general average surveys. **Risk management** encompasses: risk assessment, cargo projects, civil engineering projects, shipyard inspections, condition surveys, feasibility studies, and survey and advice for: voyage or towage, vessel lay up or reactivation, mooring arrangements, cargo load out, and stowage and towage.
* The SA is not the only organisation carrying out the types of work described above, and many private ship and cargo firms are also instructed by insurers, average adjusters, etc. See also notes on **insurance surveyors** at I03b.6.
* **SA website**: www.wreckage.org

G02b.3 Average adjusters

- are expert in the **law and practice of general average and marine insurance**. Applicants for Membership of the Association of Average Adjusters have to demonstrate their expertise by rigorous examination.
- **prepare claims** under marine insurance policies which generally involve loss or damage to marine craft, their cargoes or freight. They may also be called upon to **prepare statements of claim against third parties** and to deal with the **division of recoveries from third parties**.
- are usually instructed **to collect general average security**, and also **salvage security**, and to **prepare general average statements** and to **assist in effecting settlements** thereunder. General average is a particular area of expertise.

- **may be appointed by any party** involved in a marine claim. However, irrespective of the identity of that party, the average adjuster is bound to act in an impartial and independent manner.
- will sometimes **instruct surveyors** (and often **Salvage Association** surveyors) to represent general average interests in a marine casualty situation.
* For notes on the **role of the average adjuster following a general average incident**, see G06c.
* **Association of Average Adjusters website**: www.average-adjusters.com

G03 Insurance law and principles

* There is **no legal obligation** in English law to insure ships, goods or freight[5].
* All marine insurance contracts agreed in the UK are governed by the **Marine Insurance Act 1906**. Section 22 of the Act provides that, subject to the provisions of any statute, a contract of marine insurance is inadmissible in evidence unless it is embodied in a marine policy in accordance with the Act.

G03a MARINE INSURANCE ACT 1906

- defines a **contract of marine insurance** as a contract whereby the insurer undertakes to indemnify the assured, in manner and to the extent thereby by agreed, against marine losses, that is to say, the losses incident to marine adventure (section 1).
- provides that a **marine adventure** exists when a ship, cargo or "other moveables" are exposed to **maritime perils**, these being defined as "the perils consequent on, or incidental to, the navigation of the sea, that is to say, perils of the sea, fire, war perils, pirates, rovers, thieves, capture, seizure, restraints, and detainments of princes and peoples, jettisons, barratry, and any other perils, either of the like kind or which may be designated by the policy" (section 3).
- provides that the contract is concluded when the assured's proposal is accepted by the underwriters, whether or not the contract document (the policy) is issued at that time (section 21).
- recognises two policy types: time and voyage (section 25).
- provides for three major **principles of insurance**, i.e. **indemnity**, **insurable interest** and **utmost good faith**.
- provides for a **doctrine of proximate cause**.

G03b PRINCIPLES OF INSURANCE

G03b.1 Indemnity

* Section 1 of the Marine Insurance Act 1906 defines a **contract of marine insurance** as: "a contract whereby the insurer undertakes to indemnify the assured, in the manner and to the extent thereby agreed, against marine losses, i.e. the losses incident to a marine adventure". Thus the purpose of a marine insurance contract is **indemnity**.
* The **principle of indemnity** is that the insurer will indemnify the assured against a loss he has suffered, and will restore him (financially) to the position he was in immediately before the loss occurred. In insurance contracts where indemnity is not the purpose, such as life assurance and accident insurance contracts, the purpose is to pay a known sum of money (called "the benefit") on the happening of an event, with the possibility that the assured will, as a result, be better off than he was before the loss. In policies where indemnity is the purpose, such as motor and marine insurance, the assured should not be in a better position as a result of the loss. (If this were not the case, insurance fraud might be encouraged.)
* In **non-marine** (e.g. motor) insurance, an indemnity is for the value of the subject matter insured at the time of its loss, i.e. the insurer agrees to place the assured in the same financial position as he occupied immediately prior to his loss. Because of the difficulty of putting a value on ships at sea or on cargoes in transit (especially since cargoes normally increase in value as they near their eventual markets), Marine Insurance Act 1906 requires a **marine insurer** to indemnify the assured "in manner and to the extent thereby agreed". Ships and cargoes therefore have a value placed on them at the commencement of the risk (i.e. at the time of effecting the policy), and insurers use these values to determine the **measure of indemnity** they will give the assured. In **marine insurance**, therefore, the value of the subject-matter insured may be different from its actual value at the time of loss, depending on how the market has gone since the policy was effected. But whether or not the assured has gained or lost by a fluctuation in value will not affect what the insurer pays on the claim.

---

[5] Some countries, e.g. Australia, are considering making insurance compulsory for shipping in their waters.

* **Where there is a total loss** the measure of indemnity is 100% of the insured value. Where 50% of subject matter insured is destroyed, the measure of indemnity is 50% of the insured value, etc.
* **Contribution** is a sub-principle of indemnity whereby the assured cannot claim more than once on the same risk. Thus if the assured has policies covering the same risk with two insurers (**double insurance**), each makes a pro-rata contribution to any settlement. Double insurance is not the same as spreading the risk between several insurers, which is normally done.
* **Subrogation** is another sub-principle of indemnity whereby the assured cannot recoup his loss from another party after the insurer has settled his claim. E.g. where the insurer has paid a goods owner's claim, the goods owner cannot afterwards claim from the carrier. Instead the insurer who paid the claim **subrogates**, or takes over, the assured's rights in respect of any claim against a third party. An insurer paying a claim for goods lost or damaged on board may then claim against the carrier in his own name and can retain any sum recovered up to the amount claimed, any excess being repaid to the assured.

G03b.2 Insurable interest

* Before anyone may legally enter into a marine insurance contract he must have, or expect to acquire, an **insurable interest** in the property at risk, i.e. he must stand to benefit by the safety or due arrival of insurable property, or may be prejudiced by its loss, or damage thereto, or by the detention thereof, or may incur liability in respect thereof (section 5).
* **Essential features of insurable interest** include:
  * the subject matter insured must be a physical object exposed to peril; and
  * any assured must have some legal relationship to the subject matter insured, and must stand to benefit by its preservation or lose by its loss or damage.
* Where the assured in a marine insurance contract has no insurable interest or no expectation of acquiring one, the policy is deemed to be a "**gaming or wagering contract**". Every such contract is illegal and void (section 4). If a party with no insurable interest took out insurance on a ship or cargo, they could in effect be betting on the non-arrival of that vessel or cargo, which would probably lead to an increase in maritime fraud and piracy.
* The insurable interest of an assured is limited to the amount which he **actually stands to lose**.
* The simplest form of insurable interest is **ownership** of the subject matter insured. FOB and CIF (etc.) contracts of sale define the time of passing of risk (and therefore of insurable interest) from seller to buyer.
* A **carrier** has an insurable interest in goods because of his liability to the goods owner. A **shipper** has an insurable interest in respect of any advance freight paid but not earned (e.g. where the vessel does not complete the voyage) (section 12). The **insurer** of a subject-matter insured has an insurable interest in the risk he has written, allowing him to re-insure and spread the risk.
* The **master** or any member of the **crew** of a ship has an insurable interest in respect of his wages (section 11).

G03b.3 Utmost good faith

* A contract of marine insurance is a contract based upon the **utmost good faith**[6] and, if the utmost good faith is not observed by either party, the contract may be avoided by the other party (section 17).
* Section 18 requires the **assured to disclose** to the insurer, before the contract is concluded, every **material circumstance** which is known to the assured. Every circumstance which would influence the insurer's judgement in fixing the premium or determining whether or not he would accept the risk, would be "material". For example, it would be dishonest for a shipowner *not* to disclose that his 20-year old vessel had just failed her 5th special survey and had been rejected by a classification society. If the assured fails to make such disclosure, the insurer may "avoid the contract".
* The assured is deemed to know every circumstance which, in the ordinary course of his business, ought to be known by him (e.g. that a log carrier is more likely than most bulk carriers to get damaged by cargo). Some circumstances need not be disclosed, e.g. those that would diminish the risk.

G03b.4 Doctrine of proximate cause

* Subject to the provisions of the Act, and unless the policy otherwise provides, the insurer is liable for any loss **proximately caused** by a peril insured against, but, subject as aforesaid, he is not liable for any loss which is not proximately caused by a peril insured against (section 55(1)).

---

[6] Under the **principle of utmost good faith**, each party to an insurance policy (of any kind) has the duty of revealing to the other party all material facts, whether the other party requests the information or not. The principle is sometimes referred to by its Latin name "*uberrima fides*".

* Where there is a chain of events leading to a loss, the **proximate cause** is the most dominant and effective cause, not the nearest cause in time. For example, if a ship is scuttled, the proximate cause is the act of scuttling, although the nearest cause in time is seawater entering the ship. An assured who scuttled his ship might claim that a "peril of the seas" was the cause of his loss, but the insurer would not be liable since scuttling is wilful misconduct of the assured. See also G03d.

G03c MARINE INSURANCE ACT PROVISIONS RELATING TO POLICY

* Where the contract is to insure the subject-matter "at and from" (e.g. "goods at and from Liverpool"), or from one place to another or others (e.g. "from Liverpool to Montreal"), the policy is called a **voyage policy**, and where the contract is to insure the subject-matter for a definite period of time (e.g. 12 months) the policy is called a **time policy** (section 25). A contract for both voyage and time may be included in the same policy.

* **Hull and machinery (H&M) policies** are usually time policies, the maximum period of insurance usually being 12 months (although the Marine Insurance Act 1906 does not restrict the period). Cover usually attaches and expires at noon or midnight GMT.

* **Consignments of goods** are usually insured on voyage policies "at and from" one place to another or simply "from" a place to another. (The former type gives cover whilst awaiting shipment.) Most goods shipped are usually insured on a warehouse-to-warehouse basis rather than for the sea voyage only. Some cargoes (e.g. FOB shipments) may be covered only from the time of loading. Time policies are not normally used for goods insurance.

* The usual **policy form** used in the London marine insurance market is the **MAR Form** (see G04a.1).

* Where a ship is the subject matter insured of a voyage policy, it is unnecessary for the vessel to actually be at the place named in the policy at the time that the insurance contract is made, but there is an implied condition in the contract that the adventure will commence within a reasonable time (section 42). If it does not, the insurer can avoid the contract.

* The **risk does not attach** if:
  • the ship sails from a different place from that named in the policy (section 43); or
  • the ship proceeds to a destination other than that named in the policy (section 44).

* A policy may be either **valued** or **unvalued** (section 27). A **valued policy** is a policy which specifies the agreed value of the subject matter insured (which is the usual practice). The **insured value** is the amount stated in the policy as the calculated value of the subject matter insured, whereas the **sum insured** is the portion of the insured value actually covered by the insurance. Where the property is insured for its full value, the agreed value and the insured value will be the same. This is usually the case with cargo, so the policy might read "£20,000 on merchandise so valued".

* It is not necessary to insure property for its full value, and some assureds, in return for a lower premium, prefer to carry part of the risk themselves (thus becoming self-insurers for part of the insured value). A H&M policy might state the insured value as, for example, "£4,000,000 on Hull & Machinery valued at £5,000,000".

* An **unvalued policy** does not specify the value of the subject matter insured (section 28). Subject to a limit of the sum assured, it leaves the insurable value to be subsequently ascertained if and when a claim arises.

* Insurance policies contain **warranties** (see G03e). Insurers bind the assured to the warranties in the policy unless **amended terms** (see G03e.4) are agreed.

G03d MARINE INSURANCE ACT PROVISIONS RELATING TO INSURER'S LIABILITY

* Subject to the provisions of the Marine Insurance Act 1906, and unless the policy otherwise provides, the insurer is liable for any loss **proximately caused by a peril insured against**, but, subject to the same conditions, he is not liable for any loss not proximately caused by a peril insured against (section 55(1)).

* The insurer is not liable for any loss attributable to the **wilful misconduct of an assured**, but unless the policy otherwise provides, he is liable for any loss proximately caused by a peril insured against, even though the loss would not have occurred without the misconduct or negligence of master or crew (section 55(2)(a)). Thus, if a ship runs aground through the negligence of its master or crew, the underwriter will be liable.

* Unless the policy otherwise provides, an insurer of a ship or goods is not liable for any loss proximately caused by **delay**, although the delay may be caused by a peril insured against (section 55(2)(b)).

* Unless the policy otherwise provides, an insurer is not liable for **ordinary wear and tear**, **ordinary leakage and breakage**, **inherent vice or nature** of the subject matter insured, or for any loss proximately caused by **rats** or **vermin**, or for any **injury to machinery not proximately caused by marine perils** (section 55(2)(c)).

G03e MARINE INSURANCE ACT PROVISIONS RELATING TO WARRANTIES

* **Section 33 of the Marine Insurance Act 1906** defines a "**warranty**" as "a promissory warranty, that is to say, a warranty by which the **assured undertakes** that some particular thing shall or shall not be done, or that some condition shall be fulfilled, or whereby he affirms or negatives the existence of a particular state of facts". A warranty may be express or implied. A warranty, as above defined, is a condition which must be exactly complied with, whether it be material to the risk or not. If it be not so complied with, then, subject to any express provision in the policy, the insurer is discharged from liability as from the date of the breach of warranty, but without prejudice to any liability incurred by him before that date.
* An **express warranty** must be written into the policy or contained in some document (e.g. Institute Warranties) incorporated by reference into the policy (section 35).
* **Implied warranties** are not written in the policy but are implied by law to exist in the contract. They must be strictly complied with in the same way as express warranties. There are two major implied warranties in marine insurance policies, covering **seaworthiness** (see G03e.1 and G03e.2) and **legality** (see G03e.3).
* An express warranty does not override an implied warranty unless the two conflict.
* There may be many express warranties in a marine insurance policy, a common example in a hull and machinery policy being a warranty that the vessel is classed with a particular society, and that her class will be maintained. The wording is likely to be, for example: "Warranted LR classed and class maintained."

G03e.1 Warranty of seaworthiness in voyage policies

* In a voyage policy there is an implied warranty that at the commencement of the voyage the ship will be seaworthy for the purpose of the particular adventure (i.e. voyage) insured (section 39(1)).
* A ship is deemed to be **seaworthy** when "**reasonably fit in all respects to encounter the ordinary perils of the seas of the adventure insured**" (section 39(4)). ("Seaworthy" in insurance law thus means approximately the same as in carriage of goods law - see F07a.4 and F07c.2b).
* Where the policy attaches in port, there is also an implied warranty that the ship insured will, at the commencement of the risk, be **reasonably fit to encounter the ordinary perils of the port** (section 39(2)).
* Where the policy relates to a voyage performed in separate stages, there is an implied warranty that at the **commencement of each stage**, the ship will be **seaworthy for the purposes of that stage** (section 39(3)).
* In a policy on goods or other moveables, there is no implied warranty that the goods, etc. are seaworthy (section 40(1)).
* In a voyage policy on goods or other moveables, there is an implied warranty that at the commencement of the voyage, **the ship will be seaworthy and reasonably fit to carry the goods**, etc. to the destination stated in the policy (section 40(2)).

G03e.2 Warranty of seaworthiness in time policies

* In a time policy there is no implied warranty that the ship will be seaworthy at any stage of the adventure, but where, with the assured's privity (i.e. his knowledge and consent), the ship is sent to sea in an unseaworthy state, the **insurer is not liable for any loss attributable to unseaworthiness** (section 39(5)). This means that cover may be lost if the ship is sent to sea in an unseaworthy condition with the knowledge of the owners' senior management. "Knowledge" would include both express, clear knowledge (e.g. after defects have been reported in writing by a master or a surveyor) and deliberate "turning of a blind eye". Cover would only be lost, however, where the known unseaworthiness had caused the loss.

G03e.3 Warranty of legality in marine insurance policies

* There is an implied warranty that the **adventure insured is a lawful one** and that, so far as the assured can control it, the adventure will be carried out in a **lawful manner** (section 41). If the adventure is illegal at the time the insurance is effected, the policy will be void. Thus, drug-running or gun-running trips, or voyages to countries or ports subject to a United Nations embargo, would be deemed unlawful.

G03e.4 Breach of warranty in marine insurance policies

* A "**warranty**", as defined in section 33(1), is a condition which **must be exactly complied with**, whether it is material to the risk or not. If it is not so complied with, then, subject to any express provision in the policy, the insurer is discharged from liability as from the date of the breach of warranty, but without prejudice to any liability incurred by him before that date (section 33(3)). For example, if an owner breaches a warranty that his vessel will trade "worldwide within Institute Warranty Limits" (see G04a.4), the fact that she does not suffer any loss or damage in a prohibited area outside Institute Warranty Limits (IWLs) does not matter: there is a **breach of warranty**.
* Under section 34(1) **non-compliance with a warranty will be excused**:
  * when circumstances leading the insurer to insist on the insertion of the warranty change or cease to exist (e.g. where a war zone ceases to operate); or
  * when continued compliance with a warranty would be illegal under a new law.
* **Where a warranty is broken**, the assured cannot avail himself of the defence that the breach has been remedied, and the warranty complied with, before loss (section 34(2)). Thus, if a ship whose policy states "worldwide trading within IWLs" ventures outside IWLs, then re-enters IWLs and goes aground, the insurer is not liable for any damage claim, etc.
* Any breach of warranty may be **waived** by the insurer (section 34(3)).
* A shipowner intending to breach any warranty should **notify his insurer** of his intention, agree to any **amended conditions** imposed and pay any **additional premium** required. This is commonly done, for example, to allow vessels to trade beyond Institute Warranty Limits ("IWLs"), e.g. on a voyage to a port in one of the ice-prone areas of the world.

G03f MARINE INSURANCE ACT PROVISIONS RELATING TO CONDITIONS

G03f.1 Condition regarding deviation in marine insurance policies

* There is an **implied condition** in every marine insurance policy in respect of **deviation** in a voyage.
* When a ship, **without lawful excuse, deviates** from the voyage contemplated by the policy (i.e. the stated or customary voyage), the insurer is discharged from liability from the time (and not the date) of the deviation, and it is immaterial that the ship may have regained the proper route before any loss occurs: the insurer has no further liability from the moment of the deviation (section 46(1)).
* **There is a deviation** from the voyage contemplated by the policy when -
  * the **course** of the voyage is **specifically stated** by the policy and is **departed from** (section 46(2)(a)); or
  * the **course** of the voyage is **not specifically stated** by the policy, but the **usual and customary route is departed from** (section 46(2)(b)).
* The effect of deviating is that **any loss arising during or after the deviation will be borne by the shipowner**. Losses up to the time of the deviation will be borne by insurer, if covered by the policy.
* Where several ports of discharge are specified by the policy, the ship may proceed to all or any of them, but in the absence of any usage or sufficient cause to the contrary, she must proceed to them in the order stated on the policy; otherwise, there is a **deviation** (section 47(1)).
* Where the policy is to unnamed "ports of discharge" within a given area, the ship must, in the absence of any usage or sufficient cause to the contrary, call in their geographical order; if not there is a **deviation** (section 47)(2)).
* **Deviation is excused** under section 49(1) -
  * where authorised by any special term in the policy;
  * where caused by circumstances beyond the control of the master or employer (e.g. force majeure);
  * where reasonably necessary so as to comply with an express or implied warranty;
  * where reasonably necessary for the safety of the ship or subject matter insured;
  * for the purpose of saving human life or aiding a ship in distress where human life may be in danger;
  * where reasonably necessary for the purpose of obtaining medical or surgical aid for any person onboard; or
  * where caused by barratry of the master or crew, if barratry is an insured peril.
* When the **cause excusing the deviation ceases to operate**, the ship must resume her course and prosecute the voyage with reasonable despatch (section 49(2)).

G03f.2 Condition regarding delay in marine insurance policies

* **In a voyage policy** the adventure insured must be prosecuted throughout its course with "**reasonable dispatch**" and if it is not, the insurer is discharged from liability from the time when the delay became unreasonable (section 48). (A delay of 10 days waiting for cargo at an intermediate port has been held to be unreasonable.)
* **Delay in prosecuting the voyage is excused** under section 49(1) in the same circumstances as for deviation (see G03f.1). The voyage must be resumed with reasonable despatch once the delay has ceased to operate (section 49(2)).

G03f.3 Condition regarding change of voyage in marine insurance policies

* There is an implied condition that where, after commencement of the risk, the ship's **departure or destination port (or both) are voluntarily changed** from that stated in the policy, there is a "**change of voyage**" and unless the policy otherwise provides, the **insurer is discharged** from liability from the time of the change (section 45(1)). It is immaterial that the ship may not have left the course of the voyage contemplated by the policy when the loss occurs.

G04 Marine insurance policies

G04a HULL AND MACHINERY POLICIES

* In the **London marine insurance market**, hull and machinery (H&M) cover is usually obtained from:
    * **underwriters at Lloyd's**; and/or
    * **underwriters in the Companies market**. (See notes on the IUA at G02a.2.)
* H&M cover is generally arranged for owners or managers by **brokers** who act as agents of assureds. Broking practice and procedure is similar in both Lloyd's and Companies markets. Only Lloyd's Brokers may approach underwriters at Lloyd's to obtain insurance; no non-broker may approach an underwriter personally.
* On instructions from the assured, the broker prepares a **slip** for presentation of the subject matter details to underwriters. (The slip is equivalent to a motor insurance proposal form.) The broker supplements the basic facts on the slip with all material information about the risk as supplied by assured (under the principle of **utmost good faith** – see G03b.3).
* The broker contracts with one or more **underwriters** to pay an agreed premium for a policy covering loss or damage, etc. Unless the insured value of the vessel is small, the broker takes the slip first to an influential **lead underwriter**, then to a succession of others, until the risk is 100% covered. Some underwriters may not be interested in covering any part of the risk, while those who are interested will usually "write a line" only on a small percentage of the insured value of the ship. Each underwriter indicates acceptance of his share of the risk by writing his signature or initials against the line on the slip bearing the percentage he accepts on behalf of his syndicate or company.
* When the slip is complete, i.e. the risk is 100% covered, the broker prepares details of the cover on a **cover note** and sends this to the assured for approval.
* If the assured approves of the terms, a formal **policy** is drawn up. Some time will elapse before the policy can be signed and the contract legally made. In English contract law, presentation of the slip by the broker constitutes an offer, and the writing of each "line" constitutes acceptance. The contract is concluded when the underwriter writes his initials or signature on the slip.
* The Marine Insurance Act 1906 (see G03a) requires the contract to be embodied in a policy, so the contract is not legally enforceable until the policy is drawn up. However, under the code of ethics of the London market, once an underwriter has initialled or signed a slip he is honour-bound to pay any claim on it.

G04a.1 The MAR form

* The New Marine Policy Form, or "**MAR Form**" -
    - was first introduced by Lloyd's on 1 January 1982 to replace the antiquated and archaically worded **SG Form**;
    - is used for **ship**, **goods** or **freight** policies, whether time or voyage, effected in the London market;
    - contains a **schedule** on the outer cover with blank spaces for insertion of the relevant details, which might be as follows:

Policy number	XYZ123
Date	21.12.02
Name of assured	Hard Lines Ltd
Vessel	"Hard Luck"
Voyage or period of insurance	12 months @ 1st January 2003
Subject-matter insured	Hull & machinery etc
Agreed value (if any)	$5,000,000 $3,000,000
Amount insured hereunder	100% of value as above
Premium	4.50%
Clauses, endorsements, special conditions and warranties	Institute Time Clauses Hulls (1/10/83) Institute Warranties Institute War Clauses Institute Strike Clauses Survey and claims payable clause

* The policy form has inner sections for attaching the applicable **clauses** and **warranties**. These are printed on individual sheets for different classes of cover, e.g. for a hull and machinery policy:
  • Institute Time Clauses Hulls (1/10/83), or Institute Voyage Clauses (1/10/83);
  • Institute Strike Clauses (1/11/95);
  • Institute War and Strikes Clauses (Hulls - Time) (1/11/95) or (Hulls - Voyage) (1/11/95); and
  • Institute Warranties (1/7/76).
* A statement on the form provides that "the attached Clauses and Endorsements form part of the Policy".
* The clauses attached to the policy do not have to be Institute Clauses. American Hull Clauses are popular with many owners. If Institute Clauses are used, they do not have to be the latest edition; the Institute Time Clauses – Hulls (1/10/83) are more popular than the 1995 clauses of the same name.

G04a.2 International Hull Clauses (01/11/02)

- are a set of 53 numbered and named standard insurance clauses printed on sheets which may be attached to a Lloyd's or Companies H&M policy to form the terms and conditions of the contract.
- are in **three parts**, as follows: **Part 1**: Principal insuring conditions (clauses 1 to 33) ; **Part 2**: Additional clauses (01/11/02) (clauses 34 to 44); **Part 3**: Claims provisions (01/11/02) (clauses 45 to 53). Part 1, Clauses 34 to 39 of Part 2, and Part 3 apply to any insurance. Clauses 40 to 44 of Part 2 will only apply where the underwriters have expressly so agreed in writing.
- are **numbered and titled** as follows: **1**: General; **2**: Perils; **3**: Leased equipment; **4**: Parts Taken Off; **5**: Pollution Hazard; **6**: 3/4ths Collision Liability; **7**: Sistership; **8**: General Average and Salvage; **9**: Duty of the Assured (Sue and Labour); **10**: Navigation Provisions; **11**: Breach of Navigation Provisions; **12**: Continuation; **13**: Classification and ISM; **14**: Management; **15**: Deductible(s); **16**: New for old; **17**: Bottom Treatment; **18**: Wages and Maintenance; **19**: Agency Commission; **20**: Unrepaired Damage; **21**: Constructive Total Loss; **22**: Freight Waiver; **23**: Assignment; **24**: Disbursements Warranty; **25**: Cancelling Returns; **26**: Separate Insurances; **27**: Several Liability; **28**: Affiliated Companies; **29**: War Exclusion; **30**: Strikes Exclusion; **31**: Malicious Acts Exclusion; **32**: Radioactive Contamination Exclusion; **33**: Chemical, Biological, Bio-Chemical, Electromagnetic Weapons and Cyber Attack Exclusion; **34**: Navigating Limits; **35**: Bering Sea Transit; **36**: Recommissioning Condition; **37**: Helicopter Engagement; **38**: Premium Payment; **39**: Contracts (Rights of Third Parties) Act 1999; **40**: 4/4ths Collision Liability; **41**: Fixed and Floating Objects; **42**: Returns for Lay-Up; **43**: General Average Absorption; **44**: Additional Perils; **45**: Leading Underwriter(s); **46**: Notice of Claims; **47**: Tender Provisions; **48**: Duties of the Assured; **49**: Duties of Underwriters in Relation to Claims; **50**: Provision of Security; **51**: Payment of Claims; **52**: Recoveries; **53**: Dispute Resolution.
- have been available for use since 1 November 2002. (Despite this, many shipowners may continue to opt for the tried and tested International Time Clauses – Hulls (1/10/83).)
- are designed to replace the Institute Time Clauses – Hulls (01/11/95), which themselves were intended to replace the Institute Time Clauses – Hulls (1/10/83). (The 1995 clauses have largely been shunned by shipowners and have been blamed for losing the London market some business.)
* Alternatives to the Institute Time Clauses – Hulls and the International Hull Clauses include the American Hull Clauses and the Norwegian Hull Clauses. Without seeing the applicable H&M policy, there is no way of knowing which clauses are attached to a ship's insurance policy.

* The following notes are restricted to those International Hull Clauses likely to be of chief interest to masters and deck officers.

G04a.2a Clause 2 - Perils

- is also known as the "**Inchmaree Clause**" following a case involving a ship of that name where the insurers were held not liable for a loss that had not been caused by a peril named in the policy.
- provides that the **insurance covers loss or damage caused by**:
  - perils of the seas, rivers, lakes or other navigable waters;
  - fire, explosion;
  - violent theft by persons from outside the vessel;
  - jettison;
  - piracy;
  - contact with land conveyance, dock or harbour equipment or installation;
  - earthquake, volcanic eruption or lightning;
  - accidents in loading, discharging or shifting cargo or fuel;
  - contact with satellites, aircraft, helicopters or similar objects, or objects falling therefrom.
- also **covers loss or damage caused by**:
  - bursting of boilers or breakage of shafts (but not the cost of repairing the burst boiler or broken shaft itself);
  - latent defects in the machinery or hull;
  - negligence of master, officers, crew or pilots;
  - negligence of repairers or charterers, provided they are not an Assured under the Policy;
  - barratry of master, officers or crew (see H01d.2); and
  - **provided** that in these last 5 cases the loss or damage did not result from want of due diligence by the Assured, Owners or Managers.
- * Should masters, officers, crew or pilots hold shares in the vessel, they will not be considered as Owners.
- * Cover in the second group of perils is conditional upon **due diligence** being exercised, whereas there is no such condition for the first group.
- * Onshore managers are presumed to have a close knowledge of the condition of their companies' ships and their machinery. They cannot be both "duly diligent" and ignorant such matters at the same time.
- * The **extension of the "due diligence" requirements to onshore managers** is aimed at reducing claims on underwriters which have arisen due to owners cutting costs and allowing machinery, etc. to deteriorate to such an extent that it causes damage which is covered by the policy (i.e. making insurers pay for maintenance).
- * Cover in this clause is as per ITC 1/10/83 but with the addition of satellites.

G04a.2b Clause 6 - 3/4ths Collision Liability

- provides that underwriters will pay for **three quarters** of any:
  - **loss** of or **damage** to another vessel or property on it;
  - **delay** to or **loss of use** of another vessel or property on it;
  - **general average** of another vessel or property on it;
  - **salvage** or **salvage under contract** of another vessel or property on it –
  - where the payment by the Assured is a result of a **collision** with the other vessel.
- can be extended to 4/4ths cover (if Clause 40 is expressly agreed to in writing by the underwriters).
- was formerly called, and is still often referred to as, the **Running Down Clause** (or **RDC**).
- was originally intended by underwriters to make shipowners more careful with the navigation of their vessels, since they would be carrying a quarter of the risk themselves.
- * The one fourth of liability not covered by the underwriters under the policy is normally insured under the shipowner's **P&I club policy** (see G04b.1).

G04a.2c Clause 7 - Sister Ship

- allows vessels owned wholly or partly by the **same owners**, or under the **same management**, to be treated in the event of collision or salvage as if they were owned by **different companies**.
- * In such cases liability is to be referred to a mutually-agreed sole arbitrator.

G04a.2d Clause 8 - General Average and Salvage

- provides that –
  - the insurance covers the **vessel's proportion of salvage**, **salvage charges** and/or **general average**, reduced in respect of any under-insurance;
  - **adjustment** is to be according to the law and practice of the place where the adventure ends, as if the contract of affreightment (e.g. charter party or bill of lading contract) contained no special terms on the subject, but where the contract agrees, adjustment will be according to the York-Antwerp Rules.

G04a.2e Clause 9 - Duty of Assured (Sue and Labour)

- provides that the assured has a duty to take all reasonable steps to **avert or minimise any loss** for which a claim would be payable under the policy. In return, most costs incurred in taking such steps are recoverable from the underwriters.
- was formerly known (in ITC 1/10/83 and older policies) as the **Sue and Labour Clause**.
- * **Sue and labour charges** are not to be confused with general average expenditure (see G06b). They are incurred for the benefit of only a **single interest** (e.g. the vessel, or the cargo), whereas general average expenditure is incurred for the common benefit (e.g. of the ship, cargo and freight, if any at risk).
- * **Examples** of sue and labour charges might include costs incurred by a shipowner in recovering a lost anchor and cable, and costs incurred by a cargo owner of having a refrigerated cargo stored ashore while a ship's refrigerating machinery is under repair.

G04a.2f Clause 10 – Navigation Provisions

- applies unless and to the extent otherwise agreed by the underwriters in accordance with Clause 11.
- provides that –
  - the vessel must not sail nor be employed in breach of any provisions of the insurance as to **cargo, trade** or **locality**, including, but not limited to, **Clause 34 – Navigating Limits** (see G04a.2m);
  - the vessel may sail or navigate with or without pilots, go on trial trips and assist and tow vessels or craft in distress, but **must not be towed**, except as is customary (including customary towage in connection with loading or discharging) or to the **first safe port or place** when in need of assistance, or **undertake towage** or **salvage services under a contract previously arranged** by the Assured and/or Owners and/or Managers and/or Charterers;
  - the Assured must not enter into any **contract** with pilots or for customary towage which limits or exempts the **liability** of the pilots and/or tugs and/or towboats and/or their owners except where the Assured or their agents accept or are **compelled** to accept such contracts in accordance with established local law or practice;
  - the vessel must not be employed in trading operations which entail **cargo loading or discharging at sea** from or into another vessel (not being a harbour or inshore craft).

G04a.2g Clause 11 – Breach of Navigation Provisions

- provides that in the event of any breach of Clause 10's provisions, the underwriters will not be liable for any loss, damage, liability or expense during the period of the breach unless **notice** is given to them immediately after receipt (by the assured) of advices of the breach and any **amended terms of cover** and any **additional premium** required are agreed.

G04a.2h Clause 12 - Continuation

- provides that should the vessel be, when the insurance expires, **at sea**, or **in distress or missing**, or at a **port of refuge** or port of call she will, provided due **notice** has been given to underwriters, be **held covered** at a pro-rata monthly premium until arrival at the **next port** in good safety. (This avoids the problem of expiry of a time policy while the vessel is still at sea).

G04a.2i Clause 13 – Classification and ISM

- **will prevail** notwithstanding any other inconsistent written, typed or printed provision in the insurance.
- provides that at the inception of and throughout the period of the insurance:
  - the **vessel must be classed** with a **classification society agreed by the underwriters**;

- there must be **no change**, **suspension**, **discontinuance**, **withdrawal or expiry** of the vessel's **class** with the classification society;
- any **recommendations**, **requirements** or **restrictions** imposed by the classification society which relate to the vessel's seaworthiness or to her maintenance in a seaworthy condition (e.g. conditions of class) must be complied with by the dates required by the society;
- the **owners** or the party assuming responsibility for operation of the vessel from the owners must hold a valid **Document of Compliance** in respect of the vessel as required by SOLAS chapter IX;
- the **vessel** must have in force a valid **Safety Management Certificate** as required by SOLAS chapter IX.

* Institute Time Clauses - Hulls (1/10/83) include no standard class requirement, although in policies incorporating those clauses a class requirement is often added as a warranty by a stand-alone clause. In the International Hull Clauses (01/11/02) the class requirement is not a warranty but a condition of the insurance (i.e. the wording states "…the vessel shall be classed….").

G04a.2j Clause 14 – Management

- **will prevail** notwithstanding any other inconsistent written, typed or printed provision in the insurance.
- provides that unless the underwriters agree to the contrary in writing, the insurance will **terminate automatically** at the time of:
  - any **change**, voluntary or otherwise, in the **ownership or flag** of the vessel;
  - transfer of the vessel to **new management**;
  - **charter** of the vessel on a **bareboat** basis;
  - **requisition** of the vessel for title or use (e.g. by the flag State in times of hostilities);
  - **provided** that, if the vessel has cargo on board and has already sailed from her loading port or is at sea in ballast, the automatic termination will, if required, be **deferred** whilst the vessel continues her planned voyage, until arrival at final port of discharge, or port of destination if in ballast. However, in the event of requisition for title or use without the prior execution of a written agreement by the assured, the automatic termination will occur **fifteen days** after the requisition whether the vessel is at sea or in port.
- provides that unless the underwriters agree to the contrary in writing, the insurance will terminate automatically at the time of the vessel sailing (with or without cargo) with an intention of being **broken up**, or being **sold for breaking up**.
- provides that it is the **duty** of the assured, owners and managers at the inception of and throughout the period of the insurance to:
  - **comply with all statutory requirements of the vessel's flag State** relating to construction, adaptation, condition, fitment, equipment, operation and manning of the vessel; and
  - **comply with all requirements of the vessel's classification society** regarding the **reporting** to the society of **accidents** to and **defects** in the vessel.

  In the event of any breach of any of these duties, the underwriters will not be liable for any loss, damage, liability or expense attributable to such breach.

G04a.2k Clause 15 – Deductible(s)

- provides that no claims arising from an insured peril are payable unless the aggregate of all such claims exceeds an agreed minimum, i.e. the **deductible**.
* A **deductible** is a value, or "platform", which must be reached before a claim will be met by the insurer, and a compulsory "excess" which is deducted from every claim passing this platform. In return for agreeing to pay the first part of the claim, his **premium is reduced**.
* The deductible will not be applied to a claim for total or constructive total loss.

G04a.2l Clauses 29, 30, 31, 32 and 33 - Exclusions

- define **risks expressly excluded** from the cover, i.e.:
  - war;
  - strikes;
  - malicious acts;
  - radioactive contamination; and
  - chemical, biological, bio-chemical, electromagnetic weapons and cyber attack.
* **Clause 29 - War Exclusion** excludes loss, damage, liability or expense caused by war, civil war, revolution, etc., capture, seizure, arrest, restraint or detainment (but **not barratry and piracy**), as well as derelict mines, torpedoes, bombs, etc. Underwriters will not pay claims for damage incurred in these circumstances. War risks cover can,

however, be obtained by taking out additional **War Risks cover**, in which case the Institute War Risks Clauses would be attached to the policy. Alternatively, cover can be obtained through the owners' P&I club.

* **Clause 30 - Strikes Exclusion** excludes loss, damage, liability or expense caused by strikers, locked-out workmen, or persons taking part in labour disturbances, riots or civil commotions, or from terrorists and persons acting from a political motive. (Shipowners may obtain separate strikes cover if they wish.)
* **Clause 31 - Malicious Acts Exclusion** excludes loss, damage, liability or expense caused by the detonation of an explosive or any weapon of war.
* **Clause 32 - Radioactive Contamination Exclusion** excludes loss, damage, liability or expense caused by ionising radiations from or radioactive contamination from nuclear fuel, nuclear waste, nuclear weapons, etc.
* **Clause 33 – Chemical, Biological, Bio-Chemical, Electromagnetic Weapons and Cyber Attack Exclusion** excludes loss, damage, liability or expense caused by any chemical, biological, bio-chemical or electromagnetic weapon, or the use or operation, as a means of inflicting harm, of any computer, computer system, software, etc.

G04a.2m Clause 34 – Navigating Limits

- imposes **trading limitations**, thereby reducing the risk to the underwriters.
- prohibits the vessel from entering certain sea **areas** where ice is a hazard, or from carrying **Indian coal** in eastern waters in the summer months (when it may be prone to spontaneous combustion).
* The limitations set out in Clause 34 have been used in the London market for many years as the "**Institute Warranty Limits**", and have been applied to insurances as warranties with the words "Warranted no Baltic Sea ……" etc. As set out in the International Hull Clauses (01/11/02) the limitations are not warranties but **conditions**, each commencing with the words "The vessel shall not ….(enter the Baltic Sea, etc.)".
* For a full list of the limitations with the wording **as warranties**, see G04a.4.
* Whereas in policies incorporating the prohibitions as Institute Warranties, the prohibitions are **warranties**,

G04a.2n Clause 35 – Bering Sea Transit

- provides that the vessel may, when on through voyages to or from the Far East, navigate the **Bering Sea** provided that:
  * the vessel has on board the appropriate hydrographic **charts** corrected up to date;
  * **entry** is made through the Unimak Pass and **exit** west of Buldir Island or vice-versa;
  * the vessel is equipped and properly fitted with marine **radar**, a **satellite navigator** or Loran, **sonic depth sounding apparatus, radio direction finder** and **gyro compass**, all fully **operational** and manned by **qualified personnel**.
* **Alternatively**, the vessel may enter or leave through the Amchitka, Amukta or Attu Passes, but only when equipped and properly fitted with marine radar, Loran, a satellite navigator, sonic depth sounding apparatus, radio direction finder, gyro compass and a weather facsimile recorder, all fully operational and manned by qualified personnel.

G04a.2o Clause 37 – Helicopter Engagement

- provides that the practice of engaging **helicopters** for the transportation of **personnel, supplies and equipment** to and/or from the vessel will not prejudice the insurance, provided that the operations are carried out in accordance with the recommendations and procedures in the ICS "**Guide to Helicopter/Ship Operations**".

G04a.2p Clause 43 – General Average Absorption

- can be included in the insurance, but only with the express written agreement of the underwriters.
- provides that if the underwriters have expressly agreed in writing, and subject to the provisions of Clause 8 (General Average and Salvage) (see G04a.2d), the assured will have the option of claiming the total General Average in full (excluding only commission and interest) from the underwriters without recourse to any other contributing interests (such as cargo consignees), up to the amount expressly agreed by the underwriters.
- is not included in Institute Time Clauses - Hulls (1/10/83), but is often added to policies incorporating those clauses (see G04a.5).

G04a.2q Clause 44 – Additional Perils

- can be included, but only with the express written agreement of the underwriters.
- was not included in International Time Clauses - Hulls (1/10/83). For notes on the **Additional Perils Clause** often used, see G05c.

- provides that if the underwriters have expressly agreed in writing, the insurance covers:
  - the cost of repairing or replacing a **boiler** which bursts or **shaft** which breaks, where such bursting or breakage has caused loss of or damage to the subject matter insured covered by Clause 2.2.1;
  - the cost that would have been incurred to correct the **latent defect** where such latent defect has caused loss of or damage to the subject matter insured covered by Clause 2.2.2;
  - loss of or damage to the vessel caused by **any accident** or by **negligence**, **incompetence** or **error of judgment** of any person whatsoever.
- The Additional Perils cover provided in Clause 44.1 is subject to the **proviso** that such loss or damage has not resulted from **want of due diligence** by the assured, owners or managers. (Master, officers, crew or pilots are not to be considered "owners" under this clause should they hold shares in the vessel.)

G04a.2r Clause 46 – Notice of Claims

- provides that in the event of an accident or occurrence which may result in a **claim** under the insurance, **notice** must be given to the **leading underwriter(s)** as soon as possible after the date on which the assured, owners or managers become aware of the accident or occurrence (and within 180 days), so that a **surveyor** may be appointed if the leading underwriter(s) so desire.

G04a.2s Clause 47 – Tender Provisions

- provides that the **leading underwriter(s)** will be entitled to decide the port to which the vessel will proceed for **docking** or **repair** and will have a right of **veto** concerning a **place of repair** or a **repairing firm**.
- provides that the **leading underwriter(s)** may also take **tenders** or may require **further tenders** to be taken for the repair of the vessel.
- provides that if the assured fails to comply with Clause 47, a deduction of 15% will be made from the amount of the ascertained net claim.
- * Failure to advise the underwriters as required may create difficulties in agreeing the cause of damage or repair costs, which is essential before a claim can be met.
- * Institute Time Clauses – Hulls (1/10/83) includes a requirement to give notice to the nearest **Lloyd's Agent** (see G02b.1).

G04a.3 Risks not covered by the H&M policy

- * A shipowner is exposed to many risks not covered by his H&M policy (see G01a.1), some of which are outlined below.
- * **Increased value**, **disbursements** and **excess liabilities** are covered in separate policies designed to provide an additional source of recovery over and above the H&M value in event of a total loss. They also give cover on any balance owing of general average, salvage, sue and labour and collision liabilities which are not recoverable under the H&M policy because of under-insurance (e.g. where the "amount insured hereunder" was not the full insured value of the H&M).
- * **P&I risks** are insured with a protection and indemnity association if the vessel is fully entered with a club. For notes on P&I cover, see G04b.
- * **Loss of charter hire** may occur if a time-chartered ship is placed off-hire or is unable to trade because of damage sustained due to an insured peril. Loss of hire policies are obtainable from the Lloyd's or Companies markets.
- * **Loss of freight cover** is also available under a separate policy to which the Institute Time Clauses - Freight are usually attached.
- * **War risks cover** is a supplementary insurance against the operation of war risks which are generally excluded from H&M policies containing standard clauses such as the Institute Time Clauses - Hulls as well as many P&I policies. Standard policies generally exclude damage due to war, hostile acts, capture, seizure, arrest, strikes, etc. The London Underwriters Association decides on the operation of a war zone in any particular area from time to time and normal cover in that area is suspended and additional premiums are required for ships entering the zone. Some underwriters specialise in giving war risks cover for an additional premium. Institute War and Strikes Clauses are available for use in Lloyd's or Company policies. The P&I clubs also offer war risks cover under their own terms. Owners normally arrange for their ships to be "held covered" for war risks on a permanent worldwide basis, but should consult their broker when a vessel is going to enter a war zone.

G04a.4 Institute Warranty Limits

* The "**Institute Warranty Limits**" under the Institute Warranties, as amended 1976, are as follows:
  1. Warranted no:
     * Atlantic Coast of North America, its rivers or adjacent islands -
       - North of 52°10' N lat. and West of 50° W long.;
       - South of 52°10' N lat. in the area bounded by lines drawn between Battle Harbour/Pistolet Bay; Cape Ray/Cape North; Port Hawkesbury/Port Mulgrave and Baie Comeau/Matane, between 21st December and 30th April, both dates inclusive;
       - West of Baie Comeau/Matane (but not West of Montreal) between 1st December and 30th April both days inclusive.
     * Great Lakes or St Lawrence Seaway west of Montreal.
     * Greenland Waters.
     * Pacific Coast of North America its rivers or adjacent islands North of 54°30' N lat. or West of 130°50' W long.
  2. Warranted no Baltic Sea or adjacent waters East of 15° E long. -
     * North of a line between Mo (63°24' N lat.) and Vasa (63°06' N lat.) between 10th December and 25th May, both dates inclusive;
     * East of a line between Viipuri (Vyborg) (28°47' E long.) and Narva (28°12' E long.) between 15th December and 15th May, both dates inclusive;
     * North of a line between Stockholm (59°20' N lat.) and Tallinn (59°24' N lat.) between 8th January and 5th May, both dates inclusive;
     * East of 22° E long. and South of 59° N lat. between 28th December and 5th May, both dates inclusive.
  3. Warranted not North of 70° N lat. other than voyages direct to or from any port or place in Norway or Kola Bay.
  4. Warranted no Bering Sea, no East Asian waters North of 46° N lat. and not to enter or sail from any port or place in Siberia except Nakhodka and/or Vladivostock.
  5. Warranted not to proceed to Kerguelen and/or Croset Islands or South of 50° S except to ports and/or places in Patagonia and/or Chile and/or Falkland Islands, but liberty is given to enter waters South of 50° S lat., if en route to or from ports and/or places not excluded by this warranty.
  6. Warranted not to sail with Indian Coal as cargo:
     * between 1st March and 30th June, both dates inclusive;
     * between 1st July and 30th September, both dates inclusive, except to ports in Asia, not West of Aden or beyond Singapore.
* The Institute Warranty Limits are sometimes referred to on policy documents as the "**British Warranty Limits**" or "**IWLs**". In the "Trading" section of the policy schedule it may simply state: "Institute Warranties or held covered on payment of additional premium".
* For notes on **breach of Institute Warranty Limits** by the vessel during the voyage, see H01a.3.

G04a.5 General Average Absorption Clauses

* In cases of **small general averages**, especially in containerships and general cargo vessels where the involvement of numerous cargo interests would make the drawing up of a general average statement very difficult and uneconomic, the Hull and Machinery underwriters will often agree to bear the entire general average. An increasingly common feature of hull and machinery policies in respect of containerships and other general cargo vessels is, therefore, the inclusion of a **General Average Absorption Clause**.
* A General Average Absorption Clause will typically provide that in cases where the general average is estimated not to exceed a specified amount (e.g. USD100,000), the assured will have the option of deciding whether he will claim the whole of the general average under the Hull and Machinery insurance, or claim from the various cargo interests, as he thinks fit. The clause may also provide that it will not apply in cases where the general average consists mostly of general average sacrifices of and/or damage to cargo, in which event a full general average statement will have to be drawn up.
* The **International Hull Clauses** (01/11/02) include a General Average Absorption Clause (Clause 43) which will apply only where the underwriters have expressly so agreed in writing (see G04a.2p).
* For notes on **general average**, see G06.

G04b P&I COVER

G04b.1 P&I cover available

* P&I clubs offer shipowners and charterers various **classes of cover**, e.g. Protection; Indemnity; Strikes; Freight, Demurrage and Defence, etc. Individual clubs may offer slightly different types of cover, although in the main, most will offer the same basic cover. Most clubs offer two principal classes of cover: **Protection and Indemnity** (P&I) (known as Class 1), and **Freight, Demurrage and Defence** (FD&D) (known as Class 2).

* **Protection and Indemnity (P&I) cover** includes the following liabilities:

- **cargo claims** (e.g. for short delivery, loss or damage to cargo);
- **crew claims** (e.g. medical expenses, repatriation, substitute expenses, compensation for death or injury);
- **collision liabilities** (to the extent that the claim is not covered under the hull policy);
- "**fixed and floating objects**" (e.g. damage to docks, wharves and buoys);
- **third party injury and death claims** (e.g. from stevedores, crew members and passengers);
- **oil pollution liability** (and liability for pollution by other substances);
- **special compensation** payable in accordance with Article 14 of the International Convention on Salvage 1989 (see H05c.1), including payments assessed under the Scopic Clause (see H05d.3a);
- **miscellaneous claims** (including fines for innocent breaches of regulations, diversion and other expenses incurred in landing refugees, sick persons and stowaways, contractual liabilities including those of customary towage, unrecoverable general average contributions, ship's proportion of general average when in excess of the insured value, salvor's expenses under Lloyd's Open Form, and wreck removal costs.

* **Freight, Demurrage and Defence (FD&D) cover** indemnifies members for legal and related expenses incurred in connection with disputes under charter parties and other contracts, as defined in the club's rules, but does not extend to the principal amount in dispute.

* The UK clubs give cover normally lasting a maximum of 12 months, with renewal traditionally commencing annually at Noon GMT on February 20th.

* A **Certificate of Entry** issued by the club relates to the vessel or vessels named in it and entered for insurance in the club. The insurance is conditional on compliance with the terms and conditions of the club, as expressed in the club's handbook. The Certificate of Entry sets out the **classes of cover** in force and the **deductibles** applicable to each type of cover. It is not a legal requirement for an entered ship to carry a Certificate of Entry, but many ships carry a copy of the Certificate since this meets the recommendation contained in IMO Guidelines on Shipowners' Responsibilities in Respect of Maritime Claims, adopted by resolution A.898(21) (see G01a). Every entered ship should carry the club's **rules**, which are normally published in a small handbook.

G04b.2 Limits and restrictions on P&I cover

* The board of directors of each club will determine what limits and restrictions should be placed on the cover offered to members, their decisions usually being taken and announced shortly before the next annual renewal date of 20 February. A particular club's rule book will reflect the current position in the club.

* The following notes are **examples** of cover restrictions, but are not to be taken as currently applicable in any particular club.

* Liabilities arising during **towage of an entered ship** may only be covered if the member has become liable under the terms of a towage contract for normal port towage or towage of an entered barge. For cover on other types of towage the member must advise the club in advance.

* When the member's vessel is **towing** another vessel, loss or damage to the tow, or cargo on the tow, or wreck removal of the tow and cargo, is only covered if the towage contract has been approved by the managers.

* Liabilities arising under **indemnities** (e.g. in respect of delivery of cargo requested at a port other than that stated in the bill of lading or without production of a bill of lading) may be covered only on approval of the club's management, and if the terms of the indemnity have been approved by the club. However, club directors are unlikely to exercise their discretion in favour of giving owners cover for such liabilities, even if the indemnity is in approved form and signed by a first class bank. Owners cannot therefore rely on their club entry to protect them in these cases, and the clubs generally stress that the indemnity should be viewed as a replacement for club cover for such claims, and not as additional protection.

* Liabilities to seamen arising under a **crew contract** are covered only if the contract has been approved in writing by the managers. This also applies to cover for repatriation, loss of seamen's effects and shipwreck unemployment indemnity.

* Liabilities arising from carriage under **bills of lading** are normally only covered if the bills of lading are subject to the Hague Rules or Hague-Visby Rules.
* The Board of Directors of each club will usually determine, in accordance with the club's rules, the limits on the club's liability in respect of any and all **claims for oil pollution** for the next policy year, the decision being taken towards the end of the current year. For the policy year commencing 20 February 2002, for example, some clubs impose a limit of USD1,000 million each accident or occurrence in respect of each ship entered by or on behalf of an owner (not being a charterer other than a charterer by demise or bareboat charterer).
* Clubs will **not normally cover**:
  * ad valorem bills of lading;
  * deviation;
  * delivery of cargo at a port other the port specified in the contract of carriage;
  * failure to arrive or late arrival at the port of loading;
  * delivery of cargo without production of a bill of lading;
  * ante-dated or post-dated bills of lading;
  * clean bills of lading in respect of damaged cargo;
  * deck cargo carried on terms of an under-deck bill of lading;
  * arrest or detention of an entered ship.
* The only **fines** on an entered ship that will normally be covered are:
  * customs fines;
  * immigration fines;
  * fines for failure to have proper documentation on board;
  * fines for breach of any regulation relating to the construction, adoption, alteration or fitment of an entered ship;
  * fines incurred as a result of the conduct of the crew or other servant or agent of the member;
  * fines imposed for failure to maintain safe working conditions.

G04c CARGO INSURANCE

* **Cargo insurance** (also called **marine cargo insurance** or **goods transit insurance**) covers physical damage to or loss of goods whilst in transit by land, sea and air. There is no statutory requirement to obtain insure goods in transit, but in international sales the seller and buyer will usually agree that one party or the other will obtain cargo insurance. (See notes on INCOTERMS at F03b, especially the meanings of the CFR and CIF terms.)
* Cargo insurance can be obtained directly from an **insurance company**, from underwriters in the **Lloyd's** and/or **Companies** markets (through a broker), from **freight forwarders**, and from some **carriers** in the liner trades. (In the Lloyd's and Companies markets the broking procedure is much the same as with a ship – see G04a.)
* There is no standard cargo policy in the UK and most policies are tailored for the individual risk. However, most policies incorporate the **Institute Cargo Clauses A, B or C**.

G04c.1 Institute Cargo Clauses A, B and C

* **Institute Cargo Clauses C** give cover only against major casualties: fire, explosion, vessel or craft stranded, grounded, sunk, capsized, overturning or derailment of land conveyances, collision or contact, discharge at a port of distress, general average sacrifice and jettison. Malicious damage is excluded but can be covered by the Malicious Damage Clause for an extra premium. Theft is not covered.
* **Institute Cargo Clauses B** extend the "C" cover to include earthquake, volcanic eruption, lightning, washing overboard, entry of sea, lake or river into the vessel, craft, hold, conveyance, liftvan or place of storage, total loss of packages lost overboard or dropped overboard during loading or unloading. There is a Deliberate Damage Exclusion, requiring the addition of the Malicious Damage Clause. Theft is not covered.
* **Institute Cargo Clauses A** give cover "Against all risks of loss of or damage to the subject matter insured", making the policy almost "**fully comprehensive**". However, ordinary leakage, ordinary loss in weight or volume, ordinary wear and tear, inherent vice, and delay are excluded.
* Some conditions are common to all Institute Cargo Clauses. For cover, the **Institute Strikes Clauses** must be incorporated and the following claims are always excluded:
  * claims resulting from insufficient or unsuitable packing or preparation of the subject matter insured;
  * claims for loss or damage arising from the insolvency or financial default of the owners, managers, charterers or operators of the vessel. (The insurer cannot be responsible for the performance of the carrier and this exclusion is aimed at encouraging the use of reputable carriers);
  * claims for loss, damage or expense arising from the use of any nuclear weapon;

- claims for damage caused by terrorists or persons acting for a political motive;
- claims for loss, damage or expense arising from:
- unseaworthiness of the vessel or craft;
- unfitness of vessel, craft, conveyance or liftvan for the safe carriage of the subject-matter insured -
- where the assured or their servants are privy to such unseaworthiness or unfitness, at the time the subject-matter insured is loaded therein.

G04c.2 War and strikes cover for cargo owners

* Cargo owners normally buy cover against **war risks and strikes**.
* **Institute War Clauses** cover loss or damage caused by hostilities, warlike operations, civil war, revolution, rebellion, insurrection, etc. The cover is only for the sea passage, i.e. it attaches when the goods are loaded on an overseas vessel and terminates on discharge. It excludes loss or damage from use of atomic or nuclear weapons.
* The **Institute Strikes, Riots and Civil Commotions Clause** gives cover throughout a strike and covers physical loss or damage directly caused by strikers, locked out workmen or persons taking part in labour disturbances, riots, civil commotions, and persons acting maliciously. It excludes loss or damage caused by the passive action of strikers in withdrawing their labour (e.g. the decay of perishables), for which extra cover is required.

G04c.3 Open covers

* An **open cover** is a commonly used form of long-term cargo insurance contract covering all goods shipments forwarded by an assured during the duration of the open cover.
* The assured will usually be a regular exporter or importer.
* The open cover itself is an original slip, placed in the same way as an individual goods insurance policy. The period of the open cover is usually fixed at **12 months**, with a 30-day notice period for cancellation by either side, reduced to 7 days when there are war risks.
* The **assured is honour-bound to declare and insure all his shipments** during the term of the open cover (i.e. he cannot choose to insure some and not others) and the insurer is honour-bound to insure all the assured's shipments, whether a loss occurs before a declaration is made or not. There is no aggregate limit to the value of all shipments made, but there is a set limit on the **amount at risk in any one vessel**, and often on the **amount at risk in any one location**.
* The insurer allows the merchant to issue himself with a **certificate of insurance** "off the open cover" for each consignment shipped, as formal policy documents for each shipment would take time to draw up.
* The advantage to the insurer of an open cover is that he gets **steady business**, while for the merchant it means **speed and simplicity** in the arrangement of insurance cover.
* An **open policy** is a formal policy issued to give legality to a long-term marine insurance contract such as a cargo open cover. Without a formal policy document the contract may not be recognised by a court of law. To satisfy the requirements of marine insurance law, therefore, an open policy will be issued in which a nominal premium is specified by way of consideration.

G04c.4 Floating policies

* A **floating policy** operates rather like an open cover, but has a **fixed aggregate limit** which is gradually reduced as each shipment is made. It has largely fallen into disuse with the growth in popularity of open covers.

G04d POLLUTION LIABILITY INSURANCE, CONVENTIONS AND SCHEMES

G04d.1 Statutory requirement for oil pollution insurance

* **Under section 163(2) of the Merchant Shipping Act 1995** a ship carrying a **bulk cargo of more than 2,000 tons of oil** of a description specified in the Oil Pollution (Compulsory Insurance) Regulations (see G04d.2) must not enter or leave a UK port or a terminal in UK territorial waters or, in the case of a UK ship, a port in any other country or a terminal in the territorial sea of any other country, unless there is in force **a certificate** complying with

section 163(3) and showing that **there is in force in respect of the ship a contract of insurance or other security** satisfying the requirements of Article VII of the Civil Liability Convention (the "CLC"). The required certificate is properly called a **Certificate of Financial Responsibility in respect of Civil Liability for Oil Pollution Damage** but is more commonly known as an **Oil Pollution Insurance Certificate** or "**OPIC**". The requirement for an OPIC does not apply to "Government ships"[7].

* **Section 163(3)** provides that in respect of a UK ship, the OPIC must be **issued by the MCA**. In the case of a ship registered in a Civil Liability Convention (CLC) Party State, the OPIC must be issued by the flag State Administration, and in the case of a ship registered in a non-Party State, it must be issued either by the MCA or by or under the authority of any other CLC Party State.
* **Section 163(4)** provides that the OPIC must, where required to be in force, be **produced by the master** on the demand of any officer of Customs and Excise or of the MCA and, in the case of a UK ship, a proper officer.
* Under **section 163(5)**, if a ship **enters or leaves, or attempts to enter or leave**, a port or terminal **without a valid OPIC**, the **master or owner** will be liable on conviction on indictment to an unlimited fine, or on summary conviction to a fine not exceeding **£50,000**.
* **Section 163(6)** provides that if a ship fails to carry, or the master fails to produce, an OPIC as required, he will be liable on summary conviction to a fine not exceeding Level 4 on the Standard Scale (see B03b.3c).
* Under **section 163(7)** the ship may in these cases be **detained**.

G04d.1a Oil Pollution Insurance Certificate (OPIC)

- **is properly** called a **Certificate of Insurance or Other Financial Security in Respect of Civil Liability for Oil Pollution Damage**, but is more commonly known as an "OPIC".
- **is a requirement** under the International Convention on Civil Liability for Oil Pollution Damage (CLC). A CLC Convention Country must require certain ships, wherever registered, to show proof that there is in force a **policy of insurance or other financial security** against oil pollution liabilities when entering or leaving ports in its territory, or arriving at or leaving offshore terminals in its territorial seas.
- **is required** to be carried by all ships carrying more than 2000 tons of persistent oil in bulk as cargo. "**Persistent oil**" is defined broadly as all hydrocarbon mineral oils, residual oil (residues of distillation of or refining of crude oil) and whale oil (see G04d.1b for the UK's definition).
- **is described** in **M.1374**.
- **is obtained** by a shipowner from MCA, Greenock, Scotland, on submission of satisfactory **evidence that a suitable insurance policy or other security is in force** for the ship and payment of a fee. The required evidence is furnished in the form of a certificate called a "Blue Card" issued by the insurer or guarantor, e.g. the owner's P&I Club; proof of membership of a recognised **pollution compensation fund** (see G04d.2) also satisfies the requirements.
- **is valid** for a maximum of 12 months. The period of validity usually is usually concurrent with the period of the insurance cover. If the insurer is a P&I club, this will normally be from Noon GMT on 20 February in one year to the same time and date in the following year. (See G02a.3c for a footnote concerning the reason for use of this date.)

G04d.1b Oil Pollution (Compulsory Insurance) Regulations

* The **Oil Pollution (Compulsory Insurance) Regulations 1997** (SI 1997/1820) -
  - revoke and replace The Oil Pollution (Compulsory Insurance) Regulations 1981 (SI 1981/912), as amended, as a consequence of the UK becoming a party to the **International Convention on Civil Liability for Oil Pollution Damage 1992**.
  - define "**oil**" for the purposes of section 163(1) of the Merchant Shipping Act 1995 (see G04d.1) as "any persistent hydrocarbon mineral oil such as crude oil, fuel oil, heavy diesel oil and lubricating oil, but excluding any oil which at the time of shipment consists of hydrocarbon fractions –
    * at least 50% of which, by volume, distil at a temperature of 340°C, and
    * at least 95% of which, by volume, distil at a temperature of 370°C,
    - when tested by the ASTM Method D86/78 published by the American Society of Testing and Materials".
  - deal with the cancellation and delivery up of OPICs (in regulation 4).
* Where the person to whom an OPIC was issued by the MCA **ceases to be the owner** of the ship to which it relates, he must **deliver the OPIC** to the MCA or a proper officer for cancellation (regulation 4(1)).
* The Regulations make **no requirement** to have oil pollution insurance or to carry an **OPIC**; those requirements are made in section 163 of the Merchant Shipping Act 1995 (see G04d.1).

---

[7] Under section 167(1) "Government ships" (i.e. warships and ships being used by the government of any State for non-commercial purposes) are not required (in the UK) to have oil pollution insurance.

G04d.2 Pollution liability conventions and schemes

* For owners of **dry cargo ships** with risks of pollution liabilities, there are currently **no international liability schemes** in operation. However, individual countries whose coasts and waters are polluted will generally impose strict liability on owners and charterers under domestic legislation.

* For **tanker owners**, four liability schemes have operated, all based on the idea that the costs of an oil spill should be shared between the shipowner and the cargo owner. Two international conventions have been adopted: the **Civil Liability Convention (CLC)** and the **Fund Convention**, while there have been two voluntary schemes: **TOVALOP** and **CRISTAL**. These are outlined below.

* The **present regime** of compensation for pollution damage by persistent oil from tankers is based on a two-tier compensation scheme established under the **1992 Civil Liability Convention (CLC 1992)**, which is sometimes referred to as the CLC Protocol 1992 and supersedes the 1969 CLC, and the **Fund Convention 1992**, which is sometimes referred to as the Fund Protocol 1992 and supersedes the Fund Convention 1971.

* An individual **tanker owner** and his oil pollution liability insurer (usually his **P&I club**) are liable for the **first tier** of compensation under the CLC 1992. The tanker owner has **strict liability** for damage caused by cargo oil but can normally limit his financial liability up to an amount established according to the ship's tonnage.

* The **second tier** of compensation is supplementary to the first tier and is paid by the International Oil Pollution Compensation Fund 1992 (**IOPC Fund 1992**). This was established by the Fund Convention 1992, is financed by oil receivers in member States and is administered, independently of IMO, in London. Claims paid mainly include claims for property damage, costs of clean-up operations at sea and on shore, claims for economic losses suffered by fishermen or those engaged in mariculture and economic losses in the tourism sector.

* An **IOPC Supplementary Fund** is established under the 2000 Amendments to the Fund Convention which will supplement the compensation payable under the CLC 1992 and the Fund Convention 1992 with a **third tier** of compensation.

* **The Tanker Owners Voluntary Agreement Concerning Liability for Oil Pollution, 1969** ("**TOVALOP**") and the **Contract Regarding a Supplement to Tanker Liability for Oil Pollution** ("**CRISTAL**") were designed to be interim arrangements pending the widespread adoption by States of the CLC 1969 and Fund Convention 1971, which they respectively mirrored. The rapid growth in acceptances of the 1992 CLC and Fund conventions led to a decision to terminate TOVALOP and CRISTAL on 20 February 1997.

G04d.3 P&I pollution cover

* **P&I club cover for pollution liabilities** is generally to the extent that the pollution is a result of an escape or discharge or threatened escape or discharge of oil or any other substance. Clubs have traditionally covered:
  * liability for damages or compensation;
  * costs of reasonably-taken measures for preventing, minimising or cleaning up pollution;
  * liabilities of tanker owners as a party to the Tanker Owners' Voluntary Agreement for Liability for Oil Pollution (TOVALOP) (defunct from 20 February 1997 - see G04d.2);
  * costs or liabilities incurred as a result of compliance with government directions during a pollution incident;
  * special compensation payable to salvors under Article 14 of the International Salvage Convention 1989 (see H05c.1c).
  * fines for pollution.
* For notes on **limits on P&I pollution cover** see G04b.2.

G04d.4 Foreign pollution cover requirements

* **US federal law** requires vessels using US navigable waters to carry a Certificate of Financial Responsibility (Water Pollution) or "**COFR**" (see G04d.4a) as evidence of financial responsibility for oil pollution.

* Certain **US states** (e.g. Alaska and California) have their own coastal pollution law requiring the carriage of a **state COFR**.

G04d.4a Certificate of Financial Responsibility (Water Pollution)

* A **Certificate of Financial Responsibility (Water Pollution)**, commonly known as a "**COFR**" -
  - **is required** under Title 33, US Code of Federal Regulations 138 (33 CFR 138) to be carried by all ships over 300gt using the navigable waters of the USA or any port or place subject to the jurisdiction of the USA, including an offshore facility subject to the jurisdiction of the USA.

- **certifies** that the vessel operator has established financial responsibility in accordance with 33 CFR 138, to meet liability under section 1002 of the Oil Pollution Act of 1990, and under section 107 of the Comprehensive Environmental Response, Compensation, and Liability Act, which may result from the operation of the named vessel.
- **is issued** by the US National Pollution Funds Center, Arlington, VA following submission of evidence of suitable financial responsibility and payment of a fee. **Evidence** is normally provided by the P&I club with which the ship is entered.
- **is valid** for a maximum of 3 years.
- **must be renewed** between 21 and 90 days before expiry.
- **shows** the vessel operator; vessel; effective date; expiration date; conditions (on reverse side).
- **becomes invalid** if the named operator is not the party responsible for operating the vessel.
- **must be shown** on demand to an officer of the US Coast Guard or Customs Service.

* If evidence of financial responsibility cannot be produced by a vessel to which the above requirements apply, the US Coast Guard may:
  • **deny entry** of the vessel to any port or place in the US or US navigable waters;
  • **detain** the vessel at a port or place in the US in which it is located;
* Any vessel **found in US navigable waters** without the necessary evidence of financial responsibility is subject to **seizure by and forfeiture** to the US.

G04d.4b Australian cargo or bunker oil pollution liability insurance requirements

* **AMSA Marine Notice No. 3 of 2001** warns that, under amendments to the Protection of the Sea (Civil Liability) Act 1981, ships of 400gt or more carrying oil as **cargo or bunkers** (other than tankers carrying a valid OPIC) are required to carry a "**relevant insurance certificate**" when visiting an **Australian port**. This requirement will be met in most cases by a **P&I Club Certificate of Entry**. The certificate must be produced on request of Port State Control inspectors and Australian Customs Service officers when ships are entering and leaving Australia. **AMSA Marine Notices** can be viewed at: www.AMSA.gov.au/amsa/mn

G05 Losses

G05a CATEGORIES OF LOSS

* **Section 56(1) of the Marine Insurance Act 1906** provides that (in marine insurance), a loss may be either **total** or **partial**, and that **any loss other than a total loss**, as defined in the Act, is a "**partial loss**".
* Section 56(2) provides that a **total loss** may be either an "**actual total loss**", or a "**constructive total loss**".
* **Marine losses** may thus be categorised as:
  • **total losses**; and
  • **partial losses** (a partial loss being known as "**average**").
* **Total losses** may be categorised as:
  • **actual total losses** (sometimes written as "ATLs"); and
  • **constructive total losses** (or "CTLs").
* For notes on **total losses** see G05b.
* A **partial loss** (or "**average**") will always be categorised as either:
  • **particular average** (sometimes written as "**PA**"); or
  • **general average** (or "**GA**"),
  - depending on whether the loss meets the qualifying criteria to be treated as a general average loss or not.
* For notes on **particular average** see G05c.
* For notes on **general average** see G06.

G05b TOTAL LOSSES

G05b.1 Actual total loss

* **Section 57(1) of the Marine Insurance Act 1906** provides that there is an "**actual total loss**" where the subject-matter insured is **destroyed**, or **so damaged as to cease to be a thing of the kind insured**, or where the assured is **irretrievably deprived** of the subject-matter insured.
* **Section 58** provides that where the ship concerned in the adventure is **missing**, and after the lapse of a reasonable time no news of her has been received, an **actual total loss may be presumed**.
* An **actual total loss** may thus occur in four ways:
    * where the property insured is actually **destroyed**, e.g. where a ship is wrecked or burnt out, or where goods are crushed in the collapse of a stow of cargo;
    * where goods change their character to such a degree that they can be said to be **no longer a thing of the kind that was insured**, e.g. where dates become "mush", or where cement powder solidifies;
    * where the assured is **irretrievably deprived** of his property, e.g. where a ship is sunk in very deep water; or
    * where the insured property is posted "**missing**" at Lloyd's, e.g. where a ship has not reported for several weeks.

G05b.2 Constructive total loss

* **Section 60(1) of the Marine Insurance Act 1906** provides that, subject to any express provision in the policy, there is a **constructive total loss** where the subject matter insured is **reasonably abandoned** on account of:
    * its actual total loss appearing to be unavoidable; or
    * because it could not be preserved from actual total loss without an expenditure which would exceed its value when the expenditure had been incurred."
* **Section 60(2)** provides that, in particular, there is a constructive total loss in the following cases:
    * Where an assured is **deprived of possession** of his ship or goods by a **peril insured against** and -
        * it is **unlikely that he can recover them**; or
        * the **cost of recovering** the ship or goods, as the case may be, **would exceed their value** when recovered; and
    * In the case of **damage to goods**, where the **cost** of repairing the damage and forwarding the goods to their destination would **exceed their value** on arrival.
* Thus, where a ship that has stranded due to a "peril of the seas" is in danger of breaking up, there is a constructive total loss. The shipowner will not want to wait until she has actually broken up before claiming for a total loss, so he will normally claim a constructive total loss on the grounds that an actual total loss appears to be unavoidable.
* Where an owner who has War Risks Insurance cover is deprived of his ship by its entrapment by war-wrecked vessels, there is a constructive total loss. As time passes, it may become more unlikely that the assured can recover the vessel and she will therefore be declared a constructive total loss. The cost of recovering her (towage, etc.) after several years of idleness would exceed her market value after recovery. (The same will apply to goods on a trapped ship.)
* In the case of damage to a ship, where she is so damaged by a peril insured against, e.g. grounding damage, that the cost of repairing the damage would exceed the value of the ship when repaired, there is a constructive total loss.

G05b.3 Abandonment

* An owner of a damaged and salvaged ship will not usually spend more on repairs than the value of the ship after repair. (The ship may qualify as a constructive total loss.)
* The owner is not obliged to claim a constructive total loss; he may choose to claim a 100% partial loss, make repairs and retain the ship.
* If he wishes to claim a constructive total loss, the owner must **abandon the property to the insurer**.
* After a valid abandonment, the insurer is entitled to **take over the interest** of the assured in whatever remains of the insured property, including all proprietary rights in it, e.g.:
    * the right to any freight in the course of being earned when the casualty occurred;
    * the right to take over the ship;
    * the right to dispose of the ship as he thinks fit and retain all the proceeds (even if more than the claim paid).
* When a ship is badly damaged and the owner fears a constructive total loss the owner gives **notice of abandonment** to the underwriter. Tenders are taken from salvors and repairers. It is ascertained whether expenditure will exceed

the repaired value. Items taken into account in the calculation include estimated repair costs; the cost of future salvage operations; any general average contributions to which the ship would be liable if she were repaired. If the estimated total outlays exceed estimated repaired value, a **constructive total loss** is shown and the underwriter will be liable for a **total loss**. The insurer pays the claim and takes over proprietary rights in the vessel if she is eventually recovered.

* **Section 57(2) of the Marine Insurance Act 1906** provides that in the case of an actual total loss **no notice** of abandonment need be given.

G05c PARTICULAR AVERAGE

* Section 64 of the Marine Insurance Act 1906 defines a **particular average (PA) loss** as "a partial loss, proximately caused by a peril insured against and which is not a general average loss".
* The **insured perils** in a hull and machinery (H&M) policy are listed in a **Perils Clause** in the set of clauses attached to the policy, such as the International Hulls Clauses (01/11/02) or the Institute Time Clauses – Hulls (1/10/83). For notes on Clause 2 - Perils - of the International Hull Clauses - Hulls (01/11/02), see G04a.2a. Under such a clause, structural damage proximately caused by collision, grounding, heavy weather, etc. ("perils of the seas") would normally be classed as a **particular average loss**.
* Many owners insuring their ships under the Institute Time Clauses – Hulls prefer to extend their cover by paying an **additional premium** for clauses such as the **Institute Additional Perils Clauses – Hulls (APCs)**, which cover loss or damage caused by **any accident**. Instead of having to demonstrate the operation of one of the **perils insured against** (as with the Institute Time Clauses – Hulls (1/10/83)), the assured only has to prove that the loss or damage was caused by **an accident** during the policy term. (Both Clause 6.2 of the Institute Time Clauses (1/10/83) and the APCs are subject, however, to the **proviso** that the loss or damage has not resulted from **want of due diligence** on the part of the assured, owners or managers.)
* For notes on **Clause 44 – Additional Perils** – in the International Hull Clauses (01/11/02), see G04a.2q.

G06 General Average

G06a PRINCIPLE OF GENERAL AVERAGE

G06a.1 Principle and object of general average

* The **principle of general average** may be said simply to be: "That which has been sacrificed for the benefit of all shall be made good by the contribution of all"[8].
* The **object of general average** is to ensure that the owner of a vessel or cargo who has incurred an expenditure or suffered a sacrifice of his property in order to extricate the vessel (and consequently the cargo) from a perilous position receives a contribution to his loss from all those who have benefited from the action.
* A **general average loss** is a partial loss incurred through a **deliberate** act performed with the intention of preserving all the property involved in a voyage from a **danger** which threatens them all. General average losses are **equitably shared** by all the parties to the "**common maritime adventure**" (the voyage being the "maritime adventure") (see G06a.2), each party contributing in proportion to his share of the total values involved.
* In theory, whenever a shipowner deliberately incurs an expenditure, no matter how small, which results in the ship and its cargo being preserved from a peril (such as a fire on board), there is a **general average act** and the owners of the cargo saved by it become liable for a contribution to the shipowner's costs. In practice, however, general average is not always declared, since the calculation and collection of all the due contributions could, depending on the nature of the cargo, involve a huge amount of time, effort and expense (see notes on **General Average Absorption Clauses** in G04a.5).
* Following a general average act a ship will often make for a "port of refuge", and it is in these emergency port calls that, very often, the majority of the general average expenditure is incurred. For notes on the **procedure at a port of refuge following a general average act**, see I02i.

---

[8] The principle was applied under Rhodian law, the body of maritime law said to have been administered on the island of Rhodes from about 800 B.C.

G06a.2 Parties to the "common maritime adventure"

* The term **"maritime adventure"** comes from the days of merchant adventurers who sponsored ships' voyages to the East and West Indies, etc. A **"common maritime adventure"** is a voyage in which several parties have some financial interest, as opposed to a ballast voyage of a non-chartered liner vessel where the only party involved is the shipowner.
* The **parties to a "common maritime adventure"** could include:
  * the **shipowner**;
  * each **consignee** of cargo on board (however many these may be);
  * where the vessel is on time charter, the **owners of the bunker fuel** (time charterer); and
  * the **recipient of the freight** (who will normally be the shipowner or time charterer).
* **Where cargo is owned by more than one party**, each consignee is treated as a separate interest and is liable for his own contribution to the general average, no matter how small. The carrier usually makes this clear to the holder of a bill of lading in a General Average Clause.
* Where, on a vessel, **equipment is installed** that belongs to some third party (e.g. a diving system owned by a diving contractor or a cable-laying installation or drilling equipment fitted on a chartered vessel, etc.), the owner(s) of that equipment become a party to the common maritime adventure.
* **Where a vessel is time chartered**, the **charterer's interest** is determined by the value of his **bunkers** remaining on board at the termination of the voyage, plus **any freight at risk** (i.e. freight earned and payable). Where the time charterers own the cargo there may not be any freight at risk.

G06a.3 Essential elements of a general average act

* In order to have the right to claim a contribution from other parties to the "common maritime adventure", the owner of a vessel which, together with its cargo and any other property has been saved from danger must be able to show that there was a **"general average act"**.
* A **general average act** is defined in Rule A of the York-Antwerp Rules as follows: "There is a general average act when, and only when, any extraordinary sacrifice or expenditure is intentionally and reasonably made or incurred for the common safety for the purpose of preserving from peril the property involved in a common maritime adventure".
* The **essential elements of a general average act** are contained in the above definition, and are as follows:
  * There must be a **sacrifice or expenditure**.
  * The sacrifice or expenditure must be **extraordinary**.
  * The sacrifice or expenditure must be **intentionally** made or incurred.
  * The sacrifice or expenditure must be **reasonably** made or incurred.
  * The sacrifice or expenditure must be made for the **common safety**.
  * The sacrifice or expenditure must be made for the **purpose of preserving the property from peril**.

G06a.3a Sacrifice or expenditure

* Examples of **sacrifices** that may be allowed in general average are:
  * **cargo jettisoned** to refloat a grounded vessel or to prevent the capsize of a dangerously listed vessel.;
  * **machinery damage** sustained during refloating operations.
* Examples of **expenditure** that may be allowed in general average are:
  * costs of **salvage expenditure,** including the **salvor's reward**;
  * costs of **entering, staying at and leaving a port of refuge**.

G06a.3b Extraordinary nature of sacrifice or expenditure

* To be allowed in general average, a sacrifice or expenditure must be of an **extraordinary** nature, and not an ordinary or every-day loss or expense incurred in running a ship and carrying cargoes.
* **Losing an anchor** in attempting to prevent a ship from running aground is not "extraordinary", since that is what anchors are meant to do. **Losing an anchor laid out as ground tackle** during a refloating operation would, however, be "extraordinary", and the cost of the lost anchor may be allowed in general average.
* **Damage to a main engine** through over-working whilst trying to prevent grounding would not be "extraordinary", whereas damage done during a refloating operation would be "extraordinary" and may be allowed in general average.

* A wide variety of costs, even including small and, at first glance, insignificant expenses such as a superintendent's taxi fare to a shipyard at a port of refuge, may be regarded as "extraordinary" and may therefore be recoverable as general average expenditure.

G06a.3c Sacrifice or expenditure intentionally made or incurred

* The sacrifice or expenditure comprising the general average act must be made **intentionally**, and not by or in connection with some accident.
* **When a ship's CO_2 cylinders are discharged** in order to put out a fire on board, an intentional expenditure is incurred which will usually be allowed in general average. The costs of wetting damage done to previously undamaged cargo when a hold is flooded in a boundary cooling operation would also usually be allowed in general average. (The costs of damage done by the fire itself would not be allowed in general average, however.)
* **Beaching a leaking ship** in order to prevent her foundering is an **intentional** act, the costs of which (including costs of damage caused by the beaching operation) would normally be allowed in general average. The costs of **repairs to the damage causing the leak** would **not be allowed** in general average, but would, if caused by an insured peril, be allowed in particular average.
* The **costs of refloating an accidentally grounded ship** would be allowed in general average, since the act of refloating is **intentional**. The costs of damage done by running aground, however, would not be allowed in general average.

G06a.3d Sacrifice or expenditure reasonably made or incurred

* To be allowed in general average, the sacrifice or expenditure must be **reasonably** made or incurred. Where more cargo is jettisoned than was necessary to refloat a grounded ship, the excess would probably not be allowed in general average.
* Expenditure at a port of refuge over and above **reasonable expenditure** would not be allowed in general average.

G06a.3e Sacrifice or expenditure for the common safety

* To be allowed in general average, the sacrifice or expenditure must be made or incurred **for the benefit of all the parties** to the common maritime adventure (i.e. the "**common safety**") and not for the benefit of only one party.
* For example, where the refrigerating machinery of a loaded reefer vessel breaks down during a voyage through tropical waters, making it imperative (for the sake of the cargo) to put into a port for repairs, the threat of loss is limited to the owner(s) of the cargo and, perhaps, the freight. So far as the ship itself is concerned, the voyage could quite safely continue, so the costs of the deviation to the repair port would not be allowed in general average. (Furthermore, it would not be appropriate to call the repair port a "port of refuge" in this case (see I02i.1a).)

G06a.3f Sacrifice or expenditure to preserve the property from peril

* To be allowed in general average, a sacrifice or expenditure must have been made for the purpose of **preserving the property from peril**, i.e. great danger.
* The peril must have been **real and substantial**, although it **need not have been imminent**. A vessel which lost main engine power in mid-ocean would be "in peril", even though the weather at the time might be good and there seemed to be no immediate threat. Sooner or later, however, ship and cargo would come to grief, either by running aground and breaking up or foundering, etc., so the cost of a tow to a port of refuge would normally be allowed in general average.
* It might be argued that expenditure incurred in **taking shelter** from a tropical storm during a voyage should be allowed in general average, since any tropical storm constitutes a real and substantial peril, and the action of sheltering is for the preservation of all the property involved. Such action, however, would the **ordinary** practice of prudent seamen. It would not be "extraordinary", and would therefore not meet all of the criteria necessary to be allowed in general average.

G06b YORK-ANTWERP RULES

G06b.1 Nature and application of York-Antwerp Rules

* The **York-Antwerp Rules** -
  - are a set of internationally recognised rules, drawn up by a number of maritime countries to **enable the assessment of each party's general average contribution** following an incident in which general average was declared.
  - are (unlike the Hague-Visby Rules) **not incorporated into national law** but are voluntarily and mutually **accepted by shippers, shipowners and insurers**.
  - are generally incorporated into a contract of carriage in a **General Average Clause**. If the parties have not agreed to apply the York-Antwerp Rules, common law - usually that of the country where the voyage is terminated following the general average act - may be applied to the general average adjustment. There is a risk in such cases of wide variations from one country to another in the method of adjustment of general average).
  - consist of **7 lettered rules** (A to G) stating the **general principles** of general average, plus **22 numbered rules** (I to XXII) dealing with specific matters.
  - provide a **definition of a general average act** (in Rule A) as follows: "There is a general average act when, and only when, any extraordinary sacrifice or expenditure is intentionally and reasonably made or incurred for the common safety for the purpose of preserving from peril the property involved in a common maritime adventure".

G06b.2 Examples of general average acts allowed under York-Antwerp Rules

- include:
  - taking a tow to a port of refuge after a major machinery failure;
  - jettisoning or discharging cargo to aid refloating after stranding;
  - extinguishing a fire;
  - wetting previously undamaged cargo while extinguishing a fire. (Damage caused by the fire would be particular average, while damage by water would be general average.)
  - beaching a ship ("voluntary stranding") to avoid foundering;
  - putting into a port of refuge during a loaded voyage due to fire, shifting of cargo, collision, grounding, leakage, etc.; and
  - putting into a port of refuge to effect essential hull or machinery repairs.

G06b.3 Examples of general average sacrifices allowed under York-Antwerp Rules

- include:
  - damaging engine, propeller or hull in refloating operations;
  - jettison of cargo from underdeck;
  - jettison of cargo carried on deck by a recognised custom of the trade; and
  - slipping an anchor and cable to avoid a collision.

G06b.4 Examples of general average expenditure allowed under York-Antwerp Rules

- include:
  - cost of hiring a tug to refloat a stranded ship with cargo onboard;
  - cost of discharging cargo in order to refloat a stranded ship or to carry out repairs at a port of refuge;
  - salvage costs;
  - agency fees at a port of refuge;
  - surveyors' fees;
  - warehousing charges;
  - port charges;
  - master's and crew's wages while a ship is being repaired; and
  - average adjuster's fee.

G06b.5 Salvage claim

* General average acts often give rise to a **salvage claim**, e.g. where a ship is refloated and/or towed to a port of refuge.
* Although under the laws of many nations, salvage charges are quite **separate** from general average charges, **salvage claims are usually treated as general average expenditure** and are therefore paid by hull and cargo insurers.
* **Rule VI of the York-Antwerp Rules** provides that any salvage charges will be treated as general average.
* **Salvage security** is not to be confused with general average security. Salvage security is paid by a shipowner and cargo owners to the salvor at the place where the salvage services terminate, whereas security for general average is paid by cargo owners to the shipowner at the destination.

G06c PORT OF REFUGE BUSINESS

* For notes on action to be taken at the port of destination following a general average incident, see I02i.

G06d ADJUSTMENT OF GENERAL AVERAGE

G06d.1 Basis of general average adjustments

* Each item of property at risk in the common maritime adventure at the time of the incident giving rise to the general average act and saved by that act must **contribute** to the general average according to its value to its owner (i.e. its sound market value) at the termination of adventure (i.e. the end of the voyage, at the final destination). These values may appear in the adjustment document as "**contributory values**".
* **Calculation of contributory values** and **assessment of general average losses**, especially on vessels such as large container ships, is a complex task for an average adjuster (see G02b.3). All the property at risk in the common maritime adventure at the time of the occurrence giving rise to the general average act and saved by that act must contribute to the general average according to its sound value at destination. Cargo discharged prior to the occurrence or loaded following it will not contribute. Therefore, **if fire broke out during loading**, it would be necessary to have accurate particulars of all cargo on board **at the time of the outbreak**.
* The **value of the ship after the general average act**, and the **CIF value of sound, undamaged cargo** remaining after the general average act are calculated for general average purposes.

G06d.2 Equitable nature of general average

* There must be equality of contribution between the owner of property sacrificed and the owner of property saved, so that no interest profits by his sacrifice. **Property sacrificed** by a general average act must, therefore, always **contribute to its own loss**. This is shown in the example adjustment below.
* Any amount allowed as general average in respect of sacrifice of property is added to the damaged value of the particular property as an "amount made good". This principle preserves the **equitable nature of general average**, as shown in the following simple example.
* **A ship** valued at US$500,000 and loaded with 500 containers each worth US$1000 runs aground accidentally. During refloating operations one container is discharged, the costs of the operation being allowed as general average.

	US$
Value of ship at destination:	500,000
Sound value of cargo at destination 499 x $1,000:	499,000
Total contributory values:	999,000
(**Say**):	1,000,000
Total **General Average expenditure**:	1,000
	= 0.001% of total contributory values

Each interest must therefore contribute 0.001% of the contributory value of his property, as follows:

Consignee A's container jettisoned. Consignee A's loss:	1000
Consignee A's contribution to General Average fund = 0.001% x $1000:	1
Consignee A's contributory value at destination:	999
Consignee B's container saved intact. Value at destination:	1000
Consignee B's contribution to General Average fund = 0.001% x $1000:	1
Consignee B's contributory value at destination:	999

Ship owners will contribute 0.001% of the value of the ship = 0.001% x $500,000:   500
Cargo owners will together contribute 0.001% of the value of the saved cargo at destination = 0.001% x $499,000: 499
Total sum made good to Consignee A is therefore: 999

*   Consignee A has suffered a net loss of $1 or, like the other parties, 0.001% of the value of his interest in the adventure. He has not profited by the jettisoning of his goods, and all parties are equally out of pocket.

G06d.3 Simplified example of a general average adjustment

*   Assume that a vessel on a loaded voyage accidentally ran aground, was salvaged on a Lloyd's Open Form salvage agreement, and was towed to a port of refuge for repairs. Cargo was discharged and stored ashore to allow drydocking, bottom survey and repairs. The ship's crew was accommodated in a hotel during the drydocking.

*   The bottom was found to be damaged by the grounding, while the propeller and tailshaft were found to have been damaged during the refloating operation.

*   On completion of repairs the vessel was undocked, reloaded her cargo and continued on her voyage.

*   The salvors obtained security from the ship and cargo interests before the vessel left the port of refuge, the salvage award being set some time later by the Lloyd's Arbitration hearing.

*   The shipowners paid the costs of entering the port, discharging and reloading cargo, the costs of wages and maintenance of the crew, fuel, stores, etc. whilst making for and staying at the port of refuge.

*   The **adjustment of general average** was prepared as set out below:

	US$	General Average per YA Rules US$
Salvage awarded against ship $1,850,000 & cargo $1,295,000	3,145,000	
Allow per Rule VI		3,145,000
Port charges putting into and leaving port of refuge	165,000	
Allow per Rule X(a)		165,000
Cost of **repairs**:		
Accidental bottom damage repairs (**not allowed** as general average)	185,000	
Propeller, etc. repairs	65,000	
Allow per Rule XVIII		65,000
Cost of **drydocking**	100,000	
Allow 50%		50,000
Cost of **discharging, storage and reloading of cargo**	145,000	
Allow per Rule X(b) and (c)		145,000
Wages and maintenance of crew, fuel and stores, etc.	50,000	
Allow per Rule XI		50,000
Interest at 7% per annum and 2% commission allowed on General		
Average disbursements per Rules XX and XXI, say		510,000
		4,130,000
Ship's contributory value per Rule XVII		
Sound market value:	38,000,000	
Deduct: Damage ($185,000 + $65,000 + $100,000)	350,000	
	37,650,000	
Add: Made good ($65,000 + $50,000)	110,000	
	37,760,000	3,239,485
Cargo's contributory value per Rule XVII		
Sound CIF market value at destination:	11,000,000	

Deduct: Damage (found on arrival at destination)	620,000		
		10,380,000	890,515
		48,140,000	4,130,000

* **Ship and cargo both contribute** to the general average **equal proportions** (in this case approx. **8.6%**) of their respective contributory values. The **ship's proportion** is $3,239,485 while the **cargo's proportion** is $890,515.

G07 Claims

G07a HULL CLAIMS

* **Following any case of hull or machinery damage**, e.g. due to collision or grounding, the shipowner/manager's insurance department will normally immediately inform, via the broker, the lead hull and machinery insurer.
* If abroad, Lloyd's Agent will normally be notified.
* **Underwriters** or their agent, e.g. Lloyd's Agent, will **instruct a surveyor** to ascertain the nature, cause and extent of damage. In major casualty cases, the surveyor appointed is likely to be a **Salvage Association** surveyor.
* In the event of a **claim on a Lloyd's policy**, the client must contact the broker concerned to initiate the claims process. The broker will inform the leading underwriter at Lloyd's (who originally set the terms and conditions of the risk) and Lloyd's Claims Office, which acts on behalf of "following" Lloyd's underwriters. Once the validity of the claim has been checked and payment agreed, Lloyd's central accounting system will ensure that the claim is paid directly to the broker's account and the accounts of the underwriting syndicates are duly debited. Claims arising on syndicates no longer trading continue to be paid through a "run-off" company.

G07a.1 Documents and information required from the ship by the claims handler

* In addition to copies of the relevant insurance **policies** (which will be supplied by owners), the **documents and information listed below** may be required to accompany a claim lodged by owners against underwriters. If an **adjustment** is prepared, the **average adjuster** will extract the required information from the documents and incorporate it in the adjustment, but underwriters are in any case entitled to see the original documents and vouchers if they wish.
* Certain items forwarded will require the **endorsement of the underwriters' surveyor** as being fair and reasonable. The endorsement may be obtained either by the owners' superintendent at the time of survey or repair, or later through correspondence between the average adjuster and the surveyor.

G07a.1a General documents and information required

- include:
  - deck and engine room **log books** covering the casualty and the repair period;
  - **master's** and/or chief engineer's detailed **report** (as appropriate);
  - relevant **letters of protest**;
  - protests and extended **protests**;
  - underwriter's **surveyor's report**;
  - class **surveyor's report**;
  - owners' **superintendent's report**;
  - **receipted accounts for repairs** and/or any spare parts supplied by owners, in connection with repairs, endorsed by underwriters' surveyor as being fair and reasonable;
  - **accounts covering any drydocking and general expenses** relating to the repairs, endorsed as above;
  - accounts for all incidental disbursements at the port of repair, e.g. for port charges, watchmen, communications expenses, agency fees, etc.;
  - **details of fuel and engine room stores consumed** during the repair period (i.e. from the time of deviation to the port of refuge), together with the cost of replacement;
  - **accounts for owners' repairs effected concurrently** with damage repairs;
  - copies of **faxes and telexes sent** and details of long-distance calls made in connection with the casualty, together with their costs.
  - any **accounts rendered by surveyors, etc.**, with dates of payment where made.

G07a.1b Information required when the vessel has been removed for repairs

- includes:
  - the **reason** for the removal;
  - deck and engine room **log extracts** covering the removal passage of details of:
  - the last port prior to the repair port, and the first port thereafter;
  - details of the dates of arrival/departure at the relevant ports;
  - details of whether a **new cargo or charter** was booked on the removal to the repair port, together with information concerning any freight earned thereon;
  - details of any **new cargo** booked to be loaded following completion of repairs;
  - accounts for the **outward port charges at the last port** prior to the repair port, the **inward and outward port charges at the repair port**, and, if the vessel returns to the port from which she originally moved, the **inward port charges** at that port;
  - **portage bill** showing the wages of the officers and crew during the removal to the repair port, and also for the return passage if the vessel returns to her original port; the **cost of maintenance for the officers and crew** should also be stated;
  - details of **fuel and stores consumed** during the removal period, and the cost of their replacement;
  - accounts in respect of any **temporary repairs effected** solely to enable the vessel to move to the repair port.

G07a.1c Information required after a collision

- includes:
  - details of **steps taken to establish liability** for the collision and the eventual **settlement** made between the two parties (i.e. the apportionment of blame);
  - where a **recovery** has been attempted against the colliding vessel, a detailed copy of the **claim** put forward and all the items allowed from the claim put forward and all the items allowed from the claim by the owners of the colliding vessel together with accounts covering legal costs;
  - a detailed copy of any **claim received** from the other vessel, together with details of which items included in the claim have been agreed;
  - details of **efforts to limit liability**.

G07b P&I CLAIMS

* Where a member of a P&I club, e.g. a shipowner, makes any claim against his club, the **first $5 million** will be met by the club's own resources. In excess of $5 million, and **up to $30 million** the claim is divided among the member clubs in the **International Group Pool** (including the club making the claim), with the Pooling contribution of each club being calculated taking into account its entered tonnage, premium income and claims record in the Pool. For claims in excess of the Pool limit, the International Group arranges an **Excess of Loss reinsurance contract** in the market; this currently provides cover for **$2,000 million** ($2 billion) in excess of $30 million in relation to all types of claim except oil pollution, where the limit is $1,000 million ($1 billion)[9].

* Should a claim ever exceed the upper limit of the Excess of Loss Contract, it would then fall back on the Pool and be borne by each club *pro rata* according to its entered tonnage. Such a claim is called an "**overspill claim**", and would be funded by each club either from club reserves or by making a special "**overspill call**" on the membership. For most of the history of the P&I clubs there was no upper limit to cover, but there is now an upper limit of **$4.25 billion** on overspill claims. Some clubs have extensive reinsurance for overspill claims.

* The rules of most clubs require that a member gives **immediate notification** of any incident which could result in a claim or liability falling within the scope of the club's cover. Once a claim or potential claim has been notified, the club takes over the investigation and handling of the claim, often with the help of its correspondents, as well as surveyors and lawyers appointed by the club.

* In liaison with the member, the club will handle the claim to its conclusion. If the member proves to have a liability, the club will instruct him to **pay** the agreed amount to the third party claimant. Once the member has paid the claim, he may then seek **indemnity** (i.e. reimbursement) from the club in accordance with the club rules and the member's terms of entry.

* The **amount recoverable** from the club may be limited because of a special limit in the member's cover, or because the cover for a particular type of claim is subject to a **deductible**, i.e. an amount which the member has agreed to bear himself before he can claim from his club.

---

[9] The Excess of Loss contract, which is effected on behalf of the whole International Group, is one of the largest single insurance policies in the world and is currently led by Lloyd's, the risk being shared by a large number of major insurance companies in other leading insurance markets.

* A club may at times assist a member in handling claims which are not covered or only partially covered. An example of the latter case is **collision**, where a club will normally only cover one fourth of the member's liability for collision, with the hull underwriters cover the remaining three fourths. It is common for the hull underwriters in these cases to leave the handling of the claim to the club, so as to save duplication of action and costs, which are divided between the club and the hull underwriters in accordance with the percentage risk each is bearing.

G07c CARGO CLAIMS

* **Where cargo loss or damage is discovered** (usually by the receiver or consignee at the discharge port or destination), a Delivery Note or Consignment Note will be claused with a note of the loss or damage. The **cargo owner** will immediately inform his **insurer**; if the loss or damage is found outside the UK, this is done through the local **Lloyd's Agent** in the case of a Lloyd's policy. Where the goods were sold "CIF", the relevant Lloyd's Agent is noted on Certificate of Insurance, e.g. "Lloyd's Agent at Hong Kong", Hong Kong being the destination in this case.

* If the loss or damage value is likely to exceed about £250, underwriters will normally ask for a **Survey Report**. This is arranged by Lloyd's Agent, who can appoint surveyors and pay small claims locally.

* After the claim is quantified and documented, the **underwriter** settles the claim through Lloyd's Agent.

* The **underwriter** then decides (under the doctrine of **subrogation** (see G03b.1) whether or not claim is worth pursuing against the **carrier**. If he decides to pursue the claim, he immediately makes a written claim on the carrier; failure to claim may prejudice his right of recovery. The claim (including the surveyor's fee) is settled by the **carrier** in the currency stated in the policy or on the Certificate of Insurance.

* The **carrier**, if a P&I club member, then claims on his club policy.

* For notes on **cargo records** likely to be required by P&I club claims handlers, see H01c.3.

Section H

AT SEA

Section H Contents

H06 Communications and reports

H01 The voyage

H01a VOYAGE INSTRUCTIONS AND ADVICE

H01a.1 Company's instructions

* As part of the shipboard Safety Management System as required by the ISM Code, all shipowners and managers should issue **standing instructions** to their shipmasters.
* A company which does not issue and demand compliance with masters' standing instructions may not have a good defence to cargo and other claims in which **unseaworthiness** is alleged by a plaintiff.
* In the absence of company's standing instructions, compliance with the **ICS Bridge Procedures Guide** may be, and should be demanded by the owner and managers. Any company instructions should not conflict with the advice in the Guide. For a description of the Guide and its contents see H01a.10.

H01a.2 Charterer's instructions

* **Any charterer** should not order the vessel into:
  * the **Antarctic area**, unless the vessel meets statutory pollution requirements outlined at H01a.4;
  * the **500m safety zone** round any offshore installation, unless serving that installation (see H01a.5).
* **A voyage under a charterparty** must keep within the geographical limits of the **Voyage Clause** in the Crew Agreement (see E07c.1i). If the ship is permitted to venture beyond the agreed limits, the employer will be in **breach of contract** with each crew member who is party to the agreement.
* **A voyage charterer** generally has no authority to direct the **routeing** of the vessel. However, the vessel must always take the **shortest route** consistent with safety and the law. This is normally the **customary route** for the particular trade.
* **On a time charter**, while the **owner** is responsible for **navigational** matters, the **charterer** is normally responsible for matters connected with the ship's **employment** (i.e. commercial operations), and may lawfully give **directions** concerning her employment to the master in conformity with the charterparty's terms. This extends to directions as to the general **strategy** of the voyage, including voyage **routeing**, the law on this matter having been clarified in the *Hill Harmony* **ruling** by the House of Lords in which it was decided that the owner was in breach of his obligation to execute the voyage with the utmost despatch by refusing to follow the usual route.[1] The master may always refuse to carry out a charterer's instructions which **endanger the safety of the vessel and her cargo**. However, **safety** must always justify the master's conduct where he fails to follow the charterer's instructions. The judges referred to **guidelines** to differentiate between "**employment**" and "**navigation**" and drew a distinction between "**strategy**" (meaning the overall planning of the voyage) and "**tactics**" (meaning decisions made during the voyage, e.g. to alter course to avoid ice known to be in the vicinity). **Strategic decisions** are part of the commercial background of the charter and are therefore for the time charterer to decide. Only where a decision made by the master during the voyage includes **some element of seamanship** will it qualify as a **navigational** decision capable of overriding the time charterer's orders. The master still has a right to refuse to obey the time charterer's instructions on the grounds of **safety or other navigational hazard**, but the onus will be on the owner to justify the master's decision.
* The usual agreement in a **time charter** is that the charterer may employ the vessel only in **lawful trades**, carrying **lawful merchandise**, using only **safe ports and berths** and in some cases **safe anchorages** where the vessel can "safely lie always afloat". Ice-bound or other unsafe ports are usually expressly excluded unless the owner agrees otherwise.
* **Lightening at sea** is not normally permitted without the **permission of underwriters**, since this will usually be outside the terms of the Hull and Machinery policy.
* **Time charterers** will usually issue **instructions to the master** in an appendix to the time charterparty. Instructions may be given on matters such as sailing speed, hold or tank cleaning, bunkering scheme, loading scheme, radio communication scheme, arrival notices to be given to various parties (with addresses), accounting authority for radio messages, list of agents (with addresses), reports to be sent (e.g. log abstract, loading reports, daily reports of fuel consumption and average speed).

---

[1] The *Hill Harmony* was time-chartered for two trans-Pacific voyages. On advice from Oceanroutes, the charterer instructed the master to take the great circle route. The master decided, on the basis of personal experience, to take the longer rhumb line route, resulting in higher consumption of the charterer's bunkers. The charterer deducted his loss from the hire payment, which the owner sought to recover in an arbitration, which the charterer won. The owner won in his appeal to the High Court, and also in the Court of Appeal. The charterer then appealed to the House of Lords, which decided (in the year 2000) in the charterer's favour.

H01a.3 Breach of Institute Warranty Limits or Navigating Limits

* Where the **Institute Warranties** (sometimes called the **Institute Trading Warranties**) (see G04a.4) are attached to a Hull and Machinery insurance policy, the vessel is not permitted to trade in any of the high ice-risk areas listed, i.e. beyond "**Institute Warranty Limits**". Any venture into an excluded area will be a **breach of warranty** which should be immediately notified to the insurer (via the owner) so that **amended terms** may be agreed. The limits have been incorporated into **Clause 34 – Navigating Limits** – of the International Hull Clauses (01/11/02), but as **conditions** rather than warranties.
* Many **time charterparties** permit trading "**Worldwide within Institute Warranty Limits**" (often abbreviated to "**IWLs**") but with certain express **exclusions of countries or places of increased risk**. Common exclusions include Israel, Persian/Arabian Gulf, Cuba, Vietnam, Kampuchea, North Korea, Lebanon, Angola, Namibia, Syria, Libya, Somalia, Ethiopia, South Africa and the Orinoco.
* The master of a time-chartered ship should always check his copy of the charterparty for any such **prohibitions** and should immediately report to the owners if charterers order the vessel to an excluded country or place. (It may be agreed that time charterers have the option of breaching Institute Warranty Limits subject to prior approval of the owner and master, which is not to be unreasonably withheld, but in these cases the charterers must pay all additional expenses, including costs of additional premiums. Time charterers may also have the option of trading the vessel to certain excluded countries or places subject to the owner's prior consent, but in accordance with any recommendations of the owner's underwriters. Additional **war risk premiums**, risks of **blocking** and **trapping** and payment of any **war risk bonus to crew** will generally be for charterers' account.)
* In the event that charterers indicate their intention to breach Institute Warranty Limits (e.g. by ordering the vessel into the Great Lakes), the master should **contact the owner** for advice.

H01a.4 Statutory restrictions on ships entering Antarctic area

* The Antarctic is an area subject to special protection (including entry restrictions on ships) under the provisions of the Antarctic Treaty. For details see the **British Antarctic Survey website** at www.antarctica.ac.uk
* For details of the Protocol on Environmental Protection to the Antarctic Treaty (1991) see www.antarctica.ac.uk/AboutAntarctica/Treaty/protocol.html
* **Regulation 6A of the MS (Prevention of Pollution by Garbage) (Amendment) Regulations 1993** (SI 1993/1681) prohibits a UK ship from entering the Antarctic area (i.e. the sea area south of latitude 60° S) unless:
  * it has sufficient capacity for the retention on board of all garbage while operating in the area; and
  * it has concluded arrangements for the discharge of retained garbage at a reception facility after it has left the area.
* **Regulation 16(6) of the MS (Prevention of Oil Pollution) Regulations 1996** (SI 1996/2154) prohibits a UK ship from entering the Antarctic area unless:
  * it is fitted with a tank or tanks of sufficient capacity for the retention on board of all sludge, dirty ballast, tank washing water and other oily residues and mixtures while operating in the area; and
  * it has concluded arrangements to have such oily residues and mixtures discharged into a reception facility after it has left the area.

H01a.5 Statutory prohibition on entering offshore safety zones

* Under **sections 21-24 of the Petroleum Act 1987** all oil and gas installations on the UK Continental Shelf which project above the sea surface at any state of the tide, including those being constructed or dismantled, are automatically protected by **safety zones** extending to **500 metres** from the installation. New safety zones, where necessary, are established by statutory instruments bearing the title "The Offshore Installations (Safety Zones) Order (year)".
* In general, **all vessels are prohibited** under section 23(1) from entering any 500m safety zone established by virtue of the Act, and entry by an unauthorised vessel makes the owner, master and others who have contributed to the offence liable to a fine or imprisonment or both.
* Under **regulation 2 of the Offshore Installations (Safety Zones) Regulations 1987** (SI 1987/1331) the **prohibition** under section 23(1) on a vessel entering or remaining in a safety zone established around an installation by virtue of the Act **will not apply** to a vessel entering or remaining in the safety zone -
  * in connection with the laying, inspection, testing, repair, alteration, renewal or removal of any submarine cable or pipeline in or near that safety zone;
  * to provide services for, to transport persons or goods to or from, or under the authority of a Government department to inspect, any installation in that safety zone;

- if it is a vessel belonging to a general lighthouse authority performing duties relating to the safety of navigation; in connection with the saving or attempted saving of life or property;
- owing to stress of weather; or
- when in distress.

* **Support vessels** servicing installations, and other vessels listed above, should only enter a safety zone after consultation with the installation's offshore installation manager (OIM) to ensure that they do not endanger any other operations being carried out. OIMs may demand the **modification or termination** of any support vessel activity which they regard as hazardous.

* Masters should bear in mind that under the national laws of different coastal States, the **type of installation subject to a safety zone** may vary from State to State. It should always be assumed, therefore, that a safety zone exists unless information has been received to the contrary.

* Further details of the operation of safety zones are given in **Notice No. 20** of the Annual Summary of Notices to Mariners and **M.1290**.

H01a.6 Ships' routeing

* The **MS (Safety of Navigation) Regulations 2002** (SI 2002/1473) (see H01f.2) –
  - **revoke** and replace the MS (Mandatory Ships' Routeing) Regulations 1997 (SI 1997/1341).
  - **require compliance** by a ship to which the Regulations apply with **paragraph 7 of SOLAS regulation V/10** (which relates to **Ships' routeing**).

* **SOLAS regulation V/10.7** provides that a ship must use a mandatory ships' routeing system adopted by IMO as required for its category or cargo carried and in accordance with the relevant provisions in force unless there are compelling reasons not to use a particular ships' routeing system. Any such reason must be recorded in the ship's log.

* **SOLAS regulation V/10** and the **Guidance Notes to regulation V/10** in MCA's 2002 SOLAS Chapter V publication, including **Annex 5** (Use of IMO-Adopted Routeing Systems) supersede MGN 28 (Observance of Traffic Separation Schemes).

* The publication of *Ships' Routeing* by IMO is intended primarily for Administrations responsible for planning and supporting routeing systems for use by international shipping. **Part A** includes **the General Provisions on Ships' Routeing** which have been developed to ensure that all adopted routeing systems conform to the same general criteria and principles. **Parts B to F** include **descriptions of routeing systems** and **associated rules and recommendations on navigation** which have been adopted by IMO. There is no UK statutory requirement that a ship must carry *Ships' Routeing*.

* For notes on **adopted and unadopted traffic separation schemes**, see H02a.1b.

H01a.7 Weather routeing

* There is **no UK statutory requirement** for a ship to be weather routed. There may, however, be a contractual requirement under a charterparty for the owner to employ a routeing service.

* Some weather routeing organisations offer services providing an **analysis of a vessel's performance**, which assists the charterer and owner in showing whether there has been any **under-performance** during the charter period. For notes on the choice of route and the *Hill Harmony* ruling, see H01a.2.

H01a.8 Deep-sea pilotage

* **MGN 55** encourages masters to use the services of **deep sea pilots**, but only those who are certified by a Competent Authority in accordance with Council Directive 79/115/EEC concerning deep-sea pilotage in the North Sea and English Channel. MGN 55 lists the three UK bodies authorised under section 23(1) of the Pilotage Act 1987 to grant deep sea pilot certificates, i.e. **The Corporation of Trinity House** (in London), **The Corporation of Hull Trinity House and The Corporation of the Newcastle upon Tyne Trinity House**, as well as and the competent authorities for Belgium, France, Germany and the Netherlands.

* MGN 55 advises masters to be careful to **check the credentials** of anyone offering his services as a deep sea pilot, and draws attention to IMO Resolution A.486(XII) which recommends making use only of those pilots in possession of a **deep sea pilot's card**, an example of which is shown in the Annex to the MGN.

* **Providers of deep sea pilotage services** in the North Sea, English Channel and Skagerrak are listed in Admiralty List of Radio Signals (ALRS), Volume 6, Part 1.

H01a.9 Position reporting

* **M.1551** lists UK radio stations accepting AMVER reports from ships for transmission to the AMVER centre in New York. Ships fitted with satellite terminals can send messages direct to the AMVER centre at Southbury (USA) or via a British CES using the Inmarsat satellite system.
* For notes on the **AMVER system** see H06c.1a.

H01a.10 Bridge Procedures Guide

* The **Bridge Procedures Guide**, published by the International Chamber of Shipping, is not a statutory or mandatory document and is intended purely as guidance. Adherence to it is, however, recommended by most P&I clubs.
* **Part A** contains **Guidance to masters and navigating officers** with sections on Bridge organisation, Passage planning, Duties of the officer of the watch (OOW), and Operation and maintenance of bridge equipment. **Annexes** contain a specimen master/pilot exchange checklist, specimen wheelhouse poster, graphic card showing Required boarding arrangements for pilot, Distress alert and frequencies to use, and Guidance on steering gear test routines.
* **Part B** contains a set of **non-emergency checklists** for the following situations: B1: Familiarisation with bridge equipment; B2: Preparation for sea; B3: Preparation for arrival in port; B4: Pilotage; B5: Passage plan appraisal; B6: Navigation in coastal waters; B7: Navigation in ocean waters; B8: Anchoring and anchor watch; B9: Navigation in restricted visibility; B10: Navigation in heavy weather or in tropical storm areas; B11: Navigation in ice; B12: Changing over the watch; and B13: Calling the master.
* **Part C** contains a set of **Emergency checklists** including: C1: Main engine or steering failure; C2: Collision; C3 Stranding or grounding; C4: Man overboard; C5: Fire; C6: Flooding; C7: Search and rescue; C8: Abandoning ship. Additional appropriate checklists should be devised to suit the particular needs of the ship type and trade.

H01a.11 Master's discretion

* The **MS (Safety of Navigation) Regulations 2002** (SI 2002/1473) (see H01f.2) -
  - require compliance by a ship to which the Regulations apply with all paragraphs of **SOLAS regulation V/34**, which relates to **Safe navigation and avoidance of dangerous situations**.
  - revoke the **MS (Master's Discretion) Regulations 1997** (SI 1997/2886).
* **SOLAS regulation V/34.3** provides that the owner, charterer or the company, as defined in regulation IX/1 (i.e. the ISM Code), operating the ship or any other person must not prevent or restrict the master of a ship from taking or executing any decision which, in the master's professional judgement, is necessary for safe navigation and protection of the marine environment[2].
* The effect of **regulation V/34.3** is that the master has absolute discretion to take decisions in the interests of safe navigation and/or protection of the marine environment. (This does not mean, however, that the master of a time-chartered ship automatically has the right to take decisions as to the **voyage strategy**. For notes on the *Hill Harmony* decision, see H01a.2.)
* The **effect of regulation V/34.3** may mean that an **offence** is committed, for example -
  * where a shipowner, manager or charterer unduly pressures a master to delay accepting an offer of salvage services when a ship is in peril;
  * where a ship owner or operator unduly pressures a master of a ship navigating in fog to increase speed against the master's better judgement, in order to reach a berth by a particular time; or
  * where a ship owner or operator unduly pressures a master of a ship to sail when the master considers it imprudent to do so on account of a factor related to safe navigation, e.g. a bad weather forecast, or navigational aids out of order; or
  * where a time charterer or his supercargo pressures a master into taking a time- or fuel-saving course (say between certain islands) against the master's better judgement.

H01a.12 Temporary exclusion zones

* Section 100A of the Merchant Shipping Act 1995 -
  - was created by virtue of section 1 of the Merchant Shipping and Maritime Security Act 1997;

---

[2] **SOLAS regulation V/34.3** replaces regulation V/10.2, which was introduced following the *Amoco Cadiz* casualty, in which the decisions of the master concerning the acceptance of salvage services were unduly influenced by the charterer's instructions.

- applies where a **ship, structure** or **other thing** is in **UK waters** or in the waters above the **UK Continental Shelf** (UKCS) and is **wrecked, damaged or in distress**, and where **significant harm** (i.e. significant pollution or significant damage to persons or property) will or may occur as a direct or indirect result.
- gives the UK Secretary of State for Transport power to establish a **temporary exclusion zone** (TEZ) around the casualty, in which access is restricted.

* A TEZ will be made by the giving of a **direction** under section 100A, which must be published as soon as practicable in an appropriate manner for bringing it to the attention of persons likely to be affected by it.

* A TEZ may be identified by reference to the position of the casualty from time to time, and may be reduced in size. The direction establishing the zone may be revoked when necessary.

* Section 100B of the Merchant Shipping Act 1995 sets out **offences** in relation to TEZs.

* If a **direction** establishing a TEZ **states** that it is given for the purpose of preventing or reducing significant **pollution**, or the risk of significant pollution, in the UK, UK waters or sea over the UKCS, **no ship may enter** or remain in the TEZ (section 100B(1)).

* If a **direction** establishing a TEZ **does not state** that it is given for the purpose of preventing or reducing significant pollution, or the risk of significant pollution, in the UK, UK waters or UKCS waters, then -
- **no ship may enter** or remain in any part of the TEZ that is in **UK waters** (section 100B(3)(a));
- **no UK ship** may enter or remain in any part of a TEZ that is over the **UKCS** (section 100B(3)(b));
but -
- **a ship may enter** or remain in the TEZ only if it does so **in accordance with the direction** establishing the TEZ, or with the **consent of the MCA**, or in accordance with **Regulations** made under section 100B of the Act (section 100B(4);
- a **qualifying foreign ship** may enter a TEZ in exercise of its right of **transit passage** through straits used for international navigation (section 100B(5).

* Subject to the defence that the master did not know of the existence or area of the TEZ, the **penalty** on the owner or master of a ship that enters or remains in a TEZ in contravention of section 100B(1) or 100B(3) is, on summary conviction, a fine not exceeding **£50,000**, and on conviction on indictment, imprisonment for not more than 2 years or an unlimited fine, or both (section 100(B)(7)).

H01b SEAWORTHINESS

H01b.1 Seaworthiness at sea

* The obligation on the owner to provide a **seaworthy vessel** (i.e. a vessel that is technically seaworthy, cargo-worthy and fit for the intended voyage) *before* the voyage commences is absolute (see F07a.4). The common law recognises, however, that the merchant ship which is absolutely watertight in all weather conditions has not yet been built, since even the most well-found vessel will contort in a seaway, allowing water to penetrate the hatchcover seals, etc. Owners therefore cannot guarantee the seaworthiness of their vessels after leaving port, when they become subject to various **perils of the sea**[3].

* The requirements of the common law, as modified by Article III(1) of the Hague and Hague-Visby Rules (see F07c.2b), will be met if, at the time the vessel left her berth, she was in a seaworthy condition as far as could be ascertained by the exercise of **due diligence** (i.e. the reasonably careful inspection) by the owner, master and officers to see that she was **ready for sea**.

* The **Hamburg Rules** do not expressly mention seaworthiness or an obligation to exercise due diligence. However, the carrier's obligation under Article 5(1) to prove that he, his servants and his agents took all measures which could reasonably be required to avoid the occurrence and its consequences, would appear to impose an obligation to exercise due diligence at all times and all stages of the voyage.

* A merchant ship would probably be deemed **unseaworthy** in law if she proceeded on a voyage without:
- valid **statutory certificates**;
- a valid **Certificate (or Interim Certificate) of Class**;
- **proper stowage** and securing of cargo;
- **cargo care system** in good order;
- a **properly qualified master and crew**;
- the **proper crew complement**, as set out in the Safe Manning Document;
- appropriate **charts** and **publications** for the intended voyage, corrected up-to-date; and

---

[3] **"Perils of the sea"** have been defined as "fortuitous accidents or casualties, peculiar to transportation on navigable water, such as stranding, sinking, collision of the vessel, striking a submerged object, or encountering heavy weather or other unusual forces of nature". The ordinary corrosive action of seawater (which may cause a vessel to leak and founder) is not a peril of the sea, since it is not fortuitous, i.e. it does not happen by chance.

* sufficient **bunkers**, **stores** and **provisions** for the voyage.
* Provided the vessel **departs** on her voyage in a seaworthy condition (to the extent described above), she will normally remain covered by her insurers throughout the voyage to the next port, even when, technically, her seaworthiness may have been compromised by some accident, e.g. heavy weather damage or seawater shipped in heavy seas. The vessel would not be covered on her **next** voyage (or leg of the voyage), however, if she left the next port of call without her seaworthiness being restored.
* For seaworthiness requirements under voyage and time **marine insurance policies**, see G03e.1 and G03e.2.
* For requirements of Clause 4 – Classification and Clause 5 - Termination of the Institute Time Clauses - Hulls (1.11.95), see G04a.2d and G04a.2e respectively.
* A **passenger ship on an international voyage** might be regarded by a court as being unseaworthy if she is operated in non-emergency circumstances outside her **operational limitations**, as documented in accordance with SOLAS regulation V/30 on the **Operational Limitations Document** appended to the Passenger Ship Safety Certificate (see D03b.9).

H01b.2 Statutory implied obligation of owner in crew contracts as to ship's seaworthiness

* **Section 42 of the Merchant Shipping Act 1995** provides that in every contract of employment between the owner of a UK ship and its **master** or any **seaman** employed in it, there will be implied an obligation on the owner that the ship will be **kept in a seaworthy condition for the voyage during the voyage**. This implied obligation **cannot be contracted out of**.
* For a more detailed note on the provisions of section 42, see C03a.

H01b.3 Statutory obligation of owner or bareboat charterer as to ship's safe operation

* **Section 100 of the Merchant Shipping Act 1995** provides that it will be the duty of the **owner or bareboat charterer** of a UK ship, and the owner or bareboat charterer of any other ship within UK waters while proceeding to or from a port in the UK, to take all reasonable steps to secure that the ship is **operated in a safe manner**, unless the ship would not be proceeding to or from the port but for **weather conditions** or any other **unavoidable circumstances**.
* For a more detailed note on the provisions of section 100, see C03b.

H01c CARE OF CARGO AT SEA

H01c.1 Carrier's general duties

* The carrier must **perform the voyage agreed** in the contract of carriage, whether this is a contract evidenced by a bill of lading or a charterparty or other document.
* Where the contract of carriage is evidenced by a bill of lading or sea waybill and the **Hague Rules, Hague-Visby Rules** or **Hamburg Rules** are expressly incorporated by statute or agreement into the contract terms, the carrier's duties will be those set out in the relevant rules (see H01c.1a and F07c).
* Most P&I clubs publish **loss prevention literature** aimed at reducing cargo claims, and masters should ask their companies to place this literature on board. **Club managers** will also readily provide **information on cargo care** when requested by a master of an entered vessel.
* The carrier is a **bailee** in respect of the goods carried. For notes on **bailment** and the **master's duties as a bailee**, see E04f.1.

H01c.1a Carrier's duties under the Hague and Hague-Visby Rules

* **Article 3 of the Hague Rules** and **Article III of the Hague-Visby Rules** require the carrier to "…..properly and carefully load, handle, stow, carry, keep, care for, and discharge the goods carried". This means, for example, maintaining **proper procedures** in relation to the care of the cargo, including usual seamanlike practices such as operating ventilation systems properly and sounding bilges regularly, and also includes taking any necessary **special**

measures that may be required for particular commodities or items. The words "**properly and carefully**" mean what they say, and imply a greater degree of care than an obligation to "exercise due diligence".

H01c.1b Carrier's duties under the Hamburg Rules

* **Article 5 of the Hamburg Rules** provides that **the carrier is liable** for loss resulting from loss of or damage to the goods, as well as from delay in delivery, if the occurrence which caused the loss, damage or delay took place while the goods were in his charge as defined in Article 4, **unless** the carrier proves that he, his servants or agents took all measures that could reasonably be required to avoid the occurrence and its consequences.

H01c.2 Care and slaughter of livestock at sea

* The **Welfare of Animals (Transport) Order 1997** (SI 1997/1480) applies (subject to paragraphs (2) and (3) of the Order) to the transport of:
    * the following domestic animals: cattle, sheep, pigs, goats and horses;
    * poultry, domestic birds and domestic rabbits;
    * domestic dogs and domestic cats;
    * all other mammals (except man) and birds; and
    * other vertebrate animals and cold-blooded animals.
* **Article 4** contains **general provisions on the protection of animals in transport** and provides that no legal or natural person (i.e. company or private individual) may transport any animal in a way which causes or is likely to cause injury or unnecessary suffering to that animal (article 4(1)).
* Without prejudice to the generality of article 4(1), a **master** of a vessel must not transport any animal by sea if in his judgement the animal is **likely to be caused injury or unnecessary suffering** in the course of the transport due to adverse weather or sea conditions likely to be encountered during the voyage (article 4(2)).
* Any person transporting cattle, sheep, pigs, goats or horses must do so in accordance with Schedules 1 and 2 (article 4(3)). (Several other schedules contain transport requirements for poultry, domestic birds, rabbits, dogs, cats and other mammals or birds.)
* **Article 7** of the Order deals with the **treatment of sick animals**. Where animals fall ill or are injured during transport, the **person in charge of the animals** must ensure that they receive **first-aid treatment** as soon as possible, that they are given appropriate **veterinary treatment** and if necessary **are slaughtered** in a way which does not involve unnecessary suffering (regulation 7(1)).
* Without prejudice to the generality of regulation 7(1), where an animal which is being transported by sea **falls ill or is injured** during the journey, the **master** of the vessel must, if he considers it necessary having regard to the availability of appropriate veterinary treatment or of landing the animal without causing it unnecessary suffering, **cause it to be slaughtered** in a way which does not involve unnecessary suffering (regulation 7(2)).
* **Slaughtering** should be carried out with a "humane killer" weapon and ammunition in respect of which a **Firearms Certificate** (see D04u.1) should be in force and carried on board.
* **Article 8** of the Order sets out the **feeding and watering requirements** for different kinds of animal. In the case of cattle, sheep, pigs, goats and horses (except registered horses), the transporter must ensure that they are rested, and offered liquid and food during a journey at least in accordance with **Schedule 7** of the Order.
* **Article 9** provides that a transporter (e.g. ship operator) who transports **vertebrate animals on journeys of over 50km** must ensure that the persons to whom he entrusts the animals includes at least one "competent person" who has either specific training or "equivalent practical experience" qualifying him to handle and transport vertebrate animals and to administer, if necessary, appropriate care, and who has sufficient knowledge of and abilities in the competencies set out in Schedule 8 to enable him to safeguard the welfare of the animals being transported.
* **Article 10** provides that any person transporting animals must ensure that the animals are transported **without delay** to their place of destination.
* Government **authorisations and registrations** of transporters of vertebrate animals are dealt with by **article 12**.
* **Article 13** provides that where horses (other than registered horses), cattle, sheep, pigs or goats are traded between EU member States or exported to third countries, and the journey time exceeds 8 hours, a **route plan** is required to be made by the transporter on an official form and submitted to a Government official with an application for an Export Health Certificate. The approved documents are then returned to the transporter and must accompany the consignment throughout the journey.
* **MGN 99** advises owners and masters of their statutory responsibilities in relation to "competent persons" provided for by article 9.

H01c.3 Cargo records

* The P&I clubs stress the importance of **keeping records** in order to help defeat cargo claims. Claimants usually allege that any cargo damage noted has occurred during the loaded voyage, whereas in fact it is more likely to have occurred ashore.
* **Documentary evidence** required by P&I club claims handlers includes:
    * bilge, ballast and bunker sounding and pumping records;
    * cargo ventilation, humidity and temperature records;
    * records of unusual weather conditions, routeing details, warnings and weather reports;
    * records of hatch, access, hold and watertight door checks;
    * records of fire and safety equipment checks, including log entries of and records of training and safety exercises;
    * records of cargo securing and lashing rounds and checks;
    * records of cargo temperatures (heating or cooling) where appropriate;
    * records of inert gas and venting operations;
    * records of reefer defrosting and temperature control;
    * records of temperatures in fuel oil tanks below sensitive cargoes.
* For notes on **cargo claims**, see G07c.

H01d DEVIATION

H01d.1 Deviation references

* For notes on the **meaning of "deviation" in carriage of goods law and insurance law**, and other notes on deviation, see F07a.5.
* For notes on **use of a Deviation Clause** in a voyage charter party, see F05a.4.
* For a note on **deviations during the loaded voyage under a voyage charter**, see F05d.
* For notes on the **effect on hire of deviations under a time charter**, see F06c.6.
* For notes on **provisions relating to deviation in the Hague Rules and Hague-Visby Rules**, see F07c.2e.
* For notes on **provisions relating to deviation in the Marine Insurance Act 1906**, see G03f.1.
* For notes on deviation from a voyage for a **medical reason**, see H04c.4.

H01d.2 Barratry

- is defined in the Rules for Construction of Policy (Schedule 1, Marine Insurance Act 1906) as including "every wrongful act wilfully committed by the Master or Crew to the prejudice of the owner, or, as the case may be, the charterer".
- includes every kind of **fraud and wrong deliberately committed by the master or crew** with the intention of benefiting themselves at the expense of the shipowner or charterer.
- includes, for example:
    * **deviating** from the proper route for personal reasons;
    * **delaying the vessel's progress** for personal reasons; and
    * **selling cargo** for personal profit.
* **Clause 6 – Perils** – of the Institute Time Clauses - Hulls (1.11.95) (see G04a.2f) covers the assured for loss or damage caused by **barratry of the master, officers or crew** provided that the loss or damage did not result from want of due diligence by the Assured, Owners, Managers or Superintendents or any of their onshore management (e.g. port captains).

H01e ZONES OF COASTAL STATE JURISDICTION

H01e.1 Zones of jurisdiction established by UNCLOS

* **UNCLOS** (see A02a) provides for several **zones of coastal State jurisdiction**, including **internal waters**, **territorial sea**, **archipelagic waters**, **contiguous zone**, **fisheries zones**, **continental shelf** and **exclusive economic zone**. Waters beyond the jurisdiction of any coastal State are the **high seas**.
* **None of the coastal zones is obligatory** and coastal States may choose the types of zones they wish to claim and the distances from their coasts that they wish them to extend to, subject to **prescribed maximum limits**.
* **Jurisdiction of the coastal State** within zones other than internal waters **does not include sovereignty**; the coastal State has limited rights only.
* For a list of **claims of individual maritime States**, see **Annual Notice to Mariners No. 12** (National Claims to Maritime Jurisdiction) in the Annual Summary of Admiralty Notices to Mariners (NP247). This lists, for each State, the width of the Territorial Sea (TS), Contiguous Zone (CZ), Exclusive Economic Zone (EEZ), and (where no EEZ is claimed) Fishery Zone (FZ).
* Since the limits of the various zones as claimed by different maritime States vary from one State to another, it should never be assumed by a shipmaster that his vessel is either within or outside a particular zone simply by reference to the vessel's distance from a State's coastline.

H01e.1a Internal waters

* **Internal waters** extend from the shore to the **baseline** from which the territorial sea is measured, and form part of the **national waters** of the coastal State.
* All vessels, whether owned privately or commercially, by the act of voluntarily entering internal waters, place themselves **within the jurisdiction of the coastal State**.
* Foreign flag vessels have a right of **innocent passage** through internal waters in three cases:
  * when baselines which have been redrawn enclose waters previously to seaward of the baselines;
  * in cases of *force majeure*, i.e. when vessels enter internal waters involuntarily due to distress, stress of weather or mechanical breakdown (in such cases jurisdiction remains with the flag State);
  * in the case of **warships and other public vessels**: these are granted special status in international law as they are regarded as agents of the sovereign. All sovereigns are immune from the jurisdiction of other States and their vessels are granted immunity, provided they enter internal waters with the coastal State's consent.
* While merchant ships are subject to their jurisdiction, there is a tendency for coastal States not to enforce their own laws on foreign-flag vessels in internal waters except in cases where their "particular interests are engaged", e.g.:
  * when an offence by the vessel affects the peace and good order of the port (including breach of customs and immigration regulations);
  * when the master of the vessel requests the coastal State to assert jurisdiction (e.g. when passengers are disorderly);
  * when a person other than a crew member (e.g. a stevedore) is involved; or
  * when the vessel breaches local regulations on pollution, navigation, pilotage, etc.

H01e.1b Territorial sea

- may extend to **12 nautical miles** from the baseline. (The effect of this is that over 100 international straits between 6 and 24 miles wide, including Dover Strait, have lost their "high seas" corridors.) The UK extended its 3-mile limit to 12 miles following the passing of the Territorial Sea Act 1987.
- is also part of the **national waters** of the coastal State but has a different juridical status from internal waters, mainly in that foreign flag vessels have a right of **innocent passage** through it.
* **Passage is "innocent"** so long as it is not prejudicial to the peace, good order or security of the coastal State. Operations taking place on or from a foreign merchant ship which may be considered by coastal State authorities to be **non-innocent** include sub-sea operations (such as diving, cable-laying or maintenance, dredging, etc.) operating aircraft, research or surveying operations, ship-to-ship cargo transfer, embarking persons or goods contrary to customs, fiscal, immigration or sanitary regulations, wilful and serious pollution, etc.
* The **right of innocent passage can be suspended**, but only "temporarily in specified areas....if such suspension is essential for the protection of (the coastal State's) security, which includes the conduct (of its own) weapons exercises" (Article 25(3)).
* Vessels on passage through the territorial sea are under an obligation to ensure their **innocence**. Activities not considered "innocent" are: threat or use of force against the coastal State; weapons practices; intelligence-gathering; propaganda activities; operation of aircraft; landing or taking on board of any military device; breaches of the

customs, fiscal, immigration and sanitary laws of the coastal State; acts of wilful and serious pollution; fishing; research and surveying activities; interference with the communications and any other facilities and installations of the coastal State; any other activity not having a direct bearing on passage (Article 19).

* Vessels must also comply with legislation which further affects the conduct of innocent passage, including regulations dealing with: the safety of navigation and the regulation of maritime traffic; the protection of navigational aids and facilities and other facilities and installations; the protection of cables and pipelines; the conservation of living resources; the enforcement of fisheries laws and regulations; the protection of the marine environment; the control of scientific research and hydrographic surveying; the enforcement of customs, fiscal, immigration and sanitary laws; and vessels are also obliged to comply with the Collision Regulations (Article 19).

* Another important distinction between the territorial sea and internal waters is that, in internal waters, the coastal State can, with the exceptions listed above, exercise jurisdiction over all vessels. In the territorial sea it should not exercise criminal jurisdiction except:

  • if the consequences of a crime extend to the coastal State;
  • if a crime disturbs the peace of the country or the good order of the territorial sea;
  • if the master of a vessel or an agent of a flag State requests the coastal State to exercise jurisdiction; or
  • if jurisdiction is necessary to suppress the illicit traffic of narcotic drugs or psychotrophic substances. (Article 27).

* In civil matters the coastal State can only exercise jurisdiction over vessels if they are passing through the territorial sea after leaving internal waters (Article 28).

* **Straits transit passage** may be made by ships. States bordering straits may not impede transit passage and must give appropriate publicity to any navigational dangers. Transit passage cannot be suspended, but coastal States have a limited right to regulate passage through straits. They may establish sea lanes and traffic separation schemes which vessels must observe.

* States may also enact **legislation** concerning: the safety of navigation; the prevention, reduction and control of pollution, fishing activity, and customs, fiscal, immigration and sanitary arrangements. Vessels must comply with these laws when passing through straits; if they do not, the flag State can be held responsible. Ships on transit passage must comply with international regulations, procedures and practices for: safety at sea, collision avoidance, and the prevention, reduction and control of pollution from ships.

* The **UK Government** does not recognise claims to territorial seas exceeding 12 nautical miles.

* The **UK** claims a territorial sea of 12 miles. Waters within the seaward limits of the territorial sea of the UK (as well as waters in any area designated under section 1(7) of the Continental Shelf Act 1964) are known as "**United Kingdom controlled waters**".

H01e.1c Archipelagic waters

- can only be established for **mid-ocean archipelagic States** (e.g. Fiji) which are constituted wholly by one or more archipelagos and may include other islands (Article 46).
- have a similar status to that of the territorial sea, but the coastal State is bound by a number of additional obligations regarding access to traditional fishing grounds, for other legitimate activities and for the maintenance and replacement of existing submarine cables (Article 51).
* As in the territorial sea, foreign flag vessels have a right of **innocent passage** through archipelagic waters (Article 52).

H01e.1d Contiguous zone

- can extend **12 nautical miles beyond the territorial sea** limit.
- consists of a combination of **revenue** and **public health** or **quarantine** jurisdiction.
- allows the coastal State to detain vessels beyond the territorial sea if there are **reasonable grounds for assuming they are about to violate customs or public health regulations** (Article 33), e.g. vessels being used to smuggle narcotics, guns or illegal immigrants into the coastal State. Vessels carrying noxious or dangerous substances or waste may be turned away on public health or environmental grounds.
* **The UK Government** does not recognise claims to contiguous zones exceeding 24 nautical miles.
* The **UK** does not claim a contiguous zone.

H01e.1e Fisheries zones (IFZ and EFZ)

* Although not specifically mentioned in UNCLOS, there is a recognised **inshore fisheries zone** (IFZ) of 12 nautical miles within which the coastal State may exercise exclusive rights to living resources. Beyond this is the **extended fisheries zone** (EFZ) extending to a maximum distance of **200 miles** and within which coastal States may exercise preferential rights over fish stocks.

* Any fishing vessel, even when only transiting a zone and otherwise exercising the right of innocent passage, must observe the **fisheries regulations** in force in the zone.
* The **UK Government** does not recognise claims to fisheries zones exceeding 200 nautical miles.
* The **UK** claims an EFZ of 200 miles.

H01e.1f Continental shelf

- is **defined geologically** and may extend well beyond 200 miles from the baseline. A **maximum of 350 miles** is specified.
- is a **resource zone** (and not a security zone), and does not form part of the territory of the coastal State.
* The seas above the continental shelf remain "high seas" if an EFZ (see above) is declared, but not if an EEZ (see below) is declared.
* The **resources** covered are "mineral and other non-living resources of the sea-bed and subsoil together with living organisms belonging to sedentary species" (Article 77).
* **Rights to the resources** of the shelf are exclusive to the coastal State. The coastal State has the "exclusive right to construct and to authorise and regulate the construction, operation and use of artificial islands, installations and structures, for the purposes of exploiting the resources of the shelf" (Article 60). The coastal State has exclusive jurisdiction over these "with regard to customs, fiscal, health, safety and immigration laws and regulations".
* **Safety zones** of not more than 500 metres may be established within which the coastal State "may take appropriate measures to ensure the safety of navigation and of the artificial islands, installations and structures" within them. (Safety zones have been established around oil and gas installations on the UK Continental Shelf and criminal and civil UK jurisdiction has been extended to these zones.)
* The **UK** claims jurisdiction over its continental shelf and designates the area of its jurisdiction in the Continental Shelf Act 1964 (c.29).

H01e.1g Exclusive economic zone (EEZ)

- can extend to a maximum of **200 nautical miles** from the baseline.
* Within the EEZ the coastal State has rights and duties in relation to **natural resources**.
* Freedom of navigation is the same as on the high seas (see H01e.1h). However, in the interests **of safety near offshore installations**, coastal States may **restrict navigation** in the EEZ.
* If there is no EEZ, high seas commence where territorial seas end. If an EEZ has been declared, the coastal State's rights and jurisdiction are increased to the extent that the zone can no longer be described as "high seas".
* The **UK Government** does not recognise claims to EEZs exceeding 200 nautical miles.
* The **UK** does not claim an EEZ.

H01e.1h High seas

- are all parts of the sea that are not included in the EEZ, territorial sea or internal waters of a State, or in the archipelagic waters of an archipelagic State (Article 86).
- are open to all States, whether coastal or land-locked. **Freedom of the high seas** comprises freedom of: navigation; overflight; to lay submarine cables and pipelines; to construct artificial islands and other installations permitted under international law; fishing; and scientific research (Article 87).
* **Warships** on the high seas have complete immunity from the jurisdiction of any State other than the flag State (Article 95).
* **Ships owned or operated by a State** and used only on government non-commercial service on the high seas have complete immunity from the jurisdiction of any State other than the flag State (Article 96).
* In the event of a collision or any other incident of navigation concerning a ship on the high seas, no penal or disciplinary proceedings may be commenced against the master or any other person in the service of the ship except by the judicial or administrative authorities either of the **flag State** or **the State of which that person is a national**. Only the State which has issued a master's certificate or certificate of competence or licence shall be competent to withdraw the certificate, even if the holder is not a national of the issuing State. No arrest or detention of the ship, even as a matter of investigation, may be ordered except by the **flag State authorities** (Article 97).
* There is a **duty to render assistance** to persons in danger of being lost, to **proceed to the assistance of persons in distress** and, after a collision, to **render assistance and exchange identification information** with the other ship (Article 98).
* **Other "high seas" provisions** cover ship registration, flag State obligations, prevention of the slave trade, piracy, seizure of ships, illicit narcotics trafficking and unauthorised broadcasting. For enforcement purposes, there are provisions for relevant rights of visit, seizure, arrest and hot pursuit.

H01f SAFETY OF NAVIGATION

H01f.1 SOLAS Chapter V (Safety of Navigation)

- **was substantially revised** in 2000 to reflect advances and growth in technology. The revised Chapter V was adopted in December 2000 and came into effect on 1 July 2002. (The replaced 1974 chapter had come into effect in 1980.)
- **contains 35 regulations** (as listed below), compared to 23 in the old chapter. An Appendix to the revised Chapter V contains rules for the management, operation and financing of the North Atlantic ice patrol, while new SOLAS Appendices contain specimens of a Record of Equipment for the Passenger Ship Safety Certificate (Form P) and a Record of Equipment for the Cargo Ship Safety Equipment Certificate (Form E), which have also been revised to take account of the requirements of the new Chapter V.
- **contains new requirements** for the fitting of:
  - an **automatic identification system** (AIS) in all ships of 300gt and over on international voyages, cargo ships of 500gt and over not engaged on international voyages and passenger ships irrespective of size (regulation V/19.2.4);
  - a **global navigation satellite system** (GNSS) or terrestrial radio-navigation system, or other means to establish and update the ship's position automatically in all ships, irrespective of size (regulation V/19.2.1.6);
  - a **voyage data recorder** (VDR) in all passenger ships (of any tonnage) and other ships of 3000gt and over (regulation V/20.1);
- **is given effect in the UK** by the **MS (Safety of Navigation) Regulations 2002** (SI 2002/1473) (see H01f.2).
* **Regulations of Chapter V** are numbered as follows: **1**. Application; **2**. Definitions; **3**. Exemptions and equivalents; **4**. Navigational warnings; **5**. Meteorological services and warnings; **6**. Ice Patrol Service; **7**. Search and rescue services; **8**. Life-saving signals; **9**. Hydrographic services; **10**. Ships' routeing; **11**. Ship reporting systems; **12**. Vessel traffic services; **13**. Establishment and operation of aids to navigation; **14**. Ships' manning; **15**. Principles relating to bridge design, design and arrangement of navigational systems and equipment and bridge procedures; **16**. Maintenance of equipment; **17**. Electromagnetic compatibility; **18**. Approval, surveys and performance standards of navigational systems and equipment and voyage data recorder; **19**. Carriage requirements for shipborne navigational systems and equipment; **20**. Voyage data recorders; **21**. International Code of Signals; **22**. Navigation bridge visibility; **23**. Pilot transfer arrangements; **24**. Use of heading and/or track control systems; **25**. Operation of main source of electrical power and steering gear; **26**. Steering gear: Testing and drills; **27**. Nautical charts and nautical publications; **28**. Records of navigational activities; **29**. Life-saving signals to be used by ships, aircraft or persons in distress; **30**. Operational limitations; **31**. Danger messages; **32**. Information required in distress messages; **33**. Distress messages: Obligations and procedures; **34**. Safe navigation and avoidance of dangerous situations; **35**. Misuse of distress signals; **Appendix**; Rules for the management, operation and financing of the North Atlantic Ice Patrol. Some of the regulations apply only to Contracting Governments. Some apply only to Administrations (e.g. the MCA). Some regulations or certain paragraphs of regulations apply to ships. **Those regulations or paragraphs which apply to ships** are listed in the table at H01f.2.

H01f.2 Safety of Navigation Regulations

* The **MS (Safety of Navigation) Regulations 2002** (SI 2002/1473) -
  - **give effect** in the UK to the provisions of the revised SOLAS chapter V (see H01f.1) which came into effect on 1 July 2002.
  - **consist** of regulations numbered as follows: **1**. Citation and commencement; **2**. Interpretation; **3**. Repeals and revocations, and consequential amendments; **4**. Application; **5**. Safety of navigation requirements; **6**. Supplementary provisions on safety of navigation requirements; **7**. Exemptions and allowance for equivalents; **8**. Restrictions on the granting of exemptions; **9**. Approvals; **10**. Offences and penalties; **11**. Detention; **Schedule 1**. Classification of ships; **Schedule 2**. Repeals and revocations; **Schedule 3**. Consequential amendments; **Schedule 4**. Supplementary provisions on safety of navigation requirements; **Schedule 5**. Offences and penalties.
  - **revoke** (by virtue of regulation 3(1)) the following SIs:
    - MS (Automatic Pilot and Testing of Steering Gear) Regulations 1981 (SI 1981/571);
    - MS (Passenger Ships of Classes IV, V, VI and VI(A) – Bridge Visibility) Regulations 1992 (SI 1992/2357);
    - MS (Navigational Equipment) Regulations 1993 (SI 1993/69);
    - MS (Mandatory Ship Reporting) Regulations 1996 (SI 1996/1749);

- • MS (Navigational Warnings) Regulations 1996 (SI 1996/1815);
- • MS (Mandatory Ships' Routeing) Regulations 1997 (SI 1997/1341);
- • MS (Master's Discretion) Regulations 1997 (SI 1997/2886);
- • MS (Navigation Bridge Visibility) Regulations 1998 (SI 1998/1419);
- • MS (Distress Messages) Regulations 1998 (SI 1998/1691);
- • MS (Co-operation with Search and Rescue Services) Regulations 1998 (SI 1998/1692);
- • MS (Carriage of Nautical Publications) Regulations 1998 (SI 1998/2647); and
- • MS (Pilot Transfer Arrangements) Regulations 1999 (SI 1999/17).
- - **apply**, subject to certain provisos, to all UK ships wherever they may be and to all other ships while they are in UK waters (regulation 4(1)).
- - **replace** the requirements of the revoked regulations listed above with a requirement for ships to comply with various provisions of SOLAS Chapter V (regulation 5(1)). These requirements, which are listed in regulation 5(2), are explained in the **MCA's 2002 SOLAS Chapter V publication** (see H01f.2a).
- - **do not generally apply** to warships and naval auxiliaries, non-UK ships which are owned or operated by a SOLAS Contracting Government and are used only on government non-commercial service, or to ships which navigate solely on the Great Lakes of North America and their connecting and tributary waters.
* Certain regulations or paragraphs of regulations are not applicable to particular categories of ship. The paragraphs applying to ships, and the UK ships to which particular regulations do not apply, are set out in tabular form in Annex 2 to the MCA's 2002 SOLAS V publication (see H01f.2a).
* Under regulation 5(1), and subject to regulations 5(3) and 5(4), **a ship to which the Regulations apply must comply with those requirements referred to in regulation 5(2)** as applying in relation to a ship of its description. The requirements referred to in regulation 5(2) are set out in the MCA's 2002 SOLAS V publication (see H01f.2a) and are shown in the following table.

SOLAS V regulation	Title of regulation	Paragraphs to be complied with by ships	Associated Annexes of 2002 SOLAS V publ'n	SBC ref.
7	Search and rescue services	3	-	D04t.7, H04b.14
10	Ships' routeing	7	5	H01a.6
11	Ship reporting systems	7	-	H06c.2
17	Electromagnetic compatibility	2 and 3	-	D04b.6
18	Approval, surveys and performance standards of navigational systems and equipment and voyage data recorder	1, 2, 3, 7 and 8	8, 9, 10	D04b.3 (Equip) D05b.7 (VDR)
19	Carriage requirements for shipborne navigational systems and equipment	All	11, 12	B04a.4, D04n.1
20	Voyage data recorders	1	10, 20	D05b.7
21	International Code of Signals	All	-	D04o
22	Navigation bridge visibility	All	-	D03a.4
23	Pilot transfer arrangements	All	21	I01b.9
24	Use of heading and/or track control systems	All	18	H01f.4
25	Operation of main source of electrical power and steering gear	All	18	H01f.3
26	Steering gear: Testing and drills	All	18	I07i.4
27	Nautical charts and nautical publications	All	3	D04o
28	Records of navigational activities	All	22	D05b.8
29	Life-saving signals to be used by ships, aircraft or persons in distress	All	-	D04w
30	Operational limitations	All	23	D03b.9, H01b.1
31	Danger messages	1 and 4	-	H06d
32	Information required in danger messages	1, 2, 4 and 5	-	H06d
33	Distress messages: Obligations and procedures	1 and 2	-	H04b.1, H04b.2, H04b.3
34	Safe navigation and avoidance of dangerous situations	All	25	H01a.12, H01f.5

* A ship to which the Safety of Navigation Regulations apply must comply with such of the requirements as apply in relation to a ship of its description and are set out in any subsequent MCA publication amending or replacing the 2002 SOLAS V publication (regulation 5(3)). Requirements specified in any such subsequent publication will be alternative or additional requirements that relate to amendments of SOLAS Chapter V regulations (regulation 5(4)).

* Where there is a **footnote** to a SOLAS chapter V regulation, and the footnote specifies an **IMO recommendation, resolution, guidance, code or other document** which sets out a standard, that footnote must be treated as a **requirement** for the purposes of regulation 5(1) or (3), as the case may be (regulation 5(5))[4].
* Where a SOLAS chapter V regulation, or an IMO Recommendation, Resolution, Guidance, Code or other document setting out a standard with which a ship must comply by virtue of the Safety of Navigation Regulations, refers to "should", that word must be construed as "shall" for the purposes of the Safety of Navigation Regulations (regulation 5(6)).
* Nothing in regulations 24 to 26 of SOLAS chapter V relating to the use of an automatic pilot will override special rules made by an appropriate authority for roadsteads, harbours, rivers, lakes or inland waterways connected with the high seas and navigable by sea-going ships; for these purposes an "appropriate authority" means any person empowered by law to make the special rules (regulation 5(7)).
* **Regulation 6** provides that Schedule 4 (Supplementary provisions) will have legal effect.
* **Regulation 7** provides for the granting of **exemptions** and allows for **equivalents**, subject to regulation 8. Regulation 7(5) permits conditional exemptions for classes of ships or individual ships from the requirements of SOLAS regulations V/18, 19 or 20. Regulation 7(6) permits conditional exemptions from the requirements of SOLAS regulation V/22 for ships·of unconventional design. Regulation 7(7) The Secretary of State permits conditional exemptions from the requirements of SOLAS regulation V/26(1) and (2) for ships which regularly engage on voyages of less than 24 hours duration and which carry out checks and tests required by those paragraphs at least once every week.
* Regulation 8 sets out **conditions** for the granting of **exemptions** under regulation 7.
* Regulation 9 provides for the granting of written **approvals** by the MCA where a SOLAS chapter V regulation refers to any thing requiring approval by, the satisfaction of, or acceptance by the Administration.
* Regulation 10 provides that Schedule 5 (offences and penalties) will have legal effect.
* Regulation 11 provides for **detention** of any ship failing to comply with the Regulations.
* **Schedule 1** contains a **Classification of ships** in Classes I to XII and A, B, C and D. This is similar to the classification in the MS (Life-Saving Appliances for Ships other than Ships of Classes III to VI(A)) Regulations 1999 (SI 1999/2721), as amended by SI 2000/2687 (see D04c).
* **Schedule 2** contains a list of **Repeals and revocations** made under regulation 3(1). Four subsections of the Merchant Shipping Act 1995, concerning navigational warnings, are repealed. Twelve SIs are revoked. Regulation 38 of the MS (Life-Saving Appliances for Ships other than Ships of Classes III to VI(A)) Regulations 1999 (SI 1999/2721) is revoked.
* **Schedule 3** contains **Consequential amendments** made under regulation 3(3). Minor amendments are made to section 93 of the Merchant Shipping Act 1995, the Official Log Books Regulations and the Survey and Certification Regulations.
* **Schedule 4** contains **Supplementary provisions** on Safety of Navigation requirements made under regulation 6. These amplify certain requirements of regulations 7, 10, 11, 21, 23, 24, 25, 26, 31 and 33.
* **Schedule 5** sets out a list of **Offences and penalties** under regulation 10.

H01f.2a 2002 SOLAS Chapter V publication

* **Safety of Navigation – Implementing SOLAS Chapter V -**
  - is an **MCA publication** intended to assist understanding and compliance with the provisions of SOLAS Chapter V's regulations and giving practical guidance on how the regulations should be implemented.
  - is published on the **MCA website** in the "Campaigns and Publications" pages. (Click on "Regulations".)
  - is published on a **CD-ROM** available from the MCA at no charge.
  - is published in **book format** and is available from The Stationery Office (see B04a.3a) at the address shown in **MIN 135**.
  - **supersedes**, in conjunction with the SOLAS chapter V regulations, MGN 28, MGN 54, MGN 57, MGN 72, MGN 109, MGN 133, MGN 153, MGN 166, M.760, M.1104, M.1638, M.1641, MSN 1688 and MSN 1716.
  - for each of the thirty-five SOLAS V regulations, **contains**:
    * a **summary** of what each regulation relates to;
    * the **full text** of each regulation;
    * MCA's **guidance notes** on the regulation.
* The document contains **25 annexes**, as listed below, which are linked to the Guidance Notes for certain regulations and contain further guidance and relevant documents such as IMO resolutions.

---

[4] An example of such a footnote is in SOLAS regulation V/33, which refers to the IAMSAR Manual (see H04b.12a) and therefore makes IAMSAR a statutory requirement for the purposes of regulation 5(1) of the Safety of Navigation Regulations.

Annex	Annex title	Related SOLAS V regulations	Related M Notices	SBC ref.
1	Categories of waters and classes of ships		MSN 1758	D04c
2	Table of requirements for ships	All		H01f.2
3	Nautical charts and publications	19, 21, 27	MGN 194	D04o
4	WMO maritime services	5	-	
5	Use of IMO-adopted routeing systems	10	M.1642 MGN 128	H01a.6
6	Principles of Safe Manning	14	MSN 1682	E03b.2a
7	Equipment Manuals – IEC requirements	16	-	D04n.1
8	Performance standards and type approval	18, 19, 20	-	D04b.3
9	IMO Performance Standards for Navigational Equipment	18, 19, 20	-	D04b.3
10	Voyage data recorders (VDRs)	20	-	D05b.7
11	Navigation equipment – new ships	19, 20	-	D04n
12	Navigation equipment – existing Ships	19	-	D04n
13	Magnetic compass	19	-	D04n.2
14	Electronic charts	19	MGN 194	D04o.1
15	Radar reflectors	19	-	-
16	Radar equipment	19	-	-
17	Automatic identification systems (AIS)	19	-	D04n.1h
18	Steering gear, heading and track control systems	19, 24, 25, 26	-	I07i.4
19	High Speed Craft Code – Chapter 13	19	-	D03i
20	Inspection and survey of navigational equipment	19	-	D04n
21	Pilot transfer arrangements	23	-	I01b.9
22	Recording of navigational events	28	-	D05b.8
23	Passenger ship – operational limitations	30	-	D03b.9
24	Voyage planning	34	-	I07i.2
25	Guidelines for voyage planning – IMO Resolution A.893(21)	34	-	I07i.2

* The summaries and Guidance Notes, including any annexes, have no statutory force.

H01f.3 Operation of steering gear power units

* The **MS (Safety of Navigation) Regulations 2002** (SI 2002/1473) (see H01f.2) require compliance by a ship to which the Regulations apply with **SOLAS regulation V/25** (which relates to **Operation of main source of electrical power and steering gear**).
* **SOLAS regulation V/25.1** provides that in areas where navigation demands special caution, ships must have **more than one steering gear power unit in operation** when such units are capable of simultaneous operation.
* **SOLAS regulations V/24, V/25 and V/26**, together with the **Guidance Notes** in MCA's 2002 SOLAS Chapter V publication, including **Annex 18** (Steering Gear, Heading & Track Control Systems), supersede the MS (Automatic Pilot and Testing of Steering Gear) Regulations 1981 (SI 1981/571) and MGN 54.

H01f.4 Use of heading and/or track control systems

* The **MS (Safety of Navigation) Regulations 2002** (SI 2002/1473) (see H01f.2) require compliance by a ship to which the Regulations apply with **SOLAS regulation V/24** (which relates to **Use of heading and/or track control systems**).
* **SOLAS regulation V/24.1** provides that in areas of high traffic density, in conditions of restricted visibility and in all other hazardous navigational situations where heading and/or track control systems are in use, it must be possible to establish manual control of the ship's steering immediately.
* **SOLAS regulation V/24.2** provides that in circumstances as above, the officer in charge of the navigational watch must have available without delay the services of a qualified helmsperson who must be ready at all times to take over steering control.
* **SOLAS regulation V/24.3** provides that the change-over from automatic to manual steering and vice versa must be made by or under the supervision of a responsible officer.
* **SOLAS regulation V/24.4** provides that the manual steering must be tested after prolonged use of heading and/or track control systems, and before entering areas where navigation demands special caution.
* SOLAS regulation V/24, together with regulation V/25 (see H01f.3) and V/26 (see I07i.4) supersede the MS (Automatic Pilot and Testing of Steering Gear) Regulations 1981 (SI 1981/571).
* SOLAS regulations V/24, V/25 and V/26 and the Guidance Notes to the regulations in the MCA's 2002 SOLAS V publication supersede MGN 54.

H01f.5 Safe navigation and avoidance of dangerous situations

* The **MS (Safety of Navigation) Regulations 2002** (SI 2002/1473) (see H01f.2) require compliance by a ship to which the Regulations apply with **SOLAS regulation V/34**, which relates to **Safe navigation and avoidance of dangerous situations**.
* **SOLAS regulation V/34.1** provides that **prior to proceeding to sea**, the master must ensure that the intended voyage has been **planned** using the appropriate nautical charts and nautical publications for the area concerned, taking into account the guidelines and recommendations developed by the IMO[5].
* **SOLAS regulation V/34.2** provides that the voyage plan must identify a route which:
  * takes into account any relevant ships' routeing systems (2.1);
  * ensures sufficient sea room for the safe passage of the ship throughout the voyage (2.2);
  * anticipates all known navigational hazards and adverse weather conditions (2.3); and
  * takes into account the marine environmental protection measures that apply, and avoids, as possible, actions and activities which could cause damage to the environment (2.4).
* **Regulation V/34** and the **Guidance Notes** to regulation V/34 in MCA's 2002 SOLAS Chapter V publication, including **Annexes 24 and 25**, supersede MGN 72 and MGN 166.
* For notes on **SOLAS regulation V/34.1** and V/**34.2** (Voyage planning), see I07i.2.
* For notes on **SOLAS regulation V/34.3** (Master's discretion) see H01a.11.

H02 Collision Regulations

H02a INTERNATIONAL COLLISION PREVENTION REGULATIONS

H02a.1 International Collision Prevention Regulations

* **The International Regulations for Preventing Collisions at Sea, 1972** -
  - were made under the **Convention on the International Regulations for Preventing Collisions at Sea, 1972**, as amended (**COLREG**).
  - enhance safe navigation by (1) prescribing the conduct of vessels underway, (2) specifying the display of internationally-understood lights and sound signals, and (3) setting out collision avoidance actions in close quarter situations.
  - **are amended** by Resolutions A.464(XII), A.626(15), A.678(16) and A.736(18), are printed in full in **M.1642/COLREG 1**, which was issued in April 1996.
  - provide in Rule 38 for the granting of **exemptions** (see H02a.1a).
  - are given effect in the UK by the **MS (Distress Signals and Prevention of Collision) Regulations 1996** (SI 1996/75) (see H02a.2).

H02a.1a Exemptions under Rule 38

* **Rule 38** of the International Collision Regulations provides that **any vessel** (or **class of vessels**), provided that she complies with the requirements of the International Regulations for Preventing Collisions at Sea, 1960, the keel of which was laid or which was at a corresponding stage of construction before the entry into force of the 1972 Regulations, may be **permanently exempted** from compliance with the Regulations in three cases, as follows:
  * the **repositioning of lights** as a result of conversion from Imperial to metric units and rounding off measurement figures (Rule 38(c));
  * the **repositioning of masthead lights** on vessels of **less than 150 metres** in length, resulting from the prescriptions of Section 3(a) of Annex I[6] to the 1972 Regulations (Rule 38(d)(i)); and
  * the **repositioning of all-round lights** resulting from the prescription of Section 9(b) of Annex I to the Regulations (Rule 38(h)).

---

[5] The **Guidelines for Voyage Planning**, adopted by IMO by resolution A.893(21) are printed in Annex 25 to the Guidance Notes to the MCA's 2002 SOLAS V publication.

[6] Section 3(a) of Annex 1 provides, *inter alia*, that when two masthead lights are prescribed for a power-driven vessel, the horizontal distance between them must not be less than one-half the length of the vessel. In some offshore support vessels (which typically have a long, open working deck, and superstructure positioned well forward) it is impossible to achieve the regulatory horizontal spacing, and flag State Administration exemptions from Rule 38(d)(i) are commonly in force for such vessels.

H02a.1b Adopted and unadopted traffic separation schemes

* **Rule 10**, as amended, of the International Collision Regulations prescribes the conduct of vessels **within or near traffic separation schemes** (TSSs) which have been adopted by IMO.
* An **adopted TSS** is one recognised by IMO. An **unadopted TSS** is one not recognised by IMO. Rule 10 does not prescribe conduct in **unadopted TSSs**.
* Before adopting a TSS, IMO considers whether it meets IMO's design criteria, etc.
* Where a TSS lies wholly within national territorial waters, decisions concerning routeing lie with the coastal State government, but these schemes may also be submitted to IMO for approval and adoption. The national rules of the State may therefore differ from the "conventional" international rules.
* An **infringement of an adopted TSS** anywhere in the world is dealt with by the **flag State**.
* An **infringement of a non-adopted TSS** is dealt with by the **coastal State** in whose waters the scheme lies, in accordance with the laws of that State.
* **MGN 28** (Observance of traffic separation schemes) has been superseded by **SOLAS regulation V/10** and the **Guidance Notes to regulation V/10** in MCA's 2002 SOLAS Chapter V publication. For notes on **SOLAS regulation V/10** and **ships' routeing**, see H01a.6.

H02a.2 Distress Signals and Prevention of Collision Regulations

* The **MS (Distress Signals and Prevention of Collision) Regulations 1996** (SI 1996/75) -
  - replace the MS (Distress Signals and Prevention of Collision) Regulations 1989, as amended, and related instruments.
  - give effect in the UK to **The International Collision Prevention Regulations 1972, as amended**, made under the Convention on the International Regulations for Preventing Collisions at Sea, 1972, as amended (COLREG).
  - apply to **all UK ships** wherever they may be and to **non-UK ships** in the UK or UK territorial waters.
  - require all vessels, other than those subject to **exemptions under Rule 38**, to comply with the provisions of **Rules 1 to 36** of and **Annexes I to III** to the International Regulations for Preventing Collisions at Sea 1972, as amended (regulation 4).
* Whereas the 1989 Regulations contained the full text of the International Regulations, the 1996 Regulations do not; instead they are set out in **M.1642/COLREG 1**, which incorporates changes to Rule 26 and to Annexes I, II and IV adopted in November 1993 by IMO (Resolution A736(18)).
* **The MCA may exempt** any ship or description of ships from all or any of the provisions of the Regulations which relate to the number, position, range or arc of visibility of lights or shapes, as well as to the disposition and characteristics of sound-signalling appliances if satisfied that compliance is either impractical or unreasonable (regulation 5). For each exemption granted, the vessel must carry an **Exemption Certificate**.

H02a.2a Penalties for breach of collision regulations

* Regulation 6(1) of the **MS (Distress Signals and Prevention of Collision) Regulations 1996** provides that where any of the Regulations is contravened (e.g. by a failure to comply with any of the International Regulations), the **owner** of the vessel, the **master** and **any person for the time being responsible for the vessel's conduct** (e.g. the officer-of-the-watch) will each be guilty of an **offence** punishable on conviction on indictment by a maximum 2 years' imprisonment and a fine, or on summary conviction -
  * in the case of a breach of **Rule 10(b)(i)** (Duty to proceed with traffic flow in lanes of separation schemes) by a fine not exceeding **£50,000** (see also B03b.3e); and
  * in any other case by a fine not exceeding the **statutory maximum** (i.e. £5000).
* It will be a **defence** for the person charged to show that he took all reasonable precautions to avoid committing the offence (regulation 6(2)).
* A ship which fails to comply with any of the requirements of the Regulations is liable to be **detained** (regulation 7).

H02b FOREIGN COLLISION PREVENTION RULES

* Although Rule 1(a) of the International Regulations for Preventing Collisions at Sea 1972 provides that the Regulations will apply to all vessels on the high seas and in all waters connected therewith navigable by seagoing vessels, the COLREG Convention 1972 under which the Regulations were made is binding only on **signatory States**. A few maritime States are not parties to the Convention and vessels flying the flags of these States are therefore not strictly bound to observe the International Regulations, whether in practice they do or not.

* Rule 1(b) provides that nothing in the International Regulations shall interfere with operation of **special rules** made by an appropriate authority for **roadsteads, harbours, rivers, lakes or inland waterways** connected with the high seas and navigable by seagoing vessels, but these special rules must conform as closely as possible with the International Regulations.
* For information about **local navigation rules**, masters should consult pilot books, notices to mariners, charts and should seek advice from agents when approaching a port for the first time.

H03 Discharges of pollutants at sea

H03a DISCHARGES AT SEA OF OIL

H03a.1 MARPOL Annex I

- **contains** the Regulations for the Prevention of Pollution by Oil.
- **came into force** on 2 October 1983 and has (at 31 May 2002) 121 Contracting States representing 96.41% of world tonnage.
- **includes** a List of Oils in Appendix I, a specimen International Oil Pollution Prevention (IOPP) Certificate in Appendix II and a specimen Oil Record Book (Parts 1 and 2) in Appendix III.
- **defines** "special area" (in regulation 1) as "a sea area where for recognised technical reasons in relation to its oceanographical and ecological condition and to the particular character of its traffic the adoption of special mandatory methods for the prevention of sea pollution by oil is required".
- **designates** (in regulation 10) the following nine areas as **Annex I special areas**: the **Mediterranean Sea area**, the **Baltic Sea area**, the **Black Sea area**, the **Red Sea area**, the "**Gulfs area**", the **Gulf of Aden area**, the **Antarctic area** and the **North-West European waters**, defined as follows:
  * the **Mediterranean Sea area** means the Mediterranean Sea proper including the gulfs and seas therein with the boundary between the Mediterranean and the Black Sea constituted by the 41° N parallel and bounded to the west by the Straits of Gibraltar at the meridian of 5°36' W;
  * the **Baltic Sea area** means the Baltic Sea proper with the Gulf of Bothnia, the Gulf of Finland and the entrance to the Baltic Sea bounded by the parallel of the Skaw in the Skagerrak at 57°44.8' N;
  * the **Black Sea area** means the Black Sea proper with the boundary between the Mediterranean and the Black Sea constituted by the parallel 41° N;
  * the **Red Sea area** means the Red Sea proper including the Gulfs of Suez and Aqaba bounded at the south by the rhumb line between Ras si Ane (12°28.5' N, 43°19.6' E) and Husn Murad (12°40.4' N, 43°30.2' E);
  * the **Gulfs area** means the sea area located north-west of the rhumb line between Ras al Hadd (22°30' N, 59°48' E) and Ras al Fasteh (25°04' N, 61°25' E);
  * the **Gulf of Aden area** means that part of the Gulf of Aden between the Red Sea and the Arabian Sea bounded to the west by the rhumb line between Ras si Ane (12°28.5' N, 43°19.6' E) and Husn Murad (12°40.4' N, 43°30.2' E) and to the east by the rhumb line between Ras Asir (11°50' N, 51°16.9' E) and Ras Fartak (15°35' N, 52°13.8' E);
  * the **Antarctic area** means the sea area south of latitude 60° S;
  * the **North-West European waters** include the North Sea and its approaches, the Irish Sea and its approaches, the Celtic Sea, the English Channel and its approaches and part of the North-East Atlantic immediately to the west of Ireland. The area is bounded by lines joining the following points: 48°27' N on the French coast; 48°27' N, 6°25' W; 49°52' N, 7°44' W; 50°30'N, 12° W; 56°30' N, 12° W; 62° N, 3° W; 62° N on the Norwegian coast; 57°44.8' N on the Danish and Swedish coasts.
  - **is given effect in the UK** by the **MS (Prevention of Oil Pollution) Regulations 1996** (SI 1996/2154) (see H03a.2).
* "**From the nearest land**" means, in relation to all land other than a part of the north-eastern coast of Australia (see below), from the **nearest baseline** from which the territorial sea of any territory is established in accordance with international law.
* **Off the north-eastern coast of Australia** the term "from the nearest land" means from a line drawn from a point on the coast of Australia in latitude 11°00' S, longitude 142°08' E to a point in latitude 10° 35' S, longitude 141°55' E, thence to a point latitude 10°00' S, longitude 142°00' E, thence to a point latitude 9°10' S, longitude 143°52' E, thence to a point latitude 9°00' S, longitude 144°30' E, thence to a point latitude 13°00' S, longitude 144°00' E, thence to a point latitude 15°00' S, longitude 146°00' E, thence to a point latitude 18°00' S, longitude 147°00' E, thence to a point latitude 21°00' S, longitude 153°00' E, thence to a point on the coast of Australia in latitude 24°42' S, longitude 153°15' E. This makes the Great Barrier Reef and the north-eastern coast of Australia a **prohibited discharge area**.

H03a.2 Prevention of Oil Pollution Regulations

* The **MS (Prevention of Oil Pollution) Regulations 1996** (SI 1996/2154) -
  - **give effect** in the UK to the provisions of MARPOL Annex I.
  - **are outlined** in D03a.2 as "operational requirements applicable to all UK ships".
  - **are amended** by the MS (Prevention of Oil Pollution) (Amendment) Regulations 1997 (SI 1997/1910) and the MS (Prevention of Oil Pollution) (Amendment) Regulations 2000 (SI 2000/483), as outlined in D03a.2.
  - **contain in Part III – Requirements for control of operational pollution - control of discharge of oil** - the following regulations: **11**. General exceptions; **12**. Ships other than oil tankers and machinery space bilges of oil tankers; **13**. Oil tankers; **14**. Oil filtering equipment and oil discharge monitoring and control system; **15**. Retention of oil on board; **16**. Methods for the prevention of oil pollution from ships operating in special areas.

H03a.3 Discharge provisions of Prevention of Oil Pollution Regulations

- are contained in **regulations 12, 13 and 16** (the "discharge regulations").
- apply to two **sources of oil**, i.e.:
  * ships other than oil tankers and machinery space bilges of oil tankers (regulation 12); and
  * oil tankers (regulation 13).
- are subject to certain **general exceptions** granted by regulation 11 (see H03a.7).
* **Regulation 12** sets the criteria for legal **discharges from ships other than oil tankers**, and from the **machinery space bilges of oil tankers**.
* **Regulation 13** sets the criteria for legal **discharges from oil tankers**, other than discharges from machinery spaces.
* Regulation 16 sets the criteria for legal discharges in special areas.

H03a.4 Discharges outside special areas from ships other than oil tankers, and from machinery space bilges of oil tankers (regulation 12)

H03a.4a Ships to which regulation 12 applies

* Regulation 12(1) provides that, subject to the **general exceptions** in regulation 11, regulation 12(2) (which sets the criteria for legal discharges) applies to:
  * **UK ships other than oil tankers**;
  * **UK oil tankers**, in relation to discharges from their **machinery space bilges** (unless mixed with cargo residues), but excluding cargo pump room bilges;
  * (subject to regulation 38) **non-UK ships other than oil tankers**; and
  * (subject to regulation 38) **non-UK oil tankers**, in relation to discharges from their **machinery space bilges** (unless mixed with cargo residues), but excluding cargo pump room bilges -
  - wherever these ships are. (For an outline of requirements of regulation 38, see B03b.2j.)
* The criteria set by regulation 12 vary according to the ship's date of build and whether she is fitted with 15 ppm oil filtering equipment or not. Under regulation 12(3) a ship delivered before 6 July 1993 did not have to comply with the requirements of regulation 12(2) before 6 July 1998, but if she did not, she had to be fitted with oily-water separating equipment which restricted the oil content of any oily mixture discharged into the sea to 100 ppm or less, and she could discharge oil only when more than 12 miles from the nearest land. **All ships** are now required to have **filtering equipment**.

H03a.4b Criteria for legal discharges outside special areas from non-tankers and machinery space bilges of tankers

* Regulation 12(2) provides that a ship to which regulation 12 applies (i.e. a non-tanker, or a tanker in respect of machinery space bilge discharges only – see H03a.4a) may discharge **oil or oily mixture** into any part of the sea unless **all of the following conditions** are
  satisfied:
  * the ship is **proceeding on a voyage** (i.e. under way);
  * the ship is **not within an Annex I special area** (see H03a.6a);
  * the **oil content of the effluent does not exceed 15 ppm**; and
  * the ship has in operation the **filtering equipment** and **oil discharge monitoring and control equipment** as required by regulation 14 (see D04g.1).

* These criteria have been in force since 6 July 1998[7], by which date all ships had to be fitted with **filtering equipment** ("15 ppm equipment").

H03a.5 Discharges from oil tankers (regulation 13)

* Subject to the **general exceptions** in regulation 11, regulation 13 applies to:
  * every UK oil tanker; and
  * (subject to regulation 38) every non-UK oil tanker -
  - wherever it may be. (For an outline of requirements of regulation 38, see B03b.2j.)
* An oil tanker to which regulation 13 applies may not discharge any oil or oily mixture except from her machinery bilge spaces (see H03a.4) unless all of the following conditions are satisfied:
  * the tanker is **proceeding on a voyage** (i.e. is under way);
  * the tanker is **not within an Annex I special area**;
  * the tanker is more than **50 miles** from the nearest land;
  * the instantaneous rate of discharge of the oil content does not exceed **30 litres per mile**;
  * in the case of **tankers entering service after 31 December 1979**, the total quantity of oil discharged is not more than **1/30,000** of the total quantity of the particular cargo of which the residue formed a part; or
  * in the case of **tankers entering service before 1 January 1980**, the total quantity of oil discharged is not more than **1/15,000** of the total quantity of the particular cargo of which the residue formed a part; and
  * the tanker has in operation an **oil discharge monitoring and control system** and a **slop tank** arrangement as required by regulation 15.
* The above conditions do not apply to discharges of **clean or segregated ballast** or **unprocessed oily mixture** which without dilution has an oil content not exceeding **15 ppm** and which does not originate from cargo pump room bilges and is not mixed with cargo residues (regulation 13(3)).
* No discharge may contain **chemicals or other substances** in quantities or concentrations hazardous to the marine environment, or chemicals or other substances introduced for the purpose of circumventing the regulation (regulation 13(4)).
* Any oil or oily mixture that has not been unloaded as cargo and may not be discharged into the sea under regulation 13 must be **retained on board** and discharged into **reception facilities** (regulation 13(5)).

H03a.6 Discharges in special areas (regulation 16)

H03a.6a Special areas

* Regulation 1 defines a **special area** as "a sea area where, for recognised technical reasons in relation to its oceanographical and ecological condition and to the particular character of its traffic, the adoption of special mandatory methods for the prevention of sea pollution by oil is required, and shall include those areas listed in regulation 16".
* **Special areas for the purposes of the MS (Prevention of Oil Pollution) Regulations 1996** designated by regulation 16(1), as amended, are:
  * the **Mediterranean Sea area**, i.e. the Mediterranean Sea including the gulfs and seas therein with the boundary between the Mediterranean and the Black Sea constituted by the 41° N parallel and bounded to the west by the Straits of Gibraltar at the meridian of 5°36' W;
  * the **Baltic Sea area**, i.e. the Baltic Sea with the Gulf of Bothnia, the Gulf of Finland and the entrance to the Baltic Sea bounded by the parallel to the Skaw in the Skagerrak at 57°44.8' W;
  * the **Black Sea area**, i.e. the Black Sea with the boundary between the Mediterranean and the Black Sea constituted by the parallel 41° N;
  * the **Antarctic area**, i.e. the sea area south of 60° S latitude; and
  * the **North West European waters area**, i.e. the North Sea and its approaches, the Irish Sea and its approaches, the Celtic Sea, the English Channel and its approaches and part of the North East Atlantic immediately to the

---

[7] Under regulation 12(3), ships delivered before 6 July 1993, unless already fitted with 15 ppm filtering equipment, were permitted to discharge oily mixtures into the sea through a separator ("100 ppm equipment") until 6 July 1998, since which date all discharges must be through filtering equipment ("15 ppm equipment"). Until 6 July 1998 no vessel could discharge oil or oily mixture into any part of the sea unless all of the following conditions were satisfied: (1) the ship had to be proceeding on a voyage (i.e. be under way); (2) the ship could not be within an Annex I special area; (3) the ship had to be more than 12 miles from the nearest land; (4) the oil content of the effluent had to be less than 100 ppm; (5) the ship had to have in operation approved oily-water separating equipment ("100 ppm equipment"). The requirement to be more than 12 miles from the nearest land is no longer necessary, since a discharge containing less than 15 ppm of oil can should leave no visible trace of oil on the sea surface.

west of Ireland, being the area bounded by line joining the following points: 48°27' N on the French coast; 48°27' N; 6°25' W; 49°52' N; 7°44' W; 50°30' N; 12° W; 56°30' N; 12° W; 62° N; 3° W; 62° N on the Norwegian coast; and 57°44.8' N on the Danish and Swedish coasts.

* **Special areas designated by regulation 10 of MARPOL Annex I in addition to the above areas** are:
  * the **Red Sea area** meaning the Red Sea proper including the Gulfs of Suez and Aqaba bounded at the south by the rhumb line between Ras si Ane (12°8.5' N, 43°19.6' E) and Husn Murad (12°40.4' N, 61°25' E);
  * the **Gulfs area** meaning the sea area located north-west of the rhumb line between Ras al Hadd (22°30' N, 59°48' E) and Ras al Fasteh (25°04' N, 61°25' E); and
  * the **Gulf of Aden area** meaning that part of the Gulf of Aden between the Red Sea and the Arabian Sea bounded to the west by the rhumb line between Ras si Ane (12°28.5' N, 43°19.6' E) and Husn Murad (12°40.4' N, 43°30.2' E) and to the east by the rhumb line between Ras Asir (11°50' N, 51°16.9' E) and the Ras Fartak (15°35' N, 52°13.8' E).
* The **Red Sea area and the Gulfs area** were downgraded from special area status in UK law by **SI 1985/2040**. However, the **Red Sea Pilot** advises that in Saudi law special area status of these areas is enforced, and the **Clean Seas Guide** lists them as special areas to be observed[8].
* **Newly designated special areas** will be promulgated by Marine Information Note (MIN). (**MIN 52** promulgated the designation of the North West European waters as an Annex I special area with effect from 1 August 1999.)
* See also the notes at H03a.1 regarding **prohibited discharges** in the area of the **Great Barrier Reef and north-eastern coast of Australia**.

H03a.6b Criteria for legal discharges in special areas

* Subject to the general exceptions provided for in regulation 11 and the provisions relating to discharges of clean or segregated ballast and processed bilge water in regulation 16(3), **in the Antarctic area** it is illegal to discharge into the sea any oil or oily mixture from any UK ship (regulation 16(2)(a)).
* Regulation 16(2)(b) provides that, subject to the general exceptions provided for in regulation 11 and the provisions relating to discharges of clean or segregated ballast and processed bilge water in regulation 16(3), **in special areas other than the Antarctic area** it is illegal to discharge into the sea any oil or oily mixture from:
  * **any UK oil tanker** (of any tonnage); or
  * **any UK non-tanker of 400 GT or above**; and
  * **any UK non-tanker of less than 400 GT**, except (in the case of these small ships) when the oil content of the effluent without dilution does not exceed 15 ppm.
* The prohibitions in regulation 16(2) do not apply to the discharge of **clean or segregated ballast** (regulation 16(3)(a)).
* **Discharges of processed bilge water from machinery spaces** are permitted in special areas under regulation 16(3)(b) provided all of the following conditions are satisfied:
  * the bilge water **does not originate from cargo pump room bilges**;
  * the bilge water is **not mixed with cargo residues**;
  * the ship is **proceeding on a voyage** (i.e. under way);
  * the oil content of the effluent, without dilution, does not exceed **15 ppm** of the mixture;
  * the ship has in operation an **oil filtering system** complying with regulation 14(5) and **oil content measuring equipment** and **alarm devices** complying with regulation 14(6), i.e. of a design approved in accordance with the "Guidelines and Specifications for Pollution Prevention Equipment for Machinery Space Bilges of Ships" (MEPC.60(33));
  * the oil filtering system is equipped with a **stopping device** which will ensure that the discharge is automatically stopped if the oil content of the effluent exceeds 15 ppm.
* No discharge in a special area may contain **chemicals or other substances** in quantities or concentrations hazardous to the marine environment, or chemicals or other substances introduced for the purpose of circumventing the regulation (regulation 16(4)(a)).
* Where residues of oil or oily mixture may not be discharged into the sea under regulation 16(2) or 16(3), they must be retained on board and may be discharged only into reception facilities (regulation 16(4)(b)).
* For notes on **statutory restrictions on ships entering the Antarctic area**, see H01a.4.
* **MIN 52** (which has now expired) clarified the requirements relating to discharges in special areas.

---

[8] The effect of the "downgrading" of special area status is that a master of a UK ship contravening Annex I special area discharge prohibitions in the Red Sea of Gulfs areas would not be contravening UK regulations, but would probably be in breach of coastal State law.

H03a.7 General exceptions to the discharge regulations (regulation 11)

* Regulation 11 provides that the provisions of regulations 12, 13 and 16 ("the discharge regulations") **do not apply** to -
    - any discharge into the sea of oil or oily mixture which is necessary for the purpose of **securing the safety of a ship** or **saving life** at sea; or
    - any discharge into the sea of oil or oily mixture which **results from damage to a ship or its equipment** provided that -
        • all reasonable precautions were taken after the occurrence of the damage or discovery of the discharge for the purpose of **preventing or minimising the disc**harge; and
        • the owner or master did not act either with **intent to cause damage**, or **recklessly** and **with knowledge that damage would probably result**; or
    - any **approved discharge** into the sea of **substances containing oil**, when being used for the purpose of combating specific pollution incidents in order to minimise the damage from pollution. Any such discharge will be subject to the approval of any Government in whose jurisdiction it is contemplated the discharge will be made.

H03a.8 Penalties and defence (regulation 36)

* Under regulation 36(2), as amended by regulation 8 of the **MS (Prevention of Oil Pollution) (Amendment) Regulations 1997** (SI 1997/1910), if any ship fails to comply with **any requirement** of regulations 12, 13 or 16 (the "discharge regulations"), **the owner and the master** will each be guilty of an **offence** and both will be liable on summary conviction to a fine not exceeding **£250,000**, or on conviction on indictment to an **unlimited fine**.
* A **defence** will be to show that the person charged took all reasonable precautions and exercised all due diligence to avoid the commission of the offence.
* **Regulation 37** deals with enforcement and application of fines.

H03a.9 Oil Record Book entries (regulation 10)

* Records of all **operational** and **exceptional discharges** must be kept in the Oil Record Book (regulation 10). For notes on requirements relating to **Oil Record Books**, including **entries to be made**, see D05b.2.

H03a.10 Oil discharge criteria tables

* Permitted and prohibited discharges of oil at sea are summarised in the following tables.

DISCHARGES OF OIL FROM MACHINERY SPACES OF ALL SHIPS – IN SPECIAL AREAS		
Sea area	Ship type and size	Discharge critieria
Any special area except the Antarctic area	Oil tankers Other ships of 400gt and above	Discharge permitted if: • proceeding en route; • oil content, without dilution, is less than 15ppm; • ship has oil filtering equipment with alarm and automatic 15ppm stopping device; • (on tankers) the bilge water does not come from pump room bilges and is not mixed with cargo residue.
Any special area except the Antarctic area	Ships of less than 400gt except tankers	Discharge permitted if: • oil content of effluent is less than 15ppm • vessel is at least 12 nautical miles from nearest land
Antarctic area	All ships	No discharges permitted.

DISCHARGES OF OIL FROM MACHINERY SPACES OF ALL SHIPS – OUTSIDE SPECIAL AREAS		
Sea area	Ship type and size	Discharge critieria
Anywhere outside a special area	Oil tankers Other ships of 400gt and above	Discharge permitted if: • proceeding en route; • oil content, without dilution, is less than 15ppm; • ship has ODMCS, oil filtering equipment (with alarm and automatic 15ppm stopping device if 10,000gt or over); • (on tankers) the bilge water does not come from pump room bilges and is not mixed with cargo residue.
Anywhere outside a special area	Ships of less than 400gt except tankers	Discharge permitted if: • criteria as above are fulfilled; or • ship has means to store oily waste and discharge it to shore.

DISCHARGES OF OIL FROM CARGO TANKS AND BALLAST SPACES OF OIL TANKERS	
Sea area	Discharge criteria
Within 50 nautical miles from nearest land	No discharges permitted except for clean or segregated ballast.
Outside a special area and more than 50 nautical miles from nearest land	Discharge of clean or segregated ballast permitted.
Outside a special area and more than 50 nautical miles from nearest land	Discharge permitted if: • tanker is en route; • rate of discharge is less than 30 litres per mile; • total quantity discharged is less than 1/30,000 of previous cargo (or 1/15,000 on ship entering service before 1 January 1980); • ODMCS is in operation; • ship has slop tank.
Inside any special area	No discharge permitted except for clean or segregated ballast.

H03b DISCHARGES AT SEA OF NOXIOUS LIQUID SUBSTANCES

H03b.1 MARPOL Annex II

- **contains** the **Regulations for the Control of Pollution by Noxious Liquid Substances in Bulk**.
- **came into force** on 2 October 1983 and has (at May 2002) 120 **Contracting States** (which include the UK) representing 95.90% of world tonnage.
- **includes** Guidelines for the categorisation of noxious liquid substances in Appendix I, a list of noxious liquid substances in Appendix II, a list of "other liquid substances" in Appendix III, a specimen Cargo Record Book in Appendix IV and a specimen NLS Certificate in Appendix V.
- **defines** "special area" (in regulation 1) as "a sea area where for recognised technical reasons in relation to its oceanographic and ecological condition and to the particular character of its traffic the adoption of special mandatory methods for the prevention of sea pollution by noxious liquid substances is required".
- **designates** (in regulation 1) the following three areas as **Annex II special areas**: the **Baltic Sea area**, the **Black Sea area** and the **Antarctic area**, all defined geographically as in Annex I (see H03a.1).
- **is given effect in the UK** by the **MS (Dangerous or Noxious Liquid Substances in Bulk) Regulations 1996** (SI 1996/3010) (see H03b.2).

H03b.2 Dangerous or Noxious Liquid Substances in Bulk Regulations

* The **MS (Dangerous or Noxious Liquid Substances in Bulk) Regulations 1996** (SI 1996/3010) -
  - **give effect in the UK** and in UK waters (including controlled waters) to the requirements of MARPOL Annex II;
  - **are described** in D03e.2a.
* In outline, **discharges into the sea of NLSs or mixtures containing them** are prohibited (regulation 5); and discharges into the sea of **liquid wastes containing residues** of such substances are strictly controlled. The greater the hazard which the category of substance presents, the stricter the controls.
* Ships must follow specified **procedures** when **washing cargo tanks**. The procedures depend on the category of substance carried and on whether or not unloading takes place in a special area.
* See also **M.1438**, which lists substances contained in the Appendices to MARPOL Annex II.
* Regulation 5(1) provides that the **discharge of any noxious liquid substance into the sea is prohibited**, except where permitted by **Schedule 2** (Discharge and washing of tanks) of **M.1703/NLS 1**.
* **Tanks** must be **washed**, or **pre-washed**, and the tank washings must be dealt with, as prescribed in **Schedule 2** of **M.1703/NLS 1** (regulation 5(2)).

H03b.6 M.1703/NLS 1 Schedule 2 requirements

* For details of **tank washing requirements in port**, see I07c.1 and **Schedule 2 of M.1703/NLS1**.
* Three **special areas** are designated (as in MARPOL Annex II), as follows:
  * the **Baltic Sea area**, meaning the Baltic Sea with the Gulf of Bothnia, the Gulf of Finland and the entrance to the Baltic Sea bounded by the parallel of the Skaw in the Skagerrak at 57° 44.8' N;
  * the **Black Sea area**, meaning the Black Sea with the boundary between the Mediterranean and the Black Sea constituted by the parallel 41° N; and
  * the **Antarctic area**, meaning the sea area south of latitude 60° S.
* In the **Antarctic area** any discharge into the sea of **any noxious liquid substances** is prohibited (paragraph 1).

H03b.6a Discharge of Category A substances and residual mixtures

* The discharge into the sea of a **Category A substance** is prohibited (paragraph 2).
* The discharge into the sea of a **Category A residual mixture** is prohibited under paragraph 4 except where all the following conditions are satisfied:
  * the effluent consists solely of **water** added to the tank after it has been emptied in accordance with the Regulations;
  * the ship is proceeding at a speed of at least **7 knots** in the case of a self-propelled ship or at least 4 knots in the case of a ship which is not self-propelled;
  * the discharge is made **below the waterline**; and
  * the discharge is made at a distance of not less than **12 nautical miles** from the nearest land and in a depth of water of not less than **25 metres**.

H03b.6b Discharge of Category B and C substances and residual mixtures

* The discharge into the sea of a **Category B or Category C substance** is prohibited (paragraph 5).
* The discharge into the sea of a **Category B or Category C residual mixture** is prohibited under paragraph 10(1) except where all the following conditions are complied with:
  * all relevant requirements of **paragraphs 6 to 9 of M.1703/NLS1** have been complied with;
  * the concentration of the substance in, and the rate of discharge of, the effluent is in accordance with the procedures and arrangements specified in respect of substances of the category in question in the ship's **Procedures and Arrangements Manual**;
  * the ship is proceeding at a speed of at least **7 knots** in the case of a self-propelled ship or at least 4 knots in the case of a ship which is not self-propelled;
  * the discharge is made **below the waterline**; and
  * the discharge is made at a distance of not less than **12 nautical miles** from the nearest land and in a depth of water of not less than 25 metres; and
  * **if the ship is in a Special Area** and the substance in question is a **Category B substance**, the tank from which the discharge is made has been **pre-washed** in accordance with the procedure specified in the ship's Procedures and Arrangements Manual for the substance in question and the resulting tank washings have been discharged to a **reception facility**; or
  * **if the ship is in a Special Area** and the substance in question is a **Category C substance** the maximum quantity of the substance discharged from any one tank and its associated piping system does not exceed the **maximum quantity approved** in the ship's Procedures and Arrangements Manual for discharge of Category C substances in a Special Area.
* Where a tank which contained a **Category B or Category C residual mixture** has been emptied by a discharge made in accordance with the above requirements, **water added afterwards** to that tank may be discharged notwithstanding that the ship is not proceeding at the speed specified above, provided that all the other requirements above are complied with (paragraph 10(2).

H03b.6c Discharge of Category D substances and residual mixtures

* The discharge into the sea of a **Category D substance** is prohibited (paragraph 11).
* The discharge into the sea of a **Category D residual mixture** is prohibited under paragraph 12 except where:

- the ship is proceeding on its way at a speed of at least **7 knots** in the case of a **self-propelled ship** or at least **4 knots** in the case of a **non-self-propelled ship**;
- the concentration of the substance in the effluent is not greater than **one part of the substance to ten parts of water**; and
- the discharge is made at a distance of not less than **12 nautical miles** from the nearest land.

H03b.6d Discharge of unassessed liquid substances

* The discharge into the sea of any **unassessed liquid substance carried in bulk**, or of a **residual mixture containing any such substance**, is prohibited under paragraph 13 except where -
- the MCA has given **written approval** to its carriage; and
- any **conditions** relating to discharge and subject to which that approval was given are complied with.

H03b.6e Discharge of clean and segregated ballast and non-polluting liquid substances

* The discharge of **clean ballast**, **segregated ballast** or any **non-polluting substance** is not prohibited by Schedule 2 (paragraph 14).
* "**Clean ballast**" means ballast carried in a tank which, since it was last used to carry a noxious liquid substance in bulk, has been thoroughly cleaned and the residues resulting therefrom have been discharged and the tank emptied in accordance with Schedule 2.
* "**Segregated ballast**" means ballast water introduced into a tank which is permanently allocated to the carriage of water ballast or cargoes other than oil or noxious liquid substances and which is completely separated from the cargo pumping and piping system and from the fuel oil pumping and piping system.
* "**Non-polluting substance**" means a substance listed in Chapter 17 or 18 of the IBC Code having against it in column "c" the entry "III".

H03b.6f Emergency discharges

* The discharge restrictions set out in paragraphs 1, 2, 4, 5 and 10 to 13 of Schedule 2 (as described above) will not apply to any discharge into the sea of a **noxious liquid substance** or **unassessed liquid substance** or **mixture containing any such substance** -
  - which is necessary for the purposes of securing the **safety of a ship or saving life at sea**; or
  - which results from **damage to a ship or its equipment**, provided that all **reasonable precautions** were taken after the occurrence of the damage or discovery of the discharge to **prevent or minimise the discharge**, and neither the owner nor the master acted either **with intent** to cause damage, or **recklessly** and **with knowledge** that damage would probably result; or
  - where the **substance or mixture** in question **is approved by the MCA** for use in combating **specific pollution incidents** in order to minimise the damage from pollution and **the discharge is made with the approval of the MCA** or, if the discharge is to be made in waters within the jurisdiction of another State, with the **approval of the government of that State**.

H03b.7 Loading and carriage in bulk of dangerous or noxious liquid substances (regulation 6)

* "**Tripartite agreement**" means an agreement between flag State Administrations for the carriage of unassessed liquid substances in accordance with MEPC Circular 265.
* "**Oil-like substance**" means a substance listed as such in MEPC Circular 2/CIRC.1 or provisionally assessed as an oil-like substance.
* No ship may load in bulk or carry in bulk any **dangerous or noxious liquid substance or substances subject to a tripartite agreement** unless -
  - a valid **INLS Certificate**, a **BCH Code Certificate**, an **IBC Code Certificate** or an **appropriate Certificate** covering the substance is in force for the ship and the loading and carriage is in accordance with its terms; or
  - either the MCA or a SOLAS or MARPOL Party State government has given **written permission** for the carriage of the substance and any conditions subject to which the permission was granted are complied with; or
  - if the substance is an **oil-like substance**, a valid **IOPP Certificate** or **UKOPP Certificate**, suitably **endorsed**, is in force for that ship, and the loading and discharge of the substance is in accordance with its terms and, in the case of a Category C or D substance, the substance is handled and carried in accordance with **Schedule 3 (Oil-like substances) of M.1703/NLS 1**.
* For notes on the **certificates** mentioned above, see D04g.

H03b.8 Cargo Record Book entries (regulation 8)

* Whenever any of the above operations (i.e. **discharges of residues into the sea** in accordance with regulations, and **emergency discharges**) takes place in respect of any noxious liquid substance, a **record** of the operation must be made in the **Cargo Record Book** in relation to **each tank** affected by the operation. For notes on the requirement to carry a Cargo Record Book (NLS) and entries required, see D05b.3.

H03b.9 Penalties (regulation 14)

* If there is any **contravention of the Regulations other than of regulation 5** (Discharge of cargo tanks) the owner and master of the ship will each be guilty of an offence punishable on summary conviction by a **fine not exceeding the statutory maximum** (£5,000), or on conviction on indictment, by an **unlimited fine** (regulation 14(1), as amended).
* If there is any **contravention of regulation 5** (Discharge of cargo tanks) the owner and master will each be guilty of an offence and section 131(3) of the Merchant Shipping Act 1995 will apply as it applies to an offence under that section, so that the owner and master will each be liable on summary conviction to a fine not exceeding **£25,000**, or on conviction on indictment, to an **unlimited fine** (regulation 14(1A))[9].

H03b.10 Defence (regulation 14)

* It will be a **defence** for a person charged with an offence under the Regulations to prove that he took all reasonable steps to ensure that the regulations in question were complied with.

H03b.11 NLS discharge criteria tables

* **Permitted and prohibited discharges** of noxious liquid substances carried in bulk are summarised in the following tables.

DISCHARGE OF EFFLUENTS CONTAINING NOXIOUS LIQUID SUBSTANCES INSIDE SPECIAL AREAS				
Condition	**Substance**			
	Category A	**Category B**	**Category C**	**Category D**
Maximum concentration at time of discharge	Virtually nil	1ppm in wake of ship	1ppm in wake of ship	1 part substance in 10 parts water
Maximum quantity of cargo discharged from tank	Virtually nil; Tank washings to reception facility	Virtually nil; Tank washings to reception facility	1m^3 or 1/3,000 of tank capacity	No limit
Discharge of effluent	Below the waterline			
Minimum depth of water	25 metres			No limit
Minimum distance from land	12 nautical miles			
Minimum speed of ship	7 knots			

DISCHARGE OF EFFLUENTS CONTAINING NOXIOUS LIQUID SUBSTANCES OUTSIDE SPECIAL AREAS				
Condition	**Substance**			
	Category A	**Category B**	**Category C**	**Category D**
Maximum concentration at time of discharge	Virtually nil	1ppm in wake of ship	10ppm in wake of ship	1 part substance in 10 parts water
Maximum quantity of cargo discharged from tank	Virtually nil; Tank washings to reception facility	1m^3 or 1/3,000 of tank capacity	3m^3 or 1/1,000 of tank capacity	No limit
Discharge of effluent	Below the waterline			
Minimum depth of water	25 metres		No limit	
Minimum distance from land	12 nautical miles			
Minimum speed of ship	7 knots			

---

[9] Regulation 14(1) of the Principal Regulations (SI 1996/3010) originally set a fine of the statutory maximum (£5,000) for breach of any of the Regulations. The fivefold raising of the fine for breach of the discharge regulations was made by regulation 2 of the MS (Dangerous or Noxious Liquid Substances in Bulk) (Amendment) Regulations 1998 (SI 1998/1153).

H03c DISPOSAL AT SEA OF PACKAGED HARMFUL SUBSTANCES

H03c.1 MARPOL Annex III

- **contains** the **Regulations for the Prevention of Pollution by Harmful Substances Carried by Sea in Packaged Form**.
- **came into force** on 1 July 1992 and has (at May 2002) 101 **Contracting States** (which include the UK) representing 81.46% of world tonnage.
- **includes** Guidelines for the categorisation of noxious liquid substances (in Appendix I), a list of noxious liquid substances (in Appendix II), a list of "other liquid substances" (in Appendix III), a specimen Cargo Record Book (in Appendix IV) and a specimen NLS Certificate (in Appendix V).
- designates no "special areas" and contains no provisions relating to discharges or disposal at sea.
- **is given effect** in the UK by the **MS (Dangerous Goods and Marine Pollutants) Regulations 1997** (SI 1997/2367) (see F07f.2).

H03c.2 Prohibition of jettisoning of harmful substances at sea

* **Regulation 7(1) of MARPOL Annex III** provides that **jettisoning** of harmful substances carried in packaged form is **prohibited**, except where necessary for the purpose of **securing the safety of the ship and saving life at sea**.
* **Regulation 7(2)** provides that subject to the provisions of MARPOL, **appropriate measures** based on the physical, chemical and biological properties of harmful substances must be taken (i.e. by Party States) to **regulate the washing of leakages overboard**, provided that compliance with such measures would not impair the safety of the ship and persons on board.

H03c.3 Emergency procedures for dealing with packaged harmful substances at sea

* Where packaged harmful substances (i.e. dangerous goods or marine pollutants) become a danger to the vessel or personnel on board, the **Emergency Schedules** in the Supplement to the **IMDG Code** should be consulted for guidance on **appropriate disposal methods**. The master should also seek guidance from the owner, charterer, shipper or consignee and/or the P&I club correspondent. The Safety Management Manual may also be a source of guidance.
* In view of the prohibition in MARPOL Annex III regulation 7(1) (see H03c.2), **jettison** should be a **last resort** and disposal should, if possible, be to **shore authorities under controlled conditions**, e.g. with fire brigade attendance.
* For notes on the **statutory requirement to report a discharge** of dangerous goods or harmful substances in packaged form, or of the probability of such a discharge, including of those goods in freight containers, portable tanks, road and rail vehicles and shipborne barges, see H06e.1.

H03c.4 Disposal of expired pyrotechnics

* For notes on preferred methods of disposal of out-of-date pyrotechnics, see H03e.3.

H03d DISCHARGES AT SEA OF SEWAGE

H03d.1 MARPOL Annex IV

- **contains** the **Regulations for the Prevention of Pollution by Sewage from Ships**.
- is an **optional annex**.
- entered into force on **27 September 2003**.
- **defines "sewage"** in regulation 1(3) as:
  * drainage and other wastes from any form of toilets, urinals and WC scuppers;
  * drainage from medicinal premises (dispensary, sick bay, etc.) via wash basins, wash tubs and scuppers located in such premises;
  * drainage from spaces containing living animals; or

- • other waste waters when mixed with the drainages defined above.
- **applies** to all ships of 200gt and above, and all other ships certified to carry more than 10 persons. For **new ships**, application of Annex IV will be from the date of entry into force of the Annex; for **existing ships** (on that date) application will be 10 years later (i.e. on 27 September 2013) (regulation 2).
- **designates no special areas**.
- * **Regulation 8** sets **discharge criteria** (see H03d.2). **Regulation 9** specifies conditions under which **regulation 8 will not apply** (see H03d.3). Regulation 10 requires Governments of Party States to provide **reception facilities**. **Regulation 11** contains specifications for **standard discharge connections**.
- * For notes on the **MARPOL Annex IV** requirements for sewage pollution equipment, surveys and documentation, see D04g.8.
- * "**From the nearest land**" means, in relation to all land other than a part of the north-eastern coast of Australia (see below), from the **nearest baseline** from which the territorial sea of any territory is established in accordance with international law.
- * **Off the north-eastern coast of Australia** the term "from the nearest land" means from a line drawn from a point on the coast of Australia in latitude 11°00' S, longitude 142°08' E to a point in latitude 10°35' S, longitude 141°55' E, thence to a point latitude 10°00' S, longitude 142°00' E, thence to a point latitude 9°10' S, longitude 143°52' E, thence to a point latitude 9°00' S, longitude 144°30' E, thence to a point latitude 13°00' S, longitude 144°00' E, thence to a point latitude 15°00' S, longitude 146°00' E, thence to a point latitude 18°00' S, longitude 147°00' E, thence to a point latitude 21°00' S, longitude 153° 00' E, thence to a point on the coast of Australia in latitude 24°42' S, longitude 153°15' E. This effectively makes the north-eastern coast of Australia, including the Great Barrier Reef, a **prohibited discharge area**.

H03d.1a Legal sewage discharge criteria (regulation 8)

- * Subject to the provisions of regulation 9 (see H03d.1b), discharges of sewage into the sea are prohibited except under the following conditions.
- * **Within 4 nautical miles from the nearest land**, no discharge is permitted except from sewage treatment plant approved by the flag State Administration.
- * **Between 4 and 12 nautical miles from the nearest land**, no discharge is permitted except:
  - • from sewage treatment plant approved by the flag State Administration; or
  - • from a system approved by the flag State Administration for comminuting and disinfecting sewage.
- * **More than 12 nautical miles from the nearest land**, the following discharges are permitted:
  - • discharges from an approved sewage treatment plant or an approved system for comminuting and disinfecting sewage; or
  - • discharges of sewage which is not comminuted or disinfected, provided that the ship is proceeding at not less than 4 knots and the rate of discharge is approved by the flag State Administration.
- * **Discharges are not prohibited** when a ship is in waters under the jurisdiction of a State and is discharging sewage in accordance with such less stringent requirements as may be imposed by the State.

H03d.1b Exceptions (regulation 9)

- * **Regulation 8 does not apply** to:
  - • discharges of sewage **necessary** for the purpose of **securing the safety of a ship and those on board or saving life at sea**; or
  - • discharges of sewage **resulting from damage to the ship or its equipment** if all reasonable precautions have been taken before and after the occurrence of the damage to prevent or minimise the discharge.

H03d.1c Sewage discharge criteria table

- * The following table summarises Annex IV **sewage disposal requirements**.

Distance from the nearest land	Discharge criteria
Within 4 nautical miles	Discharge permitted only if from sewage treatment plant approved by the flag State Administration.
Between 4 and 12 nautical miles	Discharge permitted only if: • from sewage treatment plant approved by the flag State Administration; or • from a system approved by the flag State Administration for comminuting and disinfecting sewage.
More than 12 nautical miles	Discharge permitted only if: • from an approved sewage treatment plant or an approved system for comminuting and disinfecting sewage; or • sewage is not comminuted or disinfected, provided ship is proceeding at not less than 4 knots and the rate of discharge is approved by the flag State Administration.

H03d.2 Compliance with sewage pollution legislation by UK ships

* **No ship sewage pollution prevention regulations** are in force in the UK at the time of writing (June 2003). This position will change, however, before MARPOL Annex IV enters into force as described in H03d.1.
* A number of maritime States have passed domestic legislation giving effect to the provisions of MARPOL Annex IV. UK ships entering the national waters of these countries are subject to the pollution-prevention legislation of the coastal State, and many UK ships are therefore already equipped for dealing with sewage to the requirements of Annex IV. (For notes on the **Statement of Compliance with Annex IV of MARPOL 73/78** see D04g.8a.)
* The **Helsinki Convention** (the Convention on the Protection of the Marine Environment of the Baltic Sea Area, 1992) has been signed by all the countries bordering the Baltic Sea as well as the EU, and entered into force on 17 January 2000. It covers all forms of pollution from land, sea and air in the Baltic Sea.
* Regulation 4 of Annex IV to the Helsinki Convention provides that, subject to regulation 5 of Annex IV, the Contracting Parties must apply the provisions of **Annexes I-V of MARPOL 73/78**.
* Regulation 5 of Annex IV to the Helsinki Convention provides that the Contracting Parties must apply the provisions of paragraphs A to D and F and G of regulation 5 on **discharge of sewage from ships** while operating in the Baltic Sea Area. Those paragraphs apply to:
  * ships of 200gt and above;
  * ships of less than 200gt which are certified to carry more than 10 persons; and
  * ships which do not have a measured gross tonnage but are certified to carry more than 10 persons.
* Subject to paragraph D (which makes exceptions for safety and damage-caused discharges), **discharge of sewage into the sea in the Baltic Sea is prohibited** under regulation 5, except when:
  * the ship is discharging **comminuted and disinfected sewage**, using a system approved by the flag State Administration, at a distance of **more than 4 nautical miles** from the nearest land, or sewage which is **not comminuted or disinfected** at a distance of **more than 12 nautical miles** from the nearest land, (provided that in any case sewage that has been **stored in holding tanks** must not be discharged instantaneously but at a **moderate rate** when the ship is **en route** and proceeding at **not less than 4 knots**); or
  * the ship has in operation a **sewage treatment plant** which has been approved by the flag State Administration, and the **test results** of the plant are laid down in a **document** carried by the ship and the effluent produces **no visible floating solids** in, and **no discolouration** of the surrounding water.
* Paragraph G requires ships on international voyages in the Baltic Sea to be issued with a **Sewage Pollution Prevention Certificate** by the flag State Administration, valid for not longer than 5 years, subject to initial and periodical **surveys** prescribed in paragraph F.
* The full text of the **Helsinki Convention** can be seen at www.helcom.fi/convention/conven92.html

H03e DISPOSAL AT SEA OF GARBAGE

H03e.1 MARPOL Annex V

- **contains** the **Regulations for the Prevention of Pollution by Garbage from Ships**.
- **came into force** on 31 December 1988 and has (at May 2002) 106 Contracting States (which include the UK), representing 87.88% of world tonnage.
- includes a specimen Garbage Record Book.
- **defines "special area"** as "a sea area where for recognised technical reasons in relation to its oceanographical and ecological condition and to the particular character of its traffic the adoption of special mandatory methods for the prevention of sea pollution by garbage is required" (regulation 1(3)).
- **defines "garbage"** as "all kinds of victual, domestic and operational waste excluding fresh fish and parts thereof, generated during the normal operation of the ship and liable to be disposed of continuously or periodically except those substances which are defined or listed in other Annexes to the present Convention" (regulation 1(1)).
- **designates** (in regulation 5) **eight special areas**, whereas only **under UK law only three are designated** (see H03e.2a).

H03e.2 Prevention of Pollution by Garbage Regulations

* **The MS (Prevention of Pollution by Garbage) Regulations 1998** (SI 1998/1377) -
  - give effect in the UK to MARPOL Annex V.
  - apply (by virtue of regulation 3) to:
    * all **UK ships**, of any tonnage, wherever they may be;

- • **non-UK ships** while they are in UK waters, controlled waters[4] or, in relation to regulations 4 to 7 (i.e. the regulations dealing with disposal) any other waters which are at sea; and
  - • **fixed or floating installations** in controlled waters.
- * "**Garbage**" means all kinds of victual, domestic and operational wastes excluding fresh fish and parts thereof, generated during the normal operation of the ship and liable to be disposed of continuously or periodically except sewage originating from ships (regulation 2).
- * "**Operational wastes**" means all maintenance wastes, cargo associated wastes and cargo residues except residues or wastes from oil or oily mixtures, noxious liquid substances, non-polluting liquid substances or harmful substances in packaged form (regulation 2).
- * "**Required standard**" means, in relation to comminuted or ground garbage, comminuted or ground sufficiently finely to be capable of passing through a screen with openings no greater than 25 millimetres.
- * "**From the nearest land**" means, in relation to all land other than a part of the north-eastern coast of Australia (see below), from the **nearest baseline** from which the territorial sea of any territory is established in accordance with international law.
- * **Off the north-eastern coast of Australia** the term "from the nearest land" means from a line drawn from a point on the coast of Australia in latitude 11°00' S, longitude 142°08' E to a point in latitude 10°35' S, longitude 141°55' E, thence to a point latitude 10°00' S, longitude 142°00' E, thence to a point latitude 9°10' S, longitude 143°52' E, thence to a point latitude 9°00' S, longitude 144°30' E, thence to a point latitude 13°00' S, longitude 144°00' E, thence to a point latitude 15°00' S, longitude 146°00' E, thence to a point latitude 18°00' S, longitude 147°00' E, thence to a point latitude 21°00' S, longitude 153°00' E, thence to a point on the coast of Australia in latitude 24°42' S, longitude 153°15' E. This effectively makes the north-eastern coast of Australia, including the Great Barrier Reef, a **prohibited discharge area**.

H03e.2a Special areas (regulation 2)

- * **Three special areas** are designated by regulation 2 of the Prevention of Pollution by Garbage Regulations, as follows:
  - • the **Baltic sea area**, meaning the Baltic Sea proper with the Gulf of Bothnia and the Gulf of Finland and the entrance to the Baltic Sea bounded by the parallel 57°44.8' N east of the Skaw in the Skagerrak;
  - • the **North Sea area**, meaning[10] all sea areas within the following boundaries (including the North Sea proper and the English Channel and its approaches) -
    - ▪ to the north, the boundary constituted by the 62° N parallel from Norway westward to 4° W meridian and
    - ▪ thence southward to Scotland;
    - ▪ to the east, the boundary constituted by the parallel 57°44.8' N east of the Skaw in the Skagerrak;
    - ▪ to the south, the boundary constituted by the parallel 48°30' N from France westward to 5° W meridian and thence northward to England; and
  - • the **Antarctic area**, meaning the sea area south of latitude 60° S.
- * **Regulation 5(1) of MARPOL Annex II** designates **an additional five areas** as special areas, as follows:
  - • the **Mediterranean Sea area**, meaning the Mediterranean Sea proper including the gulfs and seas therein with the boundary between the Mediterranean and the Black Sea constituted by the 41° N parallel and bounded to the west by the Straits of Gibraltar at the meridian 58°36' W;
  - • the **Black Sea area**, meaning the Black Sea with the boundary between the Mediterranean and the Black Sea constituted by the parallel 41° N;
  - • the **Red Sea area**, meaning the Red Sea proper including the Gulfs of Suez and Aqaba bounded at the south by the rhumb line between Ras si Ane (12°28.5' N, 43°19.6' E) and Husn Murad (12°40.4' N, 43°30.2' E);
  - • the **Gulfs area**, meaning the sea area located north-west of the rhumb line between Ras al Hadd (22°30' N, 59°48' E) and Ras al Fasteh (25°04' N, 61°25' E); and
  - • the **Wider Caribbean Region**, meaning the Gulf of Mexico and Caribbean Sea proper including the bays and seas therein and that portion of the Atlantic Ocean within the boundary constituted by the 30° N parallel from Florida eastward to 77°30' W meridian, thence a rhumb line to the intersection of 20° N parallel and 59° W meridian, thence a rhumb line to the intersection of 7°20' N parallel and 50° W meridian, thence a rhumb line drawn south-westerly to the eastern boundary of French Guiana.
- * A discharge of garbage in excess of permitted levels **in any of the additional areas** listed in Annex II regulation 5(1) **will not be an offence under UK law**, but may be a violation of the law of the nearest **coastal State**, if that law extends to the position at which the discharge was made. In the case of a non-UK ship, it may also be an offence under the law of the **flag State**.

---

[4] "**Controlled waters**" means the waters specified as areas within which the jurisdiction and rights of the UK are exercisable by the MS (Prevention of Pollution) (Limits) Regulations 1996 (SI 1996/2128, as amended by SI 1997/506) (see I01a.1b).
[10] The wording of the definition of the North Sea Area in MARPOL Annex V regulation 5 differs slightly from the UK regulation wording.

* See also the notes at H03e.2 regarding **prohibited discharges** in the area of the **Great Barrier Reef and north-eastern coast of Australia**.

H03e.2b Disposal of garbage outside special areas (regulations 4 and 5)

* The disposal of any **plastics** from a ship to the sea outside any Special Area (designated in regulation 2) is prohibited (regulation 4).
* Subject to regulation 7, the disposal of **garbage other than plastics** from a ship into the sea outside any Special Area is prohibited except where it is made as far from the nearest land as is practicable and –
  * in the case of **dunnage, lining and packing materials which will float**, not less than **25 nautical miles** from the nearest land;
  * in the case of **food wastes and all other garbage** including paper products, rags, glass, metal, bottles, crockery and similar refuse, not less than 12 miles or, if such wastes and other garbage have been ground or comminuted to the required standard, not less than **3 miles** from the nearest land (regulation 5).

H03e.2c Disposal of garbage within special areas (regulation 6)

* Within the **Antarctic area**, no garbage of any kind may be disposed of.
* Within a special area other than the Antarctic area:
  * no garbage other than **food wastes** may be disposed of;
  * food wastes may be disposed of, **without grinding or comminution**, where the disposal is as far as practicable, and in no case less than **12 nautical miles** from, the nearest land (regulation 6).
* **MARPOL Regulation V/5** (Disposal of garbage within special areas) contains a provision concerning the **Wider Caribbean Region** that is not given effect in the UK's Regulations, i.e. that disposal into the Wider Caribbean Region of ground or comminuted food wastes must be made as far as practicable from land, but in any case not less than 3 miles from the nearest land. This requirement does not apply to disposal from fixed or floating platforms, or ships within 500m of them, which are subject to the restrictions described in H03e.2d.

H03e.2d Disposal of garbage within 500 metres of fixed or floating installations (regulation 7)

* The disposal into the sea of **any garbage** from a fixed or floating installation, or from **any ship alongside or within 500 metres** of such an installation, is prohibited except that **food wastes which have been comminuted or ground** to the required standard may be disposed of into the sea from such installations or ships if the installation in question is located more than **12 nautical miles** from the nearest land.

H03e.2e Offences and penalties (regulation 14)

* Any breach of the "**disposal regulations**" (i.e. regulations 4, 5, 6 or 7), in respect of a ship will be an **offence** on the part of the **owner, manager, demise charterer and master** of the ship, and in respect of an installation will be an **offence** on the part of the **owner and installation manager**, punishable on summary conviction by a fine not exceeding **£25,000**, or on conviction on indictment by an **unlimited fine**. (See also B03b.3f.)
* The maximum penalty on summary conviction for breach of regulations of the Prevention of Pollution by Garbage Regulations 1998 **other than regulations 4, 5, 6 or 7** is a fine not exceeding the **statutory maximum** (i.e. £5,000).

H03e.2f Defences (regulation 20)

* In any proceedings for an offence under the Prevention of Pollution by Garbage Regulations 1998 it will be a defence for the person charged to prove:
  * that he took all reasonable steps and exercised all due diligence to ensure that the Regulations were complied with;
  * that the disposal was necessary for the purpose of securing the safety of the ship or installation or those on board, or of saving life at sea; or
  * that the escape of garbage resulted from damage to the ship or installation or the ship's or installation's equipment and that all reasonable precautions were taken before and after the damage occurred to prevent or minimise the escape.

H03e.2g Garbage disposal criteria table

* The following tables summarise, in two ways, the **garbage disposal requirements** of the Regulations.

DISCHARGES OF GARBAGE		
Type of garbage	Areas where discharge is permitted outside special areas	Areas where discharge is permitted inside special areas
Plastics	Nowhere	Nowhere
Food wastes (ground or comminuted to 25mm)	As far as practicable but not less than 3 miles from the nearest land	In Wider Caribbean Region: As far as practicable but not less than 3 miles from the nearest land. Elsewhere: As far as practicable and not less than 12 miles from the nearest land.
Food wastes (unground/uncomminuted)	As far as practicable but not less than 12 miles from the nearest land	As far as practicable but not less than 12 miles from the nearest land, except in Wider Caribbean Region.
All other garbage (including paper products, rags, glass, metal, bottles, crockery and similar refuse) except dunnage, lining and packaging materials which float	As far as practicable and not less than 12 miles from the nearest land	Nowhere
Dunnage, lining and packaging materials which float	As far as practicable and not less than 25 miles from the nearest land	Nowhere

Distance from nearest land	Types of garbage which may be discharged outside special areas	Types of garbage which may be discharged inside special areas
Up to 3 miles	No garbage of any kind	No garbage of any kind
Between 3 and 12 miles (but as far from nearest land as practicable)	Food wastes only (ground or comminuted to 25mm)	In Wider Caribbean Region: Ground or comminuted food wastes only. In other areas: No garbage of any kind.
Between 12 and 25 miles (but as far from nearest land as practicable)	Food wastes and all other garbage including paper products, rags, glass, metal, bottles, crockery and similar refuse, other than dunnage, lining and packaging materials which float, and plastics	In Wider Caribbean Region: Ground or comminuted food wastes only. In other areas: Food wastes only. (Grinding or comminution not required.)
Outside 25 miles (but as far from nearest land as practicable)	Dunnage, lining and packaging materials which float, and all other garbage except plastics	In Wider Caribbean Region: Ground or comminuted food wastes only. Elsewhere: Food wastes only. (Grinding or comminution not required.)

H03e.3 Disposal of out-of-date pyrotechnics

* While for many years it was recommended in the Annual Summary of Notices to Mariners that **ship and survival craft pyrotechnics** which were past their expiry date should be dumped in deep water well away from land, that practice is now **prohibited** under MARPOL Annex IV and the MS (Prevention of Pollution by Garbage) Regulations, because of the use of plastics in pyrotechnic manufacture.
* **MGN 256** contains the MCA's advice on methods of **disposal ashore** of out-of-date pyrotechnics.
* Date-expired pyrotechnics should be disposed of ashore by one of the following means:
  • returning them to the **supplier**, directly or via the supplier's local representative;
  • requesting a **liferaft service station** in the UK or overseas to accept any of the ship's out-of-date pyrotechnics when liferafts are being sent ashore for servicing; liferaft service stations deal with the disposal of expired pyrotechnics on a regular basis and have arrangements locally to do this;
  • contacting the **local Coastguard**, who will be able to arrange disposal through a military establishment.

H03e.4 Garbage disposal records and inspection

* The MCA publication *The Prevention of Pollution by Garbage from Ships and the provision and use of Port Waste Reception facilities: Instructions for the Guidance of Surveyors* (see B05b.5) states that although no equipment requirements, record books or certificates are specified for vessels to comply with the provisions of the MS (Prevention of Pollution by Garbage) Regulations, many vessels will be fitted with equipment such as **incinerators** and **compactors**, and most ships will require **storage facilities** for garbage. When ships are visited for other purposes, the arrangements made by ships for complying with the Regulations should be examined by the surveyor and the master's attention drawn to the importance of compliance by discussion and the issue of MCA promotional material (e.g. a poster). An **assessment** should be made by the surveyor to determine if the ship is complying with the Regulations by:

- **examining ship's records**, particularly any log entries referring to garbage or any receipts for garbage discharged to shore reception facilities. Although these receipts cannot be demanded they are helpful in showing compliance with the Regulation requirements;
- ensuring that **crew have been made aware** of the Regulations;
- checking, if the ship has been at sea for some time, that **plastic garbage has accumulated** on board for disposal to shore reception facilities (provided it has **not been incinerated** during the voyage).

* For notes on **Garbage Management Plans** see D04t.4.
* For notes on **Garbage Record Books**, see D04t.5.

H03f CONTROL OF AIR POLLUTION FROM SHIPS

H03f.1 MARPOL Protocol 1997

- **adds Annex VI (Regulations for the Prevention of Air Pollution from Ships)** to the MARPOL Convention.
- **was adopted** by IMO in September 1997 but **is not yet in force** internationally. It will enter into force 12 months after acceptance by at least 15 States with a combined tonnage of at least 50% of world gross tonnage. At May 2002 there were 5 Contracting States representing 15.80% of world tonnage.
- **sets limits on emissions of sulphur oxide (SO$_x$) and nitrogen oxide (NO$_x$)** from **ship exhausts** and will prohibit deliberate emissions of **ozone-depleting substances**. Annex VI emission control requirements are in accordance with the **1987 Montreal Protocol** (a UN international environmental treaty), as amended in London in 1990.
- **includes** a specimen form of International Air Pollution Prevention (IAPP) Certificate (in Appendix I), requirements for Test Cycles and Weighting Factors (in Appendix II), Criteria and procedures for designation of SO$_x$ Emission Control Areas (in Appendix III), Type approval and operating limits for shipboard incinerators (in Appendix IV), and Information to be included in the Bunker Delivery Note (in Appendix V).

* For notes on **air pollution prevention equipment, surveys and certification** see D04g.10.
* **Chapter III of Annex VI** (regulations 12 to 19) contains **requirements for control of emissions from ships**.
* **Regulation 12(1)** prohibits **deliberate emissions of ozone-depleting substances**, except where necessary for the purpose of securing the safety of a ship or saving life, as provided in regulation 3. **Regulation 12(2)** prohibits, on all ships, new installations containing ozone-depleting substances, except that new installations containing hydrochlorofluorocarbons (HCFCs) are permitted until 1 January 2020.
* **Regulation 13** sets **NO$_x$ emission limits** for diesel engines with a power output of more than 130kW installed on ships built on or after 1 January 2000, and diesel engines of similar power undergoing a major conversion on or after 1 January 2000. It does not apply to emergency diesel engines, engines installed in lifeboats and any device or equipment intended to be used solely in case of emergency, or engines installed on ships solely engaged in voyages within waters subject to the sovereignty or jurisdiction of the flag State, provided that such engines are subject to an alternative NO$_x$ control measure established by the Administration. Notwithstanding this, the flag State Administration may allow exclusion from regulation 13 for any diesel engine installed on a ship constructed, or on a ship undergoing a major conversion, before the entry into force of the Protocol, provided that the ship is solely engaged in voyages to ports or offshore terminals within the flag State.
* **Regulation 14** provides for adoption of "**SO$_x$ Emission Control Areas**" where the adoption of special mandatory measures for SO$_x$ emissions from ships is required to prevent, reduce and control air pollution from SO$_x$ and its attendant adverse impacts on land and sea areas with more stringent control on sulphur emissions. In these areas the sulphur content of fuel oil used on ships must not exceed 1.5% m/m. Alternatively, ships in these areas must fit an **exhaust gas cleaning system** or use any other technological method to limit SO$_x$ emissions. The **Baltic Sea** is designated as a SO$_x$ Emission Control Area.
* **Regulation 15** provides that in ports or terminals in Party States any regulation of emissions of **Volatile Organic Compounds** (VOCs) from tankers must be in accordance with Annex VI.
* **Regulation 16** sets out requirements for **shipboard incineration**. Regulation 16(4) bans the incineration of:
  - MARPOL Annex I, II and III cargo residues and related contaminated packing materials;
  - polychlorinated biphenyls (PCBs);
  - garbage, as defined in MARPOL Annex V, containing more than traces of heavy metals; and
  - refined petroleum products containing halogen compounds.
* Under regulation 16(5) incineration of **sewage sludge and sludge oil** generated during the normal operation of a ship may take place in the main or auxiliary power plant or boilers (as well as in an incinerator), but in those cases, must not take place inside ports, harbours and estuaries.
* Regulation 16(6) prohibits the shipboard incineration of **polyvinyl chlorides** (PVCs), except in incinerators for which IMO Type Approval Certificates have been issued.

* Under regulation 16(7) all ships with incinerators subject to regulation 16 must possess a **manufacturer's operating manual** which must specify how to operate the incinerator within the limits described in paragraph 2 of appendix IV to Annex VI.
* Under regulation 16(8) **personnel responsible for operation of any incinerator** must be trained and capable of implementing the guidance in the manufacturer's operating manual.
* Regulation 3 provides that the regulations of Annex VI will not apply to any emission necessary for the purpose of securing the **safety of a ship or saving life at sea**, or any emission resulting from **damage** to a ship or its equipment, subject to certain conditions.
* **Regulation 19** contains the **requirements for platforms and drilling rigs**.

H03g CONTROL OF POLLUTION BY BALLAST WATER

H03g.1 The ballast water problem

* A 200,000dwt ship may discharge around 60,000 tonnes of ballast water before loading. Shipping is estimated to move between **10 and 12 billion tonnes of ballast water** across the oceans each year. In doing so it **moves thousands of marine species from one environment to another**.
* Marine life-forms moved in ballast water include bacteria and other microbes, small invertebrates and the eggs, cysts and larvae of numerous species. The problem is worsened by the fact that virtually all marine species have a **planktonic stage** in their life cycle, during which the plankton may be transported even if the adults are unlikely to because of their size or because they live on or in the seabed.
* It is estimated that at any given time **between 3000 and 4500 species** are being transported in ships' ballast tanks around the world. Many of these will not survive the voyage, but those that do may be deposited in a new environment where they may multiply to such an extent that they **compete with and displace local populations**. As a result, entire eco-systems are being changed. For example:
  * in the USA, the European zebra mussel has infested over 40% of internal waterways;
  * in southern Australia, Asian kelp has displaced local species;
  * in the Black Sea the North American jellyfish has depleted plankton stocks to such an extent that it has contributed to the collapse of entire fisheries.
* The introduction of invasive marine species into new environments is a **major threat to the world's oceans**.

H03g.2 Ballast water control measures

* **Re-ballasting at sea** (i.e. "**ballast water exchange**") is recommended by the IMO Guidelines and is currently the most practical method of reducing the transfer of harmful aquatic organisms. However, it is less than 100% effective at removing unwanted organisms, and some parties believe it may contribute to the problem by more widely dispersing the "pest" species, and in some cases depositing them in places where they may infest the waters of island States.
* **Alternative methods** are urgently being investigated by the ocean scientific community. Methods being considered include:
  * mechanical treatment methods such as filtration and separation;
  * physical treatment methods such as sterilisation by ozone, ultra-violet light, electric currents and heat treatment;
  * chemical treatment methods; and
  * combinations of the above methods.
* The IMO Marine Environment Protection Committee (MEPC) is developing **draft regulations** for ballast water management, and an IMO diplomatic conference is planned for **late 2003** to adopt the new requirements as an "International Convention for the Control and Management of Ships' Ballast Water and Sediments". (National legislation would then be required in Part States to enforce the IMO requirements.)
* Through the **Global Ballast Water Management Programme** ("GloBallast"), IMO is assisting developing countries to tackle the ballast water pollution problem. The **GloBallast website** is at: http://globallast.imo.org

H03g.3 Ballast water exchange requirements

* Pending the implementation of the internationally-agreed measures mentioned in H03g.2, several coastal States and individual ports have introduced their own requirements for ballast water management and control. In most cases

(but not all) these requirements involve the exchange of ballast water at sea, and the recording on board of certain details such as the time, location, volume and salinity of water loaded, exchanged at sea, and discharged.
* Additional States and ports will inevitably produce their own requirements before the introduction of the planned IMO Convention on Ballast Water Control and Management, resulting in a complexity of diverse requirements which will be difficult for shipowners, managers and shipmasters to ascertain.
* Ballast water requirements are currently published on the Internet for Buenos Aires, Australia, Canadian Great Lakes and St Lawrence ports west of 63°, Vancouver, Chile, Israel, New Zealand, Scapa Flow (UK), and the USA. Summary details and contact addresses are available on the GloBallast website (see H03g.2) and (for Intertanko member companies) on the Intertanko website at www.intertanko.com/tankerfacts/environmental/ballast
* Masters who do not have access to the Internet or other sources of ballast water information should **ask their agents** at ports of destination for any local ballast water requirements, as long before arrival as possible.

H03g.4 IMO Ballast Water Guidelines

* **MGN 81** superseded M.1533 and draws attention to the IMO publication "**Guidelines for the Control and Management of Ships' Ballast Water to Minimize the Transfer of Harmful Aquatic Organisms and Pathogens**" which was adopted by Resolution A.868(20)[11]. The Guidelines provide flag State administrations and port State authorities with guidance on procedures for minimising pollution by ballast water, and include **procedures for ships**.
* Where any statutory or regulatory requirements in any port or State waters conflict with the IMO Guidelines, the **statutory or regulatory requirements will prevail**.
* **Compliance with the Guidelines** is not, at present, a legal requirement in the UK. MGN 81 advises, however, that ships' agents and shipowners are strongly urged to ensure that vessels discharging ballast water in UK waters comply with the Guidelines. The UK Government is (according to the MGN) reviewing the need for regulatory controls in the UK, which would reflect the IMO Guidelines.
* Masters are advised by MGN 81 to **contact destination ports** to ascertain any local requirements relating to ballast water exchange.
* The full text of Resolution A.868(20) (i.e. the Guidelines) can be found at http://globallast.imo.org

H03h COMPLIANCE AT SEA WITH FOREIGN POLLUTION LAWS

H03h.1 US federal pollution law

* Under the US **Federal Clean Water Act** an owner, operator or person in charge of an onshore or offshore facility (including a ship) may be fined up to **USD 5,000** for oil discharged from such facility affecting US waters. Some owners and masters post "Fine 5000" warning notices on board and use the threat of this fine as a tool to prevent crew members from discharging oil overboard.
* Under the US **Oil Pollution Act 1990**, the "Fine 5000" notices are obsolete and may mislead crew members in respect of the implications of discharging oil overboard in US waters. Shipowners now carry **unlimited liability** for the clean-up operation and damage caused by an oil spill in US waters, and also face strict criminal penalties for violations of the Act. For spilling oil affecting US waters, the offender risks criminal prosecution (1) **for spilling the oil** and (2) **for failing to notify the US Government** of the spill. Both individual violators and organisations may be penalised, and individuals may be imprisoned. For "negligent violations", the maximum fine is **USD 50,000 per day** and one year imprisonment[12]. For "knowing[13] violations" imprisonment may be for up to **three years**.
* Under the **Alternative Fines Act** the maximum fine for an individual is **USD 100,000 (negligent)** and **USD 250,000 (knowingly)**. For an organisation the fines are doubled. If an individual or an organisation derives pecuniary loss to a third party, the fine will be up to **twice the gross gain or loss**, which, depending on the circumstances, could run to millions.
* US federal law requires **every ship above 26 feet** in length to have a **placard** of at least 5 x 8 inches made of durable material fixed in a conspicuous place **in each machinery space**, or at the **bilge and ballast pump station**, with the following message, in a language understood by the crew: "Discharge of Oil Prohibited. The Federal Water

---

[11] Resolution A.868(20) revoked Resolution A.774(18) which adopted earlier Guidelines which were published by the UK with M.1533.
[12] The fine is composed of a mandatory civil penalty for up to USD 25,000 per day of violation or USD 1,000 per barrel discharged, and a further USD 25,000 a day or three times the costs incurred by the Oil Spill Liability Trust Fund, for failing to clean up. The penalty for the second or subsequent offence is two years imprisonment for a negligent violation.
[13] "Knowing" requires only general intent, not specific intent to break the law.

Pollution Control Act prohibits the discharge of oil or oily waste into or upon the navigable waters of the United States, or the waters of the contiguous zone, or which may affect natural resources belonging to, appertaining to, or under the exclusive management authority of the United States, if such discharge causes a film or discoloration of the surface of the water or causes a sludge or emulsion beneath the surface of the water. Violators are subject to substantial civil penalties and/or criminal sanctions including fines and imprisonment." Old warning notices may be left in place, but the new placard should be added and all crew members should be informed of the new fines. The new placards may be obtained through US shipchandlers.

* Under the US **Oil Pollution Act 1990** (OPA 90), evidence of financial responsibility for oil pollution is required from any vessel over 300gt (except a non-self-propelled vessel which does not carry oil as cargo or fuel) using a place subject to US jurisdiction and in respect of any vessel using the waters of the US Exclusive Economic Zone (EEZ) to trans-ship or lighter oil destined for the USA. This evidence is provided by a **Certificate of Financial Responsibility (Water Pollution)**, (known as a **COFR**) issued by the US Coast Guard under Title 33 US Code, Section 1321(p). For notes on the **COFR**, see G04d.4a.

H03h.2 Pollution law of other countries

* A large number of maritime States have not ratified or yet acceded to the annexes of the MARPOL Convention, and in these countries national pollution regulations may differ from those in force in MARPOL Party States. Where there is any doubt about local regulations, the master of a ship arriving at a non-MARPOL State's port or terminal should attempt to ascertain the requirements from the agent and/or the P&I club correspondent.
* P&I club literature and club websites carry reports of marine pollution fines, usually sent by club correspondents. One report, for example, shows that the fine on tankers of over 5000gt discharging dirty ballast in Turkey is 149,438,250,000 Turkish Lira (US$273,088). Dirty ballast or "every kind of residue in liquid or solid form" discharged from any vessel over 1000gt will result in a fine of 29,887,650,000 Turkish Lira (US$54,618).
* The Australian Maritime Safety Authority (AMSA) has a good marine environment protection website at www.amsa.gov.au/amsa/env.htm

H03i UK GOVERNMENT INTERVENTION POWERS IN POLLUTION INCIDENTS

* **Section 137 of the Merchant Shipping Act 1995**[14] confers certain **powers** which are exercisable where -
  * an **accident**[15] has occurred to or in a ship; and
  * in the opinion of the Department for Transport (DfT) **oil from the ship will or may cause significant pollution in the UK, UK waters or a part of the sea specified by virtue of section 129(2)(b)**; and
  * in the opinion of the DfT the **use of the powers** conferred by this section is **urgently needed**[16].
* For the purpose of preventing or reducing oil pollution, or the risk of oil pollution, the DfT may give **directions** as respects the ship or its cargo -
  * to the **owner** of the ship, or to any person in possession of the ship;
  * to the **master** of the ship;
  * to any **pilot** of the ship;
  * to any **salvor in possession** of the ship, or to **any person who is the servant or agent of any salvor in possession** of the ship, and who is **in charge** of the salvage operation; or
  * where the ship is in waters which are regulated or managed by a harbour authority, to the **harbour master** or to the **harbour authority**.
* The directions may require the person to whom they are given **to take, or refrain from taking, any action of any kind whatsoever**, and may require -
  - that **the ship is to be, or is not to be, moved**, or is to be **moved to a specified place**, or is to be **removed from a specified place or locality**; or

[14] As amended by section 2 of the Merchant Shipping and Maritime Security Act 1997.
[15] "**Accident**" means a collision of ships, stranding or other incident of navigation, or other occurrence on board a ship or external to it resulting in material damage or imminent threat of material damage to a ship or cargo.
[16] Command and Control: Report of Lord Donaldson's Review of Salvage and Intervention and their Command and Control, paragraph 4.2 states: The statutory intervention powers of the Secretary of State empower him to take command in that, in the last resort, he is entitled to "take any such action as he has power to require to be taken by a direction under this Section". However it is difficult to envisage any scenario in which he would do so, save in the case of a master who refused to accept salvage assistance and thereby created a dangerous situation involving a threat of significant pollution. In such a case the Secretary of State might over-ride the authority of the master. That apart, the exercise of his powers will almost always be confined to exercising control of the salvage operation. Furthermore, that control will not be total. It will normally be limited to requiring certain general courses of action to be adopted or avoided.

- that the ship is **not to be moved to a specified place or area, or over a specified route**; or
- that any oil or other cargo is to be, or is not to be, unloaded or discharged; or
- that specified **salvage measures are to be, or are not to be, taken**.

* If the above powers prove to be inadequate, the DfT may, for the purposes of preventing or reducing oil pollution or its risk, take, as respects the ship or its cargo, **any action of any kind whatsoever**, including **sinking or destroying the ship**, or take over **control of the ship**.

* Every person concerned with compliance with directions given, or with action taken, must use his best endeavours to avoid any risk to human life.

* Under **section 139**, if the person to whom a direction is given as above contravenes, or fails to comply with it, he will be guilty of an **offence**. A **person intentionally obstructing** any person acting on behalf of the DfT in connection with giving or serving a direction, or acting in compliance with a direction, will be guilty of an **offence** and liable to a maximum fine of **£50,000** on summary conviction, or an **unlimited fine** on conviction on indictment.

* The **MS (Prevention of Pollution: Substances Other than Oil) (Intervention) Order 1997** (SI 1997/1869) prescribes numerous substances **other than oil** (most of which are chemicals), a threat of pollution from which (following a shipping casualty) will trigger the DfT's powers of intervention under section 137 of the Merchant Shipping Act 1995.

* The **MS (Prevention of Pollution) (Intervention) (Foreign Ships) Order 1997** (SI 1997/2568) extends the scope of the DfT's intervention powers under Merchant Shipping Act 1995, enabling it to give directions in relation to a **non-UK ship** where there is a grave and imminent threat of pollution, provided that the persons or companies directed **owe allegiance** to the UK.

* Intervention under the above powers would in most cases occur during some form of salvage operation. The **right of a coastal State to intervene** in salvage operations where pollution threatens to harm their coasts or interests is contained **in article 9 of the International Salvage Convention 1989** (see H05c.2).

* Under **section 138A**, any reference to **oil** in section 137 (or section 138) includes a reference to **any other substance which is liable to create hazards** to human health, to harm living resources and marine life, to damage amenities or to interfere with other legitimate uses of the sea.

* Powers to prevent and reduce pollution and the risk of pollution following an incident involving an **offshore installation** are contained in the Offshore Installations (Emergency Pollution Control) Regulations 2002 (SI 2002/1861), and correspond to those under sections 137 to 140 of the Merchant Shipping Act 1995 in relation to ships.

* See also notes on **Convention provisions on government intervention in maritime casualty incidents** at H05c.2.

H04 Incidents at sea

H04a MASTER'S AUTHORITY TO TAKE ACTION

* The master of a ship has **implied authority** in English law to perform whatever acts are **reasonably and ordinarily necessary** for the safe and proper prosecution of the voyage with respect to both ship and cargo. (For notes on **agency**, see B03d.3.)

* Circumstances may arise, e.g. where the vessel is in grave and imminent danger and requires immediate assistance, such that the master's implied authority becomes extended, since he cannot, in the special circumstances of the case, obtain instructions from the owner or charterer.

* At such times of peril, the master may become an **agent of necessity** of the cargo owners and has implied powers to act in their best interests. For notes on **agency of necessity**, see B03d.3b. For notes on the **master as agent of necessity**, see E04f.2.

* **Article 6.2 of the International Convention on Salvage 1989** (see H05c.1), which is given the force of law in the UK under section 224 of the Merchant Shipping Act 1995, provides that the **master of a salved vessel** will have the **authority to conclude salvage contracts on behalf of the owner**, and the **master** or the owner will have the **authority to conclude salvage contracts on behalf of the owner of property** on the vessel.

* **M.1175** states that "....the Master has complete authority to take whatever steps are necessary to ensure safety, including the engagement of salvors;" and ".....while the master will quite properly wish to keep his Owners informed as to what he is doing, it is vital that he should not feel that he is obliged to discuss with them before acting."

H04b DISTRESS, URGENCY AND SAFETY INCIDENTS

H04b.1 Assistance to persons in distress at sea

* The MS (Safety of Navigation) Regulations 2002 (SI 2002/1473) (see H01f.2) -
    - **revoke** regulations 3 to 8 of the MS (Distress Messages) Regulations 1998 (SI 1998/1691) which, until 1 July 2002, imposed on masters of UK ships a duty to assist persons in distress at sea.
    - require compliance by a ship to which the Regulations apply (from 1 July 2002) with **paragraphs 1 and 2 of SOLAS regulation V/33**, which relates to **Distress messages: Obligations and procedures**. Paragraph 1 imposes on shipmasters a duty to **respond to distress alerts**. Paragraph 2 confers on shipmasters a right to **requisition assistance from other ships**, and imposes on masters of requisitioned ships a duty to **comply with the requisition**.
* **SOLAS regulation V/33.5** provides that the provisions of regulation V/33 do not prejudice the Convention for the Unification of Certain Rules of Law relating to Assistance and Salvage at Sea, signed at Brussels on 23 September 1910, particularly the **obligation to render assistance** imposed by article 11 of that Convention[17].

H04b.1a Duty to assist persons in distress at sea

* **SOLAS regulation V/33.1** provides that the **master of a ship at sea** which is in a position to be able to be able to provide **assistance on receiving a signal from any source** that persons are in distress at sea, is bound to **proceed with all speed** to their assistance, if possible **informing them or the search and rescue service** that the ship is doing so.
* SOLAS regulation V/33.1 **does not apply** to the master of a ship which is **not at sea**.
* SOLAS regulation V/33.1 **does not impose a duty to assist aircraft in distress**; that obligation is now in section 93 of the Merchant Shipping Act 1995, as modified (see H04b.2).
* It should be noted that there is **no statutory obligation to save maritime property** in danger of being lost. Any attempt by the master of a merchant vessel to save property is a **commercial venture** and not a statutory obligation. For notes on **offering salvage assistance**, see H05e.3.

H04b.1b Action when ship is unable to assist persons in distress

* **SOLAS regulation V/33.1** (in addition to the provision described in H04b.1a) provides that if the ship receiving the distress alert is **unable** or, in the special circumstances of the case, considers it **unreasonable** or **unnecessary** to proceed to their assistance, the master must **enter in the log book the reason for failing to proceed** to the assistance of the persons in distress, taking into account the IMO recommendation[18] to inform the appropriate SAR service accordingly.

H04b.1c Right to requisition assistance from other ships

* **SOLAS regulation V/33.2** provides that the **master of a ship in distress** or the **search and rescue service** concerned, after **consultation**, so far as may be possible, with the masters of ships which answer the distress alert, has the **right to requisition** one or more of those ships as the master of the ship in distress or the SAR service considers **best able to render assistance**. The regulation further provides that it will be **the duty of the master or masters of the ship or ships requisitioned to comply with the requisition** by continuing to proceed with all speed to the assistance of the persons in distress.

H04b.1d Release from obligation to assist

* **SOLAS regulation V/33.3** provides that **masters of ships will be released** from the obligation imposed by regulation V/33.1 on learning that:
    1. **their ships have not been requisitioned**; and
    2. **one or more other ships have been requisitioned and are complying** with the requisition.

---

[17] The Brussels Salvage Convention 1910 was given effect in the UK by the now-repealed Maritime Conventions Act 1911 which is in part replaced by the provisions of the Merchant Shipping Act 1995. The 1995 Act also gives effect to the International Convention on Salvage 1989, Article 10.1 of which provides that "every master is bound, so far as he can do so without serious danger to his vessel and persons thereon, to render assistance to any person in danger of being lost at sea". Article 10.2 requires States Party to the Convention to adopt the measures necessary to enforce the duty in Article 10.1. Article 10.3 provides that the owner of the vessel will incur no liability for a breach by the master of the duty under Article 10.1.
[18] A footnote to SOLAS 74 regulation V/10, which regulation V/33 amends and replaces, states "Refer to the immediate action to be taken by each ship on receipt of a distress message in the IAMSAR Manual, as it may be amended". The same footnote does not appear in the revised regulation V/33, as printed in the MCA's 2002 SOLAS V publication.

* The regulation further provides that this decision[19] must, if possible, be **communicated** to the other requisitioned ships and to the SAR service.
* **SOLAS regulation V/33.4** provides that the **master of a ship will be released** from the obligation imposed by regulation V/33.1 and, if his ship has been requisitioned, from the obligation imposed by regulation V/33.2 **on being informed** by:
    * the **persons in distress**; or by
    * the **SAR service**; or by
    * the master of another ship which has reached the persons in distress,
    - that **assistance is no longer necessary**.

H04b.2 Statutory duty to assist aircraft in distress

* **Section 93(1) of the Merchant Shipping Act 1995**, as modified by regulation 2 of the MS (Distress Messages) Regulations 1998 (SI 1998/1691), provides that the master of a ship, on receiving at sea a **distress signal from an aircraft** or **information from any source that an aircraft is in distress**, must **proceed with all speed** to the assistance of the persons in distress, informing them, if possible, that he is doing so, unless he is **unable**, or in the special circumstances of the case considers it **unreasonable** or **unnecessary** to do so, or if he is **released** from this duty under section 93(5). Under section 93(3) the duties imposed by section 93(1) apply to masters of UK ships wherever they may be, and the masters of non-UK ships when in UK waters.
* **Section 93(5), as modified**, provides that the master will be **released** from the duty under section 93(1) if he is informed by the persons in distress, or by the master of any ship that has reached them, that assistance is no longer required.
* **Compliance** by a master with the provisions of section 93 will not affect his right, or the right of any other person, to **salvage** (section 93(7)).

H04b.3 Official Log Book entries concerning distress signals and messages

* The following Official Log Book entries relating to distress signals and messages are required to be made under paragraph 13 of the Schedule of the MS (Official Log Books) Regulations 1981 (SI 1981/569) (see D05a.3):
    * a **record of every signal of distress or a message** that a vessel, aircraft or person is in distress at sea, observed or received (entry No. 13). This entry is to be made by the master or someone authorised by the master and witnessed by a member of the crew;
    * where the master, on receiving at sea a signal of distress or information from any source that a vessel or aircraft is in distress, is **unable**, or in the special circumstances of the case considers it **unreasonable or unnecessary** to go to the assistance of the persons in distress, a statement of his **reasons for not going** to the assistance of those persons (entry No. 14). The entry is to be made by the **master in person** and witnessed by a member of the crew.

H04b.4 Statutory duties following collision

* **Section 92(1) of the Merchant Shipping Act 1995** provides that in every case of collision between two ship, it will be the duty of the master of each ship, if and so far as he can do so without danger to his own ship, crew and passengers, if any:
    * to **render** to the other ship, its master, crew and passengers (if any) such **assistance** as may be practicable, and may be necessary to save them from any danger caused by the collision (section 92(1)(a));
    * to **stay by the other ship** until he has ascertained that it has no need of further assistance (section 92(1)(a)); and
    * to **give** to the master of the other ship the **name** of his **own ship** and also the names of the **ports** from which it comes and to which it is bound (section 92(1)(b)).
* These duties apply to the master of UK ships (anywhere) and to the masters of foreign ships in UK waters (section 92(2)).
* The failure of the master of a ship to comply with the above duties will not raise any presumption of law that the **collision** was caused by his wrongful act, neglect or default (section 93(3)).
* Under section 92(4) a master who fails to comply with the requirement to render assistance to and stand by the other vessel will be liable:
    * on summary conviction, to a fine of up to **£50,000**; or

---

[19] It is not clear from the regulation what "this decision" means.

* on conviction on indictment, to an unlimited fine or imprisonment for up to 2 years, or both.
* Where the master has breached either duty, if he is a certified officer, an **inquiry** into his conduct may be held, and his certificate **cancelled** or **suspended** (section 92(4)).
* The **MS (Accident Reporting and Investigation) Regulations 1999** (SI 1999/2567) require the master to:
    * **send** a report to the MAIB (regulation 5(1)) (see E10r.4); and
    * **preserve** relevant evidence (regulation 7(1)) (see E10r.10).
* **Regulation 9 of the MS (Reporting Requirements for Ships Carrying Dangerous or Polluting Goods) Regulations 1995** (SI 1995/2498), as amended by SI 1999/2121, requires the master to send a **pollution report** where the collision results in any pollution (see H06e).
* Paragraph 12 of the Schedule of the MS (Official Log Books) Regulations 1981 (SI 1981/569) requires the master to make an **entry in the Official Log Book** (narrative section) where the ship is **in collision**, recording a description of the casualty and the place where, or the position of the ship when, it occurred (see D05a.4).

H04b.5 Non-statutory duties following a collision or other casualty

* **Emergency Check List C2** in the ICS Bridge Procedures Guide (yellow pages) relates to **collision** and should be consulted if available.
* As well as fulfilling his statutory obligations following a collision or any other casualty involving his vessel, her crew or passengers, a master should always act in the best interests of the shipowner and the owners of any cargo on board.
* The master should always obtain the assistance and advice of the P&I club's local correspondent. P&I clubs are expert in **loss prevention procedures** and will always suggest appropriate ways to safeguard the owner's interests and limit his liability.
* **Following a collision**, and after rendering assistance, etc. as outlined in H04b.4, the master should:
    * **inform** the owner or manager, as appropriate; and
    * **inform** the P&I club's local correspondent, who will advise on the best action to take in the owner's interest in the circumstances.
* Generally, **liability should never be admitted** to any other party.
* A P&I club may advise the master of a ship damaged in collision with another vessel, if able and justified, to serve **written notice** on the master of the other vessel as follows:

```
                                                        m.v. Hard Luck
                                                        Port of Seaville
                                                        1st April 1997

        The Master
        m.v. Careless
        of (port of registry/flag)


        Dear Sir

        Re: Collision Damage

        With reference to the collision which occurred between our respective vessels
        on 1st April 1997 at 0635 hours Local Time, I hereby give you, on behalf of my
        owners and their underwriters, formal notice holding you and your owners solely
        responsible for all loss or damage whatsoever sustained by my owners in
        consequence of the collision.

        Please inform your owners immediately so that they and their underwriters can
        take steps to carry out a joint survey on my vessel, m.v. Hard Luck, in order to
        establish extent and quantum of damage.

        Please let me have the name of your vessel's agents. My vessel's agents are
        Seaville Agencies Ltd.

        Please acknowledge receipt of this letter on the enclosed copy.

        Yours faithfully

        (signed)
        John Perfect
        Master, m.v. Hard Luck (Port of Registry: Glasgow; Flag: UK)
        Copies to owners, local P&I club correspondent, agents.
```

* Should the master **receive** a similar notice holding him and his owners responsible for damage to the other vessel, he should reply **denying any liability** but accepting any invitation to attend a survey on the other vessel **without prejudice**.
* The owner, agent or master should take steps to have other the vessel **arrested** (see B03h) pending payment of **security** up to the limit of liability. Alternatively, the owner may decide on an arbitration agreement using Lloyd's Form.
* In order to give the owner's solicitors enough information to pursue the claim, a **full report** should be drawn up describing all events leading to the collision, including the following:
    * deck and engine room log books, movement books and contemporaneous notes;
    * graphs and print-outs from bridge equipment in use such as course recorder, echo sounder and sat-nav;
    * statements from all witnesses to the collision including, where possible, pilots, tugmasters, etc.;
    * full details of both ships, including names (correctly spelt), ports of registry, call signs and gross tonnages;
    * exact location of the collision;
    * exact time of the collision, stating whether UTC (GMT) or local time;
    * difference between bridge and engine room clocks;
    * estimates of speeds and courses of both vessels at the time of impact;
    * estimates of angle of impact (this may have to be estimated by an expert surveyor);
    * charts in use before and up to the time of the collision (unaltered and unerased);
    * weather and tide conditions at the time of the collision;
    * list of all navigation equipment in use at the time of the collision;
    * records of all signals and communications made between the colliding ships (and any other ships in the vicinity) prior to the collision;
    * names and positions of other ships in the vicinity at the time of the collision;
    * details of any pilotage or vessel traffic control in operation at the time of the collision;
    * in the case of a collision involving a moored vessel, details of moorings deployed.
* All **evidence** gathered should be **stored securely** until it can be passed to the company's P&I club or solicitors.
* Although it is normal for lawyers and investigators representing each ship to avoid seeking to interview the crew of the other ship involved, crew members should be warned of the importance of **not giving statements to any person** other than those lawyers and investigators **acting for the owner**. The master should be able to ascertain the identity of these persons from the P&I club correspondent.

H04b.6 Notice of Claim Clause

* A Hull and Machinery insurance policy to which either the International Hull Clauses (01/11/02) or the Institute Time Clauses – Hulls (1/10/83) are attached (see G04a.2r) obliges the assured to give **notice** to the leading underwriters as soon as possible of an **accident** whereby **loss or damage may result in a claim** under the insurance (see G04a.2r).
* The **underwriters** are entitled to decide which port the vessel should proceed to for docking or repair and have a right of **veto** over the place of repair or repair firm. In the event of failure to comply with this requirement, a deduction of 15% will be made from the amount of the ascertained claim (see G04a.2s).

H04b.7 Fire

* **Emergency Check List C5** in the ICS Bridge Procedures Guide (yellow pages) relates to **fire** and should be consulted if available.
* Any fire, whether major or minor, should be reported to the owner or manager as soon as practicably possible. As soon as the fire is being tackled to the master's satisfaction, and any other actions required under the circumstances (e.g. sending a navigational warning) have been taken, the master should contact the owner for his assessment of the situation. Information which should be given to the owner includes:
    * exact position of vessel;
    * location of fire;
    * nature of cargo alight, if any;
    * nature of cargo in adjacent holds/tanks;
    * information about any other highly inflammable cargo on board;
    * remaining stock of CO_2.
* If circumstances permit, the master should discuss with the owner a **port of refuge** (if necessary), **discharging port**, **port for repairs**, and **declaration of general average**. If the situation allows, the owner will normally recommend

(in consultation with the lead underwriter) making for an effective **port of refuge**, i.e. one with several repair yards capable of carrying out temporary or permanent repairs.

* Damage done in **fighting any fire** on board will generally be allowed under general average, since if no action were taken, the "common safety" would almost certainly be jeopardised when the fire spread throughout the vessel.

* Damage done by the fire itself will normally be covered under the Institute Time Clauses - Hulls.

* Fire-fighting costs are normally allowed under **general average** where other applicable GA criteria are met (see G06). As well as accounts for repairs to the vessel and survey reports showing the division of damage caused by the fire itself and efforts to fight the fire, average adjusters will eventually want **accounts** for any fire-fighting costs, including costs of refilling extinguishers, CO_2 bottles, etc. A **tally** should therefore be made of equipment and stores used in the fire-fighting operation.

* The owner or manager should be given **statements** showing:
  * crew's overtime in connection with the incident;
  * CO_2 consumption;
  * other equipment used in connection with the incident; and
  * if the vessel calls at a port of refuge, items listed in I02i.5.

* The **MS (Accident Reporting and Investigation) Regulations 1999** (SI 1999/2567) require a **report to the MAIB** to be made within 24 hours when a ship is **materially damaged by fire or explosion**. For notes on the **procedure for reporting to MAIB** see E08k.

* The Schedule of the MS (Official Log Books) Regulations 1981 (SI 1981/569) does not require an Official Log Book entry specifically recording a **fire**. Paragraph 12, however, requires an entry to be made (in the narrative section) when the **ship is materially damaged**, which is likely to be the case in a fire (see D05a.4).

* Section 4 of the Merchant Shipping and Maritime Security Act 1997 amended section 3 of the Fire Services Act 1947 to permit UK fire authorities to employ their maintained fire brigades or use their fire brigades' equipment at sea, whether or not within the UK territorial sea.

H04b.8 Stranding or grounding

* **Emergency Check List C3** in the ICS Bridge Procedures Guide (yellow pages) relates to **stranding or grounding** and should be consulted if available.

* A vessel is **stranded** when she is aground and unable to refloat without external assistance.

* **Grounding at sea**, i.e. during the voyage, is more likely to result in hull damage, cargo loss or damage, and harm to the environment, than grounding in port, where it may even be expected and controlled to some degree.

* Many expensive salvage contracts have been entered into in circumstances where the vessel could have been refloated by her own means, and the owner will normally expect the master to **communicate** with him as soon as practicably possible after the vessel has gone aground. The following should be **reported** to the owner:
  * the exact position of the ship;
  * the part of the vessel aground;
  * conditions of weather, wind, wave height, swell, and area forecast;
  * to what extent the vessel is aground (e.g. 30%), and degree of stresses on hull and machinery;
  * details of visible damage, including leakages from tanks;
  * whether vessel's main engine can be used;
  * state of tide when vessel grounded;
  * quantity and disposition of cargo on board;
  * master's assessment of possibilities of refloating by trimming prior to next high water;
  * details of any salvage craft or tugs in vicinity.

* If circumstances permit, the master should always **consult the owner** (or manager, as appropriate) or the leading underwriter (who may be contactable through Lloyd's Casualty Department) **before agreeing** any salvage contract.

* **If it is impossible to contact the owner** or the lead underwriter, the master should consider trying for **tug tariff rates** plus 50%-100%. If the signing of a contract is demanded by salvage vessels, Lloyd's Open Form 2000 - No Cure, No Pay - is the recommended form (see H05d.1).

* During a **refloating operation** the following should be **recorded** in the deck log book, using annexed pages if necessary:
  * the times of all events during the salvage operation;
  * the progress of the operation;
  * the state of tide, wind, sea and weather;
  * the nature of any special risks faced by salvors;
  * any damage or harm suffered by salvors;
  * nature and extent of assistance given by ship's crew and equipment;

- details of any damage sustained by ship during the operation.
* A detailed **report of the operation** together with relevant log abstracts should be sent to the owner.
* A **statement** should be drawn up by the master,and sent to the owner, showing the vessel's expenditure and consumption in excess of the daily norm during the refloating operation, including:
  - crew's overtime (itemised on a separate sheet);
  - fuel oil;
  - diesel oil;
  - lubricating oil;
  - sundry engine spares, stores, wire, shackles, etc. (itemised in a separate list).
* **Expenditure** in refloating following an accidental grounding may qualify as general average if other GA criteria are met (see G06a.3).
* The master should discuss with the owner a **port of refuge** (if necessary), a **discharging port**, **port for repairs**, and **declaration of General Average**.
* If the situation allows, the owner will normally recommend (in consultation with their leading underwriters) making for an effective **port of refuge**, i.e. one with several repair yards capable of carrying out temporary or permanent repairs. The procedure for making for and arrival at a port of refuge (see I02i) should be followed as soon as the vessel is refloated.
* Regulation 5 of the **MS (Accident Reporting and Investigation) Regulations 1999** (SI 1999/2567) requires a **report to the MAIB** to be made within 24 hours whenever a ship **grounds**. For notes on the procedure for reporting to MAIB see E08k.
* Paragraph 12 of the Schedule of the MS (Official Log Books) Regulations 1981 (SI 1981/569) requires the master to make an **entry in the Official Log Book** (narrative section) where the ship **strands**, recording a description of the casualty and the place where, or the position of the ship when, it occurred (see D05a.4).

H04b.9 Mechanical breakdown and machinery damage

* **Emergency Check List C1** in the ICS Bridge Procedures Guide (yellow pages) relates to **main engine or steering failure** and should be consulted if available.
* **For every mechanical breakdown**, details including the nature of the problem and relevant times of its occurrence, etc. should always be recorded. Brief details should be entered in the deck log book, with full details in the engine room log book.
* Any **particular average repairs** carried out, and the time of the resumption of the voyage or other subsequent action such as salvage measures, should be recorded.
* **Where the vessel has suffered a major mechanical failure** the master should **contact the owner or manager** as soon as circumstances permit; the owner or manager will in turn contact the leading underwriter if necessary, and he will instruct a damage surveyor.
* Where machinery damage affects the class status of the ship, owners should inform the classification society and make arrangements for a survey on arrival in port.
* Leading underwriters will arrange a further **survey on completion of repairs**.
* Before departure for sea the vessel will require an Interim Certificate of Class from a surveyor representing her classification society.
* Regulation 5 of the **MS (Accident Reporting and Investigation) Regulations 1999** (SI 1999/2567) requires a **report to the MAIB** to be made within 24 hours whenever a ship is **disabled**[20]. For notes on the procedure for reporting to MAIB see E08k.
* Paragraph 12 of the Schedule of the MS (Official Log Books) Regulations 1981 (SI 1981/569) requires the master to make an **entry in the Official Log Book** (narrative section) where the ship **is materially damaged** and also where the **ship is disabled**, recording a description of the casualty and the place where, or the position of the ship when, it occurred (see D05a.4).
* **Where repairs have been made at sea**, a **statement** should be drawn up by the master showing:
  - crew's overtime in connection with repairs;
  - consumption of spare parts and stores.
* **Any defective and replaced parts** should be retained until they can be examined by a surveyor acting for the leading underwriter.
* **Where repairs are carried out at a repair yard**, statements will be required showing:
  - expenses and fuel/lubricating oil consumption during the deviation;
  - expenses during tank cleaning operations;
  - expenses at the repair port.

---

[20] The 1999 Regulations do not specify any particular period or circumstances of disablement. Any disablement of the ship must be reported.

H04b.10 Helicopter assistance at sea, including MEDEVAC

* **M.1506** gives advice on the provision of facilities for emergency helicopter operations on all types of sea-going ships which do not have a helideck, and guidance on:
  * the provision of areas suitable for winching and low hovering operations; and
  * the contingency plans which should be made and the drills which should be undertaken in anticipation of the need for helicopter assistance.
* **Notice No.4** in the Annual Summary of Notices to Mariners contains much useful information on **helicopter operations with merchant ships**, including routine use of helicopters and use of helicopters for rescue and medical evacuation. A Helicopter Operations – Shipborne **Safety Check List** is provided in Appendix G of Notice No.4.
* The **IAMSAR Manual, Volume III, Section 2** (pages 2-21 to 2-30) similarly contains a great deal of information on **helicopter operations**, with diagrams. In case of medical evacuation (MEDEVAC) by helicopter, Section 4, page 4-8 should be consulted. MEDICO message information as in H04c.3 may need to be prepared and given beforehand. A Shipboard **Safety Check List** is at page 4-10.
* The **Ship Captain's Medical Guide, Chapter 13 (External Assistance)** has sections on Radio medical advice and MEDEVAC service by helicopter.

H04b.11 Man overboard

* The three usual "man overboard" situations are when:
  * a person falling overboard is seen from the bridge, so that immediate action can be taken;
  * a person overboard is reported to the bridge from elsewhere, resulting in delayed action; and
  * a person is reported to the bridge as "missing", resulting in a delay of unknown duration since the mishap.
* The **IAMSAR Manual, Volume III, Section 4** (page 4-12) contains information on **person overboard** situations including initial actions and various types of turn, and should, if available, be consulted.
* **Emergency Check List C4** in the ICS Bridge Procedures Guide (yellow pages) relates to **man overboard** situations and should be consulted if available.
* For notes on reporting and other formalities relating to the loss of a person overboard see H04c.6.

H04b.12 Search and rescue operations

* Search and rescue (SAR) services may request the assistance of a merchant ship during an emergency. For notes on the **statutory duty to proceed to the aid of persons in distress at sea** see H04b.1a. For notes on the **International Convention on Maritime Search and Rescue, 1979**, see A03c.1.
* A ship's **participation in a search and rescue operation** will be regarded in law as a **justifiable deviation** (see F07a.5 and G03f.1). The date and time and reasons for any such deviation should always be fully recorded in the Official Log Book, and a detailed record kept of the ship's participation in the SAR operation.
* **Emergency Check List C7** in the ICS Bridge Procedures Guide (yellow pages) relates to **search and rescue** and should be consulted if available.
* **Notice No.4** in the Annual Summary of Notices to Mariners contains much useful information on **distress and rescue at sea**, and covers both ships in distress and aircraft casualties at sea.
* **Volume III of the IAMSAR Manual** (see H04b.12a) should be consulted during a SAR operation.
* The **AMVER** system may be utilised by SAR services during an operation. For notes on **AMVER** see H06c.1a.
* **UK passenger ships** (and non-UK passenger ships in operating in UK waters) requiring the assistance of SAR services should implement the MCA-approved **SAR Co-operation Plan** (see D04t.7).

H04b.12a IAMSAR Manual

* The **International Aeronautical and Maritime Search and Rescue (IAMSAR) Manual** -
  * is **published jointly by IMO and ICAO** (the International Civil Aviation Organization).
  * is **designed** to assist States in meeting their own SAR needs, as well as the obligations they accepted under the Convention on International Civil Aviation, the International Convention on Maritime Search and Rescue and the SOLAS Convention.
  * provides guidelines for a **common aviation and maritime approach** to organising and providing SAR services.
  * was **adopted by IMO** in 2000 by Resolution A.894(21).
  * **replaces** the Merchant Ship Search and Rescue (**MERSAR**) Manual and IMO Search and Rescue (**IMOSAR**) Manual.

- is published in **three volumes**, each specifically targeted to different levels of the SAR system. **Volume I** (Organization and Management) discusses the global SAR system concept, establishment and improvement of national and regional SAR systems and co-operation with neighbouring States to provide effective and economical SAR services. **Volume II** (Mission Co-ordination) assists personnel who plan and co-ordinate SAR operations and exercises. Volume III (Mobile Facilities) is intended to be carried aboard rescue units, aircraft and vessels to help with performance of search, rescue, or on-scene co-ordinator function and with aspects of SAR that pertain to their own emergencies.

* **Volume III** contains **four sections** as follows: Section **1**: Overview; Section **2**: Rendering Assistance; Section **3**: On-Scene Co-ordination; Section **4**: On-Board Emergencies. **Section 2** includes information on Initial action by assisting craft (page 2-1), Debriefing of survivors (page 2-37), Handling of deceased persons (page 2-38), Contact with the media (page 2-39), Training (page 2-55). **Section 3** includes information on On-Scene Co-ordination of SAR operations (page 3-1), Planning and conducting the search (page 3-14), and Conclusion of search (page 3-39). **Section 4** includes information on Distress alert notification (page 4-1), Cancellation of a distress message (page 4-7), MEDICO messages (page 4-8), Medical evacuation (MEDEVAC) (page 4-8), Person overboard (page 4-12), Ship emergencies at sea including Shipboard fire (page 4-16), Grounding (page 4-16), Hull damages (page 4-16), Abandoning ship (page 4-17), Medical emergencies (page 4-17), Unlawful acts – pirates and armed robbers (page 4-17), and Aircraft emergencies (page 4-19).

* In the MCA's 2002 SOLAS V publication, Guidance Note 4 to SOLAS regulation V/33 states that the IAMSAR Manual "should be carried on board all ships".

H04b.13 Abandoning ship

* **Emergency Check List C8** in the ICS Bridge Procedures Guide (yellow pages) relates to **abandoning ship** and should be consulted if available.
* The **decision to abandon** should only be taken as a very **last resort**; crew, passengers and other personnel may be more at risk from the abandonment process than from the hazards of remaining on the vessel, if still afloat.
* The **order to abandon** ship must be given by the master or senior surviving officer, and should be **oral**.
* An **EPIRB and at least one SART** should be activated and taken to a survival craft along with hand-held VHF radios switched to Channel 16.
* The **ship's position** should be fixed and noted before abandoning; the information may be of use to survival craft occupants.
* Personnel in charge of survival craft should be instructed that all craft are to **remain in safe proximity to the ship** following abandonment, and to attempt to secure to each other.
* Ship's personnel should be trained to attend survival craft drills with **clothing suitable for a real abandonment**, so that when the general emergency alarm signal is sounded in a real emergency, taking extra clothing to survival craft stations is as natural as taking a lifejacket.
* The master or senior surviving officer should, if possible, remove the **Official Log Book** and **deck log** when abandoning ship. The information contained in them may be of assistance in any subsequent investigation.
* Following abandonment and rescue of personnel, any "**Mayday**" relating to the abandoned vessel should be **cancelled or downgraded** as soon as possible. In certain circumstances (e.g. when adrift) an abandoned vessel should be regarded as a "dangerous derelict" and should therefore be reported as such in a danger message (formerly known as a navigational warning) (see H06d.2). If transferred from a survival craft to a rescue vessel, the master of the abandoned vessel should suggest to the host master that a navigational warning is broadcast relating to the abandoned vessel.
* Regulation 5 of the **MS (Accident Reporting and Investigation) Regulations 1999** (SI 1999/2567) requires a **report to the MAIB** to be made within 24 hours whenever a ship **is abandoned**. For notes on the **procedure for reporting to MAIB** see E08k.
* Paragraph 12 of the Schedule of the MS (Official Log Books) Regulations 1981 (SI 1981/569) requires the master to make an **entry in the Official Log Book** (narrative section) where the **ship is abandoned**, recording a description of the casualty and the place where, or the position of the ship when, it occurred (see D05a.4). (This entry would, of course, only be made if the Official Log Book was taken off the ship at the time of abandonment.)

H04c ILLNESS, INJURIES AND DEATHS AT SEA

H04c.1 Illness at sea

* For notes on **action in cases of illness** see E08j.2.
* For notes on **medical records required under the MS (Official Log Books) Regulations 1981**, see D05b.5.
* **Radio medical advice** should be obtained if necessary (see H04c.3).
* A **deviation** to land the seaman should be made if on-board treatment is insufficient (see H01d and H04c.4).
* **In all cases**, all actions taken and treatment given should be **recorded** in the Official Log Book (see D05a). (See requirement for **Entry No.38** in D05a.4.)

H04c.2 Personal injury at sea

* For notes on **action in cases of personal injury** see E08j.2.
* For notes on **medical records required under the MS (Official Log Books) Regulations 1981**, see D05b.5.
* **Radio medical advice** should be obtained if necessary (see H04c.3).
* A **deviation** to land the seaman should be made if on-board treatment is insufficient (see H01d and H04c.4).
* For notes on the ship's **safety officer's** duty to **investigate and report** on accident circumstances, see E08d.3.
* The category of the injury should be determined. If it qualifies under the MS (Accident Reporting and Investigation) Regulations as a "**major injury**" (see E08k.1b), it must be reported to the MAIB within 24 hours as an "accident". If it qualifies as a "**serious injury**" (see E08k.1b) it must be reported within 14 days. For notes on **information needed** in accident reports see E08k.1e. For **MAIB contact** details see E08k.1f.
* To enable the **P&I club** to defend any claim against the owner, as much **evidence** as possible should be obtained including:
  * full details from the accident book, any accident reports made, records of any first aid or medical treatment given, including details of how and by whom the accident victim was moved from the scene of the accident;
  * statements from the accident victim (if possible) and any witnesses;
  * photographs of the accident area (as long as they are not adverse to the owner's case);
  * log books;
  * reports, findings and/or recommendations by the ship's Safety Committee or Safety Officer;
  * relevant items of equipment, damaged or otherwise.

H04c.3 Radio medical advice (MEDICO messages)

* **Radio messages requesting or transmitting medical advice** are known internationally as "**MEDICO**" messages and should generally be prefixed "**DHMEDICO**".
* Radio medical advice **may be obtained**:
  * through any **coast radio station** listed as providing Medical Advice by Radio in the **ITU List of Radiodetermination and Special Service Stations** or in **Admiralty List of Radio Signals, Volume 1**;
  * from the **International Radio Medical Centre**, Rome, Italy (callsign **CIRM**), whose services are free of charge. Requests should be prefixed with "MEDRAD" or "DHMEDICO". Telephone +39 6 5923 331 and 332. Fax +39 6 5923 333. Telex 612068 CIRM I. The Centre can also be contacted through the US Coast Guard or coast radio stations; or
  * from a **ship carrying a registered doctor** (e.g. a cruise ship, large RFA or large warship).
* Countries with radio stations providing medical advice are listed alphabetically in **Admiralty List of Radio Signals, Volume 1**. The International Radio Medical Centre (**CIRM**) has a special entry in this list.
* **MGN 225** advises that Council Directive 92/29/EC requires EU Member States to designate one or more centres to provide radio medical advice to ships. Officially designated centres in the UK are at Queen Alexandra Hospital, Portsmouth and at Aberdeen Royal Infirmary. To obtain radio medical advice from these centres, masters should first contact HM Coastguard on either MF DSC, VHF DSC, VHF Channel 16 or INMARSAT. Urgent calls for assistance may be broadcast using the normal Urgency prowords "Pan Pan" following the example in MGN 225.
* **When considering a request** for radio medical advice, the **Ship Captain's Medical Guide, Chapter 13 (External assistance)** should be consulted.
* **When requesting medical assistance by radio** the following **information** should be provided:
  * name of ship and radio call sign;
  * position of ship, ports of departure and destination, ETA, course or route and speed;

- patient's name, nationality, age and language;
- information about breathing rate, pulse rate, temperature and blood pressure;
- description of patient's symptoms, location and type of pain, and any relevant information concerning the illness;
- in the case of an accident, a description of where and how the accident occurred, as well as the symptoms;
- patient's case history including type, time, form and amounts of all medicines given;
- ability of patient to eat, drink, walk or be moved;
- (where an accident has occurred) how the accident happened;
- information about the medicines available on board;
- information about medicines already administered;
- whether the vessel has a doctor or other medically trained person on board;
- whether a suitable clear landing area is available for helicopter winch operations or landing;
- name and contact details of ship's agent;
- last port of call, next port of call and ETA to next port of call;
- communications and homing signal available; and
- any other relevant information.
* **MSN 1726** lists medicines and medical equipment for ships of Categories A, B and C.
* **M.1633** draws the attention of ships' doctors to the section "Radio medical advice" in the Ship Captain's Medical Guide, in order to avoid the prescribing by doctors of medicines which are not carried on board.
* **AMVER** (see H06c.1a) does not provide medical advice to ships. However, a **coastguard station** which has contacted AMVER should be able to indicate whether there are any vessels in the ship's vicinity with medical facilities.

H04c.4 Deviation for a medical reason

* **Where medical facilities on board are insufficient**, the ill or injured person (i.e. the patient) should be **landed** for appropriate treatment. Any **deviation** to land an ill or injured person for urgent medical attention will always be regarded as **justifiable** in carriage of goods and marine insurance law if it is "reasonable and necessary". To avoid any dispute over its justification, however, full details should be **recorded** in the Official Log Book.
* The **owner or manager should be notified** as soon as the decision to land the patient has been taken, and a request should be made for contact details of any **agent** appointed by the company at the place of intended landing.
* The local **correspondent** of the **P&I club** should be contacted at the earliest opportunity (see Club handbook for contact details) and given full details of the patient, the nature of the illness or injury and the landing arrangements.
* The **port authority** should be contacted at the earliest opportunity and notified of the intention to land the person(s).
* The **agent** should be requested to inform the relevant shore authorities (e.g. immigration, customs, police) regarding the landing of the patient.
* In the case of a patient who is on a List of Crew, preparations should be made for **signing the patient off** as detailed in E07d.6 or, where he is unable to sign off in person, E07d.7.
* For important notes on **sailing short-handed** (which have may be contemplated) see E03d.6.
* Any **personal property** not accompanying the patient to the shore medical facility should be landed to the care of the agent. If the property is not packed by the patient, it should be tallied by two officers, one copy of the tally sheet accompanying the property and another being retained in the Official Log Book.
* **If landing a seaman/patient in a foreign country**, arrangements should also be made to notify the nearest **proper officer**, e.g. a British Consul, of the leaving behind of a seaman from a British ship, and an entry (entry No. 18) recording this notification should be made in the Official Log Book.
* The patient should be **accompanied** by:
  - their **identification documents**, e.g. passport and Discharge Book;
  - a copy of their **medical records**;
  - notes describing their **symptoms and treatment** to date.
* **Official Log Book entries** (see D05a.4) should be made recording all arrangements including:
  - the **illness or injury** of the person(s);
  - the **deviation** from the ship's ordinary course or normal operation;
  - the landing of the patient;
  - the landing of any personal property of the patient; and
  - the notification of the proper officer.
* For **P&I club purposes** a record should also be made of:
  - the position where the deviation was commenced;
  - fuel/lubricating oil consumption during the deviation;

- any expenses at the port or place where the seaman was landed.
* **Following the landing** of the patient:
  - the voyage should be **resumed**;
  - the **crew list** should be amended if the patient was listed on it;
  - the owner or manager, and any time charterer, as appropriate, should be **informed**;
  - the **time and position of rejoining the original (ordinary) route** should be noted, so that the net deviation can, if necessary be calculated.

H04c.5 Death on board at sea

* For notes on **legislation relating to deaths** in ships, see E14a.
* For notes on making **Returns of Deaths**, see E14b.
* For notes on dealing with the **property of deceased seamen**, see E14c.
* For notes on **Official Log Book entries** relating to deaths, see E14d.
* For notes on the **effect of a crew member's death** on safe manning, see E14e.
* For notes on **procedure for dealing with a body** on board, and a summary of the **procedure following a death on board**, see E14f.
* **On the ship's arrival** at the next port where there is an MCA superintendent (in the UK) or a proper officer (outside the UK), the relevant official may visit the ship to take **statements** as part of a **death inquiry** (see B07f). **Witnesses** should expect to be asked questions, and it will therefore be of assistance if relevant **notes** are made while memories are fresh. (The chief witnesses should not be permitted to leave the ship on arrival until permission has been granted by the superintendent or proper officer.)

H04c.6 Loss of a person overboard

* For notes on **search and rescue procedures when a person is overboard** see H04b.12.
* A person lost overboard should not be recorded as "**deceased**" unless that can be confirmed as a fact.
* In the event of **failure to recover a person lost overboard**, the relevant parts of the procedure following a death on board (see E14f) should be followed.
* Regulation 5 of the **MS (Accident Reporting and Investigation) Regulations 1999** (SI 1999/2567) requires a **report to the MAIB** to be made within 24 hours whenever any **person is lost or falls overboard** from a ship or ship's boat. For notes on **MAIB accident reporting requirements** see E08k.
* Paragraph 12 of the Schedule of the MS (Official Log Books) Regulations 1981 (SI 1981/569) requires the master to make an **entry in the Official Log Book** (narrative section) where a person is lost from the ship or a ship's boat, recording a description of the casualty and the place where, or the position of the ship when, it occurred (see D05a.4).
* **On the ship's arrival** at the next port where there is an MCA superintendent (in the UK) or a proper officer (outside the UK), the relevant official may visit the ship to take **statements** as part of a **death inquiry** (see B07f). Witnesses should expect to be asked questions, and it will therefore be of assistance if relevant **notes** are made while memories are fresh. (The chief witnesses should not be permitted to leave the ship on arrival until permission has been granted by the superintendent or proper officer.)
* A **full report** should be written of the efforts to find and recover the overboard person, and copies should be prepared for:
  - the owner or manager;
  - any time charterer;
  - any MCA superintendent or proper officer who may conduct an inquiry;
  - the P&I club;
  - the police, if interested.

H04d CARGO PROBLEMS AT SEA

* It is impossible in a book of this size to quote procedures for every kind of cargo problem that may arise at sea.
* In general, a major cargo problem should always be tackled in consultation with the **owner and the P&I club**. The owner may contact (or advise the master to contact) the charterer, shipper or consignee for expert advice or instructions, particularly in cases where the cargo is hazardous. Some cargo problems may be tackled by the ship's crew, while those that pose a serious threat to the safety of the ship and other property on board may necessitate an immediate **deviation** to a port of refuge, the costs of doing so qualifying as **general average expenditure**.

* In general, any cargo problem should be **fully recorded** in the appropriate log or record book. Where it has caused an **accident**, relevant **evidence**[21] **should be retained** as required by regulation 7(1) of the MS (Accident Reporting and Investigation) Regulations 1999 (see E08k.1j), as well as for P&I claims handling purposes.
* Some cargo problems will necessitate a **radio report** and/or a **written report** to be made.
* **Where any large unit of cargo that has fallen overboard or been jettisoned** will pose a hazard to other shipping (including small craft), a **danger message** (or "navigational warning") should be broadcast (see H06d).
* **Where there has been a collapse of cargo**, **unintended movement of cargo or ballast** sufficient to cause a **list**, or **loss of cargo overboard**, a **report to the MAIB** to be made within 24 hours in compliance with regulation 5 of the **MS (Accident Reporting and Investigation) Regulations 1999** (see E08k).
* A **full report** of the occurrence should in every case be sent to the owner, with copies for the P&I club and charterer where relevant.
* **Where the ship is materially damaged** (e.g. by a collapse of a stow or by a cargo explosion or fire), paragraph 12 of the Schedule of the MS (Official Log Books) Regulations 1981 requires the master to make an **entry in the Official Log Book** (narrative section) recording a description of the casualty and the place where, or the position of the ship when, it occurred (see D05a.4).
* **Where there has been**:
  * **damage or leakage to a package containing infectious substances**;
  * a **discharge of oil or noxious liquid substances above the permitted level**, or the **probability** of a discharge of oil or noxious liquid substances, for **whatever reason including** those for the purpose of securing the safety of the ship or for saving life at sea;
  * a **discharge of dangerous goods or harmful substances in packaged form**, or the **probability** of such a discharge, including those in freight containers, portable tanks, road and rail vehicles and shipborne barges;
  * a **discharge during the operation of the ship of oil or noxious liquid substances in excess of the permitted level**; or
  * a **threat of damage to the coastline or related interests** of the UK,
  - a report must be sent in accordance with the **MS (Reporting Requirements for Ships Carrying Dangerous and Polluting Goods) Regulations 1995**, as amended (see H06e.1). Supplementary reports may also be required (see H06e.1c).

H04e TERRORISM, STOWAWAYS, REFUGEES, PIRATES AND DRUGS

H04e.1 Unauthorised persons: offences related to safety

* **Section 106 of the Merchant Shipping Act 1995** provides that where any person goes to sea in a ship without the consent of the master or of any other person authorised to give it or is conveyed on a ship under section 73(5)(b), **section 58** (Conduct endangering ships, structures or individuals) and **section 59** (Concerted disobedience and neglect of duty) will apply as if he were a seaman employed in the ship.
* This may mean, for example, that a **stowaway** (i.e. a person who goes to sea in a ship without the consent of the master or of any other person authorised to give it), who interferes with, steals or damages safety equipment (such as lifeboat equipment or provisions) may be prosecuted under section 58, or that a "distressed British seaman" carried under a Conveyance Order who refuses to carry out orders may be prosecuted under section 59.

H04e.2 Ship security measures at sea

* **SOLAS chapter XI-2** (Special Measures to Enhance Maritime Security) and the International Ship and Port Facility Security Code (**ISPS Code**) apply from 1 July 2004 to ships on international voyages, as detailed in D03a.6.
* When at sea, a ship to which SOLAS chapter XI-2 and the ISPS Code applies must be operated in accordance with the **Ship Security Plan** (see D04t.10a) and at (or above) a designated **security level** (see D03a.6a) which must be set and notified by the flag State Administration. (The Company may at any time choose to operate the ship at a **higher security level**.)
* Under the provisions of SOLAS regulation XI-2/9, which is in force from 1 July 2004, when a ship is at a port or **is proceeding to a port** of a SOLAS Contracting Government, that Contracting Government will have the right, to exercise various **control and compliance measures** with respect to that ship. On arrival, the ship will be subject to port State control inspections, but such inspections will not normally extend to examination of the Ship Security Plan itself except in specific circumstances. The ship may also be subject to additional control measures if the

---

[21] This could mean, for example, a broken cargo lashing device.

Contracting Government exercising the control and compliance measures has reason to believe that the security of the ship has, or the port facilities it has served have, been compromised.

* Other relevant international instruments are the IMO **Convention for the Suppression of Unlawful Acts against the Safety of Navigation** and the **Protocol on Unlawful Acts against the Safety of Fixed Platforms** (see A03c.4). These instruments have been reviewed by the Legal Committee of IMO in the wake of the attacks in the USA on 11 September 2001.

* Shipmasters, ship security officers (SSOs) and company security officers (CSOs) can obtain useful **reports of attacks on shipping**, from any source, on two websites, as follows:

• The US Office of Naval Intelligence (ONI) weekly report, **Worldwide Threat to Shipping - Mariner Warning Information**, at http://164.214.12.145/onit/onit_j_main.html

• The **ICC Commercial Crime Services Weekly Piracy Report** at: http://www.iccwbo.org/ccs/imb_piracy/weekly_piracy_report.asp

* For notes on the **MCA's guidance** on measures to counteract piracy, armed robbery and other acts of violence against merchant shipping, contained in **MGN 241**, see H04e.5.

* Whether an **act of violence at sea** is, in law, "terrorism", "piracy" or "armed robbery" may not be clear – or important to know - at the time of the incident, and any ship security guidance will be valid in all violent situations.

* A shipowner normally has no **right of recovery from his P&I club** in respect of any liability or expenses caused by **acts of terrorism** (or by the other "war risks", i.e. war, civil war, revolution, rebellion, insurrection or civil strife arising therefrom, or any hostile act by or against a belligerent power). The majority of P&I clubs therefore have very little or no guidance or information specifically on terrorism amongst their loss prevention literature.

H04e.3 Stowaways discovered at sea

* An **international convention** relating to stowaways was adopted in Brussels in 1957, but because of a lack of signatories has not entered into force and is not likely to do so. IMO has since introduced various guidelines, the latest being in **Resolution A.871(20)**, adopted on 27 November 1997, and its Annex, "**Guidelines on the Allocation of Responsibilities to seek the Successful Resolution of Stowaway Cases**". While the UK follows the IMO Guidelines, in many countries they are not followed since they conflict with national legislation.

* IMO's Facilitation Committee agreed in 2000 to introduce procedures for dealing with stowaways into the FAL Convention (see A03c.4). Amendments to incorporate standards and recommended practices were adopted in January 2002 and are expected to come into force on 1 May 2003.

* **Current MCA guidance** on stowaway cases is in **MGN 70**, which superseded M.1660 and contains the text of **Resolution A.871(20)** and its Annex, referred to above. The **IMO Guidelines** -

  - define a "**stowaway**" (in paragraph 2) as "a person who is secreted on a ship, or in a cargo which is subsequently loaded on the ship, without the consent of the shipowner or the master or any other responsible person, and who is detected on board after the ship has departed from a port and is reported as a stowaway by the master to the appropriate authorities".

  - contain (in paragraph 4) nine **basic principles** which can be applied generally. The second of these is that stowaway/asylum-seekers should be **treated in compliance with international protection principles** as set out in international instruments[22] and relevant national legislation. The ninth is that stowaway incidents should be dealt with **humanely** by all parties involved. Due consideration should always be given to the **operational safety of the ship** and to the **well-being of the stowaway**.

  - contain (in paragraph 5.1) a list of **responsibilities of the master**, as listed below.

* **Paragraph 5.1 of the IMO Guidelines** lists the following **responsibilities of the master in stowaway cases**:

  1. to make every effort to **determine** immediately the **port of embarkation** of the stowaway;
  2. to make every effort to **establish the identity**, including the nationality/citizenship of the stowaway;
  3. to prepare a **statement** containing all information relevant to the stowaway, in accordance with information specified in the standard document annexed to these Guidelines, for presentation to the appropriate authorities;
  4. to **notify** the existence of a stowaway and any relevant details to his **shipowner** and **appropriate authorities at the port of embarkation, the next port of call and the flag State**;
  5. **not to depart from his planned voyage** to seek the disembarkation of a stowaway to any country unless repatriation has been arranged with sufficient documentation and permission for disembarkation, or unless there are extenuating security or compassionate reasons;
  6. to ensure that the **stowaway is presented to appropriate authorities at the next port of call** in accordance with their requirements;
  7. to take appropriate measures to **ensure the security, general health, welfare and safety of the stowaway** until disembarkation.

---

22 These include the UN Convention relating to the Status of Refugees of 28 July 1951 and the UN Protocol relating to the Status of Refugees of 31 January 1967.

* **On the discovery at sea of stowaways**, the following procedure should, in general, be adopted.
  1. The **owner or manager**, as appropriate, should be contacted. The owner will normally contact the P&I club's managers to decide on a **course of action**. The P&I club's **correspondent** serving the next port of call will normally be contacted by the club managers. The correspondent should be able to advise what **information** will be required by port State and other officials.
  2. An entry should be made in the **Official Log Book** recording the discovery of the stowaways.
  3. The **compartment** or area in which the stowaways were found should be **searched**. Any documents or articles of clothing, etc. may give an indication of their place of origin. (Most countries only allow a stowaway to be landed if he has the necessary travel documents to return to his own country. Stowaways rarely have any documentation, however, and some will try to destroy all clues as to their identity.)
  4. The **clothing** of the stowaways should be **searched** for indications as to their origin.
  5. The **agent** at the next port of call should be contacted and instructed to advise the appropriate authorities of the port State of the presence of stowaways on board.
  6. Each stowaway found should be individually **interviewed** in order to establish the following details:
     * name of stowaway;
     * stowaway's date and place of birth;
     * nationality of stowaway;
     * name, date and place of birth of either or both of the stowaway's parents;
     * postal and residential address of the stowaway and either parent;
     * stowaway's passport or seaman's book number, together with date and place of issue; and
     * stowaway's next of kin, if different from above.
  7. The **Stowaway Details Form** in MGN 70 should be completed. The completed form should be copied by fax or e-mail to the **agent** and the P&I **club correspondent** at the next port of call.
  8. **Photographs** of each stowaway should be taken and, where digital camera facilities are available, transmitted to the P&I club correspondent; these may enable travel documents to be obtained more quickly on the ship's arrival.
  9. All stowaways should be **housed** in some part of the crew accommodation which **can be locked when necessary**.
  10. The stowaways **should not be locked** in their accommodation when the vessel is at sea and well clear of land unless they are considered a threat to the safety of the ship or personnel on board. Consideration should be given, however, to the possibility of unguarded stowaways **launching a liferaft or boat** in an attempt to reach land.
  11. The stowaways **should be locked securely** in their accommodation when the vessel **approaches any port** or **nears any land**. (Consideration should be given to the possibility of the stowaways' escape through open scuttles.)
  12. The stowaways **should** be provided with **adequate food, water, sanitary facilities**, etc.
  13. The stowaways **should** be treated in a **humane** manner.
  14. The stowaways **should not be made to work** for their keep.
  15. The stowaways **should not** be signed on the Crew Agreement and **should not** be entered on any List of Crew. A "Stowaway List" should be made recording any known particulars, ready for production to port officials.
  16. **Evidence of costs** relating to the stowaway case, such as fuel, insurance, wages, stores, provisions and port charges, should be gathered to support the owner's claim on his P&I policy. (The **owner's costs** associated with the landing of stowaways are usually recoverable from his P&I club.)
  17. Full details of all events and particulars relating to the stowaway incident should be **recorded** in the Official Log Book, if necessary in an annexed document. (This may be used as part of any report required by owners, the club, etc.)
* **If stowaways are heard inside a cargo container** which cannot be opened in its present stowage position:
  1. Urgent efforts should be made to **communicate with the stowaways**, primarily in order to **ascertain their state of health**. If people are trapped inside a container that cannot be opened in its present stowage position, urgent consideration should be given to **diverting** to the nearest port able to handle containers. (Amongst the considerations should be the time elapsed since departure from the last port of call, time to the next scheduled port, time to a possible emergency port of call.)
  2. Attempts should be made to **ascertain the number, ages and nationalities** of the stowaways, and whether they need **air, food and water** (which is likely). It may be possible to drill holes in the container in order to supply air, food and water by hosepipe.
  3. The **container number and stowage position** should be passed to the owner or manager, as appropriate, with all other relevant information, as above.
* For notes relating to **arrival with stowaways on board**, see I01g.4. For notes relating to **pre-departure stowaway searches**, see I07e.

* **P&I club guidance on stowaway issues** can be found in circulars and bulletins on most club websites (as listed in G02a.3a).

H04e.4 Refugees encountered at sea

H04e.4a Status of refugees

* A "**refugee**" is defined in article 1 of the Convention relating to the Status of Refugees, 1951 as a person who, "owing to well-founded fear of being persecuted for reasons of race, religion, nationality, membership of a particular social group or political opinion, is outside the country of his nationality and is unable, or owing to such fear, is unwilling to avail himself of the protection of that country; or who, not having a nationality and being outside the country of his former habitual residence as a result of such events, is unable or, owing to such fear, is unwilling to return to it.". Such persons may nowadays be encountered at sea in many parts of the world, usually in small, unseaworthy craft, and will probably indicate that they are **in distress**. The master of any ship encountering people under such circumstances is therefore under a **statutory obligation to render assistance** to them (see H04b.1).
* The official body responsible for the care of refugees and implementation of the 1951 Convention is the United Nations High Commissioner for Refugees (**UNHCR**). However, the UNHCR will not usually take responsibility for a refugee until he or she has applied for asylum; until that time the person is officially termed a "**migrant**". If migrants rescued at sea request asylum, the master of the rescuing ship should make arrangements to contact the nearest UNHCR office at soon as possible.
* Once migrants have been rescued by a ship at sea, they are subject to the **jurisdiction of the ship's flag State**. However, there is no obligation on the flag State to grant asylum.

H04e.4b Care of refugees on board

* When migrants are taken on board, the following matters should be addressed as priorities:
  1. **Communication** should be established with the group.
  2. **Health problems**, e.g. dehydration, hypothermia, malnourishment, should be addressed before all others.
  3. **Radio medical advice** should be sought where necessary (see H04c.3).
  4. Precautions should be taken against the spread of **infectious disease** where this is a possibility in view of the refugees' country of origin.
  5. **Food, drink, clothing, shelter, and washing and toilet facilities** should be provided.
  6. **Emergency procedures**, partularly for fire and abandonment situations, should be established and instruction given to the migrants.

H04e.4c Landing of refugees

* Although there is no binding international convention dealing with migrants while on board rescuing ships, the accepted international practice is that migrants rescued at sea should be disembarked at the next scheduled port of call, where the port State should admit them until their status can be determined and they can be either resettled or repatriated. No port State may forcibly repatriate an asylum applicant.
* Masters should have access to the **Guidelines for the Disembarkation of Refugees**, issued by the UNHCR in 1988, which state:
  1. When a vessel picks up refugees at sea, it should normally **proceed to the first scheduled port of call**, informing the ship's agent of the **number of refugees** the vessel has on board and the **circumstances** of their rescue.
  2. The ship's **agent** should in turn inform the port and immigration authorities of the presence of refugees on board, requesting permission for the ship to enter the harbour, requesting permission for the ship to enter the harbour.
  3. The ship's **agent** should also inform the local UNHCR office and the diplomatic representative of the country whose flag the ship is flying.
  4. Should the ship be flying the flag of a country in a position to resettle refugees, the **diplomatic representative** of that country will inform the local authorities of his government's willingness to accept the refugees for resettlement, normally within 90 days of their disembarkation.
  5. If the vessel flies a flag of an open registry, or a flag of a country which cannot reasonably be expected to accept refugees for resettlement, **UNHCR** will contact countries which have contributed to a special pool of resettlement places known as Disembarkation Resettlement Offers (DISERO) to provide disembarkation guarantees and share responsibility for subsequent resettlement.

6. Once the guarantee has been conveyed by the relevant diplomatic mission to the local authorities, **immigration** and **UNHCR officials** will board the vessel to interview the refugees. Upon completion of the interviews, the refugees will be allowed to disembark, and they are no longer of concern to the vessel.

7. Upon disembarkation, each refugee will be examined by the **local health authorities** and given medical assistance as necessary. UNHCR covers all care and maintenance expenses.

* The following **information** is generally required at **all ports** before permission for the disembarkation of refugees can be granted and should be **radioed or cabled** to the next scheduled port of call as soon as possible:
  * name of the rescuing ship;
  * flag and port of registry of rescuing ship;
  * name and address of ship's owner;
  * owner's agent at next port;
  * estimated date and time of arrival at next port;
  * exact number of refugees on board;
  * date, time, latitude and longitude at time of rescue; and
  * state of health of refugees on board and whether they are in need of emergency medical treatment upon arrival.
* Disembarkation of refugees will usually be hastened if a **list of their full names**, by family groups, showing date of birth, nationality and sex, is typed out and handed to the port immigration authorities on arrival or, if possible, is transmitted to the ship's agent prior to arrival.

H04e.4d P&I club cover relating to refugees

* **P&I clubs** normally indemnify their members against the costs of proceeding to the assistance of persons in distress and the reasonable costs of caring for those persons and landing them. Diversion expenses will usually be covered where they are solely for the purpose of landing the rescued persons.
* Whilst on board, migrants will be "third parties", and the normal P&I cover against the owner's liability for personal injury, illness or death of a third party will apply.
* Fines imposed on the owner by port States for bringing the migrants into the country, or where a migrant escapes from the ship, or for absence of proper documentation, will also normally be reimbursed by the P&I club.
* In view of its degree of involvement, the P&I club should be kept advised by the ship's master throughout the period during which the migrants are on board.

H04e.5 Piracy and armed robbery

* **"Piracy"** is defined by article 101 of the UN Convention on the Law of the Sea (UNCLOS) as consisting of any of the following acts:
  (a) any illegal acts of violence and detention, or any act of depredation, committed for private ends by the crew or the passengers of a private ship or private aircraft, and directed:
  * on the high seas, against another ship or aircraft, or against persons or property on board such a ship or aircraft;
  * against a ship, aircraft, persons or property in a place outside the jurisdiction of any State;
  (a) any act of voluntary participation in the operation of a ship or of an aircraft with knowledge of facts making it a pirate ship or aircraft;
  (b) any act of inciting or of intentionally facilitating an act described in subparagraph (a) or (b).
* The **International Maritime Bureau** (**IMB**) (one of whose functions is to track down pirates and pirated ships and cargoes) defines "**piracy**" as "an act of boarding any vessel with the intent to commit theft or any other crime, and with the intent or capability to use force to further that act".
* **"Armed robbery"** takes place within the jurisdiction of a nation State, i.e. in the territorial waters of a coastal State, usually within the proximity of a port or anchorage. Responsibility for the protection of a merchant vessel against armed robbery is that of the coastal State in whose waters the vessel is.
* **MGN 241** replaced MGN 75 and draws attention to the risk of acts of piracy on the high seas (as well as armed robbery against ships at anchor off ports or when under way through a coastal State's territorial waters and other acts of violence against shipping). It outlines steps that should be taken to **reduce the risk** of such attacks, possible **responses to attacks** and the need to **report** such attacks. The contents of MGN 241 include:
  * Introduction;
  * Locations and methods of attack (including Attacks at anchor – within port limits or at anchorage; Attacks when tied alongside; Attacks when underway; Other attacks);
  * Factors encouraging or favouring attackers (including Cash in the ship's safe; Smaller crews);
  * Recommended practices (including The Anti-Attack Plan; Routeing and delaying anchoring; Prior to entering areas where attacks occur; At anchor or in port; Watchkeeping and vigilance; Radio procedures; Radio

watchkeeping and responses; Standard message formats; Secreted VHF transceiver; Lighting – when underway; Lighting – at anchor; CCTV; Secure areas; Alarms; Evasive manoeuvring and use of hoses; Use of distress flares; Firearms; If attackers board; If attackers gain control; Action after an attack and reporting incidents);

* Security measures;
* Summary of general precautions;
* Jurisdiction and intervention (including Criminal jurisdiction; Naval intervention; Role of the coastal State);
* Conclusion;
* Piracy Reporting Centre;
* Travel Advice Notices;
* Amendments.

H04e.5a Jurisdiction in cases of piracy

* **Paragraph 67 of MGN 75** states: "Piracy is an offence committed on the high seas, or in a place outside the jurisdiction of any State. A pirate who has been apprehended on the high seas therefore falls to be dealt with under the laws of the **flag State** of his captors".
* It is the view of NUMAST[23] that, since by definition piracy takes place **on the high seas or in waters outside the jurisdiction of any State**, it is the responsibility of the **naval assets of the flag State** of any merchant vessel to give protection from piracy, and in respect of a merchant vessel whose flag State has insufficient or no naval assets, the responsibility of the international maritime community to take such action (e.g. through IMO) as is necessary to reduce pirate attacks on merchant shipping.

H04e.5b Piracy information

* **Information on piracy attacks and the regions of greatest risk** can be obtained free of charge from the **Piracy Reporting Centre** operated by the ICC International Maritime Bureau at Kuala Lumpur, Malaysia. Telephone +603 201 0014. Fax +603 238 5769. Telex MA 31880 IMBPCI. E-mail ccskl@imbkl.po.my
* The Piracy Reporting Centre also issues status reports and warning messages on the SafetyNET service of Inmarsat C at 0001 UTC each day.

H04e.5c Piracy reports

* If **suspicious vessel movements** are identified which may result in imminent attack, the relevant Rescue Co-ordination Centre (RCC) for the area should be contacted. Where the master believes that these movements constitute a direct danger to navigation consideration should be given to broadcasting an "**All Stations (CQ)**" "**danger message**" as a warning to other ships as well as **advising the RCC**.
* **Should an attack occur** and, in the opinion of the master, the ship or crew are in grave and imminent danger requiring immediate assistance, he should immediately authorise the broadcasting of a **Distress message**, preceded by the appropriate distress alerts (MAYDAY, SOS, DSC, etc.) using all available communications systems.
* Appendix 1 to MGN 75 contains formats for:
  * **Initial message: Piracy/armed robbery attack alert**; and
  * **Piracy/armed robbery attack/sighting/suspicious act report**.
* An **Initial message: Piracy/armed robbery attack alert** should contain:
  * Vessel's name and callsign/INMARSAT ID (plus ocean region code);
  * "MAYDAY" (see Note below);
  * "PIRACY ATTACK";
  * Vessel's position (and time of position (UTC);
  * Nature of event.
  It is expected that this message will be a **Distress Message** because the vessel or persons will be in grave or imminent danger when under attack. **Where this is not the case**, the word MAYDAY is to be omitted. Use of distress priority (3) in the INMARSAT system will not require MAYDAY to be included.
* A **Piracy/armed robbery attack/sighting/suspicious act report** should contain:
  1. Vessel's name and call sign.
  2. Reference initial "PIRACY ALERT".
  3. Position of incident.
  4. Date/time of incident (UTC).
  5. Details of incident, e.g.:

---

[23] The UK trade union for Merchant Navy officers.

- Method of attack.
- Description of suspect craft.
- Number and brief description of pirates.
- Injuries to crew.
- Damage to ship.
- Brief details of stolen property/cargo.
6. Last observed movements of pirate/suspect vessel, e.g. Date/time/course/position/speed.
7. Assistance required.
8. Preferred communications with reporting vessel, e.g.:
   - Appropriate Coast Radio Station.
   - HF/MF/VHF.
   - INMARSAT ID (plus ocean region code).
9. Date/time of report (UTC).

H04e.5d Piracy deterrence

* Detailed advice is contained in MGN 75. In the absence of the MGN, or of any advice from the owner or charterer, the following notes summarise the chief points of the advice:
- Prepare an **anti-attack plan** and ensure each person knows what to do if the ship is attacked.
- Keep **one bridge door locked** (and both locked if pirates board the vessel).
- **Secure all doors** to accommodation spaces, engine room, steering flat and funnel.
- Lock all **store rooms** on deck.
- Set **extra watches**, e.g. two lookouts on the bridge, one looking aft to detect small craft not detected by radars.
- Assign crew members to man **searchlights**.
- Have **fire pumps** running from sunset to sunrise, with fire hoses rigged on rails around the poop deck.
- Ensure the **poop deck is well illuminated**. (At anchor or in port, keep all decks brightly lit.)
- Ensure as far as practicable that **pirates are aware that the ship is alert and prepared**.

H04e.6 Drugs

* **Drugs may be found** on board either:
- **in the possession of a seafarer** or passenger;
- or **not in the possession of any person** (e.g. hidden amongst ship's stores, cargo, etc.).

H04e.6a Action when drugs are found in the possession of a seafarer

* **When drugs are found in the possession of a seafarer**, the master should:
1. Make a **detailed record of the discovery** of the drugs in the Official Log Book.
2. Deal with the seafarer as provided in the rules or code of conduct, if any, incorporated in the Crew Agreement, or, where no such rules or code are incorporated, using the procedures of the **Merchant Navy Code of Conduct** (see E10b).

H04e.6b Action when drugs are found not in the possession of any person

* **When drugs are found not in the possession of any person** (e.g. hidden) the master should:
1. With at least one other officer as witness, **record the position** of the package and take **photographs**.
2. **Make a detailed record** of the discovery of the drugs in the **Official Log Book** (narrative pages or annex), noting:
   - the time and date of the discovery;
   - the location in which the package was found;
   - the approximate quantity of the substance or number of packages;
   - the names and rank of the finder;
   - the names and ranks of all witnesses.
   - the reason why the finder was in the location.
3. Inform the **shipowner** or manager (as appropriate).
4. Inform the **P&I club correspondent** at the next port of call.
5. Inform the **agent** at the next port of call, requesting him to inform the appropriate **shore authorities**.

6. **Retain the packages** in a secure place (e.g. ship's safe or bond locker), and ensure that the P&I club correspondent and agent are aware of their retention so that they can inform the authorities at the next port.
7. If necessary, **search other locations** for further caches.
8. **Do not permit crew to go ashore** on arrival until authorised by the appropriate authorities.
9. When handling the packages:
   * wear skin protection and a face mask;
   * do not inhale or taste fumes or powder;
   * do not allow anyone to smoke in the vicinity;
   * wash hands and brush clothing clean as soon as possible afterwards.

* The **P&I clubs** generally advise that if drugs are discovered on board by port officials, the master should co-operate fully with the authorities and seek help from the club's local correspondent to ensure the owner's interests are protected.
* The P&I clubs also stress the importance of taking all possible **precautions to avoid the concealment of drugs** on board, especially when trading to the USA. Many shipowners participate in the US Customs' **Sea Carrier Initiative Program** in which each participating carrier undertakes to take reasonable precautions against the concealment of drugs on board its ships. Although participants cannot be exempted from statutory sanctions any penalty for a participant will be limited if drugs are discovered on board by US Customs, and the existence of an agreement, and the carrier's proven adherence to it, may be important in mitigating any fine if drugs are found on the vessel or in the possession of a crew member. Participating companies should therefore maintain a well documented and enforced system of security, training and instruction on board ship.
* MGN 193 gives advice concerning the effect of alcohol or drugs on survival at sea.
* Where the **Merchant Navy Code of Conduct** is incorporated by an express term in the Crew Agreement, possession or distribution of drugs by a seafarer who is a party to the Crew Agreement will be a breach of paragraph 9 (i.e. a "dismissal breach"), and **disciplinary action** should be taken against the seafarer in accordance with the Code's provisions (see E10b).

H05 Salvage

H05a ASPECTS OF SALVAGE

* "**Salvage**" is a service rendered by a person who saves or helps to save maritime property in danger.
* Salvage must be considered from three legal aspects:
   * the **common law** aspect;
   * the **statutory** aspect; and
   * the **contractual** aspect,
   - and from a **practical seamanship** aspect.

H05b COMMON LAW ASPECTS OF SALVAGE

H05b.1 Essential elements in a salvage service

* **In common law** any salvage service rendered will not qualify for a salvage reward unless the following conditions are all met:
   * the salvage service must be **voluntary**;
   * the salvage service must be rendered to a **recognised subject of salvage**;
   * the subject of salvage must be in **danger**; and
   * the salvage service must be **successful**.
* These **common law principles** would be applied by a court in the absence of any express contract terms and where no overriding statutory provisions applied (e.g. Merchant Shipping Act 1995).

H05b.1a Voluntary service

* The person rendering the salvage service **must be a "volunteer"**, i.e. he must be under any pre-existing contract or statutory duty to render the service. The crew of a ship cannot, therefore, claim salvage in respect of their own ship

unless the Crew Agreement has been terminated either expressly or by implication or the services rendered are in excess of what could reasonably be expected of them under the contract. Harbour tugs and pilots are in a similar position.

* Tugs called out in an emergency would be "volunteers", but tugs engaged under a previously-arranged towage contract would not be "volunteers".

H05b.1b Recognised subject of salvage

* Salvage services can only be rendered to "**maritime property**", i.e. property at risk of being lost if the salvage service is not rendered.
* "**Maritime property**" includes **vessels**, their **equipment**, **cargo**, **bunkers**, **wreck** and the **freight** that stands to be lost by non-completion of the voyage.
* Salving of **ships' provisions**, passengers' and crew's **personal effects**, and **other property** saved at sea, e.g. drifting **navigation buoys**, do not qualify for salvage rewards.
* The saving of life, called "**life salvage**", may qualify, provided **property is also saved** from which a life salvage award can be made (see note on article 16.2 of the International Salvage Convention 1989 in H05c.1e).
* A salvage award is also payable in respect of **aircraft** in danger of being lost at sea.

H05b.1c In danger

* The danger must be such that any prudent master would consider it reasonable to accept an offer of salvage assistance. This means that a **real peril** must be threatening the property at the commencement of the salvage service, but it **need not be present or imminent**.
* For example. a vessel which has lost her propeller at sea will be in peril, since she will eventually either run aground or founder, etc. The danger, although not necessarily imminent, makes it imperative to call for assistance.

H05b.1d Successful

* Since the salvage reward is **payable out of value of the property saved**, it follows that unless something of value is saved, there can be no salvage reward. This is what is meant by the well-known "**no-cure, no-pay**" salvage principle.
* The service **need not be entirely successful**, however, as long as something is saved from which a reward can be paid.

H05b.2 Salvage claims under common law

* In the UK a **claim for salvage** may be dealt with:
  * by **private agreement** (e.g. between legal representatives of the salvor and other parties); or
  * by the **Admiralty Court** (part of the High Court in London), in cases where the salvage was not under Lloyd's Open Form of contract; or
  * in Scotland, by the **Court of Session** or a **sheriff**.
* **Salvage claims following services rendered under Lloyd's Open Form** (see H05d.1) are heard by arbitrators in London appointed by the Committee of Lloyd's. The **arbitrators** are normally QCs practising in the Admiralty Court.
* A salved vessel's **own master, crew and pilot** cannot normally claim salvage for saving their own vessel, since they are employed to preserve her from danger. However, any person **performing duties in excess of those expected under the terms of his contract of employment** may have a valid claim for salvage.
* When a crew properly abandons their vessel (on the orders of the master and without hope or expectation of returning to her), the crew are no longer employed under the Crew Agreement and the vessel becomes a "**derelict**". If the (former) crew members subsequently manage to re-board and save the vessel (as in the case of the tanker *San Demetrio* in World War 2[24]), they do so as **volunteers** and may have a valid claim to a salvage reward.

---

[24] In November 1940, during the Battle of the Atlantic, the British tanker *San Demetrio*, loaded with petrol, was severely damaged by enemy gunfire. The master gave orders to abandon ship and three boats got away. The ship later caught fire. The next day she was found, still on fire but afloat. Led by the second mate and chief engineer, the surviving crew boarded the ship, put out the fires, got the engine started and, with great difficulty, brought the ship to the Clyde. They claimed, and won, salvage, it being held that the ship had been **properly abandoned** on the orders of the master.

H05b.3 Salvage reward

* **To qualify** for a salvage reward, salvage services must be rendered.
* A salvage reward is not payable where a vessel stands by without actually rendering salvage services. The salvage services **must be rendered in tidal waters**, i.e. on the high seas or in waters directly connected therewith[25].
* A salvage reward is payable to the salvor on the successful conclusion of the salvage services, i.e. after some **recognised subject of salvage, of some value, has been saved**.
* No reward is payable where there is no success, giving rise to the well-known expression, "**no cure, no pay**".
* The salvage reward is **paid out of the value of the property saved** and can not, therefore, exceed this value.
* **The size of the salvage reward** will depend on many factors including the degree of danger, the enterprise and skill of the salvors, the degree of risk to which the salvors were exposed, the extent of labour of the salvors, the risk to the salvor's property, the value of property saved, and the loss, if any, incurred by the salvor.
* Where a merchant ship has performed salvage services the **salvage reward** is normally divided between the shipowner (and charterer if any), and the master and crew, the proportions varying according to the **degree of effort** by each. Although there is **no hard and fast rule**, shipowners have traditionally been awarded 3/4 of the reward, the **remaining quarter going to the master and crew**. Of that quarter, one third (i.e. one twelfth of the total) usually goes to the master, the remainder (i.e. **one sixth of the total**) being divided between the officers and crew in proportion to their rates of pay. On this basis, a salvage reward of USD120,000 would be distributed as follows:

| Owner's share | (3/4 of total) | USD90,000 |
| Master and crew's share | (1/4 of total) | USD30,000 |

* The **master and crew's share** would be distributed as follows:

| Master's share | (1/3, i.e. 1/12 of total) | USD10,000 |
| Crew's share | (2/3, i.e. 1/6 of total) | USD20,000 |

However, the payments will vary according to special circumstances, contractual provisions, etc.
* Cadets' salvage rewards are explained in **M.1227**.
* The **beneficiaries** of salvage services, and therefore the **parties liable to pay** the salvage reward, are the **owners of the property saved** by the salvor, who may include:
  * the **owner of a salved vessel**;
  * the **owners of any equipment fitted** on the vessel (e,g. diving equipment or cable-maintenance equipment fitted on a chartered ship);
  * **charterers** of a salved vessel;
  * **owners of salved cargo** (i.e. cargo salved from a vessel or from the sea);
  * the owner of salved **bunker fuel** (e.g. a time charterer); and
  * the party to whom any **freight at risk** (i.e. unpaid freight) is due.
* Where there is a "common maritime adventure", i.e. a voyage in which there are several participant owners of property at risk, each party is liable for a **contribution** to any salvage reward **in proportion to his share of the total salved values**.
* Each party involved in a voyage with property at risk, as listed above, will normally **insure against his potential liability for salvage charges**. Salvage awards are therefore **generally paid by the insurers** of the hull and machinery, cargo and freight, and these insurers will usually appoint surveyors following a salvage incident. (For notes on Clause 10 – General Average and Salvage – of the Institute Time Clauses – Hulls, see G04a.2i.)

H05b.4 Salvor's maritime lien

* A salvage reward may not be known for some months after the completion of the salvage services. In the meantime the **salvor's rights are protected by his maritime lien** on the property salved. (Where LOF has been used, the salvor also has a **contractual lien** on the salved property for his security.)
* In practice a salved cargo will have to get to its market and a salved ship will have to continue trading. Owners of salved property are therefore usually willing to pay **security to the salvor** pending the final reward being made by the court or arbitrators.
* Where no security is forthcoming, the **salvor may enforce his lien** by retaining possession of the property saved and applying to a court to have the property **arrested** and, if necessary, **sold** in order to pay the award.
* For notes on **maritime liens**, see B03g.3.
* For notes on **arrest of ships**, see B03h.

---

[25] An English court has held that salvage services rendered in non-tidal harbour waters (e.g. in docks directly connected to the high seas) will also qualify.

H05b.5 General Average and salvage

* **Salvage expenditure** is normally allowed as **General Average**. **Rule VI - Salvage Remuneration** - of the York-Antwerp Rules 1994 provides: "Expenditure incurred by the parties to the adventure on account of salvage, whether under contract or otherwise, shall be allowed in General Average to the extent that the salvage operations were undertaken for the purpose of preserving from peril the property involved in the common maritime adventure."

H05c STATUTORY ASPECTS OF SALVAGE

H05c.1 International Convention on Salvage 1989

* The **International Convention on Salvage 1989** (sometimes known as the "London Salvage Convention 1989") is an IMO Convention which entered into force on 14 July 1996. It was initially given the force of law in the UK by section 1 of the MS (Salvage and Pollution) Act 1994. That Act was repealed by the **Merchant Shipping Act 1995**, of which **section 224** now gives force of law to the Convention in the UK. The text of the Convention is contained in Schedule 12 to the 1995 Act.
* **M.1595** explains the main benefits of the Convention.
* The main provisions of the 1989 Salvage Convention of relevance to shipmasters are as follows.
* "**Salvage operation**" means any act or activity undertaken to assist a **vessel** or any other **property** in danger in navigable waters or in any other waters whatsoever (article 1(a)). "**Vessel**" means any ship or craft, or any structure capable of navigation (article 1(b)). "**Property**" means any property not permanently and intentionally attached to the shoreline and includes freight at risk (article 1(c)).
* The Convention will apply whenever **judicial or arbitral proceedings** are brought (i.e. before a court or arbitrators) in a country which is party to the Convention (article 2).
* The Convention **will not apply to mobile oil or gas rigs** when they are on location and working, but **will apply** when they are in transit between locations (article 3).
* The Convention **will not apply to warships** and other **non-commercial vessels owned or operated by a State** and entitled to sovereign immunity under international law unless the State decides otherwise (article 4.1).
* The Convention will not affect any national laws or salvage convention relating to savage operations by or under the control of public authorities (article 5).
* The Convention will apply to any salvage operations save to the extent that a contract otherwise provides, either expressly or impliedly (article 6.1).
* The **master of the salved vessel** will have the **authority to conclude salvage contracts on behalf of the owner**, and the **master or the owner** will have the **authority to conclude salvage contracts on behalf of the owner of property** on the vessel (article 6.2).
* A contract or any contract terms may be **annulled or modified** if:
    * the contract was agreed under **undue influence** or the **influence of danger** and its **terms are inequitable**; or
    * the payment agreed is **in an excessive degree too large or too small** for the services actually rendered (article 7).
* Under article 8.1 the **salvor** will owe certain duties to the owner of the vessel or other property in danger (see H05c.1a).
* Under article 8.2 the **owner and master** of the vessel or the **owner of other property in danger** will owe a duty to the salvor (see H05c.1a).

H05c.1a Duties of the salvor and of the owner and master

* Under Convention article 8.1 the **salvor** will owe a **duty** to the owner of the vessel or other property in danger -
    - to carry out the salvage operations with **due care**;
    - to exercise due care to **prevent or minimise damage to the environment**;
    - whenever circumstances reasonably require, to **seek assistance from other salvors**; and
    - to **accept the intervention of other salvors** when reasonably requested to do so by the owner or master of the vessel or other property in danger; provided that the amount of his reward will not be prejudiced if it is found that the request was unreasonable.
* Under article 8.2 the **owner and master** of the vessel or the **owner of other property in danger** will owe a duty to the salvor -
    * to **co-operate fully** with him during the salvage operations;
    * to exercise due care to **prevent or minimise damage to the environment**;

- when the vessel or property have been brought to a place of safety (see H05e.2), to **accept redelivery when reasonably requested** by the salvor.
* Every **master must**, so far as he can do so without serious danger to his vessel and persons on board, **render assistance to any person** in danger of being lost at sea (article 10.1).

H05c.1b Rights of salvors

* Salvage operations which have had a useful result give right to a **reward** (article 12.1). Except where special compensation is due, **no payment** will be due if there is **no useful result** (article 12.2).
* The salvor's rights are not affected where he owns both the salving and salved vessel (article 12.3).
* Article 13 contains the **criteria for fixing the reward**. The reward will be fixed with a view to **encouraging salvage operations**, taking into account the following criteria (without regard to the order of the list):
  - the salved value of the vessel and other property;
  - the skill and efforts of the salvors in preventing or minimising damage to the environment;
  - the measure of success obtained by the salvor;
  - the nature and degree of danger;
  - the skill and efforts of the salvors in salving the vessel, other property and life;
  - the time used and expenses and losses incurred by the salvors;
  - the risk of liability and other risks run by the salvors or their equipment;
  - the promptness of the services rendered;
  - the availability and use of vessels or other equipment intended for salvage operations;
  - the state of readiness and efficiency of the salvor's equipment and the value thereof.
* Payment of the reward will be made by the vessel and other property interests in proportion to their respective salved values (article 13.2).
* The rewards, exclusive of any interest or legal costs, will not exceed the salved value of the vessel and other property (article 13.3).

H05c.1c Special compensation

* If the salvor has carried out salvage operations in respect of a vessel which by itself or its cargo **threatened damage to the environment**, have **failed to earn a reward** at least equivalent to the special compensation assessable under the Convention (because, for example, of the low values of the vessel and/or cargo salved), the salvor will be entitled to **special compensation** from the vessel's owner equivalent to his expenses, i.e. his out-of-pocket expenses reasonably incurred in the salvage operation and a **fair rate for equipment and personnel** actually and reasonably used (article 14.1). ("**Damage to the environment**" is defined as "substantial physical damage to human health or to marine life or resources in coastal or inland waters or areas adjacent thereto, caused by pollution, contamination, fire, explosion or similar major incidents".)
* If, in the above circumstances, the **salvor has prevented or minimised damage to the environment**, the special compensation payable by the owner may be **increased** up to a maximum of 30% of the salvor's expenses (i.e. it may be 130% of his expenses) (article 14.2). However, the tribunal, if it deems it fair and just to do so, and bearing in mind the relevant criteria for fixing the reward, may increase the special compensation up to a maximum of 100% of the salvor's expenses (i.e. the salvor may recover between 130% and 200% of his expenses).
* The total special compensation under article 14 will be paid only if and to the extent that it exceeds any reward recoverable by the salvor under article 13 (article 14.4).
* If the salvor has been **negligent** and has thereby **failed to prevent or minimise damage to the environment**, he may be deprived of all or part of his special compensation (article 14.5).
* Calculation of special compensation in accordance with the provisions of Article 14 threw up some legal difficulties, resulting in salvors, P&I clubs and hull insurers devising a more "user-friendly" method of calculation, i.e. the "Scopic" Clause. For notes on the **Scopic Clause**, see H05d.3a.

H05c.1d Claims and actions

* Nothing in the Convention will affect the salvor's **maritime lien** under any international convention or national law (article 20.1). The salvor may not enforce his lien when satisfactory **security** for his claim, including interest and costs, has been paid (article 20.2).
* On the request of the salvor a person liable for a salvage reward or special compensation must provide satisfactory **security** for the claim, including interests and costs of the salvor (article 21.1). The owner of the salved vessel must use his best endeavours to ensure that the owners of the **cargo** provide satisfactory **security** for the claims against them including interest and costs before the cargo is released (article 21.2). The salved vessel and other property

must not, without the salvor's consent, be **moved** from the port or place where they first arrive after completion of the salvage operations until satisfactory security has been put up (article 21.3).
* Under paragraph 2(1) of Schedule 11 of the Merchant Shipping Act 1995, the Convention will not apply to a salvage operation in **UK inland waters** in which all the vessels involved are of **inland navigation**, or in which no vessels are involved. "**Inland waters**" does not include any waters within the ebb and flow of the tide at ordinary spring tides or the waters of any dock which is directly (by means of one or more other docks) connected with such waters.

H05c.1e Other provisions of the Salvage Convention

* The **apportionment of a reward between salvors** will be made on the basis of the criteria in article 13 of the Convention (article 15.1). The **apportionment between the owner, master and other persons in each salving vessel** will be determined by the **law of the flag State** (article 15.2).
* No remuneration is due from persons whose **lives** are saved, except where national law provides otherwise (article 16.1).
* A **salvor of human life** who has **taken part in the salvage of the vessel** will be entitled to a fair share of the salvage reward and/or special compensation (article 16.2). (See note on "**life salvage**" in H05b.1b.)
* No payment is due under the Convention unless the **services rendered exceed** what can reasonably be considered as **due performance of a contract** entered into before the danger arose (article 17). (See note on the **difference between towage and salvage** in I01c.2.)
* The salvor may be deprived of all or part of the payment due to the extent that the salvage operations have become necessary or more difficult because of **fault or neglect** on his part or if the salvor has been guilty of **fraud or dishonest conduct** (article 18).
* Services rendered notwithstanding the **express and reasonable prohibition of the owner or master** of the vessel or the owner of any other property in danger which is not and has not been on board the vessel shall not give rise to payment under the Convention (article 19).

H05c.2 Convention provisions on government intervention in maritime casualty incidents

* Nothing in the Convention will affect the **right of a coastal State** to take measures in accordance with the generally recognised principles of international law to protect its coastline or related interests from pollution upon a maritime casualty or acts relating to a maritime casualty which may reasonably be expected to result in major harmful consequences, including the **right to give directions** in relation to salvage operations (Salvage Convention, article 9).
* For notes on UK **Government intervention powers in a pollution incident** see H03i.
* For notes on the **Secretary of State's Representative for Maritime Salvage and Intervention (SOSREP)** see B05b.3a.
* **If the vessel is on the high seas**, then under the International Convention relating to Intervention on the High Seas in Cases of Oil Pollution Casualties, 1969, and the Protocol Relating to Intervention on the High Seas in Cases of Marine Pollution by Substances other than Oil, 1973, the government of any country that is threatened by pollution may take measures to prevent, mitigate or eliminate any grave and imminent danger of pollution. The government must **consult**, if possible, with other affected governments, including the ship's flag State Administration and the owners of the ship and cargo, if known. Measures taken must be **reasonably necessary** for the purpose, and **compensation** is payable if damage is caused by excessive measures.

H05d CONTRACTUAL ASPECTS OF SALVAGE

H05d.1 Salvage agreements

* Although the right to a salvage reward exists independently of contract, most salvage services are rendered under an **agreement** (i.e. a contract) of one sort or another.
* Any agreement made for salvage services **will not alter the statutory obligations** of the parties involved, as described in H05c.1a.
* There are two main **types of salvage agreement**:
  * on the basis of **ordinary tariff**, **fixed lump sum** or **daily rate**; and
  * on the basis that **remuneration will be settled later**, whether by agreement, court judgement or arbitration.

* Salvage services arranged on basis of **ordinary tariff, lump sum, etc**. is usually **cheaper** and should always be obtained if time allows, e.g. where the vessel is "soft aground" in a sheltered, non-tidal harbour and not in imminent danger. In these cases assistance will normally be arranged by the owner through negotiation with tug companies, etc. Salvage on this basis may also be used when a sunken or capsized vessel is **raised**.
* Salvage on the basis that **remuneration will be settled later** includes services rendered in times of **imminent danger** to the ship or environment.
* The agreement most often used in such cases is **Lloyd's Standard Form of Salvage Agreement**, commonly known as "Lloyd's Open Form" or "LOF" (see H05d.1).
* **Advantages of using LOF** may be summarised as:
  * agreement can be reached via radio (if witnessed) or other telecoms methods; there is no need for the form to be signed until the salvage services have been completed;
  * the agreement is not likely to be disputed;
  * LOF is basically a "no-cure, no-pay" agreement;
  * English law applies to claims;
  * the salvor has a maritime lien in the property salved, even after its sale to another party (e.g. where a salved ship or cargo is sold to try to avoid having to pay salvage charges);
  * salved property can be quickly released on payment of security to the salvor;
  * the salvor gets an **interim award**;
  * disputes are referred to arbitration in London, saving legal costs;
  * underwriters' liability cannot be increased beyond that for total loss (i.e. underwriters will not be liable for "sue and labour" costs where a total loss occurs); and
  * excessive claims by salvors are avoided.
* Various "national" forms of salvage agreement, such as the Japanese Form, the Beijing Form, the Moscow Form and the Turkish Form, are in local use around the world. The law and jurisdiction in any arbitration or litigation under these contracts will generally be the local law in the country of origin of the form.

H05d.2 Lloyd's Open Form: historical development

* The first Lloyd's Form of Salvage Agreement was adopted in 1892. Since then, LOF has undergone 10 revisions, the latest being LOF 2000 (see H05d.3).
* In its **early editions** (up to LOF 1970), LOF was a **straight "no cure, no pay"** contract.
* The 1980 edition (**LOF 80**) moved away from the traditional "no cure, no pay" principle by providing a "**safety net**" for salvors who agreed to the salvage of **loaded oil tankers**. The "safety net" guaranteed that the salvor's expenses would be paid in cases where the value of the salved property proved insufficient to provide for a normal salvage reward. In addition, the salvor could receive an an **increment** of up to a maximum of 15% of his expenses. These features were intended as incentives to persuade the declining number of professional salvors to stay in the salvage business.
* An improved incentive scheme, called "**special compensation**", was introduced in **article 14 of the International Salvage Convention, 1989**. This compensation is payable by the shipowner[26] in cases where the salvor has prevented or minimised damage to the environment but the value of the salved property is insufficient to provide for a normal salvage award. Whereas the LOF 80 "safety net" only applied in the salvage of loaded **oil** tankers, the scope of "special compensation" includes **any type of vessel or cargo which threatens damage to the environment**. In addition, the possible **increment** on the salvor's expenses was increased to a maximum of 100% of those expenses. However, whereas LOF 80 applied worldwide, special compensation payable under article 14 was restricted to salvage services in "coastal or inland waters or areas adjacent thereto". The 1990 edition of Lloyd's Open Form (**LOF 90**) contract gave immediate effect to article 14.
* Although seen by salvors as a welcome incentive, difficulties were experienced in several salvage cases in assessing the amount of special compensation due under article 14. An alternative means of assessing special compensation remuneration, known as the **Special Compensation P&I Clause** or "**Scopic Clause**", was therefore developed by salvors, P&I Clubs, underwriters and other parties. Where the Scopic Clause is incorporated into the contract, there is no geographical restriction or linkage to the existence of a pollution threat.
* The Scopic Clause came into effect in August 1999. An improved edition, "**Scopic 2000**", was introduced in September 2000 and may be used in LOF 2000 (see H05d.3).
* **LOF is administered** in London by the **Salvage Arbitration Branch** of Lloyd's whose **homepage** is at: www.lloydsoflondon.com/homepages/agencysalvage_hp.htm
* Around **120 LOF cases are notified to Lloyd's each year**, of which only a proportion have to be arbitrated. The majority of awards are settled commercially, on an amicable basis.

---

[26] The shipowner's P&I club policy usually covers special compensation payments (see G04b.1).

* Nearly **4,300 salvage operations** were performed by International Salvage Union members in the period 1978-2000, just under **60% of which were carried out under LOF**.

H05d.3 Lloyd's Open Form 2000 (LOF 2000)

* **LOF 2000 -**
  - **should be used** where the ship or marine environment are at risk and the master has **insufficient time to request the owner to arrange salvage services** on a the basis of a pre-agreed rate or sum.
  - **does not need to be on board**; the masters of the vessels involved simply need to expressly agree to its terms before the salvage services commence.
  - **superseded LOF 95**. Where a salvor offers services on LOF 95 or some other terms, the master of the vessel in difficulties should attempt to get agreement to LOF 2000 terms.
  - **is regarded** by the International Salvage Union as a major advance, with clear, user-friendly language and many innovations.
  - **is a single sheet** (2-page) document (whereas LOF 95 consists of 6 pages) in a simplified format.
  - **has a boxed front page layout** with numbered boxes for information to be entered as follows: 1. Name of the salvage contractors; 2. Property to be salved (vessel's name to be inserted); "he property" as named includes her cargo, freight, bunkers, stores and any other property thereon but excludes the personal effects or baggage of passengers, master or crew); 3. Agreed place of safety; 4. Agreed currency of any arbitral award and security (if other than US dollars); 5. Date of agreement; 6. Place of agreement; 7. "Is the Scopic Clause incorporated into this agreement?" Yes/No; 8. Name and signature of person signing for and on behalf of the Contractors; 9. Name and signature of Captain or other person signing for and on behalf of the property, with signature;
  - contains 12 clauses, A to L, as described below.
  - **contains a clear statement** – of importance to the salvor in responding to a casualty – that the **salvor** is entitled to **all information relevant to the performance of the salvage**.
  - **contains more balanced arrangements** for the termination of salvage services.
  - **defines the conditions** under which a casualty is in a **safe condition for redelivery** to the owner (which can be of crucial importance in the closing stages of a salvage operation).
* Under LOF 2000 the **Contractors** (i.e. the salvors) agrees to use their best endeavours to salve the **property** specified in Box 2 (i.e. the named vessel and/or cargo, freight, bunkers, stores and any other property on board, but excluding the personal effects of passengers, master or crew) and take the property to the **place stated** in Box 3 or to such **other place** as may be later agreed. If no place is stated, and in the absence of subsequent agreement as to the place where the property is to be taken, the Contractors must take the property to a "**place of safety**" (see H05e.2).
* **Clause A – Contractor's basic obligation** – provides that the Contractors identified in Box 1 agree to use their best endeavours to salve the property specified in Box 2 and to take the property to the place stated in Box 3 or to such other place as may be agreed after the signing of the agreement. If no place of safety is inserted in Box 3 and in the absence of any subsequent agreement as to the place where the property is to be taken the Contractors agree to take the property to a place of safety.
* **Clause B – Environmental protection** – provides that while performing the salvage services the Contractors will also use their best endeavours to prevent or minimise damage to the environment.
* **Clause C – Scopic Clause** – provides that unless the word "No" in Box 7 has been deleted, the agreement will be deemed to have been made on the basis that the Scopic Clause is **not** incorporated and forms no part of the agreement. If the word "No" is deleted, this shall not of itself be construed as a notice invoking the Scopic Clause within the meaning of sub-clause 2 of the Scopic Clause.
* **Clause D – Effect of other remedies** – provides that subject to the provisions of the International Convention on Salvage 1989 as incorporated into English law relating to special compensation and to the Scopic Clause if incorporated into the agreement, the Contractors' services will be rendered and accepted as salvage services on the principle of "no cure – no pay" and any salvage remuneration to which the Contractors become entitled will not be diminished by reason of the exception to the principle of "no cure – no pay" in the form of special compensation or remuneration payable to the Contractors under a Scopic Clause.
* **Clause E – Prior services** – provides that any salvage services rendered by the Contractors to the property before and up to the date of the agreement will be deemed to be covered by the agreement.
* **Clause F – Duties of property owners** – provides that each of the owners of the property will co-operate fully with the Contractors. In particular:
  * the Contractors may make reasonable use of the vessel's machinery, gear and equipment free of expense provided that the Contractors will not unnecessarily damage, abandon or sacrifice any property on board;
  * the Contractors will be entitled to all such information as they may reasonably require relating to the vessel or the remainder of the property provided such information is relevant to the performance of the services and is capable of being provided without undue difficulty or delay;

- the owners of the property will co-operate fully with the Contractors in obtaining entry to the place of safety stated in Box 3 or agreed or determined in accordance with Clause A.
* **Clause G – Rights of termination** – provides that where there is no longer any reasonable prospect of a useful result leading to a salvage reward in accordance with articles 12 and/or 13 of the International Salvage Convention 1989, either the owners of the vessel or the Contractors will be entitled to terminate the salvage services by giving reasonable prior written notice to the other party.
* **Clause H – Deemed performance** – provides that the Contractors' services will be deemed to have been performed when the property is in a safe condition in the place of safety stated in Box 3 or agreed or determined in accordance with Clause A. For the purpose of this provision the property will be regarded as being in safe condition notwithstanding that the property (or part thereof) is damaged or in need of maintenance if (i) the Contractors are not obliged to remain in attendance to satisfy the requirements of any port or harbour authority, governmental agency or similar authority and (ii) the continuation of skilled salvage services from the Contractors or other salvors is no longer necessary to avoid the property becoming lost or significantly further damaged or delayed.
* **Clause I – Arbitration and the LSSA Clauses** – provides that the Contractors' remuneration and/or special compensation will be determined by arbitration in London in the manner prescribed by Lloyd's Standard Salvage and Arbitration Clauses ("the LSSA Clauses') and Lloyd's Procedural Rules. The provisions of the LSSA Clauses and Lloyd's Procedural Rules are deemed to be incorporated in the agreement and form an integral part thereof. Any other difference arising out of the agreement or the operations under it will be referred to arbitration in the same way.
* **Clause J – Governing law** – provides that the agreement and any arbitration under it will be governed by English law.
* **Clause K – Scope of authority** – provides that the Master or other person signing the agreement on behalf of the property identified in Box 2 enters the agreement as agent for the respective owners of the property and binds each (but not the one for the other or himself personally) to the due performance of it.
* **Clause L – Inducements prohibited** – provides that no person signing the agreement or any party on whose behalf it is signed will at any time or in any manner whatsoever offer, provide, make, give or promise to provide or demand or take any form of inducement for entering into the agreement.
* **Two important notices** are appended, as follows: **1. Salvage security**. This states that as soon as possible the owners of the vessel should notify the owners of other property on board that the agreement has been made. If the Contractors are successful the owners of such property should note that it will become necessary to provide the Contractors with salvage security promptly in accordance with Clause 4 of the LSSA Clauses referred to in Clause I. The provision of General Average security does not relieve the salved interests of their separate obligation to provide salvage security to the Contractors. **2. Incorporated provisions**. This states that copies of the Scopic Clause, the LSSA Clauses and Lloyd's Procedural Rules may be obtained from (i) the Contractors or (ii) the Salvage Arbitration Branch at Lloyd's, One Lime Street, London EC3M 7HA. Tel No. +44(0)20 7327 5408. Fax No. +44(0)20 7327 6827. E-mail: lloyds-salvage@lloyds.com

H05d.3a SCOPIC Clause

* The **Special Compensation P&I Clause**, known as the "**Scopic Clause**" –
  - is **supplementary** to any Lloyd's Open Form Salvage Agreement "No Cure – No Pay" which incorporates the provisions of Article 14 of the International Convention on Salvage 1989.
  - **was introduced** into LOF agreements for reasons outlined in H05d.2.
  - as used with LOF 2000 is known as "**Scopic 2000**".
  - **may be invoked** at the option of the salvage contractor by written notice on the owners of the vessel being salvaged. (The Scopic Clause is not incorporated into the LOF agreement unless expressly invoked in accordance with the provisions of the Clause.)
  - **determines the method of assessing special compensation** where payable under Article 14(1) to 14(4) of the Convention. Special compensation assessed in accordance with the Scopic Clause is called "Scopic remuneration" (see below).
  - **does not change the "no cure – no pay" principle** as applying to the salvage award, since that it separate from special compensation.
  - **allows** the vessel owners, once the Clause has been invoked, to appoint at their sole option a **Shipowner's Casualty Representative** ("SCR") to attend the salvage operation in accordance with the terms and conditions in Appendix B to the Clause.
  - **allows** the Hull and Machinery underwriter (or, if more than one, the lead underwriter) and one owner or underwriter of all or part of any cargo on board to each appoint one special representative, called, respectively, the **Special Hull Representative** and the **Special Cargo Representative**, to attend the casualty to observe and report on the salvage operation in accordance with the terms in Appendix C of the Clause.

* **Scopic remuneration** -
    - **is payable only by the owners of the vessel** (and not by the cargo owners) and is only payable to the extent that it exceeds the total Article 13 award (the salvage award) or, if none, any potential Article 13 award. Where the owner of the vessel is a member of a P&I club, the club will normally pay the special compensation (hence the interest and involvement of the P&I clubs in drafting the Scopic Clause).
    - is not a General Average expense (unlike the salvage award).
    - is assessed on the basis of a tariff of rates for personnel, tugs and other craft, portable salvage equipment, out-of-pocket expenses, and bonus due. The **tariff** forms Appendix A to the Scopic Clause. (The salvage services under the main agreement continue to be assessed in accordance with Article 13 of the Convention (see H05c.1b), even if the contractor has invoked the Scopic Clause.)

H05e PRACTICAL ASPECTS OF SALVAGE

H05e.1 Considerations before accepting salvage assistance

* **When a vessel is in peril**, the master must immediately **assess the threat** and **decide urgently whether assistance, including salvage assistance, is needed** or not. The master should always **over-react on the side of safety and pollution prevention** rather than delay in the hope that the situation may improve.
* **The master** of a vessel in peril should -
    - **seek advice and instructions** from the shipowner, but **only if time allows**. If the urgency of the situation does not permit communications with the owners of the property in peril, the master will usually have authority to **act on his own initiative** (i.e. as an **agent of necessity**). For notes on **agency of necessity**, see B03d.3b, E04f.2 and H04a.
    - **immediately request assistance** if he thinks it necessary for the safety of the ship, crew and cargo.
    - accept the assistance that seems the **most reasonable**, taking into account the possible value of the assisting ships, her ability to perform the salvage services and the amount of her deviation from her intended route.
    - try to obtain agreement **to Lloyd's Open Form 2000** before accepting any salvage services offered.
    - **give the salvor all possible assistance** to enable him to do the job, remembering, however, that the more that can be done by the ship's crew, the less will be the salvor's reward and the cost to the shipowner and cargo owners. (Professional salvors may well want to do everything, in order to maximise their reward.)
    - gather contemporaneous **evidence** relating to:
        * the **terms** on which assistance was offered and accepted (e.g. witnessed log entries of radio messages);
        * details of **assisting vessels** and their **equipment** used (e.g. ropes, pumps, etc.);
        * any **measures taken before the salvor's arrival**, and measures that might have taken to save the ship had salvors not arrived (i.e. "sue and labour" cost items);
        * any **damage to the ship, injuries to crew**, etc.;
        * **assistance rendered by the ship's crew, the master and the ship's own equipment** during the salvage services.
* **If immediate assistance is not required** and time allows (e.g. where a disabled vessel is adrift in fine weather far from land and shipping lanes), **assistance should be arranged through the owner** on a contractual basis stipulating ordinary tariff, fixed lump sum or a daily rate.
* **Where safety of life, the ship, the cargo or the marine environment are in immediate peril**, however (as in the case of a disabled, laden vessel drifting onto a lee shore in a densely-trafficked area), negotiations should not delay the engagement of salvors. In this case, when one or more suitable vessels respond, they should be immediately requested to undertake **whatever action is necessary**.
* **In cases of immediate peril** there should **never be a delay to negotiate a particular form of agreement** or contract terms. Any form of contract offered (whether Lloyd's Open Form or some other form) should be **immediately agreed to** in order to get the salvage operation under way.
* In addition to any threat to life, ship and cargo, the necessity to avoid or reduce the **risk of harm to the marine environment** should be a prime consideration.
* **In deciding whether to accept salvage assistance** the master should take account of all circumstances including:
    * safety of personnel;
    * proximity to the shore or shoal water;
    * weather and sea conditions;
    * current and tide;
    * nature of sea bed and shoreline;
    * potential for safe anchoring;

- availability of assistance;
- damage already sustained by ship;
- risk of further damage to ship;
- prospect of maintaining communications;
- threat of pollution; and
- manpower and material requirements.

H05e.2 Accepting salvage assistance

* **Acceptance of an offer** of services on the basis of Lloyd's Open Form (LOF) may be made **orally** or by **radio, fax, e-mail** or **other** form of communication by sending a message as follows:
  "ACCEPT SALVAGE SERVICES ON BASIS LLOYD'S STANDARD FORM LOF NO CURE NO PAY. ACKNOWLEDGE REPEATING FOREGOING. MASTER (SHIP'S NAME)."

* **Where several prospective salvors appear on the scene**, the master has **absolute discretion** in deciding which vessel(s) will be employed. **If more assistance is required**, more salvors should be engaged. (A salvor may also engage one or more sub-contractors.) Vessels already engaged in a salvage operation have no right to object to others being brought in[27].

* **Where there is more than one salvor**, the agreement of all salvors to **co-operate** with each other should be obtained. One **leading salvor** should be appointed.

* **If the vessel offering assistance declines to accept LOF but proposes other terms**, these should be accepted. However, if the terms offered seem **unreasonable or extortionate**, the master should communicate a suitable protest and record this in the deck log and the Official Log Book.

* **The authority of the master is not reduced by engagement of salvors**; the master remains in command of his vessel, even where a salvage master is on board and is supervising the salvage operation. Even where salvage services have been accepted and assistance is being rendered, the **salvor must cease the services** if so instructed by the master.

* **The master and crew should, however, co-operate fully with professional salvors** since they are experts in salvage operations. Any **advice given by a salvage master** or other person in charge of providing or advising on salvage services[28] should be heeded.

* **The master should ensure that he is fully aware of all salvage actions** being taken.

* Salvors may not be experts in safety and handling of certain special cargoes, or be familiar with the vessel being salved. If the master is in doubt about the advisability of any action suggested by the salvors, he should challenge the advice given, bearing in mind his overriding responsibility for the safety of the ship, her cargo and the personnel on board.

* **M.1175** draws attention to "three publications which contain a great deal of information on the procedures to be followed by a ship which is in hazard and by ships giving assistance", i.e.:
  - **Notice No.4** in the Annual Summary of Admiralty Notices to Mariners;
  - the IMO **MERSAR** Manual (which has been superseded by the IMO/ICAO **IAMSAR** Manual – see H04b.12a); and
  - the ICS/OCIMF publication "**Peril at Sea and Salvage: A Guide for Masters**".

* **In deciding on a "place of safety"**, the factors to be considered include:
  - the repair facilities at the place;
  - the possibility of safely discharging and storing cargo and of forwarding it to its destination;
  - the danger of deterioration of the cargo in the place;
  - whether the place is the most suitable place at which the vessel can be repaired, with regard to nearness, convenience, cheapness and facilities; and
  - whether the vessel is capable of manoeuvring under her own power or not, and whether, therefore, she could still be regarded as being in a position of danger even though moored in a "safe port".

* Taking the above factors into account, it may be necessary for the ship to be towed past places at which she could lie in safety. Arbitrators tend to consider that unless a vessel is at a port or place where she can effect the repairs necessary for the safe continuation of the voyage, she cannot be considered to be in a "place of safety" so far as completion of the salvage services is concerned. The master should not, therefore, release the salving vessel until his ship is in a place of safety or a place named in the LOF.

---

[27] If salving a derelict vessel, however, the first salvor to take possession of the vessel has sole right to the salvage, and may not be interfered with except in the face of "manifest incompetence".
[28] Such as SOSREP (in UK waters – see B05b.3a) or a Salvage Association surveyor.

H05e.3 Offering salvage assistance

* There is a **statutory obligation** to attempt to **save the lives** of persons in distress at sea (see H04b.1a), but **no such obligation to save maritime property** in danger of being lost. Any attempt by the master of a merchant vessel to save property is a **commercial venture** and not a statutory obligation.
* A vessel requiring a tow (e.g. a disabled, drifting vessel) is **not necessarily in distress**. The master of a vessel offering a towage service should, therefore, carefully consider the following points before contracting to perform a salvage service:
    * Does the **contract of carriage** (as contained in the charter party or bill of lading) give the vessel the liberty to tow?
    * Are there sufficient **bunkers** and/or **fresh water** on board for the tow, and will sufficient reserves be maintained, throughout and after the tow, to meet the stipulations of the owner or charterers?
    * Is there a possibility of missing any **cancelling date** under a charter party? (See F05b.1.)
    * Does the nature of the **cargo** permit a lengthening of the voyage? (This is relevant especially in reefers.)
    * Is the vessel's machinery of **adequate power** and in good enough condition for towing?
    * Is the **value** of the vessel requesting the tow, plus her cargo, of sufficient value to merit a salvage service?
    * Has an agreement to salvage on **Lloyd's Open Form** terms been made? (See below.)
    * Has a port of **destination** or **place of safety** been agreed? (Where the casualty is near the UK it is preferable to tow the vessel here rather than to a Continental port.) (See H05e.2.)
    * Have the owner or manager and any time charterer been **notified**, so that additional hull insurance can be arranged if necessary?
    * Are proper **records** of all events and circumstances to date being kept? (See H05e.4.)
* **Lloyd's Open Form 2000** (LOF 2000) is the most appropriate contract to be offered to the vessel requiring assistance. An offer of salvage services on LOF 2000 terms may be agreed to by sending a message as follows:
    "OFFER SALVAGE SERVICES ON BASIS LLOYD'S OPEN FORM 2000 LOF 2000 NO CURE NO PAY. MASTER (SHIP'S NAME)".

H05e.4 Record-keeping during salvage operations

* **Detailed records** should be kept of all events associated with the accident or the breakdown of machinery or equipment, and the salvage services subsequently rendered. The records may be in any form. All contemporaneous notes, whether on scraps of paper, in movement books or log books should be retained, together with course, rudder angle, depth and other records. Appropriate entries should be made in deck and engine room logs and in the Official Log Book. Accounts should be kept of:
    * particulars of the vessel and her cargo;
    * the condition of the vessel (including its position, proximity to the shore, nature of the sea bed, the condition of the engines and anchors, the availability of crew, etc.;
    * all salvage services rendered;
    * all expenses incurred (overtime, hire of boats, etc.); and
    * the weather conditions prevailing.

H06 Communications and reports

H06a ROUTINE COMMUNICATIONS

* **Liner companies** will usually have **standing instructions to masters** regarding reporting periodically from sea.
* A conventional **time charter party** (i.e. one other than for a specialised vessel) will almost certainly incorporate a requirement, perhaps in a rider clause or side letter, stipulating **advices or notices** to be sent by the master to various parties at certain stages of any voyage. Typically, the addressees are the charterer's head office, charterer's nominated agents, consignees and receivers. Messages may have to be sent daily, or at intervals such as 72, 48, 24 and 12 hours before arrival. Non-compliance would be a breach of the charter party terms, possibly making the owner liable for damages.
* A **voyage charter party** should always be checked for any similar requirement.
* **MGN 114** draws attention to the contents of IMO circular COMSAR/Circ.17, which recommends that GMDSS equipment should be utilised for routine communications or testing in order to ensure equipment availability and operator competency, and to reduce the number of false alerts caused by inexperienced operators.

H06b DISTRESS AND SAFETY COMMUNICATIONS

H06b.1 Conventional distress signals

* **Regulation 3(1) of the MS (Distress Signals and Prevention of Collisions) Regulations 1996** (SI 1996/75) provides that the signals of distress which must be used by vessels to which regulation 2(1)(a) of the Regulations apply[29] are those set out in Annex IV to the International Regulations for Preventing Collisions at Sea, 1972.
* Merchant Shipping Notice **M.1642/COLREG 1**, which is an integral part of the MS (Distress Signals and Prevention of Collisions) Regulations 1996, contains in full the International Regulations for Preventing Collisions at Sea, 1972, as amended by Resolutions A.464(XII), A626(15), A.678(16) and A.736(18). Distress signals are listed in Annex IV of the International Regulations, which is printed on page 32 of the M.1642.
* **Paragraph 1 of Annex IV** provides that the following signals, used or exhibited either together or separately, indicate distress and need of assistance:
  * (a)   a gun or other explosive signal fired at intervals of about a minute;
  * (b)   a continuous sounding with any fog-signalling apparatus;
  * (c)   rockets or shells, throwing red stars fired one at a time at short intervals;
  * (d)   a signal made by radiotelegraphy or by any other signalling method consisting of the group . . . - - - . . . (SOS) in the Morse code;
  * (e)   a signal sent by radiotelephony consisting of the spoken word "Mayday";
  * (f)   the International Code Signal of distress indicated by N.C.;
  * (g)   a signal consisting of a square flag having above or below it a ball or anything resembling a ball;
  * (h)   flames from the vessel (as from a burning tar barrel, oil barrel, etc.);
  * (i)   a rocket parachute flare or a hand flare showing a red light;
  * (j)   a smoke signal giving off orange-coloured smoke;
  * (k)   slowly and repeatedly raising and lowering arms outstretched to each side;
  * (l)   the radiotelegraph alarm signal;
  * (m)   the radiotelephone alarm signal;
  * (n)   signals transmitted by emergency position-indicating radio beacons;
  * (o)   approved signals transmitted by radiocommunications systems, including survival craft radar transponders.
* **Paragraph 2 of Annex IV** prohibits the use or exhibition of any of the foregoing signals except for the purpose of indicating distress and need of assistance, and the use of other signals which may be confused with any of the above signals.
* Paragraph 3 of Annex IV draws attention to the relevant sections of the International Code of Signals, the Merchant Ship Search and Rescue Manual (MERSAR) and the following signals:
  * a piece of orange-coloured canvas with either a black square and circle or other appropriate symbol (for identification from the air); and
  * a dye marker.
* The signals listed above are also listed in **Notice No.4** in the Annual Summary of Admiralty Notices to Mariners.
* **Regulation 3(2)** of the Distress Signals and Prevention of Collisions Regulations provides that **no signal of distress may be used** by any vessel unless the **master** of the vessel so orders.
* **Regulation 3(3)** of the Distress Signals and Prevention of Collisions Regulations provides that the master must not order any signal of distress to be used by his vessel unless he is satisfied -
  * that his vessel is in **serious and imminent danger**, or that another ship or an aircraft or person is in serious and imminent danger and cannot send that signal; and
  * that the vessel in danger (whether his own vessel or another vessel) or the aircraft or person in danger, as the case may be, **requires immediate assistance** in addition to any assistance then available.
* Regulation 3(4) provides that the master of a vessel which has sent any signal of distress by means of radio or other means must **cause that signal to be revoked by all appropriate means** as soon as he is satisfied that the vessel or aircraft to which or the person to whom the signal relates is no longer in need of assistance as aforesaid.
* **Regulation 4 of the MS (Radio Installations) Regulations 1998** (SI 1998/2070) (see D04m.1) provides that nothing in the Regulations will prohibit any ship, survival craft or person in distress from using **any means at their disposal** to attract attention, make known their position or obtain help.
* For general notes on the **MS (Distress Signals and Prevention of Collision) Regulations 1996**, and notes on the Collision Regulations provisions of the Regulations, see H02a.2

---

[29] Regulation 2(1)(a) provides that the Regulations apply to UK ships wherever they are, and other ships while in the UK or UK territorial waters.

H06b.2 VHF safety message prefixes

* **Regulation 28(2) of the MS (Radio Installations) Regulations 1998** (SI 1998/2070) provides that a card of instructions giving a clear summary of the distress, urgency and safety procedures must be displayed at each VHF operating position on a non-GMDSS ship. The procedures are usually printed on three cards as described in Appendix F of Notice No.4 in Annual Summary of Notices to Mariners. Radio-telephone safety message prefixes are printed on "Card 2" as follows:
* "**MAYDAY**" (distress) indicates that a ship or other vehicle is threatened by grave and imminent danger and requests immediate assistance.
* "**PAN PAN**" (urgency) indicates that the calling station has a very urgent message to transmit concerning the safety of a ship, aircraft or other vehicle, or of a person.
* "**SECURITÉ**" (safety) indicates that the station is about to transmit a message concerning the safety of navigation or giving important meteorological warnings.
* The **IAMSAR** Manual, Volume III, Section 4, states that "Mayday" is used, for example, when a vessel has a person overboard and a master considers that further help is necessary. "Mayday" has priority over all other communications. The urgency signal "Pan Pan" should be used when an unsafe situation exists that may eventually involve a need for assistance, and has priority over all but distress traffic. "Securité" is used for messages concerning the safety of navigation or giving important meteorological information. Any message headed by one of these signals has priority over routine messages.

H06b.3 GMDSS distress alerts

* **MGN 67** gives advice on measures to be taken to avoid transmitting false alerts on GMDSS equipment.
* **MGN 113** advises that masters should ensure, if in distress, or if assisting in SAR operations, that measures are taken to terminate all non-emergency communications from the ship and to offer all assistance to the RCC in maintaining communications.

H06b.4 Standard Marine Navigational Vocabulary

* **M.1252** contains in its Annex the full text of the Standard Marine Navigational Vocabulary developed by IMO and recommends masters, officers and seamen, as well as the owner ashore, to use the Vocabulary to minimise the possibility of misunderstanding vital information.
* The Standard Marine Navigational Vocabulary is due to be replaced by the **Standard Marine Communication Phrases** (SMCP) (see H06b.5).

H06b.5 Standard Marine Communication Phrases

* **MGN 48** states that Administrations have been requested to conduct shipboard trials with the draft **Standard Marine Communication Phrases** (SMCP) developed by IMO, and to encourage their use by persons involved in maritime communications.
* Copies of SCMP, which were issued in MSC Circular 794, were not available from the MCA at the time of writing. In the meantime, **M.1252** (Standard Marine Navigational Vocabulary) is still valid, although it will not be re-issued or reprinted.
* The SMCPs can be viewed at www.info.gov.hk/mardep/comphrase/comphrase.htm

H06c SHIP REPORTING SYSTEMS AND REQUIREMENTS

H06c.1 Ship reporting systems

* Ships should **report** to the shore-based authority without delay when **entering** an area covered by a mandatory ship reporting system and, if necessary, when **leaving** the area. Additional reports or information may be required to update or modify a previous report.
* A technical failure preventing a ship from making a required report should be **recorded** in the deck log.

* **Admiralty List of Radio Signals (ALRS) Volume 1** contains a section on Ship Reporting Systems designed to provide information to shipping in event of a Search-and-Rescue incident. A detailed section on the AMVER service (see H06c.1a) is included.
* Ship reporting systems concerned with **traffic management** (including national reporting systems for deep-draught vessels, vessels carrying dangerous cargoes, etc.) are included in **ALRS Volume 6** along with the reporting requirements for entering ports.
* **Notice No.17A** in the Annual Summary of Notices to Mariners gives details of the UK **Automatic Ship Identification and Reporting System** (AIRS).
* Some ship reporting systems are recommendatory. **MGN 58**, for example, encourages watchkeepers on vessels using the Minches (off NW Scotland) to comply with a reporting recommendation in IMO Resolution A.768(18).

H06c.1a AMVER

- is a unique, computer-based, voluntary **global ship reporting system** used worldwide by search and rescue authorities to arrange for assistance to persons in distress at sea. Through AMVER, rescue co-ordinators can identify participating ships in the area of distress and divert the best-suited ship or ships to respond.
- **is sponsored** by the **US Coast Guard**.
- employs a large **computer database** to which any maritime rescue service in the world has access on request.
- operates with the **voluntary participation of ships**, which send details of their voyage routes.
- keeps the estimated or dead reckoning **positions** of participating ships **updated** on the computer to enable a "surpic" to be obtained for any location at a moment's notice.
- will pass, on request of a co-ordinating coastguard service, up-to-date details of all **AMVER participant vessels** on-plot in the area so that **suitable vessels for SAR or medical assistance tasks can be selected**.
- **does not take direct calls** from ships.
* Ships incur no additional obligation to respond to a "distress" beyond that already existing under international law. Since AMVER identifies the best ship or ships to respond to a distress call, it releases other vessels to continue their voyage, saving fuel, time and payroll costs.
* **ALRS** Volume 1, parts 1 and 2 contain separate sections on **Ship Reporting Systems** and contain a description of AMVER message format and a list of stations which will accept AMVER messages.
* See **M.1551** regarding costs of AMVER messages to UK coast radio stations.
* AMVER website: www.amver.com
* For a note on the role of AMVER in **radio medical assistance**, see H04c.3.

H06c.2 Mandatory ship reporting requirements

* The **MS (Safety of Navigation) Regulations 2002** (SI 2002/1473) (see H01f.2) –
  - **revoke** and replace the MS (Mandatory Ship Reporting) Regulations 1996 (SI 1996/1749).
  - **require compliance** by a ship to which the Regulations apply with **paragraph 7 of SOLAS regulation V/11** (which relates to **Ship reporting systems**).
* **SOLAS regulation V/11.7** provides that the master of a ship must comply with the requirements of adopted ship reporting systems and report to the appropriate authority all information required in accordance with the provisions of each such system.
* The **Guidance Notes to regulation V/11** in MCA's 2002 SOLAS Chapter V publication supersede MGN 153[30] (Compliance with mandatory ship reporting systems).
* **Details of mandatory ship reporting schemes** are promulgated in Admiralty List of Radio Signals (ALRS) (see D04m.3d). Locations of ship reporting schemes are shown where applicable on Admiralty charts.
* The only mandatory ship reporting scheme currently in operation in UK waters covers the Dover Strait (see **MGN 128**).

H06d DANGER MESSAGES

H06d.1 Merchant Shipping Act 1995 requirements relating to reports of dangers to navigation

* **Section 91(1), (2), (3) and (4) of the Merchant Shipping Act 1995**, which provided for the sending by a master of a **navigational warning** when specified dangers to navigation were encountered, was repealed by regulation 3(1)

---

[30] The document states that MGN 24 is the superseded notice; this was superseded in August 2000 by MGN 153.

and Schedule 2 of the MS (Safety of Navigation) Regulations 2002 (SI 2002/1473). The requirements for ships to send navigational warnings are now contained in **SOLAS regulations V/31.1 and .4** and **V/32**, as given effect in the UK by the **Safety of Navigation Regulations** (see H06d.2).

H06d.2 Safety of Navigation Regulations requirements relating to danger messages

* The **MS (Safety of Navigation) Regulations 2002** (SI 2002/1473) (see H01f.2) –
  - **revoke** and replace the MS (Navigational Warnings) Regulations 1996 (SI 1996/1815).
  - **require compliance** by a ship to which the Regulations apply with **paragraphs 1 and 4 of SOLAS regulation V/31** (which relates to **Danger messages**) and **paragraphs 1, 2, 4 and 5 of SOLAS regulation V/32** (which relates to **Information required** in danger messages) (regulation 5(1)).
* **SOLAS regulation V/31.1** provides that the master of every ship which meets with **dangerous ice**, a **dangerous derelict**, or any **other direct danger to navigation**, or a **tropical storm**, or encounters sub-freezing air temperatures associated with gale force winds causing **severe ice accretion** on superstructures, or winds of **force 10 or above** on the Beaufort scale for which **no storm warning** has been received, must communicate the information by all means at his disposal to **ships in the vicinity**, and also to the "**competent authorities**" (i.e. the appropriate national or NAVAREA Co-ordinator for navigational warnings via a coast station). The form in which the information is sent is not obligatory. It may be transmitted either in **plain language** (preferably English) or by means of the **International Code of Signals**.
* **SOLAS regulation V/31.4** provides that all radio messages issued under regulation 31.1 must be preceded by the **safety signal**, using the procedure as prescribed by the Radio Regulations as defined in SOLAS regulation IV/2.
* **SOLAS regulation V/32** sets out the details of **information to be included in danger messages** sent in compliance with regulation V/31.
* **SOLAS regulation V/32.1** provides that the following information must be sent in danger messages relating to **ice**, **derelicts** and **other direct dangers** to navigation:
  * the kind of ice, derelict or danger observed;
  * the position of the ice, derelict or danger when last observed;
  * the time and date (UTC) when the danger was last observed.
* **SOLAS regulation V/32.2** provides that the following information must be sent in danger messages relating to **tropical cyclones** (storms):
  * a statement that a tropical cyclone has been encountered. This obligation should be interpreted in a broad spirit, and information transmitted whenever the master has good reason to believe that a tropical cyclone is developing or exists in the neighbourhood.
  * time, date (UCT) and position of ship when the observation was taken;
  * as much of the following information as is practicable: barometric pressure, preferably corrected (stating millibars, millimetres, or inches, and whether corrected or uncorrected); barometric tendency (the change in barometric pressure during the past three hours); true wind direction; wind force (Beaufort scale); state of the sea (smooth, moderate, rough, high); swell (slight, moderate, heavy) and the true direction from which it comes. Period or length of swell (short, average, long) would also be of value; true course and speed of ship.
* **SOLAS regulation V/32.3** (which is not mandatory for UK ships) provides that when a master has reported a tropical cyclone or other dangerous storm, it is desirable but not obligatory that further observations be made and transmitted hourly, if practicable, but in any case at intervals of not more than 3 hours, so long as the ship remains under the influence of the storm.
* **SOLAS regulation V/32.4** relates to danger messages concerning **winds of force 10 or above** on the Beaufort scale for which **no storm warning** has been received, and is intended to deal with storms other than the tropical cyclones referred to in regulation V/32.2. When such a storm is encountered, the message should contain similar information as for tropical cyclones but excluding the details concerning sea and swell.
* **SOLAS regulation V/32.5** provides that the following information must be sent in danger messages relating to sub-freezing air temperatures associated with gale force winds causing severe ice accretion on superstructures:
  * time and date (UCT);
  * air temperature;
  * sea temperature (if practicable); and
  * wind force and direction.
* **Guidance Notes** to regulations V/31 and V/32 are contained in the MCA's 2002 SOLAS Chapter V publication. The Guidance Notes together with the two regulations supersede M.1641/NW1.
* The **Guidance Notes to regulation V/32** advise that the appropriate NAVAREA Co-ordinator for NAVAREA 1 (which includes UK waters) is, for dangers to navigation, the National Hydrographer, UKHO, Taunton. For meteorological dangers (listed in regulation V/32.2 to 32.5), it is the National Meteorological Centre of the Met Office.

* **Examples of danger messages** are shown in the following table.

Danger encountered	Message
Ice	TTT ICE. LARGE BERG SIGHTED IN 4506 N, 4410 W, AT 0800 UTC. MAY 15.
Derelict	TTT DERELICT. OBSERVED DERELICT ALMOST SUBMERGED IN 4006 N, 1243 W, AT 1630 UTC. APRIL 21.
Danger to navigation	TTT NAVIGATION. ALPHA LIGHTSHIP NOT ON STATION. 1800 UTC. JANUARY 3
Tropical storm	TTT STORM. 0030 UTC. AUGUST 18. 2004 N, 11354 E. BAROMETER CORRECTED 994 MILLIBARS. TENDENCY DOWN 6 MILLIBARS. WIND NW, FORCE 9, HEAVY SQUALLS. HEAVY EASTERLY SWELL. COURSE 067, 5 KNOTS.
Icing	TTT EXPERIENCING SEVERE ICING. 1400 UTC. MARCH 2. 69 N, 10 W. AIR TEMPERATURE 18. SEA TEMPERATURE 29. WIND NE, FORCE 8.

H06e REPORTING REQUIREMENTS FOR SHIPS CARRYING DANGEROUS AND POLLUTING GOODS

H06e.1 Reporting Requirements Regulations

* The **MS (Reporting Requirements for Ships Carrying Dangerous and Polluting Goods) Regulations 1995** (SI 1995/2498) -
   - **give effect** in the UK to Council Directive 93/75/EEC concerning minimum requirements for vessels bound for or leaving Community ports and carrying dangerous or polluting goods as amended by Council Directive 98/55/EC.
   - **revoke** the MS (Tankers) (EEC Requirements) Regulations 1981 (SI 1981/1077), the MS (Tankers) (EEC Requirements) (Amendment) Regulations 1982 (SI 1982/1637) and the MS (Reporting Requirements for Ships Carrying Dangerous and Polluting Goods) Regulations 1994 (SI 1994/3245).
   - **are amended** by the MS (Reporting Requirements for Ships Carrying Dangerous and Polluting Goods) (Amendment) Regulations 1999 (SI 1999/2121).
   - **apply to** UK ships wherever they are and to non-UK ships while they are in the UK or UK territorial waters. Regulations 9, 10 and 11 also apply to non-UK ships which are outside the UK or UK territorial waters if they are involved in an **incident or circumstance at sea mentioned in regulation 9(1)** (see H06e.1b).
   - **contain** regulations numbered as follows: **1**. Citation and commencement; **2**. Interpretation and revocation; **3**. Application; **4**. Competent authority; **5**. Notification by ships carrying dangerous or polluting goods; **6**. Notification to the State of destination or anchorage; **7**. Vessel Traffic Services; **8**. Incidents involving infectious substances; **9**. Reporting of incidents; **10**. Supplementary reports; **11**. Reporting procedures; **12**. Master to supply information to pilots; **13** and **14**. Duties of pilots; **15** and **16**. Offences; **17** and **18**. Inspection and detention of ships; **19**. Duties of the Coastguard Agency.
   - **are explained** in **MSN 1741**.
* **The "competent authority" in the UK is the MCA** for the purposes of the Council Directive and the Regulations (regulation 4(1)). Reports to the UK required under the Regulations should be sent to **Dover Coastguard**, whether directly or through any other MCA channel.
* The **competent authority in relation to any other EU member State** means any authority designated as such for the purposes of article 3 of the Council Directive in the particular State (regulation 4(2)).
* **Regulations 5 to 14** impose various requirements. For notes on requirements relating to **vessels arriving at ports**, see I01a.7. For requirements relating to **vessels departing from ports**, see I07d.
* For notes on the requirements of **regulation 5(1) (Notifications before leaving port)**, see I07d.1.
* For notes on the requirements of **regulation 5(2) (Shipper's notification of shipment of radioactive materials)**, see F07f.5.
* For notes on the requirements of **regulation 6 (Notification to the State of destination or anchorage)**, see I01a.7a.
* For notes on the requirements of **regulation 7 (Vessel Traffic Services)**, see I01b.10.
* For notes on the requirements of **regulation 8 (Incidents involving infectious substances)**, see H06e.1a.
* For notes on the requirements of **regulation 9 (Reporting of incidents)**, see H06e.1b.
* For notes on the requirements of **regulation 10 (Supplementary reports)**, see H06e.1c.
* For notes on the requirements of **regulation 11 (Reporting procedures)**, see H06e.1d.
* For notes on the requirements of **regulation 12 (Master to supply information to pilots)**, see I01a.7b.
* For notes on the requirements of **regulations 13** and **14 (Duties of pilots)**, see I01b.7.

H06e.1a Requirement to report incidents involving infectious substances (regulation 8)

* **Regulation 8** provides that in the event of **damage or leakage to a package containing infectious substances,** the master must report the incident by the **fastest telecommunications channel available** in accordance with the requirements in the **IMDG Code** for **Class 6.2** goods.

H06e.1b Requirement to report incidents (regulation 9)

* **Regulation 9(1)** provides that the master of a ship involved in an **incident or circumstance at sea** involving:
   • a **discharge of oil or noxious liquid substances above the permitted level**, or the **probability** of a discharge of oil or noxious liquid substances, for **whatever reason including** those for the purpose of securing the safety of the ship or for saving life at sea;
   • a **discharge of dangerous goods or harmful substances in packaged form**, or the **probability** of such a discharge, including those in freight containers, portable tanks, road and rail vehicles and shipborne barges;
   • any **damage, failure or breakdown of a ship of 15 metres in length or above** which –
      ▪ **affects the safety** of the ship, such as collision, grounding, fire, explosion, structural failure, flooding or cargo shifting; or
      ▪ **impairs the safety of navigation**, such as failure or breakdown of steering gear, propulsion plant, electrical generating system or essential shipborne navigational aids;
   • a **discharge during the operation of the ship of oil or noxious liquid substances in excess of the permitted level**; or
   • without prejudice to the reports of events as required above, **a threat of damage to the coastline or related interests** of the UK,
   - **must report** the particulars of the incident **without delay** and to the **fullest extent possible**, together with the **information specified in Schedule 1 to MSN 1741**, which includes the following details:
   • name and call sign of the ship and, where appropriate, the IMO identification number;
   • nationality of the ship;
   • length and draught of the ship;
   • port of destination;
   • estimated time of arrival at the port of destination or pilot station, as required by the competent authority;
   • estimated time of departure;
   • intended route;
   • the correct technical name of the dangerous or polluting goods, the United Nations (UN) numbers where they exist, the IMO hazard classes in accordance with the IMDG, IBC and IGC Codes and, where appropriate, the class of the ship as defined in the INF Code, the quantities of such goods and their location on board and, if in portable tanks or freight containers, their identification marks;
   • confirmation that a list or manifest or appropriate loading plan giving details of the dangerous or polluting goods carried and their location on the ship is on board; and
   • number of crew on board.
* **Regulation 9(2)** provides that **where the State concerned is the UK** (and the competent authority is the MCA) and the information listed in Schedule 1 of MSN 1741 has **already been reported** to the competent authority of another EU member State, the reporting requirement is satisfied if the master informs the MCA **which other competent authority** holds the required information.
* **Regulation 9(3)** provides that **where a report from the master is incomplete or unobtainable**, the **operator** must, to the fullest extent practicable, make or complete the incident report (regulation 9(3)).
* **Regulation 9(4)(a)** provides that a **report** made under regulation 9(1) or, if there is more than one, the **initial report**, must comply with the **Standard Reporting Requirements** as to form and contents. Regulation 9(4)(b) defines "Standard Reporting Requirements" as meaning the requirements stated in the Annex to Resolution A.851(20), adopted by IMO on 27 November 1997 (see H06e.4).

H06e.1c Supplementary reports (regulation 10)

* **Regulation 10** provides that any person required to make an incident report under regulation 9 (as amended) must:
   • make such a **supplementary report or reports** as may be appropriate in the circumstances -
      ▪ supplementing the information contained in the initial report as necessary; and
      ▪ complying as fully as possible with any request for additional information made by or on behalf of the government of a State whose interests may be affected by the incident; and
   • comply as fully as possible with any **request for additional information** made by or on behalf of the government of a State whose interests may be affected by the incident.

H06e.1d Reporting procedures (regulation 11)

* **Regulation 11** provides that an incident report must be made by the **fastest telecommunications channels available** with the **highest possible priority**. Where the incident or threat is to the coastline or to a related interest of the UK, the report must be made to a UK Maritime Rescue Centre (MRC) (e.g. to "Dover Coastguard") (regulation 11(a)). In any other case, the report must be made to the **competent authority of the nearest coastal State** (regulation 11(b)).

H06e.2 Reports under the Oil Pollution Preparedness, Response and Co-operation Convention Regulations

* The **MS (Oil Pollution Preparedness, Response and Co-operation Convention) Regulations 1998** (SI 1998/1056) implement, in part, the International Convention on Oil Pollution Preparedness, Response and Co-operation, 1990.
* **Regulation 5(1)** requires the master of a UK ship **in UK waters or controlled waters**[31], **or elsewhere**, who observes or otherwise becomes aware of any event involving **discharge of oil** at sea from **another ship** or from an **offshore installation**, to **report the discharge without delay**. If his ship is in UK waters or controlled waters, the master must report to **HM Coastguard**, and if his ship is elsewhere he must report to the **nearest coastal State**.

H06e.3 Pollution reports to coastal States

* **Admiralty List of Radio Signals (ALRS) Volume 1** contains a section on Pollution Reports by Radio which details procedures for reporting pollution incidents when in the waters of certain countries and territories. Countries listed are Australia, Canada, Chile, Cuba, French Antilles, French Guiana and New Caledonia, and New Zealand.

H06e.4 Standard Reporting Requirements

* **IMO's standard reporting format and procedure**, the application of which was extended to include the detailed requirements for reporting incidents involving dangerous goods, harmful substances (e.g. oil) and marine pollutants, is contained in the Annex and Appendix to **Resolution A.851(20)**, adopted on 27 November 1997. The full text of the Annex and Appendix is printed in the **Supplement to the IMDG Code** (2000 edition).
* The **Annex to Resolution A.851(20)** contains:
  * General principles for ship reporting systems and ship reporting requirements;
  * Guidelines for reporting incidents involving dangerous goods; and
  * Guidelines for reporting incidents involving harmful substances and/or marine pollutants.
* The **Appendix to Resolution A.851(20)** contains:
  * Procedures (see H06e.4a);
  * Standard reporting format and procedures; and
  * Guidelines for detailed reporting requirements.
* **M.1614,** which was published in May 1995, contains the Standard Reporting Requirements as laid down in the **Annex to Resolution A.648(16)**, which was revoked by Resolution A.851(20). The differences between the reporting requirements of the old and new Resolutions are, for practical purposes, minor.

H06e.4a Reporting procedures

* **The "Procedures"** section of the Appendix to Resolution A.851(20) lists **types of report** and when each should be sent. The information is shown in tabulated form below.

Type of report	When the report should be sent
Sailing Plan (SP)	Before or as near as possible to the time of departure from a port within a system or when entering the area covered by a system.
Position report (PR)	When necessary to ensure effective operation of the system.
Deviation report (DR)	When the ship's position varies considerably from the position that would have been predicted from previous reports, when changing the reported route, or as decided by the master.
Final report (FR)	On arrival at destination and when leaving the area covered by a system.
Dangerous goods report (DG)	When an incident takes place involving the loss or likely loss overboard of packaged dangerous goods, including those in freight containers, portable tanks, road and rail vehicles and shipborne barges, into the sea.

---

[31] **"Controlled waters"** means water specified as areas within which the jurisdiction and rights of the UK are exercisable by the MS (Prevention of Pollution) (Limits) Regulations 1996 (SI 1996/2128) as amended by SI 1997/506. See also I01a.1b.

Harmful substances report (HS)	When an incident takes place involving the discharge or probable discharge of oil (Annex I of MARPOL 73/78) or noxious liquid substances in bulk (Annex II of MARPOL 73/78).
Marine pollutants report (MP)	In case of loss or likely loss overboard of harmful substances in packaged form including those in freight containers, portable tanks, road and rail vehicles and shipborne barges, identified in the IMDG Code as marine pollutants (Annex III of MARPOL 73/78).
Any other report	Any other report should be made in accordance with the system procedures as notified.

* The **"Standard reporting format and procedures"** section contains a table comprising four columns headed "Telegraphy", "Telephone (alternative)", "Function" and "Information required". 26 **functions** (e.g. Date and time of event, Position, True course) are listed by letters **A to Z**, the "Information required" column showing the precise information needed.

* **When a report of a type listed above is to be sent**, the procedure is as follows:
1. The **Guidelines for detailed reporting requirements** should be consulted to determine which **items** (e.g. A, B, C, M, Q, etc.) must be reported. Certain items are shown with expanded, numbered details (e.g. in the case of a Harmful substances report, P 1 to 5, Q 1 and 2, R 1 to 10, T1 and X 1, 2 and 3).
2. Reports should commence with the **"system identifier"** (i.e. the ship reporting system or appropriate coast radio station, e.g. "AUSREP") and the **type of report**, e.g. "Dangerous goods report" (by telephony).
3. The **"Standard reporting format and procedures"** should be consulted to determine, for each lettered item, the information required.

H06f OTHER REPORTS FROM SEA

H06f.1 If the vessel is delayed on a preliminary voyage

* For notes on the **preliminary voyage** under a voyage charter, see F05b.2.
* **Should the vessel be delayed** for any reason when on a preliminary voyage, to the extent that there is a **risk of missing the cancelling date**, the master should:
1. Check the charter party for any related obligation to inform the charterer or charterer's agent(s), etc.
2. Check the charter party for any obligation of the charterer to declare his intention with respect to the vessel.
3. Notify the owner if the charterer unreasonably delays his contractually-required decision, where relevant.
4. Inform the charterer of the ETA.
5. Inform the owner of the ETA.
6. Pending arrival of instructions, continue with all speed to the loading port.
7. Inform the P&I club correspondent for the loading port, to put them "in the picture".
8. Tender Notice of Readiness on arrival in accordance with the charter party terms.
9. Inform the owner and P&I club correspondent of the vessel's arrival.
10. Note protest as soon as possible after arrival.
11. Await instructions from the charterer and/or owner.
12. Enter details of the circumstances of the delay in the Official Log Book (annexing a full report if required).
13. Keep hard copies of all messages received and sent relating to the matter.

H06f.2 If ordered to an unsafe port by a charterer

* For notes on **safe ports**, see F04c.
* **If ordered to an unsafe port** by a time or voyage charterer, the master should:
1. Refuse to enter the port. Necessary reasonable expenditure (e.g. hire of tugs) may be incurred in order to make the port "safe", the charterer being liable for the additional expense.
2. Inform the owner of the charterer's instruction, and the reason(s) for believing the port not to be a "safe port".
3. Inform the P&I club correspondent.
4. Protest in writing to the charterer (or his agent), pointing out the charterer's contractual obligation and requesting the charterer to nominate another (safe) port.
5. If the charterer fails to nominate another safe port, inform the owner and proceed (in the absence of contrary instructions from the owner) to the nearest safe port.
6. If the second nominated port is found unsafe on arrival, either refuse to enter or, as above, incur necessary reasonable expenditure to make the port "safe", charging the expenses of doing so to the charterer.
7. Note protest on arrival in port.
8. Enter details of the matter in the Official Log Book, annexing a full report if required.
9. Keep hard copies of all messages received and sent relating to the matter.

H06f.3 If ordered to an unsafe berth by a charterer

* For notes on **safe berths**, see F04c.
* **If ordered to an unsafe berth** by a time or voyage charterer, the master should:
    1. Refuse to use the berth.
    2. Inform the owner of the charterer's instruction, and the reason(s) for believing the berth not to be a "safe berth".
    3. Inform the P&I club correspondent.
    4. Protest in writing to the charterer (or his agent), pointing out the charterer's contractual obligation and requesting the charterer to nominate another (safe) berth.
    5. If the charterer fails to nominate another safe berth, inform the owner and proceed (in the absence of contrary instructions from the owner) to the nearest available safe berth.
    6. If the second nominated berth is found unsafe on arrival, either refuse to use it.
    7. Note protest as soon as possible on arrival.
    8. Enter details of the matter in the Official Log Book, annexing a full report if required.
    9. Keep hard copies of all messages received and sent relating to the matter.

H06f.4 Radio quarantine reports

* **Admiralty List of Radio Signals (ALRS) Volume 1** contains a section on Radio Quarantine Reports from Ships at Sea. Entries for the few countries listed vary widely in content, with the entry for Australia forming the major part of the section. International Code signals for pratique messages are also listed.

H06f.5 Reports of piracy and armed robbery

* **Admiralty List of Radio Signals (ALRS) Volume 1** contains a section on Piracy and Armed Robbery – Reports, which includes sections on **locations and methods of attack** and **recommended practices** and, in three annexes, formats for an **Initial Message** – Piracy/Armed Robbery Attack Alert, a Piracy/Armed Robbery **Attack/Sighting/Suspicious Act Report**, and a **Summary of General Precautions**. Details of the South-East Asia **Regional Piracy Countermeasures Centre** (RPCC), Kuala Lumpur, are given, together with transmission details of **piracy countermeasures broadcast messages**.

H06f.6 Reports of alien smuggling

* **Admiralty List of Radio Signals (ALRS) Volume 1** contains a small section on the reporting by masters of alien smuggling operations observed at sea. While the section refers to an IMO "Alien Smuggling Resolution", the only reporting procedures listed are those of the US Coast Guard, which requests mariners to report any vessel that is suspected of being involved with undocumented alien smuggling, and also requests merchant vessels under way within 500 nautical miles of the US coast and observing a potential smuggling situation to contact the USCG using the listed procedure.

H06f.7 Accident reports

* Accidents occurring on UK ships at sea should be reported to the MAIB in accordance with the **requirements** detailed in E08k.

H06f.8 MARS reports

* To assist in accident prevention, the Nautical Institute operates the International **Marine Accident Reporting Scheme** ("MARS"). Nautical Institute members and other professional seafarers are encouraged to share their experiences of unsafe practices, personal accidents, near-miss situations, equipment failures, etc. with other maritime professionals by sending reports of incidents to the address below. MARS reports are published in the centre pages of the Institute's monthly journal *Seaways*.
* Where used to report "unspecified hazardous incidents" (see E08k.11), MARS has the approval of the MAIB. No MARS report is, however, sent to the MAIB.
* **Address** for sending MARS reports: Captain R. Beedel FNI, 17 Estuary Drive, Felixstowe, Suffolk IP11 9TL, UK.
* **MARS fax**: +44 (0)1394 282435.
* **MARS e-mail address**: mars@nautinst.org

Section I

IN PORT

Section I Contents

I01 Arrival business

I01a APPROACHING PORT

I01a.1 Territorial and national waters

* For notes on the **zones of coastal State jurisdiction** established by UNCLOS, see H01e.1.
* **National claims to maritime jurisdiction** (i.e. territorial sea (TS), contiguous zone (CZ), exclusive economic zone (EEZ) and fisheries zone (FZ)), are listed in **Annual Notice No. 12** in Annual Summary of Admiralty Notices to Mariners.
* The UK Government does not recognise claims to **territorial seas** exceeding 12 miles, to **contiguous zones** exceeding 24 miles or to **EEZs** and **fisheries zones** exceeding 200 miles.

I01a.1a UK waters

- are **defined** in section 313(2)(a) of the Merchant Shipping Act 1995 as "the sea or other waters within the seaward limits of the territorial sea of the United Kingdom".
- **means** all waters inside the 12-mile limit of the UK's territorial sea.
* "**Other waters**" in the definition includes **categorised waters** (see D04c.2a) and **internal waters** (see H01e.1a).

I01a.1b Controlled waters

- are **defined** in regulation 5(3) of the MS (Oil Pollution Preparedness, Response and Co-operation Convention) Regulations 1998 (see H06e.2) as "water specified as areas within which the jurisdiction and rights of the UK are exercisable by the MS (Prevention of Pollution) (Limits) Regulations 1996".
- are areas forming a zone beyond the territorial sea around the UK and the Isle of Man within which the **jurisdiction and rights of the UK are exercisable** in accordance with part XII of the UN Convention on the Law of the Sea (Cmnd. 8941) (i.e. UNCLOS).
* The **limits of the UK's controlled waters** are set out in the Schedule to the **MS (Prevention of Pollution) (Limits) Regulations 1996** (SI 1996/2128) as amended by the **MS (Prevention of Pollution) (Limits) Regulations 1997** (SI 1997/506). The limits follow agreed maritime boundaries with Norway, Denmark, Germany, Netherlands, Belgium, France and the Republic of Ireland. To the west of Scotland, the limits are arcs of 200nm measured from St Kilda. Towards the Faroes, the limits coincide with the current outer limits of the Designated Area of the UK Continental Shelf, pending the establishment of an agreed boundary with Denmark (Faroes).

I01a.1c Designated waters

- are areas of sea above any of the areas for the time being designated under section 1(7) of the Continental Shelf Act 1964, i.e. the waters over the UK Continental Shelf.
* **Regulation 3(1) of the MS (Port State Control) Regulations 1995** (SI 1995/3128), as amended (see I02c.3) provides that Part I of the Regulations (which contains the inspection provisions) applies to ships which, *inter alia*, are at offshore installations, **except** in waters which are neither UK waters nor **designated waters**. In other words, Port State Control cannot be implemented under the Regulations in the case of ships which are at offshore installations on the UK Continental Shelf and beyond the seaward limit of the UK's territorial sea.

I01a.2 Coastal State law

* A coastal State whose waters a merchant vessel may enter may have different laws on navigation, pollution, etc. from those of adjacent coastal States. US marine pollution law, for example, varies in various aspects from Canadian marine pollution law, and Canadian law varies from Russian law.
* Within a coastal State there may be administrative regions in which the **regional laws** differ from the State (national) laws, as in the USA where, for example, Californian **state law** on marine pollution supplements the **federal law** in various aspects, e.g. on Vessel Response Plans. Furthermore, the **state law in different US states**, may also differ. In Australia, Commonwealth (national) law differs in many areas from the law of the various states and the Northern Territory.

* A shipmaster should consult Sailing Directions and check with **port agents** and the local **P&I club correspondent** if in doubt as to the applicable law in a coastal or port State. **P&I club bulletins and websites** (see G02a.3a) are useful sources of information on this subject.

I01a.3 War zones

* **War zones** are declared from time to time by marine insurers, including P&I clubs, who may prohibit a vessel from entering a particular area on current terms (i.e. without payment of an **additional war risks premium**). A vessel which enters a war zone **without amended cover** will usually be without hull and machinery or P&I insurance, including crew injury cover.
* The master of a vessel expected to enter a declared war zone should be made aware of the status of the zone by the owner or managers. If a war zone is confirmed the master should:
  * check the charter party (if any) and bills of lading for any **War Clause** incorporated; and
  * read the War Clause to determine:
    * whether the charterer has any right to order the vessel into the war zone;
    * what liberties the vessel has, if any, to comply with orders and directions given by the flag State and other authorities;
    * what liberties, if any, the master has to leave the war zone without completing cargo operations.
* An **additional contractual clause** may be inserted in the **Crew Agreement** of a vessel operating in a war zone, under which any crew members has the option of signing off the Agreement where he is not satisfied with conditions, etc.
* For a note on **war risks cover**, see G04a.3.

I01a.4 Pre-arrival messages

* The following will usually have to be sent or given when approaching port:
  * **ETA**, to the port agent with a request for berth details, cash requirements, crew relief arrangements, etc. Updated ETAs at agreed intervals should follow initial contact;
  * request for a **pilot**, made direct to a pilot station or harbour authority, or via the agent See **Bridge Procedures Guide** section 2.6.2 (Pre-arrival information exchange with pilot) and information exchange forms at Annexes A1 and A2;
  * **notification to port health authority** of any circumstances requiring the attention of the **port medical officer**. At a UK port the message must arrive between 4 and 12 hours before the ship. **Health clearance signals** should also be shown (see I01e.1d);
  * request for **boatmen** and/or **line handlers**, also to agent;
  * confirmation to the port authority that **all equipment is in good working order** before entering port limits (usually made by VHF when near fairway). A check list may also have to be completed.
* Special instructions about **advices or messages to be sent** in advance of the vessel's arrival may be contained in voyage instructions or the charter party.
* If the vessel is **arriving with stowaways on board**, see notes at H04e.3 and I01g.4. The **agent**, **P&I club correspondent** and **port State authorities** should be advised of the presence on board of stowaways. It may be necessary to hire special **security personnel** to guard the stowaways whilst the vessel is in port.
* The terrorist attacks of 11 September 2001 prompted changes to US Notice of Arrival Regulations. Full details of current arrival requirements can be found on the **National Vessel Movement Center website**, www.nvmc.uscg.gov

I01a.5 Port entry publications to consult

* Before entering port limits it is usually prudent to consult:
  * the **passage plan** and any associated notebook (see **Bridge Procedures Guide section 2**);
  * any **special instructions** from the owner or time charterer;
  * any **information about the port** received from the owner or charterer;
  * **port approaches charts** and **harbour charts** (corrected up to date);
  * relevant **sailing directions** ("pilot books") (corrected up to date);
  * **Guide to Port Entry** or similar publication, if on board;
  * **List of Lights** (corrected up to date);
  * **tide tables** and **tidal stream atlases**;
  * **Admiralty List of Radio Signals** (corrected up to date).

I01a.6 Pre-arrival paperwork

* **Documents** that should be prepared for the arrival of boarding officials normally include:
  * **pilot card**, updated as necessary (see I08b.8a);
  * ship to shore **master/pilot exchange information** (see I01b.8a);
  * **master's declaration** (see I01f.4);
  * **crew declaration** (see I01f.4);
  * **cargo declaration** (see I01f.4);
  * (in some countries) a separate **stores declaration** (see I01f.4a);
  * (in some countries) a **bunker declaration** (see I01f.4a);
  * **cargo documents**, e.g. bills of lading, sea waybills, manifest, Dangerous Goods Notes (see Section F);
  * several copies of the **up-to-date crew list** (preferably on IMO/FAL model form) (see I01g.1);
  * the **passenger list** or **passenger return** or declaration (PAS 15 in UK) (see I01i);
  * all **statutory and class certificates** (preferably in clear plastic pockets in a binder) (see Section D);
  * if carrying dangerous or polluting goods in EU waters, a **check list for vessels carrying dangerous or polluting goods** (see I01a.7 and **MSN 1741**);
  * **clearance from the last port** (see I01f.9 and I07h); and
  * in certain cases, a **Maritime Declaration of Health** (see I01e.1e).
* **The port agent** should be able to advise the master before arrival on documentary requirements.

I01a.7 Pre-arrival hazardous cargo notifications

* **The MS (Reporting Requirements for Ships Carrying Dangerous or Polluting Goods) Regulations 1995** (SI 1995/2498) -
  * **give effect** in the UK to Council Directive 93/75/EEC concerning minimum requirements for vessels bound for or leaving Community ports and carrying dangerous or polluting goods as amended by Council Directive 98/55/EC.
  * **require** masters to **provide details of the ship, its equipment, crew and ship certificates** to a pilot or the competent authority (e.g. the harbour master), if demanded.
  * **are explained** in **MSN 1741**.
* For notes on the **application and contents of the Regulations**, and requirements for **reports of incidents at sea**, see H06e.
* In relation to **arrival check lists**, the Regulations apply to **UK ships** wherever they may be and **non-UK ship** while they are in the UK or UK territorial waters, when **carrying dangerous or polluting goods** (which term excludes bunkers, stores and equipment for use on board). The Regulations do not apply to warships and ships being used by any government for non-commercial purposes (regulation 3(3)).

I01a.7a Notification to the State of destination or anchorage

* **Regulation 6(1)** provides that regulation 6 applies to a ship carrying **dangerous or polluting goods** which is coming from a non-EU port, and which is:
  * a **UK ship bound for a port or anchorage in any EU State** (or the State's **territorial sea**) (regulation 6(1)(a)); or
  * a **non-UK ship bound for a port or anchorage in the UK or UK territorial sea** (regulation 6(1)(b)).
* **Regulation 6(2)** provides that a ship referred to in regulation 6(1)(a) may not enter a port or use an anchorage in an EU State, or in the case of a ship referred to in regulation 6(1)(b) may not enter a port or use an anchorage in the UK or UK territorial sea, unless the operator has, on or before departure of the ship from the port of loading or, in respect of several loading ports, on or before departure from the last such port, notified all the information listed in **Schedule 1 of MSN 1741** to the **competent authority** in which the port of destination or anchorage is located, or (if there is more than one such port or anchorage of destination in one or more member States) to the competent authority of the EU State in which the **first such port or anchorage** is located. In respect of the UK, notifications must be made in accordance with **MSN 1741**.
* The **information in Schedule 1 to MSN 1741** is a list of **Information on ships carrying dangerous or polluting goods** and includes:
  1. name and call sign of vessel;
  2. nationality of vessel;
  3. length and draught of vessel in metres;
  4. port of destination;

5. ETA at port of destination or pilot station, as required by the competent authority;
6. estimated time of departure (ETD);
7. intended route;
8. correct technical name of the dangerous and polluting goods, the UN numbers (if any), the IMO hazard classes in accordance with the IMDG, IBC and IGC Codes, the quantities of such goods and their location on board (in a list, manifest or stowage plan) and, if in portable tanks or freight containers, their identification marks.

I01a.7b Notification to pilots

* **Regulation 12(1)** provides that the **master of any ship** must, before navigating in a port in the UK, and, in the case of a UK ship, before navigating in a port in another EU State, must **complete a check list** for the ship as set out in **Schedule 2 to MSN 1741**.
* **Regulation 12(2)** provides that the check list must be **made available** to:
  1. any **pilot** boarding the ship to pilot it within the port;
  2. if it so requests, the **competent authority**; and
  3. to any **other person specified** by the competent authority.
* **Schedule 2 to MSN 1741** is headed **Check list for carrying dangerous or polluting goods**. The check list has 4 parts: **A**: Vessel identification; **B**: Safety installations aboard; **C**: Documents; and **D**: Officers and ratings.
* For notes on requirements of the Regulations which are applicable **before departure of a ship** see I07d.1.
* For notes on **duties of UK pilots** under the Regulations see I01b.7.

I01b PORT AND CANAL PILOTAGE

I01b.1 Provision of pilotage services in UK ports and waters

* The **Pilotage Act 1987** (c.21) regulates the provision of pilotage services in UK ports and waters, compulsory pilotage, charging by authorities, agents and joint arrangements, accounts, rights of pilots, misconduct by pilots, limitation of liability, and deep-sea pilotage.
* Responsibility for provision of pilotage services belongs to **competent harbour authorities**, e.g. Aberdeen Harbour Board, Associated British Ports, Port of London Authority. A "**competent harbour authority**" is any harbour authority with statutory powers in relation to the regulation of shipping movements and the safety of navigation within its harbour, and whose harbour falls wholly or partly within an active former pilotage district.
* **Duties and powers of competent harbour authorities** are:
  1. to **provide for pilotage services** needed for the safety of navigation of ships within, and in the approaches to, their respective harbours;
  2. to **approve the suitability of ships** to be used as pilot boats;
  3. to **determine qualifications** required by pilots;
  4. to **authorise persons to act as pilots**;
  5. to **revoke authorisations** when necessary;
  6. to **make pilotage directions** specifying that all ships, or all of certain types of ships, are subject to compulsory pilotage in specified areas of the respective competent harbour authoritys' areas of jurisdiction;
  7. to **issue Pilotage Exemption Certificates** to the master or first mate of any ship;
  8. to **revoke Pilotage Exemption Certificates**; and
  9. to make reasonable charges for pilotage services.

I01b.2 Pilotage directions

* Under **section 7(1) of the Pilotage Act 1987**, and subject to certain provisions, if a competent harbour authority considers that in the interests of **safety** it should do so, it must direct that **pilotage will be compulsory** for ships navigating in any area or part of an area under its jurisdiction. Such directions are called **pilotage directions**.
* **A pilotage direction -**
  • may apply to **all ships or all ships of a description specified** in it (subject to any exceptions therein) (section 7(2)(a)).
  • must specify the **area and circumstances** in which it applies (section 7(2)(b)).
  • may specify the circumstances in which an authorised pilot in charge of a ship to which it applies is to be **accompanied by an assistant** who is also an authorised pilot (section 7(2)(c)).
  • may contain such **supplementary provisions** as the authority considers appropriate (section 7(2)(d)).

* will not apply to ships of **less than 20 metres** in length or to fishing boats with a registered length of less than 47.5 metres (section 7(3)).
  * may not be issued before the competent harbour authority **consults with the owners of ships regularly using the area** to which they will apply (section 7(4)(a)) and other persons who carry on harbour operations in the area (section 7(4)(b)).
* If a competent harbour authority considers that pilotage should be compulsory for ships navigating in any area outside its harbour, it must apply for a **Harbour Revision Order** to be made under section 14 of the Harbours Act 1964 or (in Northern Ireland) under section 1 of the Harbours Act (Northern Ireland) 1970, to extend the limits within which the harbour authority has jurisdiction; a pilotage direction given by it will not apply to that area unless the limits have been so extended.

I01b.3 Compulsory and non-compulsory pilotage

* **Section 15 of the Pilotage Act 1987** provides that a ship being navigated in an area and in circumstances in which **pilotage is compulsory** for it by virtue of a pilotage direction must be under the pilotage of either:
  * an **authorised pilot** (accompanied by an assistant if required by a pilotage direction); or
  * a **master or a first mate possessing a Pilotage Exemption Certificate** in respect of that area and that ship.
* **In a compulsory area unauthorised pilots may not be used** under any circumstances.

I01b.4 Rights of pilots

* **Section 17 of the Pilotage Act 1987** provides that **an authorised pilot has the right to supersede an unauthorised pilot**.
* A pilot may require the master of any ship which he is piloting to **declare its draught, length and beam**, and to provide him with such other information relating to the ship or its cargo as the pilot specifies and is necessary for him to carry out his duties (section 18(1)).
* The **master must bring to the notice of the pilot** any defect in, and any matter peculiar to, the ship and its machinery and equipment of which the master knows and which might materially affect the navigation of the ship (section 18(2)).
* An **authorised pilot must not be taken out of his area** without his consent or without reasonable cause (section 19(1)).
* The master of a ship which is subject to compulsory pilotage must **facilitate an authorised pilot boarding and subsequently leaving** the ship (section 20).

I01b.5 Pilotage offences

* **Offences** are committed under the Pilotage Act 1987 if:
  * a ship in a compulsory area is not under the pilotage of an authorised pilot or master or first mate holding a Pilotage Exemption Certificate (section 15(2));
  * the master navigates his ship in a compulsory area without first notifying the competent harbour authority that he proposes to do so (section 15(3));
  * the master navigates his non-exempt ship in a compulsory area without notifying the competent harbour authority that he proposes to do so (section 17(2));
  * an unauthorised person pilots a ship in a harbour knowing that an authorised pilot has offered to pilot it (section 17(3));
  * the master, navigating his ship in a harbour, knowingly employs an unauthorised pilot after an authorised pilot has offered his services (section 17(3));
  * the master refuses to comply with the pilot's request for information on the ship's draught, length, beam, etc. (section 18(3)(a));
  * the master makes a false statement in response to the pilot's request for information, or fails to correct a false statement made by another person (section 18(3)(b));
  * the master fails to bring the ship's defects to pilot's notice (section 18(3)(c));
  * the master takes an authorised pilot out of his district without reasonable excuse (section 19(1));
  * the master of ship not under lawful pilotage in a compulsory area fails to facilitate boarding and leaving by pilot (section 20(1)(a));

- the master accepts the services of an authorised pilot but fails to facilitate boarding and leaving by pilot (section 20(1)(b));
- a ship navigating in compulsory area is not under pilotage of an authorised pilot (section 20(1)).

I01b.6 Liability for damage done whilst under pilotage

* Under most (if not all) jurisdictions, the ship will almost certainly be held to blame, and not the pilot, for damage done to quays, bridges, locks, etc. **Section 16 of the Pilotage Act 1987** provides that "the fact that the ship is being navigated in an area and in circumstances in which pilotage is compulsory...shall not affect any liability of the owner or master of the ship for any loss or damage caused by the ship or by the manner in which it is navigated....". This would appear to mean that, even if the vessel is under compulsory pilotage, the owner or master of the ship will be held liable for loss or damage caused by negligent navigation.

* **Section 22(1) of the Pilotage Act 1987** provides that the liability of an authorised pilot for any loss or damage caused by any act or omission of his while acting as such a pilot will not exceed £1,000 and the amount of the pilotage charges in respect of the voyage during which his liability arose.

* **In the Panama Canal** all vessels in the Canal are under the absolute control of their pilots as regards navigation and manoeuvring (see I01b.8). Liability for damage sustained within the Canal locks is assumed by the Panama Canal Commission (PCC). Liability for damage sustained in the Canal outside the locks is assumed by the PCC when proximately caused by negligence of PCC personnel. In both cases, the PCC's liability is reduced in proportion to any contributory negligence of the ship's crew.

I01b.7 Duty of UK pilots under Reporting Requirements Regulations

* **Regulation 13 of the MS (Reporting Requirements for Ships Carrying Dangerous or Polluting Goods) Regulations 1995** (SI 1995/2498) provides that if a pilot engaged in berthing, unberthing or manoeuvring a ship in UK waters **learns of deficiencies** in the ship which may prejudice the safe navigation of the ship, he must immediately inform the port authority, who must immediately **inform the MCA**.

* **If a pilot**, having boarded a ship to which the Regulations apply, to pilot it into or out of a port, **knows or believes there are defects** which may prejudice the safe navigation of the ship which have not been notified to the port authority in accordance with regulations 12 or 13, he must **notify the master** of those defects (regulation 14). If the pilot knows or believes that the master, having been notified by the pilot of those defects, has failed to notify the port authority, the pilot must immediately **notify the port authority** of the defects.

* If the **master fails to make a check list available** to the pilot in accordance with regulation 12, the pilot must immediately **notify the port authority**.

* For notes on requirements of the Regulations relating to **pre-arrival hazardous cargo notifications**, see I01a.7.

I01b.8 The master/pilot relationship

* The law in most countries regards a ship's pilot as being merely an advisor to the master, without having command, navigational control or charge of the vessel. The pilot's duty is restricted to advising the master of local conditions affecting safe navigation.

* The term **"pilot"** has been defined in UK law as meaning "any person not belonging to a ship who has the conduct thereof"[1]. This makes a pilot rather more than a simple adviser, and British courts tend to take the view that a pilot's advice should be followed on account of his specialised local knowledge and special skill.

* In virtually every country (with the notable exception of Panama, where Panama Canal pilots have extraordinary responsibility and powers (see below and I01b.6), the master has full responsibility for the navigation and manoeuvring of his ship during all acts of pilotage.

* **Pilotage in the Panama Canal**: Paragraph II.6 of the *Memorandum of Understanding Between the National Response Team and the Panama Canal Commission*, dated December 12, 1997, provides: "Ships operating in the Panama Canal come under the direction of a Panama Canal Pilot who assumes operational control of the ship when it enters the Canal, unlike pilots in other locales who act as advisors to the Master of the ship. The Panama Canal Pilots are employees, or agents, of the PCC making the PCC effectively the ship operator for the time the ship is under the control of a Panama Canal Pilot"[2].

* **The rights and duties of pilots** (in English law) are the same whether a pilotage is compulsory or not, and whether the pilot is authorised or licensed or not. The pilot is charged with the safety of the ship and must use all reasonable

---

[1] The definition was contained in section 742 of the Merchant Shipping Act 1894.
[2] Control of the Panama Canal passed at noon on 31 December 2000 from the USA to the Republic of Panama, and the canal is now operated by the Panama Canal Authority (ACP).

diligence, care and skill. He is entitled to the same assistance from the crew as the master has when there is no pilot on board.

* **Generally, the master should**:
  * follow the pilot's advice unless he has good reason to believe that following it will endanger the ship;
  * see that the ship's navigation is monitored (including plotting fixes/positions on charts) as if there were no pilot on board;
  * insist that the pilot takes all reasonable precautions;
  * ensure that officers, helmsmen, etc. attend to the pilot's requests with efficiency and courtesy;
  * instruct the officer-of-the-watch that he has charge of the vessel whilst under pilotage, unless specifically informed otherwise by the master;
  * always state his opinion to the pilot on important matters of navigation and manoeuvring.
  * warn the pilot if it appears that the pilot is taking or proposing to take any action of which the master disapproves.
* Examples of cases **where the master should interfere** are:
  * where the **pilot is incapable** through apparent illness, drink or drugs;
  * where the pilot gives orders to the helmsman which will, if carried out, result in a **breach of the law**.
* MGN 72 (which has been superseded by the MCA's 2002 SOLAS Chapter V publication) contained (in paragraphs 21 to 24) some advice on the master/pilot relationship and an extract from IMO Resolution A.285(VIII) as follows: "Despite the duties and obligations of a pilot, his presence on board does not relieve the officer of the watch from his duties and obligations for the safety of the ship. He should co-operate closely with the pilot and maintain an accurate check on the vessel's position and movements. If he is in any doubt as to the pilot's actions or intentions, he should seek clarification from the pilot and if doubt still exists he should notify the master immediately and take whatever action is necessary before the master arrives."
* **The shipowner is generally liable** for the consequences of negligent navigation whilst the ship is under pilotage.

I01b.8a Master/pilot information exchange

* IMO Resolution A.601(15) recommends the use in pilotage operations of **Master/Pilot Exchange** (or "**MPX**") **information sheets**. Their use is not mandatory internationally or under UK law, although it may be under the law of certain countries.
* **MGN 201** advises that the MCA recommends that **manoeuvring information** in the form of a pilot card, wheelhouse poster and manoeuvring booklet should be provided on all ships as follows:
  * the **pilot card** on all ships to which SOLAS applies;
  * the pilot card, wheelhouse poster and manoeuvring booklet on all new ships of 100 metres in length and over, and all new chemical tankers and gas carriers regardless of size; and
  * the **pilot card, wheelhouse poster and manoeuvring booklet** on all new ships that may pose a hazard due to unusual dimensions or characteristics.
* The manoeuvring information should be **amended** after any modification or conversion of the ship that may alter its manoeuvring characteristics or extreme dimensions (MGN 201, paragraph 3).
* The three appendixes to MGN 201 contain **specimen pilot card, wheelhouse poster and recommended information** to be included in the manoeuvring booklet.
* **Annex A1 of the Bridge Procedures Guide** contains a specimen Ship to Shore Master/Pilot Exchange data sheet. On this sheet the ship's details should be given for the pilot's information.
* **Annex A2 of the Bridge Procedures Guide** contains a specimen Shore to Ship Master/Pilot Exchange data sheet. On this sheet the pilot should give information about the pilotage and berthing operation for the information of the ship's bridge team.
* **Annex A3 of the Bridge Procedures Guide** contains a specimen Pilot Card.
* **Annex A4 of the Bridge Procedures Guide** contains a specimen wheelhouse poster for the provision and display of manoeuvring information, as recommended in IMO Resolution A.601(15).
* The exchange of information between the master and pilot **does not transfer the ultimate responsibility** for the safety of the vessel from the master to the pilot.

I01b.9 Pilot transfer arrangements

* The **MS (Safety of Navigation) Regulations 2002** (SI 2002/1473) (see H01f.2) –
  - **revoke** and replace the MS (Pilot Transfer Arrangements) Regulations 1999 (SI 1999/17).
  - **require compliance** by a ship to which the Regulations apply with **SOLAS regulation V/23** (which relates to **Pilot transfer arrangements**).
* **SOLAS regulation V/23.1** relates to the **Application** of regulation V/23.

* **Regulation V/23.1.1** provides that ships engaged on voyages in the course of which pilots are likely to be employed must be provided with pilot transfer arrangements.
* **Regulation V/23.1.2** provides that pilot transfer equipment and arrangements installed on or after 1 January 1994 must comply with the requirements of regulation V/23, and due regard must be paid to the IMO standards (references for which are given in MCA's 2002 SOLAS V publication).
* **Regulation V/23.1.3** provides that pilot transfer equipment and arrangements installed before 1 January 1994 must at least comply with the requirements of regulation V/17 of SOLAS 1974 in force prior to that date, and due regard must be paid to IMO standards adopted prior to that date.
* **Regulation V/23.1.4** provides that equipment and arrangements replaced after 1 January 1994 must, as far as is reasonable and practicable, comply with the requirements of regulation V/23.
* **SOLAS regulation V/23.2** contains **General** requirements. All arrangements used for pilot transfer must efficiently fulfil their purpose of enabling pilots to embark and disembark safely. The appliances must be kept clean, properly maintained and stowed and must be regularly inspected to ensure that they are safe to use. They must be used solely for the embarkation and disembarkation of personnel (23.2.1). The rigging of the pilot transfer arrangements and the embarkation of a pilot must be supervised by a responsible officer having means of communication with the navigation bridge who must also arrange for the escort of the pilot by a safe route to and from the bridge. Personnel engaged in rigging and operating any mechanical equipment must be instructed in the safe procedures to be adopted and the equipment must be tested prior to use (23.2.2).
* **SOLAS regulation V/23.3** contains requirements for **Transfer arrangements**.
* **SOLAS regulation V/23.4** contains requirements for **Access to the ship's deck**.
* **SOLAS regulation V/23.5** contains requirements for **Shipside doors**.
* **SOLAS regulation V/23.6** contains requirements for **Mechanical pilot hoists**.
* **SOLAS regulation V/23.7** contains requirements for **Associated equipment**.
* **SOLAS regulation V/23.8** contains requirements for **Lighting**.
* Regulation V/23, together with the **Guidance Notes to regulation V/23** in MCA's 2002 SOLAS Chapter V publication, including **Annex 21** (IMO Resolution A.889(21) - Recommendation on Pilot Transfer Arrangements) supersede MSN 1716 (Pilot transfer arrangements).
* **Guidance Note 1** states that regulation V/23 **does not apply** to UK ships of less than 150gt on any voyage (domestic or international), or to UK ships of less than 500gt which are not on international voyages, or to fishing vessels, **unless** they are likely to employ a pilot. (On voyages where a pilot is likely to be employed, regulation V/23 **will** therefore apply.)

I01b.10 Use of Vessel Traffic Services in UK ports

* **Regulation 7 of the MS (Reporting Requirements for Ships Carrying Dangerous or Polluting Goods) Regulations 1995** (SI 1995/2498) provides that the master of a ship entering or leaving a port in the UK **must make use of any Vessel Traffic Services** (VTS) provided in that port[3].
* IALA standards for the **training and certification of VTS personnel** are outlined in **MGN 180**.

I01b.11 Duty of UK pilots under Port State Control Regulations

* **Regulation 15(1) of the MS (Port State Control) Regulations 1995** (SI 1995/3128), as amended, provides that a **UK pilot**[4], berthing or unberthing (in the UK) a ship to which Part I of the Regulations applies (see I02c.3), or engaged on such a ship bound for a port within an EU member State, who learns in the course of his normal duties that there are **deficiencies** which may prejudice the safe navigation of the ship, or which may pose a threat of harm to the marine environment, **must immediately inform**:
  * if the pilot is an authorised pilot, the port authority authorising him (who must in turn immediately inform the MCA);
  * if the pilot is not an authorised pilot, the MCA or the competent authority of another EU member State.

---

[3] This gives effect in the UK to SOLAS regulation V/8-2.4, which requires Contracting Governments to endeavour to secure participation in, and compliance with the provisions of, VTSs by ships entitled to fly their flags.

[4] "**UK pilot**" means a pilot authorised pursuant to the Pilotage Act 1987 and any pilot boarding a ship in UK waters (as defined in section 313(2)(a) of the Merchant Shipping Act 1995).

I01b.12 Pilotage Exemption Certificates

* A **Pilotage Exemption Certificate** (PEC) is a certificate issued by the competent harbour authority for a port in the UK, or by the port authority or pilotage authority for a port outside the UK, to a master or first mate of a ship which regularly uses that port, in order that a vessel in the charge of the holder may be exempted from taking a professional pilot when navigating in the pilotage waters under the jurisdiction of the issuing authority.
* The Pilotage Exemption Certificate system operating at UK ports is provided for in sections 8 and 15 of Part I of the Pilotage Act 1987. The Act requires competent harbour authorities to grant a PEC to any applicant who is *bona fide* the **master or first mate** of a vessel. *Bona fide* masters and first mates of ships regularly calling at a port in the UK may usually obtain a Pilotage Exemption Certificate for that port subject to their being able to satisfy the competent harbour authority for the port as to their skill, experience, local knowledge, knowledge of English, and medical fitness. Many officers in the short-sea trades therefore hold PECs for a range of ports served by their vessels, in order to save the shipowner the cost of pilotage, where this is compulsory.
* The arrangements under which applicants may qualify for, obtain, and use a PEC are generally laid down in a **pilotage direction** for the port. The pilotage direction will generally specify the type and size of vessels which are subject to pilotage and the vessels to which PECs apply.
* A PEC is valid only in respect of the **vessel or vessels named on the certificate** and only when such vessel (or any of them) is being piloted by the holder of the certificate, who must at the time be the *bona fide* **master or first mate** of the vessel. A Certificate will generally remain in force for not more than 12 months, before expiry of which the holder must undergo re-examination and prove continuing medical fitness.
* Applicants for PECs should discuss the PEC syllabus and examination arrangements with the harbour master for the port concerned.
* Different classes of PEC may be issued by the competent harbour authority, e.g. one class to masters and first mates of ordinary merchant ships, and one class to masters, first mates and persons in charge of local craft involved in sand, gravel and mineral extraction.
* Information about PECs is contained in Chapter 2.6 of the Port Marine Safety Code, which states that:
  * the standards for PECs must not be more onerous than those required for an authorised pilot, but they should be equivalent;
  * PEC holders and their employers are accountable to the issuing harbour authority for the proper use of any certificate;
  * harbour authorities should have formal written agreements with PEC holders and their employers to regulate the use of certificates.

I01b.12a Duties of a Pilotage Exemption Certificate holder

* When a ship is in the charge of a master or first mate holding a PEC and is underway within the area of jurisdiction of the issuing authority, the **pilotage flag** (H) should be displayed by day.
* Pilotage Exemption Certificate holders may be required to demonstrate their use of the certificate by submitting **monthly returns** to the competent harbour authority.
* A PEC holder who, during a pilotage act, observes any alteration to shoals or channels or that any seamarks are out of place or do not conform or show their proper distinctive character, should immediately **report** the circumstances to the competent harbour authority.

I01c HARBOUR TOWAGE

I01c.1 Towage terms and conditions

* **A shipmaster has implied authority in English law to engage a tug or tugs** whenever he deems it reasonably necessary for the safety of the ship's operations, and the shipowner (or operator or time charterer, as the case may be) will be bound by the terms of the contract he makes with the tugowner if they are reasonable. The contract may be verbal or written.
* **The terms and conditions under which towage is to be performed** are normally embodied in a printed agreement. In UK ports and harbours and many Commonwealth ports the customary agreement is the **UK Standard Conditions for Towage and Other Services (Revised 1986)**. This is heavily weighted in the tug owner's favour, but is widely accepted in the shipping industry. Other countries may have their own standard terms and conditions, and P&I clubs normally cover an owner-member's liabilities arising under customary, routine and ordinary port towage under the terms of the local agreement normally used. Where there is any doubt on the master's part as to the local terms, he should contact the club correspondent.

* **Under UK Standard Towage Conditions**, whilst towing or rendering any other service at the request of the hirer, the master and crew of the tug are deemed to be the servants of the hirer and under the control of the hirer or his servants or agents. The hirer is accordingly deemed to be vicariously liable for any act or omission by any such person deemed to be the servant of the hirer.
* **Under Clause 4 of the UK Standard Towage Conditions**, whilst towing or whilst rendering any other service at the request of the shipowner, the tugowner will not be responsible for or liable for:
  * any damage done by or to the tug, the ship, the cargo, or any other thing on board the ship or tug; or
  * for the loss of the tug, the ship, the cargo, or any other thing.
* In view of the disproportionate weight of liability borne by the shipowner under UK Standard Towage Conditions, the master of a ship under ordinary tow should be especially careful to avoid accidental contact with the tug or personal injury to tug's crew caused by towlines, heaving lines, etc.
* In English law there is an **implied condition in every towage contract** that if, in the course of the towage, the tow is placed in danger due to some extraordinary and unforeseen peril, the tug must render all necessary assistance. This does not mean, however, that the towage contract continues through any salvage operation (see I01c.2).
* P&I clubs cover liabilities arising under the terms of any contract for **"ordinary towage"**, i.e. ordinary port towage.

I01c.2 Difference between towage and salvage

* **Clause 1(b)(i) of UK Standard Towage Conditions** provides that **"towing"** means any operation in connection with the holding, pushing, pulling, moving, escorting or guiding of or standing by the Hirer's vessel, and the expressions "to tow", "being towed" and "towage" shall be defined likewise".
* **"Towage"** may, on the basis of the above definition, be defined as any operation in connection with the holding, pushing, pulling, moving, escorting or guiding of or standing by a hirer's vessel, in return for fixed remuneration.
* **"Salvage operation"** is defined in article 1, paragraph 1 of the International Convention on Salvage 1989 as any act or activity undertaken to assist a vessel or any other property in danger in navigable waters or in any other waters whatsoever. "Vessel" means any ship or craft, or any structure capable of navigation, and "property" means any property not permanently and intentionally attached to the shoreline and includes freight at risk.
* **Mere difficulty** in the performance of towage does not automatically convert towage into salvage.
* Towage and salvage **cannot be performed concurrently**. Where, for example, a ship under tow runs aground and requires salvage services, the towage contract must either terminate before the salvage services start, or must be superseded by the salvage services.
* Unless expressly stated to the contrary in the towage contract, salvage services (which are "extraordinary") will not normally be contemplated by the hirer or the tugowner as being within the services contracted for. Furthermore, the agreed towage fee will normally cover only those services described in the definition of "towing" (as above), and will not usually be regarded as reasonable remuneration for any extraordinary services, such as salvage, over and above the ordinary towage services contracted for. In determining whether services performed by the tug-owner were "towage" or "salvage", therefore, **two rules** must be applied in each case:
  1. "Were the services performed by the tug-owner of such an extraordinary nature that they could not have been within the reasonable contemplation of the parties to the original towage contract?"
  2. "Would the (salvage) services in fact performed and the risks in fact run have been reasonably remunerated if the contractual remuneration (i.e. for the towage services) only was paid?"
* **Clause 6 of UK Standard Towage Conditions** provides that nothing contained in the Conditions will limit, prejudice or preclude any legal rights which the tugowner may have against the hirer of the tug including any rights which the tugowner or his servants or agents may have to claim **salvage remuneration or special compensation** for any extraordinary services rendered to vessels or anything aboard vessels by any tug or tender.
* **Article 17 of the International Convention on Salvage 1989** provides that no payment (of salvage or special compensation) is due under the provisions of the Convention unless the **services rendered exceed** what could be reasonably considered as **due performance of a contract** entered into before the danger arose.

I01d PORT AND BERTH: LEGAL ASPECTS

I01d.1 Safe port

* For a definition of **"safe port"** and notes on **contractual requirements** relating to safe ports and berths, see F05a.2b.
* **Examples of conditions that may render a port "unsafe"** within the meaning of the contract of carriage are:
  * heavy swell preventing entry;

- unsafe river approach;
- buoys out of position;
- incorrect information (re- soundings, buoys, etc.) on chart making entry dangerous;
- need for more tugs than charterer anticipated;
- excessive ranging of vessels on berths;
- rioting;
- vessel unable to remain at the port for weather reasons (e.g. onset of ice, swell, etc.);
- vessel unable to remain at the port due to abnormal occurrence (e.g. hostilities or riots); or
- vessel unable to leave port because of blockage by other moored vessels; or
- unanticipated ice (see I01d.1a).

I01d.1a Ice

* Ice affects many ports worldwide, especially in the Baltic; St Lawrence River and St Lawrence Seaway; Hudson River and Hudson Bay; British Columbia; east coast of Russia; north China; North Korea; and the Black Sea. For times of year when ice is a threat, see Sailing Directions.
* BIMCO publishes **Ice Reports** for the benefit of its shipowner and charterer members.
* The **onset of ice** at a port at which a vessel calls may render the port legally "unsafe", in which case the master may be justified in:
  - refusing to enter the port; or
  - hiring the assistance of an icebreaker, charging the cost to the charterer.
* For notes on the **Ice Clause** in a charter party, see F05a.17.

I01d.2 Safe berth

* Any **berth** the vessel is sent to under a charter party must, in the absence of any charter party term providing otherwise, be "safe" in the same respects as a "safe port" (see F05a.2b).
* Where **passing vessels** are causing problems, e.g. ranging, the master should send a **Letter of Protest** to the harbour authority and make an appropriate entry in the Official Log Book. For notes on **Letters of Protest**, see I04b.

I01d.3 Action on being ordered to an unsafe port or berth

* **If ordered to an unsafe port or berth**, or if a port or berth is **found on arrival to be unsafe**, or if a port or berth **becomes unsafe** during the vessel's stay, the master should:
  - **communicate** with the owner and charterer;
  - **collect evidence** as detailed below;
  - **note protest** at the first opportunity;
  - where ice is the reason for the non-safety, check the contract of carriage for the provisions of any **Ice Clause**;
  - make an **Official Log Book entry** describing the conditions considered to be unsafe.
* Lawyers dealing with unsafe port or berth claims (e.g. acting for the owners' or charterer's P&I club) will usually require **evidence** from the master, including some or all of the following:
  - **photographs** or **video** film (taken by master or crew members) showing damage to vessel, berth, etc.;
  - deck and engine room **log books**, bell books, movement books, data logger charts, etc.;
  - **statements** from relevant crew members (e.g. master, OOW, chief engineer, watch ratings);
  - relevant **weather forecast**(s);
  - **note of protest** made by master following incident;
  - any **Letters of Protest** written by master relating to the port/berth before the incident;
  - **drawings of port and berth layouts**, with supplementary information;
  - **drawings of berth facilities** (including ro-ro ramps, piling, cranes, bollards, etc. where relevant);
  - relevant **published data** about the port or berth including extracts from sailing directions, *Guide to Port Entry*, etc.;
  - copy of relevant **charter party clauses**;
  - **damage survey reports** by class and/or owner's surveyors;
  - **ship's particulars**;
  - relevant **ship's plans/drawings**.
* Some of the above items may be obtained from the owner's superintendents, etc., but the ship should provide any items available.

I01d.4 Contact damage to port property

* An action to recover **costs of contact damage** may be brought against owners:
  * **under contract** (effective when the ship uses the port or terminal); or
  * **under local statute laws** under which visiting ships are responsible for damage; or
  * **in tort**, in which case **negligence** of the owners or his servants would have to be proved by the port or terminal owners.
* Most contact damage occurs while the ship is manoeuvring, often under pilotage and/or towage. However, pilotage and towage contracts usually absolve the pilotage authority and tug owner from any liability whatsoever, even where the contact may have been caused through their negligence.
* **In event of contact damage** the master should:
  * **record** in the deck log any defects or damage to berth piles, etc. noticed prior to or immediately on berthing;
  * **inform the owner** as soon as possible;
  * **inform the P&I club correspondent** as soon as possible;
  * submit a **full report** to owner as soon as possible, signed (where possible) by the pilot, tug master(s), and any eye-witnesses, e.g. linesman, and including:
    * if vessel was under way, speed and angle of approach;
    * appended extracts from logs detailing helm and engine movements;
    * weather conditions;
    * state of tide and current;
    * where the ship broke moorings before causing damage, full details of moorings and all action taken (e.g. tending moorings and fenders, etc.) up to the time of parting.
  * where any damage to ship, issue a **letter of protest** to the port or terminal operator (see I04b);
  * with assistance from the P&I club correspondent if necessary, appoint an **independent surveyor** to inspect the damage. The survey should ideally be a **joint survey** with a surveyor appointed by the port/terminal operator or their underwriters.
  * take, and submit to the owner, **photographs** of any damage to piles, dolphins, etc.;
  * if requested, give the port/terminal operator and/or their surveyors every opportunity to survey any damage to the vessel, and attempt to agree with them the cause and extent of the damage.
* Where the safety of the port or the berth are in question the master should:
  * obtain the **best information** available about weather and other hazards at a berth.
  * keep **comprehensive records** of all events relating to a "safe berth" incident.
* The owner will usually have a claim against the charterer under any Safe Berth Clause in the charter party.
* **Where port or terminal operators threaten arrest of the vessel** in an effort to obtain financial security, contact the **owner** and/or the **P&I club correspondent**. The P&I club will usually give the port/terminal operator a **Letter of Guarantee** or **Letter of Undertaking**, stating that the club will pay if the ship is legally liable. These letters are usually acceptable and will allow the ship to sail pending the outcome of the claim negotiations.
* The port/terminal operators will normally issue ship with a **Letter of Protest** (see I04b) in respect of contact damage. When signing for receipt of this, the master should sign "**for receipt only**" and thus not admit any liability, since:
  * **the ship may not, in fact, be liable**, if the reason for the damage is found to be some cause beyond the master's control such as wash from passing vessels, excessive current, etc.;
  * underwriters and P&I club rules **prohibit the shipowner from admitting liability** without their consent.

I01e PORT HEALTH CLEARANCE

I01e.1 Public Health (Ships) Regulations

* **The Public Health (Ships) Regulations 1979** (SI 1979/1435) -
  - **give effect** in the UK to the World Health Organization's **International Health Regulations**.
  - **regulate** port health control for ships arriving at or leaving ports in England and Wales.
  - **are equivalent** and, for all practical purposes, the same as regulations in force in Scotland and Northern Ireland. (Most other WHO member States have similar regulations.)
  - **do not apply** to ships forming part of the UK armed forces.

* In the Regulations:
  * "**authorised officer**" means the medical officer, the proper officer, as described by paragraph 13 of Schedule 14 of the Local Government Act 1972, or any other officer authorised by the health authority under regulation 4, to enforce and execute any of the Public Health (Ships) Regulations.
  * "**excepted port**" means any port in the "excepted area", i.e. all the territory of Belgium, Metropolitan France, Spain, Greece, the Republic of Ireland, Italy, Luxembourg, the Netherlands, and the UK, Channel Islands and Isle of Man.
  * "**free pratique**" means permission for a ship to disembark and commence operation.
  * "**medical officer**" means the medical officer for a port health district, or any other medical practitioner appointed by the health authority under regulation 5.
* For the purposes of the Regulations, a ship will not be deemed to have **been in an infected area** if, without having been itself in contact with the shore, it has landed only mail, passengers and baggage, or has taken on board there only mail, fuel, water, stores or passengers, with or without baggage, who have not themselves been in contact either with the shore or with any person from the shore. A ship will not be regarded as having **met another ship or offshore installation** unless, in the course of the encounter, a person has boarded the ship or installation from the other.

I01e.1a Powers of port health officials

* **Part III of the Regulations** deals with **Incoming Ships** and contains certain **powers of port health officials**.
* The authorised officer may inspect any ship arriving or already in the district, and must do so if her master has given notice of an infectious disease or there are reasonable grounds to suspect it (regulation 7).
* An officer may **require a ship to be brought to**, and if necessary **moored** or **anchored**, at a safe and convenient place for **medical inspection** (regulation 8).
* The medical officer may, and if requested by the master or required by the Secretary of State, must **examine suspected persons** on ships (regulation 9) and may place under surveillance those from infected areas (regulation 30).
* Where there is, or the medical officer suspects that there is, a person suffering from infectious disease on board a ship on arrival or already in the district, he may require the **person to be removed and isolated** or sent to hospital, or he may prohibit the removal (regulation 10).
* An officer may give **radio permission** to a ship from a foreign port to enter a district with **free pratique** if he is satisfied that this will not result in or contribute to the spread of disease (regulation 12).
* On the arrival of a ship which, during its voyage has been in a foreign port other than an excepted port the authorised officer, or at certain ports, a customs officer, may require **any person on board or disembarking** to produce a valid **International Vaccination Certificate** (regulation 9(3)).
* A customs officer or other authorised officer may **detain until the arrival of the medical officer** or for **three hours**, whichever is the shorter period, any such person who has been required to produce an International Vaccination Certificate and is unable to do so (regulation 9(4)). Where such a person fails to satisfy that he possesses a Certificate, the medical officer may **detain him for examination** and may apply certain additional measures (regulation 9(5)). The powers in regulation 9(3), (4) and (5) must not be exercised in respect of anyone on a ship arriving from an **excepted port** unless the Health Secretary has so directed or the medical officer is satisfied that the measures are necessary on account of danger to public health.
* The authorised officer may require the **master** of a ship which has been taken or directed to a mooring station or detained because **rodents** have been discovered or there are reasonable grounds for suspecting that there are rodents on board to take all **practicable measures to prevent the escape of rodents** from the ship (regulation 29).
* **Part IV** relates to **Outgoing Ships**. It provides for the **examination**, etc. in prescribed circumstances of **persons proposing to embark for a destination outside the UK** (regulation 33). **Part V** contains miscellaneous provisions, including a provision for the removal from a district of any ship whose **master is unwilling to comply** with the Regulations (regulation 42).

I01e.1b Supply of information, etc. by masters (regulation 11)

* The **master** of a ship on arrival or already in a district must -
  * **answer** all questions as to the health conditions on board which may be put to him by a customs officer or an authorised officer and provide the officer with all such information and assistance as reasonably required for the purposes of the Regulations (regulation 11(a)); and
  * **notify** the authorised officer immediately of any **circumstances** on board which are **likely to cause the spread of infectious disease**, including in his notification particulars as to the sanitary condition of the ship and the presence of animals and captive birds (including poultry) of any species, or mortality or sickness among such animals or birds, on the ship (regulation 11(b));

- **comply** with the Regulations and with any directions or requirements of an authorised officer or customs officer given or made for the purposes of the Regulations (regulation 11(c)).

I01e.1c Notification of infectious disease, etc. on board (regulation 13)

* **Regulation 13(1)** provides that the master of a ship must, in accordance with paragraph (2), report: the occurrence on board before arrival of:
  - the **death** of a person otherwise than as a result of an accident; or
  - **illness** where the person who is ill has or had a temperature of **38°C or greater** which was accompanied by a **rash, glandular swelling or jaundice**, or where such temperature persisted for more than **48 hours**; or
  - illness where the person has or had **diarrhoea** severe enough to interfere with work or normal activities;
  - the presence on board of a person who is suffering from an **infectious disease** or who has **symptoms** which may indicate the presence of infectious disease;
  - any other circumstances on board which are likely to cause the **spread of infectious disease**; and
  - the presence of **animals or captive birds**, and the occurrence of **mortality or sickness amongst them**.

* If the ship is equipped with radio the master must **send before arrival**, either directly to the health authority or through an agent approved by them, a **radio message** complying with paragraph (3) (regulation 13(2)(a)). If the ship does not have a radio transmitter, the master must **notify the health authority** whenever practicable before arrival and otherwise immediately **on arrival**, of the presence on board of such infectious disease, symptoms or other similar circumstances (regulation 13(2)(b)).

* Any radio message sent under regulation 13 must be sent so as to reach the **health authority** not more than **12 hours** and whenever practicable not less than **4 hours**, before the expected arrival of the ship, and if it is in code, must conform with Part VIII of the International Code of Signals, unless the health authority otherwise directs (regulation 13(3)).

* For notes on **radio quarantine reports** required when arriving in certain foreign countries, see H06f.4.

I01e.1d Signals (regulation 14)

* Where a ship is due to arrive in a district and the master has a report to make in accordance with regulation 13(1)(a), (b) or (c), the master must, when the ship comes within the district, show or give between sunrise and sunset the appropriate **day signal** set out in the part VIII of the International Code of Signals, as reproduced in Schedule 1 to the Regulations, and between sunset and sunrise the **night signal** set out in Schedule 1 to the Regulations (regulation 14).

* **Signals listed in Schedule 1** are as follows:

ZS	My vessel is "healthy" and I request free pratique.	Q
	*I require health clearance.	QQ

* By night, a red light over a white light may be shown, where it can best be seen, by vessels requiring health clearance. These lights should *only* be about 2 metres (6 feet) apart, should be exhibited within the precincts of a port, and should be visible all round the horizon as nearly as possible.

ZT	My Maritime Declaration of Health has negative answers to the six health questions.
ZU	My Maritime Declaration of Health has a positive answer to the question(s) … (indicated by appropriate number(s)).
ZV	I believe I have been in an infected area in the last thirty days.
ZW	I require Port Medical Officer.
	ZW1 Port Medical Officer will be available at (time indicated).
ZX	You should make the appropriate pratique signal.
ZY	You have pratique.
ZZ	You should proceed to anchorage for health clearance (at place indicated).
	ZZ1 Where is the anchorage for health clearance?

I have a doctor on board.	AL
Have you a doctor?	AM

I01e.1e Maritime Declaration of Health (regulations 15 and 16)

* Subject to the following proviso, where on the arrival of a ship the master either has a report to make in accordance with regulation 13(1)(a), (b) or (c), or is directed by the medical officer to complete a Maritime Declaration of Health, he must complete such a Declaration in the form set out in Schedule 2 to the Regulations, and that this Declaration must be countersigned by the ship's surgeon if one is carried (regulation 15(1)). Provided that in the case of a ship which during its voyage has not been in a foreign port other than an excepted port, and has not during its voyage met a ship which has proceeded from a foreign port outside the excepted area, the master will not be required to comply with the provisions of regulation 15 unless he has been notified by the medical officer that compliance is necessary on account of danger to public health.

* The master must deliver the Declaration to the authorised officer, who must forward it to the health authority (regulation 15(2)).
* If within 4 weeks after the master of a ship has delivered a Maritime Direction of Health under regulation 15 of a corresponding provision in force in Scotland or Northern Ireland, the ship arrives in a district or calls at another district, as the case may be, the master must report to the authorised officer any case or suspected case of infectious disease which has occurred on board since the Declaration was delivered and which has not already been reported (regulation 16).
* Maritime Declaration of Health (MDOH) forms vary in layout depending on the health authority but generally include: (1) port of arrival; (2) date; (3) name of ship; (4) ports from/to; (5) nationality of ship; (6) master's name; (7) NRT; (8) Deratting or Deratting Exemption Certificate issued (date/place); (9) number of passengers; (10) number of crew; (11) list of ports of call from commencement of voyage with dates of departure.
* **Six questions on the MDOH** require a "Yes" or "No" answer from the master:
    1. *Has there been on board during the voyage any case or suspected case of plague, cholera, or yellow fever? Give particulars in the Schedule.*
    2. *Has plague occurred or been suspected amongst the rats or mice on board during the voyage, or has there been an unusual mortality amongst them? (If more than 4 weeks have elapsed since the voyage began, only the particulars for the last 4 weeks are required.)*
    3. *Has any person died on board during the voyage otherwise than as a result of accident? Give particulars in the Schedule.*
    4. *Is there on board or has there been during the voyage any case of illness which you suspect to be of an infectious nature? Give particulars in the Schedule.*
    5. *Is there any sick person on board now? Give particulars in the Schedule.*
    6. *Are you aware of any other condition on board which may lead to infection or the spread of infectious disease?*
* **"Infectious disease"** means a quarantinable disease or any other infectious or contagious disease other than VD or TB. The following diseases must be entered on the MDOH: chicken pox; cholera; dengue; diphtheria; dysentery; encephalitis (acute); erysipelas; German measles; glandular fever; hepatitis (infectious); malaria; measles; meningitis (cerebrospinal); mumps; paratyphoid fever; pertussis; plague; pneumonia; poliomyelitis; psittacosis; relapsing fever; scarlet fever; smallpox; typhus; typhoid fever; yellow fever.
* **The MDOH may contain a note** as follows: "In the absence of a surgeon, the Master should regard the following symptoms as ground for suspecting the existence of infectious disease:
    * fever accompanied by prostration or persisting for several days, or attended with glandular swelling; or
    * any acute skin rash or eruption with or without fever; or
    * severe diarrhoea with symptoms of collapse; or
    * jaundice accompanied by fever."
* The master must sign and date a declaration that the particulars and answers to the 6 questions are true and correct to best of his knowledge and belief; his signature must be countersigned by the ship's surgeon if one is carried.
* **The Schedule to a MDOH** generally requires particulars of every case of illness or death occurring on board with: (1) name; (2) class or rating; (3) age; (4) sex; (5) nationality; (6) port of embarkation; (7) date of embarkation; (8) nature of illness; (9) date of its onset; (10) results of illness (whether recovered, still ill, or died); and (12) disposal of case (whether still on board; landed or buried at sea).
* **Other information about the crew and passengers** may be requested by the port health authority. The master should have ready a list of any passengers and crew leaving the ship together with their destination addresses. The MDOH must be returned to the boarding officer, who will either **grant health clearance** or **quarantine** the ship.

I01e.1f Restriction on boarding or leaving ships (regulation 17)

* Where the authorised officer so directs, or where the master is required to make a report under regulation 13(1)(a), (b) or (c), no person, other than a **pilot**, a **customs officer** or an **immigration officer** may, without the permission of the authorised officer, **board or leave a ship** until free pratique has been granted, and the **master** must take all reasonable steps to secure compliance with this provision (regulation 17(1)).
* Before granting permission to a person to leave the ship, the authorised officer may require him to state his **name** and **intended destination and address**, and give any **other necessary information** for transmission to the medical officer for the area of the intended destination (regulation 17(2)).
* If such a person cannot state his intended destination and address, or arrives within 14 days at a different address, he must immediately after his arrival **send particulars** to the authorised officer for the port where he left the ship (regulation 17(3)).

I01e.1g Deratting Certificates and Deratting Exemption Certificates (regulations 18, 19 and 20)

* **Regulation 18(1)** provides that if the master of a ship which during its voyage has been in a foreign port cannot produce to the authorised officer for the district in which the ship arrives or for any district at which the ship calls a valid Deratting Certificate or Deratting Exemption Certificate in respect of the ship in the form set out in Schedule 3 to the Regulations, the authorised officer must:
    * if the district is an **approved port** or a **designated approved port**[5], require the ship to be **inspected** to ascertain whether it is kept in such a condition that it is free of rodents and the plague vector; or
    * if the district is not such a port, **direct the ship to proceed** at its own risk to the **nearest approved port or a designated approved port** convenient to the ship at which a Deratting Certificate or Deratting Exemption Certificate, as the case may be, can be obtained.
* If, after the ship has been inspected, the authorised officer for the approved port or a designated approved port is satisfied that the ship is free of rodents and the plague vector, he must **issue a Deratting Exemption Certificate** (regulation 18(2)).
* Regulation 18(3) provides that if, after the ship has been inspected, the authorised officer is not so satisfied, he must:
    * if the district is a designated approved port, **require the ship to be deratted** in a manner to be determined by him; or
    * if the district is not a designated approved port, **direct the ship to proceed** at its own risk to the nearest designated approved port convenient to the ship **for deratting**.
* **Regulation 18(4)** provides that if the master produces a Deratting Certificate or Deratting Exemption Certificate, but the authorised officer has evidence that the deratting was not satisfactorily completed or that there is evidence of rodents on board the ship the authorised officer may, notwithstanding such Certificate, exercise in relation to the ship his powers under regulation 18(3).
* The master must forthwith make **arrangements for any deratting** required by the authorised officer for the designated approved port (regulation 18(5)).
* When deratting has been completed to the satisfaction of the authorised officer for the designated approved port, he must **issue a Deratting Certificate** (regulation 18(6)).
* Before the authorised officer directs that a ship must proceed to another port, he must **consult with a customs officer** for the district (regulation 18(7)).
* On receipt of an application in writing from the owner of a ship in an approved port, or from the master acting for and on behalf of the owner, for a Deratting Certificate or a Deratting Exemption Certificate in respect of the ship, the authorised officer must take any steps which he considers necessary to satisfy himself that the ship is kept in such a condition that it is free of rodents and the plague vector, or at a designated approved port give directions for the deratting of the ship, as the case may require, and, on being satisfied as to the condition of the ship or that the deratting has been properly carried out, he must **issue the appropriate Certificate** (regulation 19).
* Every Deratting Certificate and Deratting Exemption Certificate must be in the **form specified in Schedule 3** to the Regulations (regulation 20(1)). A **copy** of every certificate issued under regulation 18 or 19 must be retained by the health authority (regulation 20(2)). The owner or master of a ship must pay to the health authority the current **charge** for the inspection of the ship for the purposes of regulation 18 or 19 (regulation 20(3)).
* For notes on **Deratting and Deratting Exemption Certificates** see D04q.2.

I01e.1h Detention of ships, and ships to be taken to mooring stations (regulations 21 to 29)

* Regulations 21 to 29 contain provisions for the taking of infected and suspected ships to **mooring stations** for detention, and their **detention** pending inspection by a medical officer. ("Mooring station" is defined in regulation 2(1), and basically means a specified quarantine anchorage.)

I01e.1i Deratting

- is carried out only at **designated approved ports**. If the port of inspection is an **approved port** but not a designated approved port, the health authority will send the ship to a designated approved port for deratting.
- must be carried out using the **method determined by the health authority**.
- must be carried out **so as to avoid damage** to the ship and the cargo.
- must **not take longer than absolutely necessary**.
- must be carried out wherever possible **when the holds are empty**, and if the vessel is in ballast, must be done before loading.

---

[5] An "**approved port**" is defined in the Regulations as a port approved by the Secretary of State for Health for the issue of Deratting Exemption Certificates only. A "**designated approved port**" is a port approved by the Secretary of State for Health for the issue of both Deratting Certificates and Deratting Exemption Certificates.

I01e.2 Animal quarantine

I01e.2a Pet quarantine

* Details of the UK Government's latest rules on the import and export of live animals and animal quarantine can be found on the DEFRA[6] website at http://www.defra.gov.uk/animalh/animfrm.htm
* The UK regulations relating to animal quarantine are **in The Rabies (Importation of Dogs, Cats and other Mammals) Order 1974** (SI 1974/2211), as amended. The Order provides for an **animal landed in the UK without a licence** to be either directed to **quarantine, re-exported or destroyed** and its owner prosecuted. Serious offences may be tried on indictment at a Crown Court where offenders are liable to penalties of up to a year's imprisonment an unlimited fine or both. It is thus important to ensure that all the licensing requirements are met.
* The **Pet Travel Scheme (PETS)** is a system that allows pet animals from certain European countries to enter the UK without quarantine as long as they meet certain conditions. It also means that people in the UK can, having taken their pets to these countries, bring them back without the need for quarantine. PETS was introduced for dogs and cats travelling from certain European countries on 28 February 2000. The Scheme was extended to Cyprus, Malta and certain "long haul" countries and territories on 31 January 2001. Details can be found on the DEFRA website at www.defra.gov.uk/animalh/quarantine/index.htm

I01e.2b Imports of livestock

* In order to ensure that animal diseases are not imported into Great Britain, DEFRA enforces a system of **controls** which rely primarily on imported animals being accompanied by **health certification** and being subject to **post-import veterinary inspection**. The controls fall into two main categories: those for **imports from the European Union** and those for **imports from third countries**. Details can be found on the DEFRA website at www.defra.gov.uk/animalh/int-trde/default.htm

I01e.2c Imports of endangered species

* Under the **Convention on International Trade in Endangered Species** ("**CITES**"), to which the UK is a Party, over 800 species of animals and plants are banned from international trade and a further 30,000 are strictly controlled by CITES and EU legislation including many corals, reptiles, orchids and cacti as well as tigers, rhinos, elephants and turtles.
* Details can be found on the CITES website at www.ukcites.gov.uk

I01e.2d Carriage of animals as pets on ships

* **M.1363** brings to the attention of shipowners, masters and seamen the provisions of the **Rabies (Importation of Dogs, Cats and Other Mammals) Order 1974** (SI 1974/2211) as amended, which, for the purpose of preventing the introduction of rabies into Great Britain, controls the landing in the UK of certain animals which are listed in the Annex to the M Notice.
* In view of the PETS scheme outlined in I01e.2a, the quarantine information in M.1363 is now out of date.

I01f CUSTOMS PROCEDURES ON ARRIVAL

I01f.1 Customs Notices

* Various useful notices are available on the HM Customs and Excise website at www.hmce.gov.uk/forms/catalogue/catalogue.htm
* **Notice 69** (Sep 1994) explains the procedures for Report and Clearance by Ships' Masters. This form can be downloaded from the website or viewed on-line.
* **Notice 69A** (Jul 1989) explains the regulations on Duty-free Ships' Stores and should be read if:
  • on arriving in a UK port, duty-free stores are on board; or
  • on leaving a UK port, the master wishes to take duty-free stores on board.
* **Notice 199** (Nov 1994) explains the regulations on the Control of Imported Goods and should be read if unloading or transporting non-EC goods. This form can be downloaded from the website or viewed on-line.

---

[6] The functions of the Ministry of Agriculture, Fisheries and Food (MAFF) were taken over by the Department for Environment, Food and Rural Affairs (DEFRA) following the 2001 UK general election.

I01f.2 Vessels on intra-EC voyages

* In response to the EC Single Market, new arrangements were introduced on 1 January 1993 to eliminate the requirement for EC commercial vessels engaged solely on intra-EC voyages to report and clear as a matter of routine. No forms are therefore required to be completed by the master for Customs purposes.
* The UK Continental Shelf (UKCS) is regarded by HM Customs as a "third country", i.e. beyond the EC. Offshore supply vessels (OSVs) servicing installations on the UKCS from ports such as Aberdeen and Peterhead may be required to report and clear as if they were vessels arriving from or departing for non-EC ports.
* Other merchant vessels engaged on non-EC voyages are still required to report and clear as normal, as explained in the following notes.

I01f.3 Vessels on non-EC voyages: which vessels must report

* The master must report his ship to Customs **if arriving in a port from a place outside the EC**. Vessels on intra-EC voyages will not normally be required to report. The following vessels arriving in the UK must report:
  * vessels arriving from outside the EC;
  * vessels from another EC country, but carrying uncleared imported goods loaded in a country outside the EC, or for onward carriage to a non-EC country.
* **The Isle of Man** is included in the UK for reporting purposes, but the **Channel Islands** are not.
* Unless Customs inform the master otherwise, an **agent** may act on his behalf.

I01f.4 How to report

* The master's report must consist of the original and one copy of:
  * **Form C.13 - Master's Declaration**. On this form some general information is given about the ship and its voyage, and details of the ship's stores on arrival. The form must be signed either by the master or an authorised person. The form can be downloaded from the Customs & Excise website at www.hmce.gov.uk/forms/formsother/formsother.htm
  * **C.142 - Crew Declaration**. On this form the master crew must declare certain goods. Notes on the form explain which goods must be declared. Any small parcels of merchandise and any addressed packages not shown elsewhere on the report must also be declared. The form must be signed either by the master or an authorised person. The form can be downloaded from the Customs & Excise website at www.hmce.gov.uk/forms/formsother/formsother.htm
  * **Cargo declaration**. The master must declare the cargo. The declaration should be made in one of four ways:
    1. On a **manifest**, or other commercial or administrative document, giving the following details for each consignment, as applicable:
       * the maritime transport document reference, e.g. the bill of lading number;
       * the container identification/vehicle registration number;
       * the number, kind, marks and numbers of the packages;
       * the description and gross weight/volume of the goods;
       * the port or place where the goods were loaded on to the ship;
       * the original port or place of shipment for goods on a through transport document.
    2. If there is no manifest or other suitable document Customs will accept a cargo declaration on the **model form produced by IMO**.
    3. If the ship is carrying a **single commodity bulk cargo**, its details can be given in box 13 of Form C.13 instead of on a separate cargo declaration.
    4. Some ports in the UK operate a **computerised inventory control system** approved by Customs. The master can usually make the cargo declaration by computer at these ports. In this case the words "**Declaration of cargo by computer**" must be written in box 13 of **Form C13**.
* If applicable, a **PAS 15 (Arrival) Passenger Return** should be attached to the report.
* Customs may ask the master to give an extra copy of any or all of the report forms. In some ports they will always ask for an extra copy of the report.
* The vessel's **Oil Pollution Insurance Certificate** (OPIC), if any, must be shown.

I01f.4a Reporting to Customs in other countries

* Some foreign countries require certain other declarations, e.g. a **Stores Declaration**, a **Bunker Declaration**. Local requirements should be ascertained from the vessel's port **agent** when approaching a port for the first time.

* A document evidencing proper **clearance from the last port** may be required.
* In some ports, failure to have the correct forms prepared, or to prepare them correctly, may lead to a heavy **fine** on the ship[7].

I01f.5 When to report

* **If Customs visit the ship on arrival**, they will normally ask for the report then. The visiting officer will keep the original documents and return the duplicates.
* **If Customs do not visit the ship**, the originals only must be delivered to the designated place in the port (see below):
    * not later than 3 hours after the ship has reached its place of loading or unloading; or
    * 24 hours after arrival within port limits if by then the ship has not reached a place of loading or unloading.
  The limit of 3 hours for delivery of the report may be increased to 6 hours providing the agent tells Customs in advance whether or not the ship will be carrying livestock, including birds. The agent must declare this in writing to the designated customs office responsible for the ship's berth or dock during opening hours, and at least 6 hours before the ship's arrival in port.
* **Animals to be landed** in the UK must be distinguished in the declaration from those animals remaining on board for re-export.
* The ship might arrive at a midstream anchorage overnight ready to discharge overside. If no officer visits and takes the report, the master may wait until 0900 hours to deliver it. Enquiries should be made locally about these arrangements.
* **The master must keep the duplicate report** on board while the ship is in port. Customs may want to see it if they visit.

I01f.6 Where to report

* The designated place in the port for delivery of the report might be a **Customs office or a special post box**, and is advertised in Customs offices.

I01f.7 Passengers and crew disembarking

* The master is responsible for telling Customs **in advance** if there are on board:
    * **passengers** who are going to **disembark**; or
    * **crew members** who will be **paying off**.
* Customs may need to ask them questions and examine their baggage and any articles they are carrying. They must know of their arrival in advance so they can be present to give them clearance.

I01f.8 Bond locker

* The contents of the ship's **bonded stores locker** will be checked by the boarding Customs officer against the **Stores List** on the back of the C.13. If in order, the Customs officer will seal the door for the duration of the stay in port.
* The master should accurately **count the bond locker contents** and note them on the Stores List before the ship arrives in port.

I01f.9 "Inward clearance"

* **Clearance** is granted by the boarding officer, if satisfied with all documents and the bond locker count, by stamping the "report accepted" space at the foot of the C.13. The vessel is then said to be "**cleared inwards**" and personnel may embark and disembark and cargo operations may commence.

---

[7] In a case reported in a P&I club bulletin in 1996, an owner was threatened with a US$800,000 fine in a West African port because the master had failed to stamp and sign the bunker declaration. The fine was reduced after negotiation to $23,000.

I01f.10 UK coastwise shipping

* For ships carrying cargo between ports in the UK there are simplified Customs procedures.
* A **cargo book** must be carried by ships mainly carrying domestic goods coastwise around the UK. The book identifies the ship, the master and the POR and gives details of all domestic goods carried as cargo coastwise. The master is responsible for its accuracy and for keeping it up to date. The cargo book must show:
  * a description and the quantity of the cargo;
  * when and where the cargo was loaded;
  * where it was intended to discharge the cargo; and
  * when and where the cargo was actually discharged.
* **Uncleared foreign cargo and cargo already cleared for export** need not be shown in the cargo book, but it may avoid confusion to show them.
* The cargo book may be kept either as a register or in loose-leaf form (in which case the cargo manifest or bill of lading may form the basic record; if a bill of lading is used, it must show the 4 details as above.
* Customs officers may inspect the cargo book and make copies.
* The cargo book must be kept for at least 6 months after the date of the last entry, either on board or at an approved place.

I01f.11 Offshore supply vessels

* **Offshore supply vessels (OSVs) regularly supplying fixed offshore installations** may be allowed a variation of the normal coastwise procedures with the written agreement of the Customs officer at the place where the ship is usually based. Block or "**omnibus**" clearances valid for one month's sailings are sometimes granted in these cases.
* For notes relating to **OSVs servicing installations on the UK Continental Shelf**, see I01f.2.

I01f.12 Coastwise ships exempt from the above procedures

* **Ships exempted by HM Customs** include ships sailing within port limits, ferries (i.e. any passenger-carrying vessel operating a public service to a published timetable), dredgers, RFAs and other Armed Services vessels, vessels operated or chartered by government departments, vessels dumping rubbish calling at only one port, and fishing vessels.

I01f.13 Legal basis of Customs and Excise control

* **The Customs and Excise Management Act 1979** (CEMA) is the general basis for control, in particular sections 19, 27, 69 to 74, and 77. Under the powers contained in the legislation which preceded CEMA, the Customs and Excise Act 1952, the Commissioners of Customs and Excise have made the Carriage of Goods Coastwise Regulations 1952 which govern the movement of goods coastwise.
* **Customs officers have powers to**:
  * search a ship at any time while it is within the limits of a port; and
  * require any person concerned with the shipment for carriage coastwise of goods for which an entry is called for and to produce and to allow any officer to inspect and to take extracts from, or copy, any documents relating to the goods.

I01g IMMIGRATION CONTROL

I01g.1 Arrival at a UK port with no passengers

* Under **the Immigration (Particulars of Passengers and Crew) Orders 1972** and **1975**, the master of a ship which arrives in the UK from outside the Common Travel Area is required to furnish within 12 hours of arrival a **crew list** showing:
  * all crew members engaged outside the UK, and
  * all crew members subject to UK immigration control engaged in the UK.
* A specimen copy of the required form (i.e. the IMO/FAL form) is shown in the Schedule to **SI 1975/980**.
* **A "nil" return must be made** if appropriate, or a complete list of crew may be submitted if more convenient.

* **The master must inform an Immigration Officer** before any member of the crew who was engaged outside the UK or any member of the crew who was engaged in the UK but who is subject to immigration control is discharged from the ship's articles. The Immigration Officer will require to see all such members of the crew, and those who are subject to immigration control will require leave to enter the UK.

* **The master must report at once to an Immigration Officer** when it is necessary to land to hospital for medical treatment any member of the crew who is subject to immigration control, and must produce his document for endorsement.

* **Members of the crew may be granted temporary shore leave** during the ship's stay in port on condition that they leave in the same ship. This permission does not apply to any member of the crew who is, or has been, refused leave to enter the UK by an Immigration Officer, or to whom an Immigration Officer has given notice requiring him to submit to examination, or who is the subject of a Deportation Order.

* Any **deserter** who is subject to immigration control must be reported at once to an Immigration Officer and his documents handed to the ship's agents.

* For the purposes of preparing the crew list, of notifying crew signing off or entering hospital and of reporting deserters, **a crew member should be regarded as subject to immigration control unless** he holds:
  * a British Seaman's Card;
  * a UK passport, showing him to be born in the UK or otherwise exempt from immigration control; or
  * a passport of the Republic of Ireland.

* The above notes are on the back of the **Crew List form IS 6**, copies of which can be obtained from offices of the Home Office **Immigration and Nationality Directorate** in the UK. **IND website**: www.ind.homeoffice.gov.uk

I01g.2 Arrival at a UK port with passengers

* **The master must not allow passengers to disembark** until they have been seen by an Immigration Officer unless prior arrangements have been made with the Immigration authorities.

I01g.3 Arrival in the UK with shipwrecked seamen on board

* **Shipwrecked seamen** are usually cared for in the UK by the Shipwrecked Mariners Society, a representative of which may be found at major ports. Shipwrecked seamen are normally given permission to stay in the UK until they can be returned to their own countries.

I01g.4 Arrival with stowaways on board

* The **IMO Guidelines** on the Allocation of Responsibilities to seek the Successful Resolution of Stowaway Cases (see H04e.3) -
  - **state** (in paragraph 3) that the resolution of stowaway cases is difficult because of different national legislation in each of the potentially several countries involved: the country of embarkation, the country of disembarkation, the flag State of the vessel, the country of apparent, claimed or actual nationality/citizenship of the stowaway, and countries of transit during repatriation.
  - **contain** (in paragraph 4) certain **basic principles** which can be applied generally. The **first** of these is that there is a recognition that stowaways arriving at or entering a country without the required documents are, in general, illegal entrants. Decisions on dealing with such situations are the prerogative of the countries where such arrival or entry occurs. The **third** is that the shipowner and his representatives on the spot, the master, as well as the port authorities and national Administrations, should co-operate as far as possible in dealing with stowaway cases.

* In every case the **agent should be notified** of the presence of stowaways in advance of arrival.

* Under the **U.S. Refugee Act 1980** a stowaway who arrives in the USA can request political asylum. The Immigration and Naturalization Service (INS) has taken the position that shipowners are required to provide 24-hour armed guards during the entire asylum process which can take months. There have been cases where the owner has incurred costs in excess of $1m for such detention.

* Many countries impose very heavy **penalties** (in some cases of over US$200,000) on **masters** who fail to ensure that stowaways are kept securely on board in port.

* For notes relating to **stowaways discovered at sea**, see H04e.3.

I01g.5 Liability for illegal immigration

* For notes on **carrier's liability** for illegal immigration, see C03c.7.
* **In the USA**, the Illegal Immigration Reform and Immigrant Responsibility Act of 1996 provides that "the person providing transportation (defined as the owner, **master** or agent) of a vessel bringing an illegal immigrant to the United States, is responsible for transporting that person to the country to which he or she is expelled". A fine of $3,000 is imposed on the owner and his agent who "fails in their duty to prevent the landing of unauthorised aliens".

I01h SHIP'S AGENT

I01h.1 Appointment of agents under a voyage charter

* Under the terms of voyage charters port agents are normally **appointed**, and therefore **paid for**, by the shipowner. However, many voyage charterers insist on **nominating** port agents, and are entitled to do so if the charter party is suitably claused to that effect[8].
* Where a charter party provides that "the vessel shall be consigned to Charterers' agents....", it means that the charterer will **nominate** agents.

I01h.2 Appointment of agents under a time charter party

* When on a time charter, most of the "voyage costs" associated with earning the freight or other revenue are normally for the time charterer's account, and it can be expected that port agents will be **appointed by the charterer** in order to look after his commercial interests. The charterer's obligation to provide and pay for agents may be in a **"Charterers to provide"** clause, or a separate **Agency Clause** or **Consignment Clause**[9].
* Any **"protecting"** or **"husbandry agent"** used will be nominated and appointed by the shipowner (see I01h.4).

I01h.3 Agent's duties

* Where the charterer nominates an agent and the shipowner appoints him, the agent's **principal** is the shipowner.
* When an agent nominated by a voyage charterer, but appointed by the shipowner, appears to act primarily in the interests of the charterer and to the detriment of the interests of the shipowner, the agent should be reminded that his **prime duty is to his principal**, i.e. the shipowner.
* Any agent should primarily serve his **principal**, i.e. the party paying his fee, regardless of whether that party or some other party has nominated him. Generally, if the shipowner is paying a port agent's fee, then the shipowner is the agent's principal, regardless of whether a charterer or other party nominated the agent.
* **The chief duty of a ship's agent** is to look after the needs of his principal's ship and the ship's personnel whilst at the agent's port. In carrying out this duty the agent should:
  * represent his principal (i.e. the shipowner or time charterer, as the case may be);
  * assist the ship so as to achieve the quickest possible turn-round with the maximum efficiency, at minimum cost;
  * assist the master in his dealings with port, port State and other officials and commercial parties;
  * procure any provisions, stores or other ship-related requirements for the master;
  * communicate messages between the owner (or time charterer) and the master;
  * be reliable and energetic; and
  * use all due care, skill and diligence in the performance of the agency.

I01h.3a Agents' authority to sign bills of lading

* When the master signs a bill of lading in accordance with the terms of a charter party, he is signing on behalf of the **shipowner**, not the charterer. In practice the signing is usually done **on the master's behalf by the agent** under **authority** expressly given by a clause in the charter party. (Such a clause might read: "The master, charterers and/or their agents are hereby authorised by the owner to sign on master's and/or owner's behalf Bills of Lading as

---

[8] Clause 24 of "SHELLVOY 5", for example, provides:"The vessel's agents shall be nominated by Charterers at nominated ports of loading and discharging". Clause 14 of the BP charter party "COASTALVOY 2" provides: Charterers shall nominate Agents at loading and discharge ports but such Agents shall be employed, instructed and paid by Owners".
[9] Clause 4 (Charterers to provide) of "BALTIME 1939" provides: "The Charterers to provide and pay for.......agencies...". Clause 2 of "NYPE 1946" has similar words.

presented in accordance with Mate's receipts without prejudice to this Charter-Party".) Alternatively, a separate **letter of authority** should be signed by the master or the owner giving the charterer and his agents **authority to sign bills of lading for the master**. An example of such a letter is shown below.

```
                          (NAME OF OWNERS)

Dear Sirs

      I hereby confirm that you have authority to sign bills of lading on my behalf in strict
conformity with mate's or tally clerk's receipts signed by me or by the chief officer*, in
respect only of the following cargo loaded at this port and said to be:
                          (details of cargo)
      Please note that this authority is non-transferable, and that you do not have authority to
sign any bill of lading which does not specifically incorporate the terms, conditions and
exceptions of the Charter party dated ........................................................................................
and/or the Hague/Hague-Visby Rules (or rules having a similar effect).
      The Charterers' instructions/Charter party governing this voyage stipulate that the port of
discharge will be ........................................................................ The destination shown on the bills of
lading must be consistent with this provision.
      Please ensure that all bills of lading are properly dated.
      'Freight prepaid' bills are not to be issued unless expressly authorised by my owners.
Do not hesitate to refer to my owners on this or any other matter concerning the issue of bills
of lading.


Yours faithfully


..............................................
Master

Signature of any nominated signatory:................................................................
Signature for receipt:................................................
```

* Delete when the cargo is a bulk cargo for which no mate's or tally clerk's receipts have been issued.

I01h.4 The master/agent relationship

* The master should, if necessary, remind an agent that no matter who appointed him, **his primary duty is towards the ship**.
* A time charterer's agent automatically become the ship's agent on arrival and has an agent's usual duty to use all care, skill and diligence in the performance of the agency. The agent may, however, be concerned more with commercial matters such as cargo entry and clearance, loading and discharging, etc. than with ship's "husbandry" matters, unless specially instructed by the charterer. In these cases the time charterer is expected to instruct his agent to **act as if the shipowner was the principal**.
* Where there is a risk of a time charterer's agent acting to the detriment of the owner's interests, the owner should appoint a "**protecting agent**" (also known as a "supervising agent" or "husbandry agent") to deal exclusively with ship's affairs. (Some charter parties include a clause expressly providing for the owner to do this.)

I01i PASSENGER RETURN

* **Section 107 of the Merchant Shipping Act 1995** provides that the **master of every ship**, whether or not a UK ship, which carries any passenger to a place in the UK from any place outside the UK, or from any place in the UK to any place outside the UK, must provide a **return giving the total number of passengers carried** and distinguishing the total number of any **class** of passenger. Any passenger must furnish the master with any information required for the purpose of the return.
* **M.1101** gives directions which superseded, with effect from 1 April 1984, those set out in the MS (Passenger Returns) Regulations 1960 (SI 1960/1477). The return is to be furnished by the master of every ship, British or foreign, which carries any passenger:
  to a place in the UK from a place outside the UK; and
  from a place in the UK to a place outside the UK.
* The return must be made on form **PAS 15 (ARRIVAL)** or **PAS 15 (DEPARTURE)** as appropriate and duly completed and signed by the master or an officer of the ship or other person authorised to sign on his behalf.
* Alternatively, the information required in columns 5, 8 and 9 of the form may be supplied in a **list of passengers** showing the ports of embarkation and disembarkation of every passenger which must be appended to the form and also signed. In this case the words "Passenger list attached" must be inserted in column 5 of the form.

* The return, duly completed, must be given to the officer of Customs and Excise for the final port of destination or last port of call in the UK, as appropriate -
  * in the case of a ship arriving in the UK from a place outside the UK, as soon as reasonably practicable (and in any event within the time allowed by law for reporting the ship inwards) after the arrival of the ship at its final port of destination in the UK; and
  * in the case of a ship leaving the UK for a place outside the UK, on or within 4 working days of its departure from its last port of call in the UK; or
  * alternatively in the case of a **ship carrying passengers on a regular service to or from a UK port** the information required may be supplied in a single return for a period of not more than 1 week, listing each voyage and showing for each voyage the number of passengers carried for each port of embarkation and disembarkation.

I01j NOTING PROTEST AND OTHER CONSULAR BUSINESS

I01j.1 Reasons for contacting the consul

* For notes on **overseas representation of flag State Administrations**, see B02d. For notes on the **duties and functions of British consuls**, see B02d.2.
* A master of a UK ship may have various **reasons for visiting a British consul** at an overseas port, as shown in the following table.

Reason for contacting consul	Remarks	SBC ref.
To apply for a survey.		D04f.5
To obtain consular authentication of an extension to a certificate's validity.	Where the extension was received from the MCA by radio or fax, and difficulties are experienced with port State officials.	D04f.2p
In connection with some problem concerning the port State's acceptance of ship's certificates or seamen's documents.		-
To obtain official documents.	Crew agreement forms, Official Log Books, Radio Logs.	D05
To deliver documents after closure of Crew Agreement.		E07b.2c
To report a death occurring on board, or the death of a seaman ashore.	In accordance with the MS (Returns of Births and Deaths) Regulations 1979.	E14b
To obtain a form RBD.1 and submit a return of death.	Form RBD.1.	E14b.3
To make a statement for the purposes of the consul's inquiry into a death.		B07f
To make arrangements for the repatriation or burial of a deceased seaman or person who died on board.		E14f
To obtain advice about a seaman's wages dispute.	In accordance with the Wages Regulations.	E09b.1c
To report the leaving behind of a seaman (e.g. in hospital or prison).	In accordance with the Repatriation Regulations.	E13c.1b
To seek advice about some aspect of local law, commercial practice, port regulations, etc.		B02d.2
In connection with the detention or arrest of any person carried in the ship.		E10e
To note protest.	Where no local requirement to protest before a notary public.	I01j.2
To extend a protest.	Where no local requirement to protest before a notary public.	I01j.2c
In connection with the detention of the vessel.		I02e
In connection with the arrest of the vessel.		B03h

* It is appropriate for the master to demand to see the **consul in person**, rather than a junior member of the consulate staff.
* Any consular officer whose assistance a shipmaster seeks should generally be the official representative of the ship's **flag State**, regardless of the master's personal nationality. (An exception to this rule would be when, for example, a British master of a foreign-flag ship has personal problems concerning his own passport, etc., in which case he should seek the assistance of a British consul.)

I01j.2 Noting protest

* A "**protest**", sometimes called a "**sea protest**", is a solemn declaration, made on oath by a shipmaster before a person legally empowered to hear such declarations, that circumstances beyond his control have, or may have, caused loss of and/or damage to his ship and/or its cargo, or have caused him to take action which may render the

owner liable to another person[10]. A protest (without an extension) is a simple statement of fact, without added details.

* An "**extended protest**" is a protest to which supplementary information has been added at a later date.
* "**Noting protest**" is the act of making the protest before the appropriate person.
* **The appropriate person** before whom a protest should be noted is a **notary public** in those countries (such as the UK, USA, India, South Africa, etc.) where notaries public are appointed, or a **British consul** in other countries. A "**notary public**" or "**notary**" is a public official who is primarily concerned with the preparation and authentication of documents for use abroad and is empowered under his country's law to administer oaths (i.e. swearings to the truth of a statement), take acknowledgments, certify documents and take depositions for use in legal actions[11]. The signature and seal or stamp of a notary public is necessary to attest to the oath of truth of a person making an affidavit and to attest that a person has acknowledged that he/she executed a deed, power of attorney or other document, and is required for recording in public records.

I01j.2a When to note protest

* **Noting protest may help** to resist cargo loss or damage claims against the shipowner, and may be required in the adjustment of a general average, but is not always necessary. The local P&I club representative should be able to advise the master on the need for noting protest.
* It may be prudent to **note protest** in the following situations:
  * after every case of **general average**;
  * after wind and/or sea conditions have been encountered which **may have damaged cargo**;
  * after wind and/or sea conditions have been encountered which caused **failure to make a cancelling date**;
  * after cargo is shipped in a condition **likely to deteriorate** during the forthcoming voyage[12];
  * after the **ship has sustained material damage**;
  * after the **ship has caused material damage**;
  * after a **serious breach of the charter party** by the charterer or his agent (e.g. undue delay, refusal to load, cargo not of a sort allowed by the charter party, refusal to pay demurrage, refusal to accept bills of lading after signing because of clausing by master, sending vessel to an unsafe port, etc.);
  * after the **consignee fails to discharge or take delivery of the cargo** or **fails to pay freight**.
* **Protest should be noted as soon as possible** after arrival and always within 24 hours of arrival. If in connection with cargo, it should be noted **before breaking bulk**. If cargo for more than one discharge port is involved, the P&I club correspondent should be asked whether it will be necessary to note protest at each port in the rotation.

I01j.2b Procedure for noting protest

* The master should request the agent to arrange an **appointment** with, and transport to, a **notary public**, **British consul** or other appropriate person before whom a protest can be made. (In some countries the appropriate person may be a magistrate or other official.)
* The **master**, accompanied by one or more **witnesses** from the crew who have knowledge of the relevant facts, should take with him to the notary's office the **Official Log Book**, the **deck log** and any **other relevant information** pertaining to the matter being protested about. (Where, for example, bad weather has led to cargo damage, a record of the weather should be taken to the notary's office. Where reefer machinery has failed during the voyage, cargo temperature records should be taken.) Copies of log entries or other relevant records will be attached to the protest.
* The master will normally have to show **proof of his identity** to the notary. The notary will hear the **master's declaration** and will make a written record in a **Register of Protests**.
* **At least three certified copies** of the protest should be obtained from the notary: two for the owner and one for the ship's file.
* **A fee** will be payable for noting the protest and for each requested copy. (For notes on **fees** payable to British consuls for notarial services, see B02d.2.)
* An **example** of a protest made before a UK notary is shown below.

---

[10] An American online legal dictionary defines a "**protest**" as "a writing, attested by a justice of the peace or a consul, drawn by the master of a vessel, stating the severity of a voyage by which a ship has suffered, and showing it was not owing to the neglect or misconduct of the master".

[11] Descriptions of the services performed by notaries public in the UK can be seen on the website of Cheeswrights, the largest firm of notaries public in the City of London: www.cheeswrights.co.uk and at the website of The Notaries Society: www.thenotariessociety.org.uk

[12] In such cases, bills of lading should be appropriately claused after consultation with the shipper and the P&I club correspondent.

PROTEST

"On this day, the 1st day of April, one thousand nine hundred and ninety-six, before me, James S. Anderson of the City of Glasgow, Scotland, Notary Public duly admitted and sworn, personally appeared Angus McMillan, master of the motor vessel "Kintyre Venture" belonging to the Port of Campbeltown, official number 300123, of the burthen 593.02 tons gross, or thereabouts, which sailed from Ardrishaig on or about the 29th day of March 1996 with a cargo of timber and therewith to Glasgow, and arrived in this Port of Glasgow on the 30th day of March 1996.

It is declared that this vessel at various times on passage met very rough seas and heavy swell, pitched and rolled, shipped spray and water, and encountered heavy rain.

And fearing that damage and loss may have been sustained by the said cargo during the said voyage, he thus enters a note of HIS PROTEST against all losses, damage, etc. to be extended in due form if necessary, reserving right to extend the same at a time and place convenient.

Signed before me...
              James S. Anderson, Notary Public
at 11.00 GMT on 1st April 1996

....
Angus McMillan
Master, m.v. "Kintyre Venture"

I01j.2c Extending protest

* Since it is often impossible to ascertain the full extent of a loss or of damage at the time of noting protest, an **extended protest** should be made when the relevant facts have come to light, which may be, for example, when a surveyor's report has been received. It is therefore necessary at the time of making the original protest to "reserve the right to extend the protest at a time and place convenient".
* An **extended protest document** will usually be required by an average adjuster preparing a General Average Statement.
* Although it is good practice to always extend protest, in the UK it is not legally necessary in order to safeguard the owner's interests.

I01j.2d Procedure for extending protest

* Extension need not be made in the same place as the original protest was made, but must be in strict conformity with **local law** regarding time limits and content.
* The extension expands the bare facts of the original protest, and again, any **relevant documents** (e.g. log books and reports) should be taken to the notary's office. The extension is entered, witnessed, signed and sealed in the same manner as the initial protest.
* An American extended protest form is laid out as follows:

MARINE EXTENDED PROTEST

By this public instrument of declaration and protest be it known and made manifest to all whom these presents shall come or may concern, that on the........day of...............…, 19..., before...........................American .... for .... and dependencies thereof, personally came and appeared ...., Master of the vessel called the ...., Official No..................., of the burthen of ....tons or thereabout, then lying in this port of .... laden with .... cargo, who duly noted and entered with the said .... his protest, for the uses and purposes hereafter mentioned; and now, on this day, the .... day of ...., 19..., before me ...., American .... at ...., comes the said ...., and requires me to extend this protest; and together with the said Master also come .... and ...., all crew members of said ship, all of whom, being by me duly sworn, do voluntarily asservate as follows: That these appearers, on the .... day of ...., sailed in and with the said ....….. from the port of .... laden with ...., and bound to the port of ....……..
That the said ship was then properly manned and equipped and in every respect seaworthy; that*..
....
....
* Here insert narrative of the facts of the voyage as they occurred, with full and minute particulars, with date, latitude, longitude, etc. If additional space is required blank sheets may be used and securely attached to this document under the seal of the consular office.

And these appearers, upon their oaths aforesaid, do further declare and say: That during the said voyage they, together with the others of the said ship's company, used their utmost endeavors to preserve the said .... and cargo from all manner of loss, damage or injury. Wherefore the said ....Master, has protested in accordance with law and declares that all losses, damages, costs, charges and expenses as stated herein that have happened to the said................................... or cargo, or to either, are and ought to be borne by those to whom the same by right may appertain by way of average or otherwise, the same having occurred as before mentioned, and not by or through the insufficiency of the said ...., her tackle or apparel, or fault or neglect of this appearer, his officers, or any of his mariners, or fault or neglect in the proper loading, stowage, custody and care of the cargo.

Thus done and presented in the port of .... this .... day of .... 19........
IN TESTIMONY WHEREOF, these appearers have hereunto subscribed their names, and I, the said ....….......... have granted to the said Master this public instrument, under my hand and the seal of this .... to serve and avail him, and all others whom it does or may concern as need and occasion may require.

....
...............................……................of the United States of America
....………Master
....………First Officer
.... (Position of crew)
.... (Position of crew)

I01k SHIP SECURITY REQUIREMENTS

* **SOLAS chapter XI-2** (Special Measures to Enhance Maritime Security) and **part A of the ISPS Code** set out various requirements relating to **port security**, **security of ships arriving at and staying at port facilities** and **security of ships engaged in ship-to-ship operations**.
* A "**port facility**" is defined in SOLAS regulation XI-2/1.1 as a location, as determined by the Contracting Government or by the Designated Authority, where the ship/port interface takes place. This includes areas such as anchorages, waiting berths and approaches from seaward, as appropriate. "**Contracting Government**" means a SOLAS Party State. "**Designated Authority**" means the organisation(s) or the administration(s) identified, within the Contracting Government, as responsible for ensuring the implementation of the provisions of chapter XI-2 pertaining to port facility security and ship/port interface, from the point of view of the port facility. The "**ship/port interface**" is defined as the interactions that occur when a ship is directly and immediately affected by actions involving the movement of persons, goods or the provisions of port services to or from the ship.
* A port facility must be subject to a **port security risk assessment**, must develop and maintain a **Port Facility Security Plan**, and appoint a **port facility security officer** (PFSO) (see I01k.1).
* Under ISPS Code, part A, section 14.1, a **port facility must act upon the security levels** set by the SOLAS Contracting Government within whose territory it is located. Security measures and procedures must be applied at the port facility in such a manner as to cause a minimum of interference with, or delay to, passengers, ship, ship's personnel and visitors, goods and services.
* ISPS Code, part A, section 14.2 provides that at **security level 1**, the following activities must be carried out through **appropriate measures** in all port facilities, taking into account the guidance given in part B of the ISPS Code, in order to identify and take preventive measures against security incidents:
  * ensuring the performance of all port facility security duties;
  * **controlling access** to the port facility;
  * **monitoring** of the port facility, including anchoring and berthing area(s);
  * monitoring **restricted areas** to ensure that only authorised persons have access;
  * supervising the handling of **cargo**;
  * supervising the handling of **ship's stores**; and
  * ensuring that **security communication** is readily available.
* At **security level 2**, the additional protective measures, specified in the port facility security plan, must be implemented for each activity detailed in section 14.2, taking into account the guidance given in part B of the ISPS Code (section 14.3).
* At **security level 3**, further specific protective measures, specified in the port facility security plan, must be implemented for each activity detailed in section 14.2, taking into account the guidance given in part B of the ISPS Code (section 14.4).
* In addition, at **security level 3**, port facilities are required to respond to and implement any security instructions given by the Contracting Government within whose territory the port facility is located (section 14.4.1).
* Ships using port facilities may be subject to the **port State control inspections** and **additional control measures** outlined in regulation XI-2/9. The relevant authorities may request the provision of information regarding the ship,

its cargo, passengers and ship's personnel prior to the ship's entry into port (see D05b.9). There may be circumstances in which **entry into port could be denied**.

* When a Port Facility Security Officer is advised that a **ship encounters difficulties in complying** with the requirements of chapter XI-2 or part A of the ISPS Code **or in implementing the appropriate measures and procedures** as detailed in the Ship Security Plan, and in the case of security level 3 following any security instructions given by the SOLAS Contracting Government within whose territory the port facility is located, the **port facility security officer and ship security officer must liase and co-ordinate** appropriate actions (section 14.5).

* SOLAS regulation XI-2/9.2.4 provides that if, after receipt of the information described in regulation XI-2/9.2.1 (see D05b.9), officers duly authorised by the SOLAS Contracting Government of the port in which the ship intends to enter (i.e. port State control officers) have **clear grounds** for believing that the **ship is in non-compliance** with the requirements of SOLAS chapter XI-2 or part A of the ISPS Code, those officers must **attempt to establish communication** with and between the **ship** and the **flag State Administration** in order to rectify the non-compliance. If this communication does not result in rectification, or if the port State control officers have **clear grounds otherwise** for believing that the **ship is in non-compliance** with the requirements of SOLAS chapter XI-2 or part A of the ISPS Code, the officers **may take steps** as listed below in relation to the ship. Any such steps taken must be **proportionate**, taking into account the guidance given in part B of the ISPS Code. The steps that may be taken are:
  1. a requirement for the **rectification of the non-compliance**;
  2. a requirement that the **ship proceeds to** a location specified in the **territorial sea or internal waters** of that SOLAS Contracting Government (i.e. a location in the national waters of the port State);
  3. **inspection** of the ship, if the ship is in the territorial sea of the SOLAS Contracting Government the port of which the ship intends to enter; or
  4. **denial of entry** into port.

I01k.1 Port facility security officer

* ISPS Code, part A, section 2.1 defines a **port facility security officer** (PFSO) as the person designated as responsible for the development, implementation, revision and maintenance of the Port Facility Security Plan and for liaison with the ship security officers (SSOs) and company security officers (CSOs).

* ISPS Code, part A, section 14.5 provides that when a port facility security officer is advised that a **ship encounters difficulties in complying** with the requirements of SOLAS chapter XI-2 or part A of the ISPS Code or in **implementing the appropriate measures and procedures** as detailed in the Ship Security Plan, and in the case of security level 3 **following any security instructions** given by the SOLAS Contracting Government within whose territory the port facility is located, the **port facility security officer and ship security officer must liaise and co-ordinate** appropriate actions

* ISPS Code, part A, section 14.6 provides that when a port facility security officer is advised that a **ship is at a security level which is higher than that of the port facility**, he must **report** the matter to the competent authority and must **liaise with the Ship Security Officer and co-ordinate appropriate actions**, if necessary.

I01k.2 Declaration of Security

* SOLAS regulation XI-2.2 defines a **Declaration of Security** as an agreement reached between a ship and either a port facility or another ship with which it interfaces specifying the security measures each will implement.
* **ISPS Code, part A, section 5** makes requirements relating to a **Declaration of Security**.
* **SOLAS Contracting Governments** must determine when a Declaration of Security is required by assessing the risk the ship/port interface or ship-to-ship activity poses to people, property or the environment (section 5.1).
* Under section 5.2 a **ship can request completion of a Declaration of Security** when:
  * the ship is operating at a higher security level than the port facility or another ship it is interfacing with;
  * there is an agreement on Declaration of Security between SOLAS Contracting Governments covering certain international voyages or specific ships on those voyages;
  * there **has been a security threat or a security incident** involving the **ship** or involving the **port facility**, as applicable;
  * the ship is at a port which is not required to have and implement an approved Port Facility Security Plan; or
  * the ship is conducting ship-to-ship activities with another ship not required to have and implement an approved Ship Security Plan.
* **Requests** for the completion of a Declaration of Security, under this section, must be **acknowledged** by the applicable port facility or ship (section 5.3).

* Section 5.4 provides that the **Declaration of Security must be completed by**:
  * the **master** or the **ship security officer** on behalf of the ship(s); and, if appropriate,
  * the port facility security officer or, if the SOLAS Contracting Government determines otherwise, by any other body responsible for shore-side security, on behalf of the port facility.
* The Declaration of Security must **address the security requirements** that could be **shared** between a port facility and a ship (or between ships) and **must state the responsibility for each** (section 5.5).
* **Flag State Administrations** must specify, bearing in mind the provisions of regulation XI-2/9.2.3, the **minimum period** for which Declarations of Security must be kept by ships entitled to fly their flag (section 5.7).

I01k.3 Compliance by ships with security measures

* **Prior to entering a port or whilst in a port** within the territory of a SOLAS Contracting Government, a ship must **comply** with the requirements for the **security level** set by that Contracting Government, if such security level is higher than the security level set by the flag State Administration for that ship (SOLAS regulation XI-2/4.3).
* **Ships** must **respond** without undue delay to any **change to a higher security level** (SOLAS regulation XI-2/4.4).
* Where a ship is **not in compliance** with the requirements of SOLAS chapter XI-2 or of part A of the ISPS Code, or cannot comply with the requirements of the security level set by the flag State Administration or by another SOLAS Contracting Government and applicable to that ship, then the **ship must notify** the **appropriate competent authority** prior to conducting any **ship/port interface or prior to entry into port**, whichever occurs earlier (SOLAS regulation XI-2/4.5). A "ship/port interface" is defined in regulation XI-2/1 as "the interactions that occur involving movement of people, goods or provisions of port services to or from the ship".
* **Records** must be maintained of security measures taken, as detailed in D05b.9.

I02 Business with Port State and harbour officials

I02a COMPLIANCE WITH PORT STATE LAWS

* **All vessels**, whether owned privately or commercially, by the act of voluntarily entering the internal waters of a coastal State, place themselves **within the jurisdiction of the coastal State**. Seafarers, passengers and others going ashore from a visiting ship are subject to the laws of the port State whilst ashore in the port State.
* Whilst on board their ship when she is in a foreign port, masters and seafarers are subject both to the laws of the flag State and to the laws of the port State. The master of a UK ship must, even while in a foreign port, carry out various duties under UK Merchant Shipping legislation, such as providing means of access, making Official Log Book entries, etc., and the port State authorities will not normally interfere with the operation of the ship under those provisions so long as there is no breach of the port State's laws.
* **UNCLOS Article 218** deals with port State jurisdiction in **pollution offences**. When a vessel is voluntarily within a port or at an offshore terminal, the port State may, where the evidence warrants, begin proceedings in respect of discharges in violation of international rules (e.g. MARPOL). Another State in which a discharge violation has occurred, or the flag State, may request the port State to investigate the violation.
* **Section 281 of the Merchant Shipping Act 1995** provides that where any British citizen is charged with having committed any **offence** under the Merchant Shipping Act 1995 **in any foreign port or harbour**, or **on board any foreign ship** to which he does not belong, and he is found (in the UK) within the jurisdiction of a UK court, he may be tried in the UK (see B03b.2g).

I02b PORT STATE AUTHORITIES

I02b.1 Port State Administration

* The marine authorities of a foreign port State government (i.e. the "**port State Administration**") will usually be responsible for much the same matters in their own country as the Department for Transport (DfT) is in the UK (see B05a), and will probably have similar powers to those of MCA personnel (see B05b.4).
* Masters should bear in mind that one of the conditions of continued validity of SOLAS certificates under **regulation 8 of the MS (Survey and Certification) Regulations 1995** (SI 1995/1210) is that **any accident or defect** affecting the ship's safety or completeness (including structure, machinery and equipment) **must be reported** at the earliest

opportunity to the "**appropriate authorities of the port State**" (see D04f.2i). The ship's agent should be able to assist the master in reporting to the appropriate organisation.

I02b.2 General inspections

* **Section 258 of the Merchant Shipping Act 1995** empowers MCA surveyors (and other officials) to inspect UK ships and their equipment at any reasonable time.
* The surveyor carrying out a "**general inspection**" will generally have the freedom to use any or all of his powers under the Merchant Shipping Acts. A **port State control inspector**, on the other hand, is initially restricted as to what he may inspect (see I02c.3).

I02b.3 Inspections for purposes under the Safe Manning Regulations

* Regulation 15 of the MS (Safe Manning, Hours of Work and Watchkeeping) Regulations 1997 (SI 1997/1320) provides that an **authorised person may inspect any non-UK ship in UK waters** for the purposes of:
  * verifying that all seamen on board who are required to be certificated hold valid appropriate certificates;
  * assessing the suitability of the seamen in the ship to maintain the watchkeeping standards required by the Regulations where there are grounds for believing that these standards are not being maintained because, while in a UK port or in the approaches to that port, any of the following have occurred:
    * the ship has been involved in a collision, grounding or stranding;
    * there has been an unlawful discharge of substances from the ship when underway, at anchor or at a berth;
    * the ship has manoeuvred in an erratic or unsafe manner, or navigational course markers or traffic separation schemes have not been followed; or
    * the ship has otherwise been operated in such a manner as to pose a danger to persons, property or the environment.
* **If an authorised person finds one of the following deficiencies**, i.e.:
  * a failure of any seaman, required to hold an appropriate certificate, to have a valid appropriate certificate or a valid exemption from that requirement;
  * a failure to comply with the safe manning document;
  * a failure of navigational or engineering watch arrangements to conform to the requirements specified for the ship by the competent authority of the flag State;
  * an absence on a watch of a person qualified to operate equipment essential to safe navigation, safe radio communications or the prevention of marine pollution;
  * an inability of the master to provide adequately rested persons for the first watch at the commencement of a voyage and for subsequent relieving watches,
  - he must give written notification to the master, and in the case of a non-UK ship, to the nearest maritime, consular diplomatic representative of the flag State.
* Regulation 16 provides that when any of these deficiencies are found and there is a **consequential danger to persons, property or the environment**, the ship may, after notification to the master, be **detained**.

I02c PORT STATE CONTROL

I02c.1 Port State control

* "**Port State control**" is the inspection of foreign ships present in a nation's ports for the purpose of verifying that the condition of the ships and their equipment comply with the provisions of international conventions and codes, and that the ships are manned and operated in compliance with those provisions.
* **The primary responsibility** for maintaining ships' standards rests with their flag States, as well as their owners and masters. However, many flag States do not, for various reasons, fulfil their obligations under international maritime conventions, and port State control provides a useful "safety net" to catch substandard ships. Port State control effectively does what flag State control should, but in many cases fails, to do.
* A "**Port State Control regime**", where set up under a "**memorandum of understanding**" ("**MOU**") or similar accord between neighbouring port States, is a system of harmonised inspection procedures designed to target substandards ships with the main objective being their eventual elimination from the region covered by the MOU's participating States.

* Several of the most important IMO technical conventions such as SOLAS and MARPOL, as well as ILO Convention 147 (the "Minimum Standards Convention") contain provisions for ships to be inspected when they visit foreign ports to ensure that they meet IMO and ILO requirements. IMO has encouraged the establishment of regional port State control organisations and agreements on port State control.
* A good explanation of how Port State Control works in practice is in the section "PSC at work" in the Paris MOU website: www.parismou.org

I02c.2 Port State Control regimes

* Eight international PSC agreements are currently in force world-wide, as follows:
    * Paris Memorandum of Understanding (**Paris MOU**) (see I02c.2a);
    * Acuerdo de Viña del Mar (**Latin-American Agreement**) (see I02c.2b);
    * Tokyo Memorandum of Understanding (**Tokyo MOU**) (see I02c.2c);
    * Caribbean Memorandum of Understanding (**Caribbean MOU**) (see I02c.2d);
    * Mediterranean Memorandum of Understanding (**Mediterranean MOU**) (see I02c.2e);
    * Indian Ocean Memorandum of Understanding (**Indian Ocean MOU**) (see I02c.2f);
    * West and Central African Memorandum of Understanding (**Abuja MOU**) (see I02c.2g); and
    * Black Sea Memorandum of Understanding (**Black Sea MOU**) (see I02c.2h).
* The **US Coast Guard** operates a national **Port State Control Initiative** (see I02c.5).

I02c.2a Paris MOU

* **Participating countries** and Associate Members: Belgium, Canada, Croatia, Denmark, Finland, France, Germany, Greece, Iceland[13], Ireland, Italy, Netherlands, Norway, Poland, Portugal, Russian Federation, Spain, Sweden, and UK (19).
* **Target inspection rate**: 25% annual inspection rate per country. (UK's target is currently 30%.)
* **Relevant instruments**: LOADLINE 1966, LL PROT 1988, SOLAS 1974, SOLAS PROT 1978, 1988, MARPOL 73/78, STCW 1978, COLREG 1972, TONNAGE 1969, ILO 147.
* Ships considered as an **overriding priority for inspection** are:
    * ships which have been reported by pilots or port authorities in accordance with section 1.5 of the Memorandum;
    * ships carrying dangerous or polluting goods, which have failed to report all relevant information concerning the ship's particulars, the ship's movements and concerning the dangerous or polluting goods being carried to the competent authority of the port and coastal State;
    * ships which have been the subject of a report or notification by another Port State Control Authority;
    * ships which have been the subject of a report or complaint by the master, a crew member, or any person or organisation with a legitimate interest in the safe operation of the ship, shipboard living and working conditions or the prevention of pollution, unless the Authority concerned deems the report or complaint to be manifestly unfounded; the identity of the person lodging the report or complaint must not be revealed to the master or the shipowner of the ship concerned;
    * ships which have been:
        * involved in a collision, grounding or stranding on their way to the port;
        * accused of an alleged violation of the provisions on discharge of harmful substances or effluents;
        * manoeuvred in an erratic or unsafe manner whereby routing measures, adopted by the IMO, or safe navigation practices and procedures have not been followed; or
        * otherwise operated in such a manner as to pose a danger to persons, property or the environment;
        * ships which have been suspended or withdrawn from their class for safety reasons in the course of the preceding 6 months.
* Paris Memorandum Secretariat **website**: http://www.parismou.org
* A "no more favourable treatment" policy ensures that non-convention State vessels can not have lower standards than convention State ships.
* No ship should normally be inspected earlier than 6 months following its last inspection or certificate renewal.
* The current condition of every vessel inspected is recorded on the data bank, to which reference can be made by any national surveyor at any time.
* Factors governing selection of a ship for inspection include date of her last inspection, age, 'track record' and vessel type (e.g. oil, chemical or gas tanker).
* Documents (certificates, record books, manuals, etc.) are checked first.

---

[13] Iceland became the 19th Paris MOU member State in 2000.

* If documents are all in order and the surveyor has no misgivings concerning the condition of the ship, no further action is taken.
* If documents are all in order but the surveyor decides that there are clear grounds for believing that the ship's condition and/or equipment does not substantially correspond with the particulars on the certificates, rectifications are necessary before sailing.
* If certificates are invalid or missing, rectifications are necessary before sailing.
* If the ship is found defective in some way, the surveyor has various options:
   * if the defects are assessed as 'fairly minor', he will probably require immediate repairs but, if the ship is bound for another Paris MOU signatory State port, he may permit her to proceed there, in which case he will notify the next port State Administration;
   * if replacement items of a minor nature are required but are not immediately available, the surveyor may permit a short voyage to another MOU State port, depending on the nature of the defects;
   * if serious defects are found, the surveyor will require them to be made good before sailing, whether or not the ship is delayed;
   * if the surveyor finds the vessel "dangerously unsafe", he will detain her. The harbour master will be informed and the ship may be moved to another berth.
* On completion of the Port State Control inspection, the surveyor will issue to the master a Report showing, in a numerical code designed to overcome language problems, any defects found. The master is recommended to keep the Report for at least 6 months. A copy is kept by the surveyor and the inspection is recorded on the data bank.
* For notes on **UK Port State Control regulations and procedures**, see I02c.3.

I02c.2b Latin American Agreement (Acuerdo de Viña del Mar)

* **Participating countries** and Associate Members: Argentina, Bolivia, Brazil, Chile, Colombia, Cuba, Ecuador, Mexico, Panama, Peru, Uruguay, Venezuela (12).
* **Target inspection rate**: 15% annual inspection rate per country within 3 years.
* **Relevant instruments**: LOADLINE 1966, SOLAS 1974, SOLAS PROT 1978, MARPOL 73/78, STCW 1978, COLREG 1972.
* **Special attention** given to:
   * passenger ships, ro-ro ships, bulk carriers;
   * ships which may present a special hazard;
   * ships which have had several recent deficiencies.
* **Website**: http://www.acuerdolatino.int.ar

I02c.2c Tokyo MOU

* **Participating countries** and Associate Members: Australia, Canada, China, Fiji, Indonesia, Japan, Republic of Korea, Malaysia, New Zealand, Papua New Guinea, Philippines, Russian Federation, Singapore, Solomon Islands, Thailand, Vanuatu, Viet Nam, Hong Kong (China) (18).
* **Target inspection rate**: 50% annual regional inspection rate by the year 2000 (achieved in 1996).
* **Relevant instruments**: LOADLINE 1966, SOLAS 1974, SOLAS PROT 1978, MARPOL 73/78, STCW 1978, COLREG 1972, ILO 147.
* **Special attention** given to:
   * passenger ships, ro-ro ships, bulk carriers;
   * ships which may present a special hazard;
   * ships visiting a port for the first time or after an absence of 12 months or more;
   * ships flying the flag of a State appearing in the 3-year rolling average table of above-average detentions;
   * ships which have been permitted to leave the port of a State with deficiencies to be rectified;
   * ships which have been reported by pilots or port authorities as being deficient;
   * ships carrying dangerous or polluting goods which have failed to report relevant information.
* **Website**: http://www.tokyo-mou.org

I02c.2d Caribbean MOU

* **Participating countries** and Associate Members: Anguilla, Antigua and Barbuda, Aruba, Bahamas, Barbados, Bermuda, British Virgin Islands, Cayman Islands, Dominica, Grenada, Guyana, Jamaica, Montserrat, Netherlands Antilles (Curaçao, St Maarten), St Kitts & Nevis, Saint Lucia, Saint Vincent & the Grenadines, Suriname, Trinidad & Tobago, Turks and Caicos Islands (20).
* **Target inspection rate**: 10% annual inspection rate per country within 3 years.

* **Relevant instruments**: LOADLINE 1966, SOLAS 1974, SOLAS PROT 1978, MARPOL 73/78, STCW 1978, COLREG 1972, ILO 147.
* **Special attention** given to:
  * ships visiting a port for the first time or after an absence of 12 months or more;
  * ships which have been permitted to leave the port of a State with deficiencies to be rectified;
  * ships which have been reported by pilots or port authorities as being deficient;
  * ships whose certificates are not in order;
  * ships carrying dangerous or polluting goods which have failed to report relevant information;
  * ships which have been suspended from class in the preceding 6 months.

I02c.2e Mediterranean MOU

* **Participating countries** and Associate Members: Algeria, Cyprus, Egypt, Israel, Jordan, Malta, Lebanon, Morocco, Tunisia, Turkey, Palestinian Authority (11).
* **Target inspection rate**: 15% annual inspection rate per country within 3 years.
* **Relevant instruments**: LOADLINE 66, SOLAS 1974, SOLAS PROT 1978, MARPOL 73/78, STCW 1978, COLREG 1972, ILO 147.
* **Special attention** given to:
  * ships visiting a port of a State for the first time or after an absence of 12 months or more;
  * ships which have been permitted to leave the port of a State with deficiencies to be rectified;
  * ships which have been reported by pilots or port authorities as being deficient;
  * ships whose certificates are not in order;
  * ships carrying dangerous or polluting goods which have failed to report relevant information;
  * ships which have been suspended from class in the preceding 6 months.
* **Website**: www.medmou.org

I02c.2f Indian Ocean MOU

* **Participating countries** and Associate Members: Djibouti, Eritrea, Ethiopia, India, Iran, Kenya, Maldives, Mauritius, Mozambique, Seychelles, South Africa, Sri Lanka, Sudan, Tanzania, Yemen (15).
* **Target inspection rate**: 10% annual inspection rate per country within 3 years.
* Relevant instruments: LOADLINE 1966, SOLAS 1974, SOLAS PROT 1978, MARPOL 73/78, STCW 1978, COLREG 1972, TONNAGE 69, ILO 147.
* **Special attention** given to:
  * ships visiting a port of a State for the first time or after an absence of 12 months or more;
  * ships which have been permitted to leave the port of a State with deficiencies to be rectified;
  * ships which have been reported by pilots or port authorities as being deficient;
  * ships whose certificates are not in order;
  * ships carrying dangerous or polluting goods which have failed to report relevant information;
  * ships which have been suspended from class in the preceding 6 months.

I02c.2g West and Central African MOU (Abuja MOU)

* **Participating countries** and Associate Members: Benin, Cape Verde, Congo, Côte d'Ivoire, Gabon, Gambia, Ghana, Guinea, Liberia, Mauretania, Namibia, Nigeria, Sénégal, Sierra Leone, South Africa and Togo (16). (Angola, Cameroon and Equatorial Guinea have agreed to sign the MOU at a later date.)
* **Target inspection rate**: 15% annual inspection rate per country within 3 years.
* **Relevant instruments**: LOADLINE 1966, SOLAS 1974, SOLAS PROT 1978, MARPOL 73/78, STCW 1978, COLREG 1972, TONNAGE 69, ILO 147.
* **Special attention** given to:
  * ships visiting a port of a State for the first time or after an absence of 12 months or more;
  * ships which have been permitted to leave the port of a State with deficiencies to be rectified;
  * ships which have been reported by pilots or port authorities as being deficient;
  * ships whose certificates are not in order;
  * ships carrying dangerous or polluting goods which have failed to report relevant information;
  * ships which have been suspended from class in the preceding 6 months.

I02c.2h Black Sea MOU

* **Participating countries** and Associate Members: Bulgaria, Georgia, Romania, Russian Federation, Turkey, Ukraine (6).
* **Target inspection rate**: 15% annual inspection rate per country within 3 years.
* **Relevant instruments**: LOADLINE 1966, SOLAS 1974, SOLAS PROT 1978, MARPOL 73/78, STCW 1978, COLREG 1972, TONNAGE 69, ILO 147.
* **Special attention** given to:
  * ships visiting a port of a State for the first time or after an absence of 12 months or more;
  * ships which have been permitted to leave the port of a State with deficiencies to be rectified;
  * ships which have been reported by pilots or port authorities as being deficient;
  * ships whose certificates are not in order;
  * ships carrying dangerous or polluting goods which have failed to report relevant information;
  * ships suspended from class;
  * ships which have been subject of a report or notification by another authority.

I02c.2i Persian Gulf MOU

* Countries in the Persian Gulf region have agreed informally on the need to establish a Port State Control regime.

I02c.3 Port State Control Regulations

* **The MS (Port State Control) Regulations 1995** (SI 1995/3128) -
  - **give effect** in the UK (through Part 1) to Council Directive 95/21/EC in respect of shipping using Community ports and sailing in waters under the jurisdiction of the Member States, of international standards for ship safety, pollution prevention and shipboard living and working conditions (port State control).
  - **are amended** by the -
    * MS (Port State Control) (Amendment) Regulations 1998 (SI 1998/1433);
    * MS (Port State Control) (Amendment No.2) Regulations 1998 (SI 1998/2198); and
    * MS (Port State Control) (Amendment) Regulations 2001 (SI 2001/2349).
* The Regulations are in **3 Parts**, as follows: **Part I**. Implementation of Council Directive 95/21/EC (regulations 2 to 18); **Part II**. Rights of appeal and compensation in respect of detained ships (regulation 19); and **Part III**. Inspection of familiarity of crew with operational procedures (regulation 20).
* **Regulations** are as follows: **1**. Citation, commencement and effect; **2**. Interpretation of Part I; **3**. Application of Part I; **4**. Competent Authority; **5**. Inspection commitments; **6**. Inspection procedure; **7**. Expanded inspection of certain ships; **8**. Report of inspection to the master; **9**. Rectification and detention; **9A**. Procedure applicable in the absence of ISM certificates; **10**, **11** and **12**. Right of appeal and compensation; **13**. Follow-up to inspections and detention; **14**. Professional profile of inspectors; **15**. Reports from pilots and port authorities; **16**. Release of information; **17**. Reimbursement of costs; **18**. Offences; **19**. Rights of appeal and compensation in respect of detained ships; **20**. Inspection of familiarity of crew with operational procedures.
* Under regulation 3(1), and subject to regulation 3(2), **Part 1 applies to any ship which is not a British ship** (see D01c.4), **in a port in the UK** or **at an offshore installation**, or **anchored** off such a port or installation, **except** in waters which are neither UK waters (see I01a.1a) nor designated waters (see I01a.1c)[14]. Regulation 3(2) provides that Part 1 does not apply to British ships, fishing vessels, warships, naval auxiliaries, wooden ships of primitive build, government ships used for non-commercial purposes and pleasure yachts not engaged in trade.
* In the case of a ship below 500gt to the extent to which a Convention does not apply, an inspector may (without prejudice to any other powers under MS legislation, take such action as may be necessary to ensure that the ship is **not clearly hazardous** to safety, health or the environment (regulation 3(3)).
* When inspecting a ship, no more favourable treatment of the ship or crew will be given to a non-Convention ship than to a Convention ship or its crew (regulation 3(4)).
* Under regulation 3(5), inspectors may exercise a power of inspection or detention conferred by a Convention in relation to ships which are at offshore installations or are anchored off an offshore installation or a UK port. In view of the provision in regulation 3(1), however, this only applies where the offshore installations are within UK waters, i.e. within the UK's territorial sea.
* **The MCA** is designated by regulation 4(1) as the **competent authority** for the UK for the purposes of the Council Directive and the Regulations. The MCA will, under regulation 5(1), annually inspect at least 25% of all ships to

---

[14] An amendment to section 95 of the Merchant Shipping Act 1995 extends the powers of inspection and detention to a ship at sea in UK waters, except for a ship on innocent passage.

which the Regulations apply entering UK ports during a calendar year. In selecting ships for inspection the MCA will, under regulation 5(2), give priority to the ships listed in **Annex I, part I of MSN 1725**, as amended by **MSN 1753**; and in determining the order for priority for inspection of the other ships listed in Annex I, the MCA will use the ship's overall target factor as listed in Annex I, part II. Under regulation 5(3), the MCA must refrain from inspecting ships which have been inspected by any EU Member State in accordance with the Council Directive within the previous 6 months, provided that:
* the ship is not listed in Annex I of MSN 1725, as amended by MSN 1753; and
* no deficiencies have been reported, following a previous inspection; and
* no clear ground exist for carrying out an inspection -
- but, under regulation 5(4), these provisions will not apply to any of the operational controls specifically provided for in the Convention enactments.
* **Minimum criteria for inspectors** are set out in Annex VII of **MSN 1725**. Inspectors will carry an MCA identification card which will include the information specified in Annex VIII of MSN 1725.

I02c.3a Inspection procedure

* Under regulation 6(1), the inspector will as a minimum:
    * check the **certificates and documents** listed in Annex II of MSN 1725, as amended by MSN 1753, to the extent applicable; and
    * satisfy himself of the **overall condition of the ship**, including the engine room and accommodation and including hygienic conditions.
* The inspector may, under regulation 6(2), examine **all relevant certificates and documents**, other than those listed in Annex II of MSN 1725, as amended by MSN 1753, which are required to be carried on board in accordance with the Convention requirements.
* Whenever there are **clear grounds** for believing, after the inspection referred to above, that the condition of the ship or its equipment or crew does not substantially meet the relevant requirements of a Convention enactment, **a more detailed inspection** may be carried out under regulation 6(3), including **further checking of compliance with on-board operational requirements**. The inspector will also observe the relevant procedures and guidelines for the control of ships specified in Annex IV of MSN 1725 (regulation 6(4)).
* **"Clear grounds"** means evidence which in the professional judgement of an inspector warrants a more detailed inspection of a ship, its equipment or its crew. **Examples of clear grounds** are listed in Annex III to MSN 1725.
* **"More detailed inspection"** means an inspection where the ship, its equipment and crew as a whole or, as appropriate, parts thereof are subjected, in the circumstances specified in regulation 6(3), to an in-depth inspection covering the ship's construction, equipment, manning, living and working conditions and compliance with on-board operational procedures.

I02c.3b Expanded inspection of certain ships

* Where there are clear grounds for a more detailed inspection of a ship belonging to the categories listed in Annex V of MSN 1725, an **expanded inspection** will be carried out under regulation 7, taking into account the guidelines in Annex V, section B of MSN 1725.
* The ships listed in Annex V of MSN 1725 will be subject to an expanded inspection by any of the competent authorities of the Member States only **once during a period of 12 months**. However, these ships may be subject to the inspection provided for in regulation 6(1) and (2) (see I02c.3a).
* Subject to the provisions of the last paragraph, in the case of a passenger ship operating on a regular schedule in or out of port in the UK, an expanded inspection of the ship will be carried out **before taking up service** and **every 12 months** thereafter by the MCA subject to consultation with the competent authority of a Member State if the ship operates to ports in that Member State.
* **Regulation 7 will not apply** to a vessel which to the MCA's satisfaction has **in the last 12 months** been subject to an **initial survey** in accordance with Article 6 of Council Directive 1999/35/EC on a system of mandatory surveys for the safe operation of regular ro-ro ferry and high-speed passenger craft services or a **specific survey** in accordance with Article 8 of that directive. (The Directive is implemented by the **MS (Mandatory Surveys for Ro-Ro Ferry and High Speed Passenger Craft) Regulations 2001** (SI 2001/152) (see D04f.4).

I02c.3c Applicable conventions

* **The conventions which will be enforced** are listed in regulation 2 and are: Load Lines, 1966; SOLAS 74; MARPOL 73/78; STCW 78; COLREG 72; TONNAGE 69; and ILO 147, together with Protocols and Amendments

to these Conventions and related Codes of mandatory status (e.g. the IGC and IBC Codes), in force at the time of adoption of the EC Directive.

I02c.3d Ships to be considered for priority inspection

* Annex I of MSN 1725 contains a list of **ships to be considered for priority inspection**, as referred to in regulation 5(2). That list has been replaced by the list in **Annex 1 of MSN 1753**, which is as follows:

* **I. Overriding factors**

Regardless of the value of the target factor, the following ships shall be considered as an overriding priority for inspection.

1. Ships which have been reported by pilots or port authorities as having deficiencies which may prejudice their safe navigation (pursuant to Council Directive 93/75/EEC and regulation 15 of the Regulations).
2. Ships which have failed to comply with the obligations laid down in Council Directive 93/75/EEC (see MSN 1741).
3. Ships which have been the subject of a report or notification by another Member State.
4. Ships which have been the subject of a report or complaint by the master, a crew member, or any person or organisation with a legitimate interest in the safe operation of the ship, shipboard living and working conditions or the prevention of pollution, unless the Member State concerned deems the report or complaint to be manifestly unfounded. The identity of the person lodging the report or complaint must not be revealed to the master or the shipowner of the ship concerned.
5. Ships which have been –
   - involved in a collision, grounding or stranding on their way to the port,
   - accused of an alleged violation of the provisions on discharge of harmful substances or effluents,
   - manoeuvred in an erratic or unsafe manner whereby routing measures, adopted by the IMO, or safe navigation practices and procedures have not been followed, or
   - otherwise operated in such a manner as to pose a danger to persons, property or the environment.
6. Ships which have been suspended or withdrawn from their class for safety reasons in the course of the preceding six months.

II. Overall targeting factor

The following ships shall be considered as priority for inspection.

1. Ships visiting a port in the MOU region for the first time or after an absence of 12 months or more from a port in the MOU region. The MCA shall rely upon available SIRENAC data and inspect those ships which have not been recorded in the SIRENAC database following the entry into force of that database on 1 January 1993.
2. Ships not inspected by any Member State within the previous six months.
3. Ships whose statutory certificates on the ship's construction and equipment, issued in accordance with the Conventions, and the classification certificates, have been issued by an organisation which is not recognised under the terms of Council Directive 94/57/EC of 22 November 1994 on common rules and standards for ship inspection and survey organisations and for the relevant activities of maritime administrations.
4. Ships flying the flag of a State appearing in the 3 year rolling average table of above average detentions and delays published in the annual report of the MOU.
5. Ships which have been permitted to leave the port of a Member State on certain conditions, such as –
   - deficiencies to be rectified before departure;
   - deficiencies to be rectified at the next port;
   - deficiencies to be rectified within 14 days;
   - deficiencies for which other conditions have been specified.
   If all deficiencies have been rectified this is taken into account.
6. Ships for which deficiencies have been recorded during a previous inspection, according to the number of deficiencies.
7. Ships which have been detained in a previous port.
8. Ships flying the flag of a country which has not ratified all relevant international conventions referred to in regulation 2 of the Regulations.
9. Ships flying the flag of a country with a deficiency ratio above average.
10. Ships with class deficiency ratio above average.
11. Ships which are in a category for which an expanded inspection is required by regulation 7 of the Regulations.
12. Other ships above 13 years old.

In determining the order of priority for inspection of the ships listed above, the competent authority shall take into account the order indicated by the overall target factor shown on the SIRENAC database.

A higher target factor is indicative of a higher priority. The target factor is the sum of the applicable target factor values as defined within the framework of the MOU. Items 5, 6 and 7 shall only apply to inspections carried out in the last 12 months. The overall target factor shall not be less than the sum of the values of items 3, 4, 8, 9, 10, 11 and 12.

I02c.3e Certificates and documents inspected

* The **certificates and documents** referred to in regulation 6(1) are listed in **Annex II to MSN 1753**, and include:
1. International Tonnage Certificate (1969).
2. Passenger Ship Safety Certificate.
   Cargo Ship Safety Construction Certificate.
   Cargo Ship Safety Equipment Certificate.
   Cargo Ship Safety Radiotelegraphy Certificate.
   Cargo Ship Safety Radiotelephony Certificate.
   Cargo Ship Safety Radio Certificate.
   Exemption Certificate, including, where appropriate, the list of cargoes.
   Cargo Ship Safety Certificate.
3. International Certificate of Fitness for Carriage of Liquefied Gases in Bulk.
   Certificate of Fitness for the Carriage of Liquefied Gases in Bulk.
4. International Certificate of Fitness for the Carriage of Dangerous Chemicals in Bulk.
   Certificate of Fitness for the Carriage of Dangerous Chemicals in Bulk.
5. International Oil Pollution Prevention Certificate.
   International Pollution Prevention Certificate for the Carriage of Noxious Liquid Substance in Bulk.
6. International Load Line Certificate (1966).
   International Load Line Exemption Certificate.
7. Oil Record Book, parts I and II.
8. Cargo Record Book.
9. Minimum Safe Manning Document.
10. Certificates of Competency including Dangerous Goods Endorsement.
11. Medical Fitness Certificates.
12. Stability information including grain loading information and Document of Authorisation.
13. Document of Compliance and Safety Management Certificate issued in accordance with the ISM Code.
14. Certificates as to the ship's hull strength and the machinery installations issued by the classification society in question (only to be required if the ship maintains its class with a classification society)
15. Document of Compliance with the Special Requirements for Ships Carrying Dangerous Goods.
16. High Speed Craft Safety Certificate and Permit To Operate High Speed Craft.
17. Dangerous goods special list or manifest, or detailed stowage plan.
18. Ship's log book (OLB) with respect to the records of tests and drills and the log for records of inspection and maintenance of lifesaving appliances and arrangements.
19. Special Purpose Ship Safety Certificate.
20. Mobile Offshore Drilling Unit (MODU) Safety Certificate.
21. For oil tankers, the record of oil discharge monitoring and control system for the last ballast voyage.
22. Muster list, fire control plan, and for passenger ships, a damage control plan.
23. Shipboard Oil Pollution Emergency Plan (SOPEP).
24. Survey report files (in case of bulk carriers and oil tankers).
25. Reports of previous port State control inspections.
26. For ro-ro passenger ships, information on the A/A maximum ratio (A/Amax Certificate).
27. Document of authorisation for the carriage of grain.
28. Cargo Securing Manual.
29. Garbage Management Plan and Garbage Record Book.
30. Decision Support System for masters of passenger ships.
31. SAR Cooperation Plan for passenger ships trading on fixed routes.
32. List of operational limitations for passenger ships.
33. Bulk carrier booklet.
34. Loading and unloading plan for bulk carriers.

I02c.3f Report of inspection

* On completion of an **inspection**, a **more detailed inspection**, or an **expanded inspection**, the master of the ship will, under regulation 8(1), be provided by the inspector with a **report document** giving the **results** of the inspection and details of any **decisions** taken by the inspector, and of **corrective action** to be taken by the master, owner or operator.

* In the case of **deficiencies warranting detention** of a ship, the document to be given to the master must include information about the **future publication of the detention** in accordance with regulation 15 (regulation 8(2)).

I02c.3g Rectification and detention

* The owner must, under regulation 9(1), satisfy the MCA that any deficiencies confirmed or revealed by an inspection are or will be rectified in accordance with the Conventions.
* In the case of deficiencies which are **clearly hazardous to safety, health or the environment**, the inspector must **detain the ship**, or require the **stoppage of the operation** in the course of which the deficiencies have been revealed (regulation 9(2)). Powers of detention in the Merchant Shipping Acts, or in an SI which is a Convention enactment will be applied as appropriate. In the case of a stoppage of an operation the power to issue a **Prohibition Notice** will be applied. A **Detention Order** may include a direction that the ship must remain in a particular place or must move to a particular anchorage or berth. A Detention Order may specify circumstances when the master of the ship may move his ship from a specified place for reasons of safety or prevention of pollution.
* The Detention Order or stoppage of an operation will not be lifted until the hazard is removed or until the MCA establishes that the ship can, subject to the necessary conditions, proceed to sea or the operation be resumed without risk to the safety and health of the passengers or crew, or risk to other ships, or without there being an unreasonable threat of harm to the marine environment.
* When exercising his professional judgement as to whether or not a ship should be detained, the inspector will apply the criteria set out in **Annex VI to MSN 1725** (regulation 9(3)).
* In exceptional circumstances, where the overall condition of a ship is obviously substandard, the inspector may, in addition to detaining the ship, suspend the inspection of the ship until the responsible parties have taken the steps necessary to ensure that it complies with the relevant requirements of the Conventions (regulation 9(4)).
* Regulation 10 provides for an **owner's right of appeal against detention** of a ship.

I02c.3h Procedure applicable in the absence of ISM Certificates

* Under regulation 9A(1), where an inspection reveals that a copy of the **Document of Compliance or Safety Management Certificate** required by the ISM Code are **not on board** a vessel to which the Code is applicable, the inspector must **detain** the ship.
* Regulation 9A(2)(i) provides that, notwithstanding the absence of ISM Code certificates, if the inspection reveals no other deficiencies warranting detention, the MCA may lift the Detention Order to avoid port congestion. Where deficiencies are found which cannot be rectified in the port of detention, regulation 13 will apply.

I02c.3i Follow-up inspections and detention

* Where deficiencies referred to in regulation 9(2) (see I02c.3g) **cannot be rectified in the port of detention**, the MCA may, under regulation 13(1), allow the ship to **proceed to the nearest appropriate repair yard available**, as chosen by the master and the responsible parties, provided that the conditions determined by the competent authority of the flag Administration and agreed by the MCA are complied with. Such conditions must ensure that the ship can proceed without risk to the safety and health of passengers or crew, or risk to other ships, or without there being an unreasonable threat of harm to the marine environment.
* A ship which proceeds to sea from any EU port following release **to avoid port congestion** may not enter any UK port until the owner has provided evidence to the competent authority of the detaining EU State that the ship fully complies with all applicable requirements of the relevant Conventions (regulation 13(5)(a)). Notwithstanding this requirement, access to a specific UK port may be permitted in the event of *force majeure* or overriding safety considerations, or to reduce or minimise the risk of pollution or to have deficiencies rectified, provided adequate measures to the satisfaction of the MCA have been implemented by the owner or master of the ship to ensure safe entry (regulation 13(8)).

I02c.3j Reports from pilots and port authorities

* Regulation 15(1) provides that **pilots**, engaged in berthing or unberthing ships or engaged on ships bound for a port within the UK, must immediately **inform the port authority** who must immediately inform the **MCA**, whenever they learn in the course of their normal duties that there are **deficiencies** which may prejudice the safe navigation of the ship, or which may pose a threat of harm to the marine environment.
* If a **port authority**, when exercising its normal duties, learns that a ship within its port has **deficiencies** which may prejudice the safety of the ship or poses an unreasonable threat of harm to the marine environment, the authority must immediately inform the **MCA** (regulation 15(3)).

I02c.3k Publication of detentions

* Regulation 16 provides that the MCA will publish, at least **every month**, the information in Annex IX, Part I of MSN 1725 concerning ships detained in the UK or refused access to UK ports during the previous month.
* **Detentions** are listed on the MCA website at: www.mcga.gov.uk/news

I02c.3l Equasis

* **Equasis** is a database holding safety-related details of more than 66,000 ships[15], including a record of port State control inspections. It is on the Internet and may be viewed by any member of the public.
* The main **principles** behind the Equasis information system are that:
  * Equasis should be a tool aiming at reducing substandard shipping, and it should be limited to safety-related information on ships.
  * Equasis has no commercial purpose; it addresses a public concern and should act accordingly.
  * Equasis should be an international database covering the whole world fleet.
  * Active co-operation with all players involved in the maritime industry is needed.
  * Equasis will be a tool used for a better selection of ships, but it will be used on a voluntary basis; there will be no legal pressure for industry to use Equasis.
  * The setting-up and effective operation of Equasis will promote the exchange of unbiased information and transparency in maritime transport and thus allow persons involved in maritime transport to be better informed about the performance of ships and maritime organisations with which they are dealing.
* **Equasis** forms part of the Quality Shipping campaign launched by the EU in 1997. It is formally supported by signatories from marine Administrations, classification societies, P&I clubs and the ITF. More than 20 organisations provide information to Equasis. It is expected to be used heavily by charterers and insurers as well as marine Administrations with port State control functions.
* **Equasis website**: www.equasis.org

I02c.4 US Coast Guard Port State Control Initiative

* The US Coast Guard (USCG) exercises a **Port State Control Initiative**, the goal of which is to identify vessels not in compliance with international conventions through boardings and examinations, and to take the appropriate action to eliminate the threat that such vessels may pose to US waters, ports and citizens.
* The US Coast Guard's program is designed to effectively direct its vessel inspection resources to those vessels which may pose greater risks. As a result, a vessel making a US port call that is owned or operated by a person or entity that has had that vessel, or a different vessel, subject to more than one intervention action within the last twelve months (three for owners of large international fleets), is a higher priority for a Coast Guard port State control boarding. However, the owner/operator is only one of several factors considered by the US Coast Guard in deciding whether to actually board and inspect a vessel.
* The following sections are included in the Port State Control Initiative **webpages**:
  * **Port State Information Exchange**: This system contains vessel specific information derived from the US Coast Guard's Marine Safety Information System (MSIS);
  * **List of Detained Vessels** including vessel name, IMO number, date of detention, ship type, port, flag, classification society and deficiency summary.
  * **Port State Control Owner & Operator List**: US Coast Guard's compilation, updated monthly, of vessel owners and operators which have been associated with more than one detention under the authority of an international convention by the Coast Guard within the past 12 months. Owners and operators of large international fleets may not appear on this list unless they are associated with at least three detentions within the past 12 months.
  * **Port State Control Charterer List**: US Coast Guard's compilation, updated monthly, of charterers which have been associated with at least one detention under the authority of an international convention by the Coast Guard.
  * **List of Targeted and Non-Targeted Classification Societies**: Class societies are evaluated on their performance over the previous 3 years. Those with less than 10 distinct vessel arrivals in the previous year are filtered out. If they have been associated with any detentions in the previous three years, they receive Priority 1 Status. If they have not been associated with any detentions in the previous three years, they receive zero points. Class societies with more than 10 distinct vessel arrivals are evaluated on their performance over the previous

---

[15] In June 2001.

three years. Their performance is based on the ratio of class-related detentions and the number of distinct vessel arrivals. This ratio is then compared to the average detention ratio, and assigned points in the risk based vessel targeting matrix as follows:

- Below the average detention ratio = 0 points
- Between the average ratio and two times the average ratio = 1 point
- Between two and three times the average ratio = 3 points
- Between three and four times the average ratio = 5 points
- More than four times the average ratio = Priority 1

- **2001 Annual Flag List** of Flag State Administrations identified as having a detention ratio higher than the overall average and associated with more than one detention in the past year. Detention ratios are based on data from the previous three years.
- **ISM Denials of Entry**: Vessels detained for non-compliance with the ISM Code and ordered out of US waters. These vessels become automatic Priority 1 boardings until compliance with the ISM Code can be verified.

* The USA's equivalent to the UK's MS (Port State Control) Regulations 1995 is **Commandant Instruction 16711.12A**, which is on the webpage: www.uscg.mil/hq/g-m/nmc/compl
* **US Coast Guard Port State Control webpage**: www.uscg.mil/hq/g-m/psc/psc.htm
* **USCG Navigation and Vessel Inspection Circulars** (NVICs) are at: www.uscg.mil/hq/g-m/nvic

I02d DANGEROUSLY UNSAFE SHIPS

I02d.1 Meaning of "dangerously unsafe ship"

* **Section 94 of the Merchant Shipping Act 1995** provides that a ship is "**dangerously unsafe**" if, having regard to the nature of the service for which it is intended, the ship is, by reasons of the matters mentioned below, unfit to go to sea without serious danger to human life. Those matters are:
  - the condition, or the unsuitability for its purpose, of the ship or its machinery or equipment; or any part of the ship or its machinery or equipment;
  - undermanning;
  - overloading or unsafe or improper loading; and
  - any other matter relevant to the safety of the ship.

I02d.2 Power to detain dangerously unsafe ships

* **Section 95 of the Merchant Shipping Act 1995** provides that where any (UK or foreign) ship in a port in the UK appears to an inspector to be a dangerously unsafe ship, she may be detained. Inspectors in this context include:
  - an MCA surveyor of ships;
  - an MCA superintendent;
  - any person appointed by the Secretary of State for this duty.
* The detaining officer will serve on the master a **detention notice** which:
  - states that the inspector is of the opinion that the ship is a dangerously unsafe ship;
  - specifies the matters which, in the inspector's opinion, make the ship dangerously unsafe;
  - prohibits the ship from going to sea until it is released by a competent authority.
* In the case of a ship which is not a British ship, the detaining officer must cause a copy of the **detention notice** to be sent as soon as practicable to the nearest consular officer for the country to which the ship belongs.

I02d.3 Owner's and master's liability for dangerously unsafe ship

* Section 98(1) of the Merchant Shipping Act 1995 provides that if a ship which -
  - is in a port in the UK; or
  - is a UK ship in any other port,
  - is dangerously unsafe (as defined in I02d.1 above), then, subject to certain defences (see below), the master and the owner of the ship will each be guilty of an offence. (This is an offence of strict liability - see B03e.6.)
* Where, at the time that the ship has been found to be dangerously unsafe, any responsibilities of the owner with respect to safety matters have been assumed (either wholly or in part) by another party, either directly, under the terms of a charter-party or management agreement made with the owner, or indirectly, under the terms of a series of

charter-parties or management agreements, the "owner" will be construed as including that other party (section 98(2)).
* Section 98(3) provides that a person guilty of an offence under section 98 will be liable:
  • on summary conviction, to a fine not exceeding **£50,000**;
  • on conviction on indictment, to imprisonment for a term not exceeding 2 years, or a fine, or both.
* It will be a defence to prove that at the time of the alleged offence -
  • arrangements had been made to rectify the matters making it dangerously unsafe; or
  • it was reasonable for such arrangements not to have been made.
* It will also be a defence to prove that where the safety responsibilities of the owner had been assumed by a third party (e.g. charterer or ship manager), the accused had taken all reasonable steps to secure the proper discharge of their safety responsibilities. Regard will be had to whether the accused was or ought to have been aware of any deficiency in the discharge of the responsibilities, and the extent to which he was unable, under the terms of the agreement, to terminate the agreement or intervene in the management of the ship, and whether it was reasonable for the accused to place himself in that position.

I02e DETENTION

I02e.1 Nature of detention

* **"Detention"** of a ship lying at or off a port or terminal may be described as the prohibition, by an authorised officer of the port State Administration, of the ship's proceeding to sea or on a voyage until released by an authorised officer of the Administration.
* Detention should not be confused with **arrest**, which is the restraint of a ship (or other maritime property) on the order of a court. (For notes on **arrest of maritime property**, see B03h.) A ship which is under arrest by a court may simultaneously be detained by the port State Administration, and release from arrest will not trigger release from detention, or *vice versa*.
* In other maritime States the legislation relating to detention of ships may be more draconian than that in the UK, which is outlined below.

I02e.2 Detention provisions

* **A ship may be detained** in the UK only where there is a breach of some provision of Merchant Shipping legislation containing a provision **permitting detention** of the ship. Many such provisions can be found in the Merchant Shipping Act 1995 and in statutory instruments, e.g.:
  • **section 95(1) of the Merchant Shipping Act 1995**, which provides that "Where a ship in a port in the United Kingdom appears to a relevant inspector to be a dangerously unsafe ship the ship may be detained";
  • **regulation 9(2)(a) of the MS (Port State Control) Regulations 1995** (SI 1995/3128), which provides that "In case of deficiencies which are clearly hazardous to safety, health or the environment, the inspector shall detain the ship, or require the stoppage of the operation in the course of which the deficiencies have been revealed, using powers of detention in Convention enactments as appropriate, or using a prohibition notice under section 262 of the Act, as the case may be";
  • **regulation 35(2)(a) of the MS (Prevention of Oil Pollution) Regulations 1996** (SI 1996/2154), which provides that "In any case where a ship to which these Regulations apply is suspected of a contravention of these Regulations, the ship shall be liable to be detained";
  • **regulation 27 of the MS and FV (Health and Safety at Work) Regulations 1997** (SI 1997/2962), which provides that "A relevant inspector may inspect any United Kingdom ship and if he is satisfied that there has been a failure to comply in relation to that ship with the requirements of these Regulations may detain the ship until the health and safety of all workers and other persons aboard ship is secured, but shall not in the exercise of these powers detain or delay the ship unreasonably".
* Some detention powers, such as those in regulation 27 the Health and Safety at Work Regulations, are exercisable only in relation to a UK ship, while others, such as in the Port State Control Regulations, are also exercisable in relation to a non-UK ship in the UK.

I02e.2a Deficiencies warranting detention

* Numerous grounds for detention are set out in primary and secondary Merchant Shipping legislation, most of them featuring some deficiency or other.
* **Annex VI of MSN 1725** contains the text of the Annexes to **Council Directive 95/21/EC on Port State Control**, Annex VI of which lists numerous examples of deficiencies that may warrant detention, e.g.
  1. Failure of the proper operation of propulsion and other essential machinery, as well as electrical installations.
  2. Absence, non-compliance or serious deterioration of lights, shapes or sound signals.
  3. Absence of corrected navigational charts, and/or all other relevant nautical publications necessary for the intended voyage, taking into account that electronic charts may be used as a substitute for the charts.

I02e.3 Detaining officers

* **Section 284(1) of the Merchant Shipping Act 1995** provides that where a ship is to be or may be detained, any of the following **officers may detain the ship**:
  * any commissioned naval or military officer;
  * any "departmental officer" (i.e. any officer of the Department for Transport, including MCA superintendents and surveyors);
  * any officer of HM Customs and Excise; or
  * any British consular officer.

I02e.4 Detention Notice

* When a ship is to be detained, the detaining officer will serve an appropriate form of **Detention Notice**, which may be either:
  * **Notice of the Detention of a Ship as Dangerously Unsafe** (MCA form MSF 1700) (see I02e.4a); or
  * **Notice of the Detention of a Ship for Failure to Comply with Merchant Shipping Legislation** (MCA form MSF 1701) (see I02e.4b).

I02e.4a Notice of the Detention of a Ship as Dangerously Unsafe

- **states** that the (named) detaining officer, having inspected the (named) ship, is of the opinion that it is unfit to proceed to sea or on a voyage without serious danger to human life having regard to the nature of service for which the vessel is intended. In exercise of the powers in section 95 of the Merchant Shipping Act 1995, the ship is prohibited from going to sea or on a voyage until released by an officer of the Maritime and Coastguard Agency. If applicable, the Chief Officer of Customs will withhold clearance until he receives advice from the detaining officer that the ship has been released.
- **states** the grounds for detention, e.g. "Failure of main engines", "Inoperable emergency fire pump".
- **contains** a notice which states: "***Direction to ship****. Under regulation 9 of the Merchant Shipping (Port State Control) Regulations 1995 the detention notice may include a direction that the ship shall remain in a particular place or move to a particular anchorage or berth. It may also specify circumstances when the master may move the ship from a specified place for reasons of safety or prevention of pollution.*" A space is provided for the detaining officer to insert such a direction.
- **contains** a footnote as follows: "The master is hereby informed that there is a **right of appeal** against this detention notice. Advice on the appeals procedure is contained in a leaflet entitled "Arbitration on Detention of Merchant Ships and Fishing Vessels" which is available from the Detaining Officer".

I02e.4b Notice of the Detention of a Ship for Failure to Comply with Merchant Shipping Legislation

- **states** that the (named) detaining officer, in exercise of power contained in the legislation listed in the notice, detains the ship because it fails to comply fully with statutory requirements. The ship is prohibited from going to sea or on a voyage until released by an officer of the Maritime and Coastguard Agency. If applicable, the Chief Officer of Customs will withhold clearance until he receives advice from the detaining officer that the ship has been released.
- **contains** a two-column table in which the detaining officer will insert (in the first column) the **statutory requirements** and (in the second column) the reasons for non-compliance of the ship.

- **contains** a notice which states: "***Direction to ship***. *Under regulation 9 of the Merchant Shipping (Port State Control) Regulations 1995 the detention notice may include a direction that the ship shall remain in a particular place or move to a particular anchorage or berth. It may also specify circumstances when the master may move the ship from a specified place for reasons of safety or prevention of pollution.*" A space is provided for the detaining officer to insert such a direction.
- **contains** a footnote as follows: "The master is hereby informed that there is a **right of appeal** against this detention notice. Advice on the appeals procedure is contained in a leaflet entitled "Arbitration on Detention of Merchant Ships and Fishing Vessels" which is available from the Detaining Officer".

I02e.4c Service of documents

* **Section 291 of the Merchant Shipping Act 1995** relates to **service of documents** and provides that any document authorised or required to be served on the master of a ship may be served, where there is a master, by leaving it for him on board the ship with the person appearing to be in command or charge of the ship, and where there is no master, on the managing owner of the ship, or where there is no managing owner, on any agent of the owner, or where no such agent is known or can be found, by leaving a copy of the document fixed to the mast of the ship.

I02e.4d Refusal of outwards clearance

* **Section 284(6) of the Merchant Shipping Act 1995** confers on officers of Customs and Excise in the UK the right to **refuse to clear a ship outwards or grant a transire** to the ship in any case where she may be detained under the Act. **If she is actually detained** under the Act, an officer of HM Customs and Excise **must refuse to clear the ship outwards or grant a transire**.

I02e.5 Arbitration on detention and compensation for invalid detention

* **Section 96 of the Merchant Shipping Act 1995** contains provisions dealing with references of detention notices to **arbitration**. Section 97 contains provisions dealing with **compensation** in connection with invalid detention of a ship.

I02e.6 Breach of Detention Notice

* **Section 284(2) of the Merchant Shipping Act 1995** provides that if a ship which has been detained, or which is under notice of or order for detention, **proceeds to sea before release** by a competent authority, the master will be liable -
  * on summary conviction, to a fine not exceeding **£50,000**; and
  * on conviction on indictment, to an **unlimited fine**.
* The owner of a ship, and any person who sends to sea a ship breaching a Detention Order shall, if party or privy to the offence, will also be guilty of an **offence** and liable accordingly (section 284(3)).
* Where a ship proceeding to sea in breach of a Detention Order **takes to sea any of the detaining officers** listed in section 284(1) or any surveyor of ships in the execution of his duty, the owner and master will each be liable to pay all expenses of and incidental to the officer or surveyor being so taken to sea and be guilty of an **offence** (section 284(4)).

I02e.7 Release from detention

* Before a ship is released from detention, the detaining officer or another MCA official on his behalf will issue to the master or the owner's agent or representative a **Notice of Release from Detention under the Merchant Shipping Acts** (MCA form MSF 1702). This states that the detaining officer is satisfied that the defect/s found in the (named) ship has/have been rectified, apart from those defects (if any) which are listed, and that the ship can now be released from detention.

I02e.8 Publication of list of ships under detention in the UK

* The MCA publishes on its website (see B05b.6) a **monthly list of vessels under detention in the UK**. This fulfils the UK government's obligation under section 3.14 of the Paris Memorandum on Port State Control, which requires each participating Authority to, as a minimum, publish quarterly information concerning ships detained during the previous 3-month period and which have been detained more than once during the past 24 months.

I02f DISTRESS ON SHIP

* "**Distress**" means, in English commercial law, the **seizure of goods** for the performance of an obligation.
* **Section 285(1) of the Merchant Shipping Act 1995** provides that when a **master or owner has failed to pay** any seaman's wages, fines or other sums of money as directed by a court order, then the court may -
  * except in Scotland, direct the amount remaining unpaid to be **levied by distress**; and
  * in Scotland, grant warrant authorising the **arrestment and sale of the ship and its equipment**.

I02g HARBOUR AUTHORITY AND HARBOUR MASTER

I02g.1 Powers and duties of UK harbour authorities and harbour masters

* The powers and duties of UK harbour authorities and harbour masters are mainly derived from **statute** (e.g. the Harbours, Docks and Piers Clauses Act 1847), from **local Acts of Parliament** (e.g. the Harwich Harbour Act 1974) and from **statutory orders** (e.g. the Lerwick Harbour Revision Order 1989).
* **Powers to carry out harbour conservancy functions** such as provision of lights and buoys, dredging, and removal of wrecks and other obstructions must generally be conferred by Act of Parliament. British courts have in several cases decided that harbour authorities also have **common law duties** in respect of conservancy, e.g. ".....to take reasonable care so long as they keep a port open for the public use of all who may choose to navigate it, that they may do so without danger to their lives or property".
* In English common law there is a **public right of navigation in tidal waters** which includes a right of anchoring, mooring and grounding in the ordinary course of navigation, subject to payment of proper tolls and dues and to the provision of any statute regulating the harbour (e.g. a **byelaw**).

I02g.2 Harbour byelaws

* UK harbour authorities have wide powers under their own special secondary legislation, derived from Act of Parliament (including the Harbours, Docks and Piers Clauses Act 1847 and the Harbours Act 1964), allowing them to make **byelaws** for regulating the admission to and removal from the harbour of vessels, and for their conduct within the harbour. (For notes on **byelaws** in general, see B04a.3b.)
* **Harbour byelaws** may cover a wide range of subjects, e.g. navigational rules, general duties of masters, movement of hazardous and polluting goods, alcohol and drugs, ferries, lighters, barges and tugs, noise and smoke, recreational craft including water-skiing, jet-biking; bathing, and speed limits.
* **Examples of UK harbour byelaws** are:
  * **Harwich Harbour Byelaws 1994**, made by Harwich Haven Authority in exercise of the powers vested in it by sections 38 and 39 of the Harwich Harbour Act 1974. (See website at www.hha.co.uk/byelaws.htm)
  * **Gloucester Harbour Byelaws** made by Gloucester Harbour Trustees in exercise of the powers conferred by section 83 of the Harbour, Docks and Piers Clauses Act 1847, and article 16 of the Gloucester Harbour Revision Order 1994. (See website at www.gloucesterharbourtrustees.org.uk/laws.htm)
* **Byelaws may be enforced** by the harbour authority within its area of jurisdiction either by officers of the authority who are duly authorised in that behalf, or by any police officer. Penalties for breaches are provided for as with other secondary legislation[16].

---

[16] Section 38 (3) of the Harwich Harbour Act 1974 provides as follows: "Without prejudice to any liability of any person for an offence against any byelaws of the Authority, any person who fails to comply with any direction lawfully given by the Harbour Master under those byelaws shall be liable on summary conviction to a fine not exceeding level 3 on the standard scale".

I02g.2a General directions and special directions

* In exercise of their powers under the relevant legislation, harbour authorities and harbour masters may regulate shipping within their harbours by two kinds of **direction**[17]:
    * **general directions** under which the harbour authority may regulate the movement, etc. of shipping within the harbour (e.g. Harwich Haven Authority's *General Directions for Navigation 1994*); and
    * **special directions** which the harbour master may give to particular ships on particular occasions (e.g. to all ships in approach channels, etc. when a tanker is manoeuvring).
* **General directions** may be made for a particular harbour (for example) -
    * for designating areas, routes or channels in the harbour which vessels are to use or refrain from using for movement or mooring;
    * for securing that vessels move only at certain times or during certain periods;
    * for securing that vessels make use of descriptions of navigation aids specified in the direction;
    * for prohibiting -
    * entry into or movement in the harbour by vessels at times of poor visibility due to the weather or any other condition;
    * entry into the harbour by a vessel which for any reason would be or be likely to become a danger to other vessels in the harbour; and
    * entry into or navigation within any main navigation channel during any temporary obstruction thereof;
    * requiring the master of a vessel to give to the harbour master information relating to the vessel reasonably required by the harbour master for effecting any of the purposes of this paragraph.
* A **general direction** may apply (for example) -
    * to all vessels or to a class of vessels designated in the direction; or to the whole of the harbour or to a part designated in the direction; or
    * at all times or at times designated in the direction.
* A **special direction** may (for example) be given by the harbour master to a vessel anywhere in the harbour, requiring it to comply with a requirement made in or under a general direction and, so far as required for the ease, convenience or safety of navigation, for either of the following purposes -
    * regulating or requiring the movement, mooring or unmooring of a vessel;
    * regulating the manner in which a vessel takes in or discharges cargo, fuel, water or ship's stores otherwise than at a dock or pier.

I02g.3 Powers under the Dangerous Vessels Act 1985

* **Section 1(1) of the Dangerous Vessels Act 1985** (c.22) allows a harbour master to give **directions to a master** (or to a **salvor** in possession) prohibiting the entry into, or requiring the removal from, the harbour of any vessel if, in his opinion, the condition of the vessel, or the nature or condition of anything it contains, is such that its presence in the harbour might involve:
    * grave and imminent danger to the safety of any person or property (including ships and their crews); or
    * grave and imminent risk (i.e. not necessarily accompanied by imminent danger) that the vessel may, by sinking or foundering in the harbour, prevent or seriously prejudice the use of the harbour by other vessels.
* The directions may be given to the owner, the master or the salvor (or any servant or agent of the salvor in possession of the vessel and who is in charge of the salvage operation) (section 1(2)). They may be given in any reasonable manner (section 1(4)). The harbour master must state his grounds for giving them (section 1(5)).
* **Section 3** of the Act gives the **MCA powers to override a harbour master's directions** which have prohibited a vessel from entering a harbour, or have required its removal from the harbour. This power can only be exercised for the purpose of securing the **safety** of any person or vessel, including the vessel directed.
* The maximum penalty for failing to comply with a direction under the Dangerous Vessels Act 1985 is £25,000 on summary conviction, or on conviction on indictment, a fine.
* Masters should bear in mind that **harbour masters in foreign ports** may have wider powers than their UK counterparts, and that penalties for disobeying a harbour master's directions may be more severe than those stated above.

---

[17] Article 11 of the Gloucester Harbour Revision Order 1994 permits Gloucester Harbour Trustees to give general directions, while Article 12 allows the Gloucester harbour master to give special directions.

I02g.4 Powers under the Dangerous Substances in Harbour Areas Regulations 1987

* The carriage and handling of dangerous goods in ports is currently governed by the **Dangerous Substances in Harbours Areas Regulations 1987**[18] (SI 1987/37) (DSHAR), which are based on the **IMO Recommendations** on the Safe Transport Handling and Storage of Dangerous Substances in Port Areas.
* **Regulation 6** requires notice to be given of the **entry of dangerous goods** into a harbour or harbour area. This requirement overlaps with the requirements of the MS (Reporting Requirements for Ships Carrying Dangerous or Polluting Goods) Regulations 1995 (SI 1995/2498) (see H06e.1).
* With certain exceptions, **regulation 33** requires an explosives licence to be obtained before any explosive may be brought into or carried or handled within, a harbour or harbour area, or in certain cases loaded or unloaded outside a harbour or harbour area.

I02g.5 Power to deny entry to ports or offshore terminals

* **Regulation 35(1) of the MS (Prevention of Oil Pollution) Regulations 1996** (SI 1996/2154) provides that if a harbour master has reason to believe that a ship which he believes proposes to enter the harbour does not comply with the requirements of the Regulations, he must immediately **inform the MCA** (in exercise of the powers of "the Secretary of State"). If the MCA is satisfied that the ship presents an **unreasonable threat of harm** to the marine environment, **it may deny entry** of the ship to UK ports or offshore terminals.
* Under regulation 35(2)(a), if a vessel **enters a UK port or offshore terminal in contravention of an MCA ban**, she is liable to be **detained** (see I02e).

I02g.6 Power to inspect Oil Record Books

* Under **regulation 10(6) of the Prevention of Oil Pollution) Regulations 1996** (SI 1996/2154), authority is given to **harbour masters and any other persons employed by a harbour authority** to:
  * **inspect the Oil Record Book** on board any ship required to carry an ORB under the MS (Prevention of Oil Pollution) Regulations (i.e. tankers of 150gt and over and other ships of 400gt and over) whilst the ship is in a harbour in the UK; and
  * **make a copy of any entry** in the ORB; and
  * **require the ship's master** to certify that the copy is a true copy of that entry.
* Under section 259(6) of the Merchant Shipping Act 1995 a harbour master (or other person appointed by the DfT for the purpose) may **inspect and copy an entry in any Oil Record Book** or other document carried on any ship for the purpose of ascertaining the circumstances relating to an alleged discharge of oil or a mixture containing oil from the ship into the harbour. This provision covers tankers of under 150gt and other ships of under 400gt, which are not covered by the MS (Prevention of Oil Pollution) Regulations.

I02g.7 Power to detain ships for pollution offences

* **Section 144 of the Merchant Shipping Act 1995** provides that where a harbour master has reason to believe that the master or owner of a ship has committed an offence under section 131 of the Merchant Shipping Act 1995 by the discharge from the ship of oil, or a mixture containing oil, into the waters of the harbour, **the harbour master may detain the ship**.
* Where a harbour master detains a **non-UK ship** he must immediately notify the MCA, who must then inform the consul or diplomatic representative or maritime authorities of the flag State.
* A harbour master who detains a ship must immediately release the ship -
  * if no proceedings for the offence are instituted within 7 days from the day of detention;
  * if proceedings are concluded without the master or owner being convicted; or
  * if either:
    * £55,000 in security is paid to the harbour authority by way of security; or
    * security satisfactory to the harbour authority, but not less than £55,000 -
    is paid by or on behalf of the master or owner (e.g. by the owner's P&I club); or

---

[18] In May 2000 the Health and Safety Commission, in response to a need to update the DSHAR Regulations, produced proposals for new Regulations covering the carriage and handling of dangerous goods in harbours. The revised Regulations, to be called the Dangerous Goods in Harbours Regulations (DGHR), will incorporate the provisions of Amendment 30 to the IMDG Code, which will have the effect of bringing the Harbour Regulations in line with the legislation applicable to dangerous goods travelling by road and rail.

- where the master or owner is convicted of the offence, if any costs ordered to be paid by him, and any fine imposed on him, have been paid.
* The harbour authority must repay the security given if no proceedings are commenced within 7 days from the date of payment, or if the court fails to convict the owner or master.
* Section 144 does not apply to HM warships or UK Government ships.
* **Regulation 37 of the MS (Prevention of Oil Pollution) Regulations 1996** (SI 1996/2154) sets out the conditions for release of a ship detained for breach of the oil pollution regulations. SI 1997/1910 amends these regulations and increases the sum of security required for release from £55,000 to £255,000.

I02g.8 Power to board ships to serve documents

* **Section 143(1)(b) of the Merchant Shipping Act 1995** allows a harbour authority to bring legal **proceedings** for an offence under Part VI, Chapter II of the Act (Oil Pollution), e.g. where a ship has discharged oil into the harbour (section 131), or where pollution has not been reported to the harbour authority (section 136).
* **Section 143(7)** provides that any person authorised to serve any document for the purposes of the institution of, or otherwise in connection with, proceedings for an offence under Chapter II of the Act will, **for that purpose**, have the right to **go on board** the ship in question.

I02g.9 Port Marine Safety Code

* **The Port Marine Safety Code** -
    - was **published** by the DETR (now DfT) in March 2000.[19]
    - **introduces** a UK **national standard** for every aspect of port marine safety.
    - **aims** to improve safety for those who use or work in ports, their ships, passengers and cargoes, and the environment.
    - **establishes** a measure by which harbour authorities can be accountable for the legal powers and duties which they have to run their harbours safely.
    - **contains** two main parts. **Part 1** concerns Harbour Authorities' Duties and Powers. **Part 2** concerns Measures.
    - **contains the following sections in Part 1**: 1.1. Background; 1.2. General Duties and Powers; 1.3. Specific Duties and Powers; 1.4. Revising Duties and Powers; 1.5. Accountability for Marine Safety; 1.6. Dues.
    - **contains the following sections in Part 2**: 2.1. Setting a Standard; 2.2. Risk Assessment and Safety Management; 2.3. Conservancy Duties; 2.4. Regulation and Management of Navigation; 2.5. Pilotage; 2.6. Pilotage Exemption; 2.7. Marine Services.
* The Code contains much information of interest and relevance to **shipmasters using UK ports**, such as the sections regulation and management of navigation, and on pilotage and pilotage exemption.
* The Code is downloadable from the DfT website at www.dft.gov.uk

I02g.10 Notifications to harbour authorities

* **Section 135(1) of the Merchant Shipping Act 1995** provides that no oil may be transferred between sunset and sunrise from ship in any harbour in the UK unless the requisite **notice** has been given in accordance with section 135 or the transfer is for the purposes of a **fire brigade**. Under section 135(3) the notice must be given between 3 and 96 hours before the transfer begins. A **general notice** may be given under section 135(2) to cover frequent transfers between sunset and sunrise for a maximum of 12 months. Where oil is transferred from a ship in contravention of section 135, section 135(5) makes the master of the ship liable. Where the oil is transferred to or from a place on land, the occupier of that place (e.g. the terminal operator) will also be liable.
* **Under section 136**, if any **mixture containing oil is discharged** from a ship into the waters of a harbour in the UK, or is found **to be escaping or to have escaped** from a ship into any such waters, the owner or **master** must immediately **report the occurrence to the harbour master** or, where there is no harbour master, the **harbour authority**, stating whether it is a discharge or an escape.

---

[19] Following the grounding of the tanker *Sea Empress*, and the subsequent MAIB report of July 1997, a review of the Pilotage Act 1987 was undertaken by Lord Donaldson. His review concluded that a national standard must be set for the discharge of harbour authorities' responsibilities for marine safety. The Port Marine Safety Code was published for that purpose.

I02g.11 Duty of UK port authorities under Port State Control Regulations

* **Regulation 15(3) of the MS (Port State Control) Regulations 1995** (SI 1995/3128), as amended, provides that if a **port authority**, when exercising its normal duties, learns that a ship to which Part I of the Regulations applies (see I02c.3) within its port has **deficiencies** which may **prejudice the safety** of the ship or which pose an **unreasonable threat of harm** to the marine environment, the authority must immediately **inform the MCA**.

I02h REPORTING WRECK

I02h.1 Wreck and wreck law

* **The law on wreck** is contained in sections 231-255 of the Merchant Shipping Act 1995.
* "**Wreck**" includes **jetsam**, **flotsam**, **lagan** and **derelict** found in or on the shores of the sea or any tidal water (section 255(1) Merchant Shipping Act 1995). "**Jetsam**" means goods or cargo jettisoned from a vessel. "**Flotsam**" means floating wreckage (e.g. wreckage of a ship or cargo, such as a floating container). "**Lagan**" means goods, cargo or wreckage at the bottom of sea, including goods attached to a buoy with a view to later recovery. A "**derelict**" is an abandoned vessel, ownerless at sea without hope or intention of recovery.
* **Fishing boats or fishing gear** lost or abandoned at sea and either found or taken possession of within UK waters, or found or taken possession of beyond UK waters and brought within UK waters, must be dealt with as "wreck" for the purposes of Part IX of the Merchant Shipping Act 1995 (section 255(2), Merchant Shipping Act 1995).
* Wreck law on is closely associated with salvage law, and the **Protection of Wrecks Act 1973** and the **Protection of Military Remains Act 1986** impose duties on the finders or salvors of wreck. (These Acts are more likely to concern divers who find and salve wreck than masters.)
* **Items found in non-tidal waters** are treated as if they were found on land, and are dealt with under other legislation (e.g. the Treasure Act 1996, and the Ancient Monuments and Archaeological Areas Act 1979).

I02h.2 Receiver of Wreck

* **The UK government official in charge of wreck** is the **Receiver of Wreck**. For notes on the functions and **powers of the Receiver**, which are prescribed by the Merchant Shipping Act 1995, see B05b.3b.

I02h.3 Procedure on finding wreck

* **All wreck** (as defined in I02h.1), **found within UK national or territorial waters** (i.e. within the "12-mile limit" – see I01a.1a), or **found outside UK waters and brought within UK waters**, must, under section 236(1) of the Merchant Shipping Act 1995, be reported to the Receiver of Wreck. **All material**, from ships and cargo containers to small coins on the seabed, must be reported, no matter how small and seemingly insignificant; it is up to the Receiver to decide whether the material is important as wreck.
* **If the finder is not the owner of the wreck**, a **Report of Wreck and Salvage form** (known as a "**Droit form**") must be obtained from the Receiver, a Coastguard station or HM Customs & Excise, and must be completed and sent to the Receiver at Southampton (see address in B05b.3b). (Report forms can be downloaded from the MCA web site.) Once a report has been received, the Receiver will **investigate ownership** of the wreck items. The Receiver is required to notify **Lloyds** of recovered property considered to be in excess of the value of £5000. Finders should assume that all recovered wreck has an **owner**. This may, for example, be an individual, a company, a dive club, an insurance company, the Ministry of Defence (MOD) or the Department for Transport (DfT). The finder **may be allowed to keep** any items of wreck reported, subject to agreement with the Receiver.
* The owner has **12 months** from the date of the Report in which to come forward and **prove title** to the property. The Receiver will try to locate the owner, and the finder has a duty to assist in this task. During this period the goods are legally **under the control of the Receiver** but the finder is normally allowed to hold them on an indemnity to the MCA (see reverse page of the Report form) and may not use or dispose of them. If the owner wants the goods returned he will first have to settle **salvage** with the legal finder. If at the end of the 12-month period the owner has not been traced, the goods will be disposed of.
* The Crown makes no claim on **unclaimed wreck recovered from outside UK territorial waters** and the goods may be returned to the finder as salvor. The goods may be released to the finder, if he wishes, on payment of any related **expenses** incurred by the Receiver of Wreck in the 12-month period, and any **Customs charges** owing.

* **If the wreck was recovered from within UK territorial waters and no owner establishes a claim** to the property within one year of it being reported to the Receiver, then it generally becomes **property of the Crown** and is disposed of at the discretion of the Receiver of Wreck through **sale or auction**, or **offered to the salvor in lieu of salvage**. If the goods are sold, once all costs have been deducted from the money raised, the finder will be awarded a sum as a **salvage reward**. This does not preclude the finder from making a bid for the goods.
* **In certain cases** the **Receiver of Wreck may sell the goods before 12 months have elapsed**, but no salvage award will be made until the 12 months have expired.
* **If the owner of the goods claims them before 12 months have passed**, the finder may be entitled to a salvage reward. The goods will not be released to its owner until any outstanding charges have been paid, including any salvage award made. The level of the salvage award, if any, is a matter for a civil court to decide and not the Receiver of Wreck.
* **If the finder is also the owner of the goods** he must still advise the Receiver of Wreck of the salvage, describing how the goods can be recognised. He will also be required to pay any Customs charges on the goods.
* Goods reported to the Receiver of Wreck, the importation of which is prohibited, will be seized by Customs and not returned. If a licence is required to import the goods into the UK they will be detained by Customs until the licence has been obtained. If a licence is refused, the goods will be seized.
* **Failure to report wreck** and concealment of such goods are **offences** under Merchant Shipping legislation which may render the finder to prosecution and a fine[20].
* **Failure to declare goods** liable to charges, evasion of Customs charges and the importation of goods to which a prohibition or restriction applies are **offences** under Customs legislation and may lead to prosecution, with fine or imprisonment or both.
* **Goods found which are not wreck**, such as the property of seamen, should be handed in to the local police station.
* **It is an offence** to take into a foreign port and **sell**:
  * any vessel stranded, derelict or otherwise in distress found on or near the coasts of the UK or any tidal water within UK waters;
  * any part of the cargo or equipment of, or anything belonging to, such a vessel; or
  * any wreck found within those waters (section 245 Merchant Shipping Act 1995).
* **The master of a vessel may forcibly repel** any person boarding, or attempting to board, without the master's permission, any vessel which is wrecked, stranded or in distress (section 246 Merchant Shipping Act 1995).

I02i PORT OF REFUGE BUSINESS

I02i.1 Deviation to port of refuge

I02i.1a What constitutes a port of refuge

* A "**port of refuge**" is a port or place that a vessel diverts to when her master considers it **unsafe to continue the voyage** due to a **peril** that threatens the "**common safety**", e.g. when there is a dangerous ingress of water into the vessel, a dangerous shift of cargo, the vessel adopts an angle of loll, there is a serious fire on board, etc. Where such a deviation is **for the preservation from peril of property involved in a common maritime adventure**, it will usually constitute a **general average act** and the costs of the deviation to and stay at the port of refuge will be allowed in **general average** (see G06a).
* In recent years there have several well-publicised incidents in which **ships which have been turned away from ports** or waters to which they were making for reasons of safety[21]. In one case, where the Irish State authorities had turned a ship away from Irish territorial waters and the shipowner had sought an indemnity in respect of the refusal of refuge, the Irish court considered that, despite the established custom whereby a stricken merchant ship has a right to expect access to a port of refuge in times of peril, a new custom is evolving to **refuse access** to some ships which pose grave and imminent danger to coastal waters, particularly when a refusal of refuge would result solely in economic loss, for example where the crew has been or can be airlifted to safety.

---

[20] A **person in breach** (without reasonable excuse) of the **duty to report wreck** under section 236(1) of the Merchant Shipping Act 1995 will be liable, on summary conviction, to a maximum fine of Level 4. If he is not the owner of the wreck he will also **forfeit any claim to salvage** and be liable to **pay twice the value of the wreck to its owner** (if it is claimed) or to the person entitled to the wreck (if it is unclaimed).

[21] The most notable of these incidents is that involving the tanker *Castor* in January 2001.

I02i.1b Justifiable deviation

* Where the shipowner or carrier is a party to a contract of carriage, discontinuation of the voyage is a **deviation** from the contract. A deviation to a port of refuge will be regarded as a **justifiable deviation** if the reason can be shown to be a valid one within the terms of the contract. All contractual rights would, in that case, be unaffected.
* If the reason for deviating could not be shown to be valid, the deviation would be considered **unjustifiable** and the consequences could be severe for the shipowner or carrier, in that it would probably constitute a **repudiatory breach** of the contract, making the owner/carrier liable for all costs of any accident to ship or cargo sustained during the deviation.
* **Valid reasons** for deviating to a port of refuge usually include:
  * weather, collision or grounding damage affecting seaworthiness of the ship;
  * serious fire;
  * dangerous shift of cargo;
  * serious machinery breakdown;
  * any other accident causing some serious threat to the vessel and cargo;
  * shortage of bunkers (if it can be proved that the vessel left port with adequate bunkers for the foreseeable voyage, and ran short as a consequence of weathering exceptionally severe weather, contamination, etc.).

I02i.1c General average aspects of deviation

* "**Port of refuge**" is a term usually associated with a **general average act** since, under the York-Antwerp Rules (1974 and 1994 editions), certain **costs and expenses incurred in making for, entering, staying at and leaving** a port or place of refuge, even where the ship returns to her port or place of loading, are admitted as general average[22].
* **Paragraph (a) of Rule X (Expenses at Port of Refuge, etc.)** of the York-Antwerp Rules 1994 provides that "When a ship shall have entered a port or place of refuge or shall have returned to her port or place of loading in consequence of accident, sacrifice or other extraordinary circumstances which render that necessary for the common safety, the expenses of entering such port or place shall be admitted as general average; and when she shall have sailed thence with her original cargo, or a part of it, the corresponding expenses of leaving such port or place of refuge consequent upon such entry or return shall likewise be admitted as general average."
* **Where there is no "common maritime adventure"**, or there was a "common maritime adventure" but the cause of the deviation was not an accident, sacrifice or other extraordinary circumstance that was necessary for the common safety, the expenses will not be admitted as general average. For example, where a reefer ship's refrigerating machinery has failed during a loaded voyage, necessitating urgent repairs in order to preserve the cargo, the deviation expenses will not be admitted as general average since the safety of the ship herself is not at risk.
* Port expenses resulting from an accident to cargo that compromises the safety of the ship (e.g. a shift of a bulk cargo necessitating a re-stow) will normally be admitted as general average. Expenses resulting from a cargo fire in one hold (e.g. containing fishmeal) will be admissible as general average, since the fire threatens the safety of the entire ship and other cargo.
* **Paragraph (a) of Rule X** continues: "When a ship is at any port or place of refuge and is necessarily removed to another port or place because repairs cannot be carried out in the first port or place, the provisions of this Rule shall be applied to the second port or place as if it were a port or place of refuge and the cost of such removal including temporary repairs and towage shall be admitted as general average. The provisions of Rule XI shall be applied to the prolongation of the voyage occasioned by such removal."
* The term "**safe haven**" is often used in documents relating to "port of refuge incidents", but is not mentioned in the York-Antwerp Rules.
* **A port or place where a vessel seeks temporary shelter** from adverse weather is **not a port of refuge**, since running for shelter is "ordinary" practice and not "extraordinary" in the context of Rule A of the York-Antwerp Rules.

I02i.2 Termination of the adventure and declaration of general average

* A "common maritime adventure" is said to be **terminated** on completion of discharge of cargo (or disembarkationof passengers) at the **port of destination** following a general average act. If the voyage is **abandoned** at an intermediate port (e.g. a port of refuge), then the adventure terminates at that port.
* A **declaration of general average** should be formally made in compliance with local law and custom before delivery of cargo at the termination of the voyage, in order to initiate an adjustment. The declaration is usually made

---

[22] The term arises in two rules: Rule X. Expenses at port of refuge etc., and Rule XI. Wages and maintenance of crew and other expenses. bearing up for and in a port of refuge, etc.

by the shipowner or the master, but in some countries any one of the interested parties may make it. The owners or agent should be able to advise on local requirements.

* Following the declaration, the **adjustment** (i.e. assessment) of the general average by an **average adjuster** may begin. This may take many months. For notes on **functions of average adjuster,** see G02b.3.

I02i.3 Security for general average contributions

* A carrier or shipowner has a **common law lien** on cargo in his possession for its contribution to a general average, this being a condition of delivery of the cargo. Possession of the cargo is the carrier's/shipowner's only guarantee that the cargo owners will pay the required contributions without costly court actions to enforce this.
* **In practice**, general average contributions take months or even years to be assessed, so it is not normal for the shipowner to exercise his lien on cargo for the full contribution. Instead, he exercises the lien on some form of **security** pending the final adjustment.
* It becomes the duty of the **master** (or the ship's **agent** on behalf of the master) to obtain an **acceptable security** for the cargo's general average contribution before delivering the cargo to receivers.
* **Acceptable general average security** may be given in the form of:
  * a **general average deposit** (paid by cargo receivers) (see I02i.3a);
  * a **general average bond** (i.e. a signed promise by the receivers to pay their general average charges when known) (see I02i.3a);
  * a **general average guarantee** (a promise from cargo underwriters to pay the required contribution without the collection of a deposit) (see I02i.3b),
  - or a **combination** of two of the above, e.g. a bond backed by a guarantee.
* **Special charges** -
  - are expenses reasonably incurred for the preservation or recovery of the **cargo alone** (and not for the "common safety" as with general average), e.g. the costs of **reconditioning** damaged goods.
  - form a **direct charge against the cargo** in respect of which they were incurred; the shipowner therefore has a lien on the goods in his possession in this respect, and adequate security to cover any special charges should therefore be obtained from the receiver before delivery of the goods. (Lloyd's Average Bond and Lloyd's Average Guarantee forms cover special charges in addition to general average, avoiding the need for separate security.)

I02i.3a General average bonds and deposits

* The **average adjuster** will, on his appointment, make an **estimate** of the loss or damage and the **rate of contribution** required from each party to the common maritime adventure (e.g. 10% of the total arrived value of their property).
* **Each owner of cargo saved** by the general average act must then sign a **general average bond**, wherein, in return for delivery to them or to their order of the goods noted in the bond, they agree to pay the proper proportion of any general average charges which may later be ascertained to be due from the goods.
* **Receivers** agree also to furnish particulars of the **value** of the goods and make a **general average deposit** of an amount certified by the adjuster to be due.
* In return for the general average bond and deposit, the cargo is **delivered** to the receivers or to their order.
* **Lloyd's forms** of bond and deposit receipt are commonly used, i.e. **Lloyd's Average Bond** and **Lloyd's Average Deposit Receipt**.
* **Cargo should never be delivered** after a general average act until a **general average bond** has been signed and the required **deposit** has been collected. As evidence of their deposits, receivers are issued with a **general average deposit receipt**; these must never be issued in duplicate.

I02i.3b General average guarantees

* A **General Average Guarantee** is a **cargo underwriter's signed guarantee** given in consideration of delivery of the goods to the consignees without collection of a **general average deposit** in those cases when it is practicable to do so. The form commonly used is called an **Average Guarantee**. **Lloyd's Average Guarantee form** is commonly used.

I02i.4 Port of refuge procedure

* **Procedure at any particular port or place of refuge** will obviously vary with the circumstances surrounding the event necessitating the ship's arrival, but in general, the following basic steps should be followed.
* **As soon as the decision is taken** to discontinue the voyage and make for a port or place of refuge, (whether under tow or otherwise) **inform the owner and charterer** (if any), stating the reason for the deviation. Give relevant details to duty superintendent; he will probably call the company's insurance manager, who will contact appropriate insurers' staff. In case of hull or machinery damage, the owner's staff will contact the classification society, who will inform their local surveyor.
* Record the **ship's position**. Sound tanks for quantity of bunkers on board. From this point until departure from the port or place of refuge, **keep accurate records** of events and expenditure, etc., for eventual delivery to the owner and average adjuster.
* Request the owner to arrange the appointment of an **agent** at the port of refuge to handle the vessel's visit.
* **If under tow**, see notes on salvage at H05.
* If the cause of the deviation is an "**accident**" as defined in the **MS (Accident Reporting and Investigation) Regulations**, inform MAIB (see E08k or **MGN 115** for numbers and procedure).
* **Call the agent** as soon as his identity is known. Pass ETA and information necessary for making preparations for the vessel's arrival, including tonnage, length, flag, P&I club, classification society, etc. Request the **agent to notify**:
  * port State Administration if vessel is damaged or seaworthiness is affected;
  * harbour master or port authority. Inform port authority of the full facts, as the authority may want to keep vessel outside port until cargo discharged, etc. Give details of the nature and severity of damage, mentioning any disabled navaids, steering gear, machinery, etc. State any pollution hazard.
  * pilot station, linesmen, boatman, customs, port health, immigration, etc.
  * local correspondent of the owner's P&I club. (See club handbook for name and address, or ask owners.) A representative from the correspondent firm, or a surveyor appointed by the correspondent, should attend on arrival.
* **On arrival at the port or place of refuge**, the salvor (if any) will require **salvage security**, which should be arranged by the owner and cargo owners. Failing this, the salvor may have vessel **arrested** pending satisfaction of his claim.
* **Obtain health clearance** in accordance with local regulations (as advised by the agent).
* **Enter vessel in** with customs "under average".
* **Inform the owner** (and charterer, if any) of vessel's safe arrival.
* Owners will **declare general average**. (Any of the parties involved may declare general average, but the owners will normally do this since they are closest to "the action".)
* **Note protest** as soon as possible but in any case within 24 hours, in compliance with local custom (ask the agent about this), reserving the right "to extend at a time and place convenient".
* **Where there is hull or machinery damage**, the owner will notify his insurance broker if the port of refuge is in the UK. Abroad, the agent should be requested to **notify local Lloyd's Agent** (a requirement of the Notice of Claim and Tenders Clause in Institute Time Clauses - Hulls 1.10.83).
* **Hull and machinery underwriters** normally instruct a **surveyor**, in major cases from the **Salvage Association** (see G02b.2).
* **Where there is hull or machinery damage**, a class surveyor, if available at the port, will inspect and report on the damage, stipulating repairs necessary for the vessel to maintain class. Temporary repairs may be acceptable.
* **If no class surveyor is available**, the class society should be contacted, and will advise the appropriate steps to take in order for class to be maintained until a port can be reached for survey. (Thanks to the ease of modern communications, the old practice of requesting two independent masters or engineers to inspect temporary repairs and issue a **Certificate of Seaworthiness** should no longer be necessary. Even where a class surveyor cannot reach a damaged ship, the classification society can usually be notified of the damage and asked for instructions.)
* **If cargo damage is probable**, or cargo discharge is necessary before repairs can be made, **call a hatch survey** before commencing discharge. Employ only registered and unbiased surveyors recommended by the P&I club correspondent. Cargo interests should be notified so that they can appoint their own surveyors. Remember that cargo surveyors are appointed by cargo interests and may criticise the master's actions or allege that the vessel was unseaworthy. Be guided by the P&I club correspondent as to who to allow on board and about making statements which may adversely affect the owner's legal position (see I05g.1).
* **If the voyage is being terminated** and cargo owners are taking delivery of their consignments, **General Average Bond** and **General Average Guarantee** forms will first have to be signed (see I02i.3a and I02i.3b). The **owner's lien on cargo** should be exercised if necessary; this should be discussed with the owner and agent.
* **Arrange cargo discharge** (under survey) and either **trans-shipment or warehousing** of cargo during the repairs, if necessary. (This will depend on the length of time in port, nature of cargo, etc.)

* **On receipt of class surveyor's report** re- hull/machinery damage, the owner will advertise for tenders. (Superintendents and the Salvage Association surveyor will jointly attend to this, bearing in mind the Notice of Claim and Tenders Clause and underwriters' power of veto. Tenders should only be accepted with guidance from Salvage Association surveyor and Lloyd's or IUA Agent.)
* **Carry out repairs** under class and Salvage Association surveyors' guidance.
* **On completion of repairs**, class surveyor will carry out another survey. If, in his opinion, the vessel is seaworthy he will issue an **Interim Certificate of Class**, and will send his report to the classification society. If acceptable to the society's committee, the vessel will **retain class**. If the class surveyor is employed by an authorised society, he may also issue **provisional statutory certificates** on behalf of MCA (or other flag State Administration) to enable the vessel to continue her voyage.
* **Reload cargo** (under survey) if voyage being continued.
* **Extend Protest** to include all details of the damage and repairs. Obtain copies for owners.
* **Port agent will pay repairers.** (If unpaid, repairers will have a **maritime lien** on the vessel.) Allow general average and Salvage Association surveyors (representing H&M insurers) to see the agent's account before paying.
* **Send all relevant documents to the owner** for onwards delivery to the average adjuster.
* **Enter vessel outwards** with Customs (in accordance with local regulations, as advised by the agent). Obtain **outwards clearance**.
* Continue the voyage.

I02i.5 Evidence required at port of refuge

* In most general average cases the main evidence required for the adjustment comes from the various **survey reports**, supported by **statements by witnesses** and **ship's records**, as listed below.
* Full and accurate records should be kept of the general average incident and the call at the port of refuge, including details of all the various parties involved and their actions.
* **Photographs and video footage** may be useful; the general average statement may take more than a year to produce.
* **Where salvage services are engaged**, a full record should be kept of the salvor's actions and of the equipment used by both parties.
* In order to assess the various **contributory values**, the average adjuster will require the following documents:
  * all general average security documents including signed average bonds, average guarantees, counterfoils of average deposit receipts and cancelled deposit receipts;
  * casualty reports from the master;
  * certified extracts from deck and engine room logs;
  * copies of extended protests;
  * survey reports on hull and machinery damage;
  * survey reports on cargo lost or damaged by general average sacrifice;
  * account sales of any cargo sold;
  * copies of any shipping invoices;
  * copies of telexes;
  * accounts for disbursements incurred together with all supporting vouchers;
  * cargo valuation forms;
  * manifest of cargo onboard at time of the general average act;
  * copies of bills of lading;
  * portage account for the voyage, and an account of stores consumed;
  * any other evidence relating to the casualty.

I02i.6 Personnel likely to visit the ship in connection with a general average act

- will usually include:
  * **owners' representatives** (e.g. marine or engineer superintendents);
  * port **agent**;
  * a surveyor on behalf of combined **general average interests** (who may be referred to as the "general average surveyor");
  * a surveyor on behalf of the **hull and machinery underwriters**;
  * a surveyor on behalf of **loss-of-hire underwriters**;
  * an independent surveyor on behalf of **cargo interests**;

- a **salvage master** (who is owners' consultant);
- a **class surveyor** (from ship's classification society);
- various **contractors' representatives** (from firms involved throughout the salvage, etc.);
- various other local **officials** (marine Administration, port State control, customs, immigration, port health, etc.).

* One or more of the **surveyors** instructed are likely to be from the **Salvage Association** (see G02b.2), although each surveyor so instructed will usually be representing a different principal.

I03 Port business with commercial parties

I03a P&I CLUB CORRESPONDENT

I03a.1 When to contact the Club correspondent

* For notes on the **nature and functions of P&I club correspondents**, see G02a.3d.

* The correspondent of the P&I club in which the ship is entered should be contacted in the following circumstances:
- when the ship has been in **collision** with another vessel, or with a "fixed or floating object", such as a quay or navigation mark;
- when there has been a **bunker spill** or any other form of **pollution**;
- when any **cargo is damaged** during the voyage;
- when a crew member, passenger or other person on board (including stevedores) suffers an **injury**;
- when **stowaways** are found on board;
- when the ship is **detained**;
- when the ship is **arrested**;
- when the ship is **fined**;
- when a crew member is being **left behind** in the port (ill, injured, jailed, AWOL, etc.);
- when a crew member is to be **repatriated** after being left behind;
- when there has been a **General Average** act or sacrifice;
- when there is a problem with a **cargo document** such as a bill of lading or sea waybill;
- when in any doubt about the **identity or authority of surveyors**, lawyers or other parties claiming to have lawful access to the ship or business on board, or seeking to interview crew members, etc.

I03a.2 Identifying the Club correspondent

* The leading P&I clubs provide a **list of correspondents** in booklet form to each entered ship, listing the port, company name and contact details of every correspondent serving the club.

* In the absence of such a publication on board, the master should be able to obtain the contact details from the shipowner or manager, from the ship's agent, or from the club managers. (For website addresses of P&I clubs, see G02a.3a.)

I03b SURVEYORS

I03b.1 Identification of surveyors

* In some cases it may not be clear to the master or crew members exactly what a particular surveyor's **function** on board is, or who his **principal** is. It is always important to determine the identity of any visitor to the ship, and particularly important following an incident such as a collision or accident for which the shipowner may have some liability, when surveyors representing various parties involved may attempt to obtain information.

* All surveyors should carry an official **identification card** or document, which should be asked for and inspected by the master. Where there is any doubt about the identity or legitimate interests on board of a surveyor, the owner's P&I club correspondent should be consulted. For notes on **legal considerations** relating to visitors on board, see I05g.1.

I03b.2 Class surveyors

-   include "**exclusive**" surveyors employed by and working exclusively for one classification society, such as Lloyd's Register of Shipping.
-   include "**non-exclusive**" surveyors who may be appointed by and carry out surveys for more than one organisation.
-   are employed by classification societies to carry out both **class and statutory** survey work.
-   may issue Interim Certificates of Class after satisfactory completion of survey work in port.
-   are not permitted (by the major societies) to issue full term Certificates of Class (which can normally only be issued by the society's head office after receipt of the surveyor's report).
-   carry out **statutory surveys** and issue statutory certificates only when authorised to do so by a flag State Administration. A large society such as Lloyd's Register will usually hold authorisations from numerous governments to carry out a wide range of surveys for different international certificates, and will carry out these surveys both abroad and, in many cases, in the flag State's own ports.
*   For notes on **surveys required under classification society rules**, see D02d.

I03b.3 Marine Administration surveyors

-   include **flag State Administration surveyors** and **port State Administration surveyors**.
-   are generally employed by the marine Administration of a country, e.g. the Maritime and Coastguard Agency (MCA) on behalf of the Department for Transport in the UK, the US Coast Guard in the USA, AMSA in Australia, etc.
-   have statutory **powers to inspect and, where necessary, detain ships**, as outlined (in the case of UK surveyors) in B05b.4.
-   carry out **statutory surveys and inspections of flag State ships** as required by the State's merchant shipping law, including surveys for issue, continued validity and renewal of international and national certificates.
-   carry out **surveys of foreign vessels** for issue, continued validity and renewal of international certificates at the request of and on behalf of the flag State Administration. (Although these surveys are the responsibility of the flag State Administration, in practice they are often delegated to other bodies including overseas Administrations and classification societies.)
-   carry out **measurement surveys** for registry and tonnage purposes where these are not carried out by a classification society (e.g. on an unclassed vessel).
-   carry out **accident investigations** and inspections (although in many states this is now a function of a dedicated accident investigation agency).
-   carry out **port State control inspections** of foreign ships in the State's ports and waters.
-   carry out **inspections of ships' provisions and water**. In this case the inspector is usually employed by the flag State Administration or the central or local government food/hygiene inspectorate.

I03b.4 Chartering and cargo surveyors

-   carry out surveys and inspections of many kinds in connection with chartering and cargo.
-   are usually **independent surveyors** who are either employed by a firm or association of surveyors or are self-
-   employed.
-   include **government inspectors** employed by the **agricultural or food inspectorate** of the port or flag State, who inspect ships prior to loading cargoes such as grain;
-   carry out **on-hire and off-hire surveys** at the start and completion of a time charter period, to determine responsibility for damage during the charter, and for taking over the stocks of fuel on board. The surveyor may be hired jointly by the owner and the charterer .
-   carry out **condition surveys** of ships on behalf of prospective charterers. (For notes on OCIMF inspections, see I03b.5.)
-   carry out **draft surveys**, particularly on ships carrying dry or liquid bulk cargoes to determine the amount of cargo loaded or discharged.
-   carry out **pre-loading surveys** of various kinds on vessels carrying sensitive cargoes, to ensure that cargo spaces are fit for loading, and **pre-shipment surveys** on cargoes such as steel, while on the quayside.
-   carry out **post-loading surveys** of various kinds to determine that sensitive cargoes have been properly stowed, before issue of a certificate of stowage/loading. These are useful in resisting claims, and may therefore be required by the owner/carrier.
-   carry out **post-discharge inspections/surveys** before issue of an empty hold/tank dry certificate.

- carry out **ullage surveys** to determine quantities of liquid cargoes loaded.
- carry out **grain surveys** to verify that a grain cargo has been safely loaded in accordance with international regulations. In this case the surveyor may be a government representative.
- carry out **hatch surveys** to determine the condition of a cargo at the end of a voyage, before discharge.
- carry out **damage surveys** to determine the nature, cause and extent of damage to a ship or cargo, usually on behalf of insurers of both parties. Where a surveyor is trying to obtain information which will assist in proving ship's liability, he will be working for the claimant's lawyers or insurers and the master and crew will need guidance as to what to disclose to him. The P&I club correspondent and/or the owner should be consulted immediately in this case.
- carry out **sale and purchase inspections and valuations** before a transfer of ownership. A **ship valuer** may be a shipbroker rather than a professional surveyor.

I03b.5 OCIMF inspectors

- are professional mariners employed by **OCIMF** (see I03b.5a) to carry out inspections of oil, gas or chemical tankers under the SIRE Programme (see I03b.5b), for the benefit of OCIMF members.
- must hold, or have held, a master's licence for vessels of 3,000gt or more or certification as chief engineer officer of vessels powered by main propulsion of 3,000kW or more, plus at least 5 years' service in tankers, of which not less than 2 years must have been as senior officer in the type of tanker to be inspected, and a Dangerous Cargo Endorsement appropriate to the type of vessel to be inspected.
- must have familiarity with the international regulations, codes and guidelines applicable to the type of tanker to be inspected.
- use a standard **vessel inspection questionnaire** to question ships' personnel.

I03b.5a OCIMF

- is the **Oil Companies International Marine Forum**, which describes itself as a voluntary association of oil companies having an interest in the shipment and terminalling of crude oil and oil products with a mission "to be the foremost authority on the safe and environmentally responsible operation of oil tankers and terminals, promoting continuous improvement in standards of design and operation".
* **OCIMF website**: www.ocimf.com

I03b.5b SIRE

- is OCIMF's **Ship Inspection Report Programme**, which enables OCIMF members to submit ship inspection reports to OCIMF for distribution to OCIMF members and certain other qualifying organisations.
- is claimed by OCIMF to be a unique tanker risk assessment tool of value to charterers, ship operators, terminal operators and government bodies concerned with ship safety.
* The **SIRE system** is an up-to-date computer database of about 10,000 tanker inspection reports relating to more than 4,000 tankers. Reports are filed by inspectors direct to the computer in OCIMF's London office, from where reports are distributed to users.
* **Access to the SIRE database** is available, at a nominal cost, to OCIMF members, bulk oil terminal operators, port authorities, canal authorities, oil, power, industrial or oil trader companies which charter tankers as a normal part of their business. It is also available, free of charge, to Governmental bodies which supervise safety and/or pollution prevention in respect of oil tankers (e.g. port State control authorities, MOUs, etc.).

I03b.6 Insurance surveyors

- are instructed (i.e. appointed) by their principals (such as consignees, cargo insurers, Lloyd's Agents or P&I clubs) to carry out **cargo damage surveys** after goods arrive at a port in a damaged condition.
- are instructed by hull and machinery underwriters, P&I clubs, average adjusters, shipowners and charterers to carry out **hull and machinery damage surveys** on ships following casualties. Surveyors are instructed by underwriters (or Lloyd's Agents or IUA Agents on behalf of underwriters) in order to provide an **impartial report** of the nature, cause and extent of damage, and to recommend **measures to minimise the loss** to the underwriter.
- may be instructed by **Lloyd's Agent or IUA Agent** on behalf of underwriters where the claim value is likely to be small.
- may be instructed by the **average adjuster** where general average has been declared, e.g. where a loaded ship has been salvaged and taken to a port of refuge for essential repairs.

- are likely to be employed by the **Salvage Association (SA)** in cases of major ship or major cargo damage, where the insurer is Lloyd's or an IUA insurance company. More than one SA surveyor may attend a major casualty, representing different interests and working independently of each other. In minor damage cases, surveyors from other survey firms are more likely to be instructed.
- carry out **pre-risk surveys** to determine whether a property or operation is suitable to be insured, e.g. where a ship or floating dock is to be towed or where a barge is to be loaded with a large cargo item.
- carry out **ship inspections on behalf of P&I clubs** determined to ensure a high standard of Members' entered tonnage. In this case the inspectors are likely to be former shipmasters directly employed by the P&I club.
- may be instructed by a P&I club to carry out a **condition survey** where the club's ship inspection has been failed. In this case the surveyor may be independent, although instructed by the P&I club.
- carry out **lay-up surveys** to ensure that insurers' requirements for laying up a ship have been carried out.

I03c SUPPLIERS AND REPAIRERS

I03c.1 Goods and services ordered on behalf of shipowners

* For notes on the **master's responsibility for contracts made in his own name**, see E04e.3.
* When signing orders and receipts for goods or services on behalf of the shipowners, the master should generally always **qualify his signature** as in the following example:

      I.B.Smart
      Master
      For and on behalf of ABC Line Ltd

* A copy of any document signed on behalf of the owner (or the charterer) should be retained by the master as protection against later alteration of the original.
* **Blank or uncompleted papers should never be signed** (e.g. where the master is told that the later addition of a few words or figures is routine). Added words may alter the liability of the master, the owner or the charterer.

I03c.2 Goods ordered by time charterers

* **Bunkers** supplied to a time-chartered ship are normally for the charterer's account. However, if the charterer fails to pay for them the supplier may attempt to recover the cost from the shipowner, and may have the ship arrested to enforce his lien.
* To protect the shipowner's position the master, **before receiving bunkers** ordered by the time charterer, should issue a **notice** to the bunker supplier making it clear that:
  • the bunkers were **ordered by and solely for the account of the time charterer**, stating the name of the charterer and his agent; and
  • the bunkers are **not for the account of the ship or her owner or manager**; and
  • **no lien or other claim against the ship** can arise in respect of the supplies concerned.
* This notice may be given in the form of a **standard letter** which may be in the following style:

```
To the Supplier of the goods/services described below

TAKE NOTICE
The goods/services set out below: .....................................................................................................
(particulars of goods/services) were ordered by and for the sole account of:
.................................................................................. (charterer's name and agent's name and
address) and not for the account of the ship or her Owners.

No lien or other claim against the ship may arise in respect of the goods/services supplied.

Yours faithfully

........................................................... (Signed)
                  Master
```

I03d TIME CHARTER DELIVERY AND REDELIVERY

* For notes on charter party provisions stipulating **arrangements for delivery**, including **on-hire surveys**, see F06b.
* For notes on charter party provisions stipulating **arrangements for redelivery**, including **off-hire surveys**, see F06d.

I04 Cargo business in port

* For notes on **bill of lading-related problems**, see F07b.16
* For notes on the requirements of the **MS (Dangerous Good and Marine Pollutants) Regulations**, see F07f.2.
* For notes on the requirements of the **MS (Carriage of Cargoes) Regulations**, see F07g.

I04a CARGO-RELATED SURVEYS

* For notes on **surveyors likely to come on board**, see I03b.
* **Cargo-related surveys** include:
  * hatch surveys;
  * tank/hold clean surveys;
  * tank dry/hold empty surveys;
  * draught surveys;
  * pre-loading surveys;
  * damage surveys.
* In certain trades, e.g. the container trade, cargo surveys held on board may be rare (since containers are more easily inspected ashore), while in others, such as the oil, chemical and dry bulk trades, on-board surveys are commonplace.

I04b LETTERS OF PROTEST

I04b.1 Nature and purpose of letters of protest

* A **letter of protest**, which may also be simply called a "**protest**", is a written communication[23] intended to convey and record dissatisfaction on the part of the protester (the sender) concerning some matter over which the recipient has control, and holding the recipient responsible for any (legal or financial) consequences of the matter being complained of.
* A letter of protest may help to **substantiate a claim** by the owner, or **refute a claim** by a charterer, harbour authority, etc., and may prove useful, if properly filed, in the resolution of a dispute long after the related event[24].
* A **letter of protest** should not to be confused with a **protest** (or "**sea protest**") noted or lodged before a notary public or consul. (For notes on **noting protest**, see I01j.2.)
* Letters of protest may be sent, in appropriate circumstances, **by the master** of any ship, large or small, in any trade, and can be expected to be received by **the master** of any ship. They are especially common (in both directions) in the **tanker trades**, where a variety of reasons give occasion for their sending.
* Letters of protest are in most cases in connection with **cargo operations**, although they may be written about almost **any matter** where there may be legal **liability**, whether there is a contractual arrangement between the employers of the sender and recipient (as in the case of cargo-related protests) or not (as in the case of a protest sent to the master of a closely berthed ship that is causing damage to the sender's ship).
* For **examples** of forms of protest see I04b.3.
* Some companies, especially those in the oil, gas or chemical trades, supply their masters with a stock of printed pro-forma protest forms phrased in the company's "house" style, while others expect their masters to compose suitable protest letters when required.
* If not on a company pro-forma document, a letter of protest should be typed or hand-written by the master. The letter should always end in an appropriate formal manner, such as:

---

[23] A protest made to a notary public, by contrast, is an oral protest, recorded in a register by the notary.
[24] A master who is asked by his company or their lawyers for details surrounding a dispute may find it difficult to remember the facts several months afterwards. If they are recorded in a copy of a protest letter, he is less likely to be disturbed while on leave, etc.

- *"the undersigned hereby declares that the Bill of Lading will be signed under protest......"* or
- *"....and I hereby lodge protest accordingly, and we, including my disponent owners, hold you and/or Charterers responsible for delays and consequences."*

* The **original letter and one copy**, for return, should be sent or given to the recipient, who should be asked to sign for receipt of the letter. (A dotted line at the foot of the letter is normally provided by the writer for the recipient's signature.) The recipient will normally sign "**............for receipt only**", so as to avoid any implication that he accepts liability.

* The signed, returned copy of the protest letter should be placed in the **ship's file**, and copies of this should be sent to the **company** and the **port agent**. (It may be prudent for the master to take a personal copy off the ship when he leaves, in order to have the facts of the matter to hand if and when details are requested while on leave, etc.)

I04b.2 When to send a letter of protest

* A **letter of protest** should be sent to the **person in charge of the relevant operations** (e.g. terminal supervisor, stevedore, harbour master, etc.) in any of the following circumstances:
- when there is a discrepancy between ship's and shore cargo figures;
- when the rate of loading or discharging is too slow or too fast;
- when berth or fendering arrangements are inadequate;
- when longshoremen/dockers are misusing ships' equipment and ignoring duty officers' advice;
- when passing vessels cause ranging, wash damage, etc. whilst loading/discharging;
- in any other situation where the master wishes to formally record his dissatisfaction with arrangements over which the other party has some control.

* Circumstances may arise when it is appropriate to send a letter of protest to the **master of another vessel**, e.g.:
- when there is a discrepancy as to the quantity of cargo received from a vessel being lightened;
- when there is a discrepancy as to the quantity of bunkers received from a bunker vessel, etc.;
- when another vessel is causing, or likely to cause, damage to own ship (e.g. by mooring/berthing too close).

The text of one of the example letters in I04b.3 should be amended as necessary and the letter sent to the master of the other ship with a request for **return of the receipted copy**.

I04b.3 Examples of letters of protest

I04b.3a Letter of protest for discrepancy between ship and shore figures

```
                          LETTER OF PROTEST

M.v.                                     Voyage No.:
Cargo:
Port:                                    Berth/terminal:
Date:                                    Time:
To: (recipient's name and/or position)

Please be advised that there is a discrepancy between ship and shore figure covering
(description of cargo) loaded at your terminal this (date).

    Shore figures: ...........................................
    Ship figures: ...........................................
    Difference: ...........................................

The undersigned hereby declares that the Bill of Lading was signed under protest because of
the unreasonable difference between ship and shore figures.

Protest lodged by........................................... Master    Signed for receipt ...........................................
              (Signature and vessel's stamp)                          ...........................................Company
```

I04b.3b Letter of protest for slow discharging

LETTER OF PROTEST

M.v.   Voyage No.
Cargo:
Port: Berth/terminal:
Date: Time:
To: (recipient's name and/or position)

Please be advised that the average discharge rate has been .... mtph.

The vessel can discharge ....mtph against psi.........................kg/cm^2.

We have consequently not been allowed to use the vessel's full pumping capacity.

I hereby lodge protest accordingly, and we, including my disponent owners, hold you and/or Charterers responsible for all delays and consequences.

Protest lodged by.. Master   Signed for receipt..
                (Signature and vessel's stamp)   ....Company

I04b.3c General purpose letter of protest

LETTER OF PROTEST

M.v.   Voyage No.
Cargo:
Port: Berth/terminal:
Date: Time:
To: (recipient's name and/or position)

Please be advised that ....
....

I hereby lodge protest accordingly, and we, including my disponent owners, hold you and/or Charterers responsible for all delays and consequences.

Protest lodged by.. Master   Signed for receipt ....
                (Signature and vessel's stamp)   ....Company

I04c STEVEDORE DAMAGE REPORTS

* Stevedores may damage the ship, or its equipment (e.g. cranes, derricks and winches), or cargo. Charter parties usually contain a Stevedore Damage clause, the terms of which the master should be aware of, familiar with and adhere to.
* In case of damage to the ship or its equipment, a **stevedore damage report** in the following terms should be sent to the stevedore company management as soon as possible after the damage occurred or has been discovered.

NOTICE OF DAMAGE BY STEVEDORE TO SHIP OR EQUIPMENT

M.v.   Voyage No.
Cargo:
Port: Berth/terminal:
Date: Time:
To: (recipient's name and/or position)

You are hereby notified that I hold you responsible for the below mentioned damage which occurred on my vessel as a result of your stevedoring operations.

> The repairs of the damage are for the account of you and/or your principals, and I am authorised to have the damage repaired in my option at any convenient time and place, with any competent repair shop or yard at regular and usual rates and terms. Your liability and responsibility are not limited to payment of the repair shop's or yard's bill only, but also to any consequences of the damage, including loss of time.
>
> Time and date of damage.. 20............
> Description of damage ....
>
> .... (signed)   Witness to above ....(signed)
>   Master   (Position)
>
> The cause and extent of damage are correctly stated above, and liability acknowledged.
> ....(signed)
>   Stevedore

*   If agreement as to the cause of the damage cannot be agreed on, or damage is extensive, an **independent survey** should be arranged.

I05 Personnel business in port

I05a CREW CHANGES

*   For notes on **procedures for engaging or discharging crew**, see E07c.
*   The master should liaise with the agent on crew change requirements. The agent should be given full written details of crew joining and/or leaving the ship, with copies for immigration officers, police, etc. Several copies of the **current crew list** may be required.
*   In certain countries, personnel joining ship and personnel intending to proceed ashore, including for crew change purposes, require a **valid visa**[25].

I05b ACCIDENTS IN PORT INVOLVING PERSONNEL

I05b.1 Crew accidents

*   **Procedure** should be as follows.
    1. **Treat any injuries** as per Ship Captain's Medical Guide. If hospitalisation is thought necessary, contact **harbour authority** and/or **agent** and send victim ashore for further treatment (see E08j.) If possible, **interview victim** as to cause before he goes ashore. (The employer and/or the master may be sued for **negligence** where hospital treatment is needed but is not provided.)
    2. Have safety officer make **accident investigation** and report (see E08k.1h and E08d.3).
    3. Take steps to **prevent a recurrence** of the accident.
    4. **Inform** the **agent**.
    5. **Inform** the **owners/managers** of facts. A narrative report should be sent when time permits.
    6. **Inform** the **P&I club correspondent**. If necessary, the correspondent will send a lawyer to investigate facts, assist in dealings with local authorities and arrange a local autopsy or burial where the victim died, or repatriation where necessary. Where the victim is hospitalised locally, the P&I club correspondent should ensure the **correct treatment** is given, that **repatriation** is effected as soon as possible thereafter, and that **costs** are kept to a reasonable minimum. P&I clubs generally extend the same accident and repatriation cover to **crewmembers' wives and children**; the club correspondent should therefore be contacted even where the accident victim is such a person.
    7. Complete **Official Log Book** entries as required by the MS (Official Log Books) Regulations (see D05a).
    8. Follow procedure required under the MS (Accident Reporting and Investigation) Regulations 1999 (see E08k) including completion and sending to MAIB of form IRF.

---

[25]Since 11 September 2001, US immigration law has been tightened. Section 402 of Title IV, Inspection and Admission of Aliens, of the Enhanced Border Security and Visa Entry Reform Act 2002 requires, *inter alia*, all commercial vessels to provide crew and passenger manifest information, including: "US visa number, date, and place of issuance, where applicable". This requirement applies to all persons entering US territory, including seafarers. Personnel without valid visas will be denied entry or shore leave.

9. **Write a narrative report**, filing copies to the owner, P&I club and ship's file. Keep a personal copy: queries may arise long after the accident.
10. **Collect documentary evidence** required by the P&I club, for defending any claim against the owner (see D05d.3).

I05b.2 Passenger accidents

* **Masters of passenger ships** are especially at risk from passenger claims of negligence, although passenger tickets will usually contain a **Himalaya Clause** giving protection to the carrier's servants and sub-contractors (see F07b.9a).
* **Passengers injured whilst ashore** on an excursion from the ship may have a valid claim against the carrier.
* **Procedure in case of a passenger accident** should be broadly the same as for a crew accident (see I05b.1).
* The necessity to take steps to **prevent a recurrence** is doubly important, e.g. clearing up spilt liquids on decks. (Personal negligence of the master may include continuing to allow a passenger to be served alcoholic drinks causing the passenger's intoxication, leading to an accident.)
* **Crew should be instructed** not to indulge in practices which, if imitated by passengers, could lead to injuries (e.g. sliding down ladders without using all steps provided).
* For notes on **documentary evidence required by the P&I club** (in order to defend claims), see D05d.3.

I05b.3 Stevedore accidents and accidents to other persons in port

* The shipowner may have a liability to compensate almost any person injured on board, such as customs, immigration and port health officers, surveyors, ship's agents and cargo handlers. In some countries the owner or charterer has a **strict liability** for all accidents on board, but in others liability is based on **negligence** or **breach of statutory duty** with respect to ship's equipment. In these latter countries, evidence will be sought to prove negligence of the liable party.
* Particular care should be taken, especially at US ports and terminals, to ensure that **conditions on board are safe for stevedores** to work in. Any slippery deck surfaces, for example, should be made non-slip or fenced off, and appropriate warning signs displayed, etc.
* **In case of an accident involving a cargo handler** (i.e. stevedore, docker or longshoreman), broadly the same procedure should be adopted as for a crew accident. Where some defective part of ship's structure or equipment is involved, the item should be preserved if possible for the P&I club lawyer's attention. For other notes on **accidents to shore-based workers**, e.g. cargo handlers, see E08k.1k.
* **The following personnel should be interviewed** as soon as possible after the accident:
  * the victim;
  * any eyewitnesses;
  * the first person to arrive at the scene;
  * any persons with knowledge of the equipment or part of ship involved, or of the injured person's activities immediately before the accident.
* **Documentary evidence required by the P&I club** (for defending any claim made) includes:
  * relevant extracts from deck and engine room log books, medical log and accident book;
  * oil record book, if relevant;
  * maintenance records;
  * copies of accident report forms and reports;
  * diagrams or contemporary photographs or sketches of the accident scene and equipment involved;
  * witness statements.
* For notes on **documentary evidence required by the P&I club** (in order to defend claims), see D05d.3.

I05b.3a Accidents to shore-based workers in UK

* **Injuries to shore-based workers while a ship is in a port or shipyard within the UK** should be reported by the person's employer to the Health and Safety Executive (HSE) (see B05e). Dangerous occurrences whilst in a UK shipyard should also be reported to HSE by the shipyard operator. **Reports by the master to MAIB** of such injuries or occurrences are not required (see **MGN 115**).

I05c MEDICAL AND DENTAL TREATMENT

* If a person, while employed in a UK ship, receives outside the UK any **surgical or medical treatment**, or such **dental or optical treatment** (including the repair or replacement of any appliance) as cannot be postponed without impairing efficiency, the reasonable expenses of the treatment must be borne by his employer (section 45(1) Merchant Shipping Act 1995).
* Regardless of whether the owner was negligent in causing or contributing to a seaman's illness or accident, seamen are generally able to recover the costs of medical attention from their employers from the time of signing on the crew agreement until the time of signing off, and in some cases beyond.
* The payment of medical expenses by the owner may not preclude a **claim of negligence** made by the seaman, but P&I clubs try to ensure that any claim is reduced by the amount of any contractual benefit paid by their shipowner-members.
* The P&I clubs generally extend the same medical and dental treatment cover to crewmembers' **wives and children**.
* For notes on **medical attention**, see E08j.

I05d INDUSTRIAL ACTION BY CREW

I05d.1 Strike action in port

* For notes on the law relating to **industrial action by seamen**, and **NUMAST advice to members**, see E12a.
* Seamen employed in UK ships which go to sea (i.e. in ships which operate beyond Category A, B, C or D waters) will be committing an offence under section 59 of the Merchant Shipping Act 1995 if they go on strike at a time when their ship is **at sea**, which means (for the purposes of section 59) at any time when it is **not securely moored in a safe berth**. The Act does not appear to prohibit such action at berths in places outside the UK.

I05d.2 ITF involvement in industrial action

Home
* ITF inspectors have no statutory authority to board any ship and may only do so with the master's permission.
* In ITF "strongholds" such as Scandinavian countries and Australia, shore transport union workers, e.g. dockers, lock-keepers and tugmen, may be called on to support the crew's action, e.g. by refusing to work the ship.
* Should the ship be "blacked" by members of an ITF-affiliated union the master should:
  * produce the "**Blue Certificate**" if the owner has been awarded one (see C06a);
  * exercise extreme **restraint** and avoid worsening the situation;
  * contact the **owner** and P&I **club correspondent**;
  * contact **NUMAST** or other professional union (if a member) and follow union guidelines.

I05e DESERTERS

* "**Desertion**" is the wilful abandonment of an employment or of duty[26]. A seaman becomes a **deserter** when he is signed on a crew agreement but wilfully fails to rejoin the ship in breach of the agreement. Desertion may lead to a civil action by the employer for **breach of contract**.
* Although desertion is not a criminal offence, in a country other than his own a deserter may be violating the State's immigration laws, and may thus be liable to criminal prosecution and a fine or imprisonment, as well as deportation. Any costs, e.g. for repatriation, may be levied on the shipowner.
* **In some countries**, e.g. Canada, the shipowner is required to put up a deposit with the authorities to cover the repatriation cost, even before the deserter is found. The owner will claim for recovery of this deposit from his P&I club. If the deserter is not found within a certain time, the deposit is refunded to the owner by the government, and the owner refunds the P&I club.
* **In US ports**, if a seaman is designated as a "prohibited immigrant" by the immigration authorities (the INS) on arrival of the ship, he will not even be allowed to go down the accommodation ladder onto the quay. If he violates this rule the ship will usually incur a minimum fine of US$1000, even if the seaman subsequently returns to the ship. The INS may require security guards to be posted if there are prohibited immigrants on board, at the ship's expense.

---

[26] The Shorter Oxford English Dictionary.

* **If a seaman deserts**, or is believed to have deserted:
  1. **Check his cabin** for any indication of intent to desert.
  2. **Ask his work colleagues** if he made any indication of intent to desert, and log same in Official Log Book;
  3. **Inform the agent** immediately and request him to inform relevant local authorities e.g. immigration authorities, police, etc.;
  4. Inform the **P&I club correspondent**;
  5. Inform the **proper officer** (i.e. British consul or shipping master), and record his informing in the Official Log Book;
  6. Inform the **owner** (who will stop the seaman's pay, if paid from the office);
  7. **Discharge the seaman** (in his absence) from the Crew Agreement (see E07d.7);
  8. **Send a written report** to the owner (who will normally send a copy to the P&I club);
  9. **Tally the seaman's personal effects** (see E13c.1g), insert copies of tally in Official Log Book and kit bag and send to seaman's home address;
  10. Make **arrangements with the agent** for the seaman's **relief and repatriation** if he is eventually found to be hospitalised, in jail, etc. and not to have deserted. (The owner's obligation to provide for relief and repatriation expires after 3 months from date of leaving ship, except where the seaman's absence was not his own fault (see E13c).
  11. Make **Official Log Book** entries relating to the seaman's discharge (entry No. 16), the informing of the proper officer (entry No. 18), the tallying of the personal effects (entry No. 20), and the sending of the personal effects to the seaman's home address (see D05a.4).

I05f LEAVING A SEAMAN BEHIND

* **A seaman will be "left behind"** if he is hospitalised, absent without leave, detained by authorities, imprisoned, etc. at the time of the vessel's departure for sea.
* It is most important that the **agent**, **immigration authorities**, **P&I club correspondent**, **proper officer** (at a non-UK port) and the **shipowner or manager are informed** that the seaman has been left behind. The agent should be instructed to make the various contacts.
* Generally, a seaman left behind should be **discharged** from the Crew Agreement in his absence following the procedure in E07d.7.
* In some cases a seaman left behind may be expected to "catch up" with the ship in a few days' time, and the master may feel that it is not worth the trouble of signing him off the Crew Agreement. That would mean, however, that the List of Crew will not then accurately show the true complement, which could lead to problems with authorities, especially if the ship were diverted after departure.
* **Where a seaman is left behind at a non-UK port**, the **proper officer** must be informed (see E13c.1b) and a record of his informing (entry No. 18) made in the Official Log Book (see D05a.4).

I05g VISITORS ON BOARD

I05g.1 Legal considerations

* **P&I clubs advise masters to be careful** to verify the identity of any surveyor, lawyer or other expert coming on board. If in doubt, the owner's P&I club correspondent should be consulted. For notes on the **identification of surveyors**, see I03b.1.
* In the interests of safety and of legal propriety, surveyors and other visitors who need to move about the ship should always be **accompanied** by an officer. The **movements of visitors** on any kind of business on board should be **restricted** to those parts of the ship of legitimate interest. (If in doubt, the P&I club correspondent should be consulted.) The movements of **other visitors** (e.g. crew members' family, students, etc.) should likewise be **monitored and controlled**, and in the interests of third party claims reduction should be restricted to **non-working areas** of the vessel.
* A correspondent of the owner's P&I club should always be given every assistance and should be shown any documentation asked for.
* **Documents should never be shown** to anyone who does not have the approval of the club correspondent.
* Occasionally it may be inadvisable for the master or any crew member to give information to a particular surveyor, or to allow him free access to the vessel or its records. The local P&I club correspondent should be able to advise the master as to the correct course of action when in doubt.

I05g.2 Unauthorised persons on board

* **Section 104 of the Merchant Shipping Act 1995** provides that where a UK ship or a ship registered in any other country is in a port in the UK and a person who is neither in Her Majesty's service nor authorised by law to do so -
  * goes on board the ship without the consent of the master or of any other persons authorised to give it; or
  * remains on board the ship after being requested to leave by the master, a constable, an officer authorised by the Secretary of State or an officer of Customs and Excise –
  - he will be liable on summary conviction to a fine not exceeding level 5 on the standard scale.

I05h WATCHKEEPING ARRANGEMENTS IN PORT

I05h.1 Normal port watchkeeping arrangements

* **Regulation 12 of the MS (Safe Manning, Hours of Work and Watchkeeping) Regulations 1997** (SI 1997/1320) provides that the master of any ship which is safely moored or safely at anchor under normal circumstances in port must arrange for an **appropriate and effective watch** to be maintained for the purposes of **safety**. The arrangements must be in accordance with part 4 of section A-VIII/2 of the STCW Code and any operational guidance specified by the MCA.
* **Part 4 of section A-VIII/2 of the STCW Code** relates to **watchkeeping in port** and contains provisions as follows: Principles applying to all watchkeeping (including General; Watch arrangements; Taking over the watch; and Watch in port on ships carrying hazardous cargo).

I05h.2 Port watchkeeping arrangements in ships carrying hazardous cargo

* **Regulation 13 of the Safe Manning, etc. Regulations** provides that the master of any ship carrying hazardous cargo whilst in port, even when the ship is safely moored or safely at anchor, must, in addition to any other port watchkeeping arrangements required by the Regulations, **ensure** the following:
  * that, on a ship carrying **hazardous cargo in bulk**, a **safe deck watch and safe engineering watch** are maintained by the ready availability on board of **a duly qualified officer or officers**, and, where appropriate, **ratings**; and
  * that **in organizing safe watchkeeping arrangements** on a ship carrying **hazardous cargo other than in bulk**, he **takes account** of the nature, quantity, packing and stowage of the hazardous cargo and of any special conditions on board, afloat and ashore.
* These watchkeeping arrangements must take full account of the principles and requirements specified by the MCA.

I06 Other port business

I06a BUNKERING OPERATIONS AND HARBOUR POLLUTION

I06a.1 Discharge of oil from ships into UK national waters

* **Section 131 of the Merchant Shipping Act 1995** provides that if any oil or mixture containing oil is discharged as mentioned below into **UK national waters** navigable by sea-going ships, then, subject to certain defences (see I06a.2), the following will be guilty of an **offence**:
  * if the discharge is from a ship, the **owner or master** (unless he proves that the discharge took place and was caused as mentioned in the next sub-paragraph);
  * if the discharge is from a ship but takes place during a **transfer** of oil to or from another ship or a place on land and is caused by the act or omission of any person in charge of any apparatus in that other ship or that place, the **owner or master of the other ship** or the occupier of that place, as the case may be.
* The above provisions do not apply to any discharge which is made into the sea and is of a kind or is made in circumstances for the time being prescribed by regulations made by the DfT (i.e. permitted discharges).

* A person guilty under section 131 will be liable on summary conviction to a fine not exceeding **£50,000** or on conviction on indictment to an unlimited fine.

I06a.1a Defences of owner or master charged with offence under Section 131

* **Section 132 of the Merchant Shipping Act 1995** provides that, where an owner or master is charged with an offence under section 131, it will be a defence to prove that the oil or mixture was discharged for the purpose of:
  * securing the safety of any ship;
  * preventing damage to any ship or cargo; or
  * saving life.
* These defences may not used if the court is satisfied that the discharge of oil or mixture was not necessary in the circumstances or was not a reasonable step to take in the circumstances.
* Where an owner or master is charged with an offence under section 131, it will also be a defence to prove:
  * that the oil or mixture escaped as a result of damage to the ship, and that as soon as practicable after the damage occurred all reasonable steps were take for preventing, or (if it could not be prevented) for stopping or reducing, the escape of the oil or mixture; or
  * that the oil or mixture escaped by reason of leakage, that neither the leakage or any delay in discovering it was due to any want of reasonable care, and that as soon as practicable after the escape was discovered all reasonable steps were taken for stopping or reducing it.

I06a.2 Restrictions on transfers of oil at night

* **Section 135 of the Merchant Shipping Act 1995** provides that no oil may be transferred between sunset and sunrise to or from a ship in any harbour in the UK unless the requisite notice has been given as below, or the transfer is for the purposes of a fire brigade.
* A general notice may be given to the harbour master of a harbour that transfers oil between sunset and sunrise will be frequently carried out at a place in the harbour within such period, not ending later than 12 months after the date on which the notice is given, as is specified in the notice. If a general notice is given it will be the requisite notice for the purposes of section 135 as regards transfers of oil at that place within the period specified in the notice. (This kind of notice will generally be in force at tanker terminals.)
* In other cases, a notice must be given to the harbour master not less than three hours not more than 96 hours before the transfer of oil begins.
* In the case of a harbour which has no harbour master, references in section 131 to the harbour master are to be construed as references to the harbour authority.

I06a.3 Duty to report discharge of oil into waters of harbours

* **Section 136 of the Merchant Shipping Act 1995** provides that if any oil or mixture containing oil -
  * is discharged from a ship into the waters of a harbour in the UK; or
  * is found to be escaping or to have escaped from a ship into any such waters -
  - the owner or master must forthwith **report** the occurrence to the harbour master, or, if the harbour has no harbour master, to the harbour authority, stating the type of occurrence.

I06a.4 Bunkering procedural checks in owner's interests

* **Bunker spillage claims** account for a large proportion of all P&I claims and have an adverse effect on shipowners' deductibles and standing with their clubs. In order to minimise claims on the club and fines or arrest of the vessel (and possibly of the master himself), the master should ensure that a **proper procedure** will be strictly followed during every bunkering operation. Many companies will have such a procedure laid down in standing orders or in ISM Code Safety Management System documentation. The following notes are included mainly for the benefit of masters where no such procedure is in place.
* **Where the vessel is under a time charter** the **Bunker Clause** should be checked before ordering or taking bunkers.
* **In order to avoid claims** on the owner and his P&I club, the master of a vessel taking bunkers should ensure that:
  * bunkers are ordered specifying an **approved fuel standard**, e.g. "BSMA 100", rather than only specifying a type and viscosity, e.g. "IFO 180";
  * bunkers presented for loading match ship's requirements and **specification** ordered;

- accurate **soundings** of tanks are taken before bunkering in order to verify the amount of fuel delivered;
- a **compatibility test** is made to confirm that bunkers presented are compatible with fuel already on board;
- bunkers are loaded into **empty tanks** if possible, and kept separate from other bunkers until any analysis has been completed;
- the vessel is, so far as possible, maintained **upright** and on even keel throughout the bunkering operation;
- **samples** of oil loaded will be taken at regular intervals at the manifold;
- local and international **regulations** are complied with throughout the operation;
- scupper plugs are fitted before bunkering;
- **drain plugs** in manifold and fuel tank air pipe containment save-alls are in place before bunkering;
- **communications** are established with supply control position and signals to be used are understood by both sides;
- **maximum pumping rate and pressure** are agreed with supplier;
- condition of **hoses and couplings** are checked before (and after) bunkering;
- **blanks** and numbers of required **nuts and bolts, etc.** are checked before bunkering;
- required **hose lengths** (allowing for ranging of vessel) are checked before bunkering;
- **valves** are in required positions before bunkering and **tank vent pipes** are free from obstruction;
- **barge and shore tank soundings** and/or **meter readings** are checked before (and after) bunkering to help avert any problems concerning quantity;
- frequent **soundings** are taken during bunkering;
- rate of delivery is **slowed down** while topping off;
- ample warning is given to the supplier to **reduce delivery rate** and final shutting off;
- accurate soundings of tanks are taken after bunkering and compared with pre-loading soundings to **determine quantity delivered**;
- **Oil Record Book**, and deck and engine room **log books** are completed immediately after bunkering with accurate details of the operation.

I06a.5 Action when bunkers are spilled

* **When bunkers are spilled** during bunkering operations the master should take immediate steps to:
  1. **Stop** the bunkering operation.
  2. **Minimise the spread of oil** in the harbour, taking all possible action to contain the spillage until shore assistance arrives, but without using any dispersants for which approval has not previously been obtained.
  3. **Stop any hot work** on board or on nearby vessels and quays;
  4. **Contact**:
     - harbour authorities (on VHF if possible);
     - ship's agent;
     - P&I club correspondent;
     - owners/managers;
  5. **Obtain samples** of the oil from which the spillage came.
  6. Attempt to establish the **quantity of oil** spilled.
  7. **Establish the other facts** and (before investigators arrive, if possible) write a full **report** of the occurrence, detailing all efforts taken by ship's crew to deal with the spillage.
  8. Make a **report to the port State administration**, as required by the law of the port State (which can be ascertained by consulting the P&I club correspondent).
* The master, officers and crew should **work closely with the local authorities** in the clean-up operation. (This may help to mitigate any penalty.)

I06a.6 Bunker samples and quality analysis

* **Samples of oil loaded during bunkering** as above should be sealed, dated and signed by the chief engineer and the supplier.
* **At least two samples** should be taken during bunkering. One of these should be retained on board until all bunkers loaded have been burned without problem.
* **At least one sample** should be forwarded to any independent fuel analysis service used.
* **If the vessel carries an on-board fuel test kit**, a spot analysis should be carried out by the chief engineer and, if this indicates the fuel as being unsuitable, a full analysis should be carried out at an approved shore laboratory before the bunkers are used.

I06a.7 Bunker oil pollution insurance

* **Australian regulations** require that ships of 400gt or more carrying oil as cargo or **bunkers** are required to carry a "relevant insurance certificate" (see G04d.4b).

I06a.8 Oil Transfer Records Regulations

* The **Oil in Navigable Waters (Transfer Records) Regulations, 1957** (SI 1957/358) -
  - **apply** (in the UK) to every vessel, whether registered or not, and of any nationality, capable of carrying in bulk, whether for cargo or for bunker purposes, more than twenty-five tons of oil, or which, though not so capable, is constructed or fitted to carry in bulk more than five tons of oil in any one space or container (regulation 1).
  - **require** the master to keep a **record** of the particulars specified in regulation 4 relating to the transfer of oil to and from the vessel while it is within the seaward limits of the territorial waters of the UK (regulation 2).
* In the case of a **transfer of oil to a barge** the records must be kept by the **person supplying the oil**, and in the case of the **transfer of oil from a barge** the record must be kept by the **person to whom the oil is delivered** (regulation 3).
* The particulars specified in regulation 4 to be recorded are:
  * the name and port of registry (if any) of the vessel or barge;
  * the date and time of transfer;
  * the place of transfer;
  * the amount and description of oil transferred; and
  * from what vessel, barge or place on land, and to what vessel, barge or place the oil was transferred.
* The record of each operation must be separately **signed and dated** by the master or such other person as is referred to in regulation 3.
* If the record is kept in the Official Log of a vessel it is not necessary separately to state the name and port of registry (if any) of the vessel.

I06b DISPOSAL OF SHIP SEWAGE IN PORT

* **Ship sewage** is the subject of Annex IV to MARPOL 73/78, which enters into force on 27 September 2003. For notes on **Annex IV**, see D04g.8. At the time of writing, although the UK had ratified Annex IV, no legislation giving effect to it in the UK was in force.
* **National sewage disposal regulations** are in force in certain countries, e.g. States bordering the Baltic Sea. (For notes on the Helsinki Convention, see H03d.2.) The master of a ship at a port or terminal outside the UK should ascertain the local legal position on sewage disposal from the agent and/or the P&I club correspondent.
* Regulation 10 of Annex IV requires the government of each Party to MARPOL 73/78 accepting Annex IV to ensure the provision of adequate **sewage reception facilities** in ports.
* For notes on **ships' sewage equipment and certification**, see D04g.8.
* For notes on **discharges of ship sewage at sea**, see H03d.

I06c DISPOSAL OF WASTES IN PORT

I06c.1 Port Waste Reception Facilities Regulations

* **The MS (Port Waste Reception Facilities) Regulations 1997** (SI 1997/3018) –
  - **implement requirements of MARPOL 73/78** requiring all Contracting States to ensure the provision of reception facilities for oil residues and mixtures, noxious liquid substances carried in bulk, and garbage.
  - **apply** to any **harbour** or **terminal** within a harbour in the UK (regulation 3).
  - **revoke** and replace with amendments the Prevention of Pollution (Reception Facilities) Order 1984 (SI 1984/862) and the MS (Reception Facilities for Garbage) Regulations 1988 (SI 1988/2293) (regulation 16).
  - **amend** the MS (Fees) Regulations 1996 (SI 1996/3243) (regulation 16).
  - **require** every **harbour authority** and **terminal operator** to **prepare a Waste Management Plan** (regulation 8) which must be submitted to the MCA for approval (regulation 10).
  - **give the MCA powers of direction** in relation to the implementation of Waste Management Plans (regulation 9).

- **defines "garbage"** as "all kinds of victual domestic and operational waste excluding fresh fish and parts thereof, generated during the normal operation of the ship and liable to be disposed of continuously or periodically except sewage originating from ships" (regulation 2(1)).
- **defines "operational waste"** as "all maintenance wastes, cargo associated wastes and cargo residues or wastes from oil or oily mixtures, noxious liquid substances, non-polluting liquid substances or harmful substances in packaged form". (This means that tanker slops are "garbage" within the meaning of the Regulations.)
* **Regulation 4(1)** provides that every harbour authority and terminal operator must **provide adequate reception facilities** for the reception of **prescribed wastes** from ships using the harbour or terminal. "**Prescribed wastes**" are defined in regulation 2 as meaning any **garbage**, **waste oil** and **oily mixtures** and **waste noxious liquid substances**.
* **Regulation 7** provides that any **waste reception facilities provided must be open to all ships** which in the opinion of the harbour authority or terminal operator are using the harbour or terminal for a primary purpose other than to utilise the reception facilities, on payment of any **charges** and compliance with any **reasonable conditions** imposed.
* **MSN 1709** explains the operation of the Regulations.

I06c.2 Use of waste reception facilities

* Where **waste oil reception facilities** have been used in any port or place, a record should be made in the appropriate **Oil Record Book** (see D05b.2).
* Where **waste noxious liquid substances reception facilities** have been used in any port or place, a record should be made in the **Cargo Record Book** (Noxious Liquid Substances) (see D05b.3).
* Where **garbage reception facilities** have been used in any port or place, a record should be made in the **Garbage Record Book** (see D04t.5).
* Harbour and terminal authorities usually charge an "**environmental levy**" for the use of waste reception facilities, whether they are used by the ship or not.
* Harbour and terminal authorities **must be notified** when any waste to be landed is **contaminated by pest or disease organisms** or where its disposal on land may present a risk to human or animal health or to the environment.

I06c.3 Inadequacy of waste reception facilities in the UK

* **MGN 82** contains guidance on the action that should be taken in any port (in the UK or elsewhere) where waste oil residues, waste noxious liquid substances or garbage are to be landed, but reception facilities are found to be inadequate.
* MGN 82 points out that every port, harbour, terminal and marina in the UK is now required to have a Port Waste Management Plan, detailing how their waste is dealt with. Each plan should contain a **contact point** for reporting inadequacies in the provision of waste reception facilities, and a **means of addressing such inadequacies**.
* **The master of a ship faced with a lack of reception facilities, or reception facilities which are inadequate**, is advised to:
  * Submit to the address in paragraph 6 of MGN 82 (i.e. Chief Surveyor, MSAS(d), MCA Southampton), either directly or through the shipowner, as appropriate, details of the inadequacy using the report form annexed to MGN 82.
  * Bring the alleged inadequacy to the attention of the port concerned (i.e. the responsible port or terminal operator).
  * If the problem is not resolved to the master's satisfaction, or in UK ports, if the Port Waste Management Plan does not fully meet the master's requirements, or the consultation process is ineffective, note this in the report to the MCA.
* The annex to MGN 82 contains a specimen "**Form for reporting alleged inadequacy** of oily waste, noxious liquid substances and garbage reception facilities". This can be photocopied, completed and sent to MCA headquarters in Southampton, whether the port concerned is in the UK or not. Sections for completion in the form include: 1. Ship's particulars; 2. Port particulars; 3. Type and amount of waste for discharge to facility; 4. Type and amount of waste not accepted by the facility; 5. Special problems encountered; 6. Action taken by the port; Remarks.
* In the case of a non-UK port, the MCA will take up the matter with the port State and make a report to IMO, while in respect of a UK port the MCA will take up the matter directly with the port or terminal authority concerned.
* **M.1197** reminds masters that use of oil reception facilities should be **recorded** in the Oil Record Book.

I06c.4 Compliance with port or coastal State legislation on garbage disposal

* Most (but not quite all) maritime States are signatories to MARPOL 73/78, but not all ratifying States interpret MARPOL's provisions in the same way. While IMO sets minimum standards, individual States may set more stringent regulations.
* All maritime States set their own penalties for pollution law infringements and in many cases these will be more severe than the penalties under UK law. For example, the US Coast Guard is empowered under the **Marine Plastic Pollution Research and Control Act 1987** to issue civil penalties of **US$25,000** for each garbage law violation by a ship in US waters[27]. If a person knowingly violates MARPOL or the US Act he is subject to criminal penalties in the USA, which include fines of up to **$50,000** per violation and/or up to 5 years' imprisonment. (Up to one half of the fine may be paid to the person giving information leading to conviction.)
* **The marine pollution laws of the host State** must always be complied with by a UK vessel whilst in the State's ports or territorial waters.
* **The master should** try to ascertain (from the owner, the P&I club correspondent, agent, charterer, pilot books, etc.) which local laws apply, and be careful to observe them.
* For notes on the **Garbage Management Plan**, see D04t.4.
* For notes on the **Garbage Record Book**, see D04t.5.

I06c.5 Compliance with Environmental Protection Act 1990

* **Waste** landed under MARPOL Annexes I, II and V is classified as "**industrial waste**". As such it is a **controlled waste** under the Environmental Protection Act 1990, rendering its management and disposal subject to:
  * a duty of care under section 34 of the Act; and
  * the waste management licensing provisions of Part II of the Act.
* The **duty of care** applies to any person who imports, produces, carries, keeps, treats or disposes of controlled waste, including **masters** of ships. It requires each person to take reasonable measures to:
  * **prevent the contravention** by someone else of section 33 of the Act (e.g. the unlawful deposit, recovery or disposal of waste);
  * **prevent the escape of the waste** from his control or the control of any other person; and
  * ensure that when waste is transferred it is transferred only to an authorised person (e.g. a registered waste carrier) and that a satisfactory **written description of the waste** is transferred with it.
* **Practical guidance** on how to comply with the duty of care is provided in *The Duty of Care: A Code of Practice* (HMSO ISBN 0-11-752557-X).
* **Exemptions** available from the waste management license requirements include one for the temporary storage, at reception facilities provided within a harbour area, of waste discharged under MARPOL Annexes I, II and V.

I06c.6 Compliance with Special Waste Regulations 1996

* MARPOL 73/78 does not cover requirements for the **disposal of residues and effluent** of certain substances to reception facilities in the UK. Disposal of consignments of these "**special wastes**" is the subject of **The Special Waste Regulations 1996** (SI 1996/972). These Regulations, which are made in compliance with an EU **Hazardous Waste Directive**, apply in England, Scotland and Wales, but not in Northern Ireland.
* The Regulations define "**special waste**" as (subject to some provisos) controlled waste (as defined in the Environmental Protection Act 1990) to which a 6-digit code is assigned in a **Hazardous Waste List** set out in part I of Schedule 2 to the Regulations, or controlled waste displaying certain properties listed in a coded **Hazardous Properties List** in part II to Schedule 2. The **Hazardous Waste List** contains numerous, mainly industrial wastes, including waste from marine transport tank cleaning, containing oil or chemicals; bilge oils from inland or other navigation, oil/water separator sludges and many others likely to be carried by ships and is reproduced in **M.1678**[28].
* The Regulations affect **carriers of special waste** making either a **single journey** or a **carrier's round** where all consignments are transported to the same consignee.
* **A carrier of special waste is required** to prepare, and in some cases furnish to certain parties, a number of copies of a **consignment note**. The standard form of consignment note is shown in M.1678 and in the Regulations, and contains four parts, A to D as follows:
  * Part A: Consignment details

---

[27] After stewards threw 20 full garbage bags into the sea off the Florida Keys, Princess Cruises paid the maximum penalty of US$500,000 (20 x $25,000).

[28] M.1678 should be read with caution, since it fails to clearly explain all parts of the Regulations as they affect shipmasters, and to some extent appears to conflict with the requirements of the Special Waste Regulations.

- Part B: Carrier collection certificate
- Part C: Consignor's collection certificate
- Part D: Consignee's collection certificate

* Where special waste is being removed from a ship in a harbour area to reception facilities within the harbour area, or by pipeline to reception facilities outside the harbour area, regulation 9 applies. This requires the master of the ship from which the waste is being removed, before the removal takes place, to:
  - ensure that 3 copies of the **consignment note** are prepared, with Parts A and B completed and the relevant code (from the Hazardous Waste List or Hazardous Properties list) entered on each copy;
  - ensure that Part D is completed on each copy;
  - retain one copy (on which Parts A to D have been completed); and
  - give the two remaining copies (on which parts A to D have been completed) to the operator of the reception facilities.

* Regulation 6 lists cases in which **pre-notification** (i.e. preparation and furnishing of consignment notes before removal of a consignment) is not required. These cases include *inter alia* the removal from a ship in a harbour area of a consignment of special waste to a conveyance (which includes other ships as well as other transport forms) for transportation to a place outside that area, and the return of special wastes to their original supplier or manufacturer.

* **Standard procedure for preparation and furnishing of consignment notes** where regulation 6 is applicable is contained in regulation 7.

* **Where a carrier's round is being made**, regulation 8 sets out the requirements for consignment notes.

* Regulation 15 requires consignors and carriers to keep **registers** containing all consignment notes and carrier's schedules.

I06c.7 Inspection of Garbage Record Books and garbage-related operations

* **Regulation 12(1) of the MS (Prevention of Pollution by Garbage) Regulations 1998** (SI 1998/1377) provides that an **inspector may inspect any ship** to which the Regulations apply in any port in the UK.

* The **inspector may investigate any operation** regulated by the Regulations (e.g. garbage management on board) if he has clear grounds for believing that the **master or crew are not familiar with the ship's on-board procedures** for preventing pollution by garbage (regulation 12(2)).

* **If the inspector is satisfied** that either the **master or crew are not familiar** with the ship's on-board procedures for preventing pollution by garbage, he must take such steps as he considers necessary, including **detaining the ship**, to ensure that the **ship does not sail** until the situation has been brought into accordance with the requirements of the Regulations (regulation 12(3)).

* The **inspector may require**, in respect of a ship to which regulation 11 applies[29], the owner, **master or any member of the crew** of the ship, while the ship is in any UK port or offshore terminal to **produce the Garbage Record Book** for inspection (regulation 13(1)).

* The inspector may make a **copy of any entry in the garbage record book** and may require the master of the ship or installation manager to **certify** that the copy is a true copy of such an entry (regulation 13(2)). Any copy certified by the master or installation manager as a true copy will be admissible in any judicial proceedings as **evidence** of the facts stated in it (regulation 13(3)).

* For notes on **Garbage Record Books**, see D04t.5.

I06d CONTROL OF AIR POLLUTION IN PORT

I06d.1 Emissions of dark smoke in UK internal waters

* **Section 44 (1) of the Clean Air Act 1993** (c.11), which relates to "**Vessels**", provides that **section 1 (prohibition of emissions of dark smoke)** applies in relation to **vessels in waters to which section 44 applies** as it applies in relation to buildings.

* **The waters to which section 44 applies** are all waters not navigable by sea-going ships, and all waters navigable by sea-going ships within the seaward limits of UK territorial waters (i.e. UK **internal waters**) and which are contained within any port, harbour, river, estuary, haven, dock, canal or other place, so long as a person, or body of persons, is

---

[29] Regulation 11 applies to every ship of 400gt or above, and to every ship certified to carry 15 persons or more engaged on voyages to ports or offshore terminals of another MARPOL party State.

empowered by or under any Act to make charges[30] in respect of vessels entering it or using facilities in it (section 44(4)).

* Under **Section 1,** as amended by section 44(2) (which makes certain substitutions of expressions in the application of section 1 to a vessel), **dark smoke**[31] may not be emitted from a vessel, and if, on any day, dark smoke is emitted, the **master or other officer or person in charge** of the vessel will be guilty of an **offence** (section 1(1)).

* In proceedings for an offence under section 1, it will be a **defence** to prove that the alleged emission was solely due to the **starting** of a vessel's engine which was cold or a **failure** of an engine.and that all practicable steps had been taken to prevent or minimise the emission.

* Section 44(6) provides that, **except as provided in section 44**, nothing in Parts I to III of the Act applies to **smoke, grit** or **dust** from any vessel. (Part I deals with dark smoke; Part II deals with smoke, grit, dust and fumes; and Part III deals with smoke control areas.)

I06d.2 MARPOL Annex VI provisions

* The MARPOL Protocol of 1997 adds **Annex VI (Regulations for the Prevention of Air Pollution from Ships)** to the MARPOL Convention, but is not yet in force. For notes on its entry into force, etc., see H03f.1.

* Following entry into force of Annex VI, ships will be subject, under **regulation 10**, to inspection by Port State Control officers for **operational requirements of Annex VI** where there are clear grounds for believing that the master or crew are not familiar **with essential shipboard procedures relating to the prevention of air pollution from ships**.

* Under **regulation 17**, Annex VI Party States will undertake to provide **reception facilities** for ozone-depleting substances and equipment containing such substances when removed from ships.

* Under **regulation 18, fuel oil for combustion purposes** must meet certain minimum **quality specifications**. Details of fuel oil for combustion purposes delivered to and used on board must be recorded by means of a **Bunker Delivery Note** which must contain at least the information specified in Appendix V to Annex VI. A **sample** must also be provided.

I06d.3 EU requirements on air pollution

* **Council Directive 1999/32/EC** came into effect on 1 July 2000 and requires that the sulphur content of marine diesel oil (MDO) and marine gas oil (MGO) does not exceed 0.2% by mass. This limit does not apply to marine fuel oil (heavy fuel oil) (HFO).

* **Different EU Member States** interpret the Directive's requirements in different ways. Generally, ships trading solely within the EU should only use MDO or MGO with a sulphur content below 0.2%, and any new supplies of MDO or MGO obtained in an EU port should be below the 0.2% sulphur limit. **In most EU ports**, ships arriving from a country outside the EU will not be required to comply. In certain countries, however, such as the Netherlands, non-compliance with the sulphur limits **on any voyage or at any time** may result in a maximum fine on "the transgressor" (assumed to be the master or chief engineer) of euro 10,000 or 6 months' (maximum) imprisonment and on "the company responsible for the transgressor" of euro 45,000. The European Commission apparently shares the Netherlands' interpretation of the Directive's requirements.

* The legal position in any port in an EU Member State may be ascertained from the ship's agent or P&I club correspondent.

I06e REPAIRS AND DRYDOCKING

* Under **The Shipbuilding and Ship-repairing Regulations 1960** (SI 1960/1932)[32] the master, owner or officer is required to provide a **safe means of access** and **adequate lighting** at the place of work and to all spaces which workers may need to enter to get to and from the work. **Safe access to and from the ship** must be provided. The Shipbuilding and Ship-repairing Regulations will be complied with if the MS (Means of Access) Regulations 1988 (SI 1988/1637) are complied with (see E08e.2).

* For notes on **accidents to shore-based workers in UK ports**, see E08k.1k and I05b.3.

---

[30] "Charges" in section 44(4) means any charges with the exception of light dues, local light dues and any other charges payable in respect of lighthouses, buoys or beacons and of charges in respect of pilotage.

[31] "Dark smoke" is defined in section 3 as smoke which, if compared with a "Ringelmann Chart" would appear to be as dark as or darker than shade 2 on the chart. However, a court may be satisfied that smoke is or is not dark smoke notwithstanding that there has been no actual comparison of the smoke with a chart.

[32] The equivalent Northern Ireland regulations are The Shipbuilding and Ship-repairing Regulations (Northern Ireland) 1971.

I07 Pre-departure business

I07a ORDERS FOR SERVICES

* The master may have to order the services of:
  - a pilot;
  - tug(s); and
  - linesmen ("line-handlers") or boatmen, or both.
* Orders, which in most ports are usually made through the agent, should be made in plenty of time.

I07b LOAD LINE LAW

I07b.1 Load Line Regulations

* Relevant Regulations are the **MS (Load Line) Regulations 1998** (SI 1998/2241), as amended. For notes on the **application of and general compliance with the Regulations**, see D03a.3. For notes on requirements relating to **load line surveys and documentation**, see D04i.

I07b.1a Requirements before proceeding to sea (regulation 6)

* **Regulation 6(1)** provides that, subject to any exemption granted under the Regulations, a ship may not proceed or attempt to proceed to sea unless:
  - it has been **surveyed** in accordance with the Regulations;
  - it is **marked** with the appropriate marks (i.e. a deck line and load lines);
  - it complies with the **Conditions of Assignment** applicable to it[33]; and
  - the **information** regarding stability, loading and ballasting required by regulation 32 and 33 is provided for the master's guidance.

  These requirements do not apply to a non-UK ship in respect of which a valid Load Line Convention certificate is produced (regulation 6(2)).
* **Regulation 6(3)** provides that a ship may not be so loaded that:
  - **if the ship is in salt water and has no list**, the appropriate load line on each side of the ship is submerged; or
  - **in any other case** (e.g. where the ship is in dock water or fresh water), the appropriate load line on each side of the ship would be submerged if the ship were in salt water and had no list.
* The requirements of regulation 6(3) **apply in port as well as at sea**, and the fact that a vessel is not intending to proceed to sea is immaterial. The only exception to this rule is in respect of a vessel that is to proceed down-river to sea, which may submerge her marks to allow for the consumption of fuel, water, etc. during the river passage.
* A ship may not proceed to sea in contravention of regulation 6(3) (regulation 6(4)).
* **Regulation 6(5)** provides that before any ship proceeds to sea from a port in the UK, the master must produce to an officer of Customs from whom clearance for the ship is demanded for an international voyage:
  - in the case of a "Convention-size ship"[34], a "valid Convention certificate"[35]; or
  - in the case of any other ship, a UK Load Line Certificate or a UK Load Line Exemption Certificate,
  - which is in force in relation to the ship.

I07b.1b Appropriate load line (regulation 20)

* **Regulation 20** provides that the **appropriate load line**[36] in respect of a ship at any particular zone or area and seasonal period is to be ascertained in accordance with the provisions of Schedule 1 in **MSN 1752**.

---

[33] A ship which does not comply with the Conditions of Assignment will be deemed to be "**dangerously unsafe**". For notes on the **consequences of a ship being found "dangerously unsafe"**, see I02d.
[34] A "**Convention-size**" means in the case of an existing ship, of not less than 150 gross tonnage (ascertained in accordance with the law in force on 21st July 1968), and in the case of a new ship, of not less than 24 metres in length (regulation 2(1)).
[35] A "**valid Convention certificate**" is "valid Convention certificate" means: (a) an International Load Line Certificate (1966) or an International Load Line Exemption Certificate (1966), which is in force, or (b) an International Load Line Certificate or an International Load Line Exemption Certificate, which is in force (regulation 2(1)).

* The International Load Line Convention, 1966 provides for various **permanent zones**, **seasonal zones** and **seasonal areas**. These were shown on a coloured chart accompanying the 1968 Rules, but are not shown in the 1998 Regulations.
* "**Zones**" are bands of sea/ocean going for the most part fully around the world. They may be **permanent** or **seasonal**.
* "**Areas**" are sea areas generally confined within land masses. All the areas are seasonal.
* In any of the three **permanent zones** (i.e. one Summer zone in each hemisphere and a single Tropical zone in the equatorial belt), the **same load line** (i.e. "S" or "T") is applicable throughout the year.
* In a **seasonal zone** or a **seasonal area** (i.e. the Winter Seasonal and Seasonal Tropical Zones and Areas) the load line to be used depends on the **date**.
* In either of the two **summer zones** a ship at sea may not be loaded deeper than her summer load line.
* In the **tropical zone** a ship at sea may not be loaded deeper than her tropical load line.
* In the **winter seasonal zones** and **seasonal tropical areas** a ship may load only to the load line appropriate to the season as shown on the chart.
* In addition to the zones and areas detailed above there are five **winter seasonal areas** for ships of 100 metres or less in length. These ships may load only to the load line appropriate to the season as shown on the chart. These areas are the Baltic Sea, area of the Black Sea, area of the Mediterranean, area of the Sea of Japan and a Special Winter Seasonal Area in the North Atlantic.
* In the **North Atlantic winter seasonal area** a ship may load only to the load line appropriate to the season and size of ship as shown on the chart.
* In the case of a ship of 100 metres or less in length, the appropriate load line is the **Winter North Atlantic load line** in either of the North Atlantic Winter Seasonal Zones (I or II) as shown on the chart, during the winter seasonal periods respectively applicable in those zones.

I07b.1c Ships with timber load lines (regulation 19)

* **Regulation 19(1)** prescribes the measurements and positions of timber load lines.
* The maximum depth to which a ship may be loaded in relation to a Timber load line referred to in regulation 19(1) will be the depth indicated by the upper edge of the appropriate Timber load line (regulation 19(2)). This means that a ship marked with timber load lines and carrying a timber deck cargo **in accordance with the provisions of the Regulations** (as detailed in MSN 1752) may load to the timber load line corresponding to the applicable load line that she would use if she were not marked with timber load lines (i.e. Lumber Summer (LS) in a Summer Zone, Lumber Winter (LW) in a Winter Zone, etc.).
* **When a timber deck cargo is not carried in accordance with the Regulations**, the ordinary load lines will be applicable.

I07b.1d Load line offences and penalties (regulation 35)

* The chief **offences** committed under the MS (Load Line) Regulations 1998, and penalties prescribed by regulation 35, are summarised in the following table.

Offence (with offender shown in bold)	Legislation contravened	Penalties regulation and penalties on summary conviction (SC) & conviction on indictment (COI)
Ship proceeds or attempts to proceed to sea in contravention of regulation 6(1) (surveying and marking requirements). (**Owner and master**)	Regulation 6(1), MS (Load Line) Regulations 1998	Reg. 35(1): SC: Statutory maximum fine COI: Unlimited fine Ship may be detained until surveyed and marked
Ship is overloaded (i.e. appropriate load line is submerged (under regulation 6(3)(a)) or would have been submerged (under regulation 6(3)(b))). (**Owner and master**)	Regulation 6(3)(a) and 6(3)(b), MS (Load Line) Regulations 1998	Reg. 35(2): SC: Statutory maximum fine and additional fine[37] (max. £1,000 for each complete centimetre of overloading) COI: Unlimited fine
Master takes an overloaded ship to sea, or **any other person**, having reason to believe that ship is overloaded, sends or is party to sending her to sea overloaded.	Regulation 6(4) MS (Load Line) Regulations 1998	Reg. 35(4): SC: Statutory maximum fine COI: Unlimited fine (without prejudice to the fine for overloading)

---

[36] "**Appropriate load line**" means the load line directed to be marked on a ship pursuant to regulation 7(2)(b), or in the case of a ship not surveyed under the Regulations, pursuant to an International Load Line Certificate or an International Load Line Certificate (1966) which is in force, indicating the maximum depth to which the ship may be loaded in salt water in a particular zone or area and seasonal period (regulation 2(1)).

[37] Regulation 35(2)(a) provides for "such additional fine....... as the court thinks fit to impose, having regard to the extent to which the earning capacity of the ship was increased by reason of the contravention". Regulation 35(3) limits the additional fine to a maximum amount of £1,000 for each complete centimetre by which the appropriate load line on each side was submerged or, where the ship was not at sea, would have been submerged when at sea. The combined maximum fines on summary conviction for taking an overloaded ship to sea are, therefore, £5,000 + £1,000 per cm of overloading; in the case of a ship overloaded by 10cm, the total fine could be £15,000 on summary conviction.

Owner and master failing to keep the ship marked with the appropriate marks.	Regulation 23(1), MS (Load Line) Regulations 1998	Reg. 35(6)(a): SC: Maximum Level 5 fine
Any person concealing, removing, altering, defacing or obliterating the appropriate marks except with the authority of the Assigning Authority.	Regulation 23(2), MS (Load Line) Regulations 1998	Reg. 35(6)(b): SC: Maximum Level 5 fine
Ship proceeds or attempts to proceed to sea without the appropriate certificate in force. (Master)	Regulation 9(4), MS (Load Line) Regulations 1998	Reg. 35(7): SC: Statutory maximum fine COI: Unlimited fine
Owner and master failing to keep appropriate certificate or Exemption Certificate legible and posted up in some conspicuous place.	Regulation 13, MS (Load Line) Regulations 1998	Reg. 35(8)(a): SC: Maximum Level 3 fine
Master failing to post up Draught of Water and Freeboard Notice (FRE13) in some conspicuous place (except on ships on a near-coastal voyage).	Regulation 13, MS (Load Line) Regulations 1998	Reg. 35(8)(b): SC: Maximum Level 3 fine
Owner and master failing to keep Draught of Water and Freeboard Notice (FRE13) posted and legible until ship arrives at some other dock, wharf, harbour or place (except on ships on a near-coastal voyage).	Regulation 13, MS (Load Line) Regulations 1998	Reg. 35(8)(c): SC: Maximum Level 3 fine

I07b.1e Detention of ship (regulation 37)

* A ship may be **detained**:
  * where, in contravention of regulation 6(1) it proceeds or attempts to proceed to sea without being surveyed and marked (until it has been surveyed and marked) (regulation 37(1));
  * which **does not comply with the Conditions of Assignment** applicable to it (until it complies) (regulation 37(2));
  * without prejudice to any proceedings under regulation 33 (relating to information as to loading and ballasting), which is loaded in contravention of regulation 6(3) (i.e. **overloaded**) (until it ceases to be overloaded) (regulation 37(3)).

I07b.2 Overloading or unsafe or improper loading causing ship to be dangerously unsafe

* **Section 94 of the Merchant Shipping Act 1995** provides that **overloading or unsafe or improper loading** are matters by virtue of which a ship may be considered "dangerously unsafe", in which case the owner and the master will each be guilty of an **offence** punishable by a fine of up to **£50,000** on summary conviction, or 2 years' imprisonment plus an unlimited fine on conviction on indictment.

I07b.3 Effects of overloading on class status and insurance cover
Home
* **Significant overloading** will almost certainly **invalidate the vessel's Certificate of Class**, which will probably have the "knock-on" effects of:
  * **loss of hull and machinery insurance cover**;
  * **loss of P&I cover**;
  * rendering the vessel **unseaworthy** at common law;
  * **suspension or cancellation of statutory certificates**[38] (see D04d.2a).

I07b.4 Rectifying overloaded condition

* It is important that, where a ship becomes **overloaded** in port, her condition is rectified as soon as possible, and before sailing. The cargo or commodity unloaded should, if possible, be that which causes the minimum of commercial disruption, consistent with safety on sailing.

---

[38] Without prejudice to any requirements of a statutory instrument as to the issue of certificates, authorised organisations (i.e. the MCA-authorised classification societies) must not issue certificates to a UK ship de-classed or changing class for safety reasons before consulting the MCA to determine whether a full inspection is necessary (regulation 5, MS (Ship Inspection and Survey Organisations) Regulations 1996 (SI 1996/2908).

* **Water ballast, feed water and potable (domestic) water** should be discharged in preference to bunker fuel. **Cargo cleared for export** should be unloaded only as a last resort, due to the documentary complications and inconvenience that would be caused to the shipowner, shippers, consignees, bankers, insurance brokers, customs officials and others.

I07b.5 Draught of Water and Freeboard Notice

* **Regulation 13(2) of the MS (Load Line) Regulations 1998**, as amended, provides that before any UK ship leaves any dock, wharf, harbour or other place for the purpose of proceeding to sea, the master must ensure that a **notice** (i.e. the MCA Form "**Draught of Water and Freeboard – Notice**", formerly known as an "**FRE 13**") is posted up in some conspicuous place on board the ship, in a form and containing such particulars relating to the depth to which the ship is loaded as is specified in **Schedule 7 to MSN 1752**.
* **Regulation 13(4)** provides regulation 13(2) does not apply to a ship employed on a **near-coastal voyage**. (Under the 1968 Regulations, as amended, it did not apply to ships within the Limited European Trading Area.)
* **Regulation 13(3)** provides that where a notice has been posted up, the master must cause it to be kept posted and legible until the ship arrives at some other dock, wharf, harbour or place.
* **The Draught of Water and Freeboard Notice** is not a copy of the "freeboard sheet" on pages 30-31 of the Official Log Book; the freeboard sheet requires 19 columns to be completed, whereas the Notice has only 9 columns.
* **Entries required on the Notice** are as follows: Ship's name, port of registry and gross tonnage; freeboards and Timber freeboards assigned, and corresponding draughts, as in the Official Log Book; the FWA and timber FWA in millimetres; particulars of loading, in the following columns: 1: Date; 2: Place; 3: Actual draught forward; 4: Actual draught aft; 5: Actual mean draught; 6: Actual mean freeboard; 7: Corrected mean freeboard; 8: Signature of master; 9: Signature of an officer.
* The "**actual mean freeboard**" is the mean of the freeboards on each side of the ship when the ship is loaded and ready to leave. The "**corrected mean freeboard**" is the freeboard that the ship will have in salt water, i.e. without any dock water allowance applied. If the actual mean freeboard is greater than the appropriate salt water freeboard, Column 7 need not be filled in.
* The **date and time of posting the Notice** must be entered in column 15 of the Official Log Book departures/arrivals page or the AFS/72 form in use, or column 20 of the AFS/RO/89 used in a ro-ro passenger ship.

I07b.6 Official Log Book entries relating to draught and freeboard

* For notes on **Official Log Book entries** required to be recorded and **Additional Freeboard Sheet (AFS) forms** used in certain ships, see D05a.8 and D05a.9.

I07b.7 Recording of draughts, etc. on passenger ships

* **Regulation 42 of the MS (Passenger Ship Construction: Ships of Classes I, II and II(A)) Regulations 1998** (SI 1998/2514) provides that on completion of loading of a ship to which the Regulations apply and before it proceeds on a voyage, the master or an officer appointed for that purpose by him must **ascertain** –
  * the **draught** at the bow and stern;
  * the **trim** by the bow or the stern; and
  * the **vertical distance** from the waterline to the appropriate subdivision load line mark on each side of the ship.
* The draughts, trim and vertical distance must be recorded by the master or the appointed officer in the **Official Log Book**. For notes on completion of the **Official Log Book freeboard pages** and **Additional Freeboard Sheet** (AFS) forms see D05a.8 and D05a.9.

I07b.8 Calculation of stability on passenger ships

* **Regulation 43(1) of the MS (Passenger Ship Construction: Ships of Classes I, II and II(A)) Regulations 1998** (SI 1998/2514) provides that on completion of loading of a ship to which the Regulations apply and before it proceeds on a voyage, the master must determine the **trim and stability** and also record that the ship is in compliance with **stability criteria** in the relevant Regulations. The determination of the ship's stability must always be made by **calculation**, although use of an electronic loading and stability **computer** or equivalent means may be accepted for this purpose.

* **Regulation 43(2)** provides that, in the case of **ships of Class II or II(A)** the actual **weights** of goods vehicles and other items of cargo required to be provided for the stability calculation must be in accordance with the **MS (Weighing of Goods Vehicles and Other Cargo) Regulations 1988** (SI 1988/1275), as amended by SI 1989/270. In the case of **ships of Class I**, the actual **weights** of goods vehicles and other items of cargo must be used and determined in accordance with the **same Regulations as if the ship was a Class II ship**. For items not required to be weighed, the **declared weights or weights estimated as accurately as possible** must be used.
* **Where the calculation is made by means of a shore-based loading and stability computer system**, a **print-out** of the calculation must be presented to the master before the ship proceeds on its voyage. It is the duty of the **person responsible for the computer system** to ensure that the calculations are substantially correct (regulation 43(3)).

I07c COMPLETION OF CARGO OPERATIONS

I07c.1 Unloading and washing of NLS tanks

* **Schedule 2 of M1703/NLS1** contains the technical requirements of the **MS (Dangerous or Noxious Liquid Substances) Regulations 1996** (SI 1996/3010). For an outline of the Regulations and the **discharge requirements** applicable to vessels **at sea**, see H03b.
* A tank from which a **Category A substance** has been unloaded must be **washed before a ship leaves port**. Detailed washing requirements are given in **Schedule 2 of M1703/NLS1**.
* Whenever a **Category B or Category C substance is unloaded**, unloading must, if possible, be carried out in accordance with the ship's Procedures and Arrangements Manual.
* Where a **Category B or Category C substance is unloaded at a port outside a Special Area**, and
  * it is impossible for unloading to be carried out in accordance with the Procedures and Arrangements Manual to the satisfaction of a MARPOL surveyor; or
  * in any case where the substance in question is a high residue substance,
  - every tank unloaded must be **pre-washed** and the resulting washings must be discharged into a **reception facility** at that port.
* Where a **Category B substance is unloaded at a port in a Special Area**, every tank unloaded must be pre-washed and the resulting washings must be discharged into a reception facility at that port unless:
  * unloading was carried out in accordance with the Procedures and Arrangements Manual to the satisfaction of a MARPOL surveyor; and
  * the substance is not a high residue substance; and
  * the residues are to be retained on board for discharge outside a Special Area.
* Where a **Category C substance is unloaded at a port in a Special Area** every tank unloaded must be pre-washed and the resulting washings must be discharged into a reception facility at that port unless:
  * unloading was carried out in accordance with the Procedures and Arrangements Manual to the satisfaction of a MARPOL surveyor; and
  * either:
    * the substance is a Category C substance identified in the Procedures and Arrangements Manual as likely to result in a residue quantity from any one tank which does not exceed 1 cubic metre or $1/3000^{th}$ of the capacity of the tank, whichever is the greater; or
    * the substance is not a high residue substance and the residues are to be retained on board for discharge outside a Special Area.
* Notwithstanding the provisions of regulation 4(2) and the relevant requirements above, any tank from which a Category A, B or C substance has been unloaded will not be required to be washed and the resultant washings discharged before sailing if a MARPOL surveyor at the unloading port **exempts** the ship from those requirements on the following grounds:
  * the tank is to be re-loaded with the same substance or another substance compatible with it and the tank will not be washed or ballasted before such reloading;
  * the tank is neither to be washed or ballasted at sea; and
    * the washing and discharge requirements will be complied with in respect of that tank at another port; and
    * it has been confirmed in writing to the MCA, or (at a non-UK port) to the satisfaction of the government or proper authority of the port State, that an adequate reception facility will be available at that other port; or
  * the substance is one for which cleaning by ventilation is stated to be appropriate to the ship's P&A Manual or is approved by the MCA.

I07c.2 Cargo matters for attention before sailing

* On completion of cargo operations, and before sailing, some or all of the following **cargo-related matters** may have to be attended to:
    * **determination of cargo quantity**, in some cases by draught survey;
    * passing **cargo quantity** figures to the person responsible for completing bills of lading;
    * signing bills of lading;
    * "**early departure procedure**" for bill of lading completion (in some tanker trades/ports);
    * checking and signing the **Statement of Facts** if presented by agent;
    * checking the agent's **despatch/demurrage calculation** ("Laytime Statement");
    * **securing** of cargo;
    * **closing and sealing hatches** and shell doors;
    * receiving on board any **small parcels** for carriage between ports;
    * notifying appropriate authority of any **hazardous cargo** on board (see I07d).

I07d HAZARDOUS CARGO NOTIFICATIONS

* The **MS (Reporting Requirements for Ships Carrying Dangerous or Polluting Goods) Regulations 1995** (SI 1995/2498), as amended by SI 1999/2121, provide that certain information in respect of ships carrying hazardous cargo to be **notified** to the competent authority in the following cases:
    * where **any ship** departs from a **UK port** carrying **dangerous or polluting goods** (see I07d.1);
    * where a **UK ship** leaves a **EU port** outside the UK carrying **dangerous or polluting goods** (see I07d.2; and
    * where a **UK ship** leaves a port **outside the EU** carrying **dangerous goods or harmful substances in packaged form** (see I07d.3).
* For notes on requirements of the Regulations relating to **arrival notifications**, see I01a.7.
* For notes on requirements of the Regulations relating to **reports of incidents at sea**, see H06e.1.

I07d.1 Ships departing from UK ports carrying dangerous or polluting goods

* **Under regulation 5(1)(a) of the Reporting Requirements Regulations the operator** of a ship carrying **dangerous goods or polluting goods** must, before its departure from a **UK port**, notify all information listed in **Schedule 1 to MSN 1741** to the **competent authority** for the UK in accordance with MSN 1741. This requirement **does not apply** to any ship engaged on a **regular scheduled service of less than 1 hour's sailing** which the MCA has exempted (or on such a service of such longer period as the MCA with the consent of the EC Commission may allow), in accordance with **MSN 1741** (regulation 5(1)(c)).
* "**Dangerous goods**" means goods classified as such in the IMDG Code, including radioactive materials as referred to in the INF Code, in Chapter 19 of the IGC Code or Chapter 17 of the IBC Code.
* "**Polluting goods**" means oil as defined in MARPOL Annex I (excluding bunkers and ship's stores), noxious liquid substances, and harmful substances in packaged form.
* For the purposes of Council Directive 93/75/EC and the Regulations, the **MCA** is designated under regulation 4(1) as the "**competent authority**" for the UK.
* The **information in Schedule 1 to MSN 1741** is a list of **Information on ships carrying dangerous or polluting goods** and includes:
    1. Name and call sign of vessel.
    2. Nationality of vessel.
    3. Length and draught of vessel in metres.
    4. Port of destination.
    5. ETA at port of destination or pilot station, as required by the competent authority.
    6. Estimated time of departure (ETD).
    7. Intended route.
    8. Correct technical name of the dangerous and polluting goods, the UN numbers (if any), the IMO hazard classes in accordance with the IMDG, IBC and IGC Codes, the quantities of such goods and their location on board (in a list, manifest or stowage plan) and, if in portable tanks or freight containers, their identification marks.

I07d.2 UK ships leaving EU ports outside the UK carrying dangerous or polluting goods

* **Under regulation 5(1)(b) of the Reporting Requirements Regulations** the **operator** of a UK ship, before the ship leaves any EU port outside the UK carrying dangerous or polluting goods, must notify all information listed in **Schedule 1 to MSN 1741** (as in I07d.1) to the **competent authority of the State** in which the port is situated
* In EU member States other than the UK, the "**competent authority**" is, under regulation 4(2), any authority designated as such in conformity with article 3 of the Council Directive. (The identity of the appropriate authority may be ascertained from ships' agents.)

I07d.3 UK ships leaving ports outside the EU carrying dangerous goods or harmful substances in packaged form

* **Under regulation 5(1)(c) of the Reporting Requirements Regulations** the operator of a UK ship, before leaving a port outside the EU carrying dangerous goods or harmful substances in packaged form, must comply with the requirements set out in **paragraphs 7.2 and 7.3 of MSN 1741**.
* "**Harmful substances in packaged form**" has the meaning given by MARPOL Annex III[39].
* "**In packaged form**" an individual package or receptacle including a freight container or a portable tank or tank container or tank vehicle or shipborne barge or other cargo unit.
* In any non-EU State, the "**competent authority**" is, under regulation 4(3), any authority designated as such by that State in relation to a purpose of the Regulations, or, if none is designated, the State itself (i.e. the government of the country).
* **Paragraph 7.2 of MSN 1741** provides: "Ships carrying dangerous goods or harmful substances in packaged form have to have a **manifest or a special list or stowage plan** on board. This document must list the dangerous goods and harmful substances in packaged form on board, and give their location (and, for dangerous goods only, their classification)."
* **Paragraph 7.3 of MSN 1741** provides: The **manifest, special list or stowage plan** must be **made available**, before departure, to the person or organisation designated by the port State. When the ship has **harmful substances in packaged form** on board, the owner (or a representative) must **retain a copy** of the document on shore until they are unloaded."

I07e PRE-DEPARTURE STOWAWAY SEARCH

I07e.1 Offence of stowing away

* A person who, without the consent of the master or of any other person authorised to give consent, **goes to sea** or **attempts to go to sea** in a UK ship commits an **offence** under **section 103(1) of the Merchant Shipping Act 1995**, and will be liable on summary conviction to a fine not exceeding Level 3 on the standard scale.
* **Unauthorised presence on board** a UK ship, which is dealt with under section 104 of the Act, is not "stowing away" unless the ship goes to sea or the person attempts to go to sea.

I07e.2 High stowaway risk areas

* According to the P&I clubs (who deal with many stowaway incidents), certain parts of the world are high-risk areas for stowaways. The breakdown of borders and security in **eastern Europe** in the 1990s led to a significant increase in the number of people trying to get into the USA and Canada illegally, with **Le Havre, Antwerp, Rotterdam, Hamburg** and **Bremen** being reported as ports having an especially high risk of stowaway embarkation for these countries. The June/August 2000 issue of *Gard News*, highlighted **Africa, Central America, Colombia, Dominican Republic, India, Pakistan** and **Indonesia** as being problem areas. More recently, ports on the Continental side of the English Channel have featured in news bulletins as "asylum seekers" from middle Eastern countries and beyond attempt to gain entry to the UK, in many cases organised by "migrant smugglers".
* As the political and economic state of the world changes, patterns of stowaway movements will also change. Since the P&I clubs invariably have the latest intelligence on stowaway risks, masters should endeavour to obtain their latest club bulletins and information.

---

[39] For the purposes of MARPOL Annex III, "harmful substances" are those substances which are identified as marine pollutants in the IMDG Code.

* **At any port in a high-risk area**, great care should be taken to ensure that stowaways do not board, and the following safeguards should be observed:
  1. A watch should be kept on the **accommodation ladder or gangway**.
  2. **Stevedores** should only be allowed to work in restricted areas and a watch should be kept on them.
  3. **Open spaces** should be closed as far as possible.
  4. A **search** of the ship should be carried out before the ship sails.
  5. All **open-top containers on the quay** should be checked. **All containers** on the quay should be stacked door-to-door, if possible.
* Masters are recommended to read "*Stowaways by Sea*" published by the Nautical Institute. This recommends a number of measures to take in particularly high-risk areas including:
  * **checking everyone** embarking and disembarking;
  * **sealing off certain parts of the ship** to prevent access and reduce the areas and compartments which may need to be searched;
  * **conducting searches** of vehicles and loose cargo; and
  * **posting a lookout** to prevent people climbing aboard.

I07e.3 Stowaway search forms and procedure

* An extensive, systematic and detailed **search** of the ship should be made immediately before departure, especially from any high-risk port or place.
* Before starting a stowaway search, the master should draw up a **checklist** or lists based on his own ship or cargo. A standard ship's form can easily be drafted for modification when different cargoes are on board or in other particular circumstances. Separate parts of the ship can be detailed on separate lists, e.g. accommodation, machinery spaces, cargo spaces, open deck areas, etc.
* Some P&I clubs produce **stowaway checklist cards**, but because of the wide differences in design, cargo, etc. between individual ships, these are not always suitable for a particular ship.
* The **accommodation search form** drawn up should include (but should not necessarily be limited to) the following areas: bridge, wheelhouse, radio room, toilet, monkey island, masts; cabins, toilets, shower rooms, hospital, lockers; storerooms, linen lockers, safety gear lockers; saloon, messroom, bar, recreation rooms; galley, dry stores; laundry, changing rooms; ship's offices.
* The **machinery spaces search form** should include (but should not necessarily be limited to) the following areas: engine room, control room, under-plate spaces, emergency generator room, fiddly (funnel casing); funnel top, accesses, safety lockers, storerooms; CO_2 room; changing room; steering flat.
* The **cargo spaces search form** should include (but should not necessarily be limited to) the following areas: holds, tween decks, accesses, lockers; deck cargo stacks; hatchcover recesses; empty, unsealed containers; ventilator trunks.
* The **deck areas search form** should include (but should not necessarily be limited to) the following areas: forecastle, forecastle head spaces (including chain locker, paint locker, bosun's stores, bow thruster space, etc.), upper deck, hold accesses, fan rooms, contactor rooms, pump rooms; lifeboats; swimming pool; ropes hanging overside; spurling pipes and hawsepipes of large ships; ventilators; crane cabs, winch houses and house tops; inside coils of mooring rope, behind stacks of dunnage, etc.
* **Completed checklists** should be returned to the chief officer or master and filed. (These may later be needed by owners, the P&I club, lawyers or the shore authorities if stowaways are discovered.)
* The master should make an **entry in the deck log** recording the search and its results, with full details of date, time, spaces searched, and names and ranks of searchers.
* For procedures in connection with **stowaways discovered at sea**, see H04e.3.

I07f PASSENGERS

I07f.1 Counting and Registration of Persons on Board Passenger Ships Regulations

* **The MS (Counting and Registration of Persons on Board Passenger Ships) Regulations 1999** (SI 1999/1869) –
  - implement Council Directive 98/41/EC and SOLAS regulation III/27.
  - **revoke** the MS (Passenger Boarding Cards) Regulations 1988 (SI 1988/191), the MS (Passenger Boarding Cards) (Application to non-UK Ships) Regulations 1988 (SI 1988/641) and the MS (Passenger Counting and Recording Systems) Regulations 1990 (SI 1990/659).

- **apply to** any UK passenger ship wherever it may be, and any non-UK passenger ship while in UK waters.
- **do not apply to** any warship, any troopship or any pleasure yacht unless it is or will be crewed and carry more than 12 passengers for commercial purposes.
* "**Appropriate search and rescue services**" means, in relation to a ship involved in an emergency, the search and rescue services for the area in which the ship is located.
* "**Community ship**" means a ship registered in, or which is entitled to fly the flag of, a member State of the EU.
* "**International voyage**" in the regulations means a voyage from any SOLAS party country to a port outside that country, or conversely.
* "**Landing point**" means any berth, excursion point, floating pier or stage, link span, pier, port, stop or anchorage point from or to where passengers are embarked or disembarked.
* "**Person**" means any person on board a ship irrespective of their age.
* "**Protected sea area**" means a sea area sheltered from open sea effects where a ship is at no time more than six miles from a place of refuge where shipwrecked persons can land and in which the proximity of search and rescue facilities is ensured.
* "**Regular community service**" means a regular service in a sea area where the annual probability of the significant wave height exceeding two metres is less than 10% and-
    * the voyage does not exceed thirty miles or thereabouts from the point of departure; or
    * the primary purpose of the service is to provide regular links to outlying communities for customary purposes.
* "**Regular service**" means a series of ship crossings operated so as to serve traffic between the same two or more ports either-
    * according to a published timetable; or
    * with crossings so regular or frequent that they constitute a recognisable systematic series.
* "**Voyage**" includes an excursion.
* Where a ship is managed or operated by a person other than the owner (whether on behalf of the owner or some other person, or on his own behalf), a reference in the Regulations to the "owner" should be construed as including a reference to that other person.

I07f.1a Passenger counting (regulation 5)

* The owner of any UK passenger ship leaving any landing point (anywhere), and of any non-UK passenger ship leaving any landing point in the UK, must ensure that the ship has an MCA-approved **counting system** capable of counting all persons on board (i.e. passengers, crew and others) (regulation 5(1)). The counting system on all passenger ships must conform to the requirements of **MSN 1729**.
* In the case of a **Class II or II(A) passenger ship**, the counting system must use **individual passenger boarding cards**.
* Regulation 5(2) provides that **the counting system must be such that**:
    * all persons boarding the ship at a landing point at the beginning of a voyage are counted individually on or just prior to boarding.
    * all persons disembarking at subsequent landing points during a voyage are counted individually as they disembark;
    * all persons boarding at subsequent landing points during a voyage, are counted individually on, or just prior to, boarding; and
    * the number of persons **remaining on board at each landing point** is determined.
* As an alternative to the system required by regulation 5(2) **another system, approved by the MCA and of equivalent effectiveness**, may be used.
* If the counting system uses individual passenger boarding cards, no passenger may be permitted to board the ship unless he has been issued with an **individual boarding card** (regulation 5(3)).
* Immediately before a passenger ship leaves any landing point the **total number of persons on board at that time** as determined by means of the counting system must be **communicated to the master** of the ship **and to the passenger registrar** ashore (regulation 5(4)).
* Where, in respect of a person on board, any person (e.g. that person or their carer) has declared a **need for special care or assistance in emergency situations**, the owner must ensure that this information is properly **recorded** and **communicated to the master** (regulation 5(5)).
* Regulation 5(6) provides that no passenger ship may leave any landing point if:
    * the above requirements have not been complied with; or
    * the total number of persons on board exceeds the number of persons the ship is permitted to carry.
* The counting system arrangements must be described in **written instructions** which must be kept on board the ship at all times in the custody of the master (regulation 5(7)).

I07f.1b Counting and registration: additional requirements for voyages of more than 20 miles (regulation 6)

* Regulation 6 applies to:
    * any UK passenger ship leaving any landing point within the EU on a voyage of more than 20 miles from that landing point;
    * any UK passenger ship leaving any landing point outside the EU on an international voyage;
    * any non-UK passenger ship leaving any landing point in the UK on a voyage of more than 20 miles from that landing point.
* The owner of any passenger ship to which regulation 6 applies must ensure that the information specified below is collected, in relation to each person on board, before the ship departs from the landing point.
* The information must be communicated to the passenger registrar within 30 minutes of the ship's departure from the landing point.
* Any information regarding a person's need for special care or assistance in emergency situations, must be communicated to the master before the ship leaves the landing point.
* The following **details are to be communicated to the passenger registrar** in relation to each person on board the ship:
    * family name;
    * forenames or initials;
    * gender;
    * subject to the provision in the next paragraph, an indication of the category of age (such category being either adult, child or infant) to which the person belongs or the age or the year of birth of the person; and
    * if volunteered by a person, any information concerning the need for special care or assistance in emergency situations.
* If the information in relation to a person indicates the category of age to which the person belongs but does not indicate that person's age or year of birth, then:
    * the information must be accompanied by an indication of the age range used to define each category, and
    * the age range used must be the age range used by the system for the registration of the information established in accordance with regulation 8(1) (see I07f.1d).

I07f.1c Non-Community ships on voyages from outside the EU to the UK (regulation 7)

* Regulation 7 provides that in respect of any **non-EU passenger ship on any voyage from any landing point outside the EU to the UK**, the owner shall make:
    * information as to the total number of persons on board the ship; and
    * the information specified in regulation 6(3) above,
    * readily available to the appropriate search and rescue services for the purposes of search and rescue in the event of an emergency or in the aftermath of an accident involving the ship.

I07f.1d Registration system (regulation 8)

* The owner of a passenger ship to which regulation 5 or regulation 6 applies must establish a **system**, approved by the MCA and meeting the requirements of MSN 1729, **for the registration of passenger information** collected under the Regulations (regulation 8(1)).
* The owner must also appoint a **shore-based passenger registrar** who shall be responsible for holding the information collected pursuant to the Regulations and for its **transmission to appropriate search and rescue services** in the event of an emergency or in the aftermath of an accident involving the ship.
* The owner must ensure that the information collected under the Regulations is at all times **readily available** for transmission to the appropriate search and rescue services for use in an emergency or in the aftermath of an accident involving the ship.
* Any **personal data** collected solely pursuant to the Regulations by an owner may be **kept only for as long as is necessary** for the purposes of the Regulations.
* The MCA may appoint **persons to carry out checks** on the proper functioning of registration systems approved under this regulation. The persons appointed will be entitled to board any ship to which the registration system relates and enter any premises of the passenger registrar, and have access to any records and documents, including electronic and computer records, which comprise the owner's registration system.

I07f.1e Miscellaneous provisions

* **Exemption** from the Regulations, or any part of them, is possible under regulation 9.
* Regulation 10 prohibits the making of **false statements** when determining the total number of persons on board or in the collection of passenger information, and falsifying the information for the passenger registrar.

I07f.2 Practice passenger musters and safety briefings

* **Regulation 9 of the MS (Musters, Training and Decision Support Systems) Regulations 1999** (SI 1999/2722) provides that on any ship carrying **passengers** where the passengers are scheduled to be **on board for more than 24 hours**, musters of the passengers must take place **within 24 hours after their embarkation**. This initial muster must include instruction in the **use of a lifejacket** and the **action to be taken in an emergency**.
* If only a **small number of passengers** embarks at a port after the initial muster described above has been held, it will be sufficient, instead of holding another muster, to draw the attention of the new passengers to the **emergency instructions** required by regulation 5 (see E08l.1b).
* In any ship of **Class II, II(A) or III**, or of **Class VIII, VIII(A), VIII(A)(T) and IX in which passengers are carried**, or of **Class XI on an international voyage**, if a passenger muster is not held on departure, the attention of the passengers must be drawn to the **emergency instructions** required by regulation 5 (see E08l.1b).
* **Whenever passengers embark** on any ship, a **passenger safety briefing** must be given, either immediately before or immediately after the ship next sails, by way of an announcement which must:
  * be made on the ship's PA system or by other equivalent means likely to be heard at least by the passengers who have not yet heard the announcement during the voyage;
  * be made in English and any other appropriate language; and
  * include the emergency instructions required by regulation 5 (see E08l.1b).
* The passenger safety briefing may be included in the initial muster required within 24 hours of embarkation if this muster is held immediately before or immediately after the ship next sails.
* **Information cards**, **posters** or **video programmes** displayed on the ship's video display system may be used to supplement the passenger safety briefing, but may not be used to replace the required announcement.

I07f.3 Emergency Information for Passengers Regulations

* **The MS (Emergency Information for Passengers) Regulations 1990** (SI 1990/660) -
  - **apply to** UK passenger ships operating as passenger ships of Classes I, II, II(A), III, IV, V, VI and VI(A).
  - contain provisions requiring a **public address system** on ships carrying more than 20 passengers (regulation 4) and **marking of exits**   (regulation 6).
  - allow **exemptions** to be granted (regulation 7).
* In ships of **Class I**, if a muster of the passengers is not held on departure, the attention of the passengers must be drawn by means of an announcement at the commencement of the voyage to the emergency instructions required by the MS (Musters, Training and Decision Support Systems) Regulations 1999 (regulation 5(1)).
* In ships of **Classes IV, V, VI and VI(A)** the passengers must be informed by means of an announcement at the commencement of each voyage of the action they should take in the event of an emergency which could lead to the ship being abandoned (regulation 5(2)(a)).
* In ships of **Classes IV, V, VI and VI(A)** notices providing emergency instructions for passengers must also be displayed in each passenger compartment (regulation 5(2)(b)).
* The Regulations are explained in **M.1409**, which gives details of signs, passenger emergency instructions notices, PA systems, and means of drawing passengers' attention to passenger emergency instructions notices. An example is given of emergency instructions for passengers and an emergency instruction broadcast.

I07f.4 Passenger return

* For notes on requirements relating to **passenger returns for ships arriving in or departing from UK ports** see I01i.

I07g LIGHT DUES

I07g.1 Payment and collection of light dues in UK and Ireland

* **"General light dues"** are a service charge on ships for the maintenance of lights and marks around the UK and Irish coasts, and are payable under **section 205 of the Merchant Shipping Act 1995**. Section 205(2) provides that a general lighthouse authority may demand, take and recover general light dues in accordance with section 205 and for that purpose appoint persons to collect them. Section 205(4) provides that general light dues will be payable in respect of all ships whatever, except ships belonging to Her Majesty (i.e. Government-owned ships) and ships exempted from payment under regulations made under section 205(5).
* **Section 207(1)** provides that the light dues will be payable by the **owner or the master**, or "such **consignees or agents of the owner or master** as have paid, or made themselves liable to pay, any other charge on account of the ship in the port of her arrival and discharge". (Generally, ships' agents pay light dues at ports in all countries where they are levied.)
* **Collection of light dues** is the responsibility of the Institute of Chartered Shipbrokers, who provide **regional collectors** who visit ships' agents and other parties through whom ships' light dues are paid.
* **All light dues collected** in the UK and Ireland are pooled into a central fund called the **General Lighthouse Fund** which is administered by the Department for Transport (DfT) and meets the costs of the three General Lighthouse Authorities (GLAs), i.e. **Trinity House**, **The Commissioners of Irish Lights** and **The Northern Lighthouse Board**. Additionally, a grant in aid is made to the fund by the Irish Government's Department of the Marine and Natural Resources.
* **Light dues payable** for the current year are notified by a Statutory Instrument entitled **The MS (Light Dues) Regulations** which generally come into force on 1 April of the relevant year and are amended as necessary in subsequent years for changes in rates payable, etc.

I07g.2 Light Dues Regulations

* The **MS (Light Dues) Regulations 1997** (SI 1997/562) -
    - revoke and replace the MS (Light Dues) Regulations 1990 as amended.
    - came into force on 1 April 1997.
    - are amended by the MS (Light Dues) (Amendment) Regulations 1998 (SI 1998/495) and the MS (Light Dues) (Amendment) Regulations 2002 (SI 2002/504).
    - set out the **rates of light dues** payable by merchant ships, tugs, fishing vessels and pleasure craft.
* **Rates payable** are set out in a **scale of payments** in Part II of Schedule 2 of the Regulations (regulation 3(1)).
* **Light dues will be levied** in accordance with the **rules** in Part III of Schedule 2 (regulation 3(2)).
* **Light dues will not be levied** in the case of vessels of the descriptions listed in Part IV of Schedule 2 (regulation 3(3)).
* **Tugs, fishing vessels and pleasure vessels** are required to **make periodical payments**. Ships of other classes (including merchant ships) make **payments per voyage** (see I07g.2a).

I07g.2a Payments per voyage

* Paragraph 3(1) of Part II – Scale of payments - provides that in respect of **ships of all classes other than tugs, fishing vessels and pleasure vessels**, and subject to a **minimum charge of £60 per voyage**, a **maximum charge of £16,000** and to paragraph 3(2), the amount of light dues per voyage will be **40 pence per ton**[40]. (A ship's tonnage for light dues purposes is its net tonnage assessed in accordance with the International Convention on Tonnage Measurement of Ships 1969 and entered on its International Tonnage Certificate (1969) or, if this certificate is not available for any reason, the ship's gross registered tonnage or, in the case of an unregistered ship or a ship measured only by length, the tonnage reckoned in accordance with the Thames Measurement adopted by Lloyds Register.)
* Paragraph 3(2) provides that where a ship has paid dues under paragraph 3(1) in respect of a voyage it will not be required to pay light dues in respect of any subsequent voyage in any period of **one month** commencing with the last preceding relevant date. For this purpose, "relevant date" means the date on which a ship arrives at or departs from a port or place on a voyage in respect of which light dues were paid or payable (paragraph 3(3)).

---

[40] The cap of £16,000 and reduction from 41p to 40p per ton were introduced on 1 April 2002 and were made possible by an increase in efficiency of the General Lighthouse Authorities.

* Paragraph 3(4) provides that **in any year**, a ship will not be required to make payments of light dues for more than seven voyages in total. A voyage of a ship will be reckoned from port to port (paragraph 3(5)). (A **year** is reckoned from 1 April.)

* Paragraph 3(6) provides that a payment on account of light dues made under paragraph 3(1) in any year will not entitle the ship to any exemption from dues in accordance with the provisions of paragraph 3(2) or any limitation of liability for dues in accordance with the provisions of paragraph 3(4) above, beyond 30 April in the following year.

* **Examples of annual payments** (i.e. for 7 voyages) for different ship types at the rate of 40p per ton are as shown in the following table.

Ship type	Gross tonnage	Net tonnage	Net tonnage x 40p per ton (GBP)	Annual light dues (GBP)
Ro-ro passenger ferry	3296	988	2,766.40	2,766.40
Ro-ro passenger ferry	20446	6133	17,172.40	(Capped) 16,000.00
Mainline container ship	50350	28369	79,433.20	(Capped) 16,000.00
Cruise ship	70327	37182	104,109.60	(Capped) 16,000.00
VLCC	130145	108734	304,455.20	(Capped) 16,000.00

I07g.2b Vessels exempted from light dues

* Under **part IV of the Regulations, as amended by SI 1998/495**, the following vessels are **exempted** from payment of light dues:

1. Ships on charter to Her Majesty or used by a **Government department** or a foreign government other than for commercial purposes.
2. Ships of **less than 20 tons**, other than ships liable to pay dues by reference to their length.
3. Sailing ships used exclusively for **sail training** purposes, operating as travelling museums or vessels of historical interest.
4. **Tugs and fishing vessels** of **less than 10m** in length.
5. Ships (other than those subject to periodical payments) when navigating wholly and bona fide **in ballast** and not engaged in any other revenue earning, commercial, or passenger-carrying activity or service).
6. Ships putting in solely for **bunkers, stores, crew changes**, embarkation or disembarkation of **pilots**, a **medical emergency**, or for **provisions** for their own use on board, unless they are otherwise engaged in any revenue-earning or commercial activity or service.
7. Ships putting in from **stress of weather** or because of **damage** or on voyages solely for the purpose of **damage or running repairs**, where they are not otherwise engaged in a revenue-earning or commercial activity or service, provided they do not discharge or load cargo other than cargo discharged with a view to such repairs, and afterwards re-shipped.
8. Ships navigating solely and entirely **within the limits of a harbour authority**; except in the outer areas of the Port of London Authority and the Forth Ports Authority where aids to navigation are maintained by the General Lighthouse Authorities.
9. Any ship (including a pleasure vessel) in respect of any year during the whole of which it is **laid up**.
10. Vessels engaged solely in **harbour maintenance, dredging, building or maintenance of sea defences or land reclamation** on behalf of a statutory or harbour authority.
11. Vessels solely engaged in **pollution control, prevention or recovery** on behalf of a statutory authority.
12. Vessels engaged solely in the **transportation of sewerage waste** to spoil grounds by or on behalf of a statutory authority.
13. Vessels putting in or departing in ballast for the purpose of **modification**, **alteration**, **scrapping** or **departing as new buildings** from a shipyard, not otherwise engaged in any other revenue-earning or commercial activity or service.
14. Dumb barges, lighters, hulks, or other vessels being towed which are specifically designed and built **without a means of propulsion**.

I07g.3 Light Certificates

* **Section 209(1) of the Merchant Shipping Act 1995** provides that a **receipt** for general light dues must be given to the person paying them by the authority or person receiving them from him. A ship may be **detained** in port under section 209(2) until the receipt is **produced** to a Customs officer or the Collector.

* The ship's **agent** will normally be responsible for remitting light dues payable in respect of a merchant vessel in a UK or Irish port, and will arrange for the issue of a **Light Certificate** to the ship as a receipt[41].
* Before light dues are levied, the **last Light Certificate** received by the ship should be checked by the agent, along with the vessel's **net tonnage** as shown on the International Tonnage Certificate (1969). (The tonnage shown on the Certificate of Registry will be accepted if no ITC(1969) is held.)
* For each payment of light dues in the current year (April 1 to March 31), a ship's copy of the receipted **Light Certificate** must be given to the master. All certificates received in the current year should be retained for inspection at subsequent ports of call in the UK or Ireland.
* When all light dues payable in the current year have been paid, the **final Light Certificate issued should be stamped** "Exempt from further payment for the year (e.g.) 2002/2003". This certificate should be retained by the master for the remainder of the current year and shown to Customs at every subsequent clearance during that year from a UK or Irish port.
* **Light Certificates** are issued on behalf of the General Lighthouse Authorities of Great Britain and Ireland and show the following details:
  * year of payment (e.g. "2002/2003");
  * certificate number;
  * name and address of owner or agent paying light dues;
  * collector's stamp and signature;
  * vessel details, including full name, IMO or Lloyd's Register number, and previous name (if changed recently);
  * dates of arrival, departure and certificate expiry;
  * current year payment number;
  * last certificate number (in current year);
  * voyage details (from/to);
  * port code;
  * vessel category (e.g. 01: tanker; 02: general cargo);
  * number of voyages covered by the certificate;
  * type of payment (A = voyage rate);
  * country of registry (as per code on back of certificate);
  * source of tonnage details (ITC 1969 or national tonnage certificate);
  * tonnages (net and gross);
  * total paid;
  * currency in which paid (pounds, punts or euros).
* A note at the top of Light Certificates reads: "**Important**: All Light Certificates for the current year must be produced when Light Dues are being paid or exemption claimed. Exemption will not be granted without production of these."

I07g.4 Local light dues

* **Section 210(2) of the Merchant Shipping Act 1995** provides for local lighthouse authorities to levy "**local light dues**" on the same basis as general light dues.
* An example of a local lighthouse authority in the UK charging local light dues is Gloucester Harbour Trustees[42].

I07g.5 Foreign light dues

* **Many coastal States** other than the UK and Ireland, e.g. India, Malaysia, USA, Ukraine and Turkey (to name but a few), impose charges for the use of lights on shipping entering their ports. In the USA light dues are called "**tonnage tax**"[43], while in Australia they are officially termed the "**Marine Navigation Levy**". The basis for light dues in foreign countries may be net tonnage, internal volume or some other basis.
* The **European Union** is considering the whole topic of "User Pays Service" for marine navigation and it is thought likely that this means of financing lighthouse services may be introduced by the European Commission to other EU coastal States in future.

---

[41] The ship's agent will collect the light dues (by adding the sum due to the shipowner's disbursements account) and will contact the regional Collector to obtain a Light Certificate. In some cases the ship's agent employed, if a member of the Institute of Chartered Shipbrokers, will be the regional Collector.

[42] Cargo vessels navigating within Gloucester Harbour pay local light dues at the rate (with effect from 1 October 1991) of £0.045 per Summer DWT subject to a minimum charge based on 750 DWT, on both inward and outward passages to or from any part of Gloucester Harbour.

[43] This term means something entirely different in the UK

I07h OUTWARDS CUSTOMS CLEARANCE

I07h.1 Requirement for clearance

* **Clearance outwards** for a ship must be obtained from HM Customs before the ship leaves a UK port or terminal for an eventual destination outside the EU. Ships on UK domestic voyages or voyages to other ports in the EU do not need to obtain clearance outwards.

I07h.2 Procedure for obtaining customs clearance

* "**Clearance outwards**" must be obtained at the "proper place" before leaving a UK port for an eventual destination outside the EC, or, in the case of an offshore supply vessel, for an installation on the UKCS. The "**proper place**" is advertised in all customs port offices.
* **For clearance outwards**, the master should complete **Form C.13 (Master's Declaration)** in duplicate and give the forms to Customs. He should also:
    * give Customs a copy of the **cargo declaration** which was given for report (see I01f.4) if any imported goods remain on board for export;
    * show Customs any **clearance** given at other EU ports for the same voyage;
    * produce the following **forms** where applicable:
    * TC 12 (UK Form C73) Information Note;
    * PAS 15 (DEPARTURE) Passenger Return (see I01i).
* **TC 12 - Information Note for the Intended Port of Destination** (Customs & Excise form C73) is required under HM Customs & Excise Regulation 1214/92 and must be presented to the competent authorities for authentication at the port of departure. Information to be entered includes: vessel's name; port and date of departure; intended port of destination; probable ports of call; signature of captain of the vessel or his representative; official authentication by the competent authority at the port of departure.
* **Before giving clearance** Customs check the following statutory **ship certificates**:
    * in the case of **cargo ships over 500gt**: Loadline; IOPP; Safety Construction, Safety Equipment and Safety Radio (or Cargo Ship Safety Certificate instead of these last three, where issued);
    * in the case of **passenger ships**: Loadline; IOPP; Passenger Certificate or Passenger Ship Safety Certificate.
* Customs no longer check that **light dues** have been paid although a **Light Certificate** must still be obtained (through the agent) to show that dues have been paid or that the ship is exempt from further payment (see I07g.3).
* If all documents are in order, the vessel will be "**cleared outwards**" by the Customs officer stamping the "clearance granted" space at the foot of the C.13. **Unless she is subject to a Detention Order** the vessel may then legally sail. (The stamped C.13 should be retained as **proof of legal clearance** for production to officials in other ports and countries.)
* **Under regulation 12 of the MS (High-Speed Craft) Regulations 1996** (SI 1996/3188), the master of every high-speed craft must produce to a customs officer from whom clearance is being demanded for an international voyage, a valid High-Speed Craft Safety Certificate and a valid Permit to Operate.

I07h.3 Transires

* A "**transire**" is a permit document, issued by a customs officer or other appropriate authority in a State, to the master of a ship to sail with cargo coastwise within that State. Transires are used in various countries, including the UK and South Africa.
* In the UK a ship not regularly carrying domestic goods as cargo coastwise may still use the **cargo book system**. However, if the master chooses not to use the cargo book system, he must complete a **Transire** form (C.16) in duplicate. Both copies must be handed to a Customs officer before sailing; the officer will stamp and return one copy.
* **A Transire is not valid** until it is stamped. Once stamped, it becomes the master's authority to sail with the cargo coastwise.
* The stamped Transire must be kept onboard for at least 6 months from the date of issue for inspection.
* If the Customs office is unattended on arrival or departure and the master cannot get the Transire stamped, the vessel may still sail provided that the master enters in the "for official use" box (bottom right) the date and times of arrival and departure from that port. The second copy should be left at the Customs office and the original kept onboard. Each time the vessel makes a new voyage with coastwise cargo from a UK port, a new Transire will be required.

I07h.4 Refusal of outwards clearance

* **Section 284(6) of the Merchant Shipping Act 1995** confers on officers of Customs and Excise in the UK the right to **refuse to clear a ship outwards or grant a transire** to the ship in any case where she may be detained under the Act. **If a ship is actually detained** under the Act, an officer of Customs and Excise **must refuse to clear the ship outwards or grant a transire**.

I07i VOYAGE PREPARATIONS

I07i.1 Pre-departure checklist

* **Part B of the ICS Bridge Procedures Guide** contains a basic but useful Preparation For Sea check list (blue section check list **B2**) that can be adapted if necessary for different equipment, etc.

I07i.2 Voyage planning

* The **MS (Safety of Navigation) Regulations 2000** (SI 2000/1473) (see H01f.2) require compliance by a ship to which the Regulations apply with **SOLAS regulation V/34**, which relates to **Safe navigation and avoidance of dangerous situations** and applies to all ships which proceed to sea.
* **SOLAS regulation V/34.1** provides that **prior to proceeding to sea**, the master must ensure that the **intended voyage** has been **planned** using the appropriate nautical charts and nautical publications for the area concerned, taking into account the guidelines and recommendations developed by the IMO[44].
* **SOLAS regulation V/34.2** provides that the voyage plan must identify a route which:
  * takes into account any relevant ships' routeing systems (2.1);
  * ensures sufficient sea room for the safe passage of the ship throughout the voyage (2.2);
  * anticipates all known navigational hazards and adverse weather conditions (2.3); and
  * takes into account the marine environmental protection measures that apply, and avoids, as possible, actions and activities which could cause damage to the environment (2.4).
* **SOLAS regulation V/34.2**, together with the associated guidance notes in the MCA's 2002 SOLAS V publication, supersede MGN 166.
* **Part A, section 2 of the ICS Bridge Procedures Guide** concerns **Passage planning** and contains: 2.1. Overview; 2.2. Responsibility for passage planning; 2.3. Notes on passage planning; 2.4. Notes on passage planning in ocean waters; 2.5. Notes on passage planning in coastal or restricted waters; 2.6. Passage planning and pilotage; 2.7. Passage planning and ships' routeing; 2.8. Passage planning and ship reporting systems; 2.9. Passage planning and vessel traffic services.
* For notes on SOLAS regulation V/34.3 (Master's discretion), see H01a.11.

I07i.3 Maritime safety information (MSI)

* **MGN 44** gives guidance about the principal sources of relevant MSI, defined in the SOLAS Convention as navigational and meteorological warnings, meteorological forecasts and other related safety messages broadcast to ships. Masters should use all available means to obtain the latest MSI.

I07i.4 Steering gear tests and drills

* The **MS (Safety of Navigation) Regulations 2000** (SI 2000/1473) (see H01f.2) require compliance by a ship to which the Regulations apply with all paragraphs of **SOLAS regulation V/26**, which relates to **Steering gear: Testing and drills**.
* **SOLAS regulations V/24, V/25 and V/26**, together with the **Guidance Notes** in MCA's 2002 SOLAS Chapter V publication, including **Annex 18** (Steering Gear, Heading & Track Control Systems), supersede the MS (Automatic Pilot and Testing of Steering Gear) Regulations 1981 (SI 1981/571) and MGN 54.

---

[44] The **Guidelines for Voyage Planning**, adopted by IMO by resolution A.893(21) are printed in Annex 25 to the Guidance Notes to the MCA's 2002 SOLAS V document.

* **SOLAS regulation V/26.1** provides that within **12 hours before departure**, the ship's steering gear must be **checked and tested** by the ship's crew. The **test procedure** must include, where applicable, the operation of the following:
  * the main steering gear;
  * the auxiliary steering gear;
  * the remote steering gear control systems;
  * the steering positions located on the navigating bridge;
  * the emergency power supply;
  * the rudder angle indicators in relation to the actual position of the rudder;
  * the remote steering gear control systems power failure alarms;
  * the steering gear power unit failure alarms; and
  * automatic isolating arrangements and other automatic equipment.
* **SOLAS regulation V/26.2** provides that the **checks and tests must include**:
  * the full movement of the rudder according to the required capabilities of the steering gear (27.2.1);
  * a visual inspection of the steering gear and its connecting linkage (27.2.2); and
  * the operation of the means of communication between the navigating bridge and the steering gear compartment (27.2.3).
* **SOLAS regulation V/26.3.1** provides that **simple operating instructions** with a block diagram showing the **change-over procedures** for remote steering gear control systems and steering gear power units must be permanently displayed on the **navigation bridge** and in the **steering gear compartment**.
* **SOLAS regulation V/26.3.2** provides that all ships' **officers** concerned with the operation and/or maintenance of steering gear must be **familiar** with the **operation of the steering systems** fitted on the ship and with the **procedures for changing** from one system to another.
* **SOLAS regulation V/26.4** provides that in addition to the routine checks and tests prescribed in paragraphs 1 and 2, **emergency steering drills** must take place at least once every 3 months in order to practice emergency steering procedures. These drills must include **direct control** within the steering gear compartment, the **communications procedure** with the navigation bridge and, where applicable, the operation of **alternative power supplies**.
* **SOLAS regulation V/26.5** provides that the flag State Administration may **waive** the requirements to carry out the checks and tests prescribed in regulations V/26.1 and 26.2 for ships which regularly engage on **voyages of "short duration"**. Such ships must carry out these checks and tests at least **once every week**.
* **SOLAS regulation V/26.6** provides that the **date** on which the checks and tests prescribed in paragraphs 1 and 2 are carried out and the **date** and **details** of the emergency steering drills carried out under regulation V/26.4, must be **recorded**. (Under the **MS (Official Log Books) Regulations 1981** (SI 1981/569) (see D05a.2) the **date, time and place of each routine steering gear check and test** carried out must be recorded by the master in the Official Log Book (entry No. 25) (regulation 6(a)). A special page is provided for this purpose; when the page is full, additional pages may be annexed to the Official Log Book. On ships not required to carry an Official Log Book, a record of the tests, checks and drills should be retained on board by the master or skipper and be available for inspection on request.)
* **Annex 18** to the 2002 SOLAS V publication contains notes on application of SOLAS regulation V/26.
* **Section 4.3 of the Bridge Procedures Guide** contains advice on **testing and use of steering gear**, automatic pilot and off-course alarms.
* **Annex A7 of the Bridge Procedures Guide** contains **guidance on steering gear test routines**.

I07i.5 Testing of other equipment

* **M.1563** (which was cancelled without replacement) contained the MCA's advice on the testing of controllable pitch propellers, bridge-to-engine room communications and operation of the emergency engine stop.
* **Section 3.2.5 of the Bridge Procedures Guide** contains advice on **periodic checks on navigational equipment**.
* **Section 4.3 of the Bridge Procedures Guide** contains advice on the **operation and maintenance of bridge equipment**.

I07i.6 Master/pilot information exchange

* For notes on **master/pilot information exchange** (which should be used on **departure under pilotage** or when **shifting ship under pilotage**, as well as on arrival) see I01b.8a.

I07i.7 Master's discretion

* The **MS (Safety of Navigation) Regulations 2002** (SI 2002/1473) (see H01f.2), which require compliance with SOLAS regulation V/34.3, may mean that an owner, charterer or company, or any other person who exerts pressure on a master of a ship to depart from a port, terminal or anchorage or place of shelter against his better judgement, e.g. when the vessel can not be safely navigated due to adverse weather conditions, defective or inadequate navigational equipment or publications, etc., may be committing an offence.

I07j SEAWORTHINESS

* For notes on the **implied obligation as to seaworthiness in Crew Agreements**, under section 42 of the Merchant Shipping Act 1995, see C03a. The obligation under section 42 means that if the **master fails, at the start of the voyage**, to use all reasonable means to **ensure the seaworthiness of the ship for the voyage**, or fails to keep the ship in a seaworthy condition during the voyage, there is a breach of the Crew Agreement by the owner.
* For notes on **warranty of seaworthiness in carriage of goods contracts**, see F05a.2a.
* For notes on the **carrier's obligation as to seaworthiness under the Hague-Visby Rules**, see F07c.2b.
* For notes on **seaworthiness in voyage and time insurance policies**, see G03e.1 and G03e.2 respectively.
* For notes on **Clause 4 - Classification** of the Institute Time Clauses – Hulls - 1.11.95, see G04a.2d.
* For notes on **seaworthiness at sea**, see H01b.1.

INDEX

Index

Where there is more than one reference for an entry, the <u>principal reference</u> is shown in underlined type.

G

M

N

Z

Notes

Notes

Notes

Notes